MEDALLION EDITION • AMERICA READS

ENGLAND in Literature

MEDALLION EDITION • AMERICA READS

PURPOSE in Literature
Edmund J. Farrell
Ruth S. Cohen
L. Jane Christensen
H. Keith Wright

LITERATURE and LIFE
Helen McDonnell
Ruth S. Cohen
Thomas Gage
Alan L. Madsen

ARRANGEMENT in Literature
Edmund J. Farrell
Ouida H. Clapp
James L. Pierce
Raymond J. Rodrigues

QUESTION and FORM in Literature
James E. Miller, Jr.
Roseann Dueñas Gonzalez
Nancy C. Millett

UNITED STATES in Literature
James E. Miller, Jr.
Carlota Cárdenas de Dwyer
Robert Hayden
Russell J. Hogan
Kerry M. Wood

ENGLAND in Literature
Helen McDonnell
Neil E. Nakadate
John Pfordresher
Thomas E. Shoemate

MEDALLION EDITION • AMERICA READS

ENGLAND in Literature

Helen McDonnell
Neal E. Nakadate
John Pfordresher
Thomas E. Shoemate

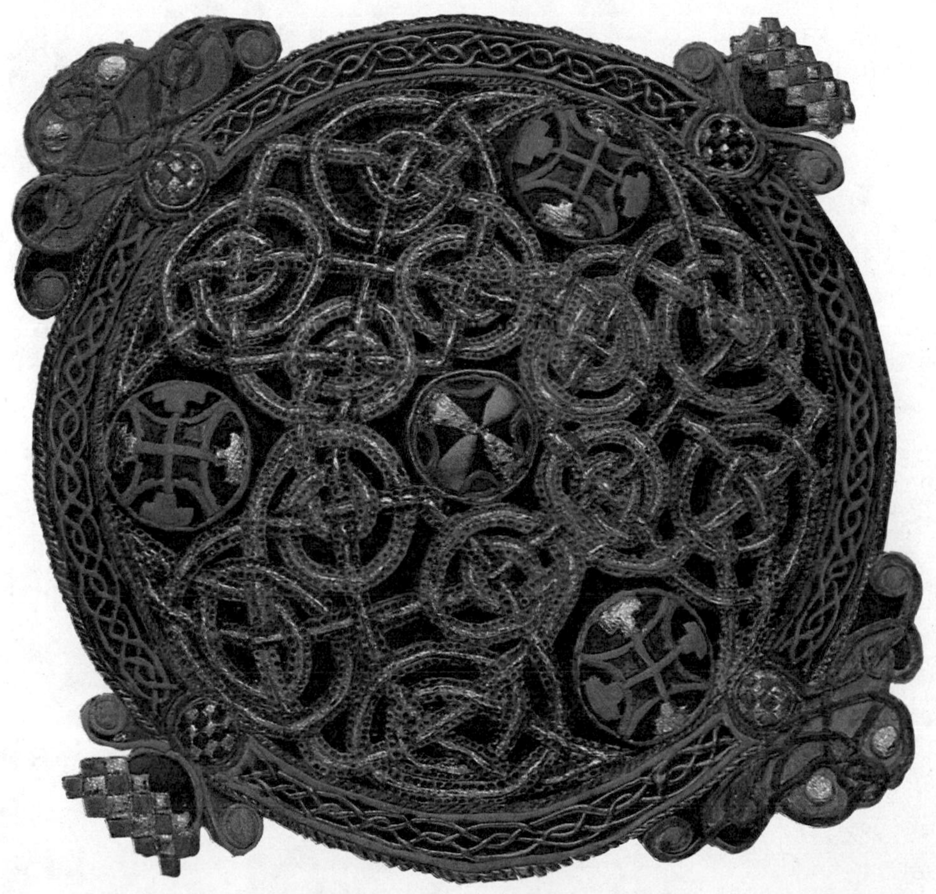

Scott, Foresman and Company

Editorial Offices: Glenview, Illinois

Regional Sales Offices: Palo Alto, California • Tucker, Georgia • Glenview, Illinois • Oakland, New Jersey • Dallas, Texas

HELEN McDONNELL English Supervisor of the Ocean Township Junior and Senior High Schools, Oakhurst, New Jersey. Formerly Chairman of the Committee on Comparative and World Literature, NCTE. Editor of *Nobel Parade* and co-author of titles in the America Reads and Fountainhead Series, Scott Foresman and Company.

NEAL E. NAKADATE Assistant Professor of English, Iowa State University. Formerly Professor of English, the University of Texas, Austin. Contributor of papers to the Modern Language Association, the South Central MLA, and the NCTE Conference of College Composition and Communication.

JOHN PFORDRESHER Associate Professor of English, Georgetown University. Formerly Assistant Professor of English, the University of New Hampshire, Durham. Editor, *Variorum Edition of the Idylls of the King.* Co-author of titles in the America Reads and Fountainhead Series, Scott Foresman and Company.

THOMAS E. SHOEMATE Language Arts Consultant and Associate Right-to-Read Director for Grades K–12 in the Marietta (Georgia) City Schools. Formerly President of the Georgia Council of Teachers of English. Formerly teacher of English, Lakeside High School, Atlanta, NCTE director representing the Georgia Council, and member Professional Practice Commission in Georgia.

ISBN: 0-673-12921-7 (Macbeth)
ISBN: 0-673-12922-5 (Hamlet)

12345678910-RRW-8584838281807978

Contents

Unit 1

The Anglo Saxons

450–1100

2 Time Line
4 Background

6–31 **Beowulf, Part I** (trans. by Kevin Crossley-Holland)
9 Notes and Comments: *The Epic*
13 Notes and Comments: *The Poetry of* BEOWULF
33 Notes and Comments: *from* GRENDEL by John Gardner
35 Notes and Comments: *Beowulf* by Richard Wilbur
37 **The Battle of Brunanburh** (trans. by Burton Raffel)
38 Notes and Comments: *Brunanburh A. D. 937* by Jorge Luis Borges
39 **The Wanderer** (trans. by Kevin Crossley-Holland)
43 Notes and Comments: *The Wanderer* by W. H. Auden
44 **The Husband's Message** (trans. by Burton Raffel)
45 **The Wife's Lament** (trans. by Charles Kennedy)
48 **Anglo-Saxon Riddles** (trans. by Michael Alexander)
49 from **Bede's History** (trans. by Leo Sherley-Price)
50 Notes and Comments: *The Exeter Book*
51 Notes and Comments: *Dark Age Glosses on the Venerable Bede* by Louis MacNeice

Unit Review/Tests
53 Review
53 Test I, **The Seafarer** (trans. by Burton Raffel)
55 Test II, Composition

Unit 2

The Medieval Period

1100–1500

56 Time Line
58 Background

60 **Lord Randal**
61 **The Unquiet Grave**
62 **Get Up and Bar the Door**
64 **Sir Patrick Spence**
65 Notes and Comments: *The Ballad*
66-80 **Prologue to the Canterbury Tales** by Geoffrey Chaucer (trans. by Nevill Coghill)
68 Notes and Comments: *The Physiognomists*
73 Notes and Comments: *Chaucer the Satirist* by Rosemary Woolf
76 Notes and Comments: *Chaucer's Words to His Scribe*
81-95 **The Wife of Bath's Tale** by Geoffrey Chaucer (trans. by Nevill Coghill)
85 Notes and Comments: *Opinions of the Wife*
89 Notes and Comments: *How Original was Chaucer?* by F. N. Robinson
96 **The Day of Destiny** from *Morte Darthur* by Sir Thomas Malory

Unit Review/Tests
104 Review
104 Test I, from **Sir Gawain and the Green Knight** (trans. by Brian Stone)
109 Test II, Composition

Unit 3

The Renaissance

1500–1650

110 Time Line
112 Background

116 **Whoso List to Hunt** by Sir Thomas Wyatt
116 **A Lover's Vow** by Henry Howard, Earl of Surrey
117 from **Certain Books of Virgil's Aeneid** by Henry Howard, Earl of Surrey
118 **When I Was Fair and Young** by Elizabeth I
119 **To Plead My Faith** by Robert Devereux, Earl of Essex
119 **What Is Our Life?** by Sir Walter Raleigh
119 Notes and Comments: *The Death of Raleigh*
120 **To Queen Elizabeth** by Sir Walter Raleigh
121 from **The Faerie Queene** by Edmund Spenser
124 Notes and Comments: *The Spenserian Stanza*
125 Notes and Comments: *Allegory*
126 **The Passionate Shepherd to His Love** by Christopher Marlowe
126 **The Nymph's Reply to the Shepherd** by Sir Walter Raleigh
127 **Sonnet 30** from *Amoretti* by Edmund Spenser
127 **Sonnet 31** from *Astrophel and Stella* by Sir Philip Sidney
128 **Heart Exchange** by Sir Philip Sidney
128 Notes and Comments: *i carry your heart* by E. E. Cummings
129 **The Man of Life Upright** by Thomas Campion
129 **Never Love Unless You Can** by Thomas Campion
129 **When to Her Lute Corinna Sings** by Thomas Campion
130 **Sonnet 18, Shall I compare thee . . .** by William Shakespeare
130 **Sonnet 130, My mistress' eyes . . .** by William Shakespeare
131 **Sonnet 29, When in disgrace . . .** by William Shakespeare
131 **Sonnet 30, When to the sessions . . .** by William Shakespeare
131 **Sonnet 55, Not marble . . .** by William Shakespeare
131 **Sonnet 71, No longer mourn for me . . .** by William Shakespeare
132 **Sonnet 73, That time of year . . .** by William Shakespeare

132 **Sonnet 116, Let me not to the marriage . . .** by William Shakespeare
136-203 **Hamlet** * by William Shakespeare
137 Act One
152 Notes and Comments: *The Creation of the First Folio*
154 Act Two
165 Act Three
179 Act Four
190 Act Five
136-203 **Macbeth** * by William Shakespeare
137 Act One
151 Act Two
154 Notes and Comments: *The Role of Lady Macbeth*
162 Act Three
172 Notes and Comments: *The Witch-Scenes in MACBETH* by A. C. Bradley
176 Act Four
188 *Shakespeare's Theater—The Globe*
190 Act Five
199 Notes and Comments: *The Character of Macbeth* by A. C. Bradley
204 **The Creation of the World** from *The King James Bible*
208 **The Twenty-third Psalm** from *The Great Bible*
208 **The Twenty-third Psalm** from *The King James Bible*
208 **The Twenty-third Psalm** from *The Bay Psalm Book*
208 **The Twenty-third Psalm** from *The New English Bible*
209 **Of Studies** by Sir Francis Bacon
211 **Song** by John Donne
211 **The Bait** by John Donne
212 **The Canonization** by John Donne
213 **A Valediction: Forbidding Mourning** by John Donne
213 Notes and Comments: *Donne's Puns*
214 **Sonnet 7** from *Holy Sonnets* by John Donne
214 **Sonnet 10** from *Holy Sonnets* by John Donne
214 **Sonnet 14** from *Holy Sonnets* by John Donne
215 **Meditation 17** by John Donne
216 **On My First Son** by Ben Jonson
216 **To Cynthia** by Ben Jonson
216 Notes and Comments: *Ben Jonson's Vision of His Son*
217 **It was a Beauty That I Saw** by Ben Jonson
217 **Song, to Celia** by Ben Jonson
218 **To Althea, from Prison** by Richard Lovelace
218 **To Lucasta, on Going to the Wars** by Richard Lovelace
219 **To the Virgins, to Make Much of Time** by Robert Herrick

*The MEDALLION EDITION of *England in Literature* is available in two versions, one containing *Hamlet*, the other *Macbeth*. Thus two listings appear in the Table of Contents and in the index although only one of the two plays will be found in this book.

219 **The Constant Lover** by Sir John Suckling
220 **What Care I?** by George Wither
221 **To His Coy Mistress** by Andrew Marvell
222 Notes and Comments: *You, Andrew Marvell* by Archibald MacLeish
223 **The Garden** by Andrew Marvell
225 **On His Having Arrived at the Age of Twenty-three** by John Milton
225 **On His Blindness** by John Milton
226 from **Paradise Lost, Book 1** by John Milton

Unit Review/Tests
235 Review
235 Test I, from **Richard II, Act Three** by William Shakespeare
239 Test II, Composition

Unit 4

The Age of Reason

1650–1780

240 Time Line
242 Background
244 from **The Hind and the Panther** by John Dryden
248 Notes and Comments: *Dryden and the Heroic Couplet*
247 **To the Memory of Mr. Oldham** by John Dryden
249 from **The Diary of Samuel Pepys**
256 **A Satirical Elegy on the Death of a Late Famous General** by Jonathan Swift
257 **A Description of a City Shower** by Jonathan Swift
259 **A Modest Proposal** by Jonathan Swift
265 from **The Spectator** by Joseph Addison and Richard Steele
271 **Epistle to Miss Blount** by Alexander Pope
272 from **An Essay on Criticism** by Alexander Pope
274 from **An Essay on Man** by Alexander Pope
275 from the **Dictionary of the English Language** by Samuel Johnson
277 **Letter to Chesterfield** by Samuel Johnson
278 from the **Life of Milton** by Samuel Johnson
281 **On the Death of Mr. Robert Levet** by Samuel Johnson

283 from **The Life of Samuel Johnson** by James Boswell
288 **Elegy Written in a Country Churchyard** by Thomas Gray
290 **Sonnet on the Death of Richard West** by Thomas Gray
291 **To a Mouse** by Robert Burns
292 **A Red, Red Rose** by Robert Burns

Unit Review/Tests
294 Review
294 Test 1, from **A Journal of the Plague Year** by Daniel Defoe
297 Test II, Composition

Unit 5

The Romantics

1780–1830

298 Time Line
300 Background

302 **Introduction** from *Songs of Innocence* by William Blake
302 **Introduction** from *Songs of Experience* by William Blake
303 **The Lamb** from *Songs of Innocence* by William Blake
303 **The Tyger** from *Songs of Experience* by William Blake
304 **Holy Thursday** from *Songs of Innocence* by William Blake
304 **Holy Thursday** from *Songs of Experience* by William Blake
305 **The Divine Image** from *Songs of Innocence* by William Blake
305 **The Human Abstract** from *Songs of Experience* by William Blake
306 **Proverbs of Hell** by William Blake
307 Notes and Comments: *What Did Blake Mean by Innocence and Experience?* by Morton D. Paley
309 **The World Is Too Much With Us** by William Wordsworth
309 **It Is a Beauteous Evening** by William Wordsworth
310 **Composed upon Westminster Bridge, September 3, 1802** by William Wordsworth
310 **London, 1802** by William Wordsworth

312 **Lines Composed a Few Miles Above Tintern Abbey** by William Wordsworth
316 **Frost at Midnight** by Samuel Taylor Coleridge
317 **Kubla Khan** by Samuel Taylor Coleridge
318 Notes and Comments: *Coleridge's Remarks About* KUBLA KHAN
320 **When We Two Parted** by George Gordon, Lord Byron
321 **She Walks in Beauty** by George Gordon, Lord Byron
321 **So, We'll Go No More A-roving** by George Gordon, Lord Byron
322 from **Canto #1, Don Juan** by George Gordon, Lord Byron
329 **England in 1819** by Percy Bysshe Shelley
329 **Ozymandias** by Percy Bysshe Shelley
330 **Ode to the West Wind** by Percy Bysshe Shelley
332 **When I Have Fears** by John Keats
332 **This Living Hand** by John Keats
333 **Ode on a Grecian Urn** by John Keats
334 **Ode to a Nightingale** by John Keats
336 **The Eve of St. Agnes** by John Keats
344 **On the Knocking at the Gate in** MACBETH by Thomas De Quincey
347 from **A Vindication of the Rights of Woman** by Mary Wollstonecraft
350 Notes and Comments: *Mary Wollstonecraft* by Virginia Woolf

Unit Review/Tests
354 Review
354 Test I, from **The Prelude, Book 1** by William Wordsworth
357 Test II, Composition

Unit 6

The Victorians

1830–1880

358 Time Line
360 Background

362 **Ulysses** by Alfred, Lord Tennyson
364 from **In Memoriam** by Alfred, Lord Tennyson
365 **The Passing of Arthur** from *Idylls of the King* by Alfred, Lord Tennyson
373 **Porphyria's Lover** by Robert Browning

374 **My Last Duchess** by Robert Browning
376 Notes and Comments: *The Dramatic Monologue*
377 **Dover Beach** by Matthew Arnold
378 **Self-Dependence** by Matthew Arnold
379 **Ah! Why, Because the Dazzling Sun** by Emily Brontë
380 **The Night Wind** by Emily Brontë
381 **I'll Not Weep** by Emily Brontë
382 **I Thought Once How . . .** from *Sonnets from the Portuguese* by Elizabeth Barrett Browning
382 **Unlike Are We . . .** from *Sonnets from the Portuguese* by Elizabeth Barrett Browning
383 **When Our Two Souls . . .** from *Sonnets from the Portuguese* by Elizabeth Barrett Browning
383 **My Letter, All Dead Paper . . .** from *Sonnets from the Portuguese* by Elizabeth Barrett Browning
383 **How Do I Love Thee . . .** from *Sonnets from the Portuguese* by Elizabeth Barrett Browning
384 from **Monna Innominata, Sonnet 2** by Christina Rossetti
384 **Shut Out** by Christina Rossetti
386 **Alice's Adventures Under Ground** by Lewis Carroll
409 **The Lifted Veil** by George Eliot

Unit Review/Tests
436 Review
436 Test I, from **On The Subjection of Women** by John Stuart Mill
439 Test II, Composition

Unit 7

New Directions

1880–1915

440 Time Line
442 Background

447 **Pied Beauty** by Gerard Manley Hopkins
447 **God's Grandeur** by Gerard Manley Hopkins
448 **Spring and Fall** by Gerard Manley Hopkins
448 **Thou Art Indeed Just, Lord** by Gerard Manley Hopkins
449 Notes and Comments: *Imagery in "God's Grandeur"*
450 **The Man He Killed** by Thomas Hardy
450 **Epitaph on a Pessimist** by Thomas Hardy
451 **Ah, Are You Digging on My Grave?** by Thomas Hardy

452 **At Castle Boterel** by Thomas Hardy
453 **Afterwards** by Thomas Hardy
454 **When I Was One-and-Twenty** by A. E. Housman
454 **Loveliest of Trees** by A. E. Housman
454 **To an Athlete Dying Young** by A. E. Housman
455 **Into My Heart an Air That Kills** by A. E. Housman
455 **Far in a Western Brookland** by A. E. Housman
456 Notes and Comments: *Housman on Writing His Poetry*
457 **The Lake Isle of Innisfree** by William Butler Yeats
457 Notes and Comments: *On* INNISFREE by William Butler Yeats
458 **When You Are Old** by William Butler Yeats
459 **Adam's Curse** by William Butler Yeats
460 **The Wild Swans at Coole** by William Butler Yeats
461 Notes and Comments: *The Second Coming*
461 **The Second Coming** by William Butler Yeats
462 **Sailing to Byzantium** by William Butler Yeats
464 Notes and Comments: *Sailing to Byzantium* by Elder Olson
466 **The Miracle of Purun Bhagat** by Rudyard Kipling
475 **The Lagoon** by Joseph Conrad
481 Notes and Comments: *On the Sources of His Fiction* by Joseph Conrad
485 **The Grave by the Handpost** by Thomas Hardy
489 Notes and Comments: *Pessimism in Literature* by E. M. Forster
493 **The Star** by H. G. Wells
496 Notes and Comments: *Science Fiction* by C. S. Lewis
502 **Spellbound** by George Gissing
511 **Pygmalion** by Bernard Shaw
512 Act One
519 Act Two
535 Act Three
547 Act Four
563 Epilogue
558 Notes and Comments: *The Comedy of Ideas*

Unit Review/Tests
571 Review
572 Test I, from **Major Barbara, Act One** by Bernard Shaw
575 Test II, Composition

Unit 8

The Twentieth Century

1915

576 Time Line
578 Background

Poetry:

582 **Suicide in the Trenches** by Siegfried Sassoon
582 **Dreamers** by Siegfried Sassoon
583 **The Next War** by Wilfred Owen
584 **The Hollow Men** by T. S. Eliot
586 **The Journey of the Magi** by T. S. Eliot
588 **The King of China's Daughter** by Edith Sitwell
589 **Intimates** by D. H. Lawrence
590 **Read Me, Please** by Robert Graves
591 **Sullen Moods** by Robert Graves
591 **She tells her love while half asleep** by Robert Graves
592 **Musée des Beaux Arts** by W. H. Auden
594 **The Unknown Citizen** by W. H. Auden
595 **Who's Who** by W. H. Auden
596 **An Elementary School Classroom in a Slum** by Stephen Spender
597 **Walking Away** by C. Day Lewis
598 **The British Museum Reading Room** by Louis MacNeice
599 **The Snow Man** by Louis MacNeice
600 **The Frog Prince** by Stevie Smith
602 **No Respect** by Stevie Smith
602 **Not Waving but Drowning** by Stevie Smith
603 **Alone in the Woods** by Stevie Smith
604 **The Force That Through The Green Fuse Drives the Flower** by Dylan Thomas
605 Notes and Comments: *The Force That Through . . .*
606 **Fern Hill** by Dylan Thomas
607 Notes and Comments: *Fern Hill*
608 **Do Not Go Gentle into That Good Night** by Dylan Thomas
609 Notes and comments: *The Villanelle*
610 **The O-Filler** by Alastair Reid
612 **At Grass** by Philip Larkin
612 **The Explosion** by Philip Larkin
613 **Homage to a Government** by Philip Larkin
614 **The Climbers** by Elizabeth Jennings

615 **Not in the Guidebooks** by Elizabeth Jennings
616 **The Secret Sharer** by Thom Gunn
617 **The Annihilation of Nothing** by Thom Gunn
618 **Fern** by Ted Hughes
618 **Bullfrog** by Ted Hughes
619 **Esther's Tomcat** by Ted Hughes
620 **Six Young Men** by Ted Hughes
622 **Journey Through the Night** by John Holloway
624 **P. C. Plod Vs. the Dale St. Dog Strangler** by Roger McGough

Fiction:
626 **Tobermory** by Saki
632 **Eveline** by James Joyce
635 **The Legacy** by Virginia Woolf
639 Notes and Comments: *Women and Fiction* by Virginia Woolf
640 **Tickets, Please** by D. H. Lawrence
647 **The Doll's House** by Katherine Mansfield
652 **Tears, Idle Tears** by Elizabeth Bowen
657 **A Shocking Accident** by Graham Greene
662 **My Oedipus Complex** by Frank O'Connor
670 **Three Shots for Charlie Betson** by Leslie Norris
679 **Three Miles Up** by Elizabeth Jane Howard

Essays:
690 **Three Pictures** by Virginia Woolf
692 **Why I Write** by George Orwell
697 **Reminiscences** by Dylan Thomas
701 from **Going Home** by Doris Lessing

Unit Review/Tests
704 Review
704 Test I, **Germans at Meat** by Katherine Mansfield
707 Test II, Composition

708 Definitions of Literary Terms*
717 Pronunciation Key
718 Glossary
733 Time Line Notes
734 Index of Authors and Titles
738 Index of Extension Assignments
738 Index of Vocabulary Exercises

*Items in *Definitions of Literary terms* when introduced in the editorial material accompanying selections are printed in **boldface.**

Unit 1:

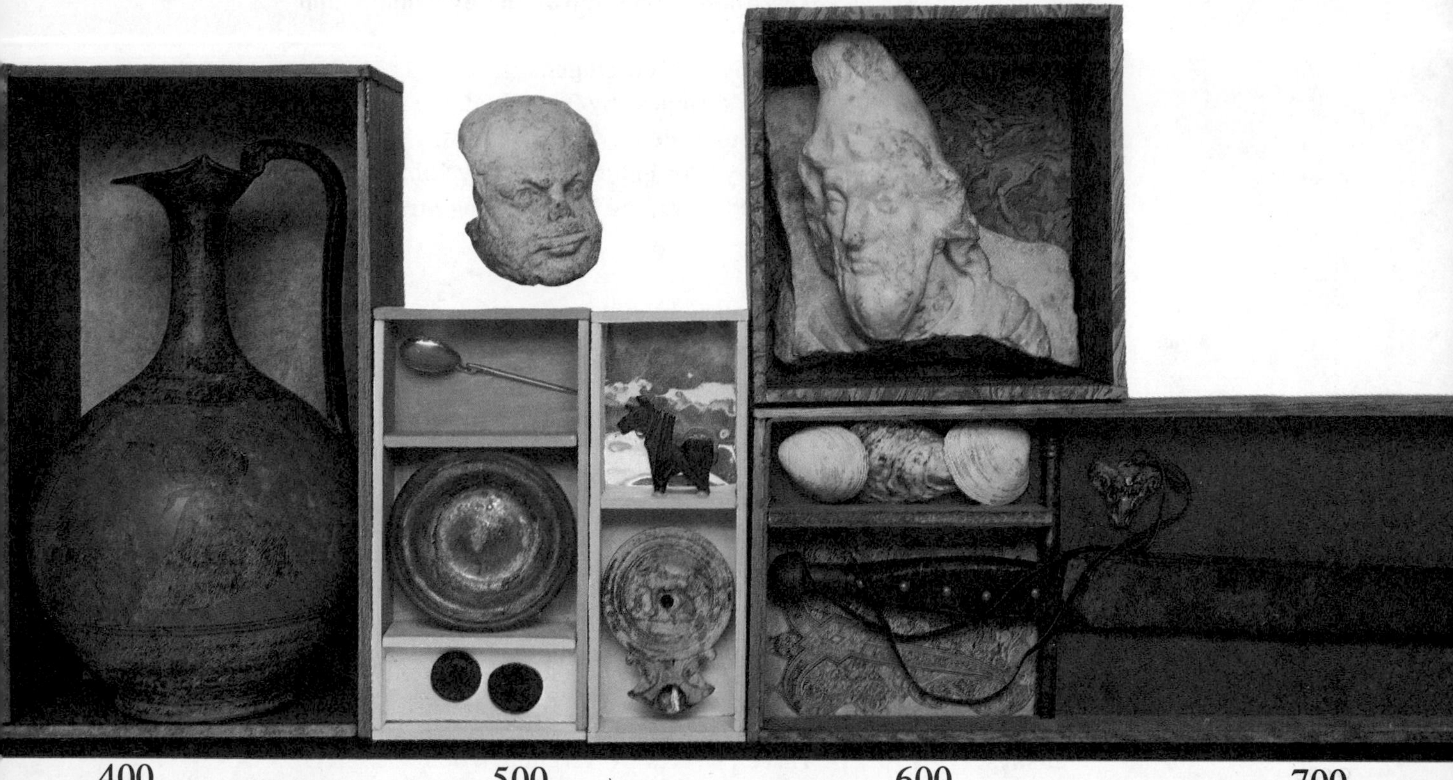

400 500 600 700

- Roman withdrawal from Britain begins
- Anglo-Saxon invasion begins
- Death of Hygelac, Beowulf's kinsman
- Roman Christian missionaries arrive
- Sutton Hoo Ship burial
- Synod of Whitby
- Bede's *History* concludes
- *Beowulf* composed

The Anglo-Saxons 450-1100

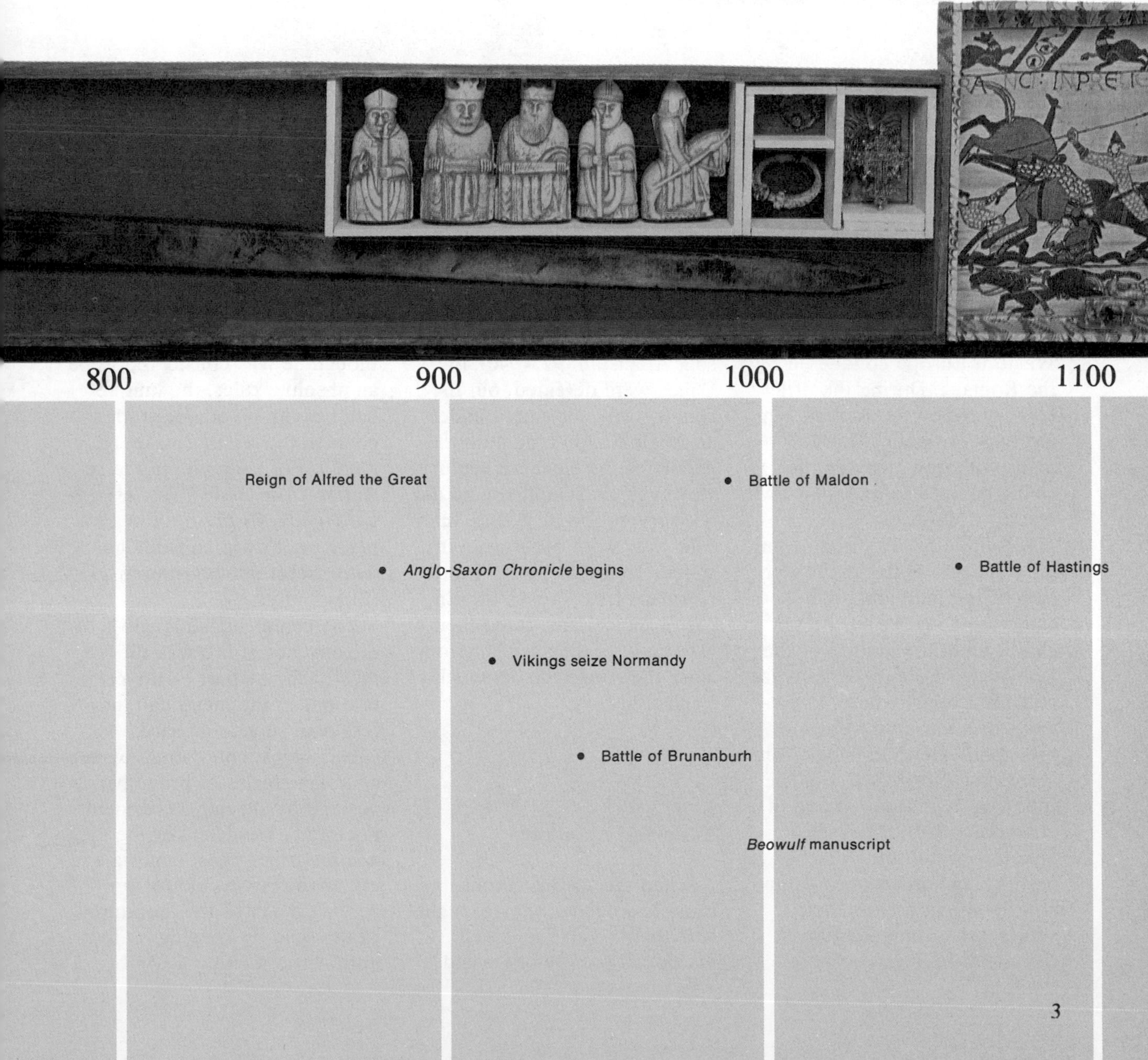

Background: The Anglo-Saxons 450-1100

Britain, as a place, was first mentioned by ancient Greek writers. To the Greeks, Britain was a legendary place—remote and mysterious. The Romans found the island occupied by Celtic Britons, who were related to the Celtic peoples of Western Europe conquered by the Romans. During the fifth century, when the Roman Empire was crumbling, the Romans withdrew, leaving the Celtic peoples to find their own means of defense.

Despite a brief period of military success under the leadership of the individual who became the King Arthur of medieval legend, the culture of the Romanized Celts of Britain had collapsed by 600 under the attacks of a variety of enemies, principally German tribes from across the North Sea. For the following two hundred and fifty years (600–850), the Anglo-Saxons—a multitude of wealthy, independent lords and kings—fought among themselves, with many kingdoms rising and falling.

To add to the plight of the Anglo-Saxons as they fought to protect their own petty kingdoms, Viking Danes began to attack during the second half of the ninth century. Under the leadership of Alfred the Great (871–899), and, later, his grandson, Athelstan (925–940), the Danes were defeated, but the country was not united under an Anglo-Saxon king until the middle of the eleventh century. However, their unified land did not survive for very long. In 1066 they were once again invaded. Their conquerers, the Normans from across the English Channel, instituted their own culture, thus bringing to a close the Anglo-Saxon epoch of English history.

Anglo-Saxon Culture

When the Anglo-Saxons came to England, they brought with them a relatively well-developed society organized around the family, the clan, the tribe, and finally the kingdom. The *eorls* (ėrlz), the ruling class, and the *ceorls* (chėrlz), bondsmen whose ancestors were former captives of the tribe, made up the two classes of Anglo-Saxon society. Although he was considered to be an absolute ruler, the king relied heavily on advice from a council, the *witan* ("wise men"). For example, in the selection from Bede's *Ecclesiastical History of the English People,* King Edwin consults his *witan* before converting to Christianity.

The center of the Anglo-Saxons' social life was the mead hall. As part of the celebrations in the mead hall, professional singers or bards, called *scops,* entertained by recounting stories of brave heroes and by serving as resident poet and chronicler for the king and his tribe. These entertainers were responsible for preserving much of the literature of the time by keeping it alive until it was written down by

Church scholars after Christianity came to England.

Until the end of the sixth century, the Anglo-Saxons worshiped various pagan gods—gods associated today with Norse mythology. Christianity did not have much impact on these pagan people until a missionary named Augustine was sent by Pope Gregory the Great to convert King Ethelbert of Kent in 597. Within one or two generations Christianity had spread throughout England.

Along with a new religion, the Christian missionaries brought education and culture. Schools grew up as monasteries were built. Young Anglo-Saxons learned not only the Scriptures but also the writing of the Roman Vergil and of the ancient Greeks. The coming of Christianity had a marked influence on literature, as the monks in the monasteries recorded the poetry that had been passed down orally from generation to generation by the mead-hall entertainers.

In spite of the widespread effects of Christianity on the Anglo-Saxons, they clung tightly to many of the superstitions and customs from their pagan past.

Anglo-Saxon Literature

English literature had its beginnings while the Anglo-Saxons were still on the Continent. When they conquered the Celts, they brought with them a rich tradition of oral literature steeped in their customs and pagan beliefs and rituals. This literature focused on the telling of the brave and heroic deeds of the warriors possessing attributes they valued and wished to emulate. The only surviving full-length epic in Old English from this tradition is *Beowulf.* The influence of the epics was sustained throughout the Anglo-Saxon period. As late as the tenth century, Christian writers produced two very excellent imitations of the battle scenes of the old heroic epics: *The Battle of Brunanburh* (page 37) and *The Battle of Maldon.* Both of these epics recount clashes between the English and the Viking Danes.

Two other important types of Anglo-Saxon poetry are the lyric and the riddle. The lyric represents a more personal and emotional form of poetry than the epic. The riddle, a form of poetry in which an object or person is described in a rather ambiguous manner, demonstrates the Anglo-Saxon fascination for manipulating words. In the lyrics and the riddles, the Anglo-Saxons expressed their terror of the northern winter, their awareness of the transitory nature of human life, and their reverence and fear of the sea because of its immensity, its mystery, and its cruelty.

Unlike Anglo-Saxon poetry, which exemplifies the highly imaginative nature of the Anglo-Saxons, the highly utilitarian prose writing from this period had its origins in the Church with the priests and monks. Because Latin was the language of the Church and because it was considered to be the language of educated men, the earliest prose writing was in Latin. The earliest recognized prose writer was the seventh-century scholar Bede. Bede's *Ecclesiastical History* was translated into Anglo-Saxon by Alfred the Great, who was the most influential prose writer of this period. One of Alfred's greatest accomplishments was the encouragement that he gave for the continuation of the *Anglo-Saxon Chronicle,* a year-by-year accounting of the events of English history. As Bede's *Ecclesiastical History* is a valuable source for Church history, the *Anglo-Saxon Chronicle* gives an accurate account of the secular events in English history.

Because Anglo-Saxon literature was preserved in a very disorganized fashion, because much of it was never written down at all, and because only four manuscripts of the poetry have survived, much of the life and literature of these people who inhabited England for approximately six centuries still is a mystery. Archaeologists and literary scholars have many questions that are yet unanswered about this Anglo-Saxon civilization. One question that certainly has not been satisfactorily answered for many is what role the monks played as they recorded the literature. Were they merely recorders or were they using the literature to inculcate Christian principles and values? What is certainly known about Anglo-Saxon literature is that it is imaginative, heroic, exciting, and rich in tradition. And like the literature of any era, its poetry and prose reveal much that is worth knowing about its creators.

Beowulf

Translated by Kevin Crossley-Holland

Beowulf,[1] *composed during the eighth century, has its origins in the traditions of the German tribes from among whom came some of the English. The poet begins in a customary way, by tracing tribal history from the reign of the first great king of the Danes, Scyld Scefing,*[2] *down to the time of Hrothgar.*

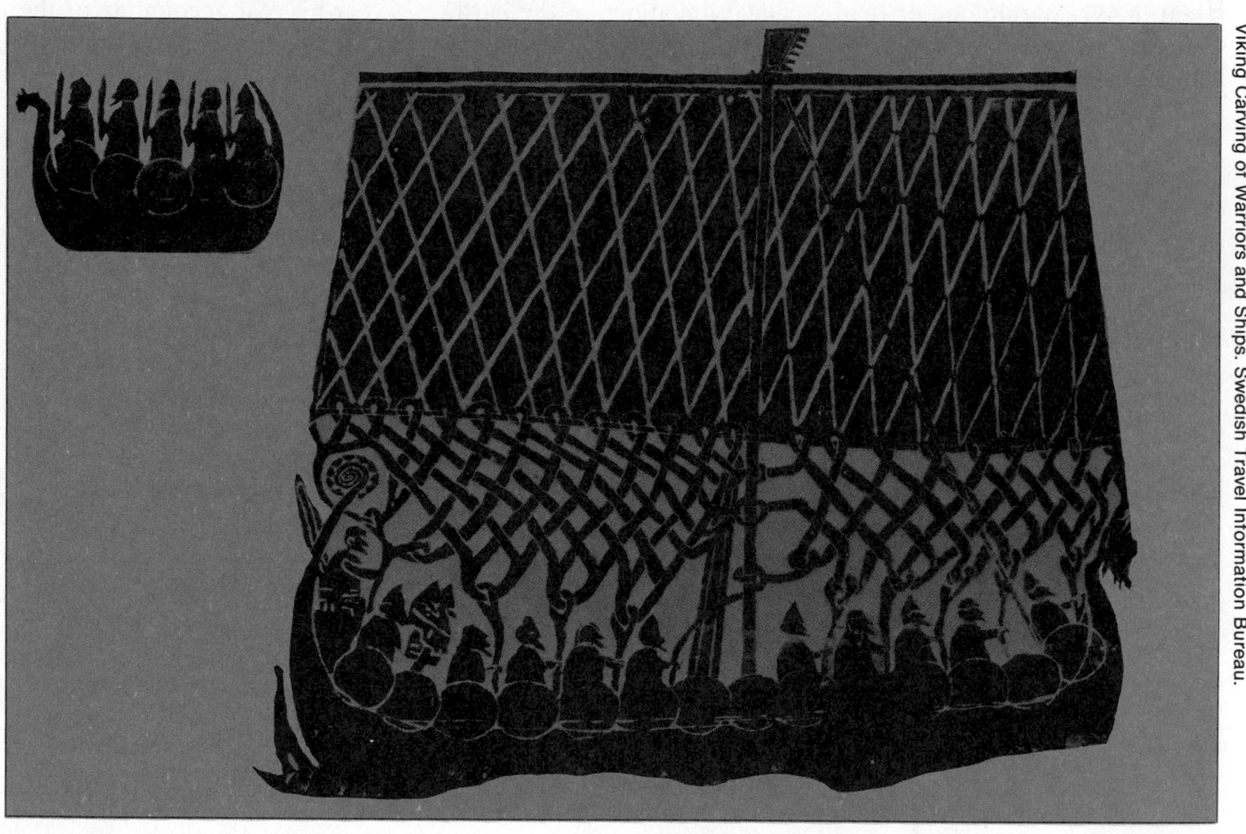

Viking Carving of Warriors and Ships. Swedish Travel Information Bureau.

Listen!
The fame of Danish kings
in days gone by, the daring feats
worked by those heroes are well known to us.
Scyld Scefing[2] often deprived his enemies,
many tribes of men, of their mead-benches.
He terrified his foes; yet he, as a boy,
had been found a waif; fate made amends for that.
He prospered under heaven, won praise and honour,
until the men of every neighbouring tribe,
across the whale's way, were obliged to obey him
and pay him tribute. He was a noble king!

---

1. ***Beowulf*** (bā′ə wu̇lf).
2. ***Scyld Scefing*** (shild′ shāf′ing).

Then a son was born to him, a child
in the court, sent by God to comfort
the Danes; for He had seen their dire distress,
that once they suffered hardship for a long while,
lacking a lord; and the Lord of Life,
King of Heaven, granted this boy glory;
Beow[3] was renowned—the name of Scyld's son
became known throughout the Norse lands. . . .
Then Scyld departed at the destined hour.
His own close companions carried him
down to the sea, as he, lord of the Danes,
had asked while he could still speak.
That well-loved man had ruled his land for many years.
There in harbour stood the ring-prowed ship,
the prince's vessel, icy, eager to sail;
and then they laid their dear lord,
the giver of rings, deep within the ship
by the mast in majesty; many treasures
and adornments from far and wide were gathered there.
I have never heard of a ship equipped
more handsomely with weapons and war-gear,
swords and corslets; on his breast
lay countless treasures that were to travel far
with him into the waves' domain.
They gave him great ornaments, gifts
no less magnificent than those men had given him
who long before had sent him alone,
child as he was, across the stretch of the seas.
Then high above his head they placed
a golden banner and let the waves bear him,
bequeathed him to the sea; their hearts were grieving,
their minds mourning. Mighty men
beneath the heavens, rulers in the hall,
cannot say who received that cargo.
When his royal father had travelled from the earth,
Beow of Denmark, a beloved king,
ruled long in the stronghold, famed
amongst men; in time Healfdene[4] the brave
was born to him; who, so long as he lived,
grey-haired and redoubtable, ruled the noble Danes.
Beow's son Healfdene, leader of men,
was favoured by fortune with four children:
Heorogar[5] and Hrothgar and Halga the good;
Yrse, the fourth, was Onela's queen,
the beloved wife of that warlike Swedish king.
Hrothgar won honour in war,
glory in battle, and so ensured
his followers' support—young men
whose number multiplied into a mighty troop.
And he resolved to build a hall,
a large and noble feasting-hall
of whose splendours men would always speak,
and there to distribute as gifts to old and young
all the things that God had given him—
but not men's lives or the public land.
Then I heard that tribes without number, even
to the ends of the earth, were given orders
to decorate the hall. And in due course
(before very long) this greatest of halls
was completed. Hrothgar, whose very word was counted
far and wide as a command, called it Heorot.[6]
He kept his promise, gave presents of rings
and treasure at the feasting. The hall towered high,
lofty and wide-gabled—fierce tongues of loathsome fire
had not yet attacked it, nor was the time yet near
when a mortal feud should flare between father-
and son-in-law, sparked off by deeds of deadly enmity. . . .
So those warrior Danes lived joyful lives,
in complete harmony, until the hellish fiend
began to perpetrate base crimes.
This gruesome creature was called Grendel,
notorious prowler of the borderland, ranger of the moors,
the fen and the fastness; this cursed creature
lived in a monster's lair for a time
after the Creator had condemned him
as one of the seed of Cain[7]—the Everlasting Lord
avenged Abel's murder. . . .

3. ***Beow*** (bā′ō).
4. ***Healfdene*** (hā′alf den ə).
5. ***Heorogar*** (hā′ə ro gär).
6. ***Heorot*** (hā′ə rot).
7. ***Cain,*** son of Adam and Eve. According to the Bible story (Genesis 4), he killed his brother Abel and was cursed by God.

Then, under cover of night, Grendel came
to Hrothgar's lofty hall to see how the Ring-Danes
were disposed after drinking ale all evening;
and he found there a band of brave warriors,
well-feasted, fast asleep, dead to worldly sorrow,
man's sad destiny. At once that hellish monster,
grim and greedy, brutally cruel,
started forward and seized thirty thanes
even as they slept; and then, gloating
over his plunder, he hurried from the hall,
made for his lair with all those slain warriors.
Then at dawn, as day first broke,
Grendel's power was at once revealed;
a great lament was lifted, after the feast
an anguished cry at that daylight discovery.
The famous prince, best of all men, sat apart in mourning;
when he saw Grendel's gruesome footprints,
that great man grieved for his retainers.
This enmity was utterly one-sided, too repulsive,
too long-lasting. Nor were the Danes allowed respite,
but the very next day Grendel committed
violent assault, murders more atrocious than before,
and he had no qualms about it. He was caught up in his crimes.
Then it was not difficult to find the man
who preferred a more distant resting-place,
a bed in the outbuildings, for the hatred
of the hall-warden was quite unmistakable.
He who had escaped the clutches of the fiend
kept further off, at a safe distance.
Thus Grendel ruled, resisted justice,
one against all, until the best of halls
stood deserted. And so it remained:
for twelve long winters the lord of the Danes
was sorely afflicted with sorrows and cares;
then men were reminded in mournful songs
that the monster Grendel fought with Hrothgar
for a long time, fought with fierce hatred
committing crime and atrocity day after day
in continual strife. He had no wish for peace
with any of the Danes, would not desist
from his deadly malice or pay wergild[8]—
No! None of the counsellors could hold out hope
of handsome compensation at that slayer's hands.
But the cruel monster constantly terrified
young and old, the dark death-shadow
lurked in ambush; he prowled the misty moors
at the dead of night; men do not know
where such hell-whisperers shrithe[9] in their wanderings.
Such were the many and outrageous injuries
that the fearful solitary, foe of all men,
endlessly inflicted; he occupied Heorot,
that hall adorned with treasures, on cloudless nights.
This caused the lord of the Danes deep,
heart-breaking grief. Strong men often sat
in consultation, trying in vain to devise
a good plan as to how best valiant men
could safeguard themselves against sudden attack. . . .
Thus Healfdene's son endlessly brooded
over the afflictions of this time; that wise warrior
was altogether helpless, for the hardship upon them—
violent visitations, evil events in the night—
was too overwhelming, loathsome, and long-lasting.
One of Hygelac's[10] thanes, Beowulf by name,
renowned among the Geats[11] for his great bravery,
heard in his own country of Grendel's crimes;
he was the strongest man alive,
princely and powerful. He gave orders
that a good ship should be prepared, said he would sail
over the sea to assist the famous leader,
the warrior king, since he needed hardy men.
Wise men admired his spirit of adventure.
Dear to them though he was, they encouraged
the warrior and consulted the omens.

---

8. ***wergild,*** the price set upon a man according to his rank, which could be claimed from the slayer by the relatives of a man wrongfully killed. If the wergild was not paid, the death could be avenged by killing the slayer. Here Grendel's refusal to pay emphasizes that he lives outside the law.
9. ***shrithe,*** an Old English word meaning "glide, wander, stride."
10. ***Hygelac,*** (hij′ə läk).
11. ***Geats*** (gā′ats).

notes and comments

The Epic

Beowulf is an **epic**—a long narrative poem presented in an elevated style, relating the heroic deeds of noble or semidivine personages. Like other traditional or folk epics (for example, the *Iliad* and the *Odyssey*), *Beowulf* originated in traditional tales or legends dating back to a remote past and handed down orally by generations of bards or singers. At some point, a literary artist put all the materials together in written form.

Literary epics developed later and were modeled on the traditional epics.

Certain features are associated with the epic. The characters are of noble birth, or they are supernatural beings from the past. If for any reason a person of lower estate is introduced, the person's name is never mentioned. The action is on an immense scale and involves the fate of a whole people or even the entire human race. Gods or semidivine creatures come to the aid of one side or another.

Certain devices also recur. The author usually announces his theme at the opening and calls on the muses to help him in his task of narration. The poem usually begins at a critical point in the action. The style is noble and majestic; the characters speak ceremoniously in long set speeches. Literary inventories—listings and descriptions of characters or objects—often form part of the descriptive passages.

Such features and devices became so predictable that there developed a kind of anti-epic, a literary form known as **mock epic.** The mock epic uses all the epic elements in wrong or bizarre ways in order to make them seem ridiculous.

Beowulf searched out the bravest of the Geats,
asked them to go with him; that seasoned sailor
led fourteen thanes to the ship at the shore.
Days went by; the boat was on the water,
moored under the cliff. The warriors, all prepared,
stepped onto the prow—the water streams eddied,
stirred up sand; the men stowed
gleaming armour, noble war-gear
deep within the ship; then those warriors launched
the well-built boat and so began their journey.
Foaming at the prow and most like a sea-bird,
the boat sped over the waves, urged on by the wind;
until next day, at the expected time,
so far had the curved prow come
that the travellers sighted land,
shining cliffs, steep hills,
broad headlands. So did they cross the sea;
their journey was at its end. Then the Geats
disembarked, lost no time in tying up
the boat—their corslets clanked;
the warriors gave thanks to God
for their safe passage over the sea.
Then, on the cliff-top, the Danish watchman
(whose duty it was to stand guard by the shore)
saw that the Geats carried flashing shields
and gleaming war-gear down the gangway,
and his mind was riddled with curiosity.
Then Hrothgar's thane leapt onto his horse
and, brandishing a spear, galloped
down to the shore; there, he asked at once:
"Warriors! Who are you, in your coats of mail,
who have steered your tall ship over the sea-lanes
to these shores? I've been a coastguard here
for many years, kept watch by the sea,
so that no enemy band should encroach
upon this Danish land and do us injury.
Never have warriors, carrying their shields,
come to this country in a more open manner.
Nor were you assured of my leaders' approval,
my kinsmen's consent. I've never set eyes
on a more noble man, a warrior in armour,
than one among your band; he's no mere retainer,

so ennobled by his weapons. May his looks never belie him,
and his lordly bearing. But now, before you step
one foot further on Danish land
like faithless spies, I must know
your lineage. Bold seafarers,
strangers from afar, mark my words
carefully: you would be best advised
quickly to tell me the cause of your coming."
The man of highest standing, leader of that troop,
unlocked his hoard of words, answered him:
"We are all Geats, hearth-companions of Hygelac;
my father was famed far and wide,
a noble lord, Ecgtheow[12] by name—
he endured many winters before he,
in great old age, went on his way; every wise man
in this world readily recalls him.
We have sailed across the sea to seek your lord,
Healfdene's son, protector of the people,
with most honourable intentions; give us your guidance!
We have come on an errand of importance
to the great Danish prince; nor, I imagine, will the cause
of our coming long remain secret. You will know
whether it is true—as we have heard tell—
that here among the Danes a certain evil-doer,
a fearful solitary, on dark nights commits deeds
of unspeakable malice—damage
and slaughter. In all good conscience
I can counsel Hrothgar, that wise and good man,
how he shall overcome the fiend,
and how his anguish shall be assuaged—
if indeed his fate ordains that these foul deeds
should ever end, and be avenged;
he will suffer endless hardship otherwise,
dire distress, as long as Heorot, best of dwellings,
stands unshaken in its lofty place."
Still mounted, the coastguard,
a courageous thane, gave him this reply:
"The discriminating warrior—one whose mind is keen—
must perceive the difference between words and deeds.
But I see you are a company well disposed
towards the Danish prince. Proceed, and bring
your weapons and armour! I shall direct you.
And I will command my companions, moreover,
to guard your ship with honour
against any foe—your beached vessel,
caulked so recently—until the day that timbered craft
with its curved prow shall carry back
the beloved man across the sea currents
to the shores of the storm-loving Geats:
he who dares deeds with such audacity and valour
shall be granted safety in the squall of battle."
Then they hurried on. The ship lay still;
securely anchored, the spacious vessel
rode on its hawser. The boar crest, brightly gleaming,
stood over their helmets: superbly tempered,
plated with glowing gold, it guarded the lives
of those grim warriors. The thanes made haste,
marched along together until they could discern
the glorious, timbered hall, adorned with gold;
they saw there the best-known building
under heaven. The ruler lived in it;
its brilliance carried across countless lands.
Then the fearless watchman pointed out the path
leading to Heorot, bright home of brave men,
so that they should not miss the way;
that bold warrior turned his horse, then said:
"I must leave you here. May the Almighty Father,
of His grace, guard you in your enterprise.
I will go back to the sea again,
and there stand watch against marauding bands."
The road was paved; it showed those warriors
the way. Their corslets were gleaming,
the strong links of shining chain-mail
clinked together. When the sea-stained travellers
had reached the hall itself in their fearsome armour,

---

12. ***Ecgtheow*** (edj′thā o).

they placed their broad shields
(worked so skilfully) against Heorot's wall.
Then they sat on a bench; the brave men's
armour sang. The seafarers' gear
stood all together, a grey-tipped forest
of ash spears; that armed troop was well equipped with weapons.
Then Wulfgar, a proud warrior,
asked the Geats about their ancestry:
"Where have you come from with these gold-plated shields,
these grey coats of mail, these visored helmets,
and this pile of spears? I am Hrothgar's
messenger, his herald. I have never seen
so large a band of strangers of such bold bearing.
You must have come to Hrothgar's court
not as exiles, but from audacity and high ambition."
Then he who feared no man, the proud leader
of the Geats, stern-faced beneath his helmet,
gave him this reply: "We are Hygelac's
companions at the bench: my name is Beowulf.
I wish to explain to Healfdene's son,
the famous prince, your lord,
why we have come if he, in his goodness,
will give us leave to speak with him."
Wulfgar replied—a prince of the Vandals,
his mettle, his wisdom and prowess in battle
were widely recognized: "I will ask
the lord of the Danes, ruler of the Scyldings,
renowned prince and ring-giver,
just as you request, regarding your journey,
and bring back to you at once whatever answer
that gracious man thinks fit to give me."
Then Wulfgar hurried to the place where Hrothgar sat,
grizzled and old, surrounded by his thanes;
the brave man moved forward until he stood
immediately before the Danish lord;
he well knew the customs of warriors.
Wulfgar addressed his friend and leader:
"Geatish men have travelled to this land,
come from far, across the stretch of the seas.
These warriors call their leader Beowulf;
they ask, my lord, that they should be allowed
to speak with you. Gracious Hrothgar,
do not give them *no* for an answer.
They, in their armour, seem altogether worthy
of the highest esteem. I have no doubt of their leader's
might, he who has brought these brave men to Heorot."
Hrothgar, defender of the Danes, answered:
"I knew him when he was a boy;
his illustrious father was called Ecgtheow;
Hrethel the Geat gave him his only daughter
in marriage; now his son, with daring spirit,
has voyaged here to visit a loyal friend.
And moreover, I have heard seafarers say—
men who have carried rich gifts to the Geats
as a mark of my esteem—that in the grasp
of his hand that man renowned in battle
has the might of thirty men. I am convinced
that Holy God, of His great mercy,
has directed him to us West-Danes[13]
and that he means to come to grips with Grendel.
I will reward this brave man with treasures.
Hurry! Tell them to come in and meet
our band of kinsmen; and make it clear, too,
that they are most welcome to the Danes!"
Then Wulfgar went to the hall door with Hrothgar's reply:
"My conquering lord, the leader of the East-Danes,[13]
commands me to tell you that he knows your lineage
and that you, so bold in mind, are welcome
to these shores from over the rolling sea.
You may see Hrothgar in your armour,
under your helmets, just as you are;
but leave your shields out here, and your deadly ashen spears,
let them await the outcome of your words."
Then noble Beowulf rose from the bench,
flanked by his fearless followers; some stayed behind
at the brave man's bidding, to stand guard over their armour.
Guided by Wulfgar, the rest hurried into Heorot
together; there went that hardy man, stern-faced

13. ***West-Danes, East-Danes.*** To make his lines alliterate (see "The Poetry of *Beowulf*" on page 13), the poet at various times refers to Hrothgar's people as North-, South-, East-, and West-Danes, and also as Bright-, Ring-, and Spear-Danes.

beneath his helmet, until he was standing under Heorot's roof.
Beowulf spoke—his corslet, cunningly linked
by the smith, was shining: "Greetings, Hrothgar!
I am Hygelac's kinsman and retainer. In my youth
I achieved many daring exploits. Word of Grendel's deeds
has come to me in my own country;
seafarers say that this hall Heorot,
best of all buildings, stands empty and useless
as soon as the evening light is hidden under the sky.
So, Lord Hrothgar, men known by my people
to be noble and wise advised me to visit you
because they knew of my great strength:
they saw me themselves when, stained by my enemies' blood,
I returned from the fight when I destroyed five,
a family of giants, and by night slew monsters
on the waves; I suffered great hardship,
avenged the affliction of the Storm-Geats and crushed
their fierce foes—they were asking for trouble.
And now, I shall crush the giant Grendel
in single combat. Lord of the mighty Danes,
guardian of the Scyldings, I ask one favour:
protector of warriors, lord beloved of your people,
now that I have sailed here from so far,
do not refuse my request—that I alone, with my band
of brave retainers, may cleanse Heorot.
I have also heard men say this monster
is so reckless he spurns the use of weapons.
Therefore (so that Hygelac, my lord,
may rest content over my conduct) I deny myself
the use of a sword and a broad yellow shield
in battle; but I shall grapple with this fiend
hand to hand; we shall fight for our lives,
foe against foe; and he whom death takes off
must resign himself to the judgment of God.
I know that Grendel, should he overcome me,
will without dread devour many Geats,
matchless warriors, in the battle-hall,
as he has often devoured Danes before. If death claims me
you will not have to cover my head,
for he already will have done so—
with a sheet of shining blood; he will carry off
the blood-stained corpse, meaning to savour it;
the solitary one will eat without sorrow
and stain his lair; no longer then
will you have to worry about burying my body.
But if battle should claim me, send this most excellent
coat of mail to Hygelac, this best of corslets
that protects my breast; it once belonged to Hrethel,
the work of Weland.[14] Fate goes ever as it must!"
Hrothgar, protector of the Scyldings, replied:
"Beowulf, my friend! So you have come here
because of past favours, to fight on our behalf! . . ."

(Hrothgar tells of a feud in which Beowulf's father, Ecgtheow, was involved and which Hrothgar settled by paying a wergild. He seems to suggest that Beowulf's fighting against Grendel would even the score of obligations, but he does not yet grant Beowulf's request. Instead, he invites Beowulf and his men to join him and his thanes in a feast.)

Then, in the feasting-hall,
a bench was cleared for the Geats all together,
and there those brave men went and sat,
delighting in their strength; a thane did his duty—
held between his hands the adorned ale-cup,
poured out gleaming liquor; now and then the poet sang,
raised his clear voice in Heorot; the warriors caroused,
no small company of Scyldings and Geats.
Ecglaf's[15] son, Unferth, who sat at the feet
of the lord of the Scyldings, unlocked his thoughts
with these unfriendly words—for the journey of Beowulf,
the brave seafarer, much displeased him
in that he was unwilling for any man

14. *Weland,* in Norse myth, the blacksmith of the gods.
15. *Ecglaf* (edj′läf).

The Poetry of *Beowulf*

To celebrate Beowulf's victory over Grendel, one of Hrothgar's thanes

"who brimmed with poetry,
 and remembered lays,
a man acquainted with ancient
 traditions
of every kind, composed a new
 song
in correct metre. Most skilfully
 that man
began to sing of Beowulf's
 feat, . . ."

This is the way Old English poetry originally was composed—orally, in front of an audience, by *scops* or bards who could draw on a vast store of traditional formula-phrases to express almost any idea in correct metrical form. Every scop also knew many ancient lays or poetic hero-tales which he recited to the warriors gathered in the mead hall of an evening, to the accompaniment of harp or lyre, varying the story each time to suit the audience and the occasion.

Beowulf must have been composed by a man who could read and write, but he used the traditional devices of the older oral poetry. Almost all the large body of Old English poetry which has survived is in a style which grew out of the oral tradition.

Above are a few lines from the Old English text of *Beowulf.*[1] (The symbol ð stands for the *th* sound.)

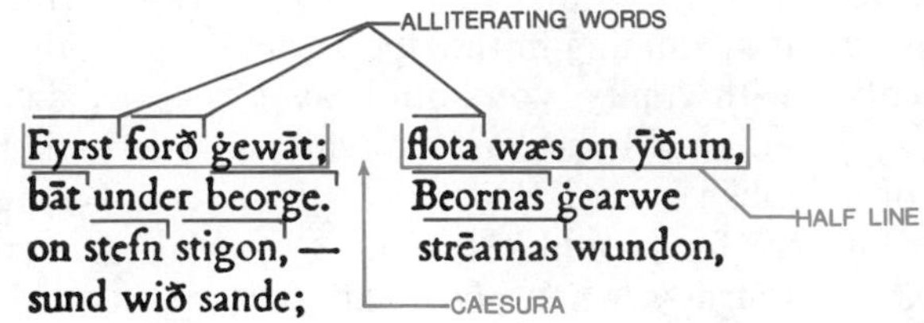

Each line has a break or *caesura* in the middle; the metrical unit is the half-line. Each half-line contains two unstressed words or syllables and an irregular number of syllables without stress. Note that there is no end rhyme to bind one line with another; rather, *alliteration* is used within the line to link important words. In a normal line, either one or two stressed words or syllables in the first half-line alliterate with one stressed word or syllable in the second half-line. Alliterating words either begin with the same consonant, or begin with a vowel; any vowel was considered as alliterating with any other.

The *Beowulf* poet, like other Old English poets, made use of the poetic conventions expected and understood by his audience. These conventions included a special poetic vocabulary, fixed expressions or formula-phrases, and poetic compounds.

The formulas are set metrical combinations that could be varied according to the needs of alliteration. For example, the phrase "on the sea" could be expressed by *on hranrade* ("on the whale-road") or by *on seglrade* ("on the sail-road"), depending on whether the poet needed a word beginning with *h* or one beginning with *s*. A person, place, or object was almost never referred to by a single, plain word, but almost always by a more elaborate expression. Hrothgar is "Healfdene's son," "ring-giver," "protector of warriors," "gold-friend," "ruler of the Scyldings," "grizzled warrior," and so on.

Most of the compounds used by the *Beowulf* poet—like "helm-bearer" or "shield-bearer" for *warrior,* or "battle-blade" for *sword*—are easily understood. The more far-fetched, riddling kind of descriptive comparisons known as kennings, so popular with other Old English and Norse poets, are used only sparingly in *Beowulf.* Examples are "battle-light" (*sword,* referring to the light reflected by the sword-blade), "candle of the sky" and "gem of heaven" *(sun),* "great sea-garment" *(sail),* "bone chamber" *(body).*

---

1. The literal translation is:
 Time forth went; floater was on waves,
 boat under cliff. Warriors eager
 on prow climbed,— streams eddied,
 sea against sand;
See lines 165–168 in the Crossley-Holland translation.

in this wide world to gain more glory than himself:
"Are you the Beowulf who competed with Breca,
vied with him at swimming in the open sea
when, swollen with vanity, you both braved
the waves, risked your lives on deep waters
because of a foolish boast? No one,
neither friend nor foe, could keep you
from your sad journey, when you swam out to sea,
clasped in your arms the water-streams,
passed over the sea-paths, swiftly moved your hands
and sped over the ocean. The sea heaved,
the winter flood; for seven nights
you both toiled in the water; but Breca outstayed you,
he was the stronger; and then, on the eighth morning,
the sea washed him up on the shores of the Heathoreams.[16]
From there he sought his own country,
the land of the Brondings who loved him well;
he went to his fair stronghold where he had a hall
and followers and treasures. In truth, Beanstan's son
fulfilled his boast that he could swim better than you.
So I am sure you will pay a heavy price—
although you have survived countless battle storms,
savage sword-play—if you dare
ambush Grendel in the watches of the night."
Beowulf, the son of Ecgtheow, replied:
"Truly, Unferth my friend, all this beer
has made you talkative: you have told us much
about Breca and his exploits. But I maintain
I showed the greater stamina, endured
hardship without equal in the heaving water.
Some years ago when we were young men,
still in our youth, Breca and I made a boast,
a solemn vow, to venture our lives
on the open sea; and we kept our word.
When we swam through the water, we each held
a naked sword with which to ward off
whales; by no means could Breca
swim faster than I, pull away from me
through the press of the waves—
I had no wish to be separated from him.
So for five nights we stayed together in the sea,
until the tides tore us apart,
the foaming water, the freezing cold,
day darkening into night—until the north wind,
that savage warrior, rounded against us.
Rough were the waves; fishes in the sea
were roused to great anger. Then my coat of mail,
hard and hand-linked, guarded me against my enemies;
the woven war-garment, adorned with gold,
covered my breast. A cruel ravager
dragged me down to the sea-bed, a fierce monster
held me tightly in its grasp; but it was given to me
to bury my sword, my battle weapon,
in its breast; the mighty sea-beast
was slain by my blow in the storm of battle.
In this manner, and many times, loathsome monsters
harassed me fiercely; with my fine sword
I served them fittingly.
I did not allow those evil destroyers to enjoy
a feast, to eat me limb by limb
seated at a banquet on the sea-bottom;
but the next morning they lay in the sand
along the shore, wounded by sword strokes,
slain by battle-blades, and from that day on
they could not hinder seafarers from sailing
over deep waters. Light came from the east,
God's bright beacon; the swell subsided,
and I saw then great headlands,
cliffs swept by the wind. Fate will often spare
an undoomed man, if his courage is good.
As it was I slew nine sea-beasts
with my sword. I have never heard
of a fiercer fight by night under heaven's vault
nor of a man who endured more on the ocean streams.
But I escaped with my life from the enemies' clutches,
worn out by my venture. Then the swift current,
the surging water, carried me
to the land of the Lapps. I have not heard tell

16. ***Heathoreams*** (hā′th ə rā′əmz).

that you have taken part in any such contests,
in the peril of sword-play. Neither you nor Breca
have yet dared such a deed with shining sword
in battle—I do not boast because of this—
though of course it is true you slew your own brothers,
your own close kinsmen. For that deed, however clever
you may be, you will suffer damnation in hell.
I tell you truly, son of Ecglaf,
that if you were in fact as unflinching
as you claim, the fearsome monster Grendel
would never have committed so many crimes
against your lord, nor created such havoc in Heorot;
but he has found he need not fear unduly
your people's enmity, fearsome assault
with swords by the victorious Scyldings.
So he spares none but takes his toll
of the Danish people, does as he will,
kills and destroys, expects no fight
from the Spear-Danes. But soon, quite soon,
I shall show him the strength, the spirit and skill
of the Geats. And thereafter, when day dawns,
when the radiant sun shines from the south
over the sons of men, he who so wishes
may enter the mead-hall without terror."
  Then the grizzled warrior, giver of gold,
was filled with joy; the lord of the Danes,
shepherd of his people, listened to Beowulf's
brave resolution and relied on his help.
The warriors laughed, there was a hum
of contentment. Wealhtheow[17] came forward,
mindful of ceremonial—she was Hrothgar's queen;
adorned with gold, that proud woman
greeted the men in the hall, then offered the cup
to the Danish king first of all.
She begged him, beloved of his people,
to enjoy the feast; the king, famed
for victory, ate and drank in happiness.
Then the lady of the Helmings walked about the hall,
offering the precious, ornamented cup
to old and young alike, until at last
the queen, excellent in mind, adorned with rings,
moved with the mead-cup towards Beowulf.
She welcomed the Geatish prince and with wise words
thanked God that her wish was granted
that she might depend on some warrior for help
against such attacks. The courageous warrior
took the cup from Wealhtheow's hands
and, eager for battle, made a speech:
Beowulf, the son of Ecgtheow, said:
"When I put to sea, sailed
through the breakers with my band of men,
I resolved to fulfil the desire
of your people, or suffer the pangs of death,
caught fast in Grendel's clutches.
Here, in Heorot, I shall either work a deed
of great daring, or lay down my life."
Beowulf's brave boast delighted Wealhtheow:
adorned with gold, the noble Danish queen
went to sit beside her lord.
  Then again, as of old, fine words were spoken
in the hall, the company rejoiced,
a conquering people, until in due course
the son of Healfdene wanted to retire
and take his rest. He realized the monster
meant to attack Heorot after the blue hour,
when black night has settled over all—
when shadowy shapes come shrithing
dark beneath the clouds. All the company rose.
Then the heroes Hrothgar and Beowulf saluted
one another; Hrothgar wished him luck
and control of Heorot, and confessed:
"Never since I could lift hand and shield,
have I entrusted this glorious Danish hall
to any man as I do now to you.
Take and guard this greatest of halls.
Make known your strength, remember your might,
stand watch against your enemy. You shall have
all you desire if you survive this enterprise."
  Then Hrothgar, defender of the Danes,
withdrew from the hall with his band of warriors.
Truly, the leader of the Geats fervently trusted
in his own great strength and in God's grace.
Then he took off his helmet and his corslet
of iron, and gave them to his servant,
with his superb, adorned sword,

---

17. ***Wealhtheow*** (wā′əl thā ō).

telling him to guard them carefully.
And then, before he went to his bed,
the brave Geat, Beowulf, made his boast:
"I count myself no less active in battle,
no less brave than Grendel himself:
thus, I will not send him to sleep with my sword,
so deprive him of life, though certainly I could.
Despite his fame for deadly deeds,
he is ignorant of these noble arts, that he might strike
at me, and hew my shield; but we, this night,
shall forego the use of weapons, if he dares fight
without them; and then may wise God,
the holy Lord, give glory in battle
to whichever of us He should think fitting."
Then the brave prince leaned back, put his head
on the pillow while, around him,
many a proud seafarer lay back on his bed.
Not one of them believed he would see
day dawn, or ever return to his family
and friends, and the place where he was born;
they well knew that in recent days
far too many Danish men had come to bloody ends
in that hall. But the Lord wove the webs of destiny,
gave the Geats success in their struggle,
help and support, in such a way
that all were enabled to overcome their enemy
through the strength of one man. We cannot doubt
that mighty God has always ruled mankind.
Then the night prowler
came shrithing through the shadows. All the Geats
guarding Heorot had fallen asleep—
all except one. Men well knew that the evil enemy
could not drag them down into the shadows
when it was against the Creator's wishes,
but Beowulf, watching grimly for his adversary Grendel,
awaited the ordeal with increasing anger.
Then, under night's shroud, Grendel walked down
from the moors; he shouldered God's anger.
The evil plunderer intended to ensnare
one of the race of men in the high hall.
He strode under the skies, until he stood
before the feasting-hall, in front of the gift-building
gleaming with gold. And this night was not the first
on which he had so honoured Hrothgar's home.
But never in his life did he find hall-wardens
more greatly to his detriment. Then the joyless warrior
journeyed to Heorot. The outer door, bolted
with iron bands, burst open at a touch from his hands:
with evil in his mind, and overriding anger,
Grendel swung open the hall's mouth itself. At once,
seething with fury, the fiend stepped onto
the tessellated floor; a horrible light,
like a lurid flame, flickered in his eyes.
He saw many men, a group of warriors,
a knot of kinsmen, sleeping in the hall.
His spirits leapt, his heart laughed;
the savage monster planned to sever,
before daybreak, the life of every warrior
from his body—he fully expected to eat
his fill at the feast. But after that night
fate decreed that he should no longer feed off
human flesh. Hygelac's kinsman,
the mighty man, watched the wicked ravager
to see how he would make his sudden attacks.
The monster was not disposed to delay;
but, for a start, he hungrily seized
a sleeping warrior, greedily wrenched him,
bit into his body, drank the blood
from his veins, devoured huge pieces;
until, in no time, he had swallowed the whole man,
even his feet and hands. Now Grendel stepped forward,
nearer and nearer, made to grasp the valiant Geat
stretched out on his bed—the fiend reached towards him

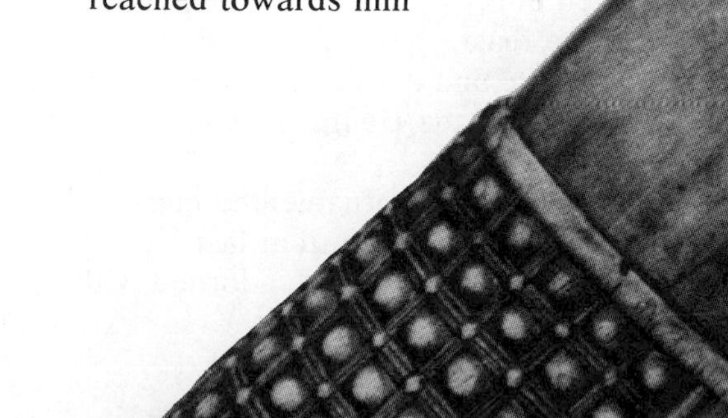

with his open hand; at once Beowulf perceived
his evil plan, sat up and stayed Grendel's outstretched arm.
Instantly that monster, hardened by crime,
realized that never had he met any man
in the regions of earth, in the whole world,
with so strong a grip. He was seized with terror.
But, for all that, he was unable to break away.
He was eager to escape to his lair, seek the company
of devils, but he was restrained as never before.
Then Hygelac's brave kinsman bore in mind
his boast: he rose from the bed and gripped
Grendel fiercely. The fiend tried to break free,
his fingers were bursting. Beowulf kept with him.
The evil giant was desperate to escape,
if indeed he could, and head for his lair
in the fens; he could feel his fingers cracking
in his adversary's grip; that was a bitter journey
that Grendel made to the ring-hall Heorot.
The great room boomed; all the proud warriors—
each and every Dane living in the stronghold—
were stricken with panic. The two hall-wardens
were enraged. The building rang with their blows.
It was a wonder the wine-hall withstood

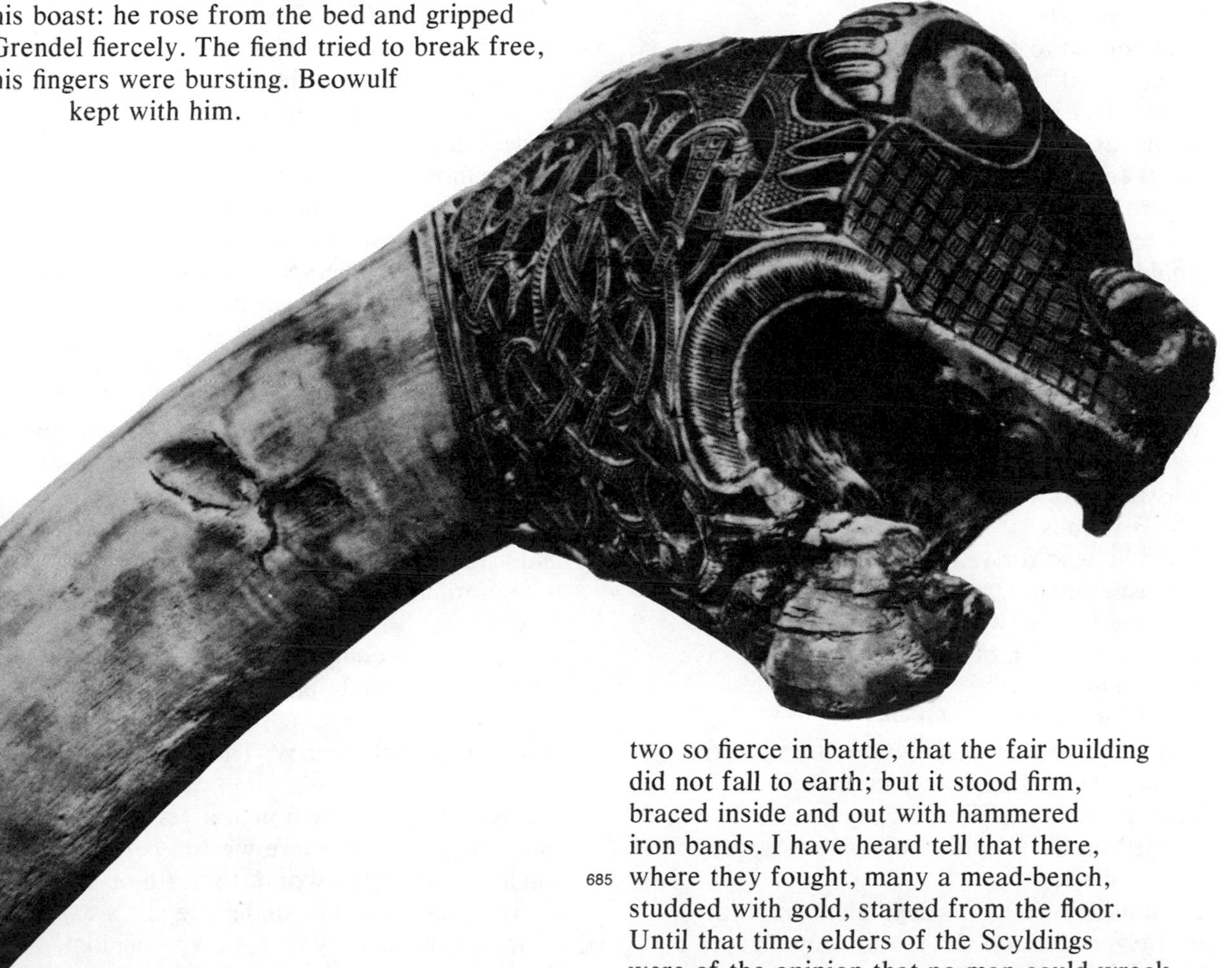

two so fierce in battle, that the fair building
did not fall to earth; but it stood firm,
braced inside and out with hammered
iron bands. I have heard tell that there,
where they fought, many a mead-bench,
studded with gold, started from the floor.
Until that time, elders of the Scyldings
were of the opinion that no man could wreck
the great hall Heorot, adorned with horns,
nor by any means destroy it unless it were gutted
by greedy tongues of flame. Again and again
clang and clatter shattered the night's silence;

Post Head of Osberg. University of National Antiquities, Oslo.

dread numbed the North-Danes, seized all
who heard the shrieking from the hall,
the enemy of God's grisly lay of terror,
his song of defeat, heard hell's captive
keening over his wound. Beowulf held him fast,
he who was the strongest of all men
ever to have seen the light of life on earth.
By no means did the defender of thanes
allow the murderous caller to escape with his life;
he reckoned that the rest of Grendel's days
were useless to anyone. Then, time and again,
Beowulf's band brandished their ancestral swords;
they longed to save the life, if they
so could, of their lord, the mighty leader.
When they did battle on Beowulf's behalf,
struck at the monster from every side,
eager for his end, those courageous warriors
were unaware that no war-sword,
not even the finest iron on earth,
could wound their evil enemy,
for he had woven a secret spell
against every kind of weapon, every battle blade.
Grendel's death, his departure from this world,
was destined to be wretched, his migrating spirit
was fated to travel far into the power of friends.
Then he who for years had committed crimes
against mankind, murderous in mind,
and had warred with God, discovered
that the strength of his body could not save him,
that Hygelac's brave kinsman held his hand
in a vise-like grip; each was a mortal enemy
to the other. The horrible monster
suffered grievous pain; a gaping wound
opened on his shoulder; the sinews sprang apart,
the muscles were bursting. Glory in battle
was given to Beowulf; fatally wounded,
Grendel was obliged to make for the marshes,
head for his joyless lair. He was
well aware that his life's days were done,
come to an end. After that deadly encounter
the desire of every Dane was at last accomplished.

In this way did the wise and fearless man
who had travelled from far cleanse Hrothgar's hall,
release it from affliction. He rejoiced in his night's work,
his glorious achievement. The leader of the Geats
made good his boast to the East-Danes;
he had removed the cause of their distress,
put an end to the sorrow every Dane had shared,
the bitter grief that they had been constrained
to suffer. When Beowulf, brave in battle,
placed hand, arm and shoulder—Grendel's
entire grasp—under Heorot's spacious roof,
that was evidence enough of victory.

Then I have heard that next morning
many warriors gathered round the gift-hall;
leaders of men came from every region,
from remote parts, to look on the wonder,
the tracks of the monster. Grendel's death
seemed no grievous loss to any of the men
who set eyes on the spoor of the defeated one,
saw how he, weary in spirit, overcome in combat,
fated and put to flight, had made for the lake
of water-demons—leaving tracks of life-blood.

There the water boiled because of the blood;
the fearful swirling waves reared up,
mingled with hot blood, battle gore;
fated, he hid himself, then joyless
laid aside his life, his heathen spirit,
in the fen lair; hell received him there.

After this, the old retainers left the lake
and so did the company of young men too;
brave warriors rode back on their gleaming horses
from this joyful journey. Then Beowulf's exploit
was acclaimed; many a man asserted
time and again that there was no better
shield-bearer in the world, to north or south
between the two seas, under the sky's expanse,
no man more worthy of his own kingdom.
Yet they found no fault at all with their friendly lord,
gracious Hrothgar—he was a great king.

At times the brave warriors spurred their bays,
horses renowned for their speed and stamina,

and raced each other where the track was suitable.
And now and then one of Hrothgar's thanes
who brimmed with poetry, and remembered lays,
a man acquainted with ancient traditions
of every kind, composed a new song
in correct meter. Most skilfully that man
began to sing of Beowulf's feat,
to weave words together, and fluently
to tell a fitting tale. . . .

(The scop weaves in stores of the exploits of Sigemund, most renowned of Germanic heroes, who slew a dragon and claimed the treasure the dragon had been guarding. He also sings about Heremod, an early Danish king, who failed to live up to the promise of his youth. These stores—no doubt familiar to the poet's original audience—were included in order to compare and contrast Sigemund and Heremod with Beowulf. Thus the hours quickly pass.)

Stout-hearted warriors
without number travelled to the high hall
to inspect that wonder; the king himself, too,
glorious Hrothgar, guardian of ring-hoards,
came from his quarters with a great company, escorted
his queen and her retinue of maidens into the mead-hall.
Hrothgar spoke—he approached Heorot,
stood on the steps, stared at the high roof
adorned with gold, and at Grendel's hand:
"Let us give thanks at once to God Almighty
for this sight. I have undergone many afflictions,
grievous outrages at Grendel's hands; but God,
Guardian of heaven, can work wonder upon wonder.
Until now, I had been resigned,
had no longer believed that my afflictions
would ever end: this finest of buildings
stood stained with battle blood,
a source of sorrow to my counsellors;
they all despaired of regaining this hall
for many years to come, of guarding it from foes,
from devils and demons. Yet now one warrior
alone, through the Almighty's power, has succeeded
where we failed for all our fine plans.
Indeed, if she is still alive,
that woman (whoever she was) who gave birth
to such a son, to be one of humankind,
may claim that the Creator was gracious to her
in her child-bearing. Now, Beowulf,
best of men, I will love you in my heart
like a son; keep to our new kinship
from this day on. You shall lack
no earthly riches I can offer you. . . ."
After this, the son of Ecglaf boasted less
about his prowess in battle—when all the warriors,
through Beowulf's might, had been enabled
to examine that hand, the fiend's fingers,
nailed up on the gables. Seen from in front,
each nail, each claw of that warlike,
heathen monster looked like steel—
a terrifying spike. Everyone said
that no weapon whatsoever, no proven sword
could possibly harm it, could damage
that battle-hardened, blood-stained hand.
Then orders were quickly given for the inside of Heorot
to be decorated; many servants, both men and women,
bustled about that wine-hall, adorned that building
of retainers. Tapestries, worked in gold,
glittered on the walls, many a fine sight
for those who have eyes to see such things. . . .Then it was time
for Healfdene's son to proceed to the hall,
the king himself was eager to attend the feast.
I have never heard of a greater band of kinsmen
gathered with such dignity around their ring-giver.
Then the glorious warriors sat on the benches,
rejoicing in the feast. Courteously
their kinsmen, Hrothgar and Hrothulf,
quaffed many a mead-cup, confident warriors
in the high hall. Heorot was packed
with feasters who were friends; the time was not yet come
when the Scyldings practised wrongful deeds.
Then Hrothgar gave Beowulf Healfdene's sword,

and a battle banner, woven with gold,
and a helmet and a corslet, as rewards for victory;
many men watched while the priceless, renowned sword
was presented to the hero. Beowulf emptied
the ale-cup in the hall; he had no cause
to be ashamed at those precious gifts.
There are few men, as far as I have heard,
who have given four such treasures, gleaming with gold,
to another on the mead-bench with equal generosity.
A jutting ridge, wound about with metal wires,
ran over the helmet's crown, protecting the skull,
so that well-ground swords, proven in battle,
could not injure the well-shielded warrior
when he advanced against his foes.
Then the guardian of thanes ordered
that eight horses with gold-plated bridles
be led into the courtyard; onto one was strapped
a saddle, inlaid with jewels, skilfully made.
That was the war-seat of the great king,
Healfdene's son, whenever he wanted
to join in the sword-play. That famous man
never lacked bravery at the front in battle,
when men about him were cut down like corn.
Then the king of the Danes, Ing's descendants,
presented the horses and weapons to Beowulf,
bade him use them well and enjoy them.
Thus the renowned prince, the retainers' gold-warden,
rewarded those fierce sallies in full measure,
with horses and treasure, so that no man
would ever find reason to reproach him fairly.
Furthermore, the guardian of warriors gave
a treasure, an heirloom at the mead-bench,
to each of those men who had crossed the sea
with Beowulf; and he ordered that gold
be paid for that warrior Grendel slew
so wickedly—as he would have slain many another,
had not foreseeing God and the warrior's courage
together forestalled him. The Creator ruled over
all humankind, even as He does today.
Wherefore a wise man will value forethought
and understanding. Whoever lives long
on earth, endures the unrest of these times,
will be involved in much good and much evil.
  Then Hrothgar, leader in battle, was entertained
with music—harp and voice in harmony. . . .

(The scop sings a lay about Finn, king of the Frisians, his Danish wife Hildeburh, and Hildeburh's brother Hnaef. While Hnaef and his followers were visiting Finn, they were treacherously attacked by Finn's thanes, in retaliation for some earlier wrong. Hnaef and Hildeburh's son were killed in the battle. An uneasy truce ensued, but in the spring the fighting was resumed. Finn was killed and the Danes returned to Denmark, taking with them Hildeburh, who had lost her husband, son, and brother. The story seems to hint at similar treachery and tragedy that will later come to the court of Hrothgar.

This same story was told in another Old English poem, "The Fight at Finnsburg.")

Thus was the lay sung,
the song of the poet. The hall echoed with joy,
waves of noise broke out along the benches;
cup-bearers carried wine in glorious vessels.
Then Wealhtheow, wearing her golden collar, walked
to where Hrothgar and Hrothulf were sitting side by side,
uncle and nephew, still friends together, true to one another.
And the spokesman Unferth sat at the feet
of the Danish lord; all men admired
his spirit and audacity, although he had deceived
his own kinsmen in a feud. Then the lady of the Scyldings
spoke these words: "Accept this cup, my loved lord,
treasure-giver; O gold-friend of men,
learn the meaning of joy again, and speak words
of gratitude to the Geats, for so one ought to do.
And be generous to them too, mindful of gifts
which you have now amassed from far and wide.

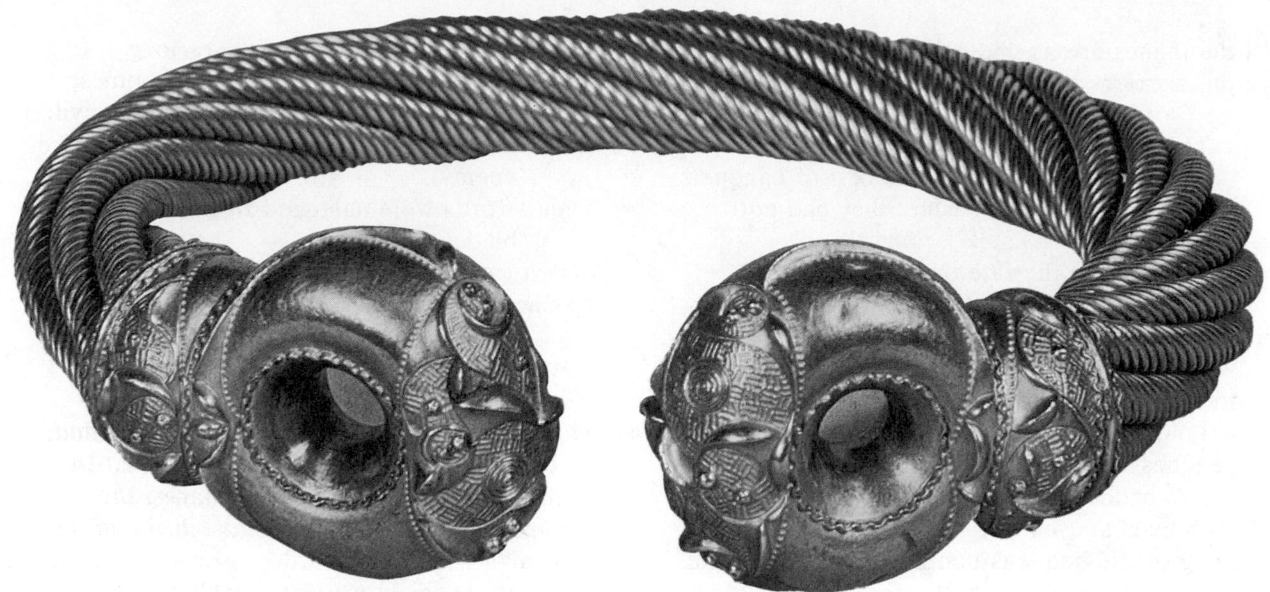

The Snettisham Torque, First Century B.C. Courtesy of the Trustees of The British Museum.

I am told you intend to adopt this warrior,
take him for your son. This resplendent ring-hall,
Heorot, has been cleansed; give many rewards
while you may, but leave this land and the Danish people
to your own descendants when the day comes
for you to die. I am convinced
that gracious Hrothulf will guard our children
justly, should he outlive you, lord of the Scyldings,
in this world; I believe he will repay our sons
most generously if he remembers all we did
for his benefit and enjoyment when he was a boy."
Then Wealhtheow walked to the bench where her sons,
Hrethric and Hrothmund, sat with the sons of thanes,
fledgling warriors; where also that brave man,
Beowulf of the Geats, sat beside the brothers.
To him she carried the cup, and asked in gracious words
if he would care to drink; and to him she presented
twisted gold with courtly ceremonial—
two armlets, a corslet and many rings,
and the most handsome collar in the world. . . .

(Here follows a brief digression telling how Beowulf's uncle, Hygelac, king of the Geats, later wore this collar when he was killed in a foolhardy raid on the Frisians and Franks.)

Applause echoed in the hall.
Wealtheow spoke these words before the company:
"May you, Beowulf, beloved youth, enjoy
with all good fortune this necklace and corslet,
treasures of the people; may you always prosper;
win renown through courage, and be kind in your counsel
to these boys; for that, I will reward you further.
You have ensured that men will always sing
your praises, even to the ends of the world,
as far as oceans still surround cliffs,
home of the winds. May you thrive, O prince,
all your life. I hope you will amass
a shining hoard of treasure. O happy Beowulf,
be gracious in your dealing with my sons.
Here, each warrior is true to the others,
gentle of mind, loyal to his lord;

the thanes are as one, the people all alert,
the warriors have drunk well. They will do as I ask."
Then Wealhtheow retired to her seat
beside her lord. That was the best of banquets,
men drank their fill of wine; they had not tasted
bitter destiny, the fate that had come and claimed
many of the heroes at the end of dark evenings,
when Hrothgar the warrior had withdrawn
to take his rest. Countless retainers
defended Heorot as they had often done before;
benches were pushed back; the floor was padded
with beds and pillows. But one of the feasters
lying on his bed was doomed, and soon to die.
They set their bright battle-shields
at their heads. Placed on the bench
above each retainer, his crested helmet,
his linked corslet and sturdy spear-shaft
were plainly to be seen. It was their habit,
both at home and in the field,
to be prepared for battle always,
for any occasion their lord might need
assistance; that was a loyal band of retainers.
And so they slept. One man paid a heavy price
for his night's rest, as often happened
after Grendel first held the gold-hall
and worked his evil in it, until he met his doom,
death for his crimes. For afterwards it became clear,
and well known to the Scyldings, that some avenger
had survived the evil-doer, still lived after
that grievous, mortal combat.
Grendel's mother
was a monster of a woman; . . .
mournful and ravenous, she resolved to go
on a grievous journey to avenge her son's death.
Thus she reached Heorot; Ring-Danes, snoring,
were sprawled about the floor. The thanes suffered
a serious reverse as soon as Grendel's mother
entered the hall. The terror she caused,
compared to her son, equalled the terror
an Amazon inspires as opposed to a man,
when the ornamented sword, forged on the anvil,
the razor-sharp blade stained with blood,
shears through the boar-crested helmets of the enemy.
Then swords were snatched from benches, blades
drawn from scabbards, many a broad shield
was held firmly in the hall; none could don helmet
or spacious corslet—that horror caught them by surprise.
The monster wanted to make off for the moors,
fly for her life, as soon as she was found out.
Firmly she grasped one of the thanes
and made for the fens as fast as she could.
That man whom she murdered even as he slept
was a brave shield-warrior, a well-known thane,
most beloved by Hrothgar of all his hall retainers
between the two seas. Beowulf was not there;
the noble Geat had been allotted another lodging
after the giving of treasure earlier that evening.
Heorot was in uproar; she seized her son's
blood-crusted hand; anguish once again
had returned to the hall. What kind of bargain
was that, in which both sides forfeited
the lives of friends?
Then the old king,
the grizzled warrior, was convulsed with grief
when he heard of the death of his dearest retainer.
Immediately Beowulf, that man blessed with victory,
was called to the chamber of the king. At dawn
the noble warrior and his friends, his followers,
hurried to the room where the wise man was waiting,
waiting and wondering whether the Almighty
would ever allow an end to their adversity.
Then Beowulf, brave in battle, crossed
the floor with his band—the timbers thundered—
and greeted the wise king, overlord of Ing's
descendants; he asked if the night had passed off
peacefully, since his summons was so urgent.
Hrothgar, guardian of the Scyldings, said:
"Do not speak of peace; grief once again

afflicts the Danish people. Yrmenlaf's
elder brother, Æschere,[18] is dead,
my closest counsellor and my comrade,
my shoulder-companion when we shielded
our heads in the fight, when soldiers clashed on foot,
slashed at boar-crests. Æschere was all
that a noble man, a warrior should be.
The wandering, murderous monster slew him
in Heorot; and I do not know where that ghoul,
drooling at her feast of flesh and blood,
made off afterwards. She has avenged her son
whom you savaged yesterday with vise-like holds
because he had impoverished and killed my people
for many long years. He fell in mortal combat,
forfeit of his life; and now another mighty
evil ravager has come to avenge her kinsman;
and many a thane, mournful in his mind
for his treasure-giver, may feel she has avenged
that feud already, indeed more than amply;
now that hand lies still which once sustained you.

I have heard my people say,
men of this country, counsellors in the hall,
that they have seen *two* such beings,
equally monstrous, rangers of the fell-country,
rulers of the moors; and these men assert
that so far as they can see one bears
a likeness to a woman; grotesque though he was,
the other who trod the paths of exile looked like a man,
though greater in height and build than a goliath;
he was christened *Grendel* by my people
many years ago; men do not know if he
had a father, a fiend once begotten
by mysterious spirits. These two live
in a little-known country, wolf-slopes, windswept headlands,
perilous paths across the boggy moors, where a mountain stream
plunges under the mist-covered cliffs,
rushes through a fissure. It is not far from here,
if measured in miles, that the lake stands
shadowed by trees stiff with hoar-frost.
A wood, firmly-rooted, frowns over the water.
There, night after night, a fearful wonder may be seen—
fire on the water; no man alive
is so wise as to know the nature of its depths.
Although the moor-stalker, the stag with strong horns,
when harried by hounds will make for the wood,
pursued from afar, he will succumb
to the hounds on the brink, rather than plunge in
and save his head. That is not a pleasant place.
When the wind arouses the wrath of the storm,
whipped waves rear up black from the lake,
reach for the skies, until the air becomes misty,
the heavens weep. Now, once again, help may be had
from you alone. As yet, you have not seen the haunt,
the perilous place where you may meet this most evil monster
face to face. Do you dare set eyes on it?
If you return unscathed, I will reward you
for your audacity, as I did before,
with ancient treasures and twisted gold."

Beowulf, the son of Ecgtheow, answered:
"Do not grieve, wise Hrothgar! Better each man
should avenge his friend than deeply mourn.
The days on earth for every one of us
are numbered; he who may should win renown
before his death; that is a warrior's
best memorial when he has departed from this world.
Come, O guardian of the kingdom, let us lose
no time but track down Grendel's kinswoman.
I promise you that wherever she turns—
to honeycomb caves, to mountain woods,
to the bottom of the lake she shall find no refuge.
Shoulder your sorrows with patience
this day; this is what I expect of you."

Then the old king leapt up, poured out his gratitude
to God Almighty for the Geat's words.
Hrothgar's horse, his stallion with plaited mane,
was saddled and bridled; the wise ruler
set out in full array; his troop of shield-bearers

---

18. ***Æschere*** (ash′her rə).

fell into step. They followed the tracks
along forest paths and over open hill-country
for mile after mile; the monster had made
for the dark moors directly, carrying
the corpse of the foremost thane of all those
who, with Hrothgar, had guarded the hall.

Viking Sword from the Ninth Century. University of National Antiquities, Oslo.

Then the man of noble lineage left Heorot far behind,
followed narrow tracks, string-thin paths
over steep, rocky slopes—remote parts
with beetling crags and many lakes
where water-demons lived. He went ahead
with a handful of scouts to explore the place;
all at once he came upon a dismal wood,
mountain trees standing on the edge
of a grey precipice; the lake lay beneath,
blood-stained and turbulent. The Danish retainers
were utterly appalled when they came upon
the severed head of their comrade Æschere
on the steep slope leading down to the lake;
all the thanes were deeply distressed.
The water boiled with blood, with hot gore;
the warriors gaped at it. At times the horn sang
an eager battle-song. The brave men all sat down;
then they saw many serpents in the water,
strange sea-dragons swimming in the lake,
and also water-demons, lying on cliff-ledges,
monsters and serpents of the same kind
as often, in the morning, molest ships
on the sail-road. They plunged to the lake bottom,
bitter and resentful, rather than listen
to the song of the horn. The leader of the Geats
picked off one with his bow and arrow,
ended its life; the metal tip
stuck in its vitals; it swam more sluggishly
after that, as the life-blood ebbed from its body;
in no time this strange sea-dragon
bristled with barbed boar-spears, was subdued
and drawn up onto the cliff; men examined
that disgusting enemy.
Beowulf donned
his coat of mail, did not fear for his own life.
His massive corslet, linked by hand
and skilfully adorned, was to essay the lake—
it knew how to guard the body, the bone-chamber,
so that his foe's grasp, in its malicious fury,
could not crush his chest, squeeze out his life;
and his head was guarded by the gleaming helmet
which was to explore the churning waters,

stir their very depths; gold decorated it,
and it was hung with chain-mail, as the weapon smith
had wrought it long before, wondrously shaped it
and beset it with boar-images, so that
afterwards no battle-blade could do it damage.
Not least amongst his might aids was Hrunting,
the long-hilted sword Unferth lent him in his need;
it was one of the finest of heirlooms; the iron blade
was engraved with deadly, twig-like patterning,
tempered with battle blood. It had not failed
any of those men who had held it in their hands,
risked themselves on hazardous exploits,
pitted themselves against foes. That was not
the first time it had to do a hard day's work.
Truly, when Ecglaf's son, himself so strong,
lent that weapon to his better as a swordsman,
he had forgotten all those taunts he flung
when tipsy with wine; he dared not chance
his own arm under the breakers, dared not
risk his life; at the lake he lost
his renown for bravery. It was not so with Beowulf
once he had armed himself for battle.

The Geat, son of Ecgtheow, spoke:
"Great son of Healfdene, gracious ruler,
gold-friend of men, remember now—
for I am now ready to go—
what we agreed if I, fighting on your behalf,
should fail to return: that you would always
be like a father to me after I had gone.
Guard my followers, my dear friends,
if I die in battle; and, beloved Hrothgar,
send to Hygelac the treasures you gave me.
When the lord of the Geats, Hrethel's son,
sees those gifts of gold, he will know
that I found a noble giver of rings
and enjoyed his favour for as long as I lived.
And, O Hrothgar, let renowned Unferth
have the ancient treasure, the razor sharp
ornamented sword; and I will make my name
with Hrunting, or death will destroy me."

After these words the leader of the Geats
dived bravely from the bank, did not even
wait for an answer; the seething water
received the warrior. A full day elapsed
before he could perceive the bottom of the lake.

She who had guarded the lake's length and breadth
for fifty years, vindictive, fiercely ravenous for blood,
soon realized that one of the race of men
was looking down into the monsters' lair.
Then she grasped him, clutched the Geat
in her ghastly claws; and yet she did not
so much as scratch his skin; his coat of mail
protected him; she could not penetrate
the linked metal rings with her loathsome fingers.
Then the sea-wolf dived to the bottom-most depths,
swept the prince to the place where she lived,
so that he, for all his courage, could not
wield a weapon; too many wondrous creatures
harassed him as he swam; many sea-serpents
with savage tusks tried to bore through his corslet,
the monsters molested him. Then the hero saw
that he had entered some loathsome hall
in which there was no water to impede him,
a vaulted chamber where the floodrush
could not touch him. A light caught his eye,
a lurid flame flickering brightly.

Then the brave man saw the sea-monster,
fearsome, infernal; he whirled his blade,
swung his arm with all his strength,
and the ring-hilted sword sang a greedy war-song
on the monster's head. Then that guest realized
that his gleaming blade could not bite into her flesh,
break open her bone-chamber; its edge failed Beowulf
when he needed it; yet it had endured
many a combat, sheared often through the helmet,
split the corslet of a fated man; for the first time
that precious sword failed to live up to its name.

Then, resolute, Hygelac's kinsman took his courage
in both hands, trusted in his own strength.
Angrily the warrior hurled Hrunting away,
the damascened sword with serpent patterns on its hilt;

tempered and steel-edged, it lay useless on the earth.
Beowulf trusted in his own strength,
the might of his hand. So must any man
who hopes to gain long-lasting fame
in battle; he must risk his life, regardless.
Then the prince of the Geats seized the shoulder
of Grendel's mother—he did not mourn their feud;
when they grappled, that brave man in his fury
flung his mortal foe to the ground.
Quickly she came back at him, locked him
in clinches and clutched at him fearsomely.
Then the greatest of warriors stumbled and fell.
She dropped on her hall-guest, drew her dagger,
broad and gleaming; she wanted to avenge her son,
her only offspring. The woven corslet
that covered his shoulders saved Beowulf's life,
denied access to both point and edge.
Then Ecgtheow's son, leader of the Geats,
would have died far under the wide earth
had not his corslet, his mighty chain-mail,
guarded him, and had not holy God
granted him victory; the wise Lord,
Ruler of the Heavens, settled the issue
easily after the hero had scrambled to his feet.
Then Beowulf saw among weapons an invincible sword
wrought by the giants, massive and double-edged,
the joy of many warriors; that sword was matchless,
well-tempered and adorned, forged in a finer age,
only it was so huge that no man but Beowulf
could hope to handle it in the quick of combat.
Ferocious in battle, the defender of the Scyldings
grasped the ringed hilt, swung the ornamented sword
despairing of his life—he struck such a savage blow
that the sharp blade slashed through her neck,
smashed the vertebrae; it severed her head
from the fated body; she fell at his feet.
The sword was bloodstained; Beowulf rejoiced.
A light gleamed; the chamber was illumined
as if the sky's bright candle were shining
from heaven. Hygelac's thane inspected
the vaulted room, then walked round the walls,
fierce and resolute, holding the weapon firmly
by the hilt. The sword was not too large
for the hero's grasp, but he was eager to avenge
at once all Grendel's atrocities, . . .
But the resolute warrior
had already repaid him to such a degree
that he now saw Grendel lying on his death-bed,
his life's-blood drained because of the wound
he had sustained in battle at Heorot. Then Grendel's corpse
received a savage blow at the hero's hands,
his body burst open: Beowulf lopped off his head.
At once the wise men, anxiously gazing at
the lake with Hrothgar, saw that the water
had begun to chop and churn, that the waves
were stained with blood. The grey-haired Scyldings
discussed that bold man's fate, agreed
there was no hope of seeing that brave thane again—
no chance that he would come, rejoicing in victory,
before their renowned king; it seemed certain
to all but a few that the sea-wolf had destroyed him.
Then the ninth hour came. The noble Scyldings
left the headland; the gold-friend of men
returned to Heorot; the Geats, sick at heart,
sat down and stared at the lake.
Hopeless, they yet hoped to set eyes
on their dear lord.
Then the battle-sword
began to melt like a gory icicle
because of the monster's blood. Indeed,
it was a miracle to see it thaw entirely,
as does ice when the Father (He who ordains
all times and seasons) breaks the bonds of frost,
unwinds the flood fetters; He is the true Lord.
The leader of the Geats took none of the treasures
away from the chamber—though he saw many there—

except the monster's head and the gold-adorned
sword-hilt; the blade itself had melted,
the patterned sword had burnt, so hot was that blood,
so poisonous the monster who had died in the cave.
He who had survived the onslaught of his enemies
was soon on his way, swimming up through the water;
when the evil monster ended his days on earth,
left this transitory life, the troubled water
and all the lake's expanse was purged of its impurity.
Then the fearless leader of the seafarers
swam to the shore, exulting in his plunder,
the heavy burdens he had brought with him.
The intrepid band of thanes hurried towards him,
giving thanks to God, rejoicing
to see their lord safe and sound of limb.
The brave man was quickly relieved of his helmet and corslet.
The angry water under the clouds,
the lake stained with battle-blood, at last became calm.
Then they left the lake with songs on their lips,
retraced their steps along the winding paths
and narrow tracks; it was no easy matter
for those courageous men, bold as kings,
to carry the head away from the cliff
overlooking the lake. With utmost difficulty
four of the thanes bore Grendel's head
to the gold-hall on a battle-pole;
thus the fourteen Geats, unbroken
in spirit and eager in battle, very soon
drew near to Heorot; with them, that bravest
of brave men crossed the plain towards the mead-hall.
Then the fearless leader of the thanes,
covered with glory, matchless in battle,
once more entered Heorot to greet Hrothgar.
Grendel's head was carried by the hair
onto the floor where the warriors were drinking,
a ghastly thing paraded before the heroes and the queen.
Men stared at that wondrous spectacle. . . .

(Beowulf tells Hrothgar about the underwater fight.)

Then the golden hilt, age-old work of giants,
was given to Hrothgar, the grizzled warrior,
the warlike lord; wrought by master-smiths,
it passed into the hands of the Danish prince
once the demons died; for that embittered fiend,
enemy of God, guilty of murder
had abandoned this world—and so had his mother.
Thus the hilt was possessed by the best
of earthly kings between the two seas,
the best of those who bestowed gold on Norse men.
Hrothgar spoke, first examining the hilt,
the ancient heirloom. On it was engraved
the origins of strife in time immemorial,
when the tide of rising water drowned
the race of giants; their end was horrible;
they were opposed to the Eternal Lord,
and their reward was the downpour and the flood.
Also, on the sword-guards of pure gold,
it was recorded in runic letters, as is the custom,
for whom that sword, finest of blades,
with twisted hilt and serpentine patterning
had first been made.
Then Healfdene's wise son
lifted his voice—everyone listened:
"This land's grizzled guardian, who promotes truth
and justice amongst his people, and forgets nothing
though the years pass, can say for certain that this man
is much favoured by fate! Beowulf my friend,
your name is echoed in every country
to earth's end. You wear your enormous might
with wisdom and with dignity. I shall keep
my promise made when last we spoke. You will
beyond doubt be the shield of the Geats
for days without number, and a source
of strength to warriors.
Heremod was hardly that
to Ecgwala's sons, the glorious Scyldings;
he grew to spread slaughter and destruction

rather than happiness amongst the Danish people.
In mad rage he murdered his table-companions,
his most loyal followers; it came about
that the great prince cut himself off
from all earthly pleasures, though God had endowed him
with strength and power above all other men,
and had sustained him. For all that, his heart
was filled with savage blood-lust. He never gave
gifts to the Danes, to gain glory. He lived joyless,
agony racked him; he was long an affliction
to his people. Be warned, Beowulf,
learn the nature of nobility. I who tell you
this story am many winters old.
It is a miracle
how the mighty Lord in his generosity
gives wisdom and land and high estate
to people on earth; all things are in His power.
At times he allows a noble man's mind to experience
happiness, grants he should rule over a pleasant,
prosperous country, a stronghold of men,
makes subject to him regions of earth,
a wide kingdom, until in his stupidity
there is no end to his ambition.
His life is unruffled—neither old age
nor illness afflict him, no unhappiness
gnaws at his heart, in his land no hatred
flares up in mortal feuds, but all the world
bends to his will. He suffers no setbacks
until the seed of arrogance is sown and grows
within him, while still the watchman slumbers;
how deeply the soul's guardian sleeps
when a man is enmeshed in matters of this world;
the evil archer stands close with his drawn bow,
his bristling quiver. Then the poisoned shaft
pierces his mind under his helmet
and he does not know how to resist
the devil's insidious, secret temptations.
What had long contented him now seems insufficient;
he becomes embittered, begins to hoard
his treasures, never parts with gold rings
in ceremonial splendour; he soon forgets
his destiny and disregards the honours
given him of God, the Ruler of Glory.
In time his transient body wizens and withers,
and dies as fate decrees; then another man
succeeds to his throne who gives treasures and heirlooms
with great generosity; *he* is not obsessed with suspicions.
Arm yourself, dear Beowulf, best of men,
against such diseased thinking; always swallow pride;
remember, renowned warrior, what is more worthwhile—
gain everlasting. Today and tomorrow
you will be in your prime; but soon you will die,
in battle or in bed; either fire or water,
the fearsome elements, will embrace you,
or you will succumb to the sword's flashing edge,
or to the arrow's flight, or to extreme old age;
then your eyes, once bright, will be clouded over;
all too soon, O warrior, death will destroy you.

I have ruled the Ring-Danes under the skies
for fifty years, shielded them in war
from many tribes of men in this world,
from swords and from ash-spears, and the time had come
when I thought I had no enemies left on earth.
All was changed utterly, gladness
became grief, after Grendel,
my deadly adversary, invaded Heorot.
His visitations caused me continual pain.
Thus I thank the Creator, the Eternal Lord,
that after our afflictions I have lived to see,
to see with my own eyes this blood-stained head.
Now, Beowulf, brave in battle,
go to your seat and enjoy the feast;
tomorrow we shall share many treasures."

The Geat, full of joy, straightway went
to find his seat as Hrothgar had suggested.
Then, once again, as so often before,
a great feast was prepared for the brave warriors sitting in the hall.
The shadows of night
settled over the retainers. The company arose;
the grey-haired man, the old Scylding,
wanted to retire. And the Geat, the shield-warrior,

was utterly exhausted, his bones ached for sleep.
At once the chamberlain—he who courteously
saw to all such needs as a thane,
a travelling warrior, had in those days—
showed him, so limb-weary, to his lodging.
Then Beowulf rested; the building soared,
spacious and adorned with gold; the guest
slept within until the black raven gaily
proclaimed sunrise. Bright light
chased away the shadows of night.
Then the warriors
hastened, the thanes were eager to return
to their own people; the brave seafarer
longed to see his ship, so far from that place.
Then the bold Geat ordered that Hrunting,
that sword beyond price, be brought before Unferth;
he begged him to take it back and thanked him
for the loan of it; he spoke of it as an ally
in battle, and assured Unferth he did not
underrate it: what a brave man he was!
After this the warriors, wearing their chain-mail,
were eager to be off; their leader,
so dear to the Danes, walked to the daïs
where Hrothgar was sitting, and greeted him.
Beowulf, the son of Ecgtheow, spoke:
"Now we seafarers, who have sailed here from far,
beg to tell you we are eager
to return to Hygelac. We have been happy here,
hospitably entertained; you have treated us kindly.
If I can in any way win more of your affection,
O ruler of men, than I have done already,
I will come at once, eager for combat.
If news reaches me over the seas
that you are threatened by those around you
(just as before enemies endangered you)
I will bring thousands of thanes,
all heroes, to help you. I know that Hygelac,
lord of the Geats, guardian of his people,
will advance me in word and deed
although he is young, so that I can back
these promises with spear shafts, and serve you
with all my strength where you need men.
Should Hrethric, Hrothgar's son, wish
to visit the court of the Geatish king,
he will be warmly welcomed. Strong men
should seek fame in far-off lands."
Hrothgar replied: "The wise Lord put these words
into your mind; I have never heard a warrior
speak more sagely while still so young.
You are very strong and very shrewd,
you speak with discerning. If your leader,
Hrethel's son, guardian of the people,
were to lose his life by illness or by iron,
by spear or grim swordplay, and if you survived him,
it seems to me that the Geats could not choose
a better man for king, should you wish to rule
the land of your kinsmen. Beloved Beowulf,
the longer I know you, the more I like your spirit.
Because of your exploit, your act of friendship,
there will be an end to the gross outrages,
the old enmity between Geats and Danes;
they will learn to live in peace. . . ."

(Hrothgar gives Beowulf twelve rich gifts and bids him an affectionate farewell.)

Then Beowulf the warrior,
proudly adorned with gold, crossed the plain,
exulting in his treasure. The ship
rode at anchor, waiting for its owner.
Then, as they walked, they often praised
Hrothgar's generosity. He was an altogether
faultless king, until old age deprived him
of his strength, as it does most men.
Then that troop of brave young retainers
came to the water's edge; they wore ring-mail,
woven corslets. And the same watchman
who had seen them arrive saw them now returning.
He did not insult them, ask for explanations,
but galloped from the cliff-top to greet the guests;
he said that those warriors in gleaming armour,
so eager to embark, would be welcomed home.
Then the spacious ship, with its curved prow,
standing ready on the shore, was laden with armour,
with horses and treasure. The mast towered
over Hrothgar's precious heirlooms.
Beowulf gave a sword bound round with gold

to the ship's watchman—a man who thereafter
was honoured on the mead-bench that much the more
on account of this heirloom.
The ship surged forward, butted the waves in deep waters;
it drew away from the shores of the Scyldings.
Then a sail, a great sea-garment, was fastened
with guys to the mast; the timbers groaned;
the boat was not blown off its course
by the stiff sea-breezes. The ship swept
over the waves; foaming at the bows,
the boat with its well-wrought prow sped
over the waters, until at last the Geats
set eyes on the cliffs of their own country,
the familiar headlands; the vessel pressed forward,
pursued by the wind—it ran up onto dry land.
The harbour guardian hurried down to the shore;
for many days he had scanned the horizon,
anxious to see those dear warriors once more.
He tethered the spacious sea-steed with ropes
(it rode on its painter restlessly)
so that the rolling waves could not wrench it away.
Then Beowulf commanded that the peerless treasures,
the jewels and plated gold, be carried up from the shore.
He had not to go far to find the treasure-giver,
Hygelac son of Hrethel, for his house and the hall
for his companions stood quite close to the sea-wall. . . .
Then Beowulf and his warrior band walked
across the sand, tramped over
the wide foreshore; the world's candle shone,
the sun hastening from the south. The men hurried too
when they were told that the guardian of thanes,
Ongentheow's slayer, the excellent young king,
held court in the hall, distributing rings.
Hygelac was informed at once of Beowulf's arrival—
that the shield of warriors, his comrade in battle,
had come back alive to the fortified enclosure,
was heading for the hall unscathed after combat.
Space on the benches for Beowulf and his band
was hastily arranged, as Hygelac ordered.
The guardian of thanes formally greeted
that loyal man; then they sat down—
the unfated hero opposite the king,
kinsman facing kinsman. Haereth's daughter[19]
carried mead-cups round the hall,
spoke kindly to the warriors, handed the stoups
of wine to the thanes. Hygelac began
to ask his companion courteous questions
in the high hall; he was anxious to hear
all that had happened to the seafaring Geats: . . .

(Beowulf begins to tell about his exploits in Denmark. He digresses to report some news that will interest Hygelac: that Hrothgar has betrothed his daughter Freawaru to Ingeld, prince of the Heathobards, in an effort to heal a long-standing feud. Beowulf predicts that this well-intentioned effort at peacemaking will fail.

He then picks up his story again and tells how he killed Grendel and Grendel's mother.)

Then Beowulf caused to be brought in
a standard bearing the image of a boar,
together with a helmet towering in battle,
a grey corslet, and a noble sword; he said:
"Hrothgar, the wise king, gave me
these trappings and purposely asked me
to tell you their history: he said that Heorogar,
lord of the Scyldings, long owned them.
Yet he has not endowed his own brave son,
Heoroweard, with this armour, much
as he loves him. Make good use of everything!"
I heard that four bays, apple-brown,
were brought into the hall after the armour—
swift as the wind, identical. Beowulf gave them
as he gave the treasures. So should a kinsman do,
and never weave nets with underhand subtlety
to ensnare others, never have designs

19. ***Haereth's daughter,*** the young queen, Hygd.

Lid and Lock for a Purse, found at Sutton Hoo in 1939.
Courtesy of the Trustees of The British Museum.

on a close comrade's life. His nephew,
brave in battle, was loyal to Hygelac;
each man was mindful of the other's pleasure.
I heard that he gave Hygd the collar,
the wondrous ornament with which Wealhtheow,
daughter of the prince, had presented him,
and gave her three horses also, graceful creatures
with brightly-coloured saddles; Hygd
wore that collar, her breast was adorned. . . .

Then the guardian of thanes, the famous king,
ordered that Hrethel's gold-adorned heirloom
be brought in; no sword was so treasured
in all Geatland; he laid it in Beowulf's lap,
and gave him seven thousand hides of land,
a hall and princely throne. Both men
had inherited land and possessions
in that country; but the more spacious kingdom
had fallen to Hygelac, who was of higher rank.

Discussion

1. Describe Beowulf's battle with Grendel and the battle with Grendel's mother with regard to **(a)** the kinds of difficulties he faces; **(b)** the preparations he makes; **(c)** the supernatural elements involved, if any; **(d)** the extent to which the poet forecasts what will happen; **(e)** the outcome of the battle.

2. In lines 452–499, Beowulf tells the story of his swimming match with Breca and the dangers he met and overcame. What foreshadowings of his future exploits are there in his early adventure?

3. Minor characters in this epic are important, both for what they reveal about Beowulf's character and the parts they play in the action of the poem. Discuss these points with regard to Hrothgar and Wealhtheow.

4. Unferth and Beowulf engage in the kind of nearly ritual name-calling that often occurs in heroic literature. Does this episode advance or retard the story? What do the two participants reveal about themselves? Can you think of any contemporary situations in which this kind of insult-match is tolerated (for example, athletic competitions or political contests)?

5. Like most epic heroes, Beowulf embodies the qualities of character that were most admired by the people of his time and place. **(a)** Reconstruct the code of conduct of an ideal Anglo-Saxon warrior and king as you see it revealed in this poem. Which parts of the code do you consider to be valid today? **(b)** What character traits are criticized in the poem, either directly or indirectly? Does Beowulf possess any of these traits? Explain.

6. One critic has commented: "*Beowulf* is at least in part a study of kingship—of the attributes of a good king, of the difficulties he faces and how he overcomes them, of the problems of succession that arise upon his death." Discuss the validity of this statement, making references to the text to support your view.

7. *Beowulf* contains characteristics associated with folklore or fairy tales—lurid and sensational events, man-eating monsters. Why, with these elements, has the poem appealed to sophisticated audiences for more than twelve hundred years? Are there counterparts to *Beowulf* in modern entertainment media?

8. The description of the place where Grendel and his mother live, beginning on line 1052, is considered one of the masterpieces of Old English poetry. Explain why this might be true.

9. Descriptive comparisons known as *kennings* were poetic devices often used by Anglo-Saxon poets. Identify and explain some of the ones you found in the poem.

10. The scholar J. R. R. Tolkien has suggested that the theme of *Beowulf* deals with "man alien in a hostile world, engaged in a struggle which he cannot win. . . ." Do you agree with this? In what way does modern "alienation" differ from the alienation depicted in *Beowulf?* In what way is it similar?

Extension • Writing

1. Pretend you are Grendel (or Grendel's mother). Write a diary from the monster's point of view, recording at least one week in his life.

2. Write a complete description of Grendel or his mother. Use details given in the poem, but fill them out with further appropriate details.

3. Prepare a dialogue in which a modern student discusses with an Anglo-Saxon youth both the content and philosophy of *Beowulf.* Each is to maintain the viewpoint of the age to which he belongs.

4. Prepare a character sketch of Beowulf in youth and old age. Discuss his physical attributes and his character, pointing out both positive and negative qualities.

5. Retell the events in *Beowulf* from the viewpoint of one of the following: **(a)** a historian writing objectively about the age; **(b)** a writer of a newspaper epitaph on Beowulf's death; **(c)** a novelist gathering material for a historical novel; **(d)** a relative of Grendel's reporting Beowulf's death to other relatives; **(e)** a television or motion picture scenario writer preparing to turn this folk epic into a TV or film epic.

6. Choose an incident in *Beowulf* and turn it into a film script. Include specific camera and lighting directions, as well as dialogue if any is needed. Try to get across the atmosphere of the scene.

7. Persons considered to possess heroic qualities reflect the values and morals of their society. Compare the Anglo-Saxon hero with a person whom you consider to be a hero in our society. React to the statement about morals and values in your essay.

Extension • Speaking

1. Kevin Crossley-Holiand has said that *Beowulf* must be read aloud to be appreciated. Join with some of your classmates in preparing a part of it for oral presentation. One or more students could serve as general narrators, and others take the parts of individual characters.

2. Prepare a portion of *Beowulf* for class presentation as it was performed by the *scop* in Anglo-Saxon England. You will need a stringed instrument to strike chords when you pronounce the accented syllables.

Vocabulary • Context, Pronunciation, Structure, and Dictionary

A. Using context—the setting in which the word appears—as an aid, write the appropriate definition for each italicized word on a separate sheet of paper.

1. "I have never heard a warrior / speak more *sagely* while still so young." **(a)** foolishly; **(b)** wisely; **(c)** rashly; **(d)** loudly.

2. "A great *lament* was lifted, after the feast / an anguished cry." **(a)** table; **(b)** weight; **(c)** wail; **(d)** cheer.

3. "May you always prosper; / win *renown* through courage, and be kind in your counsel." **(a)** fame; **(b)** disgrace; **(c)** food; **(d)** scandal.

B. Without using your Glossary, divide the following words into syllables on the same sheet of paper, then underline the syllable that has the primary stress or accent. You may then check your work with the Glossary. Be sure you understand the meaning of, and can pronounce and spell, each word.

4. damascene
5. redoubtable
6. lineage
7. assuage

C. Answer on your paper the following questions about the structure—affixes and roots—of the italicized words below. You will need to use your Glossary.

8. **(a)** When it is said of Grendel that he "left this *transitory* life," and when it is said of a noble man that his "*transient* body . . . withers," do the italicized words suggest (1) permanence or (2) instability? **(b)** What common prefix do the words share? **(c)** What is the meaning of the Latin root word that combines with the prefix to form the ultimate source of the word *transient?*

9. **(a)** What is the spelling and the meaning of the Latin root word with which the prefix *in-* combines in *insidious?* **(b)** What is the meaning of the Latin root for *intrepid?* **(c)** The spelling of prefixes in *insidious* and *intrepid* is the same. What do the prefixes mean?

D. Using the Glossary, answer on your paper the following questions about the italicized words.

10. **(a)** What is a one-word synonym for *enmity?* **(b)** From what two languages does the word derive?

11. **(a)** When it is said of Beowulf that he is "to *essay* the lake," what part of speech is *essay?* **(b)** What does the word mean as used here? **(c)** From what language does *essay* ultimately derive?

12. **(a)** What part of speech is *sinews* in the phrase "the *sinews* sprang apart"? **(b)** What is the Old English spelling of the word?

notes and comments

John Gardner
from Grendel

In John Gardner's blackly comic novel, the story is told by a disillusioned and despairing Grendel, disgusted with the senselessness and meanness of human life. He carries on his years-long massacre of Hrothgar's thanes, until one night he encounters Beowulf.

I touch the door with my fingertips and it bursts, for all its fire-forged bands—it jumps away like a terrified deer—and I plunge into the silent, hearth-lit hall with a laugh that I wouldn't much care to wake up to myself. I trample the planks that a moment before protected the hall like a hand raised in horror to a terrified mouth (sheer poetry, ah!) and the broken hinges rattle like swords down the timbered walls. The Geats are stones, and whether it's because they're numb with terror or stiff from too much mead, I cannot tell. I am swollen with excitement, bloodlust and joy and a strange fear that mingle in my chest like the twisting rage of a bonefire. I step onto the brightly shining floor and angrily advance on them. They're all asleep, the whole company! I can hardly believe my luck, and my wild heart laughs, but I let out no sound. Swiftly, softly, I will move from bed to bed and destroy them all, swallow every last man. I am blazing, half-crazy with joy. For pure, mad prank, I snatch a cloth from the nearest table and tie it around my neck to make a napkin. I delay no longer. I seize up a sleeping man, tear at him hungrily, bite through his bone-locks and suck hot, slippery blood. He goes down in huge morsels, head, chest, hips, legs, even the hands and feet. My face and arms are wet, matted. The napkin is sopping. The dark floor steams. I move on at once and I reach for another one (whispering, whispering, chewing the universe down to words), and I seize a wrist. A shock goes through me. Mistake!

It's a trick! His eyes are open, were open all the time, cold-bloodedly watching to see how I work. The eyes nail me now as his hand nails down my arm. I jump back without thinking (whispering wildly: *jump back without thinking.*) Now he's out of his bed, his hand still closed like a dragon's jaws on mine. Nowhere on middle-earth,[1] I realize, have I encountered a grip like his. My whole arm's on fire, incredible, searing pain—it's as if his crushing fingers are charged like fangs with poison. I scream, facing him, grotesquely shaking hands—dear long-lost brother, kinsman-thane—and the timbered hall screams back at me. I feel the bones go, ground from their sockets, and I scream again. I am suddenly awake. The long pale dream, my history, falls away. The meadhall is alive, great cavernous belly, gold-adorned, bloodstained, howling back at me, lit by the flickering fire in the stranger's eyes. He has wings. Is it possible? And yet it's true: out of his shoulders come terrible fiery wings. I jerk my head, trying to drive out illusion. The world is what it is and always was. That's our hope, our chance. Yet even in times of catastrophe we people it with tricks. Grendel, Grendel, hold fast to what is true!

Suddenly, darkness. My sanity has won. He's only a man; I can escape him. I plan. I feel the plan moving inside me like thaw-time waters rising between cliffs. When I'm ready, I give a ferocious kick—but something's wrong: I am spinning—*Wa!*—falling through bottomless space—*Wa!*—snatching at the huge twisted roots of an oak . . . a blinding flash of fire . . . no, darkness. I concentrate. I have fallen! Slipped on blood. He viciously twists my arm behind my back. By accident, it comes to me, I have given him a greater advantage. I could laugh. *Woe, woe!*

And now something worse. He's whispering—spilling words like showers of sleet, his mouth three inches from my ear. I will not listen. I continue whispering. As long as I whisper myself I need not hear. His syllables lick at me, chilly fire. His syllables lick at me, chilly fire. His syllables lick at me, chilly fire. His syllables lick . . .

1. ***middle-earth,*** the human world, regarded as midway between heaven and hell.

Discussion

1. In this excerpt, Grendel anticipates another confrontation with Hrothgar's warriors. How is his excitement conveyed?

2. Does this account change the traditional image of Beowulf?

3. What effect, if any, does having Grendel tell his own story have on your concept of Grendel's character as delineated in the Anglo-Saxon epic poem?

4. One critic has stated that *Grendel* "is a first-person account of Grendel the monster, a study of maniacal drive, fear, loneliness, and craving for communication." Comment as to why this might be an accurate description.

Extension • Writing

1. Write a character sketch of Grendel as he is portrayed by Gardner.

2. Write an account of the battle between Grendel's mother and Beowulf from the mother's point of view.

3. Write a film script for this incident from *Grendel.* Include all stage, camera, and lighting directions.

notes and comments

Richard Wilbur

Upon reading the account of Beowulf from the Anglo-Saxon epic, Wilbur, a contemporary American poet, was moved to write this poem analyzing some of the events of the epic twelve hundred years after they occurred.

Beowulf

The land was overmuch like scenery,
The flowers attentive, the grass too garrulous green;
In the lake like a dropped kerchief could be seen
The lark's reflection after the lark was gone;
The Roman road lay paved too shiningly
For a road so many men had traveled on.

Also the people were strange, were strangely warm.
The king recalled the father of his guest,
The queen brought mead in a studded cup, the rest
Were kind, but in all was a vagueness and a strain,
Because they lived in a land of daily harm.
And they said the same things again and again.

It was a childish country; and a child,
Grown monstrous, so besieged them in the night
That all their daytimes were a dream of fright
That it would come and own them to the bone.
The hero, to his battle reconciled,
Promised to meet that monster all alone.

So then the people wandered to their sleep
And left him standing in the echoed hall.
They heard the rafters rattle fit to fall,
The child departing with a broken groan,
And found their champion in a rest so deep
His head lay harder sealed than any stone.

Discussion

1. How does Wilbur's version differ from or extend the original story?

2. In the original version, the story is complex and suspense is created. Why did Wilbur simplify the story and deliberately leave out the element of suspense?

3. At first reading, stanzas 1 and 5 might appear to bc reversed. It seems that stanza 5 should occur before Beowulf's arrival. That it does not is a clue to the interpretation of the poem. Explain.

4. What comment does Wilbur seem to be making about human nature by describing the people "strangely warm" on Beowulf's arrival and "strangely cold" when he leaves?

5. Wilbur emphasizes that Grendel is a "child." **(a)** In so doing, what is he saying about Grendel? **(b)** What does this portrait of Grendel do to the heroic image of Beowulf?

The land was overmuch like scenery,
The lake gave up the lark, but now its song
Fell to no ear, the flowers too were wrong,
The day was fresh and pale and swiftly old,
The night put out no smiles upon the sea;
And the people were strange, the people strangely cold.

They gave him horse and harness, helmet and mail,
A jeweled shield, an ancient battle-sword,
Such gifts as are the hero's hard reward
And bid him do again what he has done.
These things he stowed beneath his parting sail,
And wept that he could share them with no son.

He died in his own country a kinless king,
A name heavy with deeds, and mourned as one
Will mourn for the frozen year when it is done.
They buried him next the sea on a thrust of land:
Twelve men rode round his barrow all in a ring,
Singing of him what they could understand.

The Battle of Brunanburh

Translated by Burton Raffel

This epic poem, celebrating the victory of Athelstan, king of Wessex, over forces of Danes, Welsh, and Scots, is a tenth-century imitation of Old English epic poetry. In the Anglo-Saxon Chronicle, *the poem appeared under the year 937. The battle scene has never been definitely determined, but is believed to be located somewhere on or near the northwest coast of England.*

This was the year when Athelstan, king
Of Wessex, prince among earls and patron
Of heroes, and his noble brother, Edmund,
Hacked a lifelong glory from a battle
Near Brunanburh. They shattered the phalanx,
Their swords splintered the linden shields,
And the sons of Edward followed their father,
Proved the blood they had tested in battle
Before, defending their land and their homes
Against every invader. The enemy ran,
All the Scotch and the ship-borne Vikings,
Ran or drowned in blood, dropped
To a land-locked fate as the glorious sun
Went gliding over the earth like a candle
In God's broad palm, blowing sublimely
Across the sky and dipping calmly
To darkness and night. The dead lay piled
Where the spears had left them, Vikings and
Scots,
Tired, now, of the struggle and wanting
Only to rest. All the battle
Became the Wessex cavalry endlessly
Hunting a broken enemy, their honed
And sparkling blades striking home
In fugitives' backs. No Mercian refused
To aim his sword at any man
Who'd shared a sail with Anlaf, shipped
Himself across a stormy sea
To a bloody port. Five young princes
Pitched their beds on the battle-ground
And would never awake, and seven of Anlaf's
Earls, and a host of invaders, Viking
And Scotch. Anlaf himself fought
His way to the prow of a ship, he
And a tiny band, forced to flee;
They pressed to sea on a dull brown tide
That floated the king to safety. Nor
Did the old one, Constantine, trailing
Defeat behind him all the way north,
Find exultation following his steps
Or boasts on his lips; he left his kinsmen
And friends scattered over the field,
Butchered to silence, and abandoned his son
On the heaps of the slain, an untried soldier
Cut into failure. No, the crafty
Grey-beard had no need to be vain, and no more
Had Anlaf: watching their wreck of an army
Nothing welled up into laughter
Or pride that they and theirs were England's
Best for the job of battle, the crashing
Of standards, the thrust of spears, the cut
And slash of dagger and sword; they felt
No pleasure at having frolicked with Edward's
Sons. They fled in their mail-clad ships,
The blood-stained Northmen, over a deep and
noisy
Sea to Dublin, back again
To Ireland, ashamed, disgraced. But those ashes
Of defeat were the sweetest taste of victory
In the brothers' mouths, Wessex king
And Wessex prince, returning home
Together. They left a gift of dismembered
Corpses to the horny beak of the black-
plumaged

Raven, and the grey-feathered eagle, splashed
white
On his tail, to the greedy war-hawk and the
grey-flanked
Forest wolf, a feast of carcasses
For lovers of carrion meat. No carnage
Had ever been bloodier, in any battle
Fought anywhere on this island, say the books
Of the old philosophers, not since the Angles
And Saxons arrived in England out of
The East, brave men trying a broad
And dangerous sea, daring warriors
Who swept away the Britons, seized
The land and made it theirs alone.

Discussion

1. Since both *Beowulf* and *The Battle of Brunanburh* are epics, the tone is heroic. Even so, the tone is different. What is the difference?

2. Critics have stated that the vividness of this epic suggests that it was composed by a person on or near the scene of the battle. Which particular lines would support this assumption?

notes and comments

Jorge Luis Borges

The Battle of Brunanburh provides the setting for Borges, a twentieth-century Argentine writer, to reflect on the personal loss that individuals experience during any war.

Brunanburh, A.D. 937

No one at your side.
Last night I did a man to death in battle.
He was spirited and tall, of the clear line of Anlaf.
He tumbled on the ground and was a thing,
an object for crows.
Vainly will you await him, woman I have not seen.
They will not bear him back, the ships which fled
over the yellow waters.
In the hour of the dawn,
out of a dream, your hand will reach for him.
Your bed is cold.
Last night I killed a man in Brunanburh.

Discussion

1. Borges focuses on the personal loss associated with war. How does he convey this loss?

2. How does the tone of this poem differ from that of the original epic?

Extension • Writing

Write a narrative or poetic response from the point of view of the wife of the dead soldier. Either keep the same outlook toward war that Borges expresses, or assume a different attitude.

The Wanderer

Translated by Kevin Crossley-Holland

"The Wanderer" consists of a monologue spoken by a character whose fate it is to roam the seas in search of a lord to replace his dead "gold-friend." The speaker acquires wisdom through his grim wanderings. This bleak monologue is flanked by two moralizing passages. It has been suggested that the monk who wrote down the poem might have been trying to make its essentially pagan spirit more acceptable to a Christian audience by adding these expressions of faith in God to the poem.

The lonely wanderer prays often for compassion
And for mercy from Lord God; but for a long time
Destiny decrees that with a heavy heart he must dip
His oars into icy waters, working his passage over the sea.
He must follow the paths of exile. Fate is inexorable!

The wanderer's mind moved upon adversity
And savage slaughter and the ruin of kinsmen. He said,
"Time and again at the day's dawning
I must mourn all my afflictions alone.
There is no one still living to whom I dare open
The doors of my heart. I have no doubt
That it is a noble habit for a man
To bind fast all his heart's feelings with silence,
Whatever his impulse, his inclinations.

The weary in spirit cannot withstand fate;
Nothing comes of rankling resentment.
For this reason any man ambitious for renown
Confines his unhappiness to his own heart.
So ever since the day I covered my gold-friend
With dark clods of earth, I have had to keep
My thoughts to myself, and this despite my grief,
Cut off from free kinsmen, so far away
From my own dear country; for I left that land,
Ploughed the icy waves with winter in my heart;
In utter dejection I journeyed far and wide
Hunting for the hall of a generous gold-giver. . . .
For a man who would welcome me into his mead-hall,
Give me good cheer, (for I boasted no friends)
Entertain me with delights. He who has experienced it
Knows what a cruel companion sorrow can be
To any man who has few loyal friends.
For him are the ways of exile, in no wise twisted gold!
For him is a frozen body, in no wise the fruits of the earth!
He remembers hall-retainers and how in his youth
He had taken treasure from the hands of his gold-friend
After the feast. Those joys have all vanished.

A man who lacks advice for a long while
From his lord and friend lives thus in his loneliness:
In restless sleep he dreams that he clasps
And kisses his lord, and lays hands and head
Upon his lord's knee just as he had done
When he approached the gift-throne previously.
Then the lonely wanderer wakes again
And sees the dark waves surging around him,
The sea-birds bathing and spreading their feathers,
Snow flakes falling mingled with hail.

Then his wounds lie more heavy in his heart,
Aching for his lord. His sorrows are renewed;
The memory of kinsmen sweeps through his mind;
He welcomes them with songs, eagerly scans
His comrade warriors. Then they melt away again.
Their spirits do not bring many old songs

The Beginning of the Gospel of Saint Mark, The Book of Durrow fol.86. The Board of Trinity College, Dublin.

To his lips. Sorrow and care constantly
Attend the man who must send time and again
His weary heart over the frozen waves.
And thus I cannot understand why in the world
My mind is not tormented
When I brood on the fate of many brave warriors,
How they have suddenly had to leave the mead-hall,
The bold friends and followers. So it is this world
Day by day dwindles, and passes away;
For a man will not be wise until he has suffered
His share of winters in the world. A wise man must be patient,
Neither passionate nor hasty of speech,
Neither rash nor irresolute in battle;
He should not be timid, despairing, grasping,
And never eager to boast before he can implement it.
When it is his turn to boast a man must bide his time
Until he has no doubt in his brave heart
That he has resolved upon the right action.
A wise man must fathom how frightening it will be
When all the riches of the world stand waste,
As now in diverse places in this middle-earth
Old walls stand, tugged at by the winds
And hung with hoar-frost, buildings in decay.
The wine-halls crumble, heartbroken lords
Lie dead, all the proud followers
Have fallen by the wall. Battle laid claim to some,
Leading them on long journeys; the raven carried one
High over the waters, and one the grey wolf
Devoured; a warrior with downcast face
Hid yet another in an earth-cave.
Thus the Creator laid this world waste
Until the ancient works of the giants were deserted,
Hushed without the hubbub of milling inhabitants.
Then he who contemplates these noble ruins,
And who deeply ponders this dark life,
Wise in his mind, will often remember
The countless slaughters of the past and speak these words:
Where has the horse gone? Where the man? Where the giver of gold?
Where is the feasting-place? And where the pleasures of the hall?
I mourn the gleaming cup, the warrior in his corselet,
The glory of the prince. How time has passed away,
Darkened under the shadow of night even as if it had never been.
Where the beloved warriors were, there now stands a wall
Of miraculous height, carved with serpent forms.
The savage ash-spears, avid for slaughter,
Have claimed all the warriors—inexorable fate!
Storms crash against these rocky slopes;
Falling sleet and snow fetter the world;
Winter howls, then darkness draws on,
The night-shadow casts gloom and brings

The Lion, Symbol of Saint Mark, The Book of Durrow fol.191v. The Board of Trinity College, Dublin.

Fierce hailstorms from the north to frighten men.
Nothing is ever easy in the kingdom of earth,
The world beneath the heavens is in the hands of fate.
Worldly possessions are ephemeral, friends pass away,
Here man is transient and kinsman transient,
The whole world becomes a wilderness."
So spoke the wise man in his heart as he sat apart in secret thought.
He who is wise adheres to his beliefs; a brave man
Will not reveal the torments in his heart
Before he knows their remedy. It is best for a man to seek
Comfort and compassion from the Father in Heaven where we will all find security.

Discussion

1. How do you explain the relationship of the beginning and ending of the poem to the rest of the poem?

2. Beginning with line 62 there is a shift in the poem. How would you relate the first part of the poem to the latter part?

Extension • Writing

The wanderer laments the harshness of the world in which he lives. He viewed both human beings and nature as cruel. In a short essay, agree or disagree with the wanderer's view of the world, and state your reasons for doing so.

Carpet page with Inlaid Panels, The Book of Durrow fol.125v. The Board of Trinity College, Dublin.

The Wanderer

W. H. Auden

The enduring appeal of Anglo-Saxon poetry is revealed in its influence on later poets. The early poetry of the modern English poet W. H. Auden, for example, reflects his appreciation of the older verse. As the title suggests, inspiration for this poem came from the Anglo-Saxon lyric of the same name.

Doom is dark and deeper than any sea-dingle.
Upon what man it fall
In spring, day-wishing flowers appearing,
Avalanche sliding, white snow from rock-face,
That he should leave his house,
No cloud-soft hand can hold him, restraint by women;
but ever that man goes
Through place-keepers, through forest trees,
A stranger to strangers over undried sea,
Houses for fishes, suffocating water,
Or lonely on fell as chat,[1]
By pot-holed becks[2]
A bird-stone-haunting, an unquiet bird.

There head falls forward, fatigued at evening,
And dreams of home,
Waving from window, spread of welcome,
Kissing of wife under single sheet;
But waking sees
Bird-flocks nameless to him, through doorway voices
Of new men making another love.

Save him from hostile capture,
From sudden tiger's spring at corner;
Protect his house,
His anxious house where days are counted
From thunderbolt protect,
From gradual ruin spreading like a stain;
Converting number from vague to certain,
Bring joy, bring day of his returning,
Lucky with day approaching, with leaning dawn.

Discussion

Like the Anglo-Saxon poem, Auden's expresses extreme loneliness and sadness. Reread lines 37–55 of the Anglo-Saxon poem and show how the Auden poem is related.

1. ***Or lonely . . . chat,*** solitary as a bird (chat) on a barren hill (fell).
2. ***becks,*** rocky-bottomed streams.

Like "The Wanderer," these two poems are examples of Anglo-Saxon lyric poetry. They are similar because they show the loneliness of separation. The wife in "The Wife's Lament" has been banished because of accusations by her husband's parents. A wooden staff conveys the loneliness of a husband exiled from his wife and his people in "The Husband's Message." Because the manuscript was torn, "The Husband's Message" contains runes (lines 49–50) that have not been deciphered.

The Man, Symbol of Saint Matthew, The Book of Durrow fol.21v. The Board of Trinity College, Dublin.

The Husband's Message

Translated by Burton Raffel

A tree grew me; I was green, and wood.
That came first. I was cut and sent
Away from my home, holding wily
Words, carried out on the ocean,
Riding a boat's back. I crossed
Stormy seas, seeking the thresholds
Where my master's message was meant to travel
And be known. And now the knotted planks
Of a ship have brought me here, and you
Shall read my lord's heart and hear
His soul's thought. I promise a glowing
Faith shall be what you find. Read.
        See: this wood has come to make you
Remember the hands that carved it, to take you
Back to the love and the pledges you shared,
You two, in that buried time when you both
Could walk unharmed across this festive
Town, the land yours, and you
Each other's. Your people fought, and the feud
Brought him exile. Now he asks you
To listen for the sad cuckoo calling
In the grove: when its song has reached the edge
Of the woods, he wants you to come to him over
The waves, letting nothing lead you
Aside and no man living stop you.
        Go down to the sea, the gull's home,
And come to a ship that can carry you south,
Away, out on the water to where
Your husband and lord longs for your coming.
Nothing the world can send him, he says
Through me, could bring him more delight
Than for Almighty God to grant him you,
And for you and he together to bless
His soldiers and friends with treasure, with hammered
Bracelets and rings. For though his home
Is with strangers, he lives in a lovely land
And is rich: shining gold surrounds him.
And though my master was driven from here,
Rushing madly down to his ship
And onto the sea, alone, only

"The Husband's Message" Reprinted from *Prairie Schooner*, Vol. XXXII, No. 2, translated by Burton Raffel, by permission of University of Nebraska Press.

Alive because he fled, and glad
To escape, yet now he is served and followed,
Loved and obeyed by many. He has beaten
Misery: there's nothing more he wants,
Oh prince's daughter, no precious gems,
No stallions, no mead-hall pleasure, no treasure
On earth, but you, you to enjoy
In spite of the ancient oath that parted you.
And I fit together an S and an R,
And E, an A, a W and D,
In an oath to prove that your pledge is sacred
To him, and his faith as steady as his heart.
As long as life shall be in him, he'll long
To fulfill the vows and the love you shared.

The Wife's Lament

Translated by Charles Kennedy

A song I sing of sorrow unceasing,
The tale of my trouble, the weight of my woe,
Woe of the present, and woe of the past,
Woe never-ending of exile and grief,
But never since girlhood greater than now.
First, the pang when my lord departed,
Far from his people, beyond the sea;
Bitter the heartache at break of dawn,
The longing for rumor in what far land
So weary a time my loved one tarried.
Far I wandered then, friendless and homeless,
Seeking for help in my heavy need.
With secret plotting his kinsmen purposed
To wedge us apart, wide worlds between,
And bitter hate. I was sick at heart.
Harshly my lord bade lodge me here.
In all this land I had few to love me,
Few that were loyal, few that were friends.
Wherefore my spirit is heavy with sorrow
To learn my beloved, my dear man and mate
Bowed by ill-fortune and bitter in heart,
Is masking his purpose and planning a wrong.
With blithe hearts often of old we boasted

That nought should part us save death alone;
All that has failed and our former love
Is now as if it had never been!
Far or near where I fly there follows
The hate of him who was once so dear.
  In this forest-grove they have fixed my abode
Under an oak in a cavern of earth,
An old cave-dwelling of ancient days,
Where my heart is crushed by the weight of my woe.
Gloomy its depths and the cliffs that o'erhang it,
Grim are its confines with thorns overgrown—
A joyless dwelling where daily the longing
For an absent loved one brings anguish of heart.
  Lovers there are who may live their love,
Joyously keeping the couch of bliss,
While I in my earth-cave under the oak
Pace to and fro in the lonely dawn.
Here must I sit through the summer-long day,
Here must I weep in affliction and woe;
Yet never, indeed, shall my heart know rest
From all its anguish, and all its ache,
Wherewith life's burdens have brought me low.
  Ever man's years are subject to sorrow,
His heart's thoughts bitter, though his bearing be blithe;
Troubled his spirit, beset with distress—
Whether all wealth of the world be his lot,
Or hunted by Fate in a far country
My beloved is sitting soul-weary and sad,
Swept by the storm, and stiff with the frost,
In a wretched cell under rocky cliffs
By severing waters encircled about—
Sharpest of sorrows my lover must suffer
Remembering always a happier home.
Woeful his fate whose doom is to wait
With longing heart for an absent love.

Discussion

1. In "The Wife's Lament" and "The Husband's Message" there are examples of alliterative verse. Identify some of the lines you consider to be good examples of this poetic device.

2. In "The Husband's Message," the narrator is the staff bearing the message from the husband. What effect, if any, does the use of this device have on the poem?

3. Later in this unit you will read examples of Anglo-Saxon riddles. Riddling was very popular with these Anglo-Saxon peoples, who were apparently fascinated with words. Why might the opening twelve lines of "The Husband's Message" be classified as a riddle?

4. As you already know, both of these poems are examples of Anglo-Saxon lyric poetry. Consult the article on lyric poetry in *Definitions of Literary Terms* (page 712), and identify those characteristics that are present in the poems.

Anglo-Saxon Riddles

Translated by Michael Alexander

The ancient custom of riddling was a popular entertainment among Anglo-Saxons. The four riddles below are a sampling of the ninety-five riddles found in the Exeter Book (See p. 50). Pretend you are an Anglo-Saxon and guess the answers. Check your answers at the bottom of the page.

26

I am the scalp of myself, skinned by my foeman:
robbed of my strength, he steeped & soaked me,
dipped me in water, whipped me out again,
set me in the sun. I soon lost there
the hairs I had had.
The hard edge
of a keen-ground knife cuts me now,
fingers fold me, and a fowl's pride
drives its treasure trail across me,
bounds again over the brown rim,
sucks the wood-dye, steps again on me,
makes his black marks.
A man then hides me
between stout shield-boards stretched with hide,
fits me with gold. There glows on me
the jewelsmith's handiwork held with wires.

Let these royal enrichments and this red dye
and splendid settings spread the glory
of the Protector of peoples—and not plague the fool.
If the sons of men will make use of me
they shall. . . .

68

The wave, over the wave, a weird thing I saw,
through-wrought, and wonderfully ornate:
a wonder on the wave—water became bone.

35

The womb of the wold, wet and cold,
bore me at first, brought me forth.
I know in my mind my making was not
through skill with fells or fleeces of wool;
there was no winding of wefts, there is no woof in me,
no thread thrumming under the thrash of strokes,
no whirring shuttle steered through me,
no weaver's reed rapped my sides.
The worms that braid the broidered silk
with Wierd cunning did not weave me;
yet anywhere over the earth's breadth
men will attest me a trustworthy garment.

Say truly, supple-minded man,
wise in words, what my name is.

47

I heard of a wonder, of words moth-eaten;
that is a strange thing, I thought, weird
that a man's song be swallowed by a worm,
his binded sentences, his bedside stand-by
rustled in the night—and the robber-guest
not one whit the wiser for the words he had mumbled.

Discussion

1. If No. 26 may be taken as typical, a riddle opens with a deliberate deception ("I am the scalp of myself") and keeps up the deception throughout. At the same time, it throws out a few clues ("fingers fold me," "a fowl's pride drives its treasure trail across me"). What are the other clues in this riddle?

2. Analyze the other riddles. Which is the most similar to No. 26 in its pattern?

26. Bible or prayer-book 35. coat of mail
47. bookworm 68. ice

Bede's History

Translated by Leo Sherley-Price

The first important writer of prose in England was a Benedictine monk—a scholar, historian, and teacher known as the Venerable Bede (673–735). Most of his many books are no longer read, but his Ecclesiastical History of the English People *is still a valuable source of information about the early history of Britain.*

Bede wrote in Latin. His History was translated into Old English by Alfred the Great (849–901), both a great king and a great man of learning. The excerpt included here tells the story of the greatest triumph achieved by the early Christian missionaries sent from Rome.

Manuscript illumination depicting the Venerable Bede. Courtesy of the Trustees of The British Museum.

While King Edwin hesitated to accept the word of God at Paulinus' preaching, he used to sit alone for hours, deliberating what religion he should follow. On one of these occasions, the man of God came to him, and laying his right hand on his head, enquired whether he remembered this sign. The king trembled, and would have fallen at his feet, but Paulinus raised him, and said in a friendly voice: "God has helped you to escape from the hands of the enemies whom you feared, and it is through His bounty that you have received the kingdom that you desired. Remember the third promise that you made, and hesitate no longer. Accept the Faith and keep the commands of Him who has delivered you from all your earthly troubles, and raised you to the glory of an earthly kingdom. If you will henceforward obey His will, which he reveals to you through me, he will save you from the everlasting doom of the wicked, and give you a place in His eternal kingdom in heaven."

When Paulinus had spoken, the king answered that he was both willing and obliged to accept the Faith which he taught, but said that he must discuss the matter with his principal advisers and friends, so that if they were in agreement, they might all be cleansed together in Christ the Fount of Life. Paulinus agreed, and the king kept his promise. He summoned a council of the wise men, and asked each in turn his opinion of this new faith and the new God being proclaimed.

Coifi, the High Priest, replied without hesitation: "Your Majesty, let us give careful consideration to this new teaching, for I frankly admit that, in my experience, the religion that we have hitherto professed seems valueless and powerless. None of your subjects has been more devoted to the service of the gods than myself, yet there are many to whom you show greater favour, and who are more successful in all their undertakings. Now, if the gods had any power, they would surely have favoured myself, who have been more zealous in their service. Therefore, if on examination these new teachings are found to be more effectual, let us not hesitate to accept them."

Another of the king's chief men signified his agreement with this prudent argument, and went on to say: "Your Majesty, when we compare the present life of man with that time of which we have no knowledge, it seems to me like the swift flight of a lone sparrow through the banqueting-hall where you sit in the winter months to dine with your thanes and counsellors. Inside there is a comforting fire to warm the room; outside the wintry storms of snow and rain are raging. This

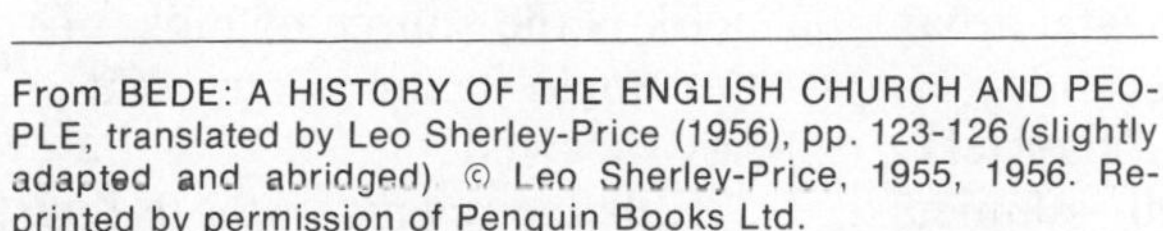

sparrow flies swiftly in through one door of the hall, and out through another. While he is inside, he is safe from the winter storms; but after a few moments of comfort, he vanishes from sight into the darkness whence he came. Similarly, man appears on earth for a little while, but we know nothing of what went before this life, and what follows. Therefore if this new teaching can reveal any more certain knowledge, it seems only right that we should follow it." The other elders and counsellors of the king, under God's guidance, gave the same advice.

Coifi then added that he wished to hear Paulinus' teaching about God in greater detail; and when, at the king's bidding, this had been given, the High Priest said: "I have long realized that there is nothing in what we worshipped. I now publicly confess that this teaching clearly reveals truths that will afford us the blessings of life, salvation, and eternal happiness. Therefore, Your Majesty, I submit that the temples and altars that we had dedicated to no advantage be immediately desecrated and burned."

And when the king asked the High Priest who should be the first to profane the altars and shrines of the idols, Coifi replied: "I will do this myself, for now that the true God has granted me knowledge, who more suitably than I can set a public example, and destroy the idols that I worshipped in ignorance?" So he asked the king to give him arms and a stallion—for hitherto it had not been lawful for the High Priest to carry arms, or to ride anything but a mare—and, thus equipped, he set out to destroy the idols. Girded with a sword and with a spear in his hand, he mounted the king's stallion and rode up to the idols.

When the crowd saw him, they thought he had gone mad, but without hesitation, as soon as he reached the temple, he cast a spear into it and profaned it. Then, full of joy at his knowledge of the worship of the true God, he told his companions to set fire to the temple. The site where these idols once stood is still shown, not far east of York, beyond the river Derwent, and is known as Goodmanham. □□

Discussion

1. In Anglo-Saxon times, the king consulted a group of wise men—the *witan*—before making any decisions. What reasons did the wise men give in Bede's version for King Edwin to adopt Christianity?

2. What can be learned about the Anglo-Saxon pagan religion from Bede's History?

3. How does the story of the bird function in Bede's account?

notes and comments

The Exeter Book

Around the year 1070, Leofric, the first bishop of Exeter Cathedral, presented to the cathedral library an old manuscript which the library catalogue described as "a big English book about every sort of thing, wrought in song-wise." Into this book, monks had copied (sometimes carelessly), a miscellaneous collection of Anglo-Saxon poems.

Because Exeter is inland, it escaped the destructions of the Danish raids on coastal areas. However, the vicissitudes of a thousand years had their effects on the ancient volume. The front was used at one time as a cutting-board and as a beer mat, and the back fourteen pages were burned through by a brand. Nevertheless, this book is the source of most of the Anglo-Saxon poetry that has survived.

Half the poems in the Exeter

Book are paraphrases of Old Testament stories or lives of the saints; the others are on secular subjects out of the pagan past. Several of the most important poems are **elegies**—melancholy thoughts about loneliness, the mutability of earthly things, the terrors of the northern winter, the immensity and cruelty of the sea, and impending fate. The lyrics do not sing of the deeds of courageous heroes as do the epics; instead they reflect in a personal tone the somberer aspects of Anglo-Saxon life. Like *Beowulf* and other early epic poems, these lyrics developed orally, and use the same alliterative verse, kennings, and other poetic devices.

nuscript Illumination of Alfred the Great, Cotton MS. D II, f.8.
produced by permission of the British Library Board.

Louis MacNeice

Bede's story of the briefly glimpsed bird has haunted English writers ever since it was told. Here is one retelling in modern English by a contemporary poet, Louis MacNeice.

Dark Age Glosses on the Venerable Bede

Birds flitting in and out of the barn
Bring back an Anglo-Saxon story:
The great wooden hall with long fires down the centre,
Their feet in the rushes, their hands tearing the meat.
Suddenly high above them they notice a swallow enter
Then out once more into the unknown night;
And that, someone remarks, is the life of man.
But now it is time to sleep; one by one
They rise from the bench and their gigantic shadows
Lurch on the shuddering walls. How can the world

Or the non-world beyond harbour a bird?
They close their eyes that smart from the woodsmoke: how
Can anyone even guess his whence and whither?
This indoors flying makes it seem absurd,
Although it itches and nags and flutters and yearns,
To postulate any other life than now.

Discussion

1. **(a)** In the Bede version, what are the various elements of analogy between the bird's flight and man's life? **(b)** Which lines convey the same elements of analogy in the MacNeice version?

2. In both versions, the time is night and the weather stormy. How would it change the effect to make the time daylight and the weather sunny?

Extension • Writing

1. Find an analogy for life (like the bird) and write a narrative or poem of its effect on you or someone else. Life is like an electric light bulb . . . a book . . . a bee snatching honey from a flower . . . a moth fluttering briefly at the light . . . a jet zooming overhead . . . Create your own analogy.

2. Bede's account seems to convey religious affirmation, while MacNeice's version expresses religious doubt. If you agree with this statement, write an essay defending the statement; if you do not agree, write an essay giving your reasons for not supporting the statement.

Vocabulary
Structure, Pronunciation, and Dictionary

A. Use your Glossary and its pronunciation key to answer the following questions about the pronunciation of the italicized words. If more than one pronunciation is given, use the first (the more common) one. Write your answers on a separate sheet of paper. Be sure that you know the meaning of, and can pronounce and spell, each italicized word.

1. The vowel sound in *blithe* is the same as in which of the following words? **(a)** strive; **(b)** free; **(c)** give; **(d)** proof; **(e)** let.

2. **(a)** How many syllables does *effectual* have? **(b)** Which syllable receives the primary or main stress? **(c)** Write a rhyme word for the *third syllable only.*

3. When the word *postulate* is used as a verb, which of the following is a rhyme word for the last syllable? **(a)** fit; **(b)** bat; **(c)** treat; **(d)** great; **(e)** hot.

4. **(a)** How many schwa (ə) sounds does *inexorable* have? **(b)** Which syllable receives the main stress? **(c)** Write a rhyme word for that syllable.

B. Use your Glossary to answer the following questions about the history or structure of the words given below. Read each clue and then write on your paper the matching word from the list.

attest	ephemeral	hone
profane	supple	tarry

5. Which word has as its root a Latin word that could mean someone who appears in a courtroom?

6. Which refers to an object that could be used to make weapons more deadly?

7. Which word is based upon a Greek root that refers to a part of the week?

8. Which word has a root that refers to a place of worship?

9. Which word, in an out-of-date meaning no longer in ordinary use, might describe what one does at a bus stop?

10. Which comes from a Latin word that could describe an action one might perform while getting exercise?

Unit Review Tests 1: The Anglo-Saxons

CONTENT REVIEW

Choose the letter that represents the best answer for each statement.

1. The only full-length epic poem extant from the Anglo-Saxon period is **(a)** *"The Husband's Message"*; **(b)** *Beowulf;* **(c)** "The Battle of Brunanburh"; **(d)** "The Wanderer."

2. Which of the following statements about Anglo-Saxon lyric poetry is incorrect? **(a)** Most of it was preserved in the Exeter Book. **(b)** The tone of Anglo-Saxon lyric poetry was often elegiac. **(c)** "The Wanderer" is an Anglo-Saxon lyric poem. **(d)** None of the poetic devices found in *Beowulf* are also found in Anglo-Saxon lyric poetry.

3. *Beowulf* contains all of the following poetic devices except **(a)** alliteration; **(b)** kennings; **(c)** end rhyme; **(d)** caesuras.

4. *Beowulf* can best be described as **(a)** a historical account; **(b)** a pagan epic with Christian references; **(c)** a Christian epic with pagan references; **(d)** a lyric poem about an Anglo-Saxon hero.

5. "Ring-giver," "Spear-Danes," and "whale-road" are all examples of **(a)** alliteration; **(b)** personification; **(c)** kennings; **(d)** caesuras.

6. In Anglo-Saxon lyric poetry, the elements of nature are usually described as **(a)** peaceful; **(b)** constantly changing; **(c)** kind; **(d)** cruel.

Unit 1, Test I
INTERPRETATION: NEW MATERIAL

The Seafarer

Translated by Burton Raffel

This poem was probably composed early in the eighth century. It is found in the Exeter Book—one of the four important collections of the surviving poetry of the Anglo-Saxon period. It stresses a theme or motif that has recurred throughout the ages of English literature—the haunting beauty, the foreboding terror, and the unfathomed mystery of the sea. The poem is the monologue of an old sailor.

This tale is true, and mine. It tells
How the sea took me, swept me back
And forth in sorrow and fear and pain,
Showed me suffering in a hundred ships,
In a thousand ports, and in me. It tells
Of smashing surf when I sweated in the cold
Of an anxious watch, perched in the bow
As it dashed under cliffs. My feet were cast
In icy bands, bound with frost,
With frozen chains, and hardship groaned
Around my heart. Hunger tore
At my sea-weary soul. No man sheltered
On the quiet fairness of earth can feel
How wretched I was, drifting through winter
On an ice-cold sea, whirled in sorrow,
Alone in a world blown clear of love,
Hung with icicles. The hailstorms flew.
The only sound was the roaring sea,
The freezing waves. The song of the swan
Might serve for pleasure, the cry of the sea-fowl,

The death-noise of birds instead of laughter,
The mewing of gulls instead of mead.
Storms beat on the rocky cliffs and were echoed
By icy-feathered terns and the eagle's screams;
No kinsman could offer comfort there,
To a soul left drowning in desolation.
And who could believe, knowing but
The passion of cities, swelled proud with wine
And no taste of misfortune, how often, how wearily,
I put myself back on the paths of the sea.
Night would blacken; it would snow from the north;
Frost bound the earth and hail would fall,
The coldest seeds. And how my heart
Would begin to beat, knowing once more
The salt waves tossing and the towering sea!
The time for journeys would come and my soul
Called me eagerly out, sent me over
The horizon, seeking foreigners' homes.
But there isn't a man on earth so proud,
So born to greatness, so bold with his youth,
Grown so brave, or so graced by God,
That he feels no fear as the sails unfurl,
Wondering what Fate has willed and will do.
No harps ring in his heart, no rewards,
No passion for women, no worldly pleasures,
Nothing, only the ocean's heave;
But longing wraps itself around him.
Orchards blossom, the towns bloom,
Fields grow lovely as the world springs fresh,
And all these admonish that willing mind
Leaping to journeys, always set
In thoughts travelling on a quickening tide.
So summer's sentinel, the cuckoo, sings
In his murmuring voice, and our hearts mourn
As he urges. Who could understand,
In ignorant ease, what we others suffer
As the paths of exile stretch endlessly on?
And yet my heart wanders away,
My soul roams with the sea, the whales'
Home, wandering to the widest corners
Of the world, returning ravenous with desire,
Flying solitary, screaming, exciting me
To the open ocean, breaking oaths
On the curve of a wave.
Thus the joys of God
Are fervent with life, where life itself
Fades quickly into the earth. The wealth
Of the world neither reaches to Heaven nor remains.
No man has ever faced the dawn
Certain which of Fate's three threats
Would fall: illness, or age, or an enemy's
Sword, snatching the life from his soul.
The praise the living pour on the dead
Flowers from reputation: plant
An earthly life of profit reaped
Even from hatred and rancour, of bravery
Flung in the devil's face, and death
Can only bring you earthly praise
And a song to celebrate a place
With the angels, life eternally blessed
In the hosts of Heaven.
The days are gone
When the kingdoms of earth flourished in glory;
Now there are no rulers, no emperors,
No givers of gold, as once there were,
When wonderful things were worked among them
And they lived in lordly magnificence.
Those powers have vanished, those pleasures are dead,
The weakest survives and the world continues,
Kept spinning by toil. All glory is tarnished,
The world's honor ages and shrinks,
Bent like the men who mould it. Their faces
Blanch as time advances, their beards
Wither and they mourn the memory of friends,
The sons of princes, sown in the dust.
The soul stripped of its flesh knows nothing
Of sweetness or sour, feels no pain,
Bends neither its hand nor its brain. A brother
Opens his palms and pours down gold
On his kinsman's grave, strewing his coffin
With treasures intended for Heaven, but nothing
Golden shakes the wrath of God
For a soul overflowing with sin, and nothing
Hidden on earth rises to Heaven.
We all fear God. He turns the earth,
He set it swinging firmly in space,
Gave life to the world and light to the sky.
Death leaps at the fools who forget their God.
He who lives humbly has angels from Heaven
To carry him courage and strength and belief.
A man must conquer pride, not kill it,
Be firm with his fellows, chaste for himself,
Treat all the world as the world deserves,
With love or with hate but never with harm,
Though an enemy seek to scorch him in hell,
Or set the flames of a funeral pyre
Under his lord. Fate is stronger
And God mightier than any man's mind.

Our thoughts should turn to where our home is,
Consider the ways of coming there,
Then strive for sure permission for us
To rise to that eternal joy,
That life born in the love of God
And the hope of Heaven. Praise the Holy
Grace of He who honored us,
Eternal, unchanging creator of earth. Amen.

On a separate sheet of paper write your answers to the following questions. Do not write in your book.

1. What kind of poem is "The Seafarer"? **(a)** epic; **(b)** lyric; **(c)** riddle.

2. Rewrite only the alliterating words from the following line: "Showed me suffering in a hundred ships."

3. What is the break or pause in the middle of the following line called: "How wretched I was, drifting through winter"? **(a)** kenning; **(b)** scop; **(c)** alliteration; **(d)** caesura.

4. **(a)** What season of the year is described in lines 48–49? **(b)** What effect does the speaker say the season has on the seafarer's thoughts of travel?

5. What does the phrase "whales' home" (lines 59–60) refer to?

6. What are some of the reasons the speaker gives to explain why he goes to sea?

7. What three threats does the speaker say every person faces with the dawn of each day?

8. How does the speaker say earthly praise is to be won (lines 72–80)?

9. The phrase "givers of gold" (line 83) probably means which of the following? **(a)** jewelers; **(b)** kings; **(c)** warriors; **(d)** sailors.

10. What does the speaker say has happened to the great kingdoms of the world?

11. What does the speaker mean when he says "a man must conquer pride, not kill it" (line 109)?

12. What was the speaker's attitude toward worldly glory?

13. What is the nature or quality of the natural world in its relationship to humanity as it appears in this poem?

14. What is the predominant tone of this poem? **(a)** melancholy; **(b)** fierce; **(c)** joyful; **(d)** humorous.

15. What was the speaker's view of life?

Unit 1, Test II
COMPOSITION

You may choose any *one* of the following assignments. Assume that you are writing for your classmates.

1. Describe the differences in the portraits of Grendel presented by the *Beowulf* poet, Richard Wilbur, and John Gardner.

2. Compare and contrast the scene in which Grendel appears in the mead hall of Heorot as it is presented in Gardner's *Grendel* and in *Beowulf* (lines 631–730).

3. Discuss where humanity is to find solace or comfort according to "The Wanderer" and "The Seafarer."

4. Discuss the views of the world of ancient cities and kingdoms expressed in "The Wanderer" (lines 71–91), and in "The Seafarer" (lines 80–90).

5. Compare and contrast the views of the relationship between humans and God that conclude "The Wanderer" and "The Seafarer."

6. Discuss the concept of fate or destiny as it appears in the following poems: "The Wanderer," Auden's poem of the same title, and "The Wife's Lament."

7. Imagine that you are a member of the crowd mentioned in the last paragraph of Bede's *Ecclesiastical History.* What might you make of the actions of the High Priest Coifi—how would you interpret his actions?

8. Describe, in general, the Anglo-Saxon view of life based on the material you have read in this unit. Give examples as evidence to support your opinions.

Unit 2:

1100	1150	1200	1250	1300

- Henry II marries Eleanor of Aquitaine
- The Model Parliament
- *Magna Carta*
- Geoffrey of Monmouth: *Historia Regum Britanniae*
- Founding of Oxford
- The Third Crusade

The Medieval Period 1100-1500

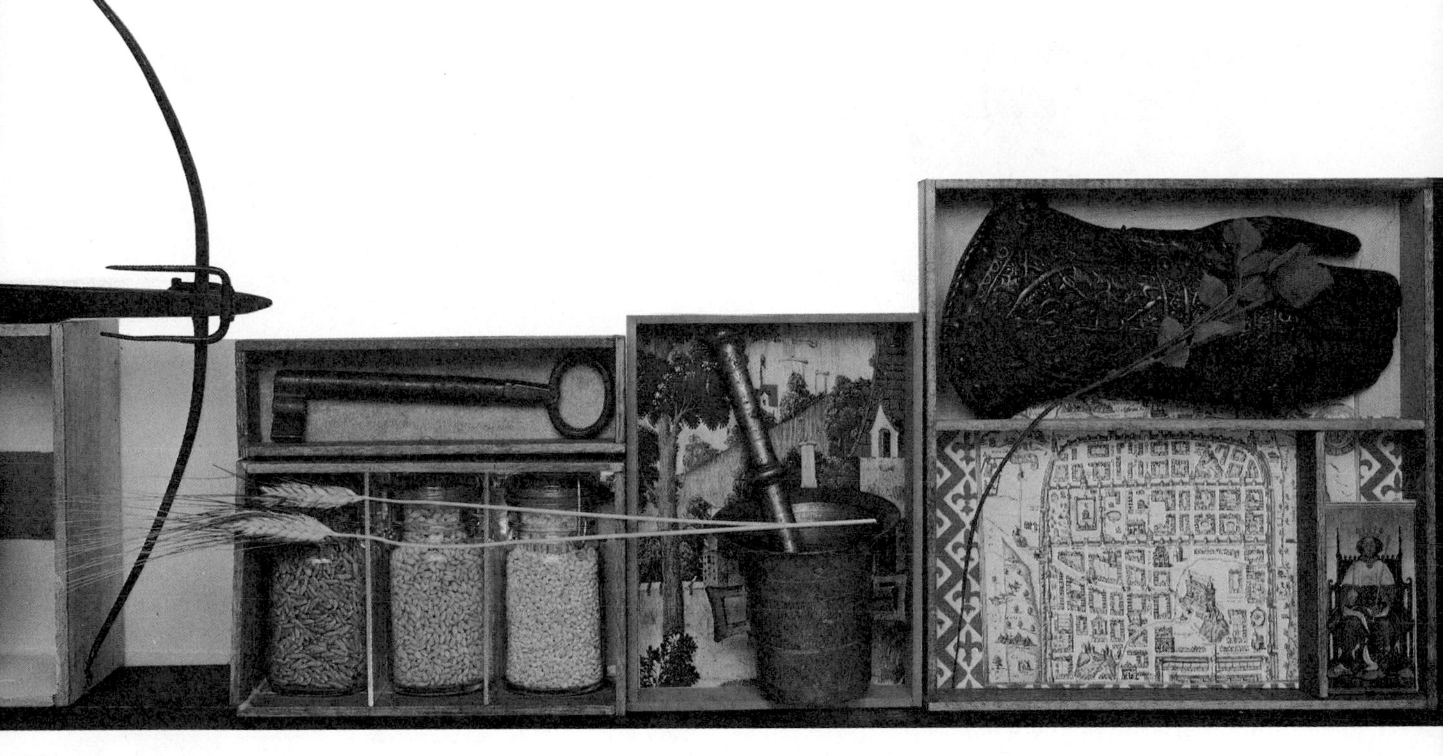

1350	1400	1450	1500

- *Vision of Piers Plowman*
- Malory: *Morte Darthur*
- Chaucer's Death
- Battle of Crécy
- *Sir Gawain and the Green Knight*
- Caxton's press
- First appearance of the Black Death
- Peasants' Revolt
- Wycliffe's Bible

Background: The Medieval Period 1100-1500

For a thousand years England had been vulnerable to invasion from the Continent. But the last invaders changed all that. They were the Normans, descended from Germanic tribes that had invaded a broad stretch of northern France early in the tenth century. They adopted the French language and owed nominal allegiance to the French king. For this reason their ruler held the title of duke. But he was, in fact, more powerful than many kings.

When the English king Edward the Confessor died without an heir in 1066 the Norman duke William claimed the English throne. But, as always, there were other contenders. William invaded England and won a decisive victory at the Battle of Hastings in 1066.

Norman Society

William, now called "the Conqueror," proceeded to transform England. He declared that every inch of English soil belonged to him. Much of it he gave to his men, but only in exchange for a promise of absolute loyalty. Englishmen who wished to retain their lands had to repurchase them from the king.

To ensure his firm control, William compiled an exacting survey of every bit of property on the island, recorded in the *Domesday Book* (1086). He ejected the old Anglo-Saxon leaders and substituted his own people.

Most of the people were *serfs,* permanent servants of the Norman lords. To them they owed obedience, the performance of specific duties, and taxes.

There was also another important segment of society, large in number and significant in influence—the clergy. The Church owned vast tracts of land, maintained its own separate legal system, its own taxes (tithes), and communicated with ecclesiastical leaders in Rome and on the Continent without consulting the king or his ministers. It supervised the education of most of the people who were educated, and continually competed in political matters with civil authority.

In the Norman English society William initiated, there were three languages. The Norman rulers spoke and wrote French. The clergy and the members of the legal profession spoke and wrote Latin. The common people and the old, displaced English nobility still spoke an evolving version of Anglo-Saxon.

Medieval Literature

For the history of English literature, the Norman invasion meant the disappearance of almost any record of literary activity for over a century. But this does not mean that English literature died. It must be kept in mind that until what must be called "recent" history, literature has primarily been oral. In both Anglo-Saxon and medieval times very few people could read at all and those who did, read aloud.

They did this for good reasons. People then lived in clusters, not in the tiny groups typical of our modern day. Whether it was in the hall of a noble lord's castle, the great refectory room of a monastery, or by the kitchen fire of a country cottage, people worked, ate, and lived together. For them entertainment almost always meant singing or listening to someone tell a story. Both, of course, are forms of literature. So literature, the primary entertainment, was usually a shared experience.

The Norman invasion did not stop English literature; it only temporarily prevented people from writing it down. When, about a century later, literary works reappear, the surviving copies have a verve and style which suggest that during the period in between, vigorous literary traditions continued in their oral form.

What were they? Here are some typical examples. For the nobility the retelling of heroic adventures about King Arthur, Charlemagne, and Alexander the Great. For the clergy, and through them for everyone, sermons and saints' lives. For the common folk, ballads and carols. As medieval culture evolved, these forms and many others developed.

And the English language itself developed. Over the course of the four centuries which followed the Norman invasion, the Germanic Anglo-Saxon language, so alien to us that no modern English speaker can read it without training, began to combine with Norman French into a synthesis of the two, which by Chaucer's day looked much like our language. As this process evolved, the Latin terms of the lawyer and scholar continually entered the language. In this way Modern English came into being.

Most medieval literature is now lost. What has survived is varied in form and content and tells us about the vitality of that era in many ways. From the surviving works this book offers three brief but typical selections.

First, there are the folk ballads. These song lyrics, probably invented by humble singers for people of small communities, have survived for centuries by word of mouth. No one knows who made them up, or when.

Quite different are the poems of Geoffrey Chaucer. He grew up during medieval England's period of greatest prosperity and influence. A man trained in the royal court and close to the most intelligent and powerful people of his day, Chaucer was able to travel widely throughout Europe and to study the literature of France and Italy. With striking success, he combined his wide-ranging learning with an enthusiastic love for the everyday lives of ordinary English people into his masterpiece, *The Canterbury Tales.* This is a poem which the learned could admire for its careful development of current literary forms, while ordinary listeners could relish its comedy, adventure, and pathos. It became one of the most popular poems of its day.

Geoffrey Chaucer

Our final selection comes from a different world. During the century following Chaucer's death, England tore itself apart in the civil warfare of the "Wars of the Roses." The ideals of the medieval knight were all but forgotten in the bitter cruelty of that struggle over which aristocratic faction would govern England. A man who was caught up in the confusion, Sir Thomas Malory, tried to regain the vision of what was already a lost medieval perfection in his prose retelling of the story of King Arthur and his knights.

Malory's was one of the first English books to appear in print. William Caxton, an ingenious English traveler, saw the newly invented system of printing from movable type in Germany and set up his own press in London in 1476. This initiated a major change in English literature. Now books didn't have to be laboriously copied by hand. Soon, they would be relatively cheap. With books easily obtainable more people could learn to read, and more books would be produced. The experience of literature would soon shift from the breathless group of listeners gathered in a hall or around a fire, hearing an old tale told once more, to the solitary individual, alone with the thoughts and feelings of another person speaking from the printed page.

Popular Ballads

Lord Randal

1

"O where hae ye been, Lord Randal, my son?
  O where hae ye been, my handsome young man?"
"I hae been to the wild wood; mother, make my bed soon,
  For I'm weary wi hunting, and fain wald lie down."

2

"Where gat ye your dinner, Lord Randal, my son?
  Where gat ye your dinner, my handsome young man?"
"I din'd wi my true-love; mother, make my bed soon,
  For I'm weary wi hunting, and fain wald lie down."

3

"What gat ye to your dinner, Lord Randal, my son?
  What gat ye to your dinner, my handsome young man?"
"I gat eels boild in broo; mother, make my bed soon,
  For I'm weary wi hunting, and fain wald lie down."

4

"What became of your bloodhounds, Lord Randal, my son?
  What became of your bloodhounds, my handsome young man?"
"O they swelld and they died; mother, make my bed soon,
  For I'm weary wi hunting, and fain wald lie down."

5

"O I fear ye are poisond, Lord Randal, my son!
  O I fear ye are poisond, my handsome young man!"
"O yes! I am poisond; mother, make my bed soon,
  For I'm sick at the heart, and I fain wald lie down."

From Scott's *Ministrelsy of the Scottish Border,* 1803.[1]

---

1. ***From Scott's . . . Border, 1803.*** There are German and Italian versions of this ballad, even older than the English. The novelist Sir Walter Scott, who spent ten years collecting ballads from singers in isolated Scottish villages, discovered this one.

Medieval Hunting Scene. The Bettmann Archive, Inc.

The Unquiet Grave

1

"The wind doth blow today, my love,
  And a few small drops of rain;
I never had but one true-love,
  In cold grave she was lain.

2

"I'll do as much for my true-love
  As any young man may;
I'll sit and mourn all at her grave
  For a twelvemonth and a day."

3

The twelvemonth and a day being up,
  The dead began to speak:
"Oh who sits weeping on my grave,
  And will not let me sleep?"

4

"'Tis I, my love, sits on your grave,
  And will not let you sleep;
For I crave one kiss of your clay-cold lips,
  And that is all I seek."

5

"You crave one kiss of my clay-cold lips;
  But my breath smells earthy strong;
If you have one kiss of my clay-cold lips,
  Your time will not be long.

6

"'Tis down in yonder garden green,
  Love, where we used to walk,
The finest flower that ere was seen
  Is withered to a stalk.

7

"The stalk is withered dry, my love,
  So will our hearts decay;
So make yourself content, my love,
  Till God calls you away."

Detail, Medieval Hunting Scene. The Bettmann Archive, Inc.

Communicated orally by a young
girl in Sussex; published 1868.

Get Up and Bar the Door

1

It fell about the Martinmas time,
And a gay time it was then,
When our goodwife got puddings[1] to make,
And she's boild them in the pan.

2

The wind sae cauld blew south and north,
And blew into the floor;
Quoth our goodman to our goodwife,
"Gae out and bar the door."

3

"My hand is in my hussyfskap,[2]
Goodman, as ye may see;
An it shoud nae be barrd this hundred year,
It's no be barrd for me."

4

They made a paction tween them twa,[3]
They made it firm and sure,
That the first word whaeer shoud speak,
Shoud rise and bar the door.

5

Then by there came two gentlemen,
At twelve o clock at night,
And they could neither see house nor hall,
Nor coal nor candle-light.

6

"Now whether is this a rich man's house,
Or whether is it a poor?"
But neer a word wad ane o them speak,
For barring of the door.

1. ***puddings,*** sausages.
2. ***hussyfskap,*** housewife's work.
3. ***paction . . . twa,*** agreement between themselves.

7

And first they[4] ate the white puddings,
  And then they ate the black;
Tho muckle[5] thought the goodwife to hersel,
  Yet neer a word she spake.

8

Then said the one unto the other,
  "Here, man, tak ye my knife;
Do ye tak aff the auld man's beard,
  And I'll kiss the goodwife."

9

"But there's nae water in the house,
  And what shall we do than?"
"What ails ye at the pudding-broo,
  That boils into the pan?"

10

O up then started our goodman,
  An angry man was he:
"Will ye kiss my wife before my een,
  And scad me wi pudding-bree?"

11

Then up and started our goodwife,
  Gied three skips on the floor:
"Goodman, you've spoken the foremost word,
  Get up and bar the door."

Herd, *The Ancient and Modern Scots Songs,* 1769.

---

4. ***they,*** gentlemen.
5. ***muckle,*** a great deal.

"Double Portrait of Israhel van Mechenem and His Wife Ida" by Israhel van Meckenem. National Gallery of Art, Washington. Rosenwald Collection.

Sir Patrick Spence[1]

1

The king sits in Dumferling[2] toune,
  Drinking the blude-reid wine:
"O whar will I get guid sailor,
  To sail this schip of mine?"

2

Up and spak an eldern knicht,
  Sat at the kings richt kne:
"Sir Patrick Spence is the best sailor
  That sails upon the se."

3

The king has written a braid letter,[3]
  And signed it wi his hand,
And sent it to Sir Patrick Spence,
  Was walking on the sand.

4

The first line that Sir Patrick red,
  A loud lauch[4] lauched he;
The next line that Sir Patrick red,
  The teir blinded his ee.

5

"O wha is this has don this deid,
  This ill deid don to me,
To send me out this time o' the yeir,
  To sail upon the se!

6

"Mak hast, mak haste, my mirry men all,
  Our guid schip sails the morne":
"O say na sae, my master deir,
  For I feir a deadlie storme.

7

"Late late yestreen I saw the new moone,
  Wi the auld moone in hir arme,
And I feir, I feir, my deir master,
  That we will cum to harme."

8

O our Scots nobles wer richt laith
  To weet their cork-heild schoone;
But lang owre a' the play wer playd,
  Their hats they swam aboone.[5]

9

O lang, lang may their ladies sit,
  Wi their fans into their hand,
Or eir they se Sir Patrick Spence
  Cum sailing to the land.

10

O lang, lang may the ladies stand,
  Wi their gold kems in their hair,
Waiting for thair ain deir lords,
  For they'll se thame na mair.

11

Haf owre, haf owre to Aberdour,[6]
  It's fiftie fadom deip,
And thair lies guid Sir Patrick Spence,
  Wi the Scots lords at his feit.

From Percy's *Reliques,* 1765.

---

1. Some scholars think this ballad is based on actual historical events. In 1281, the Scottish king's daughter Margaret was married to Eric, King of Norway. She crossed safely to Norway in August, but on the return journey the ship, carrying many knights and nobles, was lost.
2. ***Dumferling,*** residence of the Scottish kings.
3. ***braid letter,*** letter of command.
4. ***lauch,*** laugh.
5. ***laith . . . aboone.*** The sense of this passage is that the Scottish nobles did not want to get their feet (cork-heeled shoes) wet, but before the voyage was over, they were in water over their heads (their hats swam about).
6. ***Haf . . . Aberdour,*** halfway home to Aberdeen.

notes and comments

The Ballad

The folk **ballads** were songs sung by the common people of England. Their origins remain a mystery. Most seem to have been composed between 1200 and 1500, and while there has been much argument, no one is exactly sure how they were created. Present-day theories suggest that many were invented by local minstrels, descendants of the Anglo-Saxon scops, who entertained the humble people of a village by making up songs.

Multiple versions of most ballads exist, for at least two reasons. Singers felt free to alter parts of a ballad to fit the time, place, and audience. And undoubtedly some singers would change a detail or two to improve the song.

So for most ballads there are no "earliest" or "correct" versions, only variety to match the requirements of performance.

The fact that ballads were originally songs committed to memory has a crucial effect on their form and content. The ballad stanza—usually four lines alternating between four and three iambic feet, the second and fourth lines rhyming—fits the simple tunes to which it was sung. The frequent use of refrains—repetition of one or more lines, as in "Lord Randal"—suggests the use of a chorus; perhaps those listening who knew the song joining in with the minstrel. The ballad form does not allow elaborate detail in plot, setting, or character. Ballads focus on crises in the actions they record, depending on dialogue between characters rather than a narrator. The subjects are universal themes: love, death, revenge. After all, they had to be easy to understand, since they were sung to an audience, and they had to be easy to remember, since they were not written down.

No one knows how many ballads have been lost. Those which survive do so by accident. In the eighteenth century, people interested in medieval culture began trying to collect these songs of the common people. They found a few in old manuscripts, and they found others by going to remote villages and writing down the versions recalled by local singers.

In ballads we come as close to a true folk literature as we can find in English.

Discussion

1. (a) At what point in "Lord Randal" do you begin to guess what has happened? When are you certain? **(b)** Now go back to earlier passages in the poem. Once you know the conclusion, can you see hints near its beginning? What are they? **(c)** What is the effect of the shift in wording of line 20?

2. (a) Why does the young man mourn by "The Unquiet Grave"? **(b)** Why does the dead girl refer to the flower (lines 21–26)? **(c)** What sort of atmosphere do natural details give?

3. (a) Why won't the wife "get up and bar the door"? Why does the husband refuse? **(b)** Given their actions, how would you characterize the "two gentlemen"? **(c)** Why does the wife skip?

4. (a) Unlike the other three ballads in this unit, "Sir Patrick Spence" describes several different moments in time. What are they, and where do the shifts from one time to another take place? **(b)** Why does Sir Patrick accept the king's command? What does this tell us about him?

5. (a) What does the "blude-reid wine" in line 2 of "Sir Patrick Spence" add to the poem's emotional tone? What would be the effect of using "clear white wine" instead? **(b)** Find other examples of emotionally weighted detail in these ballads.

Extension • Writing

Retell the events narrated in a ballad as a short story. When you have finished, underline those parts of your story which were not in the original and explain why you thought they had to be included.

Geoffrey Chaucer

The Canterbury Tales

translated by Nevill Coghill

The Prologue

Whan that Aprill with his shoures soote
The droghte of March hath perced to the roote,
And bathed every veyne in swich licour
Of which vertu engendred is the flour;
Whan Zephirus eek with his sweete breeth
Inspired hath in every holt and heeth
The tendre croppes, and the yonge sonne
Hath in the Ram his halve cours yronne,
And smale foweles maken melodye,
That slepen al the nyght with open ye
(So priketh hem nature in hir corages);
Thanne longen folk to goon on pilgrimages,
And palmeres for to seken straunge strondes,
To ferne halwes, kowthe in sondry londes;
And specially from every shires ende
Of Engelond to Caunterbury they wende,
The hooly blisful martir for to seke,
That hem hath holpen whan that they were
seeke.

When in April the sweet showers fall
And pierce the drought of March to the root, and all
The veins are bathed in liquor of such power
As brings about the engendering of the flower,
When also Zephyrus[1] with his sweet breath
Exhales an air in every grove and heath
Upon the tender shoots, and the young sun
His half-course in the sign of the *Ram* has run,[2]
And the small fowl are making melody
That sleep away the night with open eye
(So nature pricks them and their heart engages)
Then people long to go on pilgrimages
And palmers[3] long to seek the stranger strands
Of far-off saints, hallowed in sundry lands,
And specially, from every shire's end
In England, down to Canterbury they wend
To seek the holy blissful martyr,[4] quick
To give his help to them when they were sick.
It happened in that season that one day
In Southwark, at *The Tabard,*[5] as I lay
Ready to go on pilgrimage and start
For Canterbury, most devout at heart,
At night there came into that hostelry
Some nine and twenty in a company
Of sundry folk happening then to fall
In fellowship, and they were pilgrims all
That towards Canterbury meant to ride.
The rooms and stables of the inn were wide;
They made us easy, all was of the best.
And shortly, when the sun had gone to rest,
By speaking to them all upon the trip
I soon was one of them in fellowship
And promised to rise early and take the way
To Canterbury, as you heard me say.
But none the less, while I have time and space,
Before my story takes a further pace,
It seems a reasonable thing to say
What their condition was, the full array
Of each of them, as it appeared to me
According to profession and degree,
And what apparel they were riding in;
And at a Knight I therefore will begin.
There was a *Knight,* a most distinguished man,
Who from the day on which he first began
To ride abroad had followed chivalry,
Truth, honour, generousness, and courtesy.
He had done nobly in his sovereign's war
And ridden into battle, no man more,
As well in christian as in heathen places,
And ever honoured for his noble graces.
When we took Alexandria,[6] he was there.
He often sat at table in the chair
Of honour, above all nations, when in Prussia.
In Lithuania he had ridden, and Russia,
No christian man so often, of his rank.
When, in Granada, Algeciras sank
Under assault, he had been there, and in
North Africa, raiding Benamarin;
In Anatolia he had been as well
And fought when Ayas and Attalia fell,

1. ***Zephyrus,*** the west wind.
2. ***young sun . . . has run.*** Since the Ram, the first sign of the Zodiac, begins its run about March 21, Chaucer dates the pilgrimage in early April.
3. ***palmers,*** pilgrims to the Holy Land wore the image of crossed palm leaves as their emblem.
4. ***martyr,*** St. Thomas à Becket, murdered in Canterbury Cathedral in 1170. His tomb was a favorite destination for medieval English pilgrims.
5. ***Southwark, at The Tabard.*** *The Tabard* was a famous inn at the beginning of the road from London to Canterbury, located in a suburb south of London.
6. ***Alexandria.*** Here and in the following lines the narrator refers to battles against the major non-Christian enemies of Chaucer's era.

For all along the Mediterranean coast
He had embarked with many a noble host.
In fifteen mortal battles he had been
And jousted for our faith at Tramissene
Thrice in the lists, and always killed his man.
This same distinguished knight had led the van
Once with the Bey of Balat, doing work
For him against another heathen Turk;
He was of sovereign value in all eyes.
And though so much distinguished, he was wise
And in his bearing modest as a maid.
He never yet a boorish thing had said
In all his life to any, come what might;
He was a true, a perfect gentle-knight.
  Speaking of his equipment, he possessed
Fine horses, but he was not gaily dressed.
He wore a fustian tunic stained and dark
With smudges where his armour had left mark;
Just home from service, he had joined our ranks
To do his pilgrimage and render thanks.
  He had his son with him, a fine young *Squire,*[7]
A lover and cadet, a lad of fire
With locks as curly as if they had been pressed.
He was some twenty years of age, I guessed.
In stature he was of a moderate length,
With wonderful agility and strength.
He'd seen some service with the cavalry
In Flanders and Artois and Picardy[8]
And had done valiantly in little space
Of time, in hope to win his lady's grace.
He was embroidered like a meadow bright
And full of freshest flowers, red and white.
Singing he was, or fluting all the day;
He was as fresh as is the month of May.
Short was his gown, the sleeves were long and wide;
He knew the way to sit a horse and ride.
He could make songs and poems and recite,
Knew how to joust and dance, to draw and write.
He loved so hotly that till dawn grew pale
He slept as little as a nightingale.
Courteous he was, lowly and serviceable,
And carved to serve his father at the table.
  There was a *Yeoman*[9] with him at his side,
No other servant; so he chose to ride.

7. ***Squire,*** a young man learning to be a knight through service.
8. ***Flanders and Artois and Picardy,*** battles much closer to home than those the knight has seen.
9. ***Yeoman.*** A free man and a commoner, servant to the knight.

notes and comments

The Physiognomists

In the Middle Ages, a "science" called physiognomy became popular. It was based on the idea that the mental and emotional characteristics of an individual could be determined from physical characteristics like physique, hair, and voice quality. Chaucer, like his readers, must have been familiar with these ideas.

The details in the description of the Pardoner, for example (lines 693–709), conveyed to Chaucer's audience information that a modern reader might miss. In medieval physiognomical lore, sparse yellow hair, soft and long, was a token of effeminacy, cunning, and deceptiveness. Hare-eyes that bulge and glitter indicated shameless effrontery, gluttony, and drunkenness. The goat-voice and beardlessness confirmed the Pardoner's lack of manhood and implied craftiness and treachery.

To a fourteenth-century audience, the fact that the Wife of Bath's teeth were set wide apart might indicate that she was envious, irreverent, bold, deceitful, and fond of luxury; or it might be interpreted as a sign that she was destined to do much traveling.

Two other significant descriptions are those of the Miller and the Reeve. According to the physiognomists, the Miller's broad, thickset physique, red beard, and large nostrils, as well as the bristly wart at the tip of his nose, indicated his bold, garrulous, quarrelsome nature. The Reeve's thin body and calfless legs were associated with the choleric humor, which denoted quick temper, sharp wit, and wantonness.

This Yeoman wore a coat and hood of green,
And peacock-feathered arrows, bright and keen
And neatly sheathed, hung at his belt the while
—For he could dress his gear in yeoman style,
His arrows never drooped their feathers low—
And in his hand he bore a mighty bow.
His head was like a nut, his face was brown.
He knew the whole of woodcraft up and down.
A saucy brace was on his arm to ward
It from the bow-string, and a shield and sword
Hung at one side, and at the other slipped
A jaunty dirk, spear-sharp and well-equipped.
A medal of St Christopher[10] he wore
Of shining silver on his breast, and bore
A hunting-horn, well slung and burnished clean,
That dangled from a baldrick of bright green.
He was a proper forester I guess.
  There also was a *Nun,* a Prioress,[11]
Her way of smiling very simple and coy.
Her greatest oath was only "By St Loy!"[12]
And she was known as Madam Eglantyne.[13]
And well she sang a service, with a fine
Intoning through her nose, as was most seemly,
And she spoke daintily in French, extremely,
After the school of Stratford-atte-Bowe;[14]
French in the Paris style she did not know.
At meat her manners were well-taught withal;
No morsel from her lips did she let fall,
Nor dipped her fingers in the sauce too deep;
But she could carry a morsel up and keep
The smallest drop from falling on her breast.
For courtliness she had a special zest,
And she would wipe her upper lip so clean
That not a trace of grease was to be seen
Upon the cup when she had drunk; to eat,
She reached a hand sedately for the meat.
She certainly was very entertaining,
Pleasant and friendly in her ways, and straining
To counterfeit a courtly kind of grace,
A stately bearing fitting to her place,
And to seem dignified in all her dealings.
As for her sympathies and tender feelings,
She was so charitably solicitous
She used to weep if she but saw a mouse
Caught in a trap, if it were dead or bleeding.
And she had little dogs she would be feeding
With roasted flesh, or milk, or fine white bread.
And bitterly she wept if one were dead
Or someone took a stick and made it smart;
She was all sentiment and tender heart.
Her veil was gathered in a seemly way,
Her nose was elegant, her eyes glass-grey;
Her mouth was very small, but soft and red,
Her forehead, certainly, was fair of spread,
Almost a span across the brows, I own;
She was indeed by no means undergrown.
Her cloak, I noticed, had a graceful charm.
She wore a coral trinket on her arm,
A set of beads, the gaudies tricked in green,[15]
Whence hung a golden brooch of brightest
    sheen
On which there first was graven a crowned A,
And lower, *Amor vincit omnia.*[16]
  Another *Nun,* the chaplain at her cell,
Was riding with her, and *three Priests* as well.
  A *Monk* there was, one of the finest sort
Who rode the country; hunting was his sport.
A manly man, to be an Abbot[17] able;
Many a dainty horse he had in stable.
His bridle, when he rode, a man might hear
Jingling in a whistling wind as clear,
Aye, and as loud as does the chapel bell
Where my lord Monk was Prior of the cell.
The Rule[18] of good St Benet or St Maur
As old and strict he tended to ignore;
He let go by the things of yesterday
And took the modern world's more spacious
    way.
He did not rate that text at a plucked hen
Which says that hunters are not holy men
And that a monk uncloistered is a mere
Fish out of water, flapping on the pier,
That is to say a monk out of his cloister.
That was a text he held not worth an oyster;
And I agreed and said his views were sound;
Was he to study till his head went round
Poring over books in cloisters? Must he toil
As Austin[19] bade and till the very soil?

---

10. ***St Christopher,*** patron of travelers and foresters.
11. ***Prioress,*** religious woman who runs a convent.
12. ***St Loy.*** This saint refused to swear on sacred relics. To swear by him was to swear mildly or not at all.
13. ***Eglantyne,*** sweet briar.
14. ***daintily . . . Stratford-atte-Bowe,*** inferior French learned in an English convent.
15. ***A set . . . green,*** coral rosary beads with every larger tenth bead ("gaudies") made from a different stone.
16. ***Amor . . . omnia.*** "Love overcomes all." The phrase might be used for sacred or secular love.
17. ***Abbot,*** director of a monastery.
18. ***The Rule,*** ancient laws governing the life of a monk, first established by St. Benedict and his disciple St. Maur.
19. ***Austin.*** St. Augustine (d. A.D. 430) advised to engage in manual labor.

The Wife of Bath, the Franklin, the Pardoner, and Chaucer, from the Ellesmere Chaucer. By permission of the Huntington Library, San Marino, California.

Was he to leave the world upon the shelf?
Let Austin have his labour to himself.
  This Monk was therefore a good man to horse;
Greyhounds he had, as swift as birds, to course.
Hunting a hare or riding at a fence
Was all his fun, he spared for no expense.
I saw his sleeves were garnished at the hand
With fine grey fur, the finest in the land,
And on his hood, to fasten it at his chin
He had a wrought-gold cunningly fashioned pin;
Into a lover's knot it seemed to pass.
His head was bald and shone like looking-glass;
So did his face, as if it had been greased.
He was a fat and personable priest;
His prominent eyeballs never seemed to settle;
They glittered like the flames beneath a kettle;
Supple his boots, his horse in fine condition.
He was a prelate fit for exhibition,
He was not pale like a tormented soul.
He liked a fat swan best, and roasted whole.
His palfrey was as brown as is a berry.
  There was a *Friar,* a wanton one and merry,
A Limiter,[20] a very festive fellow.
In all Four Orders[21] there was none so mellow
So glib with gallant phrase and well-turned speech.
He'd fixed up many a marriage, giving each
Of his young women what he could afford her.
He was a noble pillar to his Order.
Highly beloved and intimate was he
With County folk within his boundary,
And city dames of honour and possessions;
For he was qualified to hear confessions,
Or so he said, with more than priestly scope;
He had a special license from the Pope.
Sweetly he heard his penitents at shrift[22]
With pleasant absolution, for a gift.
He was an easy man in penance-giving
Where he could hope to make a decent living;
It's a sure sign whenever gifts are given
To a poor Order that a man's well shriven,
And should he give enough he knew in verity
The penitent repented in sincerity.
For many a fellow is so hard of heart
He cannot weep, for all his inward smart.
Therefore instead of weeping and of prayer
One should give silver for a poor Friar's care.
He kept his tippet[23] stuffed with pins for curls,
And pocket-knives, to give to pretty girls.
And certainly his voice was gay and sturdy,
For he sang well and played the hurdy-gurdy.[24]
At sing-songs he was champion of the hour.
His neck was whiter than a lily-flower
But strong enough to butt a bruiser down.
He knew the taverns well in every town
And every innkeeper and barmaid too
Better than lepers, beggars and that crew,
For in so eminent a man as he
It was not fitting with the dignity
Of his position, dealing with a scum
Of wretched lepers; nothing good can come
Of dealings with the slum-and-gutter dwellers,
But only with the rich and victual-sellers.
But anywhere a profit might accrue
Courteous he was and lowly of service too.
Natural gifts like his were hard to match.
He was the finest beggar of his batch,
And, for his begging-district, payed a rent;
His brethren did no poaching where he went.
For though a widow mightn't have a shoe,
So pleasant was his holy how-d'ye-do

20. ***Limiter.*** Within a specific district ("limitatio") such a friar would beg for donations, preach, and bury the dead.
21. ***Four Orders,*** the four groups of begging friars: Dominicans, Franciscans, Carmelites, Augustinians.
22. ***shrift,*** confession of sins.
23. ***tippet,*** a narrow part of hood or sleeve used as a pocket.
24. ***hurdy-gurdy.*** Chaucer's term, "rote," describes a stringed instrument.

He got his farthing from her just the same
Before he left, and so his income came
To more than he laid out. And how he romped,
Just like a puppy! He was ever prompt
To arbitrate disputes on settling days[25]
(For a small fee) in many helpful ways,
Not then appearing as your cloistered scholar
With threadbare habit hardly worth a dollar,
But much more like a Doctor or a Pope.
Of double-worsted was the semi-cope
Upon his shoulders, and the swelling fold
About him, like a bell about its mould
When it is casting, rounded out his dress.
He lisped a little out of wantonness
To make his English sweet upon his tongue.
When he had played his harp, or having sung,
His eyes would twinkle in his head as bright
As any star upon a frosty night.
This worthy's name was Hubert, it appeared.

There was a *Merchant* with a forking beard
And motley[26] dress; high on his horse he sat,
Upon his head a Flemish beaver hat
And on his feet daintily buckled boots.
He told of his opinions and pursuits
In solemn tones, and how he never lost.
The sea should be kept free at any cost
(He thought) upon the Harwich-Holland range,[27]
He was expert at currency exchange.
This estimable Merchant so had set
His wits to work, none knew he was in debt,
He was so stately in negotiation,
Loan, bargain and commercial obligation.
He was an excellent fellow all the same;
To tell the truth I do not know his name.

An *Oxford Cleric,* still a student though,
One who had taken logic long ago,
Was there; his horse was thinner than a rake,
And he was not too fat, I undertake,
But had a hollow look, a sober stare;
The thread upon his overcoat was bare.
He had found no preferment in the church
And he was too unworldly to make search
For secular employment. By his bed
He preferred having twenty books in red
And black, of Aristotle's philosophy,
To having fine clothes, fiddle or psaltery.[28]
Though a philosopher, as I have told,
He had not found the stone for making gold.[29]
Whatever money from his friends he took
He spent on learning or another book
And prayed for them most earnestly, returning
Thanks to them thus for paying for his learning.
His only care was study, and indeed
He never spoke a word more than was need,
Formal at that, respectful in the extreme,
Short, to the point, and lofty in his theme.
The thought of moral virtue filled his speech
And he would gladly learn, and gladly teach.

A *Serjeant at the Law*[30] who paid his calls,
Wary and wise, for clients at St Paul's[31]
There also was, of noted excellence.
Discreet he was, a man to reverence,
Or so he seemed, his sayings were so wise.
He often had been Justice of Assize

---

25. ***settling days,*** on which disputes could be settled by independent negotiators out of court. Friars often acted in this capacity and received "gifts" for their services. In Chaucer's day this was officially forbidden.
26. ***motley,*** here, cloth woven with a figured design.
27. ***The sea . . . Harwich-Holland range.*** He wants ships sailing the England-to-Holland route protected at any cost.
28. ***psaltery,*** stringed instrument played with the hand.
29. ***stone for making gold.*** In alchemy the philosopher's stone was supposed to turn ordinary metals into gold. No one ever found it.
30. ***Serjeant at the Law,*** one of the king's legal servants. There were only twenty such men in Chaucer's day. They were chosen from lawyers with over 16 years experience, and sat as judges both in London and in the traveling courts, the assizes (l. 324) which met at various country towns.
31. ***St Paul's.*** During the afternoon, when the courts were closed, lawyers would meet clients on church porches to discuss business.

By letters patent,[32] and in full commission.
His fame and learning and his high position
Had won him many a robe and many a fee.
There was no such conveyancer as he;
All was fee-simple[33] to his strong digestion,
Not one conveyance could be called in
question.
Nowhere there was so busy a man as he;
But was less busy than he seemed to be.
He knew of every judgement, case and crime
Recorded, ever since King William's time.[34]
He could dictate defences or draft deeds;
No one could pinch a comma from his screeds,[35]
And he knew every statute off by rote.
He wore a homely parti-coloured coat
Girt with a silken belt of pin-stripe stuff;
Of his appearance I have said enough.
There was a *Franklin*[36] with him, it appeared;
White as a daisy-petal was his beard.
A sanguine man, high-coloured and benign,
He loved a morning sop of cake in wine.
He lived for pleasure and had always done,
For he was Epicurus'[37] very son,
In whose opinion sensual delight
Was the one true felicity in sight.
As noted as St Julian[38] was for bounty
He made his household free to all the County.
His bread, his ale were finest of the fine
And no one had a better stock of wine.
His house was never short of bake-meat pies,
Of fish and flesh, and these in such supplies
It positively snowed with meat and drink
And all the dainties that a man could think.
According to the seasons of the year
Changes of dish were ordered to appear.
He kept fat partridges in coops, beyond,
Many a bream and pike were in his pond.
Woe to the cook whose sauces had no sting
Or who was unprepared in anything!
And in his hall a table stood arrayed
And ready all day long, with places laid.
As Justice at the Sessions none stood higher;[39]
He often had been Member for the Shire.[40]
A dagger and a little purse of silk
Hung at his girdle, white as morning milk.
As Sheriff[41] he checked audit, every entry.
He was a model among landed gentry.
A *Haberdasher*, a *Dyer*, a *Carpenter*,
A *Weaver* and a *Carpet-maker* were
Among our ranks, all in the livery
Of one impressive guild-fraternity.[42]
They were so trim and fresh their gear would
pass
For new. Their knives were not tricked out
with brass
But wrought with purest silver, which avouches
A like display on girdles and on pouches.
Each seemed a worthy burgess, fit to grace
A guild-hall with a seat upon the dais.[43]
Their wisdom would have justified a plan
To make each one of them an alderman;[44]
They had the capital and revenue,
Besides their wives declared it was their due.
And if they did not think so, then they ought;
To be called *"Madam"* is a glorious thought,
And so is going to church and being seen
Having your mantle carried like a queen.
They had a *Cook* with them who stood alone
For boiling chicken with a marrow-bone,
Sharp flavouring-powder and a spice for
savour.
He could distinguish London ale by flavour,
And he could roast and seethe and broil and
fry,
Make good thick soup and bake a tasty pie.
But what a pity—so it seemed to me,
That he should have an ulcer on his knee.
As for blancmange,[45] he made it with the best.
There was a *Skipper* hailing from far west;
He came from Dartmouth, so I understood.
He rode a farmer's horse as best he could,
In a woollen gown that reached his knee.
A dagger on a lanyard falling free
Hung from his neck under his arm and down.

32. ***letters patent,*** official documents from the king empowering an individual to act as Judge of the Assize.
33. ***fee simple,*** land owned outright. The Serjeant is obtaining as much of this as he can.
34. ***King William's time,*** era of William the Conqueror (1066–1087), when systematic legal records were first kept.
35. ***screeds,*** writing.
36. ***Franklin.*** Literally the term means "free man." Here we have a wealthy landowner.
37. ***Epicurus,*** Greek philosopher (342? –270 B.C.) whose ideas seemed to urge pursuit of pleasure.
38. ***St. Julian,*** patron of hospitality.
39. ***Justice . . . higher.*** When the Justices of the Peace sat in session, he presided.
40. ***Member . . . Shire,*** member of Parliament for his county.
41. ***Sheriff,*** royal administrator who collected taxes and delivered them to the king's exchequer.
42. ***Guild-fraternity.*** Since these men came from different trades, this refers to a club they all joined.
43. ***guildhall . . . dais,*** worthy to preside at meetings of the guild.
44. ***alderman,*** leading member of a town council.
45. ***blancmange,*** chicken stew flavored with spices.

Chaucer the Satirist

Rosemary Woolf

Chaucer was writing at a time when a poet never made his individual emotions the subject-matter of his poetry. Though the personal pronoun 'I' is used frequently in medieval narrative and lyric poetry, it is usually a dramatic 'I', that is, the 'I' is a character in the poem, bearing no different relation to the poet from that of the other characters. Chaucer's use of an 'I' character belongs to the tradition of such characters, but with an ingenious variation that the character appears naive, well-meaning, and obtuse, and the joke thus depends on the discrepancy between this figure in the poetry and the poet of wit and intelligence who wrote the whole.

"It is through this character that both the apparently vivid individuality of the pilgrims and the satiric aim are achieved. It is through the eyes of Chaucer the pilgrim, not Chaucer the poet, that the characters are chiefly presented. Obviously the choice of detail shows the sharp selectiveness of the satirist, but the friendly, enthusiastic, unsophisticated, unjudging tone is that of Chaucer the pilgrim.

"By his fiction of having been a close companion of his characters, Chaucer suggests their reality and individuality. He implies that most of the information which he gives us derives, not from a narrative-writer's omniscience but from the characters' own conversation. Chaucer makes his response that of a man who accepts and repeats with enthusiasm, and without criticism, whatever he is told."

Abridged from "Chaucer as Satirist in the *General Prologue* of *The Canterbury Tales* from *Critical Quarterly*, Vol. 1, 1959. Reprinted by the permission of the author, Rosemary Woolf.

The summer heat had tanned his colour brown,
And certainly he was an excellent fellow.
Many a draught of vintage, red and yellow,
He'd drawn at Bordeaux, while the trader snored.
The nicer rules of conscience he ignored.
If, when he fought, the enemy vessel sank,
He sent his prisoners home; they walked the plank.
As for his skill in reckoning his tides,
Currents, and many another risk besides,
Moons, harbours, pilots, he had such dispatch
That none from Hull to Carthage[46] was his match.
Hardy he was, prudent in undertaking;
His beard in many a tempest had its shaking,
And he knew all the havens as they were
From Gottland to the Cape of Finisterre,
And every creek in Brittany and Spain;
The barge he owned was called *The Maudelayne.*
A *Doctor* too emerged as we proceeded;
No one alive could talk as well as he did
On points of medicine and of surgery,
For, being grounded in astronomy,[47]
He watched his patient's favourable star
And, by his Natural Magic, knew what are
The lucky hours and planetary degrees
For making charms and magic effigies.
The cause of every malady you'd got
He knew, and whether dry, cold, moist, or hot;[48]
He knew their seat, their humour, and condition.
He was a perfect practising physician.
These causes being known for what they were,
He gave the man his medicine then and there.
All his apothecaries in a tribe
Were ready with the drugs he would prescribe,
And each made money from the other's guile;

46. *Hull to Carthage.* These and subsequent references indicate how widely the skipper has traveled.
47. *astronomy.* Here, astrology. It was believed that the position of the planets determined the best time to treat a patient.
48. *dry . . . hot.* In the Middle Ages people thought the human body was composed of the four elements: earth, air, fire, and water. Sickness came from too much of any one element. Character traits, too, could be explained by a slight excess of an element: too much fire produced a hot temper, etc. Such traits were called humors (line 431).

The Nun's Priest, the Miller, and the Merchant, from the Ellesmere Chaucer. By permission of The Huntington Library, San Marino, California

They had been friendly for a goodish while.
He was well-versed in Esculapius[49] too
And what Hippocrates and Rufus knew
And Dioscorides, now dead and gone,
Galen and Rhazes, Hali, Serapion,
Averroes, Avicenna, Constantine,
Scotch Bernard, John of Gaddesden, Gilbertine.
In his own diet he observed some measure;
There were no superfluities for pleasure,
Only digestives, nutritives, and such.
He did not read the Bible very much.
In blood-red garments, slashed with bluish-grey
And lined with taffeta, he rode his way;
Yet he was rather close as to expenses
And kept the gold he won in pestilences.[50]
Gold stimulates the heart, or so we're told.
He therefore had a special love of gold.
  A worthy *Woman* from beside *Bath* city
Was with us, somewhat deaf, which was a pity.
In making cloth she showed so great a bent
She bettered those of Ypres and of Ghent.[51]
In all the parish not a dame dared stir
Towards the altar steps in front of her,
And if indeed they did, so wrath was she
As to be quite put out of charity.
Her kerchiefs were of finely woven ground;
I dared have sworn they weighed a good ten
    pound,
The ones she wore on Sunday, on her head.
Her hose were of the finest scarlet red
And gartered tight; her shoes were soft and
    new.
Bold was her face, handsome, and red in hue.
A worthy woman all her life, what's more
She'd had five husbands, all at the church
    door,[52]
Apart from other company in youth;
No need just now to speak of that, forsooth.
And she had thrice been to Jerusalem,
Seen many strange rivers and passed over them;
She'd been to Rome and also to Boulogne,
St James of Compostella and Cologne,[53]
And she was skilled in wandering by the way.
She had gap-teeth, set widely, truth to say.
Easily on an ambling horse she sat
Well wimpled up,[54] and on her head a hat
As broad as is a buckler or a shield;
She had a flowing mantle that concealed
Large hips, her heels spurred sharply under
    that.
In company she liked to laugh and chat
And knew the remedies for love's mischances,
An art in which she knew the oldest dances.
  A holy-minded man of good renown
There was, and poor, the *Parson* to a town,
Yet he was rich in holy thought and work.
He also was a learned man, a clerk,
Who truly knew Christ's gospel and would
    preach it
Devoutly to parishioners, and teach it.
Benign and wonderfully diligent,
And patient when adversity was sent
(For so he proved in great adversity)
He much disliked extorting tithe or fee,
Nay rather he preferred beyond a doubt
Giving to poor parishioners round about
From his own goods and Easter offerings.
He found sufficiency in little things.
Wide was his parish, with houses far asunder,
Yet he neglected not in rain or thunder,

---

49. ***Esculapius.*** This and the names that follow belong to eminent medical authorities from ancient times to Chaucer's day. The Doctor was well-read in his profession.

50. ***pestilences,*** plagues.

51. ***Ypres . . . Ghent,*** Flemish cities famous for their weavers, and markets for the wool trade.

52. ***at the church door.*** In Chaucer's day marriage services were held at the church door, and the subsequent nuptial Mass inside.

53. ***Rome . . . Cologne.*** The Wife has visited most of the important shrines in Italy, France, Spain, and Germany.

54. ***well wimpled up.*** A linen garment covered her head, neck, and the sides of her face.

In sickness or in grief, to pay a call
On the remotest, whether great or small,
Upon his feet, and in his hand a stave.
This noble example to his sheep he gave,
First following the word before he taught it,
And it was from the gospel he had caught it.
This little proverb he would add thereto
That if gold rust, what then will iron do?
For if a priest be foul in whom we trust
No wonder that a common man should rust.
The true example that a priest should give
Is one of cleanness, how the sheep should live.
He did not set his benefice to hire
And leave his sheep encumbered in the mire
Or run to London to earn easy bread
By singing masses for the wealthy dead,
Or find some Brotherhood and get enrolled.[55]
He stayed at home and watched over his fold
So that no wolf should make the sheep
    miscarry.
He was a shepherd and no mercenary.
Holy and virtuous he was, but then
Never contemptuous of sinful men,
Never disdainful, never too proud or fine,
But was discreet in teaching and benign.
His business was to show a fair behaviour
And draw men thus to Heaven and their
    Saviour,
Unless indeed a man were obstinate;
And such, whether of high or low estate,
He put to sharp rebuke to say the least.
I think there never was a better priest.
He sought no pomp or glory in his dealings,
No scrupulosity had spiced his feelings.
Christ and His Twelve Apostles and their lore
He taught, but followed it himself before.
  There was a *Plowman* with him there, his
    brother.
Many a load of dung one time or other
He must have carted through the morning dew.
He was an honest worker, good and true,
Living in peace and perfect charity,
And, as the gospel bade him, so did he,
Loving God best with all his heart and mind
And then his neighbour as himself, repined
At no misfortune, slacked for no content,
For steadily about his work he went
To thrash his corn, to dig or to manure
Or make a ditch; and he would help the poor
For love of Christ and never take a penny
If he could help it, and, as prompt as any,
He paid his tithes in full when they were due
On what he owned, and on his earnings too.
He wore a tabard smock and rode a mare.
  There was a *Reeve,* also a *Miller,* there,
A College *Manciple* from the Inns of Court,
A papal *Pardoner* and, in close consort,
A Church-Court *Summoner,* riding at a trot,
And finally myself—that was the lot.
  The *Miller* was a chap of sixteen stone,[56]
A great stout fellow big in brawn and bone.
He did well out of them, for he could go
And win the ram at any wrestling show.
Broad, knotty, and short-shouldered, he would
    boast
He could heave any door off hinge and post,
Or take a run and break it with his head.
His beard, like any sow or fox, was red
And broad as well, as though it were a spade;
And, at its very tip, his nose displayed
A wart on which there stood a tuft of hair
Red as the bristles in an old sow's ear.
His nostrils were as black as they were wide.
He had a sword and buckler at his side,
His mighty mouth was like a furnace door.
A wrangler and buffoon, he had a store
Of tavern stories, filthy in the main.

---

55. ***find . . . enrolled.*** The Parson refuses the easy work of the paid chaplain for a London guild.
56. ***sixteen stone,*** two hundred twenty-four pounds.

notes and comments

Chaucer's Words to His Scribe

Chaucer's worry about scribal errors and their distortions of meaning is apparent in this half-humorous curse addressed to the man who copied his manuscripts. *Boece* and *Troilus* are two of Chaucer's works.

Adam scriveyn, if ever it thee bifalle
Boece or Troilus to wryten newe,
Under thy long lokkes° thou most have the scalle°, — locks/
But after my makyn thou wryte more trewe; — mange
So oft a-days I mot thy werk renewe,
It to correcte and eek to rubbe and scrape°; — erase
And al is thorough thy negligence and rape.° — haste

His was a master-hand at stealing grain.
He felt it with his thumb and thus he knew
Its quality and took three times his due—
A thumb of gold,[57] by God, to gauge an oat!
He wore a hood of blue and a white coat.
He liked to play his bagpipes up and down
And that was how he brought us out of town.
  The *Manciple* came from the Inner Temple;[58]
All caterers might follow his example
In buying victuals; he was never rash
Whether he bought on credit or paid cash.
He used to watch the market most precisely
And got in first, and so he did quite nicely.
Now isn't it a marvel of God's grace
That an illiterate fellow can outpace
The wisdom of a heap of learned men?
His masters—he had more than thirty then—
All versed in the abstrusest legal knowledge,
Could have produced a dozen from their College
Fit to be stewards in land and rents and game
To any Peer in England you could name,
And show him how to live on what he had
Debt-free (unless of course the Peer were mad)
Or be as frugal as he might desire,
And they were fit to help about the Shire
In any legal case there was to try;
And yet this Manciple could wipe their eye.
  The *Reeve*[59] was old and choleric and thin;
His beard was shaven closely to the skin,
His shorn hair came abruptly to a stop
Above his ears, and he was docked on top
Just like a priest in front; his legs were lean,
Like sticks they were, no calf was to be seen.
He kept his bins and garners very trim;
No auditor could gain a point on him.
And he could judge by watching drought and rain
The yield he might expect from seed and grain.
His master's sheep, his animals and hens,
Pigs, horses, dairies, stores and cattle-pens
Were wholly trusted to his government.
And he was under contract to present
The accounts, right from his master's earliest years.
No one had ever caught him in arrears.
No bailiff,[60] serf, or herdsman dared to kick,
He knew their dodges, knew their every trick;
Feared like the plague he was, by those beneath.
He had a lovely dwelling on a heath,
Shadowed in green by trees above the sward.
A better hand at bargains than his lord,
He had grown rich and had a store of treasure
Well tucked away, yet out it came to pleasure
His lord with subtle loans or gifts of goods,
To earn his thanks and even coats and hoods.

57. ***thumb of gold.*** Unscrupulous millers would secretly press their thumbs down on their scales when weighing grain to take more for themselves.
58. ***Manciple . . . from the Inner Temple.*** London lawyers formed themselves into societies which inhabited buildings once owned by the ancient society of Knights of the Temple. They hired administrators, called manciples, to purchase food for their meals.
59. ***Reeve,*** a minor official on a country estate who served as an intermediary between the lord of the manor and his serfs.
60. ***bailiff,*** a servant of the lord of the manor whose job was to help direct the maintenance of farms. Traditionally a superior to the reeve.

When young he'd learnt a useful trade and still
He was a carpenter of first-rate skill.
The stallion-cob he rode at a slow trot
Was dapple-grey and bore the name of Scot.
He wore an overcoat of bluish shade
And rather long; he had a rusty blade
Slung at his side. He came, as I heard tell,
From Norfolk, near a place called Baldeswell.
His coat was tucked under his belt and splayed.
He rode the hindmost of our cavalcade.
There was a *Summoner*[61] with us in the place
Who had a fire-red cherubinnish face,
For he had carbuncles.[62] His eyes were narrow,
He was as hot and lecherous as a sparrow.
Black, scabby brows he had, and a thin beard.
Children were afraid when he appeared.
No quicksilver, lead ointments, tartar creams,
Boracic, no, nor brimstone, so it seems,
Could make a salve that had the power to bite,
Clean up or cure his whelks of knobby white
Or purge the pimples sitting on his cheeks.
Garlic he loved, and onions too, and leeks,
And drinking strong wine till all was hazy.
Then he would shout and jabber as if crazy,
And wouldn't speak a word except in Latin
When he was drunk, such tags as he was pat in;
He only had a few, say two or three,
That he had mugged up out of some decree;
No wonder, for he heard them every day.
And, as you know, a man can teach a jay
To call out "Walter" better than the Pope.
But had you tried to test his wits and grope
For more, you'd have found nothing in the bag.
Then *"Questio quid juris"*[63] was his tag.
He was a gentle varlet and a kind one,
No better fellow if you went to find one.
He would allow—just for a quart of wine—
Any good lad to keep a concubine
A twelvemonth and dispense it altogether!
Yet he could pluck a finch to leave no feather.[64]
And if he found some rascal with a maid
He would instruct him not to be afraid
In such a case of the Archdeacon's curse
(Unless the rascal's soul were in his purse)
For in his purse the punishment should be.
"Purse is the good Archdeacon's Hell," said he.
But well I know he lied in what he said;
A curse should put a guilty man in dread,
For curses kill, as shriving brings, salvation.
We should beware of excommunication.
Thus, as he pleased, the man could bring duress
On any young fellow in the diocese.
He knew their secrets, they did what he said.
He wore a garland set upon his head
Large as the holly-bush upon a stake
Outside an ale-house;[65] and he had a cake,
A round one, which it was his joke to wield
As if it were intended for a shield.
He and a gentle *Pardoner*[66] rode together,
A bird from Charing Cross[67] of the same feather,
Just back from visiting the Court of Rome.
He loudly sang *"Come hither, love, come home!"*
The Summoner sang deep seconds to this song,
No trumpet ever sounded half so strong.
This Pardoner had hair as yellow as wax,
Hanging down smoothly like a hank of flax.
In driblets fell his locks behind his head
Down to his shoulders which they overspread;
Thinly they fell, like rat-tails, one by one.
He wore no hood upon his head, for fun;
The hood inside his wallet[68] had been stowed,
He aimed at riding in the latest mode;
But for a little cap his head was bare
And he had bulging eye-balls, like a hare.
He'd sewed a holy relic on his cap;
His wallet lay before him on his lap,
Brimful of pardons come from Rome all hot.
He had the same small voice a goat has got.
His chin no beard had harboured, nor would harbour,

---

61. ***Summoner,*** a paid messenger who summoned "sinners" to appear before an ecclesiastical court.
62. ***carbuncles,*** pimples.
63. ***"Questio quid juris."*** "The question is, what part of the law applies?"
64. ***Yet . . . feather.*** The Summoner indulged in the same sins he is just said to have excused in others.
65. ***Large . . . ale-house.*** A tavern was customarily identified by such a bush on a stake.
66. ***Pardoner.*** In the Middle Ages sinners under sentence of an extended penance could purchase a remittance of their penance duties from official pardoners. This soon led to corrupt practices, the ignorant believing they could buy complete forgiveness for a sin. Fake pardoners were only too willing to exploit such people.
67. ***Charing Cross,*** district of London in which was located the hospital of the Blessed Mary of Rouncivalle. In Chaucer's time unauthorized pardons were sold by persons claiming they were collecting money for the hospital, and Pardoners of Rouncivalle were often satirized.
68. ***wallet,*** pack.

Smoother than ever chin was left by barber.
I judge he was a gelding, or a mare.
As to his trade, from Berwick down to Ware
There was no pardoner of equal grace,
For in his trunk he had a pillow-case
Which he asserted was Our Lady's veil.
He said he had a gobbet[69] of the sail
Saint Peter had the time when he made bold
To walk the waves, till Jesu Christ took hold.
He had a cross of metal set with stones
And, in a glass, a rubble of pigs' bones.
And with these relics, any time he found
Some poor up-country parson to astound,
On one short day, in money down, he drew
More than the parson in a month or two,
And by his flatteries and prevarication
Made monkeys of the priest and congregation.
But still to do him justice first and last
In church he was a noble ecclesiast.
How well he read a lesson or told a story!
But best of all he sang an Offertory,
For well he knew that when that song was sung
He'd have to preach and tune his honey-tongue
And (well he could) win silver from the crowd.
That's why he sang so merrily and loud.
Now I have told you shortly, in a clause,
The rank, the array, the number and the cause
Of our assembly in this company
In Southwark, at that high-class hostelry
Known as *The Tabard,* close beside *The Bell.*
And now the time has come for me to tell
How we behaved that evening; I'll begin
After we had alighted at the Inn,
Then I'll report our journey, stage by stage,
All the remainder of our pilgrimage.
But first I beg of you, in courtesy,
Not to condemn me as unmannerly
If I speak plainly and with no concealings
And give account of all their words and dealings,
Using their very phrases as they fell.
For certainly, as you all know so well,
He who repeats a tale after a man
Is bound to say, as nearly as he can,
Each single word, if he remembers it,
However rudely spoken or unfit,
Or else the tale he tells will be untrue,
The things invented and the phrases new.
He may not flinch although it were his brother,
If he says one word he must say the other.
And Christ Himself spoke broad in Holy Writ,
And as you know there's nothing there unfit,
And Plato says, for those with power to read,
"The word should be as cousin to the deed."
Further I beg you to forgive it me
If I neglect the order and degree
And what is due to rank in what I've planned.
I'm short of wit as you will understand.
Our *Host* gave us great welcome; everyone
Was given a place and supper was begun.
He served the finest victuals you could think,
The wine was strong and we were glad to drink.
A very striking man our Host withal,
And fit to be a marshal in a hall.
His eyes were bright, his girth a little wide;
There is no finer burgess in Cheapside.[70]
Bold in his speech, yet wise and full of tact,
There was no manly attribute he lacked,
What's more he was a merry-hearted man.
After our meal he jokingly began
To talk of sport, and, among other things
After we'd settled up our reckonings,
He said as follows: "Truly, gentlemen,
You're very welcome and I can't think when
—Upon my word I'm telling you no lie—
I've seen a gathering here that looked so spry,
No, not this year, as in this tavern now.
I'd think you up some fun if I knew how.
And, as it happens, a thought has just occurred
And it will cost you nothing, on my word.
You're off to Canterbury—well, God speed!
Blessed St. Thomas answer to your need!
And I don't doubt, before the journey's done
You mean to while the time in tales and fun.
Indeed, there's little pleasure for your bones
Riding along and all as dumb as stones.
So let me then propose for your enjoyment,
Just as I said, a suitable employment.
And if my notion suits and you agree
And promise to submit yourselves to me
Playing your parts exactly as I say
Tomorrow as you ride along the way,
Then by my father's soul (and he is dead)
If you don't like it you can have my head!
Hold up your hands, and not another word."
Well, our consent of course was not deferred,

69. ***gobbet,*** piece.
70. ***burgess in Cheapside,*** citizen of a district in London.

It seemed not worth a serious debate;
We all agreed to it at any rate
And bade him issue what commands he would.
"My lords," he said, "now listen for your good,
And please don't treat my notion with disdain.
This is the point. I'll make it short and plain.
Each one of you shall help to make things slip
By telling two stories on the outward trip
To Canterbury, that's what I intend,
And, on the homeward way to journey's end
Another two, tales from the days of old;
And then the man whose story is best told,
That is to say who gives the fullest measure
Of good morality and general pleasure,
He shall be given a supper, paid by all,
Here in this tavern, in this very hall,
When we come back again from Canterbury.
And in the hope to keep you bright and merry
I'll go along with you myself and ride
All at my own expense and serve as guide.
I'll be the judge, and those who won't obey
Shall pay for what we spend upon the way.
Now if you all agree to what you've heard
Tell me at once without another word,
And I will make arrangements early for it."
  Of course we all agreed, in fact we swore it
Delightedly, and made entreaty too
That he should act as he proposed to do,
Become our Governor in short, and be
Judge of our tales and general referee,
And set the supper at a certain price.
We promised to be ruled by his advice
Come high, come low; unanimously thus
We set him up in judgement over us.
More wine was fetched, the business being done;
We drank it off and up went everyone
To bed without a moment of delay.
  Early next morning at the spring of day
Up rose our Host and roused us like a cock,
Gathering us together in a flock,
And off we rode at slightly faster pace

Detail, Tavern Scene, from the Luttrell Psalter. Reproduced by permission of the British Library Board.

Than walking to St Thomas' watering-place;[71]
And there our Host drew up, began to ease
His horse, and said, "Now, listen if you please,
My lords! Remember what you promised me.
If evensong and matins will agree[72]
Let's see who shall be first to tell a tale.
And as I hope to drink good wine and ale
I'll be your judge. The rebel who disobeys,
However much the journey costs, he pays.
Now draw for cut and then we can depart;
The man who draws the shortest cut shall
start. . . ."

71. ***St Thomas' watering-place,*** a brook on the pilgrimage route to Canterbury.
72. ***If evensong . . . agree.*** If you feel in the morning (matins) as you did the night before (evensong).

Discussion

1. **(a)** The narrator describes the first pilgrim as "a true, a perfect gentle-knight." (line 74) What characteristics of the man qualify him for such praise? How do his clothes hint at his virtues? **(b)** By contrast, what motivates the Knight's Squire? How do his clothes suggest this?

2. What do the Prioress's pet dogs tell us about her?

3. **(a)** What details in the character sketch of the poor Parson show that Chaucer regards him as the ideal priest? **(b)** What is Chaucer's opinion of the Monk, the Friar, the Summoner, and the Pardoner? Why do the sketches of these four amuse us while that of the Parson does not?

4. **(a)** In what ways are the Merchant, Oxford Cleric, Serjeant at Law, and the Doctor typical of their professions? **(b)** If you had to deal with each, which would you trust and which would you watch cautiously?

5. **(a)** In what ways do the Skipper and Miller cheat others? Could they trick the Reeve? **(b)** Given these examples, would you call Chaucer's age more corrupt than ours?

6. In lines 743–764 Chaucer disclaims responsibility for anything offensive in what he is about to present. **(a)** How do you feel about his statement that an author "is bound to say, as nearly as he can, each single word, if he remembers it, however rudely spoken or unfit"? **(b)** What might have been Chaucer's reason for ending this passage with the line "I'm short of wit as you will understand"? **(c)** Considered in its entirety, does the passage reflect the views of Chaucer the pilgrim, Chaucer the poet-satirist, or both?

Vocabulary
Context and Dictionary

A. Use context as an aid to interpret the italicized word in each of the following passages; then on a separate sheet of paper use the italicized word in a sentence of your own that shows you understand the meaning of the word. You may use your Glossary if you are not entirely certain of the meaning. Be sure you can pronounce and spell all italicized words.

1. "When in April the sweet showers fall / And pierce the drought of March to the root, and all / The veins are bathed in liquor of such power / As brings about the *engendering* of the flower. . . ."

2. "Our Host gave us great welcome; everyone / Was given a place and supper was begun. / He served the finest *victuals* you could think. . . ."

3. "As for her sympathies and tender feelings, / She was so charitably *solicitous* / She used to weep if she but saw a mouse / Caught in a trap, if it were dead or bleeding."

4. "I saw his sleeves were *garnished* at the hand / With fine grey fur, the finest in the land. . . ."

B. Use your Glossary to answer the following questions on your paper.

5. **(a)** The word *boor* comes from one of two languages. What are they? **(b)** What did the word originally mean?

6. What specific epidemic disease can *pestilence* refer to?

7. What is the Latin word from which *eminent* comes?

8. Give the Old French and Latin words from which *accrue* comes.

The Wife of Bath's Tale

The Wife of Bath's Prologue

If there were no authority on earth
Except experience, mine, for what it's worth,
And that's enough for me, all goes to show
That marriage is a misery and a woe;
For let me say, if I may make so bold,
My lords, since when I was but twelve years old,
Thanks be to God Eternal evermore,
Five husbands have I had at the church door;
Yes, it's a fact that I have had so many,
All worthy in their way, as good as any. . . .
Welcome the sixth, whenever he appears.
I can't keep continent for years and years.
No sooner than one husband's dead and gone
Some other christian man shall take me on,
For then, so says the Apostle,[1] I am free
To wed, o'God's name, where it pleases me.
Wedding's no sin, so far as I can learn.
Better it is to marry than to burn. . . .
Show me a time or text where God disparages,
Or sets a prohibition upon marriages
Expressly, let me have it! Show it me!
And where did He command virginity?
I know as well as you do, never doubt it,
All the Apostle Paul has said about it;
He said that as for precepts he had none.
One may advise a woman to be one;
Advice is no commandment in my view.
He left it in our judgement what to do. . . .
And as for being married, he lets me do it
Out of indulgence, so there's nothing to it
In marrying me, suppose my husband dead;
There's nothing bigamous in such a bed. . . .
"I grant it you. I'll never say a word
Decrying maidenhood although preferred
To frequent marriage; there are those who mean
To live in their virginity, as clean
In body as in soul, and never mate.
I'll make no boast about my own estate.
As in a noble household, we are told,
Not every dish and vessel's made of gold,
Some are of wood, yet earn their master's praise,
God calls His folk to Him in many ways.
To each of them God gave His proper gift,
Some this, some that, and left them to make shift.
Virginity is indeed a great perfection,
And married continence, for God's dilection,
But Christ, who of perfection is the well,
Bade not that everyone should go and sell
All that he had and give it to the poor
To follow in His footsteps, that is sure.
He spoke to those that would live perfectly,
And by your leave, my lords, that's not for me.
I will bestow the flower of life, the honey,
Upon the acts and fruit of matrimony.
". . . I'll have a husband yet
Who shall be both my debtor and my slave
And bear his tribulation to the grave
Upon his flesh, as long as I'm his wife.
For mine shall be the power all his life
Over his proper body, and not he,
Thus the Apostle Paul has told it me,
In bidding husbands love their wives, I say.
That's an opinion suits me every way."
The Pardoner started up, and thereupon
"Madam," he said, "by God and by St John,
That's noble preaching no one could surpass!
I was about to take a wife; alas!
Am I to buy it on my flesh so dear?
There'll be no marrying for me this year!"
"You wait," she said, "my story's not begun.
You'll taste another brew before I've done;
You'll find it isn't quite so nice as beer.
For while the tale is telling you shall hear
Of all the tribulations man and wife
Can have; I've been an expert all my life,
That is to say, myself have been the whip.
So please yourself whether you want to sip
At that same cask of marriage I shall broach;
Be cautious before making the approach. . . ."
"Madam, I put it to you as a prayer,"
The Pardoner said, "go on as you began!
Tell us your tale, spare not for any man.
Instruct us younger men in your technique."
"Gladly," she answered, "if I am to speak.
But still I hope the company won't reprove me
Though I should speak as fantasy may move me,
And please don't be offended at my views;
They're really only offered to amuse.

---

1. ***Apostle,*** St. Paul. In the passages that follow, the Wife quotes scripture freely—but not always accurately—to support her arguments.

"Now, gentlemen, I'll on and tell my tale
And as I hope to drink good wine and ale
I'll tell the truth. Those husbands that I had,
Three of them were good and two were bad.
The three that I call 'good' were rich and old. . . .
I governed them so well and held the rein
So firmly they were rapturously fain
To go and buy me pretty things to wear;
They were delighted if I spoke them fair.
God knows how spitefully I used to scold them.
"Listen, I'll tell you how I used to hold them,
You knowing women, who can understand.
First put them in the wrong, and out of hand.
No one can be so bold—I mean no man—
At lies and swearing as a woman can.
This is no news, as you'll have realized,
To knowing ones, but to the misadvised.
A knowing wife if she is worth her salt
Can always prove her husband is at fault,
And even though the fellow may have heard
Some story told him by a little bird
She knows enough to prove the bird is crazy
And get her maid to witness she's a daisy,
With full agreement, scarce solicited.
But listen. Here's the sort of thing I said:
" 'Now, sir old dotard, what is that you say?
Why is my neighbour's wife so smart and gay?
She is respected everywhere she goes.
I sit at home and have no decent clothes.
Why haunt her house? What are you doing there?
Are you so amorous? Is she so fair?
What, whispering secrets to our maid? For shame,
Sir ancient lecher! Time you dropped that game.
And if I see my gossip or a friend
You scold me like a devil! There's no end
If I as much as stroll towards his house.
Then you come home as drunken as a mouse,
You mount your throne and preach, chapter and verse
—All nonsense—and you tell me it's a curse
To marry a poor woman—she's expensive;
Or if her family's wealthy and extensive
You say it's torture to endure her pride
And melancholy airs, and more beside. . . .
" 'You say that some desire us for our wealth,
Some for our shapeliness, our looks, our health,
Some for our singing, others for our dancing,
Some for our gentleness and dalliant glancing,
And some because our hands are soft and small;
By your account the devil gets us all.
That's what you say as you stump off to bed,
You brute! You say no man of sense would wed,
That is, not if he wants to go to Heaven.
Wild thunderbolts and fire from the seven
Planets descend and break your withered neck!
" 'You say that buildings falling into wreck,
And smoke, and scolding women, are the three
Things that will drive a man from home. Dear me!
What ails the poor old man to grumble so?
" 'We women hide our faults to let them show
Once we are safely married, so you say.
There's a fine proverb for a popinjay![2]
" 'You say that oxen, asses, hounds and horses
Can be tried out on various ploys and courses;
And basins too, and dishes when you buy them,
Spoons, chairs and furnishings, a man can try them
As he can try a suit of clothes, no doubt,
But no one ever tries a woman out
Until he's married her; old dotard crow!
And then you say she lets her vices show.
" 'You also say we count it for a crime
Unless you praise our beauty all the time,
Unless you're always poring on our faces
And call us pretty names in public places;
Or if you fail to treat me to a feast
Upon my birthday—presents at the least—
Or to respect my nurse and her grey hairs,
Or be polite to all my maids upstairs
And to my father's cronies and his spies.
That's what you say, old barrelful of lies!
" 'Then there's our young apprentice, handsome Johnny;
Because he has crisp hair that shines as bonny
As finest gold, and squires me up and down
You show your low suspicions in a frown.
I wouldn't have him, not if you died to-morrow!

2. ***popinjay,*** parrot.

" 'And tell me this, God punish you with sorrow,
Why do you hide the keys of coffer doors?
It's just as much my property as yours.
Do you want to make an idiot of your wife?
Now, by the Lord that gave me soul and life,
I think you'd like to lock me in your coffer!
"Go where you please, dear wife," you ought to offer,
"Amuse yourself! I shan't give ear to malice,
I know you for a virtuous wife, Dame Alice."
We cannot love a husband who takes charge
Of where we go. We like to be at large. . . .
" 'And when a woman tries a mild display
In dress or costly ornament, you say
It is a danger to her chastity,
And then, bad luck to you, start making free
With Bible tags in the Apostle's name;[3]
"And in like manner, chastely and with shame,
You women should adorn yourselves," said he,
"And not with braided hair or jewelry
With pearl or golden ornament." What next!
I'll pay as much attention to your text
And rubric in such things as would a gnat.
" 'And once you said that I was like a cat,
For if you singe a cat it will not roam
And that's the way to keep a cat at home.
But when she feels her fur is sleek and gay
She can't be kept indoors for half a day
But off she takes herself as dusk is falling
To show her fur and go a-caterwauling.
Which means if I feel gay, as you suppose,
I shall run out to show my poor old clothes.
" 'Silly old fool! You and your private spies!
Go on, beg Argus[4] with his hundred eyes
To be my bodyguard, that's better still!
But yet he shan't, I say, against my will.
I'll pull him by the beard, believe you me!
" 'And once you said that principally three
Misfortunes[5] trouble earth, east, west and north,
And no man living could endure a fourth.
My dear sir shrew, Jesu cut short your life!
You preach away and say a hateful wife
Is reckoned to be one of these misfortunes.
Is there no other trouble that importunes
The world and that your parables could condemn?
Must an unhappy wife be one of them?
" 'Then you compared a woman's love to Hell,
To barren land where water will not dwell,
And you compared it to a quenchless fire,
The more it burns the more is its desire
To burn up everything that burnt can be.
You say that just as worms destroy a tree
A wife destroys her husband and contrives,
As husbands know, the ruin of their lives.'
"Such was the way, my lords, you understand
I kept my older husbands well in hand.
I told them they were drunk and their unfitness
To judge my conduct forced me to take witness
That they were lying. Johnny and my niece
Would back me up. O Lord, I wrecked their peace,
Innocent as they were, without remorse!
For I could bite and whinney like a horse
And launch complaints when things were all my fault;
I'd have been lost if I had called a halt.
First to the mill is first to grind your corn;
I attacked first and they were overborne,
Glad to apologize and even suing
Pardon for what they'd never thought of doing.
"I'd tackle one for wenching, out of hand,
Although so ill the man could hardly stand,
Yet he felt flattered in his heart because
He thought it showed how fond of him I was.
I swore that all my walking out at night
Was just to keep his wenching well in sight.
That was a dodge that made me shake with mirth;
But all such wit is given us at birth.
Lies, tears, and spinning are the things God gives
By nature to a woman, while she lives.
So there's one thing at least that I can boast,
That in the end I always ruled the roost;
Cunning or force was sure to make them stumble,
And always keeping up a steady grumble. . . .

3. ***Apostle's name.*** The reference is to 1 Timothy 2:9. Note that the Wife is accusing her husband of using the same tactics that she constantly uses herself.
4. ***Argus,*** in Greek legend, a hundred-eyed giant who never closed all his eyes in sleep at the same time and therefore kept constant watch.
5. ***three/Misfortunes.*** She is alluding to Proverbs 3:21–23: "For three things the earth is disquieted, and for four which it cannot bear: for a servant when he reigneth; and a fool when he is filled with meat; for an odious woman when she is married; and an handmaid that is heir to her mistress."

"I then would say, 'My dear, just take a peep!
What a meek look on Willikin our sheep!
Comc nearer, husband, let me kiss your cheek;
You should be just as patient, just as meek;
Sweeten your heart. Your conscience needs a probe.
You're fond of preaching patience out of Job,
And so be patient; practise what you preach,
And if you don't, my dear, we'll have to teach
You that it's nice to have a quiet life.
One of us must be master, man or wife,
And since a man's more reasonable, he
Should be the patient one, you must agree. . .
"That's how my first three husbands were undone.
Now let me tell you of my last but one.
"He was a reveller, was number four;
That is to say he kept a paramour.
And I was young, ah, ragery's the word,
Stubborn and strong and jolly as a bird.
Play me the harp and I would dance and sing,
Believe me, like a nightingale in spring,
If I had had a draught of sweetened wine. . . .
"But . . . ! Whenever it comes back to me,
When I recall my youth and jollity,
It fairly warms the cockles of my heart!
This very day I feel a pleasure start,
Yes, I can feel it tickling at the root.
Lord, how it does me good! I've had my fruit,
I've had my world and time, I've had my fling!
But age that comes to poison everything
Has taken all my beauty and my pith.
Well, let it go, the devil go therewith!
The flour is gone, there is no more to say,
And I must sell the bran as best I may;
But still I mean to find my way to fun. . . .
Now let me tell you of my last but one.
"I told you how it filled my heart with spite
To see another woman his delight,
By God and all His saints I made it good!
I carved him out a cross of the same wood,
Not with my body in a filthy way,
But certainly by seeming rather gay
To others, frying him in his own grease
Of jealousy and rage; he got no peace.
By God on earth I was his purgatory,
For which I hope his soul may be in glory.
God knows he sang a sorry tune, he flinched,
And bitterly enough, when the shoe pinched.
And God and he alone can say how grim,
How many were the ways I tortured him.
"He died when I came back from Jordan Stream[6]
And he lies buried under the rood-beam,[7]
Albeit that his tomb can scarce supply us
With such a show as that of King Darius
—Apelles sculped it in a sumptuous taste—
But costly burial would have been mere waste.
Farewell to him, God give his spirit rest!
He's in his grave, he's nailed up in his chest.
"Now of my fifth, last husband let me tell.
God never let his soul be sent to Hell!
And yet he was my worst, and many a blow
He struck me still can ache along my row
Of ribs, and will until my dying day. . . .
Though he had beaten me in every bone
He still could wheedle me to love, I own.
I think I loved him best, I'll tell no lie.
He was disdainful in his love, that's why.
We women have a curious fantasy
In such affairs, or so it seems to me.
When something's difficult, or can't be had,
We crave and cry for it all day like mad.
Forbid a thing, we pine for it all night,
Press fast upon us and we take to flight;
We use disdain in offering our wares.
A throng of buyers sends prices up at fairs,
Cheap goods have little value, they suppose;
And that's a thing that every woman knows.
"My fifth and last—God keep his soul in health!
The one I took for love and not for wealth,
Had been at Oxford not so long before
But had left school and gone to lodge next door,
Yes, it was to my godmother's he'd gone.
God bless her soul! *Her* name was Alison.
She knew my heart and more of what I thought
Than did the parish priest, and so she ought!
"And so one time it happened that in Lent,
As I so often did, I rose and went
To see her, ever wanting to be gay
And go a-strolling, March, April, and May,
From house to house for chat and village malice.

6. ***When I . . . Jordan Stream,*** when she returned from one of her pilgrimages to the Holy Land.

7. ***rood-beam,*** a beam, usually between the chancel and the nave of a church, on which was placed a rood or crucifix. Burial within the chancel itself would have been more expensive.

notes and comments

Opinions of the Wife

"I translated Chaucer . . . and, amongst the rest, pitched on the *Wife of Bath's Tale;* not daring, as I have said, to adventure on her *Prologue* because 'tis too licentious."

John Dryden, in his Preface to *Fables,* 1700

"The Characters of Women Chaucer has divided into two classes, the Lady Prioress and the Wife of Bath. Are not these leaders of the ages of men? The lady prioress, in some ages, predominates; and in some the wife of Bath, in whose character Chaucer has been . . . minute and exact, because she is . . . a scourge and a blight. I shall say no more of her, nor expose what Chaucer has left hidden; let the young reader study what he has said of her: it is useful as a scarecrow. There are of such characters born too many for the peace of the world."

William Blake, in *A Descriptive Catalogue of Pictures, Poetical and Historical Inventions,* 1809.

"The Wife of Bath is without doubt the most outrageous woman who ever walked into immortality. . . . Chaucer has given her his own irrepressible delight in living, and her whole discourse is one whoop of satisfaction over the fun she has had."

Marchette Chute in *Geoffrey Chaucer of England,* 1946.

"Johnny (the boy from Oxford) and Dame Alice
And I myself, into the fields we went.
My husband was in London all that Lent;
All the more fun for me—I only mean
The fun of seeing people and being seen
By cocky lads; for how was I to know
Where or what graces Fortune might bestow?
And so I made a round of visitations,
Went to processions, festivals, orations,
Preachments and pilgrimages, watched the carriages
They use for plays and pageants, went to marriages,
And always wore my gayest scarlet dress.
"These worms, these moths, these mites, I must confess,
Got little chance to eat it, by the way.
Why not? Because I wore it every day.
"Now let me tell you all that came to pass.
We sauntered in the meadows through the grass
Toying and dallying to such extent,
Johnny and I, that I grew provident
And I suggested, were I ever free
And made a widow, he should marry me.
And certainly—I do not mean to boast—
I ever was more provident than most
In marriage matters and in other such.
I never think a mouse is up to much
That only has one hole in all the house;
If that should fail, well, it's good-bye the mouse.
"I let him think I was as one enchanted
(That was a trick my godmother implanted)
And told him I had dreamt the night away
Thinking of him, and dreamt that as I lay
He tried to kill me. Blood had drenched the bed.
'But still it was a lucky dream,' I said,
'For blood betokens money, I recall.'
It was a lie. I hadn't dreamt at all.
'Twas from my godmother I learnt my lore
In matters such as that, and many more.
"Well, let me see . . . what had I to explain?
Aha! By God, I've got the thread again.
"When my fourth husband lay upon his bier
I wept all day and looked as drear as drear,
As widows must, for it is quite in place,
And with a handkerchief I hid my face.
Now that I felt provided with a mate
I wept but little, I need hardly state.
"To church they bore my husband on the morrow

With all the neighbours round him venting sorrow,
And one of them of course was handsome Johnny.
So help me God, I thought he looked so bonny
Behind the coffin! Heavens, what a pair
Of legs he had! Such feet, so clean and fair!
I gave my whole heart up, for him to hold.
He was, I think, some twenty winters old,
And I was forty then, to tell the truth.
But still, I always had a coltish tooth.
Yes, I'm gap-toothed; it suits me well I feel,
It is the print of Venus and her seal.
So help me God I was a lusty one,
Fair, young and well-to-do, and full of fun!
"What shall I say? Before the month was gone
This gay young student, my delightful John,
Had married me in solemn festival.
I handed him the money, lands, and all
That ever had been given me before;
This I repented later, more and more.
None of my pleasures would he let me seek.
By God, he smote me once upon the cheek
Because I tore a page out of his book,
And that's the reason why I'm deaf. But look,
Stubborn I was, just like a lioness;
As to my tongue, a very wrangleness.
I went off gadding as I had before
From house to house, however much he swore.
Because of that he used to preach and scold,
Drag Roman history up from days of old,
How one Simplicius Gallus left his wife,
Deserting her completely all his life,
Only for poking out her head one day
Without a hat, upon the public way.
"Some other Roman—I forget his name—
Because his wife went to a summer's game
Without his knowledge, left her in the lurch.
"And he would take the Bible up and search
For proverbs in Ecclesiasticus,
Particularly one that has it thus:
'Suffer no wicked woman to gad about.'
And then would come the saying (need you doubt?)
A man who seeks to build his house of sallows,
A man who spurs a blind horse over fallows,
Or lets his wife make pilgrimage to Hallows,
Is worthy to be hanged upon the gallows.[8]
But all for naught. I didn't give a hen
For all his proverbs and his wise old men.
Nor would I take rebuke at any price;
I hate a man who points me out my vice,
And so, God knows, do many more than I.
That drove him raging mad, you may rely.
No more would I forbear him, I can promise.
"Now let me tell you truly by St Thomas
About that book and why I tore the page
And how he smote me deaf in very rage.
"He had a book, he kept it on his shelf,
And night and day he read it to himself
And laughed aloud, although it was quite serious.
He called it *Theophrastus and Valerius*.[9] . . .
"It was a book that dealt with wicked wives;
He knew more legends of them and their lives
Than there are good ones mentioned in the Bible.
For take my word for it, there is no libel
On women that the clergy will not paint,
Except when writing of a woman-saint,
But never good of other women, though.
Who called the lion savage? Do you know?
By God, if women had but written stories
Like those the clergy keep in oratories,
More had been written of man's wickedness
Than all the sons of Adam could redress.
"Now to my purpose as I told you; look,
Here's how I got a beating for a book.
One evening Johnny, glowering with ire,
Sat with his book and read it by the fire.
And first he read of Eve whose wickedness
Brought all mankind to sorrow and distress,
Root-cause why Jesus Christ Himself was slain
And gave His blood to buy us back again.
Aye, there's the text where you expressly find
That woman brought the loss of all mankind.
"He read me then how Samson as he slept
Was shorn of all his hair by her he kept,
And by that treachery Samson lost his eyes.
And then he read me, if I tell no lies,
All about Hercules and Deianire;
She tricked him into setting himself on fire.
"He left out nothing of the miseries
Occasioned by his wives to Socrates. . . .

---

8. ***A man . . . gallows,*** a proverbial saying that apparently reflects Johnny's opinion of the Wife's pilgrimages. *Sallows* are willow twigs; *fallows* are fields that have been plowed but left unseeded.

9. ***Theophrastus and Valerius,*** a satire on matrimony attributed to Walter Map, a wit and cynic who lived about A.D. 1200.

"The Cook and His Wife" by Albrecht Durer, c. 1496. Kupferstichkabinett.

"And then he told how one Latumius
Lamented to his comrade Arrius
That in his orchard-plot there grew a tree
On which his wives had hanged themselves, all three,
Or so he said, out of some spite or other;
To which this Arrius replied, 'Dear brother,
Give me a cutting from that blessed tree
And planted in my garden it shall be!' . . .
"Who could imagine, who could figure out
The torture in my heart? It reached the top
And when I saw that he would never stop
Reading this cursed book, all night no doubt,
I suddenly grabbed and tore three pages out
Where he was reading, at the very place,
And fisted such a buffet in his face
That backwards down into our fire he fell.
"Then like a maddened lion, with a yell
He started up and smote me on the head,
And down I fell upon the floor for dead.
"And when he saw how motionless I lay
He was aghast and would have fled away,
But in the end I started to come to.
'O have you murdered me, you robber, you,
To get my land?' I said. 'Was that the game?
Before I'm dead I'll kiss you all the same.'
"He came up close and kneeling gently down
He said, 'My love, my dearest Alison,
So help me God, I never again will hit
You, love; and if I did, you asked for it.
Forgive me!' But for all he was so meek
I up at once and smote him on the cheek
And said, 'Take that to level up the score!
Now let me die. I can't speak any more.'
"We had a mort of trouble and heavy weather
But in the end we made it up together.
He gave the bridle over to my hand,
Gave me the government of house and land,
Of tongue and fist, indeed of all he'd got.
I made him burn that book upon the spot.
And when I'd mastered him, and out of deadlock
Secured myself the sovereignty in wedlock,
And when he said, 'My own and truest wife,
Do as you please for all the rest of life,
But guard your honour and my good estate,'
From that day forward there was no debate.
So help me God I was as kind to him
As any wife from Denmark to the rim
Of India, and as true. And he to me.
And I pray God that sits in majesty
To bless his soul and fill it with his glory.
Now, if you'll listen, I will tell my story."

Words between the Summoner and the Friar

The Friar laughed when he had heard all this.
"Well, Ma'am," he said, "as God may send me bliss,
This is a long preamble to a tale!"
But when the Summoner heard the Frair rail,
"Just look at that!" he cried. "God's arms and skin!
These meddling friars are always butting in!
Don't we all know a friar and a fly
Go buzzing into every dish and pie!
What do you mean with your 'preambulation'?
Amble yourself, trot, do a meditation!
You're spoiling all our fun with your commotion."
The Friar smiled and said, "Is that your notion?
I promise on my word before I go
To find occasion for a tale or so

About a summoner that will make us laugh."
"Well, damn your eyes, and on my own behalf,"
The Summoner answered, "mine be damned as well
If I can't think of several tales to tell
About the friars that will make you mourn
Before we get as far as Sittingbourne.
Have you no patience? Look, he's in a huff!"
Our Host called out, "Be quiet, that's enough!
Shut up, and let the woman tell her tale.
You must be drunk, you've taken too much ale.
Now, Ma'am, you go ahead and no demur."
"All right," she said, "it's just as you prefer,
If I have licence from this worthy friar."
"Nothing," said he, "that I should more desire."

The Wife of Bath's Tale

When good King Arthur ruled in ancient days,
(A king that every Briton loves to praise)
This was a land brim-full of fairy folk.
The Elf-Queen and her courtiers joined and broke
Their elfin dance on many a green mead,
Or so was the opinion once, I read,
Hundreds of years ago, in days of yore.
But no one now sees fairies any more,
For now the saintly charity and prayer
Of holy friars seem to have purged the air;
They search the countryside through field and stream
As thick as motes that speckle a sunbeam,
Blessing the halls, the chambers, kitchens, bowers,
Cities and boroughs, castles, courts, and towers,
Thorpes,[10] barns and stables, outhouses and dairies,
And that's the reason why there are no fairies. . . .
Now it so happened, I began to say,
Long, long ago in good King Arthur's day,
There was a knight who was a lusty liver.
One day as he came riding from the river
He saw a maiden walking all forlorn
Ahead of him, alone as she was born.

Detail from a miniature by Vrelant, Arthur and Guinevere are married by the Archbishop of Cantebury (MS. 9243, fol. 39v). Copyright Bibliothèque Royale Albert Ier, Bruxelles

And of that maiden, spite of all she said,
By very force he took her maidenhead.
This act of violence made such a stir,
So much petitioning of the king for her,
That he condemned the knight to lose his head
By course of law. He was as good as dead
(It seems that then the statutes took that view)
But that the queen, and other ladies too,
Implored the king to exercise his grace
So ceaselessly, he gave the queen the case
And granted her his life, and she could choose
Whether to show him mercy or refuse.
The queen returned him thanks with all her might,

10. ***thorpes,*** agricultural villages.

And then she sent a summons to the knight
At her convenience, and expressed her will:
"You stand, for such is the position still,
In no way certain of your life," said she,
"Yet you shall live if you can answer me:
What is the thing that women most desire?
Beware the axe and say as I require.
"If you can't answer on the moment, though,
I will concede you this: you are to go
A twelve month and a day to seek and learn
Sufficient answer, then you shall return.
I shall take gages[11] from you to extort
Surrender of your body to the court."

Sad was the knight and sorrowfully sighed,
But there! All other choices were denied,
And in the end he chose to go away
And to return after a year and day
Armed with such answer as there might be sent
To him by God. He took his leave and went.
He knocked at every house, searched every place,
Yes, anywhere that offered hope of grace.
What could it be that women wanted most?
But all the same he never touched a coast,

11. ***gages,*** pledges, guarantees.

notes and comments

How Original Was Chaucer?

F. N. Robinson

There has been much speculation as to what suggested to Chaucer the idea of a pilgrimage. He may, of course, have been describing an actual experience. At all events he had no occasion to resort to books for knowledge of the pilgrimage as an institution. In the general device of a frame story, or series of tales within an enclosing narrative, it has often been thought that he imitated the *Decameron*.[1] But it now appears improbable that Chaucer knew Boccaccio's great collection of tales, and the idea of tales within a tale was so familiar that no particular model need be sought. Popular from antiquity in the Orient (from which Europe derived in modern times one of the most famous examples, *The Thousand and One Nights),* the type was well known in classical and medieval literature. But the *Canterbury Tales* are unlike most collections of the sort in the fact that the enclosing narrative is not formal or mechanical or merely introductory, but provides, and keeps in action, a social group engaged naturally in mutual entertainment.

Whatever the reason for its adoption, the device of the pilgrimage is one of the happiest ever employed in a collection of stories. It afforded Chaucer an opportunity to bring together a representative group of various classes of society, united by a common religious purpose, yet not so dominated by that purpose as to be unable to give themselves over to enjoyment. Whether such a company would ever have mingled as Chaucer's pilgrims do, or would have entered upon such a round of storytelling, it is idle to discuss, as idle as to question whether the speakers could have been heard from horseback on the road. Literal truth to fact the *Canterbury Tales* obviously do not represent. In their very metrical form there is, if one chooses to be literal-minded, a convention of unreality. But there is essential poetic truth in the portrayal of the characters, in their sentiments and personal relations, and, no less, in the representation of the pilgrimage as a social assemblage.

For the General Prologue, as for the general device of the Canterbury pilgrimage, no real model has been found. Individual sketches of knights or

1. ***Decameron,*** a collection of tales by the Italian writer Giovanni Boccaccio, written 1351–1353. The frame story tells how ten young people who have gone to the country to escape the Black Death pass the time by telling stories. The hundred tales range widely in length, mood, and effect, but tend to be earthy in nature and to emphasize the role of fortune and the triumph of shrewdness in human affairs.

priests or peasants are common enough in medieval literature of France and England, and some of them—like the lazy priest in *Piers Plowman*,[2] who knew his Robin Hood better than his paternoster—have often been adduced to illustrate one or another of Chaucer's characters. Whole works, too, were devoted to the description of the various orders of society, and others to the classification of men and women by physical and temperamental characteristics. With this lore of the physiognomists and social philosophers Chaucer was doubtless familiar. But in none of his predecessors has there been found a gallery of portraits like that in the *Prologue*, and there is very little that is comparable in later English poetry except in Chaucer's avowed imitators.

Chaucer's pilgrims are far more vivid and personal than the usual personified types in medieval allegories. This is perhaps sufficiently accounted for by Chaucer's creative imagination. But it is hard to believe that his men and women were not in some measure drawn from life, and a number of facts confirm this suspicion. Harry Bailly, the Host, has the same name as a contemporary innkeeper in Southwark. In several other instances, details of locality, occupation, and character are given with so much particularity that the temptation has proved irresistible to look for historical counterparts. The probability is strong that Chaucer had contemporary models for his characters. And curiosity on this subject, it is proper to add, is not merely trivial. Such inquiries and conjectures, like the search for literary sources, help toward an understanding of the poet's imagination and of the material on which it worked.

Individual as the pilgrims are, they are also representative. Many of them exhibit types of character or of professional conduct—the gentle Knight, the venal Friar, the hypocrite in the person of the Pardoner—such as were familiar in the literature of the age. And taken together, they cover nearly the whole range of life in Chaucer's England. The circle of royalty and the higher nobility, to be sure, is not directly represented. Men of such rank and station could hardly have been included in the company. But the mind and manners of courtly society are well expressed by the Knight, who had seen honorable service at home and abroad; by his son the Squire, the typical courtly lover; again, from a different angle, by the Prioress; and, best of all, by Chaucer himself, the accomplished courtier and man of the world, who as author creates the atmosphere and medium of the whole narrative. The clergy, regular and secular, are included in liberal number, and there are also represented the learned professions of law and medicine, the merchants and the craftsmen of the guild, officials of the manor, the sailor, and the common peasant farmer. It would be hard to find such a description of English society between the *Beowulf*, with its picture of the heroic age, and the broader canvas of the Elizabethan drama.

In keeping with the miscellaneous character of the company is the wide range of tastes and interests represented by the stories they relate. Nearly every type of medieval fiction appears, and appears at its best. In almost every case Chaucer assigned to a pilgrim a tale suited to his character and vocation. He represents the party as engaged in free and natural social intercourse, and oftener than not the tales are evoked by the talks along the way. In fact, from one point of view, the pilgrimage is a continuous and lively drama, in which the stories themselves contribute to the action.

2. ***Piers Plowman***, a long allegorical poem, contemporary with Chaucer's work, but written in alliterative verse. It is a moral and social satire in the familiar medieval form of a dream-vision. Though usually attributed to a hypothetical William Langland, it seems to be by at least two, perhaps even five, different writers.

Country, or town in which there seemed to be
Any two people willing to agree.
Some say the things we most desire are these:
Freedom to do exactly as we please,
With no one to reprove our faults and lies,
Rather to have one call us good and wise.
Truly there's not a woman in ten score

Who has a fault, and someone rubs the sore,
But she will kick if what he says is true;
You try it out and you will find so too.
However vicious we may be within
We like to be thought wise and void of sin.
Others assert we women find it sweet
When we are thought dependable, discreet
And secret, firm of purpose and controlled,
Never betraying things that we are told.
But that's not worth the handle of a rake;
Women conceal a thing? For Heaven's sake!
Remember Midas?[12] Will you hear the tale?
  Among some other little things, now stale,
Ovid relates that under his long hair
The unhappy Midas grew a splendid pair
Of ass's ears; as subtly as he might,
He kept his foul deformity from sight;
Save for his wife, there was not one that knew.
He loved her best, and trusted in her too.
He begged her not to tell a living creature
That he possessed so horrible a feature.
And she—she swore, were all the world to win,
She would not do such villainy and sin
As saddle her husband with so foul a name;
Besides to speak would be to share the shame.
Nevertheless she thought she would have died
Keeping this secret bottled up inside;
It seemed to swell her heart and she, no doubt
Thought it was on the point of bursting out.
  Fearing to speak of it to woman or man
Down to a reedy marsh she quickly ran
And reached the sedge. Her heart was all on fire
And, as a bittern bumbles in the mire,
She whispered to the water, near the ground
"Betray me not, O water, with thy sound!
To thee alone I tell it: it appears
My husband has a pair of ass's ears!
Ah! My heart's well again, the secret's out!
I could no longer keep it, not a doubt."
And so you see, although we may hold fast
A little while, it must come out at last.
We can't keep secrets; as for Midas, well,
Read Ovid for his story; he will tell.
  This knight that I am telling you about
Perceived at last he never would find out
What it could be that women loved the best.
Faint was the soul within his sorrowful breast
As home he went, he dared no longer stay;
His year was up and now it was the day.
  As he rode home in a dejected mood,
Suddenly, at the margin of a wood,
He saw a dance upon the leafy floor
Of four and twenty ladies,[13] nay, and more.
Eagerly he approached, in hope to learn
Some words of wisdom ere he should return;
But lo! Before he came to where they were,
Dancers and dance all vanished into air!
There wasn't a living creature to be seen
Save one old woman crouched upon the green.
A fouler-looking creature I suppose
Could scarcely be imagined. She arose
And said, "Sir knight, there's no way on from here.
Tell me what you are looking for, my dear,
For peradventure that were best for you;
We old, old women know a thing or two."
  "Dear Mother," said the knight, "alack the day!
I am as good as dead if I can't say
What thing it is that women most desire;
If you could tell me I would pay your hire."
"Give me your hand," she said, "and swear to do
Whatever I shall next require of you
—If so to do should lie within your might—
And you shall know the answer before night."
"Upon my honour," he answered, "I agree."
"Then," said the crone, "I dare to guarantee
Your life is safe; I shall make good my claim.
Upon my life the queen will say the same.
Show me the very proudest of them all
In costly coverchief or jewelled caul[14]
That dare say no to what I have to teach.
Let us go forward without further speech."
And then she crooned her gospel in his ear
And told him to be glad and not to fear.
  They came to court. This knight, in full array,
Stood forth and said, "O Queen, I've kept my day
And kept my word and have my answer ready."
  There sat the noble matrons and the heady
Young girls, and widows too, that have the grace

12. ***Midas.*** The source is Ovid's *Metamorphoses,* in which, however, the secret is known by Midas's barber, not his wife.
13. ***dance . . . ladies,*** the fairy ring, a familiar element in Celtic folklore.
14. ***caul,*** a netted cap worn by women.

"January" from Les Très Riches Heures. The Bettmann Archive, Inc.

Of wisdom, all assembled in that place,
And there the queen herself was throned to hear
And judge his answer. Then the knight drew near
And silence was commanded through the hall.
  The queen then bade the knight to tell them all
What thing it was that women wanted most.
He stood not silent like a beast or post,
But gave his answer with the ringing word
Of a man's voice and the assembly heard:
  "My liege and lady, in general," said he,
"A woman wants the self-same sovereignty
Over her husband as over her lover,
And master him; he must not be above her.

That is your greatest wish, whether you kill
Or spare me; please yourself. I wait your will."
In all the court not one that shook her head
Or contradicted what the knight had said;
Maid, wife, and widow cried, "He's saved his life!"
And on the word up started the old wife,
The one the knight saw sitting on the green,
And cried, "Your mercy, sovereign lady queen!
Before the court disperses, do me right!
'Twas I who taught this answer to the knight,
For which he swore, and pledged his honour to it,
That the first thing I asked of him he'd do it,
So far as it should lie within his might.
Before this court I ask you then, sir knight,
To keep your word and take me for your wife;
For well you know that I have saved your life.
If this be false, deny it on your sword!"
"Alas!" he said, "Old lady, by the Lord
I know indeed that such was my behest,
But for God's love think of a new request,
Take all my goods, but leave my body free."
"A curse on us," she said, "if I agree!
I may be foul, I may be poor and old,
Yet will not choose to be, for all the gold
That's bedded in the earth or lies above,
Less than your wife, nay, than your very love!"
"My love?" said he. "By Heaven, my damnation!
Alas that any of my race and station
Should ever make so foul a misalliance!"
Yet in the end his pleading and defiance
All went for nothing, he was forced to wed.
He takes his ancient wife and goes to bed.
Now peradventure some may well suspect
A lack of care in me since I neglect
To tell of the rejoicings and display
Made at the feast upon their wedding-day.
I have but a short answer to let fall;
I say there was no joy or feast at all,
Nothing but heaviness of heart and sorrow.
He married her in private on the morrow
And all day long stayed hidden like an owl,
It was such torture that his wife looked foul.
Great was the anguish churning in his head
When he and she were piloted to bed;
He wallowed back and forth in desperate style.
His ancient wife lay smiling all the while;
At last she said "Bless us! Is this, my dear,
How knights and wives get on together here?
Are these the laws of good King Arthur's house?
Are knights of his all so contemptuous?
I am your own beloved and your wife,
And I am she, indeed, that saved your life;
And certainly I never did you wrong.
Then why, this first of nights, so sad a song?
You're carrying on as if you were half-witted!
Say, for God's love, what sin have I committed?
I'll put things right if you will tell me how."
"Put right?" he cried. "That never can be now!
Nothing can ever be put right again!
You're old, and so abominably plain,
So poor to start with, so low-bred to follow;
It's little wonder if I twist and wallow!
God, that my heart would burst within my breast!"
"Is that," said she, "the cause of your unrest?"
"Yes, certainly," he said, "and can you wonder?"
"I could set right what you suppose a blunder,
That's if I cared to, in a day or two,
If I were shown more courtesy by you.
Just now," she said, "you spoke of gentle birth,
Such as descends from ancient wealth and worth.
If that's the claim you make for gentlemen
Such arrogance is hardly worth a hen.
Whoever loves to work for virtuous ends,
Public and private, and who most intends
To do what deeds of gentleness he can,
Take him to be the greatest gentleman.
Christ wills we take our gentleness from Him,
Not from a wealth of ancestry long dim,
Though they bequeath their whole establishment
By which we claim to be of high descent.
Our fathers cannot make us a bequest
Of all those virtues that became them best
And earned for them the name of gentleman,
But bade us follow them as best we can. . . .
For of our parents nothing can we claim
Save temporal things, and these may hurt and maim.
"But everyone knows this as well as I;
For if gentility were implanted by

The natural course of lineage down the line,
Public or private, could it cease to shine
In doing the fair work of gentle deed?
No vice or villainy could then bear seed. . . .
"Gentility is only the renown
For bounty that your fathers handed down,
Quite foreign to your person, not your own;
Gentility must come from God alone.
That we are gentle comes to us by grace
And by no means is it bequeathed with place. . . .
And therefore, my dear husband, I conclude
That even if my ancestors were rude,
Yet God on high—and so I hope He will—
Can grant me grace to live in virtue still,
A gentlewoman only when beginning
To live in virtue and to shrink from sinning.
"As for my poverty which you reprove,
Almighty God Himself in whom we move,
Believe, and have our being, chose a life
Of poverty, and every man or wife,
Nay, every child can see our Heavenly King
Would never stoop to choose a shameful thing.
No shame in poverty if the heart is gay,
As Seneca and all the learned say.
He who accepts his poverty unhurt
I'd say is rich although he lacked a shirt.
But truly poor are they who whine and fret
And covet what they cannot hope to get.
And he that, having nothing, covets not,
Is rich, though you may think he is a sot. . . .
And since it's no offence, let me be plain;
Do not rebuke my poverty again.
"Lastly you taxed me, sir, with being old.
Yet even if you never had been told
By ancient books, you gentlemen engage
Yourselves in honour to respect old age.
To call an old man 'father' shows good breeding,
And this could be supported from my reading.
"You say I'm old and fouler than a fen.
You need not fear to be a cuckold, then.
Filth and old age, I'm sure you will agree,
Are powerful wardens upon chastity.
Nevertheless, well knowing your delights,
I shall fulfil your worldly appetites.
"You have two choices; which one will you try?
To have me old and ugly till I die,
But still a loyal, true, and humble wife
That never will displease you all her life,
Or would you rather I were young and pretty
And take your chance what happens in a city
Where friends will visit you because of me,
Yes, and in other places too, maybe.
Which would you have? The choice is all your own."
The knight thought long, and with a piteous groan
At last he said, with all the care in life,
"My lady and my love, my dearest wife,
I leave the matter to your wise decision.
You make the choice yourself, for the provision
Of what may be agreeable and rich
In honour to us both, I don't care which;
Whatever pleases you suffices me."
"And have I won the mastery?" said she,
"Since I'm to choose and rule as I think fit?"
"Certainly, wife," he answered her, "that's it."
"Kiss me," she cried. "No quarrels! On my oath
And word of honour, you shall find me both,
That is, both fair and faithful as a wife;
May I go howling mad and take my life
Unless I prove to be as good and true
As ever wife was since the world was new!
And if tomorrow when the sun's above
I seem less fair than any lady-love,
Than any queen or empress east or west,
Do with my life and death as you think best.
Cast up the curtain, husband. Look at me!"
And when indeed the knight had looked to see,
Lo, she was young and lovely, rich in charms.
In ecstasy he caught her in his arms,
His heart went bathing in a bath of blisses
And melted in a hundred thousand kisses,
And she responded in the fullest measure
With all that could delight or give him pleasure.
So they lived ever after to the end
In perfect bliss; and may Christ Jesus send
Us husbands meek and young and fresh in bed,
And grace to overbid them when we wed.
And—Jesu hear my prayer!—cut short the lives
Of those who won't be governed by their wives;
And all old, angry niggards of their pence,
God send them soon a very pestilence!

Discussion

1. The Wife, at the beginning of her Prologue, says "please don't be offended at my views; / They're really only offered to amuse" (87–88). Does she really mean it? What is her purpose in this long speech?

2. From the Wife's point of view, what is a good husband? How does she keep him that way?

3. While the Wife's fourth husband was in London on business, she tells us she "Went to processions, festivals, orations, / Preachments and pilgrimages" (352–353). Why did she go? For what reason, do you think, is she currently traveling to Canterbury?

4. What point of view does the fifth husband's favorite book take on the woman question? How does that book argue its case? How does the wife defeat the book?

5. At the beginning of her tale the Wife of Bath mockingly describes the "holy friars" who, she says, now throng the countryside (lines 8–16). Why does she say this?

6. In what ways does the Wife of Bath's tale fit her personality and attitudes? Consider, in particular, the secret which the old hag tells the guilty knight, and the knight's solution to the problem of choosing an ugly, loyal wife or a beautiful, unfaithful one.

7. Do you find yourself liking or disliking the Wife of Bath? Point to specific personality traits which affect your judgment.

Vocabulary • Structure and Dictionary

A. Use the Glossary to answer the following questions about the structure of the following words. Read each clue, then write on your paper the matching word from the list. Be sure you can spell and pronounce each word.

bequeath	extort
disperse	continent
caterwaul	preamble

1. Which word has two roots that describe something that might keep you awake?

2. Which has a root that might describe a sight-seeing activity?

3. Which has a prefix and root that might describe what happens to a crowd sprayed with tear gas?

4. Which has a prefix and root that might describe what a prison does with inmates?

5. Which has a root that might describe an exercise motion?

B. Use your Glossary to answer the following questions about the italicized words on your paper.

6. The prefix *dis-* in *disparage* means "opposite of, lack of, not." What is the meaning of the Old French word from which *disparage* comes?

7. (a) What is the meaning of the obsolete word related to *aghast?* What does the Old English root word mean? **(b)** What is this root related to?

8. The prefix *re-* means "again, anew, once more." What is the meaning of the root word in *reprove,* and what phrase do prefix and root form joined together?

Geoffrey Chaucer
1340? • 1400

The son of a prosperous London wine merchant, Chaucer was trained from an early age for a court career. By 1357 he was a page in the service of the wife of King Edward III's third son. While serving with the army in France in 1359 he was taken prisoner, but was freed the following year upon payment of a ransom to which the king made a sizable contribution. He married one of the queen's ladies-in-waiting, and from that time on was in the employ of the king. He was frequently sent abroad on diplomatic missions, notably to France, the Low Countries, and Italy.

His earliest works were translations from the French *(The Romance of the Rose)* or showed the influence of French authors *(The Book of the Duchess, The House of Fame).* In these long poems, as well as in a later work, *The Legend of Good Women,* Chaucer used a form popular with medieval French writers, the dream-vision.

During his first trip to Italy, Chaucer became acquainted with the writings of Dante, Petrarch, and Boccaccio. In his greatest works, *Troilus and Criseyde* and *The Canterbury Tales,* he used stories Boccaccio and other Italian storytellers used, although he probably did not know Boccaccio's *Decameron* directly.

Chaucer was buried in Westminster Abbey (an honor accorded him because of his government appointments).

Sir Thomas Malory

"The Day of Destiny" describes the end of King Arthur's reign and the dissolution of the order which he, along with his Knights of the Round Table, had established. This end grows out of the corruption within the royal court itself. Arthur's illegitimate son Mordred seeks to kill his father. He knows of the secret love between Arthur's wife, Queen Guinevere, and his best friend, the knight Lancelot. One night Mordred leads a band of knights to Guinevere's chamber. They find the Queen with Lancelot.

Although he is reluctant, Arthur feels obligated to burn his wife at the stake. But at the last minute Lancelot rescues her, killing the two knights Gaherys and Gareth, who were guarding the queen. Lancelot subsequently flees to a castle in France and Arthur forgives Guinevere; but Gawain, the brother of the dead knights, demands vengeance on Lancelot.

His hatred forces Arthur to lead his men on an attack against Lancelot's French fortress. In the ensuing battles Lancelot seriously wounds Gawain but refuses to kill him.

Meanwhile, Mordred senses his chance. With Arthur in France he leads a rebellion in England claiming the throne and trying to seize Guinevere as his queen. She flees to the Tower of London and Arthur, lifting the siege on Lancelot's castle, returns to defend his crown.

At Dover Arthur's forces battle Mordred for the first time and Gawain is fatally wounded. Before his death he writes a letter to Lancelot ending their feud and asking Lancelot to return to England to help Arthur. After a second, inconclusive battle with Mordred's forces, Arthur regroups his men and moves westward.

The Day of Destiny
from Morte Darthur[1]

And quickly King Arthur moved himself with his army along the coastline westward, toward Salisbury. And there was a day assigned betwixt King Arthur and Sir Mordred, that they should meet upon a field beside Salisbury and not far from the coast. And this day was assigned as Monday after Trinity Sunday, whereof King Arthur was passing glad that he might be avenged upon Sir Mordred.

Then Sir Mordred stirred up a crowd of people around London, for those from Kent, Sussex and Surrey, Essex, Suffolk, and Norfolk stayed for the most part with Sir Mordred. And many a full noble knight drew unto him and also to the King; but they that loved Sir Lancelot drew unto Sir Mordred.

So upon Trinity Sunday at night King Arthur dreamed a wonderful dream, and in his dream it seemed that he saw upon a platform a chair, and the chair was fixed to a wheel, and there upon sat King Arthur in richest cloth of gold that might be made. And the King dreamed there was under him, far below him, a hideous deep black water, and therein were all kinds of serpents and dragons and wild beasts foul and horrible. And suddenly the King dreamed that the wheel turned up side down, and he fell among the serpents, and every beast took him by a limb. And then the King cried out as he lay in his bed,

"Help! help!"

And then knights, squires and yeomen awaked the King, and then he was so amazed that he knew not where he was. And so he remained awake until it was nearly day, and then he fell into a slumber again, neither sleeping nor completely awake.

1. From Part IV of *The Most Piteous Tale of the Morte Darthur Saunz Guerdon*, slightly modernized, from the Winchester MS. version in *The Works of Thomas Malory* edited by Eugène Vinaver (Oxford University Press, 1947, 1967).

Arthur Unhorses One of the Ten Rebels MS. FR. 95 fol. 236. Bibliothèque Nationale, Paris

Then it seemed to the King that there came Sir Gawain unto him with a number of fair ladies with him. So when King Arthur saw him he said,

"Welcome, my sister's son, I thought you had died! And now I see thee alive, great is my debt to Almighty Jesus. Ah, fair nephew, who be these ladies that come hither with you?"

"Sir," said Sir Gawain, "all these be fair ladies for whom I have fought for, when I was a living man. And all these are those that I did battle for in righteous quarrels, and God hath given them that aid for their earnest prayers; and because I did battle for them for their rights, they brought me hither unto you. Thus hath God given me leave for to warn you of your death: for if ye fight tomorrow with Sir Mordred, as ye both have agreed, doubt ye not ye shall be slain, and the greatest part of your people on both sides. And for the great concern and good that Almighty Jesus has had for you, and for pity of you and many other good men that shall be slain, God

King Arthur's Last Battle with Mordred. The Royal Library, The Hague.

hath sent me to you of His special grace to give you warning that in no way ye do battle tomorrow, but instead that ye make a treaty for a month and a day. And request this urgently, so that tomorrow you can delay. For within a month shall come Sir Lancelot with all his noble knights, and rescue you loyally, and slay Sir Mordred and all that ever will stay with him."

Then Sir Gawain and all the ladies vanished, and at once the King called upon his knights, squires, and yeomen, and charged them quickly to fetch his noble lords and wise bishops unto him. And when they were come the King told them of his vision; that Sir Gawain had told him and warned him that if he fought on the morn, he should be slain. Then the King commanded Sir Lucan the Butler and his brother Sir Bedivere the Bold, with two bishops with them, and charged them in any way to make a treaty for a month and a day with Sir Mordred:

"And spare not, offer him lands and goods as much as ye think reasonable."

So then they departed and came to Sir Mordred where he had a grim host of a hundred thousand, and there they entreated Sir Mordred a long time. And at the last Sir Mordred agreed for to take over Cornwall and Kent during King Arthur's lifetime; and after that all England, after the days of King Arthur.

Then were they agreed that King Arthur and Sir Mordred should meet betwixt both their hosts, and each of them should bring fourteen persons. And so they came with this word unto Arthur. Then he said,

"I am glad that this is done"; and so he went into the field.

And when King Arthur departed he warned all his host that if they saw any sword drawn, "look ye come on fiercely and slay that traitor, Sir Mordred, for I in no way trust him." In like manner Sir Mordred warned his host that "and ye see any manner of sword drawn, look that ye come on fiercely and so slay all that before you stand, for in no way will I trust in this treaty." And in the same way said Sir Mordred unto his host: "for I know well my father will be avenged upon me."

And so they met as they had arranged, and were agreed and accorded thoroughly. And wine was fetched, and they drank together. Just then came an adder out of a little heath-bush, and it stung a knight in the foot. And so when the knight felt himself so stung, he looked down and saw the adder; and at once he drew his sword to slay the adder, and thought of no other harm. And when the host on both sides saw that sword drawn, then they blew trumpets and horns, and shouted grimly, and so both hosts attacked each other. And King Arthur mounted his horse and said, "Alas, this unhappy day!" and so rode to his men, and Sir Mordred in like wise.

And never since was there seen a more grievous battle in no Christian land, for there was only slashing and riding, thrusting and striking, and many a grim word was there spoken of one to the other, and many a deadly stroke. But ever King Arthur rode through the battle against Sir Mordred many times and acted full nobly, as a noble king should do, and at all times he never hesitated. And Sir Mordred did his utmost that day and put himself in great peril.

And thus they fought all the day long, and never ceased 'till the noble knights were fallen on the cold earth. And yet they fought still 'till it was near night, and by then was there a hundred thousand lay dead upon the earth. Then was King Arthur wild with wrath beyond measure, when he saw his people so slain because of him.

And so he looked about himself and could see no more of all his host and of good knights left no more alive but two knights: Sir Lucan the Butler and his brother, Sir Bedivere; and yet they were very badly wounded.

"Jesus have mercy!" said the King, "where are all my noble knights gone? Alas, that ever I should see this grievous day! For now," said King Arthur, "I am come to mine end. But would to God," said he, "that I knew now where were that traitor Sir Mordred that hath caused all this mischief."

Then King Arthur looked about and was aware where stood Sir Mordred leaning upon his sword among a great heap of dead men.

"Now give me my spear," said King Arthur unto Sir Lucan, "for yonder I have seen the traitor that all this woe hath wrought."

"Sir, let him be," said Sir Lucan, "for he brings misfortune. And if ye pass this unfortunate day ye shall be right well revenged. And, good lord, remember ye of your night's dream and what the spirit of Sir Gawain told you last night, and God of His great goodness hath preserved you hitherto. And for God's sake, my lord, leave this battle, for, blessed be God, ye have won the field: for yet be here three alive, and with Sir Mordred is not one alive. And therefore if ye leave now, this wicked day of Destiny is past!"

"Now come death, come life," said the King, "now I see him yonder alone, he shall never escape my hands! For at a better advantage shall I never have him."

"God speed you well!" said Sir Bedivere.

Then the King took his spear in both his hands, and ran towards Sir Mordred, crying out and saying,

"Traitor, now is thy death-day come!"

And when Sir Mordred saw King Arthur he ran towards him with his sword drawn in his hands, and there King Arthur struck Sir Mordred under the shield, with a thrust of his spear, through and beyond the body more than a foot. And when Sir Mordred felt that he had his death's wound he thrust himself with the might that he had up to the hand guard of King Arthur's spear, and then he smote his father, King Arthur, with his sword holding it in both his hands, upon the side of the head, so that the sword pierced the helmet and the outer membrane of the brain. And with that Sir Mordred dashed down stark dead to the earth.

And noble King Arthur fell in a swoon to the earth, and there he swooned several times, and Sir Lucan and Sir Bedivere several times lifted him up. And so weakly betwixt them they led him to a little chapel not far from the sea, and when the King was there, he thought himself reasonably eased.

Then heard they people cry in the field.

"Now go thou, Sir Lucan," said the King, "and help me to learn what means that noise in the field."

So Sir Lucan departed, though he was grievously wounded in many places; and as he rode he saw and noticed by the moonlight how the plunderers and robbers were come into the field to plunder and to rob many a full noble knight of brooches and bracelets and of many a good ring and many a rich jewel. And those that were not yet dead, there they slew them for their armor and their gold.

When Sir Lucan understood this he came to the King as soon as he might, and told him all which he had heard and seen.

"Therefore by my advice," said Sir Lucan, "it is best that we bring you to some town."

"I would that it were so," said the King, "but I may not stand, my head fails so. . . . Ah, Sir Lancelot!" said King Arthur, "this day have I missed thee! And alas, that ever I was against thee! For now I have my death, whereof Sir Gawain warned me in my dream."

Then Sir Lucan took up the King on one side and Sir Bedivere the other side, and in the lifting up the King swooned, and in the lifting Sir Lucan fell in a swoon, and part of his guts fell out of his body, and with that the noble knight's heart burst. And when the King awoke he beheld Sir

Lucan, how he lay foaming at the mouth and part of his guts lay at his feet.

"Alas," said the King, "this is to me a very sad sight, to see this noble duke die so for my sake, for he would have helped me that had more need of help than I! Alas, that he would not complain for himself, for his heart was so set to help me. Now Jesu have mercy upon his soul!"

Then Sir Bedivere wept for the death of his brother.

"Now leave this mourning and this weeping, gentle knight," said the King, "for all this will not help me. For know thou well, if I might live myself, the death of Sir Lucan would grieve me evermore. But my time passeth on fast," said the King. "Therefore," said King Arthur unto Sir Bedivere, "take thou here Excalibur, my good sword, and go with it to the yonder water side; and when thou comest there, I charge thee throw my sword in that water, and come again and tell me what thou seest there."

"My lord," said Sir Bedivere, "your commandment shall be done, and lightly bring you word again."

So Sir Bedivere departed. And on the way he beheld that noble sword, and the pommel and the haft was all precious stones. And then he said to himself, "If I throw this rich sword in the water, of this shall never come good, but harm and loss." And then Sir Bedivere hid Excalibur under a tree, and so as soon as he might he came again unto the King and said he had been at the water and had thrown the sword into the water.

"What saw thou there?" said the King.

"Sir," he said, "I saw nothing but waves and wind."

"That is untruly said by thee," said the King. "And therefore go thou lightly again, and do my commandment; as thou art to me beloved and dear, spare not, but throw it in."

Then Sir Bedivere returned again and took the sword in his hand; and yet he thought it a sin and shame to throw away that noble sword. And so again he hid the sword and returned again and told the King that he had been at the water and done his commandment.

"What sawest thou there?" said the King.

"Sir," he said, "I saw nothing but lapping waters and darkening waves."

"Ah, traitor unto me and untrue," said King

"Excalibur" from Le Roman du Lancelot du Lac et de la Mort du Roi Artu. Reproduced by permission of the British Library Board

Arthur, "now hast thou betrayed me twice! Who would believe that thou hast been to me so beloved and dear, and also named so noble a knight, that thou would betray me for the wealth of this sword? But now go again lightly; for thy long tarrying putteth me in great jeopardy of my life, for I am growing cold. And if thou do not now as I bid thee, if ever I may see thee, I shall slay thee by mine own hands, for thou wouldst for my rich sword see me dead."

Then Sir Bedivere departed and went to the sword and lightly took it up, and so he went unto the water side. And there he bound the belt about the hilt, and threw the sword as far into the water as he might. And there came an arm and an hand above the water, and took it and seized it, and shook it thrice and brandished, and then vanished with the sword into the water.

So Sir Bedivere came again to the King and told him what he saw.

"Alas," said the King, "help me hence, for I dread me I have tarried over long."

Then Sir Bedivere took the King upon his back and so went with him to the water side. And when they were there, even close by the bank floated a little barge with many fair ladies on it, and among them all was a queen, and all of them had black hoods. And all of them wept and shrieked when they saw King Arthur.

"Now put me into that barge," said the King.

And so he did softly, and there received him

three ladies with great mourning. And so they set him down, and in one of their laps King Arthur laid his head. And then the queen said,

"Ah, my dear brother! Why have ye tarried so long from me? Alas, this wound on your head hath caught overmuch cold!"

And then they rowed away from the land, and Sir Bedivere beheld all those ladies go away from him. Then Sir Bedivere cried out and said,

"Ah, my lord Arthur, what shall become of me, now ye go from me and leave me here alone among mine enemies?"

"Comfort thyself," said the King, "and do as well as thou mayest, for in me is no trust for to trust in. For I must go into the vale of Avilion to heal me of my grievous wound. And if thou hear never more of me, pray for my soul!"

But ever the queen and ladies wept and shrieked, that it was pitiful to hear. As soon as Sir Bedivere had lost sight of the barge he wept and wailed, and so entered the forest and traveled all night.

And in the morning he was aware, betwixt two wan woods, of a chapel and a hermitage. Then was Sir Bedivere fearful, and thither he went, and when he came into the chapel he saw where lay a hermit groveling on all fours, close there by a tomb was new dug. When the hermit saw Sir Bedivere he knew him well, for he was but little before Bishop of Canterbury that Sir Mordred put to flight.

"Sir," said Sir Bedivere, "what man is there here buried that ye pray so earnestly for?"

"Fair son," said the hermit, "I know not truly but only guess. But this same night, at midnight, there came a number of ladies and brought here a dead corpse and prayed me to bury him. And here they offered a hundred candles, and they gave me a thousand coins."

"Alas!" said Sir Bedivere, "that was my lord King Arthur, which lieth here buried in this chapel."

Then Sir Bedivere swooned, and when he awoke he prayed the hermit that he might stay with him still, there to live with fasting and prayers:

"For from hence will I never go," said Sir Bedivere, "by my will, but all days of my life stay here to pray for my lord Arthur."

"Sir, ye are welcome to me," said the hermit, "for I know you better than you think that I do: for ye are Sir Bedivere the Bold, and the full noble Duke Sir Lucan the Butler was your brother."

Then Sir Bedivere told the hermit all as ye have heard before, and so he remained with the hermit that was before the Bishop of Canterbury. And there Sir Bedivere put upon himself poor clothes, and served the hermit full lowly in fasting and in prayers.

Thus of Arthur I find no more written in books that have been written, nothing more of the very certainty of his brave death I never read . . .

Yet some men say in many parts of England that King Arthur is not dead, but had by the will of Our Lord Jesu gone into another place; and men say that he shall come again, and he shall win the Holy Cross. Yet I will not say that it shall be so, but rather would I say: here in this world he changed his life. And many men say that there is written upon the tomb this:

HIC IACET ARTHURUS,
REX QUONDAM REXQUE FUTURUS.

Here lies Arthur, King Once and King That Will Be. □□

Discussion

1. What do you think is the meaning of Arthur's first dream on the night before the battle? In what way is it related to his second dream of that night?

2. What breaks the truce between Arthur and Mordred? What does this imply about Arthur's efforts to avoid the battle?

3. Arthur insists on fighting Mordred after the battle has ended. What does this tell us about his character?

4. What do the plunderers

Sir Lucan sees on the battlefield suggest about England's future after Arthur's death?

5. When Sir Bedivere twice hides Excalibur, what do we learn about Arthur's kingship?

6. From movies and television we get a general idea of medieval heroism. Do Arthur and his knights do or say anything which surprised you at first, because it doesn't seem to match the heroic ideal? Describe such incidents and try to explain them.

Extension • Writing

1. The story of Arthur and the Round Table was already old when Malory took it up. He saw in the heroes of this archaic tale virtues lacking in his own era. In a short essay describe to your reader the kinds of heroism you find in "The Day of Destiny." Are they still important in our day?

2. Write an account of Arthur's last days. As a modern biographer you must sift fact from legend. Is there any way to scientifically explain some of the legendary elements—as disguised facts, for instance? Malory is your only source, but you must use him skeptically.

Vocabulary
Pronunciation and Dictionary

Use your Glossary to answer the following questions on a separate sheet of paper. Be sure you understand the meaning of each word.

1. (a) What part of speech is the word *passing* in the following line?: " . . . whereof King Arthur was *passing* glad that he might be avenged upon Sir Mordred." **(b)** What is its meaning in this line?

2. Which of the following words rhymes with the first syllable of *hideous?* **(a)** speed; **(b)** lied; **(c)** lid; **(d)** trod.

3. (a) From what two Old French words does *jeopardy* come? **(b)** How do you suppose the literal meaning of the original French phrase developed into the present meaning of the word? **(c)** How many syllables does the word have?

4. (a) Write a rhyming word for the first pronunciation given for *grovel.* **(b)** What part of speech was it originally?

5. (a) Which of the three definitions given in the entry applies to the way *yeoman* is used by Malory? **(b)** What label is attached to that definition?

6. (a) How many syllables does the word *grievous* have? **(b)** Write a rhyme word for the first syllable.

7. What two objects does the word *pommel* describe?

8. (a) From what two languages does *peril* come? **(b)** What is the adjective form of the word?

Sir Thomas Malory
c.1395 • 1471

The author Sir Thomas Malory is usually identified with a Warwickshire knight of that name. Malory lived during the turbulent period of the Wars of the Roses, a series of vicious conflicts which split England into two factions organized around the rival houses of York and Lancaster. He spent most of the last twenty years of his life in prison on one charge or another. During his imprisonment he worked on his compilation of the Arthurian legends. Newgate, where he was imprisoned, was near the house of the Grey Friars, which had a large library. Probably Malory obtained his source materials from that library.

His writings contain several references to his imprisonment. In particular, he ends his book on the Arthurian legends with these words: "I pray you all, gentlemen and gentlewomen, that readeth this book of Arthur and his knights from the beginning to the ending, pray for me while I am on live that God send me good deliverance [from prison]; and when I am dead, I pray you all pray for my soul." When Malory died, he was buried in the chapel of the Grey Friars.

Unit Review Tests 2: The Medieval Period

CONTENT REVIEW

1. Medieval literature was written a long time ago. Do you find the people you encounter there strikingly different from the people of our own day? Give the examples on which you base your conclusions. In particular, you might consider the so-called "battle of the sexes," heroism in the face of danger, and jealousy in love.

2. In Anglo-Saxon literature Nature is usually hostile toward people. Is this still true in medieval literature? Does it offer any examples of a benevolent Nature?

3. Compare King Arthur with Beowulf. What similarities and differences do you see in these two warrior heroes?

4. In what various ways does medieval literature use ghosts and other supernatural powers?

5. In what ways do medieval writers use common, everyday details to develop a sense of character or situation?

6. Which of the selections in this unit used each of the following most effectively: **(a)** refrains, **(b)** irony, **(c)** naturalistic dialogue? Explain.

Unit 2, Test I

INTERPRETATION: NEW MATERIAL

from Sir Gawain and the Green Knight

Translated by Brian Stone

The following excerpt is from a medieval romance—a story of knights and their deeds—by an author whose name is unknown. He was probably Chaucer's contemporary, but because he lived in a provincial center far from Chaucer's world of London and the court, the poet worked in an older tradition of alliterative meter that had its roots in Anglo-Saxon verse. In the following scene King Arthur and his knights of the Round Table are celebrating in Camelot during the Christmas season. Their banquet is interrupted by a giant knight of fierce appearance, on horseback, his body and clothes all "glittering green." The horseman has asked for "good sport," and since he is not wearing armor, and carries no weapons except an axe, Arthur assumes that the stranger seeks "unarmoured combat." The Green Knight is speaking as the scene opens.

I

"No, it is not combat I crave, for come to that,
On this bench only beardless boys are sitting.
If I were hasped[1] in armour on a high steed,
No man among you could match me, your might being meagre.
So I crave in this court a Christmas game,
For it is Yuletide and New Year, and young men abound here.
If any in this household is so hardy in spirit,
Of such mettlesome mind and so madly rash
As to strike a strong blow in return for another,
I shall offer to him this fine axe freely;
This axe, which is heavy enough, to handle as he please.
And I shall bide the first blow, as bare as I sit here.
If some intrepid man is tempted to try what I suggest,
Let him leap towards me and lay hold of this weapon,
Acquiring clear possession of it, no claim from me ensuing.

1. ***hasped,*** fastened.

Then shall I stand up to his stroke, quite still on this floor—
So long as I shall have leave to launch a return blow
Unchecked.
Yet he shall have a year
And a day's reprieve,[2] I direct.
Now hasten and let me hear
Who answers, to what effect."

II

If he had astonished them at the start, yet stiller now
Were the henchmen[3] in hall, both high and low.
The rider wrenched himself round in his saddle
And rolled his red eyes about roughly and strangely,
Bending[4] his brows, bristling and bright, on all,
His beard swaying as he strained to see who would rise.
When none came to accord with him, he coughed aloud,
Then pulled himself up proudly, and spoke as follows:
"What, is this Arthur's house, the honour of which
Is bruited abroad so abundantly?
Has your pride disappeared? Your prowess gone?
Your victories, your valour, your vaunts, where are they?
The revel and renown of the Round Table
Is now overwhelmed by a word from one man's voice,
For all flinch for fear from a fight not begun!"
Upon this, he laughed so loudly that the lord[5] grieved.
His fair features filled with blood
For shame.
He raged as roaring gale;
His followers felt the same.
The King, not one to quail,
To that cavalier then came.

III

"By heaven," then said Arthur, "What you ask is foolish,
But as you firmly seek folly, find it you shall.
No good man here is aghast at your great words.
Hand me your axe now, for heaven's sake,
And I shall bestow the boon you bid us give."
He sprang towards him swiftly, seized it from his hand,
And fiercely the other fellow footed the floor.[6]
Now Arthur had his axe, and holding it by the haft
Swung it about sternly, as if to strike with it.
The strong man stood before him, stretched to his full height,
Higher than any in the hall by a head and more.
Stern of face he stood there, stroking his beard,
Turning down his tunic in a tranquil manner,

---

2. ***year . . . reprieve,*** the usual period for a legal contract.
3. ***henchmen,*** trusted followers.
4. ***Bending,*** directing.
5. ***lord,*** King Arthur.
6. ***footed the floor,*** jumped off his horse.

Less unmanned and dismayed by the mighty strokes
Than if a banqueter at the bench[7] had brought him a drink
Of wine.
Then Gawain at Guinevere's[8] side
Bowed and spoke his design:
"Before all, King, confide
This fight to me. May it be mine."

IV

"If you would, worthy lord," said Gawain to the king,
"Bid me stir from this seat and stand beside you,
Allowing me without lese-majesty[9] to leave the table,
And if my liege lady were not displeased thereby,
I should come there to counsel you before this court of nobles.
For it appears unmeet[10] to me, as manners go,
When your hall hears uttered such a haughty request,
Though you gladly agree, for you to grant it yourself,
When on the benches about you many such bold men sit,
Under heaven, I hold, the highest-mettled,
There being no braver knights when battle is joined.
I am the weakest, the most wanting in wisdom, I know,
And my life, if lost, would be least missed, truly.
Only through your being my uncle, am I to be valued;
No bounty but your blood in my body do I know.[11]
And since this affair is too foolish to fall to you,
And I first asked it of you, make it over to me;
And if I fail to speak fittingly, let this full court judge
Without blame."
Then wisely they whispered of it,
And after, all said the same:
That the crowned king should be quit,[12]
And Gawain given the game.

V

Then the King commanded the courtly knight to rise.
He directly uprose, approached courteously,
Knelt low to his liege lord, laid hold of the weapon;
And he graciously let him have it, lifted up his hand
And gave him God's blessing, gladly urging him
To be strong in spirit and stout of sinew.
"Cousin, take care," said the King, "To chop once,
And if you strike with success, certainly I think
You will take the return blow without trouble in time."
Gripping the great axe, Gawain goes to the man

---

7. ***banqueter . . . bench,*** a man at his seat.
8. ***Gawain*** (gä′wān, gä′win), nephew of Arthur and his noblest knight, ***Guinevere*** (gwin′ə vir), Arthur's queen.
9. ***lese-majesty,*** offense against the dignity of a ruler, severe discourtesy.
10. ***unmeet,*** unsuitable, improper.
11. ***No bounty . . . know,*** that is, the only good in my body comes from your blood.
12. ***quit,*** excused from the contest.

Who awaits him unwavering, not quailing at all.
Then said to Sir Gawain the stout knight in green,
"Let us affirm our pact freshly, before going farther.
I beg you, bold sir, to be so good
As to tell me your true name, as I trust you to."
"In good faith," said the good knight, "Gawain is my name,
And whatever happens after, I offer you this blow,
And in twelve months' time I shall take the return blow
With whatever weapon you wish, and with no one else
Shall I strive."
The other with pledge replied,
"I'm the merriest man alive
It's a blow from you I must bide,
Sir Gawain, so may I thrive."

VI

"By God," said the Green Knight, "Sir Gawain, I rejoice
That I shall have from your hand what I have asked for here.
And you have gladly gone over, in good discourse,
The convenant I requested of the King in full,
Except that you shall assent, swearing in truth,
To seek me yourself, in such place as you think
To find me under the firmament,[13] and fetch your payment
For what you deal me today before this dignified gathering."
"How shall I hunt for you? How find your home?"
Said Gawain, "By God that made me, I go in ignorance;
Nor, knight, do I know your name or your court.
But instruct me truly thereof, and tell me your name,
And I shall wear out my wits to find my way there;
Here is my oath on it, in absolute honour!"
"That is enough this New Year,[14] no more is needed,"
Said the gallant in green to Gawain the courteous,
"To tell you the truth, when I have taken the blow
After you have duly dealt it, I shall directly inform you
About my house and my home and my own name.
Then you may keep your covenant, and call on me,
And if I waft you no words, then well may you prosper,
Stay long in your own land and look for no further
Trial.
Now grip your weapon grim;
Let us see your fighting style."
"Gladly," said Gawain to him,
Stroking the steel the while.

VII

On the ground the Green Knight graciously stood,
With head slightly slanting to expose the flesh.

---

13. ***firmament,*** heavens, sky.
14. ***New Year,*** a time associated with friendship and piety.

King Arthur's Knight Sir Gawain Cotton MS. Nero A X f. 94v. Reproduced by permission of the British Library Board

His long and lovely locks he laid over his crown,
Baring the naked neck for the business now due.
Gawain gripped his axe and gathered it on high,
Advanced the left foot before him on the ground,
And slashed swiftly down on the exposed part,
So that the sharp blade sheared through, shattering the bones,
Sank deep in the sleek flesh, split it in two,
And the scintillating steel struck the ground.
The fair head fell from the neck, struck the floor,
And people spurned it as it rolled around.
Blood spurted from the body, bright against the green.
Yet the fellow did not fall, nor falter one whit,
But stoutly sprang forward on legs still sturdy,
Roughly reached out among thc ranks of nobles,
Seized his splendid head and straightway lifted it.
Then he strode to his steed, snatched the bridle,
Stepped into the stirrup and swung aloft,
Holding his head in his hand by the hair.
He settled himself in the saddle as steadily
As if nothing had happened to him, though he had
No head.

He twisted his trunk about,
That gruesome body that bled;
He caused much dread and doubt
By the time his say was said.

On a separate sheet of paper, write your answers to the following questions. Do not write in your book.

1. Where does this scene take place?

2. Who proposes the "Christmas game" in the first stanza?

3. What is the attitude of the knights and ladies toward the Green Knight in stanza II?

4. How would you characterize the Green Knight's statements in stanza II?

5. What effect do the Green Knight's words have on Arthur?

6. Rewrite *only* the alliterative words in the following line: "When your hall hears uttered such a haughty request."

7. What kind of character does Gawain reveal in stanza IV?

8. In stanza VI, when does the Green Knight promise to reveal his name and home to Gawain?

9. What evidence of the supernatural is there in the last stanza?

10. Among the Green Knight's outstanding characteristics is: **(a)** humility; **(b)** dishonesty; **(c)** arrogance; **(d)** devotion.

Unit 2, Test II

COMPOSITION

You may choose any *one* of the following assignments. Assume that you are writing for your classmates.

1. Compare and contrast the character of Sir Patrick Spence in the ballad of that title with the character of Sir Mordred in Malory's "The Day of Destiny."

2. Discuss the various treatments of the theme of death in "Lord Randal," "The Unquiet Grave," and "Sir Patrick Spence."

3. Compare and contrast the behavior of Sir Patrick Spence in carrying out his king's command with that of Sir Bedivere in regard to King Arthur's command in "The Day of Destiny."

4. Which of the pilgrims described by the narrator in "The Prologue" to *The Canterbury Tales* do you find most appealing? Which least appealing? Explain.

5. Write a detailed description of the Host's character based upon his words, actions, and appearance in lines 765–854 in "The Prologue" and lines 22–25 in the "Words between the Summoner and the Friar."

6. Compare and contrast the characters of the Prioress (lines 122–166) and the Wife of Bath (lines 455–486) as they are described in "The Prologue" to *The Canterbury Tales.*

7. Discuss the character of knighthood as it is revealed in the portraits of the Knight and Squire in "The Prologue" to *The Canterbury Tales* (lines 43–102), and the knight in "The Wife of Bath's Tale."

8. Discuss the character of the Plowman described in "The Prologue" (lines 537–553) as an example of the virtuous man.

9. Compare and contrast the five husbands of the Wife of Bath as described in the prologue to her tale.

10. Compare and contrast the description of Arthur and his knights in Malory's "The Day of Destiny" with the world of Arthur's Round Table described in the excerpt from *Sir Gawain and the Green Knight* in Test I.

Unit 3:

1500 1525 1550 1

- Columbus to West Indies
- Henry VIII: *Defense of the Seven Sacraments*
- Golding's *Ovid*
- Cabot to North America
- Act of Supremacy
- Surrey's *Virgil*
- Vasco da Gama to India
- Copernicus's theory
- Cortez in Mexico
- *Book of Common Prayer*

The Renaissance 1500-1650

1600 1625 1650

ned: *Chronicles*

• Shakespeare: *Hamlet*

s voyage

of the Armada •

• Marlowe: *Dr. Faustus*

• Spenser: *The Faerie Queene*

• Sidney: *Astrophel and Stella*

• Bacon: *Essays*

• Hakluyt: *Voyages*

• The Globe Theater opens

• Battle of Naseby

Herrick: *Hesperides* •

Execution of Charles I •

Puritans close the theaters

• Browne: *Religio Medici* •

Background: The Renaissance 1500-1650

In the opening years of the fourteenth century, there began to develop in Italy an increasing interest in the manuscripts that had survived from ancient Greece and Rome. As more and more of these were unearthed in libraries and monasteries, Italy fell under the spell of the intellectual movement we have come to call the Renaissance—the rebirth of scholarship based on classical learning and philosophy. Spreading westward across Europe, the phenomenon of the Renaissance touched England lightly and fleetingly during the time of Chaucer. As far as England was concerned, however, this early contact was negligible, largely because external wars and internal strife ravaged the country for almost a century and a half, from 1337 to 1485.

As the Renaissance developed in Italy and other European countries, it began to take on added dimensions. Perhaps stimulated by the discovery that the men and women of ancient Greece and Rome were intelligent, cultured, and creative, the Renaissance gradually became also a rebirth of the human spirit, a realization of the human potential for development. This realization led eventually to many discoveries—geographical, religious, and scientific, as well as artistic and philosophical. Both the Age of Discovery, including the exploration of America, and the Protestant Reformation had their origins in the Renaissance spirit. To the same spirit may be attributed Copernicus' assertion that the earth was not the center of the universe. Upsetting traditional religious teachings, this discovery indirectly fostered the Renaissance belief that life in this world was not merely a preparation for the next world, as taught by medieval Christianity; but that, on the contrary, an active life in this world had value in itself.

The Renaissance in England

The Renaissance period in England may conveniently be divided into three parts: the rise of the Renaissance under the early Tudor monarchs (1500–1558), the height of the Renaissance under Elizabeth I (1558–1603), and the decline of the Renaissance under the Stuart monarchs (1603–1649).

In 1485, with the end of the Wars of the Roses and the crowning of Henry VII, domestic unrest ended. Henry immediately set about unifying the country, strengthening the crown, and replenishing the royal treasury.

Under the reign of his son, Henry VIII (1509–1547), England was ripe for the intellectual ferment of the Renaissance. The population had begun to increase rapidly, feudalism was on its deathbed, and there was a steady movement of population to the larger towns and cities, especially London. The population of London, only 93,000 in 1563, had by 1605 more than doubled, to 224,000.

In addition, the invention of the printing press, together with improved methods of manufacturing paper, made possible the rapid spread of knowledge. In 1476, during the Wars of the Roses, William Caxton had set up England's first printing press at Westminster, a part of London. By 1640, that press and others had printed more than 26,000 different works and editions. With the advent of the printing press and the increased availability of books, literacy increased. It is estimated that by 1530 more than half the population of England was literate.

Near the end of the fifteenth century, Renaissance learning made its tardy entry into England, carried home by scholars who had traveled in Italy. Earliest among these was the Oxford Group, which introduced the new learning of the Renaissance to Oxford in the 1490's and 1500's. A decade later, the great Dutch humanist, Desiderius Erasmus, was teaching Greek at Cambridge.

The first major impact of the Renaissance on English literature is observable in the poetry of Wyatt and Surrey, who introduced and Anglicized the sonnet, a verse form that has proved to be both popular and durable. Surrey is credited also with inventing English blank verse. Other verse forms, borrowed from the Italian and the French, had a lesser impact. Elaborate Renaissance conventions of love poetry were also transplanted, finding their outlet chiefly in sonnets and sonnet sequences.

Though the non-native influence was strong insofar as poetry was concerned, the native drama continued to develop and gain popularity. Miracle and morality plays remained a favorite form of entertainment, while a new dramatic form, the *interlude,* developed. One of the important ancestors of Elizabethan drama, the interlude was a short play designed to be presented between the courses of a banquet.

While the Renaissance was gathering strength in England, two events occurred that were inimical to the influence of the Catholic Church. The first was Martin Luther's posting of his Ninety-five Theses on a church door in Wittenberg, Germany, in 1517, an act which heralded the Reformation. The second event was brought about by the desire of Henry VIII for a male heir and his wish to divorce Catherine of Aragon, who had borne only one child, Mary. When the Pope refused to end the marriage, Henry, with an eye also to seizing the vast and wealthy holdings of the Church, overthrew papal jurisdiction, married Anne Boleyn, and was declared, with Parliament's help, head of the English Church. Thus England became a Protestant nation.

During the reign of his successor, the child king Edward VI, the movement toward Protestantism continued. However, Queen Mary, the next monarch, was a devout Catholic. Her attempts to restore Catholicism to the country resulted in internal turmoil and much bloodshed.

The Height of the Renaissance

Under Elizabeth I (1558–1603), the next monarch, order was restored and England entered upon her most glorious age. Only twenty-five when she assumed the throne, Elizabeth, who never married, was to rule wisely and well for forty-five years. Through her policy of middle-of-the-road Protestantism, she held in check throughout her reign the proponents of Catholicism on one hand and the growing numbers of Puritan extremists on the other. A master politician, wise in the choice of her councilors, Elizabeth established a strong central government that received the loyal support of her subjects.

During her reign, England began to gain supremacy on the seas. Threatened by an invasion from her long-time enemy, the King of Spain, Elizabeth sent Hawkins and Drake out to destroy the Spanish Armada. Her words upon that occasion are noteworthy: ". . . I know I have the body of a weak feeble woman, but I have the heart and stomach of a king—and a king of England, too, and think foul scorn that . . . Spain or any Prince of Europe should dare to invade the borders of my realm."

England's increasing population created new markets and brought about the exploitation of new sources of raw materials, among them those of the New World. The commercial ventures of the Virginia Company in North America and of the East India Company in the Orient were aspects of this expansion. Riches also came from ventures like those of the pirate-patriot Sir Francis Drake, whom Elizabeth commissioned to intercept Spanish treasure ships on the high seas and relieve them of the heavy burden of gold they had stolen from the Indians of South America. Such ventures generated as much as 5000 percent return, which went to swell the royal treasury.

Elizabeth's reign was the age of courtiers. The serious aspects of court life, those that led to England's becoming a world power, were tempered somewhat by the lighter aspects. The queen loved music and dancing, and her court entertainments were notable. Educated in both the classical and modern languages, Elizabeth was not only a master politician, but also a poet of no mean ability. Many of the men of her court did live up to the Renaissance ideal (as expressed in *Hamlet*) of courtier, soldier, and scholar. Most famous of the courtier poets were the Earl of Essex, Sir Walter Raleigh, and Sir Philip Sidney. Edmund Spenser, unsuccessfully seeking court preferment, wrote *The Faerie Queene,* a long allegorical epic in which Gloriana, the Faerie Queene, represented Elizabeth.

During Elizabeth's reign, the popularity of the sonnet led to the writing of sonnet sequences, usually telling the story of unrequited love. Sir Philip Sidney set the vogue for these with *Astrophel and Stella.* Among his more famous followers were Edmund Spenser, with *Amoretti,* and William Shakespeare, with an untitled, enigmatic series of 154 sonnets.

Most of Elizabeth's courtiers did not want their work published, preferring to limit their audience to a small group of the *cognoscenti,* or educated class.

Lyric poetry and song also flourished in Elizabethan England, as courtier and commoner alike found in song an outlet for the exuberant Renaissance spirit. Most famous of the songwriters was Thomas Campion, whose five collections of songs with lute accompaniment were printed and made available to Elizabethans at all social levels. Another source of popular music was the drama. Songs were an integral part not only of comedies, but on occasion also of tragedies.

Beyond question the Elizabethan period was the golden age of English drama, including among its dramatists Christopher Marlowe, William Shakespeare, and Ben Jonson, along with more than a dozen other first-rate playwrights. Under the skillful handling of these dramatists, blank verse, introduced into the language by Surrey, became the main vehicle for tragedy and comedy. *Hamlet, Macbeth,* and Shakespeare's other tragedies were cast in blank verse, as were his comedies.

Native English drama, which had existed at least since medieval times, was the wellspring of Elizabethan drama. Although Classical drama had been known earlier, its initial influence came in the 1560's, with the translation of Latin drama, especially the revenge tragedies of Seneca and the comedies of Plautus and Terence. Somehow everything coalesced, and Elizabethan England saw the theater develop to an unprecedented degree. The plays of the great dramatists contained something for everyone: low comedy for the groundlings, elevated philosophical concepts for the educated, and strong story lines to engage the attention of everyone. Public theaters, such as Shakespeare's

Globe, competed with one another outside the limits of London. Within the city itself, private theaters, charging higher admissions and offering more sophisticated entertainment, provided further competition.

Because the public theaters attracted large audiences from all levels of society, pickpockets and other criminals were drawn there. As Puritan influence grew in England, more and more complaints were made about the ungodliness of the theaters, and they were occasionally closed. In time of plague, too, their operations were suspended, and the acting companies went on tour.

The Puritan influence that forced the occasional closing of the theaters was symptomatic of what was to come. Renaissance exuberance was the exuberance of youth, and as Elizabethan poets warned, youth cannot last forever. Queen Elizabeth's middle-of-the-road Protestantism and personal presence had maintained England's domestic stability. In 1600, however, when the new century began, Elizabeth was in her late sixties, an aging queen not in the best of health. Despite the urging of her councilors, not until she was on her deathbed in 1603 did she name her successor, King James of Scotland.

The Decline of the Renaissance

James I had little firsthand knowledge of England, nor was he equipped with leadership traits to rouse patriotic fervor and bind his new subjects to him. Elizabeth had managed to maintain religious balance, but under the Stuarts, James and his son Charles I, who succeeded him, that balance was lost. Both monarchs were firm Anglicans, opposed to Puritanism. James' active persecution of the Puritans, in fact, led to the founding of Plymouth in New England.

Both monarchs also engaged in struggles with Parliament, notably the House of Commons, over finances and their divine right to rule absolutely. The increasing strength of the predominantly Puritan middle class in the House of Commons made confrontation inevitable. This did not occur until the reign of Charles, who settled his disputes with his Parliaments by high-handedly dismissing them. In 1642, civil war erupted, with the King and his supporters, called Royalists or Cavaliers, ranged against the Parliamentary forces, called Puritans or Roundheads. The king was defeated, tried, found guilty of treason, and executed in 1649. England was declared a commonwealth under the jurisdiction of Parliament.

At the beginning of the Stuart period, poetry was only a little less exuberant, a little more cynical and introspective than it had been earlier under Elizabeth. A major development was the growth of a group of metaphysical poets, led by John Donne. For emphasis, they used "strong" or harsh lines, overriding regular meter; they employed strained metaphors (or **conceits**); and they were intellectual rather than romantic, even in their love poetry. The lyrics of Ben Jonson, spanning the Elizabethan and Stuart periods, show the gradual movement toward the metaphysical.

With the outbreak of the Puritan revolution, literature polarized. A number of young Cavaliers, loyal to the king, wrote lyrics about love and loyalty, but even in the love poems it is evident that the freshness of the Elizabethan era had passed. Among the best of these poets were Richard Lovelace, Robert Herrick, Sir John Suckling, and George Wither (who later became a Puritan).

King James performed a great service to literature as well as to the Protestant cause when he commissioned a new English translation of the Bible. Completed in 1611, the King James Bible influenced English prose for generations.

A major accomplishment in English prose occurred with the publication, over a period of years, of the essays of Francis Bacon. Their insights into human nature and their clear style make them popular to this day.

Drama continued to flourish in England under the Stuarts. Shakespeare's great tragedies were written during the reign of King James, and Shakespeare's acting company, taken under the patronage of the king, became known as the King's Men. The theater did in fact remain a popular form of entertainment until the Puritan government closed all playhouses in 1649.

The greatest of the Puritan poets, and one of the greatest English poets, was John Milton, Latin Secretary to the Puritan Commonwealth. He continued in this position when his sight began to fail, eventually becoming blind. Sightless, he composed *Paradise Lost,* his greatest work and the only successful English epic, choosing for his subject the fall of man. Although Milton's great epic was written after the fall of the Puritan Commonwealth, he is included in the Renaissance unit because he did his early work during that period, and because his output looks back toward the Renaissance rather than ahead to the Age of Reason. The same is true of Andrew Marvell, Puritan and close friend of Milton.

The Renaissance might be called the age of the **sonnet,** *for it was during this period that this short, highly structured poetic form was introduced into England, and flourished.*

The sonnet form originated in Italy, probably in the thirteenth century, and was used by two Italian masters, Dante (1265–1321) and Petrarch (1304-1374). Sir Thomas Wyatt and Henry Howard, Earl of Surrey, are credited with introducing and establishing the form in England early in the sixteenth century. It soon became fashionable in England to write love sonnets to a beloved—usually idealized—lady, after the manner of Petrarch's sonnets to his mistress Laura.

Thomas Wyatt

Whoso List to Hunt

Whoso list[1] to hunt, I know where is an hind,[2]
But as for me, alas, I may no more.
The vain travail hath wearied me so sore
I am of them that furthest come behind
Yet may I, by no means, my wearied mind
Draw from the deer: but as she fleeth afore
Fainting I follow. I leave off therefore,
Since in a net I seek to hold the wind.
Whoso list her hunt, I put him out of doubt,
As well as I, may spend his time in vain:
And graven with diamonds in letters plain
There is written, her fair neck round about,
"*Noli me tangere,*[3] for Caesar's I am,
And wild for to hold, though I seem tame."

1. ***list,*** likes.
2. ***hind,*** female deer.
3. ***Noli me tangere,*** do not touch me. [Latin] Tradition has it that the subject of this sonnet was Anne Boleyn, Wyatt's first cousin, with whom he was reputed to be in love. Anne was the wife of Henry VIII and Queen of England.

Henry Howard, Earl of Surrey

A Lover's Vow

Set me whereas the sun doth parch the green,
Or where his beams may not dissolve the ice,
In temperate heat, where he is felt and seen;
With proud people, in presence sad and wise,
Set me in base, or yet in high degree;
In the long night, or in the shortest day;
In clear weather, or where mists thickest be;
In lusty youth, or when my hairs be gray;
Set me in earth, in heaven, or yet in hell;
In hill, in dale, or in the foaming flood;
Thrall,[1] or at large, alive whereso I dwell;
Sick or in health, in ill fame or in good;
Yours will I be, and with that only thought
Comfort myself when that my hap[2] is naught.

1. ***Thrall,*** enslaved.
2. ***hap,*** good fortune.

Discussion

1. Sonneteers liked to speak in elaborate metaphors, in which one set of terms stands for another. What is the central metaphor in Wyatt's "Whoso List to Hunt," and how far is it extended?

2. The last two lines of Surrey's "A Lover's Vow" appear to explain the somewhat frenzied tone of the preceding lines. What is the explanation, and how persuasive is it?

3. As a literary exercise, determine how well "Whoso List

Besides establishing the English form of the sonnet, Surrey made another major contribution to English poetry. It was he who introduced **blank verse** *into England in 1554, with his translation of parts of Virgil's* Aeneid. *In the first edition, his work is picturesquely described as: ". . . translated into English and drawn into a strange meter by Henry late Earl of Surrey, worthy to be embraced." Other poets did find the new verse form "worthy to be embraced"—the great dramas of Marlowe and Shakespeare are written in blank verse, as is Milton's* Paradise Lost, *and it has remained a popular verse form to this day.*

from Certain Books of Virgil's Aeneid

The passage that follows describes the building of the Trojan horse. Aeneas of Troy is the speaker:

The Greeks' chieftains, all irked with the war
Wherein they wasted had so many years,
And oft repulsed by fatal destiny,
A huge horse made, high raised like a hill,
By the divine science of Minerva;[1]
Of cloven fir compacted were his ribs;
For their return a feigned sacrifice,
The fame whereof so wandered it at point.[2]
In the dark bulk they closed bodies of men
Chosen by lot, and did enstuff by stealth
The hollow womb with armed soldiers.
There stands in sight an isle hight Tenedon,[3]
Rich and of fame while Priam's kingdom[4] stood,
Now but a bay, and road[5] unsure for ship.
Hither them secretly the Greeks withdrew,
Shrouding themselves under the desert shore.
And, weening we[6] they had been fled and gone,
And with that wind had fet[7] the land of Greece,
Troye discharged her long continued dole.[8]
The gates cast up, we issued out to play,
The Greekish camp desirous to behold,
The places void and the forsaken coasts.
Here Pyrrhus' band, there fierce Achilles' pight,[9]
Here rode their ships, there did their battles join.
Astonied, some the scatheful[10] gift beheld,
Behight[11] by vow unto the chaste Minerve,
All wond'ring at the hugeness of the horse.

1. ***Minerva,*** a Roman goddess identified with the Greek goddess of wisdom, Athena.
2. ***The fame . . . at point,*** the rumor of which circulated readily.
3. ***hight Tenedon,*** named ***Tenedon*** (ten′ə don), or Tenedos, an island in the Aegean Sea.
4. ***Priam's kingdom,*** Troy.
5. ***road,*** harbor.
6. ***weening we,*** we supposed.
7. ***fet,*** reached.
8. ***dole,*** sorrow.
9. ***pight*** (pit), camp.
10. ***scatheful,*** harmful.
11. ***Behight,*** promised.

---

to Hunt" conforms to the rhyme scheme and thought division of the Italian sonnet, and "A Lover's Vow" conforms to those of the English sonnet.

4. (a) In the translation from the *Aeneid,* how effective is the blank verse description of the Trojan horse? **(b)** Do you find this to be a "strange meter"? Support your answer by one or two examples from the text.

Something of Queen Elizabeth's attitude toward the arts is indicated by her own efforts as a poet, and by the efforts of the men of action who surrounded her at court. Some examples of this courtly poetry are presented in these three pages. Sir Walter Raleigh and the Earl of Essex were among Elizabeth's most influential advisers. Raleigh, who was first in the queen's favor, fell out when Essex became a favorite, and then returned to his position when Essex fell. Both men were dashing adventurers, soldier-statesmen, and poets.

Portrait of Elizabeth I. Prints Division, The New York Public Library, Astor, Lenox, and Tilden Foundations.

Queen Elizabeth

When I Was Fair and Young

When I was fair and young, and favor gracèd me,
  Of many was I sought, their mistress for to be;
But I did scorn them all, and answered them therefore,
  "Go, go, go, seek some otherwhere,
    Impòrtune me no more!"

How many weeping eyes I made to pine with woe,
  How many sighing hearts, I have no skill to show;
Yet I the prouder grew, and answered them therefore,
  "Go, go, go, seek some otherwhere,
    Impòrtune me no more!"

Then spake fair Venus' son, that proud victorious boy,[1]
  And said, "Fine dame, since that you be so coy,
I will so pluck your plumes that you shall say no more,
  'Go, go, go, seek some otherwhere,
    Impòrtune me no more!'

When he had spake these words, such change grew in my breast,
  That neither night nor day since that, I could take any rest,
Then lo! I did repent that I had said before,
  "Go, go, go, seek some otherwhere,
    Impòrtune me no more!"

1. ***Venus' son . . . boy.*** Cupid and his mother Venus were the patrons of lovers in Classical mythology.

Discussion

1. **(a)** What is the tone of this poem? **(b)** In the last stanza, what has occurred in the speaker's life? **(c)** Do you think that Queen Elizabeth intended this poem to be autobiographical? Explain.

2. Queen Elizabeth never married—some say for reasons of state—but down through the ages rumors have persisted, romantically linking her and Essex. **(a)** How may "To Plead My Faith" be read in the light of these rumors? **(b)** Compare the tone of this poem with that of "When I Was Fair and Young." Which seems more sincere? Why?

Robert Devereux, Earl of Essex

To Plead My Faith Where Faith Had No Reward

To plead my faith where faith had no reward,
To move remorse where favor is not borne,
To heap complaints where she doth not regard—
Were fruitless, bootless, vain, and yield
but scorn.

I lovèd her whom all the world admired,
I was refused of her that can love none;
And my vain hopes, which far too high aspired,
Is dead, and buried, and for ever gone.

Forget my name, since you have scorned
my love,
And womanlike do not too late lament;
Since for your sake I do all mischief prove,
I none accuse nor nothing do repent.

I was as fond as ever she was fair,
Yet loved I not more than I now despair.

Sir Walter Raleigh

What Is Our Life?

What is our life? a play of passion;
Our mirth, the music of division;[1]
Our mothers' wombs the tiring-houses[2] be
Where we are dressed for this short comedy.
Heaven the judicious sharp spectator is,
That sits and marks still[3] who doth act amiss;
Our graves that hide us from the searching sun
Are like drawn curtains when the play is done.
Thus march we playing to our latest rest;
Only we die in earnest—that's no jest.

1. ***music of division,*** music played between acts or other divisions of a play.
2. ***tiring houses,*** dressing rooms.
3. ***still,*** continuously.

notes and comments

The death of Raleigh

A Scaffold was erected in the old Palace yard, upon which after 14 yeares reprivement, [Sir Walter Raleigh's] head was cutt off; at which time, such abundance of bloud issued from his veines, that shewed he had stock of nature enough left to have continued him many yeares in life, though now above three score yeares old, if it had not been taken away by the hand of Violence. And this was the end of the great Sir Walter Raleigh: great sometimes in the favour of Queen Elizabeth, and next to Sir Francis Drake, the great Scourge and hate of the Spaniard. . . ."

To Queen Elizabeth

Our passions are most like to floods and streams,
The shallow murmur, but the deep are dumb;
So, when affections yield discourse, it seems
The bottom is but shallow whence they come.
  They that are rich in words must needs discover
  That they are poor in that which makes a lover.

Wrong not, dear empress of my heart,
  The merit of true passion
With thinking that he feels no smart
  That sues for no compassion;
Since, if my plaints serve not to prove
  The conquest of your beauty,
They come not from defect of love
  But from excess of duty.

For knowing that I sue to serve
  A saint of such perfection
As all desire, yet none deserve,
  A place in her affection,
I rather choose to want[1] relief
  Than venture the revealing;
When glory recommends the grief,
  Despair distrusts the healing.

Thus those desires that aim too high
  For any mortal lover,
When reason cannot make them die
  Discretion doth them cover.
Yet, when discretion doth bereave
  The plaints that they should utter,
Then your discretion may perceive
  That silence is a suitor.

Silence in love bewrays[2] more woe
  Than words, though ne'er so witty;
A beggar that is dumb, you know,
  Deserveth double pity.
Then misconceive not, dearest heart,
  My true though secret passion;
He smarteth[3] most that hides his smart
  And sues for no compassion.

---

1. ***want,*** lack.
2. ***bewrays,*** betrays, reveals.
3. ***smarteth,*** hurts.

Discussion

1. **(a)** Is "To Queen Elizabeth" reminiscent of the Raleigh who, according to tradition, spread out his cloak for Queen Elizabeth to walk on? Explain. **(b)** Both this poem and "To Plead My Faith" were addressed to Queen Elizabeth. To which do you think she would respond more favorably? Why?

2. Relate the last words of "What Is Our Life?" ("Only we die in earnest—that's no jest") to the rest of the poem.

Extension • Writing

Assume that you are new at Queen Elizabeth's court, and write a note to a friend or relative describing what it is like.

Edmund Spenser

from The Faerie Queene

Edmund Spenser's plan for his allegorical epic, *The Faerie Queen* (published 1590–1595), was remarkably elaborate: there were to be twelve books, each book to be devoted to one of the twelve virtues of chivalry, such as Holiness, Temperance, Chastity. Spenser completed only half of his projected plan, or a total of six books with twelve cantos each. Even so, the poem is the longest noteworthy poem in the English language.

In order to illustrate moral virutes, Spenser fashioned his poem as an **allegory,** letting his characters stand for particular abstract qualities. But the allegorical purposes fused with political and other purposes, and the characters became identifiable not only with virtues but with historical personages. The Faerie Queene herself, Gloriana, is a guiding presence throughout the work who dispatches her knights on errands and quests in the service of virtue. Gloriana represents glory in a general sense, but she also represents Queen Elizabeth.

But it is a mistake to get bogged down in allegorical and political references when reading *The Faerie Queene.* Spenser's poetry has a vivid, physical quality that gives it tremendous force on a simple narrative level. The poem should be read first for this quality and the allegory left to fend for itself.

The Knight Slays a Monster

(from Canto I)

The Faerie Queene opens with a description of a knight riding his steed across a plain. He is followed by a lovely lady who is attended by a dwarf carrying her "needments" on his back. The knight is venturing forth to prove his power in battle and thus to win the favor of his queen and the admiration of the lady. This strange group soon loses its way and comes by accident upon an ominous-looking cave. Inside lurks an ugly monster, half serpent, half woman—"most loathsome, filthy, foul." Thus the knight is given his first opportunity to test his strength and bravery.

14

But full of fire and greedy hardiment,[1]
The youthful knight could not for aught be stayed,
But forth unto the darksome hole he went,
And looked in: his glistering armor made
A little glooming light, much like a shade,
By which he saw the ugly monster plain,
Half like a serpent horribly displayed,
But th'other half did woman's shape retain,
Most loathsome, filthy, foul, and full of vile disdain.

15

And as she lay upon the dirty ground,
Her huge long tail her den all overspread,
Yet was in knots and many broughtes[2] upwound,
Pointed with mortal sting. Of her there bred
A thousand young ones, which she daily fed,
Sucking upon her poisonous dugs, each one
Of sundry shapes, yet all ill favored:
Soon as that uncouth light upon them shone,
Into her mouth they crept, and sudden all were gone.

1. ***greedy hardiment,*** eager courage.

2. ***broughtes,*** coils.

16

Their dam upstart, out of her den affrayed,[3]
And rushed forth, hurling her hideous tail
About her cursed head, whose folds displayed
Were stretched now forth at length without entrail.[4]
She looked about, and seeing one in mail
Armed to point,[5] sought back to turn again;
For light she hated as the deadly bale,
Ay wont in desert darkness to remain,
Where plain none might her see, nor she see any plain.

17

Which when the valiant Elf[6] perceived, he leapt
As lion fierce upon the flying prey,
And with his trenchant blade her boldly kept
From turning back, and forced her to stay:
Therewith enraged she loudly 'gan to bray,
And turning fierce, her speckled tail advanced,
Threatening her angry sting, him to dismay:
Who naught aghast, his mighty hand enhanced:[7]
The stroke down from her head unto her shoulder glanced.

18

Much daunted with that dint,[8] her sense was dazed,
Yet kindling rage, herself she gathered round,
And all at once her beastly body raised
With doubled forces high above the ground:
Then wrapping up her wreathed stern around,
Leaped fierce upon his shield, and her huge train[9]
All suddenly about his body wound,
That hand or foot to stir he strove in vain:
God help the man so wrapped in Error's endless train.[10]

3. ***affrayed,*** frightened away.
4. ***entrail,*** coiling, folding.
5. ***to point,*** completely.
6. ***Elf,*** the knight; he was described as coming from Faerie.
7. ***enhanced,*** lifted.
8. ***dint,*** blow.
9. ***train,*** long trailing tail.
10. ***train,*** snare.

19

His Lady sad to see his sore constraint,
Cried out, "Now, now, Sir knight, show what ye be.
Add faith unto your force, and be not faint:
Strangle her, else she sure will strangle thee."
That when he heard, in great perplexity,
His gall did grate for grief[11] and high disdain,
And knitting all his force got one hand free,
Wherewith he gripped her gorge with so great pain,
That soon to loose her wicked bands did her constrain.

20

Therewith she spewed out of her filthy maw
A flood of poison horrible and black,
Full of great lumps of flesh and gobbets raw,
Which stunk so vilely, that it forced him slack
His grasping hold, and from her turn him back:
Her vomit full of books and papers was,
With loathly frogs and toads, which eyes did lack,
And creeping sought way in the weedy grass:
Her filthy parbreake[12] all the place defiled has.

21

As when old father Nilus 'gins to swell
With timely pride above the Egyptian vale,
His fatty waves do fertile slime outwell,
And overflow each plain and lowly dale:
But when his later spring 'gins to avale,[13]
Huge heaps of mud he leaves, wherein there breed
Ten thousand kinds of creatures, partly male
And partly female of his fruitful seed;
Such ugly monstrous shapes elsewhere may no man reed.[14]

22

The same so sore annoyed has the knight,
That well nigh choked with the deadly stink,
His forces fail, nor can no longer fight.

11. ***His gall . . . grief,*** his anger was stirred.
12. ***parbreake,*** vomit.
13. ***avale,*** subside.
14. ***reed,*** see.

Whose courage when the fiend perceived to
shrink,
She poured forth out of her hellish sink
Her fruitful cursed spawn of serpents small,
Deformed monsters, foul, and black as ink,
Which swarming all about his legs did crawl,
And him encumbered sore, but could not hurt
at all.

23

As gentle Shepherd in sweet eventide,
When ruddy Phoebus[15] 'gins to welke[16] in
west,
High on an hill, his flock to viewen wide,
Marks which do bite their hasty supper best;
A cloud of cumbrous[17] gnats do him molest,
All striving to infix their feeble stings,
That from their 'noyance he no where can
rest,
But with his clownish hands their tender
wings
He brusheth oft, and oft doth mar their
murmurings.

15. ***Phoebus*** (fē′bəs), Apollo, the Greek god of the sun.
16. ***welke,*** diminish.

17. ***cumbrous,*** bothersome, annoying.

24

Thus ill bestead,[18] and fearful more of shame,
Than of the certain peril he stood in,
Half furious unto his foe he came,
Resolved in mind all suddenly to win,
Or soon to lose, before he once would lin;[19]
And struck at her with more than manly force,
That from her body full of filthy sin
He raft[20] her hateful head without remorse;
A stream of coal-black blood forth gushed from her corse.[21]

25

Her scattered brood, soon as their Parent dear
They saw so rudely falling to the ground,
Groaning full deadly, all with troublous fear,
Gathered themselves about her body round,
Weening their wonted entrance to have found
At her wide mouth: but being there withstood
They flocked all about her bleeding wound,
And sucked up their dying mother's blood,
Making her death their life, and eke[22] her hurt their good.

18. ***bestead,*** situated.
19. ***lin,*** stop.
20. ***raft,*** took off.
21. ***corse,*** body.
22. ***eke,*** also.

26

That detestable sight him much amazed,
To see th'unkindly Imps of heaven accursed,
Devour their dam; on whom while so he gazed,
Having all satisfied their bloody thirst,
Their bellies swollen he saw with fullness burst,
And bowels gushing forth: well worthy end
Of such as drunk her life, the which them nursed:
Now needeth him no longer labor spend,
His foes have slain themselves, with whom he should contend.

27

His Lady seeing all that chanced, from far
Approached in haste to greet his victory,
And said, "Fair knight, born under happy star,
Who see your vanquished foes before you lie:
Well worthy be you of that Armory,[23]
Wherein you have great glory won this day,
And proved your strength on a strong enemy,
Your first adventure: many such I pray,
And henceforth ever wish, that like succeed it may."

23. ***Armory,*** i.e., the armor of a Christian man (a reference to Ephesians 6:13-14).

notes and comments

The Spenserian Stanza

Edmund Spenser devised a special stanza for *The Faerie Queene*. It has a total of nine lines, the first eight in **iambic pentameter** (five feet of unaccented-accented syllables), and the last an **alexandrine,** made of *iambic hexameter* (i.e., with one additional foot). The rhyme scheme is highly interlocking: ababbcbcc. The tightness of the form, and especially the finality of the long last line, tends to make each stanza self-contained. The result, when used in narrative poetry (at least in Spenser's hands) is a sequence of densely packed, richly woven images, almost like miniatures flashing by one at a time, vividly present and then gone. Many poets after Spenser have tried to write in this stanza form, but none with so much success as John Keats in "The Eve of St. Agnes." (See pages 336–342.)

28

Then mounted he upon his Steed again,
And with the Lady backward sought to wend;
That path he kept, which beaten was most plain,
Nor ever would to any byway bend,
But still did follow one unto the end,
The which at last out of the wood them brought.
So forward on his way (with God to friend)[24]
He passed forth, and new adventure sought;
Long way he traveled, before he heard of aught.

24. ***to friend,*** as a friend.

Discussion

1. First read this passage as an exciting action, ignoring for the moment the allegorical elements. **(a)** Many readers of *The Faerie Queene* have noted its dreamlike quality. What elements in this passage suggest a dream? **(b)** Are the characters individuals or types?

2. The knight represents Holiness, the lady Truth, the monster Error. Holiness, with the aid of Truth, crushes Error. Look at this passage now as allegory. **(a)** In stanza 16, why is the monster afraid of light? **(b)** Discuss the children of the monster—their creation and their death—in allegorical terms.

3. The form, imagery, and language of *The Faerie Queene* are in large part the secret of its success. **(a)** What is the effect in the Spenserian stanza (see page 124) of the long last (ninth) line, with six feet (an *alexandrine*)? Does it convey a sense of rapidity and openness, or the opposite? How does this sense affect the narrative flow? **(b)** stanzas 25 and 26 present a repulsive sight of the monster's children thriving on their mother's death and then expiring. Examine the imagery and diction to discover how Spenser achieves this effect. **(c)** Show how the Shepherd metaphor in stanza 23 functions in the passage.

notes and comments

Allegory

An **allegory** is a narrative in which the characters, events, or settings stand for something other than simply themselves. Very frequently they represent abstract ideas such as Faith, Honor, Virtue, but sometimes political, religious, or professional attitudes, beliefs, or personages. Allegory is not, therefore, a literary type in the sense of "sonnet" or "short story." It is, rather, a strategy or technique that can be used in any literary type, poetry or prose. The most famous allegories in English literature are the medieval morality play, *Everyman,* Edmund Spenser's long poem, *The Faerie Queene,* and John Bunyan's prose narrative, *Pilgrim's Progress.*

An allegorical meaning or an allegorical dimension may be found in works that do not comply fully with the traditional definition of allegory, such as the Bible (Jonah and the whale), Herman Melville's *Moby Dick,* or Joseph Heller's *Catch-22.* George Orwell's *Animal Farm* is an allegory in the form of a satire, ridiculing an entire political system. The modern theater of the absurd is strongly allegorical. Samuel Beckett's *Waiting for Godot,* Eugene Ionesco's *The Bald Soprano,* Harold Pinter's *The Caretaker,* and Edward Albee's *The Zoo Story* all contain enigmatic situations that appear to stand for the enigmatic situation of modern man.

Christopher Marlowe

The Passionate Shepherd to his Love

Come live with me and be my Love,
And we will all the pleasures prove
That hills and valleys, dales and fields,
Or woods or steepy mountain yields.

And we will sit upon the rocks,
And see the shepherds feed their flocks
By shallow rivers, to whose falls
Melodious birds sing madrigals.

And I will make thee beds of roses
And a thousand fragrant posies;
A cap of flowers, and a kirtle
Embroidered all with leaves of myrtle;

A gown made of the finest wool
Which from our pretty lambs we pull;
Fair-lined slippers for the cold,
With buckles of the purest gold;

A belt of straw and ivy buds
With coral clasps and amber studs—
And if these pleasures may thee move,
Come live with me and be my Love.

The shepherd swains shall dance and sing
For thy delight each May morning—
If these delights thy mind may move,
Then live with me and be my Love.

1. ***kirtle,*** a skirt or dress.

Sir Walter Raleigh

The Nymph's Reply to the Shepherd

If all the world and love were young,
And truth in every shepherd's tongue,
These pretty pleasures might me move,
To live with thee and be thy love.

Time drives the flocks from field to fold,
When rivers rage, and rocks grow cold;
And Philomel[1] becometh dumb;
The rest complain of cares to come.

The flowers do fade, and wanton fields
To wayward winter reckoning yields;
A honey tongue, a heart of gall,
Is fancy's spring, but sorrow's fall.

Thy gowns, thy shoes, thy bed of roses,
Thy cap, thy kirtle, and thy posies,
Soon break, soon wither, soon forgotten;
In folly ripe, in reason rotten.

Thy belt of straw and ivy buds,
Thy coral clasps and amber studs,
All these in me no means can move,
To come to thee and be thy love.

But could youth last, and love still breed,
Had joys no date, nor age no need,
Then these delights my mind might move
To live with thee and be thy love.

1. ***Philomel,*** the nightingale.

Edmund Spenser

from Amoretti

30

My love is like to ice, and I to fire:
How comes it then that this her cold so great
Is not dissolved through my so hot desire,
But harder grows the more I her entreat?
Or how comes it that my exceeding heat
Is not allayed by her heart-frozen cold,
But that I burn much more in boiling sweat,
And feel my flames augmented manifold?
What more miraculous thing may be told,
That fire, which all things melts, should harden ice,
And ice, which is congeal'd with senseless cold,
Should kindle fire by wonderful device?
Such is the power of love in gentle mind,
That it can alter all the course of kind.[1]

1. ***kind,*** nature.

Sir Philip Sidney

from Astrophel and Stella

31

With how sad steps, O moon, thou climb'st the skies!
How silently, and with how wan a face!
What! may it be that even in heavenly place
That busy archer[1] his sharp arrows tries?
Sure, if that long-with-love-acquainted eyes
Can judge of love, thou feel'st a lover's case;
I read it in thy looks—thy languished grace
To me, that feel the like, thy state descries.[2]
Then, even of fellowship, O moon, tell me,
Is constant love deemed there but want of wit?
Are beauties there as proud as here they be?
Do they above love to be loved, and yet
Those lovers scorn whom that love doth possess?
Do they call virtue there ungratefulness?[3]

1. ***archer,*** Cupid.
2. ***descries,*** reveals.
3. ***Do . . . ungratefulness?*** Do they call ungratefulness a virtue there?

Discussion

1. (a) How persuasive is the passionate Shepherd? **(b)** What sort of "delights" does he offer the Nymph—sophisticated, simple, or what?

2. (a) Under what circumstances does the Nymph say she would consent to be the Shepherd's love? **(b)** Do you think she really means this, or is just being coy?

3. It has been said that the Shepherd is a romantic, the Nymph a realist. Do the poems indicate this? Explain.

4. The central paradoxical metaphor of "My Love Is Like to Ice" is clear enough (she is ice, he is fire). The wonder is that it sustains the poem for fourteen lines. How?

5. What does Sonnet 31 imply about the speaker's experience with love?

Extension • Writing

Write a script for a modern version of the shepherd-nymph exchange, in prose or poetry, in formal language, or in whatever is the current style. Describe the setting for the dramatic scene, and provide instructions for your actors.

Extension • Speaking

Set up a dialogue in class in which one student plays the role of the Shepherd, the other the Nymph. They should read alternately, the Shepherd the first stanza of his poem, the Nymph the first stanza of her poem, etc.

Sir Philip Sidney

Heart Exchange

My true love hath my heart, and I have his,
By just exchange one for the other given:
I hold his dear, and mine he cannot miss;
There never was a bargain better driven.
His heart in me keeps me and him in one;
My heart in him his thoughts and senses guides:
He loves my heart, for once it was his own;
I cherish his, because in me it bides.
His heart his wound received from my sight;
My heart was wounded with his wounded heart;
For, as from me on him his hurt did light,
So still me-thought in me his hurt did smart:
Both equal hurt in this change sought our bliss:
My true love hath my heart and I have his.

From *Arcadia* (1590).

Discussion

Both the Sidney and the Cummings poem make use of a single **conceit** (a fanciful and sometimes far-fetched image) in which there is much play on the word "heart," moving without warning from its metaphorical to its physical and then back to its metaphorical meaning. **(a)** Explore the ways in which the two poems are alike and how they differ in wittily developing this conceit. **(b)** Explain line 4 in the Sidney poem: "His heart in me keeps me and him in one." **(c)** Explain lines 3–4 in the Cummings poem: "whatever is done/by only me is your doing, my darling)."

notes and comments

E. E. Cummings

The modern American poet E. E. Cummings (1894–1962) has written a poem astonishingly close in meaning and metaphor to Sidney's "Heart Exchange."

i carry your heart

i carry your heart with me(i carry it in
my heart)i am never without it(anywhere
i go you go,my dear;and whatever is done
by only me is your doing,my darling)
                                                      i fear
no fate(for you are my fate,my sweet)i want
no world(for beautiful you are my world,my true)
and it's you are whatever a moon has always meant
and whatever a sun will always sing is you

here is the deepest secret nobody knows
(here is the root of the root and the bud of the bud
and the sky of the sky of a tree called life;which grows
higher than soul can hope or mind can hide)
and this is the wonder that's keeping the stars apart

i carry your heart(i carry it in my heart)

Thomas Campion

The Man of Life Upright

The man of life upright,
  Whose guiltless heart is free
From all dishonest deeds,
  Or thought of vanity;

The man whose silent days
  In harmless joys are spent,
Whom hopes cannot delude,
  Nor sorrow discontent;

That man needs neither towers
  Nor armor for defence,
Nor secret vaults to fly
  From thunder's violence.

He only can behold
  With unaffrighted eyes
The horrors of the deep
  And terrors of the skies.

Thus, scorning all the cares
  That fate or fortune brings,
He makes the heav'n his book,
  His wisdom heav'nly things,

Good thoughts his only friends,
  His wealth a well-spent age,
The earth his sober inn
  And quiet pilgrimage.

Discussion

1. In what respects is "When to Her Lute" a love poem?

2. Could the person described in "The Man of Life Upright" live in today's world?

3. (a) What is the tone of "Never Love Unless You Can"? **(b)** Who comes off better, the man or the woman?

Never Love Unless You Can

Never love unless you can
Bear with all the faults of man;
Men sometimes will jealous be,
Though but little cause they see,
  And hang the head, as discontent,
  And speak what straight they will repent.

Men that but one saint adore
Make a show of love to more;
Beauty must be scorned in none,
Though but truly served in one;
  For what is courtship but disguise?
  True hearts may have dissembling eyes.

Men when their affairs require
Must a while themselves retire,
Sometimes hunt, and sometimes hawk,
And not ever sit and talk,
  If these and such like you can bear,
  Then like, and love, and never fear.

When to Her Lute Corinna Sings

When to her lute Corrina sings,
Her voice revives the leaden stringes,
And doth in highest notes appeare
As any challeng'd echo cleere;
But when she doth of mourning speake,
Ev'n with her sighes the strings do breake.

And, as her lute doth live or die,
Led by her passion, so must I:
For when of pleasure she doth sing,
My thoughts enjoy a sudden spring;
But if she doth of sorrow speake,
Ev'n from my hart the strings doe breake.

Shakespeare's Sonnets

During the Elizabethan era, love poetry tended to follow certain conventions, one of which was an exaggerated description of the beauty of the beloved. She was usually blonde and fair, with a peaches-and-cream complexion—and disdainful. Common themes were fame, mutability (changes worked by time), and the coldness of the beloved. A poet generally felt obligated to work within these conventions, but he tried to achieve originality in spite of them—through ingenuity in devising comparisons, through cleverness of phrasing, or even by turning the conventions upside down.

Detail from a painting showing a nobleman's feast. National Portrait Gallery, London.

18

Shall I compare thee to a summer's day?
Thou art more lovely and more temperate.
Rough winds do shake the darling buds of May.
And summer's lease hath all too short a date.
Sometime too hot the eye of heaven shines,
And often is his gold complexion dimmed.
And every fair from fair sometimes declines,
By chance or nature's changing course untrimmed.[1]
But thy eternal summer shall not fade,
Nor lose possession of that fair thou owest,[2]
Nor shall Death brag thou wander'st in his shade,
When in eternal lines to time thou growest.
  So long as men can breathe, or eyes can see,
  So long lives this, and this gives life to thee.

1. ***untrimmed,*** reduced; shorn of beauty.
2. ***fair thou owest,*** beauty you possess.

130

My mistress' eyes are nothing like the sun,
Coral is far more red than her lips' red.
If snow be white, why then her breasts are dun,
If hairs be wires, black wires grow on her head.
I have seen roses damasked,[1] red and white,
But no such roses see I in her cheeks.
And in some perfumes is there more delight
Than in the breath that from my mistress reeks.
I love to hear her speak, yet well I know
That music hath a far more pleasing sound.
I grant I never saw a goddess go,[2]
My mistress, when she walks, treads on the ground.
  And yet, by Heaven, I think my love as rare
  As any she[3] belied with false compare.

1. ***damasked,*** mingled.
2. ***go,*** walk.
3. ***any she,*** any woman.

29

When in disgrace with fortune and men's eyes
I all alone beweep my outcast state,
And trouble deaf Heaven with my bootless[1]
cries
And look upon myself and curse my fate,
Wishing me like to one more rich in hope,
Featured like him, like him with friends
possessed,
Desiring this man's art and that man's scope,
With what I most enjoy contented least—
Yet in these thoughts myself almost despising,
Haply I think on thee, and then my state,
Like to the lark at break of day arising
From sullen earth, sings hymns at Heaven's
gate.
For thy sweet love remembered such wealth
brings
That then I scorn to change my state with
kings.

1. ***bootless,*** useless.

30

When to the sessions[1] of sweet silent thought
I summon up remembrance of things past,
I sigh the lack of many a thing I sought,
And with old woes new wail my dear time's
waste.
Then can I drown an eye, unused to flow,
For precious friends hid in death's dateless[2]
night,
And weep afresh love's long since canceled
woe,
And moan the expense[3] of many a vanished
sight.
Then can I grieve at grievances foregone,[4]
And heavily from woe to woe tell o'er
The sad account of forebemoaned moan,
Which I new-pay as if not paid before.
But if the while I think on thee, dear friend,
All losses are restored and sorrows end.

1. ***sessions,*** literally, the sittings of a law court.
2. ***dateless,*** endless.
3. ***expense,*** loss.
4. ***foregone,*** past.

55

Not marble, nor the gilded monuments
Of princes, shall outlive this powerful rhyme.
But you shall shine more bright in these
contents
Than unswept stone,[1] besmeared with sluttish
time.
When wasteful war shall statues overturn,
And broils root out the work of masonry,
Nor Mars his sword nor war's quick fire shall
burn
The living record of your memory.
'Gainst death and all-oblivious enmity
Shall you pace forth. Your praise shall still find
room
Even in the eyes of all posterity
That wear this world out to the ending doom.
So, till the judgment[2] that[3] yourself arise,
You live in this, and dwell in lovers' eyes.

1. ***unswept stone,*** dusty slab over a grave (in the floor of a church, where prominent people were often buried.
2. ***judgment,*** Day of Judgment at the end of the world.
3. ***that,*** when.

71

No longer mourn for me when I am dead
Than you shall hear the surly sullen bell
Give warning to the world that I am fled
From this vile world, with vilest worms to
dwell.
Nay, if you read this line, remember not
The hand that writ it, for I love you so
That I in your sweet thoughts would be forgot
If thinking on me then should make you woe.
Oh, if, I say, you look upon this verse
When I perhaps compounded am with clay,
Do not so much as my poor name rehearse,
But let your love even with my life decay,
Lest the wise world should look into your
moan,
And mock you with me after I am gone.

73

That time of year thou mayst in me behold
When yellow leaves, or none, of few, do hang
Upon those boughs which shake against the cold,
Bare ruined choirs[1] where late the sweet birds sang.
In me thou see'st the twilight of such day
As after sunset fadeth in the west,
Which by and by black night doth take away,
Death's second self, that seals up[2] all in rest.
In me thou see'st the glowing of such fire,
That on the ashes of his youth doth lie
As the deathbed whereon it must expire,
Consumed with that which it was nourished by.
This thou perceivest, which makes thy love more strong,
To love that well which thou must leave ere long.

1. ***choir,*** part of a cathedral where services are held.
2. ***seals up,*** ends, concludes.

116

Let me not to the marriage of true minds
Admit impediments. Love is not love
Which alters when it alteration finds,
Or bends with the remover to remove.[1]
Oh no! It is an ever-fixed mark,
That looks on tempests and is never shaken.
It is the star to every wandering bark,
Whose worth's unknown, although his height be taken.
Love's not Time's fool, though rosy lips and cheeks
Within his bending sickle's compass come.
Love alters not with his brief hours and weeks,
But bears it out even to the edge of doom.
If this be error and upon me proved,
I never writ, nor no man ever loved.

1. ***Or bends . . . remove,*** or changes when the loved one is inconstant.

Discussion

1. (a) In Sonnet 18, why does Shakespeare begin by asking a question? **(b)** How consistent is he in carrying through the comparison of his love with a summer's day? **(c)** In the last line, what does "this" refer to, and how does it give life to the beloved? **(d)** Some readers believe that Shakespeare was, in this and other sonnets, paying greater tribute to his poetry than to his love. Explain. What do you think?

2. (a) What conventions are turned upside down in Sonnet 130? **(b)** Explore the effect of the use of "dun" in line 3; of "reeks" in line 8. **(c)** The final couplet opens "And yet," signifying a reversal of some sort. Explain the impact of this couplet on the preceding 12 lines.

3. Which of the previously discussed sonnets strikes you as the more sincere? Why?

4. Sonnets 29 and 30 are sequential. **(a)** What is the situation of the speaker in 29? **(b)** In 30? **(c)** Despite the different situations, how are they similar?

5. How has history borne out the truth of Sonnet 55?

6. (a) How sound is the advice with which Sonnet 71 ends? **(b)** Both Sonnets 71 and 55 deal with the speaker's post-humous memory. Which response to death seems more sincere. Why?

7. Sonnet 73 is a superb example of the English sonnet, with its theme being developed in three stages (lines 1–4, 5–8, and 9–12) and brought to a conclusion in the final couplet. By specific references to the sonnet, show how this is so.

8. Comment upon the effectiveness of the closing couplet in Sonnet 116.

Vocabulary

Structure and Dictionary

Use your Glossary to answer the following questions about the structure of the words listed below. Read each clue and then write on a separate sheet of paper the matching word from the list. *Then write a one-word synonym for each word.*

allay bereave compound
delude discourse encumber
remorse travail

1. Which word has a Latin root that means a kind of exercise?

2. Which word has a prefix and root the literal meanings of which when joined together might describe what one does to individual ingredients to make a stew?

3. Which word has a prefix and root whose literal meanings describe what a dog might do if attacked?

4. Which word has a root that describes something that anchors a tent rope?

5. Which word has an Old English prefix and root, the literal meanings of which you might use in an informal phrase telling someone to stop bothering you?

6. Which has a root that describes what keeps an animal in the zoo?

7. Which has an Old English root that describes a kind of theft?

8. Which has a root the literal meaning of which might describe what a child does?

Extension • Writing

1. Write an evaluation of a sonnet of your choice. Discuss tone, theme, imagery, and conformance to the standards of the English sonnet.

2. Try your hand at writing a sonnet of your own—serious or otherwise.

Thomas Campion 1567 • 1620

Physician, lawyer, poet, musicologist, and outstanding songwriter, Campion embodied the idea of the "Renaissance man." He disliked meaningless rhyming for sheer style, and his sensitivity to both music and language is illustrated in his poetic work. He also wrote a prose discourse, *Observations on the Art of English Poesy,* in which he argued against "the vulgar and unartificial (clumsy) custom of riming," and in favor of rhymeless verse in the classical Latin style.

Robert Devereux, Earl of Essex 1566 • 1601

Devereux is probably best known as one of Queen Elizabeth's favorites. Like many of the other gallant young men at Court, he was both a military adventurer and a poet. He was more childish and impetuous than others in his relations with the queen, and this resulted in his ultimate disfavor.

In 1599, after being involved in military adventures in France and Spain, he was sent to Ireland to command an army against the rebels. Hearing reports of the popularity of his rivals at Court, he made a hasty and unauthorized treaty with the leader of the rebellion and rushed back to the queen, hoping to regain the status he feared he had lost. Elizabeth banished him from Court for disobeying orders, and also deprived him of his license to collect a tax on sweet wines, the mainstay of his finances. Resentful, Devereux organized a plot against the queen which was discovered. He was charged with treason and executed—a sentence which Elizabeth decreed only reluctantly.

Christopher Marlowe 1564 • 1593

Marlowe's unconventional life ended at twenty-nine; all his writings were produced in a period of four years.

He was a professional writer, a University Wit (see Shakespeare), and a classical scholar who produced works—both translations and original writings—that were very popular in his day. Among his most powerful plays are *Tamburlaine, The Tragical History of Dr. Faustus,* and *The Jew of Malta.* Some scholars think he may have had a hand in some of Shakespeare's plays. He was also an occasional actor for the Lord Admiral's Men.

In addition to being a professional dramatist, Marlowe is believed to have been a secret agent for the government. One reason for this theory is that the hesitancy of Cambridge University to grant him an M.A. degree (because of his long absences from his studies) was overridden by an order from the Queen's Privy Council. Another supporting fact is that on the day he was killed he was in the company of proven spies.

Some of the details of Marlowe's death are still mysterious. He died of stab wounds inflicted at an inn. Many scholars believe he was the victim of a political murder. Others think his death may simply have been the result of a quarrel. Still a third theory holds that the scene at the inn was actually a plot to produce the rumor of his death, enabling him to go on a secret mission of espionage.

William Shakespeare

1564 • 1616

Shakespeare was descended from Warwickshire Farmers. His father, John, a glover by trade, owned property and by election or appointment held important city offices. Shakespeare's mother, Mary Arden, was a member of the Warwickshire gentry.

Born in Stratford probably on April 23 (his baptismal record still survives in the Stratford Church), Shakespeare probably attended the Stratford grammar school, where he received a classical education under its excellent schoolmaster.

The years from the mid 1580's to about 1592 are called the "lost years" in Shakespeare's life because nothing is known of him. By 1592, at any rate, he was a rising young playwright in London.

This was an exciting period in the English theater, mainly because of a group known as the University Wits, which included Marlowe, Nashe, and others. These brilliant young men turned out sophisticated plays for the courtiers and sensational plays for the general public. Though not a university man like the rest, Shakespeare stepped into this tradition and carried it forward with great success, producing a tremendous variety of plays—thirty-seven in all—within two decades.

Play-writing as such was usually a poorly paid business, but because of his success as a playwright, Shakespeare held a full share in the profits of the Lord Chamberlain's Men, an acting company later called the King's Men. He occasionally acted with the company, taking minor parts (e.g., King Duncan in *Macbeth* and the Ghost in *Hamlet*). When Shakespeare retired to Stratford a few years before his death, it was to the second-largest house in town, proudly displaying the family's coat-of-arms.

Sir Walter Raleigh

1552 • 1618

Raleigh was an outstanding example of the versatile renaissance man. Though he was active in the service of Queen Elizabeth for over ten years, his importance lies more in his other accomplishments than in his influence upon her. He was a poet, a dabbler in music and science, a historian, a pirate, a landowner, a member of Parliament, and a colonizer of the New World.

He was several times imprisoned in the Tower of London —the first time, in 1592 at the Queen's displeasure over his having seduced one of her ladies-in-waiting. Later, during James I's reign, he spent fifteen years in the Tower on a charge of treason. While there, he wrote and performed scientific experiments. He finally obtained his release to go on an expedition to find gold in South America. Raleigh disobeyed instructions on the journey, and also failed to find gold. Upon returning to England, he was again charged with treason, and beheaded.

Sir Philip Sidney 1554 • 1586

Though Wyatt and Surrey were responsible for introducing the sonnet into England, the great popularity of the form was the result of the publication, in 1591, of Sidney's sonnet sequence *Astrophel and Stella.*

Sidney came from an intellectual and aristocratic background and was well-connected in England and on the continent. He was a soldier, scholar, poet, critic, courtier, and diplomat.

Sidney's *Defense of Poesie,* written in reply to a Puritan fanatic's attack on literature, is considered the best critical work written in the Elizabethan period. His *Arcadia,* a florid prose romance interspersed with lyrics, was an early forerunner of the modern novel.

Sidney's last act, according to his friend and biographer, Fulke Greville, was typically gallant. Though fatally wounded in a battle in Holland, Sidney passed his water bottle to a wounded foot-soldier, saying "Thy necessity is greater than mine."

Edmund Spenser 1552 • 1599

Spenser was born in London of middle-class parents, but early in his career, through his literary interests and talents, became associated with members of the nobility. In 1580 he won a government post in Ireland. There he pursued his literary career, and published the first three books of *The Faerie Queene* in 1590. Like other writers of the period, Spenser composed a sonnet sequence —*Amoretti,* dedicated to his future bride, Elizabeth Boyle. Along with other works, he finished another three books of *The Faerie Queene* by 1596. Although he did not live to complete the additional six books planned, *The Faerie Queene* is considered one of the great works of English poetry, and has influenced many of the major English poets who followed him.

Henry Howard, Earl of Surrey 1517 • 1547

The aristocratic Howard family boasted two of the queens of Henry VIII, a Tudor in-law, and an assortment of dukes and earls. Among the latter was the poet Henry Howard. His father, the Duke of Norfolk, was a close adviser of Henry VIII, and Surrey himself was considered as a possible husband for the princess Mary (later queen), at the suggestion of his cousin, Anne Boleyn.

Henry Howard is known, along with Thomas Wyatt, as being one of the first English sonnet writers and for having established the English or Shakespearean sonnet form. He was the first proponent of blank verse (unrhymed lines of iambic pentameter). At this time it was customary for poetry to be circulated in manuscript, and Howard's works were not published until ten years after his death.

The Howard family's rivalry with the equally powerful Seymour family was probably responsible for Surrey's several political imprisonments during the last ten years of his life, and for his eventual execution.

Sir Thomas Wyatt 1503 • 1542

Only thirteen when he made his first appearance at Court, and later educated at Cambridge, Wyatt spent most of his life in the service of the crown. Various diplomatic posts took him to Spain, France, and Italy, where he had personal contact with the continental Renaissance. Twice imprisoned by Henry VIII for political reasons, he was twice pardoned. Anne Boleyn, his first cousin, with whom he had grown up and apparently been in love, became Henry VIII's wife in 1533; Wyatt's political problems tended to follow her fortunes at court.

Wyatt's greatest contribution to English literature is his introduction of the Italian sonnet into England. None of Wyatt's poetry was published during his lifetime; like other courtiers, he circulated his work in manuscript form. Although known for his sonnets, Wyatt did his best work when he wrote native English lyrics.

HAMLET

Prince of Denmark

William Shakespeare

Characters

CLAUDIUS, King of Denmark.
HAMLET, son to the late, and nephew to the present King.
POLONIUS, Lord Chamberlain.
HORATIO, friend to *Hamlet.*
LAERTES, son to *Polonius.*
VOLTIMAND, CORNELIUS, ROSENCRANTZ, GUILDENSTERN, OSRIC, A GENTLEMAN, } courtiers.
MARCELLUS, BERNARDO, } officers.
FRANCISCO, a soldier.
REYNALDO, servant to *Polonius.*
A PRIEST.
PLAYERS.
TWO CLOWNS, grave-diggers.
FORTINBRAS, Prince of Norway.
A CAPTAIN.
ENGLISH AMBASSADORS.

GERTRUDE, Queen of Denmark, and mother to *Hamlet.*
OPHELIA, daughter to *Polonius.*

GHOST of *Hamlet's* Father.

LORDS, LADIES, OFFICERS, SOLDIERS, SAILORS, MESSENGERS, and other ATTENDANTS.

SCENE
Denmark

Act One

SCENE 1.

Elsinore. A platform[1] before the castle. FRANCISCO *at his post. Enter to him* BERNARDO.

BER. Who's there?
FRAN. Nay, answer me: stand, and unfold yourself.
BER. Long live the king!
FRAN. Bernardo?
BER. He.
FRAN. You come most carefully upon your hour.
BER. 'Tis now struck twelve; get thee to bed, Francisco.
FRAN. For this relief much thanks; 'tis bitter cold,
And I am sick at heart.
BER. Have you had quiet guard?
FRAN. Not a mouse stirring.
BER. Well, good night.
If you do meet Horatio and Marcellus,
The rivals[2] of my watch, bid them make haste.
FRAN. I think I hear them. Stand, ho! Who's there?

Enter HORATIO *and* MARCELLUS.

HOR. Friends to this ground.
MAR. And liegemen to the Dane.
FRAN. Give you good night.
MAR. O, farewell, honest soldier:
Who hath relieved you?
FRAN. Bernardo has my place.
Give you good night. *(Exit.)*
MAR. Holla! Bernardo!
BER. Say,
What, is Horatio there?
HOR. A piece of him.
BER. Welcome, Horatio: welcome, good Marcellus.
MAR. What, has this thing appear'd again to-night?
BER. I have seen nothing.
MAR. Horatio says 'tis but our fantasy,
And will not let belief take hold of him
Touching this dreaded sight, twice seen of us:
Therefore I have entreated him along
With us to watch the minutes of this night;
That if again this apparition come,
He may approve[3] our eyes and speak to it.
HOR. Tush, tush, 'twill not appear.

Enter GHOST.

MAR. Peace, break thee off; look, where it comes again!
BER. In the same figure, like the king that's dead.
MAR. Thou art a scholar[4]; speak to it, Horatio.
BER. Looks it not like the king? mark it, Horatio.
HOR. Most like: it harrows me with fear and wonder.
BER. It would be spoke to.
MAR. Question it, Horatio.
HOR. What art thou that usurp'st this time of night,
Together with that fair and warlike form
In which the majesty of buried Denmark
Did sometimes march? by heaven I charge thee, speak!
MAR. It is offended.
BER. See, it stalks away!
HOR. Stay! speak, speak! I charge thee, speak! *(Exit* GHOST.*)*
MAR. 'Tis gone, and will not answer.
BER. How now, Horatio! you tremble and look pale:
Is not this something more than fantasy?
What think you on 't?
HOR. Before my God, I might not this believe
Without the sensible and true avouch
Of mine own eyes.
MAR. Is it not like the king?
HOR. As thou art to thyself:
Such was the very armor he had on
When he the ambitious Norway[5] combated;
So frown'd he once, when, in an angry parle,
He smote the sledded Polacks[6] on the ice.
'Tis strange.

---

1. ***platform,*** a level space on the battlements of the royal castle at Elsinore, a Danish seaport; now Helsignör.
2. ***rivals,*** partners.
3. ***approve,*** confirm.
4. ***scholar,*** a man who can speak Latin, which was the language used to exorcise, or drive out, evil spirits.
5. ***Norway,*** the king of Norway. It was customary to refer to the king of a country by the name of the country.
6. ***when . . . sledded Polacks,*** when in an encounter he struck down the Polish soldiers in sleds.

MAR. Thus twice before, and jump[7] at this dead hour,
With martial stalk hath he gone by our watch.
HOR. In what particular thought to work I know not;
But in the gross and scope[8] of my opinion,
This bodes some strange eruption to our state.
MAR. Good now, sit down, and tell me, he that knows,
Why this same strict and most observant watch
So nightly toils the subject of the land,[9]
And why such daily cast[10] of brazen cannon
And foreign mart[11] for implements of war;
Why such impress[12] of shipwrights, whose sore task
Does not divide the Sunday from the week;
What might be toward, that this sweaty haste
Doth make the night joint-laborer with the day:
Who is 't that can inform me?
HOR. That can I;
At least, the whisper goes so.
Now, sir, young Fortinbras,
Of unimproved mettle[13] hot and full,
Hath in the skirts of Norway here and there
Shark'd up a list of lawless resolutes,[14]
For food and diet, to some enterprise
That hath a stomach in 't; which is no other—
As it doth well appear unto our state—
But to recover of us, by strong hand
And terms compulsatory, those lands
So by his father lost: and this, I take it,
Is the main motive of our preparations,
The source of this our watch and the chief head
Of this post-haste and romage[15] in the land.
BER. I think it be no other but e'en so:
Well may it sort[16] that this portentous figure
Comes armed through our watch; so like the king
That was and is the question of these wars.
HOR. A mote it is to trouble the mind's eye.
In the most high and palmy state of Rome,
A little ere the mightiest Julius fell,
The graves stood tenantless and the sheeted dead
Did squeak and gibber in the Roman streets:
As stars with trains of fire[17] and dews of blood,
Disasters in the sun; and the moist star
Upon whose influence Neptune's empire stands.[18]
Was sick almost to doomsday with eclipse:
And even the like precurse of fear'd events,
But soft, behold! lo, where it comes again!
(Re-enter GHOST.*)*
I'll cross[19] it, though it blast me. Stay, illusion!
If thou hast any sound, or use of voice,
Speak to me:
If there be any good thing to be done,
That may to thee do ease and grace to me,
Speak to me: *(Cock crows.)*
If thou art privy to thy country's fate,
Which, happily, foreknowing may avoid,
O, speak!
Or if thou hast uphoarded in thy life
Extorted treasure in the womb of earth,
For which, they say, you spirits oft walk in death,
Speak of it: stay, and speak![20] Stop it, Marcellus.
MAR. Shall I strike at it with my partisan?[21]
HOR. Do, if it will not stand.
BER. 'Tis here!
HOR. 'Tis here!
MAR. 'Tis gone! *(Exit* GHOST.*)*
We do it wrong, being so majestical,
To offer it the show of violence;
For it is, as the air, invulnerable,
And our vain blows malicious mockery.

---

7. ***jump,*** precisely.
8. ***gross and scope,*** general drift.
9. ***toils . . . land,*** wearies the Danish people.
10. ***cast,*** casting, founding.
11. ***foreign mart,*** trade abroad.
12. ***impress,*** conscription.
13. ***unimproved mettle,*** courage not hitherto turned to account.
14. ***Shark'd up . . . resolutes,*** got together in haphazard fashion a group of lawless men.
15. ***romage,*** bustle, commotion.
16. ***Well may it sort,*** it may well be appropriate.
17. ***stars with trains of fire,*** meteors.
18. ***moist star . . . stands.*** The "moist star" is the moon, so called because it affects the tides. Thus it governs the empire of Neptune, Roman god of the sea.
19. ***cross,*** meet, face.
20. ***stay, and speak!*** Horatio is enumerating three reasons ghosts were believed to return from the grave: to perform a good deed left undone at death, to warn of danger to the country, or to reveal the whereabouts of hidden treasure. Horatio fails to mention a fourth reason: to reveal the particulars of the ghost's death.
21. ***partisan,*** long-handled weapon, like a pike or spear.

BER. It was about to speak, when the cock crew.
HOR. And then it started like a guilty thing
Upon a fearful summons. I have heard,
The cock, that is the trumpet to the morn,
Doth with his lofty and shrill-sounding throat
Awake the god of day; and, at his warning,
Whether in sea or fire, in earth or air,
The extravagant and erring[22] spirit hies
To his confine: and of the truth herein
This present object made probation.[23]
MAR. It faded on the crowing of the cock.
Some say that ever 'gainst[24] that season comes
Wherein our Saviour's birth is celebrated,
The bird of dawning singeth all night long:
And then, they say, no spirit dare stir abroad;
The nights are wholesome; then no planets strike,[25]
No fairy takes, nor witch hath power to charm,
So hallow'd and so gracious is the time.
HOR. So have I heard and do in part believe it.
But, look, the morn, in russet mantle clad,
Walks o'er the dew of yon high eastward hill:
Break we our watch up; and by my advice,
Let us impart what we have seen to-night
Unto young Hamlet; for, upon my life,
This spirit, dumb to us, will speak to him.
Do you consent we shall acquaint him with it,
As needful in our loves, fitting our duty?[26]
MAR. Let's do 't, I pray; and I this morning know
Where we shall find him most conveniently.
(Exeunt.)

SCENE 2.

A room of state in the castle.
Enter the KING, QUEEN, HAMLET, POLONIUS, LAERTES, VOLTIMAND, CORNELIUS, LORDS *and* ATTENDANTS.

KING. Though yet of Hamlet[1] our dear brother's death
The memory be green, and that it us befitted
To bear our hearts in grief and our whole kingdom
To be contracted in one brow of woe,
Yet so far hath discretion fought with nature
That we with wisest sorrow think on him,
Together with remembrance of ourselves.
Therefore our sometime[2] sister, now our queen,
The imperial jointress[3] to this warlike state,
Have we, as 'twere with a defeated joy,—
With an auspicious and a dropping eye,[4]
With mirth in funeral and with dirge in marriage,
In equal scale weighing delight and dole,—
Taken to wife: nor have we herein barr'd
Your better wisdoms, which have freely gone
With this affair along. For all, our thanks.
Now follows, that you know, young Fortinbras,
Holding a weak supposal of our worth,
Or thinking by our late dear brother's death
Our state to be disjoint and out of frame,
Colleagued with the dream of his advantage,[5]
He hath not fail'd to pester us with message,
Importing[6] the surrender of those lands
Lost by his father, with all bonds of law,
To our most valiant brother. So much for him.
Now for ourself and for this time of meeting:
Thus much the business is: we have here writ
To Norway, uncle of young Fortinbras,—
Who, impotent and bed-rid, scarcely hears
Of this his nephew's purpose,—to suppress
His further gait[7] herein; in that the levies,
The lists and full proportions, are all made
Out of his subject[8]: and we here dispatch
You, good Cornelius, and you, Voltimand,
For bearers of this greeting to old Norway;
Giving to you no further personal power

SCENE 1 22. ***extravagant and erring,*** wandering. Both words mean the same thing.
23. ***made probation,*** proved.
24. ***'gainst,*** just before.
25. ***planets strike.*** It was believed that planets could exert an evil influence on men.
26. ***As needful . . . duty,*** as befitting the behavior of friends.

SCENE 2 1. ***Hamlet,*** the elder Hamlet, brother of the present king, the father of young Hamlet, Prince of Denmark.
2. ***sometime,*** former.
3. ***jointress,*** dowager, wife who holds an estate settled on her to be enjoyed after her husband's death.
4. ***With . . . dropping eye,*** joyfully yet tearfully.
5. ***Colleagued . . . advantage,*** allied with his visionary hope of success.
6. ***Importing,*** pertaining to.
7. ***gait,*** proceeding.
8. ***subject,*** people of Norway.

To business with the king, more than the scope
Of these delated[9] articles allow.
Farewell, and let your haste commend your duty.

COR.
VOL. In that and all things will we show our duty.

KING. We doubt it nothing: heartily farewell.
(Exeunt VOLTIMAND *and* CORNELIUS.*)*
And now, Laertes, what 's the news with you?
You told us of some suit; what is 't, Laertes?
You cannot speak of reason to the Dane,
And lose your voice[10]: what wouldst thou beg, Laertes,
That shall not be my offer, not thy asking?
The head is not more native to the heart,
The hand more instrumental to the mouth,
Than is the throne of Denmark to thy father.
What wouldst thou have, Laertes?

LAER. My dread lord,
Your leave and favor to return to France;
From whence though willingly I came to Denmark,
To show my duty in your coronation,
Yet now, I must confess, that duty done,
My thoughts and wishes bend again toward France
And bow them to your gracious leave and pardon.

KING. Have you your father's leave? What says Polonius?

POL. He hath, my lord, wrung from me my slow leave
By laborsome petition, and at last
Upon his will I seal'd my hard consent:
I do beseech you, give him leave to go.

KING. Take thy fair hour,[11] Laertes; time be thine,
And thy best graces spend it at thy will!
But now, my cousin Hamlet, and my son,—

HAM. *(Aside)* A little more than kin, and less than kind.[12]

KING. How is it that the clouds still hang on you?[13]

HAM. Not so, my lord; I am too much i' the sun.[14]

QUEEN. Good Hamlet, cast thy nighted color off,
And let thine eye look like a friend on Denmark.
Do not for ever with thy vailed lids
Seek for thy noble father in the dust:
Thou know'st 'tis common; all that lives must die,
Passing through nature to eternity.

HAM. Ay, madam, it is common.

QUEEN. If it be,
Why seems it so particular with thee?

HAM. Seems, madam! nay, it is; I know not "seems."
'Tis not alone my inky cloak, good mother,
Nor customary suits of solemn black,
Nor windy suspiration of forced breath,
No, nor the fruitful river in the eye,
Nor the dejected 'havior of the visage,
Together with all forms, moods, shapes of grief,
That can denote me truly: these indeed seem,
For they are actions that a man might play:
But I have that within which passeth show;
These but the trappings and the suits of woe.

KING. 'Tis sweet and commendable in your nature, Hamlet,
To give these mourning duties to your father:
But, you must know, your father lost a father;
That father lost, lost his, and the survivor bound
In filial obligation for some term
To do obsequious[15] sorrow: but to persever
In obstinate condolement[16] is a course
Of impious stubbornness; 'tis unmanly grief;
It shows a will most incorrect to heaven,

---

9. ***delated,*** expressly stated.
10. ***speak of . . . voice,*** speak reasonably to the King of Denmark and not be heeded.
11. ***Take thy fair hour,*** make the most of your youth.
12. ***A little more . . . kind.*** Hamlet and the King are a little more than kin in that to the previous uncle/nephew relationship has been added the stepfather/stepson relationship. A marriage between a widow and her brother-in-law was at that time regarded as incestuous; hence Hamlet's "less than kind," "kind" at that time meaning "natural" or "according to nature."
13. ***How is it . . . you?*** Claudius refers to Hamlet's mourning. Hamlet is still wearing black, while the other members of the court have resumed their normal garb.
14. ***I am . . . sun.*** Hamlet is punning on sun-son, a monarch often being referred to as the sun; Hamlet is also "son" (stepson) to Claudius.
15. ***obsequious,*** dutiful.
16. ***obstinate condolement,*** Hamlet's stubborn persistence in observing the rites of mourning, referring especially to his black garb.

A heart unfortified, a mind impatient,
An understanding simple and unschool'd:
For what we know must be and is as common
As any the most vulgar thing to sense,[17]
Why should we in our peevish opposition
Take it to heart? Fie! 'tis a fault to heaven,
A fault against the dead, a fault to nature,
To reason most absurd; whose common theme
Is death of fathers, and who still hath cried,
From the first corse till he that died to-day,
"This must be so." We pray you, throw to earth
This unprevailing woe, and think of us
As of a father: for let the world take note,
You are the most immediate to our throne;
And with no less nobility of love
Than that which dearest father bears his son,
Do I impart toward you. For your intent
In going back to school in Wittenberg,[18]
It is most retrograde[19] to our desire:
And we beseech you, bend you to remain
Here, in the cheer and comfort of our eye,
Our chiefest courtier, cousin, and our son.

QUEEN. Let not thy mother lose her prayers, Hamlet:
I pray thee, stay with us; go not to Wittenberg.

HAM. I shall in all my best obey you, madam.[20]

KING. Why, 'tis a loving and a fair reply:
Be as ourself[21] in Denmark. Madam, come;
This gentle and unforced accord of Hamlet
Sits smiling to my heart: in grace whereof,[22]
No jocund health that Denmark drinks to-day,
But the great cannon to the clouds shall tell,
And the king's rouse[23] the heaven shall bruit[24] again,
Re-speaking earthly thunder. Come away.
(Exeunt all but HAMLET*.)*

HAM. O, that this too too solid flesh would melt,
Thaw and resolve itself into a dew!
Or that the Everlasting had not fix'd
His canon 'gainst self-slaughter! O God! God!
How weary, stale, flat and unprofitable,
Seem to me all the uses of this world!
Fie on 't! ah fie! 'tis an unweeded garden,
That grows to seed; things rank and gross in nature
Possess it merely. That it should come to this!
But two months dead: nay, not so much, not two:
So excellent a king; that was, to this,
Hyperion[25] to a satyr[26]; so loving to my mother
That he might not beteem[27] the winds of heaven
Visit her face too roughly. Heaven and earth!
Must I remember? why, she would hang on him,
As if increase of appetite had grown
By what it fed on: and yet, within a month—
Let me not think on 't—Frailty, thy name is woman!—
A little month, or ere those shoes were old
With which she follow'd my poor father's body,
Like Niobe,[28] all tears:—why she, even she—
O God! a beast, that wants discourse of reason,
Would have mourn'd longer—married with my uncle,
My father's brother, but no more like my father
Than I to Hercules[29]: within a month:
Ere yet the salt of most unrighteous tears
Had left the flushing in her galled eyes,
She married. O, most wicked speed, to post
With such dexterity to incestuous[30] sheets!

---

17. ***the most . . . sense,*** the most familiar thing in our experience.
18. ***Wittenberg,*** famous German university founded in 1502.
19. ***retrograde,*** contrary.
20. ***I shall . . . madam.*** Hamlet is indirectly telling Claudius that he will ignore Claudius' wishes but honor Gertrude's.
21. ***Be as ourself,*** behave with the freedom of the king himself.
22. ***in grace whereof,*** in honor of which.
23. ***rouse,*** toast.
24. ***bruit,*** echo, report.
25. ***Hyperion*** (hī pēr′i ən), the sun god.
26. ***satyr,*** a creature half man, half goat, ugly and lecherous.
27. ***might not beteem,*** could not permit.
28. ***Niobe*** (nī′ō bē), in Greek mythology a mother whose fourteen beautiful children were slain because she boasted about them. She was changed by Zeus into a stone that appeared to weep continually.
29. ***Hercules,*** in Greek and Roman mythology, a hero famous for his great strength.
30. ***incestuous.*** Marriage with a deceased husband's brother was forbidden by the medieval Church.

It is not nor it cannot come to good:
But break, my heart; for I must hold my tongue.

Enter HORATIO, MARCELLUS, *and* BERNARDO

HOR. Hail to your lordship!
HAM. I am glad to see you well:
Horatio,—or I do forget myself.
HOR. The same, my lord, and your poor servant ever.
HAM. Sir, my good friend; I'll change that name with you[31]:
And what make you from Wittenberg,[32] Horatio? Marcellus?
MAR. My good lord—
HAM. I am very glad to see you. Good even, sir.
But what, in faith, make you from Wittenberg?
HOR. A truant disposition, good my lord.
HAM. I would not hear your enemy say so,
Nor shall you do mine ear that violence,
To make it truster of your own report
Against yourself: I know you are no truant.
But what is your affair in Elsinore?
We'll teach you to drink deep ere you depart.
HOR. My lord, I came to see your father's funeral.
HAM. I pray thee, do not mock me, fellow-student;
I think it was to see my mother's wedding.
HOR. Indeed, my lord, it follow'd hard upon.
HAM. Thrift, thrift, Horatio! the funeral baked meats
Did coldly furnish forth the marriage tables.
Would I had met my dearest foe in heaven
Or ever I had seen that day, Horatio!
My father!—methinks I see my father.
HOR. Where, my lord?
HAM. In my mind's eye, Horatio.
HOR. I saw him once; he was a goodly king.
HAM. He was a man, take him for all in all,
I shall not look upon his like again.
HOR. My lord, I think I saw him yesternight
HAM. Saw? who?
HOR. My lord, the king your father.
HAM. The king my father!
HOR. Season your admiration[33] for a while
With an attent ear, till I may deliver,
Upon the witness of these gentlemen,
This marvel to you.
HAM. For God's love, let me hear.
HOR. Two nights together had these gentlemen,
Marcellus and Bernardo, on their watch,
In the dead vast and middle of the night,
Been thus encounter'd. A figure like your father,
Armed at point exactly cap-a-pe,[34]
Appears before them, and with solemn march
Goes slow and stately by them: thrice he walk'd
By their oppress'd and fear-surprised eyes,
Within his truncheon's length; whilst they, distill'd
Almost to jelly with the act of fear,
Stand dumb and speak not to him. This to me
In dreadful secrecy impart they did;
And I with them the third night kept the watch:
Where, as they had deliver'd, both in time,
Form of the thing, each word made true and good,
The apparition comes: I knew your father;
These hands are not more like.
HAM. But where was this?
MAR. My lord, upon the platform where we watch'd.
HAM. Did you not speak to it?
HOR. My lord, I did;
But answer made it none: yet once methought
It lifted up it head and did address
Itself to motion, like as it would speak;
But even then the morning cock crew loud,
And at the sound it shrunk in haste away,
And vanish'd from our sight.
HAM. 'Tis very strange.
HOR. As I do live, my honor'd lord, 'tis true;
And we did think it writ down in our duty
To let you know of it.
HAM. Indeed, indeed, sirs, but this troubles me.
Hold you the watch to'night?
MAR.
BER. } We do, my lord.

---

31. ***I'll change . . . you,*** I'll exchange the name of friend with you.
32. ***what . . . Wittenberg,*** what are you doing away from Wittenberg.
33. ***Season your admiration,*** restrain your astonishment.
34. ***cap-a-pe*** (kap′a pe′), head to foot.

HAM. Arm'd, say you?
MAR.
BER. } Arm'd, my lord.
HAM. From top to toe?
MAR.
BER. } My lord, from head to foot.
HAM. Then saw you not his face?
HOR. O yes, my lord; he wore his beaver[35] up.
HAM. What, look'd he frowningly?
HOR. A countenance more in sorrow than in anger.
HAM. Pale or red?
HOR. Nay, very pale.
HAM. And fix'd his eyes upon you?
HOR. Most constantly.
HAM. I would I had been there.
HOR. It would have much amazed you.
HAM. Very like, very like. Stay'd it long?
HOR. While one with moderate haste might tell a hundred.
MAR.
BER. } Longer, longer.
HOR. Not when I saw 't.
HAM. His beard was grizzled,—no?
HOR. It was, as I have seen it in his life,
A sable silver'd.
HAM. I will watch to-night;
Perchance 'twill walk again.
HOR. I warrant it will.
HAM. If it assume my noble father's person,
I'll speak to it, though hell itself should gape
And bid me hold my peace. I pray you all,
If you have hitherto conceal'd this sight,
Let it be tenable[36] in your silence still;
And whatsoever else shall hap to-night,
Give it an understanding, but no tongue:
I will requite your loves. So, fare you well:
Upon the platform, 'twixt eleven and twelve,
I'll visit you.
ALL. Our duty to your honor.
HAM. Your loves, as mine to you: farewell.
(Exeunt all but HAMLET.*)*
My father's spirit in arms! all is not well;
I doubt some foul play: would the night were come!
Till then sit still, my soul: foul deeds will rise,
Though all the earth o'erwhelm them, to men's eyes.
(Exit.)

SCENE 3.

A room in Polonius' house.
Enter LAERTES *and* OPHELIA.

LAER. My necessaries are embark'd: farewell:
And, sister, as the winds give benefit
And convoy is assistant,[1] do not sleep,
But let me hear from you.
OPH. Do you doubt that?
LAER. For Hamlet and the trifling of his favor,
Hold it a fashion[2] and a toy in blood,[3]
A violet in the youth of primy nature,
Forward,[4] not permanent, sweet, not lasting,
The perfume and suppliance of a minute[5];
No more.
OPH. No more but so?
LAER. Think it no more:
For nature, crescent,[6] does not grow alone
In thews and bulk, but, as this temple[7] waxes,
The inward service of the mind and soul
Grows wide withal. Perhaps he loves you now,
And now no soil nor cautel[8] doth besmirch
The virtue of his will: but you must fear,
His greatness weigh'd,[9] his will is not his own;
For he himself is subject to his birth:
He may not, as unvalued persons do,
Carve for himself[10]; for on his choice depends
The sanity and health of this whole state;
And therefore must his choice be circumscribed
Unto the voice and yielding of that body
Whereof he is the head. Then if he says he loves you,
It fits your wisdom so far to believe it
As he in his particular act and place

---

35. ***beaver,*** visor on the helmet.
36. ***tenable,*** held, contained.

SCENE 3 1. ***as the winds . . . assistant,*** when the winds are favorable and convoy is available.
2. ***fashion,*** custom, fad.
3. ***toy in blood,*** a passing fancy rather than true love.
4. ***Forward,*** early, precocious.
5. ***suppliance of a minute,*** pastime.
6. ***crescent,*** growing, waxing.
7. ***temple,*** body.
8. ***no soil nor cautel,*** no blemish or crafty device.
9. ***His greatness weigh'd,*** considering his noble birth.
10. ***Carve for himself,*** follow his own inclination.

May give his saying deed; which is no further
Than the main voice of Denmark goes withal.
Then weigh what loss your honor may sustain,
If with too credent ear you list his songs,
Fear it, Ophelia, fear it, my dear sister,
And keep you in the rear of your affection,[11]
Out of the shot and danger of desire.
The chariest maid is prodigal enough,
If she unmask her beauty to the moon:
Be wary then; best safety lies in fear:
Youth to itself rebels, though none else near.[12]

OPH. I shall the effect of this good lesson keep,
As watchman to my heart. But, good my brother,
Do not, as some ungracious pastors do,
Show me the steep and thorny way to heaven;
Whiles, like a puff'd and reckless libertine,
Himself the primrose path of dalliance treads,
And recks not his own rede.[13]

LAER. O, fear me not.
I stay too long: but here my father comes.

Enter POLONIUS.

A double blessing is a double grace;
Occasion smiles upon a second leave.

POL. Yet here, Laertes! aboard, aboard, for shame!
The wind sits in the shoulder of your sail,
And you are stay'd for. There; my blessing with thee!
And these few precepts in thy memory
Look thou character.[14] Give thy thoughts no tongue,
Nor any unproportion'd thought his act.[15]
Be thou familiar, but by no means vulgar.
Those friends thou hast, and their adoption tried,
Grapple them to thy soul with hoops of steel;
But do not dull thy palm with entertainment
Of each new-hatch'd, unfledged comrade. Beware
Of entrance to a quarrel, but being in,
Bear 't that the opposed may beware of thee.
Give every man thy ear, but few thy voice;
Take each man's censure,[16] but reserve thy judgment.
Costly thy habit as thy purse can buy,
But not express'd in fancy; rich, not gaudy;
For the apparel oft proclaims the man,
And they in France of the best rank and station
Are of a most select and generous chief in that.
Neither a borrower nor a lender be;
For loan oft loses both itself and friend,
And borrowing dulls the edge of husbandry.
This above all: to thine own self be true,
And it must follow, as the night the day,
Thou canst not then be false to any man.
Farewell: my blessing season this in thee!

LAER. Most humbly do I take my leave, my lord.

POL. The time invites you; go; your servants tend.

LAER. Farewell, Ophelia; and remember well
What I have said to you.

OPH. 'Tis in my memory lock'd,
And you yourself shall keep the key of it.

LAER. Farewell. *(Exit.)*

POL. What is 't, Ophelia, he hath said to you?

OPH. So please you, something touching the Lord Hamlet.

POL. Marry, well bethought:
'Tis told me, he hath very oft of late
Given private time to you; and you yourself
Have of your audience been most free and bounteous:
If it be so, as so 't is put on me,
And that in way of caution, I must tell you,
You do not understand yourself so clearly
As it behooves my daughter and your honor.
What is between you? give me up the truth.

OPH. He hath, my lord, of late made many tenders[17]
Of his affection to me.

POL. Affection! pooh! you speak like a green girl,

---

11. ***keep you in the rear of your affection,*** don't let your emotions lead you astray.
12. ***Youth to itself . . . near,*** youth tends to do what it shouldn't at the slightest temptation.
13. ***recks . . . rede,*** heeds not his own counsel.
14. ***precepts . . . character,*** be certain you inscribe these precepts in your memory.
15. ***Nor . . . act,*** nor act upon any unrestrained thought.
16. ***censure,*** opinion.
17. ***tenders,*** offers. Note how Shakespeare plays on the word *tenders* in the following lines.

Unsifted[18] in such perilous circumstance.
Do you believe his tenders, as you call them?
OPH. I do not know, my lord, what I should think.
POL. Marry, I'll teach you: think yourself a baby;
That you have ta'en these tenders[19] for true pay,
Which are not sterling. Tender yourself more dearly;
Or—not to crack the wind of the poor phrase,
Running it thus—you'll tender me a fool.[20]
OPH. My lord, he hath importuned me with love
In honorable fashion.
POL. Ay, fashion you may call it; go to, go to.
OPH. And hath given countenance to his speech, my lord,
With almost all the holy vows of heaven.
POL. Ay, springes to catch woodcocks.[21] I do know,
When the blood burns, how prodigal the soul
Lends the tongue vows: these blazes, daughter,
Giving more light than heat, extinct in both,
Even in their promise, as it is a-making,
You must not take for fire. From this time
Be somewhat scanter of your maiden presence;
Set your entreatments[22] at a higher rate
Than a command to parley.[23] For Lord Hamlet,
Believe so much in him, that he is young,
And with a larger tether may he walk
Than may be given you: in few, Ophelia,
Do not believe his vows; for they are brokers,[24]
Not of that dye[25] which their investments[26] show,
But mere implorators[27] of unholy suits,
Breathing like sanctified and pious bawds,
The better to beguile. This is for all[28]:
I would not, in plain terms, from this time forth,
Have you so slander any moment leisure,
As to give words or talk with the Lord Hamlet.
Look to 't, I charge you: come your ways.
OPH. I shall obey, my lord. *(Exeunt.)*

SCENE 4.

The platform.
Enter HAMLET, HORATIO, *and* MARCELLUS.

HAM. The air bites shrewdly; it is very cold.
HOR. It is a nipping and an eager air.
HAM. What hour now?
HOR. I think it lacks of twelve.
MAR. No, it is struck.
HOR. Indeed? I heard it not: then it draws near the season
Wherein the spirit held his wont to walk.
(A flourish of trumpets, and ordnance shot off, within.)
What does this mean, my lord?
HAM. The king doth wake[1] to-night and takes his rouse,
Keeps wassail, and the swaggering up-spring[2] reels;
And, as he drains his draughts of Rhenish down,
The kettle-drum and trumpet thus bray out
The triumph of his pledge.[3]
HOR. Is it a custom?
HAM. Ay, marry, is 't:
But to my mind, though I am native here
And to the manner born, it is a custom
More honor'd in the breach than the observance.
This heavy-headed revel east and west
Makes us traduced and tax'd[4] of other nations:
They clepe[5] us drunkards, and with swinish phrase[6]

---

18. ***Unsifted,*** untried.
19. ***tenders,*** promises to pay.
20. ***tender me a fool,*** offer me a fool for a daughter.
21. ***springes . . . woodcocks.*** Since woodcocks are supposedly stupid birds who are easily trapped, Polonius is suggesting Ophelia is stupid in believing Hamlet's vows.
22. ***entreatments,*** negotiations to surrender.
23. ***command to parley,*** mere invitation to talk.
24. ***brokers,*** go-betweens, procurers.
25. ***dye,*** color or sort.
26. ***investments,*** clothing.
27. ***implorators,*** solicitors.
28. ***This is for all,*** these are your orders.

SCENE 4 1. ***doth wake,*** stays awake, celebrates.
2. ***up-spring,*** a German dance, particularly associated with drunken parties.
3. ***pledge,*** a pledge of health and then a draining of the drinking cup in one swallow.
4. ***traduced and tax'd,*** slandered and censured.
5. ***clepe,*** call.
6. ***with swinish phrase,*** by speaking of us as swine.

Soil our addition[7]; and indeed it takes
From our achievements, though perform'd at height,
The pith and marrow of our attribute.[8]
So, oft it chances in particular men,
That for some vicious mole of nature[9] in them,
As, in their birth—wherein they are not guilty,
Since nature cannot choose his origin—
By the o'ergrowth of some complexion,[10]
Oft breaking down the pales and forts of reason,
Or by some habit that too much o'er-leavens
The form of plausive[11] manners, that these men,
Carrying, I say, the stamp of one defect,
Being nature's livery,[12] or fortune's star,[13]—
Their virtues else—be they as pure as grace,
As infinite as man may undergo—
Shall in the general censure take corruption
From that particular fault: the dram of eale[14]
Doth all the noble substance of a doubt[15]
To his own scandal.

HOR. Look, my lord, it comes!

Enter GHOST.

HAM. Angels and ministers of grace defend us!
Be thou a spirit of health or goblin damn'd,
Bring with thee airs from heaven or blasts from hell,
Be thy intents wicked or charitable,
Thou comest in such a questionable shape
That I will speak to thee: I'll call thee Hamlet,
King, father, royal Dane: O, answer me!
Let me not burst in ignorance; but tell
Why thy canonized bones, hearsed in death,
Have burst their cerements; why the sepulchre,
Wherein we saw thee quietly interr'd,
Hath oped his ponderous and marble jaws,
To cast thee up again. What may this mean,
That thou, dead corse, again in complete steel
Revisit'st thus the glimpses of the moon,[16]
Making night hideous; and we fools of nature
So horridly to shake our disposition
With thoughts beyond the reaches of our souls?
Say, why is this? wherefore? what should we do?

(GHOST *beckons* HAMLET.)

HOR. It beckons you to go away with it,
As if it some impartment[17] did desire
To you alone.

MAR. Look, with what courteous action
It waves you to a more removed ground:
But do not go with it.

HOR. No, by no means.

HAM. It will not speak; then I will follow it.

HOR. Do not, my lord.

HAM. Why, what should be the fear?
I do not set my life at a pin's fee;
And for my soul, what can it do to that,
Being a thing immortal as itself?
It waves me forth again: I'll follow it.

HOR. What if it tempt you toward the flood, my lord,
Or to the dreadful summit of the cliff
That beetles o'er his base into the sea,
And there assume some other horrible form,
Which might deprive your sovereignty of reason[18]
And draw you into madness? think of it:
The very place puts toys of desperation,[19]
Without more motive, into every brain
That looks so many fathoms to the sea
And hears it roar beneath.

HAM. It waves me still.
Go on; I'll follow thee.

MAR. You shall not go, my lord.

HAM. Hold off your hands.

HOR. Be ruled; you shall not go.

HAM. My fate cries out,
And makes each petty artery in this body
As hardy as the Nemean lion's[20] nerve.
Still am I call'd. Unhand me, gentlemen.

---

7. ***addition,*** title.
8. ***attribute,*** reputation.
9. ***mole of nature,*** natural blemish in one's constitution.
10. ***complexion,*** temperament, trait.
11. ***plausive,*** pleasing.
12. ***nature's livery,*** nature's endowment.
13. ***fortune's star,*** the position in which one is placed by fortune.
14. ***dram of eale,*** small measure of evil.
15. ***of a doubt.*** There have been several readings of this phrase. The meaning is probably in the sense of "erase" or "counteract."
16. ***the glimpses of the moon,*** the earth by night.
17. ***impartment,*** communication.
18. ***deprive . . . reason,*** take away the supremacy of your reason.
19. ***toys of desperation,*** notions of suicide.
20. ***Nemean*** (ni mē′ən) ***lion's.*** According to Greek and Roman mythology, Hercules, a hero famous for his strength, had to slay the Nemean lion as one of his twelve tasks.

By heaven, I'll make a ghost of him that lets me!
I say, away! Go on: I'll follow thee.
(Exeunt GHOST *and* HAMLET.*)*

HOR. He waxes desperate with imagination.

MAR. Let's follow; 'tis not fit thus to obey him.

HOR. Have after. To what issue will this come?

MAR. Something is rotten in the state of Denmark.[21]

HOR. Heaven will direct it.

MAR. Nay, let's follow him.
(Exeunt.)

SCENE 5.

Another part of the platform.
Enter GHOST *and* HAMLET.

HAM. Whither wilt thou lead me? speak; I'll go no further.

GHOST. Mark me.

HAM. I will.

GHOST. My hour is almost come,
When I to sulphurous and tormenting flames
Must render up myself.

HAM. Alas, poor ghost!

GHOST. Pity me not, but lend thy serious hearing
To what I shall unfold.

HAM. Speak; I am bound to hear.

GHOST. So art thou to revenge, when thou shalt hear.

HAM. What?

GHOST. I am thy father's spirit,
Doom'd for a certain term to walk the night,
And for the day confined to fast in fires,
Till the foul crimes done in my days of nature
Are burnt and purged away. But that I am forbid
To tell the secrets of my prison-house,
I could a tale unfold whose lightest word
Would harrow up thy soul, freeze thy young blood,
Make thy two eyes, like stars, start from their spheres,
Thy knotted and combined locks to part
And each particular hair to stand an end,
Like quills upon the fretful porpentine[1]:
But this eternal blazon[2] must not be
To ears of flesh and blood. List, list, O, list!
If thou didst ever thy dear father love—

HAM. O God!

GHOST. Revenge his foul and most unnatural murder.[3]

HAM. Murder!

GHOST. Murder most foul, as in the best it is;
But this most foul, strange and unnatural.

HAM. Haste me to know 't, that I, with wings as swift
As meditation or the thought of love,
May sweep to my revenge.

GHOST. I find thee apt;
And duller shouldst thou be than the fat weed
That roots itself in ease on Lethe wharf,[4]
Wouldst thou not stir in this. Now, Hamlet, hear:
'Tis given out that, sleeping in my orchard,
A serpent stung me; so the whole ear of Denmark
Is by a forged process of my death
Rankly abused: but know, thou noble youth,
The serpent that did sting thy father's life
Now wears his crown.

HAM. O my prophetic soul![5]
My uncle!

GHOST. Ay, that incestuous, that adulterate[6] beast,
With witchcraft of his wit, with traitorous gifts,—
O wicked wit and gifts, that have the power
So to seduce!—won to his shameful lust
The will of my most seeming-virtuous queen:
O Hamlet, what a falling-off was there!

---

21. ***Something . . . Denmark.*** One of the most quoted lines in the play. It is part of an overall theme of corruption and rottenness, the imagery of which is prevalent throughout the play.

SCENE 5 1. ***porpentine,*** porcupine.
2. ***eternal blazon,*** revelation of the hereafter.
3. ***unnatural murder,*** murder of a brother, fratricide.
4. ***fat weed . . . Lethe*** (lē′thi) ***wharf,*** a plant growing along the wharves of Lethe, the river of forgetfulness in Hades.
5. ***O . . . soul!*** Hamlet has apparently had earlier suspicions about his father's death.
6. ***adulterate,*** adulterous.

From me, whose love was of that dignity
That it went hand in hand even with the vow
I made to her in marriage, and to decline
Upon a wretch whose natural gifts were poor
To those of mine!
But, soft! methinks I scent the morning air;
Brief let me be. Sleeping within my orchard,
My custom always of the afternoon,
Upon my secure hour thy uncle stole,
With juice of cursed hebenon[7] in a vial,
And in the porches of my ears did pour
The leperous distillment; whose effect
Holds such an enmity with blood of man
That swift as quicksilver it courses through
The natural gates and alleys of the body,
And with a sudden vigor it doth posset[8]
And curd, like eager droppings into milk,
The thin and wholesome blood: so did it mine:
And a most instant tetter bark'd about,
Most lazar-like,[9] with vile and loathsome crust,
All my smooth body.
Thus was I, sleeping, by a brother's hand
Of life, of crown, of queen, at once dispatch'd[10]:
Cut off even in the blossoms of my sin,
Unhousel'd, disappointed, unaneled,[11]
No reckoning made, but sent to my account
With all my imperfections on my head:
O, horrible! O, horrible! most horrible!
If thou hast nature in thee, bear it not;
Let not the royal bed of Denmark be
A couch for luxury and damned incest.
But, howsoever thou pursuest this act,
Taint not thy mind, nor let thy soul contrive
Against thy mother aught: leave her to heaven
And to those thorns that in her bosom lodge,
To prick and sting her. Fare thee well at once!
The glow-worm shows the matin to be near,
And 'gins to pale his uneffectual fire:
Adieu, adieu! Hamlet, remember me.
(Exit.)

HAM. O all you host of heaven! O earth! what else?
And shall I couple hell? O, fie! Hold, hold, my heart;
And you, my sinews, grow not instant old,
But bear me stiffly up. Remember thee!
Ay, thou poor ghost, while memory holds a seat
In this distracted globe.[12] Remember thee!
Yea, from the table of my memory
I'll wipe away all trivial fond[13] records,
All saws of books, all forms, all pressures[14] past,
That youth and observation copied there;
And thy commandment all alone shall live
Within the book and volume of my brain,
Unmix'd with baser matter: yes, by heaven!
O most pernicious woman!
O villain, villain, smiling, damned villain!
My tables,[15]—meet it is I set it down,
That one may smile; and smile, and be a villain;
At least I'm sure it may be so in Denmark:
(Writing.)
So, uncle, there you are. Now to my word;
It is "Adieu, adieu! remember me."
I have sworn 't.

MAR., **HOR.** *(Within)* My lord, my lord,—

MAR. *(Within)* Lord Hamlet,—

HOR. *(Within)* Heaven secure him!

HAM. So be it!

MAR. *(Within)* Hillo, ho, ho,[16] my lord!

HAM. Hillo, ho, ho, boy! come, bird, come.

Enter HORATIO *and* MARCELLUS.

MAR. How is 't, my noble lord?

HOR. What news, my lord?

HAM. O, wonderful!

HOR. Good my lord, tell it.

HAM. No; you'll reveal it.

HOR. Not I, my lord, by heaven.

MAR. Nor I, my lord.

HAM. How say you, then; would heart of man once think it?
But you'll be secret?

---

7. ***hebenon,*** probably *henbane,* a poisonous plant, coarse and bad-smelling.
8. ***posset,*** coagulate, curdle.
9. ***tetter bark'd about . . . lazar-like,*** the skin became covered with a barklike substance similar to leprosy.
10. ***dispatch'd,*** deprived of.
11. ***Unhousel'd . . . unaneled,*** without having received Communion, unprepared to death, without having received extreme unction.
12. ***distracted globe,*** confused head.
13. ***fond,*** foolish.
14. ***saws . . . pressures,*** maxims, images, impressions.
15. ***tables,*** writing tablet.
16. ***Hillo, ho, ho,*** a falconer's call to a hawk in air.

HOR.
MAR. Ay, by heaven, my lord.
HAM. There's ne'er a villain dwelling in all Denmark
But he's an arrant knave.
HOR. There needs no ghost, my lord, come from the grave
To tell us this.
HAM. Why, right; you are i' the right;
And so, without more circumstance at all,
I hold it fit that we shake hands and part:
You, as your business and desire shall point you;
For every man has business and desire,
Such as it is; and for mine own poor part,
Look you, I'll go pray.
HOR. These are but wild and whirling words, my lord.
HAM. I'm sorry they offend you, heartily;
Yes, 'faith, heartily.
HOR. There's no offence, my lord.
HAM. Yes, by Saint Patrick,[17] but there is, Horatio,
And much offence too. Touching this vision here,
It is an honest ghost, that let me tell you:
For your desire to know what is between us,
O'ermaster 't as you may. And now, good friends,
As you are friends, scholars and soldiers,
Give me one poor request.
HOR. What is 't, my lord? we will.
HAM. Never make known what you have seen to-night.
HOR.
MAR. My lord, we will not.
HAM. Nay, but swear 't.
HOR. In faith,
My lord, not I.
MAR. Nor I, my lord, in faith.
HAM. Upon my sword.[18]
MAR. We have sworn, my lord, already.
HAM. Indeed, upon my sword, indeed.
GHOST. *(Beneath)* Swear.
HAM. Ah, ha, boy! say'st thou so? art thou there, truepenny?[19]
Come on—you hear this fellow in the cellarage—
Consent to swear.
HOR. Propose the oath, my lord.
HAM. Never to speak of this that you have seen,
Swear by my sword.
GHOST. *(Beneath)* Swear.
HAM. *Hic et ubique?*[20] then we'll shift our ground.
Come hither, gentlemen,
And lay your hands again upon my sword:
Swear by my sword,
Never to speak of this that you have heard.
GHOST. *(Beneath)* Swear by his sword.
HAM. Well said, old mole! canst work i' the earth so fast?
A worthy pioner![21] Once more remove, good friends.
HOR. O day and night, but this is wondrous strange!
HAM. And therefore as a stranger give it welcome.
There are more things in heaven and earth, Horatio,
Than are dreamt of in your philosophy.
But come;
Here, as before, never, so help you mercy,
How strange or odd soe'er I bear myself,
As I perchance hereafter shall think meet
To put an antic[22] disposition on,
That you, at such times seeing me, never shall,
With arms encumber'd[23] thus, or this head-shake,
Or by pronouncing of some doubtful phrase,
As "Well, well, we know," or "We could, an if we would,"
Or "If we list to speak," or "There be, an if they might,"
Or such ambiguous giving out, to note
That you know aught of me: this not to do,
So grace and mercy at your most need help you,
Swear.

---

17. ***Saint Patrick.*** St. Patrick was keeper of Purgatory and patron saint of all blunders and confusion.
18. ***Upon my sword.*** Hamlet asks Horatio and Marcellus to swear on his sword, a far more serious oath, because the hilt gives the sword the shape of a cross and the oath thus becomes sacred. Note Marcellus' initial hesitation to do so.
19. ***truepenny,*** good old boy, or the like.
20. ***Hic et ubique,*** (hik et u′bē kwā), here and everywhere. [*Latin*]
21. ***pioner,*** digger, miner.
22. ***antic,*** fantastic.
23. ***encumber'd,*** folded or entwined.

GHOST. *(Beneath)* Swear.
HAM. Rest, rest, perturbed spirit! *(They swear.)* So, gentlemen,
With all my love I do commend me to you:
And what so poor a man as Hamlet is
May do, to express his love and friending to you,
God willing, shall not lack. Let us go in together;
And still your fingers on your lips, I pray.
The time is out of joint: O cursed spite,
That ever I was born to set it right!
Nay, come, let's go together. *(Exeunt.)*

Discussion

Act One, Scene 1

The mood of this scene is dominated by fear—both of natural and supernatural events. Indicate lines which contribute to the development of this mood.

Scene 2

1. Claudius is holding his first court since being crowned King. **(a)** How does he justify his hasty and incestuous marriage to Gertrude? **(b)** What matter of state does he handle? **(c)** What petition does he approve?

2. **(a)** How do Claudius and Gertrude treat Hamlet in this scene? **(b)** How does he react?

3. In a soliloquy, the character in speaking to himself must also speak the truth to the audience as he sees it. **(a)** What does Hamlet's soliloquy "O, that this too too solid flesh would melt" (lines 129–158) tell about his state of mind? **(b)** What events have caused him to feel that way? **(c)** Put yourself in his place. Would you feel as he does? Explain.

Scene 3

1. What do Polonius' endless sermons to his children suggest about his relationships with them?

2. **(a)** What do Polonius and Laertes warn Ophelia about? **(b)** How does she react? Explain.

Scene 4

1. What is the effect of having the sounds of Claudius' carousing reach the watchers on the platform?

2. **(a)** Why does Horatio warn Hamlet not to follow the Ghost? **(b)** What does Hamlet's reaction to the warning indicate about his state of mind?

Scene 5

1. **(a)** Does the Ghost ask Hamlet to take any specific action? Explain. **(b)** To forego any specific action? Explain.

2. When the Ghost exits, Hamlet is left to soliloquize. What does the soliloquy tell us about his reaction to the Ghost?

3. **(a)** Is Hamlet's behavior to Horatio and Marcellus different after he has seen the Ghost? Explain. **(b)** How do you account for Hamlet's behavior to the Ghost when it speaks "beneath" the stage?

4. At the end of the scene (lines 184–185) Hamlet says, "The time is out of joint: O cursed spite, / That ever I was born to set it right!" **(a)** What does this tell about his state of mind? **(b)** How does it relate to his "O, that this too too solid flesh would melt" soliloquy in Scene 2?

Act One In Review

1. Act One contains five scenes, each of which introduces or forwards a major action of the play with regard to Hamlet. Take the scenes in order and discuss the major action in each.

2. By the end of Act One, how would you assess the state of affairs in Denmark **(a)** politically; **(b)** militarily; **(c)** morally?

notes and comments

The First Folio

Published in 1623, seven years after Shakespeare's death, the First Folio collection of his plays is recognized today as a truly monumental achievement. The first attempt to collect in a single volume all the plays that could be directly ascribed to Shakespeare, it was undertaken by his long-time friends and fellow actors, John Heminge and Henry Condell. Members of Shakespeare's acting company for more than twenty years, these two men were qualified by experience and motivated by affection to include only authorized texts. According to their testimony in its subtitle, the First Folio was prepared from "the True Originall Copies" of Shakespeare's plays.

From the perspective of the present day, more than 350 years after the First Folio was published, it is difficult to appreciate the magnitude of that feat—assembling and seeing through the press more than nine hundred oversized double-column pages of text in an age that knew nothing of the aids to publication that we today take for granted: photocopies, typewriters, or even carbon paper. In the early seventeenth century, type had to be set by hand, backwards (from right to left), oftentimes from hard-to-decipher handwritten copy.

Shakespearean scholars estimate that between 1,000 and 1,200 copies of the First Folio were printed. Today approximately 230 copies are known to be in existence, a remarkable rate of survival that in itself testifies to the great respect and care this volume received from those fortunate enough to possess a copy of it. Of the copies still extant, eighty are owned by the Folger Shakespeare Library in Washington, D.C., the world's largest single repository.

The facts underlying the publication of the First Folio are interesting, not only as a tribute to Shakespeare, but in their own right. The First Folio is itself the only source for eighteen of Shakespeare's plays, among them *Macbeth.* Had it not been printed, these masterpieces would probably have been lost forever.

Work on the First Folio began at least as early as the summer of 1621, under the direction of William and Isaac Jaggard, the printers selected by Heminge and Condell, and continued for about two years. A project of such magnitude naturally involved financial uncertainties for the printer, for the size of the volume meant that it would have to sell for an unusually high price. A partial solution was apparently reached by dividing the plays into three categories—comedies, histories, and tragedies, each with its own pagination, in order that, if necessary, each part might be bound and sold separately. Fortunately, this expedient was not necessary.

Mr. WILLIAM
SHAKESPEARES
COMEDIES,
HISTORIES, &
TRAGEDIES.
Published according to the True Originall Copies.
LONDON
Printed by Isaac Iaggard, and Ed. Blount. 1623.

Title page of a copy of the First Folio of Shakespeare. Reproduced by permission of the British Library Board.

The source of the First Folio was, as promised by Heminge and Condell, "the True Originall Copies." Although eighteen of the plays had been published earlier in quarto form (a quarto is a page half the size of those used for the First Folio), none of these was copied exactly in the First Folio.

To understand the text that underlies the Folio, it is necessary to know something about the procedure followed by Elizabethan dramatists. When Shakespeare had completed the final draft of a play (drafts were referred to as "foul papers"), he had it copied by a scribe. This copy (known as the "fair copy," because it was free from authors' corrections) became the promptbook and was annotated by a man known as the "prompter" or the "bookkeeper," to include additional instructions for actually performing the play.

Probably because of the time required to copy an entire play over and over again (remember, there was no carbon paper), each actor received only his own "part," limited to his speeches and any necessary cues.

Most of the plays in the First Folio were printed either from the promptbook copy or from Shakespeare's foul papers. Although eleven of the plays were probably set from earlier quarto versions, changes were made in all of them, probably as a result of consulting the promptbook as well as the quarto.

The high quality of the First Folio is evident when six plays in it are compared with their quarto versions, those usually referred to as the "bad" quartos. In Shakespeare's day acting companies were hesitant about publishing the plays they owned, presumably because they were afraid attendance might drop if the plays were available to other companies in printed form. Copyright procedure then differed from that of today, but there did exist a Stationer's Register, in which a work proposed for printing and publication was supposed to be listed. This procedure made the work the legal property of the person, usually the printer, under whose name it was registered.

Despite all precautions, however, some of Shakespeare's plays fell into the possession of unscrupulous persons and were published in pirated or "bad" quarto editions. No one today knows exactly how this occurred. Some theories are that these are "memorial" versions, surreptitiously reconstructed by actors who memorized their own parts and then tried to memorize those of the other actors as well; that shorthand versions of the plays were taken down as they were acted; or that some "parts" were copied and the balance dubbed.

Shortly after the "bad" quarto of *Hamlet* was published, Shakespeare's acting company did authorize a corrected copy. The "bad" quarto of *Hamlet* is dated 1603; the corrected quarto is dated 1604.

Although many questions remain to be answered about the preparation of the First Folio, there can be no doubt as to its authority. It is probably the second most important volume to be published in the English language, yielding place only to the King James Version of the Bible, published a dozen years earlier.

The difference in quality between the "bad" quartos and the First Folio plays becomes clear if the two versions of the "To be or not to be" soliloquy in *Hamlet* are compared. For the First Folio version, see *Hamlet,* Act Three, Scene 1, lines 56–88. The "bad" quarto version reads as follows:

HAMLET. To be, or not to be, I there's the point,
To Die, to sleepe, is that all? I all:
No, to sleepe, to dreame, I mary there it goes,
For in that dreame of death, when wee awake,
And borne before an everlasting Judge,
From whence no passenger ever retur'nd,
The undiscovered country, at whose sight
The happy smile, and the accursed damn'd.
But for this, the joyful hope of this,
Whol'd beare the scornes and flattery of the world,
Scorned by the right rich, the rich curssed of the poore?
The widow being oppressed, the orphan wrong'd,
The taste of hunger, or a tirants raigne,
And thousand more calamities besides,
To grunte and sweate under this weary life,
When that he may his full *Quietus* make,
With a bare bodkin, who would this indure,
But for a hope of something after death?
Which pusles [puzzles] the braine, and doth confound the sense,
Which makes us rather beare those evilles we have,
Than flie to others that we know not of.
I that, O this conscience makes cowardes of us all.

Act Two

SCENE 1

A room in Polonius' house.
Enter POLONIUS *and* REYNALDO.

POL. Give him this money and these notes, Reynaldo.
REY. I will, my lord.
POL. You shall do marvelous wisely, good Reynaldo,
Before you visit him, to make inquire
Of his behavior.
REY. My lord, I did intend it.
POL. Marry, well said; very well said. Look you, sir,
Inquire me first what Danskers[1] are in Paris;
And how, and who, what means, and where they keep,
What company, at what expense; and finding
By this encompassment and drift of question[2]
That they do know my son, come you more nearer
Than your particular demands[3] will touch it:
Take you, as 'twere, some distant knowledge of him;
As thus, "I know his father and his friends,
And in part him:" do you mark this, Reynaldo?
REY. Ay, very well, my lord.
POL. "And in part him; but" you may say "not well:
But, if 't be he I mean, he's very wild;
Addicted so and so:" and there put on him
What forgeries[4] you please; marry, none so rank
As may dishonor him; take heed of that;
But, sir, such wanton, wild and usual slips
As are companions noted and most known
To youth and liberty.
REY. As gaming, my lord.
POL. Ay, or drinking, fencing, swearing, quarreling,
Drabbing[5]: you may go so far.
REY. My lord, that would dishonor him.
POL. 'Faith, no; as you may season it in the charge.[6]
You must not put another scandal on him,
That he is open to incontinency;
That's not my meaning: but breathe his faults so quaintly
That they may seem the taints of liberty,
The flash and outbreak of a fiery mind,
A savageness in unreclaimed blood,
Of general assault.[7]
REY. But, my good lord,—
POL. Wherefore should you do this?
REY. Ay my lord,
I would know that.
POL. Marry, sir, here's my drift;
And, I believe, it is a fetch of wit[8]:
You laying these slight sullies on my son,
As 'twere a thing a little soil'd i' the working,
Mark you,
Your party in converse, him you would sound,
Having ever seen in the prenominate[9] crimes
The youth you breathe of guilty, be assured
He closes with you in this consequence[10];
"Good sir," or so, or "friend," or "gentleman,"
According to the phrase or the addition
Of man and country.
REY. Very good, my lord.
POL. And then, sir, does he this—he does—what was I about to say? By the mass, I was about to say something: where did I leave?
REY. At "closes in the consequence," at "friend or so," and "gentleman."
POL. At "closes in the consequence," ay, marry;
He closes thus: "I know the gentleman;
I saw him yesterday, or t' other day,
Or then, or then; with such, or such; and, as you say,
There was a' gaming; there o'ertook in 's rouse[11];
There falling out at tennis." See you now;
Your bait of falsehood takes this carp of truth:

1. ***Danskers,*** Danes.
2. ***encompassment and drift of question,*** roundabout, gradual inquiry.
3. ***particular demands,*** direct questions.
4. ***forgeries,*** fabrications.
5. ***Drabbing,*** associating with immoral women.
6. ***season it in the charge,*** soften the charge by the way in which you state it.
7. ***savageness . . . general assault,*** a tendency common to untamed youth.
8. ***fetch of wit,*** clever trick.
9. ***prenominate,*** previously named.
10. ***closes . . . consequence,*** agrees with you as follows.
11. ***o'ertook in's rouse,*** overcome by liquor.

And thus do we of wisdom and of reach,[12]
With windlasses[13] and with assays of bias,[14]
By indirections find directions out:
So by my former lecture and advice,
Shall you my son. You have me, have you not?

REY. My lord, I have.

POL. God be wi' you; fare you well.

REY. Good my lord!

POL. Observe his inclination in yourself.[15]

REY. I shall, my lord

POL. And let him ply his music.

REY. Well, my lord.

POL. Farewell! *(Exit* REYNALDO.*)*

Enter OPHELIA.

How now, Ophelia! what's the matter?

OPH. O, my lord, my lord, I have been so affrighted!

POL. With what, i' the name of God?

OPH. My lord, as I was sewing in my closet,[16]
Lord Hamlet, with his doublet all unbraced;
No hat upon his head; his stockings foul'd,
Ungarter'd, and down-gyved[17] to his ankle;
Pale as his shirt; his knees knocking each other;
And with a look so piteous in purport
As if he had been loosed out of hell
To speak of horrors,—he comes before me.

POL. Mad for thy love?

OPH. My lord, I do not know;
But truly, I do fear it.

POL. What said he?

OPH. He took me by the wrist and held me hard;
Then goes he to the length of all his arm;
And, with his other hand thus o'er his brow,
He falls to such perusal of my face
As he would draw it. Long stay'd he so;
At last, a little shaking of mine arm
And thrice his head thus waving up and down,
He raised a sigh so piteous and profound
As it did seem to shatter all his bulk
And end his being[18]: that done, he lets me go:
And, with his head over his shoulder turn'd,
He seem'd to find his way without his eyes;
For out o' doors he went without their helps,
And, to the last, bended their light on me.

POL. Come, go with me: I will go seek the king.
This is the very ecstasy of love,
Whose violent property fordoes itself[19]
And leads the will to desperate undertakings
As oft as any passion under heaven
That does afflict our natures. I am sorry.
What, have you given him any hard words of late?

OPH. No, my good lord, but, as you did command,
I did repel his letters and denied
His access to me.

POL. That hath made him mad.
I am sorry that with better heed and judgment
I had not quoted[20] him: I fear'd he did but trifle,
And meant to wreck thee; but, beshrew my jealousy![21]
By heaven, it is as proper to our age
To cast beyond ourselves in our opinions
As it is common for the younger sort
To lack discretion. Come, go we to the king:
This must be known; which, being kept close, might move
More grief to hide than hate to utter love.[22]

(Exeunt.)

SCENE 2.

A room in the castle.

Enter KING, QUEEN, ROSENCRANTZ, GUILDENSTERN, *and* ATTENDANTS.

KING. Welcome, dear Rosencrantz and Guildenstern!
Moreover that we much did long to see you,
The need we have to use you did provoke

---

12. ***reach,*** comprehension.
13. ***windlasses,*** here used to mean "circuitous paths."
14. ***assays of bias,*** oblique approaches (a term from bowling).
15. ***in yourself,*** with your own eyes.
16. ***closet,*** private chamber.
17. ***down-gyved,*** fallen.
18. ***At last . . . being.*** What Hamlet sees in Ophelia's face confirms his suspicion that she is acting under her father's influence, therefore, Hamlet is no longer able to trust her.
19. ***Whose violent property fordoes itself,*** whose violent nature destroys itself.
20. ***quoted,*** observed.
21. ***beshrew my jealousy,*** curse my suspicion.
22. ***might move . . . love,*** might cause more grief to others than hatred of me and my family. Polonius is worried that the king and queen will disapprove of Hamlet's loving someone of a lower rank.

Our hasty sending. Something have you heard
Of Hamlet's transformation; so call it,
Sith nor the exterior nor the inward man
Resembles that it was. What it should be,
More than his father's death, that thus hath put him
So much from the understanding of himself,
I cannot dream of: I entreat you both,
That, being of so young days brought up with him,
And sith so neighbor'd to his youth and havior,
That you vouchsafe your rest[1] here in our court
Some little time: so by your companies
To draw him on to pleasures, and to gather,
So much as from occasion you may glean,
Whether aught, to us unknown, afflicts him thus,
That, open'd, lies within our remedy.

QUEEN. Good gentlemen, he hath much talk'd of you;
And sure I am two men there are not living
To whom he more adheres. If it will please you
To show us so much gentry and good will
As to expend your time with us awhile,
For the supply and profit of our hope,
Your visitation shall receive such thanks
As fits a king's remembrance.

ROS. Both your majesties
Might, by the sovereign power you have of us,
Put your dread pleasures more into command
Than to entreaty.

GUIL. But we both obey,
And here give up ourselves, in the full bent
To lay our service freely at your feet,
To be commanded.

KING. Thanks, Rosencrantz and gentle Guildenstern.

QUEEN. Thanks, Guildenstern and gentle Rosencrantz:
And I beseech you instantly to visit
My too much changed son. Go, some of you,
And bring these gentlemen where Hamlet is.

GUIL. Heavens make our presence and our practices
Pleasant and helpful to him!

QUEEN. Ay, amen!

(Exeunt ROSENCRANTZ, GUILDENSTERN, *and some* ATTENDANTS.*)*

Enter POLONIUS.

POL. The ambassadors from Norway, my good lord,
Are joyfully return'd.

KING. Thou still has been the father of good news.

POL. Have I, my lord? I assure my good liege,
I hold my duty, as I hold my soul,
Both to my God and to my gracious king:
And I do think, or else this brain of mine
Hunts not the trail of policy so sure
As it hath used to do, that I have found
The very cause of Hamlet's lunacy.

KING. O, speak of that; that do I long to hear.

POL. Give first admittance to the ambassadors;
My news shall be the fruit[2] to that great feast.

KING. Thyself do grace to them, and bring them in. *(Exit* POLONIUS.*)*
He tells me, my dear Gertrude, he hath found
The head and source of all your son's distemper.

QUEEN. I doubt it is no other but the main;
His father's death, and our o'erhasty marriage.

KING. Well, we shall sift him.

Re-enter POLONIUS, *with* VOLTIMAND *and* CORNELIUS.

Welcome, my good friends!
Say, Voltimand, what from our brother Norway?

VOLT. Most fair return of greetings and desires.
Upon our first,[3] he sent out to suppress
His nephew's levies; which to him appear'd
To be a preparation 'gainst the Polack;
But, better look'd into, he truly found
It was against your highness: whereat grieved,
That so his sickness, age and impotence
Was falsely borne in hand,[4] sends out arrests
On Fortinbras; which he, in brief, obeys;
Receives rebuke from Norway, and in fine

1. ***vouschsafe your rest,*** agree to stay.
2. ***fruit,*** dessert.
3. ***Upon our first,*** at our first audience.
4. ***falsely borne in hand,*** deceived.

Makes vow before his uncle never more
To give the assay of arms against your majesty.
Whereon old Norway, overcome with joy,
Gives him three score thousand crowns in annual fee,
And his commission to employ those soldiers,
So levied as before, against the Polack:
With an entreaty, herein further shown,
(Giving a paper.)
That it might please you to give quiet pass
Through your dominions for this enterprise,
On such regards of safety and allowance
As therein are set down.

KING. It likes[5] us well;
And at our more consider'd time we'll read,
Answer, and think upon this business.
Meantime we thank you for your well-took labor:
Go to your rest; at night we'll feast together:
Most welcome home!

(Exeunt VOLTIMAND *and* CORNELIUS.*)*

POL. This business is well ended.
My liege, and madam, to expostulate
What majesty should be, what duty is,
Why day is day, night night, and time is time,
Were nothing but to waste night, day and time.
Therefore, since brevity is the soul of wit,[6]
And tediousness the limbs and outward flourishes,
I will be brief: your noble son is mad:
Mad call I it; for, to define true madness,
What is 't but to be nothing else but mad?
But let that go.

QUEEN. More matter, with less art.

POL. Madam, I swear I use no art at all.
That he is mad, 'tis true: 'tis true 'tis pity;
And pity 'tis 'tis true: a foolish figure[7];
But farewell it, for I will use no art.
Mad let us grant him, then: and now remains
That we find out the cause of this effect,
Or rather say, the cause of this defect,
For this effect defective comes by cause:
Thus it remains, and the remainder thus.
Perpend.[8]
I have a daughter—have while she is mine—
Who, in her duty and obedience, mark,
Hath given me this: now gather, and surmise. *(Reads.)*
To the celestial and my soul's idol, the most beautified Ophelia—
That's an ill phrase, a vile phrase; *beautified* is a vile phrase: but you shall hear. Thus:
(Reads.)
In her excellent white bosom, these, &c.

QUEEN. Came this from Hamlet to her?

POL. Good madam, stay awhile; I will be faithful. *(Reads.)*
Doubt thou the stars are fire;
Doubt that the sun doth move;
Doubt truth to be a liar;
But never doubt I love.
O dear Ophelia, I am ill at these numbers[9]; I have not art to reckon my groans[10]: but that I love thee best, O most best, believe it. Adieu.
Thine evermore, most dear lady, whilst this machine[11] is to him, HAMLET.
This, in obedience, hath my daughter shown me,
And more above, hath his solicitings,
As they fell out by time, by means and place,
All given to mine ear.

KING. But how hath she
Received his love?

POL. What do you think of me?

KING. As of a man faithful and honorable.

POL. I would fain prove so. But what might you think,
When I had seen this hot love on the wing—
As I perceived it, I must tell you that,
Before my daughter told me—what might you,
Or my dear majesty your queen here, think,
If I had play'd the desk or table-book,[12]
Or given my heart a winking,[13] mute and dumb,
Or look'd upon this love with idle sight;
What might you think? No, I went round to work,
And my young mistress thus I did bespeak:

---

5. ***likes,*** pleases.
6. ***wit,*** wisdom, understanding. Note the irony of *Polonius'* saying this.
7. ***figure,*** figure of speech.
8. ***Perpend,*** consider.
9. ***ill at these numbers,*** unskilled in writing verses.
10. ***reckon my groans,*** sum up my love.
11. ***machine,*** body.
12. ***play'd the desk or table-book,*** remained shut up, concealed the information.
13. ***given my heart a winking,*** given my heart a signal to keep quiet.

"Lord Hamlet is a prince, out of thy star[14];
This must not be:" and then I prescripts gave her,
That she should lock herself from his resort,
Admit no messengers, receive no tokens.
Which done, she took the fruits of my advice;
And he, repelled—a short tale to make—
Fell into a sadness, then into a fast,
Thence to a watch, thence into a weakness,
Thence to a lightness, and, by this declension,[15]
Into the madness wherein now he raves,
And all we mourn for.

KING. Do you think 'tis this?

QUEEN. It may be, very like.

POL. Hath there been such a time—I'd fain know that—
That I have positively said " 'Tis so,"
When it proved otherwise?

KING. Not that I know.

POL. *(Pointing to his head and shoulder)*
Take this from this, if this be otherwise:
If circumstances lead me, I will find
Where truth is hid, though it were hid indeed
Within the center.

KING. How may we try it further?

POL. You know, sometimes he walks four hours together
Here in the lobby.

QUEEN. So he does indeed.

POL. At such a time I'll loose my daughter to him:
Be you and I behind an arras then;
Mark the encounter: if he love her not
And be not from his reason fall'n thereon,
Let me be no assistant for a state,
But keep a farm and carters.

KING. We will try it.

QUEEN. But, look, where sadly the poor wretch comes reading.

POL. Away, I do beseech you, both away:
I'll board[16] him presently.

(Exeunt KING, QUEEN, *and* ATTENDANTS.*)*

Enter HAMLET, *reading.*

O, give me leave:
How does my good Lord Hamlet?

HAM. Well, God-a-mercy.

POL. Do you know me, my lord?

HAM. Excellent well; you are a fishmonger.

POL. Not I, my lord.

HAM. Then I would you were so honest a man.

POL. Honest, my lord!

HAM. Ay, sir; to be honest, as this world goes, is to be one man picked out of ten thousand.

POL. That 's very true, my lord.

HAM. For if the sun breed maggots in a dead dog, being a god kissing carrion,[17]—Have you a daughter?

POL. I have, my lord.

HAM. Let her not walk i' the sun: conception is a blessing: but not as your daughter may conceive. Friend, look to 't.

POL. *(Aside)* How say you by that? Still harping on my daughter: yet he knew me not at first; he said I was a fishmonger: he is far gone: and truly in my youth I suffered much extremity for love; very near this. I'll speak to him again. What do you read, my lord?

HAM. Words, words, words.

POL. What is the matter, my lord?

HAM. Between who?

POL. I mean, the matter that you read, my lord.

HAM. Slanders, sir: for the satirical rogue says here that old men have grey beards, that their faces are wrinkled, their eyes purging thick amber and plum-tree gum and that they have a plentiful lack of wit, together with most weak hams: all which, sir, though I most powerfully and potently believe, yet I hold it not honesty to have it thus set down, for yourself, sir, should be old as I am, if like a crab you could go backward.

POL. *(Aside)* Though this be madness, yet there is method in 't. Will you walk out of the air, my lord?

HAM. Into my grave.

POL. Indeed, that is out o' the air. *(Aside)* How pregnant sometimes his replies are! a happiness that often madness hits on, which reason and sanity could not so prosperously be delivered of. I will leave him, and suddenly contrive the means of meeting between him and my daughter.—My honorable lord, I will most humbly take my leave of you.

HAM. You cannot, sir, take from me any thing

---

14. ***out of thy star,*** above you in rank.
15. ***declension,*** decline.
16. ***board,*** intercept.
17. ***god kissing carrion,*** the sun god shining on a dead body.

that I will more willingly part withal: except my life, except my life, except my life.

POL. Fare you well, my lord.

HAM. These tedious old fools!

Enter ROSENCRANTZ *and* GUILDENSTERN.

POL. You go to seek the Lord Hamlet; there he is.

ROS. *(To Polonius)* God save you, sir!

(Exit POLONIUS.*)*

GUIL. My honored lord!

ROS. My most dear lord!

HAM. My excellent good friends! How dost thou, Guildenstern? Ah, Rosencrantz! Good lads, how do ye both?

ROS. As the indifferent children of the earth.

GUIL. Happy, in that we are not over-happy; On fortune's cap we are not the very button.

HAM. Nor the soles of her shoe?

ROS. Neither, my lord.

HAM. What's the news?

ROS. None, my lord, but that the world's grown honest.

HAM. Then is doomsday near: but your news is not true. Let me question more in particular: what have you, my good friends, deserved at the hands of fortune, that she sends you to prison hither?

GUIL. Prison, my lord!

HAM. Denmark's a prison.[18]

ROS. Then is the world one.

HAM. A goodly one; in which there are many confines, wards and dungeons, Denmark being one o' the worst.

ROS. We think not so, my lord.

HAM. Why, then, 'tis none to you; for there is nothing either good or bad, but thinking makes it so: to me it is a prison.

ROS. Why then, your ambition makes it one; 'tis too narrow for your mind.

HAM. O God, I could be bounded in a nutshell and count myself a king of infinite space, were it not that I have bad dreams.

GUIL. Which dreams indeed are ambition, for the very substance of the ambitious is merely the shadow of a dream.

HAM. A dream itself is but a shadow.

ROS. Truly, and I hold ambition of so airy and light a quality that it is but a shadow's shadow.

HAM. Then are our beggars bodies, and our monarchs and outstretched heroes the beggars' shadows.[19] Shall we to the court? for, by my fay, I cannot reason.

ROS.
GUIL. } We'll wait upon you.

HAM. No such matter: I will not sort you with the rest of my servants, for, to speak to you like an honest man, I am most dreadfully attended. But, in the beaten way of friendship,[20] what make you at Elsinore?

ROS. To visit you, my lord; no other occasion.

HAM. Beggar that I am, I am even poor in thanks; but I thank you: and sure, dear friends, my thanks are too dear a halfpenny. Were you not sent for? Is it your own inclining? Is it a free visitation? Come, deal justly with me: come, come; nay, speak.

GUIL. What should we say, my lord?

HAM. Why, any thing, but to the purpose. You were sent for; and there is a kind of confession in your looks which your modesties have not craft enough to color: I know the good king and queen have sent for you.

ROS. To what end, my lord?

HAM. That you must teach me. But let me conjure you, by the rights of our fellowship, by the consonancy of our youth, by the obligation of our ever-preserved love, and by what more dear a better proposer could charge you withal, be even and direct with me, whether you were sent for, or no?

ROS. *(Aside to Guil.)* What say you?

HAM. *(Aside)* Nay, then, I have an eye of you.—If you love me, hold not off.

GUIL. My lord, we were sent for.

HAM. I will tell you why; so shall my anticipation prevent your discovery, and your secrecy to the king and queen moult no feather. I have of late—but wherefore I know not—lost all my mirth, forgone all custom of exercises; and indeed it goes so heavily with my disposition that this goodly frame, the earth, seems to me a sterile promontory, this most excellent canopy, the air, look you, this brave o'erhanging firmament, this majestical roof fretted with golden

---

18. ***Denmark's a prison.*** Denmark is indeed a prison to Hamlet, since Claudius has refused his request to return to Wittenberg.
19. ***beggars bodies . . . beggars' shadows,*** if ambition is but the shadow of a shadow, then beggars, who have no ambition, are solid substance and kings and heroes, who are ruled by ambition, are shadows.
20. ***in the . . . friendship,*** as old friends.

fire, why, it appears no other thing to me than a foul and pestilent congregation of vapors.[21] What a piece of work is a man! how noble in reason! how infinite in faculty! in form and moving how express and admirable! in action how like an angel! in apprehension how like a god! the beauty of the world! the paragon of animals! And yet, to me, what is this quintessence of dust? man delights not me: no, nor woman neither, though by your smiling you seem to say so.

ROS. My lord, there was no such stuff in my thoughts.

HAM. Why did you laugh then, when I said "man delights not me"?

ROS. To think, my lord, if you delight not in man, what lenten entertainment the players shall receive from you: we coted[22] them on the way; and hither are they coming, to offer you service.

HAM. He that plays the king shall be welcome; his majesty shall have tribute of me; the adventurous knight shall use his foil and target[23]; the lover shall not sigh gratis; the humorous man[24] shall end his part in peace; the clown shall make those laugh whose lungs are tickle o' the sere[25]; and the lady shall say her mind freely, or the blank verse shall halt for 't. What players are they?

ROS. Even those you were wont to take delight in, the tragedians of the city.

HAM. How chances it they travel? their residence, both in reputation and profit, was better both ways.

ROS. I think their inhibition[26] comes by the means of the late innovation.[27]

HAM. Do they hold the same estimation they did when I was in the city? are they so followed?

ROS. No, indeed, are they not.

HAM. How comes it? do they grow rusty?

ROS. Nay, their endeavor keeps in the wonted pace: but there is, sir, an aery[28] of children, little eyases,[29] that cry out on the top of question,[30] and are most tyrannically clapped for 't: these are now the fashion, and so berattle the common stages—so they call them—that many wearing rapiers are afraid of goosequills and dare scarce come thither.[31]

HAM. What, are they children? who maintains 'em? how are they escoted?[32] Will they pursue the quality no longer than they can sing?[33] will they not say afterwards, if they should grow themselves to common players—as it is most like, if their means are no better—their writers do them wrong, to make them exclaim against their own succession?

ROS. 'Faith, there has been much to do on both sides; and the nation holds it no sin to tarre[34] them to controversy: there was, for a while, no money bid for argument,[35] unless the poet and the player went to cuffs in the question.

HAM. Is 't possible?

GUIL. O, there has been much throwing about of brains.

HAM. Do the boys carry it away?

ROS. Ay, that they do, my lord; Hercules and his load too.[36]

HAM. It is not very strange; for mine uncle is king of Denmark, and those that would make mows[37] at him while my father lived, give twenty, forty, fifty, an hundred ducats a-piece for his picture in little.[38] 'Sblood, there is something in this more than natural, if philosophy could find it out.

(Flourish of trumpets within.)

GUIL. There are the players.

HAM. Gentlemen, you are welcome to Elsinore. Your hands, come then: the appurtenance of welcome is fashion and ceremony: let me comply with you in this garb,[39] lest my extent[40]

---

21. ***I have . . . vapors.*** This is almost a classic description of melancholy, an ailment familiar to Elizabethans.
22. ***coted,*** passed.
23. ***foil and target,*** sword and shield.
24. ***humorous man,*** the man who plays a particular "humor" (disposition) as, for example, "melancholy."
25. ***tickle o' the sere,*** easy on the trigger.
26. ***inhibition,*** prevention from acting in the city.
27. ***innovation,*** the increased popularity of the Blackfriars Theatre acting company, composed entirely of children.
28. ***aery,*** eagle's nest.
29. ***eyases,*** eaglets; young eagles.
30. ***cry out on the top of question,*** declaim in shrill voices.
31. ***many wearing . . . thither,*** many men of fashion do not attend the public playhouses for fear of being satirized by the poets writing for the boy actors at Blackfriars.
32. ***escoted,*** supported.
33. ***pursue . . . can sing,*** follow the profession only until their voices change.
34. ***tarre,*** incite.
35. ***no money . . . argument,*** the plot of a play could not be sold.
36. ***Hercules and his load too.*** Shakespeare's own company (the Globe Theater, whose sign was that of Hercules bearing the world on his shoulders) seems to have suffered from the competition of the boy actors.
37. ***mows,*** grimaces.
38. ***picture in little,*** miniature.
39. ***comply . . . garb,*** observe the formalities of courtesy.
40. ***extent,*** extension of courtesy.

to the players, which, I tell you, must show fairly outward, should more appear like entertainment than yours. You are welcome: but my uncle-father and aunt-mother are deceived.

GUIL. In what, my dear lord?

HAM. I am but mad north-north-west: when the wind is southerly I know a hawk from a handsaw.[41]

Re-enter POLONIUS.

POL. Well be with you, gentlemen!

HAM. Hark you, Guildenstern; and you too: at each ear a hearer: that great baby you see there is not yet out of his swaddling-clouts.

ROS. Happily[42] he's the second time come to them; for they say an old man is twice a child.

HAM. I will prophesy he comes to tell me of the players; mark it.—You say right, sir: o' Monday morning; 'twas so indeed.

POL. My lord, I have news to tell you.

HAM. My lord, I have news to tell you. When Roscius[43] was an actor in Rome,—

POL. The actors are come hither, my lord.

HAM. Buz, buz!

POL. Upon mine honor,—

HAM. Then came each actor on his ass,—

POL. The best actors in the world, either for tragedy, comedy, history, pastoral, pastoral-comical, historical-pastoral, tragical-historical, tragical-comical-historical-pastoral, scene individable,[44] or poem unlimited[45]: Seneca[46] cannot be too heavy, nor Plautus[47] too light. For the law of writ and the liberty,[48] these are the only men.

HAM. O Jephthah,[49] judge of Israel, what a treasure hadst thou!

POL. What a treasure had he, my lord?

HAM. Why,

One fair daughter, and no more,
The which he loved passing well.

POL. *(Aside)* Still on my daughter.

HAM. Am I not i' the right, old Jephthah?

POL. If you call me Jephthah, my lord, I have a daughter that I love passing well.

HAM. Nay, that follows not.

POL. What follows, then, my lord?

HAM. Why,

As by lot, God wot,

and then, you know,

It came to pass, as most like it was,—

the first row[50] of the pious chanson will show you more; for look, where my abridgement[51] comes.

Enter four or five PLAYERS.

You are welcome, masters; welcome, all. I am glad to see thee well. Welcome, good friends. O, my old friend! thy face is valanced[52] since I saw thee last: comest thou to beard me in Denmark? What, my young lady and mistress![53] By 'r lady, your ladyship is nearer to heaven than when I saw you last, by the altitude of a chopine.[54] Pray God, your voice, like a piece of uncurrent gold, be not cracked within the ring.[55] Masters, you are all welcome. We'll e'en to 't like French falconers, fly at any thing we see: we'll have a speech straight: come, give us a taste of your quality; come, a passionate speech.

FIRST PLAY. What speech, my lord?

HAM. I heard thee speak me a speech once, but it was never acted; or, if it was, not above once; for the play, I remember, pleased not the million; 'twas caviare to the general: but it was—as I received it, and others, whose judgments in such matters cried in the top of mine[56]—an excellent play, well digested in the scenes, set down with as much modesty as cunning. I remember, one said there were no sallets[57] in the lines to make the matter savory,

---

41. ***I am but . . . handsaw,*** I am only partly mad; at times I am as clear-headed as anyone.
42. ***Happily,*** perhaps.
43. ***Roscius,*** a famous Roman actor. This is Hamlet's way of saying that Polonius' news is old.
44. ***scene individable,*** a play that observes the Classical principles of unified time, place, and action in drama.
45. ***poem unlimited,*** a play that disregards the above.
46. ***Seneca*** (sen′ə kə), Roman dramatist whose "blood-and-thunder" tragedies were imitated by Elizabethan playwrights.
47. ***Plautus*** (plô′təs), Roman writer of farcical comedies.
48. ***law of writ and the liberty,*** following the rules faithfully or improvising.
49. ***Jephthah*** (jef′thə), Hamlet proceeds to quote a ballad about Jephthah's sacrifice of his daughter. (Judges 11:34–39) Jephthah had promised if successful in battle to sacrifice the first creature that met him on his return; his daughter was the first. Hamlet is implying that Polonius is willing to sacrifice Ophelia to gain his own ends.
50. ***row,*** stanza.
51. ***abridgement,*** opportunity for cutting the conversation short.
52. ***valanced,*** fringed (with a beard).
53. ***mistress.*** Women's parts were played by boys in Elizabethan times.
54. ***chopine,*** a shoe with a thick sole.
55. ***uncurrent gold . . . ring.*** Gold pieces that were cracked through the ring surrounding the image of the ruling sovereign could not be lawfully passed.
56. ***cried in the top of mine,*** exceeded mine.
57. ***sallets,*** spicy bits.

nor no matter in the phrase that might indict the author of affectation; but called it an honest method, as wholesome as sweet, and by very much more handsome than fine. One speech in it I chiefly loved: 'twas Æneas'[58] tale to Dido[59]; and thereabout of it especially, where he speaks of Priam's[60] slaughter: if it live in your memory, begin at this line: let me see, let me see—

The rugged Pyrrhus,[61] *like the Hyrcanian beast,*[62]—

It is not so:—it begins with Pyrrhus:—

The rugged Pyrrhus, he whose sable arms,[63]
Black as his purpose, did the night resemble
When he lay couched in the ominous horse,[64]
Hath now this dread and black complexion smear'd
With heraldry more dismal; head to foot
Now is he total gules; horridly trick'd
With blood of fathers, mothers, daughters, sons,
Baked and impasted with the parching streets,
That lend a tyrannous and damned light
To their lord's murder: roasted in wrath and fire,
And thus o'er-sized with coagulate gore,
With his eyes like carbuncles,[65] *the hellish Pyrrhus*
Old grandsire Priam seeks.
So, proceed you.

POL. 'Fore God, my lord, well spoken, with good accent and good discretion.

FIRST PLAY. *Anon he finds him*
Striking too short at Greeks; his antique sword,
Rebellious to his arm, lies where it falls,
Repugnant to command: unequal match'd,
Pyrrhus at Priam drives; in rage strikes wide;
But with the whiff and wind of his fell sword
The unnerved father falls. Then senseless Ilium,[66]
Seeming to feel this blow, with flaming top
Stoops to his base, and with a hideous crash
Takes prisoner Pyrrhus' ear; for, lo! his sword,
Which was declining on the milky head
Of reverend Priam, seem'd i' the air to stick:
So, as a painted tyrant, Pyrrhus stood,
And like a neutral to his will and matter,
Did nothing.
But, as we often see, against some storm,
A silence in the heavens, the rack stand still,
The bold winds speechless and the orb below
As hush as death, anon the dreadful thunder
Doth rend the region, so, after Pyrrhus' pause,
Aroused vengeance sets him new a-work;
And never did the Cyclops' hammers fall
On Mars's armor forged for proof eterne[67]
With less remorse than Pyrrhus' bleeding sword
Now falls on Priam.
Out, out, thou strumpet, Fortune! All you gods,
In general synod, take away her power;
Break all the spokes and fellies[68] *from her wheel,*
And bowl the round nave down the hill of heaven,
As low as to the fiends!

POL. This is too long.

HAM. It shall be to the barber's, with your beard. Prithee, say on: he's for a jig or a tale of bawdry, or he sleeps: say on: come to Hecuba.[69]

FIRST PLAY. *But who, O, who had seen the mobled*[70] *queen—*

HAM. "The mobled queen?"

POL. That 's good; "mobled queen" is good.

FIRST PLAY. *Run barefoot up and down, threatening the flames*
With bisson rheum,[71] *a clout upon that head*
Where late the diadem stood, and for a robe,
A blanket, in the alarm of fear caught up;
Who this had seen, with tongue in venom steep'd,
'Gainst Fortune's state would treason have pronounced:

---

58. ***Aeneas*** (i nē′əs), the Trojan hero of Vergil's *Aeneid.*
59. ***Dido*** (dī′dō), queen of Carthage.
60. ***Priam*** (prī′əm), king of Troy.
61. ***Pyrrhus*** (pir′əs), a Greek hero of the Trojan War.
62. ***Hyrcanian*** (hėr kā ni ən) **beast,** the tiger.
63. ***sable arms,*** the black heraldic device used on his shield.
64. ***ominous horse,*** the wooden horse used by the Greeks to trick the Trojans.
65. ***like carbuncles,*** glowing red.
66. ***senseless Ilium,*** insensible Troy, the city now in flames.
67. ***Cyclops' . . . proof eterne.*** In Greek mythology, the Cyclops, or one-eyed giants, assisted Vulcan, the blacksmith for the other gods.
68. ***fellies,*** sections forming the rim of a wheel.
69. ***Hecuba*** (hek′ū bə), wife of Priam.
70. ***mobled,*** muffled.
71. ***bisson rheum,*** blinding tears.

But if the gods themselves did see her then
When she saw Pyrrhus make malicious sport
In mincing with his sword her husband's limbs,
The instant burst of clamor that she made,
Unless things mortal move them not at all,
Would have made milch[72] *the burning eyes of heaven,*
And passion in the gods.

POL. Look, whether he has not turned his color and has tears in 's eyes. Pray you, no more.

HAM. 'Tis well; I'll have thee speak out the rest soon. Good my lord, will you see the players well bestowed? Do you hear, let them be well used; for they are the abstract and brief chronicles of the time: after your death you were better have a bad epitaph than their ill report while you live.

POL. My lord, I will use them according to their desert.

HAM. God's bodykins, man, much better: use every man after his desert, and who should 'scape whipping? Use them after your own honor and dignity: the less they deserve, the more merit is in your bounty. Take them in.

POL. Come, sirs.

HAM. Follow him, friends: we'll hear a play to-morrow. *(Exit* POLONIUS *with all the* PLAYERS *but the* FIRST.*)* Dost thou hear me, old friend; can you play the Murder of Gonzago?

FIRST PLAY. Ay, my lord.

HAM. We'll ha 't to-morrow night. You could, for a need, study a speech of some dozen or sixteen lines, which I would set down and insert in 't, could you not?

FIRST PLAY. Ay, my lord.

HAM. Very well. Follow that lord; and look you mock him not. *(Exit* FIRST PLAYER.*)* My good friends, I'll leave you till night: you are welcome to Elsinore.

ROS. Good my lord!

HAM. Ay, so, God be wi' ye; *(Exeunt* ROSENCRANTZ *and* GUILDENSTERN.*)* Now I am alone.
O, What a rogue and peasant slave am I!
Is it not monstrous that this player here,
But in a fiction, in a dream of passion,
Could force his soul so to his own conceit[73]
That from her working all his visage wann'd,
Tears in his eyes, distraction in 's aspect,
A broken voice, and his whole function suiting
With forms to his conceit? and all for nothing!
For Hecuba!
What 's Hecuba to him, or he to Hecuba,
That he should weep for her? What would he do,
Had he the motive and the cue for passion
That I have? He would drown the stage with tears
And cleave the general ear with horrid speech,
Make mad the guilty and appal the free,
Confound the ignorant, and amaze indeed
The very faculties of eyes and ears.
Yet I,
A dull and muddy-mettled rascal, peak,[74]
Like John-a-dreams,[75] unpregnant of[76] my cause,
And can say nothing; no, not for a king,
Upon whose property and most dear life
A damn'd defeat was made. Am I a coward?
Who calls me villain? breaks my pate across?
Plucks off my beard, and blows it in my face?
Tweaks me by the nose? gives me the lie i' the throat,
As deep as to the lungs? who does me this?
Ha!
'Swounds, I should take it: for it cannot be
But I am pigeon-liver'd and lack gall
To make oppression bitter,[77] or ere this
I should have fatted all the region kites
With this slave's offal: bloody, bawdy villain!
Remorseless, treacherous, lecherous, kindless[78] villain!
O, vengeance!
Why, what an ass am I! This is most brave,
That I, the son of a dear father murder'd,
Prompted to my revenge by heaven and hell,
Must, like a whore, unpack my heart with words,
And fall a-cursing, like a very drab,
A scullion!

---

72. ***milch,*** moist with tears.
73. ***Could force his soul . . . conceit,*** could make his whole being respond to his thought.
74. ***peak,*** mope.
75. ***John-a-dreams,*** Elizabethan expression for a dreamer.
76. ***unpregnant of,*** not quickened by.
77. ***I am . . . bitter,*** I am unable to feel the bitterness of oppression.
78. ***kindless,*** unnatural.

Fie upon 't! foh! About, my brain! I have heard
That guilty creatures sitting at a play
Have by the very cunning of the scene
Been struck so to the soul that presently
They have proclaim'd their malefactions;
For murder, though it have no tongue, will speak
With most miraculous organ. I'll have these players
Play something like the murder of my father
Before mine uncle: I'll observe his looks;
I'll tent[79] him to the quick: if he but blench,
I know my course. The spirit that I have seen
May be the devil: and the devil hath power
To assume a pleasing shape; yea, and perhaps
Out of my weakness and my melancholy,
As he is very potent with such spirits,[80]
Abuses[81] me to damn me: I'll have grounds
More relative[82] than this: the play's the thing
Wherein I'll catch the conscience of the king.
(Exit.)

---

79. ***tent,*** probe.
80. ***spirits,*** moods.
81. ***Abuses,*** deceives.
82. ***relative,*** definite.

Discussion

Act Two, Scene 1

1. What does Polonius' sending Reynaldo to ferret out information about Laertes say about Polonius as a father? How does this action compare with his treatment of Ophelia in Act One, Scene 3?

2. **(a)** What sort of interview does Ophelia report she has had with Hamlet? **(b)** What does this indicate about Hamlet? **(c)** About Ophelia's love for him? **(d)** How does Polonius react to this news?

Scene 2

1. This scene introduces Rosencrantz and Guildenstern, Hamlet's schoolfellows. **(a)** Why have they been summoned to the court? **(b)** How does Hamlet react to their visit? **(c)** What sort of friends are they to Hamlet?

2. **(a)** What evidence of Hamlet's love for Ophelia does Polonius give to the King? **(b)** What do you think of the quality of this evidence? **(c)** Should Ophelia have given it to Polonius? **(d)** Should he have shown it to the King? **(e)** How might Hamlet feel if he found out?

3. **(a)** Describe the encounter between Hamlet and Polonius. **(b)** What is Hamlet's attitude toward Polonius at this time?

4. **(a)** How does the King of Norway stop Fortinbras from making his proposed attack on Denmark? **(b)** In return, what is Claudius to allow Fortinbras?

5. **(a)** How does Hamlet react to the news of the acting company's visit? **(b)** What bit of topical news (topical in Shakespeare's day) does the acting company bring with it? **(c)** Shakespeare apparently uses this scene to interject some of his own comments on acting. What do they indicate about the theater in his day? **(d)** What play does Hamlet ask the company to do? **(e)** What is Hamlet himself going to do first?

6. The scene ends with a long soliloquy by Hamlet, "O, What a rogue and peasant slave am I!" **(a)** What has occasioned this? **(b)** How does Hamlet feel about his failure to exact vengeance on Claudius? **(c)** What does he now plan to do?

Act Two in Review

1. There are in this act at least four attempts by characters to trip or entrap other characters. **(a)** Describe these in detail, explaining who is doing the trapping, who the intended victim is, and why the trap is set. **(b)** What does such intriguing indicate about the situation in Denmark at this time?

2. This act opens after Hamlet has told Horatio and Marcellus that he intends to feign insanity. **(a)** To whom does he pretend to be insane? **(b)** Do they appear to be convinced? Explain.

3. With a single exception, every action in the play thus far has affected Hamlet in one way or another; the same is true for the rest of the play. The single exception is the conversation between Polonius and Reynaldo in Act Two, Scene 1. If you were directing the play, would you include it? Why, or why not?

Act Three

SCENE 1.

A room in the castle.
Enter KING, QUEEN, POLONIUS, OPHELIA, ROSENCRANTZ, *and* GUILDENSTERN.

KING. And can you, by no drift of conference,[1]
Get from him why he puts on this confusion,
Grating so harshly all his days of quiet
With turbulent and dangerous lunacy?
ROS. He does confess he feels himself distracted;
But from what cause he will by no means speak.
GUIL. Nor do we find him forward[2] to be sounded,
But, with a crafty madness, keeps aloof,
When we would bring him on to some confession
Of his true state.
QUEEN. Did he receive you well?
ROS. Most like a gentleman.
GUIL. But with much forcing of his disposition.
ROS. Niggard of question[3]; but, of our demands,
Most free in his reply.
QUEEN. Did you assay[4] him
To any pastime?
ROS. Madam, it so fell out, that certain players
We o'er-raught[5] on the way: of these we told him;
And there did seem in him a kind of joy
To hear of it: they are about the court,
And, as I think, they have already order
This night to play before him.
POL. 'Tis most true:
And he beseech'd me to entreat your majesties
To hear and see the matter.
KING. With all my heart; and it doth much content me
To hear him so inclined.
Good gentlemen, give him a further edge,[6]
And drive his purpose on to these delights.
ROS. We shall, my lord.
(Exeunt ROSENCRANTZ *and* GUILDENSTERN.*)*
KING. Sweet Gertrude, leave us too;
For we have closely[7] sent for Hamlet hither,
That he, as 'twere by accident, may here
Affront Ophelia:
Her father and myself, lawful espials,[8]
Will so bestow ourselves that, seeing, unseen,
We may of their encounter frankly judge,
And gather by him, as he is behaved,
If 't be the affliction of his love or no
That thus he suffers for.
QUEEN. I shall obey you.
And for your part, Ophelia, I do wish
That your good beauties be the happy cause
Of Hamlet's wildness: so shall I hope your virtues
Will bring him to his wonted way again,
To both your honors.
OPH. Madam, I wish it may.
(Exit QUEEN.*)*
POL. Ophelia, walk you here. Gracious,[9] so please you,
We will bestow ourselves. *(To Ophelia)* Read on this book;
That show of such an exercise may color
Your loneliness.[10] We are oft to blame in this,—
'Tis too much proved—that with devotion's visage
And pious action we do sugar o'er
The devil himself.
KING. *(Aside)* O, 'tis too true!
How smart a lash that speech doth give my conscience!
The harlot's cheek, beautied with plastering art,
Is not more ugly to the thing[11] that helps it
Than is my deed to my most painted word:
O heavy burthen!
POL. I hear him coming; let's withdraw, my lord. *(Exeunt* KING *and* POLONIUS.*)*
Enter HAMLET.

---

1. ***drift of conference,*** device of conversation.
2. ***forward,*** willing.
3. ***Niggard of question,*** sparing of conversation.
4. ***assay,*** tempt, challenge.
5. ***o'er-raught,*** overtook.
6. ***edge,*** incitement, urging on.
7. ***closely,*** secretly.
8. ***espials,*** spies.
9. ***Gracious,*** your grace. Polonius is addressing the king.
10. ***That show . . . loneliness,*** that your solitude may appear more natural.
11. ***to the thing,*** compared to the cosmetic.

HAM. To be, or not to be: that is the question:
Whether 'tis nobler in the mind to suffer
The slings and arrows of outrageous fortune,
Or to take arms against a sea of troubles,
And by opposing end them? To die: to sleep;
No more; and by a sleep to say we end
The heart-ache and the thousand natural shocks
That flesh is heir to, 'tis a consummation
Devoutly to be wish'd. To die, to sleep;
To sleep: perchance to dream: ay, there 's the rub;
For in that sleep of death what dreams may come
When we have shuffled off this mortal coil,[12]
Must give us pause: there 's the respect
That makes calamity of so long life[13];
For who would bear the whips and scorns of time,
The oppressor's wrong, the proud man's contumely,
The pangs of despised love, the law's delay,
The insolence of office and the spurns
That patient merit of the unworthy takes,
When he himself might his quietus[14] make
With a bare bodkin?[15] who would fardels[16] bear,
To grunt and sweat under a weary life,
But that the dread of something after death,
The undiscover'd country from whose bourn
No traveler returns, puzzles the will
And makes us rather bear those ills we have
Than fly to others that we know not of?
Thus conscience does make cowards of us all;
And thus the native hue of resolution
Is sicklied o'er with the pale cast of thought,
And enterprises of great pitch and moment
With this regard their currents turn awry,
And lose the name of action.—Soft you now!
The fair Ophelia! Nymph, in thy orisons
Be all my sins remember'd.

OPH. Good my lord.
How does your honor for this many a day?

HAM. I humbly thank you; well, well, well.

OPH. My lord, I have remembrances of yours,
That I have longed long to re-deliver;
I pray you, now receive them.

HAM. No, not I:
I never gave you aught.

OPH. My honor'd lord, you know right well you did;
And, with them, words of so sweet breath composed
As made the things more rich: their perfume lost,
Take these again; for to the noble mind
Rich gifts wax poor when givers prove unkind.
There, my lord.

HAM. Ha, ha! are you honest?

OPH. My lord?

HAM. Are you fair?

OPH. What means your lordship?

HAM. That if you be honest and fair, your honesty should admit no discourse to your beauty.[17]

OPH. Could beauty, my lord, have better commerce than with honesty?

HAM. Ay, truly; for the power of beauty will sooner transform honesty from what it is to a bawd than the force of honesty can translate beauty into his likeness: this was sometime a paradox, but now the time gives it proof. I did love you once.

OPH. Indeed, my lord, you made me believe so.

HAM. You should not have believed me; for virtue cannot so inoculate our old stock but we shall relish of it[18]: I loved you not.

OPH. I was the more deceived.

HAM. Get thee to a nunnery: why wouldst thou be a breeder of sinners? I am myself indifferent honest[19]; but yet I could accuse me of such things that it were better my mother had not borne me: I am very proud, revengeful, ambitious, with more offences at my beck[20] than I have thoughts to put them in, imagination to give them shape, or time to act them in. What

---

12. ***shuffled off this mortal coil,*** sloughed off this turmoil that is life. *Coil* might mean "body" in the sense that it is wound around the soul like a rope.
13. ***That makes . . . life,*** that makes us live out a long life of calamity.
14. ***quietus*** (kwi ē′təs), acquittance; here, death.
15. ***bare bodkin,*** mere (or unsheathed) dagger.
16. ***fardels,*** burdens.
17. ***That if you . . . beauty.*** In Elizabethan times *honest* meant both "truthful" and "pure." *Fair* meant both "honorable" and "beautiful." Hamlet is saying to Ophelia that if she is pure and beautiful, she had better not let beauty destroy her purity.
18. ***virtue . . . of it,*** virtue cannot be grafted upon old stock to thereby change its wickedness.
19. ***indifferent honest,*** reasonably virtuous.
20. ***beck,*** command.

should such fellows as I do crawling between earth and heaven? We are arrant knaves, all; believe none of us. Go thy ways to a nunnery. Where 's your father?

OPH. At home, my lord.

HAM. Let the doors be shut upon him, that he may play the fool no where but in 's own house. Farewell.

OPH. O, help him, you sweet heavens!

HAM. If thou dost marry, I'll give thee this plague for thy dowry: be thou as chaste as ice, as pure as snow, thou shalt not escape calumny. Get thee to a nunnery, go: farewell. Or, if thou wilt needs marry, marry a fool; for wise men know well enough what monsters[21] you make of them. To a nunnery, go, and quickly too. Farewell.

OPH. O heavenly powers, restore him!

HAM. I have heard of your paintings too, well enough; God has given you one face, and you make yourselves another: you jig, you amble, and you lisp, and nick-name God's creatures, and make your wantonness your ignorance.[22] Go to, I'll no more on 't; it hath made me mad. I say, we will have no more marriages: those that are married already, all but one, shall live; the rest shall keep as they are. To a nunnery, go. *(Exit.)*

OPH. O, what a noble mind is here o'er-thrown!
The courtier's, soldier's, scholar's, eye, tongue, sword;
The expectancy and rose of the fair state,
The glass of fashion and the mould of form,
The observed of all observers, quite, quite down!
And I, of ladies most deject and wretched,
That suck'd the honey of his music vows,
Now see that noble and most sovereign reason,
Like sweet bells jangled, out of tune and harsh;
That unmatch'd form and feature of blown[23] youth
Blasted with ecstasy[24]: O, woe is me,
To have seen what I have seen, see what I see!

Re-enter KING *and* POLONIUS.

KING. Love! his affections do not that way tend;
Nor what he spake, though it lack'd form a little,
Was not like madness. There 's something in his soul,
O'er which his melancholy sits on brood;
And I do doubt the hatch and the disclose
Will be some danger: which for to prevent,
I have in quick determination
Thus set it down: he shall with speed to England,
For the demand of our neglected tribute:
Haply the seas and countries different
With variable objects shall expel
This something-settled matter in his heart,
Whereon his brains still beating puts him thus
From fashion of himself. What think you on 't?

POL. It shall do well: but yet do I believe
The origin and commencement of his grief
Sprung from neglected love. How now, Ophelia!
You need not tell us what Lord Hamlet said;
We heard it all. My lord, do as you please;
But, if you hold it fit, after the play
Let his queen mother all alone entreat him
To show his grief: let her be round[25] with him;
And I'll be placed, so please you, in the ear
Of all their conference. If she find him not,
To England send him, or confine him where
Your wisdom best shall think.

KING. It shall be so:
Madness in great ones must not unwatch'd go. *(Exeunt.)*

SCENE 2.

A hall in the castle.

Enter HAMLET *and* PLAYERS.

HAM. Speak the speech, I pray you, as I pronounced it to you, trippingly on the tongue: but if you mouth it, as many of your players do, I had as lief the town-crier spoke my lines. Nor do not saw the air too much with your hand, thus, but use all gently; for in the very torrent, tempest, and, as I may say, the whirlwind of

---

21. ***monsters,*** an allusion to the horns of the cuckold.
22. ***make your wantonness your ignorance,*** excuse your wantonness on the grounds of ignorance.
23. ***blown,*** blooming.
24. ***ecstasy,*** madness.
25. ***round,*** plain-spoken.

your passion, you must acquire and beget a temperance that may give it smoothness. O, it offends me to the soul to hear a robustious periwig-pated[1] fellow tear a passion to tatters, to very rags, to split the ears of the groundlings, who for the most part are capable of nothing but inexplicable dumb-shows and noise: I would have such a fellow whipped for o'er-doing Termagant[2]; it out-herods Herod[3]: pray you, avoid it.

FIRST PLAY. I warrant[4] your honor.

HAM. Be not too tame neither, but let your own discretion be your tutor: suit the action to the word, the word to the action; with this special observance, that you o'er-step not the modesty of nature: for any thing so overdone is from the purpose of playing, whose end, both at the first and now, was and is, to hold, as 't were, the mirror up to nature; to show virtue her own feature, scorn her own image, and the very age and body of the time his form and pressure. Now this overdone, or come tardy off, though it make the unskillful laugh, cannot but make the judicious grieve; the censure of the which one must in your allowance o'erweigh a whole theater of others. O, there be players that I have seen play, and heard others praise, and that highly, not to speak it profanely, that, neither having the accent of Christians nor the gait of Christian, pagan, nor man, have so strutted and bellowed that I have thought some of nature's journeymen[5] had made men and not made them well, they imitated humanity so abominably.

FIRST PLAY. I hope we have reformed that indifferently[6] with us, sir.

HAM. O, reform it altogether. And let those that play your clowns speak no more than is set down for them; for there be of them that will themselves laugh, to set on some quantity of barren[7] spectators to laugh too; though, in the mean time, some necessary question of the play be then to be considered: that 's villainous, and shows a most pitiful ambition in the fool that uses it. Go, make you ready.

(Exeunt PLAYERS.*)*

Enter POLONIUS, ROSENCRANTZ, *and* GUILDENSTERN.

How now, my lord! will the king hear this piece of work?

POL. And the queen too, and that presently.

HAM. Bid the players make haste.

(Exit POLONIUS.*)*

Will you two help to hasten them?

ROS. }
GUIL. } We will, my lord.

(Exeunt ROSENCRANTZ *and* GUILDENSTERN.*)*

HAM. What ho! Horatio!

Enter HORATIO.

HOR. Here, sweet lord, at your service.

HAM. Horatio, thou art e'en as just a man
As e'er my conversation coped withal.

HOR. O, my dear lord,—

HAM. Nay, do not think I flatter;
For what advancement may I hope from thee
That no revenue hast but thy good spirits,
To feed and clothe thee? Why should the poor be flatter'd?
No, let the candied[8] tongue lick absurd pomp,
And crook the pregnant hinges of the knee
Where thrift may follow fawning. Dost thou hear?
Since my dear soul was mistress of her choice
And could of men distinguish her election,
S' hath seal'd thee for herself; for thou hast been
As one, in suffering all, that suffers nothing,
A man that fortune's buffets and rewards
Hast ta'en with equal thanks: and blest are those
Whose blood and judgment are so well commeddled,[9]
That they are not a pipe for fortune's finger
To sound what stop she please. Give me that man
That is not passion's slave, and I will wear him
In my heart's core, ay, in my heart of heart,
As I do thee.—Something too much of this.—

1. ***periwig-pated,*** wig-wearing.
2. ***Termagant*** (ter′mə gənt), Saracen god who was depicted in early morality plays as a roaring tyrant.
3. ***Herod,*** a role played with great noise and fury in early drama.
4. ***warrant,*** promise.
5. ***journeymen,*** laborers not yet masters in their trade.
6. ***indifferently,*** fairly, tolerably.
7. ***barren,*** i.e., of wit.
8. ***candied,*** sugared, honeyed.
9. ***commeddled,*** comingled, blended.

There is a play to-night before the king;
One scene of it comes near the circumstance
Which I have told thee of my father's death:
I prithee, when thou seest that act afoot,
Even with the very comment of thy soul
Observe mine uncle: if his occulted[10] guilt
Do not itself unkennel in one speech,
It is a damned[11] ghost that we have seen,
And my imaginations are as foul
As Vulcan's stithy.[12] Give him heedful note;
For I mine eyes will rivet to his face,
And after we will both our judgments join
In censure of his seeming.[13]

HOR. Well, my lord:
If he steal aught the whilst this play is playing,
And 'scape detecting, I will pay the theft.

HAM. They are coming to the play; I must be idle[14]:
Get you a place.

Danish march. A flourish. Enter KING, QUEEN, POLONIUS, OPHELIA, ROSENCRANTZ, GUILDENSTERN, *and others.*

KING. How fares our cousin Hamlet?

HAM. Excellent, i' faith; of the chameleon's dish[15]: I eat the air, promise-crammed: you cannot feed capons so.

KING. I have nothing with this answer, Hamlet; these words are not mine.[16]

HAM. No, nor mine now. *(To Polonius)* My lord, you played once i' the university, you say?

POL. That did I, my lord; and was accounted a good actor.

HAM. What did you enact?

POL. I did enact Julius Cæsar: I was killed i' the Capitol; Brutus killed me.

HAM. It was a brute part of him to kill so capital a calf there. Be the players ready?

ROS. Ay, my lord; they stay upon your patience.

QUEEN. Come hither, my dear Hamlet, sit by me.

HAM. No, good mother, here's metal more attractive.

POL. *(To the King)* O, ho! do you mark that?

HAM. Lady, shall I lie in your lap?
(Lying down at Ophelia's feet.)

OPH. No, my lord.

HAM. I mean, my head upon your lap?

OPH. You are merry, my lord.

HAM. Who, I?

OPH. Ay, my lord.

HAM. O God, your only jig-maker.[17] What should a man do but be merry? for, look you, how cheerfully my mother looks, and my father died within these two hours.

OPH. Nay, 'tis twice two months, my lord.

HAM. So long? Nay then, let the devil wear black, for I'll have a suit of sables. O heavens! die two months ago, and not forgotten yet? Then there 's hope a great man's memory may outlive his life half a year: but, by 'r lady, he must build churches, then; or else shall he suffer not thinking on, with the hobby-horse, whose epitaph is "For, O, for, O, the hobby-horse is forgot."[18]

Hautboys play. The dumb-show enters.
Enter a KING *and a* QUEEN *very lovingly; the* QUEEN *embracing him, and he her. She kneels, and makes show of protestation unto him. He takes her up, and declines his head upon her neck: lays him down upon a bank of flowers: she, seeing him asleep, leaves him. Anon comes in a fellow, takes off his crown, kisses it, and pours poison in the* KING*'s ears, and exit. The* QUEEN *returns; finds the* KING *dead, and makes passionate action. The* POISONER, *with some two or three* MUTES, *comes in again, seeming to lament with her. The dead body is carried away. The* POISONER *wooes the* QUEEN *with gifts: she seems loath and unwilling awhile, but in the end accepts his love.* *(Exeunt.)*

OPH. What means this, my lord?

HAM. Marry, this is miching mallecho[19]; it means mischief.

OPH. Belike this show imports the argument of the play.

---

10. ***occulted,*** hidden.
11. ***damned,*** in league with Satan.
12. ***Vulcan's stithy,*** the forge of Vulcan, the Roman god of fire and metal-working.
13. ***In censure of his seeming,*** in judgment of his appearance or behavior.
14. ***I must be idle,*** I must pretend to be mad.
15. ***chameleon's dish.*** The chameleon, a type of lizard, was supposed to feed on air.
16. ***are not mine,*** do not fit my question.
17. ***your only jig-maker,*** only your composer of jigs.
18. ***For . . . forgot,*** line from a song occurring in *Love's Labours Lost.*
19. ***miching mallecho,*** sneaking mischief.

Robin Nunn as the Player Queen, Graeme Campbell as the First Player, Eric Donkin as Polonius, Michael Liscinsky as Claudius.

Enter PROLOGUE.

HAM. We shall know by this fellow: the players cannot keep counsel; they'll tell all.

Pro. *For us, and for our tragedy,*
Here stooping to your clemency
We beg your hearing patiently. *(Exit.)*

HAM. Is this a prologue, or the posy[20] of a ring?

OPH. 'Tis brief, my lord.

HAM. As woman's love.

Enter two PLAYERS, KING *and* QUEEN.

P. King. *Full thirty times hath Phoebus' cart[21] gone round*
Neptune's salt wash[22] and Tellus' orbed ground,[23]
And thirty dozen moons with borrow'd sheen
About the world have times twelve thirties been,
Since love our hearts and Hymen[24] did our hands
Unite commutual[25] in most sacred bonds.

P. Queen. *So many journeys may the sun and moon*
Make us again count o'er ere love be done!
But, woe is me, you are so sick of late,
So far from cheer and from your former state,
That I distrust you.[26] Yet, though I distrust,
Discomfort you, my lord, it nothing must:
For women's fear and love holds quantity;

---

20. ***posy,*** motto.
21. ***Phoebus'*** (fē′bəs) ***cart,*** the chariot of the sun god.
22. ***Neptune's salt wash,*** the sea.
23. ***Tellus' orbed ground,*** the earth (Tellus was the Roman goddess of the earth).
24. ***Hymen*** (hī′men), god of matrimony.
25. ***commutual,*** intensely mutual.
26. ***distrust you,*** am anxious about you.

In neither aught, or in extremity.
Now, what my love is, proof hath made you know;
And as my love is sized, my fear is so:
Where love is great, the littlest doubts are fear;
Where little fears grow great, great love grows there.

P. King. *'Faith, I must leave thee, love, and shortly too;*
My operant[27] powers their functions leave[28] to do:
And thou shalt live in this fair world behind,
Honor'd, beloved; and haply one as kind
For husband shalt thou—

P. Queen. *O, confound the rest!*
Such love must needs be treason in my breast:
In second husband let me be accurst!
None wed the second but who kill'd the first.

HAM. *(Aside)* Wormwood, wormwood.[29]

P. Queen. *The instances that second marriage move*
Are base respects of thrift, but none of love:
A second time I kill my husband dead,
When second husband kisses me in bed.

P. King. *I do believe you think what now you speak;*
But what we do determine oft we break.
What to ourselves in passion we propose,
The passion ending, doth the purpose lose.
The violence of either grief or joy
Their own enactures with themselves destroy:
Where joy most revels, grief doth most lament;
Grief joys, joy grieves, on slender accident.
This world is not for aye, nor 'tis not strange
That even our loves should with our fortunes change;
For 'tis a question left us yet to prove,
Whether love lead fortune, or else fortune love.
The great man down, you mark his favorite flies;
The poor advanced makes friends of enemies.
And hitherto doth love on fortune tend;
For who not needs shall never lack a friend,
And who in want a hollow friend doth try,
Directly seasons him his enemy.
But, orderly to end where I begun,
Our wills and fates do so contrary run
That our devices still are overthrown;
Our thoughts are ours, their ends none of our own:
So think thou wilt no second husband wed;
But die thy thoughts when thy first lord is dead.

P. Queen. *Nor earth to me give food, nor heaven light!*
Sport and repose lock from me day and night!
To desperation turn my trust and hope!
An anchor's[30] cheer in prison be my scope!
Each opposite[31] that blanks the face of joy
Meet what I would have well and it destroy!
Both here and hence pursue me lasting strife,
If, once a widow, ever I be wife!

HAM. If she should break it now![32]

P. King. *'Tis deeply sworn. Sweet, leave me here awhile;*
My spirits grow dull, and fain I would beguile
The tedious day with sleep. *(Sleeps.)*

P. Queen. *Sleep rock thy brain;*
And never come mischance between us twain! *(Exit.)*

HAM. Madam, how like you this play?

QUEEN. The lady doth protest too much, methinks.

HAM. O, but she'll keep her word.

KING. Have you heard the argument? Is there no offence in 't?

HAM. No, no, they do but jest, poison in jest; no offence i' the world.

KING. What do you call the play?

HAM. The Mouse-trap. Marry, how? Tropically.[33] This play is the image of a murder done in Vienna: Gonzago is the duke's name; his wife, Baptista: you shall see anon; 't is a knavish piece of work: but what o' that? your majesty and we that have free souls, it touches us not: let the galled jade wince, our withers are unwrung.[34]

---

27. ***operant,*** active.
28. ***leave,*** cease.
29. ***Wormwood, wormwood.*** Hamlet means that these lines should taste bitter to Gertrude.
30. ***anchor,*** anchorite, or hermit.
31. ***opposite,*** adversary.
32. ***If she . . . now.*** Hamlet is hoping that Gertrude will be so emotionally overwrought that she will reveal whether she was involved in the murder of King Hamlet.
33. ***Tropically,*** figuratively.
34. ***let the . . . unwrung,*** let the guilty worry; our consciences are clear.

Enter LUCIANUS.

This is one Lucianus, nephew to the king.

OPH. You are as good as a chorus, my lord.

HAM. Begin, murderer; pox, leave thy damnable faces, and begin. Come: "the croaking raven doth bellow for revenge."

LUC. *Thoughts black, hands apt, drugs fit, and*
time agreeing;
Confederate season, else no creature seeing;
Thou mixture rank, of midnight weeds
collected,
With Hecate's ban[35] *thrice blasted, thrice*
infected,
Thy natural magic and dire property,
On wholesome life usurp immediately.

(Pours the poison into the sleeper's ears.)

HAM. He poisons him i' the garden for 's estate. His name 's Gonzago: the story is extant, and writ in choice Italian: you shall see anon how the murderer gets the love of Gonzago's wife.

OPH. The king rises.

HAM. What, frighted with false fire![36]

QUEEN. How fares my lord?

POL. Give o'er the play.

KING. Give me some light: away!

ALL. Lights, lights, lights!

(Exeunt all but HAMLET *and* HORATIO.*)*

HAM. *Why, let the stricken deer go weep,*
The hart ungalled play;
For some must watch, while some must sleep:
So runs the world away.

Would not this, sir, and a forest of feathers[37]—if the rest of my fortunes turn Turk with[38] me—with two Provincial roses on my razed shoes,[39] get me a fellowship in a cry[40] of players, sir?

HOR. Half a share.[41]

HAM. A whole one, I.
For thou dost know, O Damon[42] *dear,*
This realm dismantled was
Of Jove himself; and now reigns here
A very, very—pajock.[43]

HOR. You might have rhymed.

HAM. O good Horatio, I'll take the ghost's word for a thousand pound. Didst perceive?

HOR. Very well, my lord.

HAM. Upon the talk of the poisoning?

HOR. I did very well note him.

HAM. Ah, ah! Come, some music! come, the recorders!
For if the king like not the comedy,
Why then, belike, he likes it not, perdy.
Come, some music!

Re-enter ROSENCRANTZ *and* GUILDENSTERN.

GUIL. Good my lord, vouchsafe me a word with you.

HAM. Sir, a whole history.

GUIL. The king, sir,—

HAM. Ay, sir, what of him?

GUIL. Is in his retirement marvelous distempered.

HAM. With drink, sir?

GUIL. No, my lord, rather with choler.

HAM. Your wisdom should show itself more richer to signify this to his doctor; for, for me to put him to his purgation would perhaps plunge him into far more choler.

GUIL. Good my lord, put your discourse into some frame[44] and start not so wildly from my affair.

HAM. I am tame, sir: pronounce.

GUIL. The queen, your mother, in most great affliction of spirit, hath sent me to you.

HAM. You are welcome.

GUIL. Nay, good my lord, this courtesy is not of the right breed. If it shall please you to make me a wholesome[45] answer, I will do your mother's commandment: if not, your pardon and my return shall be the end of my business.

HAM. Sir, I cannot.

GUIL. What, my lord?

HAM. Make you a wholesome answer; my wit 's diseased: but, sir, such answer as I can make, you shall command; or, rather, as you say, my mother: therefore no more, but to the matter: my mother, you say,—

---

35. ***Hecate's*** (hek′ə tiz) ***ban,*** the curse of Hecate, goddess of witchcraft.
36. ***false fire,*** a will-o-the-wisp, imitation.
37. ***forest of feathers,*** an allusion to the plumes that Elizabethan actors were fond of wearing.
38. ***turn Turk with,*** go back on.
39. ***Provincial . . . shoes,*** rosettes of ribbons on my slashed shoes (by way of ornament).
40. ***cry,*** pack (as of hounds).
41. ***Half a share,*** i.e., in the acting company.
42. ***Damon*** (da′mən). In Roman legend, Damon and Pythias (pith′iəs) were noted for their close friendship.
43. ***pajock,*** peacock, a repulsive creature according to Elizabethan natural history.
44. ***frame,*** order.
45. ***wholesome,*** sensible.

ROS. Then thus she says; your behavior hath struck her into amazement and admiration.

HAM. O wonderful son, that can so astonish a mother! But is there no sequel at the heels of this mother's admiration? Impart.

ROS. She desires to speak with you in her closet, ere you go to bed.

HAM. We shall obey, were she ten times our mother. Have you any further trade with us?

ROS. My lord, you once did love me.

HAM. So I do still, by these pickers and stealers.[46]

ROS. Good my lord, what is your cause of distemper? You do, surely, bar the door upon your own liberty, if you deny your griefs to your friend.

HAM. Sir, I lack advancement.

ROS. How can that be, when you have the voice of the king himself for your succession in Denmark?

HAM. Ay, sir, but "While the grass grows,"[47]—the proverb is something musty.

Re-enter PLAYERS *with recorders.*

O, the recorders! let me see one. To withdraw[48] with you:—why do you go about to recover the wind of me, as if you would drive me into a toil?[49]

GUIL. O, my lord, if my duty be too bold, my love is too unmannerly.[50]

HAM. I do not well understand that. Will you play upon this pipe?

GUIL. My lord, I cannot.

HAM. I pray you.

GUIL. Believe me, I cannot.

HAM. I do beseech you.

GUIL. I know no touch of it, my lord.

HAM. 'Tis as easy as lying: govern these ventages with your fingers and thumb, give it breath with your mouth, and it will discourse most eloquent music. Look you, these are the stops.

GUIL. But these cannot I command to any utterance of harmony; I have not the skill.

HAM. Why, look you now, how unworthy a thing you make of me! You would play upon me; you would seem to know my stops; you would pluck out the heart of my mystery; you would sound me from my lowest note to the top of my compass: and there is much music, excellent voice, in this little organ; yet cannot you make it speak. 'Sblood, do you think I am easier to be played on than a pipe? Call me what instrument you will, though you can fret[51] me, yet you cannot play upon me.

Enter POLONIUS.

God bless you, sir!

POL. My lord, the queen would speak with you, and presently.

HAM. Do you see yonder cloud that's almost in shape of a camel?

POL. By the mass, and 'tis like a camel, indeed.

HAM. Methinks it is like a weasel.

POL. It is backed like a weasel.

HAM. Or like a whale?

POL. Very like a whale.

HAM. Then I will come to my mother by and by. They fool me to the top of my bent.[52] I will come by and by.

POL. I will say so.

HAM. By and by is easily said.

(Exit POLONIUS.*)*

Leave me, friends. *(Exeunt all but* HAMLET.*)*

'Tis now the very witching time of night,
When churchyards yawn and hell itself
breathes out
Contagion to this world: now could I drink
hot blood,
And do such bitter business as the day
Would quake to look on. Soft! now to my
mother.
O heart, lose not thy nature; let not ever
The soul of Nero[53] enter this firm bosom:
Let me be cruel, not unnatural:
I will speak daggers to her, but use none;
My tongue and soul in this be hypocrites;
How in my words soever she be shent,[54]
To give them seals[55] never, my soul, consent!

(Exit.)

---

46. ***these pickers and stealers,*** hands, so called from the catechism, "to keep my hands from picking and stealing."
47. ***While the grass grows.*** The proverb continues "the silly horse starves."
48. ***withdraw,*** speak in private.
49. ***why . . . into a toil,*** why do you try to maneuver about me as if to drive me into a trap.
50. ***if . . . unmannerly,*** if I am using an unmannerly boldness, it is my love that causes it.
51. ***fret,*** quibble on meaning "irritate" and the raised parts of stringed instruments that regulate fingering.
52. ***top of my bent,*** limit of my endurance.
53. ***Nero,*** Roman emperor who murdered his mother.
54. ***shent,*** rebuked.
55. ***give them seals,*** confirm them with deeds.

SCENE 3.

A room in the castle.

Enter KING, ROSENCRANTZ, *and* GUILDENSTERN.

KING. I like him not, nor stands it safe with us
To let his madness range. Therefore prepare you;
I your commission will forthwith dispatch,
And he to England shall along with you:
The terms of our estate[1] may not endure
Hazard so near us as doth hourly grow
Out of his lunacies.

GUIL. We will ourselves provide:
Most holy and religious fear it is
To keep those many many bodies safe
That live and feed upon your majesty.

ROS. The single and peculiar[2] life is bound,
With all the strength and armor of the mind,
To keep itself from noyance[3]; but much more
That spirit upon whose weal depend and rest
The lives of many. Never alone
Did the king sigh, but with a general groan.

KING. Arm[4] you, I pray you, to this speedy voyage;
For we will fetters put about this fear,
Which now goes too free-footed.

ROS.
GUIL. We will haste us.

(Exeunt ROSENCRANTZ *and* GUILDENSTERN.*)*

Enter POLONIUS.

POL. My lord, he 's going to his mother's closet:
Behind the arras I'll convey myself,
To hear the process; I'll warrant she'll tax him home[5]:
And as you said, and wisely was it said,
'Tis meet that some more audience than a mother,
Since nature makes them partial, should o'erhear
The speech, of vantage. Fare you well, my liege:
I'll call upon you ere you go to bed,
And tell you what I know.

KING. Thanks, dear my lord.

(Exit POLONIUS.*)*

O, my offence is rank, it smells to heaven;
It hath the primal eldest curse[6] upon 't,
A brother's murder. Pray can I not,
Though inclination be as sharp as will:
My stronger guilt defeats my strong intent;
And, like a man to double business bound,
I stand in pause where I shall first begin,
And both neglect. What if this cursed hand
Were thicker than itself with brother's blood,
Is there not rain enough in the sweet heavens
To wash it white as snow? Whereto serves mercy
But to confront the visage of offence?
And what 's in prayer but this two-fold force,
To be forestalled ere we come to fall,
Or pardon'd being down? Then I'll look up;
My fault is past. But, O, what form of prayer
Can serve my turn? "Forgive me my foul murder"?
That cannot be: since I am still possess'd
Of those effects for which I did the murder,
My crown, mine own ambition and my queen.
May one be pardon'd and retain the offence?
In the corrupted currents of this world
Offence's gilded hand[7] may shove by justice,
And oft 'tis seen the wicked prize itself
Buys out the law: but 'tis not so above;
There is no shuffling,[8] there the action lies
In his true nature; and we ourselves compell'd,
Even to the teeth and forehead of our faults,
To give in evidence. What then? what rests?
Try what repentance can: what can it not?
Yet what can it when one can not repent?
O wretched state! O bosom black as death!
O limed[9] soul, that, struggling to be free,
Art more engaged! Help, angels! Make assay,
Bow, stubborn knees; and, heart with strings of steel,
Be soft as sinews of the new-born babe!
All may be well. *(Retires and kneels.)*

---

1. ***terms . . . estate,*** the circumstances of our state (as king).
2. ***peculiar,*** personal, private.
3. ***noyance,*** harm.
4. ***Arm,*** prepare.
5. ***tax him home,*** rebuke him severely.
6. ***primal eldest curse,*** the curse put upon Cain for slaying his brother Abel.
7. ***Offence's gilded hand,*** hand offering a bribe.
8. ***shuffling,*** escape by trickery.
9. ***limed,*** caught, as a bird is caught with birdlime.

Enter HAMLET.

HAM. Now might I do it pat, now he is praying;
And now I'll do 't. And so he goes to heaven;
And so am I revenged. That would be scann'd[10]:
A villain kills my father; and for that,
I, his sole son, do this same villain send
To heaven.
O, this is hire and salary, not revenge.
He took my father grossly, full of bread[11];
With all his crimes broad blown, as flush as May;
And how his audit stands who knows save heaven?
But in our circumstance and course of thought,
'Tis heavy with him: and am I then revenged,
To take him in the purging of his soul,
When he is fit and season'd for his passage?
No!
Up, sword; and know thou a more horrid hent:
When he is drunk asleep, or in his rage.
Or in the incestuous pleasure of his bed;
At gaming, swearing, or about some act
That has no relish of salvation in 't;
Then trip him, that his heels may kick at heaven,
And that his soul may be as damn'd and black
As hell, whereto it goes. My mother stays[12]:
This physic[13] but prolongs thy sickly days.
(Exit.)

KING. *(Rising)* My words fly up, my thoughts remain below:
Words without thoughts never to heaven go.[14]
(Exit.)

SCENE 4.

The QUEEN'*s closet.*
Enter QUEEN *and* POLONIUS.

POL. He will come straight. Look you lay home to him:
Tell him his pranks have been too broad to bear with,
And that your grace hath screen'd and stood between
Much heat and him. I'll sconce[1] me even here.
Pray you, be round with him.

HAM. *(Within)* Mother, mother, mother!

QUEEN. I'll warrant you,
Fear me not: withdraw, I hear him coming.
(POLONIUS hides behind the arras.)

Enter HAMLET.

HAM. Now, mother, what 's the matter?

QUEEN. Hamlet, thou hast thy father much offended.

HAM. Mother, you have my father much offended.

QUEEN. Come, come, you answer with an idle tongue.

HAM. Go, go, you question with a wicked tongue.

QUEEN. Why, how now, Hamlet!

HAM. What's the matter now?

QUEEN. Have you forgot me?

HAM. No, by the rood,[2] not so:
You are the queen, your husband's brother's wife;
And—would it were not so!—you are my mother.

QUEEN. Nay, then, I'll set those to you that can speak.

HAM. Come, come, and sit you down; you shall not budge;
You go not till I set you up a glass[3]
Where you may see the inmost part of you.

QUEEN. What wilt thou do? thou will not murder me?
Help, help, ho!

POL. *(Behind)* What, ho! help, help, help!

HAM. *(Drawing)* How now! a rat? Dead, for a ducat, dead!
(Makes a pass through the arras.)

POL. *(Behind)* O, I am slain! *(Falls and dies.)*

---

10. ***would be scann'd,*** needs to be looked into.
11. ***grossly, full of bread,*** still attached to this earthly life; without confession and absolution.
12. ***stays,*** awaits.
13. ***physic,*** purging; in the case of the king, by prayer.
14. ***My words . . . go.*** Claudius is unable to repent his crime; had Hamlet known this, he would have been able to exact his revenge.

SCENE 4 1. ***sconce,*** hide.
2. ***rood,*** cross.
3. ***glass,*** mirror.

QUEEN. O me, what hast thou done?
HAM. Nay, I know not:
Is it the king?
QUEEN. O, what a rash and bloody deed is this!
HAM. A bloody deed! almost as bad, good mother,
As kill a king, and marry with his brother.
QUEEN. As kill a king!
HAM. Ay, lady, 'twas my word.
(Lifts up the arras and discovers POLONIUS.*)*
Thou wretched, rash, intruding fool, farewell!
I took thee for thy better: take thy fortune;
Thou find'st to be too busy is some danger.
Leave wringing of your hands: peace! sit you down,
And let me wring your heart; for so I shall,
If it be made of penetrable stuff,
If damned custom have not brass'd it so
That it be proof and bulwark against sense.
QUEEN. What have I done, that thou darest wag thy tongue
In noise so rude against me?
HAM. Such an act
That blurs the grace and blush of modesty,
Calls virtue hypocrite, takes off the rose
From the fair forehead of an innocent love
And sets a blister there, makes marriage-vows
As false as dicers' oaths: O, such a deed
As from the body of contraction[4] plucks
The very soul, and sweet religion makes
A rhapsody of words: heaven's face doth glow;
Yea, this solidity and compound mass,[5]
With heated visage, as against the doom,
Is thought-sick at the act.
QUEEN. Ay me, what act,
That roars so loud, and thunders in the index?[6]
HAM. Look here, upon this picture, and on this.
The counterfeit presentment[7] of two brothers.
See, what a grace was seated on this brow;
Hyperion's[8] curls; the front of Jove himself;
An eye like Mars, to threaten and command;
A station[9] like the herald Mercury
New-lighted on a heaven-kissing hill;
A combination and a form indeed,
Where every god did seem to set his seal,
To give the world assurance of a man:
This was your husband. Look you now, what follows:
Here is your husband; like a mildew'd ear,[10]
Blasting his wholesome brother. Have you eyes?
Could you on this fair mountain leave to feed,
And batten on this moor?[11] Ha! have you eyes?
You cannot call it love; for at your age
The hey-day in the blood is tame, it 's humble,
And waits upon the judgment: and what judgment
Would step from this to this? Sense,[12] sure, you have,
Else could you not have motion; but sure, that sense
Is apoplex'd[13]; for madness would not err,
Nor sense to ecstasy was ne'er so thrall'd
But it reserved some quantity of choice,
To serve in such a difference. What devil was 't
That thus hath cozen'd you at hoodman-blind?[14]
Eyes without feeling, feeling without sight,
Ears without hands or eyes, smelling sans[15] all,
Or but a sickly part of one true sense
Could not so mope.
O shame! where is thy blush! Rebellious hell,
If thou canst mutine[16] in a matron's bones,
To flaming youth let virtue be as wax,
And melt in her own fire.
QUEEN. O Hamlet, speak no more:
Thou turn'st mine eyes into my very soul;
And there I see such black and grained spots

4. ***body of contraction,*** marriage contract.
5. ***solidity and compound mass,*** the earth.
6. ***index,*** prelude or preface.
7. ***counterfeit presentment,*** portrait. On stage the portraits are presented as miniatures or as pictures on the wall.
8. ***Hyperion,*** the sun god.
9. ***station,*** manner of standing, bearing.
10. ***mildew'd ear.*** (See Genesis 41:5–7.)
11. ***batten on this moor,*** feed gluttonously on this wasteland.
12. ***Sense,*** sensory perception.
13. ***apoplex'd,*** paralyzed.
14. ***hoodman-blind,*** blindman's bluff.
15. ***sans,*** without.
16. ***mutine,*** muting, rebellion.

As will not leave their tinct.
These words, like daggers, enter in mine ears;
No more, sweet Hamlet!
HAM. A murderer and a villain;
A slave that is not twentieth part the tithe
Of your precedent lord; a vice of kings[17];
A cutpurse of the empire and the rule,
That from a shelf the precious diadem stole,
And put it in his pocket!
QUEEN. No more!
HAM. A king of shreds and patches,[18]—
Enter GHOST.
Save me, and hover o'er me with your wings,
You heavenly guards! What would your gracious figure?
QUEEN. Alas, he 's mad!
HAM. Do you not come your tardy son to chide,
That, lapsed in time and passion, lets go by
The important acting of your dread command?
O, say!
GHOST. Do not forget: this visitation
Is but to whet thy almost blunted purpose.
But, look, amazement[19] on thy mother sits:
O, step between her and her fighting soul:
Conceit[20] in weakest bodies strongest works:
Speak to her, Hamlet.
HAM. How is it with you, lady?
QUEEN. Alas, how is 't with you,
That you do bend your eye on vacancy
And with the incorporal air do hold discourse?
Forth at your eyes your spirits wildly peep;
And, as the sleeping soldiers in the alarm,
Your bedded[21] hair, like life in excrements,[22]
Start up, and stand an end. O gentle son,
Upon the heat and flame of thy distemper
Sprinkle cool patience. Whereon do you look?
HAM. On him, on him! Look you, how pale he glares!
His form and cause conjoin'd, preaching to stones,
Would make them capable.[23] Do not look upon me;
Lest with this piteous action you convert
My stern effects[24]: then what I have to do
Will want true color; tears perchance for blood.
QUEEN. To whom do you speak this?
HAM. Do you see nothing there?
QUEEN. Nothing at all; yet all that is I see.
HAM. Nor did you nothing hear?
QUEEN. No, nothing but ourselves.
HAM. Why, look you there! look, how it steals away!
My father, in his habit[25] as he lived!
Look, where he goes, even now, out at the portal! *(Exit* GHOST.*)*
QUEEN. This is the very coinage of your brain:
This bodiless creation ecstasy[26]
Is very cunning in.
HAM. Ecstasy!
My pulse, as yours, doth temperately keep time,
And makes as healthful music: it is not madness
That I have utter'd: bring me to the test,
And I the matter will re-word, which madness
Would gambol from. Mother, for love of grace,
Lay not that flattering unction to your soul,
That not your trespass, but my madness speaks:
It will but skin and film the ulcerous place,
Whiles rank corruption, mining all within,
Infects unseen. Confess yourself to heaven;
Repent what 's past; avoid what is to come;
And do not spread the compost on the weeds,
To make them ranker. Forgive me this my virtue;
For in the fatness of these pursy[27] times
Virtue itself of vice must pardon beg,
Yea, curb[28] and woo for leave to do him good.

---

17. ***vice of kings,*** buffoon of kings, a reference to the Vice, or clown, of the morality plays.
18. ***shreds and patches,*** i.e., motley, the traditional costume of the Vice.
19. ***amazement,*** frenzy, distraction.
20. ***Conceit,*** imagination.
21. ***bedded,*** laid smoothly.
22. ***excrements.*** The hair was considered an excrement or void-ed part of the body.
23. ***capable,*** susceptible to emotional appeal.
24. ***convert my stern effects,*** divert me from stern duty.
25. ***habit,*** dress.
26. ***ecstasy,*** frenzy, madness.
27. ***pursy,*** physically and morally slack.
28. ***curb,*** bow.

QUEEN. O Hamlet, thou hast cleft my heart in twain.
HAM. O, throw away the worser part of it,
And live the purer with the other half.
Good night: but go not to mine uncle's bed;
Assume a virtue, if you have it not,
That monster, custom, who all sense doth eat,
Of habits devil, is angel yet in this,
That to the use of actions fair and good
He likewise gives a frock or livery,
That aptly is put on. Refrain to-night,
And that shall lend a kind of easiness
To the next abstinence: the next more easy;
For use almost can change the stamp of nature,
And either . . . the devil,[29] or throw him out
With wondrous potency. Once more, good night:
And when you are desirous to be bless'd,
I'll blessing beg of you. For this same lord,
(Pointing to POLONIUS.*)*
I do repent: but heaven hath pleased it so,
To punish me with this and this with me,
That I must be their scourge and minister.
I will bestow him, and will answer well
The death I gave him. So, again, good night.
I must be cruel, only to be kind:
Thus bad begins and worse remains behind.
One word more, good lady.
QUEEN. What shall I do?
HAM. Not this, by no means, that I bid you do:
Let the bloat king tempt you again to bed;
Make you to ravel all this matter out,
That I essentially am not in madness,
But mad in craft.[30] 'Twere good you let him know;
For who, that 's but a queen, fair, sober, wise,
Would from a paddock,[31] from a bat, a gib,[32]
Such dear concernings hide? who would do so?
QUEEN. Be thou assured, if words be made of breath,
And breath of life, I have no life to breathe
What thou hast said to me.
HAM. I must to England; you know that?
QUEEN. Alack,
I had forgot: 'tis so concluded on.
HAM. There 's letters seal'd: and my two schoolfellows,
Whom I will trust as I will adders fang'd,
They bear the mandate; they must sweep my way,
And marshal me to knavery. Let it work;
For 'tis the sport to have the enginer
Hoise with his own petar[33] and 't shall go hard
But I will delve one yard below their mines,
And blow them at the moon: O, 'tis most sweet,
When in one line two crafts directly meet.
This man shall set me packing:
I'll lug the guts into the neighbor room.
Mother, good night. Indeed this counselor
Is now most still, most secret and most grave,
Who was in life a foolish prating knave.
Come, sir, to draw toward an end with you.
Good night, mother.
(Exeunt severally; HAMLET *dragging in* POLONIUS.*)*

---

29. ***either . . . the devil,*** defective line usually emended by inserting *master* after *either*.
30. ***Make you . . . mad in craft.*** Hamlet asks Gertrude to keep his secret: that he is not really mad, but pretending to be.
31. ***paddock,*** toad.
32. ***gib,*** tomcat.
33. ***enginer . . . petar,*** artilleryman blown up with his own explosives.

Discussion

Act Three, Scene 1

1. Hamlet's "To be, or not to be" soliloquy is probably the most famous in all literature. What does it indicate about Hamlet's state of mind?

2. (a) How mad does Hamlet appear to be in his scene with Ophelia? **(b)** Might his behavior be based on the realization that he is being spied upon? Explain. **(c)** Does Ophelia show him any sign of affection? **(d)** What remark does he make that might serve as a warning to Claudius?

3. What does Ophelia's soliloquy near the end of the scene reveal about her feeling for Hamlet?

4. After Hamlet has left Ophelia, Claudius and Polonius discuss what is wrong with Hamlet and what action to take. **(a)** What is Claudius' viewpoint? **(b)** What is Polonius' viewpoint?

Scene 2

1. (a) In Hamlet's advice to the players what standard does Hamlet propose as the test of dramatic art? **(b)** What section of the audience does Hamlet feel the actors should strive most to please?

2. The play-within-a-play is usually referred to as the Mousetrap Scene. **(a)** What instructions has Hamlet given the actors earlier? **(b)** What is Horatio to do while the scene is being played? **(c)** Why might Hamlet have placed himself by Ophelia?

Scene 3

(a) Why doesn't Hamlet kill Claudius when he has the opportunity? **(b)** Do you think more or less of Hamlet for this? Explain. **(c)** What is the state of Claudius' conscience at the end of the scene?

Scene 4

1. (a) How does Polonius meet his death? **(b)** Do you think it is an appropriate ending for him? Explain.

2. (a) With what sin does Hamlet charge Gertrude most strongly? **(b)** How does she react? **(c)** What is the effect on Hamlet of the Ghost's appearance?

3. What indication is there that Hamlet will take matters into his own hands in regard to Rosencrantz and Guildenstern?

Act Three in Review

1. By the end of this act, Hamlet has become disillusioned with his mother, his sweetheart, his school friends, and the Danish people. **(a)** Explain each. **(b)** What is their cumulative effect on Hamlet?

2. The structural climax of an Elizabethan tragedy occurs in the third act. This is the point at which the fortunes of the protagonist are at their highest. Then there occurs some action (called the dramatic reverse) at which they start downhill. Where does the structural climax occur? The dramatic reverse?

Act Four

SCENE 1.

A room in the castle.
Enter KING, QUEEN, ROSENCRANTZ, *and* GUILDENSTERN.

KING. There 's matter in these sighs, these profound heaves:
You must translate: 'tis fit we understand them.
Where is your son?
QUEEN. Bestow this place on us a little while.
(Exeunt ROSENCRANTZ *and* GUILDENSTERN.*)*
Ah, mine own lord, what have I seen to-night!
KING. What, Gertrude? How does Hamlet?
QUEEN. Mad as the sea and wind, when both contend
Which is the mightier: in his lawless fit,[1]
Behind the arras hearing something stir,
Whips out his rapier, cries, "A rat, a rat!"
And, in this brainish apprehension,[2] kills
The unseen good old man.
KING. O heavy deed!
It had been so with us, had we been there:
His liberty is full of threats to all;
To you yourself, to us, to every one.
Alas, how shall this bloody deed be answer'd?
It will be laid to us, whose providence
Should have kept short,[3] restrain'd and out of haunt,[4]
This mad young man: but so much was our love,
We would not understand what was most fit;
But, like the owner of a foul disease,
To keep it from divulging,[5] let it feed
Even on the pith of life. Where is he gone?

1. ***Mad as . . . fit.*** Gertrude is protecting Hamlet by claiming that he is mad; thus she is following the instructions he gave her in the preceding scene.
2. ***brainish apprehension,*** brainsick imagination.
3. ***kept short,*** i.e., kept on a short tether.
4. ***out of haunt,*** secluded.
5. ***divulging,*** becoming evident.

QUEEN. To draw apart the body he hath kill'd:
O'er whom his very madness, like some ore
Among a mineral of metals base,
Shows itself pure; he weeps for what is done.[6]

KING. O Gertrude, come away!
The sun no sooner shall the mountains touch,
But we will ship him hence: and this vile deed
We must, with all our majesty and skill,
Both countenance and excuse. Ho, Guildenstern!

Re-enter ROSENCRANTZ *and* GUILDENSTERN.

Friends both, go join you with some further aid:
Hamlet in madness hath Polonius slain,
And from his mother's closet hath he dragg'd him:
Go seek him out; speak fair, and bring the body
Into the chapel. I pray you, haste in this.

(Exeunt ROSENCRANTZ *and* GUILDENSTERN.*)*

Come, Gertrude, we'll call up our wisest friends;
And let them know, both what we mean to do,
And what 's untimely done
Whose whisper o'er the world's diameter,
As level as the cannon to his blank,[7]
Transports his poison'd shot, may miss our name,
And hit the woundless[8] air. O, come away!
My soul is full of discord and dismay.

(Exeunt.)

SCENE 2.

Another room in the castle.
Enter HAMLET.

HAM. Safely stowed.

ROS.
GUIL. } *(Within)* Hamlet! Lord Hamlet!

HAM. But soft, what noise? who calls on Hamlet? O, here they come.

Enter ROSENCRANTZ *and* GUILDENSTERN.

ROS. What have you done, my lord, with the dead body?

HAM. Compounded it with dust, whereto 'tis kin.

ROS. Tell us where 'tis, that we may take it thence
And bear it to the chapel.

HAM. Do not believe it.

ROS. Believe what?

HAM. That I can keep your counsel[1] and not mine own. Besides, to be demanded of[2] a sponge! what replication[3] should be made by the son of a king?

ROS. Take you me for a sponge, my lord?

HAM. Ay, sir, that soaks up the king's countenance, his rewards, his authorities. But such officers do the king best service in the end: he keeps them, like an ape an apple, in the corner of his jaw; first mouthed, to be last swallowed: when he needs what you have gleaned, it is but squeezing you, and sponge, you shall be dry again.

ROS. I understand you not, my lord.

HAM. I am glad of it: a knavish speech sleeps in a foolish ear.

ROS. My lord, you must tell us where the body is, and go with us to the king.

HAM. The body is with the king, but the king is not with the body. The king is a thing—

GUIL. A thing, my lord!

HAM. Of nothing: bring me to him. Hide fox, and all after.[4] *(Exeunt.)*

SCENE 3.

Another room in the castle.
Enter KING, *attended.*

KING. I have sent to seek him, and to find the body.
How dangerous is it that this man goes loose!
Yet must not we put the strong law on him:
He's loved of the distracted multitude,

---

6. ***he weeps . . . done.*** Again, Gertrude is protecting Hamlet.
7. ***As level . . . blank,*** as well aimed as the cannon to its target.
8. ***woundless,*** invulnerable.

SCENE 2 1. ***keep your counsel.*** Hamlet is aware of their treachery but says nothing of it.
2. ***to be demanded of,*** being questioned by.
3. ***replication,*** reply.
4. ***Hide fox and all after,*** an old signal cry in the game of hide-and-seek.

Who like not in their judgment, but their eyes;
And where 'tis so, the offender's scourge is weigh'd,
But never the offence. To bear all smooth and even,
This sudden sending him away must seem
Deliberate pause[1]: diseases desperate grown
By desperate appliance are relieved,
Or not at all.

Enter ROSENCRANTZ.

How now! what hath befall'n?

ROS. Where the dead body is bestow'd, my lord,
We cannot get from him.

KING. But where is he?

ROS. Without, my lord; guarded, to know your pleasure.

KING. Bring him before us.

ROS. Ho, Guildenstern! bring in my lord.

Enter HAMLET *and* GUILDENSTERN.

KING. Now, Hamlet, where 's Polonius?

HAM. At supper.

KING. At supper! where?

HAM. Not where he eats, but where he is eaten: a certain convocation of politic worms are e'en at him. Your worm is your only emperor for diet: we fat all creatures else to fat us, and we fat ourselves for maggots: your fat king and your lean beggar is but variable service, two dishes, but to one table: that's the end.

KING. Alas, alas!

HAM. A man may fish with the worm that hath eat of a king, and eat of the fish that hath fed of that worm.

KING. What dost thou mean by this?

HAM. Nothing but to show you how a king may go a progress[2] through the guts of a beggar.

KING. Where is Polonius?

HAM. In heaven; send thither to see: if your messenger find him not there, seek him i' the other place yourself. But indeed, if you find him not within this month, you shall nose him as you go up the stairs into the lobby.

KING. Go seek him there.

(To some ATTENDANTS.*)*

HAM. He will stay till you come.

(Exeunt ATTENDANTS.*)*

KING. Hamlet, this deed, for thine especial safety,—
Which we do tender,[3] as we dearly grieve
For that which thou hast done,—must send thee hence
With fiery quickness: therefore prepare thyself;
The bark is ready, and the wind at help,
The associates tend, and everything is bent
For England.

HAM. For England!

KING. Ay, Hamlet.

HAM. Good.

KING. So is it, if thou knew'st our purposes.

HAM. I see a cherub that sees them.[4] But, come; for England! Farewell, dear mother.

KING. Thy loving father, Hamlet.

HAM. My mother: father and mother is man and wife; man and wife is one flesh; and so, my mother. Come, for England! *(Exit.)*

KING. Follow him at foot; tempt him with speed aboard;
Delay it not; I'll have him hence to-night;
Away! for every thing is seal'd and done
That else leans on the affair: pray you, make haste.

(Exeunt ROSENCRANTZ *and* GUILDENSTERN.*)*

And, England, if my love thou hold'st at aught—
As my great power thereof may give thee sense,
Since yet thy cicatrice looks raw and red
After the Danish sword, and thy free awe
Pays homage to us—thou mayst not coldly set
Our sovereign process; which imports at full,
By letters congruing[5] to that effect,
The present death of Hamlet. Do it, England;
For like the hectic[6] in my blood he rages,
And thou must cure me: till I know 'tis done,
Howe'er my haps,[7] my joys were ne'er begun.

(Exit.)

1. ***Deliberate pause,*** considered action.
2. ***progress,*** royal journey of state.
3. ***tender,*** regard, hold dear.
4. ***I see . . . them,*** I suspect your real intentions.
5. ***congruing,*** according.
6. ***hectic,*** fever.
7. ***haps,*** fortunes.

SCENE 4.

A plain in Denmark.
Enter FORTINBRAS, *a* CAPTAIN, *and* SOLDIERS, *marching.*

FOR. Go, captain, from me greet the Danish king;
Tell him that, by his license, Fortinbras
Craves the conveyance of a promised march
Over his kingdom. You know the rendezvous.
If that his majesty would aught with us,
We shall express our duty in his eye[1];
And let him know so.
CAP. I will do 't, my lord.
FOR. Go softly[2] on.
(Exeunt FORTINBRAS *and* SOLDIERS.*)*
Enter HAMLET, ROSENCRANTZ, GUILDENSTERN, *and others.*
HAM. Good sir, whose powers are these?
CAP. They are of Norway, sir.
HAM. How purposed, sir, I pray you?
CAP. Against some part of Poland.
HAM. Who commands them, sir?
CAP. The nephew to old Norway, Fortinbras.
HAM. Goes it against the main of Poland, sir,
Or for some frontier?
CAP. Truly to speak, and with no addition,
We go to gain a little patch of ground
That hath in it no profit but the name.
To pay five ducats, five, I would not farm it[3];
Nor will it yield to Norway or the Pole
A ranker rate, should it be sold in fee.[4]
HAM. Why, then the Polack never will defend it.
CAP. Yes, it is already garrison'd.
HAM. Two thousand souls and twenty thousand ducats
Will not debate the question of this straw[5]:
This is the imposthume[6] of much wealth and peace,
That inward breaks, and shows no cause without
Why the man dies. I humbly thank you, sir.
CAP. God be wi' you, sir. *(Exit.)*
ROS. Will 't please you go, my lord?
HAM. I'll be with you straight. Go a little before. *(Exeunt all except* HAMLET.*)*
How all occasions do inform against me,[7]
And spur my dull revenge! What is a man,
If his chief good and market of his time
Be but to sleep and feed? a beast, no more.
Sure, he that made us with such large discourse,[8]
Looking before and after, gave us not
That capability and god-like reason
To fust[9] in us unused. Now, whether it be
Bestial oblivion, or some craven scruple
Of thinking too precisely on the event,
A thought which, quarter'd, hath but one part wisdom
And ever three parts coward, I do not know
Why yet I live to say "This thing 's to do;"
Sith[10] I have cause and will and strength and means
To do 't. Examples gross as earth exhort me:
Witness this army of such mass and charge
Led by a delicate and tender prince,
Whose spirit with divine ambition puff'd
Makes mouths at the invisible event,
Exposing what is mortal and unsure
To all that fortune, death and danger dare,
Even for an egg-shell. Rightly to be great
Is not to stir without great argument,
But greatly to find quarrel in a straw
When honor's at the stake. How stand I then,
That have a father kill'd, a mother stain'd,
Excitements of my reason and my blood,
And let all asleep? while, to my shame, I see
The imminent death of twenty thousand men,
That, for a fantasy and trick of fame,
Go to their graves like beds, fight for a plot
Whereon the numbers cannot try the cause,
Which is not tomb enough and continent
To hide the slain? O, from this time forth,
My thoughts be bloody, or be nothing worth!
(Exit.)

SCENE 5.

Elsinore. A room in the castle.
Enter QUEEN, HORATIO, *and a* GENTLEMAN.

1. ***in his eye,*** in his presence.
2. ***softly,*** slowly.
3. ***farm it,*** take a least of it.
4. ***in fee,*** outright.
5. ***debate the . . . straw,*** settle this trifling matter.
6. ***imposthume,*** festering abscess.
7. ***How all . . . me,*** how all events conspire against me.
8. ***discourse,*** power of thought.
9. ***fust,*** grow moldy.
10. ***Sith,*** since.

QUEEN. I will not speak with her.
GENT. She is importunate, indeed distract:
Her mood will needs be pitied.
QUEEN. What would she have?
GENT. She speaks much of her father; says she hears
There 's tricks i' the world; and hems, and beats her heart;
Spurns enviously at straws[1]; speaks things in doubt,
That carry but half sense: her speech is nothing,
Yet the unshaped[2] use of it doth move
The hearers to collection[3]; they yawn[4] at it,
And botch the words up fit to their own thoughts;
Which, as her winks, and nods, and gestures yield them,
Indeed would make one think there might be thought,
Though nothing sure, yet much unhappily.[5]
HOR. 'Twere good she were spoken with: for she may strew
Dangerous conjectures in ill-breeding minds.
QUEEN. Let her come in. *(Exit* HORATIO.*)*
To my sick soul, as sin's true nature is,
Each toy seems prologue to some great amiss:
So full of artless jealousy is guilt,
It spills itself in fearing to be spilt.[6]
Re-enter HORATIO, *with* OPHELIA.
OPH. Where is the beauteous majesty of Denmark?
QUEEN. How now, Ophelia!
OPH. *(Sings)*
How should I your true love know
From another one?
By his cockle hat and staff,
And his sandal shoon.[7]
QUEEN. Alas, sweet lady, what imports this song?
OPH. Say, you? nay, pray you, mark.
(Sings) He is dead and gone, lady,
He is dead and gone;
At his head a grass-green turf,
At his heels a stone.
QUEEN. Nay, but, Ophelia,—
OPH. Pray you, mark.
(Sings) White his shroud as the mountain snow,—

Enter KING.
QUEEN. Alas, look here, my lord.
OPH. *(Sings) Larded*[8] *all with flowers;*
Which bewept to the grave did not go with true-love showers.
KING. How do you do, pretty lady?
OPH. Well, God 'ild[9] you! They say the owl was a baker's daughter.[10] Lord, we know what we are, but know not what we may be. God be at your table!
KING. How long hath she been thus?
OPH. I hope all will be well. We must be patient: but I cannot choose but weep, to think they should lay him i' the cold ground.[11] My brother shall know of it: and so I thank you for your good counsel. Come, my coach! Good night, ladies; good night, sweet ladies; good night, good night. *(Exit.)*
KING. Follow her close; give her good watch, I pray you. *(Exit* HORATIO.*)*
O, this is the poison of deep grief; it springs
All from her father's death. O Gertrude, Gertrude,
When sorrows come, they come not single spies,
But in battalions. First, her father slain:
Next, your son gone; and he most violent author
Of his own just remove: the people muddied,
Thick and unwholesome in their thoughts and whispers,
For good Polonius' death; and we have done but greenly,[12]
In hugger-mugger[13] to inter him: poor Ophelia

---

1. ***Spurns enviously at straws,*** shies suspiciously at trifles.
2. ***unshaped,*** artless, unformed.
3. ***collection,*** inference.
4. ***yawn,*** wonder.
5. ***much unhappily,*** expression of much unhappiness.
6. ***So full . . . spilt,*** guilt betrays itself in fearing to be betrayed.
7. ***cockle hat . . . shoon.*** A hat with a cockleshell (the shell indicating travel across the sea), a staff, and sandals were the traditional garb of religious pilgrims. The disguise was also used by lovers to carry on their intrigues.
8. ***Larded,*** decorated.
9. ***God 'ild,*** God yield or reward.
10. ***They say . . . daughter.*** Reference to a legend about a baker's daughter being changed into an owl because of her selfishness.
11. ***cold ground.*** A courtier of Polonius' rank should have been interred inside the church. Burial in the ground was for common people, not for the nobility.
12. ***greenly,*** foolishly.
13. ***hugger-mugger,*** unseemly haste and secrecy.

Divided from herself and her fair judgment,
Without the which we are pictures, or mere beasts:
Last, and as much containing as all these,
Her brother is in secret come from France;
Feeds on his wonder, keeps himself in clouds,
And wants not buzzers[14] to infect his ear
With pestilent speeches of his father's death;
Wherein necessity, of matter beggar'd,
Will nothing stick[15] our person to arraign
In ear and ear. O my dear Gertrude, this,
Like to a murdering-piece,[16] in many places
Gives me superfluous death. *(A noise within.)*

QUEEN. Alack, what noise is this?

KING. Where are my Switzers?[17] Let them guard the door.

Enter another GENTLEMAN.

What is the matter?

GENT. Save yourself, my lord:
The ocean, overpeering of his list,[18]
Eats not the flats with more impetuous haste
Than young Laertes, in a riotous head,[19]
O'erbears your officers. The rabble call him lord;
And, as the world were now but to begin,
Antiquity forgot, custom not known,
The ratifiers and props of every word,[20]
They cry "Choose we: Laertes shall be king":
Caps, hands, and tongues, applaud it to the clouds:
"Laertes shall be king, Laertes king!"

QUEEN. How cheerfully on the false trail they cry!
O, this is counter, you false Danish dogs!

KING. The doors are broke. *(Noise within.)*

Enter LAERTES, *armed;* DANES *following.*

LAER. Where is this king? Sirs, stand you all without.

DANES. No, let's come in.

LAER. I pray you, give me leave.

DANES. We will, we will.

(They retire without the door.)

LAER. I thank you: keep the door. O thou vile king,
Give me my father!

QUEEN. Calmly, good Laertes.

KING. What is the cause, Laertes,
That thy rebellion looks so giant-like?
Let him go, Gertrude; do not fear our person:
There 's such divinity doth hedge a king,
That treason can but peep[21] to what it would,
Acts little of his will. Tell me, Laertes,
Why thou art thus incensed. Let him go, Gertrude.
Speak, man.

LAER. Where is my father?

KING. Dead.

QUEEN. But not by him.

KING. Let him demand his fill.

LAER. How came he dead? I'll not be juggled with:
To hell, allegiance! vows, to the blackest devil![22]
Conscience and grace, to the profoundest pit!
I dare damnation. To this point I stand,
That both the worlds I give to negligence,[23]
Let come what comes; only I'll be revenged
Most throughly[24] for my father.

KING. Who shall stay you?

LAER. My will, not all the world:
And for my means, I'll husband them so well,
They shall go far with little.

KING. Good Laertes,
If you desire to know the certainty
Of your dear father's death, is 't writ in your revenge,
That, swoopstake,[25] you will draw both friend and foe,
Winner and loser?

LAER. None but his enemies.

KING. Will you know them then?

LAER. To his good friends thus wide I'll ope my arms;

---

14. ***wants not buzzers,*** is not lacking for gossips.
15. ***nothing stick,*** not hesitate.
16. ***murdering-piece,*** a cannon using scattered shot.
17. ***Switzers,*** Swiss guards.
18. ***overpeering of his list,*** overflowing its boundary.
19. ***in a riotous head,*** heading a riotous force.
20. ***ratifiers and . . . word,*** i.e., antiquity and custom are the foundation of civil life, or government.
21. ***peep,*** look from a distance.
22. ***To hell . . . blackest devil.*** Laertes is referring to his sacred vow to be loyal to Claudius, an oath taken by court members as part of a king's coronation ceremony.
23. ***both the worlds . . . negligence,*** I despise both this world and the one to come.
24. ***throughly,*** thoroughly.
25. ***swoopstake,*** indiscriminately.

And like the kind life-rendering pelican,[26]
Repast them with my blood.

KING. Why, now you speak
Like a good child and a true gentleman.
That I am guiltless of your father's death,
And am most sensibly in grief for it,
It shall as level to your judgment 'pear
As day does to your eye.

DANES. *(Within)* Let her come in.

LAER. How now! what noise is that?

Re-enter OPHELIA.

O heat, dry up my brains! tears seven times salt,
Burn out the sense and virtue of mine eye!
By heaven, thy madness shall be paid with weight,
Till our scale turn the beam. O rose of May!
Dear maid, kind sister, sweet Ophelia!
O heavens! is 't possible, a young maid's wits
Should be as mortal as an old man's life?
Nature is fine in love, and where 'tis fine,
It sends some precious instance of itself
After the thing it loves.[27]

OPH. *(Sings)*
They bore him barefaced on the bier;
Hey non nonny, nonny, hey nonny;
And in his grave rain'd many a tear:—
Fare you well, my dove!

LAER. Hadst thou thy wits, and didst persuade revenge,
It could not move thus.

OPH. *(Sings)*
You must sing a-down a-down,
An you call him a-down-a.
O, how the wheel[28] becomes it! It is the false steward, that stole his master's daughter.

LAER. This nothing 's more than matter.

OPH. There 's rosemary, that 's for remembrance; pray, love, remember: and there is pansies, that 's for thoughts.

LAER. A document in madness, thoughts and remembrance fitted.

OPH. There 's fennel for you, and columbines: there 's rue for you; and here 's some for me: we may call it herb of grace o' Sundays: O, you must wear your rue with a difference. There 's a daisy: I would give you some violets,[29] but they withered all when my father died: they say he made a good end,—
(Sings) For bonny sweet Robin is all my joy.

LAER. Thought and affliction, passion, hell itself,
She turns to favor and to prettiness.

OPH. *(Sings)*
And will he not come again?
And will he not come again?
No, No, he is dead:
Go to thy death-bed:
He never will come again.

His beard was as white as snow,
All flaxen was his poll:
He is gone, he is gone,
And we cast away moan:
God ha' mercy on his soul!
And of all Christian souls, I pray God. God be wi' ye. *(Exit.)*

LAER. Do you see this, O God?

KING. Laertes, I must commune with your grief,
Or you deny me right. Go but apart,
Make choice of whom your wisest friends you will,
And they shall hear and judge 'twixt you and me:
If by direct or by collateral hand
They find us touch'd,[30] we will our kingdom give,
Our crown, our life, and all that we call ours,
To you in satisfaction; but if not,
Be you content to lend your patience to us,
And we shall jointly labor with your soul
To give it due content.

LAER. Let this be so;
His means of death, his obscure funeral—
No trophy, sword, nor hatchment o'er his bones,
No noble rite nor formal ostentation—
Cry to be heard, as 'twere from heaven to earth,
That I must call 't in question.

---

26. ***pelican,*** a reference to the belief that the pelican feeds its young with its own blood.
27. ***Nature is . . . loves.*** Ophelia's great love for her father has caused her to send her sanity after him in death.
28. ***wheel,*** refrain.
29. ***fennel . . . violets.*** Since Ophelia is distributing flowers, the season must be spring or summer. Each flower had for the Elizabethans its own meaning, and Ophelia distributes them appropriately: rosemary (remembrance) and pansies (thoughts) to her brother; fennel (flattery) and columbine (disloyalty and ingratitude) to Claudius; rue (sorrow) and daisies (infidelity) to Gertrude. Ophelia gives her violets (faithfulness) to no one.
30. ***touch'd,*** implicated.

KING. So you shall
And where the offence is let the great axe fall.
I pray you, go with me. *(Exeunt.)*

SCENE 6.

Another room in the castle.
Enter HORATIO *and a* SERVANT.

HOR. What are they that would speak with me?
SERV. Sailors, sir: they say they have letters for you.
HOR. Let them come in. *(Exit* SERVANT.*)*
I do not know from what part of the world
I should be greeted, if not from lord Hamlet.
Enter SAILORS.
FIRST SAIL. God bless you, sir.
HOR. Let him bless thee too.
FIRST SAIL. He shall, sir, an 't please him. There 's a letter for you, sir; it comes from the ambassador that was bound for England; if your name be Horatio, as I am let to know it is.

HOR. *(Reads) Horatio, when thou shalt have overlooked this, give these fellows some means*[1] *to the king: they have letters for him. Ere we were two days old at sea, a pirate of very warlike appointment gave us chase. Finding ourselves too slow of sail, we put on a compelled valor, and in the grapple I boarded them: on the instant they got clear of our ship; so I alone became their prisoner. They have dealt with me like thieves of mercy*[2]*: but they knew what they did; I am to do a good turn for them. Let the king have the letters I have sent; and repair thou to me with as much speed as thou wouldst fly death. I have words to speak in thine ear will make thee dumb; yet are they much too light for the bore*[3] *of the matter. These good fellows will bring thee where I am. Rosencrantz and Guildenstern hold their course for England: of them I have much to tell thee. Farewell.*
He that thou knowest thine, HAMLET.

Come, I will make you way for these your letters;
And do 't the speedier, that you may direct me
To him from whom you brought them.
(Exeunt.)

SCENE 7.

Another room in the castle.
Enter KING *and* LAERTES.

KING. Now must your conscience my acquittance seal,
And you must put me in your heart for friend,
Sith you have heard, and with a knowing ear,
That he which hath your noble father slain
Pursued my life.
LAER. It well appears: but tell me
Why you proceeded not against these feats,
So criminal and so capital in nature,
As by your safety, wisdom, all things else,
You mainly[1] were stirr'd up.
KING. O, for two special reasons;
Which may to you, perhaps, seem much unsinew'd,
But yet to me they are strong. The queen his mother
Lives almost by his looks; and for myself—
My virtue or my plague, be it either which—
She 's so conjunctive[2] to my life and soul,
That, as the star moves not but in his sphere,[3]
I could not but by her. The other motive,
Why to a public count I might not go,
Is the great love the general gender[4] bear him;
Who, dipping all his faults in their affection,
Would, like the spring that turneth wood to stone,[5]
Convert his gyves[6] to graces; so that my arrows,
Too slightly timber'd[7] for so loud a wind,
Would have reverted to my bow again,
And not where I had aim'd them.
LAER. And so have I a noble father lost;
A sister driven into desperate terms,

---

1. ***means,*** means of access.
2. ***thieves of mercy,*** merciful thieves.
3. ***bore,*** caliber, importance.

SCENE 7 1. ***mainly,*** greatly.
2. ***conjunctive,*** joined with.
3. ***sphere.*** According to the Ptolemaic (tōl′ə mā′ik) system of astronomy (which held that the earth was the fixed center of the universe), the planets moved within a hollow sphere.
4. ***general gender,*** common people.
5. ***the spring . . . stone,*** i.e., one heavily charged with lime.
6. ***gyves*** (jivz), fetters
7. ***slightly timber'd,*** light.

Whose worth, if praises may go back again,
Stood challenger on mount of all the age
For her perfections: but my revenge will come.

KING. Break not your sleeps for that: you must not think
That we are made of stuff so flat and dull
That we can let our beard be shook with danger
And think it pastime. You shortly shall hear more:
I loved your father, and we love ourself;
And that, I hope, will teach you to imagine—

Enter a MESSENGER.

How now! what news?

MESS. Letters, my lord, from Hamlet:
This to your majesty; this to the queen.

KING. From Hamlet! who brought them?

MESS. Sailors, my lord, they say; I saw them not:
They were given me by Claudio; he received them
Of him that brought them.

KING. Laertes, you shall hear them.
Leave us. *(Exit* MESSENGER.*)*

(Reads) High and mighty, You shall know I am set naked[8] *on your kingdom. To-morrow shall I beg leave to see your kingly eyes: when I shall, first asking your pardon thereunto, recount the occasion of my sudden and more strange return.* *Hamlet.*

What should this mean? Are all the rest come back?
Or is it some abuse, and no such thing?

LAER. Know you the hand?

KING. 'Tis Hamlet's character. "Naked!"
And in a postscript here, he says "alone."
Can you advise me?

LAER. I 'm lost in it, my lord. But let him come;
It warms the very sickness in my heart,
That I shall live and tell him to his teeth,
"Thus didst thou."

KING. If it be so, Laertes—
As how should it be so? how otherwise?—
Will you be ruled by me?

LAER. Ay, my lord;
So you will not o'errule me to a peace.

KING. To thine own peace. If he be now return'd,
As checking at[9] his voyage, and that he means
No more to undertake it, I will work him
To an exploit, now ripe in my device,
Under the which he shall not choose but fall:
And for his death no wind of blame shall breathe,
But even his mother shall uncharge the practice[10]
And call it accident.

LAER. My lord, I will be ruled;
The rather, if you could devise it so
That I might be the organ.[11]

KING. It falls right.
You have been talk'd of since your travel much,
And that in Hamlet's hearing, for a quality
Wherein, they say, you shine: your sum of parts
Did not together pluck such envy from him
As did that one, and that, in my regard,
Of the unworthiest siege.[12]

LAER. What part is that, my lord?

KING. A very riband in the cap of youth,
Yet needful too; for youth no less becomes
The light and careless livery that it wears
Than settled age his sables and his weeds,
Importing health and graveness. Two months since,
Here was a gentleman of Normandy:—
I've seen myself, and served against, the French,
And they can well on horseback: but this gallant
Had witchcraft in 't; he grew unto his seat;
And to such wondrous doing brought his horse,
As had he been incorpsed and demi-natured[13]
With the brave beast: so far he topp'd my thought,
That I, in forgery of shapes and tricks,[14]
Come short of what he did.

LAER. A Norman was 't?

KING. A Norman.

---

8. ***naked,*** unprovided (with retinue).
9. ***checking at,*** shying from.
10. ***uncharge the practice,*** acquit the method.
11. ***organ,*** agent.
12. ***siege,*** rank.
13. ***incorpsed and demi-natured,*** of one body and nearly of one nature.
14. ***in forgery . . . tricks,*** in imagining feats of horsemanship.

LAER. Upon my life, Lamond.
KING. The very same.
LAER. I know him well: he is the brooch indeed
And gem of all the nation.
KING. He made confession of you,[15]
And gave you such a masterly report
For art and exercise in your defense
And for your rapier most especial,
That he cried out, 'twould be a sight indeed,
If one could match you: the scrimers[16] of their nation,
He swore, had neither motion, guard, nor eye,
If you opposed them. Sir, this report of his
Did Hamlet so envenom with his envy
That he could nothing do but wish and beg
Your sudden coming o'er, to play with him.
Now, out of this,—
LAER. What out of this, my lord?
KING. Laertes, was your father dear to you?
Or are you like the painting of a sorrow,
A face without a heart?
LAER. Why ask you this?
KING. Not that I think you did not love your father;
But that I know love is begun by time;
And that I see, in passages of proof,[17]
Time qualifies the spark and fire of it.
There lives within the very flame of love
A kind of wick or snuff that will abate it;
And nothing is at a like goodness still;
For goodness, growing to a plurisy,[18]
Dies in his own too much: that we would do,
We should do when we would; for this "would" changes
And hath abatements and delays as many
As there are tongues, are hands, are accidents;
And then this "should" is like a spendthrift sigh,
That hurts by easing. But, to the quick o' the ulcer[19]:—
Hamlet comes back: what would you undertake,
To show yourself your father's son in deed
More than in words?
LAER. To cut his throat i' the church.
KING. No place, indeed, should murder sanctuarize[20];
Revenge should have no bounds. But, good Laertes,
Will you do this, keep close within your chamber.
Hamlet return'd shall know you are come home:
We'll put on those shall praise your excellence
And set a double varnish on the fame
The Frenchman gave you, bring you in fine together
And wager on your heads: he, being remiss,
Most generous and free from all contriving,
Will not peruse the foils; so that, with ease,
Or with a little shuffling, you may choose
A sword unbated,[21] and in a pass of practice[22]
Requite him for your father.
LAER. I will do 't:
And, for that purpose, I'll anoint my sword.
I bought an unction of a mountebank,
So mortal that, but dip a knife in it,
Where it draws blood no cataplasm[23] so rare,
Collected from all simples[24] that have virtue
Under the moon, can save the thing from death
That is but scratched withal: I'll touch my point
With this contagion, that, if I gall[25] him slightly,
It may be death.
KING. Let 's further think of this;
Weigh what convenience both of time and means
May fit us to our shape[26]: if this should fail,
And that our drift[27] look through our bad performance,
'Twere better not assay'd: therefore this project

---

15. ***made confession of you,*** said he knew you.
16. ***scrimers*** (skrim′érz), fencers.
17. ***passages of proof,*** proved instances.
18. ***plurisy,*** excess.
19. ***quick o' the ulcer,*** heart of the difficulty.
20. ***sanctuarize,*** protect from punishment, an allusion to the fact that religious places were sacred and protected.
21. ***unbated,*** not blunted.
22. ***pass of practice,*** treacherous thrust.
23. ***cataplasm,*** plaster or poultice.
24. ***simples,*** herbs.
25. ***gall,*** graze, wound.
26. ***shape,*** part we propose to act.
27. ***drift,*** intention.

Should have a back or second, that might hold,
If this should blast in proof. Soft! let me see:
We'll make a solemn wager on your cunnings:
I ha 't:
When in your motion you are hot and dry—
As make your bouts more violent to that end—
And that he calls for drink, I'll have prepared him
A chalice for the nonce,[28] whereon but sipping,
If he by chance escape your venom'd stuck,
Our purpose may hold there.
Enter QUEEN.
How now, sweet queen!

QUEEN. One woe doth tread upon another's heel,
So fast they follow: your sister 's drown'd, Laertes.

LAER. Drown'd! O, where?

QUEEN. There is a willow grows aslant a brook,
That shows his hoar leaves in the glassy stream;
There with fantastic garlands did she make
Of crow-flowers, nettles, daisies, and long purples:
There, on the pendent boughs her coronet weeds
Clambering to hang, an envious sliver[29] broke;
When down her weedy trophies and herself
Fell in the weeping brook. Her clothes spread wide;
And, mermaid-like, awhile they bore her up:
Which time she chanted snatches of old tunes;
As one incapable[30] of her own distress,
Or like a creature native and indued
Unto that element: but long it could not be
Till that her garments, heavy with their drink,
Pull'd the poor wretch from her melodious lay
To muddy death.

LAER. Alas then, she is drown'd?

QUEEN. Drown'd, drown'd.

LAER. Too much of water hast thou, poor Ophelia,
And therefore I forbid my tears: but yet
It is our trick[31]; nature her custom holds,
Let shame say what it will: when these are gone,
The woman will be out. Adieu, my lord:
I have a speech of fire, that fain would blaze,
But that this folly douts[32] it. *(Exit.)*

KING. Let's follow, Gertrude:
How much I had to do to calm his rage!
Now fear I this will give it start again;
Therefore let 's follow. *(Exeunt.)*

---

28. ***for the nonce,*** for such an occasion.
29. ***sliver,*** branch.
30. ***incapable,*** unaware.
31. ***trick,*** way.
32. ***douts,*** extinguishes.

Discussion

Act Four, Scenes 1–3

1. What actions does Claudius take to reduce the effect of Polonius' murder?

2. Describe Hamlet's behavior when Rosencrantz and Guildenstern bring him before the King after Polonius' murder.

3. Why does Claudius now desire Hamlet's death?

Scene 4

1. What does the soldier questioned by Hamlet suggest about the expedition of Fortinbras?

2. What effect does this have upon Hamlet's thinking?

Scene 5

1. We must assume that some time has passed between Scene 4 and this scene. **(a)** What has caused Ophelia to lose her mind? **(b)** What words and actions demonstrate she is mad? **(c)** Does her madness resemble Hamlet's, or is it different? Explain.

2. Laertes has returned to Denmark after receiving news of his father's death. **(a)** How has he been received by the Danish people? **(b)** What does he demand of Claudius? **(c)** How does Gertrude behave when Claudius is threatened? **(d)** What does this tell us about her? **(e)** Describe or explain Laertes' reaction to Ophelia's madness. **(f)** How does Claudius placate Laertes? **(g)** Does this appear to be a wise move? Explain.

Scene 6

(a) What news do the sailors bring Horatio? **(b)** Does Hamlet appear to have changed at all? Explain.

Scene 7

1. (a) What two reasons does Claudius give Laertes for not taking legal action against Hamlet for the murder of Polonius? **(b)** What do you think of his reasons? **(c)** When Claudius receives the news that Hamlet is not dead, what plot does he hatch? **(d)** What does Laertes add to it? **(e)** Would Hamlet have acted like either man? Explain.

2. (a) What dramatic purpose is served by having the news of Ophelia's drowning come after Claudius and Laertes have hatched their plot against Hamlet? **(b)** Do you think Ophelia's death was a deliberate suicide? Explain.

Act Four in Review

The fourth act of an Elizabethan tragedy is usually short, consisting of many brief scenes, as the different threads are tied together in preparation for the last act. We can assume that the last act of *Hamlet* will result in a confrontation between Hamlet and Claudius. How does Act Four prepare for this?

Act Five

SCENE 1.

A churchyard.
Enter two CLOWNS,[1] *with spades, &c.*

FIRST CLO. Is she to be buried in Christian burial that willfully seeks her own salvation?[2]

SEC. CLO. I tell thee she is; and therefore make her grave straight:[3] the crowner[4] hath sat on her, and finds it Christian burial.

FIRST CLO. How can that be, unless she drowned herself in her own defense?

SEC. CLO. Why, 'tis found so.

FIRST CLO. It must be *se offendendo*[5]; it cannot be else. For here lies the point: if I drown myself wittingly, it argues an act: and an act hath three branches; it is, to act, to do, and to perform: argal,[6] she drowned herself wittingly.

SEC. CLO. Nay, but hear you, goodman delver,—

FIRST CLO. Give me leave. Here lies the water; good: here stands the man; good: if the man go to this water, and drown himself, it is, will he, nill he, he goes,—mark you that; but if the water come to him and drown him, he drowns not himself: argal, he that is not guilty of his own death shortens not his own life.

SEC. CLO. But is this law?

FIRST CLO. Ay, marry, is 't; crowner's quest[7] law.

SEC. CLO. Will you ha' the truth on 't? If this had not been a gentlewoman, she should have been buried out o' Christian burial.

FIRST CLO. Why, there thou say'st: and the more pity that great folk should have countenance[8] in this world to drown or hang themselves, more than their even[9] Christian. Come, my spade. There is no ancient gentlemen but gardeners, ditchers, and grave-makers: they hold up Adam's profession.

SEC. CLO. Was he a gentleman?

FIRST CLO. A' was the first that ever bore arms.

---

1. ***Clowns.*** The word *clown* was used to denote peasants as well as humorous characters; here applied to the rustic type of clown. In Shakespeare's plays, very often the low comedy scenes re-echo the theme (or themes) of the play.
2. ***willfully . . . salvation.*** The First Clown continually mistakes his words. What he means is "willingly seeks her own damnation."
3. ***straight,*** straightway.
4. ***crowner,*** coroner.
5. ***se offendendo,*** for *se defendendo,* a common legal phrase meaning "in self-defense."
6. ***argal,*** corruption of *ergo,* Latin for "therefore."
7. ***crowner's quest,*** coroner's inquest.
8. ***countenance,*** privilege.
9. ***even,*** fellow.

SEC. CLO. Why, he had none.

FIRST CLO. What, art a heathen? How dost thou understand the Scripture? The Scripture says "Adam digged": could he dig without arms? I'll put another question to thee: if thou answerest me not to the purpose, confess thyself[10]—

SEC. CLO. Go to.

FIRST CLO. What is he that builds stronger than either the mason, the shipwright, or the carpenter?

SEC. CLO. The gallows-maker: for that frame outlives a thousand tenants.

FIRST CLO. I like thy wit well, in good faith: the gallows does well; but how does it well? it does well to those that do ill: now thou dost ill to say the gallows is built stronger than the church: argal, the gallows may do well to thee. To 't again, come.

SEC. CLO. 'Who builds stronger than a mason, a shipwright, or a carpenter?'

FIRST CLO. Ay, tell me that, and unyoke.[11]

SEC. CLO. Marry, now I can tell.

FIRST CLO. To 't.

SEC. CLO. Mass,[12] I cannot tell.

Enter HAMLET *and* HORATIO, *at a distance.*

FIRST CLO. Cudgel thy brains no more about it, for your dull ass will not mend his pace with beating; and, when you are asked this question next, say "a grave-maker": the houses that he makes last till doomsday. Go, get thee in, and fetch me a stoup of liquor. *(Exit* SEC. CLOWN.*)*

(He digs, and sings.)

In youth,[13] *when I did love, did love,*
Methought it was very sweet,
To contract, O, the time, for, ah, my behove,
O, methought, there was nothing meet.

HAM. Has this fellow no feeling of his business, that he sings at grave-making?

HOR. Custom hath made it in him a property of easiness.[14]

HAM. 'Tis e'en so: the hand of little employment hath the daintier sense.

FIRST CLO. *(Sings)*

But age, with his stealing steps,
Hath claw'd me in his clutch,
And hath shipped me into the land,
As if I had never been such.

(Throws up a skull.)

HAM. That skull had a tongue in it, and could sing once: how the knave jowls it to the ground, as if it were Cain's jaw-bone,[15] that did the first murder! It might be the pate of a politician, which this ass now o'er-reaches; one that would circumvent God, might it not?

HOR. It might, my lord.

HAM. Or of a courtier; which could say "Good morrow, sweet lord! How dost thou, good lord?" This might be my lord such-a-one, that praised my lord such-a-one's horse, when he meant to beg it; might it not?

HOR. Ay, my lord.

HAM. Why, e'en so: and now my Lady Worm's; chapless,[16] and knocked about the mazzard[17] with a sexton's spade: here 's fine revolution, an we had the trick to see 't. Did these bones cost no more the breeding, but to play at loggats[18] with 'em? mine ache to think on 't.

FIRST CLO. *(Sings)*

A pick-axe, and a spade, a spade,
For and a shrouding sheet:
O, a pit of clay for to be made
For such a guest is meet.

(Throws up another skull.)

HAM. There 's another: why may not that be the skull of a lawyer? Where be his quiddities now, his quillets,[19] his cases, his tenures, and his tricks? why does he suffer this rude knave now to knock him about the sconce[20] with a dirty shovel, and will not tell him of his action of battery? Hum! This fellow might be in 's time a great buyer of land, with his statutes, his recognizances, his fines, his double vouchers, his recoveries: is this the fine[21] of his fines, and

---

10. ***confess thyself,*** " . . . and be hanged" completes the proverb.
11. ***unyoke,*** unharness, your work's done.
12. ***Mass,*** by the Mass.
13. ***In youth.*** This and the two following stanzas, with nonsensical variations, are from *Tottel's Miscellany,* the first of many collections of Elizabethan lyrics.
14. ***Custom . . . easiness,*** it is a matter of habit with him now.
15. ***jowls . . . Cain's jaw-bone,*** throws it down as though it were the jaw-bone with which Cain killed his brother Abel. Hamlet is also punning on *jowl* meaning "jaw."
16. ***chapless,*** having no lower jaw.
17. ***mazzard,*** head.
18. ***loggats,*** a game in which sticks are thrown as near a fixed stake as possible.
19. ***quiddities . . . quillets,*** logical subtleties and quibbles.
20. ***sconce,*** head.
21. ***fine,*** end. Notice that Hamlet plays with four different meanings of *fine* in this sentence.

the recovery of his recoveries, to have his fine pate full of fine dirt? will his vouchers vouch him no more of his purchases, and double ones too, than the length and breadth of a pair of indentures? The very conveyances of his lands will hardly lie in this box; and must the inheritor himself have no more, ha?

HOR. Not a jot more, my lord.

HAM. Is not parchment made of sheepskins?

HOR. Ay, my lord, and of calf-skins too.

HAM. They are sheep and calves which seek out assurance in that. I will speak to this fellow. Whose grave 's this, sirrah?

FIRST CLO. Mine, sir.
(Sings) O, a pit of clay for to be made
For such a guest is meet.

HAM. I think it be thine, indeed; for thou liest in 't.

FIRST CLO. You lie out on 't, sir, and therefore it is not yours: for my part, I do not lie in 't, and yet it is mine.

HAM. Thou dost lie in 't, to be in 't and say it is thine: 'tis for the dead, not for the quick; therefore thou liest.

FIRST CLO. 'Tis a quick lie, sir; 'twill away again, from me to you.

HAM. What man dost thou dig it for?

FIRST CLO. For no man, sir.

HAM. What woman, then?

FIRST CLO. For none, neither.

HAM. Who is to be buried in 't?

FIRST CLO. One that was a woman, sir: but, rest her soul, she 's dead.

HAM. How absolute[22] the knave is! we must speak by the card,[23] or equivocation will undo us. By the Lord, Horatio, these three years I have taken note of it; the age is grown so picked[24] that the toe of the peasant comes so near the heel of the courtier, he galls his kibe.[25] How long hast thou been a grave-maker?

FIRST CLO. Of all the days i' the year, I came to 't that day that our last king Hamlet overcame Fortinbras.

HAM. How long is that since?

FIRST CLO. Cannot you tell that? every fool can tell that: it was the very day that young Hamlet was born; he that is mad, and sent into England.

HAM. Ay, marry, why was he sent into England?

FIRST CLO. Why, because he was mad: he shall recover his wits there; of, if he do not, it 's no great matter there.

HAM. Why?

FIRST CLO. 'Twill not be seen in him there; there the men are as mad as he.

HAM. How came he mad?

FIRST CLO. Very strangely, they say.

HAM. How strangely?

FIRST CLO. Faith, e'en with losing his wits.

HAM. Upon what ground?

FIRST CLO. Why, here in Denmark: I have been sexton here, man and boy, thirty years.

HAM. How long will a man lie i' the earth ere he rot?

FIRST CLO. I' faith, if he be not rotten before he die—as we have many pocky[26] corses now-a-days, that will scarce hold the laying in—he will last you some eight year or nine year: a tanner will last you nine year.

HAM. Why he more than another?

FIRST CLO. Why, sir, his hide is so tanned with his trade, that he will keep out water a great while; and your water is a sore decayer of your dead body. Here's a skull now hath lain you i' th' earth three and twenty years.

HAM. Whose was it?

FIRST CLO. A mad fellow's it was: whose do you think it was?

HAM. Nay, I know not.

FIRST CLO. A pestilence on him for a mad rogue! a' poured a flagon of Rhenish on my head once. This same skull, sir, was Yorick's skull, the king's jester.

HAM. This?

FIRST CLO. E'en that.

HAM. Let me see. *(Takes the skull.)* Alas, poor Yorick! I knew him, Horatio: a fellow of infinite jest, of most excellent fancy: he hath borne me on his back a thousand times; and now, how abhorred in my imagination it is! my gorge rises at it. Here hung those lips that I have kissed I know not how oft. Where be your gibes now? your gambols? your songs? your flashes of merriment, that were wont to set the table on a roar? Not one now, to mock your own grinning? quite chap-fallen? Now get you

---

22. ***absolute,*** positive.
23. ***by the card,*** to the point.
24. ***picked,*** refined, fastidious.
25. ***galls his kibe,*** rubs a blister on his heel.
26. ***pocky,*** diseased.

Richard Monette

to my lady's chamber, and tell her, let her paint an inch thick, to this favor she must come; make her laugh at that. Prithee, Horatio, tell me one thing.

HOR. What 's that, my lord?

HAM. Dost thou think Alexander[27] looked o' this fashion i' the earth?

HOR. E'en so.

HAM. And smelt so? pah!

(Puts down the skull.)

HOR. E'en so, my lord.

HAM. To what base uses we may return, Horatio! Why may not imagination trace the noble dust of Alexander, till he find it stopping a bung-hole?

HOR. 'Twere to consider too curiously,[28] to consider so.

HAM. No, faith, not a jot; but to follow him thither with modesty enough, and likelihood to lead it: as thus: Alexander died, Alexander was buried, Alexander returneth into dust; the dust is earth; of earth we make loam[29]; and why of that loam, whereto he was converted, might they not stop a beer-barrel?

Imperious Caesar, dead and turn'd to clay,
Might stop a hole to keep the wind away:
O, that that earth, which kept the world in awe,
Should patch a wall to expel the winter's flaw![30]
But soft! but soft! aside: here comes the king,

Enter PRIESTS, *&c. in procession; the Corpse of* OPHELIA, LAERTES *and* MOURNERS, *following;* KING, QUEEN, *their trains, &c.*

The queen, the courtiers: who is this they follow?
And with such maimed rites? This doth betoken
The corse they follow did with desperate hand
Fordo it[31] own life: 'twas of some estate.
Couch[32] we awhile, and mark.

(Retiring with HORATIO.*)*

LAER. What ceremony else?

HAM. That is Laertes,
A very noble youth: mark.

---

27. ***Alexander,*** Alexander the Great, King of Macedonia from 336 to 323 B.C. He conquered the Greek city-states and the whole Persian empire, from the coasts of Asia Minor and Egypt to India.
28. ***curiously,*** ingeniously.
29. ***loam,*** clay paste for brickmaking.
30. ***flaw,*** gust of wind.
31. ***Fordo it,*** destroy it.
32. ***Couch,*** hide.

LAER. What ceremony else?
FIRST PRIEST. Her obsequies have been as far enlarged[33]
As we have warranty: her death was doubtful;
And, but that great command o'ersways the order,[34]
She should in ground unsanctified have lodged
Till the last trumpet; for charitable prayers,
Shards, flints and pebbles should be thrown on her:
Yet here she is allow'd her virgin crants,[35]
Her maiden strewments and the bringing home
Of bell and burial.
LAER. Must there no more be done?
FIRST PRIEST. No more be done:
We should profane the service of the dead
To sing a requiem and such rest to her
As to peace-parted souls.
LAER. Lay her i' the earth:
And from her fair and unpolluted flesh
May violets spring! I tell thee, churlish priest,
A ministering angel shall my sister be,
When thou liest howling.[36]
HAM. What, the fair Ophelia!
QUEEN. Sweets to the sweet: farewell! *(Scattering flowers.)*
I hoped thou shouldst have been my Hamlet's wife;
I thought thy bride-bed to have deck'd, sweet maid,
And not have strew'd thy grave.
LAER. O, treble woe
Fall ten times treble on that cursed head,
Whose wicked deed thy most ingenious sense[37]
Deprived thee of! Hold off the earth awhile,
Till I have caught her once more in mine arms: *(Leaps into the grave.)*
Now pile your dust upon the quick and dead,
Till of this flat a mountain you have made,
To o'ertop old Pelion,[38] or the skyish head
Of blue Olympus.
HAM. *(Advancing)* What is he whose grief
Bears such an emphasis? whose phrase of sorrow
Conjures the wandering stars, and makes them stand
Like wonder-wounded hearers? This is I,
Hamlet the Dane. *(Leaps into the grave.)*
LAER. The devil take thy soul! *(Grappling with him.)*
HAM. Thou pray'st not well.
I prithee, take thy fingers from my throat;
For, though I am not splenitive[39] and rash,
Yet have I in me something dangerous,
Which let thy wisenes fear: hold off thy hand.
KING. Pluck them asunder.
QUEEN. Hamlet, Hamlet!
ALL. Gentlemen,—
HOR. Good my lord, be quiet.
(The Attendants part them, and they come out of the grave.)
HAM. Why, I will fight with him upon this theme
Until my eyelids will no longer wag.
QUEEN. O my son, what theme?
HAM. I loved Ophelia: forty thousand brothers
Could not, with all their quantity of love,
Make up my sum. What wilt thou do for her?
KING. O, he is mad, Laertes.
QUEEN. For love of God, forbear him.[40]
HAM. 'Swounds, show me what thou 'lt do:
Woo 't weep? woo 't fight? woo 't fast? woo 't tear thyself?
Woo 't drink up eisel?[41] eat a crocodile?
I'll do 't. Dost thou come here to whine?
To outface me with leaping in her grave?
Be buried quick with her, and so will I:
And, if thou prate of mountains, let them throw
Millions of acres on us, till our ground,
Singeing his pate against the burning zone,
Make Ossa like a wart! Nay, an thou 'lt mouth,
I'll rant as well as thou.

---

33. ***enlarged,*** extended, referring to the fact that suicides are not given full burial rites.
34. ***death . . . order.*** The priest reluctantly accepts the king's claim that Ophelia died by accident and not by suicide.
35. ***crants,*** garlands customarily hung upon the bier of an unmarried woman.
36. ***howling,*** i.e., in hell.
37. ***thy most ingenious sense,*** thy reason.
38. ***Pelion.*** The giants in Greek mythology piled Mount Pelion on Mount Ossa in an effort to reach Olympus. This exaggerated statement is Laertes' way of expressing his utter grief at Ophelia's death.
39. ***splenitive,*** quick-tempered.
40. ***forbear him,*** let him alone.
41. ***eisel,*** vinegar.

QUEEN. This is mere madness:
And thus awhile the fit will work on him;
Anon, as patient as the female dove,
When that her golden couplets[42] are disclosed,
His silence will sit drooping.

HAM. Hear you, sir;
What is the reason that you use me thus?
I loved you ever: but it is no matter;
Let Hercules himself do what he may,
The cat will mew and dog will have his day.
(Exit.)

KING. I pray you, good Horatio, wait upon him.
(Exit HORATIO.*)*
(To Laertes) Strengthen your patience in our last night's speech;
We'll put the matter to the present push.
Good Gertrude, set some watch over your son.
This grave shall have a living monument:
An hour of quiet shortly shall we see;
Till then, in patience our proceeding be.
(Exeunt.)

SCENE 2.

A hall in the castle.
Enter HAMLET *and* HORATIO.

HAM. So much for this, sir: now shall you see the other;
You do remember all the circumstance?

HOR. Remember it, my lord!

HAM. Sir, in my heart there was a kind of fighting,
That would not let me sleep: methought I lay
Worse than the mutines in the bilboes.[1] Rashly,
And praised be rashness for it, let us know,
Our indiscretion sometimes serves us well,
When our deep plots do pall[2]: and that should teach us
There 's a divinity that shapes our ends,
Rough-hew them how we will,—

HOR. That is most certain.

HAM. Up from my cabin,
My sea-gown scarf'd about me, in the dark
Groped I to find out them; had my desire,
Finger'd[3] their packet, and in fine withdrew
To mine own room again; making so bold,
My fears forgetting manners, to unseal
Their grand commission; where I found, Horatio,—
O royal knavery!—an exact command,
Larded with many several sorts of reasons
Importing Denmark's health and England's too,
With, ho! such bugs and goblins in my life,[4]
That, on the supervise, no leisure bated,[5]
No, not to stay the grinding of the axe,
My head should be struck off.

HOR. Is 't possible?

HAM. Here 's the commission: read it at more leisure.
But wilt thou hear me how I did proceed?

HOR. I beseech you.

HAM. Being thus be-netted round with villainies,—
Ere I could make a prologue to my brains,
They had begun the play[6]—I sat me down,
Devised a new commission, wrote it fair[7]:
I once did hold it, as our statists[8] do,
A baseness to write fair and labor'd much
How to forget that learning, but, sir, now
It did me yeoman's[9] service: wilt thou know
The effect of what I wrote?

HOR. Ay, good my lord.

HAM. An earnest conjuration from the king,
As England was his faithful tributary,
As love between them like the palm might flourish,
As peace should still her wheaten garland wear
And stand a comma[10] 'tween their amities,
And many such-like "As"es[11] of great charge,
That, on the view and knowing of these contents,

---

42. ***golden couplets.*** The dove's two fledglings are covered with golden down.

SCENE 2 1. ***mutines in the bilboes,*** mutineers in shackles.
2. ***pall,*** fail.
3. ***Finger'd,*** pilfered.
4. ***such . . . life,*** such exaggerated dangers in my continued existence.
5. ***on the supervise . . . bated,*** on perusing it no delay was allowable.
6. ***Ere . . . play,*** before I could begin to think, my mind had made its decision.
7. ***fair,*** in the hand of a professional clerk.
8. ***statists,*** statesmen.
9. ***yeoman's,*** faithful.
10. ***comma,*** i.e., connector.
11. ***"As"es,*** probably the "whereases" of a formal document.

Without debatement further, more or less,
He should the bearers put to sudden death,
Not shriving-time[12] allow'd.

HOR. How was this seal'd?

HAM. Why, even in that was heaven ordinant.[13]
I had my father's signet in my purse,
Which was the model of that Danish seal;
Folded the writ up in form of the other,
Subscribed it, gave 't the impression, placed it safely,
The changeling[14] never known. Now, the next day
Was our sea-fight; and what to this was sequent
Thou know'st already.

HOR. So Guildenstern and Rosencrantz go to 't.

HAM. Why, man, they did make love to this employment;
They are not near my conscience; their defeat
Does by their own insinuation[15] grow:
'Tis dangerous when the baser nature comes
Between the pass and fell incensed[16] points
Of mighty opposites.

HOR. Why, what a king is this!

HAM. Does it not, thinks 't thee, stand me now upon[17]—
He that hath kill'd my king and whored my mother,
Popp'd in between the election[18] and my hopes,
Thrown out his angle[19] for my proper life,
And with such cozenage[20]—is 't not perfect conscience,
To quit him with this arm? and is 't not to be damn'd,
To let this canker of our nature come
In further evil?

HOR. It must be shortly known to him from England
What is the issue of the business there.

HAM. It will be short: the interim is mine;
And a man's life 's no more than to say "One."
But I am very sorry, good Horatio,
That to Laertes I forgot myself;
For, by the image of my cause, I see
The portraiture of his: I'll court his favors:
But, sure, the bravery[21] of his grief did put me
Into a towering passion.

HOR. Peace! who comes here?

Enter OSRIC.

OSR. Your lordship is right welcome back to Denmark.

HAM. I humbly thank you, sir. Dost know this water-fly?[22]

HOR. No, my good lord.

HAM. Thy state is the more gracious; for 'tis a vice to know him. He hath much land, and fertile: let a beast be lord of beasts, and his crib shall stand at the king's mess[23]: 'tis a chough[24]; but, as I say, spacious in the possession of dirt.

OSR. Sweet lord, if your lordship were at leisure, I should impart a thing to you from his majesty.

HAM. I will receive it, sir, with all diligence of spirit. Put your bonnet to his right use; 'tis for the head.

OSR. I thank your lordship, it is very hot.

HAM. No, believe me, 'tis very cold; the wind is northerly.

OSR. It is indifferent[25] cold, my lord, indeed.

HAM. But yet methinks it is very sultry and hot for my complexion.

OSR. Exceedingly, my lord; it is very sultry,—as 'twere,—I cannot tell how. But, my lord, his majesty bade me signify to you that he has laid a great wager on your head: sir, this is the matter,—

HAM. I beseech you, remember—

(HAMLET *moves him to put on his hat.)*

OSR. Nay, good my lord; for mine ease, in good faith. Sir, here is newly come to court Laertes; believe me, an absolute gentleman, full of most excellent differences,[26] of very soft society

---

12. ***shriving-time,*** time for absolution. Hamlet is doing what he said he wanted to do to Claudius: not giving Rosencrantz and Guildenstern time to confess and repent their sins.
13. ***ordinant,*** direction.
14. ***changeling,*** exchange.
15. ***insinuation,*** inference.
16. ***pass and fell incensed,*** thrust and fiercely angered.
17. ***Does it . . . upon,*** it is not now my obligation.
18. ***election,*** a reference to the fact that the Danish throne was filled by election.
19. ***angle,*** fishhook.
20. ***cozenage,*** trickery.
21. ***bravery,*** showiness.
22. ***water-fly,*** showy idler.
23. ***let a beast . . . mess,*** any fool with enough money can get admired at court.
24. ***chough,*** chattering jackdaw.
25. ***indifferent,*** somewhat.
26. ***differences,*** distinguishing qualities.

and great showing: indeed, to speak feelingly of him, he is the card or calendar of gentry,[27] for you shall find in him the continent of what part a gentleman would see.[28]

HAM. Sir, his definement[29] suffers no perdition in you; though, I know, to divide him inventorially would dizzy the arithmetic of memory, and yet but yaw neither, in respect of his quick sail.[30] But, in the verity of extolment, I take him to be a soul of great article[31]; and his infusion[32] of such dearth and rareness, as, to make true diction[33] of him, his semblable[34] is his mirror; and who else would trace[3] him, his umbrage,[36] nothing more.

OSR. Your lordship speaks most infallibly of him.

HAM. The concernancy,[37] sir? why do we wrap the gentleman in our more rawer breath?[38]

OSR. Sir?

HOR. Is 't not possible to understand in another tongue? You will do 't,[39] sir, really.

HAM. What imports the nomination of this gentleman?

OSR. Of Laertes?

HOR. His purse is empty already; all 's golden words are spent.

HAM. Of him, sir.

OSR. I know you are not ignorant—

HAM. I would you did, sir; yet, in faith, if you did, it would not much approve me. Well, sir?

OSR. You are not ignorant of what excellence Laertes is—

HAM. I dare not confess that, lest I should compare with him in excellence; but, to know a man well, were to know himself.

OSR. I mean, sir, for his weapon; but in the imputation laid on him by them, in his meed[40] he 's unfellowed.[41]

HAM. What 's his weapon?

OSR. Rapier and dagger.

HAM. That 's two of his weapons: but, well.

OSR. The king, sir, hath wagered with him six Barbary horses; against the which he has imponed,[42] as I take it, six French rapiers and poniards, with their assigns,[43] as girdle, hangers, and so: three of the carriages, in faith, are very dear to fancy,[44] very responsive[45] to the hilts, most delicate carriages, and of very liberal conceit.[46]

HAM. What call you the carriages?

HOR. I knew you must be edified by the margent[47] ere you had done.

OSR. The carriages, sir, are the hangers.

HAM. The phrase would be more german[48] to the matter, if we could carry cannon by our sides: I would it might be hangers till then. But, on: six Barbary horses against six French swords, their assigns, and three liberal-conceited carriages; that 's the French bet against the Danish. Why is this "imponed," as you call it?

OSR. The king, sir, hath laid, that in a dozen passes between yourself and him, he shall not exceed you three hits: he hath laid on twelve for nine; and it would come to immediate trial, if your lordship would vouchsafe the answer.

HAM. How if I answer "no"?

OSR. I mean, my lord, the opposition of your person in trial.

HAM. Sir, I will walk here in the hall: if it please his majesty, 't is the breathing time[49] of day with me; let the foils be brought, the gentleman willing, and the king hold his purpose, I will win for him an I can; if not, I will gain nothing but my shame and the odd hits.

OSR. Shall I re-deliver you e'en so?

HAM. To this effect, sir; after what flourish your nature will.

OSR. I commend my duty to your lordship.

---

27. ***card or calendar of gentry,*** a veritable handbook of good breeding.
28. ***the continent . . . see,*** to possess those qualities one gentleman expects of another.
29. ***definement,*** definition.
30. ***to divide . . . sail,*** one would get dizzy before coming to the end of a list of all his qualities.
31. ***great article,*** many excellencies.
32. ***infusion,*** character.
33. ***diction,*** description.
34. ***semblable,*** only true image.
35. ***trace,*** emulate.
36. ***umbrage,*** shadow.
37. ***concernancy,*** import, meaning.
38. ***why . . . breath,*** why do we speak of him in words, which cannot match his fineness.
39. ***do't,*** out do Osric by using language even more extravagant than he uses.
40. ***meed,*** merit.
41. ***unfellowed,*** unmatched.
42. ***imponed,*** wagered.
43. ***assigns,*** accessories. *Girdle* (sword belt) and *hangers* (straps) were regarded as accessories of the rapier.
44. ***dear to fancy,*** fancifully made.
45. ***responsive,*** close in design.
46. ***liberal conceit,*** elaborate design.
47. ***margent,*** marginal comment.
48. ***german,*** germane, appropriate.
49. ***breathing time,*** time for exercise.

HAM. Yours, yours. *(Exit* OSRIC.*)* He does well to commend it himself; there are no tongues else for 's turn. *Enter a* LORD.

LORD. My lord, his majesty commended him to you by young Osric, who brings back to him, that you attend him in the hall: he sends to know if your pleasure hold to play with Laertes, or that you will take longer time.

HAM. I am constant to my purposes; they follow the king's pleasure: if his fitness speaks, mine is ready; now or whensoever, provided I be so able as now.

LORD. The king and queen and all are coming down.

HAM. In happy time.

LORD. The queen desires you to use some gentle entertainment[50] to Laertes before you fall to play.

HAM. She well instructs me. *(Exit* LORD.*)*

HOR. You will lose this wager, my lord.

HAM. I do not think so; since he went into France, I have been in continual practice; I shall win at the odds. But thou wouldst not think how ill all 's here about my heart: but it is no matter.

HOR. Nay, good my lord,—

HAM. It is but foolery; but it is such a kind of gain-giving,[51] as would perhaps trouble a woman.

HOR. If your mind dislike any thing, obey it: I will forestall their repair hither, and say you are not fit.

HAM. Not a whit, we defy augury: there 's a special providence in the fall of a sparrow. If it be now, 'tis not to come; if it be not to come, it will be now; if it be not now, yet it will come: the readiness is all: since no man has aught of what he leaves, what is 't to leave betimes? Let be.

Enter KING, QUEEN, LAERTES, LORDS, OSRIC, *and* ATTENDANTS *with foils, &c.*

KING. Come, Hamlet, come, and take this hand from me.

(The King puts Laertes' hand into Hamlet's.)

HAM. Give me your pardon, sir: I've done you wrong;
But pardon 't, as you are a gentleman.
This presence[52] knows,
And you must needs have heard, how I am punish'd
With sore distraction. What I have done,
That might your nature, honor and exception[53]
Roughly awake, I here proclaim was madness.
Was 't Hamlet wrong'd Laertes? Never Hamlet:
If Hamlet from himself be ta'en away,
And when he 's not himself does wrong Laertes,
Then Hamlet does it not, Hamlet denies it.
Who does it, then? His madness: if 't be so,
Hamlet is of the faction that is wrong'd;
His madness is poor Hamlet's enemy.
Sir, in this audience,
Let my disclaiming from a purposed evil
Free me so far in your most generous thoughts,
That I have shot mine arrow o'er the house,
And hurt my brother.

LAER. I am satisfied in nature,[54]
Whose motive, in this case, should stir me most
To my revenge: but in my terms of honor
I stand aloof; and will no reconcilement,
Till by some elder masters, of known honor,
I have a voice and precedent of peace,
To keep my name ungored.[55] But till that time,
I do receive your offer'd love like love,
And will not wrong it.

HAM. I embrace it freely;
And will this brother's wager frankly play.
Give us the foils. Come on.

LAER. Come, one for me.

HAM. I'll be your foil,[56] Laertes: in mine ignorance
Your skill shall, like a star i' the darkest night,
Stick fiery off indeed.

LAER. You mock me, sir.

HAM. No, by this hand.

KING. Give them the foils, young Osric. Cousin Hamlet,
You know the wager?

---

50. ***use some gentle entertainment,*** greet with courtesy.
51. ***gain-giving,*** misgiving.
52. ***presence,*** royal assembly.
53. ***exception,*** disapproval.
54. ***in nature,*** as far as my personal feelings are concerned.
55. ***ungored,*** unmarred.
56. ***foil,*** rapier; also a background which sets something off.

HAM. Very well, my lord;
Your grace hath laid the odds o' the weaker side.
KING. I do not fear it; I have seen you both:
But since he is better'd, we have therefore odds.
LAER. This is too heavy, let me see another.
HAM. This likes me well. These foils have all a length?[57] *(They prepare to play.)*
OSR. Ay, my good lord.
KING. Set me the stoups of wine upon that table.
If Hamlet give the first or second hit,
Or quit[58] in answer of the third exchange,
Let all the battlements their ordnance fire;
The king shall drink to Hamlet's better breath;
And in the cup an union[59] shall he throw,
Richer than that which four successive kings
In Denmark's crown have worn. Give me the cups;
And let the kettle[60] to the trumpet speak,
The trumpet to the cannoneer without,
The cannons to the heavens, the heavens to earth,
"Now the king drinks to Hamlet." Come, begin:
And you, the judges, bear a wary eye.
HAM. Come on, sir.
LAER. Come, my lord. *(They play.)*
HAM. One.
LAER. No.
HAM. Judgment.
OSR. A hit, a very palpable hit.
LAER. Well; again.
KING. Stay; give me drink. Hamlet, this pearl[61] is thine;
Here 's to thy health.
(Trumpets sound, and cannon shot off within.)
Give him the cup.
HAM. I'll play this bout first; set it by awhile.
Come. *(They play.)* Another hit; what say you?
LAER. A touch, a touch, I do confess 't.
KING. Our son shall win.
QUEEN. He 's fat,[62] and scant of breath.
Here, Hamlet, take my napkin, rub thy brows:
The queen carouses to thy fortune, Hamlet.
HAM. Good madam!
KING. Gertrude, do not drink.
QUEEN. I will, my lord; I pray you, pardon me.
KING. *(Aside)* It is the poison'd cup: it is too late.
HAM. I dare not drink yet, madam; by and by.
QUEEN. Come, let me wipe thy face.
LAER. My lord, I'll hit him now.
KING. I do not think 't.
LAER. *(Aside)* And yet 'tis almost 'gainst my conscience.[63]
HAM. Come, for the third, Laertes: you but dally;
I pray you, pass with your best violence;
I am afeard you make a wanton of me.[64]
LAER. Say you so? come on. *(They play.)*
OSR. Nothing, neither way.
LAER. Have at you now!
*(*LAERTES *wounds* HAMLET*; then, in scuffling, they change rapiers, and* HAMLET *wounds* LAERTES*.)*
KING. Part them; they are incensed.
HAM. Nay, come, again. *(The Queen falls.)*
OSR. Look to the queen there, ho!
HOR. They bleed on both sides. How is it, my lord?
OSR. How is 't, Laertes?
LAER. Why, as a woodcock to mine own springe, Osric;
I am justly kill'd with mine own treachery.
HAM. How does the queen?
KING. She swounds to see them bleed.
QUEEN. No, no, the drink, the drink,—O my dear Hamlet,—
The drink, the drink! I am poison'd. *(Dies.)*
HAM. O villainy! Ho! let the door be lock'd:
Treachery! Seek it out.
LAER. It is here, Hamlet: Hamlet, thou art slain;
No medicine in the world can do thee good;
In thee there is not half an hour of life;
The treacherous instrument is in thy hand,

---

57. ***have all a length,*** are all the same length.
58. ***quit,*** repay.
59. ***union,*** pearl.
60. ***kettle,*** kettledrum.
61. ***pearl,*** The pearl carried the poison.
62. ***fat,*** perspiring.
63. ***and yet . . . conscience,*** Laertes has had compunctions about wounding Hamlet with the poisoned foil.
64. ***make a wanton of me,*** toy with me. Hamlet believes Laertes can win the match whenever he really tries.

Unbated and envenom'd: the foul practice
Hath turn'd itself on me; lo, here I lie,
Never to rise again: thy mother 's poison'd:
I can no more: the king, the king 's to blame.

HAM. The point envenom'd too!
Then, venom, to thy work. *(Stabs the King.)*

ALL. Treason! treason!

KING. O, yet defend me, friends; I am but hurt.

HAM. Here, thou incestuous, murderous, damned Dane,
Drink off this potion. Is thy union here?
Follow my mother. *(King dies.)*

LAER. He is justly served;
It is a poison temper'd by himself.
Exchange forgiveness with me, noble Hamlet:
Mine and my father's death come not upon thee,
Nor thine on me! *(Dies.)*

HAM. Heaven make thee free of it! I follow thee.
I am dead, Horatio. Wretched queen, adieu!
You that look pale and tremble at this chance,
That are but mutes or audience to this act,
Had I but time—as this fell sergeant, death,
Is strict in his arrest—O, I could tell you—
But let it be. Horatio, I am dead;
Thou livest; report me and my cause aright
To the unsatisfied.

HOR. Never believe it:
I am more an antique Roman[65] than a Dane:
Here 's yet some liquor left.

HAM. As thou 'rt a man,
Give me the cup: let go; by heaven, I'll have 't.
O God! Horatio, what a wounded name,
Things standing thus unknown, shall live behind me!
If thou didst ever hold me in thy heart,
Absent thee from felicity awhile,
And in this harsh world draw thy breath in pain,
To tell my story.
(March afar off, and shot within.)
What warlike noise is this?

OSR. Young Fortinbras, with conquest come from Poland,
To the ambassadors of England gives
This warlike volley.

HAM. O, I die, Horatio;
The potent poison quite o'er-crows[66] my spirit:
I cannot live to hear the news from England;
But I do prophesy the election lights
On Fortinbras: he has my dying voice;
So tell him, with the occurrents,[67] more and less,
Which have solicited.[68] The rest is silence.[69] *(Dies.)*

HOR. Now cracks a noble heart. Good night, sweet prince;
And flights of angels sing thee to thy rest!
Why does the drum come hither?
(March within.)

Enter FORTINBRAS, *the* ENGLISH AMBASSADORS, *and others.*

FORT. Where is this sight?

HOR. What is it ye would see?
If aught of woe or wonder, cease your search.

FORT. This quarry cries on havoc.[70] O proud death,
What feast is toward in thine eternal cell,
That thou so many princes at a shot
So bloodily hast struck?

FIRST AMB. The sight is dismal;
And our affairs from England come too late:
The ears are senseless that should give us hearing,
To tell him his commandment is fulfill'd,
That Rosencrantz and Guildenstern are dead:
Where should we have our thanks?

HOR. Not from his mouth,
Had it the ability of life to thank you:
He never gave commandment for their death.
But since, so jump[71] upon this bloody question,

---

65. ***antique Roman,*** Horatio is referring to the practice common in ancient Rome of servants or slaves following their masters in death.
66. ***o'er-crows,*** triumphs over.
67. ***occurrents,*** events, incidents.
68. ***solicited,*** brought this about.
69. ***The rest is silence.*** The most common interpretation of Hamlet's dying words is that he is welcoming his death. There is, however, another interpretation: that he is following the Ghost's injunction to "leave her to heaven," and does not want Horatio to reveal Gertrude's sins.
70. ***This . . . havoc,*** this heap of bodies bespeaks merciless slaughter.
71. ***jump,*** exactly.

You from the Polack wars, and you from England,
Are here arrived, give order that these bodies
High on a stage be placed to the view;
And let me speak to the yet unknowing world
How these things came about: so shall you hear
Of carnal, bloody, and unnatural acts,
Of accidental judgments, casual slaughters,
Of deaths put on by cunning and forced cause,
And, in this upshot, purposes mistook
Fall'n on the inventors' heads: all this can I
Truly deliver.

FORT. Let us haste to hear it,
And call the noblest to the audience.
For me, with sorrow I embrace my fortune:
I have some rights of memory in this kingdom,
Which now to claim my vantage doth invite me.

HOR. Of that I shall have also cause to speak,
And from his mouth whose voice will draw on more[72]:
But let this same be presently perform'd,
Even while men's minds are wild; lest more mischance,
On plots and errors, happen.

FORT. Let four captains
Bear Hamlet, like a soldier, to the stage;
For he was likely, had he been put on,[73]
To have proved most royal: and, for his passage,
The soldiers' music and the rites of war
Speak loudly for him.
Take up the bodies: such a sight as this
Becomes the field, but here shows much amiss.
Go, bid the soldiers shoot.

(A dead march. Exeunt, bearing off the dead bodies; after which a peal of ordnance is shot off.)

---

72. ***whose . . . more,*** whose authority will cause others to follow.
73. ***put on,*** tried.

Discussion

Act Five, Scene 1

1. (a) One of the principal themes in *Hamlet* is corruption. Describe the attitudes toward physical corruption expressed by the Gravedigger, Hamlet, and Horatio in lines 196–260. **(b)** What sort of humor does this scene express?

2. (a) Describe the encounter between Hamlet and Laertes at Ophelia's grave. **(b)** Do you think Hamlet's wild words here real or feigned? Explain.

Scene 2

1. (a) Explain the trick which Hamlet played on Rosencrantz and Guildenstern on board the ship. **(b)** Would the Hamlet we met earlier in the play have been capable of such a trick? Explain.

2. (a) Characterize Osric. **(b)** Why does Hamlet use such ostentatious language in his conversation with him?

3. (a) Describe the duel between Hamlet and Laertes, and the deaths that take place in connection with it. **(b)** Why doesn't Horatio kill himself as he had at first intended?

4. (a) After the duel and its concomitant deaths, with what action does the play end? **(b)** Has any foundation been laid earlier for this ending? If so, where? Explain.

Act Five in Review

1. The act ends with four corpses on the stage. Explain how the deaths befit the characters. You might wish to consider the order of the deaths.

2. Does the ending of the play satisfy the conventions of a tragedy? Explain.

3. After Hamlet's death, Horatio calls him "sweet prince" and Fortinbras says of him, "He was likely, had he been put on, / To have proved most royal." **(a)** Are both eulogies appropriate? Explain. **(b)** How do they compare with Hamlet's opinion of himself?

The Play in Review

1. According to the classical view. the undoing or downfall of the main character in a tragedy is brought about through a tragic flaw in his character, or through a tragic error. What brought about Hamlet's downfall?

2. **(a)** Do you think that Hamlet was justified in plotting against and killing the King? Why or why not? **(b)** Can you find any evidence in the play that Hamlet also desired his own death? Explain.

3. According to the classical view, tragedy should arouse feelings of pity and fear in its audience. Do you think this is true of *Hamlet?* Explain.

4. In literature, characters are frequently used as foils; that is, the character traits of one person point up by contrast the character traits of another. **(a)** What traits of Hamlet are pointed up by contrast with Fortinbras? **(b)** With Laertes? **(c)** With Horatio? **(d)** With Rosencrantz and Guildenstern?

5. Review the scenes in which the acting company appears. Other than the obvious purpose of the Mousetrap Scene, what other functions does the acting company have? You might consider the content of the lines recited by the First Actor when the company arrives at Elsinore.

6. The Gravediggers' Scene is the only instance of low comedy in the play. **(a)** What purposes does it serve in addition to the burial of Ophelia? **(b)** How important are these purposes? Explain.

7. The Ghost is obviously the prime mover of the play (the character who sets the action in motion). **(a)** How pervasive is his presence throughout the play? Explain. **(b)** Would he have been satisfied with the outcome of the action? Explain.

8. Reread Hamlet's six soliloquies (pages 141, 149, 163, 166, 175, 182). **(a)** Explain how each shows Hamlet's reactions to what is occurring in the play. **(b)** Explain how they also reveal Hamlet's various—sometimes conflicting—character traits. **(c)** Which of the two functions of the soliloquies, **(a)** or **(b)** do you consider more important? Why?

Vocabulary
Context, Structure, and Pronunciation

A. Use context and structure as aids to figure out the meaning of the italicized word in each passage below, then write on a separate sheet of paper the word and its meaning in the passage.

1. "I have heard / That guilty creatures sitting at a play / Have by the very cunning of the scene / Been struck so to the soul that presently / They have proclaim'd their *malefactions.*"

2. "We should profane the service of the dead / To sing a *requiem* and such rest to her / As to peace-parted souls."

3. "The graves stood *tenantless* and the shattered dead / Did squeak and gibber in the Roman streets."

B. On the same sheet of paper, use your Glossary to divide the following words into syllables, and then underline the syllable that has the primary accent or stress. If more than one pronunciation is given, use the first (the more common) one. Then use the pronunciation key in the Glossary to think up a rhyme word of your own for the *stressed syllable only.* Example: *libertine, lib* er tine—*fib.* Be sure you know the meaning of each word.

4. contumely	**5.** superfluous
6. collateral	**7.** consummation
8. augury	**9.** judicious
10. quintessence	**11.** ambiguous
12. oblivion	**13.** unction
14. diligence	**15.** lecherous

Extension • Writing

1. "The role of Hamlet is the greatest role in all theater." Consider Hamlet's character and actions during the play and then discuss in detail why you agree or disagree with the above statement. In your answer include some of the following:

Hamlet's betrayals and his reactions to them;

Hamlet's "madness";

Skills other than acting required for the role;

Scenes you consider to be the greatest.

2. The major theme of *Hamlet* is corruption in all its aspects: political, physical (including the deterioration of dead bodies), mental, moral, and spiritual corruption. Discuss each of these aspects of corruption, giving specific examples (you need not cover them in the order given). It might be wise to begin with Claudius' pouring poison in King Hamlet's ear and the changes this corruption (the introduction of the poison) worked on his body.

3. *Hamlet* provides many examples of loyalty and many examples of its direct opposite, betrayal. Discuss these opposing traits in detail, being sure to provide specific examples of each.

4. Assume that you are a spy in the employ of Fortinbras. You are at Elsinore three months before the play *Hamlet* opens. Write a report to Fortinbras in which you describe what is happening in Denmark, with particular emphasis on the major characters: King Hamlet, Gertrude, Hamlet, Claudius, Polonius, Laertes, Ophelia, Horatio. You may have to use your imagination in some cases.

5. Assume that you are Ophelia, writing to Hamlet at school. You are at Elsinore, three months before the play *Hamlet* opens. Describe what is happening in Denmark, inquire about Hamlet and his friends at school, and show that you have some interest in Hamlet. Be sure to include information about all the major characters: yourself, King Hamlet, Gertrude, Hamlet himself, Claudius, Polonius, Laertes, Horatio, Fortinbras.

6. Assume that you are Horatio, at the end of the play, carrying out Hamlet's dying request to tell his story. Write a report to Fortinbras in which you do this.

7. One critic has said that Hamlet's problem is not "to be, or not to be," but rather "to do, or not to do." Do you agree or disagree? Write a composition in which you support your viewpoint. Use specific examples from the play to justify your position.

8. It is possible to attain greater insight into any Shakespearean drama by viewing the action from the standpoint of any major character other than the protagonist. Select any one of the following and write a description of the action of the play as he/she would see it: Claudius, Gertrude, Ophelia, Laertes, Horatio.

9. Select any one of the following character study questions and write a composition following the suggestions made in it. **(a)** Characterize Gertrude. Consider her behavior toward King Hamlet, Claudius, and Hamlet. Point out her weaknesses and her sins. Does she have any redeeming virtues? If you were called upon to pronounce final judgment of her life, what would you say, and why? **(b)** Characterize Claudius. Point out his weaknesses and his sins. What character trait do you think led him into sin? Did he have any redeeming virtues? If you were called upon to pronounce final judgment on his life, what would you say, and why? **(c)** It has been said that Ophelia is the most pathetic character in *Hamlet*, that she inspires more pity than anyone else. Explain specifically and in detail why you agree or disagree with this statement. A key factor may well be Ophelia's age. Decide how old she might be and marshal your evidence from that point. **(d)** Explain specifically and in detail why Horatio is an important character in *Hamlet*. You might begin by considering what would be missing from the play if his role were omitted. **(e)** Characterize Polonius. Is he more foolish than dangerous, or more dangerous than foolish? How old might he be? What might have been his position at court before Claudius became king? What part might he have had in Claudius' election?

Extension • Speaking

1. *Hamlet* contains many of the most famous soliloquies ever written. Select one of these; imagine that you *are* the character, with all the problems the character faces; and prepare it for delivery in class. You may wish to memorize it, or to read it directly from the text.

2. The "Mousetrap Scene" is not only a fascinating bit of drama, but also is ideal for presentation in class because of the number of characters actively involved: Hamlet, Horatio, Claudius, Gertrude, Polonius, Ophelia, Rosencrantz, Guildenstern, and at least three Players. Prepare this scene for presentation in class, with the teacher and remaining students as audience.

3. Prepare any scene or episode of the play for class presentation. You may read or memorize the lines.

The King James Bible

No complete translation of the Bible was made into English until the late fourteenth century, when John Wycliffe, a theologian and church reformer who was condemned as a heretic, oversaw a translation. Other "unauthorized" translations appeared in the early sixteenth century, including versions by William Tyndale and Miles Coverdale. Finally, in 1539, the "Great Bible" appeared, under the auspices of the reigning monarch, Henry VIII. This was the first English Bible with official endorsement.

In 1604, James I convened a conference at Hampton Court at which plans were laid for a new version of the Bible by a group of translators. Some fifty or so theologians and scholars began work in various centers of learning (Oxford, Cambridge, Westminster), making extensive use of previous translations, especially those of Tyndale and Wycliffe. The work was issued in 1611 as the "Authorized Version" and has fixed itself so firmly in the imagination of the English-speaking world that no other translation seems able to challenge it.

The King James Bible has been called "the noblest monument of English prose," and deserves the epithet because of the sheer brilliance of its language. Its extensive use of concrete terms and images, its straightforward phrases and sentences, its balance and parallelism in many passages—all make for a dignified simplicity eminently compatible with religious feeling and ritual. Indeed, the language of the King James Bible has so profoundly affected succeeding generations of writers and has so thoroughly stamped itself in the minds of ordinary people that today it forms a basic part of our everyday speech.

For a comparison of translations of the Bible, see the various versions of the Twenty-third Psalm on page 208.

The Creation of the World

(Genesis, Chapters 1–3)

In the beginning God created the heaven and the earth. And the earth was without form, and void; and darkness was upon the face of the deep. And the Spirit of God moved upon the face of the waters. And God said, "Let there be light": and there was light. And God saw the light, that it was good: and God divided the light from the darkness. And God called the light Day, and the darkness he called Night. And the evening and the morning were the first day.

And God said, "Let there be a firmament in the midst of the waters, and let it divide the waters from the waters." And God made the firmament, and divided the waters which were under the firmament from the waters which were above the firmament: and it was so. And God called the firmament Heaven. And the evening and the morning were the second day.

And God said, "Let the waters under the heaven be gathered together unto one place, and let the dry land appear": and it was so. And God called the dry land Earth; and the gathering together of the waters called he Seas: and God saw that it was good. And God said, "Let the earth bring forth grass, the herb yielding seed, and the fruit tree yielding fruit after his kind, whose seed is in itself, upon the earth": and it was so. And the earth brought forth grass, and herb yielding seed after his kind, and the tree yielding fruit, whose seed was in itself, after his kind: and God saw that it was good. And the evening and the morning were the third day.

And God said, "Let there be lights in the firmament of the heaven to divide the day from the night; and let them be for signs, and for seasons, and for days, and years: and let them be for lights in the firmament of the heaven to give light upon the earth": and it was so. And God made two great lights; the greater light to rule the day, and the lesser light to rule the night: he made the stars also. And God set them in the firmament of the heaven to give light upon the earth. And to rule over the day and over the night, and to divide the light from the darkness: and God saw that it was good. And the evening and the morning were the fourth day.

And God said, "Let the waters bring forth abundantly the moving creature that hath life, and fowl that may fly above the earth in the open firmament of heaven." And God created great whales, and every living creature that moveth, which the waters brought forth abundantly, after their kind, and every winged fowl after his kind: and God saw that it was good. And God blessed them, saying, "Be fruitful, and multiply, and fill the waters in the seas, and let fowl multiply in the earth." And the evening and the morning were the fifth day.

And God said, "Let the earth bring forth the living creature after his kind, cattle, and creeping thing, and beast of the earth after his kind": and it was so. And God made the beast of the earth after his kind, and cattle after their kind, and every thing that creepeth upon the earth after his kind: and God saw that it was good.

And God said, "Let us make man in our image, after our likeness; and let them have dominion over the fish of the sea, and over the fowl of the air, and over the cattle, and over all the earth, and over every creeping thing that creepeth upon the earth." So God created man in his own image, in the image of God created he him; male and female created he them. And God blessed them, and God said unto them, "Be fruitful, and multiply, and replenish the earth, and subdue it: and have dominion over the fish of the sea, and over the fowl of the air, and over every living thing that moveth upon the earth."

And God said, "Behold, I have given you every herb bearing seed, which is upon the face of all the earth, and every tree, in the which is the fruit of a tree yielding seed; to you it shall be for meat. And to every beast of the earth, and to every fowl of the air, and to every thing that creepeth upon the earth, wherein there is life, I have given every green herb for meat": and it was so.

And God saw every thing that he had made, and behold, it was very good. And the evening and the morning were the sixth day.

Thus the heavens and the earth were finished, and all the host of them. And on the seventh day God ended his work which he had made; and he rested on the seventh day from all his work which he had made. And God blessed the seventh day, and sanctified it: because that in it he had rested from all his work which God created and made.

The Creation of Adam and Eve

These are the generations of the heavens and of the earth when they were created, in the day that the Lord God made the earth and the heavens, and every plant of the field before it grew: for the Lord God had not caused it to rain upon the earth, and there was not a man to till the ground. But there went up a mist from the earth, and watered the whole face of the ground. And the Lord God formed man of the dust of the ground, and breathed into his nostrils the breath of life; and man became a living soul.

And the Lord God planted a garden eastward in Eden; and there he put the man whom he had formed. And out of the ground made the Lord God to grow every tree that is pleasant to the sight, and good for food; the tree of life also in the midst of the garden, and the tree of knowledge of good and evil. . . .

And the Lord God took the man, and put him into the garden of Eden to dress it and to keep it. And the Lord God commanded the man, saying, "Of every tree of the garden thou mayest freely eat: but of the tree of the knowledge of good and evil, thou shalt not eat of it: for in the day that thou eatest thereof thou shalt surely die."

And the Lord God said, "It is not good that the man should be alone; I will make him an help meet for him." And out of the ground the Lord God formed every beast of the field, and every fowl of the air; and brought them unto Adam to see what he would call them: and whatsoever Adam called every living creature, that was the name thereof. And Adam gave names to all cattle, and to the fowl of the air, and to every beast of the field; but for Adam there was not found an help meet for him.

And the Lord God caused a deep sleep to fall upon Adam, and he slept: and he took one of his

ribs, and closed up the flesh instead thereof; and the rib, which the Lord God had taken from man, made he a woman, and brought her unto the man.

And Adam said, "This is now bone of my bones, and flesh of my flesh: she shall be called Woman, because she was taken out of Man."

Therefore shall a man leave his father and his mother, and shall cleave unto his wife: and they shall be one flesh. And they were both naked, the man and his wife, and were not ashamed.

The Fall of Man

Now the serpent was more subtil than any beast of the field which the Lord God had made.

And he said unto the woman, "Yea, hath God said, 'Ye shall not eat of every tree of the garden'?"

And the woman said unto the serpent, "We may eat of the fruit of the trees of the garden: but of the fruit of the tree which is in the midst of the garden, God hath said, 'Ye shall not eat of it, neither shall ye touch it, lest ye die.'"

And the serpent said unto the woman, "Ye shall not surely die: for God doth know that in the day ye eat thereof, then your eyes shall be opened, and ye shall be as gods, knowing good and evil."

And when the woman saw that the tree was good for food, and that it was pleasant to the eyes, and a tree to be desired to make one wise, she took of the fruit thereof, and did eat, and gave also unto her husband with her; and he did eat. And the eyes of them both were opened, and they knew that they were naked; and they sewed fig leaves together, and made themselves aprons.

And they heard the voice of the Lord God

walking in the garden in the cool of the day: and Adam and his wife hid themselves from the presence of the Lord God amongst the trees of the garden.

And the Lord God called unto Adam, and said unto him, "Where art thou?"

And he said, "I heard thy voice in the garden, and I was afraid, because I was naked; and I hid myself."

And he said, "Who told thee that thou wast naked? Hast thou eaten of the tree, whereof I commanded thee that thou shouldest not eat?"

And the man said, "The woman whom thou gavest to be with me, she gave me of the tree, and I did eat."

And the Lord God said unto the woman, "What is this that thou hast done?"

And the woman said, "The serpent beguiled me, and I did eat."

And the Lord God said unto the serpent, "Because thou hast done this, thou art cursed above all cattle, and above every beast of the field; upon thy belly shalt thou go, and dust shalt thou eat all the days of thy life: and I will put enmity between thee and the woman, and between thy seed and her seed; it shall bruise thy head, and thou shalt bruise his heel."

Unto the woman he said, "I will greatly multiply thy sorrow and thy conception; in sorrow thou shalt bring forth children; and thy desire shall be to thy husband, and he shall rule over thee."

And unto Adam he said, "Because thou hast hearkened unto the voice of thy wife, and hast eaten of the tree, of which I commanded thee, saying, 'Thou shalt not eat of it': cursed is the ground for thy sake; in sorrow shalt thou eat of it all the days of thy life. Thorns also and thistles shall it bring forth to thee; and thou shalt eat the herb of the field; in the sweat of thy face shalt thou eat bread, till thou return unto the ground; for out of it wast thou taken: for dust thou art, and unto dust shalt thou return."

And Adam called his wife's name Eve; because she was the mother of all living. Unto Adam also and to his wife did the Lord God make coats of skins, and clothed them.

And the Lord God said, "Behold, the man is become as one of us, to know good and evil: and now, lest he put forth his hand, and take also of the tree of life, and eat, and live for ever": therefore the Lord God sent him forth from the garden of Eden, to till the ground from whence he was taken. So he drove out the man; and he placed at the east of the garden of Eden Cherubims, and a flaming sword which turned every way, to keep the way of the tree of life. □□

Discussion

1. Imagine that a child, beginning to be fully conscious of the world that surrounds him, asks: "Who created the world? How? Why? How long did it take? What about whales? How about man himself?" Show how the opening of Genesis answers these questions.

2. Do some research on other stories of the creation. (For example, Ovid's *Metamorphoses,* Book I, gives the Greek conception of the beginning of the world. For an American Indian version of creation, see John G. Neihardt's *Black Elk Speaks,* Chapter III: "The Great Vision." You will be able to find others, too.)

3. According to Genesis, why did God create man? woman?

4. Analyze the behavior of Adam and Eve after the Fall, and indicate how they have changed.

5. The repetition of certain words and phrases gives these passages a sonorousness and solemnity. What are some of them?

6. The style of the King James Bible has appeared to be unsurpassable. Find a passage you consider particularly effective and explore the reasons for its effectiveness. For example, analyze: "In the beginning God created the heaven and the earth."

The Bible has been the best seller of all time, and translations of it have been numerous. The achievement of the King James version can best be judged by comparing it with some of the others. Here are four versions of the Twenty-third Psalm: the King James translation, one published before it, and two published later.

from **The Great Bible** (1539)

The Lord is my shepherd; therefore can I lack nothing. He shall feed me in a green pasture, and lead me forth beside the waters of comfort. He shall convert my soul, and bring me forth in the paths of righteousness for his name's sake. Yea, though I walk through the valley of the shadow of death, I will fear no evil, for thou art with me. Thy rod and thy staff comfort me. Thou shalt prepare a table before me against them that trouble me; thou has anointed my head with oil, and my cup shall be full. But thy loving-kindness and mercy shall follow me all the days of my life and I will dwell in the house of the Lord forever.

from **The King James Bible** (1611)

The Lord is my shepherd: I shall not want.
He maketh me to lie down in green pastures:
he leadeth me beside the still waters.
He restoreth my soul: he leadeth me in the
paths of righteousness for his name's sake.
Yea, though I walk through the valley of the
shadow of death, I will fear no evil: for thou
art with me; thy rod and thy staff they
comfort me.
Thou preparest a table before me in the
presence of mine enemies: thou anointest my
head with oil; my cup runneth over.
Surely goodness and mercy shall follow me all
the days of my life: and I will dwell in the
house of the Lord forever.

from **The Bay Psalm Book** (1640)[1]

The Lord to me a shepherd is,
want therefore shall not I.
He in the folds of tender grass,
doth cause me down to lie:
To waters calm me gently leads,
Restore my soul doth he:
He doth in paths of righteousness
for his name's sake lead me.
Yea though in valley of death's shade
I walk, none ill I'll fear:
Because thou art with me, thy rod
and staff my comfort are.
For me a table thou hast spread,
in presence of my foes:
Thou dost anoint my head with oil,
my cup it overflows.
Goodness and mercy surely shall
all my days follow me:
And in the Lord's house I shall dwell
so long as days shall be.

1. The Bay Psalm Book was the first book published in the American Colonies.

from **The New English Bible** (1970)

The LORD is my shepherd; I shall want
nothing.
He makes me lie down in green pastures,
and leads me beside the waters of peace;
he renews life within me,
and for his name's sake guides me in the
right path.
Even though I walk through a valley dark as
death
I fear no evil, for thou art with me,
thy staff and thy crook are my comfort.

Thou spreadest a table for me in the sight of
my enemies;
thou hast richly bathed my head with oil,
and my cup runs over.
Goodness and love unfailing, these will
follow me
all the days of my life,
and I shall dwell in the house of the LORD
my whole life long.

Sir Francis Bacon

Sir Francis Bacon's Essays *were published in three installments over a period of a quarter-century (1597–1625) to a total of fifty-eight essays. Bacon introduced the essay form into England, and through his genius with the language made it popular. His essays were short, treated a variety of subjects of universal interest, and were written in epigrammatic, sharply honed style. His individual sentences are memorable and are still frequently quoted.*

Detail, "The Library" by Oudry. The Bettman Archive, Inc.

Of Studies

Studies serve for delight, for ornament, and for ability. Their chief use for delight is in privateness and retiring; for ornament, is in discourse; and for ability, is in the judgment and disposition of business; for expert[1] men can execute, and perhaps judge of particulars, one by one; but the general counsels, and the plots and marshaling of affairs come best from those that are learned. To spend too much time in studies is sloth; to use them too much for ornament is affectation; to make judgment wholly by their rules is the humor[2] of a scholar. They perfect nature, and are perfected by experience; for natural abilities are like natural plants, that need pruning by study; and studies themselves do give forth directions too much at large, except they be bounded in by experience. Crafty[3] men contemn studies, simple

1. ***expert,*** experienced; practical.
2. ***humor,*** whim, disposition.
3. ***Crafty,*** skilled in crafts; practical.

men admire them, and wise men use them; for they teach not their own use; but that is a wisdom without them and above them, won by observation.

Read not to contradict and confute, nor to believe and take for granted, nor to find talk and discourse, but to weigh and consider. Some books are to be tasted, others to be swallowed, and some few to be chewed and digested; that is, some books are to be read only in parts; others to be read but not curiously,[4] and some few to be read wholly, and with diligence and attention. Some books also may be read by deputy, and extracts made of them by others; but that would be only in the less important arguments and the meaner sort of books; else distilled books are, like common distilled waters, flashy[5] things.

Reading maketh a full man; conference a ready man; and writing an exact man. And, therefore, if a man write little, he had need have a great memory; if he confer little, he had need have a present wit;[6] and if he read little, he had need have much cunning, to seem to know what he doth not. Histories make men wise; poets, witty; the mathematics, subtile; natural philosophy, deep; moral, grave; logic and rhetoric, able to contend: *Abeunt studia in mores!*[7] Nay, there is no stand or impediment in the wit but may be wrought out by fit studies; like as diseases of the body may have appropriate exercises. Bowling is good for the stone[8] and reins, shooting for the lungs and breast, gentle walking for the stomach, riding for the head, and the like. So if a man's wit be wandering, let him study mathematics; for in demonstrations, if his wit be called away never so little, he must begin again. If his wit be not apt to distinguish or find differences, let him study the schoolmen,[9] for they are *cymini sectores!*[10] If he be not apt to beat over matters, and to call up one thing to prove and illustrate another, let him study the lawyers' cases. So every defect of the mind may have a special receipt. □□

4. ***curiously,*** thoroughly.
5. ***flashy,*** tasteless, flat.
6. ***wit,*** intelligence; the word is used throughout the essay in this sense.
7. ***Abeunt . . . mores!*** Studies develop into habits. [*Latin*]
8. ***stone,*** a disease of the kidneys (reins).
9. ***schoolmen,*** medieval scholars.
10. ***cymini sectores,*** hairsplitters (literally, splitters of cumin-seeds.) [*Latin*]

Discussion

1. This essay is so closely written that for you to understand and appreciate it fully you must stop and consider the meaning of almost every sentence. Explain in your own words the following: **(a)** Studies serve for delight, for ornament, and for ability. **(b)** To spend too much time in studies is sloth; to use them too much for ornament is affectation; to make judgment wholly by their rules is the humor of a scholar. **(c)** Reading maketh a full man; and writing an exact man.

2. Discuss books that you would put in the following categories: "Some books are to be tasted, others to be swallowed, and some few to be chewed and digested."

Extension • Writing

1. Some of the other essays Bacon wrote are titled "Of Parents and Children," "Of Truth," "Of Envy," and "Of Cunning." Select one of these titles, or one of your own choice, and write a short essay about it.

2. Write a familiar (that is, an informal) essay, in the first person, in which you discuss some personal observations about people or the world around you. Some suggested titles follow; you may select one of these or use your own. "On Waiting in Line," "On Riding in an Elevator," "On Waiting for a Bus," "On Riding a Bicycle (or Motorcycle, or Moped)"

John Donne

Dr. Samuel Johnson, in one of his series The Lives of the Poets, *following a suggestion by John Dryden, labeled a school of poets of the early seventeenth century the* metaphysical poets, *because of their emphasis on the intellect or wit as against feeling and emotion.*

Metaphysical poetry has come to be defined by its style rather than its content. The total effect of a metaphysical poem at its best is to startle the reader into seeing and knowing what he has not really noticed or thought about before.

Song

Go and catch a falling star,
  Get with child a mandrake root,[1]
Tell me where all past years are,
  Or who cleft the devil's foot;
Teach me to hear mermaids singing,
Or to keep off envy's stinging,
    And find
    What wind
Serves to advance an honest mind.

If thou be'st born to strange sights,
  Things invisible to see,
Ride ten thousand days and nights,
  Till Age snow white hairs on thee;
Thou, when thou return'st, will tell me
All strange wonders that befell thee,
    And swear
    No where
Lives a woman true, and fair.

If thou find'st one, let me know;
  Such a pilgrimage were sweet.
Yet do not; I would not go,
  Though at next door we might meet.
Though she were true, when you met her,
And last, till you write your letter,
    Yet she
    Will be
False, ere I come, to two or three.

1. ***Get . . . mandrake root.*** Mandrake is a European herb with a forked root, fancied to resemble the figure of a man. [Recognizing the resemblance as well as the impossiblity of a plant's reproducing as humans do, Donne includes this in his catalogue of fantastic achievements.]

The Bait

Come live with me, and be my love,
And we will some new pleasures prove
Of golden sands, and crystal brooks,
With silken lines, and silver hooks.

There will the river whispering run
Warmed by thy eyes, more than the sun.
And there th' enamoured fish will stay,
Begging themselves they may betray.

When thou wilt swim in that live bath,
Each fish, which every channel hath,
Will amorously to thee swim,
Gladder to catch thee, than thou him.

If thou, to be so seen, be'st loath,
By sun, or moon, thou darkenest both,
And if myself have leave to see,
I need not their light, having thee.

Let others freeze with angling reeds,
And cut their legs, with shells and weeds,
Or treacherously poor fish beset,
With strangling snare, or windowy net:

Let coarse bold hands, from slimy nest
The bedded fish in banks out-wrest,
Or curious traitors, sleave silk flies
Bewitch poor fishes' wandering eyes.

For thee, thou need'st no such deceit,
For thou thyself art thine own bait;
That fish, that is not catched thereby,
Alas, is wiser far than I.

The Canonization[1]

For God's sake, hold your tongue, and let me love,
Or chide my palsy, or my gout,
My five gray hairs, or ruined fortune flout,
With wealth your state, your mind with arts improve,
Take you a course,[2] get you a place,[3]
Observe his Honor, or his Grace,[4]
Or the King's real, or his stamped face[5]
Contemplate; what you will, approve,[6]
So you will let me love.

Alas, alas, who's injured by my love?
What merchant's ships have my sighs drowned?
Who says my tears have overflowed his ground?
When did my colds a forward spring remove?[7]
When did the heats which my veins fill
Add one more to the plaguy bill?[8]
Soldiers find wars, and lawyers find out still
Litigious men, which quarrels move,
Though she and I do love.

Call us what you will, we are made such by love;
Call her one, me another fly,
We are tapers too, and at our own cost die,[9]
And we in us find the eagle and the dove,[10]
The phoenix riddle[11] hath more wit[12]
By us; we two being one, are it.

So to one neutral thing both sexes fit.
We die and rise the same, and prove
Mysterious by this love.[13]

We can die by it, if not live by love,
And if unfit for tombs and hearse
Our legend be, it will be fit for verse;
And if no piece of chronicle we prove,
We'll build in sonnets pretty rooms;
As well a well-wrought urn becomes
The greatest ashes, as half-acre tombs,
And by these hymns, all shall approve
Us canonized for love:

And thus invoke us; "You whom reverend love
Made one another's hermitage;[14]
You, to whom love was peace, that now is rage;
Who did the whole world's soul contract, and
drove
Into the glasses of your eyes
(So made such mirrors and such spies,
That they did all to you epitomize)
Countries, towns, courts: beg from above
A pattern of your love!"[15]

---

1. ***Canonization,*** declaring a deceased person to be a saint; also, to make something divine.
2. ***Take you a course,*** follow some way of advancing yourself.
3. ***place,*** position at Court.
4. ***Observe . . . Grace,*** cultivate some lord or bishop.
5. ***stamped face,*** the face of the king stamped on coins.
6. ***approve,*** try out.
7. ***a forward spring remove,*** hold back an early spring.
8. ***plaguy bill,*** a list of plague victims, published weekly.
9. ***at our . . . die.*** Dying was a widely used metaphor for the consummation of physical love. The expression refers to the popular belief that each episode shortened one's life by a day.
10. ***eagle . . . dove.*** The eagle symbolized strength or the masculine quality; the dove, gentleness or the feminine element.
11. ***phoenix riddle,*** the mystery of the legendary bird which was said to burn itself to death every five hundred years and then rise again from its own ashes. It is used as a symbol both of immortality and of desire rising from its own exhaustion.
12. ***hath more wit,*** makes more sense.
13. ***We die . . . this love.*** Because physical consummation does not change or diminish our love, we are different from ordinary humans (as saints are).
14. ***hermitage,*** refuge from the world.
15. ***beg . . . love.*** The poet and his mistress, having died and become saints, are implored by the world to beg from Heaven a pattern of their love, so that later lovers may model their loves on this one.

A Valediction: Forbidding Mourning

As virtuous men pass mildly away,
And whisper to their souls to go,
Whilst some of their sad friends do say
The breath goes now, and some say, No:

So let us melt, and make no noise,
No tear-floods, nor sigh-tempests move,
'Twere profanation of our joys
To tell the laity our love.

Moving of th' earth brings harms and fears,
Men reckon what it did and meant,
But trepidation of the spheres,
Though greater far, is innocent.[1]

Dull sublunary[2] lovers' love
(Whose soul is sense) cannot admit
Absence, because it doth remove
Those things which elemented[3] it.

But we by a love so much refined
That our selves know not what it is,
Inter-assurèd of the mind,
Care less, eyes, lips, and hands to miss.

Our two souls therefore, which are one,
Though I must go, endure not yet
A breach, but an expansion,
Like gold to aery thinness beat.

If they be two, they are two so
As stiff twin compasses[4] are two;
Thy soul, the fixed foot, makes no show
To move, but doth, if th' other do.

And though it in the centre sit,
Yet when the other far doth roam,
It leans and hearkens after it,
And grows erect, as that comes home.

Such wilt thou be to me, who must
Liketh' other foot, obliquely run;
Thy firmness makes my circle[5] just,
And makes me end where I begun.

---

1. ***trepidation . . . innocent.*** Movements (trepidation) of the heavenly spheres, though greater than those of an earthquake, provoke no fears in (nor danger to) man.
2. ***sublunary,*** beneath the moon, i.e., earthly and subject to change.
3. ***elemented,*** composed.
4. ***compasses.*** The image is of the instrument used for describing a circle. One branch or leg of the compass is held steady, as a pivot, while the other leg is rotated to draw the circle.
5. ***circle,*** The circle was a symbol of perfection.

Discussion

1. (a) What quality do all the instructions in Donne's "Song" Share? **(b)** What is the state of mind of the speaker of the poem, and what do you think has happened to him?

2. "The Bait" is Donne's updating of Marlowe's "Come Live with Me and Be My Love" (page 124). Reread the original poem, and then discuss the differences introduced in "The Bait."

3. Donne is said to use "strong lines" (lines that disregard natural rhythm and stress), rather than regular, lyrical lines in his poetry. Show how he does this in "The Canonization."

4. "A Valediction: Forbidding Mourning" employs one of the most unusual conceits (extended metaphors) in all literature: "If they be . . . I begun" (lines 25-36). Explain how the conceit operates in this poem.

notes and comments

Donne's Puns

In 1601 Donne was secretly married to Anne More, the sixteen-year-old niece of his patron, Sir Thomas Egerton. Enraged when he discovered the marriage, Anne's father had Donne imprisoned. Tradition has it that from prison Donne addressed the following note to his bride: "John Donne, Anne Donne, Undone."

from Holy Sonnets

7

At the round earth's imagined corners, blow
Your trumpets, angels; and arise, arise
From death, you numberless infinities
Of souls, and to your scattered bodies go;
All whom the flood did, and fire shall, o'erthrow,
All whom war, dearth, age, agues, tyrannies,
Despair, law, chance, hath slain, and you whose eyes
Shall behold God, and never taste death's woe.[1]
But let them sleep, Lord, and me mourn a space;
For, if above all these, my sins abound,
'Tis late to ask abundance of Thy grace
When we are there. Here on this lowly ground,
Teach me how to repent; for that's as good
As if Thou hadst sealed my pardon with Thy blood.

1. ***and you . . . woe,*** those still alive at the Last Judgment and the end of the world, who will be judged without having died.

10

Death, be not proud, though some have called thee
Mighty and dreadful, for thou art not so;
For those whom thou think'st thou dost overthrow
Die not, poor Death, nor yet canst thou kill me.
From rest and sleep, which but thy pictures be,
Much pleasure; then from thee much more must flow,
And soonest our best men with thee do go,
Rest of their bones, and soul's delivery.
Thou art slave to fate, chance, kings, and desperate men,
And dost with poison, war, and sickness dwell,
And poppy[1] or charms can make us sleep as well
And better than thy stroke; why swell'st[2] thou then?
One short sleep past, we wake eternally,
And death shall be no more; Death, thou shalt die.

1. ***poppy,*** the source of various narcotic drugs.
2. ***swell'st,*** puff up with pride.

14

Batter my heart, three-personed God;[1] for You
As yet but knock, breathe, shine, and seek to mend;
That I may rise and stand, o'erthrow me, and bend
Your force to break, blow, burn, and make me new.
I, like an usurped town, to another due,
Labour to admit You, but O, to no end;
Reason, Your viceroy in me, me should defend,
But is captived, and proves weak or untrue.
Yet dearly I love You, and would be loved fain,
But am betrothed unto Your enemy.
Divorce me, untie or break that knot again;
Take me to You, imprison me, for I,
Except You enthral me, never shall be free,
Nor ever chaste, except You ravish me.

1. ***three-personed God,*** the Trinity of the Father, the Son, and the Holy Spirit.

Discussion

1. Sonnet 7 describes the end of the world, when the trumpet of doom sounds and the dead rise for the Last Judgment. Why does the speaker say, "But let them sleep, Lord, and me mourn a space"?

2. In Sonnet 10, the speaker scorns Death. **(a)** How does he cast aspersions on Death's powers? **(b)** What is meant by the last line, "And death shall be no more; Death, thou shalt die"?

3. **(a)** Why does the speaker in Sonnet 14 ask God to batter his heart? **(b)** Explain the striking paradoxes of the last two lines—enthrallment leading to freedom, ravishing to chastity.

Meditation 17

Nunc lento sonitu dicunt, morieris.
(Now this bell tolling softly for another, says to me, Thou must die.)

Perchance he for whom this bell tolls may be so ill as that he knows not it tolls for him; and perchance I may think myself so much better than I am, as that they who are about me and see my state may have caused it to toll for me, and I know not that. The church is catholic, universal, so are all her actions; all that she does belongs to all. When she baptizes a child, that action concerns me; for that child is thereby connected to that head which is my head too, and ingrafted into that body whereof I am a member.[1] And when she buries a man, that action concerns me: all mankind is of one author and is one volume; when one man dies, one chapter is not torn out of the book, but translated into a better language; and every chapter must be so translated. God employs several translators; some pieces are translated by age, some by sickness, some by war, some by justice; but God's hand is in every translation, and his hand shall bind up all our scattered leaves again for that library where every book shall lie open to one another. As therefore the bell that rings to a sermon calls not upon the preacher only, but upon the congregation to come, so this bell calls us all; but how much more me, who am brought so near the door by this sickness.

There was a contention as far as a suit[2] (in which piety and dignity, religion and estimation,[3] were mingled) which of the religious orders should ring to prayers first in the morning; and it was determined that they should ring first that rose earliest. If we understand aright the dignity of this bell that tolls for our evening prayer, we would be glad to make it ours by rising early, in that application, that it might be ours as well as his whose indeed it is. The bell doth toll for him that thinks it doth; and though it intermit again, yet from that minute that that occasion wrought upon him, he is united to God. Who casts not up his eye to the sun when it rises? but who takes off his eye from a comet when that breaks out? Who bends not his ear to any bell which upon any occasion rings? but who can remove it from that bell which is passing a piece of himself out of this world? No man is an island, entire of itself; every man is a piece of the continent, a part of the main. If a clod be washed away by the sea, Europe is the less, as well as if a promontory were, as well as if a manor of thy friend's or of thine own were. Any man's death diminishes me because I am involved in mankind, and therefore never send to know for whom the bell tolls; it tolls for thee. . . . □□

1. ***head . . . member.*** That is, the Christian church is the head of all men, as well as a body made up of its members.
2. ***contention . . . suit,*** a controversy that went as far as a lawsuit.
3. ***estimation,*** self-esteem.

Discussion

At the time Donne wrote "Meditation 17," he was recovering from a serious illness, so in one sense the selection is autobiographical. **(a)** How might that fact have influenced the entire Meditation? **(b)** Discuss the meaning and effectiveness of the two main metaphors: man as a chapter in a book and man as a piece of a continent. **(c)** Explain in your own words: ". . . never send to know for whom the bell tolls; it tolls for thee."

Ben Jonson

Poet, playwright, and friend of Shakespeare, Jonson is known as a lyric poet of the first order. His work so influenced many young poets that they called themselves the Tribe of Ben. The Cavalier Poets (page 218) owe much to Jonson's lyrics.

Jonson's eldest son, Benjamin, died of the plague in 1603 at the age of seven.

On My First Son

Farewell, thou child of my right hand,[1] and joy;
   My sin was too much hope of thee, loved boy.
Seven years thou wert lent to me, and I thee pay,
   Exacted by thy fate, on the just day.
O, could I lose all father, now! For why
   Will man lament the state he should envy?
To have so soon 'scaped world's and flesh's rage,
   And, if no other misery, yet age!
Rest in soft peace; and, asked, say: Here doth lie
   Ben Jonson his best piece of poetry—
For whose sake, henceforth, all his vows be such,
   As what he loves may never like too much.

1. ***child of my right hand,*** the meaning of the Hebrew name Benjamin.

This song, from the comedy Cynthia's Revels, *is sung by Hesperus, the evening star, to Diana, virgin goddess of the moon and the hunt. Cynthia was an epithet of Diana's and to the Elizabethans also represented their "Virgin Queen," Elizabeth.*

To Cynthia

Queen and huntress, chaste and fair,
Now the sun is laid to sleep,
Seated in thy silver chair
State in wonted[1] manner keep;
   Hesperus entreats thy light,
   Goddess excellently bright.

Earth, let not thy envious shade
Dare itself to interpose;
Cynthia's shining orb was made
Heaven to clear, when day did close;
   Bless us then with wished sight,
   Goddess excellently bright.

Lay thy bow of pearl apart,
And thy crystal shining quiver;
Give unto the flying hart
Space to breathe, how short soever,
   Thou that mak'st a day of night,
   Goddess excellently bright.

1. ***wonted,*** habitual.

notes and comment

Ben Jonson's Vision of His Son

At that time [plague] was in London, [Jonson] being in the country at Sir Robert Cotton's house with old Camden, he saw in a vision his eldest son, then a child and at London, appear unto him with the mark of a bloody cross on his forehead, as if it had been cutted with a sword; at which amazed he prayed unto God, and in the morning he came to Mr. Camden's chamber to tell him, who persuaded him it was but an apprehension of his fantasy at which he should not be disjected. In the mean time comes there letters from his wife of the death of that boy in the plague. He appeared to him (he said) of a manly shape, and of that growth that he thinks he shall be at the resurrection.

It Was a Beauty That I Saw

It was a beauty that I saw
So pure, so perfect, as the frame
Of all the universe was lame,
To that one figure, could I draw,
Or give least line of it a law!

A skein of silk without a knot,
A fair march made without a halt,
A curious[1] form without a fault,
A printed book without a blot,
All beauty, and without a spot!

1. *curious,* carefully constructed.

Song, to Celia

Drink to me only with thine eyes,
  And I will pledge with mine;
Or leave a kiss but in the cup,
  And I'll not look for wine.
The thirst that from the soul doth rise
  Doth ask a drink divine;
But might I of Jove's nectar[1] sup,
  I would not change for thine.
I sent thee late a rosy wreath,
  Not so much honoring thee
As giving it a hope, that there
  It could not withered be.
But thou thereon didst only breathe,
  And sent'st it back to me;
Since when it grows, and smells, I swear,
  Not of itself but thee.

1. *nectar,* the drink of the gods.

Discussion

1. In "To Cynthia," Cynthia has two major functions: goddess of the hunt, and goddess of the moon. How are the two interwined in the third stanza, and which does the speaker ask to have prevail?

2. **(a)** Comment upon the effectiveness of the epitaph, "Here doth lie / Ben Jonson his best piece of poetry." **(b)** Using direct references to the poem, discuss the extent of the speaker's grief.

3. "It Was a Beauty" was written late in Jonson's career, when the exuberance of earlier Elizabethan lyrics was, in many cases, being affected by the metaphysical poets. **(a)** How does this lyric show elements of both? **(b)** How does its style compare with that of "To Cynthia," written early in his career?

4. "To Celia" is one of the most famous lyrics in the book. It consists of two **conceits** (extended metaphors), one in the first stanza and the other in the second. **(a)** What are they? **(b)** Which do you think is more effective? Why?

Richard Lovelace

To Althea, from Prison

When Love with unconfinèd wings
  Hovers within my gates,
And my divine Althea brings
  To whisper at the grates;
When I lie tangled in her hair
  And fettered to her eye,
The birds that wanton in the air
  Know no such liberty.

When flowing cups run swiftly round
  With no allaying Thames,[1]
Our careless heads with roses bound,
  Our hearts with loyal flames;
When thirsty grief in wine we steep,
  When healths and drafts go free,
Fishes that tipple in the deep
  Know no such liberty.

When, like committed linnets, I
  With shriller throat will sing
The sweetness, mercy, majesty,
  And glories of my King;
When I shall voice aloud how good
  He is, how great should be,
Enlargèd winds, that curl the flood,
  Know no such liberty.

Stone walls do not a prison make,
  Nor iron bars a cage;
Minds innocent and quiet take
  That for an hermitage;
If I have freedom in my love
  And in my soul am free,
Angels alone, that soar above,
  Enjoy such liberty.

1. ***no allaying Thames,*** no diluting water from the Thames River.

To Lucasta, on Going to the Wars

Tell me not, sweet, I am unkind,
  That from the nunnery
Of thy chaste breast and quiet mind
  To war and arms I fly.

True, a new mistress now I chase,
  The first foe in the field;
And with a stronger faith embrace
  A sword, a horse, a shield.

Yet this inconstancy is such
  As thou too shalt adore;
I could not love thee, dear, so much
  Loved I not honor more.

Robert Herrick

To the Virgins, To Make Much of Time

Gather ye rosebuds while ye may,
Old time is still a-flying;
And this same flower that smiles today
Tomorrow will be dying.

The glorious lamp of heaven, the sun,
The higher he's a-getting
The sooner will his race be run,
And nearer he's to setting.

That age is best which is the first,
When youth and blood are warmer;
But being spent, the worse, and worst
Times still succeed the former.

Then be not coy, but use your time,
And, while ye may, go marry;
For, having lost but once your prime,
You may forever tarry.

Sir John Suckling

The Constant Lover

Out upon it! I have loved
Three whole days together;
And am like to love three more,
If it prove fair weather.

Time shall molt away his wings
Ere he shall discover,
In the whole wide world again,
Such a constant lover.

But the spite on't is, no praise
Is due at all to me:
Love with me had made no stays
Had it any been but she.

Had it any been but she,
And that very face,
There had been at least ere this
A dozen dozen in her place.

George Wither

What Care I?

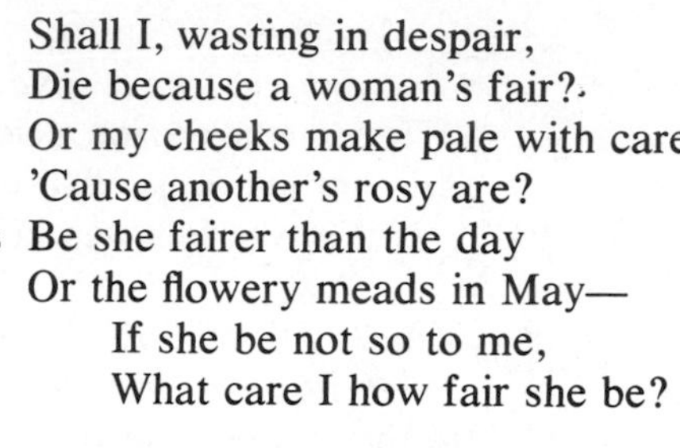
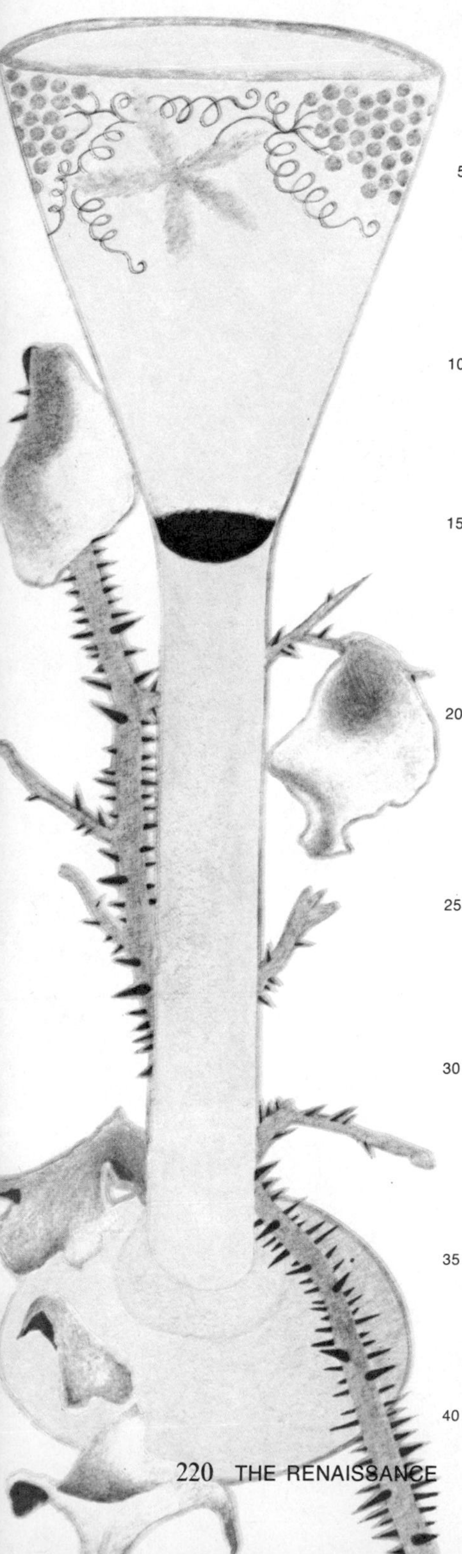

Shall I, wasting in despair,
Die because a woman's fair?
Or my cheeks make pale with care
'Cause another's rosy are?
Be she fairer than the day
Or the flowery meads in May—
If she be not so to me,
What care I how fair she be?

Shall my foolish heart be pined
'Cause I see a woman kind?
Or a well disposèd nature
Joinèd with a lovely feature?
Be she meeker, kinder, than
Turtle-dove or pelican,
If she be not so to me,
What care I how kind she be?

Shall a woman's virtues move
Me to perish for her love?
Or her merits' value known
Make me quite forget mine own?
Be she with that goodness blest
Which may gain her name of best;
If she seem not such to me,
What care I how good she be?

'Cause her fortune seems too high,
Shall I play the fool and die?
Those that bear a noble mind
Where they want of riches find,
Think what with them they would do
Who without them dare to woo;
And unless that mind I see,
What care I how great she be?

Great or good, or kind or fair,
I will ne'er the more despair;
If she love me, this believe,
I will die ere she shall grieve;
If she slight me when I woo,
I can scorn and let her go.
For if she be not for me,
What care I for whom she be?

Discussion

1. Despite its easy lyricism, "To Althea, from Prison" is a poem about three important things: love, imprisonment, and loyalty. What is the speaker's attitude toward each?

2. What might Lucasta's reaction be to the poem addressed to her?

3. **(a)** What is the advice given to young women in "To the Virgins, to Make Much of Time"? **(b)** Is the advice as sound today as it was then? Why?

4. The point of "The Constant Lover" depends upon two almost opposite meanings of the word *constant:* "faithful" and "continuous." Which applies to the speaker of this poem? Cite lines from the poem to prove your point.

5. **(a)** Is the subject of "What Care I?" one woman, or many? Explain. **(b)** What is the tone of the poem?

6. **(a)** Which of these Cavalier lyrics strikes you as the most sincere? Why? **(b)** If you could ask one of these poets to write a love poem to your sweetheart for you, which would you select, and why?

Extension • Writing

Prepare an answer, serious or otherwise, in prose or verse, to one of these five poems.

Andrew Marvell

To His Coy Mistress

Had we but world enough, and time,[1]
This coyness, lady, were no crime.
We would sit down, and think which way
To walk, and pass our long love's day.
Thou by the Indian Ganges' side
Shouldst rubies find: I by the tide
Of Humber[2] would complain[3] I would
Love you ten years before the flood,[4]
And you should, if you please, refuse
Till the conversion of the Jews,[5]
My vegetable[6] love should grow
Vaster than empires and more slow;
An hundred years should go to praise
Thine eyes, and on thy forehead gaze;
Two hundred to adore each breast,
But thirty thousand to the rest;
An age at least to every part,
And the last age should show your heart,
For, lady, you deserve this state;[7]
Nor would I love at lower rate.

But[8] at my back I always hear
Time's wingèd chariot hurrying near;
And yonder all before us lie
Deserts of vast eternity.
Thy beauty shall no more be found,
Nor in thy marble vault shall sound
My echoing song; then worms shall try
That long preserved virginity;
And your quaint[9] honor turn to dust.
And into ashes all my lust:
The grave's a fine and private place,
But none, I think, do there embrace.

Now therefore,[10] while the youthful hue
Sits on thy skin like morning dew,
And while thy willing soul transpires[11]
At every pore with instant fires,
Now let us sport us while we may,
And now, like amorous birds of prey,
Rather at once our time devour
Than languish in his slow-chapped[12] power,
Let us roll all our strength and all
Our sweetness up into one ball,
And tear our pleasures with rough strife
Thorough[13] the iron gates of life:
Thus, though we cannot make our sun
Stand still, yet we will make him run.[14]

---

1. ***time.*** Note that the poem opens with a situation contrary to fact.
2. ***Humber,*** the river that flows through Marvell's home town of Hull.
3. ***complain,*** i.e., sing plaintive love songs.
4. ***flood,*** the Biblical flood.
5. ***conversion of the Jews.*** It was a popular belief that this would occur just before the Last Judgment and the end of the world.
6. ***vegetable,*** not in the modern sense, but in the sense of living growth.
7. ***state,*** dignity.
8. ***But.*** This word reverses the situation contrary to fact of stanza 1, and returns to the real world.
9. ***quaint,*** fastidious, out-of-fashion.
10. ***Now, therefore.*** With these words, the speaker proposes a scheme of action.
11. ***transpires,*** breathes out.
12. ***slow-chapped,*** slow-jawed.
13. ***Thorough,.*** through.
14. ***Thus, though . . . run.*** Since the sun will not stand still for use, let us make him run to keep up with us.

Discussion

1. The first stanza of "To His Coy Mistress" sounds like a traditional love poem urging the lady to make the most of time. However, something frightening happens in the second stanza. What is it?

2. Relate the last two lines of "To His Coy Mistress" ("Thus, though we cannot make our sun/ Stand still, yet we will make him run") to the rest of the poem.

Contemporary writers have found Marvell's "To His Coy Mistress" a fascinating poem—not so much about love as about time. The contemporary American poet Archibald MacLeish was moved to write a poem directly to Marvell.

Archibald MacLeish

You, Andrew Marvell

And here face down beneath the sun
And here upon earth's noonward height
To feel the always coming on
The always rising of the night:

To feel creep up the curving east
The earthy chill of dusk and slow
Upon those under lands the vast
And ever climbing shadow grow

And strange at Ecbatan[1] the trees
Take leaf by leaf the evening strange
The flooding dark about their knees
The mountains over Persia change

And now at Kermanshah[2] the gate
Dark empty and the withered grass
And through the twilight now the late
Few travelers in the westward pass

And Baghdad[3] darken and the bridge
Across the silent river gone
And through Arabia the edge
Of evening widen and steal on

And deepen on Palmyra's[4] street
The wheel rut in the ruined stone
And Lebanon fade out and Crete[5]
High through the clouds and overblown

And over Sicily the air
Still flashing with the landward gulls
And loom and slowly disappear
The sails above the shadowy hulls

And Spain go under and the shore
Of Africa the gilded sand
And evening vanish and no more
The low pale light across that land

Nor now the long light on the sea:

And here face downward in the sun
To feel how swift how secretly
The shadow of the night comes on . . .

1. ***Ectaban,*** city in old Persia, now in modern Iran. (Note that MacLeish names cities from east to west, just as the sun seems to move and the shadow of dusk moves.
2. ***Kermanshah,*** ancient province and town in Iran.
3. ***Baghdad,*** most important city in Mesopotamia, now the capital of Iraq.
4. ***Palmyra,*** ancient city of central Syria.
5. ***Crete,*** an island of Greece, in the Mediterranean.

Discussion

1. Lines 21–22 of "To His Coy Mistress" are two of the most famous lines of English poetry: "But at my back I always hear/ Time's wingéd chariot hurrying near." **(a)** Discuss the meaning and effect of the lines. **(b)** How do they relate to Archibald MacLeish's poem?

3. **(a)** How much time actually elapses between lines 1 and 34–36 of the MacLeish poem? **(b)** Why does the MacLeish poem seem to begin in the middle of something, opening with the conjunction *And,* and to break off without actually concluding?

The Garden

How vainly men themselves amaze
To win the palm, the oak, or bays,[1]
And their uncessant labors see
Crowned from some single herb or tree,[2]
Whose short and narrow-verged shade
Does prudently their toils upbraid;
While all the flowers and trees do close
To weave the garlands of repose![3]

Fair Quiet, have I found thee here,
And Innocence thy sister dear?
Mistaken long, I sought you then
In busy companies of men:
Your sacred plants, if here below,
Only among the plants will grow:
Society is all but rude[4]
To this delicious solitude.

No white nor red[5] was ever seen
So amorous as this lovely green.
Fond[6] lovers, cruel as their flame,
Cut in these trees their mistress' name:
Little, alas! they know or heed
How far these beauties hers exceed!
Fair trees! wheres'e'er your barks I wound,
No name shall but your own be found.[7]

---

1. ***the palm, the oak, or bays,*** wreaths awarded for outstanding achievement in athletics, politics, or poetry.
2. ***tree,*** sources of the wreaths mentioned in line 2.
3. ***repose.*** The sense is that repose is rewarded by all flowers and trees, not merely by a single one.
4. ***rude,*** uncouth.
5. ***white nor red,*** variously explained as either signifying a woman's complexion, or the qualities of innocence and passion.
6. ***Fond,*** foolish.
7. ***found.*** The sense is that instead of carving girls' names on trees, the speaker will carve their own, i.e., "oak" on an oak, "elm" on an elm, etc.

When we have run our passions' heat,
Love hither makes his best retreat:
The gods, that mortal beauty chase,
Still in a tree did end their race;
Apollo hunted Daphne so
Only that she might laurel grow;
And Pan did after Syrinx speed
Not as a nymph, but for a reed.[8]

What wondrous life is this I lead!
Ripe apples drop about my head;
The luscious clusters of the vine
Upon my mouth do crush their wine;
The nectarine and curious[9] peach
Into my hands themselves do reach;
Stumbling on melons, as I pass,
Ensnared with flowers, I fall on grass.

Meanwhile the mind from pleasure less[10]
Withdraws into its happiness;
The mind, that Ocean where each kind
Does straight its own resemblance find;[11]
Yet it creates, transcending these,
Far other worlds, and other seas—
Annihilating all that's made
To a green thought in a green shade.[12]

Here at the fountain's sliding foot,
Or at some fruit-tree's mossy root,
Casting the body's vest aside,
My soul into the boughs does glide;[13]
There, like a bird, it sits and sings,
Then whets and combs its silver wings,
And, till prepared for longer flight,
Waves in its plumes the various light.[14]

Such was that happy Garden-state[15]
While man there walked without a mate:
After a place so pure and sweet,
What other help could yet be meet!
But 'twas beyond a mortal's share
To wander solitary there:
Two paradises 'twere in one,
To live in Paradise alone.[16]

How well the skillful gardener drew
Of flowers and herbs this dial[17] new!
Where, from above, the milder sun
Does through a fragrant zodiac run:
And, as it works, the industrious bee
Computes its time[18] as well as we.
How could such sweet and wholesome hours
Be reckoned, but with herbs and flowers!

---

8. ***reed.*** To escape Apollo, Daphne was changed into a laurel; to escape Pan, Syrinx was changed into a reed, from which he then made his panpipes.
9. ***curious,*** exquisite.
10. ***pleasure less,*** pleasure of a lesser kind.
11. ***The mind . . . find.*** It was thought that every creature on earth had its counterpart in the sea.
12. ***Yet it . . . green shade.*** The sense is that as the mind draws more into itself, its creations (thought and imagination) close out (or annihilate) those of the outside world. The last two lines (47–48) have many possibilities, and scholars have argued long over the meaning of "green thought in a green shade" without convincing one another.
13. ***glide.*** Here the speaker completely identifies himself with Nature.
14. ***And, till . . . light.*** The "longer flight" is to the next world, which it was believed was illuminated by a white radiance, as contrasted with the "various light" or rainbow colors of this world.
15. ***Garden-state,*** the Garden of Eden.
16. ***alone.*** If the speaker is serious, he prefers Eden without Eve.
17. ***dial.*** The gardener has designed a floral sun dial.
18. ***time.*** A pun on thyme-time.

Discussion

1. "At its simplest level, this poem contrasts the active and the contemplative life, preferring the latter." Cite some details to support or refute this statement.

2. **(a)** Comment upon the sensuous effects of stanza five. **(b)** What is the effect of the exaggeration?

3. The most quoted lines of the poem are the last two of Stanza 6: "Annihilating all that's made / To a green thought in a green shade." How do they uphold the contemplative life rather than the active life?

4. The concept of the passage of time occurs in the last stanza. How does it here differ from the treatment of time in "To His Coy Mistress"?

John Milton

On His Having Arrive at the Age of Twenty-Three

How soon hath Time, the subtle thief of youth
Stolen on his wing my three and twentieth year!
My hasting days fly on with full career,
But my late spring no bud or blossom shew'th.[1]
Perhaps my semblance[2] might deceive the truth
That I to manhood am arrived so near;
And inward ripeness doth much less appear,
That some more timely-happy spirits endu'th.[3]
Yet be it less or more, or soon or slow,
It shall be still in strictest measure even[4]
To that same lot, however mean or high,
Toward which Time leads me, and the will of Heaven;
All is, if I have grace to use it so,
As ever in my great Task-Master's eye.

1. ***shew'th,*** shows.
2. ***semblance,*** youthful appearance.
3. ***endu'th,*** endows.
4. ***even,*** adequate; i.e., his "inward ripeness," or inner readiness, will be adequate to whatever destiny Time and Heaven are leading him.

On His Blindness

When I consider how my light is spent
Ere half my days in this dark world and wide,
And that one talent[1] which is death to hide
Lodged with me useless, though my soul more bent
To serve therewith my Maker, and present
My true account, lest He returning chide;
"Doth God exact day-labor, light denied?"
I fondly[2] ask. But Patience, to prevent
That murmur, soon replies, "God doth not need
Either man's work or His own gifts. Who best
Bear His mild yoke, they serve Him best. His state
Is kingly: thousands at His bidding speed,
And post o'er land and ocean without rest;
They also serve who only stand and wait."

1. ***talent,*** the gift of writing. This refers to Jesus's parable of the "unprofitable servant," condemned for burying his one talent, or coin, instead of spending it. (Matt. 25:15-30)
2. ***fondly,*** foolishly.

Discussion

1. (a) In "On His Having Arrived at the Age of Twenty-Three," what complaint does Milton make in the first eight lines (the "proposition")? **(b)** How is it resolved in the last six lines (the "resolution")?

2. (a) In "On His Blindness," what solace does Milton find in the final line, "They also serve who only stand and wait"? **(b)** Who in today's world might also derive solace from them?

3. Compare "On His Blindness" with the sonnet written at the age of twenty-three (more than two decades earlier), both of which are concerned with Milton's achievements.

from Paradise Lost

Like all epic poems, Milton's *Paradise Lost* is a long narrative of events on a grand scale. In the case of *Paradise Lost,* the scale is one of the grandest possible, for the poem has as its setting the entire universe. The main characters are God, His Son, Adam and Eve, and Satan. And the theme is the fall of man as embodied in the Biblical story of the temptation of Adam and Eve and their expulsion from Paradise.

As if inspired by the earthly event of civil war in his own time and place, Milton envisions a civil war in Heaven, arising over God's appointment of His Son to the seat of honor and power at His right hand. Satan, one of the archangels, desires the exalted position for himself, and with a third of the other angels he wages war against God and His followers. God's forces prove superior; Satan and his rebel host are sent plunging down into Hell, the place that God had prepared for them, as far removed from Heaven as possible.

From this point on Satan vows eternal vengeance. He has heard of God's plan to fashion a new creature called man and to place him in a new region called the world. Why not strike back at God through the corruption of this latest creature of His handiwork?

The story of Satan's meeting with Adam and Eve in the Garden of Eden follows, in the main, the Bible story. Satan tempts Eve, who in turn persuades Adam to eat the forbidden fruit of the Tree of Knowledge. For their disobedience, Adam and Eve are driven from Paradise out into the world. The twelfth and last book of the poem closes with the pair standing hand in hand upon the threshold of the world. Paradise, "so late their happy home," lies behind them. Sadly and penitently they face the future, their punishment softened only by the promise of the ultimate redemption of man by Christ.

Milton did not develop his story chronologically. Instead he adopted the traditional epic technique of beginning *in medias res,* or in the middle of the action, waiting until later in the poem to provide a narrative of the earlier events of his story. Thus in Book I the reader is confronted with the terrifying scenes of Satan and his "horrid crew" "rolling in the fiery gulf" of Hell and of Satan hurling thundering speeches of defiance at the Almighty.

from **Book I**

Of man's first disobedience, and the fruit
Of that forbidden tree, whose mortal taste
Brought death into the world, and all our woe,
With loss of Eden, till one greater Man[1]
Restore us, and regain the blissful seat,
Sing Heavenly Muse,[2] that on the secret top
Of Oreb, or of Sinai,[3] didst inspire
That shepherd,[4] who first taught the chosen
seed,[5]
In the beginning[6] how the heavens and earth
Rose out of Chaos: Or if Sion hill[7]
Delight thee more, and Siloa's brook[8] that
flowed
Fast by the oracle of God; I thence
Invoke thy aid to my adventurous song,
That with no middle flight intends to soar

1. ***Man,*** the Messiah.
2. ***Heavenly Muse.*** Milton does not name his muse directly here, but later (Book VII) calls her Urania, meaning "Heavenly," which is the name of the Muse of Astronomy, though Milton is careful to state there is no connection between his muse and the pagan Nine Muses.
3. ***Oreb . . . Sinai,*** twin peaks in Arabia.
4. ***shepherd,*** Moses, who on Mt. Sinai received the Word of God.
5. ***chosen seed,*** the Israelites.
6. ***beginning,*** a punning reference to the Book of Genesis, supposedly composed by Moses.
7. ***Sion Hill,*** the height upon which Jerusalem was built.
8. ***Siloa's brook,*** the stream which flowed near the hill on which the temple was erected in Jerusalem.

Above the Aonian mount,[9] while it pursues
Things unattempted yet in prose or rhyme.
And chiefly Thou, O Spirit, that dost prefer
Before all temples the upright heart and pure,
Instruct me, for Thou knowest; Thou from the first
Wast present, and, with mighty wings outspread,
Dovelike sat'st brooding on the vast Abyss
And mad'st it pregnant: What in me is dark
Illumine, what is low raise and support;
That to the height of this great argument
I may assert Eternal Providence,
And justify the ways of God to men.[10]
  Say first,[11] for Heaven hides nothing from thy view,
Nor the deep tract of Hell, say first what cause
Moved our grand Parents in that happy state,
Favored of Heaven so highly, to fall off
From their Creator, and transgress His will
For one restraint, lords of the world besides?
Who first seduced them to that foul revolt?[12]
The infernal Serpent; he it was, whose guile
Stirred up with envy and revenge, deceived
The mother of mankind, what time his pride[13]
Had cast him out from Heaven, with all his host
Of rebel Angels, by whose aid aspiring
To set himself in glory above his peers,
He trusted to have equaled the Most High,
If He opposed; and with ambitious aim
Against the throne and monarchy of God
Raised impious war in Heaven and battle proud
With vain attempt. Him the Almighty Power
Hurled headlong flaming from the ethereal sky,
With hideous ruin and combustion down
To bottomless perdition, there to dwell
In adamantine chains and penal fire,
Who durst defy the Omnipotent to arms.
Nine times the space that measures day and night
To mortal men, he with his horrid crew
Lay vanquished, rolling in the fiery gulf,
Confounded though immortal: But his doom
Reserved him to more wrath; for now the thought
Both of lost happiness and lasting pain
Torments him; round he throws his baleful eyes
That witnessed[14] huge affliction and dismay
Mixed with obdurate pride and steadfast hate:
At once as far as angel's ken he views
The dismal situation waste and wild;
A dungeon horrible, on all sides round
As one great furnace flamed, yet from those flames
No light, but rather darkness visible[15]
Served only to discover sights of woe,
Regions of sorrow, doleful shades, where peace
And rest can never dwell, hope never comes
That comes to all;[16] but torture without end
Still urges, and a fiery deluge, fed
With ever-burning sulphur unconsumed:
Such place Eternal Justice had prepared
For those rebellious, here their prison ordained
In utter darkness, and their portion set
As far removed from God and light of Heaven
As from the center thrice to the utmost pole.
O how unlike the place from whence they fell!
There the companions of his fall, o'erwhelmed
With floods and whirlwinds of tempestuous fire,
He soon discerns, and weltering[17] by his side
One next himself in power, and next in crime,
Long after known in Palestine, and named
Beelzebub.[18] To whom the Arch-Enemy,
And thence in Heaven called Satan,[19] with bold words
Breaking the horrid silence thus began:

Addressing Beelzebub, Satan boldly declares that though he has been thrown into Hell, he will continue to fight God with all his might. Beelzebub is afraid that God is too strong to be overcome. Satan, chiding him for his fears, begins to make plans.

---

9. ***Aonian*** (ā ō′ni ən) ***mount,*** Mount Helicon, representing Greek poetry, which Milton, by writing a Christian poem, endeavored to surpass.
10. ***men.*** This concludes the invocation (lines 1–26).
11. ***Say first.*** Here begins the epic question.
12. ***revolt.*** The epic question ends here.
13. ***pride,*** Satan's sin, the most deadly of the Seven Deadly Sins.
14. ***witnessed,*** gave evidence of.
15. ***darkness visible.*** It was thought that the flames of hell gave no light.
16. ***to all,*** The greatest torment of Hell was the total absence of hope of salvation.
17. ***weltering,*** tossing.
18. ***Beelzebub*** (bi el′zə bub), from Hebrew meaning "Lord of Flies." In the time of Jesus, Beelzebub was "prince of the demons." (Matthew 12:24; Luke 11:15) In certain medieval literature he was a chief associate of Satan.
19. ***Satan,*** "the Adversary."

"Seest thou yon dreary plain, forlorn and wild,
The seat of desolation, void of light,
Save what the glimmering of these livid flames
Casts pale and dreadful? Thither let us tend
From off the tossing of these fiery waves,
There rest, if any rest can harbor there,
And reassembling our afflicted powers,
Consult how we may henceforth most offend
Our Enemy,[20] our own loss how repair,
How overcome this dire calamity,
What reinforcement we may gain from hope,
If not what resolution from despair."
Thus Satan, talking to his nearest mate,
With head uplift above the wave, and eyes
That sparkling blazed; his other parts besides
Prone on the flood, extended long and large,
Lay floating many a rood,[21] in bulk as huge
As whom the fables name of monstrous size,
Titanian, or Earth-born,[22] that warred on Jove,
Briareos or Typhon,[23] whom the den
By ancient Tarsus held, or that sea-beast
Leviathan,[24] which God of all His works
Created hugest that swim the ocean-stream:
Him, haply slumbering on the Norway foam,
The pilot of some small night-foundered skiff
Deeming some island, oft, as seamen tell,
With fixèd anchor in his scaly rind
Moors by his side under the lee, while night
Invests the sea, and wishèd morn delays:
So stretched out huge in length the Arch-Fiend lay
Chained on the burning lake, nor ever thence
Had risen or heaved his head, but that the will
And high permission of all-ruling Heaven
Left him at large to his own dark designs,
That with reiterated crimes he might
Heap on himself damnation, while he sought
Evil to others, and enraged might see
How all his malice served but to bring forth
Infinite goodness, grace, and mercy shown
On Man by him seduced, but on himself
Treble confusion, wrath, and vengeance poured.
Forthwith upright he rears from off the pool
His mighty stature; on each hand the flames,
Driven backward, slope their pointing spires, and rolled
In billows, leave in the midst a horrid vale.
Then with expanded wings he steers his flight
Aloft, incumbent on the dusky air
That felt unusual weight, till on dry land
He lights; if it were land that ever burned
With solid, as the lake with liquid fire;
And such appeared in hue, as when the force
Of subterranean wind transports a hill
Torn from Pelorus,[25] or the shattered side
Of thundering Etna, whose combustible
And fueled entrails thence conceiving fire,
Sublimed with mineral fury, aid the winds.
And leave a singèd bottom all involved
With stench and smoke: Such resting found the sole
Of unblest feet. Him followed his next mate,
Both glorying to have 'scaped the Stygian flood[26]
As gods, and by their own recovered strength,
Not by the sufferance of Supernal Power.
"Is this the region, this the soil, the clime,"
Said then the lost Archangel, "this the seat
That we must change for Heaven, this mournful gloom
For that celestial light? Be it so, since He
Who now is sovereign can dispose and bid
What shall be right: Farthest from Him is best,
Whom reason hath equaled, force hath made supreme
Above His equals.[27] Farewell happy fields,
Where joy forever dwells: Hail horrors! hail
Infernal world! and thou profoundest Hell
Receive thy new possessor: One who brings
A mind not to be changed by place or time.
The mind is its own place, and in itself
Can make a Heaven of Hell, a Hell of Heaven.
What matter where, if I be still the same,
And what I should be, all but less than He
Whom thunder hath made greater? Here at least

---

20. ***Enemy,*** God.
21. ***rood,*** usually seven or eight yards.
22. ***Earth-born.*** Both the Titans (giants descended from Heaven) and the earth-born (giants) "warred on Jove."
23. ***Briareos*** (brī ar′i əs) ***or Typhon*** (tī′fən), in Greek mythology, two monsters, the first with a hundred hands, the second with a hundred fire-breathing heads, who attempted to overthrow the dynasty of Jove. Typhon lived in Cilicia (sə lish′ə), of which *Tarsus* (tär′səs) (line 104) was the capital.
24. ***Leviathan,*** huge sea-monster mentioned in the Bible.
25. ***Pelorus*** (pə lor′əs), the northeastern promontory of Sicily near the volcano of Mount Etna (line 137).
26. ***Stygian*** (stij′i ən) ***flood,*** the river Styx, one of the four rivers in Hades.
27. ***equals.*** Note that Satan equates his reason with that of God, and attributes his defeat to the larger number of angels that remained loyal to God.

We shall be free; the Almighty hath not built
Here for His envy, will not drive us hence:
Here we may reign secure, and in my choice
To reign is worth ambition though in Hell:
Better to reign in Hell, than serve in Heaven.
But wherefore let we then our faithful friends,
The associates and copartners of our loss,
Lie thus astonished on the oblivious pool,
And call them not to share with us their part
In this unhappy mansion, or once more
With rallied arms to try what may be yet
Regained in Heaven, or what more lost in Hell?"
So Satan spake, and him Beelzebub
Thus answered: "Leader of those armies bright,
Which, but the Omnipotent, none could have foiled,
If once they hear that voice, their liveliest pledge
Of hope in fears and dangers, heard so oft
In worst extremes, and on the perilous edge
Of battle when it raged, in all assaults
Their surest signal, they will soon resume
New courage and revive, though now they lie
Groveling and prostrate on yon lake of fire,
As we erewhile, astounded and amazed,
No wonder, fallen such a pernicious height."
He scarce had ceased when the superior Fiend
Was moving toward the shore; his ponderous shield,
Ethereal temper, massy, large, and round,
Behind him cast; the broad circumference
Hung on his shoulders like the moon, whose orb
Through optic glass the Tuscan artist views
At evening from the top of Fesole,
Or in Valdarno,[28] to descry new lands,
Rivers, or mountains in her spotty globe.
His spear, to equal which the tallest pine
Hewn on Norwegian hills, to be the mast
Of some great ammiral,[29] were but a wand,
He walked with to support uneasy steps
Over the burning marl, not like those steps
On Heaven's azure, and the torrid clime
Smote on him sore besides, vaulted with fire;
Nathless[30] he so endured, till on the beach
Of that inflamed sea, he stood and called
His legions, Angel forms, who lay entranced
Thick as autumnal leaves that strew the brooks.
In Vallombrosa,[31] where the Etrurian shades
High overarched embower; or scattered sedge
Afloat, when with fierce winds Orion[32] armed
Hath vexed the Red Sea coast, whose waves o'erthrew
Busiris and his Memphian chivalry,
While with perfidious hatred they pursued
The sojourners of Goshen,[33] who beheld
From the safe shore their floating carcasses
And broken chariot wheels—so thick bestrewn,
Abject and lost, lay these, covering the flood,
Under amazement of their hideous change.
He called so loud, that all the hollow deep
Of Hell resounded: "Princes, Potentates,
Warriors, the Flower of Heaven, once yours, now lost,
If such astonishment as this can seize
Eternal Spirits; or have ye chosen this place
After the toil of battle to repose
Your wearied virtue, for the ease you find
To slumber here, as in the vales of Heaven?
Or in this abject posture have ye sworn
To adore the Conqueror? Who now beholds
Cherub and Seraph rolling in the flood
With scattered arms and ensigns, till anon
His swift pursuers from Heaven gates discern
The advantage, and discending, tread us down
Thus drooping, or with linked thunderbolts
Transfix us to the bottom of this gulf.
Awake, arise, or be forever fallen."

First to rise from the burning lake are the leaders of the fallen angels. Followed by the multitude, they wing their way to the plain and assemble in military formation before their "dread Commander," Satan.

---

28. ***optic . . . Valdarno.*** The optic glass is the telescope of Galileo, whom Milton refers to as Tuscan because he lived in Tuscany, a region in central Italy which includes Florence. Fesole (Fiesole, fē e′zō lā) is a city on a hill near Florence. Valdarno (val där′no) is the valley of the River Arno in which Florence is situated.

29. ***ammiral,*** admiral, the flagship bearing the admiral of the fleet.

30. ***Nathless,*** nevertheless.

31. ***Vallombrosa*** (val lom brō′sə), a valley twenty miles east of Florence. Florence and the surrounding country are in ancient Etruria (i trür′iə) (line 207).

32. ***Orion,*** in Greek mythology, a hunter who became a constellation after his death. When the constellation rises late (in November), it is supposed to cause storms.

33. ***Goshen*** (gō′shən) Busiris was a mythical king of Egypt (Goshen). Milton considers him the Pharaoh who with his cavalry pursued the children of Israel into the Red Sea (Exodus 14).

He, above the rest
In shape and gesture proudly eminent,
Stood like a tower; his form had yet not lost
All her original brightness, nor appeared
Less than Archangel ruined, and the excess
Of glory obscured: As when the sun new-risen
Looks through the horizontal misty air
Shorn of his beams, or from behind the moon
In dim eclipse, disastrous twilight sheds
On half the nations, and with fear of change
Perplexes monarchs. Darkened so, yet shone
Above them all the Archangel; but his face
Deep scars of thunder had intrenched, and care
Sat on his faded cheek, but under brows
Of dauntless courage, and considerate pride
Waiting revenge: Cruel his eye, but cast
Signs of remorse and passion to behold
The fellows of his crime, the followers rather
(Far other once beheld in bliss), condemned
Forever now to have their lot in pain.

In his speech to the army, Satan announces his intention of seeking revenge by fraud or guile, not force. Book I ends with the building of the palace of Pandemonium (that is, "All Demons"*), and with preparations for a council of war.*

Discussion

Understanding Structure

Paradise Lost is the greatest epic in the English language. Although it observes the conventions of the Classical epic, pagan elements have been Christianized. To appreciate the excerpt you have just read, you should become aware of its epic conventions.

1. "Of man's first disobedience . . . ways of God to men" (lines 1–26) constitutes the invocation, which, in the Classical tradition, begins the epic. In them the poet invokes the aid of a muse and states the theme of his work. **(a)** What muse does Milton invoke? Account for that choice. **(b)** What is the theme of the epic? **(c)** What in the invocation is in the Classical tradition, and what is Christian?

2. "Say first . . . revolt" (lines 27–33) poses the epic question, the question that the epic will deal with. In *Paradise Lost,* the epic question has two parts. What are they?

3. To aid in the visualization and understanding of scenes, persons, and events, the epic employs many similes. Because we are dealing with the introductory phases of the poem, only one appears in the first hundred lines. What is it?

4. The epic achieves much of its effect by the use of the epic simile, which consists of multiple comparisons (usually two), and is introduced by "like," "as," or, more commonly, "as whom," "as when," "as where," etc. The first of these epic similes, referred to as the Leviathan Simile, occurs in lines 101–112 (*As whom . . . morn delays).* **(a)** To what beings is Satan being compared? **(b)** Which image remains the strongest in your mind? Why? **(c)** There are three more of these epic similes in the selection. List them and explain the function of each.

5. Epic speeches are usually in elevated language, are usually introduced by the name of the person(s) being addressed, and are often boastful. Ignore Satan's first speech (lines 84–95), because space limitations necessitated that its beginning be cut, but reread the following speeches and indicate the presence or absence of elevated language, epithets, and boastfulness: Satan to Beelzebub (lines 146–174); Beelzebub to Satan (lines 176–187); Satan to his followers (lines 219–234).

6. A Classical epic always

includes detailed descriptions of the armor and weapons of the combatants and descriptions of their battles. Find the equivalent in *Paradise Lost.*

Comprehending Meaning and Artistry

1. In the invocation, Milton asks to be able to "assert Eternal Providence" (line 25)—meaning that God controls everything. How do the lines "So stretched out . . . vengeance poured" (113–124) support Milton's assertion? **(b)** Account then for the following lines: "Both glorying to have 'scaped the Stygian flood / As gods, and by their own recovered strength, / Not by the sufferance of Supernal Power" (143–145).

2. Summarize briefly the action of these excerpts.

3. All readers must marvel at the range of visual detail that the blind Milton incorporated in his epic. Find a quiet place where you can read without interruption, and reread the following passages so that you may visualize the images: **(a)** The description of Hell (lines 61–69) and scattered references elsewhere. What are the most striking images? **(b)** The descriptions of Satan (lines 96–101; 126–128; 187–202; 235–250). Condense these into a single-sentence description of him.

4. *Paradise Lost* abounds in quotable lines. Explain in your own words the meaning of the following: **(a)** "The mind is its own place, and in itself / Can make a Heaven of Hell, a Hell of Heaven" (lines 158–159). **(b)** "Better to reign in Hell than serve in Heaven" (line 167).

5. Milton did not intend that Satan be the protagonist of *Paradise Lost,* as the later books of his epic show. He did, however, paint Satan's character so strongly that generations of readers have become fascinated by him. Using what you have gleaned from the excerpts you have read, discuss the character traits of Satan that make him seem almost an antihero (a protagonist with character traits opposed to those of the conventional hero).

Vocabulary
Context, Pronunciation, and Dictionary

A. Using context as an aid, write the most appropriate definition for each italicized word on a separate sheet of paper.

1. "Read not to contradict and *confute,* nor to believe and take for granted, nor to find talk and discourse, but to weigh and consider." **(a)** prove true; **(b)** prove false; **(c)** applaud.

2. "Hail Horrors! hail / *Infernal* world! and thou profoundest Hell / Receive thy new possessor." **(a)** hellish; **(b)** heavenly; **(c)** peaceful.

3. "And God said unto them, 'Be fruitful, and multiply, and *replenish* the earth.'" **(a)** waste; **(b)** plunder; **(c)** refill.

B. Use your Glossary and its pronunciation key to answer on the same sheet of paper the following questions about the pronunciation of the italicized words.

4. **(a)** How many schwa (ə) sounds are there in *litigious?* **(b)** Does *bite* or *bit* have the same vowel sound as the accented syllable?

5. **(a)** How many syllables does *annihilate* have? **(b)** Does *guy* or *eight* rhyme with the accented syllable?

C. Use your Glossary to answer the following questions about the words listed below. Read each clue and then write the matching word from the list on your paper.

fetter	oracle
nectar	torrid

6. Which comes from a word related to a part of the body?

7. Which can mean an answer, a place, or a person?

8. Which refers to a substance gathered by bees?

Extension • Writing

1. Satan's sin, the deadliest of all sins, was pride. Write a short composition in which you point out evidence of his pride and discuss the effects of it on him and his followers.

2. *Paradise Lost* abounds in images of light and darkness, perhaps suggested or supported by Milton's consciousness of his own blindness. Write a short paper in which you discuss these images.

Extension • Speaking

Read aloud to yourself a passage of your own choosing to savor the full resonance of what Tennyson called "the organ voice" of Milton. You might wish to prepare this passage for classroom presentation.

Sir Francis Bacon 1561 • 1626

Bacon was a courtier to the manner born. His father had been one of Queen Elizabeth's important ministers, and he was kinsman to the influential and noble Cecil family. In the Renaissance tradition, Bacon successfully coordinated a life of politics with the life of the mind. He rose from a minor embassy post, during Elizabeth's reign, to the position of Lord Chancellor under James I. He was one of the first English essayists, and also wrote a fictional account of an ideal state, *The New Atlantis.* Scientific thinking, with its logical, empirical, and inductive reasoning, was championed by Bacon. His *Instauratio Magna*, or Great Renewal of Science, proposed a revision of the field of exact knowledge through experimentation and observation—the background for modern science.

Bacon's devotion to science was literally the death of him. After stuffing a chicken with snow, as an experiment in preserving meat by freezing, he contracted a fatal case of pneumonia.

John Donne 1572 • 1631

The dichotomy of flesh and spirit found in Donne's work reflects the sequence of styles in his own life. He came from a prosperous Catholic family, studied at both Oxford and Cambridge, and began to read law. As a young man his main interests seem to have been the theater, women, and the writing of bawdy and cynical verse. In 1596 he joined a military campaign and journeyed to Cádiz; the following year he went on another campaign to the Azores. In 1598 he was appointed secretary to one of the Queen's ministers, but he eloped with the minister's niece three years later and lost favor and his position.

Among the various means by which Donne tried to support his growing family (he eventually fathered twelve children) was pamphlet writing. Some of his tracts were in support of the Anglican Church. In 1607 King James, impressed by these works, urged Donne to take holy orders. (Donne had converted to the established Church before 1600.) Since the King refused to grant him any other position, Donne finally joined the clergy in 1615.

Donne preached regularly before members of the court and London's wealthy merchant class, and the literary and dramatic flair of his sermons made him widely admired. In 1621 he was appointed Dean of St. Paul's Cathedral, and he was in line for a bishopric when he died.

During his later years, Donne became obsessed with the idea of death. He is said to have preached his own funeral oration several weeks before his death, and he posed, wrapped in a shroud, for the effigy on his own tomb.

Robert Herrick 1591 • 1674

Like Donne, Herrick turned from a worldly life to holy orders. He loved London and the society of poets and wits like Ben Jonson, and when in 1629 he was appointed to a country parish in Devonshire, he considered it a better exile. Gradually, though, he came to delight in the life and customs of the West Country. As a Royalist, he lost his post during the Puritan upheaval and returned to London in 1647. The next year he published his only book, a collection of 1200 poems. Because the times were tempestuous (the country was obsessed with the trial and execution of King Charles I), Herrick's book was soon lost to public view. After the Restoration, Herrick was reinstated in his parish and resumed his quiet country life. His poetry was rediscovered only in the Nineteenth century.

Ben Jonson 1572 • 1637

Jonson was a charismatic person who fascinated his contemporaries. His work was scholarly, the result, perhaps, of several years of classical schooling he received as a boy and many years of self-tutelage in later life. He never went to university (though both Oxford and Cambridge later awarded him honorary degrees). Instead he took up his stepfather's trade, bricklaying, and then entered the army. During service in Flanders he killed a Spaniard in single-handed combat as both English and Spanish armies looked on.

On his return to London in 1595 he became an actor and a playwright. He produced his first successful play, *Every Man in His Humour,* in 1598 (Shakespeare, a friend, acted in it). Shortly after this, Jonson, always hot-headed, was imprisoned and nearly executed for killing a fellow actor in a duel. Once released, he continued his career in the theater, gained the favor of James I, and became a writer of court masques—elaborate spectacles which involved music, dancing, and pageantry. During this period he also wrote a number of sa-

tiric comedies, two of which—*Volpone* and *The Alchemist*—are still considered among the supreme satiric achievements of the English stage.

After the death of James I, Jonson was neglected by both the public and the court, for Charles I patronized painters rather than writers. Nevertheless, he became the center of a circle of young poets who dubbed themselves "The Tribe of Ben" and regularly joined him at the Mermaid Tavern for feasts of wine and wit. At his death Jonson was widely mourned as the last of the great Elizabethans. He lies buried in Westminster Abbey under the inscription "O Rare Ben Jonson."

Richard Lovelace 1618 • 1657

Handsome and clever, the eldest son of a wealthy family, Richard Lovelace was very much the courtly Cavalier poet. When King Charles and his queen visited Oxford in 1636, they were so favorably impressed by undergraduate Lovelace's demeanor that they commanded he be given an M.A. on the spot. However, his allegiance to King Charles during the Civil Wars caused him several stays in prison (during the first of which he wrote "To Althea").

His periods of imprisonment and his adventures in the French campaign against the Spanish, during which he was wounded, exhausted his inheritance. He spent the last years of his life impoverished and depressed, and died at the age of 39 in a London slum.

Andrew Marvell 1621 • 1678

Marvell was a quiet and sensible man with Puritan leanings who became devoted to Cromwell's cause. Yet he was so extremely tolerant of others' opinions that as a student at Cambridge he allowed a Jesuit to persuade him to quit his studies. (The senior Marvell, an Anglican minister, found his son in a London bookshop and convinced him to return to the university.) After earning his degree, he traveled abroad for several years and then became a tutor to the daughter of Sir Thomas Fairfax, Lord-General of the Parliamentary Forces.

In 1657 Marvell was appointed assistant to Milton, who was then Latin Secretary. Two years later Marvell was elected to the House of Commons, where he served his constituents conscientiously, refusing all bribes and writing frequent newsletters. These newsletters, together with some satires and religious tracts, made up most of the writings for which he was known during his lifetime. Three years after his death a volume of his poetry was published by a woman who claimed to be his widow, but who later turned out to be his housekeeper.

John Milton 1608 • 1674

In his parents' cultured Puritan home, Milton began to write poetry at the age of ten. After finishing his formal education with an M.A. from Cambridge, he returned to his family's country home at Horton to study under his own direction. There he read almost everything available in Latin, Greek, Italian, and English, and wrote the elegy *Lycidas* and the masque *Comus.* After five years at Horton, Milton embarked on a two-year tour of Europe, where he found his literary reputation had already begun to spread. With the outbreak of the Civil Wars, he returned to England, where he tutored and wrote pamphlets. Among these was *Areopagitica,* a strong argument for freedom of the press. When his first marriage went awry, he became an early and vehement advocate of divorce on the grounds of incompatibility, a cause which he championed in his pamphlets and which many people in Puritan England found reprehensible. (Milton was married three times, widowed twice.)

Under the new Commonwealth, Milton was appointed Latin Secretary (a post comparable to Secretary of Foreign Affairs). While he held this office, eyestrain from years of reading late into the night caused him to become totally blind.

Despite a brief imprisonment, the seizure of most of his property, and the destruction of some of his pamphlets, Milton survived the Restoration essentially unharmed. He and his daughters retired to a quiet life. Accounts tell of tension between the stern and dictorial Milton and his unsympathetic daughters, who resented having to read aloud in languages they did not understand and take dictation for hours on end. But the final years of Milton's life were productive, if not completely peaceful. During his last decade he wrote (through dictation) *Paradise Lost, Paradise Regained,* and *Samson Agonistes.*

Sir John Suckling 1609 • 1642

Suckling, like Lovelace, was a graceful and carefree Cavalier dandy. Living mainly off a sizable inheritance, he cut a dashing figure at court. He preferred women, music, and gambling to the refinements of wit and intellect. During the Civil Wars he raised a gaudily outfitted company of "gentlemen" for a campaign against the Scots, but the whole company withdrew swiftly if not graciously on first contact with the enemy.

In 1641 Suckling, a Loyalist, became involved in a plot to free one of the King's imprisoned ministers. The plot was discovered; Suckling was accused of conspiracy to overthrow Parliament. Realizing that the King could no longer provide protection, he fled to France. There he died in poverty the following year, possibly by his own hand.

George Wither 1588 • 1667

Wither first made his reputation as a poet and satirist. His satires were considered libelous and several times landed him in prison. He was in London during the plague of 1625 and wrote a lengthy poem about it. During the Civil Wars he served as a military commander, first on the side of King Charles I, later on the side of the Puritans. In 1642 he sold his estate to raise a troop of horse and was placed in charge of Farnham Castle. A few days later he set off for London, leaving the castle undefended, and was captured by Royalists. He would have been hanged except for the intervention of Sir John Denham, who said that so long as Wither lived, he himself would not be the worst poet in England.

As a convinced Puritan, Wither wrote many hymns and religious tracts. After the Restoration he spent another three years in jail, but passed the last years of his life quietly in London.

Unit Review Tests 3: The Renaissance

Content Review

1. The introduction to this unit mentions that the exuberance expressed in early Renaissance poetry gave way to a more cynical and introspective outlook as the Renaissance waned. Select three or four poets whose works may be used to demonstrate these changes, and explain how at least one poem by each typifies exuberance, cynicism, or introspection.

2. One of the major achievements of Renaissance literature was the introduction and development of the sonnet. Among its major practitioners were Wyatt, Surrey, Sidney, Spenser, Shakespeare, Donne, and Milton. Select any three sonnets, each written by a different author from this group, and discuss similarities and differences in structure and content.

3. Many of the selections in this unit treat the *carpe diem* theme, which translated from Latin to English means "seize [enjoy] the day," and in poetry usually functions to urge the young to take advantage of love while they may, before their youth and beauty have succumbed to the swift and inexorable passage of time. The first examples in this unit are the paired poems, "The Passionate Shepherd to His Love" (p. 126) and "The Nymph's Reply" (p. 126). Find two or three of the others and compare their treatment of the theme with those of the Marlowe and Raleigh poems.

4. "Poetry with ingenious comparisons, farfetched assertions, and extraordinarily clever phrasing may be interesting but cannot be sincere as genuine love poetry because it does not express deep feeling or profound emotion." Defend or attack this statement, using examples from the poetry of the Renaissance period.

5. The Renaissance has been described as consisting of "a rebirth of the human spirit, a realization of the human potential for development." Select one major author from this unit and discuss how his works illustrate that Renaissance ideal.

6. It has been said that Shakespeare stands at the pinnacle of Renaissance artistry. Support or attack this claim, using as your basis the works included in this unit.

7. Invented by Surrey at the beginning of the Renaissance period, blank verse flourished throughout the period. Discuss its versatility, using the following examples from this unit: Surrey's use of it for translation, Shakespeare's use for tragic drama, and Milton's use for epic poetry.

8. Write a composition of 400–500 words on any one of the topics listed below. (Your major source will be this unit, but you may, if you wish, use further sources.) **(a)** The Renaissance: The Golden Age of English Drama; **(b)** Queen Elizabeth and the Courtier Poets; **(c)** Prose Literature of the Renaissance Period; **(d)** Sonnet Sequences; **(e)** *Paradise Lost*: A Renaissance Epic; **(f)** *The Faerie Queene*: A Renaissance Allegory; **(g)** Metaphysical Poetry; **(h)** Thomas Campion's Songbooks (this topic will require further research); **(i)** The Growth of the Public Theater in Renaissance England (this topic will require further research).

Unit 3, Test I

INTERPRETATION: NEW MATERIAL

from Richard II, Act Three

William Shakespeare

The scene you are about to read comes from *Richard II,* one of Shakespeare's history plays. King Richard's rule is being challenged by his cousin Henry Bolingbroke, Duke of Hereford.

As the following scene opens Richard has returned to his kingdom from a war in Ireland. He finds Bolingbroke, whom he had earlier exiled, back in England at the head of a large army leading a rebellion. The Elizabethans, in general, believed that a king received his right to rule directly from God, and not from the people governed. A king was considered to be God's deputy on earth, and therefore rebellion was a moral as well as a political issue.

Characters:

KING RICHARD II
DUKE OF AUMERLE, *son to the Duke of York*
BISHOP OF CARLISLE
EARL OF SALISBURY
SIR STEPHEN SCROOP

SCENE 2.

The coast of Wales, near Barkloughly castle. Drum: flourish and colours. Enter the KING, AUMERLE, *the* BISHOP OF CARLISLE, *with* Soldiers.

K. RICH. Barkloughly castle call they this at hand?
AUM. Yea, my lord. How brooks[1] your grace the air,
After your late[2] tossing on the breaking seas?
K. RICH. Needs must I like it well: I weep for joy
To stand upon my kingdom once again.
Dear earth, I do salute thee with my hand,
Though rebels wound thee with their horses' hoofs:
As a long-parted mother with her child
Plays fondly with her tears and smiles in meeting,
So, weeping, smiling, greet I thee, my earth,
And do thee favours with my royal hands.
Feed not thy sovereign's foe, my gentle earth,
Nor with thy sweets comfort his ravenous[3] sense;
But let thy spiders, that suck up thy venom,
And heavy-gaited toads lie in their way,
Doing annoyance to the treacherous feet
Which with usurping[4] steps do trample thee:
Yield stinging nettles to mine enemies;
And when they from thy bosom pluck a flower,
Guard it, I pray thee, with a lurking adder[5]
Whose double[6] tongue may with a mortal touch
Throw death upon thy sovereign's enemies.
Mock not my senseless conjuration,[7] lords:
This earth shall have a feeling and these stones
Prove armed soldiers, ere her native[8] king
Shall falter under foul rebellion's arms.
CAR. Fear not, my lord: that Power that made you king
Hath power to keep you king in spite of all.
The means that heaven yields must be embrac'd,
And not neglected; else, if heaven would,
And we will not, heaven's offer we refuse,
The proffered means of succour and redress.
AUM. He means, my lord, that we are too remiss[9];
Whilst Bolingbroke, through our security,[10]
Grows strong and great in substance and in power.
K. RICH. Discomfortable[11] cousin! know'st thou not
That when the searching eye of heaven[12] is hid,
Behind the globe, that lights the lower world,[13]
Then thieves and robbers range abroad unseen
In murders and in outrage, boldly here;
But when from under this terrestrial ball
He fires the proud tops of the eastern pines
And darts his light through every guilty hole,
Then murders, treasons and detested sins,
The cloak of night being pluck'd from off their backs,

---

1. ***brooks,*** enjoys.
2. ***late,*** recent.
3. ***ravenous,*** greedy.
4. ***usurping,*** seizing by force.
5. ***adder,*** poisonous snake.
6. ***double,*** forked.
7. ***senseless conjuration,*** appeal to unfeeling things.
8. ***native,*** entitled to the crown by birth.
9. ***remiss,*** careless.
10. ***security,*** confidence.
11. ***Discomfortable,*** uncomforting.
12. ***searching eye of heaven,*** the sun.
13. ***that lights the lower world.*** This clause modifies *eye of heaven.*

Stand bare and naked, trembling at themselves?
So when this thief, this traitor, Bolingbroke,
Who all this while hath revell'd in the night
Whilst we were wand'ring with the antipodes,[14]
Shall see us rising in our throne, the east,
His treasons will sit blushing in his face,
Not able to endure the sight of day,
But self-affrighted tremble at his sin.
Not all the water in the rough rude sea
Can wash the balm[15] off from an anointed king;
The breath of worldly men cannot depose
The deputy elected by the Lord:
For every man that Bolingbroke hath press'd[16]
To lift shrewd steel against our golden crown,
God for his Richard hath in heavenly pay
A glorious angel: then, if angels fight,
Weak men must fall, for heaven still guards the right.

Enter SALISBURY.

Welcome, my lord: how far off lies your power?

SAL. Nor near[17] nor farther off, my gracious lord,
Than this weak arm: discomfort[18] guides my tongue
And bids me speak of nothing but despair.
One day too late, I fear me, noble lord,
Hath clouded all thy happy days on earth:
O, call back yesterday, bid time return,
And thou shalt have twelve thousand fighting men!
To-day, to-day, unhappy day, too late,
O'erthrows thy joys, friends, fortune and thy state:
For all the Welshmen, hearing thou wert dead,
Are gone to Bolingbroke, dispers'd and fled.

AUM. Comfort, my liege: why looks your grace so pale?

K. RICH. But now the blood of twenty thousand men
Did triumph in my face, and they are fled;
And, till so much blood thither come again,
Have I not reason to look pale and dead?
All souls that will be safe fly from my side,
For time hath set a blot upon my pride.

AUM. Comfort, my liege; remember who you are.

K. RICH. I had forgot myself: am I not king?
Awake, thou coward majesty! thou sleepest.
Is not the king's name twenty thousand names?
Arm, arm, my name! a puny subject strikes
At thy great glory. Look not to the ground,
Ye favourites of a king: are we not high?
High be our thoughts: I know my uncle York
Hath power enough to serve our turn. But who comes here?

Enter SCROOP.

SCROOP. More health and happiness betide[19] my liege
Than can my care-tun'd tongue deliver him!

K. RICH. Mine ear is open and my heart prepar'd:
The worst is worldly loss thou canst unfold.
Say, is my kingdom lost? why, 'twas my care;
And what loss is it to be rid of care?
Strives Bolingbroke to be as great as we?
Greater he shall not be; if he serve God,
We'll serve Him too and be his fellow so:
Revolt our subjects? that we cannot mend;
They break their faith to God as well as us:
Cry woe, destruction, ruin and decay;
The worst is death, and death will have his day.

SCROOP. Glad am I that your highness is so arm'd
To bear the tidings of calamity.
Like an unseasonable stormy day,
Which makes the silver rivers drown their shores,
As if the world were all dissolv'd to tears,
So high above his limits swells the rage
Of Bolingbroke, covering your fearful land
With hard bright steel and hearts harder than steel.
White-beards have arm'd their thin and hairless scalps
Against thy majesty; boys, with women's voices,

---

14. ***antipodes,*** opposite points on the globe.
15. ***balm,*** consecrated oil used in anointing a king.
16. ***press'd,*** forced into the ranks.
17. ***near,*** nearer.
18. ***discomfort,*** discouragement.
19. ***betide,*** happen to.

Strive to speak big and clap[20] their female[21] joints
In stiff unwieldy arms against thy crown:
Thy very beadsmen[22] learn to bend their bows
Of double-fatal[23] yew against thy state;
Yea, distaff-women manage[24] rusty bills[25]
Against thy seat: both young and old rebel,
And all goes worse than I have power to tell.

K. RICH. Too well, too well thou tell'st a tale so ill.
Where is the Earl of Wiltshire? where is Bagot?
What is become of Bushy? where is Green?
That they have let the dangerous enemy
Measure our confines with such peaceful[26] steps?
If we prevail, their heads shall pay for it:
I warrant they have made peace with Bolingbroke.

SCROOP. Peace have they made with him indeed, my lord.

K. RICH. O villains, vipers, damn'd without redemption!
Dogs, easily won to fawn on any man!
Snakes, in my heart-blood warm'd, that sting my heart!
Three Judases, each one thrice worse than Judas!
Would they make peace? terrible hell make war
Upon their spotted souls for this offence!

SCROOP. Sweet love, I see, changing his property,[27]
Turns to the sourest and most deadly hate:
Again uncurse their souls; their peace is made
With heads, and not with hands: those whom you curse
Have felt the worst of death's destroying wound
And lie full low, grav'd in the hollow ground.

AUM. Is Bushy, Green, and the Earl of Wiltshire dead?

SCROOP. Ay, all of them at Bristow lost their heads.

AUM. Where is the duke my father with his power?

K. RICH. No matter where; of comfort no man speak:
Let's talk of graves, of worms and epitaphs;
Make dust our paper and with rainy eyes
Write sorrow on the bosom of the carth,
Let's choose executors[28] and talk of wills:
And yet not so, for what can we bequeath
Save our deposed bodies to the ground?
Our lands, our lives and all are Bolingbroke's,
And nothing can we call our own but death
And that small model[29] of the barren earth
Which serves as paste and cover to our bones,
For God's sake, let us sit upon the ground
And tell sad stories of the death of kings:
How some have been depos'd; some slain in war;
Some haunted by the ghosts they have depos'd;
Some poisoned by their wives; some sleeping kill'd;
All murdered: for within the hollow crown
That rounds the mortal temples of a king
Keeps Death his court[30] and there the antic[31] sits,
Scoffing his state and grinning at his[32] pomp,
Allowing him a breath,[33] a little scene,
To monarchize, be fear'd and kill with looks,
Infusing him with self and vain conceit,
As if this flesh which walls about our life
Were brass impregnable, and humour'd[34] thus
Comes at the last and with a little pin
Bores through his castle wall, and farewell king!
Cover your heads and mock not flesh and blood
With solemn reverence: throw away respect,
Tradition, form and ceremonious duty,
For you have but mistook me all this while:
I live with bread like you, feel want,
Taste grief, need friends: subjected[35] thus,
How can you say to me, I am a king?

---

20. ***clap,*** thrust.
21. ***female,*** youthful.
22. ***beadsmen,*** people whose duty it was to pray for the king.
23. ***double-fatal.*** The wood was used for bows and the berry as poison.
24. ***manage,*** wield.
25. ***bills,*** weapons.
26. ***peaceful,*** unopposed.
27. ***property,*** distinctive quality.
28. ***executors,*** persons named to carry out the provisions of a will.
29. ***model,*** the body or the grave mound.
30. ***Keeps Death his court,*** death presides over the king's court.
31. ***antic,*** grotesque figure.
32. ***his,*** the king's.
33. ***breath,*** breathing space, moment.
34. ***humour'd,*** Death's having satisfied his humor or whim.
35. ***subjected,*** made subject to grief, want, etc. (with pun on "being treated like a subject").

On a separate sheet of paper, write your answers to the following questions. Do not write in your book.

1. Does Richard's rival to the throne appear in this scene?

2. To whom is Richard speaking in lines 6–22?

3. Who or what is the "Power" referred to by the Bishop of Carlisle in line 27?

4. Why does Richard refer to Bolingbroke as a "thief" (line 47)?

5. To what object does Richard compare himself in the metaphor in line 50?

6. Who does Richard say God will give him to fight on his side for every man that fights for Bolingbroke?

7. What has happened to the Earl of Salisbury's forces?

8. Most of this scene is in blank verse, but rhyme is often used. What is the rhyme scheme of Richard's speech in lines 76–81?

9. From the description of the kinds of people who rally to Bolingbroke (lines 112–120), what might you reasonably infer about Richard's popularity?

10. List the persons and things to which Richard compares those who have betrayed him in lines 129–132.

11. What has happened to the men Richard curses in these lines?

12. In the metaphor in lines 146–147, dust is said to be "paper." What is the implement that is to write upon that "paper"? What is to be written?

13. How has Shakespeare personified death in lines 162–170?

14. What is the "castle wall" that is bored through with a pin? What then happens to the king?

15. **(a)** How would you describe the tone of Richard's final speech? **(b)** How does it compare to the tone of his preceding speech?

Unit 3, Test II

COMPOSITION

You may choose any *one* of the following assignments. Assume that you are writing for your classmates.

1. Discuss the different attitudes toward love in Surrey's "A Lover's Vow" and Wither's "What Care I?"

2. Discuss the various attitudes toward death in Donne's "Death Be Not Proud" (Holy Sonnet No. 10) and Jonson's "On My First Son."

3. At the first mention of the monster in *The Faerie Queene* and Satan in *Paradise Lost* both creatures are described as serpents. Compare and contrast the two, including in your discussion the images of darkness and light and what these images represent.

4. Samuel Taylor Coleridge has said of Hamlet that he is an intellectual called upon to act decisively for human and divine reasons who keeps resolving to act and yet always delays action. Agree or disagree with this analysis, and give reasons to support your answer.

5. *Macbeth* is, first of all, a play about the murder of a king. This act destroys harmony not only in the character of Macbeth, but also in the society at large. Discuss Macbeth as an agent of disintegration and disorder.

6. Discuss the different attitudes toward the world of affairs, business, and the court in Bacon's essay "Of Studies" and Marvell's poem "The Garden."

7. Discuss the attitudes toward time expressed in Herrick's "To the Virgins, to Make Much of Time," Milton's "On His Having Arrived at the Age of Twenty-Three," and Marvell's "To His Coy Mistress."

8. Compare the character of Richard II in the scene in Test I with the main character in the Shakespeare play in this unit.

9. A *syllogism* is a form of reasoning that contains three propositions. For example: All men are mortal (major premise); Socrates is a man (minor premise); Therefore, Socrates is mortal (conclusion). Discuss the structure of Marvell's "To His Coy Mistress" as a kind of syllogism.

Unit 4:

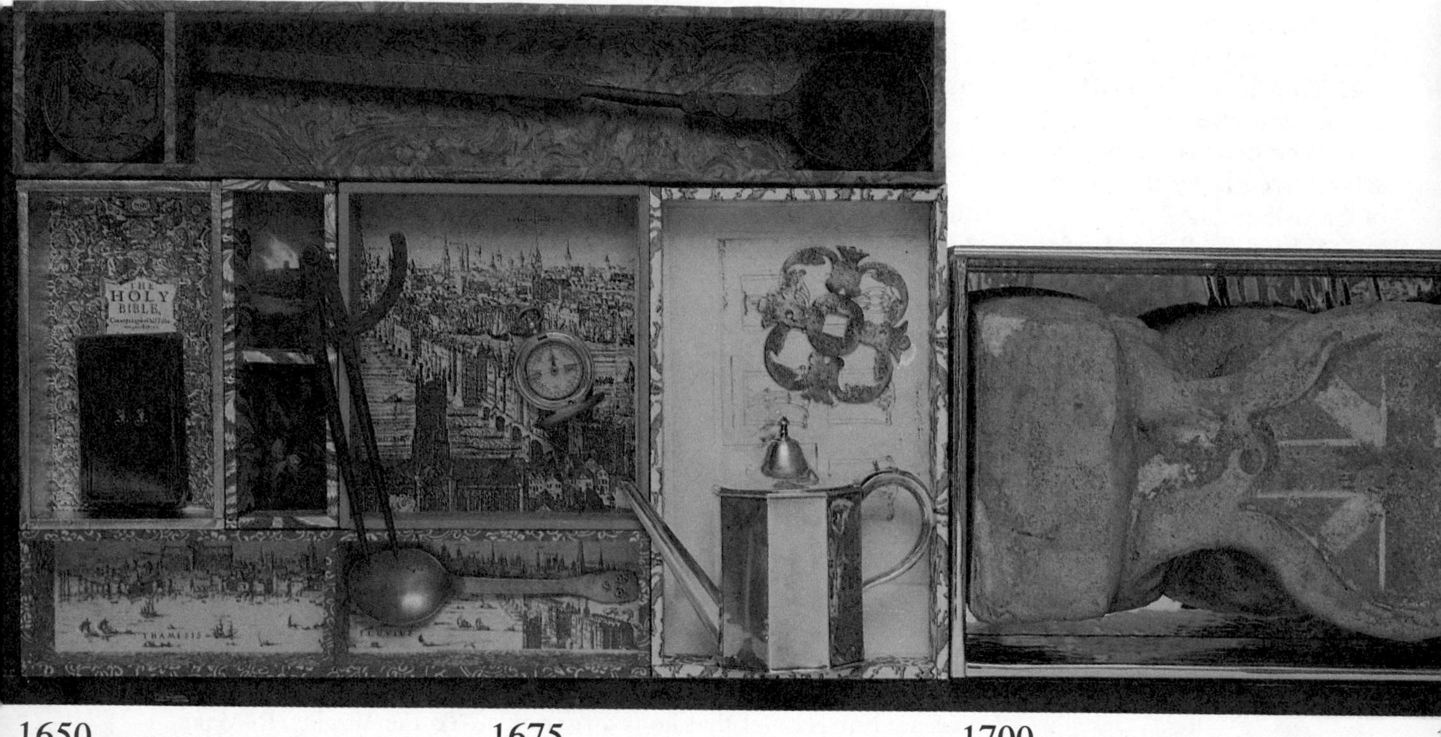

1650 | 1675 | 1700

- Hobbes: *Leviathan*
- Bunyan: *Pilgrim's Progress*
- Congreve: *The Way of the World*
- Restoration of Stuart Monarchy
- Swift: *Tale of a Tub*
- Swift: *Gulliver's Travel*
- Society of Friends founded
- Royal Society founded
- Dryden: *The Hind and the Panther*
- Theaters reopened
- Newton: *Principia*
- First Copyright Act
- The Diary of Samuel Pepys
- Pope: *An Essay on Criticism*
- The Glorious Revolution
- The Puritan Commonwealth
- Pope: *The Rape of the Lock*
- The Great Plague
- Locke: *Essay Concerning Human Understanding*
- The Fire of London
- Addison: *The Spectator*
- Milton: *Paradise Lost*
- DeFoe: *A Journal of the Plague Year*
- Dryden: *Essay of Dramatic Poesy*

The Age of Reason 1650-1780

1750 1775 1800

- Pope: *The Dunciad*
- Swift: *A Modest Proposal*
- Pope: *An Essay on Man*
- Richardson: *Pamela*
- Fielding: *Tom Jones*
- Gray: *Elegy Written in a Country Churchyard*
- Johnson's *Dictionary*
- The Lisbon Earthquake
- British Museum opens
- Sterne: *Tristram Shandy*
- Johnson and Boswell meet
- Percy's *Reliques*
- Royal Academy founded
- First edition of the *Encyclopedia Britannica*
- Goldsmith: *She Stoops to Conquer*
- Paine: *Common Sense*
- Smith: *Wealth of Nations*
- Sheridan: *The School for Scandal*
- Burns: *Poems*

American Revolution

Background: The Age of Reason 1650–1780

An Intellectual Revolution

The phrase "Age of Reason" describes an emphasis in attitudes and beliefs. People may not have been more reasonable between 1650 and 1780 than at any other time, but during that period great claims were made for reason and for what it might achieve. This attitude can be seen most clearly in the way the people of the period thought about nature.

For centuries people had believed that natural phenomena were the result of some kind of direct interference with nature. Comets and eclipses of the sun were ominous warnings from God, earthquakes and plagues the proof of His wrath. Witches and fairies caused blighted crops, deformed babies, sudden deaths. Early scientists had to work against such assumptions. Their radically different vision of nature, developed throughout the seventeenth century, triumphed with the publication, in 1687, of Isaac Newton's *Principia Mathematica.*

In the new scientific method which Newton practiced, one began with an analysis of all the facts relevant to a phenomenon, then developed an explanation, formulated that explanation mathematically, and finally tested it by experiment. The implication was that events in nature are not the result of external influence. Rather, nature now appeared to be a system governed by laws which are simple in form, apply uniformly to everything, and can be expressed in mathematical language.

While this new way of looking at nature resolved old fears and anxieties, it also created problems. The new scientific method of thinking raised serious questions about old religious assumptions. Other intellectual disciplines, dazzled by such a success, sought to achieve similar results, but it was much more difficult to create a scientific explanation for human nature or society. Yet the ideal of systematic, rational thought based on empirical fact continued to dominate the era.

The Restoration

In England the Age of Reason begins with the final rejection of the Puritans and religious extremism. On May 29, 1660, Charles Stuart, long an exile in France, finally returned to London as Charles II. In accepting his return the English people, exhausted with twenty years of religious and political strife, restored the old monarchy and the old church.

A writer's life during the Restoration was not easy. First, there was the problem of money. A writer could not yet make a living through the sale of his books. An aristocratic patron was still the usual source of extra income. Second, literary fashion was changing. Restoration readers were no longer interested in the complicated syntax and lofty themes of Elizabethan prose. Their new interest in science required a prose style using ". . . a close, naked, natural way of speaking. . . ." In the end poetry too shifted from the intensely personal subject matter and the complex imagery of the Metaphysical poets to a poetry about public issues written in plain-spoken, reasoned English, and frequently in the newly popular heroic couplet, whose formality and order seemed in tune with the era.

Remarkably, the Restoration worked for twenty-five years. But on the death of Charles II the old spectre of religious war reappeared. The new king, James II, was a Roman Catholic, and seemed intemperately determined to force a crisis. In 1688 the English responded by expelling him from the country in the Glorious Revolution. Parliament invited his daughter and her Protestant husband, William of Orange, to take the throne. They accepted, confirming Parliament's power over the monarchy. William and Mary ruled from 1689 to 1702, followed by Mary's sister, Anne, who occupied the throne until 1714. When she died without an heir Parliament again had to invite in a king, this time George I from the German duchy of Hanover. Since George and his son could barely speak English, Parliament ruled England.

The Augustans

The writers of the era of Queen Anne and George I styled theirs the *Augustan* Age because they saw a parallel between the new political and social stability of their day and Rome under Caesar Augustus. Hoping to equal the literary achievements of the Romans, the English Augustans wrote epics, satires, elegies, and tragedies just as their Roman predecessors had, and exercised great care in paralleling the form and content of their work with that of "the ancients." This did not inhibit their brilliance or their vigor. For one thing, much Augustan literature is written from a middle-class point of view. The bitter satire of Swift's "Modest Proposal," the gentler moral persuasion of *The Spectator,* even Johnson's defiant letter to Lord Chesterfield are all directed against aristocrats.

Samuel Johnson

This was the era when the middle class, the shopkeepers, traders, merchants, and government bureaucrats not only grew in numbers and in economic power, but also grew in self-consciousness and self-confidence: ". . . the middle state," says Robinson Crusoe's father (in *Robinson Crusoe,* 1719) is ". . . the best State in the World. . . ."

The middle class exercised a growing influence on literature. Their new wealth now permitted them to buy books, and writers turned from the demands of aristocratic patrons to the open market, hoping to make a living there.

The middle-class readers preferred to read about people like themselves, so heroic tragedies give way to novels, and much Augustan literature is about London, the town where so many hack writers scraped a living with their pens and middle-class readers idled with a book.

Augustan values continued to dominate the work of many writers during the second half of the century. Their prime exponent is Samuel Johnson, whose criticism articulates neo-classical artistic ideals, while his biographical work measures men by the stringent middle-class ethical code.

But simultaneously, new ideas were developing. Again, this is evidenced in a new way of looking at nature. Newtonian science seemed to take the mystery out of natural events. But people still sensed a power and saw a special kind of beauty in forest and mountain. Not everyone lived in middle-class London, and the lives of farmer and worker did not strike everyone as meaningless. The poetry of the second half of the eighteenth century, such as the work of Gray and Burns, turns more and more to rural subjects, finding in them fresh sources of emotion. This development leads, by the end of the period, toward the Romantic Revolution.

John Dryden

Much of Dryden's poetry is concerned with the events of his day. He was a topical poet, the kind of artist, to use the modern poet W. H. Auden's terms, "whose imagination was excited by actual occasions." Poetry of this sort usually dies within a year of its writing, as current events become past (and forgotten) history. Only a great writer can maintain interest in such material long after the events.

Dryden's own era was full of tumultuous change—civil war, frequent shifts in royal power, and the constant threat that political and religious principles accepted one year would be condemned the next. Dryden switched from the Church of England to the Roman Catholic Church, raising doubts about his religious sincerity. The king at the time (James II) was Roman Catholic, but faced the unyielding opposition of a Protestant parliament and population. James kept trying to advance Catholic interests, even though he infuriated the majority of his people in the attempt. One of his advisors, a Jesuit priest, kept encouraging him in these ill-considered efforts. Many English Catholics feared the results of James's efforts and wished that he would leave matters as they were. Dryden was one of these conservatives. In *The Hind and the Panther* he included the following allegory, in which the swifts, migratory birds who must flee the cold of winter, represent the endangered English Catholics, and the Martin represents the bad advice of James's Jesuit counsellor. The fatal winter storm which overwhelms the foolish swallows constitutes Dryden's ominous warning to his fellow Catholics of what may occur if they don't live cautiously within a country dominated by a Protestant majority.

from The Hind and the Panther

"The Swallow,[1] privileg'd above the rest
Of all the birds, as man's familiar guest,
Pursues the sun in summer brisk and bold,
But wisely shuns the persecuting cold:
Is well to chancels and to chimneys known,
Tho' 'tis not thought she feeds on smoke alone.
From hence she has been held of heav'nly line,
Endued with particles of soul divine.
This merry chorister had long possess'd
Her summer seat, and feather'd well her nest:
Till frowning skies began to change their cheer,
And time turn'd up the wrong side of the year;
The shedding trees began the ground to strow
With yellow leaves, and bitter blasts to blow.
Sad auguries of winter thence she drew,
Which by instinct, or prophecy, she knew:
When prudence warn'd her to remove betimes,
And seek a better heav'n and warmer climes.
"Her sons were summon'd on a steeple's height,
And, call'd in common council, vote a flight;
The day was nam'd, the next that should be fair;
All to the gen'ral rendezvous repair;
They try their flutt'ring wings, and trust themselves in air.
"Southwards, you may be sure, they bent their flight,
And harbor'd in a hollow rock at night:
Next morn they rose, and set up ev'ry sail;
The wind was fair, but blew a mack'rel gale:
The sickly young sat shiv'ring on the shore,
Abhorr'd salt water never seen before,
And pray'd their tender mothers to delay
The passage, and expect a fairer day.
"With these the Martin readily concurr'd,
A church-begot, and church-believing bird;
Of little body, but of lofty mind,

1. ***Swallow.*** Swallows live in communities, building their nests on the sides of buildings. They migrate south annually. Martins are members of the swallow family having purple plumage. Swifts, though of a different genus, are frequently confused with swallows.

Round-bellied, for a dignity design'd,
And much a dunce, as Martins are by kind.
Yet often quoted canon-laws,[2] and code
And Fathers[3] which he never understood;
But little learning needs in noble blood.
For, sooth to say, the Swallow brought him in,
Her household chaplain, and her next of kin;
In superstition silly to excess,
And casting schemes by planetary guess[4]:
In fine, short-wing'd, unfit himself to fly,
His fear foretold foul weather in the sky.
"Besides, a Raven from a wither'd oak
Left of their lodging was observ'd to croak.
That omen lik'd him[5] not; so his advice
Was present safety, bought at any price;
(A seeming pious care that cover'd cowardice).
To strengthen this, he told a boding dream
Of rising waters and a troubled stream,
Sure signs of anguish, dangers, and distress,
With something more, not lawful to express,
By which he slily seem'd to intimate
Some secret revelation of their fate.
At this, some shook for fear; the more devout
Arose, and bless'd themselves from head to foot.
"'Tis true, some stagers[6] of the wiser sort
Made all these idle wonderments their sport:
They said, their only danger was delay,
And he who heard what ev'ry fool could say
Would never fix his thoughts, but trim[7] his time away.
The passage yet was good; the wind, 't is true,
Was somewhat high, but that was nothing new,
Nor more than usual equinoxes[8] blew.
The sun (already from the Scales declin'd)
Gave little hopes of better days behind,
But change from bad to worse of weather and of wind.
Nor need they fear the dampness of the sky
Should flag their wings, and hinder them to fly,
'T was only water thrown on sails too dry.
"Th' advice was true; but fear had seiz'd the most,
And all good counsel is on cowards lost.
The question crudely put, to shun delay,
'T was carried by the major part to stay.
"His point thus gain'd, Sir Martin dated thence
His pow'r, and from a priest became a prince.
He order'd all things with a busy care,
And cells and refectories did prepare,
And large provisions laid of winter fare.
But now and then let fall a word or two
Of hope that Heav'n some miracle might show,
And, for their sakes, the sun should backward go.
In expectation of such times as these,
A chapel hous'd 'em, truly call'd of ease:
For Martin much devotion did not ask;
They pray'd sometimes, and that was all their task.
"It happen'd (as beyond the reach of wit
Blind prophecies may have a lucky hit)
That this accomplish'd, or at least in part,
Gave great repute to their new Merlin's[9] art.
Some Swifts,[10] the giants of the swallow kind,
Large-limb'd, stout-hearted, but of stupid mind,
These lubbers, peeping thro' a broken pane,
To suck fresh air, survey'd the neighboring plain
And saw (but scarcely could believe their eyes)
New blossoms flourish, and new flow'rs arise;
As God had been abroad, and, walking there
Had left his footsteps, and reform'd the year.
The sunning hills from far were seen to glow
With glittering beams, and in the meads below
The burnish'd brooks appear'd with liquid gold to flow.
At last they heard the foolish Cuckoo sing,
Whose note proclaim'd the holiday of spring.
"No longer doubting, all prepare to fly,
And repossess their patrimonial sky.
The priest before 'em did his wings display;
And that good omens might attend their way,
As luck would have it, 't was St. Martin's day.
"Who but the Swallow now triumphs alone?
The canopy of heaven is all her own;
Her youthful offspring to their haunts repair,
And glide along in glades, and skim in air,
And dip for insects in the purling springs,
And stoop on rivers to refresh their wings.

2. ***canon-laws,*** the laws of the Church.
3. ***Fathers,*** the early Christian theologians, the "Fathers of the Church."
4. ***planetary guess,*** astrology.
5. ***him,*** the Martin.
6. ***stagers,*** persons of experience. Here, the more intelligent swallows.
7. ***trim,*** to accommodate one's views to prevailing opinion, without concern for the best course of action.
8. ***equinoxes,*** winds of late September.
9. ***new Merlin,*** the Martin seems to the foolish swallows as wise as King Arthur's famed magician.
10. ***Swifts,*** otherwise call'd Martlets. (Dryden's note)

Their mothers think a fair provision made,
That ev'ry son can live upon his trade,
And, now the careful charge is off their hands,
Look out for husbands, and new nuptial bands:
The youthful widow longs to be supplied;
But first the lover is by lawyers tied
To settle jointure[11]-chimneys on the bride.
So thick they couple, in so short a space,
That Martin's marriage-off'rings[12] rise apace;
Their ancient houses, running to decay,
Are furbish'd up, and cemented with clay:
They teem already; store of eggs are laid,
And brooding mothers call Lucina's[13] aid.
Fame spreads the news, and foreign fowls appear
In flocks to greet the new returning year,
To bless the founder, and partake the cheer.
"And now 't was time (so fast their numbers rise)
To plant abroad, and people colonies.
The youth drawn forth, as Martin had desir'd,
(For so their cruel destiny requir'd),
Were sent far off on an ill-fated day;
The rest would need conduct 'em on their way,
And Martin went, because he fear'd alone to stay.
"So long they flew with inconsiderate haste
That now their afternoon began to waste;
And, what was ominous, that very morn
The sun was enter'd into Capricorn[14];
An infant moon eclips'd him in his way,
And hid the small remainders of his day.
The crowd, amaz'd, pursued no certain mark,
But birds met birds, and justled in the dark:
Few mind the public in a panic fright,
And fear increas'd the horror of the night.
Night came, but unattended with repose;
Alone she came, no sleep their eyes to close:
Alone, and black she came; no friendly stars arose.
"What should they do, beset with dangers round,
No neighb'ring dorp,[15] no lodging to be found,
But bleaky plains, and bare unhospitable ground?
The latter brood, who just began to fly,
Sick-feather'd, and unpractic'd in the sky,
For succor to their helpless mother call;
She spread her wings; some few beneath 'em crawl;
She spread 'em wider yet, but could not cover all.
T' augment their woes, the winds began to move
Debate in air, for empty fields above,
Till Boreas[16] got the skies, and pour'd amain
His rattling hailstones mix'd with snow and rain.
"The joyless morning late arose, and found
A dreadful desolation reign around,
Some buried in the snow, some frozen to the ground.
The rest were struggling still with death, and lay
The Crows' and Ravens' rights, an undefended prey:
Excepting Martin's race; for they and he
Had gain'd the shelter of a hollow tree:
But, soon discover'd by a sturdy clown,[17]
He headed all the rabble of a town,
And finish'd 'em with bats, or poll'd 'em down.
Martin himself was caught alive, and tried
For treas'nous crimes, because the laws provide
No Martin there in winter shall abide.
High on an oak, which never leaf shall bear,
He breath'd his last, expos'd to open air;
And there his corps, unblest, are hanging still,
To show the change of winds with his prophetic bill."[18]

---

11. ***jointure,*** property given a woman in marriage which she legally owns even after her husband's death. The female swifts make careful financial preparations before marriage.
12. ***marriage-off'rings,*** money given to the priest or minister who performs a marriage ceremony.
13. ***Lucina,*** Roman goddess of childbirth.
14. ***Capricorn,*** astrological description of the seasons. The sun enters this area of the heavens at the winter solstice.
15. ***dorp,*** village.
16. ***Boreas,*** the north wind.
17. ***clown,*** farm laborer.
18. ***And there . . . prophetic bill.*** The body of the Martin serves as a weather vane.

To the Memory of Mr. Oldham

Farewell, too little and too lately known,
Whom I began to think and call my own;
For sure our souls were near allied, and thine
Cast in the same poetic mould with mine.
One common note on either lyre did strike,
And knaves and fools we both abhorred alike:
To the same goal did both our studies drive,
The last set out the soonest did arrive.[1]
Thus Nisus[2] fell upon the slippery place,
While his young friend performed and won the race.
O early ripe! to thy abundant store
What could advancing age have added more?
It might (what Nature never gives the young)
Have taught the numbers[3] of thy native tongue.
But Satire needs not those, and Wit will shine
Through the harsh cadence[4] of a rugged line.
A noble error, and but seldom made,
When poets are by too much force betrayed.
Thy generous fruits, though gathered ere their prime
Still showed a quickness; and maturing time
But mellows what we write to the dull sweets of Rhyme.
Once more, hail and farewell[5]; farewell, thou young,
But ah too short, Marcellus[6] of our tongue;
Thy brows with ivy, and with laurels bound;
But Fate and gloomy Night encompass thee around.

---

1. ***The last . . . arrive.*** Oldham, born in 1653, was 22 years younger than Dryden, but gained fame for his satirical poetry before Dryden.
2. ***Nisus.*** Virgil (*Aeneid* V, 315–39) describes a race in which two friends compete. Nisus is ahead until he accidentally slips. He then trips another contender so his friend Euryalus can win.
3. ***numbers,*** ability to write in meter.
4. ***harsh cadence,*** irregular meter.
5. ***hail and farewell,*** translation of a Latin phrase used when friends part.
6. ***Marcellus,*** nephew and promising heir of Caeser Augustus, who died at the age of nineteen.

Discussion

from The Hind and the Panther

1. This animal tale serves as a warning. Ignore what you know about Dryden's era and his personal reasons for writing it. Instead, consider this tale by itself, and explain the kind of warning it gives. Be sure to include the swallows, the Martin, and the change of seasons in your explanation.

2. Examine the first description of the Martin (lines 32–45). What elements of his appearance and what mannerisms alert us to the dangers in following his advice?

3. Beast fables mix human and animal characteristics, frequently with amusing results. Look closely at the description of the swallows' return to their old haunts (lines 111–129) and disentangle human attributes from those peculiar to birds. How does Dryden employ the beast fable framework here?

Discussion

To the Memory of Mr. Oldham

1. What parallels does the speaker of the poem perceive between himself and Mr. Oldham? What differences?

2. What words in lines 19–21 contribute to the development of a single image? What does this image illustrate?

3. Compare this poem with A. E. Housman's "To an Athlete Dying Young" (p. 454). What themes and imagery do they share?

John Dryden 1631 • 1700

Contemporary records have preserved scarcely any details about Dryden's personality. He seems to have been outwardly affable but quiet, a man who poured his ambitions, his loves, and his fears into his carefully detailed poetry, rather than into his life. This was probably wise. Never in modern times did the English power elite change as rapidly and as frequently as it did during Dryden's life. He lived under four very different rulers, when his income, and perhaps his freedom, might depend upon pleasing, or at least not offending, each of them.

During the latter part of the reign of Charles II, political unrest developed over the question of his successor. Various factions supported various candidates, approaching rebellion in some cases. Dryden attacked the king's enemies in a series of satiric political poems that modern readers consider his finest work.

He followed his political satires with two religious poems. The first, *Religio Laici,* ("Beliefs of a Layman"), defended the Anglican position—the middle way between Roman Catholicism and Puritanism. In 1685 Charles died and was succeeded by his Catholic brother as James II. Shortly afterward Dryden became a Catholic, prompting charges of opportunism. He defended his new faith in his second religious poem, *The Hind and the Panther.*

Did Dryden change religion to suit his king, as his enemies charged? His motives remain a mystery. He did stick to his decision, although it shortly afterward meant the loss of all his political favors and the laureatship awarded him by Charles II, when in 1688 the English expelled James in favor of his daughter Mary and her Protestant husband, William of Orange.

notes and comments

Dryden and the Heroic Couplet

Although the use of the rhyming iambic pentameter **couplet** was not original with him, it was Dryden who used it so effectively that it became the preferred way to write for the next three generations of poets.

Dryden's predecessors developed the habit of finishing some unit of thought with the last word of the couplet's second line. The advantage of this practice is the highly condensed content of these "closed" couplets.

Within the two lines of the heroic couplet Dryden and his successors like Swift and Pope explored a number of intriguing structural possibilities. The two lines could be used in parallel forms to reinforce an idea, as in this description of oncoming autumn (drawn, as all the examples here will be, from *The Hind and the Panther*):

> Till frowning skies began to change their cheer,
> And time turn'd up the wrong side of the year;
> (lines 11–12)

The pair of lines could be used just as easily to express contrast, as in this description of the swallow:

> Pursues the sun in summer brisk and bold,
> But wisely shuns the persecuting cold:
> (lines 3-4)

These are but the most obvious devices. Ingenious poets of Dryden's era found many ways to work in this form.

But hundreds of lines following the same pattern can get monotonous. Dryden was an expert at varying the pace of his lines, many times running the idea of the first line over into the second, to break up excessive parallelism, as in:

> This merry chorister had long possess'd
> Her summer seat, and feather'd well her nest:
> (lines 9–10)

Here the poet uses balanced syntax, but not strictly according to the way the line breaks. Dryden also varies the movement of lines by using **triplets** or by attaching two extra syllables to the line, creating an **alexandrine** line of six stresses.

The Great Fire swept London when Pepys was thirty-three, working for the Royal Navy and living in a house next to its London offices. The fire began in a baker's shop and seemed at first to be inconseqential. But the weather had been hot and dry, and the section of London in which it began was full of old wooden buildings, some coated with pitch, and all jumbled close together. A high wind carried burning embers to the roofs of distant homes, and the fire spread rapidly. Primitive fire-fighting techniques such as chains of men passing buckets of water could not stop it. The Mayor was reluctant to pull down houses in the fire's path for fear of subsequent lawsuits. However, as the days passed, and the circle of destruction widened, desperate measures such as blowing up whole blocks of houses with gunpowder to create gaps between the fire and the city seemed the only solution. And they did succeed, helped by the cessation of the wind. But by this time four-fifths of the city was cinders and nearly a quarter of a million people homeless.

The Diary of Samuel Pepys

September 2, 1666

Lords day. Some of our maids sitting up late last night to get things ready against our feast today, Jane called us up, about 3 in the morning, to tell us of a great fire they saw in the City. So I rose, and slipped on my nightgown and went to her window, and thought it to be on the back side of Markelane at the furthest; but being unused to such fires as followed, I thought it far enough off, and so went to bed again and to sleep. About 7 rose again to dress myself, and there looked out at the window and saw the fire not so much as it was, and further off. So to my closet[1] to set

1. *closet,* his study.

things to rights after yesterday's cleaning. By and by Jane comes and tells me that she hears that above 300 houses have been burned down tonight by the fire we saw, and that it was now burning down all Fishstreet by London Bridge. So I made myself ready presently, and walked to the Tower[2] and there got up upon one of the high places, Sir J Robinsons little son going up with me; and there I did see the houses at that end of the bridge all on fire, and an infinite great fire on this and the other side the end of the bridge—which, among other people, did trouble me for poor little Michell and our Sarah on the Bridge. So down, with my heart full of trouble, to the Lieutenant of the Tower, who tells me that it begun this morning in the King's bakers house in Pudding-lane, and that it hath burned down St. Magnes Church and most part of Fishstreete already. So I down to the water-side and there got a boat[3] and through bridge, and there saw a lamentable fire. Poor Michells house, as far as the Old Swan, already burned that way and the fire running further, that in a very little time it got as far as the Stillyard while I was there. Everybody endeavouring to remove their goods, and flinging into the River or bringing them into lighters[4] that lay off. Poor people staying in their houses as long as till the very fire touched them, and then running into boats or clambering from one pair of stair by the water-side to another. And among other things, the poor pigeons I perceive were loath to leave their houses, but hovered about the windows and balconies till they were some of them burned their wings, and fell down.

Having stayed, and in an hour's time seen the fire rage every way, and nobody to my sight endeavouring to quench it, but to remove their goods and leave all to the fire; and having seen it get as far as the Steeleyard, and the wind mighty high and driving it into the city, and everything, after so long a drougth, proving combustible, even the very stones of churches, and among other things, the poor steeple by which pretty Mrs. — lives, and whereof my old school-fellow Elborough is parson, taken fire in the very top and there burned till it fall down—I to Whitehall[5] with a gentleman with me who desired to go off from the Tower to see the fire in my boat—to White-hall, and there up to the King's closet in the chapel, where people came about me and I did give them an account dismayed them all; and word was carried in to the King, so I was called for and did tell the King and Duke of York what I saw, and that unless his Majesty did command houses to be pulled down, nothing could stop the fire. They seemed much troubled, and the King commanded me to go to my Lord Mayor[6] from him and command him to spare no houses but to pull down before the fire every way. The Duke of York bid me tell him that if he would have any more soldiers, he shall; and so did my Lord Arlington afterward, as a great secret. Here meeting with Captain Cocke, I in his coach, which he lent me, and Creed with me, to Pauls[7]; and there walked along Watling-street as well as I could, every creature coming away loaden with goods to save—and here and there sick people carried away in beds. Extraordinary good goods carried in carts and on backs. At last met my Lord Mayor in Canning Streete, like a man spent, with a hankercher about his neck. To the King's message, he cried like a fainting woman, "Lord, what can I do? I am spent. People will not obey me. I have been pull[ing] down houses. But the fire overtakes us faster than we can do it." That he needed no more soldiers; and that for himself, he must go and refresh himself, having been up all night. So he left me, and I him, and walked home—seeing people all almost distracted and no manner of means used to quench the fire. The houses too, so very thick thereabouts, and full of matter for burning, as pitch and tar, in Thames-street—and warehouses of oyle and wines and Brandy and other things. Here I saw Mr. Isaccke Houblon, that handsome man—prettily dressed and dirty at his door at Dowgate, receiving some of his brothers things whose houses were on fire; and as he says, have been removed twice already, and he doubts (as it soon proved) that they must be in a little time removed from his house also—which was a sad consideration. And to see

---

2. ***Tower,*** the ancient fort on the Thames called the Tower of London.
3. ***boat.*** In Pepys's day small boats rowed by "watermen" were a common form of transportation in the city.
4. ***lighters,*** small, flat-bottomed boats.
5. ***Whitehall,*** king's residence and offices in London, upriver from the Tower and the fire.
6. ***Lord Mayor,*** of London.
7. ***Pauls.*** Pepys travels back towards the fire, to one of the largest churches in London, which the fire is soon to destroy.

the churches all filling with goods, by people who themselfs should have been quietly there at this time.

By this time it was about 12 a-clock, and so home and there find my guests, which was Mr. Wood and his wife, Barbary Shelden, and also Mr. Moone—she mighty fine, and her husband, for aught I see, a likely man. But Mr. Moones design and mine, which was to look over my closet and please him with the sight thereof, which he hath long desired, was wholly disappointed, for we were in great trouble and disturbance at this fire, not knowing what to think of it. However, we had an extraordinary good dinner, and as merry as at this time we could be.

While at dinner, Mrs. Batelier came to enquire after Mr. Woolfe and Stanes (who it seems are related to them), whose houses in Fishstreet are all burned, and they in a sad condition. She would not stay in the fright.

As soon as dined, I and Moone away and walked through the City,[8] the streets full of nothing but people and horses and carts loaden with goods, ready to run over one another, and removing goods from one burned house to another—they now removing out of Canning-street (which received goods in the morning) into Lumbard Streete and further; and among others, I now saw my little goldsmith Stokes receiving some friend's goods, whose house itself was burned the day after. We parted at Pauls, he home and I to Pauls-Wharf, where I had appointed a boat to attend me; and took in Mr. Carcasse and his brother, whom I met in the street, and carried them below and above bridge, to and again, to see the fire, which was now got further, both below and above, and no likelihood of stopping it. Met with the King and Duke of York in their Barge, and with them to Queen-Hith and there called Sr Rd. Browne to them. Their order was only to pull down houses apace, and so below bridge at the water-side; but little was or could be done, the fire coming upon them so fast. Good hopes there was of stopping it at the Three Cranes above, and at Buttolphs-Wharf below bridge, if care be used; but the wind carries it into the City, so as we know not by the water-side what it doth there. River full of lighter[s] and boats taking in goods, and good goods swimming in the water; and only, I observed that hardly one lighter or boat in three that had the goods of a house in, but there was a pair of virginalls in it. Having seen as much as I could now, I away to White-hall by appointment, and there walked to St. James's Park, and there met my wife and Creed and Wood and his wife and walked to my boat, and there upon the water again, and to the fire up and down, it still increasing and the wind great. So near the fire as we could for smoke; and all over the Thames, with one's face in the wind you were almost burned with a shower of Firedrops—this is very true—so as houses were burned by these drops and flakes of fire, three or four, nay five or six houses, one from another. When we could endure no more upon the water, we to a little alehouse on the Bankside over against the Three Cranes, and there stayed till it was dark almost and saw the fire grow; and as it grow darker, appeared more and more, and in Corners and upon steeples and between churches and houses, as far as we could see up the hill of the City, in a most horrid malicious bloody flame, not like the fine flame of an ordinary fire. Barbary and her husband away before us. We stayed till, it being darkish, we saw the fire as only one entire arch of fire from this to the other side the bridge, and in a bow up the hill, for an arch of above a mile long. It made me weep to see it. The churches, houses, and all on fire and flaming at once, and a horrid noise the flames made, and the cracking of houses at their ruine. So home with a sad heart, and there find everybody discoursing and lamenting the fire; and poor Tom Hater came with some few of his goods saved out of his house, which is burned upon Fish-street hill. I invited him to lie at my house, and did receive his goods: but was deceived in his lying there, the noise coming every moment of the growth of the Fire, so as we were forced to begin to pack up our own goods and prepare for their removal. And did by Moone-shine (it being brave, dry, and moonshine and warm weather) carry much of my goods into the garden, and Mr. Hater and I did remove my money and Iron-chests into my cellar—as thinking that the safest place. And got my bags of gold into my office ready to carry away, and my chief papers of accounts also there, and my tallies into

---

8. ***the City,*** the business district. The fire is moving northwest.

a box by themselfs. So great was our fear, as Sir W. Batten had carts come out of the country to fetch away his goods this night. We did put Mr. Hater, poor man, to bed a little; but he got but very little rest, so much noise being in my house, taking down of goods.

3. About 4 a-clock in the morning, my Lady Batten sent me a cart to carry away all my money and plate and best things to Sir W Riders at Bednall greene; which I did, riding myself in my nightgown in the Cart; and Lord, to see how the streets and the highways are crowded with people, running and riding and getting of carts at any rate to fetch away thing[s]. I find Sir W Rider tired with being called up all night and receiving things from several friends. His house full of goods—and much of Sir W. Batten and Sir W. Penn's. I am eased at my heart to have my treasure so well secured. Then home with much ado to find a way. Nor any sleep all this night to me nor my poor wife. But then, and all this day, she and I and all my people[9] labouring to get away the rest of our things, and did get Mr. Tooker to get me a lighter to take them in, and we did carry them (myself some) over Tower-hill, which was by this time full of people's goods, bringing their goods thither. And down to the lighter, which lay at the next quay above the Towerdock. And here was my neighbour's wife, Mrs. —, with her pretty child and some few of her things, which I did willingly give way to be saved with mine. But there was no passing with anything through the postern, the crowd was so great. At night, lay down a little upon a quilt of W. Hewer in the office (all my own things being packed up or gone); and after me, my poor wife did the like—we having fed upon the remains of yesterday's dinner, having no fire nor dishes, nor any opportunity of dressing anything.

4. Up by break of day to get away the remainder of my things, which I did by a lighter at the Iron-gate; and my hands so few, that it was the afternoon before we could get them all away.

Sir W. Penn and I to Tower-street, and there met the fire Burning three or four doors beyond Mr. Howells; whose goods, poor man (his trayes and dishes, Shovells &c., were flung all along Tower-street in the kennels,[10] and people working therewith from one end to the other), the fire coming on in that narrow street, on both sides, with infinite fury. Sir W. Batten, not knowing how to remove his wine, did dig a pit in the garden and laid it in there; and I took the opportunity of laying all the papers of my office that I could not otherwise dispose of. And in the evening Sir W. Penn and I did dig another and put our wine in it, and I my parmazan cheese as well as my wine and some other things.

This night Mrs. Turner (who, poor woman, was removing her goods all this day—good goods, into the garden, and knew not how to dispose of them)—and her husband supped with my wife and I at night in the office, upon a shoulder of mutton from the cook's, without any napkin or anything, in a sad manner but were merry. Only, now and then walking into the garden and saw how horridly the sky looks, all on a fire in the night, was enough to put us out of our wits; and endeed it was extremely dreadfull—for it looks just as if it was at us, and the whole heaven on fire. I after supper walked in the dark down to Tower-street, and there saw it all on fire at the Trinity house on that side and the Dolphin tavern on this side, which was very near us—and the fire with extraordinary vehemence. Now begins the practice of blowing up of houses in Tower-street, those next the Tower, which at first did frighten people more than anything; but it stop[ped] the fire where it was done—it bringing down the houses to the ground in the same places they stood, and then it was easy to quench what little fire was in it, though it kindled nothing almost. W. Hewer this day went to see how his mother did, and comes late home, but telling us how he hath been forced to remove her to Islington, her house in pye-Corner being burned. So that it is got so far that way and all the Old Bayly, and was running down to Fleetestreete. And Pauls is burned, and all Cheapside. I wrote to my father this night; but the post-house being burned, the letter could not go.

5. I lay down in the office again upon W. Hewer's quilt, being mighty weary and sore in my feet with going till I was hardly able to stand.

---

9. ***my people,*** Pepys's servants.
10. ***kennels,*** ditch down the center of the road.

About 2 in the morning my wife calls me up and tells of new Cryes of "Fyre!"—it being come to Barkeing Church, which is the bottom of our lane. I up; and finding it so, resolved presently to take her away; and did, and took my gold (which was about £2350), W. Hewer, and Jane down by Poundy's boat to Woolwich. But Lord, what a sad sight it was by moonlight to see the whole City almost on fire—that you might see it plain at Woolwich, as if you were by it. There when I came, I find the gates[11] shut, but no guard kept at all; which troubled me, because of discourses now begun that there is plot in it[12] and that the French had done it. I got the gates open, and to Mr. Shelden's, where I locked up my gold and charged my wife and W. Hewer never to leave the room without one of them in it night nor day. So back again, by the way seeing my goods well in the lighters at Deptford and watched well by people. Home, and whereas I expected to have seen our house on fire, it being now about 7 a-clock, it was not. But to the Fyre, and there find greater hopes than I expected; for my confidence of finding our office on fire was such, that I durst not ask anybody how it was with us, till I came and saw it not burned. But going to the fire, I find, by the blowing up of houses and the great help given by the workmen out of the King's yards, sent up by Sir W. Penn, there is a good stop given to it, as well at Marke-lane end as ours—it having only burned the Dyall of Barkeing Church, and part of the porch, and was there quenched. I up to the top of Barkeing steeple, and there saw the saddest sight of desolation that I ever saw. Everywhere great fires. Oyle-cellars and brimstone and other things burning. I became afeared to stay there long; and therefore down again as fast as I could, the fire being spread as far as I could see it, and to Sir W. Penn's and there eat a piece of cold meat, having eaten nothing since Sunday but the remains of Sunday's dinner.

Here I met with Mr. Young and Whistler; and having removed all my things, and received good hopes that the fire at our end is stopped, they and I walked into the town and find Fanchurch-street, Gracious-street, and Lumbard-street all in dust. The Exchange[13] a sad sight, nothing standing there of all the statues or pillars but Sir Tho. Gresham's picture in the corner. Walked into Moore-fields (our feet ready to burn, walking through the town among the hot coles) and find that full of people, and poor wretches carrying their goods there, and everybody keeping his goods together by themselfs (and a great blessing it is to them that it is fair weather for them to keep abroad night and day); drank there, and paid twopence for a plain penny loaf.

Thence homeward, having passed through Cheapside and Newgate-market, all burned—and seen Anthony Joyces house in fire. And took up (which I keep by me) a piece of glass of Mercer's chapel in the street, where much more was, so melted and buckled with the heat of the fire, like parchment. I also did see a poor Catt taken out of a hole in the chimney joyning to the wall of the Exchange, with the hair all burned off the body and yet alive. So home at night, and find there good hopes of saving our office—but great endeavours of watching all night and having men ready; and so we lodged them in the office, and had drink and bread and cheese for them. And I lay down and slept a good night about midnight—though when I rose, I hear that there had been a great alarme of French and Dutch[14] being risen—which proved nothing. But it is a strange thing to see how long this time did look since Sunday, having been alway full of variety of actions, and little sleep, that it looked like a week or more. And I had forgot almost the day of the week.

6. Up about 5 a-clock, and there met Mr Gawden at the gate of the office (I entending to go out, as I used every now and then to do, to see how the fire is) to call our men to Bishoppsgate, where no fire had yet been near, and there is now one broke out—which did give great grounds to people, and to me too, to think that there is some kind of plott in this (on which many by this time have been taken, and it hath been dangerous for any stranger to walk in the streets); but I went with the men and we did put it out in a little time, so that that was well again. It was pretty to see how hard the women did work in the cannells

11. ***gates,*** to the dockyard.
12. ***plot in it,*** i.e., the fire.
13. ***The Exchange,*** a large building in which merchants met to discuss business. Built in 1576 by Sir Thomas Gresham.
14. ***French and Dutch,*** England's enemies at the time.

sweeping of water; but then they would scold for drink and be as drunk as devils. I saw good Butts of sugar broke open in the street, and people go and take handfuls out and put into beer and drink it. And now all being pretty well, I took boat and over to Southwarke, and took boat on the other side the bridge and so to Westminster, thinking to Shift myself, being all in dirt from top to bottom. But could not there find any place to buy a Shirt or pair of gloves, Westminster-hall being full of people's goods—those in Westminster having removed all their goods, and the Exchequer money put into vessels to carry to Nonsuch. But to the Swan, and there was trimmed. And then to White-hall, but saw nobody, and so home. A sad sight to see how the River looks—no houses nor church near it to the Temple—where it stopped. At home did go with Sir W. Batten and our neighbour Knightly (who, with one more, was the only man of any fashion left in all the neighbourhood hereabouts, they all removing their goods and leaving their houses to the mercy of the fire) to Sir R. Ford's, and there dined, in an earthen platter a fried breast of mutton, a great many of us. But very merry; and endeed as good a meal, though as ugly a one, as ever I had in my life. Thence down to Deptford, and there with great satisfaction landed all my goods at Sir G Carteret's, safe, and nothing missed I could see, or hurt. This being done to my great content, I home; and to Sir W. Batten's, and there with Sir R. Ford, Mr Knightly, and one Withers, a professed lying rogue, supped well; and mighty merry and our fears over. From them to the office and there slept, with the office full of labourers, who talked and slept and walked all night long there. But strange it was to see Cloathworkers-hall on fire these three days and nights in one body of Flame—it being the cellar, full of Oyle.

7. Up by 5 a-clock and, blessed be God, find all well, and by water to Paul's wharfe. Walked thence and saw all the town burned, and a miserable sight of Pauls church, with all the roofs fallen and the body of the Quire fallen into St. Fayths[15]—Paul's school also—Ludgate—Fleet street—my father's house, and the church, and a good part of the Temple the like. So to Creeds lodging near the New Exchange, and there find him laid down upon a bed—the house all unfurnished, there being fears of the fire's coming to them. There borrowed a shirt of him—and washed. To Sir W. Coventry at St. James's, who lay without Curtains, having removed all his goods—as the King at White-hall and everybody had done and was doing. He hopes we shall have no public distractions upon this fire, which is what everybody fears—because of the talk of the French having a hand in it. And it is a proper time for discontents—but all men's minds are full of care to protect themselfs and save their goods. The Militia is in armes everywhere.

This day our Merchants first met at Gresham College, which by proclamation is to be their Exchange. Strange to hear what is bid for houses all up and down here—a friend of Sir W Riders having £150 for what he used to let for £40/per annum. Much dispute where the Custome-house shall be; thereby the growth of the City again to be foreseen. My Lord Treasurer, they say, and others, would have it at the other end of the town. I home late to Sir W. Penn, who did give me a bed—but without curtains or hangings, all being down. So here I went the first time into a naked bed, only my drawers on—and did sleep pretty well; but still, both sleeping and waking, had a fear of fire in my heart, that I took little rest. □□

15. ***St. Fayths,*** a chapel under St. Paul's Cathedral.

Discussion

1. Describe how Pepys's attitude toward the fire evolves as the days pass.

2. What do the fleeing citizens and Pepys himself seem to worry about most? Do their concerns surprise you? Explain.

3. What official acts does Pepys perform during this crisis? In what way does he describe them? What does this tell you about his character?

4. At the end of the fourth

of September Pepys tells us, "I wrote to my father this night; but the post-house being burned, the letter could not go." What does this suggest about Pepys's state of mind?

5. Pepys's diary is noted for its striking details of everyday life. Are there any from this passage which stick in your mind? What are they?

Extension • Reading

The Great Fire was a central event in the lives of many English people besides Pepys. You can read a different account of its progress in the diary of John Evelyn. (Look for entries on and after September 2, 1666.) You can also study the difference between these factual accounts and John Dryden's poetic version, written a year later in his *Annus Mirabilis* ("The Year of Wonders"), sections 209 to 304.

Extension • Writing

Imagine that you are, like Pepys, a resident of seventeenth-century London, but that your house is destroyed by the Great Fire. Write a narrative in which you describe how you first notice the oncoming danger, what you do to save your house and its "goods," and your feelings after the fire has been controlled and you return to the ruins. As a conclusion, tell Pepys what you think those fortunate enough to escape the fire should do for people like you.

Samuel Pepys 1633 • 1703

In his own day Pepys was a man of importance. Though he was born fairly poor, his relatives helped him through col-

lege and a cousin, Admiral Montague, took him along as a secretary on the fleet which brought King Charles II from exile. Pepys's close relationship to the new king and his men led quickly to lucrative and responsible jobs as an administrator for the Royal Navy. A smart man with a taste for work, Pepys soon made himself valuable and, except for periods when his political enemies were in power, he remained at the Naval Office for the rest of his working life.

This is Pepys' public reputation, one honored in his day and soon forgotten after his death. In 1825, however, Pepys was, in a sense, reborn. In that year an edition of his secret diary first appeared. Pepys wrote this diary for himself only. The manuscript is practically without revision, indicating that he gave no care to polishing what he wrote. In the diary he recorded whatever mattered to him—petty details of daily life as well as the major events of his era. He wrote in cipher because he told everything about himself—his many faults as well as his successes.

This absolute candor makes the diary fascinating. It suddenly opens up to us the mind and daily experiences of a man who died nearly three hundred years ago. By accident the diary has both form and substance. Pepys began keeping it January 1, 1660 when, a young and nearly penniless young man, he and his wife were struggling to survive a cold London winter. But, as in typical success tales, chance soon catapaults him into lucrative work. Several events of major importance occur during the ten years of the diary and Pepys shows us how one man lived through them—the installation of a new and alien king, sea wars with the Dutch, a horrendous attack of bubonic plague, and an unprecedented fire which nearly destroys London itself. Pepys weathers all. Failing eyesight finally forced him to cease keeping his diary. He was to have thirty-three more years of active, successful life, but so attached was he to the diary that to cease writing it seemed, he wrote, "almost as much as to see myself go into my grave. . . ."

Jonathan Swift

At the height of his success as a writer of political pamphlets Swift attacked the most celebrated and popular general in the British army, the Duke of Marlborough. While granting him great military skill, Swift accused the duke of prolonging a war in order to make money. Eventually Marlborough was dismissed (1711). When he died (June 16, 1722) Swift wrote this poem.

A Satirical Elegy on the Death of a Late Famous General

His Grace! impossible! what, dead!
Of old age, too, and in his bed!
And could that Mighty Warrior fall?
And so inglorious, after all!
Well, since he's gone, no matter how,
The last loud trump[1] must wake him now;
And, trust me, as the noise grows stronger,
He'd wish to sleep a little longer.
And could he be indeed so old
As by the newspapers we're told?
Threescore, I think, is pretty high;
'Twas time in conscience he should die.
This world he cumbered long enough;
He burnt his candle to the snuff;
And that's the reason some folks think,
He left behind so great a stink.
Behold his funeral appears,
Nor widow's sighs, nor orphan's tears,
Wont at such times each heart to pierce,
Attend the progress of his hearse.
But what of that, his friends may say,
He had those honours in his day.
True to his profit and his pride,
He made them weep before he died.

Come hither, all ye empty things,
Ye bubbles raised by breath of Kings;
Who float upon the tide of state,
Come hither, and behold your fate.
Let Pride be taught by this rebuke,
How very mean a thing's a duke;
From all his ill-got honours flung,
Turned to that dirt from whence he sprung.

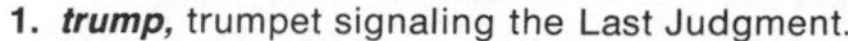

1. ***trump,*** trumpet signaling the Last Judgment.

44
III
The D of Marl: famous Mar
Into Germany to Reduce the
El: of Bavaria

Discussion

1. From the way Swift writes the first few lines of this poem—the exclamations, the questions—what appears to have happened just before the poem begins? What kind of tone does this give the poem as a whole?

2. Why does the poem's speaker think the late general would prefer to sleep through the Last Judgment (lines 7-8)?

3. What images does the speaker use in the last stanza to describe the general? What do they suggest about the dead man?

A Description of a City Shower

Careful observers may foretell the hour
(By sure prognostics) when to dread a shower:
While rain depends,[1] the pensive cat gives o'er
Her frolics, and pursues her tail no more.
Returning home at night, you'll find the sink[2]
Strike your offended sense with double stink.
If you be wise, then go not far to dine;
You'll spend in coach hire more than save in wine.
A coming shower your shooting corns presage,
Old achés throb, your hollow tooth will rage.
Sauntering in coffeehouse is Dulman seen;
He damns the climate and complains of spleen.[3]
Meanwhile the South, rising with dabbled wings,
A sable cloud athwart the welkin[4] flings,
That swilled more liquor than it could contain,
And, like a drunkard, gives it up again.
Brisk Susan[5] whips her linen from the rope,
While the first drizzling shower is borne aslope:
Such is that sprinkling which some careless quean[6]
Flirts on you from her mop, but not so clean:
You fly, invoke the gods; then turning, stop
To rail; she singing, still whirls on her mop.
Not yet the dust had shunned the unequal strife,
But, aided by the wind, fought still for life,
And wafted with its foe by violent gust,
'Twas doubtful which was rain and which was dust.
Ah! where must needy poet seek for aid,
When dust and rain at once his coat invade?
Sole coat, where dust cemented by the rain
Erects the nap, and leaves a mingled stain.
Now in contiguous drops the flood comes down,
Threatening with deluge this devoted[7] town.
To shops in crowds the daggled[8] females fly,
Pretend to cheapen[9] goods, but nothing buy.
The Templar[10] spruce, while every spout's abroach,
Stays till 'tis fair, yet seems to call a coach.
The tucked-up sempstress walks with hasty-strides,
While streams run down her oiled umbrella's sides.

---

1. ***depends,*** literally, hangs overhead, i.e., is imminent.
2. ***sink,*** sewer.
3. ***Dulman . . . spleen.*** Dulman (dull man) describes a type. Spleen (melancholy) was commonly attributed to rainy weather.
4. ***welkin,*** sky.
5. ***Susan,*** a servant.
6. ***quean,*** wench.
7. ***devoted,*** doomed.
8. ***daggled,*** mud spattered.
9. ***cheapen,*** bargain over.
10. ***Templar,*** law student.

Here various kinds, by various fortunes led,
Commence acquaintance underneath a shed.
Triumphant Tories and desponding Whigs[11]
Forget their feuds, and join to save their wigs.
Boxed in a chair[12] the beau impatient sits,
While spouts run clattering o'er the roof by fits,
And ever and anon with frightful din
The leather[13] sounds; he trembles from within.
So when Troy chairmen bore the wooden steed,[14]
Pregnant with Greeks impatient to be freed
(Those bully Greeks, who, as the moderns do,
Instead of paying chairmen, run them through),[15]
Laocoön[16] struck the outside with his spear,
And each imprisoned hero quaked for fear.
Now from all parts the swelling kennels[17] flow,
And bear their trophies with them as they go:
Filth of all hues and odors seem to tell
What street they sailed from, by their sight and smell.
They, as each torrent drives with rapid force,
From Smithfield or St. Pulchre's shape their course,
And in huge confluence joined at Snow Hill ridge,
Fall from the conduit prone to Holborn Bridge.
Sweepings from butchers' stalls, dung, guts, and blood,
Drowned puppies, stinking sprats,[18] all drenched in mud,
Dead cats, and turnip tops, come tumbling down the flood.

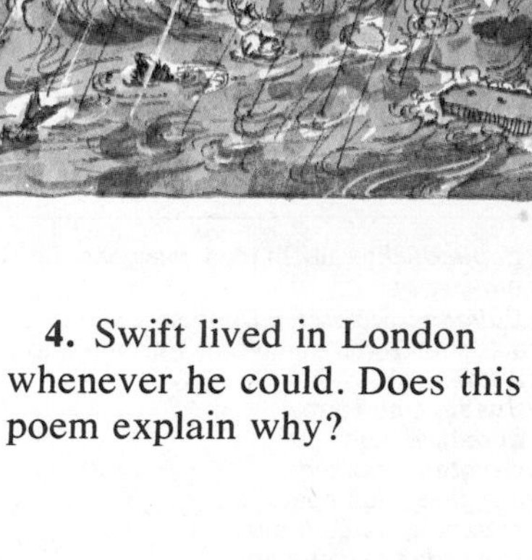

11. ***Tories, Whigs,*** two leading political parties. The former had just won power.
12. ***chair,*** sedan chair, an enclosed seat carried on poles by two men. A common form of city transportation for the rich.
13. ***leather,*** roof of the sedan chair.
14. ***Troy chairmen . . . steed,*** humorous reference to the Trojan horse, a wooden idol which the Greeks used to sneak some hidden warriors into Troy.
15. ***run them through,*** with swords.
16. ***Laocoön,*** Trojan priest who sensed the Greek plot and struck the Trojan horse with his spear. His comrades ignored his warning.
17. ***kennels,*** street gutters.
18. ***sprats,*** herrings.

Discussion

1. In the country, one watches the sky for hints of an oncoming storm. According to Swift, what warnings can one find in the city?

2. What happens to the rainwater when it falls on the city?

3. How do the following people respond to the rain: **(a)** Dulman; **(b)** the Templar; **(c)** the sempstress.

4. Swift lived in London whenever he could. Does this poem explain why?

A Modest Proposal

For Preventing the Children of Poor People in Ireland from Being a Burden to Their Parents or Country, and for Making Them Beneficial to the Public

It is a melancholy object to those who walk through this great town,[1] or travel in the country, when they see the streets, the roads, and cabin doors crowded with beggars of the female sex, followed by three, four, or six children, all in rags and importuning every passenger for an alms. These mothers, instead of being able to work for their honest livelihood, are forced to employ all their time in strolling to beg sustenance for their helpless infants; who as they grow up either turn thieves, for want of work, or leave their dear native country to fight for the pretender[2] in Spain, or sell themselves to the Barbados.[3]

I think it is agreed by all parties that this prodigious number of children in the arms, or on the backs, or at the heels of their mothers, and frequently of their fathers, is, in the present deplorable state of the kingdom, a very great additional grievance; and therefore whoever could find out a fair, cheap, and easy method of making these children sound, useful members of the commonwealth would deserve so well of the public as to have his statue set up for a preserver of the nation.

But my intention is very far from being confined to provide only for the children of professed beggars: it is of a much greater extent and shall take in the whole number of infants at a certain age who are born of parents in effect as little able to support them as those who demand our charity in the streets.

As to my own part, having turned my thoughts for many years upon this important subject and maturely weighed the several schemes of our projectors, I have always found them grossly mistaken in their computation. It is true, a child just dropped from its dam may be supported by her milk for a solar year, with little other nourishment: at most not above the value of two shillings which the mother may certainly get, or the value in scraps, by her lawful occupation of begging; and it is exactly at one year old that I propose to provide for them in such a manner, as, instead of being a charge upon their parents or the parish, or wanting food and raiment for the rest of their lives, they shall, on the contrary, contribute to the feeding and partly to the clothing of many thousands.

There is likewise another great advantage in my scheme, that it will prevent those voluntary abortions and that horrid practice of women murdering their bastard children, alas! too frequent among us, sacrificing the poor innocent babes, I doubt more to avoid the expense than the shame, which would move tears and pity in the most savage and inhuman breast.

The number of souls in this kingdom being usually reckoned one million and a half, of these I calculate there may be about two hundred thousand couple, whose wives are breeders; from which number I subtract thirty thousand couple, who are able to maintain their own children (although I apprehend there cannot be so many, under the present distresses of the kingdom), but this being granted, there will remain an hundred and seventy thousand breeders. I again subtract fifty thousand for those women who miscarry, or whose children die by accident or disease within the year. There only remains one hundred and twenty thousand children of poor parents annually born. The question therefore is, How this number shall be reared and provided for? which, as I have already said, under the present situation of affairs, is utterly impossible by all the methods hitherto proposed. For we can neither employ them in handicraft or agriculture; we neither build houses (I mean in

1. ***this great town,*** Dublin.
2. ***the pretender,*** James Stuart (1688–1766), son of King James II, "pretender" or claimant to the throne which his father had lost in the Revolution of 1688. He was Catholic, and Ireland was loyal to him.
3. ***sell . . . Barbados.*** Because of extreme poverty, many of the Irish bound or "sold" themselves to obtain passage to the West Indies or other British possessions in North America. They agreed to work for their new masters, usually planters, for a specified number of years.

the country) nor cultivate land: they can very seldom pick up a livelihood by stealing till they arrive at six years old, except where they are of towardly[4] parts; although I confess they learn the rudiments much earlier; during which time they can, however, be properly looked upon only as probationers; as I have been informed by a principal gentleman in the county of Cavan, who protested to me that he never knew above one or two instances under the age of six, even in a part of the kingdom so renowned for the quickest proficiency in that art.

I am assured by our merchants that a boy or a girl before twelve years old is no salable commodity; and even when they come to this age they will not yield above three pounds, or three pounds and half a crown at most, on the exchange; which cannot turn to account either to the parents or kingdom, the charge of nutriment and rags having been at least four times that value.

I shall now therefore humbly propose my own thoughts, which I hope will not be liable to the least objection.

I have been assured by a very knowing American of my acquaintance in London that a young healthy child well nursed is at a year old a most delicious, nourishing, and wholesome food, whether stewed, roasted, baked, or boiled; and I make no doubt that it will equally serve in a fricassee or a ragout.[5]

I do therefore humbly offer it to public consideration that of the hundred and twenty thousand children already computed, twenty thousand may be reserved for breed, whereof only one-fourth part to be males; which is more than we allow to sheep, black cattle, or swine; and my reason is that these children are seldom the fruits of marriage, a circumstance not much regarded by our savages; therefore one male will be sufficient to serve four females. That the remaining hundred thousand may, at a year old, be offered in sale to the persons of quality and fortune through the kingdom; always advising the mother to let them suck plentifully in the last month, so as to render them plump and fat for a good table. A child will make two dishes at an entertainment for friends; and when the family dines alone, the fore or hind quarter will make a reasonable dish, and seasoned with a little pepper or salt will be very good boiled on the fourth day, especially in winter.

I have reckoned upon a medium that a child just born will weigh twelve pounds, and in a solar year, if tolerably nursed, will increase to twenty-eight pounds.

I grant this food will be somewhat dear, and therefore very proper for landlords, who, as they have already devoured most of the parents, seem to have the best title to the children.

Infant's flesh will be in season throughout the year, but more plentifully in March, and a little before and after: for we are told by a grave author, an eminent French physician,[6] that fish being a prolific diet, there are more children born in Roman Catholic countries about nine months after Lent than at any other season; therefore, reckoning a year after Lent, the markets will be more glutted than usual, because the number of popish infants is at least three to one in this kingdom: and therefore it will have one other collateral advantage, by lessening the number of papists among us.

I have already computed the charge of nursing a beggar's child (in which list I reckon all cottagers, laborers, and four-fifths of the farmers) to be about two shillings per annum, rags included; and I believe no gentleman would repine to give ten shillings for the carcass of a good fat child, which, as I have said, will make four dishes of excellent nutritive meat, when he has only some particular friend or his own family to dine with him. Thus the squire will learn to be a good landlord and grow popular among his tenants; the mother will have eight shillings net profit and be fit for work till she produces another child.

Those who are more thrifty (as I must confess the times require) may flay the carcass; the skin of which artifically[7] dressed will make admirable gloves for ladies and summer boots for fine gentlemen.

As to our city of Dublin, shambles[8] may be appointed for this purpose in the most convenient parts of it, and butchers we may be assured

4. ***towardly,*** dutiful; easily managed.
5. ***ragout*** (ra gü'), a highly seasoned meat stew.
6. ***grave author . . . physician,*** Francois Rabelais (c. 1494-1553), who was anything but a "grave author."
7. ***artificially,*** artfully; skillfully.
8. ***shambles,*** slaughterhouses.

will not be wanting; although I rather recommend buying the children alive and dressing them hot from the knife as we do roasting pigs.

A very worthy person, a true lover of his country, and whose virtues I highly esteem, was lately pleased, in discoursing on this matter, to offer a refinement upon my scheme. He said that many gentlemen of this kingdom, having of late destroyed their deer, he conceived that the want of venison might be well supplied by the bodies of young lads and maidens, not exceeding fourteen years of age nor under twelve; so great a number of both sexes in every country being now ready to starve for want of work and service; and these to be disposed of by their parents, if alive, or otherwise by their nearest relations. But with due deference to so excellent a friend and so deserving a patriot, I cannot be altogether in his sentiments; for as to the males, my American acquaintance assured me from frequent experience that their flesh was generally tough and lean, like that of our schoolboys, by continual exercise, and their taste disagreeable; and to fatten them would not answer the charge. Then as to the females, it would, I think, with humble submission be a loss to the public, because they soon would become breeders themselves: and besides, it is not improbable that some scrupulous people might be apt to censure such a practice (although indeed very unjustly), as a little bordering upon cruelty; which, I confess, has always been with me the strongest objection against any project, however so well intended.

But in order to justify my friend, he confessed that this expedient was put into his head by the famous Psalmanazar,[9] a native of the island Formosa, who came from thence to London above twenty years ago: and in conversation told my friend that in his country when any young person happened to be put to death, the executioner sold the carcass to persons of quality as a prime dainty; and that in his time the body of a plump girl of fifteen, who was crucified for an attempt to poison the emperor, was sold to his imperial majesty's prime minister of state, and other great mandarins of the court, in joints from the gibbet, at four hundred crowns. Neither indeed can I deny that if the same use were made of several plump girls in this town, who, without one single groat to their fortunes, cannot stir abroad without a chair, and appear at a playhouse and assemblies in foreign fineries which they never will pay for, the kingdom would not be the worse.

Some persons of a desponding spirit are in great concern about that vast number of poor people, who are aged, diseased, or maimed; and I have been desired to employ my thoughts, what course may be taken to ease the nation of so grievous an incumbrance. But I am not in the least pain upon that matter, because it is very well known that they are every day dying and rotting, by cold and famine, and filth and vermin, as fast as can be reasonably expected. And as to the young laborers, they are now in almost as hopeful a condition: they cannot get work, and consequently pine away for want of nourishment to a degree that if at any time they are accidentally hired to common labor, they have not strength to perform it; and thus the country and themselves are happily delivered from the evils to come.

I have too long digressed and therefore shall return to my subject. I think the advantages, by the proposal which I have made, are obvious and many, as well as of the highest importance.

For first, as I have already observed, it would greatly lessen the number of papists, with whom we are yearly overrun, being the principal breeders of the nation, as well as our most dangerous enemies; and who stay at home on purpose to deliver the kingdom to the pretender, hoping to take their advantage by the absence of so many

9. ***Psalmanazar,*** the imposter George Psalmanazar (c. 1679–1763), a Frenchman who passed himself off in England as a Formosan, and wrote a totally fictional "true" account of Formosa, in which he described cannibalism.

good protestants, who have chosen rather to leave their country than stay at home and pay tithes against their conscience to an episcopal curate.[10]

Secondly, the poorer tenants will have something valuable of their own, which by law may be made liable to distress,[11] and help to pay their landlord's rent; their corn and cattle being already seized, and money a thing unknown.

Thirdly, whereas the maintenance of a hundred thousand children, from two years old and upwards, cannot be computed at less than ten shillings a piece per annum, the nation's stock will be thereby increased fifty thousand pounds per annum, beside the profit of a new dish introduced to the tables of all gentlemen of fortune in the kingdom, who have any refinement in taste. And the money will circulate among ourselves, the goods being entirely of our own growth and manufacture.

Fourthly, the constant breeders, beside the gain of eight shillings sterling per annum by the sale of their children, will be rid of the charge of maintaining them after the first year.

Fifthly, this food would likewise bring great custom to taverns: where the vintners will certainly be so prudent as to procure the best receipts for dressing it to perfection, and consequently have their houses frequented by all the fine gentlemen, who justly value themselves upon their knowledge in good eating: and a skilful cook, who understands how to oblige his guests, will contrive to make it as expensive as they please.

Sixthly, this would be a great inducement to marriage, which all wise nations have either encouraged by rewards or enforced by laws and penalties. It would increase the care and tenderness of mothers toward their children, when they were sure of a settlement for life to the poor babes, provided in some sort by the public, to their annual profit instead of expense. We should see an honest emulation among the married women, which of them could bring the fattest child to the market. Men would become as fond of their wives during the time of their pregnancy as they are now of their mares in foal, their cows in calf, or sows when they are ready to farrow; nor offer to beat or kick them (as is too frequent a practice) for fear of a miscarriage.

Many other advantages might be enumerated. For instance, the addition of some thousand carcasses in our exportation of barreled beef, the propagation of swine's flesh, and improvement in the art of making good bacon, so much wanted among us by the great destruction of pigs, too frequent at our tables; which are no way comparable in taste or magnificence to a well-grown, fat, yearling child, which roasted whole will make a considerable figure at a lord mayor's feast, or any other public entertainment. But this and many others I omit, being studious of brevity.

Supposing that one thousand families in this city would be constant customers for infants' flesh, besides others who might have it at merry-meetings, particularly weddings and christenings, I compute that Dublin would take off annually about twenty thousand carcasses; and the rest of the kingdom (where probably they will be sold somewhat cheaper) the remaining eighty thousand.

I can think of no one objection that will possibly be raised against this proposal, unless it should be urged that the number of people will be thereby much lessened in the kingdom. This I freely own, and it was indeed one principal design in offering it to the world. I desire the reader will observe that I calculate my remedy for this one individual kingdom of Ireland, and for no other that ever was, is, or, I think, ever can be upon earth. Therefore let no man talk to me of other expedients: of taxing our absentees at five shillings a pound: of using neither clothes nor household furniture, except what is of our own growth and manufacture: of utterly rejecting the materials and instruments that promote foreign luxury: of curing the expensiveness of pride, vanity, idleness, and gaming in our women: of introducing a vein of parsimony, prudence, and temperance: of learning to love our country in the want of which we differ even from LAPLANDERS and the inhabitants of TOPINAMBOO:[12] of quitting our animosities and factions, nor acting any longer like the Jews, who were mur-

---

10. ***protestants . . . curate.*** Swift is here attacking the absentee landlords.

11. ***distress,*** distraint, the legal seizure of property for payment of debts.

12. ***Topinamboo,*** a savage area of Brazil.

dering one another at the very moment their city was taken:[13] of being a little cautious not to sell our country and conscience for nothing: of teaching landlords to have at least one degree of mercy toward their tenants: lastly, of putting a spirit of honesty, industry, and skill into our shop-keepers; who, if a resolution could now be taken to buy only our native goods, would immediately unite to cheat and exact upon us in the price, the measure, and the goodness, nor could ever yet be brought to make one fair proposal of just dealing, though often and earnestly invited to it.[14]

Therefore, I repeat, let no man talk to me of these and the like expedients, till he has at least some glimpse of hope that there will be ever some hearty and sincere attempt to put them in practice.

But as to myself, having been wearied out for many years with offering vain, idle, visionary thoughts, and at length utterly despairing of success, I fortunately fell upon this proposal; which, as it is wholly new, so it has something solid and real, of no expense and little trouble, full in our own power, and whereby we can incur no danger in disobliging ENGLAND. For this kind of commodity will not bear exportation, the flesh being of too tender a consistence to admit a long continuance in salt, although perhaps I could name a country which would be glad to eat up our whole nation without it.[15]

After all, I am not so violently bent upon my own opinion as to reject any offer proposed by wise men, which shall be found equally innocent, cheap, easy, and effectual. But before something of that kind shall be advanced in contradiction to my scheme, and offering a better, I desire the author or authors will be pleased maturely to consider two points. First, as things now stand, how they will be able to find food and raiment for an hundred thousand useless mouths and backs. And secondly, there being a round million of creatures in human figure throughout this kingdom, whose whole subsistence put into a common stock would leave them in debt two millions of pounds sterling, adding those who are beggars by profession to the bulk of farmers, cottagers, and laborers, with their wives and children, who are beggars in effect; I desire those politicians, who dislike my overture, and may perhaps be so bold as to attempt an answer, that they will first ask the parents of these mortals, whether they would not at this day think it a great happiness to have been sold for food at a year old in the manner I prescribe, and thereby have avoided such a perpetual scene of misfortunes as they have since gone through by the oppression of landlords, the impossibility of paying rent without money or trade, the want of common sustenance, with neither house nor clothes to cover them from the inclemencies of the weather, and the most inevitable prospect of entailing the like or greater miseries upon their breed for ever.

I profess, in the sincerity of my heart, that I have not the least personal interest in endeavoring to promote this necessary work, having no other motive than the public good of my country, by advancing our trade, providing for infants, relieving the poor, and giving some pleasure to the rich. I have no children by which I can propose to get a single penny; the youngest being nine years old, and my wife past childbearing. □□

---

13. ***city was taken.*** While the Roman Emperor Titus was besieging Jerusalem, which he took and destroyed in A.D. 70, within the city factions of fanatics were waging bloody warfare.
14. ***invited to it.*** Swift had already made all these proposals in various pamphlets.
15. ***a country . . . without it.*** England; this is another way of saying, "The British are devouring the Irish."

Discussion

1. According to the initiator of this proposal, what are the worst problems of the moment? What do the issues which trouble him tell us about his values?

2. In what tone does he explain his solution? What methods does he use to persuade his readers to accept this proposal?

3. What word frequently replaces "mother" in this proposal? What does this tell us about the attitudes of the inventor of these ideas?

4. There are several references to an expert who has provided special information. What would you call this expert? What does his friendship with such an expert suggest about the person making this proposal?

5. Why call the proposal "Modest"? What values lie behind this term?

6. (a) List some of the shocking details of life in Ireland the essay casually reveals. **(b)** What is their cumulative effect on the reader?

7. Which solution do you think Swift intends his readers to choose: the "modest proposal," or the list of alternatives on pp. 260–261? Justify your answer.

8. Who are the major targets of this satire? In what ways are the Irish themselves responsible for their plight?

Vocabulary

Context and Dictionary

Use context and your Glossary to match the words listed below with the quotes that follow. On a separate sheet of paper, write the word (or words if more than one seems to fit) next to the number for each quote.

abhorred	combustible
contiguous	expedients
loath	particles
rebuke	repose
succor	

1. "Night came, but unattended with ______."

2. "The poor pigeons I perceive were ______ to leave their houses."

3. "Therefore let no man talk to me of other ______."

4. "And knaves and fools we both ______ alike."

5. "Now in ______ drops the flood comes down."

6. "The latter brood, who just began to fly, / . . . For ______ to their helpless mother call."

7. ". . . And the wind mighty high and driving it [the fire] into the city, and everything . . . proving ______, even the very stones of churches. . . ."

8. "Let Pride be taught by this ______, / How very mean a thing's a duke."

For those quotes for which you have listed more than one word, use the following page references to locate the quote. Then put a star next to the correct word on your paper. **1.** page 244; **2.** page 248; **3.** page 260; **4.** page 245; **5.** page 255; **6.** page 244; **7.** page 248; **8.** page 254.

Jonathan Swift 1667 • 1745

Born in Dublin of English parents, Swift was educated in Ireland, receiving his degree from Trinity College, Dublin, "by special grace" after he had been censured for offenses against college discipline. He fled with many of his fellow Anglo-Irish when James II invaded Ireland and took refuge in England in the household of a kinsman, Sir William Temple. There he remained, with only a few visits to Ireland, from 1689 to 1699, reading widely and writing his first powerful satires. At some point during his stay with Temple he decided, with some reluctance, to make the Church his career, and so was ordained an Anglican minister in 1694.

Swift soon became a convinced churchman and upheld in spirited pamphlets and conversation the causes of both the Anglican Church and the Crown against all dissenters. In 1710 he became a Tory, and in 1713 was appointed Dean of St. Patrick's Cathedral in Dublin. There he established himself as an able administrator, though he disliked living in Ireland, largely because he had formed friendships with many prominent men in England and found his Irish friends less polished.

In his later years, Swift was afflicted with a rare disease which caused dizziness, deafness, and nausea. Nevertheless he continued to write prolifically and kept his wit and his extraordinarily keen eye for human foibles and social corruption until the last few years of his life, when disease and old age closed in. *Gulliver's Travels* (1726), the only work for which he ever received payment, and *A Modest Proposal* (1729) were written at the height of his mature years.

Joseph Addison and Richard Steele

On Thursday, the First of March, 1711, the first number of The Spectator *appeared. A collaboration by Joseph Addison and Richard Steele,* The Spectator *was a single large sheet, printed on both sides, which was published every day but Sunday, running eventually to 555 issues by December 6, 1712, when it ceased publication.*

In the second number the Spectator, the fictitious author created by Addison and Steele, introduces his friends, stock characters representing typical figures of the day—a merchant, a military man, a law student, and so on. As the weeks went by, some of these stereotypical figures acquired human traits, particularly the country squire, Sir Roger de Coverly.

from The Spectator

Sir Roger de Coverley

The first of our Society[1] is a Gentleman of *Worcestershire,* of antient Descent, a Baronet, his Name Sir Roger de Coverley. His great Grandfather was Inventor of that famous Country-Dance which is call'd after him. All who know that Shire, are very well acquainted with the Parts and Merits of Sir Roger. He is a Gentleman that is very singular in his Behaviour, but his Singularities proceed from his good Sense, and are Contradictions to the Manners of the World, only as he thinks the World is in the wrong. However, this Humour creates him no Enemies, for he does nothing with Sowrness or Obstinacy; and his being unconfined to Modes and Forms, makes him but the readier and more capable to please and oblige all who know him. When he is in Town he lives in *Soho-Square:*[2] It is said he keeps himself a Batchelour by reason he was crossed in Love, by a perverse beautiful Widow of the next County to him. Before this Disappointment, Sir Roger was what you call a fine Gentleman, had often supped with my Lord *Rochester* and Sir *George Etherege,* fought a Duel upon his first coming to Town, and kick'd Bully *Dawson*[3] in a publick Coffee-house for calling him Youngster. But being ill used by the abovementioned Widow, he was very serious for a Year and a half; and tho' his Temper being naturally jovial, he at last got over it, he grew careless of himself and never dressed afterwards; he continues to wear a Coat and Doublet of the same Cut that were in Fashion at the Time of his Repulse, which, in his merry Humours, he tells us, has been in and out twelve Times since he first wore it. Sir Roger grew humble in his Desires after he had forgot this cruel Beauty. He is now in his Fifty sixth Year, cheerful, gay, and hearty, keeps a good House both in Town and Country; a great Lover of Mankind; but there is such a mirthful Cast in his Behaviour, that he is rather beloved than esteemed: His Tenants grow rich, his Servants look satisfied, all the young Women profess Love to him, and the young Men are glad of his Company: When he comes into a House he calls the Servants by their Names, and talks all the way up Stairs to a Visit. I must not omit that Sir Roger is a Justice of the *Quorum;*[4] that he fills the Chair at a Quarter-Session with great Abilities, and three Months ago gain'd universal Applause by explaining a Passage in the Game-Act.[5]

---

1. ***Society,*** the Spectator Club, formed by the fictitious author and his friends.
2. ***Soho-Square,*** a district in London.
3. ***Lord Rochester and Sir George Etherege . . . Bully Dawson.*** John Wilmot, the Earl of Rochester (1647–1680), was a courtier, a man of fashion, and a poet. Sir George Etherege (1635–1691) was a Restoration playwright, famous for his comedies. Bully Dawson was a notorious gambler of the period.
4. ***Justice of the Quorum,*** justice of the peace in a county.
5. ***the Game-Act,*** the complicated laws that protected the upper-class monopoly of wild game.

In July of 1711 Addison and Steele sent their fictitious Spectator to visit his old friend, the squire Sir Roger de Coverley, at his country estate. During his stay the Spectator gets a chance to attend a Sunday service at Sir Roger's rural parish church, to observe the local law courts in action, to stroll through the countryside, and to talk at length with country people. This visit not only gives freshness and variety to The Spectator, *but also permits a comparison of, as Addison put it, "the different Manners of the People . . . in the Town and in the Country."*

The Family

I am the more at Ease in Sir Roger's Family, because it consists of sober and staid Persons; for as the Knight is the best Master in the World, he seldom changes his Servants; and as he is beloved by all about him, his Servants never care for leaving him: By this Means his Domesticks are all in Years, and grown old with their Master. You would take his Valet de Chambre[6] for his Brother, his Butler is grey-headed, his Groom is one of the gravest Men that I have ever seen, and his Coachman has the Looks of a Privy-Counsellor. You see the Goodness of the Master even in the old House-dog, and in a grey Pad that is kept in the Stable with great Care and Tenderness out of regard to his past Services, tho' he has been useless for several Years.

I could not but observe with a great deal of Pleasure the Joy that appeared in the Countenances of these ancient Domesticks upon my Friend's Arrival at his Country-Seat. Some of them could not refrain from Tears at the Sight of their old Master; every one of them press'd forward to do something for him, and seemed discouraged if they were not employed. At the same Time the good old Knight, with a Mixture of the Father and the Master of the Family, tempered the Enquiries after his own Affairs with several kind Questions relating to themselves. This Humanity and good Nature engages every Body to him, so that when he is pleasant upon any of them, all his Family are in good Humour, and none so much as the Person whom he diverts himself with: On the Contrary, if he coughs or betrays any Infirmity of old Age, it is easy for a Stander-by to observe a secret Concern in the Looks of all his Servants.

In Church

As Sir Roger is Landlord to the whole Congregation, he keeps them in very good Order, and will suffer no Body to sleep in it besides himself; for if by Chance he has been surprized into a short Nap at Sermon, upon recovering out of it he stands up and looks about him, and if he sees any Body else nodding, either wakes them himself, or sends his Servant to them. Several other of the old Knight's Particularities break out upon these Occasions: Sometimes he will be lengthening out a Verse in the Singing-Psalms half a Minute after the rest of the Congregation have done with it; sometimes, when he is pleased with the Matter of his Devotion, he pronounces *Amen* three or four times to the same Prayer; and sometimes stands up when every Body else is upon their Knees, to count the Congregation, or see if any of his Tenants are missing.

I was Yesterday very much surprized to hear my old Friend, in the Midst of the Service, calling out to one *John Mathews* to mind what he was about, and not disturb the Congregation. This *John Mathews* it seems is remarkable for being an idle Fellow, and at that Time was kicking his Heels for his Diversion. This Authority of the Knight, though exerted in that odd Manner which accompanies him in all Circumstances of Life, has a very good Effect upon the Parish, who are not polite enough to see any thing ridiculous in his Behaviour; besides that, the general good Sense and Worthiness of his Character, make his Friends observe these little Singularities as Foils that rather set off than blemish his good Qualities.

As soon as the Sermon is finished, no Body presumes to stir till Sir Roger is gone out of the Church. The Knight walks down from his Seat in the Chancel, between a double Row of his Tenants, that stand bowing to him on each Side; and every now and then inquires how such an one's Wife or Mother, or Son, or Father do whom he does not see at Church; which is understood as a secret Reprimand to the Person that is absent.

---

6. ***Valet de Chambre,*** personal servant.

The Sleeping Congregation. Historical Pictures Service, Inc.

In Court

The Court was sat before Sir Roger came, but notwithstanding all the Justices had taken their Places upon the Bench, they made Room for the old Knight at the Head of them; who for his Reputation in the Country took Occasion to whisper in the Judge's Ear, That *he was glad his Lordship had met with so much good Weather in his Circuit*. I was listening to the Proceedings of the Court with much Attention, and infinitely pleased with that great Appearance and Solemnity which so properly accompanies such a publick Administration of our Laws; when, after about an Hour's Sitting, I observed to my great Surprize, in the Midst of a Trial, that my Friend Sir Roger was getting up to speak. I was in some Pain for him, till I found he had acquitted himself of two or three Sentences, with a Look of much Business and great Intrepidity.

Upon his first Rising the Court was hushed, and a general Whisper ran among the Country-People that Sir Roger *was up*. The Speech he made was so little to the Purpose, that I shall not trouble my Readers with an Account of it; and I believe was not so much designed by the Knight himself to inform the Court, as to give him a Figure in my Eye, and keep up his Credit in the Country.

I was highly delighted, when the Court rose, to see the Gentlemen of the Country gathering about my old Friend, and striving who should compliment him most; at the same Time that the ordinary People gazed upon him at a Distance, not a little admiring his Courage, that was not afraid to speak to the Judge.

The following essay, typical of the series, begins with a chance incident, but leads to a serious issue. And in this case it appears the city-bred reason of the Spectator is needed to control Sir Roger's old country superstititions.

Witchcraft

There are some Opinions in which a Man should stand Neuter, without engaging his Assent to one side or the other. Such a hovering Faith as this, which refuses to settle upon any Determination, is absolutely necessary in a Mind that is carefull to avoid Errors and Prepossessions. When the Arguments press equally on both sides in matters that are indifferent to us, the safest Method is to give up our selves to neither.

It is with this Temper of Mind that I consider the Subject of Witch-craft. When I hear the Relations that are made from all parts of the World, not only from *Norway* and *Lapland,* from the *East* and *West Indies,* but from every particular Nation in *Europe,* I cannot forbear thinking that there is such an Intercourse and Commerce with Evil Spirits, as that which we express by the name of Witch-craft. But when I consider that the ignorant and credulous Parts of the World abound most in these Relations, and that the Persons among us who are supposed to engage in such an Infernal Commerce are People of a weak Understanding and crazed Imagination, and at the same time reflect upon the many Impostures and Delusions of this Nature that have been detected in all Ages, I endeavour to suspend my Belief till I hear more certain Accounts than any which have yet come to my Knowledge. In short, when I consider the Question, Whether there are such Persons in the World as those we call Witches? my Mind is divided between the two opposite Opinions, or rather (to speak my Thoughts freely) I believe in general that there is and has been such a thing as Witch-craft; but at the same time can give no Credit to any Particular Instance of it.

I am engaged in this Speculation, by some Occurrences that I met with Yesterday, which I shall give my Reader an Account of at large. As I was walking with my Friend Sir Roger by the side of one of his Woods, an old Woman applied her self to me for my Charity. Her Dress and Figure put me in mind of the following Description in *Otway.*[7]

In a close Lane as I pursu'd my Journey,
I spy'd a wrinkled Hag, with Age grown double,
Picking dry Sticks, and mumbling to her self.
Her Eyes with scalding Rheum were gall'd and red,
Cold Palsy shook her Head; her Hands seem'd wither'd;
And on her crooked Shoulders had she wrap'd
The tatter'd Remnants of an old striped Hanging,
Which serv'd to keep her Carcass from the Cold:
So there was nothing of a-piece about her.
Her lower Weeds were all o'er coarsly patch'd
With diff'rent-colour'd Rags, black, red, white, yellow,
And seem'd to speak Variety of Wretchedness.

As I was musing on this Description, and comparing it with the Object before me, the Knight told me, that this very old Woman had the Reputation of a Witch all over the Country, that her Lips were observed to be always in Motion, and that there was not a Switch about her House which her Neighbours did not believe had carried her several hundreds of Miles. If she chanced to stumble, they always found Sticks or Straws that lay in the Figure of a Cross before her. If she made any Mistake at Church, and cryed *Amen* in a wrong place, they never failed to conclude that she was saying her Prayers backwards. There was not a Maid in the Parish that would take a Pinn of her, though she should offer a Bag of Mony with it. She goes by the Name of *Moll White,* and has made the Country ring with several imaginary Exploits which are palmed upon her. If the Dairy Maid does not make her

7. ***Otway.*** Thomas Otway (1652–1685) was a Restoration dramatist.

Butter come so soon as she would have it, *Moll White* is at the bottom of the Churne. If a Horse sweats in the Stable, *Moll White* has been upon his Back. If a Hare makes an unexpected Escape from the Hounds, the Huntsman curses *Moll White.* Nay, (says Sir Roger) I have known the Master of the Pack, upon such an Occasion, send one of his Servants to see if *Moll White* had been out that Morning.

This Account raised my Curiosity so far, that I beg'd my Friend Sir Roger to go with me into her Hovel, which stood in a solitary Corner under the side of the Wood. Upon our first entering Sir Roger winked to me, and pointed at something that stood behind the Door, which upon looking that way I found to be an old Broomstaff. At the same time he whispered me in the Ear to take notice of a Tabby Cat that sate in the Chimny-Corner, which, as the Knight told me, lay under as bad a Report as *Moll White* her self; for besides that *Moll* is said often to accompany her in the same Shape, the Cat is reported to have spoken twice or thrice in her Life, and to have played several Pranks above the Capacity of an ordinary Cat.

I was secretly concerned to see Human Nature in so much Wretchedness and Disgrace, but at the same time could not forbear smiling to hear Sir Roger, who is a little puzzled about the old Woman, advising her as a Justice of Peace to avoid all Communication with the Devil, and never to hurt any of her Neighbours Cattle. We concluded our Visit with a Bounty,[8] which was very acceptable.

In our return home, Sir Roger told me that old *Moll* had been often brought before him for making Children spit Pins, and giving Maids the Night-Mare; and that the Country People would be tossing her into a Pond, and trying Experiments with her every Day, if it was not for him and his Chaplain.

I have since found, upon Enquiry, that Sir Roger was several times staggered with the Reports that had been brought him concerning this old Woman, and would frequently have bound her over to the County Sessions, had not his Chaplain with much ado perswaded him to the contrary.

I have been the more particular in this Account, because I hear there is scarce a Village in *England* that has not a *Moll White* in it. When an old Woman begins to doat, and grow chargeable to a Parish, she is generally turned into a Witch, and fills the whole Country with extravagant Fancies, imaginary Distempers, and terrifying Dreams. In the mean time, the poor Wretch that is the innocent Occasion of so many Evils begins to be frighted at her self, and sometimes confesses secret Commerces and Familiarities that her Imagination forms in a delirious old Age. This frequently cuts off Charity from the greatest Objects of Compassion, and inspires People with a Malevolence towards those poor decrepid Parts of our Species, in whom Human Nature is defaced by Infirmity and Dotage. □□

8. ***Bounty,*** they give her some money.

Discussion

1. Why do Sir Roger's "singularities"—quirks or eccentricities—of behavior not alienate people?

2. What is the relationship between Sir Roger and his servants as described in "The Family"?

3. Based on Sir Roger's behavior "In Church," is he tolerant of other people's peculiarities of behavior? Is there a contradiction between his own behavior in church (and the way it is regarded by the parishoners) and his attitude toward others' eccentricities?

4. What do you think motivates Sir Roger's behavior "In Court"? Why does he seem to do and say what he does?

5. Does Sir Roger's behavior as a master, landlord, and churchgoer seem arbitrary or essentially fair and generous?

6. Since the Spectator was concerned with correcting some of the follies of the age, do you think the description of Sir Roger is meant as an example of admirable behavior, or behavior needing correction?

7. What does the Spectator mean by "a hovering Faith"? Why does he take this approach to witchcraft? In what ways do you think his attitude typical of a "reasonable" era?

8. Contrast the reactions of Sir Roger and the Spectator to the sight of Moll's "Hovel." Can you forgive Sir Roger for his superstitions? Why?

9. Given the fact that belief in witches was widespread when this essay first appeared, what do you think was Addison's purpose in writing it?

Extension • Writing

Write an essay in which you, as a modern Spectator, encounter someone suspected of witchcraft. What kinds of evidence lead to this belief? Do you give it credence? How do you act towards this person? Finish your essay with some general observations which seem to come from the specific facts.

Joseph Addison 1672 • 1719

Addison was the son of a clergyman. He was educated at the Charterhouse, where he met Richard Steele, and at Oxford, where he distinguished himself as a classical scholar, his Latin poems attracting the attention of Dryden. He prepared himself for the diplomatic service by traveling on the Continent between 1699 and 1703. He was elected a Member of Parliament in 1708 and remained in the House of Commons until his death. He varied his political activity with literary endeavors, contributing political essays to Richard Steele's *Tatler,* and later joining with Steele to produce *The Spectator.* Addison's life was an epitome of neoclassical virtues: he sought in his writings to reform the manners and tastes of his time, "to enliven morality with wit, and to temper wit with morality"; he was politically active, as an M.P. and as an official of the colonial government in Ireland. Almost from the first, readers considered *The Spectator* (to which Addison contributed the majority of the papers) a model of fine literary style as well as a guide to sensible social and ethical conduct. His periodical essays are polished, gently humorous, and unobtrusively moral in tone.

Richard Steele 1672 • 1729

In Richard Steele the new middle-class reading public found a spokesman. Born in Ireland, educated at the Charterhouse and Oxford, he spent some years in the army before beginning his literary career with two didactic efforts—a pamphlet called "The Christian Hero" and a comedy entitled *The Funeral*—both opposing Restoration morality. A few years later Steele came up with *The Tatler,* a thrice-weekly news-sheet written largely by himself. It pretended to report on current events and ideas by summarizing what was being said in the leading coffeehouses of London.

The Tatler's success caught the eye of a friend of Steele's from the Charterhouse, Joseph Addison. He contributed papers to *The Tatler* and when it folded joined Steele in developing a successor, which they called *The Spectator.* Steele continued to write increasingly political news-sheets in the years that followed, and became politically active himself, being elected a Member of Parliament and holding several government posts.

Alexander Pope

Epistle to Miss Blount

As some fond virgin,[1] whom her mother's care
Drags from the town to wholesome country air,
Just when she learns to roll a melting eye,
And hear a spark,[2] yet think no danger nigh,
From the dear man unwilling she must sever,
Yet takes one kiss before she parts for ever;
Thus from the world fair Zephalinda[3] flew,
Saw others happy, and with sighs withdrew;
Not that their pleasures caus'd her discontent;
She sigh'd not that they stay'd, but that she went.

She went to plain work,[4] and to purling brooks,
Old-fashion'd halls, dull aunts, and croaking rooks;
She went from opera, park, assembly, play,
To morning walks, and prayers three hours a-day;
To part her time 'twixt reading and bohea,[5]
To muse, and spill her solitary tea,
Or o'er cold coffee trifle with the spoon,
Count the slow clock, and dine exact at noon[6];
Divert her eyes with pictures in the fire,
Hum half a tune, tell stories to the squire;
Up to her godly garret after seven,
There starve and pray, for that's the way to heaven.

Some squire, perhaps, you take delight to rack,
Whose game is whist,[7] whose treat a toast in sack[8];
Who visits with a gun, presents you birds,
Then gives a smacking buss, and cries—no words!
Or with his hounds comes hallooing from the stable,
Makes love with nods, and knees beneath a table;
Whose laughs are hearty, though his jests are coarse,
And loves you best of all things—but his horse.

In some fair evening, on your elbow laid,
Your dream of triumphs in the rural shade;
In pensive thought recall the fancied scene,
See coronations rise on every green:
Before you pass the imaginary sights
Of lords, and earls, and dukes, and garter'd knights,
While the spread fan o'ershades your closing eyes,
Then give one flirt,[9] and all the vision flies.

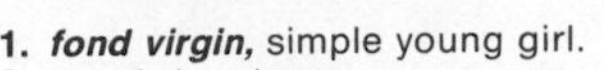

1. ***fond virgin,*** simple young girl.
2. ***spark,*** handsome young man.
3. ***Zephalinda,*** a pet name for Miss Blount.
4. ***plain work,*** sewing.
5. ***bohea,*** a variety of tea.
6. ***at noon,*** fashionable people dined at three or four P.M.
7. ***whist,*** a card game.
8. ***sack,*** sherry, or other strong, light-colored wine.
9. ***flirt,*** closing a fan.

Thus vanish sceptres, coronets and balls,
And leave you in lone woods or empty walls!
  So when your slave,[10] at some dear idle time,
(Not plagued with headaches or the want of rhyme),
Stands in the streets abstracted from the crew,
And while he seems to study, thinks of you;
Just when his fancy paints[11] your sprightly eyes,
Or sees the blush of soft Parthenia[12] rise,
Gay[13] pats my shoulder, and you vanish quite,
Streets, chairs, and coxcombs, rush upon my sight:
Vex'd to be still in town I knit my brow,
Look sour, and hum a tune, as you may now.

10. ***slave,*** Pope himself.
11. ***paints,*** imagines.
12. ***Parthenia,*** a pet name for Miss Blount's sister.
13. ***Gay,*** John Gay (1685–1732), English poet and dramatist, and friend of Pope's.

Discussion

1. In the last paragraph of the "Epistle to Miss Blount" we learn a little about the poem's speaker. When and where does he think about Miss Blount? In what ways is this moment of reverie different from that which he imagines her to have in the preceding paragraph?

2. What are the speaker's feelings towards Miss Blount? How would they affect the way he describes the imagined country squire (lines 23–30)?

3. This poem is full of assumptions about the kind of life the speaker thinks Miss Blount would like to lead. List as many of these assumptions as you can.

Extension • Writing

Imagine that Pope's friend, the young Miss Blount, really enjoys living in the country. Write her letter responding to Pope's "Epistle."

from An Essay on Criticism

Next to Shakespeare, Pope is probably the most frequently quoted of English poets. The following remarks are from his Essay on Criticism, *a long poem which expressed in polished heroic couplets (pairs of rhyming lines in iambic pentameter) the eighteenth century's basic rules for poetry.*

1. 'Tis with our judgments as our watches; none
   Go just alike, yet each believes his own.

2. Let such teach others who themselves excel,
   And censure freely who have written well.

3. Music resembles poetry; in each
   Are nameless graces which no methods teach.

4. Those oft are stratagems which errors seem,
   Nor is it Homer nods, but we that dream.

5. Of all the causes which conspire to blind
Man's erring judgment, and misguide the mind,
What the weak head with strongest bias rules,
Is pride, the never-failing vice of fools.

6. Trust not yourself: but your defects to know,
Make use of every friend—and every foe.

7. A little learning is a dangerous thing;
Drink deep, or taste not the Pierian spring.[1]
There shallow draughts intoxicate the brain,
And drinking largely sobers us again.

8. 'Tis not a lip, or eye, we beauty call,
But the joint force and full result of all.

9. True wit is Nature to advantage dressed,
What oft was thought, but ne'er so well expressed.

10. As shades more sweetly recommend the light,
So modest plainness sets off sprightly wit.

11. Words are like leaves; and where they most abound,
Much fruit of sense beneath is rarely found.

12. True ease in writing comes from art, not chance,
As those move easiest who have learned to dance.

13. Those heads, as stomachs, are not sure the best
Which nauseate all, and nothing can digest.

14. Be not the first by whom the new are tried,
Nor yet the last to lay the old aside.

15. Where'er you find "the cooling western breeze,"
In the next line, it "whispers through the trees;"
If crystal streams "with pleasing murmurs creep,"
The reader's threatened (not in vain) with "sleep."

16. Some praise at morning what they blame at night,
But always think the last opinion right.

17. We think our fathers fools, so wise we grow;
Our wiser sons, no doubt, will think us so.

18. Good nature and good sense must ever join;
To err is human, to forgive divine.

---

1. ***Pierian*** (pī ir′ ē ən) ***spring,*** i.e., inspiration; from Pieria, where the Muses were born.

from An Essay on Man

Know then thyself, presume not God to scan:
The proper study of mankind is man.
Placed on this isthmus of a middle state,
A being darkly wise, and rudely great:
With too much knowledge for the skeptic side,
With too much weakness for the Stoic's pride,
He hangs between: in doubt to act, or rest;
In doubt to deem himself a god, or beast;
In doubt his mind or body to prefer;
Born but to die, and reas'ning but to err;
Alike in ignorance, his reason such,
Whether he thinks too little, or too much:
Chaos of thought and passion, all confused;
Still by himself abused, or disabused;
Created half to rise, and half to fall;
Great lord of all things, yet a prey to all;
Sole judge of truth, in endless error hurled:
The glory, jest, and riddle of the world!

Discussion

1. Many of the excerpts from *An Essay on Criticism* can be read in two senses: as advice to writers or critics, and as general maxims for living. Select three of them and explain their use in both senses.

2. In *An Essay on Man* Pope describes human nature as "a middle state" (line 3). In what ways, according to Pope, does our nature stand between extremes? What does this imply about our relationship to the rest of creation?

Alexander Pope 1688 • 1744

Despite personal handicaps that would have caused a man of less determination to give up, Pope rose to be the leading literary figure of his day. He was a Roman Catholic in an age when adherence to the "Old Faith" prevented him from receiving a university education, voting, or holding public office, and when the tax burden on Roman Catholics was sufficiently high to drive many once well-to-do families into bankruptcy. In addition, at the age of 12 Pope was stricken with a disease that left him dwarfed, crippled, and in almost constant pain. By sheer power of will, he managed to educate himself and to become admired as a poet and feared as a satirist, boasting in a late poem "I must be proud to see/ Men not afraid of God, afraid of me."

Pope earned a large income through his poetry, editorial work, and translations of the *Iliad* and the *Odyssey,* sufficient to "Maintain a poet's dignity and ease, /And see what friends and read what books I please."

He was instrumental in forming the Scriblerus Club, a group of writers (including Swift) who met on occasion to satirize the pretensions of learned men. In an age of satire Pope was often subjected to vituperative literary attacks, but he always gave at least as good as he got, cutting down his enemies with sharply-honed heroic couplets. Among his best-known works are *An Essay on Criticism* (1711), published when he was only 23; *The Rape of the Lock* (1714): *An Essay on Man* (1733–34); and *Moral Essays* (1731–35), all written in heroic couplets.

Samuel Johnson

When Johnson began working on the *Dictionary,* he had fond dreams about the fun he would have preparing it. But what he hoped would be fun soon became drudgery. Johnson thought the work would take three years. In fact it took nine.

Johnson worked hard to achieve accuracy, but soon encountered the problems which face all students: ". . . I saw that one enquiry only gave occasion to another, that book referred to book, that to search was not always to find, and to find was not always to be informed. . . ."

With no tradition of dictionary-making to rely on, Johnson usually had to strike out on his own, establishing spelling (at times unsuccessfully, as in *chirurgeon*) and etymology (see *bully*). And for an era lacking anything like an encyclopedia, at times he tried to offer extended background information (see *alligator* and *shrewmouse*).

Johnson gave vent to his fatigue and exasperation in his definitions of *dull, grubstreet,* and *lexicographer.* And the most famous aspect of Johnson's *Dictionary* today is its personal nature.

from the Dictionary of the English Language

alliga′tor. The crocodile. This name is chiefly used for the crocodile of America, between which, and that of Africa, naturalists have laid down this difference, that one moves the upper, and the other the lower jaw; but this is now known to be chimerical, the lower jaw being equally moved by both.

bu′lly. (Skinner derives this word from *burly,* as a corruption in the pronunciation; which is very probably right; or from *bulky,* or *bull-eyed;* which are less probable. May it not come from *bull,* the pope's letter, implying the insolence of those who came invested with authority from the papal court?) A noisy, blustering, quarrelling fellow: it is generally taken for a man that has only the appearance of courage.

bu′tterfly. A beautiful insect, so named because it first appears at the beginning of the season for butter.

chi′cken. (3) A term for a young girl.

chiru′rgeon. One that cures ailments, not by internal medicines, but outward applications. It is now generally pronounced, and by many written, *surgeon.*

cough. A convulsion of the lungs, vellicated by some sharp serosity. It is pronounced *coff.*

cu′ckoo. (1) A bird which appears in the spring; and is said to suck the eggs of other birds, and lay her own to be hatched in their place; from which practice, it was usual to alarm a husband at the approach of an adulterer by calling *cuckoo,* which, by mistake, was in time applied to the husband. This bird is remarkable for the uniformity of his note, from which his name in most tongues seems to have been formed.

to cu′rtail. (*curto,* Latin. It was anciently written *curtal,* which perhaps is more proper; but dogs that had their tails cut, being called *curtal* dogs, the word was vulgarly conceived to mean originally *to cut the tail,* and was in time written according to that notion.) (1) To cut off; to cut short; to shorten.

dedica′tion. (2) A servile address to a patron.

den. (1) A cavern or hollow running horizontally,

or with a small obliquity, under ground; distinct from a hole, which runs down perpendicularly.

dull. (8) Not exhilarating; not delightful; as, *to make dictionaries is* dull *work.*

e′ssay. (2) A loose sally of the mind; an irregular indigested piece; not a regular and orderly composition.

exci′se.[1] A hateful tax levied upon commodities, and adjudged not by the common judges of property, but wretches hired by those to whom excise is paid.

fa′vourite. (2) One chosen as a companion by his superiour; a mean wretch whose whole business is by any means to please.

fun. (A low cant word.) Sport; high merriment; frolicksome delight.

ga′mbler. (A cant word, I suppose, for *game,* or *gamester.*) A knave whose practice it is to invite the unwary to game and cheat them.

to gi′ggle. To laugh idly; to titter; to grin with merry levity. It is retained in Scotland.

goat. A ruminant animal that seems a middle species between deer and sheep.

gob. A small quantity. A low word.

gra′vy. The serous juice that runs from flesh not much dried by the fire.

gru′bstreet. Originally the name of a street in Moorfields in London, much inhabited by writers of small histories, dictionaries, and temporary poems; whence any mean production is called grubstreet.

to hiss. To utter a noise like that of a serpent and some other animals. It is remarkable, that this word cannot be pronounced without making the noise which it signifies.

itch. (1) A cutaneous disease extremely contagious, which overspreads the body with small pustules filled with a thin serum, and raised as microscopes have discovered by a small animal. It is cured by sulphur.

lexico′grapher. A writer of dictionaries; a harmless drudge, that busies himself in tracing the original, and detailing the signification of words.

lunch, lu′ncheon. As much food as one's hand can hold.

ne′twork. Any thing reticulated or decussated, at equal distances, with interstices between the intersections.

oats. A grain, which in England is generally given to horses, but in Scotland supports the people.

pa′rasite. One that frequents rich tables, and earns his welcome by flattery.

pa′stern.[2] (1) The knee of an horse.

pa′tron. (1) One who countenances, supports, or protects. Commonly a wretch who supports with insolence, and is paid with flattery.

pe′nsion. An allowance made to any one without an equivalent. In England it is generally understood to mean pay given to a state hireling for treason to his country.

pe′nsioner. (2) A slave of state hired by a stipend to obey his master.

sa′tire. A poem in which wickedness or folly is censured. Proper *satire* is distinguished, by the generality of the reflections, from a *lampoon* which is aimed against a particular person; but they are too frequently confounded.

shre′wmouse. A mouse of which the bite is generally supposed venomous, and to which vulgar tradition assigns such malignity, that she is said to lame the foot over which she runs. I am informed that all these reports are calumnious, and that her feet and teeth are equally harmless with those of any other little mouse. Our ancestors however looked on her with such terrour, that they are supposed to have given her name to a scolding woman, whom for her venom they call a *shrew.*

so′nnet. (1) A short poem consisting of fourteen lines, of which the rhymes are adjusted by a particular rule. It is not very suitable to the English language, and has not been used by any man of eminence since Milton.

to′ry. (A cant term, derived, I suppose, from an Irish word signifying a savage.) One who adheres to the ancient constitution of the state, and the apostolical hierarchy of the church of England, opposed to a whig.[3]

whig. (2) The name of a faction.

---

1. ***excise.*** Johnson's father had had trouble with the commissioners of excise, in the conduct of his business as a bookseller and maker of parchment.
2. ***pastern.*** In fact, part of the foot of a horse. When a lady asked Johnson how he came to define the word in this way, he answered, "Ignorance, Madam, pure ignorance." But he didn't bother to correct his definition until eighteen years later.
3. ***whig.*** Johnson himself was a Tory.

wi′tticism. A mean attempt at wit.

to worm. (2) To deprive a dog of something, nobody knows what, under his tongue, which is said to prevent him, nobody knows why, from running mad. □□

Discussion

The excerpts from the *Dictionary* provide a cross-section of Johnson's personality as well as his work. Find examples that: **(a)** illustrate his irony; **(b)** show his learning; **(c)** display the beliefs of his age; **(d)** reveal his prejudices; **(e)** show his ability to enjoy a joke at his own expense; **(f)** illustrate his love for Latin-derived diction.

Johnson's Letter to Chesterfield

Johnson had approached Lord Chesterfield for aid in the preparation of his Dictionary. *Chesterfield encouraged him and gave him a token sum of money. Johnson went to call a second time but was kept waiting. With the* Dictionary *complete, Chesterfield wrote two short articles praising it, clearly hoping Johnson would dedicate the book to him. Johnson's response came in the following, probably the most famous letter in English literature.*

To the Right Honorable
the Earl of Chesterfield

February 7, 1755.

My Lord: I have lately been informed by the proprietor of *The World,*[1] that two papers, in which my *Dictionary* is recommended to the public, were written by your lordship. To be so distinguished is an honor which, being very little accustomed to favors from the great, I know not well how to receive, or in what terms to acknowledge.

When, upon some slight encouragement, I first visited your lordship, I was overpowered, like the rest of mankind, by the enchantment of your address; and I could not forbear to wish that I might boast myself *"Le vainqueur du vainqueur de la terre,"*[2] that I might obtain that regard for which I saw the world contending; but I found my attendance so little encouraged, that neither pride nor modesty would suffer me to continue it. When I had once addressed your lordship in public, I had exhausted all the art of pleasing which a retired and uncourtly scholar can possess. I had done all that I could; and no man is well pleased to have his all neglected, be it ever so little.

Seven years, my lord, have now passed, since I waited in your outward rooms, or was repulsed from your door; during which time I have been pushing on my work through difficulties, of which it is useless to complain, and have brought it at last to the verge of publication, without one act of assistance, one word of encouragement, or one smile of favor. Such treatment I did not expect, for I never had a patron before.

The shepherd in Vergil grew at last acquaint-

1. ***The World,*** a newspaper run by a friend of Johnson's.
2. ***Le vainquer . . . de la terre.*** "the conqueror of the conqueror of the world." [French]

ed with Love, and found him a native of the rocks.[3]

Is not a patron, my lord, one who looks with unconcern on a man struggling for life in the water, and, when he has reached ground, encumbers him with help? The notice which you have been pleased to take of my labors, had it been early, had been kind; but it has been delayed till I am indifferent and cannot enjoy it; till I am solitary, and cannot impart it; till I am known, and do not want it. I hope it is no very cynical asperity not to confess obligations where no benefit has been received, or to be unwilling that the public should consider me as owing that to a patron, which Providence has enabled me to do for myself.

Having carried on my work thus far with so little obligation to any favorer of learning, I shall not be disappointed though I should conclude it, if less be possible, with less; for I have been long wakened from that dream of hope, in which I once boasted myself with so much exaltation.

My Lord

Your Lordship's most humble,

Most Obedient servant,

Sam. Johnson

3. ***The shepherd . . . rocks.*** Johnson is referring to a passage in the *Eclogues* a collection of pastorals by the Latin poet Virgil (70–19 B.C.), that speaks of the cruelty of love.

Discussion

1. Johnson uses irony as a weapon in his letter to Chesterfield. But the reader feels the cutting edge only as the letter slowly reveals the injustices he has suffered. Examine each of the following phrases in context and explain what the reader might think it means when first reading it, and what, as the letter continues, the reader discovers to be Johnson's actual meaning: **(a)** "favors from the great"; **(b)** "the enchantment of your address"; **(c)** "Such treatment I did not expect, for I never had a patron before"; **(d)** "favorer of learning."

2. Compare the *Dictionary* definition of *patron* with that in the letter. Which do you prefer? Why?

from Milton

Milton has the reputation of having been in his youth eminently beautiful, so as to have been called the Lady of his college. His hair, which was of a light brown, parted at the foretop, and hung down upon his shoulders, according to the picture which he has given of Adam. He was, however, not of the heroick stature, but rather below the middle size, according to Mr. Richardson, who mentions him as having narrowly escaped from being "short and thick." He was vigorous and active, and delighted in the exercise of the sword, in which he is related to have been eminently skillful. His weapon was, I believe, not the rapier, but the backsword, of which he recommends the use in his book on Education.

His eyes are said never to have been bright; but, if he was a dexterous fencer, they must have been once quick.

His domestick habits, so far as they are known, were those of a severe student. He drank little strong drink of any kind, and fed without excess in quantity, and in his earlier years without delicacy of choice. In his youth he studied late at night; but afterwards changed his hours, and rested in bed from nine to four in the summer, and five in winter. The course of his day was best known after he was blind. When he first rose he heard a chapter in the Hebrew Bible, and then studied till twelve; then took some exercise for an hour; then dined; then played on the

"Milton Dictating to His Daughters" by George Romney. Courtauld Institute of Art, London.

organ, and sung, or heard another sing; then studied to six; then entertained his visiters till eight; then supped, and, after a pipe of tobacco and a glass of water, went to bed.

So is his life described; but this even tenour appears attainable only in Colleges. He that lives in the world will sometimes have the succession of his practice broken and confused. Visiters, of whom Milton is represented to have had great numbers, will come and stay unseasonably; business, of which every man has some, must be done when others will do it.

When he did not care to rise early he had something read to him by his bedside; perhaps at this time his daughters were employed. He composed much in the morning and dictated in the day, sitting obliquely in an elbow-chair, with his leg thrown over the arm.

Fortune appears not to have had much of his care. In the civil wars he lent his personal estate to the parliament, but when, after the contest was decided, he solicited repayment, he met not only with neglect, but "sharp rebuke"; and, having tired both himself and his friends, was given up to poverty and hopeless indignation, till he shewed how able he was to do greater service. He was then made Latin secretary, with two hundred pounds a year, and had a thousand pounds for his *Defence of the People.* His widow, who after his death retired to Namptwich in Cheshire, and died about 1729, is said to have reported that he lost two thousand pounds by entrusting it to a scrivener;[1] and that, in the general depredation upon the Church, he had grasped an estate of about sixty pounds a year belonging to Westminster Abbey, which, like other sharers of the plunder of rebellion, he was afterwards obliged to return. Two thousand pounds, which he had placed in the Excise-office, were also lost. There is yet no reason to believe that he was ever reduced to indigence: his wants being few were competently supplied. He sold his library before his death, and left his family fifteen hundred pounds; on which his widow laid hold, and only gave one hundred to each of his daughters.

1. ***scrivener,*** here probably a notary.

His literature was unquestionably great. He read all the languages which are considered either as learned or polite: Hebrew, with its two dialects, Greek, Latin, Italian, French, and Spanish. In Latin his skill was such as places him in the first rank of writers and criticks; and he appears to have cultivated Italian with uncommon diligence. The books in which his daughter, who used to read to him, represented him as most delighting, after Homer, which he could almost repeat, were Ovid's *Metamorphoses* and Euripides. His Euripides is, by Mr. Cradock's kindness, now in my hands: the margin is sometimes noted; but I have found nothing remarkable.

Of the English poets he set most value upon Spenser, Shakespeare, and Cowley. Spenser was apparently his favourite; Shakespeare he may easily be supposed to like, with every other skilful reader, but I should not have expected that Cowley, whose ideas of excellence were different from his own, would have had much of his approbation. His character of Dryden, who sometimes visited him, was that he was a good rhymist, but no poet.

His theological opinions are said to have been first Calvinistical, and afterwards, perhaps when he began to hate the Presbyterians, to have extended towards Arminianism.[2] In the mixed questions of theology and government he never thinks that he can recede far enough from popery or prelacy; but what Baudius says of Erasmus seems applicable to him: "magis habuit quod fugeret, quam quod sequeretur."[3] He had determined rather what to condemn than what to approve. He has not associated himself with any denomination of Protestants: we know rather what he was not, than what he was. He was not of the church of Rome; he was not of the church of England.

To be of no church is dangerous. Religion, of which the rewards are distant and which is animated only by Faith and Hope, will glide by degrees out of the mind unless it be invigorated and reimpressed by external ordinances, by stated calls to worship, and the salutary influence of example. Milton, who appears to have had full conviction of the truth of Christianity, and to have regarded the Holy Scriptures with the profoundest veneration, to have been untainted by any heretical peculiarity of opinion, and to have lived in a confirmed belief of the immediate and occasional agency of Providence, yet grew old without any visible worship. In the distribution of his hours, there was no hour of prayer, either solitary or with his household; omitting publick prayers, he omitted all.

Of this omission the reason has been sought, upon a supposition which ought never to be made, that men live with their own approbation, and justify their conduct to themselves. Prayer certainly was not thought superfluous by him, who represents our first parents as praying acceptably in the state of innocence, and efficaciously after their fall. That he lived without prayer can hardly be affirmed; his studies and meditations were an habitual prayer. The neglect of it in his family was probably a fault for which he condemned himself, and which he intended to correct, but that death, as too often happens, intercepted his reformation.

His political notions were those of an acrimonious and surly republican, for which it is not known that he gave any better reason than that "a popular government was the most frugal; for the trappings of a monarchy would set up an ordinary commonwealth." It is surely very shallow policy, that supposes money to be the chief good; and even this without considering that the support and expence of a Court is for the most part only a particular kind of traffick, by which money is circulated without any national impoverishment.

Milton's republicanism was, I am afraid, founded in an envious hatred of greatness, and a sullen desire of independence; in petulance impatient of controul, and pride disdainful of superiority. He hated monarchs in the state and prelates in the church; for he hated all whom he was required to obey. It is to be suspected that his predominant desire was to destroy rather than establish, and that he felt not so much the the love of liberty as repugnance to authority.

It has been observed that they who most loudly clamour for liberty do not most liberally

2. ***Calvinistical, Presbyterians, Arminianism,*** complex theological positions. Simply put, Johnson alludes to Milton's early belief in predestination, shared by Calvin and a sect of his followers, the Presbyterians, and to Milton's later doubts about the same subject, shared by the followers of Jacobus Arminius.

3. ***"magis habuit . . . sequerentur."*** "He was possessed more by what he fled than by what he followed." [Latin] Erasmus (?1466–1536) expressed his humanistic outlook in frequent attacks on the medieval pieties of his time.

grant it. What we know of Milton's character in domestick relations is, that he was severe and arbitrary. His family consisted of women; and there appears in his books something like a Turkish contempt of females, as subordinate and inferior beings. That his own daughters might not break the ranks, he suffered them to be depressed by a mean and penurious education. He thought woman made only for obedience, and man only for rebellion. . . . □□

Discussion

1. What details of Milton's appearance does Johnson describe in the first two paragraphs of the excerpt from his *Milton*? What do they imply about Milton as a person?

2. How does Johnson react to the traditional description of the way Milton spent his day? What does this tell us about Johnson as a biographer?

3. How does Johnson reach the conclusion that Milton did not lead a life "without prayer"? Why would Johnson want to arrive at such a conclusion?

4. From his discussion of Milton's politics, what do you think Johnson's werc? Should Johnson write this way in a biography? Explain your answer.

One of Johnson's most admirable qualities was his generosity. For over twenty years he let an obscure doctor, Mr. Levet, who cared mostly for the poor, live with him. When Levet suddenly died, Johnson, nearing his own death, wrote the following poem.

On the Death of Mr. Robert Levet, A Practiser in Physic

Condemned to Hope's delusive mine,
  As on we toil from day to day,
By sudden blasts or slow decline
  Our social comforts drop away.

Well tried through many a varying year,
  See Levet to the grave descend;
Officious,[1] innocent, sincere,
  Of every friendless name the friend.

Yet still he fills affection's eye,
  Obscurely wise and coarsely kind;
Nor, lettered Arrogance, deny
  Thy praise to merit unrefined.

When fainting nature called for aid,
  And hovering death prepared the blow,
His vigorous remedy displayed
  The power of art without the show.

In Misery's darkest cavern known,
  His useful care was ever nigh,
Where hopeless Anguish poured his groan,
  And lonely Want retired to die.

No summons mocked by chill delay,
  No petty gain disdained by pride;
The modest wants of every day
  The toil of every day supplied.

His virtues walked their narrow round,
  Nor made a pause, nor left a void;
And sure the Eternal Master found
  The single talent well employed.[2]

The busy day, the peaceful night,
  Unfelt, uncounted, glided by;
His frame was firm—his powers were bright,
  Though now his eightieth year was nigh.

Then with no fiery throbbing pain,
  No cold gradations of decay,
Death broke at once the vital chain,
  And freed his soul the nearest way.

1. ***Officious,*** charitable.
2. ***the Eternal Master . . . well employed.*** In Christ's parable of the talents, those with even few natural gifts are exhorted to regard their development as a divine trust. (Matt. 25:14–30)

Discussion

1. In praising Mr. Levet, Johnson implicitly criticizes another, different kind of doctor. Using details from the poem, describe Levet's opposite.

2. In what ways does the account of Levet's last days function as an ideal for the aged Johnson?

Vocabulary • Dictionary

Some of the words that you have encountered in the selections from *The Spectator,* Pope, and Johnson are italicized in the following questions. Answer these questions on a separate sheet of paper. If you need help, consult the Glossary. Give reasons for your answers.

1. If someone is involved in deep *speculation* would he or she be more likely to be riding in a rodeo, skiing, or sitting at a desk?

2. What sort of waterway might be dug across an *isthmus* for ships to go through—a lake, a canal, a pond?

3. If someone displays *asperity,* is he or she more likely to be smiling, frowning, or nodding?

4. Is someone who is *credulous* likely to be taken in by an imposter, investigated by the FBI, or admitted to the hall of fame?

5. If you lived in a *garret* and had been out for the evening, would you have to go upstairs or downstairs to go to bed?

6. If you knew that a report about someone was *calumnious,* would you think less of that person?

7. Are the young or the old more likely to experience *infirmity*?

8. Is someone who is *pensive* more likely to be thinking about plans for the weekend, a relationship that's ended, or a favorite kind of pie?

9. Is an act of *depredation* if discovered likely to be punished or rewarded?

10. Is a *penurious* person more likely to be a miser, a gambler, or a spendthrift?

Samuel Johnson 1709 • 1784

Samuel Johnson dominated the English literary scene during the second half of the eighteenth century. His fame came from his work as a scholar and from his vital personality, transmitted to us primarily through James Boswell's famous biography.

An attack of scrofula in childhood left young Samuel half-blind, half-deaf, his face scarred for life. For consolation he turned to literature, reading through the books in his father's bookshop. At age 19 Johnson went to Oxford. He left Oxford without a degree and from 1731 to 1737 worked as a bookseller and school teacher.

In 1737 Johnson, twenty-five and married to a middle-aged widow with three children, went to London to seek fame and fortune.

In 1746 his chance came. He entered into a contract to prepare a dictionary of the English language. Today only corporations, aided by computers, take on such a task. In Johnson's day it was even more daring. While he had a few predecessors, no one had ever tried to prepare the kind of dictionary Johnson had in mind. He wanted to list all the words currently found in English books, to establish how they should be correctly spelled, to suggest proper pronunciation, to give their history (etymology), and to give each a complete and exact definition. This last task was the most demanding. For example, Johnson's most recent predecessor had listed eighteen meanings for the verb "to take." Johnson found 134.

Finally, in 1755, after a period of nine years, the dictionary was complete. It was a resounding success and was to become the standard of the language for the next one hundred years.

The dictionary made an international reputation for Johnson, but no fortune. He had used up all his money preparing it, and a year after its appearance he was imprisoned for debt. He had to return to hack writing to pay his bills, but quickly inaugurated a new project: an edition of Shakespeare's works which took ten years to complete. His finances much improved, Johnson's last published work, considered by many a masterpiece, was *The Lives of the Poets.*

In Boswell's biography of Johnson, he emerges not only as a man of genius but as a man of essential kindness and generosity.

James Boswell

from The Life of Samuel Johnson, LL.D.

As I had the honor and happiness of enjoying Dr. Johnson's friendship for upwards of twenty years; as I had the scheme of writing his life constantly in view; as he was well apprised of this circumstance, and from time to time obligingly satisfied my inquiries by communicating to me the incidents of his early years; as I acquired a facility in recollecting, and was very assiduous in recording, his conversation, of which the extraordinary vigor and vivacity constituted one of the first features of his character; and as I have spared no pains in obtaining materials concerning him from every quarter where I could discover that they were to be found, and have been favored with the most liberal communications by his friends, I flatter myself that few biographers have entered upon such a work as this with more advantages; independent of literary abilities, in which I am not vain enough to compare myself with some great names who have gone before me in this kind of writing. . . .

Boswell Arranging Dr. Johnson's Writing. The Bettman Archive, Inc.

Boswell's Introduction to Johnson (1763)

This is to me a memorable year, for in it I had the happiness to obtain the acquaintance of that extraordinary man whose memoirs I am now writing; an acquaintance which I shall ever esteem as one of the most fortunate circumstances in my life. . . .

Mr. Thomas Davies the actor, who then kept a bookseller's shop in Russel-street, Covent-garden, told me that Johnson was very much his friend, and came frequently to his house, where he more than once invited me to meet him; but by some unlucky accident or other he was prevented from coming to us.

At last, on Monday the 16th of May, when I was sitting in Mr. Davies's back-parlor, after having drunk tea with him and Mrs. Davies, Johnson unexpectedly came into the shop; and Mr. Davies having perceived him through the glass-door in the room in which we were sitting, advancing towards us—he announced his aweful approach to me, somewhat in the manner of an actor in the part of Horatio, when he addresses Hamlet on the appearance of his father's ghost, "Look, my Lord, it comes."

I found that I had a very perfect idea of Johnson's figure, from the portrait of him painted by Sir Joshua Reynolds soon after he had published his *Dictionary*, in the attitude of sitting in his easy chair in deep meditation, which was the first picture his friend did for him, which Sir Joshua kindly presented to me. Mr. Davies mentioned my name, and respectfully introduced me to him. I was much agitated, and recollecting his prejudice against the Scotch, of which I had heard much, I said to Davies, "Don't tell where I come from."

"From Scotland," cried Davies roguishly.

"Mr. Johnson, (said I) I do indeed come from Scotland, but I cannot help it." I am willing to flatter myself that I meant this as light pleasantry to soothe and conciliate him, and not as an humiliating abasement at the expense of my country. But however that might be, this speech was somewhat unlucky, for with that quickness of wit for which he was so remarkable, he seized the expression "come from Scotland" which I used in the sense of being of that country, and, as if I had said that I had come away from it, or left it, retorted, "That, Sir, I find, is what a very great many of your countrymen cannot help."

This stroke stunned me a good deal; and when we had sat down, I felt myself not a little embarrassed, and apprehensive of what might come next. He then addressed himself to Davies: "What do you think of Garrick?[1] He has refused me an order for the play for Miss Williams,[2] because he knows the house will be full, and that an order would be worth three shillings."

Eager to take any opening to get into conversation with him, I ventured to say, "O, Sir, I cannot think Mr. Garrick would grudge such a trifle to you."

"Sir (said he, with a stern look), I have known David Garrick longer than you have done: and I know no right you have to talk to me on the subject."

Perhaps I deserved this check, for it was rather presumptuous in me, an entire stranger, to express any doubt of the justice of his animadversion upon his old acquaintance and pupil. I now felt myself much mortified, and began to think that the hope which I had long indulged of obtaining his acquaintance was blasted. And, in truth, had not my ardor been uncommonly strong, and my resolution uncommonly persevering, so rough a reception might have deterred me for ever from making any further attempts. Fortunately, however, I remained upon the field not wholly discomfited; and was soon rewarded by hearing some of his conversation, of which I preserved the following short minute, without marking the questions and observations by which it was produced.

"People (he remarked) may be taken in once, who imagine that an author is greater in private life than other men. Uncommon parts[3] require uncommon opportunities for their exertion."

"In barbarous society, superiority of parts is of real consequence. Great strength or great wisdom is of much value to an individual. But in more polished times there are people to do every thing for money; and then there are a number of other superiorities, such as those of birth and fortune, and rank, that dissipate men's attention, and leave no extraordinary share of respect for personal and intellectual superiority. This is wisely ordered by Providence, to preserve some equality among mankind." . . .

I was highly pleased with the extraordinary vigor of his conversation, and regretted that I was drawn away from it by an engagement at another place. I had, for a part of the evening, been left alone with him, and had ventured to make an observation now and then, which he received very civilly; so that I was satisfied that though there was a roughness in his manner, there was no ill-nature in his disposition. Davies followed me to the door, and when I complained to him a little of the hard blows which the great man had given me, he kindly took upon him to console me by saying, "Don't be uneasy. I can see he likes you very well."

A few days afterwards I called on Davies, and asked him if he thought I might take the liberty of waiting on Mr. Johnson at his Chambers in the Temple. He said I certainly might, and that Mr. Johnson would take it as a compliment. So upon Tuesday the 24th of May, I boldly repaired to Johnson. His Chambers were on the first floor of No. 1, Inner-Temple-lane, and I entered them with an impression given me by the Reverend Dr. Blair, of Edinburgh, who had been introduced to him not long before, and described his having "found the Giant in his den"; an expression which, when I came to be pretty well acquainted with Johnson, I repeated to him, and he was diverted by this picturesque account of himself.

He received me very courteously; but it must be confessed that his apartment, and furniture, and morning dress were sufficiently uncouth. His brown suit of clothes looked very rusty; he had

1. ***Garrick,*** David Garrick, the most famous actor of his day, and a former pupil of Johnson's.
2. ***Miss Williams,*** an indigent elderly lady who lived in Johnson's household and on his bounty.
3. ***parts,*** personal qualities; abilities or talents.

on a little old shrivelled unpowdered wig, which was too small for his head; his shirt-neck and knees of his breeches were loose; his black worsted stockings ill drawn up; and he had a pair of unbuckled shoes by way of slippers. But all these slovenly peculiarities were forgotten the moment that he began to talk. Some gentlemen whom I do not recollect were sitting with him; and when they went away, I also rose; but he said to me, "Nay, don't go."

"Sir, (said I) I am afraid that I intrude upon you. It is benevolent to allow me to sit and hear you."

He seemed pleased with this compliment, which I sincerely paid him, and answered, "Sir, I am obliged to any man who visits me." I have preserved the following short minute of what passed this day:

"Madness frequently discovers itself merely by unnecessary deviation from the usual modes of the world. My poor friend Smart shewed the disturbance of his mind by falling upon his knees and saying his prayers in the street or in any other unusual place. Now although, rationally speaking, it is greater madness not to pray at all than to pray as Smart did, I am afraid there are so many who do not pray that their understanding is not called in question."

Concerning this unfortunate poet, Christopher Smart, who was confined in a mad-house, he had, at another time, the following conversation with Dr. Burney:

BURNEY. "How does poor Smart do, Sir; is he likely to recover?"

JOHNSON. "It seems as if his mind had ceased to struggle with the disease, for he grows fat upon it."

BURNEY. "Perhaps, Sir, that may be from want of exercise."

JOHNSON. "No, Sir; he has partly as much exercise as he used to have, for he digs in the garden. Indeed, before his confinement, he used for exercise to walk to the ale-house; but he was *carried* back again. I did not think he ought to be shut up. His infirmities were not noxious to society. He insisted on people praying with him; and I'd as lief pray with Kit Smart as any one else. Another charge was that he did not love clean linen; and I have no passion for it."

Johnson continued, "Mankind have a great aversion to intellectual labor; but even supposing knowledge to be easily attainable, more people would be content to be ignorant than would take even a little trouble to acquire it."

"The morality of an action depends on the motive from which we act. If I fling half a crown to a beggar with intention to break his head, and he picks it up and buys victuals with it, the physical effect is good; but, with respect to me, the action is very wrong."

Johnson on Fathers and Sons (July 1763)

Feeling myself now quite at ease as his companion, though I had all possible reverence for him, I expressed a regret that I could not be so easy with my father, though he was not much older than Johnson, and certainly however respectable had not more learning and greater abilities to depress me. I asked him the reason of this.

JOHNSON. "Why, Sir, I am a man of the world. I live in the world, and I take, in some degree, the color of the world as it moves along. Your father is a Judge in a remote part of the island, and all his notions are taken from the old world. Besides, Sir, there must always be a struggle between a father and son, while one aims at power and the other at independence."

I said I was afraid my father would force me to be a lawyer.

JOHNSON. "Sir, you need not be afraid of his forcing you to be a laborious practising lawyer; that is not in his power. For as the proverb says, 'One man may lead a horse to the water, but twenty cannot make him drink.' He may be displeased that you are not what he wishes you to be; but that displeasure will not go far. If he insists only on your having as much law as is necessary for a man of property, and then endeavors to get you into Parliament, he is quite right."

On Young People

At night Mr. Johnson and I supped in a private room at the Turk's Head coffee-house in the Strand. "I encourage this house (said he) for the mistress of it is a good civil woman, and has not much business.

"Sir, I love the acquaintance of young people; because, in the first place, I don't like to think myself growing old. In the next place, young acquaintances must last longest, if they do last; and then, Sir, young men have more virtue than old men; they have more generous sentiments in every respect. I love the young dogs of this age: they have more wit and humor and knowledge of life than we had; but then the dogs are not so good scholars. Sir, in my early years I read very hard. It is a sad reflection, but a true one, that I knew almost as much at eighteen as I do now. My judgment, to be sure, was not so good; but I had all the facts. I remember very well, when I was at Oxford, an old gentleman said to me, 'Young man, ply your book diligently now, and acquire a stock of knowledge; for when years come upon you, you will find that poring upon books will be but an irksome task.'"

On Eating (August 1763)

At supper this night he talked of good eating with uncommon satisfaction. "Some people (said he) have a foolish way of not minding, or pretending not to mind, what they eat. For my part, I mind my belly very studiously, and very carefully; for I look upon it that he who does not mind his belly will hardly mind anything else."

He now appeared to me *Jean Bull philosophe,*[4] and he was, for the moment, not only serious but vehement. Yet I have heard him, upon other occasions, talk with great contempt of people who were anxious to gratify their palates; and the 206th number of his *Rambler* is a masterly essay against gulosity. His practice, indeed, I must acknowledge, may be considered as casting the balance of his different opinions upon this subject, for I never knew any man who relished good eating more than he did. When at table, he was totally absorbed in the business of the moment; his looks seemed rivetted to his plate; nor would he, unless when in very high company, say one word, or even pay the least attention to what was said by others, till he had satisfied his appetite, which was so fierce, and indulged with such intenseness, that while in the act of eating, the veins of his forehead swelled, and generally a strong perspiration was visible. To those whose sensations were delicate, this could not but be disgusting; and it was doubtless not very suitable to the character of a philosopher, who should be distinguished by self-command. But it must be owned that Johnson, though he could be rigidly *abstemious*, was not a *temperate* man either in eating or drinking. He could refrain, but he could not use moderately. He told me that he had fasted two days without inconvenience, and that he had never been hungry but once. They who beheld with wonder how much he eat upon all occasions when his dinner was to his taste could not easily conceive what he must have meant by hunger, and not only was he remarkable for the extraordinary quantity which he eat, but he was, or affected to be, a man of very nice discernment in the science of cookery. He used to descant critically on the dishes which had been at table where he had dined or supped, and to recollect minutely what he had liked.

When invited to dine, even with an intimate friend, he was not pleased if something better than a plain dinner was not prepared for him. I have heard him say on such an occasion, "This was a good dinner enough, to be sure; but it was not a dinner to *ask* a man to." On the other hand, he was wont to express, with great glee, his satisfaction when he had been entertained quite to his mind.

On Equality of the Sexes (April 1778)

Mrs. Knowles affected to complain that men had much more liberty allowed them than women.

JOHNSON. "Why, Madam, women have all the liberty they should wish to have. We have all the labor and the danger, and the women all the advantage. We go to sea, we build houses, we do everything, in short, to pay our court to the women."

MRS. KNOWLES. "The Doctor reasons very wittily, but not convincingly. Now, take the instance of building; the mason's wife, if she is ever seen in liquor, is ruined; the mason may get himself drunk as often as he pleases, with little loss of character; nay, may let his wife and children starve."

JOHNSON. "Madam, you must consider, if the mason does get himself drunk, and let his wife and children starve, the parish will oblige him to

4. ***Jean Bull philosophe,*** John Bull the philosopher. [French] John Bull is the personification of the British nation, the typical Englishman.

find security for their maintenance. We have different modes of restraining evil. Stocks for the men, a ducking-stool for women, and a pound for beasts. If we require more perfection from women than from ourselves, it is doing them honor. And women have not the same temptations that we have: they may always live in virtuous company; men must mix in the world indiscriminately. If a woman has no inclination to do what is wrong, being secured from it is no restraint to her. I am at liberty to walk into the Thames; but if I were to try it, my friends would restrain me in Bedlam,[5] and I should be obliged to them."

MRS. KNOWLES. "Still, Doctor, I cannot help thinking it a hardship that more indulgence is allowed to men than to women. It gives a superiority to men, to which I do not see how they are entitled."

JOHNSON. "It is plain, Madam, one or other must have the superiority. As Shakespeare says, 'If two men ride on a horse, one must ride behind.' "

DILLY. "I suppose, Sir, Mrs. Knowles would have them to ride in panniers,[6] one on each side."

JOHNSON. "Then, Sir, the horse would throw them both."

MRS. KNOWLES. "Well, I hope that in another world the sexes will be equal."

BOSWELL. "That is being too ambitious, Madam. *We* might as well desire to be equal with the angels. We shall all, I hope, be happy in a future state, but we must not expect to be all happy in the same degree. It is enough if we be happy according to our several capacities. A worthy carman will get to heaven as well as Sir Isaac Newton. Yet, though equally good, they will not have the same degrees of happiness."

JOHNSON. "Probably not." □□

5. ***Bedlam,*** a madhouse.
6. ***panniers,*** a pair of baskets carried on both sides of a pack animal.

Discussion

1. In *The Life of Samuel Johnson,* Boswell's professed objective is to write Johnson's biography so that "he will be seen as he really was," to "delineate him without reserve." **(a)** What are some of the unpleasant aspects of the picture of Johnson that Boswell presents? **(b)** What admirable characteristics do you find in Boswell's Johnson?

2. What kind of a role does Boswell play in these scenes? Why does he act this way?

3. Why does Boswell sometimes report Johnson's conversations as if they were a part of a play?

4. Why do you think people desired Johnson's company?

James Boswell 1740 • 1795

The discovery and recent publication of Boswell's personal journals have done much to correct the caricature of Boswell, pencil in hand and ear cocked, dancing attendance on the great Samuel Johnson and his circle. It is now clear that there was mutual respect and affection between the two, in spite of Boswell's sometimes absurd antics which drew harsh words from Johnson.

The son of a judge with the honorary title Lord Auchinleck, Boswell studied law at the University of Edinburgh, traveled widely on the continent, where he met and captivated Rousseau and Voltaire, and was technically a member of the gentry who could meet Johnson's circle on equal footing. He was also a man of genius with a remarkable memory and an instinct for unsparing portrayal of himself and others. His *Life of Johnson* (1791) and *Journal of a Tour to the Hebrides* (1785) reveal Johnson the whole man, not only the public figure in its most favorable aspects.

Thomas Gray

Elegy Written in a Country Churchyard

The curfew tolls the knell of parting day,
  The lowing herd wind slowly o'er the lea,
The plowman homeward plods his weary way,
  And leaves the world to darkness and to me.

Now fades the glimmering landscape on the sight,
  And all the air a solemn stillness holds,
Save where the beetle wheels his droning flight,
  And drowsy tinklings lull the distant folds;

Save that from yonder ivy-mantled tower
  The moping owl does to the moon complain
Of such as, wandering near her secret bower,
  Molest her ancient solitary reign.

Beneath those rugged elms, that yew-tree's shade,
  Where heaves the turf in many a moldering heap,
Each in his narrow cell forever laid,
  The rude forefathers of the hamlet sleep.

The breezy call of incense-breathing Morn,
  The swallow twittering from the strawbuilt shed,
The cock's shrill clarion, or the echoing horn,[1]
  No more shall rouse them from their lowly bed.

For them no more the blazing hearth shall burn,
  Or busy housewife ply her evening care;
No children run to lisp their sire's return,
  Or climb his knees the envied kiss to share.

Oft did the harvest to their sickle yield,
  Their furrow oft the stubborn glebe has broke;
How jocund did they drive their team afield!
  How bowed the woods beneath their sturdy stroke!

Let not Ambition mock their useful toil,
  Their homely joys, and destiny obscure;
Nor Grandeur hear, with a disdainful smile,
  The short and simple annals of the poor.

The boast of heraldry, the pomp of power,
  And all that beauty, all that wealth e'er gave,
Awaits alike the inevitable hour:
  The paths of glory lead but to the grave.

Nor you, ye proud, impute to these the fault,
  If Memory o'er their tomb no trophies raise,
Where through the long-drawn aisle and fretted vault
  The pealing anthem swells the note of praise.

Can storied urn[2] or animated[3] bust
  Back to its mansion call the fleeting breath?
Can Honor's voice provoke the silent dust,
  Or Flattery soothe the dull cold ear of Death?

Perhaps in this neglected spot is laid
  Some heart once pregnant with celestial fire;
Hands that the rod of empire might have swayed,
  Or waked to ecstasy the living lyre.

But Knowledge to their eyes her ample page
  Rich with the spoils of time did ne'er unroll;
Chill Penury repressed their noble rage,
  And froze the genial current of the soul.

Full many a gem of purest ray serene
  The dark unfathomed caves of ocean bear;
Full many a flower is born to blush unseen,
  And waste its sweetness on the desert air.

Some village Hampden[4] that with dauntless breast
  The little tyrant of his fields withstood;

---

1. ***horn,*** the huntsman's horn.
2. ***storied urn,*** an urn decorated with pictures that tell a story.
3. ***animated,*** lifelike.
4. ***Hampden,*** John Hampden (1594–1643), member of the Puritan or Roundhead party who spoke out against royal taxes.

Some mute inglorious Milton here may rest,
Some Cromwell[5] guiltless of his country's blood.

The applause of listening senates to command,
The threats of pain and ruin to despise,
To scatter plenty o'er a smiling land,
And read their history in a nation's eyes,

Their lot forbade; nor circumscribed alone
Their growing virtues, but their crimes confined;
Forbade to wade through slaughter to a throne,
And shut the gates of mercy on mankind,

The struggling pangs of conscious truth to hide,
To quench the blushes of ingenuous shame,
Or heap the shrine of Luxury and Pride
With incense kindled at the Muse's flame.

Far from the madding crowd's ignoble strife,
Their sober wishes never learned to stray;
Along the cool sequestered vale of life
They kept the noiseless tenor of their way.

Yet ev'n these bones from insult to protect
Some frail memorial still erected nigh,
With uncouth[6] rimes and shapeless sculpture decked,
Implores the passing tribute of a sigh.

Their name, their years, spelt by the unlettered Muse,
The place of fame and elegy supply;
And many a holy text around she strews,
That teach the rustic moralist to die.

For who, to dumb Forgetfulness a prey,
This pleasing anxious being e'er resigned,
Left the warm precincts of the cheerful day,
Nor cast one longing, lingering look behind?

On some fond breast the parting soul relies,
Some pious drops the closing eye requires;
Ev'n from the tomb the voice of Nature cries,
Ev'n in our ashes live their wonted fires.

For thee,[7] who mindful of the unhonored dead
Dost in these lines their artless tale relate;
If chance, by lonely Contemplation led,
Some kindred spirit shall inquire thy fate,

Haply some hoary-headed swain may say,
"Oft have we seen him at the peep of dawn
Brushing with hasty steps the dews away
To meet the sun upon the upland lawn,

"There at the foot of yonder nodding beech,
That wreathes its old fantastic roots so high,
His listless length at noontide would he stretch,
And pore upon the brook that babbles by.

"Hard by yon wood, now smiling as in scorn,
Muttering his wayward fancies he would rove,
Now drooping, woeful wan, like one forlorn,
Or crazed with care, or crossed in hopeless love.

"One morn I missed him on the customed hill,
Along the heath, and near his favorite tree;
Another came; nor yet beside the rill,
Nor up the lawn, nor at the wood was he;

"The next with dirges due in sad array
Slow through the church-way path we saw him borne.
Approach and read (for thou canst read) the lay,
Graved on the stone beneath yon aged thorn."

The Epitaph

Here rests his head upon the lap of Earth
A youth to Fortune and to Fame unknown.
Fair Science frowned not on his humble birth,
And Melancholy marked him for her own.

Large was his bounty, and his soul sincere,
Heaven did a recompense as largely send;
He gave to Misery all he had, a tear,
He gained from Heaven ('twas all he wished) a friend.

No farther seek his merits to disclose,
Or draw his frailties from their dread abode.
(There they alike in trembling hope repose),
The bosom of his Father and his God.

---

5. ***Cromwell.*** Oliver Cromwell (1599–1658) was a Puritan military leader whom became Lord Protector of the Commonwealth after the execution of Charles I.
6. ***uncouth,*** strange, odd.
7. ***thee,*** Gray himself.

Discussion

1. How do the sounds of nature help to establish this poem's mood in the first three stanzas?

2. What kind of life does the speaker imagine these dead people once enjoyed?

3. When the speaker considers those who might mock these humble lives, what sort of critic is he imagining?

4. What prevented the villagers from achieving the great successes of a Cromwell or a Milton? Could the villagers be happy that they have missed such opportunities? Explain.

5. What kind of life does the speaker himself live? How do we learn about it? In what ways does it parallel the lives of the villagers? In what ways is it different?

Sonnet on the Death of Richard West[1]

In vain to me the smiling mornings shine,
  And reddening Phoebus[2] lifts his golden fire:
The birds in vain their amorous descant join,
  Or cheerful fields resume their green attire;
These ears, alas! for other notes repine,
  A different object do these eyes require;
My lonely anguish melts no heart but mine,
  And in my breast th' imperfect joys expire.
Yet morning smiles the busy race to cheer,
  And new-born pleasure brings to happier men;
The fields to all their wonted tribute bear;
  To warm their little loves the birds complain:
I fruitless mourn to him that cannot hear,
  And weep the more because I weep in vain.

1. ***Richard West*** (1716–1742), poet and friend of Gray's, who died at the age of thirty-six.
2. ***Phoebus*** (fē'bəs), an epithet of Apollo, the Greek god of the sun, meaning "bright." Here, the sun.

Discussion

1. In the first four lines, three elements of nature that should give happiness are mentioned. What are they?

2. Each of these natural elements is mentioned at least once again—where, and to what effect?

3. The phrase "in vain" occurs at the beginning and end of the poem. It means "without result, fruitless." What might this (and "fruitless" in line 13) suggest about the contrast between the poet's feelings and the external world of nature?

Thomas Gray 1716 • 1771

Gray is known today primarily for his "Elegy Written in a Country Churchyard" which, when it was published in 1750, immediately established his reputation. Its supposed setting, the churchyard of Stoke Poges, a village in Buckinghamshire, became Gray's own final resting place.

Gray studied at Cambridge, left without a degree to travel abroad, and then returned to the university where he completed his studies and lived for the rest of his life. In his later years he was appointed Professor of Modern History, but he never felt called upon to give a lecture in that subject, devoting himself instead to a life of quiet retirement and various scholarly pursuits. His poetic output was relatively small. His shy, affectionate nature and gentle humor are preserved in his letters, now considered among the best from an age in which letter writing was an art.

Robert Burns

To a Mouse

on turning her up in her nest
with the plow, November, 1785

Wee, sleekit,° cow'rin', tim'rous beastie, — sleek
O what a panic's in thy breastie!
Thou need na start awa sae hasty,
Wi' bickering brattle!° — short race
I wad be laith to rin an' chase thee
Wi' murd'ring pattle!° — plow-spade

I'm truly sorry man's dominion
Has broken Nature's social union,
An' justifies that ill opinion
Which makes thee startle
At me, thy poor earth-born companion,
An' fellow-mortal!

I doubt na, whiles,° but thou may thieve; sometimes
What then? poor beastie, thou maun live!
A daimen-icker in a thrave[1]
'S a sma' request:
I'll get a blessin' wi' the lave,° the rest
And never miss 't!

Thy wee bit housie, too, in ruin!
Its silly wa's° the win's are strewin'! simple walls
An' naething, now, to big° a new ane, build
O' foggage° green! coarse grass
An' bleak December's win's ensuin',
Baith snell° an' keen! biting

Thou saw the fields laid bare and waste.
An' weary winter comin' fast,
An' cozie here, beneath the blast,
Thou thought to dwell,
Till crash! the cruel coulter° past plowshare
Out-thro' thy cell.

That wee bit heap o' leaves an' stibble
Has cost thee mony a weary nibble!
Now thou's turn'd out, for a' thy trouble,
But house or hald,° abode
To thole the winter's sleety dribble,
An' cranreuch° cauld! hoarfrost

But, Mousie, thou art no thy lane,° alone
In proving foresight may be vain:
The best laid schemes o' mice an' men
Gang aft a-gley,° go awry
An' lea'e us nought but grief an' pain
For promis'd joy.

Still thou art blest compar'd wi' me!
The present only toucheth thee:
But oh! I backward cast my e'e
On prospects drear!
An' forward tho' I canna see,
I guess an' fear!

1. ***A daimen-icker in a thrave,*** an occasional ear or head of grain in a shock.

A Red, Red Rose

O my luve is like a red, red rose
That's newly sprung in June.
O my luve is like the melodie
That's sweetly played in tune.

As fair art thou, my bonie lass,
So deep in luve am I,
And I will luve thee still, my dear,
Till a' the seas gang dry.

Till a' the seas gang dry, my dear,
And the rocks melt wi' the sun!
And I will luve thee still, my dear,
While the sands o' life shall run.

And fare thee weel, my only luve,
And fare thee weel a while!
And I will come again, my luve,
Tho' it were ten thousand mile!

Discussion

1. (a) What bit of philosophy is contained in the second stanza of "To a Mouse"? in the seventh? in the eighth? (b) What is gained by having such philosophical thoughts initiated by the plight of the mouse?

2. How would an ordinary farmer react to the discovery of a mouse nest? What does this speaker's unusual reaction tell us about him?

3. Explain what oncoming winter suggests to the speaker.

4. What is the speaker of "A Red, Red Rose" about to do?

5. What are the qualities in his beloved that his imagery suggests?

6. How serious is the speaker? Explain.

Vocabulary • Pronunciation

Following each of the sentences below are the pronunciations of two different words. One of these pronunciations is for the word that belongs in the blank. Use the pronunciation key in the Glossary to choose the correct pronunciation. Copy the letter of the correct choice on a separate sheet of paper, after the sentence number. Then write the word as it would appear in each sentence. Be sure you understand the meaning of each word.

1. "Madness frequently discovers itself by unnecessary ______ from the usual modes of the world." (a) dē′vē ā′shən; (b) dev′ə lü′shən.

2. "To quench the blushes of ______ shame . . ." (a) in jē′nyəs; (b) in jen′yü əs.

3. "I'm truly sorry man's ______ / Has broken Nature's social union." (a) dom′ə nē; (b) də min′yən.

4. "But it must be owned that Johnson, though he could be rigidly ______, was not a temperate man either in eating or drinking." (a) ab stē′mē əs; (b) ab′stə nəns.

5. "Heaven did a ______ as largely send." (a) rek′əm pens; (b) rek′ən dīt.

6. "His infirmities were not ______ to society." (a) nô′shəs; (b) nok′shəs.

7. "Some heart once pregnant with ______ fire." ((a) sə les′chəl; (b) sel′ə brāt.

8. "I am willing to flatter myself that I meant this as light pleasantry to soothe and ______ him. . . ." (a) kən sep′chü əl; ((b) kən sil′ē āt.

Robert Burns 1759 • 1796

Unlike fashionable, "citified" poets like Alexander Pope, Scotland's "Bobbie" Burns led a vigorous, earthy kind of life. Until the age of sixteen he worked, as he himself said, "with the unceasing toil of a galley slave" on the farms his father rented in the rocky Scottish Lowlands. By the time he was in his twenties, he had been in and out of several love affairs—and an even greater number of taverns. And though his last years were marked by poverty and illness, Burns undertook two rough journeys, one through northern England and the other through the Scottish Highlands, in an effort to uncover traditional songs and ballads.

Such a strenuous life was bound to be short, but before his death at thirty-seven, Burns was hailed as a new and exciting poet. His *Poems: Chiefly in the Scottish Dialect,* which he published in 1786 in hopes of getting enough money to start a new life in Jamaica, were so well received that he called off his Jamaica trip and accepted an invitation to join the fashionable, literary salons in Edinburgh. Edinburgh society, however, was still too enamored of the pedantry and polish of Alexander Pope to regard Burns as anything more than a rustic novelty, and Burns only made matters worse by acting the part of the arrogant, overly eager literary darling. He soon left the city to rejoin the "sons and daughters of labor and poverty" with whom he had grown up. In their eyes he was a great man—someone who not only spoke of the common people (as men like Thomas Gray were doing) but one who also spoke up for them in their own vigorous idiom of speech.

Unit Review Tests 4: The Age of Reason

CONTENT REVIEW

1. Poets of the Age of Reason frequently wrote about public issues. **(a)** To what extent is this the case in Dryden's *The Hind and the Panther* and Pope's *An Essay on Man?* **(b)** Though about the deaths of specific men, in what ways can Swift's "Satirical Elegy" and Johnson's "On the Death of Mr. Levet" be considered "public" poetry?

2. (a) To which social class did Johnson belong? What permits him to write Chesterfield in this way? In what works of Swift do you find a similar independence? **(b)** Which writers in this unit speak respectfully to or about their social "superiors"? Why do they adopt this tone?

3. Faced with the inevitability of death, in what different ways do the people of this "reasoned" age react? List the appropriate selections and characterize each response.

4. In what ways does London's growth in size and power during this period of history appear in the literature of the era? In answering, consider: **(a)** Which selections from the unit describe London? **(b)** Which writers seem to like city life? Why? **(c)** Which do not? What repels them?

5. (a) In his "Epistle to Miss Blount" Pope etches a satiric caricature of country life. What does he mock? **(b)** What other selection in this unit shares his attitude?

Unit 4, Test 1

INTERPRETATION: NEW MATERIAL

Journal of the Plague Year

Daniel Defoe

Daniel Defoe (1659–1731) was only a child during the Great Plague of London in 1665, and had no detailed recollection of the events he described in the *Journal of the Plague Year* (1722). The book was, in part, written and published in response to the widespread alarm about a new outbreak of the plague that had occurred in Europe in 1721. Defoe did a great deal of research to make his account of the London plague of 1665 accurate and convincing to readers concerned about a possible new outbreak in England.

I

It pleased God that I was still spared, and very hearty and sound in health, but very impatient of being pent up within doors without air, as I have been for fourteen days or thereabouts, and I could not restrain myself, but I would go to carry a letter for my brother to the post-house. Then it was indeed that I observed a profound silence in the streets. When I came to the post-house, as I went to put in my letter, I saw a man stand in one corner of the yard and talking to another at a window, and a third had opened a door belonging to the office. In the middle of the yard lay a small leather purse with two keys hanging at it, with money in it, but nobody would meddle with it. I asked how long it had lain there; the man at the window said it had lain almost an hour, but that they had not meddled with it, because they did not know but the person who dropped it might come back to look for it. I had no such need of money, nor was the sum so big that I had any inclination to meddle with it, or to get the money at the hazard it might be attended with; so I seemed to go away, when the man who had opened the door said he would take it up, but so that if the right owner came for it he should be sure to have it. So he went in and fetched a pail of water, and set it down hard by the purse, then went again and fetched some gunpowder, and cast a good deal of powder upon the purse, and then made a train from that which he had thrown loose upon the purse. The train reached about two yards. After this he goes in a third time and fetches out a pair of tongs red hot, and which he had prepared, I suppose, on purpose, and first setting fire to the train of powder, that singed the purse, and also smoked the air sufficiently. But he was not content with that, but he then takes up the purse with the tongs, holding it so long till the tongs burnt through the purse, and then he shook the money out into the pail of water, so he carried it in. The money, as I remember, was about thirteen shillings and some smooth groats and brass farthings.[1] . . .

II

Passing through Tokenhouse Yard, in Lothbury, of a sudden a casement[2] violently opened just over my head, and a woman gave three frightful screeches, and then cried, "Oh! death, death, death!" in a most inimitable[3] tone, and which struck me with horror and a chillness in my very blood. There was nobody to be seen in the whole street, neither did any other window open, for people had no curiosity now in any case, nor could anybody help one another, so I went on to pass into Bell Alley.

Just in Bell Alley, on the right hand of the passage, there was a more terrible cry than that, though it was not so directed out at the window; but the whole family was in a terrible fright, and I could hear women and children run screaming about the rooms like distracted, when a garret-window opened, and somebody from a window on the other side the alley called and asked, "What is the matter?" upon which, from the first window it was answered, "O Lord, my old master has hanged himself!" The other asked again, "Is he quite dead?" and the first answered, "Ay, ay, quite dead; quite dead and cold!" This person was a merchant and a deputy alderman, and very rich. I care not to mention the name, though I knew his name too, but that would be an hardship to the family, which is now flourishing again.

But this is but one; it is scarce credible what dreadful cases happened in particular families every day. People in the rage of the distemper, or in the torment of their swellings, which was indeed intolerable, running out of their own government,[4] raving and distracted, and oftentimes laying violent hands upon themselves, throwing themselves out at their windows, shooting themselves, &c.; mothers murdering their own children in their lunacy, some dying of mere grief as a passion, some of mere fright and surprise without any infection at all, others frighted into idiotism and foolish distractions, some into despair and lunacy, others into melancholy madness. . . .

III

. . . here I must observe also that the plague, as I suppose all distempers do, operated in a different manner on differing constitutions;[5] some were immediately overwhelmed with it, and it came to violent fevers, vomitings, insufferable headaches, pains in the back, and so up to ravings and ragings with those pains; others with swellings and tumours in the neck or groin, or armpits, which till they could be broke put them into insufferable agonies and torment; while others, as I have observed, were silently infected, the fever preying upon their spirits insensibly, and they seeing little of it till they fell into swooning, and faintings, and death without pain.

I am not physician enough to enter into the particular reasons and manner of these differing effects of one and the same distemper. . . . I am only relating what I know, or have heard, or believe of the particular cases, and what fell within the compass of my view; but this may be added too, that though the former sort of those cases, namely, those openly visited, were the worst for themselves as to pain . . . yet the latter had the worst state of the disease; for in the former they frequently recovered, especially if the swellings broke, but the latter was inevitable

---

1. ***groats, farthings,*** coins worth a small sum.
2. ***casement,*** window that opens on hinges.
3. ***inimitable,*** impossible to imitate.
4. ***government,*** control.
5. ***constitutions,*** physical makeups, natures.

death; no cure, no help could be possible, nothing could follow but death. . . .

IV

. . . the shutting up of houses, so as to confine those that were well with those that were sick, had very great inconveniences in it, and some that were very tragical. . . . But it was authorised by a law, it had the public good in view as the end chiefly aimed at, and all the private injuries that were done by the putting it in execution must be put to the account of the public benefit.

It is doubtful to this day whether, in the whole, it contributed anything to the stop of the infection. . . . Certain it is that if all the infected persons were effectually shut in, no sound person could have been infected by them, because they could not have come near them. But the case was this, and I shall only touch it here, namely, that the infection was propagated insensibly,[6] and by such persons as were not visibly infected, who neither knew whom they infected or who they were infected by. . . .

V

. . . the common people, who, ignorant and stupid in their reflections, as they were brutishly wicked and thoughtless before, were now led by their fright to extremes of folly; and, as I have said before that they ran to conjurers[7] and witches, and all sorts of deceivers, to know what should become of them (who fed their fears, and kept them always alarmed and awake on purpose to delude them and pick their pockets), so they were as mad upon their running after quacks and mountebanks,[8] and every practising old woman, for medicines and remedies; storing themselves with such multitudes of pills, potions, and preservatives, as they were called, that they not only spent their money, but even poisoned themselves beforehand, for fear of the poison of the infection, and prepared their bodies for the plague, instead of preserving them against it. On the other hand, it is incredible, and scarce to be imagined, how the posts of houses and corners of streets were plastered over with doctors' bills and papers of ignorant fellows, quacking and tampering in physic, and inviting the people to come to them for remedies, which was generally set off with such flourishes as these, viz.[9]: "Infallible preventive pills against the plague." "Never-failing preservatives against the infection." "Sovereign cordials against the corruption of the air." "Exact regulations for the conduct of the body in case of an infection." "Antipestilential pills." "Incomparable drink against the plague, never found out before." "An universal remedy for the plague." "The only true plague water." "The royal antidote against all kinds of infection"; and such a number more that I cannot reckon up; and if I could, would fill a book of themselves to set them down. . . .

VI

It is here to be observed that after the funerals became so many that people could not toll the bell, mourn or weep, or wear black for one another, as they did before; no, nor so much as make coffins for those that died; so after a while the fury of the infection appeared to be so increased that, in short, they shut up no houses at all. It seemed enough that all the remedies of that kind had been used till they were found fruitless, and that the plague spread itself with an irresistible fury; so that as the fire that succeeding year spread itself, and burned with such violence that the citizens, in despair, gave over their endeavours to extinguish it, so in the plague it came at last to such violence that the people sat still looking at one another, and seemed quite abandoned to despair. . . .

VII

In the middle of their distress, when the condition of the city of London was so truly calamitous,[10] just then it pleased God, as it were, by His immediate hand to disarm this enemy; the poison was taken out of the sting. It was wonderful; even the physicians themselves were surprised at it. Wherever they visited they found their patients better; either they had sweated kindly, or the tumours were broke, or the car-

---

6. ***propagated insensibly,*** reproduced, multiplied, or passed on unknowingly.
7. ***conjurers,*** tricksters, magicians.
8. ***mountebanks,*** person who sells useless medicines in public.
9. ***viz.,*** namely.
10. ***calamitous,*** disastrous.

buncles went down, and the inflammations round them changed colour, or the fever was gone, or the violent headache was assuaged, or some good symptom was in the case; so that in a few days everybody was recovering, whole families that were infected and down, that had ministers praying with them, and expected death every hour, were revived and healed, and none died at all out of them.

Nor was this by any new medicine found out, or new method of cure discovered, or by any experience in the operation which the physicians or surgeons attained to; but it was evidently from the secret invisible hand of Him that had at first sent this disease as a judgment upon us; and let the atheistic part of mankind call my saying what they please, it is no enthusiasm; it was acknowledged at that time by all mankind. □ □

On a separate sheet of paper, write your answers to the following questions. Do not write in your book.

1. Why does the man use gunpowder and tongs to get the money in the purse?

2. In section II the narrator says: ". . . it is scarce credible what dreadful cases happened in particular families every day." List some examples he gives to illustrate his statement.

3. When the narrator uses the phrase "the latter" in the second paragraph of section III to whom is he referring?

4. What does the narrator say was the effect on the spread of plague of shutting up houses?

5. What effect did taking "pills, potions, and preservatives" have on people's health?

6. Of what are the items in the list at the end of section V examples?

7. Did the fire described by Pepys take place before or after the plague?

8. What analogy does the narrator draw between the fire and the plague in section VI?

9. To what two things is the plague figuratively compared in the first sentence of section VII?

10. What is the dominant tone in this passage? **(a)** fearful; **(b)** angry; **(c)** factual; **(d)** puzzled.

Unit 4, Test II
COMPOSITION

You may choose any *one* of the following assignments. Write your essay on a separate sheet or sheets of paper. Assume that you are writing for your classmates.

1. Compare and contrast John Dryden's "To the Memory of Mr. Oldham" with Jonathan Swift's "A Satirical Elegy" in terms of their subject matter and tone, or attitude toward the subject.

2. Compare and contrast Defoe's description of the plague in Test II to Pepys's description of the fire in terms of the immediacy of the accounts, the emphasis on the psychological, the use of physical detail or fact, the audience addressed, and the formality of the writing style.

3. Discuss Swift's use of irony in the selections from his work in this unit. (See entry for *irony* in the *Definitions of Literary Terms.)*

4. Discuss Johnson's views on prayer as revealed in his "Life of Milton" and in the comments on Christopher Smart recorded by Boswell. What do these opinions imply about his views of popular opinion and personal eccentricity?

5. Discuss Johnson's attitude toward authority as revealed in his "Letter to Chesterfield," the dictionary entries for *pension* and *pensioner, tory* and *whig,* and the selection from "The Life of Milton."

6. Contrast Dryden's *The Hind and the Panther* with Burns's "To a Mouse" in the way each describes human characteristics and situations, in the style and tone, and in the directness with which parallels are drawn.

7. Robert Burns's "A Red, Red Rose" is unlike any other work in this unit. Describe in what ways it is different, considering in addition to other factors such things as the subject and tone.

8. Discuss the appropriateness of the label "The Age of Reason" to describe the selections you have read in this unit. Cite examples to support your argument.

Unit 5:

1780 | 1790 | 1800

French Revolution

- Beckford: *Vathek*
- Death of Louis XVI
- Napoleonic Wars begin
- Blake: *Songs of Innocence*
- Radcliffe: *The Mysteries of Udolpho*
- Wordsworth and Coleridge: *Lyrical Ballads*

Blake: *Jerusalem*

The Romantics 1780-1830

1810 | 1820 | 1830

- Nelson's naval victory at Trafalgar
- Byron: *Childe Harold's Pilgrimage*
- Austen: *Pride and Prejudice*
- Battle of Waterloo
- Coleridge: *Biographia Literaria*
- Keats: *Endymion*
- Scott: *Ivanhoe*
- Peterloo Massacre
- Byron: *Don Juan*
- Shelley: *Prometheus Unbound*
- Keats: *The Eve of St. Agnes*
- Lamb: *Essays of Elia*
- *Catholic Emancipation Act*

Background: The Romantics 1780–1830

The Romantic Age is a term used to describe life and literature in England in the late eighteenth and early nineteenth centuries. Many of the most important English writers of the period turned away from the values and ideas characteristic of the Age of Reason toward what they perceived as a more daring, individual, and imaginative approach to both literature and life.

In general, the Romantic writers placed the individual, rather than society, at the center of their vision. They tended to be optimists who believed in the possibility of progress and improvement, for humanity as well as for individuals; thus, most espoused democratic values.

By and large, the Romantic writers understood the greatness of the writers of the Age of Reason, but they felt the need to strike out in new directions in search of fresh ideas and forms compatible with a new, developing sensibility.

They tended to believe that the Augustan dedication to common sense and experience, reasonableness, and tradition, though in many ways admirable, had resulted in a limitation of vision, an inability to transcend the hard facts of the real world to glimpse an ideal order of possibility.

These new attitudes and approaches were closely linked to a political event of great importance—the French Revolution, which began in 1789. English history in this period is largely the story of England's involvement with the Revolution. For a time, almost every important British writer responded warmly to the cry of the French people for "Liberty, Equality, Fraternity." William Wordsworth later declared: "Bliss was it in that dawn to be alive, / But to be young was very heaven!"

Whereas the writers of the Age of Reason tended to regard evil as a basic part of human nature, the Romantic writers generally saw humanity as naturally good, but corrupted by society and its institutions of religion, education, and government. The French Revolution gave life and breath to the dreams of some Romantic writers for a society in which there would be liberty and equality for all.

One of the most significant aspects of nineteenth-century English life was the slow but steady application of the principles of democracy. England emerged from the eighteenth century a parliamentary state in which the monarchy was largely a figurehead. The English Parliament was far from a truly representative body, however, until, after years of popular agitation, Parliament finally passed the First Reform Bill of 1832. This bill extended the franchise, or right to vote, to virtually all the middle class; it did not enfranchise the working class.

The Industrial Revolution, which flanked the Romantic Age, involved the change that took place in England (from about 1750–1850) from an agricultural to an industrial society and from home manufacturing to factory production. The Industrial Revolution helped make England prosperous and powerful, but it involved exploitation of the workers, who lived under deplorable conditions.

As the Industrial Revolution gathered force, towns became cities; more and more villagers, forced by economic necessity to seek work in the growing factories, huddled together in filthy slums. Workers—men, women, and children—labored from sunrise to sunset for meager wages. No child able to pull a cart in the suffocating coal mines or to sweep a floor in the textile factories was considered too young to work by many employers and some parents. For the children of the poor, religious training, medical care, and education were practically nonexistent.

Gradually English society began to awaken to its obligations to the miserable and helpless. Through the efforts of reformers, the church and government assumed their responsibilities. Sunday schools were organized; hospitals were built; movements were begun to reform the prisons and regulate the conditions of child labor.

The effects of revolution abroad, the demand for a more democratic government, and a growing awareness of social injustice at home were all reflected in a new spirit that over a period of years affected practically every aspect of English life.

The Romantic Age in England was part of a movement that affected all the countries of the Western World. The forms of romanticism were so many and varied that it is difficult to speak of the movement as a whole. It tended to align itself with the humanitarian spirit of the democratic revolutionaries, but romantics were not always democrats and democrats were not always revolutionaries. Perhaps the safest thing to say is that romanticism represented an attempt to rediscover the mystery and wonder of the world, an attempt to go beyond ordinary reality into the deeper, less obvious, and more elusive levels of individual human existence.

John Keats

It is in literature that we can best see the emergence and growth of this romantic spirit in England. In the eighteenth century Robert Burns had written of the joys and sorrows of humble village folk. Thomas Gray had written of the life and work of plain country people, as well as of the beauties of nature. Various elements present in the eighteenth century—the belief in intuition, the emphasis on individual emotion rather than common experience, the interest in humble life, a belief in the healing power of the natural world—became progressively more important as the Romantic movement flourished in the early nineteenth century in the poetry of Blake, Wordsworth, Coleridge, Byron, Shelley, and Keats.

Throughout the Age of Reason interest centered in the ancient classics of Greece and Rome as models for writers. However, a few authors turned to other aspects of the past. Among them was Bishop Thomas Percy who, in 1765, published *Reliques of Ancient English Poetry,* a collection of ballads dating back to medieval times. These forgotten evidences of England's past became extremely popular with the Romantics. They relished the medieval atmosphere, the sense of mystery and the supernatural, the elemental themes of courage and valor, hatred and revenge, love and death.

The literature of this brief period has about it a sense of the uniqueness of the individual, a deep personal earnestness, a sensuous delight in both the common and exotic things of this world, a blend of intensely lived joy and dejection, a yearning for ideal states of being, and a probing interest in mysterious and mystical experience. If the Romantic vision of the world was occasionally tinged with bitterness or outrage, it was because the Romantic confronted an increasingly mechanical and materialistic society which threatened to extinguish humanity's awareness of the vital relationships among its members, and its awareness of the rhythms of nature that shape all life.

William Blake

Songs of Innocence first appeared in 1789. Five years later Blake published a second volume which he titled *Songs of Innocence and Experience: Shewing the Two Contrary States of the Human Soul.* Although not all the *Songs of Innocence* have counterparts in the *Songs of Experience,* the subtitle, as well as the fact that he never published the *Songs of Experience* as a separate volume, suggest that he intended the poems to be matched.

from Songs of Innocence

Introduction

Piping down the valleys wild,
Piping songs of pleasant glee
On a cloud I saw a child,
And he laughing said to me:

Pipe a song about a Lamb!
So I piped with merry cheer.
Piper pipe that song again—
So I piped, he wept to hear.

Drop thy pipe thy happy pipe
Sing thy songs of happy cheer.
So I sung the same again
While he wept with joy to hear.

Piper sit thee down and write
In a book that all may read—
So he vanished from my sight,
And I plucked a hollow reed,

And I made a rural pen,
And I stained the water clear,
And I wrote my happy songs,
Every child may joy to hear.

from Songs of Experience

Introduction

Hear the voice of the Bard!
Who Present, Past, and Future sees
Whose ears have heard
The Holy Word,
That walk'd among the ancient trees.

Calling the lapsed Soul[1]
And weeping in the evening dew:
That might controll
The starry pole:
And fallen fallen light renew!

O Earth O Earth return!
Arise from out the dewy grass:
Night is worn,
And the morn
Rises from the slumberous mass.

Turn away no more:
Why wilt thou turn away
The starry floor
The wat'ry shore
Is giv'n thee till the break of day.

1. ***lapsed Soul,*** soul fallen from grace after the fall of Adam and Eve.

Discussion

1. In the Introduction to *Songs of Innocence,* the speaker is both piper and poet. In the Introduction to *Songs of Experience,* there is no identifiable speaker, but the reader is instructed to listen to the voice of the bard, who is also a prophet. How is each an appropriate figure for the group of poems he introduces?

2. The Introduction to *Ex-*

The Lamb

Little Lamb, who made thee?
Dost thou know who made thee?
Gave thee life, & bid thee feed
By the stream & o'er the mead;
Gave thee clothing of delight,
Softest clothing, wooly, bright;
Gave thee such a tender voice,
Making all the vales rejoice?
Little Lamb, who made thee?
Dost thou know who made thee?

Little Lamb, I'll tell thee,
Little Lamb, I'll tell thee:
He is callèd by thy name,
For he calls himself a Lamb.
He is meek, & he is mild;
He became a little child.
I a child, & thou a lamb,
We are callèd by his name.
Little Lamb, God bless thee!
Little Lamb, God bless thee!

The Tyger

Tyger! Tyger! burning bright
In the forests of the night,
What immortal hand or eye
Could frame thy fearful symmetry?

In what distant deeps or skies
Burnt the fire of thine eyes?
On what wings dare he aspire?
What the hand dare seize the fire?

And what shoulder, & what art,
Could twist the sinews of thy heart?
And when thy heart began to beat,
What dread hand? & what dread feet?

What the hammer? what the chain?
In what furnace was thy brain?
What the anvil? what dread grasp
Dare its deadly terrors clasp?

When the stars threw down their spears,
And watered heaven with their tears,
Did he smile his work to see?
Did he who made the Lamb make thee?

Tyger! Tyger! burning bright
In the forests of the night,
What immortal hand or eye
Dare frame thy fearful symmetry?

---

perience contains indications, other than the setting, that the lapsed soul is not entirely lost, that the situation may be reversed. What are some of these indications?

3. "The Lamb" and "The Tyger" are matched poems. How is each connected with the Introduction to its category?

Holy Thursday

'Twas on a Holy Thursday,[1] their innocent faces clean,
The children walking two & two, in red & blue & green,
Grey-headed beadles walked before, with wands as white as snow,
Till into the high dome of Paul's they like Thames' waters flow.

O what a multitude they seemed, these flowers of London town!
Seated in companies they sit with radiance all their own.
The hum of multitudes was there, but multitudes of lambs,
Thousands of little boys & girls raising their innocent hands.

Now like a mighty wind they raise to heaven the voice of song,
Or like harmonious thunderings the seats of Heaven among.
Beneath them sit the agèd men, wise guardians of the poor;
Then cherish pity, lest you drive an angel from your door.

1. ***Holy Thursday,*** Ascension Day, the fortieth day after Easter, when children in orphanages were brought to St. Paul's Cathedral to give thanks for the charity of God, of which human charity is supposedly a reflection.

Holy Thursday

Is this a holy thing to see
In a rich and fruitful land,
Babes reduced to misery,
Fed with cold and usurous hand?

Is that trembling cry a song?
Can it be a song of joy?
And so many children poor?
It is a land of poverty!

And their sun does never shine,
And their fields are bleak & bare,
And their ways are filled with thorns:
It is eternal winter there.

For where-e'er the sun does shine,
And where-e'er the rain does fall,
Babe can never hunger there,
Nor poverty the mind appall.

Discussion

1. What effect does Blake gain through the contrasting views of the children in the matched "Holy Thursday" poems?

2. What do the "Holy Thursday" poems reveal about the life of London's poor in Blake's day?

3. Would you consider "The Human Abstract" from *Songs of Experience* to be an appropriate contrast to "The Divine Image" from *Songs of Innocence?*

Extension • Writing

1. Choose the meanings that you consider to be the most appropriate for Blake's symbols of lamb and tiger and write a defense of your choice.

2. Write an essay defining "Experience" as you think Blake defined it in *Songs of Experience.*

3. Write an essay explaining whether you would consider Blake's style to be simple and

The Divine Image

To Mercy, Pity, Peace, and Love
All pray in their distress;
And to these virtues of delight
Return their thankfulness.

For Mercy, Pity, Peace, and Love
Is God, our father dear,
And Mercy, Pity, Peace, and Love
Is Man, his child and care.

For Mercy has a human heart,
Pity a human face,
And Love, the human form divine,
And Peace, the human dress.

Then every man, of every clime,
That prays in his distress,
Prays to the human form divine,
Love, Mercy, Pity, Peace.

And all must love the human form,
In heathen, turk, or jew;
Where Mercy, Love, & Pity dwell
There God is dwelling too.

The Human Abstract

Pity would be no more
If we did not make somebody Poor;
And Mercy no more could be
If all were as happy as we.

And mutual fear brings peace,
Till the selfish loves increase:
Then Cruelty knits a snare,
And spreads his baits with care.

He sits down with holy fears,
And waters the ground with tears;
Then Humility takes its root
Underneath his foot.

Soon spreads the dismal shade
Of Mystery over his head;
And the Catterpiller and Fly
Feed on the Mystery.

And it bears the fruit of Deceit,
Ruddy and sweet to eat;
And the Raven his nest has made
In its thickest shade.

The Gods of the earth and sea
Sought thro' Nature to find this Tree;
But their search was all in vain:
There grows one in the Human Brain.

---

direct or complicated and elaborate. Consider subject matter, imagery, meter, and rhyme scheme.

4. Write an overall comparison of *Songs of Innocence* and *Songs of Experience,* focusing on any of the following: tone, major symbols, or verse forms and rhythm—or another area of focus approved by your teacher.

Extension • Speaking

1. Prepare the matched poems in *Songs of Innocence* and *Songs of Experience* for dramatic reading in class. Be careful to select voices appropriate to each poem.

2. Present a "Blake Poetry Festival," in which one student serves as Blake, introducing other students who read selected poems, perhaps with a musical background.

"God Creating Adam," a watercolor by William Blake. The Tate Gallery, London.

Proverbs of Hell

In seed time learn, in harvest teach, in winter enjoy.
Drive your cart and your plow over the bones of the dead.
The road of excess leads to the palace of wisdom.
Prudence is a rich, ugly old maid courted by Incapacity.
The cut worm forgives the plow.
A fool sees not the same tree that a wise man sees.
He whose face gives no light, shall never become a star.
Eternity is in love with the productions of time.
All wholesome food is caught without a net or a trap.
No bird soars too high, if he soars with his own wings.
If the fool would persist in his folly he would become wise.
Shame is pride's cloak.
Excess of sorrow laughs. Excess of joy weeps.
The roaring of lions, the howling of wolves, the raging of the stormy sea,
    and the destructive sword, are portions of eternity, too great for the eye of man.
Let man wear the fell of the lion, woman the fleece of the sheep.
The bird a nest, the spider a web, man friendship.
What is now proved was once only imagined.
Every thing possible to be believed is an image of truth.
The fox provides for himself, but God provides for the lion.
Think in the morning. Act in the noon. Eat in the evening. Sleep in the night.
The tygers of wrath are wiser than the horses of instruction.

Expect poison from the standing water.
You never know what is enough unless you know what
is more than enough.
The weak in courage is strong in cunning.
Damn braces. Bless relaxes.
The crow wished every thing was black, the owl that
every thing was white.
Improvement makes strait roads; but the crooked roads
without improvement are roads of Genius.
Truth can never be told so as to be understood, and not
be believed.

from **The Marriage of Heaven and Hell**

Discussion

If, as Blake claims, the "Proverbs of Hell" do "show the nature of Infernal wisdom," what is the nature of that wisdom?

Extension • Writing

Select any of the "Proverbs of Hell" and write a composition illustrating it. If you wish, your composition may take the form of a fable or illustrative anecdote.

notes and comments

Morton D. Paley: What Did Blake Mean by Innocence and Experience?

What are the two Contrary States and what is the relationship between them? *Innocence* and *Experience* are not, first of all, a direct record of Blake's spiritual autobiography. Anyone who thinks the *Songs of Innocence* reflect Blake's own world view at the time of composition should carefully read the prose satire *An Island in the Moon*, which Blake wrote in 1784 and in which versions of three *Songs of Innocence* first appear. In this anything-but-innocent narrative, the simplicity of "Holy Thursday," "Nurse's Song," and "Little Boy Lost" contrast sharply with the egotism and pretentiousness of the characters. Of course we cannot know whether Blake had the *Songs of Experience* in mind when he wrote the *Songs of Innocence*, but we do know that four of the earlier group seemed to him sufficiently poems of Experience to be shifted to the latter group in 1794: "The School Boy," "The Little Girl Lost," "The Little Girl Found," and "The Voice of the Ancient Bard." These poems had already burst the bounds of the state of Innocence, all of them presenting themes more appropriate to the Contrary State—institutional restraint, the prophetic function of the poet, the growth of self-awareness. Innocence *demands* Experience: both are phases in the spiritual development of man and, at the same time, perennial ways of looking at the world.

The state of Innocence is compounded of the pagan Age of Gold and the Judeo-Christian Eden. Externally and generically, it applies to the condition of man before the Fall; internally and psychologically to the child who has not yet experienced the inner divisions of human life. Its literary forebears are the worlds of the pastoral and the Psalms. Blake's Innocence also has a special relationship to the thought of the Swedish visionary Emanuel Swedenborg, whose works Blake annotated with great interest in the 1780s and who conceived of Innocence in terms peculiarly appropriate to Blake's: as an inner state, taking images such as the child and the lamb as correspondences.

Experience, too, is an inner state externalized in a world of images—chains, thorns, spears, graves, briars, blood, and roots, to name a few—all of which correspond to felt qualities in life. In Experience, which is

---

Morton D. Paley, editor, TWENTIETH CENTURY INTERPRETATIONS OF SONGS OF INNOCENCE AND OF EXPERIENCE, © 1969, pp. 1–9. Reprinted by permission of Prentice-Hall, Inc., Englewood Cliffs, New Jersey.

the world of normal adult life, people try to analyze and codify their feelings, and as a result they become incapable of spontaneity. The traditional hierarchy of society, seen as benevolent in *Innocence*, is now regarded as a vast exploitative deceit. With all this suffering, however, Experience also brings a bitter wisdom. Experience, then, is not wholly negative. The harmony of Innocence has been lost, but insight comes in its place. In the wisdom of Experience, as embodied in the voice of the prophetic Bard of the second group of Songs, lies the possibility of reorganizing man's divided self and, if not of regaining the lost world of Innocence, then of forging a new unity. "Man is so created," Swedenborg wrote, "as to be during his childhood in external innocence, and when he becomes old in internal innocence, to the end that he may come by means of the former into the latter, and from the latter into the former." "Unorganized Innocence," according to Blake, is "an Impossibility. Innocence dwells with Wisdom, but never with Ignorance."

The transition from Innocence to Experience may be seen as a version of what medieval theologians call The Fortunate Fall—the idea that the fall of Adam and Eve was in a paradoxical sense a "happy sin," in that otherwise Christ would not have been born to save mankind. For Blake, the fall into Experience was if not happy at least necessary.

As Blake tells us in *The Marriage of Heaven and Hell*, "without Contraries is no progression." In this case, progression is toward a condition of being in which the harmony lost in the fall from Innocence is regained. The agent of regeneration is Energy. In the fallen world of Experience, this Energy is present as the wrath of the Tyger.

The Victorians at times mistook Blake's simplicity for naivete and were, accordingly, disposed toward an overly literal view of the poems. We, by contrast, may be tempted to find complexities that are not there, to over-read, to discover myths hidden in the shrubbery as if the poem were an ingenious puzzle.

William Blake 1757 • 1827

William Blake, considered by some to have been mad, was not only a poet, but a painter, an engraver, and a spiritual visionary. At the age of only ten, having become interested in painting, Blake went to drawing school and then became an apprentice to an engraver. At this time he also began writing verse. As a child, he was deeply religious. He claimed to have seen the prophet Ezekiel in a tree, and on another occasion he said that he saw a tree filled with angels. By the time he married, Blake had become so consumed in mystical beliefs and had withdrawn so completely into his own visionary world that his wife is said to have remarked: "I have very little of Mr. Blake's company. He is always in Paradise."

He lived all but three years of his life in London, where he earned a moderate living as an engraver. During his lifetime, his pictures and poetry were not popularly received. Between 1783 and 1793 he wrote, illustrated, and printed his most famous lyrics, *Songs of Innocence* and *Songs of Experience.* He prepared his own illustrative engravings for these poems by a process he himself developed, and either he or his wife tinted each illustration. The result was something comparable to the illuminated manuscripts of medieval times. During this time, he also completed one major prose work, *The Marriage of Heaven and Hell.*

Giving up poetry after he reached the age of sixty, Blake turned exclusively to painting. He illustrated the poetry of Dante, Chaucer, Milton, and the *Book of Job.*

William Wordsworth

The World Is Too Much with Us

The world is too much with us; late and soon,
Getting and spending, we lay waste our powers:
Little we see in Nature that is ours;
We have given our hearts away, a sordid boon!
The sea that bares her bosom to the moon;
The winds that will be howling at all hours,
And are up-gathered now like sleeping flowers;
For this, for everything, we are out of tune;
It moves us not.—Great God! I'd rather be
A Pagan suckled in a creed outworn;
So might I, standing on this pleasant lea,
Have glimpses that would make me less forlorn;
Have sight of Proteus rising from the sea;
Or hear old Triton[1] blow his wreathèd horn.

1. ***Proteus*** (prō′tē əs) . . . ***Triton*** (trit′n), sea god in Classical mythology.

It Is a Beauteous Evening

It is a beauteous evening, calm and free,
The holy time is quiet as a Nun
Breathless with adoration; the broad sun
Is sinking down in its tranquillity;
The gentleness of heaven broods o'er the Sea:
Listen! the mighty Being is awake,
And doth with his eternal motion make
A sound like thunder—everlastingly.
Dear Child![1] dear Girl; that walkest with me here,
If thou appear untouched by solemn thought,
Thy nature is not therefore less divine:
Thou liest in Abraham's bosom[2] all the year;
And worshipp'st at the temple's inner shrine,
God being with thee when we know it not.

1. ***Dear Child,*** Wordsworth's French daughter, Caroline.
2. ***in Abraham's bosom,*** in the presence of God. See Luke 16:22.

Discussion

"The World Is Too Much with Us"

1. What aspects of the world does Wordsworth view as positive, and what as negative? With what aspects are we "out of tune"? What aspects are "too much with us"?

2. What are the "glimpses" that might make the poet "less forlorn"?

3. What personifications does Wordsworth use to present various aspects of nature? Does his use of personification make the natural world seem more intimate, or more distant?

"It Is a Beauteous Evening"

1. Describe the setting of the poem. How does the setting affect the poet?

2. What effect does Wordsworth create through the evening/Nun simile?

3. What explanation does Wordsworth give for the child's attitude being different from his?

Extension • Writing

Write your own version of "The World Is Too Much with Us" (in free verse), commenting on aspects of the modern world with which you feel we are "out of tune."

Composed upon Westminster Bridge, September 3, 1802

Earth has not anything to show more fair:
Dull would he be of soul who could pass by
A sight so touching in its majesty:
This City now doth, like a garment, wear
The beauty of the morning; silent, bare,
Ships, towers, domes, theaters, and temples lie
Open unto the fields, and to the sky;
All bright and glittering in the smokeless air.
Never did sun more beautifully steep
In his first splendor, valley, rock, or hill;
Ne'er saw I, never felt, a calm so deep!
The river glideth at his own sweet will:
Dear God! the very houses seem asleep;
And all that mighty heart is lying still!

"Westminster Bridge," a watercolor by J. M. W. Turner. Courtesy of the Trustees of The British Museum.

London, 1802

Milton! thou shouldst be living at this hour.
England hath need of thee; she is a fen
Of stagnant waters: altar, sword, and pen,
Fireside, the heroic wealth of hall and bower,
Have forfeited their ancient English dower
Of inward happiness. We are selfish men;
Oh! raise us up, return to us again,
And give us manners, virtue, freedom, power.
Thy soul was like a star, and dwelt apart:
Thou hadst a voice whose sound was like the sea;
Pure as the naked heavens, majestic, free,
So didst thou travel on life's common way,
In cheerful godliness; and yet thy heart
The lowliest duties on herself did lay.

Discussion

"Composed upon Westminster Bridge"

1. What qualities in the sleeping city would you describe as natural rather than artificial? How is Wordsworth's view of the sleeping city related to his view of nature?

2. The poem ends with an exclamation. What motivates this exclamation?

3. How does the mood of this sonnet compare with "It Is a Beauteous Evening"?

"London, 1802"

1. What qualities does Wordsworth ascribe to Milton? What qualities of life in 1802 does he mention as contrast?

2. How does this sonnet resemble "The World Is Too Much with Us" in theme and tone?

Lines Composed a Few Miles Above Tintern Abbey

Five years have past; five summers, with the length
Of five long winters! and again I hear
These waters, rolling from their mountain springs
With a soft inland murmur. Once again
Do I behold these steep and lofty cliffs
That on a wild secluded scene impress
Thoughts of more deep seclusion and connect
The landscape with the quiet of the sky.
The day is come when I again repose
Here, under this dark sycamore, and view
These plots of cottage ground, these orchard tufts,
Which at this season, with their unripe fruits,
Are clad in one green hue, and lose themselves
Mid groves and copses. Once again I see
These hedgerows, hardly hedgerows, little lines
Of sportive wood run wild; these pastoral farms,
Green to the very door; and wreaths of smoke
Sent up, in silence, from among the trees,
With some uncertain notice, as might seem
Of vagrant dwellers in the houseless woods,
Or of some hermit's cave, where by his fire
The hermit sits alone.
These beauteous forms,
Through a long absence, have not been to me
As is a landscape to a blind man's eye;
But oft, in lonely rooms, and 'mid the din
Of towns and cities, I have owed to them,
In hours of weariness, sensations sweet,
Felt in the blood, and felt along the heart;
And passing even into my purer mind,
With tranquil restoration—feelings too
Of unremembered pleasure, such, perhaps,
As have no slight or trivial influence
On that best portion of a good man's life,
His little, nameless, unremembered acts
Of kindness and of love. Nor less, I trust,
To them I may have owed another gift,
Of aspect more sublime; that blessèd mood,
In which the burthen of the mystery,
In which the heavy and the weary weight
Of all this unintelligible world,
Is lightened—that serene and blessèd mood,
In which the affections gently lead us on—
Until, the breath of this corporeal frame
And even the motion of our human blood
Almost suspended, we are laid asleep
In body, and become a living soul;

Culver Pictures

While with an eye made quiet by the power
Of harmony, and the deep power of joy,
We see into the life of things.
If this
Be but a vain belief, yet, oh! how oft—
In darkness and amid the many shapes
Of joyless daylight; when the fretful stir
Unprofitable, and the fever of the world,
Have hung upon the beatings of my heart—
How oft, in spirit, have I turned to thee,
O sylvan Wye! thou wanderer through the
woods,
How often has my spirit turned to thee!
And now, with gleams of half-extinguished
thought,
With many recognitions dim and faint,
And somewhat of a sad perplexity,
The picture of the mind revives again;
While here I stand, not only with the sense
Of present pleasure, but with pleasing thoughts
That in this moment there is life and food
For future years. And so I dare to hope,
Though changed, no doubt, from what I was
when first
I came among these hills, when like a roe
I bounded o'er the mountains, by the sides
Of the deep rivers, and the lonely streams,
Wherever nature led—more like a man
Flying from something that he dreads than one
Who sought the thing he loved. For nature then
(The coarser pleasures of my boyish days,
And their glad animal movements all gone by)
To me was all in all. —I cannot paint
What then I was. The sounding cataract
Haunted me like a passion; the tall rock,
The mountain, and the deep and gloomy wood,
Their colors and their forms, were then to me
An appetite, a feeling and a love,
That had no need of a remoter charm,
By thought supplied, nor any interest
Unborrowed from the eye.—That time is past,
And all its aching joys are now no more,
And all its dizzy raptures. Not for this
Faint I, nor mourn nor murmur; other gifts
Have followed; for such loss, I would believe,
Abundant recompense. For I have learned
To look on nature, not as in the hour
Of thoughtless youth, but hearing often times
The still, sad music of humanity,
Nor harsh nor grating, though of ample power

To chasten and subdue. And I have felt
A presence that disturbs me with the joy
Of elevated thoughts; a sense sublime
Of something far more deeply interfused,
Whose dwelling is the light of setting suns,
And the round ocean and the living air,
And the blue sky, and in the mind of man;
A motion and a spirit, that impels
All thinking things, all objects of all thought,
And rolls through all things. Therefore am I still
A lover of the meadows and the woods,
And mountains; and of all that we behold
From this green earth; of all the mighty world
Of eye, and ear—both what they half create,
And what perceive; well pleased to recognize
In nature and the language of the sense
The anchor of my purest thoughts, the nurse,
The guide, the guardian of my heart, and soul
Of all my moral being.
                    Nor perchance,
If I were not thus taught, should I the more
Suffer my genial spirits to decay;
For thou art with me here upon the banks
Of this fair river; thou my dearest friend,[1]
My dear, dear friend; and in thy voice I catch
The language of my former heart, and read
My former pleasures in the shooting lights
Of thy wild eyes. Oh! yet a little while
May I behold in thee what I was once,
My dear, dear sister! and this prayer I make,
Knowing that nature never did betray
The heart that loved her; 'tis her privilege,
Through all the years of this our life, to lead
From joy to joy; for she can so inform
The mind that is within us, so impress
With quietness and beauty, and so feed
With lofty thoughts, that neither evil tongues,
Rash judgments, nor the sneers of selfish men,
Nor greetings where no kindness is, nor all
The dreary intercourse of daily life,
Shall e'er prevail against us, or disturb
Our cheerful faith, that all which we behold
Is full of blessings. Therefore let the moon
Shine on thee in thy solitary walk;
And let the misty mountain winds be free
To blow against thee; and, in after years,
When these wild ecstasies shall be matured
Into a sober pleasure, when thy mind
Shall be a mansion for all lovely forms,
Thy memory be as a dwelling place
For all sweet sounds and harmonies; oh! then,
If solitude, or fear, or pain, or grief,
Should be thy portion, with what healing thoughts
Of tender joy wilt thou remember me,
And these my exhortations! Nor, perchance—
If I should be where I no more can hear
Thy voice, nor catch from thy wild eyes these gleams
Of past existence—wilt thou then forget
That on the banks of this delightful stream
We stood together; and that I, so long
A worshiper of nature, hither came
Unwearied in that service—rather say
With warmer love—oh! with far deeper zeal
Of holier love. Nor wilt thou then forget
That after many wanderings, many years
Of absence, these steep woods and lofty cliffs,
And this green pastoral landscape, were to me
More dear, both for themselves and for thy sake!

1. ***my dearest friend,*** Wordsworth's sister, Dorothy.

Discussion

1. In lines 1–22, the countryside is described. Are there any signs of human habitation? How is nature presented?

2. Read the sonnet "The World Is Too Much with Us" and compare with lines 22–65. What similarities of theme can you detect? What "gifts" or sustenance does Wordsworth find in nature? How does he view city life?

3. In lines 65–111, the poet describes two phases of his developing attitude toward nature. What was his attitude when he first visited the Wye? How does his present attitude differ from his feelings then?

4. In the last section of the

poem, Wordsworth turns his attention to his sister Dorothy and her attitude toward nature. At which phase of development in relation to nature does Dorothy now stand? What are her brother's wishes for her? How is Wordsworth's affection for his sister connected with the themes of the poem?

Extension • Writing

In a sense this poem is about the passage of time and the changes in attitude toward nature that Wordsworth experienced between boyhood and manhood. In lines 65–111, trace the stages of his development. What did nature mean to him as a boy? as a grown man? (In your essay, you might use the contrast between "powerful feelings" and "tranquillity" which Wordsworth brings up in his definition of poetry in the "Preface to Lyrical Ballads.")

William Wordsworth
1770 • 1850

As a restless young man, Wordsworth championed the radical causes of the French Revolution; as an old man, established as poet laureate, he voiced ultraconservative views that many found offensive.

Wordsworth's early life was spent in the mountains of the Lake District of northern England. As a young boy, he did not fully appreciate the beauty of his surroundings. The understanding and appreciation of nature that is reflected in his poetry did not develop until he was seventeen and in his first year at Cambridge University. The four years spent at Cambridge were lonely and restless years. Unimpressed with the classical curriculum, he found his independent reading much more satisfying.

While he was at Cambridge, he had taken a walking tour in France and his sympathies for the French Revolution had been aroused. After graduation he returned to France. During his stay he fell in love with Annette Vallon, who bore him a daughter, Caroline. In 1792, he was forced to return to England because his parents, who disapproved of his life in France, cut off his funds. The outbreak of war between France and England in 1793 made return to France impossible.

The first years back in England were spent searching for employment. Wordsworth's radical views and his failure to enter into a respected profession had alienated almost everyone but his sister Dorothy. He was rescued from his financial distress in 1795 by a friend's gift of nine hundred pounds. At the same time, another friend offered him a house, rent free, thus enabling him to establish a home for Dorothy and himself. Later, he returned to the Lake Country where he lived for the rest of his life.

Wordsworth's most productive writing period was from 1797 to 1807. During this time, he worked closely with Coleridge. The most significant outcome of their collaboration was *Lyrical Ballads,* published anonymously in 1798, containing poems according to the following scheme: Wordsworth was to "give the charm of novelty to subjects of everyday life"; Coleridge was to let his imagination roam over more unusual and supernatural subject matter. Though the book included such poems as Coleridge's "Rime of the Ancient Mariner" and Wordsworth's "Tintern Abbey" (now considered among the finest in the English language), it was at first contemptuously received. In 1800 an expanded edition was published with a preface written by Wordsworth to explain his theories of poetry, in which he stated that "all good poetry is the spontaneous overflow of powerful feeling."

By 1810 Wordsworth's extraordinary powers of awareness had begun to fade. He became estranged from Coleridge for several years; he lost most of his revolutionary zeal, and he rarely achieved the intensity of his earlier work.

Samuel Taylor Coleridge

Frost at Midnight

The Frost performs its secret ministry,
Unhelped by any wind. The owlet's cry
Came loud—and hark, again! loud as before.
The inmates of my cottage, all at rest,
Have left me to that solitude, which suits
Abstruser musings: save that at my side
My cradled infant[1] slumbers peacefully.
'Tis calm indeed! so calm, that it disturbs
And vexes meditation with its strange
And extreme silentness. Sea, hill, and wood,
This populous village! Sea, and hill, and wood,
With all the numberless goings-on of life,
Inaudible as dreams! the thin blue flame
Lies on my low-burnt fire, and quivers not;
Only that film,[2] which fluttered on the grate,
Still flutters there, the sole unquiet thing.
Methinks its motion in this hush of nature
Gives it dim sympathies with me who live,
Making it a companionable form,
Whose puny flaps and freaks the idling Spirit
By its own moods interprets, everywhere
Echo or mirror seeking of itself,
And makes a toy of Thought.

But O! how oft,
How oft, at school, with most believing mind,
Presageful, have I gazed upon the bars,
To watch that fluttering *stranger!* and as oft
With unclosed lids, already had I dreamt
Of my sweet birthplace, and the old church tower,
Whose bells, the poor man's only music, rang
From morn to evening, all the hot fair-day,
So sweetly, that they stirred and haunted me
With a wild pleasure, falling on mine ear
Most like articulate sounds of things to come!
So gazed I, till the soothing things, I dreamt,
Lulled me to sleep, and sleep prolonged my dreams!
And so I brooded all the following morn,
Awed by the stern preceptor's face, mine eye
Fixed with mock study on my swimming book:
Save if the door half opened, and I snatched
A hasty glance, and still my heart leaped up,
For still I hoped to see the *stranger's* face,
Townsman, or aunt, or sister more beloved,
My playmate when we both were clothed alike![3]

Dear Babe, that sleepest cradled by my side,
Whose gentle breathings, heard in this deep calm,
Fill up the interspersèd vacancies
And momentary pauses of the thought!
My babe so beautiful! it thrills my heart
With tender gladness, thus to look at thee,
And think that thou shalt learn far other lore,
And in far other scenes! For I was reared
In the great city, pent 'mid cloisters dim,
And saw nought lovely but the sky and stars.
But *thou,* my babe! shalt wander like a breeze
By lakes and sandy shores, beneath the crags
Of ancient mountain, and beneath the clouds,
Which image in their bulk both lakes and shores
And mountain crags: so shalt thou see and hear
The lovely shapes and sounds intelligible
Of that eternal language, which thy God
Utters, who from eternity doth teach
Himself in all, and all things in himself.
Great universal Teacher! he shall mold
Thy spirit, and by giving make it ask.

Therefore all seasons shall be sweet to thee,
Whether the summer clothe the general earth
With greenness, or the redbreast sit and sing
Betwixt the tufts of snow on the bare branch
Of mossy apple tree, while the nigh thatch
Smokes in the sun-thaw; whether the eave-drops fall
Heard only in the trances of the blast,
Or if the secret ministry of frost
Shall hang them up in silent icicles,
Quietly shining to the quiet Moon.

---

1. ***My cradled infant,*** Coleridge's son, Hartley.
2. ***film,*** a film of soot. Coleridge's note on this reads: "In all parts of the kingdom these films are called *strangers* and are supposed to portend the arrival of some absent friend."
3. ***when we both were clothed alike,*** i.e., when both Coleridge and his sister Ann wore infant clothes.

Kubla Khan

In Xanadu did Kubla Khan
A stately pleasure dome decree:
Where Alph, the sacred river, ran
Through caverns measureless to man
Down to a sunless sea.
So twice five miles of fertile ground
With walls and towers were girdled round:
And there were gardens bright with sinuous rills,
Where blossomed many an incense-bearing tree:
And here were forests ancient as the hills,
Enfolding sunny spots of greenery.

But oh! that deep romantic chasm which slanted
Down the green hill athwart a cedarn cover!
A savage place! as holy and enchanted
As e'er beneath a waning moon was haunted

By woman wailing for her demon lover!
And from this chasm, with ceaseless turmoil seething,
As if this earth in fast thick pants were breathing,
A mighty fountain momently was forced:
Amid whose swift half-intermitted burst
Huge fragments vaulted like rebounding hail,
Or chaffy grain beneath the thresher's flail:
And 'mid these dancing rocks at once and ever
It flung up momently the sacred river.
Five miles meandering with a mazy motion
Through wood and dale the sacred river ran,
Then reached the caverns measureless to man,
And sank in tumult to a lifeless ocean:
And 'mid this tumult Kubla heard from far
Ancestral voices prophesying war!
  The shadow of the dome of pleasure
  Floated midway on the waves;
  Where was heard the mingled measure
  From the fountain and the caves.
It was a miracle of rare device,
A sunny pleasure dome with caves of ice!

  A damsel with a dulcimer
  In a vision once I saw:
  It was an Abyssinian maid,
  And on her dulcimer she played,
  Singing of Mount Abora.
Could I revive within me
Her symphony and song,
To such a deep delight 'twould win me,
That with music loud and long,
I would build that dome in air,
That sunny dome! those caves of ice!
And all who heard should see them there,
And all should cry, Beware! Beware!
His flashing eyes, his floating hair!
Weave a circle round him thrice,
And close your eyes with holy dread,
For he on honeydew hath fed,
And drunk the milk of Paradise.

notes and comments

Coleridge's Remarks about "Kubla Khan"

In the summer of the year 1797 [Coleridge], then in ill health, had retired to a lonely farmhouse between Porlock and Linton, on the Exmoor confines of Somerset and Devonshire. In consequence of a slight indisposition, an anodyne had been prescribed, from the effects of which he fell asleep in his chair at the moment that he was reading the following sentence, or words of the same substance, in *Purchas's Pilgrimage:* "Here the Khan Kubla commanded a palace to be built, and a stately garden thereunto. And thus ten miles of fertile ground were inclosed with a wall." The author continued for about three hours in a profound sleep, at least of the external senses, during which time he has the most vivid confidence that he could not have composed less than from two to three hundred lines; if that indeed can be called composition in which all the images rose up before him as *things,* with a parallel production of the correspondent expressions, without any sensation or consciousness of effort. On awaking he appeared to himself to have a distinct recollection of the whole, and taking his pen, ink, and paper, instantly and eagerly wrote down the lines that are here preserved. At this moment he was unfortunately called out by a person on business from Porlock, and detained by him above an hour, and on his return to his room, found, to his no small surprise and mortification, that though he still retained some vague and dim recollection of the general purport of the vision, yet, with the exception of some eight or ten scattered lines and images, all the rest had passed away like the images on the surface of a stream into which a stone has been cast. . . .

Discussion

"Frost at Midnight"

1. What is the pervasive mood of this poem? What types of imagery help convey this mood?

2. What role does the "stranger" play? What memories does it recall?

3. What do Coleridge's memories suggest about his boyhood? In what ways are they related to (or contrasted with) his wishes for his infant son?

4. In the first and last lines of the poem, Coleridge refers to the "secret ministry of frost." What are the implications of this phrase? What particular overtones do you find in the word "ministry"?

Discussion

"Kubla Khan"

1. What contributes to the dreamlike quality of this poem?

2. Readers of "Kubla Khan" have often commented that in spite of the luxuriance of the scenes described, the poem has sinister undertones. Do you find any? What lines or phrases suggest them to you?

3. Rhyme, alliteration, and assonance are all used by Coleridge to achieve the musical quality for which this poem is noted. Cite examples of each.

Vocabulary

Structure and Dictionary

A. The prefix *inter-* comes from the Latin word *inter* which means "between." On a separate sheet of paper, show how this meaning joins with the root in each of the following italicized words by giving the literal combined meaning in English. Then write a one-word synonym for the present meaning of the word. For example: *interdict—inter-* between + *dicere* speak, speak between; "prohibit" or "forbid." You will need to use your Glossary.

1. "A sense sublime / Of something far more deeply *interfused.*"

2. "Amid whose swift half-*intermitted* burst / Huge fragments vaulted like rebounding hail."

3. "Dear Babe, that sleepest cradled by my side, / Whose gentle breathings, heard in this deep calm, / Fill up the *interspersèd* vacancies."

B. Use your Glossary to answer the following questions about the etymology or history of the words given below. Read each clue and then write on your paper the matching word from the list.

bard beadle boon genial sinuous

4. Which word comes from Old French and means a kind of official person?

5. Which comes from a word in Latin that originally meant "curve"?

6. Which refers to singers of a sort who entertained from before recorded history to the Middle Ages?

7. Which comes from an Old Icelandic word that meant "petition"?

8. Which comes from a Latin word the original form of which we use to mean someone brilliant?

Samuel Taylor Coleridge
1772 • 1834

Coleridge was the youngest of twelve children. Spoiled, precocious, and restless, he was continually living in a dream world. Although his family was poor, money was found to send Coleridge to Cambridge. Like Wordsworth, he enjoyed his independent reading, and read everything that he thought worthwhile. His fellow students were fascinated with his eloquent monologues, full of mysticism and radical politics.

In 1797, Coleridge met Wordsworth. Inspired by Wordsworth and enthusiastic about their joint plans for *Lyrical Ballads,* he wrote most of his greatest poetry, including "The Rime of the Ancient Mariner," "Christabel," and "Kubla Khan," in one year. Suffering from neuralgia and other ailments, a marriage gone sour, and recurrent feelings of personal inadequacy, Coleridge began taking opium. By the age of thirty he was no longer capable of sustained creative effort; at thirty-five he separated from his wife. An agonizing struggle against the addictive powers of opium occupied the remainder of his life. Nevertheless, he produced during his later years significant works of literary criticism and philosophy. He was also recognized as a brilliant lecturer and conversationalist during the last years of his life.

George Gordon, Lord Byron

When We Two Parted

When we two parted
  In silence and tears,
Half broken-hearted
  To sever for years,
Pale grew thy cheek and cold,
  Colder thy kiss;
Truly that hour foretold
  Sorrow to this.

The dew of the morning
  Sunk chill on my brow—
It felt like the warning
  Of what I feel now.
Thy vows are all broken,
  And light is thy fame;
I hear thy name spoken,
  And share in its shame.

They name thee before me,
  A knell to mine ear;
A shudder comes o'er me—
  Why wert thou so dear?
They know not I knew thee,
  Who knew thee too well:—
Long, long shall I rue thee,
  Too deeply to tell.

In secret we met—
  In silence I grieve
That thy heart could forget,
  Thy spirit deceive.
If I should meet thee
  After long years,
How should I greet thee?—
  With silence and tears.

She Walks in Beauty

She walks in beauty, like the night,
  Of cloudless climes and starry skies;
And all that's best of dark and bright
  Meet in her aspect and her eyes:
Thus mellowed to that tender light
  Which heaven to gaudy day denies.

One shade the more, one ray the less,
  Had half impaired the nameless grace
Which waves in every raven tress,
  Or softly lightens o'er her face;
Where thoughts serenely sweet express
  How pure, how dear their dwelling place.

And on that cheek, and o'er that brow,
  So soft, so calm, yet eloquent,
The smiles that win, the tints that glow,
  But tell of days in goodness spent,
A mind at peace with all below,
  A heart whose love is innocent!

So We'll Go No More A-Roving

So we'll go no more a-roving
  So late into the night,
Though the heart be still as loving,
  And the moon be still as bright.

For the sword outwears its sheath,
  And the soul wears out the breast,
And the heart must pause to breathe,
  And Love itself have rest.

Though the night was made for loving,
  And the day returns too soon,
Yet we'll go no more a-roving
  By the light of the moon.

Discussion

"When We Two Parted"

1. What words or phrases most vividly convey the feelings experienced by the speaker? What specifically is the feeling—has the speaker completely rejected the person addressed in the poem?

2. Is there any evidence that the woman shared Byron's feelings?

"She Walks in Beauty"

What quality of beauty, spiritual or physical, does Byron emphasize in this poem?

"So We'll Go No More A-Roving"

1. "Mutability" (the changes brought by time) is a favorite subject of poets (for example, see W. B. Yeats's "When You Are Old," page 458). What is the basic mood of Byron's poem? Does it differ significantly from Yeats's poem?

2. Disregarding what you may know about Byron's life (he died at the age of thirty-six), what evidence is there in this poem that it is the work of a young man?

from Don Juan, Canto 1

1

I want a hero: an uncommon want,
When every year and month sends forth a new one,
Till, after cloying the gazettes with cant,
The age discovers he is not the true one;
Of such as these I should not care to vaunt,
I'll therefore take our ancient friend Don Juan—
We all have seen him, in the pantomime,
Sent to the devil somewhat ere his time.

6

Most epic poets plunge "in medias res"
(Horace makes this the heroic turnpike road),
And then your hero tells, whene'er you please,
What went before—by way of episode,
While seated after dinner at his ease,
Beside his mistress in some soft abode,
Palace, or garden, paradise, or cavern,
Which serves the happy couple for a tavern.

7

That is the usual method, but not mine—
My way is to begin with the beginning;
The regularity of my design
Forbids all wandering as the worst of sinning,
And therefore I shall open with a line
(Although it cost me half an hour in spinning)
Narrating somewhat of Don Juan's father,
And also of his mother, if you'd rather.

8

In Seville was he born, a pleasant city,
Famous for oranges and women—he
Who has not seen it will be much to pity,
So says the proverb—and I quite agree;
Of all the Spanish towns is none more pretty,
Cadiz, perhaps—but that you soon may see:—
Don Juan's parents lived beside the river,
A noble stream, and called the Guadalquivir.

9

His father's name was Jóse—*Don*, of course,
A true Hidalgo,[1] free from every stain
Of Moor or Hebrew blood, he traced his source
Through the most Gothic gentlemen of Spain;
A better cavalier ne'er mounted horse,
Or, being mounted, e'er got down again,
Than Jóse, who begot our hero, who
Begot—but that's to come—Well, to renew:

10

His mother was a learned lady, famed
For every branch of every science known—
In every Christian language ever named,
With virtues equalled by her wit alone:
She made the cleverest people quite ashamed,
And even the good with inward envy groan,
Finding themselves so very much exceeded
In their own way by all the things that she did.

13

She knew the Latin—that is, "the Lord's prayer,"
And Greek—the alphabet—I'm nearly sure;
She read some French romances here and there,
Although her mode of speaking was not pure;
For native Spanish she had no great care,
At least her conversation was obscure;
Her thoughts were theorems, her words a problem,
As if she deemed that mystery would ennoble 'em.

---

1. ***Hidalgo,*** a member of the lower Spanish nobility.

15

Some women use their tongues—she *looked* a lecture,
Each eye a sermon, and her brow a homily,
An all-in-all sufficient self-director,
Like the lamented late Sir Samuel Romilly,[2]
The Law's expounder, and the State's corrector,
Whose suicide was almost an anomaly—
One sad example more, that "All is vanity,"—
(The jury brought their verdict in "Insanity.")

17

Oh! she was perfect past all parallel—
Of any modern female saint's comparison;
So far above the cunning powers of hell,
Her guardian angel had given up his garrison;
Even her minutest motions went as well
As those of the best time-piece made by Harrison:[3]
In virtues nothing earthly could surpass her,
Save thine "incomparable oil," Macassar![4]

18

Perfect she was, but as perfection is
Insipid in this naughty world of ours,
Where our first parents never learned to kiss
Till they were exiled from their earlier bowers,
Where all was peace, and innocence, and bliss
(I wonder how they got through the twelve hours),
Don Jóse, like a lineal son of Eve,
Went plucking various fruit without her leave.

19

He was a mortal of the careless kind,
With no great love for learning, or the learned,
Who chose to go where'er he had a mind,
And never dreamed his lady was concerned;
The world, as usual, wickedly inclined
To see a kingdom or a house o'erturned,
Whispered he had a mistress, some said *two*,
But for domestic quarrels *one* will do.

20

Now Donna Inez had, with all her merit,
A great opinion of her own good qualities;
Neglect, indeed, requires a saint to bear it,
And such, indeed, she was in her moralities;
But then she had a devil of a spirit,
And sometimes mixed up fancies with realities,
And let few opportunities escape
Of getting her liege lord into a scrape.

23

Don Jóse and his lady quarrelled—*why*,
Not any of the many could divine,
Though several thousand people chose to try,
'Twas surely no concern of theirs nor mine;
I loathe that low vice—curiosity;
But if there's anything in which I shine,
'Tis in arranging all my friends' affairs,
Not having, of my own, domestic cares.

24

And so I interfered, and with the best
Intentions, but their treatment was not kind;
I think the foolish people were possessed,
For neither of them could I ever find,
Although their porter afterwards confessed—
But that's no matter, and the worst's behind,
For little Juan o'er me threw, down stairs,
A pail of housemaid's water unawares.

25

A little curly-headed, good-for-nothing,
And mischief-making monkey from his birth;
His parents ne'er agreed except in doting
Upon the most unquiet imp on earth;
Instead of quarrelling, had they been but both in
Their senses, they'd have sent young master forth
To school, or had him soundly whipped at home,
To teach him manners for the time to come.

26

Don Jóse and the Donna Inez led
For some time an unhappy sort of life,
Wishing each other, not divorced, but dead;
They lived respectably as man and wife,
Their conduct was exceedingly well-bred,

2. ***Sir Samuel Romilly,*** an English lawyer who represented Byron's wife in her suit for divorce; he committed suicide in 1818.
3. ***Harrison,*** John Harrison (1693-1776), English watchmaker who invented the first practical marine chronometer, enabling sailors to compute accurately their longitude at sea.
4. ***Macassar,*** a fragrant oil used as a hair dressing.

And gave no outward signs of inward strife,
Until at length the smothered fire broke out,
And put the business past all kind of doubt.

27

For Inez called some druggists and physicians,
And tried to prove her loving lord was *mad*,
But as he had some lucid intermissions,
She next decided he was only *bad;*
Yet when they asked her for her depositions,
No sort of explanation could be had,
Save that her duty both to man and God
Required this conduct—which seemed very odd.

32

Their friends had tried at reconcilation,
Then their relations, who made matters worse,
('Twere hard to tell upon a like occasion
To whom it may be best to have recourse—
I can't say much for friend or yet relation):
The lawyers did their utmost for divorce,
But scarce a fee was paid on either side
Before, unluckily, Don Jóse died.

33

He died: and most unluckily, because,
According to all hints I could collect
From counsel learned in those kinds of laws
(Although their talk's obscure and circumspect),
His death contrived to spoil a charming cause;
A thousand pities also with respect
To public feeling, which on this occasion
Was manifested in a great sensation.

37

Dying intestate, Juan was sole heir
To a chancery suit, and messuages,[5] and lands,
Which, with a long minority and care,
Promised to turn out well in proper hands:
Inez became sole guardian, which was fair,
And answered but to nature's just demands;
An only son left with an only mother
Is brought up much more wisely than another.

38

Sagest of women, even of widows, she
Resolved that Juan should be quite a paragon,
And worthy of the noblest pedigree:
(His sire was of Castile, his dam from Aragon).
Then for accomplishments of chivalry,
In case our lord the king should go to war again,
He learned the arts of riding, fencing, gunnery,
And how to scale a fortress—or a nunnery.

39

But that which Donna Inez most desired,
And saw into herself each day before all
The learned tutors whom for him she hired,
Was, that his breeding should be strictly moral:
Much into all his studies she inquired,
And so they were submitted first to her, all,
Arts, sciences, no branch was made a mystery
To Juan's eyes, excepting natural history.

40

The languages, especially the dead,
The sciences, and most of all the abstruse,
The arts, at least all such as could be said
To be the most remote from common use,
In all these he was much and deeply read;
But not a page of anything that's loose,
Or hints continuation of the species,
Was ever suffered, lest he should grow vicious.

41

His classic studies made a little puzzle,
Because of filthy loves of gods and goddesses,
Who in the earlier ages raised a bustle,
But never put on pantaloons or bodices;
His reverend tutors had at times a tussle,
And for their Æneids, Iliads, and Odysseys,
Were forced to make an odd sort of apology,
For Donna Inez dreaded the Mythology.

44

Juan was taught from out the best edition,
Expurgated by learned men, who place,
Judiciously, from out the schoolboy's vision,
The grosser parts; but, fearful to deface
Too much their modest bard by this omission,
And pitying sore this mutilated case,
They only add them all in an appendix,
Which saves, in fact, the trouble of an index;

---

5. ***messuages*** (mes′wij əz), hoises together with adjacent buildings.

45

For there we have them all "at one fell swoop,"
  Instead of being scattered through the pages;
They stand forth marshalled in a handsome troop,
  To meet the ingenuous youth of future ages,
Till some less rigid editor shall stoop
  To call them back into their separate cages,
Instead of standing staring all together,
Like garden gods—and not so decent either.

47

Sermons he read, and lectures he endured,
  And homilies, and lives of all the saints;
To Jerome and to Chrysostom inured,
  He did not take such studies for restraints;
But how faith is acquired, and then ensured,
  So well not one of the aforesaid paints
As Saint Augustine in his fine Confessions,[6]
Which make the reader envy his transgressions.

48

This, too was a sealed book to little Juan—
  I can't but say that his mamma was right,
If such an education was the true one.
  She scarcely trusted him from out her sight;
Her maids were old, and if she took a new one,
  You might be sure she was a perfect fright;
She did this during even her husband's life—
I recommend as much to every wife.

49

Young Juan waxed in godliness and grace;
  At six a charming child, and at eleven
With all the promise of as fine a face
  As e'er to man's maturer growth was given:
He studied steadily and grew apace,
  And seemed, at least, in the right road to heaven,
For half his days were passed at church, the other
Between his tutors, confessor, and mother.

50

At six, I said, he was a charming child,
  At twelve he was a fine, but quiet boy;
Although in infancy a little wild,
  They tamed him down amongst them: to destroy
His natural spirit not in vain they toiled.
  At least it seemed so; and his mother's joy
Was to declare how sage, and still, and steady,
Her young philosopher was grown already.

54

Young Juan now was sixteen years of age,
  Tall, handsome, slender, but well knit: he seemed
Active, though not so sprightly, as a page;
  And everybody but his mother deemed
Him almost man; but she flew in a rage
  And bit her lips (for else she might have screamed)
If any said so, for to be precocious
Was in her eyes a thing the most atrocious.

55

Amongst her numerous acquaintance, all
  Selected for discretion and devotion,
There was the Donna Julia, whom to call
  Pretty were but to give a feeble notion
Of many charms in her as natural
  As sweetness to the flower, or salt to ocean,
Her zone to Venus, or his bow to Cupid,
(But this last simile is trite and stupid).

60

Her eye (I'm very fond of handsome eyes)
  Was large and dark, suppressing half its fire
Until she spoke, then through its soft disguise
  Flashed an expression more of pride than ire,
And love than either; and there would arise
  A something in them which was not desire,
But would have been, perhaps, but for the soul
Which struggled through and chastened down the whole.

61

Her glossy hair was clustered o'er a brow
  Bright with intelligence, and fair, and smooth;
Her eyebrow's shape was like the aërial bow,
  Her cheek all purple with the beam of youth,
Mounting, at times, to a transparent glow,
  As if her veins ran lightning; she, in sooth,
Possessed an air and grace by no means common:
Her stature tall—I hate a dumpy woman.

---

6. ***Saint Augustine . . . Confessions.*** In his *Confessions* Saint Augustine (354–430) describes a variety of his youthful sins.

Detail from "Señora Sabasa Garcia," by Francisco de Goya. National Gallery of Art, Washington. Andrew W. Mellon Collection.

62

Wedded she was some years, and to a man
  Of fifty, and such husbands are in plenty;
And yet, I think, instead of such a ONE
  'Twere better to have TWO of five-and-twenty,
Especially in countries near the sun:
  And now I think on't, "mi vien in mente,"[7]
Ladies even of the most uneasy virtue
Prefer a spouse whose age is short of thirty.

69

Juan she saw, and, as a pretty child,
  Caressed him often—such a thing might be
Quite innocently done, and harmless styled,
  When she had twenty years, and thirteen he;
But I am not so sure I should have smiled
  When he was sixteen, Julia twenty-three;
These few short years make wondrous alterations,
Particularly amongst sun-burnt nations.

70

Whate'er the cause might be, they had become
  Changed; for the dame grew distant, the youth shy,
Their looks cast down, their greetings almost dumb,
  And much embarrassment in either eye;
There surely will be little doubt with some
  That Donna Julia knew the reason why,
But as for Juan, he had no more notion
Than he who never saw the sea of ocean.

71

Yet Julia's very coldness still was kind,
  And tremulously gentle her small hand
Withdrew itself from his, but left behind
  A little pressure, thrilling, and so bland
And slight, so very slight, that to the mind
  'Twas but a doubt; but ne'er magician's wand
Wrought change with all Armida's[8] fairy art
  Like what this light touch left on Juan's heart.

72

And if she met him, though she smiled no more,
  She looked a sadness sweeter than her smile,
As if her heart had deeper thoughts in store
  She must not own, but cherished more the while
For that compression in its burning core;
  Even innocence itself has many a wile,
And will not dare to trust itself with truth,
And love is taught hypocrisy from youth.

75

Poor Julia's heart was in an awkward state;
  She felt it going, and resolved to make
The noblest efforts for herself and mate,
  For honour's, pride's, religion's, virtue's sake.
Her resolutions were most truly great,
  And almost might have made a Tarquin[9] quake:
She prayed the Virgin Mary for her grace,
As being the best judge of a lady's case.

---

7. ***"mi vien in mente,"*** "it comes to mind." [Italian]
8. ***Armida,*** a sorceress mentioned in *Jerusalem Delivered,* an epic poem by the Italian Renaissance poet Torquoto Tasso (1544-1595).
9. ***a Tarquin,*** one of the legendary kings of ancient Rome, noted for their lustiness.

76

She vowed she never would see Juan more,
  And next day paid a visit to his mother,
And looked extremely at the opening door,
  Which, by the Virgin's grace, let in another;
Grateful she was, and yet a little sore—
  Again it opens, it can be no other,
'Tis surely Juan now—No! I'm afraid
That night the Virgin was no further prayed.

77

She now determined that a virtuous woman
  Should rather face and overcome temptation,
That flight was base and dastardly, and no man
  Should ever give her heart the least sensation;
That is to say, a thought beyond the common
  Preference, that we must feel upon occasion,
For people who are pleasanter than others,
But then they only seem so many brothers.

78

And even if by chance—and who can tell?
  The devil's so very sly—she should discover
That all within was not so very well,
  And, if still free, that such or such a lover
Might please perhaps, a virtuous wife can quell
  Such thoughts, and be the better when they're over;
And if the man should ask, 'tis but denial:
I recommend young ladies to make trial.

79

And then there are such things as love divine,
  Bright and immaculate, unmixed and pure,
Such as the angels think so very fine,
  And matrons, who would be no less secure,
Platonic, perfect, "just such love as mine":
  Thus Julia said—and thought so, to be sure;
And so I'd have her think, were I the man
On whom her reveries celestial ran.

86

So much for Julia. Now we'll turn to Juan.
  Poor little fellow! he had no idea
Of his own case, and never hit the true one;
  In feelings quick as Ovid's Miss Medea,[10]
He puzzled over what he found a new one,
  But not as yet imagined it could be a
Thing quite in course, and not at all alarming,
Which, with a little patience, might grow charming.

87

Silent and pensive, idle, restless, slow,
  His home deserted for the lonely wood,
Tormented with a wound he could not know,
  His, like all deep grief, plunged in solitude:
I'm fond myself of solitude or so,
  But then, I beg it may be understood,
By solitude I mean a Sultan's, not
A hermit's, with a harem for a grot.

90

Young Juan wandered by the glassy brooks,
  Thinking unutterable things; he threw
Himself at length within the leafy nooks
  Where the wild branch of the cork forest grew;
There poets find materials for their books,
  And every now and then we read them through,
So that their plan and prosody are eligible,
Unless, like Wordsworth, they prove unintelligible.

91

He, Juan (and not Wordsworth), so pursued
  His self-communion with his own high soul,
Until his mighty heart, in its great mood,
  Had mitigated part, though not the whole
Of its disease; he did the best he could
  With things not very subject to control,
And turned, without perceiving his condition,
Like Coleridge, into a metaphysician.

92

He thought about himself, and the whole earth,
  Of man the wonderful, and of the stars,
And how the deuce they ever could have birth;
  And then he thought of earthquakes, and of wars,
How many miles the moon might have in girth,
  Of air-balloons, and of the many bars
To perfect knowledge of the boundless skies;—
And then he thought of Donna Julia's eyes.

There are 132 more stanzas in the remainder of Canto I of Don Juan. *Between 1819 and 1823 Byron added fifteen more cantos to the poem.*

---

10. ***Ovid's Miss Medea.*** In the *Metamorphoses,* Ovid presents Medea as a quick-tempered woman who took dreadful revenge on Jason for deserting her.

Discussion

1. In stanza 6, Byron refers to one of the epic conventions. What is the convention?

2. In stanza 7, Byron states that the regularity of his plans for his epic poem "Forbids all wandering as the worst of sinning." Is his poem that formal? Does he digress? How is the formality, or informality, reflected in his "poetic" diction?

3. In stanzas 10–18 Donna Inez is described. Byron says "Oh! she was perfect past all parallel." Was she?

4. Donna Inez has ambitiously moral plans for her son. What is Byron's attitude toward these plans? Is there any suggestion that Don Juan might become the kind of "paragon" his mother has in mind?

5. Most of Byron's stanzas contain some sort of "punch line." Locate a few examples. What is their effect? Describe the effect in terms of any of the following words: mild, sharp, stinging, savage, childish, clever, showy, profound.

Extension • Writing

In a one-act play, write about the adventures of a modern roguish hero, such as Don Juan.

Lord Byron 1788 • 1824

George Gordon, who became Lord Byron at the age of 11 on the death of a great-uncle whose title he inherited, was born lame, a fate to which he never quite adjusted. Byron's father, a spendthrift army captain and playboy, died when his son was three years old. Byron's mother, a descendant of James I of Scotland, was vain, tempestuous, proud, and somewhat mad. When Byron entered Cambridge at 17, he was well-read in both Latin and Greek, excelled in swimming and boxing, and had already fallen in love twice. After graduation he took the customary Grand Tour of Europe. Returning to London at age 23, he published the first two cantos of *Childe Harold,* took his seat in the House of Lords, made a brilliant speech defending workers who had wrecked machinery that threatened their jobs, and became famous overnight.

Enjoying his role as the "fair-haired boy" of London society, he dressed as he felt a poet should and tried diligently to create a mysterious air about himself. After several love affairs, he married the nobly born, very proper Annabella Milbanke in order to secure his place in society, but at the end of the first year of marriage Annabella returned to her parents with their newborn daughter. Byron was indignant. Londoners, shocked by the stories of his egotistical behavior told by Annabella, ostracized him. Bitterly disgusted with what he considered to be the hypocrisies of society, he left England in 1816, never to return.

Byron wandered about the Continent, socialized with prominent people, and carried on intrigues with ladies, one of whom, Claire Claremont, bore him a daughter. The paths of Byron and Shelley crossed during this time, and Byron befriended Shelley. He finished *Childe Harold,* began *Don Juan,* considered to be his masterpiece, and wrote many shorter poems. His poetry sold well, but while his wealth increased, his health, always poor, began to fail.

A foe of despotism anywhere, Byron was eager to fight for the oppressed. In 1823, he joined the Greek war for independence from the Turks, devoting much time and money to the cause. But before he saw battle, he caught fever and died in camp at Missolonghi, embittered and old at 36. Even today Byron remains a legend. To his own contemporaries, he was more a colorful and scandalous personality than he was a poet. The paradoxes of his life are reflected in his poetry. He was impulsive, with his impulses constantly in opposition. He was a fiery rebel and a conventional aristocrat, an idealist and a cynic, a playboy to his countrymen and a hero to the Greeks.

Percy Bysshe Shelley

England in 1819

An old, mad, blind, despised, and dying king[1]—
Princes, the dregs of their dull race, who flow
Through public scorn—mud from a muddy spring;
Rulers who neither see, nor feel, nor know,
But leechlike to their fainting country cling,
Till they drop, blind in blood, without a blow;
A people starved and stabbed in the untilled field—
An army, which liberticide and prey
Makes as a two-edged sword to all who wield;
Golden and sanguine laws which tempt and slay;
Religion Christless, Godless—a book sealed;
A Senate—Time's worst statute[2] unrepealed—
Are graves, from which a glorious Phantom[3] may
Burst, to illumine our tempestuous day.

1. ***An old . . . king,*** George III, who died in 1820, blind and insane.
2. ***Time's worst statute,*** the law restricting the civil liberties of Roman Catholics, which was not repealed until 1829.
3. ***Phantom,*** revolution.

Ozymandias

I met a traveller from an antique land
Who said: Two vast and trunkless legs of stone
Stand in the desert . . . Near them, on the sand,
Half sunk, a shattered visage lies, whose frown,
And wrinkled lip, and sneer of cold command,
Tell that its sculptor well those passions read
Which yet survive, stamped on these lifeless things,
The hand that mocked them, and the heart that fed:
And on the pedestal these words appear:
"My name is Ozymandias, king of kings:
Look on my works, ye Mighty, and despair!"
Nothing beside remains. Round the decay
Of that colossal wreck, boundless and bare
The lone and level sands stretch far away.

Discussion

"England in 1819"

1. What is the condition of England at this time as Shelley views it?

2. In the last two lines, what is predicted?

3. What figure of speech in the sonnet gives the argument its strongest impact, in your opinion?

"Ozymandias"

1. What is the irony of the inscription on the pedestal?

2. How does the imagery of the poem reinforce the double meaning of the word "despair"?

3. What comment is Shelley making about tyranny?

Ode to the West Wind

1

O wild West Wind, thou breath of Autumn's being,
Thou, from whose unseen presence the leaves dead
Are driven, like ghosts from an enchanter fleeing,

Yellow, and black, and pale, and hectic red,
Pestilence-stricken multitudes: O thou,
Who chariotest to their dark wintry bed

The wingèd seeds, where they lie cold and low,
Each like a corpse within its grave, until
Thine azure sister of the Spring shall blow

Her clarion o'er the dreaming earth, and fill
(Driving sweet buds like flocks to feed in air)
With living hues and odors plain and hill:

Wild Spirit, which art moving everywhere;
Destroyer and preserver; hear, oh, hear!

2

Thou on whose stream, mid the steep sky's commotion,
Loose clouds like earth's decaying leaves are shed,
Shook from the tangled boughs of Heaven and Ocean,

Angels of rain and lightning: there are spread
On the blue surface of thine aëry surge,
Like the bright hair uplifted from the head

Of some fierce Maenad,[1] even from the dim verge
Of the horizon to the zenith's height,
The locks of the approaching storm. Thou dirge

Of the dying year, to which this closing night
Will be the dome of a vast sepulcher,
Vaulted with all thy congregated might

Of vapors, from whose solid atmosphere
Black rain, and fire, and hail will burst: oh hear!

3

Thou who didst waken from his summer dreams
The blue Mediterranean, where he lay,
Lulled by the coil of his crystalline streams,

Beside a pumice isle in Baiae's bay,[2]
And saw in sleep old palaces and towers
Quivering within the wave's intenser day,

All overgrown with azure moss and flowers
So sweet, the sense faints picturing them! Thou
For whose path the Atlantic's level powers

Cleave themselves into chasms, while far below
The sea-blooms and the oozy woods which wear
The sapless foliage of the ocean, know

Thy voice, and suddenly grow gray with fear,
And tremble and despoil themselves: oh, hear!

4

If I were a dead leaf thou mightest bear,
If I were a swift cloud to fly with thee;
A wave to pant beneath thy power, and share

The impulse of thy strength, only less free
Than thou, O uncontrollable! If even
I were as in my boyhood, and could be

The comrade of thy wanderings over Heaven,
As then, when to outstrip thy skyey speed
Scarce seemed a vision; I would ne'er have striven

As thus with thee in prayer in my sore need.
Oh, lift me as a wave, a leaf, a cloud!
I fall upon the thorns of life! I bleed!

A heavy weight of hours has chained and bowed
One too like thee: tameless, and swift, and proud.

---

1. ***Maenad*** (mē′nad), a priestess of Dionysus, Greek god of wine, who was worshiped with savage, orgiastic rites.
2. ***Baiae's*** (bä′yäz) ***bay.*** The village of Baia is a seaport about ten miles from Naples in Italy.

5

Make me thy lyre, even as the forest is:
What if my leaves are falling like its own!
The tumult of thy mighty harmonies

Will take from both a deep, autumnal tone,
Sweet though in sadness. Be thou, Spirit fierce,
My spirit! Be thou me, impetuous one!

Drive my dead thoughts over the universe
Like withered leaves to quicken a new birth!
And, by the incantation of this verse,

Scatter, as from an unextinguished hearth
Ashes and sparks, my words among mankind!
Be through my lips to unawakened earth

The trumpet of a prophecy! O Wind,
If Winter comes, can Spring be far behind?

Discussion

1. The poem is divided into five sections. What is the topic of each section?

2. What two contradictory forces does the West Wind represent? What echoes of this paradox do you find throughout the poem? In what sense is the West Wind a spirit "moving everywhere"?

3. What does Shelley see in the West Wind that he envies and desires for himself as a poet?

4. Does the poem end on an optimistic or pessimistic note?

Percy Bysshe Shelley

1792 • 1822

Percy Shelley was the black sheep of a conventional, wealthy family; he stepped lightly over religious, political, social, and moral boundaries. Even as early as his days at Eton, a fashionable boys' school, he disgraced his parents with his unconventional views. He was a brilliant student, but very resentful of any authority. At Oxford, his views once again caused him problems. This time he was expelled for publishing a pamphlet entitled "The Necessity of Atheism."

By the age of twenty-one he was married (to Harriet Westbrooke), and a father, and had already published his first important poem, *Queen Mab,* a diatribe against orthodox religion and morality. After several years he began to find his marriage dull, and eloped with Mary Godwin, daughter of the radical William Godwin, whose revolutionary zeal Shelley shared. In 1816 Harriet committed suicide, and shortly thereafter Shelley married Mary (with whom he already had two children), but he never fully recovered from the scorn the English public heaped upon him for his actions.

In 1818 he and Mary moved to Italy. Byron, along with other English friends, spent time with them. During the next four years, Shelley produced his best poetry. In 1822, when Shelley was approaching his thirtieth birthday, he was drowned while sailing off the Italian coast. His body washed ashore ten days later and was cremated by Shelley's friends on a funeral pyre on the beach. Byron was present and swam out to watch the flames that devoured his friend and fellow exile. Mary, according to some accounts, snatched her husband's heart from the ashes. The heart is buried in the Protestant Cemetery in Rome under the inscription "Cor Cordium!" (Heart of Hearts!).

John Keats

When I Have Fears

When I have fears that I may cease to be
Before my pen has gleaned my teeming brain,
Before high-pilèd books, in charact'ry,
Hold like rich garners the full-ripened grain;
When I behold, upon the night's starred face,
Huge cloudy symbols of a high romance,
And think that I may never live to trace
Their shadows, with the magic hand of chance;
And when I feel, fair creature of an hour,
That I shall never look upon thee more,
Never have relish in the faery power
Of unreflecting love!—then on the shore
Of the wide world I stand alone, and think
Till Love and Fame to nothingness do sink.

Dan Morrill

This Living Hand[1]

This living hand, now warm and capable
Of earnest grasping, would, if it were cold
And in the icy silence of the tomb,
So haunt thy days and chill thy dreaming nights
That thou would[st] wish thine own heart dry of blood
So in my veins red life might stream again,
And thou be conscience-calm'd—see here it is—
I hold it towards you.

1. This poem was supposedly written for Fanny Brawne, with whom Keats was in love.

Discussion

"When I Have Fears"

1. In a traditional Shakespearean sonnet, the theme usually comes in the final couplet. How does the structure of this sonnet differ from the traditional? What is the grammatical structure of the sonnet?

2. What are the fears that the poet is expressing? How does he accept these fears?

"This Living Hand"
Compare these lines with the sonnet "When I Have Fears." Which is the more direct statement of "unreflecting love"?

Ode on a Grecian Urn

Thou still unravished bride of quietness,
  Thou foster child of Silence and slow Time,
Sylvan historian, who canst thus express
  A flowery tale more sweetly than our rime—
What leaf-fringed legend haunts about thy shape
  Of deities or mortals, or of both,
    In Tempe[1] or the dales of Arcady?[2]
  What men or gods are these? What maidens loath?
What mad pursuit? What struggle to escape?
    What pipes and timbrels? What wild ecstasy?

Heard melodies are sweet, but those unheard
  Are sweeter; therefore, ye soft pipes, play on;
Not to the sensual ear, but, more endeared,
  Pipe to the spirit ditties of no tone.
Fair youth, beneath the trees, thou canst not leave
  Thy song, nor ever can those trees be bare;
    Bold lover, never, never canst thou kiss,
  Though winning near the goal—yet, do not grieve;
She cannot fade, though thou hast not thy bliss,
    Forever wilt thou love, and she be fair!

Ah, happy, happy boughs! that cannot shed
  Your leaves, not ever bid the spring adieu;
And, happy melodist, unwearièd,
  Forever piping songs forever new.
More happy love! more happy, happy love!
  Forever warm and still to be enjoyed,
    Forever panting, and forever young;
  All breathing human passion far above,
That leaves a heart high-sorrowful and cloyed,
    A burning forehead, and a parching tongue.

Who are these coming to the sacrifice?
  To what green altar, O mysterious priest,
Lead'st thou that heifer lowing at the skies,
  And all her silken flanks with garlands dressed?
What little town by river or seashore,
  Or mountain-built with peaceful citadel,
    Is emptied of this folk, this pious morn?
  And, little town, thy streets forevermore
Will silent be; and not a soul to tell
    Why thou art desolate, can e'er return.

O Attic shape![3] Fair attitude! with brede[4]
  Of marble men and maidens overwrought,
With forest branches and the trodden weed;
  Thou, silent form! dost tease us out of thought
As doth eternity: Cold pastoral!
  When old age shall this generation waste,
    Thou shalt remain, in midst of other woe
  Than ours, a friend to man, to whom thou say'st,
"Beauty is truth, truth beauty—that is all
    Ye know on earth, and all ye need to know."

---

1. ***Tempe*** (tem′pē), a beautiful valley in Thessaly in Greece.
2. ***Arcady,*** Arcadia, a part of ancient Greece, celebrated in pastoral poetry as the home of an ideal shepherd life.
3. ***Attic shape,*** a shape representing the simple, elegant taste of Athens.
4. ***brede,*** embroidery.

Discussion

1. Describe the scenes pictured on the urn. Do you get a clear picture, or an indistinct one?

2. In lines 11–12, Keats said, "Heard melodies are sweet, but those unheard / Are sweeter." Explain.

3. What specifically is the source of the "happiness" that Keats sees in the scenes on the urn?

4. Why might Keats's final judgment of the urn—"Cold pastoral"—be valid?

5. What truths do you think the urn conveys about the human condition? What might Keats mean by "beauty"?

6. According to some critics, one theme of the Ode is the relationship between art and life. How would you explain this theme?

Ode to a Nightingale

My heart aches, and a drowsy numbness pains
My sense, as though of hemlock[1] I had drunk,
Or emptied some dull opiate to the drains
One minute past, and Lethe-wards[2] had sunk.
'Tis not through envy of thy happy lot,
But being too happy in thine happiness—
That thou, light-wingèd Dryad[3] of the trees,
In some melodious plot
Of beechen green, and shadows numberless,
Singest of summer in full-throated ease.

O for a draft of vintage! that hath been
Cooled a long age in the deep-delvèd earth,
Tasting of Flora[4] and the country green,
Dance, and Provencal song,[5] and sunburnt mirth!
O for a beaker full of the warm South,
Full of the true, the blushful Hippocrene,[6]
With beaded bubbles winking at the brim,
And purple-stainèd mouth;
That I might drink, and leave the world unseen,
And with thee fade away into the forest dim—

Fade far away, dissolve, and quite forget
What thou among the leaves hast never known,
The weariness, the fever, and the fret
Here, where men sit and hear each other groan;
Where palsy shakes a few, sad, last gray hairs,
Where youth grows pale, and specter-thin, and dies;
Where but to think is to be full of sorrow
And leaden-eyed despairs,
Where Beauty cannot keep her lustrous eyes,
Or new love pine at them beyond tomorrow.

Away! away! for I will fly to thee,
Not charioted by Bacchus[7] and his pards,
But on the viewless[8] wings of poesy,
Though the dull brain perplexes and retards.
Already with thee! tender is the night,
And haply the Queen-Moon is on her throne,
Clustered around by all her starry fays;
But here there is no light,
Save what from heaven is with the breezes blown
Through verdurous glooms and winding mossy ways.

---

1. ***hemlock,*** a poison.
2. ***Lethe-wards,*** towards Lethe, the river of forgetfulness in Hades.
3. ***Dryad,*** a tree nymph.
4. ***Flora,*** goddess of the flowers and the spring.
5. ***Provencal song.*** Provence in southern France was famous in the Middle Ages for the songs of its troubadours.
6. ***Hippocrene,*** a fountain on Mt. Helicon in Greece, sacred to the Muses.
7. ***Bacchus,*** god of wine, who was often represented as riding in a carriage drawn by leopards (pards).
8. ***viewless,*** invisible.

I cannot see what flowers are at my feet,
Nor what soft incense hangs upon the boughs,
But, in embalmèd darkness, guess each sweet
Wherewith the seasonable month endows
The grass, the thicket, and the fruit tree wild;
White hawthorn, and the pastoral eglantine;
Fast fading violets covered up in leaves;
And mid-May's eldest child,
The coming muskrose, full of dewy wine,
The murmurous haunt of flies on summer eves.

Darkling I listen; and, for many a time,
I have been half in love with easeful Death,
Called him soft names in many a musèd rime,
To take into the air my quiet breath;
Now more than ever seems it rich to die,
To cease upon the midnight with no pain,
While thou art pouring forth thy soul abroad
In such an ecstasy!
Still wouldst thou sing, and I have ears in vain—
To thy high requiem become a sod.

Thou wast not born for death, immortal Bird!
No hungry generations tread thee down;
The voice I hear this passing night was heard
In ancient days by emperor and clown;[9]
Perhaps the selfsame song that found a path
Through the sad heart of Ruth, when sick for home,
She stood in tears amid the alien corn;[10]
The same that ofttimes hath
Charmed magic casements, opening on the foam
Of perilous seas, in faery lands forlorn.

Forlorn! the very word is like a bell
To toll me back from thee to my sole self.
Adieu! the fancy cannot cheat so well
As she is famed to do, deceiving elf.
Adieu! adieu! thy plaintive anthem fades
Past the near meadows, over the still stream,
Up the hillside; and now 'tis buried deep
In the next valley glades.
Was it a vision, or a waking dream?
Fled is that music.—Do I wake or sleep?

---

9. ***clown,*** peasant.
10. ***Ruth . . . corn.*** According to the Bible story, Ruth left her homeland to go with Naomi, her mother-in-law, to Judah, a foreign country to her, where she worked in the corn (wheat) fields (Ruth 2:1-23).

Discussion

1. What effect does the nightingale have on Keats?

2. In what sense can this poem be called a reverie about "escaping" from the world? What possible means of escape are suggested? Why does Keats finally reject them all?

3. What roles do the poet, the nightingale, and Ruth play?

4. One of Keats's basic ideas—the permanence and changelessness of beauty—is developed in stanza 7. Explain how this idea is developed.

5. What does Keats mean by lines 73–74: "the fancy cannot cheat so well / As she is famed to do"? How is this related to his "forlorn" state?

St. Agnes, who was martyred in Rome around A.D. *300 at the age of thirteen, was the patron saint of virgins. In the Middle Ages there developed the legend on which this poem is based—that by following a certain ritual on St. Agnes's Eve (January 20), a virtuous maiden might see her future husband in a dream.*

The Eve of St. Agnes

1

St. Agnes' Eve—Ah, bitter chill it was!
The owl, for all his feathers, was a-cold;
The hare limped trembling through the frozen grass,
And silent was the flock in woolly fold:
Numb were the Beadsman's[1] fingers while he told
His rosary, and while his frosted breath,
Like pious incense from a censer old,
Seemed taking flight for heaven, without a death,
Past the sweet Virgin's picture, while his prayer he saith.

2

His prayer he saith, this patient, holy man;
Then takes his lamp, and riseth from his knees,
And back returneth, meager, barefoot, wan,
Along the chapel aisle by slow degrees:
The sculptured dead, on each side, seem to freeze,
Imprisoned in black, purgatorial rails:
Knights, ladies, praying in dumb orat'ries,
He passeth by, and his weak spirit fails
To think how they may ache in icy hoods and mails.

3

Northward he turneth through a little door,
And scarce three steps, ere Music's golden tongue
Flattered to tears this aged man and poor;
But no—already had his death-bell rung:
The joys of all his life were said and sung;
His was harsh penance on St. Agnes' Eve:
Another way he went, and soon among
Rough ashes sat he for his soul's reprieve,
And all night kept awake, for sinners' sake to grieve.

4

That ancient Beadsman heard the prelude soft;
And so it chanced, for many a door was wide,
From hurry to and fro. Soon, up aloft,
The silver, snarling trumpets 'gan to chide:
The level chambers, ready with their pride,
Were glowing to receive a thousand guests.
The carved angels, ever eager-eyed,
Stared, where upon their heads the cornice rests,
With hair blown back, and wings put crosswise on their breasts.

1. ***Beadsman,*** a dependent whose duty was to pray for his benefactor.

5

At length burst in the argent revelry,
With plume, tiara, and all rich array,
Numerous as shadows haunting faerily
The brain new-stuffed, in youth, with triumphs gay
Of old romance. These let us wish away,
And turn, sole-thoughted, to one Lady there,
Whose heart had brooded, all that wintry day,
On love, and winged St. Agnes' saintly care,
As she had heard old dames full many times declare.

6

They told her how, upon St. Agnes' Eve,
Young virgins might have visions of delight,
And soft adorings from their loves receive
Upon the honeyed middle of the night,
If ceremonies due they did aright;
As, supperless to bed they must retire,
And couch supine their beauties, lily white;
Nor look behind, nor sideways, but require
Of Heaven with upward eyes for all that they desire.

7

Full of this whim was thoughtful Madeline:
The music, yearning like a God in pain,
She scarcely heard: her maiden eyes divine,
Fixed on the floor, saw many a sweeping train
Pass by—she heeded not at all: in vain
Came many a tiptoe, amorous cavalier,
And back retired; not cooled by high disdain,
But she saw not: her heart was otherwhere;
She sighed for Agnes' dreams, the sweetest of the year.

8

She danced along with vague, regardless eyes,
Anxious her lips, her breathing quick and short:
The hallowed hour was near at hand: she sighs
Amid the timbrels, and the thronged resort
Of whisperers in anger or in sport;
'Mid looks of love, defiance, hate, and scorn,
Hoodwinked with faery fancy; all amort,[2]
Save to St. Agnes and her lambs unshorn,[3]
And all the bliss to be before tomorrow morn.

9

So, purposing each moment to retire,
She lingered still. Meantime, across the moors,
Had come young Porphyro, with heart on fire
For Madeline. Beside the portal doors,
Buttressed from moonlight, stands he, and implores
All saints to give him sight of Madeline,
But for one moment in the tedious hours,
That he might gaze and worship all unseen;
Perchance speak, kneel, touch, kiss—in sooth such things have been.

10

He ventures in: let no buzzed whisper tell,
All eyes be muffled, or a hundred swords
Will storm his heart, Love's feverous citadel:
For him, those chambers held barbarian hordes,
Hyena foemen, and hot-blooded lords,
Whose very dogs would execrations howl
Against his lineage; not one breast affords
Him any mercy in that mansion foul,
Save one old beldame, weak in body and in soul.

11

Ah, happy chance! the aged creature came,
Shuffling along with ivory-headed wand,
To where he stood, hid from the torch's flame,
Behind a broad hall pillar, far beyond
The sound of merriment and chorus bland.
He startled her: but soon she knew his face,
And grasped his fingers in her palsied hand,
Saying, "Mercy, Porphyro! hie thee from this place;
They are all here tonight, the whole blood-thirsty race!

12

"Get hence! get hence! there's dwarfish Hildebrand:
He had a fever late, and in the fit
He cursed thee and thine, both house and land:
Then there's that old Lord Maurice, not a whit
More tame for his gray hairs—Alas me! flit!
Flit like a ghost away."—"Ah, Gossip[4] dear,
We're safe enough; here in this arm-chair sit,
And tell me how—" "Good saints! not here, not here!
Follow me, child, or else these stones will be thy bier."

---

2. ***amort,*** deadened.
3. ***St. Agnes and her lambs unshorn.*** St. Agnes's day was originally celebrated by the sacrifice of two lambs, their wool to be woven later by chosen nuns.
4. ***Gossip,*** friend.

13

He followed through a lowly archèd way,
Brushing the cobwebs with his lofty plume;
And as she muttered "Well-a—well-a-day!"
He found him in a little moonlight room,
Pale, latticed, chill, and silent as a tomb.
"Now tell me where is Madeline," said he,
"O tell me, Angela, by the holy loom
Which none but secret sisterhood may see,
When they St. Agnes' wool are weaving piously."

14

"St. Agnes! Ah! it is St. Agnes' Eve—
Yet men will murder upon holy days.
Thou must hold water in a witch's sieve,[5]
And be liege-lord of all the Elves and Fays
To venture so: it fills me with amaze
To see thee, Porphyro!—St. Agnes' Eve!
God's help! my lady fair the conjurer plays
This very night: good angels her deceive!
But let me laugh awhile,—I've mickle time to grieve."

15

Feebly she laugheth in the languid moon,
While Porphyro upon her face doth look,
Like puzzled urchin on an aged crone
Who keepeth closed a wondrous riddlebook,
As spectacled she sits in chimney nook.
But soon his eyes grew brilliant, when she told
His lady's purpose; and he scarce could brook
Tears, at the thought of those enchantments cold,
And Madeline asleep in lap of legends old.

16

Sudden a thought came like a full-blown rose,
Flushing his brow, and in his pained heart
Made purple riot: then doth he propose
A stratagem, that makes the beldame start:
"A cruel man and impious thou art!
Sweet lady, let her pray, and sleep and dream
Alone with her good angels, far apart
From wicked men like thee. Go, go! I deem
Thou canst not surely be the same that thou didst seem."

17

"I will not harm her, by all saints I swear!"
Quoth Porphyro: "O may I ne'er find grace
When my weak voice shall whisper its last prayer,
If one of her soft ringlets I displace,
Or look with ruffian passion in her face.
Good Angela, believe me, by these tears;
Or I will, even in moment's space,
Awake, with horrid shout, my foemen's ears,
And beard them, though they be more fanged than wolves and bears."

18

"Ah! why wilt thou affright a feeble soul?
A poor, weak, palsy-stricken, churchyard thing,
Whose passing-bell may ere the midnight toll;
Whose prayers for thee, each morn and evening,
Were never missed." Thus plaining, doth she bring
A gentler speech from burning Porphyro;
So woeful, and of such deep sorrowing,
That Angela gives promise she will do
Whatever he shall wish, betide her weal or woe.

19

Which was, to lead him, in close secrecy,
Even to Madeline's chamber, and there hide
Him in a closet, of such privacy
That he might see her beauty unespied,
And win perhaps that night a peerless bride,
While legioned fairies paced the coverlet,
And pale enchantment held her sleepy-eyed.
Never on such a night have lovers met,
Since Merlin paid his Demon all the monstrous debt.[6]

20

"It shall be as thou wishest," said the Dame:
"All cates and dainties shall be stored there
Quickly on this feast-night: by the tambour frame
Her own lute thou wilt see: no time to spare,
For I am slow and feeble, and scarce dare
On such a catering trust my dizzy head.
Wait here, my child, with patience: kneel in prayer
The while. Ah! thou must needs the lady wed,
Or may I never leave my grave among the dead."

5. ***hold water . . . sieve,*** a sign of supernatural power.
6. ***Since Merlin . . . debt.*** Merlin, the famous wizard of King Arthur's Court, was the son of a demon. He was imprisoned magically by the sorceress Vivian who used a spell he himself had taught her.

21

So saying she hobbled off with busy fear.
The lover's endless minutes slowly passed;
The dame returned, and whispered in his ear
To follow her; with aged eyes aghast
From fright of dim espial. Safe at last
Through many a dusky gallery, they gain
The maiden's chamber, silken, hushed and chaste;
Where Porphyro took covert, pleased amain.
His poor guide hurried back with agues in her brain.

22

Her faltering hand upon the balustrade,
Old Angela was feeling for the stair,
When Madeline, St. Agnes' charmed maid,
Rose, like a missioned spirit, unaware:
With silver taper's light, and pious care,
She turned and down the aged gossip led
To a safe level matting. Now prepare,
Young Porphyro, for gazing on that bed;
She comes, she comes again, like ring-dove frayed[7] and fled.

23

Out went the taper as she hurried in;
Its little smoke, in pallid moonshine, died:
She closed the door, she panted, all akin
To spirits of the air, and visions wide:
No uttered syllable, or, woe betide!
But to her heart, her heart was voluble,
Paining with eloquence her balmy side;
As though a tongueless nightingale should swell
Her throat in vain, and die, heart-stifled, in her dell.

24

A casement high and triple-arched there was,
All garlanded with carven imageries,
Of fruits, and flowers, and bunches of knotgrass,
And diamonded with panes of quaint device,
Innumerable of stains and splendid dyes,
As are the tiger-moth's deep-damasked wings,
And in the midst, 'mong thousand heraldries,
And twilight saints, and dim emblazonings,
A shielded scutcheon blushed with blood of queens and kings.

25

Full on this casement shone the wintry moon,
And threw warm gules[8] on Madeline's fair breast,
As down she knelt for Heaven's grace and boon;
Rose-bloom fell on her hands, together prest,
And on her silver cross soft amethyst,
And on her hair a glory, like a saint:
She seemed a splendid angel, newly drest,
Save wings, for heaven:—Porphyro grew faint:
She knelt, so pure a thing, so free from mortal taint.

26

Anon his heart revives: her vespers done,
Of all its wreathed pearls her hair she frees;
Unclasps her warmed jewels one by one;
Loosens her fragrant bodice; by degrees
Her rich attire creeps rustling to her knees:
Half-hidden, like a mermaid in sea-weed,
Pensive awhile she dreams awake, and sees,
In fancy, fair St. Agnes in her bed,
But dares not look behind, or all the charm is fled.

27

Soon, trembling in her soft and chilly nest,
In sort of wakeful swoon, perplexed she lay,
Until the poppied warmth of sleep oppressed
Her soothed limbs, and soul fatigued away;
Flown, like a thought, until the morrow-day;
Blissfully havened both from joy and pain;
Clasped like a missal where swart Paynims pray;[9]
Blinded alike from sunshine and from rain,
As though a rose should shut, and be a bud again.

28

Stolen to this paradise, and so entranced,
Porphyro gazed upon her empty dress,
And listened to her breathing, if it chanced
To wake into a slumberous tenderness;
Which when he heard, that minute did he bless,

---

7. ***frayed,*** frightened.
8. ***gules*** (gyülz), red colors from the stained glass. *Gules* is a heraldic term.
9. ***Clasped . . . pray,*** shut like a prayer book which pagans would have no occasion to open.

And breathed himself: then from the closet crept,
Noiseless as fear in a wide wilderness,
And over the hushed carpet, silent, stept,
And 'tween the curtains peeped, where, lo!—how fast she slept.

29

Then by the bed-side, where the faded moon
Made a dim, silver twilight, soft he set
A table, and, half anguished, threw thereon
A cloth of woven crimson, gold and jet:—
O for some drowsy Morphean amulet![10]
The boisterous, midnight, festive clarion,
The kettle-drum, and far-heard clarinet,
Affray his ears, though but in dying tone:—
The hall-door shuts again, and all the noise is gone.

30

And still she slept an azure-lidded sleep,
In blanched linen, smooth, and lavendered,
While he from forth the closet brought a heap
Of candied apple, quince, and plum, and gourd;
With jellies soother than the creamy curd,
And lucent syrops, tinct with cinnamon;
Manna and dates, in argosy transferred
From Fez; and spiced dainties, every one,
From silken Samarcand to cedared Lebanon.

31

These delicates he heaped with glowing hand
On golden dishes and in baskets bright
Of wreathed silver: sumptuous they stand
In the retired quiet of the night,
Filling the chilly room with perfume light.—
"And now, my love, my seraph fair, awake!
Thou art my heaven, and I thine eremite:[11]
Open thine eyes, for meek St. Agnes' sake,
Or I shall drowse beside thee, so my soul doth ache."

32

Thus whispering, his warm, unnerved arm
Sank in her pillow. Shaded was her dream
By the dusk curtains:—'twas a midnight charm
Impossible to melt as iced stream:
The lustrous salvers in the moonlight gleam;
Broad golden fringe upon the carpet lies:
It seemed he never, never could redeem
From such a stedfast spell his lady's eyes;
So mused awhile, entoiled in woofèd phantasies.

33

Awakening up, he took her hollow lute,—
Tumultuous,—and, in chords that tenderest be,
He played an ancient ditty, long since mute,
In Provence called, "La belle dame sans mercy":
Close to her ear touching the melody;—
Wherewith disturbed, she uttered a soft moan;
He ceased—she panted quick—and suddenly
Her blue affrayed eyes wide open shone:
Upon his knees he sank, pale as smooth-sculptured stone.

34

Her eyes were open, but she still beheld,
Now wide awake, the vision of her sleep:
There was a painful change, that nigh expelled
The blisses of her dream so pure and deep
At which fair Madeline began to weep,
And moan forth witless words with many a sigh,
While still her gaze on Porphyro would keep:
Who knelt, with joined hands and piteous eye,
Fearing to move or speak, she looked so dreamingly.

35

"Ah, Porphyro!" said she, "but even now
Thy voice was at sweet tremble in mine ear,
Made tuneable with every sweetest vow:
And those sad eyes were spiritual and clear:
How changed thou art! how pallid, chill, and drear!
Give me that voice again, my Porphyro,
Those looks immortal, those complainings dear!
Oh, leave me not in this eternal woe,
For if thou diest, my Love, I know not where to go."

36

Beyond a mortal man impassioned far
At these voluptuous accents, he arose,

---

10. ***Morphean amulet,*** a sleep-producing charm. Morpheus was the Greek god of dreams.
11. ***eremite*** (er′ə mīt′), a hermit. The sense here is of a devoted worshipper.

Ethereal, flushed, and like a throbbing star
Seen 'mid the sapphire heaven's deep repose;
Into her dream he melted, as the rose
Blendeth its odor with the violet,—
Solution sweet: meantime the frost-wind blows
Like Love's alarum, pattering the sharp sleet
Against the window-panes; St. Agnes' moon hath set.

37

'Tis dark: quick pattereth the flaw-blown sleet.
"This is no dream, my bride, my Madeline!"
'Tis dark: the iced gusts still rave and beat:
"No dream, alas! alas! and woe is mine!
Porphyro will leave me here to fade and pine.
Cruel! what traitor could thee hither bring?
I curse not, for my heart is lost in thine,
Though thou forsakest a deceived thing;—
A dove forlorn and lost with sick unpruned wing."

38

"My Madeline! sweet dreamer! lovely bride!
Say, may I be for aye thy vassal blest?
Thy beauty's shield, heart-shaped and vermeil-dyed?
Ah, silver shrine, here will I take my rest
After so many hours of toil and quest,
A famished pilgrim,—saved by miracle.
Though I have found, I will not rob thy nest,
Saving of thy sweet self; if thou think'st well
To trust, fair Madeline, to no rude infidel.

39

"Hark! 'tis an elfin-storm from faery land,
Of haggard seeming, but a boon indeed:
Arise—arise! the morning is at hand;—
The bloated wassailers will never heed;—
Let us away, my love, with happy speed;
There are no ears to hear, or eyes to see,—
Drowned all in Rhenish and the sleepy mead:
Awake! arise! my love, and fearless be,
For o'er the southern moors I have a home for thee."

40

She hurried at his words, beset with fears,
For there were sleeping dragons all around,
At glaring watch, perhaps, with ready spears—
Down the wide stairs a darkling way they found;
In all the house was heard no human sound.
A chain-drooped lamp was flickering by each door;
The arras, rich with horseman, hawk, and hound,
Fluttered in the besieging wind's uproar;
And the long carpets rose along the gusty floor.

41

They glide, like phantoms, into the wide hall;
Like phantoms, to the iron porch they glide,
Where lay the Porter, in uneasy sprawl,
With a huge empty flagon by his side:
The wakeful bloodhound rose, and shook his hide,
But his sagacious eye an inmate owns:
By one, and one the bolts full easy slide:—
The chains lie silent on the footworn stones;
The key turns, and the door upon its hinges groans.

42

And they are gone: aye, ages long ago
These lovers fled away into the storm.
That night the Baron dreamt of many a woe,
And all his warrior-guests with shade and form
Of witch, and demon, and large coffin-worm,
Were long be-nightmared. Angela the old
Died palsy-twitched, with meager face deform;
The Beadsman, after thousand aves told,
For aye unsought-for slept among his ashes cold.

Discussion

1. The first four stanzas are devoted to setting the scene. What kinds of images appear most frequently in these stanzas? What general effect do these stanzas have on you?

2. What might the Beadsman represent? Angela is the one other character in the poem closely associated with the Beadsman. With whom are these two most strongly contrasted?

3. Why do you think Keats describes the casement (stanza 24) in such detail?

4. Stanzas 40–41 describe the escape of the lovers. Keats mentions that the lovers will face dangers, such as "sleeping dragons," "ready spears," and lamps at every door that would reveal their identity. What other details are added to create an atmosphere of danger?

Extension • Writing

If you had to interpret "The Eve of St. Agnes" as either "dream" or "reality," which would you choose? Write a brief essay defending your choice.

Vocabulary

Context and Structure

A. Use context and structure as aids to interpreting the meaning of the italicized word in each passage. Then on a separate sheet of paper rewrite the phrase that contains the italicized word, substituting a synonymous word or expression for that word. Try to keep the basic meaning of the phrase.

1. "Scatter, as from an *unextinguished* hearth / Ashes and sparks, my words among mankind!"

2. ". . . Near them, on the sand, / Half sunk, a shattered *visage* lies, whose frown, / And wrinkled lip, and sneer of cold command, / Tell that its sculptor well those passions read . . ."

B. Many English words include the root *sol,* which comes from the Latin word *solus,* meaning "alone." On your paper, show where this root appears in each of the following passages. You may use your Glossary.

3. "And, little town, thy streets forevermore / Will silent be; and not a soul to tell / Why thou art desolate, can e'er return."

4. "Silent and pensive, idle, restless, slow, / His home deserted for the lonely wood, / Tormented with a wound he could not know, / His, like all deep grief, plunged in solitude."

5. "These let us wish away, / And turn, sole-thoughted, to one Lady there, / Whose heart had brooded, all that wintry day, / On love. . . ."

John Keats 1795 • 1821

John Keats was born in London, the eldest of four children. His father, a cockney stable keeper, was killed in a riding accident when John was 9; six years later his mother died of tuberculosis. At the age of 15, soon after his mother's death, he was taken out of school (where he had become passionately interested in English poetry) and apprenticed to a physician. Although he spent some time working in London hospitals and qualified to practice as an apothecary, he soon abandoned this profession to devote his time to literature.

With support from the literary critic Leigh Hunt, Wordsworth, and Charles Lamb, a writer of familiar essays, Keats at age 21 began his literary career in earnest. Suddenly disappointment and tragedy entered his life: one brother left for America, the other died of tuberculosis. The publication of *Endymion,* his first sustained poetic effort, was received with vicious and unwarranted criticism. Critics, mocking his cockney heritage and his medical training, advised him to return to medicine and leave the writing of poetry to the educated and cultured. This adverse publicity kept his poetry from selling and he was soon destitute. In 1818, his suspicion that he had tuberculosis was confirmed. Ill, depressed, and poverty-stricken, Keats still fell in love with Fanny Brawne. Knowing that he could never marry, and under instructions from his physician to curtail all work, he left England to seek the warmer climate of Italy in one last desperate attempt to regain his health. Only six months after his arrival in Italy, Keats died in February 1821. He was buried in the Protestant Cemetery in Rome under the epitaph he had composed: "Here lies one whose name was writ in water."

Thomas De Quincey

On the Knocking at the Gate in *Macbeth*

From my boyish days I had always felt a great perplexity on one point in *Macbeth*. It was this: the knocking at the gate which succeeds to the murder of Duncan produced to my feelings an effect for which I never could account. The effect was that it reflected back upon the murderer a peculiar awfulness and a depth of solemnity; yet, however obstinately I endeavored with my understanding to comprehend this, for many years I never could see *why* it should produce such an effect.

Here I pause for one moment to exhort the reader never to pay any attention to his understanding[1] when it stands in opposition to any other faculty of his mind. The mere understanding, however useful and indispensable, is the meanest faculty in the human mind and the most to be distrusted; and yet the great majority of people trust to nothing else,—which may do for ordinary life, but not for philosophical purposes. Of this, out of ten thousand instances that I might produce, I will cite one. Ask of any person whatsoever who is not previously prepared for the demand by a knowledge of perspective, to draw in the rudest way the commonest appearance which depends upon the laws of that science,—as, for instance, to represent the effect of two walls standing at right angles to each other, or the appearance of the houses on each side of a street, as seen by a person looking down the street from one extremity. Now, in all cases, unless the person has happened to observe in pictures how it is that artists produce these effects, he will be utterly unable to make the smallest approximation to it. Yet why? For he has actually seen the effect every day of his life. The reason is that he allows his understanding to overrule his eyes. His understanding, which includes no intuitive knowledge of the laws of vision, can furnish him with no reason why a line which is known and can be proved to be a horizontal line should not *appear* a horizontal line. A line that made any angle with the perpendicular less than a right angle would seem to him to indicate that his houses were all tumbling down together. Accordingly he makes the line of his houses a horizontal line, and fails of course to produce the effect demanded. Here then is one instance out of many in which not only the understanding is allowed to overrule the eyes, but where the understanding is positively allowed to obliterate the eyes, as it were; for not only does the man believe the evidence of his understanding in opposition to that of his eyes, but (which is monstrous) the idiot is not aware that his eyes ever gave such evidence. He does not know that he has seen (and therefore, *quoad*,[2] his consciousness has *not* seen) that which he *has* seen every day of his life. But to return from this digression. My understanding could furnish no reason why the knocking at the gate in *Macbeth* should produce any effect, direct or reflected. In fact, my understanding said positively that it could *not* produce any effect. But I knew better; I felt that it did; and I waited and clung to the problem until further knowledge should enable me to solve it. At length, in 1812, Mr. Williams made his *début* on the stage of Ratcliffe Highway, and executed those unparalleled murders which have procured for him such a brilliant and undying reputation.[3] On which murders, by the way, I must observe, that in one respect they have had an ill effect, by making the connoisseur in murder very fastidious in his taste, and dissatisfied with anything that has been since done in that line. All other murders look

1. ***understanding,*** intellect; the reasoning faculty.
2. ***quoad*** (kwō′ad), relative to. (Latin)
3. ***Mr. Williams . . . reputation.*** In fact, it was in December, 1811, that John Williams, a seaman, murdered two families in the Ratcliffe Highway, a street in the slums of the East End of London.

pale by the deep crimson of his; and, as an amateur once said to me in a querulous tone, "There has been absolutely nothing *doing* since his time, or nothing that's worth speaking of." But this is wrong, for it is unreasonable to expect all men to be great artists, and born with the genius of Mr. Williams. Now it will be remembered that in the first of these murders (that of the Marrs) the same incident (of a knocking at the door soon after the work of extermination was complete) did actually occur which the genius of Shakespeare has invented; and all good judges, and the most eminent dilettanti,[4] acknowledged the felicity of Shakespeare's suggestion as soon as it was actually realized. Here then was a fresh proof that I had been right in relying on my own feeling in opposition to my understanding; and again I set myself to study the problem. At length I solved it to my own satisfaction; and my solution is this—Murder, in ordinary cases, where the sympathy is wholly directed to the case of the murdered person, is an incident of coarse and vulgar horror; and for this reason—that it flings the interest exclusively upon the natural but ignoble instinct by which we cleave to life: an instinct which, as being indispensable to the primal law of self-preservation, is the same in kind (though different in degree) amongst all living creatures. This instinct, therefore, because it annihilates all distinctions, and degrades the greatest of men to the level of "the poor beetle that we tread on,"[5] exhibits human nature in its most abject and humiliating attitude. Such an attitude would little suit the purposes of the poet. What then must he do? He must throw the interest on the murderer. Our sympathy must be with *him* (of course I mean a sympathy of comprehension, a sympathy by which we enter into his feelings, and are made to understand them—not a sympathy of pity or approbation). In the murdered person all strife of thought, all flux and reflux of passion and of purpose, are crushed by one overwhelming panic; the fear of instant death smites him "with its petrific mace."[6] But in the murderer, such a murderer as a poet will condescend to, there must be raging some great storm of passion—jealousy, ambition, vengeance, hatred—which will create a hell within him; and into this hell we are to look.

In *Macbeth*, for the sake of gratifying his own enormous and teeming faculty of creation, Shakespeare has introduced two murderers. And, as usual in his hands, they are remarkably discriminated. But—though in Macbeth the strife of mind is greater than in his wife, the tiger spirit not so awake, and his feelings caught chiefly by contagion from her—yet, as both were finally involved in the guilt of murder, the murderous mind of necessity is finally to be presumed in both. This was to be expressed; and on its own account, as well as to make it a more proportionable antagonist to the unoffending nature of their victim, "the gracious Duncan,"[7] and adequately to expound "the deep damnation of his taking off,"[8] this was to be expressed with peculiar energy. We were to be made to feel that the human nature,—*i.e.*, the divine nature of love and mercy, spread through the hearts of all creatures, and seldom utterly withdrawn from man—was gone, vanished, extinct, and that the fiendish nature had taken its place. And, as this effect is marvellously accomplished in the *dialogues* and *soliloquies* themselves, so it is finally consummated by the expedient under consideration; and it is to this that I now solicit the reader's attention. If the reader has ever witnessed a wife, daughter, or sister, in a fainting fit, he may chance to have observed that the most affecting moment in such a spectacle is *that* in which a sigh and a stirring announce the recommencement of suspended life. Or, if the reader has ever been present in a vast metropolis on the day when some great national idol was carried in funeral pomp to his grave, and, chancing to walk near the course through which it passed, has felt powerfully, in the silence and desertion of the streets and in the stagnation of ordinary business, the deep interest which at that moment was possessing the heart of man—if all at once he should hear the death-like stillness broken up by the sound of wheels rattling away from the scene, and making known that the transitory

---

4. ***dilettanti,*** literally, lovers of art; here, lovers of the art of murder.

5. ***"the poor beetle . . . on,"*** Shakespeare, *Measure for Measure*, Act Three, Scene 1, line 78.

6. ***"with its petrific mace,"*** Milton, *Paradise Lost*, Book Ten, line 293. *Petrific* means "petrifying."

7. ***"the gracious Duncan,"*** Shakespeare, *Macbeth*, Act Three, Scene 1, line 66.

8. ***"the deep . . . taking off,"*** Shakespeare, *Macbeth*, Act One, Scene 7, line 20. "Taking off" means murder.

vision was dissolved, he will be aware that at no moment was his sense of the complete suspension and pause in ordinary human concerns so full and affecting as at that moment when the suspension ceases, and the goings-on of human life are suddenly resumed. All action in any direction is best expounded, measured, and made apprehensible, by reaction. Now apply this to the case in *Macbeth*. Here, as I have said, the retiring of the human heart and the entrance of the fiendish heart was to be expressed and made sensible. Another world has stepped in; and the murderers are taken out of the region of human things, human purposes, human desires. They are transfigured: Lady Macbeth is "unsexed";[9] Macbeth has forgot that he was born of woman; both are conformed to the image of devils; and the world of devils is suddenly revealed. But how shall this be conveyed and made palpable? In order that a new world may step in, this world must for a time disappear. The murderers, and the murder, must be insulated—cut off by an immeasurable gulf from the ordinary tide and succession of human affairs—locked up and sequestered in some deep recess; we must be made sensible that the world of ordinary life is suddenly arrested—laid asleep—tranced—racked into a dread armistice; time must be annihilated; relation to things without abolished; and all must pass self-withdrawn into a deep syncope and suspension of earthly passion. Hence it is that, when the deed is done, when the work of darkness is perfect, then the world of darkness passes away like a pageantry in the clouds: the knocking at the gate is heard, and it makes known audibly that the reaction has commenced; the human has made its reflux upon the fiendish: the pulses of life are beginning to beat again; and the reestablishment of the goings-on of the world in which we live first makes us profoundly sensible of the awful parenthesis that had suspended them.

O mighty poet! Thy works are not as those of other men, simply and merely great works of art, but are also like the phenomena of nature, like the sun and the sea, the stars and the flowers, like frost and snow, rain and dew, hail storm and thunder, which are to be studied with entire submission of our own faculties, and in the perfect faith that in them there can be no too much or too little, nothing useless or inert, but that, the farther we press in our discoveries, the more we shall see proofs of design and self-supporting arrangement where the careless eye had seen nothing but accident! □□

9. ***"unsexed,"*** a reference to *Macbeth*, Act One, Scene 5, line 38.

Discussion

1. What perplexed the author of the essay about *Macbeth?*

2. What happened that caused De Quincey to understand the effect that the knocking had on him?

3. What explanation did De Quincey give for the emotional impact of the knocking at the gate?

Thomas De Quincey
1785 • 1859

De Quincey, the son of a wealthy Manchester merchant, was educated at Oxford. While at the university he studied German literature and philosophy and read English literature extensively.

He came into an inheritance, took up residence in the Lake District, and began a close relationship with those Romantic poets living in the area. De Quincey was among the first to recognize the importance of Wordsworth's and Coleridge's *Lyrical Ballads,* and he became an enthusiastic advocate of Romantic literature. After having been warmly accepted by Coleridge, De Quincey anonymously gave a gift of money to him. By this time, he, like Coleridge, had become addicted to opium to relieve the pains of neuralgia and other ailments, including a gastric disorder that he had acquired when, as a teenager, he lived in poverty in London awaiting his inheritance.

In 1821, part of the *Confessions of an English Opium-Eater* was published in periodical form. The work, considered to be his most significant, was published in its entirety the following year. He continued writing, chiefly essays for periodicals, throughout his life until his death at age 74 in 1859.

Mary Wollstonecraft

from A Vindication of the Rights of Woman

Chapter 2

To account for, and excuse the tyranny of man, many ingenious arguments have been brought forward to prove, that the two sexes, in the acquirement of virtue, ought to aim at attaining a very different character: or, to speak explicitly, women are not allowed to have sufficient strength of mind to acquire what really deserves the name of virtue. Yet it should seem, allowing them to have souls, that there is but one way appointed by providence to lead *mankind* to either virtue or happiness.

If then women are not a swarm of ephemeron[1] triflers, why should they be kept in ignorance under the specious name of innocence? Men complain, and with reason, of the follies and caprices of our sex, when they do not keenly satirize our headstrong passions and grovelling vices. Behold, I should answer, the natural effect of ignorance! The mind will ever be unstable that has only prejudices to rest on, and the current will run with destructive fury when there are no barriers to break its force. Women are told from their infancy, and taught by the example of their mothers, that a little knowledge of human weakness, justly termed cunning, softness of temper, *outward* obedience, and a scrupulous attention to a puerile kind of propriety, will obtain for them the protection of man; and should they be beautiful, every thing else is needless, for at least twenty years of their lives. . . .

The most perfect education, in my opinion is, such an exercise of the understanding as is best calculated to strengthen the body and form the heart. Or, in other words, to enable the individual to attain such habits of virtue as will render it independent. In fact, it is a farce to call any being virtuous whose virtues do not result from the exercise of its own reason. This was Rousseau's opinion respecting men:[2] I extend it to women, and confidently assert, that they have been drawn out of their sphere by false refinement, and not by an endeavour to acquire masculine qualities. Still the regal homage which they receive is so intoxicating, that till the manners of the times are changed, and formed on more reasonable principles, it may be impossible to convince them, that the illegitimate power, which they obtain by degrading themselves, is a curse, and that they must return to nature and equality, if they wish to secure the placid satisfaction that unsophisticated affections impart. But for this epoch we must wait—wait, perhaps, till kings and nobles, enlightened by reason, and, preferring the real dignity of man to childish state, throw off their gaudy hereditary trappings; and if

The Bettman Archive, Inc.

1. ***ephemeron,*** short-lived.
2. ***Rousseau's opinion . . . men.*** Jean Jacques Rousseau (1712–1778) argued that the individual's natural goodness is distorted by the false values of civilization.

then women do not resign the arbitrary power of beauty, they will prove that they have *less* mind than man. . . .

Many are the causes that, in the present corrupt state of society, contribute to enslave women by cramping their understandings and sharpening their senses. One, perhaps, that silently does more mischief than all the rest, is their disregard of order.

To do every thing in an orderly manner, is a most important precept, which women, who, generally speaking, receive only a disorderly kind of education, seldom attend to with that degree of exactness that men, who from their infancy are broken into method, observe. This negligent kind of guesswork, for what other epithet can be used to point out the random exertions of a sort of instinctive common sense, never brought to the test of reason? prevents their generalizing matters of fact, so they do to-day what they did yesterday, merely because they did it yesterday. . . .

Women are, therefore, to be considered either as moral beings, or so weak that they must be entirely subjected to the superior faculties of men.

Let us examine this question. Rousseau declares, that a woman should never, for a moment feel herself independent, that she should be governed by fear to exercise her *natural* cunning, and made a coquetish slave in order to render her a more alluring object of desire, a *sweeter* companion to man, whenever he chooses to relax himself. He carries the arguments, which he pretends to draw from the indications of nature, still further, and insinuates that truth and fortitude, the corner stones of all human virtue, shall be cultivated with certain restrictions, because with respect to the female character, obedience is the grand lesson which ought to be impressed with unrelenting rigour.

What nonsense! when will a great man arise with sufficient strength of mind to puff away the fumes which pride and sensuality have thus spread over the subject! If women are by nature inferior to men, their virtues must be the same in quality, if not in degree, or virtue is a relative idea; consequently, their conduct should be founded on the same principles and have the same aim.

Connected with man as daughters, wives, and mothers, their moral character may be estimated by their manner of fulfilling those simple duties; but the end, the grand end of their exertions should be to unfold their own faculties, and acquire the dignity of conscious virtue. They may try to render their road pleasant; but ought never to forget, in common with man, that life yields not the felicity which can satisfy an immortal soul. I do not mean to insinuate, that either sex should be so lost, in abstract reflections or distant views, as to forget the affections and duties that lie before them, and are in truth, the means appointed to produce the fruit of life; on the contrary, I would warmly recommend them, even while I assert, that they afford most satisfaction when they are considered in their true subordinate light.

Chapter 9

. . . But what have women to do in society? I may be asked, but to loiter with easy grace; surely you would not condemn them all to suckle fools and chronicle small beer![3] No. Women might certainly study the art of healing, and be physicians as well as nurses.

How much more respectable is the woman who earns her own bread by fulfilling any duty, than the most accomplished beauty!—beauty did I say?—so sensible am I of the beauty of moral loveliness, or the harmonious propriety that attunes the passions of a well-regulated mind, that I blush at making the comparison; yet I sigh to think how few women aim at attaining this respectability by withdrawing from the giddy whirl of pleasure, or the indolent calm that stupifies the good sort of women it sucks in.

Proud of their weakness, however, they must always be protected, guarded from care, and all the rough toils that dignify the mind.—If this be the fiat[4] of fate, if they will make themselves insignificant and contemptible, sweetly to waste 'life away,' let them not expect to be valued when their beauty fades, for it is the fate of the fairest flowers to be admired and pulled to pieces by the careless hand that plucked them. In how many ways do I wish, from the purest benevo-

3. ***to suckle . . . beer,*** Shakespeare, *Othello,* Act 2, Scene 1, line 161.
4. ***fiat,*** dictate, command.

lence, to impress this truth on my sex; yet I fear that they will not listen to a truth that dear bought experience has brought home to many an agitated bosom, nor willingly resign the privileges of rank and sex for the privileges of humanity, to which those have no claim who do not discharge its duties.

Those writers are particularly useful, in my opinion, who make man feel for man, independent of the station he fills, or the drapery of factitious sentiments. I then would fain convince reasonable men of the importance of some of my remarks, and prevail on them to weigh dispassionately the whole tenor of my observations.—I appeal to their understandings; and, as a fellow-creature, claim, in the name of my sex, some interest in their hearts. I entreat them to assist to emancipate their companion, to make her a *help meet* for them!

Would men but generously snap our chains, and be content with rational fellowship instead of slavish obedience, they would find us more observant daughters, more affectionate sisters, more faithful wives, more reasonable mothers—in a word, better citizens. We should then love them with true affection, because we should learn to respect ourselves; and the peace of mind of a worthy man would not be interrupted by the idle vanity of his wife, nor the babes sent to nestle in a strange bosom, having never found a home in their mother's.[5] □□

5. ***nestle . . . mother's,*** given to a nurse to be cared for.

Discussion

1. What does the author consider to be a perfect education?

2. What is a reason cited for the enslavement of women?

3. Which writers does Wollstonecraft consider to be particularly useful?

4. In the concluding paragraph, what does the author indicate will be the result of man releasing woman from "slavish obedience"?

Extension • Writing

1. If you feel that women are still enslaved today, write an essay pleading for women's rights.

2. In an essay, agree or disagree with the reasons given by Mary Wollstonecraft for releasing women from "slavish obedience."

3. Describe the life of a woman in the latter part of the eighteenth century in England, using Mary Wollstonecraft's work, the material in the text, the comments about Wollstonecraft by Virginia Woolf (pages 350–353), and your own knowledge of this period.

Mary Wollstonecraft
1759 • 1797

Mary Wollstonecraft had many experiences as she was growing up and during her early adult life that led her to voice objections to what she considered to be the oppression of women. Her father was an alcoholic and a brute. As a child, she moved often and had to depend on her own resources for most of her schooling. As a young adult, she helped her sister rid herself of an unhappy marriage and had a close friend die in childbirth. These experiences, along with others, caused her to be critical of the traditional relationships between men and women.

Attempting occupations that were considered appropriate for females, she met with little success. Giving up these "acceptable" occupations, she journeyed to London to begin her writing career. Her writings include essays, reviews, novels, letters, and educational and political books. Her most famous book, *A Vindication of the Rights of Woman,* was an appeal for women's independence. The work caused great furor, arousing attacks on the socially unacceptable life of the author and on the straightforward style of the book since, when this work was published, people were not accustomed to this style of writing.

Mary Wollstonecraft

by Virginia Woolf

Great wars are strangely intermittent in their effects. The French Revolution took some people and tore them asunder; others it passed over without disturbing a hair of their heads. Jane Austen, it is said, never mentioned it; Charles Lamb ignored it; Beau Brummell never gave the matter a thought. But to Wordsworth and to Godwin[1] it was the dawn; unmistakably they saw

> France standing on the top of golden hours,
> And human nature seeming born again.[2]

Thus it would be easy for a picturesque historian to lay side by side the most glaring contrasts—here in Chesterfield Street was Beau Brummell letting his chin fall carefully upon his cravat and discussing in a tone studiously free from vulgar emphasis the proper cut of the lapel of a coat; and here in Somers Town was a party of ill-dressed, excited young men, one with a head too big for his body and a nose too long for his face, holding forth day by day over the tea-cups upon human perfectibility, ideal unity, and the rights of man. There was also a woman present with very bright eyes and a very eager tongue, and the young men, who had middle-class names, like Barlow and Holcroft and Godwin, called her simply "Wollstonecraft," as if it did not matter whether she were married or unmarried, as if she were a young man like themselves.

Such glaring discords among intelligent people—for Charles Lamb and Godwin, Jane Austen and Mary Wollstonecraft were all highly intelligent—suggest how much influence circumstances have upon opinions. If Godwin had been brought up in the precincts of the Temple and had drunk deep of antiquity and old letters at Christ's Hospital,[3] he might never have cared a straw for the future of man and his rights in general. If Jane Austen had lain as a child on the landing to prevent her father from thrashing her mother, her soul might have burnt with such a passion against tyranny that all her novels might have been consumed in one cry for justice.

Such had been Mary Wollstonecraft's first experience of the joys of married life. And then her sister Everina had been married miserably and had bitten her wedding ring to pieces in the coach. Her brother had been a burden on her; her father's farm had failed, and in order to start that disreputable man with the red face and the violent temper and the dirty hair in life again she had gone into bondage among the aristocracy as a governess—in short, she had never known what happiness was, and, in its default, had fabricated a creed fitted to meet the sordid misery of real human life. The staple of her doctrine was that nothing mattered save independence. "Every obligation we receive from our fellow-creatures is a new shackle, takes from our native freedom, and debases the mind." Independence was the first necessity for a woman; not grace or charm, but energy and courage and the power to put her will into effect were her necessary qualities. It was her highest boast to be able to say, "I never yet resolved to do anything of consequence that I did not adhere readily to it." Certainly Mary could say this with truth. When she was a little more than thirty she could look back upon a series of actions which she had carried out in the teeth of opposition. She had taken a house by prodigious efforts for her friend Fanny, only to find that Fanny's mind was changed and she did not want a house after all. She had started a school. She had persuaded

---

1. ***Jane Austen . . . Charles Lamb . . . Beau Brummel . . . Godwin.*** Jane Austen (1775-1817) was an English novelist whose specialty was the comedy of manners. Charles Lamb (1775-1834) is best known for his essays on homely topics. George Brummell (1778-1840) was a famous dandy. William Godwin (1756-1836) was a philosophical writer and novelist.
2. ***France . . . again,*** Wordsworth, *The Prelude,* Book Six, lines 339-340.
3. ***Christ's Hospital,*** a famous school, founded in 1552. Lamb attended school there between 1782 and 1789.

Fanny into marrying Mr. Skeys. She had thrown up her school and gone to Lisbon alone to nurse Fanny when she died. On the voyage back she had forced the captain of the ship to rescue a wrecked French vessel by threatening to expose him if he refused. And when, overcome by a passion for Fuseli,[4] she declared her wish to live with him and was refused flatly by his wife, she had put her principle of decisive action instantly into effect, and had gone to Paris determined to make her living by her pen.

The Revolution thus was not merely an event that had happened outside her; it was an active agent in her own blood. She had been in revolt all her life—against tyranny, against law, against convention. The reformer's love of humanity, which has so much of hatred in it as well as love, fermented within her. The outbreak of revolution in France expressed some of her deepest theories and convictions, and she dashed off in the heat of that extraordinary moment those two eloquent and daring books—the *Reply to Burke* and the *Vindication of the Rights of Woman*, which are so true that they seem now to contain nothing new in them—their originality has become our commonplace. But when she was in Paris lodging by herself in a great house, and saw with her own eyes the King whom she despised driving past surrounded by National Guards and holding himself with greater dignity than she expected, then, "I can scarcely tell you why," the tears came to her eyes.[5] "I am going to bed," the letter ended, "and, for the first time in my life, I cannot put out the candle." Things were not so simple after all. She could not understand even her own feelings. She saw the most cherished of her convictions put into practice—and her eyes filled with tears. She had won fame and independence and the right to live her own life—and she wanted something different. "I do not want to be loved like a goddess," she wrote, "but I wish to be necessary to you." For Imlay, the fascinating American to whom her letter was addressed, had been very good to her. Indeed, she had fallen passionately in love with him. But it was one of her theories that love should be free—"that mutual affection was marriage and that the marriage tie should not bind after the death of love, if love should die." And yet at the same time that she wanted freedom she wanted certainty. "I like the word affection," she wrote, "because it signifies something habitual."

The conflict of all these contradictions shows itself in her face, at once so resolute and so dreamy, so sensual and so intelligent, and beautiful into the bargain with its great coils of hair and the large bright eyes that Southey[6] thought the most expressive he had ever seen. The life of such a woman was bound to be tempestuous. Every day she made theories by which life should be lived; and every day she came smack against the rock of other people's prejudices. Every day too—for she was no pedant, no cold-blooded theorist—something was born in her that thrust aside her theories and forced her to model them afresh. She acted upon her theory that she had no legal claim upon Imlay; she refused to marry him; but when he left her alone week after week with the child she had borne him her agony was unendurable.

Thus distracted, thus puzzling even to herself, the plausible and treacherous Imlay cannot be altogether blamed for failing to follow the rapidity of her changes and the alternate reason and unreason of her moods. Even friends whose liking was impartial were disturbed by her discrepancies. Mary had a passionate, an exuberant, love of Nature, and yet one night when the colours in the sky were so exquisite that Madeleine Schweizer could not help saying to her, "Come, Mary—come, nature lover—and enjoy this wonderful spectacle—this constant transition from colour to colour," Mary never took her eyes off the Baron de Wolzogen. "I must confess," wrote Madame Schweizer, "that this erotic absorption made such a disagreeable impression on me, that all my pleasure vanished." But if the sentimental Swiss was disconcerted by Mary's sensuality, Imlay, the shrewd man of business, was exasperated by her intelligence. Whenever he saw her he yielded to her charm, but then her quickness, her penetration, her uncompromising idealism harassed him. She saw through his excuses; she met all his reasons; she was even capable of managing his business.

---

4. ***Fuseli*** (?1742-1825), a Swiss painter living in England.
5. ***the King . . . to her eyes.*** The king was Louis XVI, who was guillotined by the revolutionary government in France in 1793.
6. ***Southey*** (suTH′ē), Robert Southey (1774-1843), English poet.

There was no peace with her—he must be off again. And then her letters followed him, torturing him with their sincerity and their insight. They were so outspoken; they pleaded so passionately to be told the truth; they showed such a contempt for soap and alum and wealth and comfort; they repeated, as he suspected, so truthfully that he had only to say the word, "and you shall never hear of me more," that he could not endure it. Tickling minnows he had hooked a dolphin, and the creature rushed him through the waters till he was dizzy and only wanted to escape. After all, though he had played at theory-making too, he was a business man, he depended upon soap and alum; "the secondary pleasures of life," he had to admit, "are very necessary to my comfort." And among them was one that for ever evaded Mary's jealous scrutiny. Was it business, was it politics, was it a woman that perpetually took him away from her? He shillied and shallied; he was very charming when they met; then he disappeared again. Exasperated at last, and half insane with suspicion, she forced the truth from the cook. A little actress in a strolling company was his mistress, she learnt. True to her own creed of decisive action, Mary at once soaked her skirts so that she might sink unfailingly, and threw herself from Putney Bridge. But she was rescued; after unspeakable agony she recovered, and then her "unconquerable greatness of mind," her girlish creed of independence, asserted itself again, and she determined to make another bid for happiness and to earn her living without taking a penny from Imlay for herself or their child.

It was in this crisis that she again saw Godwin, the little man with the big head, whom she had met when the French Revolution was making the young men in Somers Town think that a new world was being born. She met him—but that is a euphemism, for in fact Mary Wollstonecraft actually visited him in his own house. Was it the effect of the French Revolution? Was it the blood she had seen spilt on the pavement and the cries of the furious crowd that had rung in her ears that made it seem a matter of no importance whether she put on her cloak and went to visit Godwin in Somers Town, or waited in Judd Street West for Godwin to come to her? And what strange upheaval of human life was it that inspired that curious man, who was so queer a mixture of meanness and magnanimity, of coldness and deep feeling—for the memoir of his wife could not have been written without unusual depth of heart—to hold the view that she did right—that he respected Mary for trampling upon the idiotic convention by which women's lives were tied down? He held the most extraordinary views on many subjects, and upon the relations of the sexes in particular. He thought that reason should influence even the love between men and women. He thought that there was something spiritual in their relationship. He had written that "marriage is a law, and the worst of all laws . . . marriage is an affair of property, and the worst of all properties." He held the belief that if two people of the opposite sex like each other, they should live together without any ceremony, or, for living together is apt to blunt love, twenty doors off, say, in the same street. And he went further; he said that if another man liked your wife "this will create no difficulty. We may all enjoy her conversation, and we shall all be wise enough to consider the sensual intercourse a very trivial object." True, when he wrote those words he had never been in love; now for the first time he was to experience that sensation. It came very quietly and naturally, growing "with equal advances in the mind of each" from those talks in Somers Town, from those discussions upon everything under the sun which they held so improperly alone in his rooms. "It was friendship melting into love . . .," he wrote. "When, in the course of things, the disclosure came, there was nothing in a manner for either party to disclose to the other." Certainly they were in agreement upon the most essential points; they were both of opinion, for instance, that marriage was unnecessary. They would continue to live apart. Only when Nature again intervened, and Mary found herself with child, was it worth while to lose valued friends, she asked, for the sake of a theory? She thought not, and they were married. And then that other theory—that it is best for husband and wife to live apart—was not that also incompatible with other feelings that were coming to birth in her? "A husband is a convenient part of the furniture of the house," she wrote. Indeed, she discovered that she was passionately domestic. Why not, then, revise that theory too, and share the same roof? Godwin should have a room some doors off to work in; and they should dine out separately if they liked—their work, their friends, should be separate. Thus they settled it, and the plan worked admirably. The arrangement combined "the novelty and lively sensation of a visit with the more delicious and heartfelt pleasures of domestic life." Mary admitted that she was happy; Godwin confessed that, after all one's philosophy, it was "extremely gratifying" to find that "there is some one who takes an interest in one's happiness." All sorts of powers and emotions were liberated in Mary by her new satisfaction. Trifles gave her an exquisite pleasure—the sight of Godwin and Imlay's child playing together; the thought of their own child who was to be born; a day's jaunt into the country. One day, meeting Imlay in the New Road, she greeted him without bitterness. But, as Godwin wrote, "Ours is not an idle happiness, a paradise of selfish and transitory pleasures." No, it too was an experiment, as Mary's life had been an experiment from the start, an attempt to make human conventions conform more closely to human needs. And their marriage was only a beginning; all sorts of things were to follow after. Mary was going to have a child. She was going to write a book to be called *The Wrongs of Women.* She was going to reform education. She was going to come down to dinner the day after her child was born. She was going to employ a midwife and not a doctor at her confinement—but that experiment was her last. She died in child-birth. She whose sense of her own existence was so intense, who had cried out even in her misery, "I cannot bear to think of being no more—of losing myself—nay, it appears to me impossible that I should cease to exist," died at the age of thirty-six. But she has her revenge. Many millions have died and been forgotten in the hundred and thirty years that have passed since she was buried; and yet as we read her letters and listen to her arguments and consider her experiments, above all that most fruitful experiment, her relation with Godwin, and realise the high-handed and hot-blooded manner in which she cut her way to the quick of life, one form of immortality is hers undoubtedly: she is alive and active, she argues and experiments, we hear her voice and trace her influence even now among the living. □□

Extension • Writing

In her essay on Mary Wollstonecraft, Virginia Woolf gives a number of the earlier writer's views, some of them contradictory. In a short essay, attack or defend one of the opinions expressed by Wollstonecraft.

Vocabulary • Dictionary

Determine the relationship between the two italicized words listed in each question. Then select, from the pairs of words that follow, the words which are related in the same way as the words in the first pair. Write your choice on a separate sheet of paper. Example—*hot : cold* (the colon means "is related to") as (a) weather : storm; (b) day : night; (c) desert: sand. In the example, *hot* is the opposite of *cold;* therefore, the correct answer is *day : night.* In each item, there is a word in each pair that you will probably have to check in the Glossary.

1. *primal : modern* as **(a)** exhort : encourage; **(b)** happy : abject; **(c)** epoch : time.

2. *careful : scrupulous* as **(a)** negligent : careless; **(b)** placid : stormy; **(c)** indolent : busy.

3. *specious : real* as **(a)** sequester : withdraw; **(b)** procure : obtain; **(c)** ignoble : noble.

4. *abound : teem* as **(a)** free : slavish; **(b)** lifeless : inert; **(c)** tragedy : farce.

5. *obstinate : flexible* as **(a)** fastidious : sloppy; **(b)** allure : attract; **(c)** precept : rule.

6. *peaceful : querulous* as **(a)** fitness : propriety; **(b)** childish : puerile; **(c)** hidden : palpable.

7. *factitious : artificial* as **(a)** approbation : criticism; **(b)** caprice : whim; **(c)** intuitive : rational.

8. *understanding : perplexity* as **(a)** rest : exertion; **(b)** hint : insinuate; **(c)** seriousness : solemnity.

Unit Review Tests 5: The Romantics

CONTENT REVIEW

1. Which one of the following statements does not characterize the Romantic Period? **(a)** The Romantic poets often wrote about the untamed aspects of nature. **(b)** Many of the Romantic poets expressed sympathy with the French Revolution. **(c)** The writers followed the form of writing of eighteenth-century authors. **(d)** Poetry, not fiction, was the dominant mode of expression.

2. Among those nature poets who foreshadowed the Romantic Period were all of the following poets except **(a)** Gray **(b)** Johnson **(c)** Burns.

3. Who was the poet who said that "all good poetry is the spontaneous overflow of powerful feeling"? **(a)** Coleridge **(b)** Wordsworth **(c)** Blake **(d)** Keats.

4. Which poet stated that in his poetry he would "give the charm of novelty to subjects of everyday life"? **(a)** Shelley **(b)** Keats **(c)** Wordsworth **(d)** Blake.

5. The Romantic poet who wrote about the permanence and changelessness of beauty was **(a)** Blake **(b)** Wordsworth **(c)** Shelley **(d)** Keats.

6. The poet whose works were the most mystical of all the Romantic poets was **(a)** Blake **(b)** Shelley **(c)** Byron **(d)** Keats.

7. Nature was described as both nurse and teacher by **(a)** Byron **(b)** Wordsworth **(c)** Shelley **(d)** Blake.

8. Most of the poets of the Romantic Period used their poetry as a vehicle for expressing their revolutionary ideas except **(a)** Keats **(b)** Wordsworth **(c)** Shelley **(d)** Byron.

9. Most of the writers of the Romantic Period found **(a)** lyric poetry **(b)** narrative poetry **(c)** drama **(d)** essays to be the best mode for expressing their emotions.

10. Which poet, before he disgraced himself, was known as the "fair-haired boy" of London society? **(a)** Keats **(b)** Shelley **(c)** Blake **(d)** Byron.

Unit 5, Test I
Interpretation: New Material

From the Prelude, Book I
William Wordsworth

Wordsworth referred to *The Prelude,* on which he worked for almost fifty years, as "a history of the author's mind." This excerpt describes boyhood adventures which made a profound impression on him. After you have read the selection, answer the questions that follow on a separate sheet of paper.

I

Fair seed-time had my soul, and I grew up
Fostered alike by beauty and by fear:
Much favoured in my birth-place, and no less
In that belovèd Vale[1] to which erelong
We were transplanted;—there were we let
loose

1. ***Vale,*** Esthwaite Vale in Lancashire, near Wordsworth's boyhood home.

For sports of wider range. Ere I had told
Ten birth-days, when among the mountain slopes
Frost, and the breath of frosty wind, had snapped
The last autumnal crocus, 't was my joy
With store of springes[2] o'er my shoulder hung
To range the open heights where woodcocks run
Along the smooth green turf. Through half the night,
Scudding[3] away from snare to snare, I plied
That anxious visitation;—moon and stars
Were shining o'er my head. I was alone,
And seemed to be a trouble to the peace
That dwelt among them. Sometimes it befell
In these night wanderings, that a strong desire
O'erpowered my better reason, and the bird
Which was the captive of another's toil
Became my prey; and when the deed was done
I heard among the solitary hills
Low breathings coming after me, and sounds
Of undistinguishable motion, steps
Almost as silent as the turf they trod.

II

Nor less, when spring had warmed the cultured Vale,
Moved we as plunderers where the motherbird
Had in high places built her lodge; though mean
Our object and inglorious, yet the end
Was not ignoble. Oh! when I have hung
Above the raven's nest, by knots of grass
And half-inch fissures in the slippery rock
But ill sustained, and almost (so it seemed)
Suspended by the blast that blew amain,[4]
Shouldering the naked crag, oh, at that time
While on the perilous ridge I hung alone,
With what strange utterance did the loud dry wind
Blow through my ear! the sky seemed not a sky
Of earth—and with what motion moved the clouds!

III

Dust as we are, the immortal spirit grows
Like harmony in music; there is a dark
Inscrutable workmanship that reconciles
Discordant elements, makes them cling together
In one society. How strange, that all
The terrors, pains, and early miseries,
Regrets, vexations, lassitudes interfused
Within my mind, should e'er have borne a part,
And that a needful part, in making up
The calm existence that is mine when I
Am worthy of myself! Praise to the end!
Thanks to the means which Nature deigned to employ;
Whether her fearless visitings, or those
That came with soft alarm, like hurtless light
Opening the peaceful clouds; or she would use
Severer interventions, ministry
More palpable, as best might suit her aim.

IV

One summer evening (led by her) I found
A little boat tied to a willow tree
Within a rocky cove, its usual home.
Straight I unloosed her chain, and stepping in
Pushed from the shore. It was an act of stealth
And troubled pleasure, nor without the voice
Of mountain-echoes did my boat move on;
Leaving behind her still, on either side,
Small circles glittering idly in the moon,
Until they melted all into one track
Of sparkling light. But now, like one who rows,
Proud of his skill, to reach a chosen point
With an unswerving line, I fixed my view
Upon the summit of a craggy ridge,
The horizon's utmost boundary; far above
Was nothing but the stars and the grey sky.
She was an elfin pinnace;[5] lustily
I dipped my oars into the silent lake,
And, as I rose upon the stroke, my boat
Went heaving through the water like a swan;
When, from behind that craggy steep till then
The horizon's bound, a huge peak, black and huge,
As if with voluntary power instinct,
Upreared its head. I struck and struck again,
And growing still in stature the grim shape
Towered up between me and the stars, and still,
For so it seemed, with purpose of its own
And measured motion like a living thing,

2. ***springes,*** snares for catching birds.
3. ***Scudding,*** moving swiftly.
4. ***amain,*** with full force, violently.
5. ***pinnace,*** a light boat or vessel.

Strode after me. With trembling oars I turned,
And through the silent water stole my way
Back to the covert of the willow tree;
There in her mooring-place I left my bark,[6]
And through the meadows homeward went, in grave
And serious mood; but after I had seen
That spectacle, for many days, my brain
Worked with a dim and undetermined sense
Of unknown modes of being; o'er my thoughts
There hung a darkness, call it solitude
Or blank desertion. No familiar shapes
Remained, no pleasant images of trees,
Of sea or sky, no colours of green fields;
But huge and mighty forms, that do not live
Like living men, moved slowly through the mind
By day, and were a trouble to my dreams.

V

Wisdom and Spirit of the universe!
Thou Soul that art the eternity of thought
That givest to forms and images a breath
And everlasting motion, not in vain
By day or star-light thus from my first dawn
Of childhood didst thou intertwine for me
The passions that build up our human soul;
Not with the mean and vulgar works of man,
But with high objects, with enduring things—
With life and nature—purifying thus
The elements of feeling and of thought,
And sanctifying, by such discipline,
Both pain and fear, until we recognise
A grandeur in the beatings of the heart.
Nor was this fellowship vouchsafed[7] to me
With stinted kindness. In November days,
When vapours rolling down the valley made
A lonely scene more lonesome, among woods,
At noon and 'mid the calm of summer nights,
When, by the margin of the trembling lake,
Beneath the gloomy hills homeward I went
In solitude, such intercourse was mine;
Mine was it in the fields both day and night,
And by the waters, all the summer long.

VI

And in the frosty season, when the sun
Was set, and visible for many a mile
The cottage windows blazed through twilight gloom,
I heeded not their summons: happy time
It was indeed for all of us—for me
It was a time of rapture! Clear and loud
The village clock tolled six,—I wheeled about,
Proud and exulting like an untired horse
That cares not for his home. All shod with steel,
We hissed along the polished ice in games
Confederate,[8] imitative of the chase
And woodland pleasures,—the resounding horn,
The pack loud chiming, and the hunted hare.
So through the darkness and the cold we flew,
And not a voice was idle; with the din
Smitten, the precipices rang aloud;
The leafless trees and every icy crag
Tinkled like iron; while far distant hills
Into the tumult sent an alien sound
Of melancholy not unnoticed, while the stars
Eastward were sparkling clear, and in the west
The orange sky of evening died away.
Not seldom from the uproar I retired
Into a silent bay, or sportively
Glanced sideway, leaving the tumultuous throng,
To cut across the reflex[9] of a star
That fled, and, flying still before me, gleamed
Upon the glassy plain; and oftentimes,
When we had given our bodies to the wind,
And all the shadowy banks on either side
Came sweeping through the darkness, spinning still
The rapid line of motion, then at once
Have I, reclining back upon my heels,
Stopped short; yet still the solitary cliffs
Wheeled by me—even as if the earth had rolled
With visible motion her diurnal round!
Behind me did they stretch in solemn train,
Feebler and feebler, and I stood and watched
Till all was tranquil as a dreamless sleep.

6. ***bark,*** boat.
7. ***vouchsafed,*** granted or given.
8. ***confederate,*** joined or allied.
9. ***reflex,*** reflection.

1. What has the speaker done, as described in the first verse paragraph, that makes him feel he is being pursued?

2. What main action does the speaker describe in lines 26–39?

3. To what does the speaker compare the growth of the immortal spirit at the beginning of the third verse paragraph?

4. At the end of the same paragraph, the speaker refers to three means which Nature may employ to form and shape the growing spirit: "fearless visitings," "those [visitings] / That came with soft alarm," and "Severer interventions." Which one of these is exemplified in the account the speaker gives in the fourth verse paragraph?

5. Describe in your own words the apparition that disturbs the speaker in the fourth paragraph? What does it seem to be to him?

6. (a) What simile does the speaker use in describing his boat in lines 75–76? (b) Explain why you think the simile is or is not effective.

7. In the fifth verse paragraph, with what did the "Wisdom and Spirit of the universe" intertwine the passions that went to make up the speaker's soul—the "work of man," or "life and nature"?

8. What simile does the speaker use in lines 131–133?

9. (a) What game or activity is described in lines 133–135? (b) What metaphor does the speaker use (lines 136–137) to expand this description?

10. What change is described in lines 144–146?

11. What do lines 147–149 imply about the character or personality of the speaker?

12. In a sentence or two of your own, summarize the speaker's attitude toward the natural world.

Unit 5, Test II
Composition

You may choose any *one* of the following assignments. Assume that you are writing your essay for your classmates.

1. Compare and contrast the various views of the evils that afflict society expressed in Blake's "Holy Thursday" (from *Songs of Experience*), Wordsworth's "London, 1802," and Shelley's "England in 1819." Discuss what solutions, if any, to society's ills are suggested in the poems.

2. Interpret Blake's "The Tyger" in the light of the following quotation from the "Proverbs of Hell": "The tygers of wrath are wiser than the horses of instruction."

3. Compare and contrast the attitudes toward the city and urban life expressed in Wordsworth's "Tintern Abbey" (lines 22–27 and 49–54), Coleridge's "Frost at Midnight (lines 48–53), and Byron's *Don Juan* (stanza 8).

4. Based upon stanzas 90 and 91 in *Don Juan,* discuss Byron's view of Wordsworth and Coleridge. Specifically, what attitudes in these two poets does Byron seem to be satirizing? Based upon your reading of *Don Juan,* how does Byron seem to differ from these two poets?

5. Discuss Blake's use of paradox (a statement that may be true but seems to say two opposite things) in the "Proverbs of Hell."

6. Discuss the relationship between art and death as revealed by Keats in "When I Have Fears," "Ode on a Grecian Urn," and "Ode to a Nightingale."

7. Contrast the education of a youth that Byron describes in *Don Juan* with that which Wordsworth describes in *The Prelude* (Test I), with particular attention to the different tones of the two selections.

8. Explain why the term the "Age of Revolt" might be a fair label for the Romantic period. Cite specific works to support your argument.

9. Discuss how each of the Romantic poets viewed the natural world. Use examples from each poet's work to illustrate the view of nature.

Unit 6:

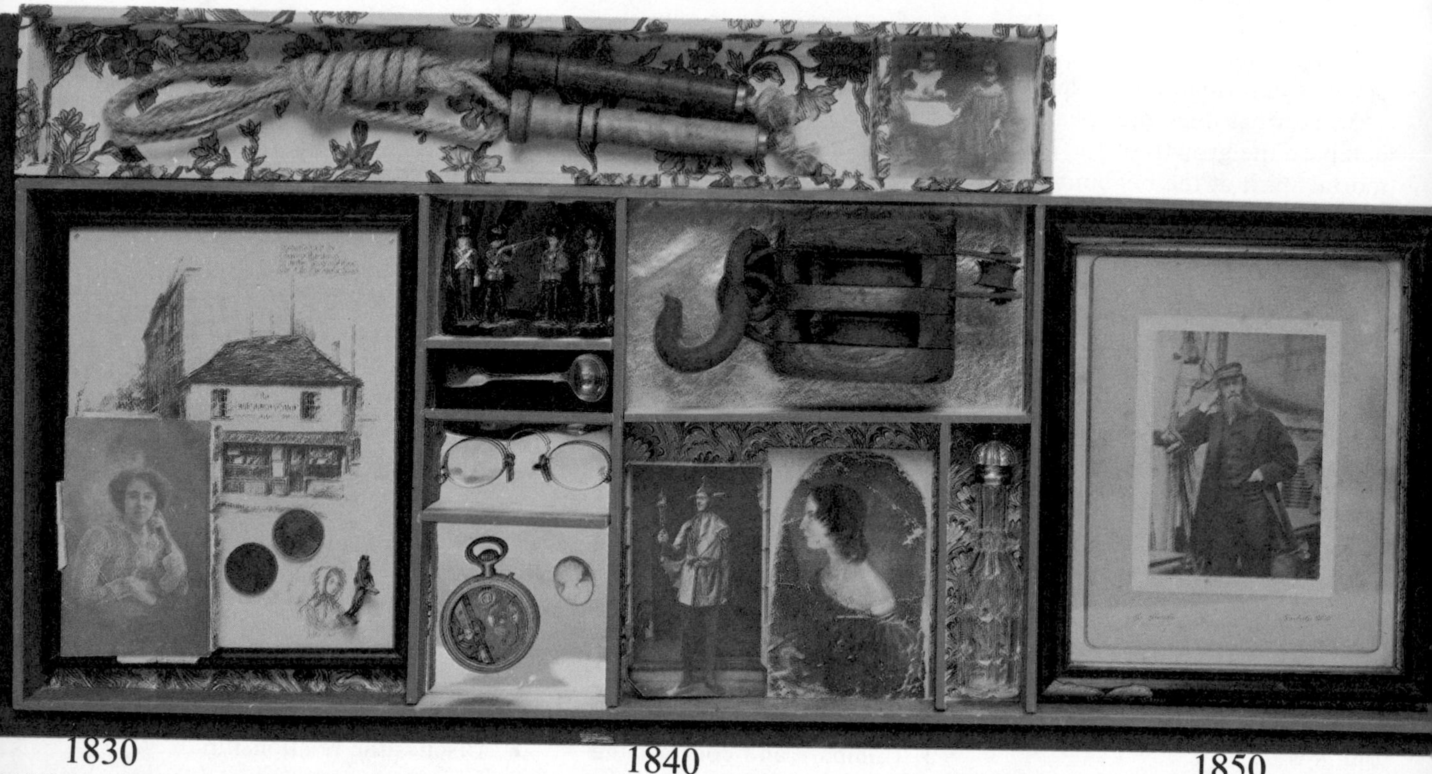

1830 1840 1850

- The Reform Bill
- Macaulay: *History of England*
- Tennyson: *In Memoriam*
- Newman *et al: Tracts for the Times*
- E. Brontë: *Wuthering Heights*
- Dickens: *Pickwick Papers*
- C. Brontë: *Jane Eyre*
- Dickens: *David Copperfield*
- Lady Charlotte Guest: *Mabinogion*
- Thackery: *Vanity Fair*
- Ruskin: *Modern Painters*
- The Crimean War
- E. B. Browning: *Sonnets from the Portuguese*
- The Great Exhibition opens

The Victorians 1830-1880

1860 | 1870 | 1880

R. Browning: *Men and Women*

• Eliot: *Silas Marner*

• C. Rossetti: *Goblin Market*

• Carroll: *Alice in Wonderland*

• Browning: *The Ring and the Book*

• Arnold: *Culture and Anarchy*

• Eliot: *Middlemarch*

• Pater: *Studies in the History of the Renaissance*

Hardy: *Return of the Native* •

• Fitzgerald: *Rubáiyát of Omar Khayyam*

• Darwin: *Origin of Species*

• Tennyson: *Idylls of the King*

• Mill: *On Liberty*

Background: The Victorians 1830-1880

In the minds of many, Queen Victoria personified the spirit of nineteenth-century England: she was Queen of the United Kingdom of Great Britain and Ireland, Empress of India, and mother of nine children; her monarchy was a model of respectability, self-righteousness, conservatism, and the domestic virtues.

By the middle of the nineteenth century, England dominated the world. Many English people were acutely conscious of their success and self-confidently pleased by it. The essayist and historian T. B. Macaulay spoke for them when he argued (in 1846) that the English had become "the greatest and most highly civilized people that ever the world saw, [they] have spread their dominion over every quarter of the globe . . . have created a maritime power which would annihilate in a quarter of an hour the navies of Tyre, Athens, Carthage, Venice, and Genoa together, have carried the science of healing, the means of locomotion and correspondence, every mechanical art, every manufacture, every thing that promotes the convenience of life, to a perfection which our ancestors would have thought magical."

When he wrote of British "dominion" Macaulay alluded to the British empire. By the Victorian era England controlled more of the earth than had any country in history.

England's world power grew out of the critical role she played in the beginning of the century. While Napoleon kept Europe embroiled in a series of bloody wars, England, isolated by the Channel, was developing into the first modern industrial state. Ready money, a skilled work force, and a government dedicated to leaving business alone, enabled ambitious middle-class factory owners to invent and develop modern production methods. During the period from 1780 to 1840 the British perfected the factory system for mass-producing goods, the practice of making interchangeable parts, and a system of railroads to carry raw materials to the factories and finished goods to the seaports. By 1850 England had eighteen thousand cotton mills, made half the pig iron in the world, and had five thousand miles of railroad track. It was the most modern, the most powerful, and the most wealthy land on earth.

Who reaped the profits? First, the middle class. They had been a small but important segment of the population for centuries. Now their numbers ballooned and their economic power dominated England commercially. These were self-made men and women, proud of the thrift, the hard work, the strict moral discipline of their lives. Most were intensely religious, sure that their success was a result of God's favor.

For hundreds of years English politics had been the playground of the aristocrats. The newly powerful middle class now demanded a share in governing, and got it in the Reform Bill of 1832 which gave them the right to vote and hold elective office.

The working class was without any political power at all, and in times of economic hardship, particularly in the late 1830s and early 1840s, England, for all of its power and success, came perilously close to a working-class revolution. A boom in the market saved the country, labor unions grew slowly but steadily, and by 1867 the British were ready, with the Second Reform Bill, to let some of the workers vote.

The tension between financial growth and social instability in Victorian England affected its literature. Prosperity brought a great number of new readers, with money to spend on books and periodicals. In a pre-electronic era, when few people went to the theater or concerts, literature functioned as a primary source of entertainment. Writers had available an audience eager to read and willing to pay. In addition, writers were respected more than at any time in English literary history. The masses knew and loved the works of the most famous, while the wealthy and titled sought their company. Major Victorian writers had the attention of political and social leaders—when they spoke, they were listened to.

The most popular, and many might say the most successful, form of writing in this era was the novel. Reading novels seems to have been an addiction for most Victorians. The most successful novelists—Dickens, Thackeray, Eliot, and Charlotte Brontë—enjoyed great fame during their lifetimes and have remained permanently popular with subsequent generations. But Victorian novels were usually long—"loose, baggy monsters" Henry James was to call them—frequently running nine-hundred pages or more.

Robert Browning

Poets faced more demanding problems than novelists. Readers frequently wanted "relevance" in what they read. The glorification of the scientific and the practical during this period made many readers and some writers sceptical about the "usefulness" of poetry.

There was, in addition, the burden of trying to continue the enormous successes of the Romantic poets. Ideas and values had shifted. Social rebellion was altogether too likely in the 1840s to make its appearance in poetry tolerable. It was less easy to praise people, now that they had become threatening industrial workers. The Romantic cult of emotion seemed dangerously excessive, and Victorian poets frequently responded with carefully balanced rationality. The Romantic love of nature remained, but frequently with a new, scientific precision of observation that replaced the old love of wildness for its own sake. Fascination with the medieval past continued, though now it was given a contemporary social significance. While in "The Eve of St. Agnes" Keats reveled in the delight of pure imagination, Tennyson in "The Passing of Arthur" saw in the trials of a medieval hero the challenges which faced the political leaders of his own era. This strong sense of public responsibility pervaded much Victorian poetry, and at times gave it an integrity missing from poetry that served only private ends.

The Victorian compromise between public concerns and private urge did not last long. By the 1860s and 1870s a rebellious new generation of writers began to break away from the conventions of midcentury.

Alfred, Lord Tennyson

Alfred, Lord Tennyson

Ulysses is one of the heroic leaders of the Greek forces during the Trojan war. In the Odyssey *Homer describes what happens to him after the Greek victory. Ulysses sails for home, but because he angers Poseidon, the god of the sea, he must wander for ten years. When he finally reaches his island kingdom he must fight to regain his crown and queen. With his victory the traditional story ends. Tennyson's poem explores the question: "But, what happened next?"*

Ulysses

It little profits that an idle king,
By this still hearth, among these barren crags,
Matched with an aged wife, I mete and dole
Unequal laws unto a savage race,
That hoard, and sleep, and feed, and know not me.
I cannot rest from travel; I will drink
Life to the lees. All times I have enjoyed
Greatly, have suffered greatly, both with those
That loved me, and alone; on shore, and when
Through scudding drifts the rainy Hyades[1]
Vexed the dim sea. I am become a name;
For always roaming with a hungry heart
Much have I seen and known—cities of men
And manners, climates, councils, governments,
Myself not least, but honored of them all—
And drunk delight of battle with my peers,
Far on the ringing plains of windy Troy.
I am part of all that I have met;
Yet all experience is an arch wherethrough
Gleams that untraveled world whose margin fades
Forever and forever when I move.
How dull it is to pause, to make an end,
To rust unburnished, not to shine in use!
As though to breathe were life! Life piled on life
Were all too little, and of one to me

1. ***rainy Hyades*** (hī′ə dēz′), constellation of stars whose appearance brought rainy weather.

Discussion

1. What does Ulysses think of **(a)** the people of his kingdom, **(b)** his wife, and **(c)** his son? Point to specific phrases which suggest his attitudes.
2. **(a)** Why does Ulysses decide to sail westward? **(b)** Do

you think his decision irresponsible? Explain your answer.

3. In what specific setting does Ulysses utter the words of this poem? How does this setting symbolize his attitude towards his own life?

Little remains; but every hour is saved
From that eternal silence, something more,
A bringer of new things; and vile it were
For some three suns to store and hoard myself,
And this gray spirit yearning in desire
To follow knowledge like a sinking star,
Beyond the utmost bound of human thought.
  This is my son, mine own Telemachus,
To whom I leave the scepter and the isle—
Well-loved of me, discerning to fulfill
This labor, by slow prudence to make mild
A rugged people, and through soft degrees
Subdue them to the useful and the good.
Most blameless is he, centered in the sphere
Of common duties, decent not to fail
In offices of tenderness, and pay
Meet adoration to my household gods,
When I am gone. He works his work, I mine.
  There lies the port; the vessel puffs her sail;
There gloom the dark, broad seas. My mariners,
Souls that have toiled, and wrought, and thought with me—
That ever with a frolic welcome took
The thunder and the sunshine, and opposed
Free hearts, free foreheads—you and I are old;
Old age hath yet his honor and his toil.
Death closes all; but something ere the end,
Some work of noble note, may yet be done,
Not unbecoming men that strove with gods.
The lights begin to twinkle from the rocks;
The long day wanes; the slow moon climbs; the deep
Moans round with many voices. Come, my friends.
'Tis not too late to seek a newer world.
Push off, and sitting well in order smite
The sounding furrows; for my purpose holds
To sail beyond the sunset, and the baths
Of all the western stars, until I die.
It may be that the gulfs will wash us down;
It may be we shall touch the Happy Isles,[2]
And see the great Achilles, whom we knew.
Though much is taken, much abides; and though
We are not now that strength which in old days
Moved earth and heaven, that which we are, we are—
One equal temper of heroic hearts,
Made weak by time and fate, but strong in will
To strive, to seek, to find, and not to yield.

2. ***To sail . . . Happy Isles.*** Ulysses conceives of the world in terms of ancient geography. The stars literally plunge into the sea (lines 60–61), boats can fall off the edge of the earth into an abyss (line 62), and somewhere in the West are the Happy Islands, a paradise for heroes now dead, like Achilles who fought with Ulysses at Troy (lines 63–64).

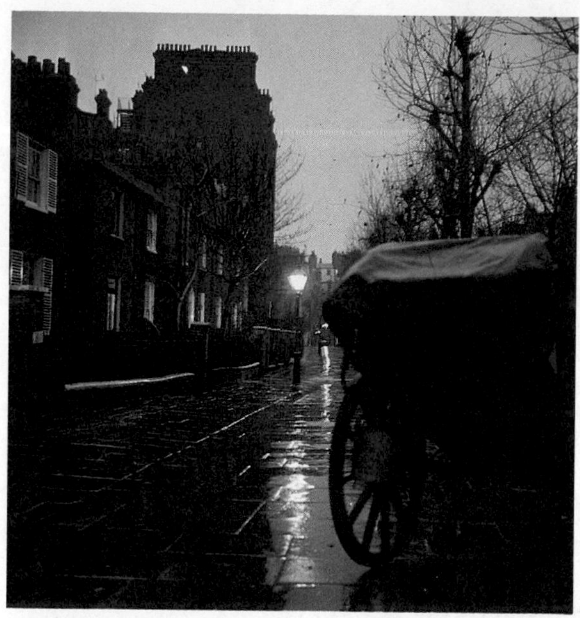
Victorian row houses. Susan MacCartney/Photo Researchers, Inc.

from In Memoriam

7

Dark house, by which once more I stand
  Here in the long unlovely street,
  Doors, where my heart was used to beat
So quickly, waiting for a hand,

A hand that can be clasped no more—
  Behold me, for I cannot sleep,
  And like a guilty thing I creep
At earliest morning to the door.

He is not here; but far away
  The noise of life begins again,
  And ghastly thro' the drizzling rain
On the bald street breaks the blank day.

34

My own dim life should teach me this,
  That life shall live for evermore,
  Else earth is darkness at the core,
And dust and ashes all that is;

This round of green, this orb of flame,
  Fantastic beauty; such as lurks
  In some wild poet, when he works
Without a conscience or an aim.

What then were God to such as I?
  'T were hardly worth my while to choose
  Of things all mortal, or to use
A little patience ere I die;

'T were best at once to sink to peace,
  Like birds the charming serpent draws,
  To drop head-foremost in the jaws
Of vacant darkness and to cease.

Discussion

1. **(a)** What does the "dark house" mean to the speaker in *In Memoriam* # 7? **(b)** How do the sounds of this lyric's third stanza suggest the speaker's feelings?

2. **(a)** In the first stanza of lyric # 34 from *In Memoriam* the speaker presents two opposing views on life's meaning. What are they? **(b)** Which of them would suggest the response described in the last stanza? Why? **(c)** Why would the conclusion that the universe has been made by a "wild poet" (line 7), rather than a benevolent God, reinforce such despair?

from Idylls of the King

"The Passing of Arthur" is the last of Tennyson's twelve Idylls of the King. *Each tells a self-contained story. Together they recount the history of Arthur and his kingdom.*

Crowned King of England, Arthur rules from Camelot and presides over his Knights of the Round Table. But success breeds jealousy. Modred seeks a way to overthrow Arthur. He discovers the guilty love between Arthur's closest friend, Lancelot, and Queen Guinevere. When he reveals this secret Guinevere flees to a convent at Almesbury where Arthur finds her "lying in the dust," repentent. Arthur must fight Lancelot, and in his absence Modred launches a rebellion. Arthur returns to defend his crown, and the following Idyll begins on the night before his last battle.

The Passing of Arthur

That story which the bold Sir Bedivere,
First made and latest left of all the knights,
Told, when the man was no more than a voice
In the white winter of his age, to those
With whom he dwelt, new faces, other minds.

For on their march to westward, Bedivere,
Who slowly paced among the slumbering host,
Heard in his tent the moanings of the King:
"I found Him in the shining of the stars,
I mark'd Him in the flowering of His fields,
But in His ways with men I find Him not.
I waged His wars, and now I pass and die.
O me! for why is all around us here
As if some lesser god had made the world,
But had not force to shape it as he would,
Till the High God behold it from beyond,
And enter it, and make it beautiful?
Or else as if the world were wholly fair,
But that these eyes of men are dense and dim,
And have not power to see it as it is.
Perchance, because we see not to the close—
For I, being simple, thought to work His will,
And have but stricken with the sword in vain;
And all whereon I lean'd in wife and friend
Is traitor to my peace, and all my realm
Reels back into the beast, and is no more.
My God, thou hast forgotten me in my death;
Nay—God my Christ—I pass but shall not die."
Then, ere that last weird battle in the West,
There came on Arthur sleeping, Gawain kill'd
In Lancelot's war,[1] the ghost of Gawain blown
Along a wandering wind, and past his ear
Went shrilling, "Hollow, hollow all delight!
Hail, King! to-morrow thou shalt pass away.
Farewell! there is an isle of rest for thee.
And I am blown along a wandering wind,
And hollow, hollow, hollow all delight."
And fainter onward, like wild birds that change
Their season[2] in the night and wail their way
From cloud to cloud, down the long wind the dream
Shrill'd; but in going mingled with dim cries
Far in the moonlit haze among the hills,
As of some lonely city sack'd by night,
When all is lost, and wife and child with wail
Pass to new lords; and Arthur woke and call'd,
"Who spake? A dream. O light upon the wind,
Thine, Gawain, was the voice—are these dim cries
Thine? or doth all that haunts the waste and wild
Mourn, knowing it will go along with me?"
This heard the bold Sir Bedivere and spake:
"O me, my King, let pass whatever will,
Elves,[3] and the harmless glamour of the field;
But in their stead thy name and glory cling
To all high places like a golden cloud
For ever; but as yet thou shalt not pass.
Light was Gawain in life, and light in death

1. ***Gawain . . . Lancelot's war.*** See headnote page 96.
2. ***wild birds . . . season,*** migrating birds flying north or south according to the season of the year.
3. ***Elves,*** elemental spirits of the wild, according to medieval folk belief; one of the peoples of Fairyland.

Illustration by Howard Pyle from *The Story of King Arthur and His Knights* (1903).

Is Gawain, for the ghost is as the man;
And care not thou for dreams from him, but rise—
I hear the steps of Modred in the West,
And with him many of thy people, and knights
Once thine, whom thou hast loved, but grosser grown
Than heathen, spitting at their vows and thee.
Right well in heart they know thee for the King.
Arise, go forth and conquer as of old."
Then spake King Arthur to Sir Bedivere:
"Far other is this battle in the West
Whereto we move, than when we strove in youth,
And brake the petty kings, and fought with Rome,
Or thrust the heathen from the Roman wall,
And shook him thro' the North. Ill doom is mine
To war against my people and my knights.
The king who fights his people fights himself.
And they my knights, who loved me once, the stroke
That strikes them dead is as my death to me.
Yet let us hence, and find or feel a way
Thro' this blind haze, which ever since I saw
One lying in the dust at Almesbury,[4]
Hath folded in the passes of the world."

Then rose the King and moved his host by night,
And ever push'd Sir Modred, league by league,
Back to the sunset bound of Lyonesse[5]—
A land of old upheaven from the abyss
By fire, to sink into the abyss again;
Where fragments of forgotten peoples dwelt,
And the long mountains ended in a coast
Of ever-shifting sand, and far away
The phantom circle of a moaning sea.
There the pursuer could pursue no more,
And he that fled no further fly the King;
And there, that day when the great light of heaven
Burn'd at his lowest[6] in the rolling year,

4. ***One . . . Almesbury*** (ämz′bėr ē). According to Tennyson, Queen Guinevere fled to the nunnery at Almesbury. Arthur pursued her there. When she heard his steps approaching the door of her nun's cell, she fell from her chair "And grovell'd with her face against the floor." (*Guinevere,* line 412)

5. ***Lyonesse*** (lī′ō nes′), a legendary country supposed to have once been attached to the peninsula of Cornwall, but long since sunk under the sea. Lyonesse is sometimes identified with Cornwall itself.

6. ***Burn'd at his lowest,*** the time of the winter solstice.

On the waste sand by the waste sea they closed.
Nor ever yet had Arthur fought a fight
Like this last, dim, weird battle of the West.
A deathwhite mist slept over sand and sea;
Whereof the chill, to him who breathed it, drew
Down with his blood, till all his heart was cold
With formless fear. And ev'n on Arthur fell
Confusion, since he saw not whom he fought.
For friend and foe were shadows in the mist,
And friend slew friend not knowing whom he slew;
And some had visions out of golden youth,
And some beheld the faces of old ghosts
Look in upon the battle. And in the mist
Was many a noble deed, many a base,
And chance and craft and strength in single fights,
And ever and anon with host to host
Shocks, and the splintering spear, the hard mail hewn,
Shield-breakings, and the clash of brands,[7] the crash
Of battleaxes on shatter'd helms, and shrieks
After the Christ, of those who falling down
Look'd up for heaven, and only saw the mist;
And shouts of heathen and the traitor knights,
Oaths, insult, filth, and monstrous blasphemies,
Sweat, writhings, anguish, labouring of the lungs
In that close mist, and cryings of the light,
Moans of the dying, and voices of the dead.
Last, as by some one deathbed after wail
Of suffering, silence follows, or thro' death
Or deathlike swoon, thus over all that shore,
Save for some whisper of the seething seas,
A dead hush fell; but when the dolorous day
Grew drearier toward twilight falling, came
A bitter wind, clear from the North, and blew
The mist aside, and with that wind the tide
Rose, and the pale King glanced across the field
Of battle: but no man was moving there;
Nor any cry of Christian heard thereon,
Nor yet of heathen; only the wan wave
Brake in among dead faces, to and fro
Swaying the helpless hands, and up and down
Tumbling the hollow helmets of the fallen,
And shiver'd brands that once had fought with Rome,
And rolling far along the gloomy shores
The voice of days of old and days to be.
Then spake King Arthur to Sir Bedivere,
And whiter than the mist that all day long
Had held the field of battle was the King:
"Hearest thou this great voice that shakes the world,
And wastes the narrow realm whereon we move,
And beats upon the faces of the dead,
My dead, as tho' they had not died for me?—
O Bedivere, for on my heart hath fall'n
Confusion, till I know not what I am,
Nor whence I am, nor whether I be King,
Behold, I seem but King among the dead."
  Then spake the bold Sir Bedivere: "My King,
King everywhere! and so the dead have kings,
There also will I worship thee as King.
Yet still thy life is whole, and still I live
Who love thee; but who hates thee, he that brought
The heathen back among us, yonder stands,
Modred unharm'd, the traitor of thine house."
  Then spake the King: "My house hath been my doom.
But call not thou this traitor of my house
Who hath but dwelt beneath one roof with me.
My house are rather they who sware my vows,
Yea, even while they brake them, own'd me King.
And well for thee, saying in my dark hour,
When all the purport of my throne hath fail'd,
That quick or dead thou holdest me for King.
King am I, whatsoever be their cry;
And one last act of knighthood shalt thou see
Yet, ere I pass." And uttering this the King
Made at the man: then Modred smote his liege
Hard on that helm which many a heathen sword
Had beaten thin; while Arthur at one blow,
Striking the last stroke with Excalibur,
Slew him, and all but slain himself, he fell.
  So all day long the noise of battle roll'd
Among the mountains by the winter sea;
Until King Arthur's Table, man by man,
Had fall'n in Lyonesse about their lord,
King Arthur. Then, because his wound was deep,
The bold Sir Bedivere uplifted him,
And bore him to a chapel nigh the field,

7. ***brands,*** swords.

A broken chancel[8] with a broken cross,
That stood on a dark strait of barren land:
On one side lay the Ocean, and on one
Lay a great water, and the moon was full.
Then spake King Arthur to Sir Bedivere:
"The sequel of to-day unsolders all
The goodliest fellowship of famous knights
Whereof this world holds record. Such a sleep
They sleep—the men I loved. I think that we
Shall never more, at any future time,
Delight our souls with talk of knightly deeds,
Walking about the gardens and the halls
Of Camelot, as in the days that were.
I perish by this people which I made,—
Tho' Merlin[9] sware that I should come again
To rule once more; but, let what will be, be,
I am so deeply smitten thro' the helm
That without help I cannot last till morn.
Thou therefore take my brand Excalibur,
Which was my pride: for thou rememberest how
In those old days, one summer noon, an arm
Rose up from out the bosom of the lake,
Clothed in white samite,[10] mystic, wonderful,
Holding the sword—and how I row'd across
And took it, and have worn it, like a king;
And, wheresoever I am sung or told
In aftertime, this also shall be known;
But now delay not: take Excalibur,
And fling him far into the middle mere:
Watch what thou seest, and lightly bring me word."
To him replied the bold Sir Bedivere:
"It is not meet, Sir King, to leave thee thus,
Aidless, alone, and smitten thro' the helm—
A little thing may harm a wounded man;
Yet I thy hest will all perform at full,
Watch what I see, and lightly bring thee word."
So saying, from the ruin'd shrine he stept,
And in the moon athwart the place of tombs,
Where lay the mighty bones of ancient men,
Old knights, and over them the sea wind sang
Shrill, chill, with flakes of foam. He, stepping down
By zigzag paths, and juts of pointed rock,
Came on the shining levels of the lake.
There drew he forth the brand Excalibur,
And o'er him, drawing it, the winter moon,
Brightening the skirts of a long cloud, ran forth
And sparkled keen with frost against the hilt;
For all the haft twinkled with diamond sparks,
Myriads of topaz lights, and jacinth work
Of subtlest jewellery. He gazed so long
That both his eyes were dazzled as he stood,
This way and that dividing the swift mind,
In act to throw: but at the last it seem'd
Better to leave Excalibur conceal'd
There in the many-knotted waterflags,
That whistled stiff and dry about the marge.
So strode he back slow to the wounded King.
Then spake King Arthur to Sir Bedivere:
"Hast thou perform'd my mission which I gave?
What is it thou hast seen? or what hast heard?"
And answer made the bold Sir Bedivere:
"I heard the ripple washing in the reeds,
And the wild water lapping on the crag."
To whom replied King Arthur, faint and pale:
"Thou hast betray'd thy nature and thy name,
Not rendering true answer, as beseem'd
Thy fealty, nor like a noble knight:
For surer sign had follow'd, either hand,
Or voice, or else a motion of the mere.
This is a shameful thing for men to lie.
Yet now, I charge thee, quickly go again,
As thou art lief[11] and dear, and do the thing
I bade thee, watch, and lightly bring me word."
Then went Sir Bedivere the second time
Across the ridge, and paced beside the mere,
Counting the dewy pebbles, fix'd in thought;
But when he saw the wonder of the hilt,
How curiously and strangely chased,[12] he smote
His palms together, and he cried aloud:
"And if indeed I cast the brand away,
Surely a precious thing, one worthy note,
Should thus be lost for ever from the earth,
Which might have pleased the eyes of many men.
What good should follow this, if this were done?
What harm, undone? Deep harm to disobey,
Seeing obedience is the bond of rule.
Were it well to obey then, if a king demand
An act unprofitable, against himself?

---

8. ***chancel*** (chan′sel), the space around the altar of a church.
9. ***Merlin*** (mėr′lən), a magician and prophet who was Arthur's chief advisor. At the beginning of the king's reign, Merlin had prophesied that Arthur would not die, but return to rule.
10. ***samite*** (sam′it), a rich, heavy silk fabric.
11. ***lief*** (lēf), beloved.
12. ***chased*** (chāsd′d) carved or engraved.

The King is sick, and knows not what he does.
What record, or what relic of my lord
Should be to aftertime, but empty breath
And rumours of a doubt? But were this kept,
Stored in some treasure-house of mighty kings,
Some one might show it at a joust of arms,
Saying, 'King Arthur's sword, Excalibur,
Wrought by the lonely maiden of the Lake.
Nine years she wrought it, sitting in the deeps
Upon the hidden bases of the hills.'
So might some old man speak in the aftertime
To all the people, winning reverence.
But now much honour and much fame were
lost."
So spake he, clouded with his own conceit,[13]
And hid Excalibur the second time,
And so strode back slow to the wounded King.
Then spoke King Arthur, breathing heavily:
"What is it thou hast seen? or what hast heard?"
And answer made the bold Sir Bedivere:
"I heard the water lapping on the crag,
And the long ripple washing in the reeds."
To whom replied King Arthur, much in wrath:
"Ah, miserable and unkind, untrue,
Unknightly, traitor-hearted! Woe is me!
Authority forgets a dying king,
Laid widow'd of the power in his eye
That bow'd the will. I see thee what thou art,
For thou, the latest-left of all my knights,
In whom should meet the offices of all,
Thou wouldst betray me for the precious hilt;
Either from lust of gold, or like a girl
Valuing the giddy pleasure of the eyes.
Yet, for a man may fail in duty twice,
And the third time may prosper, get thee hence.
But, if thou spare to fling Excalibur,
I will arise and slay thee with my hands."
Then quickly rose Sir Bedivere, and ran,
And, leaping down the ridges lightly, plunged
Among the bulrush beds, and clutch'd the
sword,
And strongly wheel'd and threw it. The great
brand
Made lightnings in the splendour of the moon,
And flashing round and round, and whirl'd in
an arch,
Shot like a streamer of the northern morn,
Seen where the moving isles of winter shock
By night, with noises of the Northern Sea.[14]
So flash'd and fell the brand Excalibur.
But ere he dipt the surface, rose an arm
Clothed in white samite, mystic, wonderful,
And caught him by the hilt, and brandish'd him
Three times, and drew him under in the mere.
And lightly went the other to the King.
Then spoke King Arthur, drawing thicker breath:
"Now see I by thine eyes that this is done.
Speak out: what is it thou hast heard, or seen?"
And answer made the bold Sir Bedivere:
"Sir King, I closed mine eyelids, lest the gems
Should blind my purpose, for I never saw,
Nor shall see, here or elsewhere, till I die,
Not tho' I live three lives of mortal men,
So great a miracle as yonder hilt.
Then with both hands I flung him, wheeling him;
But when I look'd again, behold an arm,
Clothed in white samite, mystic, wonderful,
That caught him by the hilt, and brandish'd him
Three times, and drew him under in the mere."
And answer made King Arthur, breathing hard:
"My end draws nigh; 'tis time that I were gone.
Make broad thy shoulders to receive my weight,
And bear me to the margin; yet I fear
My wound hath taken cold, and I shall die."
So saying, from the pavement he half rose,
Slowly, with pain, reclining on his arm,
And looking wistfully with wide blue eyes
As in a picture. Him Sir Bedivere
Remorsefully regarded thro' his tears,
And would have spoken, but he found not
words;
Then took with care, and kneeling on one knee,
O'er both his shoulders drew the languid hands,
And rising bore him thro' the place of tombs.
But, as he walk'd, King Arthur panted hard,
Like one that feels a nightmare on his bed
When all the house is mute. So sigh'd the King,
Muttering and murmuring at his ear, "Quick,
quick!
I fear it is too late, and I shall die."
But the other swiftly strode from ridge to ridge,
Clothed with his breath, and looking, as he
walk'd,
Larger than human on the frozen hills.
He heard the deep behind him, and a cry

13. ***conceit,*** an idea or notion, often a farfetched one.
14. ***Shot like a streamer . . . the Northern Sea.*** The comparison here is between the flight of the sword and the aurora borealis, the "northern lights," bands of light appearing in the sky around the polar regions. The "moving isles of winter" are icebergs.

Before. His own thought drove him like a goad.
Dry clash'd his harness in the icy caves
And barren chasms, and all to left and right
The bare black cliff clang'd round him, as he based
His feet on juts of slippery crag that rang
Sharp-smitten with the dint of armed heels—
And on a sudden, lo! the level lake,
And the long glories of the winter moon.
Then saw they how there hove a dusky barge,
Dark as a funeral scarf from stem to stern,
Beneath them; and descending they were ware[15]
That all the decks were dense with stately forms,
Black-stoled, black-hooded, like a dream—by these
Three Queens with crowns of gold. And from them rose
A cry that shiver'd to the tingling stars,
And, as it were one voice, an agony
Of lamentation, like a wind that shrills
All night in a waste land, where no one comes,
Or hath come, since the making of the world.
Then murmur'd Arthur, "Place me in the barge."
So to the barge they came. There those three Queens
Put forth their hands, and took the King, and wept.
But she, that rose the tallest of them all
And fairest, laid his head upon her lap,
And loosed the shatter'd casque, and chafed his hands,
And call'd him by his name, complaining loud,
And dropping bitter tears against a brow
Striped with dark blood: for all his face was white
And colourless, and like the wither'd moon
Smote by the fresh beam of the springing east;
And all his greaves and cuisses dash'd with drops
Of onset;[16] and the light and lustrous curls—
That made his forehead like a rising sun
High from the dais-throne—were parch'd with dust;
Or clotted into points and hanging loose,
Mix'd with the knightly growth that fringed his lips.
So like a shatter'd column lay the King;
Not like that Arthur who, with lance in rest,
From spur to plume a star of tournament,
Shot thro' the lists at Camelot, and charged
Before the eyes of ladies and of kings.
Then loudly cried the bold Sir Bedivere:
"Ah! my Lord Arthur, whither shall I go?
Where shall I hide my forehead and my eyes?
For now I see the true old times are dead,
When every morning brought a noble chance,
And every chance brought out a noble knight.
Such times have been not since the light that led
The holy Elders with the gift of myrrh.[17]
But now the whole Round Table is dissolved
Which was an image of the mighty world,
And I, the last, go forth companionless,
And the days darken round me, and the years,
Among new men, strange faces, other minds."
And slowly answer'd Arthur from the barge:
"The old order changeth, yielding place to new,
And God fulfils himself in many ways,
Lest one good custom should corrupt the world.
Comfort thyself; what comfort is in me?
I have lived my life, and that which I have done
May He within himself make pure! but thou,
If thou shouldst never see my face again,
Pray for my soul. More things are wrought by prayer
Than this world dreams of. Wherefore, let thy voice
Rise like a fountain for me night and day.
For what are men better than sheep or goats
That nourish a blind life within the brain,
If, knowing God, they lift not hands of prayer
Both for themselves and those who call them friend?
For so the whole round earth is every way
Bound by gold chains about the feet of God.
But now farewell. I am going a long way
With these thou seest—if indeed I go
(For all my mind is clouded with a doubt)—
To the island-valley of Avilion;[18]
Where falls not hail, or rain, or any snow.
Nor ever wind blows loudly; but it lies
Deep-meadow'd, happy, fair with orchard lawns
And bowery hollows crown'd with summer sea,
Where I will heal me of my grievous wound."
So said he, and the barge with oar and sail

---

15. ***ware,*** aware.
16. ***onset,*** combat; "drops / Of onset" are of blood.
17. ***holy Elders . . . myrrh.*** The three Magi, or priestly kings, were led by a star to the birthplace of Christ, each carrying a gift. One of the gifts was *myrrh* (mėr), a fragrant resin.
18. ***Avilion*** (ə vil′ē ən), or *Avalon,* one of the paradisiacal isles of Celtic legend, located in the West.

Moved from the brink, like some full-breasted swan
That, fluting a wild carol ere her death,
Ruffles her pure cold plume, and takes the flood
With swarthy webs. Long stood Sir Bedivere
Revolving many memories, till the hull
Look'd one black dot against the verge of dawn,
And on the mere the wailing died away.
But when that moan had past for ever more,
The stillness of the dead world's winter dawn
Amazed him, and he groan'd, "The King is gone."
And therewithal came on him the weird rhyme,
"From the great deep to the great deep he goes."
Whereat he slowly turn'd and slowly clomb
The last hard footstep of that iron crag;
Thence mark'd the black hull moving yet, and cried,
"He passes to be King among the dead,
And after healing of his grievous wound
He comes again; but—if he come no more—
O me, be yon dark Queens in yon black boat,
Who shriek'd and wail'd, the three whereat we gazed
On that high day, when, clothed with living light,
They stood before his throne in silence, friends
Of Arthur, who should help him at his need?"
Then from the dawn it seem'd there came, but faint
As from beyond the limit of the world,
Like the last echo born of a great cry,
Sounds, as if some fair city were one voice
Around a king returning from his wars.
Thereat once more he moved about, and clomb
Ev'n to the highest he could climb, and saw,
Straining his eyes beneath an arch of hand,
Or thought he saw, the speck that bare the King,
Down that long water opening on the deep
Somewhere far off, pass on and on, and go
From less to less and vanish into light.
And the new sun rose bringing the new year.

Discussion

1. In "The Passing of Arthur," what kind of spiritual crisis does Arthur face the night before the battle? Consider, in particular, lines 9–17.

2. In what ways does the setting of the battle in the west underscore its finality?

3. **(a)** What are Bedivere's reasons for twice refusing to throw away Excalibur? **(b)** How is he able, finally, to do it? **(c)** What do Bedivere's failures suggest?

4. In his final speech (especially lines 408–410) how does Arthur account for the failure of his realm?

5. What does Tennyson suggest about the future in the way he describes the departure of Arthur's mysterious barge?

Alfred Tennyson 1809 • 1892

The most important event in the life of Alfred Tennyson was the death of his friend, Arthur Henry Hallam. The months following the tragedy were, for Tennyson, the most poetically fruitful of his life. Rather than yield to his suicidal inclinations, he turned to his poetry as a vent for his despair and as a source for hope. Along with short, lyric poems about Hallam's death and his own grief he also wrote most of "The Passing of Arthur," a poem in which the medieval king's death parallels the loss of his own Arthur Hallam. At the same time Tennyson sought new hope through poems such as "Ulysses," in which the protagonist counters despair with energy, resolution, and hope.

These were lean years. His poetry was almost completely unknown. Yet he was determined to become a great poet. Living on a tiny annuity, in love with a girl he couldn't afford to marry, he disciplined himself and his art. In 1842 he published two volumes of poetry which met with some success.

But his first great triumph came in 1850 with the publication of *In Memoriam.* In this book Tennyson welds together over a hundred of the separate lyric poems he had written about Hallam's death into a single, unified work. The book was an immediate success with critics and readers. Tennyson could now afford to marry, and later in the same year Queen Victoria named him poet laureate. Tennyson lived until 1892, the most famous, respected, and popular poet of his century.

Robert Browning

Porphyria's Lover

The rain set early in tonight,
  The sullen wind was soon awake,
It tore the elm-tops down for spite,
  And did its worst to vex the lake:
  I listened with heart fit to break.
When glided in Porphyria; straight
  She shut the cold out and the storm,
And kneeled and made the cheerless grate
  Blaze up, and all the cottage warm;
  Which done, she rose, and from her form
Withdrew the dripping cloak and shawl,
  And laid her soiled gloves by, untied
Her hat and let the damp hair fall,
  And, last, she sat down by my side
  And called me. When no voice replied,
She put my arm about her waist,
  And made her smooth white shoulder bare,
And all her yellow hair displaced,
  And, stooping, made my cheek lie there,
  And spread, o'er all, her yellow hair,
Murmuring how she loved me—she
  Too weak, for all her heart's endeavor,
To set its struggling passion free
  From pride, and vainer ties dissever,
  And give herself to me forever.
But passion sometimes would prevail,
  Nor could tonight's gay feast restrain
A sudden thought of one so pale
  For love of her, and all in vain:
  So, she was come through wind and rain.
Be sure I looked up at her eyes
  Happy and proud; at last I knew
Porphyria worshiped me: surprise
  Made my heart swell, and still it grew
  While I debated what to do.
That moment she was mine, mine, fair,
  Perfectly pure and good: I found
A thing to do, and all her hair
  In one long yellow string I wound
  Three times her little throat around,
And strangled her. No pain felt she;
  I am quite sure she felt no pain.
As a shut bud that holds a bee,
  I warily oped her lids: again
  Laughed the blue eyes without a stain.
And I untightened next the tress
  About her neck; her cheek once more
Blushed bright beneath my burning kiss:
  I propped her head up as before,
  Only, this time my shoulder bore
Her head, which droops upon it still:
  The smiling rosy little head,
So glad it has its utmost will,
  That all it scorned at once is fled,
  And I, its love, am gained instead!
Porphyria's love: she guessed not how
  Her darling one wish would be heard.
And thus we sit together now,
  And all night long we have not stirred,
  And yet God has not said a word!

Discussion

1. (a) What is odd about the way Porphyria's Lover welcomes her when she enters? (b) Why does he act this way?

2. How does the lover describe the way he murdered Porphyria? Why does he talk this way?

The time is the 16th century, the scene the city of Ferrara in northern Italy. The speaker is the Duke of Ferrara.

My Last Duchess

That's my last duchess painted on the wall,
Looking as if she were alive. I call
That piece a wonder, now: Frà Pandolf's hands
Worked busily a day, and there she stands.
Will 't please you sit and look at her? I said
"Frà Pandolf" by design, for never read
Strangers like you that pictured countenance,
The depth and passion of its earnest glance,
But to myself they turned (since none puts by
The curtain I have drawn for you, but I)
And seemed as they would ask me, if they durst,
How such a glance came there; so, not the first
Are you to turn and ask thus. Sir, 'twas not
Her husband's presence only, called that spot
Of joy into the Duchess' cheek: perhaps
Frà Pandolf chanced to say "Her mantle laps
Over my lady's wrist too much," or "Paint
Must never hope to reproduce the faint
Half-flush that dies along her throat": such stuff
Was courtesy, she thought, and cause enough
For calling up that spot of joy. She had
A heart—how shall I say?—too soon made glad,
Too easily impressed; she liked whate'er
She looked on, and her looks went everywhere.
Sir, 'twas all one! My favor at her breast,
The dropping of the daylight in the West,
The bough of cherries some officious fool
Broke in the orchard for her, the white mule
She rode with round the terrace—all and each
Would draw from her alike the approving speech,
Or blush, at least. She thanked men—good! but thanked
Somehow—I know not how—as if she ranked
My gift of a nine-hundred-years-old name
With anybody's gift. Who'd stoop to blame
This sort of trifling? Even had you skill
In speech—which I have not—to make your will
Quite clear to such an one, and say, "Just this
Or that in you disgusts me; here you miss,
Or there exceed the mark"—and if she let
Herself be lessoned so, nor plainly set

Her wits to yours, forsooth, and made excuse—
E'en then would be some stooping; and I choose
Never to stoop. Oh sir, she smiled, no doubt,
Whene'er I passed her; but who passed without
Much the same smile? This grew; I gave commands;
Then all smiles stopped together. There she stands
As if alive. Will 't please you rise? We'll meet
The company below, then. I repeat,
The Count your master's known munificence
Is ample warrant that no just pretense
Of mine for dowry will be disallowed;
Though his fair daughter's self, as I avowed
At starting, is my object. Nay, we'll go
Together down, sir. Notice Neptune, though,
Taming a sea-horse, thought a rarity,
Which Claus of Innsbruck cast in bronze for me!

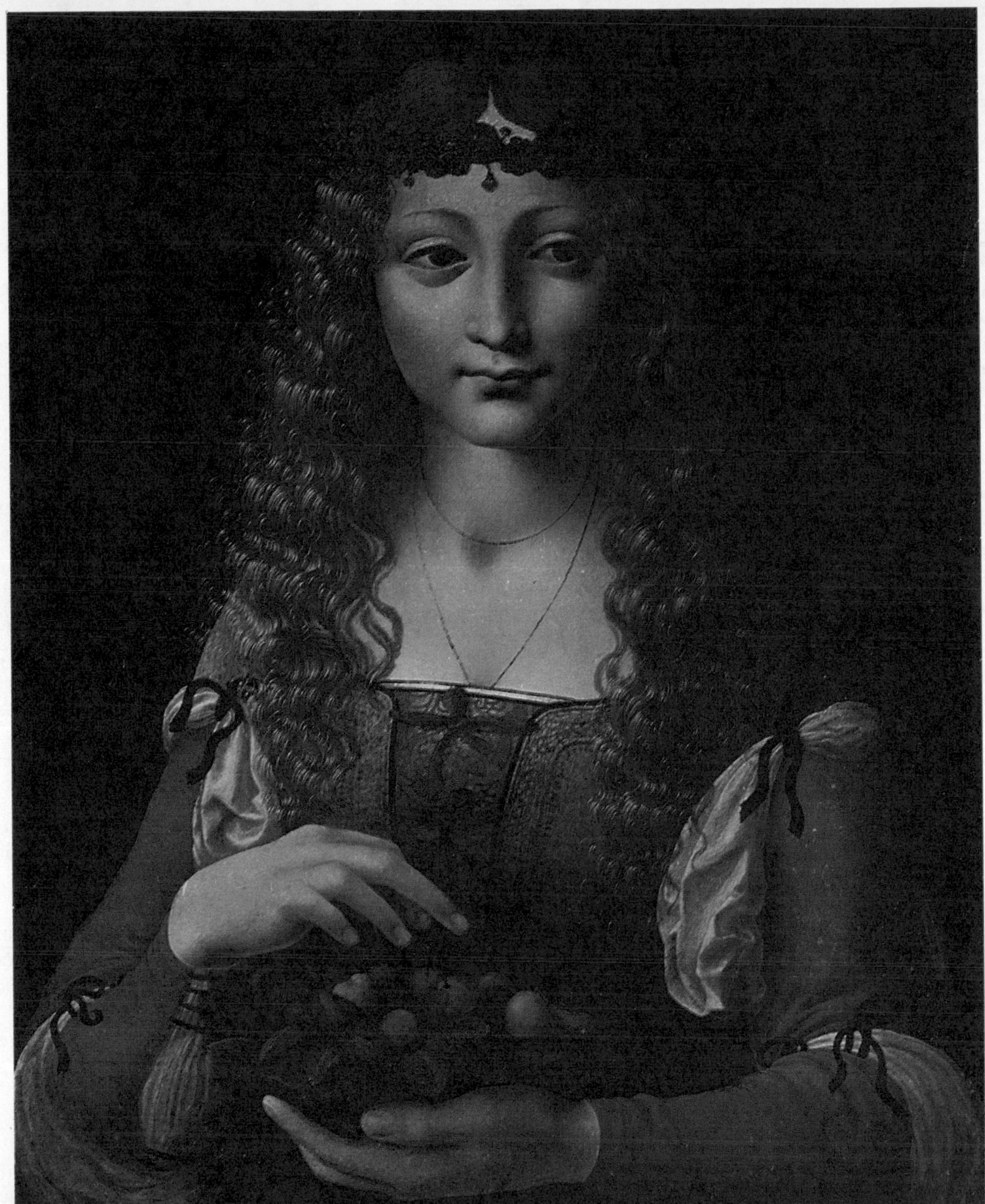

Discussion

1. "My Last Duchess" is Browning's portrait of the Duke. Point out the details which suggest his: **(a)** good taste in art; **(b)** polished manners; **(c)** pride; **(d)** insecurity; **(e)** ruthless authority. Are there still other important characteristics in this portrait?

2. **(a)** What did the Duke not like about his last Duchess? Would you criticize her for this characteristic? Why? **(b)** Why did the Duchess die? **(c)** To whom is the Duke talking now? **(d)** Why does he show this person the portrait?

The Dramatic Monologue

See if you can answer the following questions about Tennyson's "Ulysses" and Browning's "My Last Duchess." **(1)** Who is talking? **(2)** Whom is he addressing? **(3)** Where are they? **(4)** Why is the speaker talking?

You will note that all these questions can be readily answered through information supplied by the poem's speaker. In a play a character can simply talk about ideas and feelings. But in poems such as these the characters' *own words* must also create a sense of place, occasion, and purpose. Such a poem is then called a **dramatic monologue.**

Creating a character who says things with the intention of getting one kind of reaction, but who actually creates an opposite reaction in his listeners, requires particular skill. The trick of making a character unconsciously demonstrate flaws is called *undercutting.* Do you think Tennyson undercuts Ulysses? Or can we accept his statements literally?

Presumably the nature of the person listening to the speaker's words, and the occasion for their conversation, affects how the speaker talks. To test this in the poems under consideration ask yourself how the Duke would talk if he were speaking not to an official emissary from a nobleman but to a young girl he wants to marry.

Robert Browning 1812 • 1889

Browning was lucky in his parents. His father, employed in a bank, was a man of genuine intelligence, who owned a library of six thousand volumes and seems to have read them all. His mother, a devoutly religious woman, gave Browning a tenderness and optimism he would need frequently in life.

The poems came early—a book of them when he was thirteen and another, his first published volume, when he was twenty-one (1833). Not one copy sold. But a sharp-eyed reviewer noted the "intense and morbid self-consciousness" of the book. Deeply pained by the accuracy of this criticism, Browning began to discipline his writing. Instead of revealing his private emotions he strove to create characters quite different from himself who spoke on their own. He began with plays, most of them unsuccessful. But by the 1840s he was also writing dramatic monologues in which invented characters tell the reader about their personalities and their worlds through what they say.

In 1844 Browning read the newly published *Poems* of Elizabeth Barrett and found there a kind reference to his own, virtually unknown work. He wrote her a letter and soon they were corresponding. Four months later they met for the first time. She was thirty-nine at the time, six years Browning's senior, and considered a permanent invalid. The day after they met he sent her a passionate love letter.

Her domineering father refused to consider the possibility of marriage. Finally, Browning persuaded her to marry him and they eloped, escaping to Italy during the autumn of 1846. Her father never forgave her, never opened a letter from her for the rest of his life.

In Italy they settled in Florence where, for fourteen years, they lived a happy and productive life. Elizabeth Barrett was a famous, respected, and successful poet, Browning relatively unknown. Under Elizabeth's encouragement he now wrote his first complete masterpiece, *Men and Women,* fifty dramatic monologues uttered by fifty different characters. Another collection of dramatic monologues, *Dramatis Personae* (1864), ran into a second edition. Finally, critical adulation and genuine popularity met Browning's retelling of a Roman murder in *The Ring and the Book* (1868–69).

Matthew Arnold

Dover Beach

The sea is calm tonight,
The tide is full, the moon lies fair
Upon the straits; on the French coast the light
Gleams and is gone; the cliffs of England stand,
Glimmering and vast, out in the tranquil bay.
Come to the window, sweet is the night air!

Only, from the long line of spray
Where the sea meets the moon-blanched land,
Listen! you hear the grating roar
Of pebbles which the waves draw back, and fling,
At their return, up the high strand,
Begin, and cease, and then again begin,
With tremulous cadence slow, and bring
The eternal note of sadness in.

Sophocles[1] long ago
Heard it on the Aegean, and it brought
Into his mind the turbid ebb and flow
Of human misery; we
Find also in the sound a thought,
Hearing it by this distant northern sea.

The Sea of Faith
Was once, too, at the full, and round earth's shore
Lay like the folds of a bright girdle furled.
But now I only hear
Its melancholy, long, withdrawing roar,
Retreating, to the breath
Of the night wind, down the vast edges drear
And naked shingles[2] of the world.

Ah, love, let us be true
To one another! for the world, which seems
To lie before us like a land of dreams,
So various, so beautiful, so new,
Hath really neither joy, nor love, nor light,
Nor certitude, nor peace, nor help for pain;
And we are here as on a darkling plain
Swept with confused alarms of struggle and flight,
Where ignorant armies clash by night.

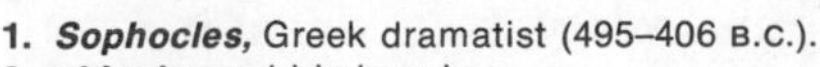

1. ***Sophocles,*** Greek dramatist (495–406 B.C.).
2. ***shingles,*** pebble beaches.

Norfolk Coast. Erich Hartmann/Magnum Photos.

Self-Dependence

1

Weary of myself, and sick of asking
What I am, and what I ought to be,
At this vessel's prow I stand, which bears me
Forwards, forwards o'er the starlit sea.

2

And a look of passionate desire
O'er the sea and to the stars I send:
"Ye who from my childhood up have
calmed me,
Calm me, ah, compose me to the end!

3

"Ah, once more," I cried, "ye stars, ye waters,
On my heart your mighty charm renew;
Still, still let me, as I gaze upon you,
Feel my soul becoming vast like you!"

4

From the intense, clear, star-sown vault of
heaven,
Over the lit sea's unquiet way,
In the rustling night-air came the answer:
"Wouldst thou *be* as these are? *Live* as they.

5

"Unaffrighted by the silence round them,
Undistracted by the sights they see,
These demand not that the things without them
Yield them love, amusement, sympathy.

6

"And with joy the stars perform their shining,
And the sea its long moon-silvered roll;
For self-poised they live, nor pine with noting
All the fever of some differing soul.

7

"Bounded by themselves, and unregardful
In what state God's other works may be,
In their own tasks all their powers pouring,
These attain the mighty life you see."

8

O air-born voice! long since, severely clear,
A cry like thine in mine own heart I hear:
"Resolve to be thyself; and know that he
Who finds himself loses his misery!"

Discussion

1. In what ways does the image of the moon-lit ocean change in the first four stanzas of "Dover Beach"?

2. Why does the speaker of "Dover Beach" beg his "love" to "be true" (line 29)?

3. How does the natural scene the speaker is looking at suggest the final image of "Dover Beach"?

4. **(a)** What spiritual malady afflicts the speaker at the beginning of "Self-Dependence"? **(b)** Why does he turn to the stars for help?

Matthew Arnold 1822 • 1888

Almost all of Arnold's poetry comes from the years of his young manhood. After four years at Oxford (1841–1844) and a couple of years as a poet-graduate fellow, he served as private secretary to an English nobleman (1847) until, in order to marry the woman he loved, he took a government job (1851). During these years Arnold read a great deal, thought with pain about the confusion and division of his own era, and wrote about his emotional and intellectual tensions in the lyrics which have preserved his reputation as a poet. "Self-Dependence" (written around 1850) and "Dover Beach" (written around 1851) are typical of both the content and the style of Arnold's best poetry.

For the government he served as an inspector of schools, and for many years he traveled back and forth across England giving tests, visiting classrooms, and writing official reports. It was taxing, usually dull work. But Arnold's sense of public obligation, of the significant role the schools played in society, kept him at it.

Emily Brontë

Ah! Why, Because the Dazzling Sun

Ah! why, because the dazzling sun
Restored my earth to joy
Have you departed, every one,
And left a desert sky?

All through the night, your glorious eyes
Were gazing down in mine,
And with a full heart's thankful sighs
I blessed that watch divine!

I was at peace, and drank your beams
As they were life to me
And revelled in my changeful dreams
Like petrel on the sea.

Thought followed thought—star followed star
Through boundless regions on,
While one sweet influence, near and far,
Thrilled through and proved us one.

Why did the morning rise to break
So great, so pure a spell,
And scorch with fire the tranquil cheek
Where your cool radiance fell?

Blood-red he rose, and arrow-straight
His fierce beams struck my brow:
The soul of Nature sprang elate,
But mine sank sad and low!

My lids closed down—yet through their veil
I saw him blazing still;
And bathe in gold the misty dale,
And flash upon the hill.

I turned me to the pillow then
To call back Night, and see
Your worlds of solemn light, again
Throb with my heart and me!

It would not do—the pillow glowed
And glowed both roof and floor,
And birds sang loudly in the wood,
And fresh winds shook the door.

The curtains waved, the wakened flies
Were murmuring round my room,
Imprisoned there, till I should rise
And give them leave to roam.

O Stars and Dreams and Gentle Night;
O Night and Stars return!
And hide me from the hostile light
That does not warm, but burn—

That drains the blood of suffering men;
Drinks tears, instead of dew:
Let me sleep through his blinding reign,
And only wake with you!

Discussion

For what reasons does the speaker of "Ah! why, because the dazzling sun. . ." hate the sunlight? Why does she like the night and the starlight?

The Night Wind

In summer's mellow midnight,
A cloudless moon shone through
Our open parlour window
And rosetrees wet with dew.

I sat in silent musing,
The soft wind waved my hair:
It told me Heaven was glorious.
And sleeping Earth was fair.

I needed not its breathing
To bring such thoughts to me,
But still it whispered lowly,
"How dark the woods will be!

"The thick leaves in my murmur
Are rustling like a dream,
And all their myriad voices
Instinct with spirit seem."

I said, "Go, gentle singer,
Thy wooing voice is kind,
But do not think its music
Has power to reach my mind.

"Play with the scented flower,
The young tree's supple bough,
And leave my human feelings
In their own course to flow."

The wanderer would not leave me;
Its kiss grew warmer still—
"O come," it sighed so sweetly,
"I'll win thee 'gainst thy will.

"Have we not been from childhood
friends?
Have I not loved thee long?
As long as thou hast loved the night
Whose silence wakes my song.

"And when thy heart is laid at rest
Beneath the church-yard stone
I shall have time enough to mourn
And thou to be alone."

I'll Not Weep

I'll not weep that thou art going to leave me,
There's nothing lovely here;
And doubly will the dark world grieve me
While thy heart suffers there.

I'll not weep, because the summer's glory
Must always end in gloom;
And, follow out the happiest story—
It closes with the tomb!

And I am weary of the anguish
Increasing winters bear;
I'm sick to see the spirit languish
Through years of dead despair.

So, if a tear, when thou art dying,
Should haply fall from me,
It is but that my soul is sighing
To go and rest with thee.

Discussion

1. What sort of human role does the wind play in "The Night Wind"? Why does the speaker want to be left alone?

2. In "I'll not weep . . ." why is it that the speaker cries? What leads her to this?

3. In what ways do each of these poems suggest a preference for passivity? What emotional tone do they seem to share?

Emily Brontë 1818 • 1848

In July of 1826 an obscure English parson bought his children a set of wooden toy soldiers. Their young lives had already witnessed a series of grim tragedies: the death of their mother in 1821 and of two sisters in 1825. He probably thought the children needed a little indulging.

There were four of them—a boy named Branwell (b. 1816) and three sisters, Charlotte (b. 1815), Emily (b. 1818), and Ann (b. 1820). They lived in a small parsonage perched on the top of a hill overlooking a factory town in the English midlands. They didn't go to school—their father tutored them—and had no friends. At the same time all were intensely emotional and intellectually precocious.

They seized upon the toy soldiers as a way of developing an imaginary play-world of their own. For the soldiers they invented a town, a country, and soon an elaborate past history. They wrote magazines, poems, novels, geography books, even multiple-volume historical chronicles about their other world.

By their mid-twenties all three of the girls were writing poems and novels. In 1846 they had a small collection of their verse printed at their own expense, and in 1847 all three published novels under male pseudonyms. Charlotte's novel was *Jane Eyre,* Ann's *Agnes Grey,* and Emily's *Wuthering Heights.*

Of the four children Emily was the quietest and the most passionate. Intense love for her family made it nearly impossible for her to ever live apart from them. Overwhelming homesickness drove her back. When her brother Branwell died (September 1848) just a half year after the appearance of her novel, Emily evidently no longer cared to live. She soon contracted tuberculosis, refused any medical aid, and died on December 19, 1848, aged thirty.

Elizabeth Barrett Browning

from Sonnets from the Portuguese

1

I thought once how Theocritus[1] had sung
Of the sweet years, the dear and wished-for years,
Who each one in a gracious hand appears
To bear a gift for mortals, old or young;
And, as I mused it in his antique tongue,
I saw in gradual vision, through my tears,
The sweet, sad years, the melancholy years,
Those of my own life, who by turns had flung
A shadow across me. Straightway I was 'ware,
So weeping, how a mystic shape did move
Behind me, and drew me backward by the hair;
And a voice said in mastery, while I strove,
"Guess now who holds thee?"—"Death," I said. But there
The silver answer rang, "Not Death, but Love."

1. ***Theocritus,*** Greek writer of the third century B.C. One of his poems personified the hours.

3

Unlike are we, unlike, O princely Heart!
Unlike our uses and our destinies.
Our ministering two angels look surprise
On one another as they strike athwart
Their wings in passing. Thou, bethink thee, art
A guest for queens to social pageantries,
With gages[1] from a hundred brighter eyes
Than tears even can make mine, to play thy part
Of chief musician. What hast *thou* to do
With looking from the lattice-lights at me,
A poor, tired, wandering singer, singing through
The dark, and leaning up a cypress-tree?[2]
The chrism[3] is on thine head; on mine the dew:
And Death must dig the level where these agree.

1. ***gages,*** tokens of promises made.
2. ***cypress-tree,*** a traditional symbol for death.
3. ***chrism.*** Consecrating ointment—he is formally annointed as a prince (line 1).

Discussion

1. **(a)** What had the past years given the speaker of sonnet number one? **(b)** What does she think the "mystic shape" (line 10) is? **(c)** Why does the actual identity of this "shape" surprise the reader?

2. In sonnet number three, what characteristics seem to separate these two people? At this point in the development of her love, what is the only thing she believes can bring them together?

3. Compare sonnet twenty-two to sonnet three. **(a)** How has their love developed? **(b)** Why does she now want to live and not to die?

4. What do you think it is that she refuses to say, at the end of sonnet twenty-eight?

5. Sonnet forty-three is the next-to-last sonnet of the cycle. In what ways does it provide a conclusion to the themes of the previous sonnets you have read?

Elizabeth Barrett Browning
1806 • 1861

Keen independence of spirit seems to have been typical of Elizabeth Barrett from her earliest years. Not content with the meager education given Victorian girls, she insisted on learning French, Latin, and

Greek from tutors while studying history and philosophy on her own. The studies for young ladies of her era didn't interest her. "I abhor music," she wrote, and described her piano practice this way: "I sit down discontented and I rise up disgusted." Dancing she called "mere idleness."

At age fourteen she saw her first poem published anonymously, and for the next twelve years she continued to publish this way—both in magazines and books. Her first translation of Aeschylus's *Prometheus Bound* appeared in 1833. In 1838 she published the first book bearing her name and by 1844 she was able to gather all her poetry to date into a two-volume edition of her work. She was, by this time, one of the best-known and most popular poets of her day.

It is this book which attracted Robert Browning to her. In 1846, during their secret courtship, Elizabeth wrote the *Sonnets from the Portuguese*. In 1849, after several years of marriage, she finally showed them to Robert. The next year she published them in a collection of her work.

The title of this sonnet sequence refers to one of Browning's pet names for his wife. They describe, in vivid, frequently unusual ways, the growth of her love for him. While many of the longer poems of Elizabeth Barrett Browning published during her life were far more popular with Victorian readers, it is this sonnet sequence which has retained an audience into our day.

22

When our two souls stand up[1] erect and strong,
Face to face, silent, drawing nigh and nigher,
Until the lengthening wings break into fire
At either curvèd point—what bitter wrong
Can the earth do to us, that we should not long
Be here contented? Think. In mounting higher,
The angels would press on us and aspire
To drop some golden orb of perfect song
Into our deep, dear silence. Let us stay
Rather on earth, Beloved—where the unfit
Contrarious moods of men recoil away
And isolate pure spirits, and permit
A place to stand and love in for a day,
With darkness and the death-hour rounding it.

1. ***souls stand up,*** that is, after death.

28

My letters! all dead paper, mute and white!
And yet they seem alive and quivering
Against my tremulous hands which loose the string
And let them drop down on my knee to-night.
This said—he wished to have me in his sight
Once, as a friend: this fixed a day in spring
To come and touch my hand . . . a simple thing,
Yet I wept for it!—this, . . . the paper's light . . .
Said, *Dear I love thee;* and I sank and quailed
As if God's future thundered on my past.
This said, *I am thine*—and so its ink has paled
With lying at my heart that beat too fast.
And this . . . O Love, thy words have ill availed
If, what this said, I dared repeat at last!

43

How do I love thee? Let me count the ways.
I love thee to the depth and breadth and height
My soul can reach, when feeling out of sight
For the ends of Being and ideal Grace.
I love thee to the level of everyday's
Most quiet need, by sun and candlelight.
I love thee freely, as men strive for Right;
I love thee purely, as they turn from Praise.
I love thee with the passion put to use
In my old griefs, and with my childhood's faith,
I love thee with a love I seemed to lose
With my lost saints—I love thee with the breadth,
Smiles, tears, of all my life!—and, if God choose,
I shall but love thee better after death.

Christina Rossetti

from Monna Innominata[1]

2

I wish I could remember that first day,
First hour, first moment of your meeting me,
If bright or dim the season, it might be
Summer or Winter for aught I can say;
So unrecorded did it slip away,
So blind was I to see and to foresee,
So dull to mark the budding of my tree
That would not blossom yet for many a May.
If only I could recollect it, such
A day of days! I let it come and go
As traceless as a thaw of bygone snow;
It seemed to mean so little, meant so much;
If only now I could recall that touch,
First touch of hand in hand—Did one but know!

1. ***Monna Innominata*** (mō′nä ē nō′mē nä′tä) "Nameless Lady." [Italian] Christina Rossetti explained that the fourteen sonnets of this sequence were supposed to have been spoken by one of the unknown ladies exalted by poets before the Italian poets Dante (1265–1321) and Petrarch (1304–1374) wrote of Beatrice and Laura by name.

Shut Out

The door was shut. I looked between
Its iron bars; and saw it lie,
My garden, mine, beneath the sky,
Pied with all flowers bedewed and green.

From bough to bough the song-birds crossed,
From flower to flower the moths and bees:
With all its nests and stately trees
It had been mine, and it was lost.

A shadowless spirit kept the gate,
Blank and unchanging like the grave.
I, peering through, said: "Let me have
Some buds to cheer my outcast state."

He answered not. "Or give me, then,
But one small twig from shrub or tree;
And bid my home remember me
Until I come to it again."

The spirit was silent; but he took
Mortar and stone to build a wall;
He left no loophole great or small
Through which my straining eyes might look.

So now I sit here quite alone,
Blinded with tears; nor grieve for that,
For nought is left worth looking at
Since my delightful land is gone.

Discussion

1. In sonnet two Christina Rossetti uses the images of a "budding . . . tree" (line 7) and the "thaw of bygone snow" (line 11). Why are these images particularly appropriate to the sonnet's subject?

2. In the poem "Shut Out" the speaker never explains the significance behind her emblematic tale. What do you think it is about?

3. How many times does the speaker in "Shut Out" repeat some form of the word "my"? What is the effect of this repetition?

Vocabulary • Structure, Pronunciation, and Dictionary

Use your Glossary to answer the following questions about the structure or pronunciation of the italicized words. Be sure you know the meaning of each word.

1. What structural element (root or affix) do *discern* and *dissever* share, and what is its spelling and meaning?

2. (a) How many syllables does the word *myriad* have? **(b)** What word designating a punctuation mark rhymes with *myriad?*

3. (a) What are the Old French and Latin words that form the root in *avail?* **(b)** With what prefix does the root combine, and what is its meaning?

4. Write a rhyme word for the first syllable in *tremulous.*

5. (a) What are the two Latin words that combine to form *munificence?* **(b)** What is the phrase that results if the meanings of the two Latin words are joined together?

6. (a) How many syllables has *officious?* **(b)** Write two rhyme words for the accented syllable.

7. (a) What is the original spelling and meaning of the Latin prefix in *elate?* **(b)** What is the spelling and meaning of the Latin root?

8. (a) Write a rhyme word for *vile* that means a unit of measurement; **(b)** write another rhyme word that means a tool used to smooth rough surfaces.

Christina Rossetti 1830 • 1894

"I always had a passion for intellect, and my wish was that my husband should be distinguished for intellect, and my children too. I have had my wish; and now I wish that there were a little less intellect in the family, so as to allow for a little more common sense." This is what Christina Rossetti's mother said, at age seventy. A remarkable woman, she taught Christina, the youngest of her four children, as well as the other three, English, French, and Italian literature, while encouraging Christina's father in his study of the Italian poet Dante. But above all, Frances Rossetti taught her children the Bible and orthodox Anglican religion. And, as she ruefully remarks, some of them needed less intellect, more common sense. Her husband and her two sons dropped away from religion altogether. Her older daughter became a nun. Christina, torn by doubt, stayed in the middle.

This close family environment, with its emphasis on learning and its religious disputes, formed Christina's mature character. Loyalty to her mother led her to live her entire life at home, caring for the household. Loyalty to her mother's religious convictions led her to refuse offers of marriage from two men she loved. Both were not members of the Church of England.

Into her poetry, which she began to publish at the age of twenty, she poured her love for her family, her religious devotion, and her despair at the painful self-denial which family and religion forced upon her. "Monna Innominata" is a sequence of sonnets modeled after Elizabeth Barrett Browning's *Sonnets from the Portugese.* But Christina Rossetti's cycle is different—these are poems written by a woman who has lost her love, not won him. "Shut Out" is even more bleak in its despair. In the manuscript for that poem Christina wrote, "What happened to me?"

Though frequently ill, Christina Rossetti continued to write poetry, stories, and books on religion throughout her life, leaving in the end over one thousand poems and eight volumes of prose.

Lewis Carroll

Alice's Adventures Under Ground grew out of the Reverend Charles Lutwidge Dodgson's affection for one little girl, Alice Liddell, daughter of the Dean of Christ Church College, Oxford, where Dodgson taught mathematics. On the afternoon of July 4, 1862, Dodgson and a friend, the Reverend Duckworth, took three of the Liddell girls, Alice among them, boating on the river Thames. As they rowed along, Dodgson began to tell extemporaneous stories of Alice's adventures; at the end of the day Alice Liddell asked him to write them out for her. He did and by February of 1863 he had finished, titling the story "Alice's Adventures Under Ground." He showed it to friends who urged him to publish it. Intrigued by the idea Dodgson went back to work, revising and expanding his original until the second version was twice as long as the first. This he now renamed Alice in Wonderland. *Dodgson gave his manuscript of the first version to Alice Liddell. And that is the version printed here. The more well-known, expanded version, with the famous illustrations by John Tenniel, was published at Dodgson's own expense in 1865.*

Alice's Adventures Under Ground

Chapter I

Alice was beginning to get very tired of sitting by her sister on the bank, and of having nothing to do; once or twice she had peeped into the book her sister was reading, but it had no pictures or conversations in it, and where is the use of a book, thought Alice, without pictures or conversations? So she was considering in her own mind (as well as she could, for the hot day made her feel very sleepy and stupid) whether the pleasure of making a daisy-chain was worth the trouble of getting up and picking the daisies, when a white rabbit with pink eyes ran close by her.

There was nothing very remarkable in that, nor did Alice think it so *very* much out of the way to hear the rabbit say to itself "dear, dear! I shall be too late!" (When she thought it over afterwards, it occurred to her that she ought to have wondered at this, but at the time it all seemed quite natural.) But when the rabbit actually *took a watch out of its waistcoat pocket,* looked at it, and then hurried on, Alice started to her feet, for it flashed across her mind that she had never before seen a rabbit with either a waistcoat pocket or a watch to take out of it, and full of curiosity, she hurried across the field after it, and

On this page are a few of the original illustrations for Alice in Wonderland, *drawn by John Tenniel, a cartoonist on the staff of the British humor magazine* Punch. *He worked closely with Dodgson (Lewis Carroll), and his interpretations of the characters have defined the way most readers visualize them. Since then, however, many other artists—including Arthur Rackham, N. C. Wyeth, and Salvador Dali—have pictured the characters in a variety of styles. The illustrations in this volume were done by the French artist Jean-Michel Folon.*

was just in time to see it pop down a large rabbit-hole under the hedge. In a moment down went Alice after it, never once considering how in the world she was to get out again.

The rabbit-hole went straight on like a tunnel for some way, and then dipped suddenly down, so suddenly that Alice had not a moment to think about stopping herself before she found herself falling down what seemed a deep well. Either the well was very deep, or she fell very slowly, for she had plenty of time as she went down to look about her and to wonder what would happen next. First, she tried to look down and make out what she was coming to, but it was too dark to see anything. Then, she looked at the sides of the well and noticed that they were filled with cupboards and bookshelves. Here and there were maps and pictures hung on pegs. She took a jar down off one of the shelves as she passed; it was labelled "Orange Marmalade," but to her great disappointment it was empty. She did not like to drop the jar for fear of killing somebody underneath, so managed to put it into one of the cupboards as she fell past it.

"Well!" thought Alice to herself, "after such a fall as this, I shall think nothing of tumbling down stairs! How brave they'll all think me at home! Why, I wouldn't say anything about it, even if I fell off the top of the house!" (Which was most likely true.)

Down, down, down. Would the fall *never* come to an end? "I wonder how many miles I've fallen by this time?" she said aloud. "I must be getting somewhere near the center of the earth. Let me see; that would be four thousand miles down, I think—" (You see Alice had learnt several things of this sort in her lessons in the schoolroom, and though this was not a *very* good opportunity of showing off her knowledge, as there was no one to hear her, still it was good practice to say it over.) "Yes, that's the right distance, but then what Longitude or Latitude line shall I be in?" (Alice had no idea what Longitude was, or Latitude either, but she thought they were nice grand words to say.)

Presently she began again, "I wonder if I shall fall right *through* the earth! How funny it'll be to come out among the people that walk with their heads downwards! But I shall have to ask them what the name of the country is, you know. Please, Ma'am, is this New Zealand or Australia?" She tried to curtsey as she spoke, (fancy *curtseying* as you're falling through the air! do you think you could manage it?) "And what an ignorant little girl she'll think me for asking! No, it'll never do to ask; perhaps I shall see it written up somewhere."

Down, down, down: there was nothing else to do, so Alice soon began talking again. "Dinah will miss me very much tonight, I should think!" (Dinah was the cat.) "I hope they'll remember her saucer of milk at tea-time! Oh, dear Dinah, I wish I had you here! There are no mice in the air, I'm afraid, but you might catch a bat, and that's very like a mouse, you know, my dear. But do cats eat bats, I wonder?" And here Alice began to get rather sleepy and kept on saying to herself in a dreamy sort of way, "Do cats eat bats? Do cats eat bats?" and sometimes, "Do bats eat cats?" For, as she couldn't answer either question, it didn't much matter which way she put it. She felt that she was dozing off, and had just begun to dream that she was walking hand in hand with Dinah, and was saying to her very earnestly, "Now, Dinah, my dear, tell me the truth. Did you ever eat a bat?" When suddenly, bump! bump! down she came upon a heap of sticks and shavings, and the fall was over.

Alice was not a bit hurt and jumped on to her feet directly. She looked up, but it was all dark overhead; before her was another long passage, and the white rabbit was still in sight, hurrying down it. There was not a moment to be lost; away went Alice like the wind, and just heard it say, as it turned a corner, "My ears and whiskers, how late it's getting!" She turned the corner after it and instantly found herself in a long, low hall, lit up by a row of lamps which hung from the roof.

There were doors all round the hall, but they were all locked, and when Alice had been all round it and tried them all, she walked sadly down the middle, wondering how she was ever to get out again. Suddenly she came upon a little three-legged table, all made of solid glass; there was nothing lying upon it but a tiny golden key, and Alice's first idea was that it might belong to one of the doors of the hall, but alas! either the locks were too large, or the key too small, but at any rate it would open none of them. However, on the second time round, she came to a low curtain behind which was a door about eighteen inches high. She tried the little key in the keyhole, and it fitted! Alice opened the door and looked down a small passage not larger than a rat hole, into the loveliest garden you ever saw. How she longed to get out of that dark hall and wander about those beds of bright flowers and those cool fountains, but she could not even get her head through the doorway. "And even if my head would go through," thought poor Alice, "it would be very little use without my shoulders. Oh, how I wish I could shut up like a telescope! I think I could, if I only knew how to begin." For, you see, so many out-of-the-way things had happened lately that Alice began to think very few things indeed were really impossible.

There was nothing else to do so she went back to the table half hoping she might find another key on it, or at any rate a book of rules for shutting up people like telescopes. This time there was a little bottle on it—"which certainly was not there before," said Alice—and tied round the neck of the bottle was a paper label with the words DRINK ME beautifully printed on it in large letters.

It was all very well to say DRINK ME, "but I'll look first," said the wise little Alice, "and see whether the bottle's marked 'poison' or not," for Alice had read several nice little stories about children that got burnt and eaten up by wild beasts and other unpleasant things, because they *would* not remember the simple rules their friends had given them, such as, that, if you get into the fire, it will burn you, and that, if you cut your finger very deeply with a knife, it generally bleeds; and she had never forgotten that if you drink a bottle marked "poison," it is almost certain to disagree with you sooner or later.

However, this bottle was *not* marked "poison," so Alice tasted it and finding it very nice (it had, in fact, a sort of mixed flavour of cherry-tart, custard, pineapple, roast turkey, toffy, and hot buttered toast) she very soon finished it off.

* * * * *

"What a curious feeling!" said Alice. "I must be shutting up like a telescope."

It was so indeed; she was now only ten inches high, and her face brightened up as it occurred to her that she was now the right size for going through the little door into that lovely garden. First, however, she waited for a few minutes to see whether she was going to shrink any further. She felt a little nervous about this, "for it might end, you know," said Alice to herself, "in my going out altogether, like a candle, and what should I be like then, I wonder?" She tried to fancy what the flame of a candle is like after the candle is blown out, for she could not remember having ever seen one. However, nothing more happened so she decided on going into the garden at once, but, alas for poor Alice! When she got to the door, she found she had forgotten the little golden key, and when she went back to the table for the key, she found she could not possibly reach it. She could see it plainly enough through the glass, and she tried her best to climb up one of the legs of the table, but it was too slippery, and when she had tired herself out with trying, the poor little thing sat down and cried.

"Come! There's no use in crying!" said Alice to herself rather sharply. "I advise you to leave off this minute!" (She generally gave herself very good advice and sometimes scolded herself so severely as to bring tears into her eyes, and once she remembered boxing her own ears for having been unkind to herself in a game of croquet she was playing with herself, for this curious child was very fond of pretending to be two people.) "But it's no use now," thought poor Alice, "to pretend to be two people! Why, there's hardly enough of me left to make one respectable person!"

Soon her eyes fell on a little ebony box lying under the table. She opened it, and found in it a very small cake on which was lying a card with the words EAT ME beautifully printed on it in large letters. "I'll eat," said Alice, "and if it makes me larger, I can reach the key, and if it makes me smaller, I can creep under the door, so either way I'll get into the garden, and I don't care which happens!"

She ate a little bit and said anxiously to herself, "Which way? Which way?" She laid her hand on the top of her head to feel which way it was growing and was quite surprised to find that she remained the same size. To be sure this is what generally happens when one eats cake, but

Alice had got into the way of expecting nothing but out-of-the way things to happen, and it seemed quite dull and stupid for things to go on in the common way.

So she set to work, and very soon finished off the cake.

* * * * *

"Curiouser and curiouser!" cried Alice. (She was so surprised that she quite forgot how to speak good English.) "Now I'm opening out like the largest telescope that ever was! Goodbye, feet!" (for when she looked down at her feet, they seemed almost out of sight, they were getting so far off). "Oh, my poor little feet, I wonder who will put on your shoes and stockings for you now, dears? I'm sure *I* can't! I shall be a great deal too far off to bother myself about you; you must manage the best way you can. But I must be kind to them," thought Alice, "or perhaps they won't walk the way I want to go! Let me see, I'll give them a new pair of boots every Christmas."

And she went on planning to herself how she would manage it. "They must go by the carrier," she thought, "and how funny it'll seem, sending presents to one's own feet! And how odd the directions will look.

ALICE'S RIGHT FOOT, ESQ.
THE CARPET,
with ALICE'S LOVE

Oh dear! what nonsense I am talking!"

Just at this moment her head struck against the roof of the hall; in fact, she was now rather more than nine feet high, and she at once took up the little golden key and hurried off to the garden door.

Poor Alice! It was as much as she could do, lying down on one side, to look through into the garden with one eye, but to get through was more hopeless than ever; she sat down and cried again.

"You ought to be ashamed of yourself," said Alice, "a great girl like you," (she might well say this) "to cry in this way! Stop this instant, I tell you!" But she cried on all the same, shedding gallons of tears, until there was a large pool about four inches deep all round her and reaching half way across the hall. After a time, she heard a little pattering of feet in the distance and dried her eyes to see what was coming. It was the white rabbit coming back again, spendidly dressed, with a pair of white kid gloves in one hand and a nosegay in the other. Alice was ready to ask help of any one, she felt so desperate, and as the rabbit passed her, she said in a low, timid voice, "If you please, Sir—" The rabbit started violently, looked up once into the roof of the hall, from which the voice seemed to come, and then dropped the nosegay and the white kid gloves and scurried away into the darkness as hard as it could go.

Alice took up the nosegay and gloves and found the nosegay so delicious that she kept smelling at it all the time she went on talking to herself. "Dear, dear! How queer everything is today! And yesterday everything happened just as usual; I wonder if I was changed in the night? Let me think. Was I the same when I got up this morning? I think I remember feeling rather different. But if I'm not the same, who in the world am I? Ah, that's the great puzzle!" And she began thinking over all the children she knew of the same age as herself to see if she could have been changed for any of them.

"I'm sure I'm not Gertrude," she said, "for her hair goes in such long ringlets, and mine doesn't go in ringlets at all—and I'm sure I can't be Florence, for I know all sorts of things, and she, oh, she knows such a very little! Besides, *she's* she, and *I'm* I, and—oh dear! how puzzling it all is! I'll try if I know all the things I used to know. Let me see: four times five is twelve, and four times six is thirteen, and four times seven is fourteen—oh dear! I shall never get to twenty at this rate! But the Multiplication Table don't signify—let's try Geography. London is the capital of France, and Rome is the capital of Yorkshire, and Paris—oh dear! dear! *That's* all wrong, I'm certain! I must have been changed for Florence! I'll try and say "How doth the little," and she crossed her hands on her lap and began, but her voice sounded hoarse and strange, and the words did not sound the same as they used to do.

"How doth the little crocodile
Improve its shining tail,
And pour the waters of the Nile
On every golden scale!

How cheerfully it seems to grin!
    How neatly spreads its claws!
And welcomes little fishes in
    With gently smiling jaws!"[1]

"I'm sure those are not the right words," said poor Alice, and her eyes filled with tears as she thought, "I must be Florence after all, and I shall have to go and live in that poky little house, and have next to no toys to play with, and oh, ever so many lessons to learn! No! I've made up my mind about it; if I'm Florence, I'll stay down here! It'll be no use their putting their heads down and saying 'come up, dear!' I shall only look up and say 'who am I, then? Answer me that first, and then, if I like being that person, I'll come up; if not, I'll stay down here till I'm somebody else—but, oh dear!" cried Alice with a sudden burst of tears, "I do wish they *would* put their heads down! I am so tired of being all alone here!"

As she said this, she looked down at her hands, and was surprised to find she had put on one of the rabbit's little gloves while she was talking. "How *can* I have done that?" thought she, "I must be growing small again." She got up and went to the table to measure herself by it, and found that, as nearly as she could guess, she was now about two feet high and was going on shrinking rapidly. Soon she found out that the reason of it was the nosegay she held in her hand. She dropped it hastily just in time to save herself from shrinking away altogether and found that she was now only three inches high.

"Now for the garden!" cried Alice, as she hurried back to the little door, but the little door was locked again, and the little gold key was lying on the glass table as before. "Things are worse than ever!" thought the poor little girl, "for I never was as small as this before, never! And I declare it's too bad, it is!" At this moment her foot slipped, and splash! she was up to her chin in salt water. Her first idea was that she had fallen into the sea; then she remembered that she was under ground, and she soon made out that it was the pool of tears she had wept when she was nine feet high. "I wish I hadn't cried so much!" said Alice, as she swam about, trying to find her way out. "I shall be punished for it now, I suppose, by being drowned in my own tears! Well! That'll be a queer thing, to be sure! However, everything is queer today." Very soon she saw something splashing about in the pool near her. At first she thought it must be a walrus or a hippopotamus, but then she remembered how small she was herself and soon made out that it was only a mouse that had slipped in like herself.

"Would it be any use, now," thought Alice, "to speak to this mouse? The rabbit is something quite out-of-the-way, no doubt, and so have I been, ever since I came down here, but that is no reason why the mouse should not be able to talk. I think I may as well try."

So she began: "Oh Mouse, do you know how to get out of this pool? I am very tired of swimming about here, oh Mouse!" The mouse looked at her rather inquisitively and seemed to her to wink with one of its little eyes, but it said nothing.

"Perhaps it doesn't understand English," thought Alice. "I daresay it's a French mouse, come over with William the Conqueror!"[2] (For, with all her knowledge of history, Alice had no very clear notion how long ago anything had happened.) So she began again, "Oú est ma chatte?"[3] which was the first sentence out of her French lesson-book. The mouse gave a sudden jump in the pool and seemed to quiver with fright. "Oh, I beg your pardon!" cried Alice

---

1. ***"How doth . . . jaws!"*** This is the first of many parodies of familiar poems that Carroll included in *Alice*. The poems and songs he chose were those that Victorian children were frequently required to memorize as part of their lessons. The original of "How doth the little crocodile" is a moralistic poem by Isaac Watts (1674–1748), titled "Against Idleness and Mischief." It runs as follows:

How doth the little busy bee
  Improve each shining hour
And gather honey all the day
  From every opening flower!

How skillfully she builds her cell!
  How neat she spreads her wax!
And labors hard to store it well
  With the sweet food she makes.

In works of labour or of skill
  I would be busy too;
For Satan finds some mischief still
  For idle hands to do.

In books, or work, or healthful play
  Let my first years be passed
That I may give for every day
  Some good account at last.

2. ***William the Conqueror*** (1027–1087), first Norman king of England.

3. ***"Oú . . . chatte?"*** "Where is my cat?" [French]

hastily, afraid that she had hurt the poor animal's feelings. "I quite forgot you didn't like cats!"

"Not like cats!" cried the mouse, in a shrill, passionate voice, "Would *you* like cats if you were me?"

"Well, perhaps not," said Alice in a soothing tone, "don't be angry about it. And yet I wish I could show you our cat Dinah, I think you'd take a fancy to cats if you could only see her. She is such a dear quiet thing," said Alice, half to herself, as she swam lazily about in the pool. "She sits purring so nicely by the fire, licking her paws and washing her face; and she is such a nice soft thing to nurse, and she's such a capital one for catching mice—oh! I beg your pardon!" cried poor Alice again, for this time the mouse was bristling all over, and she felt certain that it was really offended. "Have I offended you?"

"Offended, indeed!" cried the mouse, who seemed to be positively trembling with rage. "Our family always *hated* cats! Nasty, low, vulgar things! Don't talk to me about them any more!"

"I won't indeed!" said Alice, in a great hurry to change the conversation. "Are you—are you—fond of—dogs?" The mouse did not answer, so Alice went on eagerly, "There is such a nice little dog near our house I should like to show you! A little bright-eyed terrier, you know, with oh! such long curly brown hair! And it'll fetch things when you throw them, and it'll sit up and beg for its dinner, and all sorts of things—I can't remember half of them—and it belongs to a farmer, and he says it kills all the rats and—oh dear!" said Alice sadly, "I'm afraid I've offended it again!" For the mouse was swimming away from her as hard as it could go and making quite a commotion in the pool as it went.

So she called softly after it, "Mouse dear! Do come back again, and we won't talk about cats and dogs any more, if you don't like them!" When the mouse heard this it turned and swam slowly back to her; its face was quite pale (with passion, Alice thought) and it said in a trembling low voice, "Let's get to the shore, and then I'll tell you my history, and you'll understand why it is I hate cats and dogs."

It was high time to go, for the pool was getting quite full of birds and animals that had fallen into it. There was a Duck and a Dodo, a Lory and an Eaglet,[4] and several other curious creatures. Alice led the way, and the whole party swam to the shore.

Chapter II

They were indeed a curious looking party that assembled on the bank—the birds with draggled feathers, the animals with their fur clinging close to them—all dripping wet, cross, and uncomfortable. The first question of course was how to get dry; they had a consultation about this, and Alice hardly felt at all surprised at finding herself talking familiarly with the birds as if she had known them all her life. Indeed, she had quite a long argument with the Lory, who at last turned sulky and would only say, "I am older than you, and must know best," and this Alice would not admit without knowing how old the Lory was, and as the Lory positively refused to tell its age, there was nothing more to be said.

At last the mouse, who seemed to have some authority among them, called out "Sit down, all of you, and attend to me! I'll soon make you dry enough!" They all sat down at once, shivering, in a large ring, Alice in the middle, with her eyes anxiously fixed on the mouse, for she felt sure she would catch a bad cold if she did not get dry very soon.

"Ahem." said the mouse, with a self-important air, "are you all ready? This is the driest thing I know. Silence all round, if you please!

"William the Conqueror, whose cause was favoured by the pope, was soon submitted to by the English, who wanted leaders, and had been of late much accustomed to usurpation and conquest. Edwin and Morcar, the earls of Mercia and Northumbria—"[5]

"Ugh!" said the Lory with a shiver.

"I beg your pardon?" said the mouse, frowning, but very politely, "did you speak?"

"Not I!" said the Lory hastily.

"I thought you did," said the mouse, "I

---

4. ***a Duck . . . Eaglet.*** The animals mentioned are thinly disguised representations of members of the party which boated on the Thames in 1862. The Duck is the Reverend Duckworth; the Dodo (a flightless bird already extinct by the 1860s) is Lewis Carroll (Charles Dodgson); the Lory (an Australian parrot) is Lorina Liddell; the Eaglet, Edith Liddell.

5. The passage that the mouse recites is probably from a contemporary English history textbook.

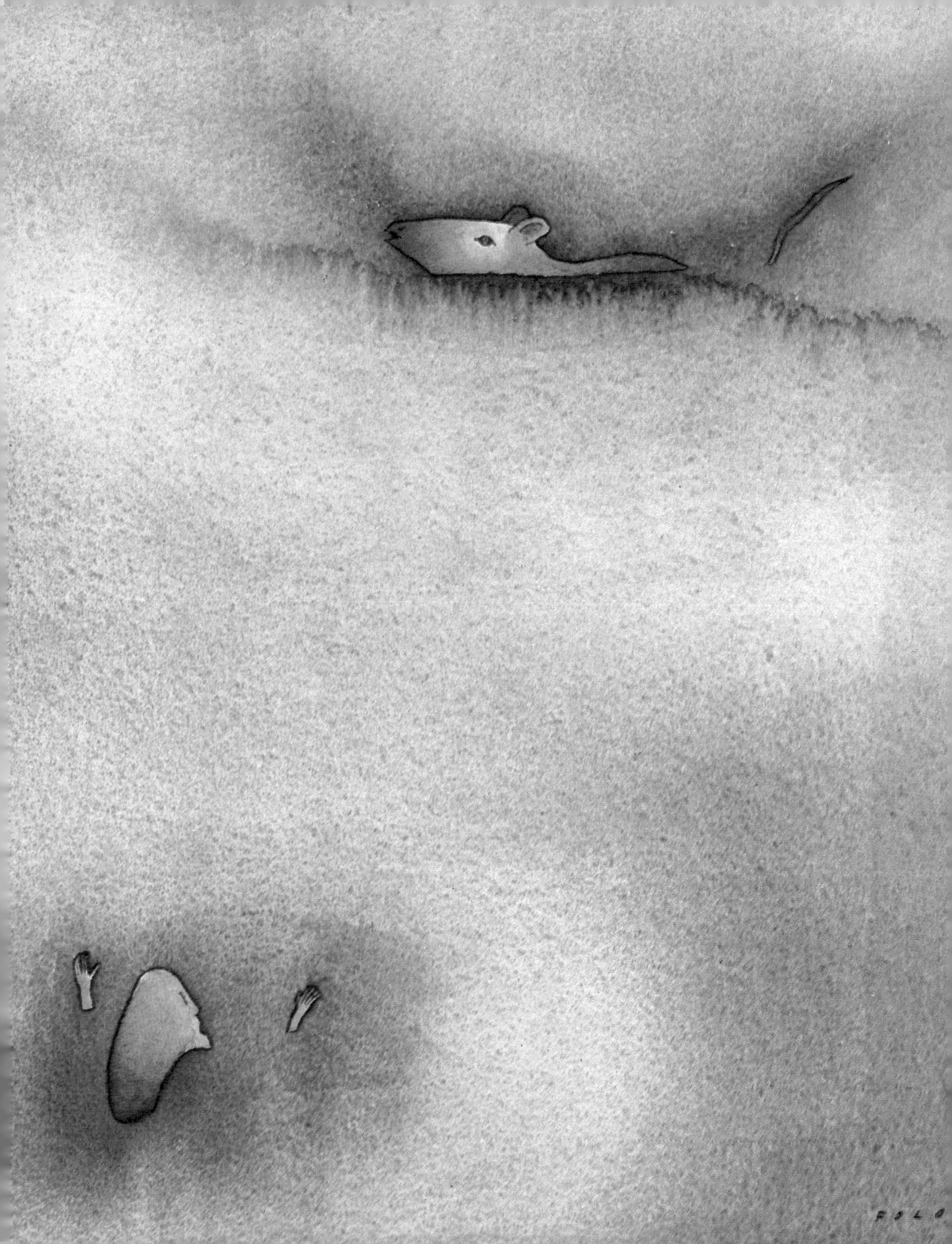

proceed. Edwin and Morcar, the earls of Mercia and Northumbria, declared for him; and even Stigand, the patriotic archbishop of Canterbury, found it advisable to go with Edgar Atheling to meet William and offer him the crown. William's conduct was at first moderate—How are you getting on now, dear?" said the mouse, turning to Alice as it spoke.

"As wet as ever," said poor Alice, "it doesn't seem to dry me at all."

"In that case," said the Dodo solemnly, rising to his feet, "I move that the meeting adjourn, for the immediate adoption of more energetic remedies—"

"Speak English!" said the Duck, "I don't know the meaning of half those long words, and what's more, I don't believe you do either!" And the Duck quacked a comfortable laugh to itself. Some of the other birds tittered audibly.

"I only meant to say," said the Dodo in a rather offended tone, "that I know of a house near here, where we could get the young lady and the rest of the party dried, and then we could listen comfortably to the story which I think you were good enough to promise to tell us," bowing gravely to the mouse.

The mouse made no objection to this, and the whole party moved along the river bank, (for the pool had by this time begun to flow out of the hall, and the edge of it was fringed with rushes and forget-me-nots), in a slow procession, the Dodo leading the way. After a time the Dodo became impatient, and, leaving the Duck to bring up the rest of the party, moved on at a quicker pace with Alice, the Lory, and the Eaglet, and soon brought them to a little cottage, and there they sat snugly by the fire, wrapped up in blankets, until the rest of the party had arrived and they were all dry again.

Then they all sat down again in a large ring on the bank and begged the mouse to begin his story.

"Mine is a long and a sad tale!" said the mouse, turning to Alice, and sighing.

"It *is* a long tail, certainly," said Alice, looking down with wonder at the mouse's tail, which was coiled nearly all round the party, "but why do you call it sad?" and she went on puzzling about this as the mouse went on speaking, so that her idea of the tale was something like this:

We lived beneath the mat
Warm and snug and fat
But one woe, & that
Was the cat!
To our joys
a clog, In
our eyes a
fog, On our
hearts a log
Was the dog!
When the
cat's away,
Then
the mice
will
play,
But, alas!
one day, (So they say)
Came the dog and
cat, Hunting
for a
rat,
Crushed
the mice
all flat,
Each
one
as
he
sat
un-
der-
neath
the
mat,
Warm,
& snug,
& fat—
Think
of
that!

"You are not attending!" said the mouse to Alice severely. "What are you thinking of?"

"I beg your pardon," said Alice very humbly, "you had got to the fifth bend, I think?"

"I had *not!*" cried the mouse, sharply and very angrily.

"A knot!" said Alice, always ready to make herself useful, and looking anxiously about her. "Oh, do let me help to undo it!"

"I shall do nothing of the sort!" said the mouse, getting up and walking away from the party. "You insult me by talking such nonsense!"

"I didn't mean it!" pleaded poor Alice, "but you're so easily offended, you know."

The mouse only growled in reply.

"Please come back and finish your story!" Alice called after it, and the others all joined in chorus "Yes, please do!" but the mouse only shook its ears and walked quickly away and was soon out of sight.

"What a pity it wouldn't stay!" sighed the Lory, and an old Crab took the opportunity of saying to its daughter, "Ah, my dear! let this be a lesson to you never to lose *your* temper!" "Hold your tongue, Ma!" said the young Crab, a little snappishly, "you're enough to try the patience of an oyster!"

"I wish I had our Dinah here, I know I do!" said Alice aloud, addressing no one in particular. "*She'd* soon fetch it back!"

"And who is Dinah, if I might venture to ask the question?" said the Lory.

Alice replied eagerly, for she was always ready to talk about her pet, "Dinah's our cat. And she's such a capital one for catching mice, you can't think! And oh! I wish you could see her after the birds! Why, she'll eat a little bird as soon as look at it!"

This answer caused a remarkable sensation among the party; some of the birds hurried off at once; one old magpie began wrapping itself up very carefully, remarking, "I really must be getting home, the night air does not suit my throat," and a canary called out in a trembling voice to its children, "Come away from her, my dears, she's no fit company for you!" On various pretexts they all moved off, and Alice was soon left alone.

She sat for some while sorrowful and silent, but she was not long before she recovered her spirits and began talking to herself again as usual. "I do wish some of them had stayed a little longer! and I was getting to be such friends with them—really the Lory and I were almost like sisters! and so was that dear little Eaglet! And then the Duck and the Dodo! How nicely the Duck sang to us as we came along through the water; and if the Dodo hadn't known the way to that nice little cottage, I don't know when we should have got dry again—" and there is no knowing how long she might have prattled on in this way if she had not suddenly caught the sound of pattering feet.

It was the white rabbit, trotting slowly back again and looking anxiously about it as it went, as if it had lost something, and she heard it muttering to itself, "the Marchioness? the Marchioness! Oh my dear paws! Oh my fur and whiskers! She'll have me executed as sure as ferrets are ferrets! Where *can* I have dropped them, I wonder?" Alice guessed in a moment that it was looking for the nosegay and the pair of white kid gloves, and she began hunting for them, but they were now nowhere to be seen—everything seemed to have changed since her swim in the pool and her walk along the river-bank with its fringe of rushes and forget-me-nots, and the glass table and the little door had vanished.

Soon the rabbit noticed Alice, as she stood looking curiously about her, and at once said in a quick angry tone, "Why, Mary Ann! what *are* you doing out here? Go home this moment, and look on my dressing-table for my gloves and nosegay, and fetch them here, as quick as you can run, do you hear?" And Alice was so much frightened that she ran off at once, without saying a word, in the direction which the rabbit had pointed out.

She soon found herself in front of a neat little house on the door of which was a bright brass plate with the name W. RABBIT, ESQ. She went in, and hurried upstairs for fear she should meet the real Mary Ann and be turned out of the house before she had found the gloves; she knew that one pair had been lost in the hall. "But of course," thought Alice, "it has plenty more of them in its house. How queer it seems to be going messages for a rabbit! I suppose Dinah'll be sending me messages next!" And she began fancying the sort of things that would happen: "Miss Alice! come here directly and get ready for your walk!" "Coming in a minute, nurse! But I've got to watch this mousehole till Dinah comes back, and see that the mouse doesn't get out— Only I don't think," Alice went on, "that they'd let Dinah stop in the house if it began ordering people about like that!"

By this time she had found her way into a tidy little room with a table in the window on which was a looking-glass and, (as Alice had hoped) two or three pairs of tiny white kid gloves. She took up a pair of gloves and was just going to leave the room when her eye fell upon a little bottle that stood near the looking-glass. There was no label on it this time with the words "Drink me," but nevertheless she uncorked it and put it to her lips. "I know something interesting is sure to happen," she said to herself, "whenever I eat or drink anything, so I'll see what this bottle does. I do hope it'll make me grow larger, for I'm quite tired of being such a tiny little thing!"

It did so indeed, and much sooner than she expected; before she had drunk half the bottle, she found her head pressing against the ceiling, and she stooped to save her neck from being broken and hastily put down the bottle, saying to herself, "That's quite enough—I hope I sha'n't grow any more—I wish I hadn't drunk so much!"

Alas! It was too late. She went on growing and growing and very soon had to kneel down. In another minute there was not room even for this, and she tried the effect of lying down with one elbow against the door and the other arm curled round her head. Still she went on growing, and as a last resource she put one arm out of the window and one foot up the chimney and said to herself, "Now I can do no more—what *will* become of me?"

Luckily for Alice, the little magic bottle had now had its full effect, and she grew no larger. Still it was very uncomfortable, and as there seemed to be no sort of chance of ever getting out of the room again, no wonder she felt unhappy. "It was much pleasanter at home," thought poor Alice, "when one wasn't always growing larger and smaller and being ordered about by mice and rabbits—I almost wish I hadn't gone down that rabbit-hole, and yet, and yet—it's rather curious, you know, this sort of life. I do wonder what *can* have happened to me! When I used to read fairy-tales, I fancied that sort of thing never happened, and now here I am in the middle of one! There ought to be a book written about me, that there ought! And when I grow up I'll write one—but I'm grown up now," said she in a sorrowful tone, "at least there's no room to grow up any more *here*."

"But then," thought Alice, "shall I *never* get any older than I am now? That'll be a comfort, one way—never to be an old woman—but then—always to have lessons to learn! Oh, I shouldn't like *that!*"

"Oh, you foolish Alice!" she said again. "How can you learn lessons in here? Why, there's hardly room for you and no room at all for any lesson-books!"

And so she went on, taking first one side and then the other and making quite a conversation of it altogether, but after a few minutes she heard a voice outside which made her stop to listen.

"Mary Ann! Mary Ann!" said the voice. "Fetch me my gloves this moment!" Then came a little pattering of feet on the stairs. Alice knew it was the rabbit coming to look for her, and she trembled till she shook the house, quite forgetting that she was now about a thousand times as large as the rabbit and had no reason to be afraid of it. Presently the rabbit came to the door and tried to open it, but as it opened inwards, and Alice's elbow was against it, the attempt proved a failure. Alice heard it say to itself, "Then I'll go round and get in at the window."

"*That* you won't!" thought Alice, and, after waiting till she fancied she heard the rabbit just under the window, she suddenly spread out her hand and made a snatch in the air. She did not get hold of anything, but she heard a little shriek and a fall and a crash of breaking glass, from which she concluded that it was just possible it had fallen into a cucumber-frame, or something of the sort.

Next came an angry voice—the rabbit's—"Pat, Pat! Where are you?" And then a voice she had never heard before, "Shure then I'm here! Digging for apples, anyway, yer honour!"

"Digging for apples indeed!" said the rabbit angrily. "Here, come and help me out of *this!*"—Sound of more breaking glass.

"Now, tell me, Pat, what is that coming out of the window?"

"Shure it's an arm, yer honour!" (He pronounced it "arrum.")

"An arm, you goose! Who ever saw an arm that size? Why, it fills the whole window, don't you see?"

"Shure, it does, yer honour, but it's an arm for all that."

"Well, it's no business there; go and take it away!"

There was a long silence after this, and Alice could only hear whispers now and then, such as, "Shure I don't like it, yer honour, at all at all!" "Do as I tell you, you coward!" and at last she spread out her hand again and made another snatch in the air. This time there were *two* little shrieks and more breaking glass—"What a number of cucumber-frames there must be!" thought Alice, "I wonder what they'll do next! As for pulling me out of the window, I only wish they *could!* I'm sure *I* don't want to stop in here any longer!"

She waited for some time without hearing anything more: at last came a rumbling of little cart-wheels and the sound of a good many voices all talking together. She made out the words, "Where's the other ladder?—Why, I hadn't to bring but one, Bill's got the other—here, put 'em up at this corner—No, tie 'em together first—they don't reach high enough yet—Oh, they'll do well enough, don't be particular—here, Bill! catch hold of this rope—Will the roof bear?—Mind that loose slate—Oh, it's coming down! Heads below!—" (a loud crash) "Now, who did that?—It was Bill, I fancy—Who's to go down the chimney?—Nay, *I* sha'n't! *You* do it!—*That* I won't then—Bill's got to go down—here, Bill! The master says you've to go down the chimney!"

"Oh, so Bill's got to come down the chimney, has he?" said Alice to herself. "Why, they seem to put everything upon Bill! I wouldn't be in Bill's place for a good deal; the fireplace is a pretty tight one, but I *think* I can kick a little."

She drew her foot as far down the chimney as she could, and waited till she heard a little animal (she couldn't guess what sort it was) scratching and scrambling in the chimney close above her, then, saying to herself, "This is Bill," she gave one sharp kick and waited again to see what would happen next.

The first thing was a general chorus of, "There goes Bill!" then the rabbit's voice alone, "Catch him, you by the hedge!" then silence, and then another confusion of voices, "How was it, old fellow? What happened to you? Tell us all about it."

Last came a little feeble squeaking voice, ("That's Bill" thought Alice) which said, "Well, I hardly know—I'm all of a fluster myself—something comes at me like a Jack-in-the-box, and the next minute up I goes like a rocket!" "And so you did, old fellow!" said the other voices.

"We must burn the house down!" said the voice of the rabbit, and Alice called out as loud as she could: "If you do, I'll set Dinah at you!" This caused silence again, and while Alice was thinking, "But how can I get Dinah here?" she found to her great delight that she was getting smaller; very soon she was able to get up out of the uncomfortable position in which she had been lying, and in two or three minutes more she was once more three inches high.

She ran out of the house as quick as she could and found quite a crowd of little animals waiting outside—guinea-pigs, white mice, squirrels, and "Bill," a little green lizard, that was being supported in the arms of one of the guinea-pigs while another was giving it something out of a bottle. They all made a rush at her the moment she appeared, but Alice ran her hardest and soon found herself in a thick wood.

Chapter III

"The first thing I've got to do," said Alice to herself, as she wandered about in the wood, "is to grow to my right size, and the second thing is to find my way into that lovely garden. I think that will be the best plan."

It sounded an excellent plan, no doubt, and very neatly and simply arranged; the only difficulty was, that she had not the smallest idea how to set about it, and while she was peering anxiously among the trees round her, a little sharp bark just over her head made her look up in a great hurry.

An enormous puppy was looking down at her with large round eyes, and feebly stretching out one paw, trying to reach her. "Poor thing!" said Alice in a coaxing tone, and she tried hard to whistle to it, but she was terribly alarmed all the while at the thought that it might be hungry, in which case it would probably devour her in spite of all her coaxing. Hardly knowing what she did, she picked up a little bit of stick, and held it out to the puppy. Whereupon the puppy jumped into the air off all its feet at once, and with a yelp of delight rushed at the stick, and made believe to worry it. Then Alice dodged behind a great thistle to keep herself from being run over, and, the moment she appeared at the other side, the puppy made another dart at the stick, and tumbled head over heels in its hurry to get hold. Then Alice, thinking it was very like having a game of play with a cart-horse, and expecting every moment to be trampled under its feet, ran round the thistle again. Then the puppy began a series of short charges at the stick, running a very little way forwards each time and a long way back and barking hoarsely all the while, till at last it sat down a good way off, panting, with its tongue hanging out of its mouth and its great eyes half shut.

This seemed to Alice a good opportunity for making her escape. She set off at once, and ran till the puppy's bark sounded quite faint in the distance, and till she was quite tired and out of breath.

"And yet what a dear little puppy it was!" said Alice, as she leant against a buttercup to rest herself, and fanned herself with her hat, "I should have liked teaching it tricks, if—if I'd only been the right size to do it! Oh! I'd nearly forgotten that I've got to grow up again! Let me see; how *is* it to be managed? I suppose I ought to eat or drink something or other, but the great question is, what?"

The great question certainly was, what? Alice looked all round her at the flowers and the blades of grass, but could not see anything that looked like the right thing to eat under the circumstances. There was a large mushroom near her, about the same height as herself, and when she had looked under it, and on both sides of it, and behind it, it occurred to her to look and see what was on the top of it.

She stretched herself up on tiptoe, and peeped over the edge of the mushroom, and her eyes immediately met those of a large blue caterpillar, which was sitting with its arms folded, quietly smoking a long hookah;[6] and taking not the least notice of her or of anything else.

For some time they looked at each other in silence. At last the caterpillar took the hookah out of its mouth, and languidly addressed her.

"Who are you?" said the caterpillar.

This was not an encouraging opening for a conversation. Alice replied rather shyly, "I—I hardly know, sir, just at present—at least I know who I *was* when I got up this morning, but I think I must have been changed several times since that."

"What do you mean by that?" said the caterpillar, "explain yourself!"

"I can't explain *myself*, I'm afraid, sir," said Alice, "because I'm not myself, you see."

"I don't see," said the caterpillar.

"I'm afraid I can't put it more clearly," Alice replied very politely, "for I can't understand it myself, and really to be so many different sizes in one day is very confusing."

"It isn't," said the caterpillar.

"Well, perhaps you haven't found it so yet," said Alice, "but when you have to turn into a chrysalis, you know, and then after that into a butterfly, I should think it'll feel a little queer, don't you think so?"

"Not a bit," said the caterpillar.

"All I know is," said Alice, "it would feel queer to *me*."

"*You!*" said the caterpillar contemptuously, "Who are you?"

Which brought them back again to the beginning of the conversation. Alice felt a little irritated at the caterpillar making such *very* short remarks, and she drew herself up and said very gravely, "I think you ought to tell me who *you* are, first."

"Why?" said the caterpillar.

Here was another puzzling question. And as Alice had no reason ready, and the caterpillar seemed to be in a *very* bad temper, she turned round and walked away.

"Come back!" the caterpillar called after her, "I've something important to say!"

This sounded promising. Alice turned and came back again.

"Keep your temper," said the caterpillar.

"Is that all?" said Alice, swallowing down her anger as well as she could.

"No," said the caterpillar.

Alice thought she might as well wait, as she had nothing else to do, and perhaps after all the caterpillar might tell her something worth hearing. For some minutes it puffed away at its hookah without speaking, but at last it unfolded its arms, took the hookah out of its mouth again,

---

6. ***hookah*** (hůk′ə), a tobacco pipe with a long flexible tube by which the smoke is drawn through water and cooled. Hookahs are used in the Orient.

and said: "So you think you're changed, do you?"

"Yes, sir," said Alice, "I can't remember the things I used to know—I've tried to say "How doth the little busy bee" and it came all different!"

"Try and repeat "You are old, father William,"[7] said the caterpillar.

Alice folded her hands, and began:

1.

"You are old, father William," the young man said,
"And your hair is exceedingly white;
And yet you incessantly stand on your head—
Do you think, at your age, it is right?"

2.

"In my youth," father William replied to his son,
"I feared it *might* injure the brain;
But now that I'm perfectly sure I have none,
Why, I do it again and again."

3.

"You are old," said the youth, "as I mentioned before,
"And have grown most uncommonly fat;
Yet you turned a back-somersault in at the door—
Pray what is the reason of that?"

4.

"In my youth," said the sage, as he shook his gray locks,
"I kept all my limbs very supple
By the use of this ointment, five shillings the box—
Allow me to sell you a couple."

5.

"You are old," said the youth, "and your jaws are too weak
For anything tougher than suet;
Yet you eat all the goose, with the bones and the beak—
Pray, how did you manage to do it?"

6.

"In my youth," said the old man, "I took to the law,
And argued each case with my wife,
And *the muscular strength, which it gave to my jaw,*
Has lasted the rest of my life."

7.

"You are old," said the youth, "one would hardly suppose
"That your eye was as steady as ever;
Yet you balanced an eel on the end of your nose—
What made you so *awfully* clever?"

8.

"I have answered three questions, and that is enough,"
Said his father, "don't give yourself airs!
"Do you think I can listen all day to such stuff?
Be off, or I'll kick you down stairs!"

"That is not said right," said the caterpillar.

"Not *quite* right, I'm afraid," said Alice timidly, "some of the words have got altered."

"It is wrong from beginning to end," said the caterpillar decidedly, and there was silence for some minutes. The caterpillar was the first to speak.

---

7. "You are old, father William" is a parody of a didactic poem by Robert Southey (1774–1843), "The Old Man's Comforts and How He Gained Them."

"You are old, father William," the young man cried,
"The few locks which are left you are gray;
You are hale, father William, a hearty old man;
Now tell me the reason, I pray."

"In the days of my youth," father William replied,
"I remember'd that youth would fly fast,
And abus'd not my health and my vigour at first,
That I never might need them at last."

"You are old, father William," the young man cried,
"And pleasures with youth pass away.
And yet you lament not the days that are gone;
Now tell me the reason, I pray."

"In the days of my youth," father William replied,
I remember'd that youth could not last;
I thought of the future, whatever I did,
That I never might grieve for the past."

"You are old, father William," the young man cried,
"And life must be hast'ning away;
You are cheerful and love to converse upon death;
Now tell me the reason, I pray."

"I am cheerful, young man," father William replied,
"Let the cause thy attention engage;
In the days of my youth I remember'd my God!
And he hath not forgotten my age."

"What size do you want to be?" it asked.

"Oh, I'm not particular as to size," Alice hastily replied, "only one doesn't like changing so often, you know."

"Are you content now?" said the caterpillar.

"Well, I should like to be a *little* larger, sir, if you wouldn't mind," said Alice, "three inches is such a wretched height to be."

"It is a very good height indeed!" said the caterpillar loudly and angrily, rearing itself straight up as it spoke (it was exactly three inches high).

"But I'm not used to it!" pleaded poor Alice in a piteous tone, and she thought to herself, "I wish the creatures wouldn't be so easily offended!"

"You'll get used to it in time," said the caterpillar, and it put the hookah into its mouth, and began smoking again.

This time Alice waited quietly until it chose to speak again: In a few minutes the caterpillar took the hookah out of its mouth, and got down off the mushroom, and crawled away into the grass, merely remarking as it went: "The top will make you grow taller, and the stalk will make you grow shorter."

"The top of *what?* The stalk of *what?*" thought Alice.

"Of the mushroom," said the caterpillar, just as if she had asked it aloud, and in another moment it was out of sight.

Alice remained looking thoughtfully at the mushroom for a minute, and then picked it and carefully broke it in two, taking the stalk in one hand, and the top in the other. "*Which* does the stalk do?" she said, and nibbled a little bit of it to try: the next moment she felt a violent blow on her chin; it had struck her foot!

She was a good deal frightened by this very sudden change, but as she did not shrink any further, and had not dropped the top of the mushroom, she did not give up hope yet. There was hardly room to open her mouth, with her chin pressing against her foot, but she did it at last, and managed to bite off a little bit of the top of the mushroom.

* * * * *

"Come! my head's free at last!" said Alice in a tone of delight, which changed into alarm in another moment, when she found that her shoulders were nowhere to be seen: She looked down upon an immense length of neck, which seemed to rise like a stalk out of a sea of green leaves that lay far below her.

"What *can* all that green stuff be?" said Alice, "and where *have* my shoulders got to? And oh! my poor hands! how is it I can't see you?" She was moving them about as she spoke, but no result seemed to follow, except a little rustling among the leaves. Then she tried to bring her head down to her hands, and was delighted to find that her neck would bend about easily in every direction, like a serpent. She had just succeeded in bending it down in a beautiful zigzag, and was going to dive in among the leaves, which she found to be the tops of the trees of the wood she had been wandering in, when a sharp hiss made her draw back. A large pigeon had flown into her face, and was violently beating her with its wings.

"Serpent!" screamed the pigeon.

"I'm *not* a serpent!" said Alice indignantly, "Let me alone!"

"I've tried every way!" the pigeon said desperately, with a kind of sob: "nothing seems to suit 'em!"

"I haven't the least idea what you mean," said Alice.

"I've tried the roots of trees, and I've tried banks, and I've tried hedges," the pigeon went on without attending to her, "but them serpents. There's no pleasing 'em!"

Alice was more and more puzzled, but she thought there was no use in saying anything till the pigeon had finished.

"As if it wasn't trouble enough hatching the eggs!" said the pigeon, "without being on the look out for serpents, day and night! Why, I haven't had a wink of sleep these three weeks!"

"I'm very sorry you've been annoyed," said Alice, beginning to see its meaning.

"And just as I'd taken the highest tree in the wood," said the pigeon raising its voice to a shriek, "and was just thinking I was free of 'em at last, they must needs come down from the sky! Ugh! Serpent!"

"But I'm *not* a serpent," said Alice, "I'm a—I'm a—"

"Well! *What* are you?" said the pigeon, "I see you're trying to invent something."

"I—I'm a little girl," said Alice, rather doubtfully, as she remembered the number of changes she had gone through.

"A likely story indeed!" said the pigeon, "I've seen a good many of them in my time, but never *one* with such a neck as yours! No, you're a serpent, I know *that* well enough! I suppose you'll tell me next that you never tasted an egg!"

"I *have* tasted eggs, certainly," said Alice, who was a very truthful child, "but indeed I don't want any of yours. I don't like them raw."

"Well, be off, then!" said the pigeon, and settled down into its nest again. Alice crouched down among the trees, as well as she could, as her neck kept getting entangled among the branches, and several times she had to stop and untwist it. Soon she remembered the pieces of mushroom which she still held in her hands, and set to work very carefully, nibbling first at one and then at the other, and growing sometimes taller and sometimes shorter, until she had succeeded in bringing herself down to her usual size.

It was so long since she had been of the right size that it felt quite strange at first, but she got quite used to it in a minute or two, and began talking to herself as usual. "Well! there's half my plan done now! How puzzling all these changes are! I'm never sure what I'm going to be, from one minute to another! However, I've got to my right size again. The next thing is, to get into that beautiful garden—how *is* that to be done, I wonder?"

Just as she said this, she noticed that one of the trees had a doorway leading right into it. "That's very curious!" she thought, "but everything's curious today. I may as well go in." And in she went.

Once more she found herself in the long hall, and close to the little glass table. "Now, I'll manage better this time," she said to herself, and began by taking the little golden key, and unlocking the door that led into the garden. Then she set to work eating the pieces of mushroom till she was about fifteen inches high: then she walked down the little passage: and *then*—she found herself at last in the beautiful garden, among the bright flowerbeds and the cool fountains.

Chapter IV

A large rose tree stood near the entrance of the garden. The roses on it were white, but there were three gardeners at it, busily painting them red. This Alice thought a very curious thing, and she went near to watch them, and just as she came up she heard one of them say, "Look out, Five! Don't go splashing paint over me like that!"

"I couldn't help it," said Five in a sulky tone, "Seven jogged my elbow."

On which Seven lifted up his head and said, "That's right, Five! Always lay the blame on others!"

"*You'd* better not talk!" said Five, "I heard the Queen say only yesterday she thought of having you beheaded!"

"What for?" said the one who had spoken first.

"That's not your business, Two!" said Seven.

"Yes, it *is* his business!" said Five, "and I'll tell him: it was for bringing tulip-roots to the cook instead of potatoes."

Seven flung down his brush, and had just begun, "Well! of all the unjust things—" when his eye fell upon Alice, and he stopped suddenly. The others looked round, and all of them took off their hats and bowed low.

"Would you tell me, please," said Alice timidly, "why you are painting those roses?"

Five and Seven looked at Two, but said nothing. Two began, in a low voice, "Why, Miss, the fact is, this ought to have been a red rose tree, and we put a white one in by mistake, and if the Queen was to find it out, we should all have our heads cut off. So, you see, we're doing our best, before she comes, to—" At this moment Five, who had been looking anxiously across the garden, called out "the Queen! the Queen!" and the three gardeners instantly threw themselves flat upon their faces. There was a sound of many footsteps, and Alice looked round, eager to see the Queen.

First came ten soldiers carrying clubs. These were all shaped like the three gardeners, flat and oblong, with their hands and feet at the corners. Next the ten courtiers; these were all ornamented with diamonds, and walked two and two, as the soldiers did. After these came the Royal children. There were ten of them, and the little dears came jumping merrily along, hand in hand, in couples; they were all ornamented with hearts. Next came the guests, mostly kings and queens, among whom Alice recognized the white rabbit. It was talking in a hurried nervous manner, smiling at everything that was said, and went by without noticing her. Then followed the Knave of Hearts, carrying the King's crown on a cushion, and, last of all this grand procession, came THE KING AND QUEEN OF HEARTS.

When the procession came opposite to Alice, they all stopped and looked at her, and the Queen said severely "Who is this?" She said it to the Knave of Hearts, who only bowed and smiled in reply.

"Idiot!" said the Queen, turning up her nose, and asked Alice "What's your name?"

"My name is Alice, so please your Majesty," said Alice boldly, for she thought to herself, "Why, they're only a pack of cards! I needn't be afraid of them!"

"Who are these?" said the Queen, pointing to the three gardeners lying round the rose tree, for, as they were lying on their faces, and the pattern on their backs was the same as the rest of the pack, she could not tell whether they were gardeners, or soldiers, or courtiers, or three of her own children.

"How should *I* know?" said Alice, surprised at her own courage, "it's no business of *mine*."

The Queen turned crimson with fury, and, after glaring at her for a minute, began in a voice of thunder, "Off with her—"

"Nonsense!" said Alice, very loudly and decidedly, and the Queen was silent.

The King laid his hand upon her arm, and said timidly, "Remember, my dear! She is only a child!"

The Queen turned angrily away from him, and said to the Knave, "Turn them over!"

The Knave did so, very carefully, with one foot.

"Get up!" said the Queen, in a shrill loud voice, and the three gardeners instantly jumped up, and began bowing to the King, the Queen, the Royal children, and everybody else.

"Leave off that!" screamed the Queen, "you make me giddy." And then, turning to the rose tree, she went on, "What *have* you been doing here?"

"May it please your Majesty," said Two very humbly, going down on one knee as he spoke, "we were trying—"

"*I* see!" said the Queen, who had meantime been examining the roses. "Off with their heads!" and the procession moved on, three of the soldiers remaining behind to execute the three unfortunate gardeners, who ran to Alice for protection.

"You shan't be beheaded!" said Alice, and she put them into her pocket. The three soldiers marched once round her, looking for them, and then quietly marched after the others.

"Are their heads off?" shouted the Queen.

"Their heads are gone," the soldiers shouted in reply, "if it please your Majesty!"

"That's right!" shouted the Queen. "Can you play croquet?"

The soldiers were silent, and looked at Alice, as the question was evidently meant for her.

"Yes!" shouted Alice at the top of her voice.

"Come on then!" roared the Queen, and Alice joined the procession, wondering very much what would happen next.

"It's—it's a very fine day." said a timid little voice. She was walking by the white rabbit, who was peeping anxiously into her face.

"Very," said Alice, "where's the Marchioness?"

"Hush, hush!" said the rabbit in a low voice, "she'll hear you. The Queen's the Marchioness: didn't you know that?"

"No, I didn't," said Alice. "What of?"

"Queen of Hearts," said the rabbit in a whisper, putting its mouth close to her ear, "and Marchioness of Mock Turtles."

"What are *they?*" said Alice, but there was no time for the answer, for they had reached the croquet-ground, and the game began instantly.

Alice thought she had never seen such a curious croquet-ground in all her life. It was all in ridges and furrows. The croquet-balls were live hedgehogs, the mallets live ostriches, and the soldiers had to double themselves up, and stand on their feet and hands, to make the arches.

The chief difficulty which Alice found at first was to manage her ostrich. She got its body tucked away, comfortably enough, under her arm, with its legs hanging down, but generally, just as she had got its neck straightened out nicely, and was going to give a blow with its head, it *would* twist itself round, and look up into her face, with such a puzzled expression that she could not help bursting out laughing. And when she had got its head down, and was going to begin again, it was very confusing to find that the hedgehog had unrolled itself, and was in the act of crawling away. Besides all this, there was generally a ridge or a furrow in her way, wherever she wanted to send the hedgehog to, and as the doubled-up soldiers were always getting up and walking off to other parts of the ground, Alice soon came to the conclusion that it was a very difficult game indeed.

The players all played at once without waiting for turns, and quarrelled all the while at the tops of their voices, and in a very few minutes the Queen was in a furious passion, and went stamping about and shouting "Off with his head!" or "Off with her head!" about once in a minute. All those whom she sentenced were taken into custody by the soldiers, who of course had to leave off being arches to do this, so that, by the end of half an hour or so, there were no arches left, and all the players, except the King, the Queen, and Alice, were in custody, and under sentence of execution.

Then the Queen left off, quite out of breath, and said to Alice, "Have you seen the Mock Turtle?"

"No," said Alice, "I don't even know what a Mock Turtle is."

"Come on then," said the Queen, "and it shall tell you its history."

As they walked off together, Alice heard the King say in a low voice, to the company generally, "You are all pardoned."

"Come, that's a good thing!" thought Alice, who had felt quite grieved at the number of executions which the Queen had ordered.

They very soon came upon a Gryphon,[8] which lay fast asleep in the sun. "Up, lazy thing!" said the Queen, "and take this young lady to see the Mock Turtle, and to hear its history. I must go back and see after some executions I ordered"; and she walked off, leaving Alice with the Gryphon. Alice did not quite like the look of the creature, but on the whole she thought it quite as safe to stay as to go after that savage Queen. So she waited.

The Gryphon sat up and rubbed its eyes. Then it watched the Queen till she was out of sight. Then it chuckled. "What fun!" said the Gryphon, half to itself, half to Alice.

"What *is* the fun?" said Alice.

"Why, *she*," said the Gryphon, "it's all her fancy, that. They never executes nobody, you know. Come on!"

"Everybody says 'Come on!' here," thought Alice, as she walked slowly after the Gryphon: "I never was ordered about so before in all my life—never!"

They had not gone far before they saw the Mock Turtle in the distance, sitting sad and lonely on a little ledge of rock, and, as they came nearer, Alice could hear it sighing as if its heart would break. She pitied it deeply. "What is its sorrow?" she asked the Gryphon, and the Gryphon answered, very nearly in the same words as before, "It's all its fancy, that. It hasn't got no sorrow, you know. Come on!"

So they went up to the Mock Turtle, who looked at them with large eyes full of tears, but said nothing.

"This here young lady," said the Gryphon, "wants for to know your history, she do."

"I'll tell it," said the Mock Turtle, in a deep hollow tone, "sit down, and don't speak till I've finished."

So they sat down, and no one spoke for some minutes. Alice thought to herself, "I don't see how it can *ever* finish, if it doesn't begin." But she waited patiently.

"Once," said the Mock Turtle at last, with a deep sigh, "I was a real Turtle."

These words were followed by a very long silence, broken only by an occasional exclamation of "hjckrrh!" from the Gryphon, and the constant heavy sobbing of the Mock Turtle. Alice was very nearly getting up and saying, "Thank you, sir, for your interesting story," but she could not help thinking there *must* be more to come, so she sat still and said nothing.

"When we were little," the Mock Turtle went on, more calmly, though still sobbing a little now and then, "we went to school in the sea. The master was an old Turtle—we used to call him Tortoise—"

---

8. ***Gryphon*** (grif′ən), a mythical creature with the head, wings, and forelegs of an eagle, and the body, hind legs, and tail of a lion.

"Why did you call him Tortoise, if he wasn't one?" asked Alice.

"We called him Tortoise because he taught us," said the Mock Turtle angrily, "really you are very dull!"

"You ought to be ashamed of yourself for asking such a simple question," added the Gryphon, and then they both sat silent and looked at poor Alice, who felt ready to sink into the earth. At last the Gryphon said to the Mock Turtle, "Get on, old fellow! Don't be all day!" and the Mock Turtle went on in these words:

"You may not have lived much under the sea—" ("I haven't," said Alice,) "and perhaps you were never even introduced to a lobster—" (Alice began to say "I once tasted—" but hastily checked herself, and said "No, never," instead), "so you can have no idea what a delightful thing a Lobster Quadrille[9] is!"

"No, indeed," said Alice. "What sort of a thing is it?"

"Why," said the Gryphon, "you form into a line along the sea shore——"

"Two lines!" cried the Mock Turtle, "Seals, turtles, salmon, and so on—advance twice—"

"Each with a lobster as partner!" cried the Gryphon.

"Of course," the Mock Turtle said, "advance twice, set to partners——"

"Change lobsters, and retire in same order——" interrupted the Gryphon.

"Then, you know," continued the Mock Turtle, "you throw the——"

"The lobsters!" shouted the Gryphon, with a bound into the air.

"As far out to sea as you can——"

"Swim after them!" screamed the Gryphon.

"Turn a somersault in the sea!" cried the Mock Turtle, capering wildly about.

"Change lobsters again!" yelled the Gryphon at the top of its voice, "and then——"

"That's all," said the Mock Turtle, suddenly dropping its voice, and the two creatures, who had been jumping about like mad things all this time, sat down again very sadly and quietly, and looked at Alice.

"It must be a very pretty dance," said Alice timidly.

"Would you like to see a little of it?" said the Mock Turtle.

"Very much indeed," said Alice.

"Come, let's try the first figure!" said the Mock Turtle to the Gryphon. "We can do it without lobsters, you know. Which shall sing?"

"Oh! *you* sing!" said the Gryphon, "I've forgotten the words."

So they began solemnly dancing round and round Alice, every now and then treading on her toes when they came too close, and waving their forepaws to mark the time, while the Mock Turtle sang slowly and sadly, these words:

"Beneath the waters *of* the sea
Are lobsters thick as thick can be—
They love to dance with you and me,
My own, my gentle Salmon!"

The Gryphon joined in singing the chorus, which was:

"Salmon come up! Salmon go down!
Salmon come twist your tail around!
Of all the fishes *of* the sea
There's none so good as Salmon!"

"Thank you," said Alice, feeling very glad that the figure was over.

"Shall we try the second figure?" said the Gryphon. "Or would you prefer a song?"

"Oh, a song, please!" Alice replied, so eagerly, that the Gryphon said, in a rather offended tone, "Hm! no accounting for tastes! Sing her 'Mock Turtle Soup,' will you, old fellow!"

The Mock Turtle sighed deeply, and began, in a voice sometimes choked with sobs, to sing this:[10]

"Beautiful Soup, so rich and green,
Waiting in a hot tureen!
Who for such dainties would not stoop?
Soup of the evening, beautiful Soup!
Soup of the evening, beautiful Soup!
Beau—ootiful Soo—oop!

---

9. *Lobster Quadrille.* The *quadrille* (kwə dril′) was a kind of square dance fashionable in Victorian England.

10. The Mock Turtle's tribute to real turtle soup is a parody of a popular contemporary song, "Star of the Evening," with words and music by James Sayles. The first verse of the original runs as follows:

Beautiful star in heav'n so bright,
Softly falls the silv'ry light,
As thou movest from earth afar,
Star of the evening, beautiful star.

CHORUS:
Beautiful star,
Beautiful star,
Star of the evening, beautiful star.

FOLON

Beau—ootiful Soo—oop!
Soo—oop of the e-e-evening,
Beautiful beautiful Soup!

"Chorus again!" cried the Gryphon, and the Mock Turtle had just begun to repeat it, when a cry of "The trial's beginning!" was heard in the distance.

"Come on!" cried the Gryphon, and, taking Alice by the hand, he hurried off, without waiting for the end of the song.

"What trial is it?" panted Alice as she ran, but the Gryphon only answered "Come on!" and ran the faster, and more and more faintly came, borne on the breeze that followed them, the melancholy words:

"Soo—oop of the e-e-evening,
Beautiful beautiful Soup!"

The King and Queen were seated on their throne when they arrived, with a great crowd assembled around them: the Knave was in custody: and before the King stood the white rabbit, with a trumpet in one hand, and a scroll of parchment in the other.

"Herald! read the accusation!" said the King.

On this the white rabbit blew three blasts on the trumpet, and then unrolled the parchment scroll, and read as follows:

"The Queen of Hearts she made some tarts
All on a summer day:
The Knave of Hearts he stole those tarts,
And took them quite away!"

"Now for the evidence," said the King, "and then the sentence!"

"No!" said the Queen. "First the sentence, and then the evidence!"

"Nonsense!" cried Alice, so loudly that everybody jumped. "The idea of having the sentence first!"

"Hold your tongue!" said the Queen.

"I won't!" said Alice. "You're nothing but a pack of cards! Who cares for you?"

At this the whole pack rose up into the air, and came flying down upon her. She gave a little scream of fright, and tried to beat them off, and found herself lying on the bank, with her head in the lap of her sister, who was gently brushing away some leaves that had fluttered down from the trees on to her face.

"Wake up, Alice dear!" said her sister, "what a nice long sleep you've had!"

"Oh, I've had such a curious dream!" said Alice, and she told her sister all her Adventures Under Ground, as you have read them, and when she had finished, her sister kissed her and said, "It *was* a curious dream, dear, certainly! But now run in to your tea; it's getting late."

So Alice ran off, thinking while she ran (as well she might) what a wonderful dream it had been.

But her sister sat there some while longer, watching the setting sun, and thinking of little Alice and her Adventures, till she too began dreaming after a fashion, and this was her dream:

She saw an ancient city, and a quiet river winding near it along the plain, and up the stream went slowly gliding a boat with a merry party of children on board—she could hear their voices and laughter like music over the water—and among them was another Little Alice, who sat listening with bright eager eyes to a tale that was being told, and she listened for the words of the tale, and lo! it was the dream of her own little sister. So the boat wound slowly along, beneath the bright summer-day, with its merry crew and its music of voices and laughter, till it passed round one of the many turnings of the stream, and she saw it no more.

Then she thought, (in a dream within the dream, as it were,) how this same little Alice would, in the after-time, be herself a grown woman, and how she would keep, through her riper years, the simple and loving heart of her childhood; and how she would gather around her other little children, and make *their* eyes bright and eager with many a wonderful tale, perhaps even with these very adventures of the little Alice of long-ago; and how she would feel with all their simple sorrows, and find a pleasure in all their simple joys, remembering her own child-life, and the happy summer days. □□

Discussion

1. Angela Pietropinto, the actress who played Alice in the Manhattan Project theater production of *Alice in Wonderland* said, "I knew I didn't want to be Alice. I found her a drag. In the book she came across to me as very staid, almost prudish. She's always trying to fit things into what she's been taught. She seemed like a stiff little English girl, and I had no cerebral or visceral contact with her. She was everything I hated." **(a)** Do you like Alice? In responding to her, do you find that you have the same problems as Ms. Pietropinto, or do you think she is wrong in her assessment? **(b)** Are there times when Alice breaks the rules of proper behavior? If so, why does she do it? **(c)** Does Alice always try to "fit things into what she's been taught"? Use carefully chosen examples to explain your ideas. **(d)** Do you think that Lewis Carroll wanted his readers to like Alice? Where does he hint at his own feelings?

2. Certain readers think that during her underground journey Alice faces some of the ordinary problems of growing up, but in new forms. To test this hypothesis, try to explain how the following experiences might suggest challenges that confront all children: **(a)** Mysterious food, with instructions such as "Eat me." **(b)** Sudden alterations in bodily size and form. **(c)** Slips of the tongue; moments of forgetfulness.

3. How does each of the following characters treat Alice: The mouse, the white rabbit, the caterpillar, the pigeon, the Queen of Hearts, the Gryphon, the Mock Turtle. In each case try to decide whether the character acts as if Alice is a child and the character is an adult. What can you learn about adults from the way these creatures treat Alice?

4. In what instances does Alice muse over or struggle with questions about her identity? How are these questions answered?

5. **(a)** At one point Alice overhears Pat, one of the white rabbit's servants, report that he has been "digging for apples." What principles of the ordinary physical world do you find violated in this story? **(b)** Are such irregularities typical of the way children see the world? **(c)** Do they give the story the quality of a dream, or of a nightmare?

6. If there is anything that can be called a "plot" in *Alice's Adventures Under Ground,* it concerns Alice's attempts to enter the beautiful garden. How does the garden look to her when she first looks at it longingly through the small door? What is it like when she finally comes to inspect it closely? What might the garden symbolize?

Charles Lutwidge Dodgson
1832 • 1898

While he is known today primarily as Lewis Carroll, the author of *Alice in Wonderland, Through the Looking-Glass,* and *The Hunting of the Snark,* Charles Lutwidge Dodgson was for the greater part of his life a Lecturer in Mathematics at Christ Church. He was the author of abstruse works on mathematics and logic, booklets of games and puzzles, some light poetry, and a variety of witty pamphlets on contemporary affairs at Oxford.

Yet there were other facets to Dodgson's donnish existence. He was an expert photographer who took exceptional portraits of children and adults at a time when photography was a new art. He was personally acquainted with Tennyson, Rossetti, Thackeray, Ruskin, and other notables of the day. He regularly walked a dozen miles before retiring. But his favorite pastime was the entertainment of young children. *Alice's Adventures Under Ground,* the first version of *Alice in Wonderland,* was written for one of these children, Alice Liddell.

George Eliot

The Lifted Veil

Chapter I

The time of my end approaches. I have lately been subject to attacks of *angina pectoris;*[1] and in the ordinary course of things, my physician tells me, I may fairly hope that my life will not be protracted many months. Unless, then, I am cursed with an exceptional physical constitution, as I am cursed with an exceptional mental character, I shall not much longer groan under the wearisome burden of this earthly existence. If it were to be otherwise—if I were to live on to the age most men desire and provide for—I should, for once, have known whether the miseries of delusive expectation can outweigh the miseries of true prevision. For I forsee when I shall die, and everything that will happen in my last moments.

Just a month from this day, on the twentieth of September, 1850, I shall be sitting in this chair, in this study, at ten o'clock at night, longing to die, weary of incessant insight and foresight, without delusions and without hope. Just as I am watching a tongue of blue flame rising in the fire, and my lamp is burning low, the horrible contraction will begin at my chest. I shall only have time to reach the bell and pull it violently, before the sense of suffocation will come. No one will answer my bell. I know why. My two servants are lovers, and will have quarreled. My housekeeper will have rushed out of the house, in a fury, two hours before, hoping that Perry will believe she has gone to drown herself. Perry is alarmed at last, and is gone out after her. The little scullery-maid is asleep on a bench: she never answers the bell; it does not wake her. The sense of suffocation increases: my lamp goes out with a horrible stench: I make a great effort and snatch at the bell again. I long for life, and there is no help. I thirsted for the unknown: the thirst is gone. O God, let me stay with the known, and be weary of it: I am content. Agony of pain and suffocation—and all the while the earth, the fields, the pebbly brook at the bottom of the rookery, the fresh scent after the rain, the light of the morning through my chamber window, the warmth of the hearth after the frosty air—will darkness close over them forever?

Darkness—darkness—no pain—nothing but darkness: but I am passing on and on through the darkness: my thought stays in the darkness, but always with a sense of moving onward—

Before that time comes, I wish to use my last hours of ease and strength in telling the strange story of my experience. I have never fully unbosomed myself to any human being; I have never been encouraged to trust much in the sympathy of my fellowmen. But we have all a chance of meeting with some pity, some tenderness, some charity when we are dead; it is the living only who cannot be forgiven—the living only from whom men's indulgence and reverence are held off, like the rain by the hard east wind. While the heart beats, bruise it—it is your only opportunity; while the eye can still turn toward you with moist, timid entreaty, freeze it with an icy, unanswering gaze; while the ear, that delicate messenger to the inmost sanctuary of the soul, can still take in the tones of kindness, put it off with hard civility, or sneering compliment, or envious affectation of indifference; while the creative brain can still throb with the sense of injustice, with the yearning for brotherly recognition—make haste—oppress it with your ill-considered judgments, your trivial comparisons, your careless misrepresentations. The heart

1. ***angina pectoris,*** acute chest pain caused by heart disease.

will by-and-by be still—*ubi sœva indignatio ulterius cor lacerare nequit;*[2] the eye will cease to entreat; the ear will be deaf; the brain will have ceased from all wants as well as from all work. Then your charitable speeches may find vent; then you may remember and pity the toil and the struggle and the failure; then you may give due honor to the work achieved; then you may find extenuation for errors, and may consent to bury them.

That is a trivial schoolboy text; why do I dwell on it? It has little reference to me, for I shall leave no works behind me for men to honor. I have no near relatives who will make up, by weeping over my grave, for the wounds they inflicted on me when I was among them. It is only the story of my life that will perhaps win a little more sympathy from strangers when I am dead, than I ever believed it would obtain from my friends while I was living.

My childhood perhaps seems happier to me than it really was, by contrast with all the after-years. For then the curtain of the future was as impenetrable to me as to other children: I had all their delight in the present hour, their sweet indefinite hopes for the morrow; and I had a tender mother: even now, after the dreary lapse of long years, a slight trace of sensation accompanies the remembrance of her caress as she held me on her knee—her arms round my little body, her cheek pressed against mine. I had a complaint of the eyes that made me blind for a little while, and she kept me on her knee from morning till night. That unequaled love soon vanished out of my life, and even to my childish consciousness it was as if that life had become more chill. I rode my little white pony with the groom by my side as before, but there were no loving eyes looking at me as I mounted, no glad arms open to me when I came back. Perhaps I missed my mother's love more than most children of seven or eight would have done, to whom the other pleasures of life remained as before; for I was certainly a very sensitive child. I remember still the mingled trepidation and delicious excitement with which I was affected by the tramping of the horses on the pavement in the echoing stables, by the loud resonance of the grooms' voices, by the booming bark of the dogs as my father's carriage thundered under the archway of the courtyard, by the din of the gong as it gave notice of luncheon and dinner. The measured tramp of soldiery which I sometimes heard—for my father's house lay near a county town where there were large barracks—made me sob and tremble; and yet when they were gone past, I longed for them to come back again.

I fancy my father thought me an odd child, and had little fondness for me; though he was very careful in fulfilling what he regarded as a parent's duties. But he was already past the middle of life, and I was not his only son. My mother had been his second wife, and he was five-and-forty when he married her. He was a firm, unbending, intensely orderly man, in root and stem a banker, but with a flourishing graft of the active landholder, aspiring to county influence: one of those people who are always like themselves from day to day, who are uninfluenced by the weather, and neither know melancholy nor high spirits. I held him in great awe, and appeared more timid and sensitive in his presence than at other times; a circumstance which, perhaps, helped to confirm him in the intention to educate me on a different plan from the prescriptive one with which he had complied in the case of my elder brother, already a tall youth at Eton. My brother was to be his representative and successor; he must go to Eton and Oxford, for the sake of making connections, of course: my father was not a man to underrate the bearing of Latin satirists or Greek dramatists on the attainment of an aristocratic position. But, intrinsically, he had slight esteem for "those dead but sceptred spirits"; having qualified himself for forming an independent opinion by reading Potter's "Æschylus," and dipping into Francis's "Horace."[3] To this negative view he added a positive one, derived from a recent connection with mining speculations; namely, that a scientific education was the really useful training for a younger son. Moreover, it was clear that a shy, sensitive boy like me was not fit to encounter the

---

2. ***"ubi . . . nequit."*** ". . . where savage indignation cannot lacerate his heart any longer." This line comes from the Latin epitaph of Jonathan Swift, which he composed himself.
3. ***Potter's "Aeschylus." . . . Francis's "Horace."*** Latimer's father has his eldest son study at Eton for a traditional education in the classics. He does not do this out of any appreciation for learning, but because such training is the first step to social acceptance.

rough experience of a public school. Mr. Letherall had said so very decidedly. Mr. Letherall was a large man in spectacles, who one day took my small head between his large hands, and pressed it here and there in an exploratory, suspicious manner—then placed each of his great thumbs on my temples, and pushed me a little way from him, and stared at me with glittering spectacles. The contemplation appeared to displease him, for he frowned sternly, and said to my father, drawing his thumbs across my eyebrows—

"The deficiency is there, sir—there; and here," he added, touching the upper sides of my head, "here is the excess.[4] That must be brought out, sir, and this must be laid to sleep."

I was in a state of tremor, partly at the vague idea that I was the object of reprobation, partly in the agitation of my first hatred—hatred of this big, spectacled man, who pulled my head about as if he wanted to buy and cheapen it.

I am not aware how much Mr. Letherall had to do with the system afterward adopted toward me, but it was presently clear that private tutors, natural history, science, and the modern languages, were the appliances by which the defects of my organization were to be remedied. I was very stupid about machines, so I was to be greatly occupied with them; I had no memory for classification, so it was particularly necessary that I should study systematic zoology and botany; I was hungry for human deeds and human emotions, so I was to be plentifully crammed with the mechanical powers, the elementary bodies, and the phenomena of electricity and magnetism. A better-constituted boy would certainly have profited under my intelligent tutors, with their scientific apparatus; and would, doubtless, have found the phenomena of electricity and magnetism as fascinating as I was, every Thursday, assured they were. As it was, I could have paired off, for ignorance of whatever was taught me, with the worst Latin scholar that was ever turned out of a classic academy. I read Plutarch, and Shakespeare, and Don Quixote by the sly, and supplied myself in that way with wandering thoughts, while my tutor was assuring me that "an improved man, as distinguished from an ignorant one, was a man who knew the reason why water ran downhill." I had no desire to be this improved man; I was glad of the running water; I could watch it and listen to it gurgling among the pebbles, and bathing the bright green water-plants, by the hour together. I did not want to know *why* it ran; I had perfect confidence that there were good reasons for what was so very beautiful.

There is no need to dwell on this part of my life. I have said enough to indicate that my nature was of the sensitive, unpractical order, and that it grew up in an uncongenial medium, which could never foster it into happy, healthy development. When I was sixteen I was sent to Geneva to complete my course of education; and the change was a very happy one to me, for the first sight of the Alps, with the setting sun on them, as we descended the Jura, seemed to me like an entrance into heaven; and the three years of my life there were spent in a perpetual sense of exaltation, as if from a draught of delicious wine, at the presence of Nature in all her awful loveliness. You will think, perhaps, that I must have been a poet, from this early sensibility to Nature. But my lot was not so happy as that. A poet pours forth his song and *believes* in the listening ear and the answering soul, to which his song will be floated sooner or later. But the poet's sensibility without his voice—the poet's sensibility that finds no vent but in silent tears on the sunny bank, when the noonday light sparkles on the water, or in an inward shudder at the sound of harsh human tones, the sight of a cold human eye—this dumb passion brings with it a fatal solitude of soul in the society of one's fellowmen. My least solitary moments were those in which I pushed off in my boat, at evening, toward the center of the lake; it seemed to me that the sky, and the glowing mountaintops, and the wide blue water, surrounded me with a cherishing love such as no human face had shed on me since my mother's love had vanished out of my life. I used to do as Jean Jacques[5] did—lie down in my boat

4. ***the excess.*** During the nineteenth century there were a number of practitioners of the pseudo-science of *phrenology.* Phrenology involved the study of the bumps and depressions of the skull as indicative of various personality traits, according to the theories of Franz Joseph Gall (1758–1828), a German physician.

5. ***Jean Jacques.*** The French philosopher Jean Jacques Rousseau (1712–1778) was born in Geneva, and lived there until 1728, when he left the city to begin the wanderings he later recorded in his *Confessions.* Rousseau's thought was influential throughout the later eighteenth and early nineteenth centuries, the period of the French Revolution and the Romantic Movement.

and let it glide where it would, while I looked up at the departing glow leaving one mountaintop after the other, as if the prophet's chariot of fire were passing over them on its way to the home of light.[6] Then when the white summits were all sad and corpse-like, I had to push homeward, for I was under careful surveillance, and was allowed no late wanderings. This disposition of mine was not favorable to the formation of intimate friendships among the numerous youths of my own age who are always to be found studying at Geneva. Yet I made *one* such friendship; and, singularly enough, it was with a youth whose intellectual tendencies were the very reverse of my own. I shall call him Charles Meunier; his real surname—an English one, for he was of English extraction—having since become celebrated. He was an orphan, who lived on a miserable pittance while he pursued the medical studies for which he had a special genius. Strange! that with my vague mind, susceptible and unobservant, hating inquiry and given up to contemplation, I should have been drawn toward a youth whose strongest passion was science. But the bond was not an intellectual one; it came from a source that can happily blend the stupid with the brilliant, the dreamy with the practical: it came from community of feeling. Charles was poor and ugly, derided by Genevese *gamins*,[7] and not acceptable in drawing rooms. I saw that he was isolated, as I was, though from a different cause, and, stimulated by a sympathetic resentment, I made timid advances toward him. It is enough to say that there sprang up as much comradeship between us as our different habits would allow; and in Charles's rare holidays we went up the Salève together, or took the boat to Vevay, while I listened dreamily to the monologues in which he unfolded his bold conceptions of future experiment and discovery. I mingled them confusedly in my thought with glimpses of blue water and delicate floating cloud, with the notes of birds and the distant glitter of the glacier. He knew quite well that my mind was half absent, yet he liked to talk to me in this way; for don't we talk of our hopes and our projects even to dogs and birds, when they love us? I have mentioned this one friendship because of its connection with a strange and terrible scene which I shall have to narrate in my subsequent life.

This happier life at Geneva was put an end to by a severe illness, which is partly a blank to me, partly a time of dimly-remembered suffering, with the presence of my father by my bed from time to time. Then came the languid monotony of convalescence, the days gradually breaking into variety and distinctness as my strength enabled me to take longer and longer drives. On one of these more vividly remembered days, my father said to me, as he sat beside my sofa—

"When you are quite well enough to travel, Latimer, I shall take you home with me. The journey will amuse you and do you good, for I shall go through the Tyrol and Austria, and you will see many new places. Our neighbors, the Filmores, are come; Alfred will join us at Basle, and we shall all go together to Vienna, and back by Prague——"

My father was called away before he had finished his sentence, and he left my mind resting on the word *Prague*, with a strange sense that a new and wondrous scene was breaking upon me: a city under the broad sunshine; that seemed to me as if it were the summer sunshine of a long-past century arrested in its course—unrefreshed for ages by the dews of night, or the rushing rain-cloud; scorching the dusty, weary, time-eaten grandeur of a people doomed to live on in the stale repetition of memories, like deposed and superannuated kings in their real gold-inwoven tatters. The city looked so thirsty that the broad river seemed to me a sheet of metal; and the blackened statues, as I passed under their blank gaze, along the unending bridge, with their ancient garments and their saintly crowns, seemed to me the real inhabitants and owners of this place, while the busy, trivial men and women, hurrying to and fro, were a swarm of ephemeral visitants infesting it for a day. It is such grim, stony beings as these, I thought, who are the fathers of ancient faded children, in those tanned time-fretted dwellings that crowd the steep before me; who pay their court in the worn and crumbling pomp of the

---

6. ***the prophet's chariot . . . light.*** The setting sun reminds Latimer of the Hebrew prophet Elijah who was taken up to heaven in a fiery chariot.
7. ***gamins*** (gam′əns), neglected children who wander the city streets.

palace which stretches its monotonous length on the height; who worship wearily in the stifling air of the churches, urged by no fear or hope, but compelled by their doom to be ever old and undying, to live on in the rigidity of habit, as they live on in perpetual midday, without the repose of night or the new birth of morning.

A stunning clang of metal suddenly thrilled through me, and I became conscious of the objects in my room again: one of the fire irons had fallen as Pierre opened the door to bring me my draught. My heart was palpitating violently, and I begged Pierre to leave my draught beside me: I would take it presently.

As soon as I was alone again, I began to ask myself whether I had been sleeping. Was this a dream—this wonderfully distinct vision—minute in its distinctness down to a patch of rainbow light on the pavement, transmitted through a colored lamp in the shape of a star—of a strange city, quite unfamiliar to my imagination? I had seen no picture of Prague: it lay in my mind as a mere name, with vaguely-remembered historical associations—ill-defined memories of imperial grandeur and religious wars.

Nothing of this sort had ever occurred in my dreaming experience before, for I had often been humiliated because my dreams were only saved from being utterly disjointed and commonplace by the frequent terrors of nightmare. But I could not believe that I had been asleep, for I remembered distinctly the gradual breaking-in of the vision upon me, like the new images in a dissolving view, or the growing distinctness of the landscape as the sun lifts up the veil of the morning mist. And while I was conscious of this incipient vision, I was also conscious that Pierre came to tell my father Mr. Filmore was waiting for him, and that my father hurried out of the room. No, it was not a dream; was it—the thought was full of tremulous exultation—was it the poet's nature in me, hitherto only a troubled, yearning sensibility, now manifesting itself suddenly as spontaneous creation? Surely it was in this way that Homer saw the plain of Troy, that Dante saw the abodes of the departed, that Milton saw the earthward flight of the Tempter. Was it that my illness had wrought some happy change in my organization—given a firmer tension to my nerves—carried off some dull obstruction? I had often read of such effects—in works of fiction at least. Nay; in genuine biographies I had read of the subtilizing or exalting influence of some diseases on the mental powers. Did not Novalis feel his inspiration intensified under the progress of consumption?[8]

When my mind had dwelt for some time on this blissful idea, it seemed to me that I might perhaps test it by an exertion of my will. The vision had begun when my father was speaking of our going to Prague. I did not for a moment believe it was really a representation of that city; I believed—I hoped it was a picture that my newly-liberated genius had painted in fiery haste, with the colors snatched from lazy memory. Suppose I were to fix my mind on some other place—Venice, for example, which was far more familiar to my imagination than Prague; perhaps the same sort of result would follow. I concentrated my thoughts on Venice; I stimulated my imagination with poetic memories, and strove to feel myself present in Venice, as I had felt myself present in Prague. But in vain. I was only coloring the Canaletto engravings[9] that hung in my old bedroom at home; the picture was a shifting one, my mind wandering uncertainly in search of more vivid images; I could see no accident or form of shadow without conscious labor after the necessary conditions. It was all prosaic effort, not rapt passivity, such as I had experienced half an hour before. I was discouraged; but I remembered that inspiration was fitful.

For several days I was in a state of excited expectation, watching for a recurrence of my new gift. I sent my thoughts ranging over my world of knowledge, in the hope that they would find some object which would send a reawakening vibration through my slumbering genius. But no; my world remained as dim as ever, and that flash of strange light refused to come again, though I watched for it with palpitating eagerness.

---

8. ***Novalis . . . consumption.*** Novalis was the pseudonym used by the German romantic writer Friedrich von Hardenberg (1772–1801), who died of tuberculosis. The belief that tuberculosis intensified the powers of the imagination was widely held in the nineteenth century.

9. ***Canaletto engravings.*** Antonio Canaletto (1697–1768) was an Italian painter famous for his scenes of Venice.

My father accompanied me every day in a drive, and a gradually lengthening walk as my powers of walking increased; and one evening he had agreed to come and fetch me at twelve the next day, that we might go together to select a musical box, and other purchases rigorously demanded of a rich Englishman visiting Geneva. He was one of the most punctual of men and bankers, and I was always nervously anxious to be quite ready for him at the appointed time. But, to my surprise, at a quarter past twelve he had not appeared. I felt all the impatience of a convalescent who has nothing particular to do, and who has just taken a tonic in the prospect of immediate exercise that would carry off the stimulus.

Unable to sit still and reserve my strength, I walked up and down the room, looking out on the current of the Rhone, just where it leaves the dark-blue lake; but thinking all the while of the possible causes that could detain my father.

Suddenly I was conscious that my father was in the room, but not alone: there were two persons with him. Strange! I had heard no footstep, I had not seen the door open; but I saw my father, and at his right hand our neighbor Mrs. Filmore, whom I remembered very well, though I had not seen her for five years. She was a commonplace middle-aged woman, in silk and cashmere; but the lady on the left of my father was not more than twenty, a tall, slim, willowy figure, with luxuriant blonde hair, arranged in cunning braids and folds that looked almost too massive for the slight figure and the small-featured, thin-lipped face they crowned. But the face had not a girlish expression: the features were sharp, the pale gray eyes at once acute, restless, and sarcastic. They were fixed on me in half-smiling curiosity, and I felt a painful sensation as if a sharp wind were cutting me. The pale-green dress, and the green leaves that seemed to form a border about her pale blonde hair, made me think of a Water-Nixie—for my mind was full of German lyrics,[10] and this pale, fatal-eyed woman, with the green weeds, looked like a birth from some cold sedgy stream, the daughter of an aged river.

"Well, Latimer, you thought me long," my father said——.

But while the last word was in my ears, the whole group vanished, and there was nothing between me and the Chinese painted folding-screen that stood before the door. I was cold and trembling; I could only totter forward and throw myself on the sofa. This strange new power had manifested itself again—. But was it a power? Might it not rather be a disease—a sort of intermittent delirium, concentrating my energy of brain into moments of unhealthy activity, and leaving my saner hours all the more barren? I felt a dizzy sense of unreality in what my eye rested on; I grasped the bell convulsively, like one trying to free himself from nightmare, and rang it twice. Pierre came with a look of alarm in his face.

"Monsieur ne se trouve pas bien?"[11] he said, anxiously.

"I'm tired of waiting, Pierre," I said, as distinctly and emphatically as I could, like a man determined to be sober in spite of wine; "I'm afraid something has happened to my father—he's usually so punctual. Run to the Hôtel des Bergues and see if he is there."

Pierre left the room at once, with a soothing "Bien, Monsieur"; and I felt the better for this scene of simple waking prose. Seeking to calm myself still further, I went into my bedroom, adjoining the *salon,* and opened a case of eau de Cologne; took out a bottle; went through the process of taking out the cork very neatly, and then rubbed the reviving spirit over my hands and forehead, and under my nostrils, drawing a new delight from the scent because I had procured it by slow details of labor, and by no strange sudden madness. Already I had begun to taste something of the horror that belongs to the lot of a human being whose nature is not adjusted to simple human conditions.

Still enjoying the scent, I returned to the *salon*, but it was not unoccupied, as it had been before I left it. In front of the Chinese folding-screen there was my father, with Mrs. Filmore on his right hand, and on his left—the slim blonde-haired girl, with the keen face and the keen eyes fixed on me in half-smiling curiosity.

---

10. ***Water-Nixie . . . German lyrics.*** The nixie was a water-sprite from German folklore celebrated by various German romantic poets. She was presented as a sirenlike woman who lives in a river and lures boatmen to destruction.
11. ***"Monsieur . . . bien?"*** "Sir, don't you feel well?" [French]

"Well, Latimer, you thought me long," my father said——

I heard no more, felt no more, till I became conscious that I was lying with my head low on the sofa, Pierre and my father by my side. As soon as I was thoroughly revived, my father left the room, and presently returned, saying——

"I've been to tell the ladies how you are, Latimer. They were waiting in the next room. We shall put off our shopping expedition to-day."

Presently he said, "That young lady is Bertha Grant, Mrs. Filmore's orphan niece. Filmore has adopted her, and she lives with them, so you will have her for a neighbor when we go home—perhaps for a near relation; for there is a tenderness between her and Alfred, I suspect, and I should be gratified by the match, since Filmore means to provide for her in every way as if she were his daughter. It had not occurred to me that you knew nothing about her living with the Filmores."

He made no further allusion to the fact of my having fainted at the moment of seeing her, and I would not for the world have told him the reason: I shrank from the idea of disclosing to anyone what might be regarded as a pitiable peculiarity, most of all from betraying it to my father, who would have suspected my sanity ever after.

I do not mean to dwell with particularity on the details of my experience. I have described these two cases at length; because they had definite, clearly traceable results in my after-lot.

Shortly after this last occurrence—I think the very next day—I began to be aware of a phase in my abnormal sensibility, to which, from the languid and slight nature of my intercourse with others since my illness, I had not been alive before. This was the obtrusion on my mind of the mental process going forward in first one person, and then another, with whom I happened to be in contact: the vagrant, frivolous ideas and emotions of some uninteresting acquaintance—Mrs. Filmore, for example—would force themselves on my consciousness like an importunate, ill-played musical instrument, or the loud activity of an imprisoned insect. But this unpleasant sensibility was fitful, and left me moments of rest, when the souls of my companions were once more shut out from me, and I felt a relief such as silence brings to wearied nerves. I might have believed this importunate insight to be merely a diseased activity of the imagination, but that my prevision of incalculable words and actions proved it to have a fixed relation to the mental process in other minds. But this superadded consciousness, wearying and annoying enough when it urged on me the trivial experience of indifferent people became an intense pain and grief when it seemed to be opening to me the souls of those who were in a close relation to me—when the rational talk, the graceful attentions, the wittily-turned phrases, and the kindly deeds, which used to make the web of their characters, were seen as if thrust asunder by a microscopic vision, that showed all the intermediate frivolities, all the suppressed egoism, all the struggling chaos of puerilities, meanness, vague capricious memories, and indolent makeshift thoughts, from which human words and deeds emerge like leaflets covering a fermenting heap.

At Basle we were joined by my brother Alfred, now a handsome self-confident man of six-and-twenty—a thorough contrast to my fragile, nervous, ineffectual self. I believe I was held to have a sort of half-womanish, half-ghostly beauty; for the portrait-painters, who are thick as weeds at Geneva, had often asked me to sit to them, and I had been the model of a dying minstrel in a fancy picture. But I thoroughly disliked my own *physique*, and nothing but the belief that it was a condition of poetic genius would have reconciled me to it. That brief hope was quite fled, and I saw in my face now nothing but the stamp of a morbid organization, framed for passive suffering—too feeble for the sublime resistance of poetic production. Alfred, from whom I had been almost constantly separated, and who, in his present stage of character and appearance, came before me as a perfect stranger, was bent on being extremely friendly and brother-like to me. He had the superficial kindness of a good-humored, self-satisfied nature, that fears no rivalry, and has encountered no contrarieties. I am not sure that my disposition was good enough for me to have been quite free from envy toward him, even if our desires had not clashed, and if I had been in the healthy human condition which admits of generous confidence and charitable construction. There must always have been an antipathy between our natures. As it was, he became in a few weeks an object of intense hatred to me; and when he entered the room, still more when he spoke, it was as if a sensation of grating metal had set my teeth on edge. My diseased consciousness was more intensely and continually occupied with his thoughts and emotions than with those of any other person who came in my way. I was perpetually exasperated with the petty promptings of his conceit and his love of patronage, with his self-complacent belief in Bertha Grant's passion for him, with his half-pitying contempt for me—seen not in the ordinary indications of intonation and phrase and slight action, which an acute and suspicious mind is on the watch for, but in all their naked skinless complication.

For we were rivals, and our desires clashed, though he was not aware of it. I have said nothing yet of the effect Bertha Grant produced in me on a nearer acquaintance. That effect was chiefly determined by the fact that she made the only exception, among all the human beings about me, to my unhappy gift of insight. About Bertha I was always in a state of uncertainty: I could watch the expression of her face, and speculate on its meaning; I could ask for her opinion with the real interest of ignorance; I could listen for her words and watch for her smile with hope and fear: she had for me the fascination of an unraveled destiny. I say it was this fact that chiefly determined the strong effect she produced on me: for, in the abstract, no womanly character could seem to have less affinity for that of a shrinking, romantic, passionate youth than Bertha's. She was keen, sarcastic, unimaginative, prematurely cynical, remaining critical and unmoved in the most impressive scenes, inclined to dissect all my favorite poems, and especially contemptuous toward the German lyrics which were my pet literature at that time. To this moment I am unable to define my feeling toward her: it was not ordinary boyish admiration, for she was the very opposite, even to the color of her hair, of the ideal woman who still remained to me the type of loveliness; and she was without that enthusiasm for the great and good, which, even at the moment of her strongest dominion over me, I should have declared to be the highest element of character. But there is no tyranny more complete than that which a self-centred negative nature exercises over a morbidly sensitive nature perpetually craving sympathy and support. The most independent people feel the effect of a man's silence in heightening their value for his opinion—feel an additional triumph in conquering the reverence of a critic habitually captious and satirical: no wonder, then, that an enthusiastic, self-distrusting youth should watch and wait before the closed secret of a sarcastic woman's face, as if it were the shrine of the doubtfully benignant deity who ruled his destiny. For a young enthusiast is unable to imagine the total negation in another mind of the emotions which are stirring his own: they may be feeble, latent, inactive, he thinks, but they are there—they may be called forth; sometimes, in moments of happy hallucination, he believes they may be there in all the greater strength because he sees no outward sign of them. And this effect, as I have intimated, was heightened to its utmost intensity in me, because Bertha was the only being who remained for me in the mysterious seclusion of soul that renders such youthful delusion possible. Doubtless there was another sort of fascination at work—that subtle physical attraction which delights in cheating our psychological predictions, and in compelling the men who paint sylphs to fall in love with some *bonne et brave femme*,[12] heavy-heeled and freckled.

Bertha's behavior toward me was such as to encourage all my illusions, to heighten my boyish passion, and make me more and more dependent on her smiles. Looking back with my present wretched knowledge, I conclude that her vanity and love of power were intensely gratified by the belief that I had fainted on first seeing her purely from the strong impression her person had produced on me. The most prosaic woman likes to believe herself the object of a violent, a poetic passion; and without a grain of romance in her, Bertha had that spirit of intrigue which gave piquancy to the idea that the brother of the man she meant to marry was dying with love and jealousy for her sake. That she meant to marry

---

12. ***sylphs . . . bonne et brave femme.*** Sylphs are imaginary beings inhabiting the air, apparently named by the alchemist Paracelsus (1493–1541). The word is applied to a slender, graceful girl or woman. The phrase *bonne et brave femme* (literally, "good and brave woman") describes a good-natured, robust individual.

my brother, was what at that time I did not believe; for though he was assiduous in his attentions to her, and I knew well enough that both he and my father had made up their minds to this result, there was not yet an understood engagement—there had been no explicit declaration; and Bertha habitually, while she flirted with my brother, and accepted his homage in a way that implied to him a thorough recognition of its intention, made me believe, by the subtlest looks and phrases—feminine nothings which could never be quoted against her—that he was really the object of her secret ridicule; that she thought him, as I did, a coxcomb, whom she would have pleasure in disappointing. Me she openly petted in my brother's presence, as if I were too young and sickly ever to be thought of as a lover; and that was the view he took of me. But I believe she must inwardly have delighted in the tremors into which she threw me by the coaxing way in which she patted my curls, while she laughed at my quotations. Such caresses were always given in the presence of our friends; for when we were alone together she affected a much greater distance toward me, and now and then took the opportunity, by words or slight actions, to stimulate my foolish timid hope that she really preferred me. And why should she not follow her inclination? I was not in so advantageous a position as my brother, but I had fortune, I was not a year younger than she was, and she was an heiress, who would soon be of age to decide for herself.

The fluctuations of hope and fear, confined to this one channel, made each day in her presence a delicious torment. There was one deliberate act of hers which especially helped to intoxicate me. When we were at Vienna her twentieth birthday occurred, and as she was very fond of ornaments, we all took the opportunity of the splendid jewelers' shops in that Teutonic Paris to purchase her a birthday present of jewelry. Mine, naturally, was the least expensive; it was an opal ring—the opal was my favorite stone, because it seemed to blush and turn pale as if it had a soul. I told Bertha so when I gave it her, and said that it was an emblem of the poetic nature, changing with the changing light of heaven and of woman's eyes. In the evening she appeared elegantly dressed, and wearing conspicuously all the birthday presents except mine. I looked eagerly at her fingers, but saw no opal. I had no opportunity of noticing this to her during the evening; but the next day, when I found her seated near the window alone, after breakfast, I said, "You scorn to wear my poor opal. I should have remembered that you despised poetic natures, and should have given you coral or turquoise, or some other opaque, unresponsive stone." "Do I despise it?" she answered, taking hold of a delicate gold chain which she always wore round her neck and drawing out the end from her bosom with my ring hanging to it; "it hurts me a little, I can tell you," she said, with her usual dubious smile, "to wear it in that secret place; and since your poetical nature is so stupid as to prefer a more public position, I shall not endure the pain any longer."

She took off the ring from the chain and put it on her finger, smiling still, while the blood rushed to my cheeks, and I could not trust myself to say a word of entreaty that she would keep the ring where it was before.

I was completely fooled by this, and for two days shut myself up in my room whenever Bertha was absent, that I might intoxicate myself afresh with the thought of this scene and all it implied.

I should mention that during these two months—which seemed a long life to me from the novelty and intensity of the pleasures and pains I underwent—my diseased participation in other people's consciousness continued to torment me; now it was my father, and now my brother, now Mrs. Filmore or her husband, and now our German courier, whose stream of thought rushed upon me like a ringing in the ears not to be got rid of, though it allowed my own impulses and ideas to continue their uninterrupted course. It was like a preternaturally heightened sense of hearing, making audible to one a roar of sound where others find perfect stillness. The weariness and disgust of this involuntary intrusion into other souls was counteracted only by my ignorance of Bertha, and my growing passion for her; a passion enormously stimulated, if not produced, by that ignorance. She was my oasis of mystery in the dreary desert of knowledge. I had never allowed my diseased condition to betray itself, or to drive me into any

unusual speech or action, except once, when, in a moment of peculiar bitterness against my brother, I had forestalled some words which I knew he was going to utter—a clever observation, which he had prepared beforehand. He had occasionally a slightly-affected hesitation in his speech, and when he paused an instant after the second word, my impatience and jealousy impelled me to continue the speech for him, as if it were something we both had learned by rote. He colored and looked astonished, as well as annoyed; and the words had no sooner escaped my lips than I felt a shock of alarm lest such an anticipation of words—very far from being words of course, easy to divine—should have betrayed me as an exceptional being, a sort of quiet energumen,[13] whom every one, Bertha, above all, would shudder at and avoid. But I magnified, as usual, the impression any word or deed of mine could produce on others; for no one gave any sign of having noticed my interruption as more than a rudeness, to be forgiven me on the score of my feeble nervous condition.

While this superadded consciousness of the actual was almost constant with me, I had never had a recurrence of that distinct prevision which I have described in relation to my first interview with Bertha; and I was waiting with eager curiosity to know whether or not my vision of Prague would prove to have been an instance of the same kind. A few days after the incident of the opal ring, we were paying one of our frequent visits to the Lichtenberg Palace. I could never look at many pictures in succession; for pictures, when they are at all powerful, affect me so strongly that one or two exhaust all my capability of contemplation. This morning I had been looking at Giorgione's picture of the cruel-eyed woman, said to be a likeness of Lucrezia Borgia.[14] I had stood long alone before it, fascinated by the terrible reality of that cunning, relentless face, till I felt a strange poisoned sensation, as if I had long been inhaling a fatal odor, and was just beginning to be conscious of its effects. Perhaps even then I should not have moved away, if the rest of the party had not returned to this room, and announced that they were going to the Belvedere Gallery to settle a bet which had arisen between my brother and Mr. Filmore about a portrait. I followed them dreamily, and was hardly alive to what occurred till they had all gone up to the gallery, leaving me below; for I refused to come within sight of another picture that day. I made my way to the Grand Terrace, since it was agreed that we should saunter in the gardens when the dispute had been decided. I had been sitting here a short space, vaguely conscious of trim gardens, with a city and green hills in the distance, when, wishing to avoid the proximity of the sentinel, I rose and walked down the broad stone steps, intending to seat myself farther on in the gardens. Just as I reached the gravel walk, I felt an arm slipped within mine, and a light hand gently pressing my wrist. In the same instant a strange intoxicating numbness passed over me, like the continuance or climax of the sensation I was still feeling from the gaze of Lucrezia Borgia. The gardens, the summer sky, the consciousness of Bertha's arm being within mine, all vanished, and I seemed to be suddenly in darkness, out of which there gradually broke a dim firelight, and I felt myself sitting in my father's leather chair in the library at home. I knew the fireplace—the dogs for the wood-fire—the black marble chimney-piece with the white marble medallion of the dying Cleopatra in the centre. Intense and hopeless misery was pressing on my soul; the light became stronger, for Bertha was entering with a candle in her hand—Bertha, my wife—with cruel eyes, with green jewels and green leaves on her white ball-dress; every hateful thought within her present to me——"Madman, idiot! why don't you kill yourself, then?" It was a moment of hell. I saw into her pitiless soul—saw its barren worldliness, its scorching hate—and felt it clothe me round like an air I was obliged to breathe. She came with her candle and stood over me with a bitter smile of contempt; I saw the great emerald brooch on her bosom, a studded serpent with diamond eyes. I shuddered—I despised this woman with the barren soul and mean thoughts; but I felt helpless before her, as if she clutched my bleeding heart, and would clutch it till the last

---

13. ***energumen*** (en′ėr gü′men), a person possessed by the devil. In the early Church, a person declared an energumen was barred from worship, pending exorcism.

14. ***Giorgione's picture . . . Lucrezia Borgia.*** Giorgione (?1478–1511) was a Venetian painter. Lucrezia Borgia (1480–1519) was an Italian noblewoman rumored to have poisoned her enemies.

drop of life-blood ebbed away. She was my wife, and we hated each other. Gradually the hearth, the dim library, the candlelight disappeared—seemed to melt away into a background of light, the green serpent with the diamond eyes remaining a dark image on the retina. Then I had a sense of my eyelids quivering, and the living daylight broke in upon me; I saw gardens, and heard voices; I was seated on the steps of the Belvedere Terrace, and my friends were round me.

The tumult of mind into which I was thrown by this hideous vision made me ill for several days, and prolonged our stay at Vienna. I shuddered with horror as the scene recurred to me; and it recurred constantly, with all its minutiæ, as if they had been burned into my memory; and yet, such is the madness of the human heart under the influence of its immediate desires, I felt a wild hell-braving joy that Bertha was to be mine; for the fulfillment of my former prevision concerning her first appearance before me, left me little hope that this last hideous glimpse of the future was the mere diseased play of my own mind, and had no relation to external realities. One thing alone I looked toward as a possible means of casting doubt on my terrible conviction—the discovery that my vision of Prague had been false—and Prague was the next city on our route.

Meanwhile, I was no sooner in Bertha's society again, than I was as completely under her sway as before. What if I saw into the heart of Bertha, the matured woman—Bertha, my wife? Bertha, the *girl*, was a fascinating secret to me still: I trembled under her touch; I felt the witchery of her presence; I yearned to be assured of her love. The fear of poison is feeble against the sense of thirst. Nay, I was just as jealous of my brother as before—just as much irritated by his small patronizing ways; for my pride, my diseased sensibility, were there as they had always been, and winced as inevitably under every offense as my eye winced from an intruding mote. The future, even when brought within the compass of feeling by a vision that made me shudder, had still no more than the force of an idea, compared with the force of present emotion—of my love for Bertha, of my dislike and jealousy toward my brother.

It is an old story, that men sell themselves to the tempter, and sign a bond with their blood, because it is only to take effect at a distant day; then rush on to snatch the cup their souls thirst after with an impulse not the less savage because there is a dark shadow beside them forevermore. There is no short cut, no patent tram-road,[15] to wisdom: after all the centuries of invention, the soul's path lies through the thorny wilderness which must be still trodden in solitude, with bleeding feet, with sobs for help, as it was trodden by them of old time.

My mind speculated eagerly on the means by which I should become my brother's successful rival, for I was still too timid, in my ignorance of Bertha's actual feeling, to venture on any step that would urge from her an avowal of it. I thought I should gain confidence even for this, if my vision of Prague proved to have been veracious; and yet, the horror of that certitude! Behind the slim girl Bertha, whose words and looks I watched for, whose touch was bliss, there stood continually that Bertha with the fuller form, the harder eyes, the more rigid mouth,—with the barren selfish soul laid bare; no longer a fascinating secret, but a measured fact, urging itself perpetually on my unwilling sight. Are you unable to give me your sympathy—you who read this? Are you unable to imagine this double consciousness at work within me, flowing on like two parallel streams which never mingle their waters and blend into a common hue? Yet you must have known something of the presentiments that spring from an insight at war with passion; and my visions were only like presentiments intensified to horror. You have known the powerlessness of ideas before the might of impulse; and my visions, when once they had passed into memory, were mere ideas—pale shadows that beckoned in vain, while my hand was grasped by the living and the loved.

In after-days I thought with bitter regret that if I had foreseen something more or something different—if instead of that hideous vision which poisoned the passion it could not destroy, or if even along with it I could have had a foreshadowing of that moment when I looked on my brother's face for the last time, some softening influence would have been shed over my feeling

15. ***patent tram-road,*** the newly invented street car.

toward him: pride and hatred would surely have been subdued into pity, and the record of those hidden sins would have been shortened. But this is one of the vain thoughts with which we men flatter ourselves. We try to believe that the egoism within us would have easily been melted, and that it was only the narrowness of our knowledge which hemmed in our generosity, our awe, our human piety, and hindered them from submerging our hard indifference to the sensations and emotions of our fellow. Our tenderness and self-renunciation seem strong when our egoism has had its day—when, after our mean striving for a triumph that is to be another's loss, the triumph comes suddenly, and we shudder at it, because it is held out by the chill hand of death.

Our arrival in Prague happened at night, and I was glad of this, for it seemed like a deferring of a terribly decisive moment, to be in the city for hours without seeing it. As we were not to remain long in Prague, but to go on speedily to Dresden, it was proposed that we should drive out the next morning and take a general view of the place, as well as visit some of its specially interesting spots, before the heat became oppressive—for we were in August, and the season was hot and dry. But it happened that the ladies were rather late at their morning toilet, and to my father's politely-repressed but perceptible annoyance, we were not in the carriage till the morning was far advanced. I thought with a sense of relief, as we entered the Jews' quarter, where we were to visit the old synagogue, that we should be kept in this flat, shut-up part of the city, until we should all be too tired and too warm to go farther, and so we should return without seeing more than the streets through which we had already passed. That would give me another day's suspense—suspense, the only form in which a fearful spirit knows the solace of hope. But, as I stood under the blackened, groined arches of that old synagogue, made dimly visible by the seven thin candles in the sacred lamp, while our Jewish cicerone[16] reached down the Book of the Law, and read to us in its ancient tongue,—I felt a shuddering impression that this strange building, with its shrunken lights, this surviving withered remnant of mediæval Judaism, was of a piece with my vision. Those darkened dusty Christian saints, with their loftier arches and their larger candles, needed the consolatory scorn with which they might point to a more shriveled death-in-life than their own.

As I expected, when we left the Jews' quarter the elders of our party wished to return to the hotel. But now, instead of rejoicing in this, as I had done beforehand, I felt a sudden overpowering impulse to go on at once to the bridge, and put an end to the suspense I had been wishing to protract. I declared, with unusual decision, that I would get out of the carriage and walk on alone; they might return without me. My father, thinking this merely a sample of my usual "poetic nonsense," objected that I should only do myself harm by walking in the heat; but when I persisted, he said angrily that I might follow my own absurd devices, but that Schmidt (our courier) must go with me. I assented to this, and set off with Schmidt toward the bridge. I had no sooner passed from under the archway of the grand old gate leading on to the bridge than a trembling seized me, and I turned cold under the midday sun; yet I went on; I was in search of something—a small detail which I remembered with special intensity as part of my vision. There it was, the patch of rainbow light on the pavement transmitted through a lamp in the shape of a star.

Chapter II

Before the autumn was at an end, and while the brown leaves still stood thick on the beeches in our park, my brother and Bertha were engaged to each other, and it was understood that their marriage was to take place early in the next spring. In spite of the certainty I had felt from that moment on the bridge at Prague, that Bertha would one day be my wife, my constitutional timidity and distrust had continued to benumb me, and the words in which I had sometimes premeditated a confession of my love had died away unuttered. The same conflict had gone on within me as before—the longing for an assur-

---

16. ***cicerone*** (sis′ə rō′nē), a guide for sightseers.

ance of love from Bertha's lips, the dread lest a word of contempt and denial should fall upon me like a corrosive acid. What was the conviction of a distant necessity to me? I trembled under a present glance, I hungered after a present joy, I was clogged and chilled by a present fear. And so the days passed on: I witnessed Bertha's engagement and heard her marriage discussed as if I were under a conscious nightmare—knowing it was a dream that would vanish, but feeling stifled under the grasp of hard-clutching fingers.

When I was not in Bertha's presence—and I was with her very often, for she continued to treat me with a playful patronage that wakened no jealousy in my brother—I spent my time chiefly in wandering, in strolling, or taking long rides while the daylight lasted, and then shutting myself up with my unread books; for books had lost the power of chaining my attention. My self-consciousness was heightened to that pitch of intensity in which our own emotions take the form of a drama which urges itself imperatively on our contemplation, and we begin to weep, less under the sense of our suffering than at the thought of it. I felt a sort of pitying anguish over the pathos of my own lot: the lot of a being finely organized for pain, but with hardly any fibers that responded to pleasure—to whom the idea of future evil robbed the present of its joy, and for whom the idea of future good did not still the uneasiness of a present yearning or a present dread. I went dumbly through that stage of the poet's suffering, in which he feels the delicious pang of utterance, and makes an image of his sorrows.

I was left entirely without remonstrance concerning this dreamy wayward life: I knew my father's thought about me: "That lad will never be good for anything in life: he may waste his years in an insignificant way on the income that falls to him: I shall not trouble myself about a career for him."

One mild morning in the beginning of November, it happened that I was standing outside the portico patting lazy old Cæsar, a Newfoundland almost blind with age, the only dog that ever took any notice of me—for the very dogs shunned me, and fawned on the happier people about me—when the groom brought up my brother's horse which was to carry him to the hunt, and my brother himself appeared at the door, florid, broad-chested, and self-complacent, feeling what a good-natured fellow he was not to behave insolently to us all on the strength of his great advantages.

"Latimer, old boy," he said to me in a tone of compassionate cordiality, "what a pity it is you don't have a run with the hounds now and then! The finest thing in the world for low spirits!"

"Low spirits!" I thought bitterly, as he rode away; "that is the sort of phrase with which coarse, narrow natures like yours think to describe experience of which you can know no more than your horse knows. It is to such as you that the good of this world falls: ready dullness, healthy selfishness, good-tempered conceit—these are the keys to happiness."

The quick thought came that my selfishness was even stronger than his—it was only a suffering selfishness instead of an enjoying one. But then, again, my exasperating insight into Alfred's self-complacent soul, his freedom from all the doubts and fears, the unsatisfied yearnings, the exquisite tortures of sensitiveness, that had made the web of my life, seemed to absolve me from all bonds toward him. This man needed no pity, no love; those fine influences would have been as little felt by him as the delicate white mist is felt by the rock it caresses. There was no evil in store for *him*: if he was not to marry Bertha, it would be because he had found a lot pleasanter to himself.

Mr. Filmore's house lay not more than a half a mile beyond our own gates, and whenever I knew my brother was gone in another direction, I went there for the chance of finding Bertha at home. Later on in the day I walked thither. By a rare accident she was alone, and we walked out in the grounds together, for she seldom went on foot beyond the trimly-swept gravel-walks. I remember what a beautiful sylph she looked to me as the low November sun shone on her blonde hair, and she tripped along teasing me with her usual light banter, to which I listened half fondly, half moodily; it was all the sign Bertha's mysterious inner self ever made to me. To-day perhaps the moodiness predominated, for I had not yet shaken off the access of jealous hate which my brother had raised in me by his parting patronage. Suddenly I interrupted and startled her by saying, almost fiercely, "Bertha, how can you love Alfred?"

She looked at me with surprise for a moment, but soon her light smile came again, and she answered sarcastically, "Why do you suppose I love him?"

"How can you ask that, Bertha?"

"What! your wisdom thinks I must love the man I'm going to marry? The most unpleasant thing in the world. I should quarrel with him; I should be jealous of him; our *ménage*[17] would be conducted in a very ill-bred manner. A little quiet contempt contributes greatly to the elegance of life."

"Bertha, that is not your real feeling. Why do you delight in trying to deceive me by inventing such cynical speeches?"

"I need never take the trouble of invention in order to deceive you, my small Tasso"[18]—(that was the mocking name she usually gave me). "The easiest way to deceive a poet is to tell him the truth."

She was testing the validity of her epigram in a daring way, and for a moment the shadow of my vision—the Bertha whose soul was no secret to me—passed between me and the radiant girl, the playful sylph whose feelings were a fascinating mystery. I suppose I must have shuddered, or betrayed in some other way my momentary chill of horror.

"Tasso!" she said, seizing my wrist, and peeping round into my face, "are you really beginning to discern what a heartless girl I am? Why, you are not half the poet I thought you were; you are actually capable of believing the truth about me."

The shadow passed from between us, and was no longer the object nearest to me. The girl whose light fingers grasped me, whose elfish, charming face looked into mine—who, I thought, was betraying an interest in my feelings that she would not have directly avowed,—this warm-breathing presence again possessed my senses and imagination like a returning siren melody which had been overpowered for an instant by the roar of threatening waves. It was a moment as delicious to me as the waking up to a consciousness of youth after a dream of middle age. I forgot everything but my passion, and said with swimming eyes—

"Bertha, shall you love me when we are first married? I wouldn't mind if you really loved me only for a little while."

Her look of astonishment, as she loosed my hand and started away from me recalled me to a sense of my strange, my criminal indiscretion.

"Forgive me," I said, hurriedly, as soon as I could speak again; "I did not know what I was saying."

"Ah, Tasso's mad fit has come on, I see," she answered, quietly, for she had recovered herself sooner than I had. "Let him go home and keep his head cool. I must go in, for the sun is setting."

I left her—full of indignation against myself. I had let slip words, which, if she reflected on them, might rouse in her a suspicion of my abnormal mental condition—a suspicion which of all things I dreaded. And besides that, I was ashamed of the apparent baseness I had committed in uttering them to my brother's betrothed wife. I wandered home slowly, entering our park through a private gate instead of by the lodges. As I approached the house, I saw a man dashing off at full speed from the stable-yard across the park. Had any accident happened at home? No; perhaps it was one of my father's peremptory business errands that required this headlong haste. Nevertheless I quickened my pace without any distinct motive, and was soon at the house. I will not dwell on the scene I found there. My brother was dead—had been pitched from his horse, and killed on the spot by a concussion of the brain.

I went up to the room where he lay, and where my father was seated beside him with a look of rigid despair. I had shunned my father more than any one since our return home, for the radical antipathy between our natures made my insight into his inner self a constant affliction to me. But now, as I went up to him, and stood beside him in sad silence, I felt the presence of a new element that blended us as we had never been blent before. My father had been one of the most successful men in the money-getting world,

---

17. ***ménage,*** household. [French]
18. ***Tasso.*** Torquato Tasso (1544–1595) was an Italian poet and the author of the epic *Jerusalem Delivered* (1575), which tells of the capture of Jerusalem from the Saracens by the Crusaders under Godfrey of Bouillon. One of the principal characters in the poem is the beautiful sorceress Armida, who is employed by Satan to seduce the Crusaders.

he had had no sentimental sufferings, no illness. The heaviest trouble that had befallen him was the death of his first wife. But he married my mother soon after and I remember he seemed exactly the same, to my keen childish observation, the week after her death as before. But now, at last, a sorrow had come—the sorrow of old age, which suffers the more from the crushing of its pride and its hopes, in proportion as the pride and hope are narrow and prosaic. His son was to have been married soon—would probably have stood for the borough at the next election. That son's existence was the best motive that could be alleged for making new purchases of land every year to round off the estate. It is a dreary thing to live on doing the same things year after year, without knowing why we do them. Perhaps the tragedy of disappointed youth and passion is less piteous than the tragedy of disappointed age and worldliness.

As I saw into the desolation of my father's heart, I felt a movement of deep pity toward him, which was the beginning of a new affection—an affection that grew and strengthened in spite of the strange bitterness with which he regarded me in the first month or two after my brother's death. If it had not been for the softening influence of my compassion for him—the first deep compassion I had ever felt—I should have been stung by the perception that my father transferred the inheritance of an eldest son to me with a mortified sense that fate had compelled him to the unwelcome course of caring for me as an important being. It was only in spite of himself that he began to think of me with anxious regard. There is hardly any neglected child for whom death has made vacant a more favored place, who will not understand what I mean.

Gradually, however, my new deference to his wishes, the effect of that patience which was born of my pity for him, won upon his affection, and he began to please himself with the endeavor to make me fill my brother's place as fully as my feebler personality would admit. I saw that the prospect which by-and-by presented itself of my becoming Bertha's husband was welcome to him, and he even contemplated in my case what he had not intended in my brother's—that his son and daughter-in-law should make one household with him. My softened feeling toward my father made this the happiest time I had known since childhood;—these last months in which I retained the delicious illusion of loving Bertha, of longing and doubting and hoping that she might love me. She behaved with a certain new consciousness and distance toward me after my brother's death; and I too was under a double constraint—that of delicacy toward my brother's memory, and of anxiety as to the impression my abrupt words had left on her mind. But the additional screen this mutual reserve erected between us only brought me more completely under her power: no matter how empty the adytum,[19] so that the veil be thick enough. So absolute is our soul's need of something hidden and uncertain for the maintenance of that doubt and hope and effort which are the breath of its life, that if the whole future were laid bare to us beyond to-day, the interest of all mankind would be bent on the hours that lie between; we should pant after the uncertainties of our one morning and our one afternoon; we should rush fiercely to the Exchange for our last possibility of speculation, of success, of disappointment; we should have a glut of political prophets foretelling a crisis or a no-crisis within the only twenty-four hours left open to prophecy. Conceive the condition of the human mind if all propositions whatsoever were self-evident except one, which was to become self-evident at the close of a summer's day, but in the meantime might be the subject of question, of hypothesis, of debate. Art and philosophy, literature and science, would fasten like bees on that one proposition which had the honey of probability in it, and be the more eager because their enjoyment would end with sunset. Our impulses, our spiritual activities, no more adjust themselves to the idea of their future nullity, than the beating of our heart, or the irritability of our muscles.

Bertha, the slim, fair-haired girl, whose present thoughts and emotions were an enigma to me amidst the fatiguing obviousness of the other minds around me, was as absorbing to me as a single unknown to-day—as a single hypothetic proposition to remain problematic till sunset; and all the cramped, hemmed-in belief and disbelief,

---

19. ***adytum*** (ad′ē tum), the innermost shrine of a sacred place, open only to the priesthood, and barred from public access by some kind of screen.

trust and distrust, of my nature, welled out in this one narrow channel.

And she made me believe that she loved me. Without ever quitting her tone of *badinage*[20] and playful superiority, she intoxicated me with the sense that I was necessary to her, that she was never at ease unless I was near her, submitting to her playful tyranny. It costs a woman so little effort to besot us in this way! A half-repressed word, a moment's unexpected silence, even an easy fit of petulance on our account, will serve us as *hashish* for a long while. Out of the subtlest web of scarcely perceptible signs, she set me weaving the fancy that she had always unconsciously loved me better than Alfred, but that, with the ignorant fluttered sensibility of a young girl, she had been imposed on by the charm that lay for her in the distinction of being admired and chosen by a man who made so brilliant a figure in the world as my brother. She satirized herself in a very graceful way for her vanity and ambition. What was it to me that I had the light of my wretched prevision on the fact that now it was I who possessed at least all but the personal part of my brother's adventures? Our sweet illusions are half of them conscious illusions, like effects of color that we know to be made up of tinsel, broken glass, and rags.

We were married eighteen months after Alfred's death, one cold, clear morning in April, when there came hail and sunshine both together; and Bertha, in her white silk and pale-green leaves, and the pale hues of her hair and face, looked like the spirit of the morning. My father was happier than he had thought of being again: my marriage, he felt sure, would complete the desirable modification of my character, and make me practical and worldly enough to take my place in society among sane men. For he delighted in Bertha's tact and acuteness, and felt sure she would be mistress of me, and make me what she chose: I was only twenty-one, and madly in love with her. Poor father! He kept that hope a little while after our first year of marriage, and it was not quite extinct when paralysis came and saved him from utter disappointment.

I shall hurry through the rest of my story, not dwelling so much as I have hitherto done on my inward experience. When people are well known to each other, they talk rather of what befalls them externally, leaving their feelings and sentiments to be inferred.

We lived in a round of visits for some time after our return home, giving splendid dinner-parties, and making a sensation in our neighborhood by the new luster of our equipage, for my father had reserved this display of his increased wealth for the period of his son's marriage; and we gave our acquaintances liberal opportunity for remarking that it was a pity I made so poor a figure as an heir and a bridegroom. The nervous fatigue of this existence, the insincerities and platitudes which I had to live through twice over—through my inner and outward sense—would have been maddening to me, if I had not had that sort of intoxicated callousness which came from the delights of a first passion. A bride and bridegroom surrounded by all the appliances of wealth, hurried through the day by the whirl of society, filling their solitary moments with hastily-snatched caresses, are prepared for their future life together as the novice is prepared for the cloister—by experiencing its utmost contrast.

Through all these crowded excited months, Bertha's inward self remained shrouded from me, and I still read her thoughts only through the language of her lips and demeanor: I had still the human interest of wondering whether what I did and said pleased her, of longing to hear a word of affection, of giving a delicious exaggeration of meaning to her smile. But I was conscious of a growing difference in her manner toward me; sometimes strong enough to be called haughty coldness, cutting and chilling me as the hail had done that came across the sunshine on our marriage morning; sometimes only perceptible in the dexterous avoidance of a *tête-à-tête*[21] walk or dinner to which I had been looking forward. I had been deeply pained by this—had even felt a sort of crushing of the heart, from the sense that my brief day of happiness was near its setting; but still I remained dependent on Bertha, eager for the last rays of a bliss that would soon be gone forever, hoping and watching for some after-glow more beautiful from the impending night.

---

20. ***badinage*** (bad′n äzh′), playful, teasing chatter.

21. ***tête-à-tête*** (tāt′ə tāt′), intimate, private; literally, "head to head." [French]

I remember—how should I not remember?—the time when that dependence and hope utterly left me, when the sadness I had felt in Bertha's growing estrangement became a joy that I looked back upon with longing, as a man might look back on the last pains in a paralyzed limb. It was just after the close of my father's last illness, which had necessarily withdrawn us from society and thrown us more upon each other. It was the evening of my father's death. On that evening the veil which had shrouded Bertha's soul from me—had made me find in her alone among my fellow-beings the blessed possibility of mystery, and doubt, and expectation—was first withdrawn. Perhaps it was the first day since the beginning of my passion for her, in which that passion was completely neutralized by the presence of an absorbing feeling of another kind. I had been watching by my father's deathbed: I had been witnessing the last fitful yearning glance his soul had cast back on the spent inheritance of life—the last faint consciousness of love he had gathered from the pressure of my hand. What are all our personal loves when we have been sharing in that supreme agony? In the first moments when we come away from the presence of death, every other relation to the living is merged, to our feeling, in the great relation of a common nature and a common destiny.

In that state of mind I joined Bertha in her private sitting-room. She was seated in a leaning posture on a settee, with her back toward the door; the great rich coils of her pale blonde hair surmounting her small neck, visible above the back of the settee. I remember, as I closed the door behind me, a cold tremulousness seizing me, and a vague sense of being hated and lonely—vague and strong, like a presentiment. I know how I looked at that moment, for I saw myself in Bertha's thought as she lifted her cutting gray eyes and looked at me: a miserable ghost-seer, surrounded by phantoms in the noonday, trembling under a breeze when the leaves were still, without appetite for the common objects of human desire, but pining after the moonbeams. We were front to front with each other, and judged each other. The terrible moment of complete illumination had come to me, and I saw that the darkness had hidden no landscape from me, but only a blank prosaic wall: from that evening forth, through the sickening years which followed, I saw all round the narrow room of this woman's soul—saw petty artifice and mere negation where I had delighted to believe in coy sensibilities and in wit at war with latent feeling—saw the light floating vanities of the girl defining themselves into the systematic coquetry, the scheming selfishness, of the woman—saw repulsion and antipathy harden into cruel hatred, giving pain only for the sake of wreaking itself.

For Bertha, too, after her kind, felt the bitterness of disillusion. She had believed that my wild poet's passion for her would make me her slave; and that, being her slave, I should execute her will in all things. With the essential shallowness of a negative, unimaginative nature, she was unable to conceive the fact that sensibilities were anything else than weaknesses. She had thought my weaknesses would put me in her power, and she found them unmanageable forces. Our positions were reversed. Before marriage she had completely mastered my imagination, for she was a secret to me; and I created the unknown thought before which I trembled as if it were hers. But now that her soul was laid open to me, now that I was compelled to share the privacy of her motives, to follow all the petty devices that preceded her words and acts, she found herself powerless with me, except to produce in me the chill shudder of repulsion—powerless, because I could be acted on by no lever within her reach. I was dead to worldly ambitions, to social vanities, to all the incentives within the compass of her narrow imagination, and I lived under influences utterly invisible to her.

She was really pitiable to have such a husband, and so all the world thought. A graceful, brilliant woman, like Bertha, who smiled on morning callers, made a figure in ballrooms, and was capable of that light repartee which, from such a woman, is accepted as wit, was secure of carrying off all sympathy from a husband who was sickly, abstracted, and, as some suspected, crack-brained. Even the servants in our house gave her the balance of their regard and pity. For there were no audible quarrels between us; our alienation, our repulsion from each other, lay within the silence of our own hearts; and if the mistress went out a great deal, and seemed to dislike the master's society, was it not natural, poor thing? The master was odd. I was kind and just to my dependents, but I excited in them a shrinking, half-contemptuous pity; for this class of men and women are but slightly determined in their estimate of others by general considerations, or even experience, of character. They judge of persons as they judge of coins, and value those who pass current at a high rate.

After a time I interfered so little with Bertha's habits, that it might seem wonderful how her hatred toward me could grow so intense and active as it did. But she had begun to suspect, by some involuntary betrayals of mine, that there was an abnormal power of penetration in me—that fitfully, at least, I was strangely cognizant of her thoughts and intentions, and she began to be haunted by a terror of me, which alternated every now and then with defiance. She meditated continually how the incubus[22] could be shaken off her life—how she could be freed from this hateful bond to a being whom she at once despised as an imbecile, and dreaded as an inquisitor. For a long while she lived in the hope that my evident wretchedness would drive me to the commission of suicide; but suicide was not in my nature. I was too completely swayed by the sense that I was in the grasp of unknown forces, to believe in my power the self-release. Toward my own destiny I had become entirely passive; for my one ardent desire had spent itself, and impulse no longer predominated over knowledge. For this reason I never thought of taking any steps toward a complete separation, which would have made our alienation evident to the world. Why should I rush for help to a new course, when I was only suffering from the consequences of a deed which had been the act of my intensest will? That would have been the logic of one who had desires to gratify, and I had no desires. But Bertha and I lived more and more aloof from each other. The rich find it easy to live married and apart.

That course of our life which I have indicated in a few sentences filled the space of years. So much misery—so slow and hideous a growth of hatred and sin, may be compressed into a sentence! And men judge of each other's lives through this summary medium. They epitomize the experience of their fellow-mortal, and pronounce judgment on him in neat syntax, and feel themselves wise and virtuous—conquerors over the temptations they define in well-selected predicates. Seven years of wretchedness glide glibly over the lips of the man who has never counted them out in moments of chill disappointment, of head and heart throbbings, of dread and vain wrestling, of remorse and despair. We learn *words* by rote, but not their meaning; *that* must be paid for with our life-blood, and printed in the subtle fibres of our nerves.

But I will hasten to finish my story. Brevity is justified at once to those who readily understand, and to those who will never understand.

Some years after my father's death, I was sitting by the dim firelight in my library one January evening—sitting in the leather chair that used to be my father's—when Bertha appeared at the door, with a candle in her hand, and advanced toward me. I knew the ball-dress she had on—the white ball-dress, with the green jewels, shone upon by the light of the wax candle which lit up the medallion of the dying Cleopatra on the mantelpiece. Why did she come to me before going out? I had not seen her in the library, which was my habitual place, for months. Why did she stand before me with the candle in her hand, with her cruel contemptuous eyes fixed on me, and the glittering serpent, like a familiar demon, on her breast. For a moment I thought this fulfillment of my vision at Vienna marked some dreadful crisis in my fate, but I saw nothing in Bertha's mind, as she stood before me, except scorn for the look of overwhelming misery with which I sat before her.——"Fool, idiot, why don't you kill yourself, then?"—that was her thought. But at length her thoughts reverted to her errand, and she spoke aloud. The apparently indifferent nature of the errand seemed to make a ridiculous anticlimax to my prevision and my agitation.

"I have had to hire a new maid. Fletcher is going to be married, and she wants me to ask you to let her husband have the public-house and farm at Molton. I wish him to have it. You must give the promise now, because Fletcher is going

---

22. ***incubus*** (ing′kyə bəs), an evil spirit supposed to descend upon sleeping persons.

to-morrow morning—and quickly, because I'm in a hurry."

"Very well; you may promise her," I said, indifferently, and Bertha swept out of the library again.

I always shrank from the sight of a new person, and all the more when it was a person whose mental life was likely to weary my reluctant insight with worldly ignorant trivialities. But I shrank especially from the sight of this new maid, because her advent had been announced to me at a moment to which I could not cease to attach some fatality: I had a vague dread that I should find her mixed up with the dreary drama of my life—that some new sickening vision would reveal her to me as an evil genius. When at last I did unavoidably meet her, the vague dread was changed into definite disgust. She was a tall, wiry, dark-eyed woman, this Mrs. Archer, with a face handsome enough to give her coarse hard nature the odious finish of bold, self-confident coquetry. That was enough to make me avoid her, quite apart from the contemptuous feeling with which she contemplated me. I seldom saw her; but I perceived that she rapidly became a favorite with her mistress, and, after the lapse of eight or nine months, I began to be aware that there had arisen in Bertha's mind toward this woman a mingled feeling of fear and dependence, and that this feeling was associated with ill-defined images of candlelight scenes in her dressing-room, and the locking-up of something in Bertha's cabinet. My interviews with my wife had become so brief and so rarely solitary, that I had no opportunity of perceiving these images in her mind with more definiteness. The recollections of the past become contracted in the rapidity of thought till they sometimes bear hardly a more distinct resemblance to the external reality than the forms of an oriental alphabet to the objects that suggested them.

Besides, for the last year or more a modification had been going forward in my mental condition, and was growing more and more marked. My insight into the minds of those around me was becoming dimmer and more fitful, and the ideas that crowded my double consciousness became less and less dependent on any personal contact. All that was personal in me seemed to be suffering a gradual death, so that I was losing the organ through which the personal agitations and projects of others could affect me. But along with this relief from wearisome insight, there was a new development of what I concluded—as I have since found rightly—to be a prevision of external scenes. It was as if the relation between me and my fellowmen was more and more deadened, and my relation to what we call the inanimate was quickened into new life. The more I lived apart from society, and in proportion as my wretchedness subsided from the violent throb of agonized passion into the dullness of habitual pain, the more frequent and vivid became such visions as that I had had of Prague—of strange cities, of sandy plains, of gigantic ruins, of midnight skies with strange bright constellations, of mountain passes, of grassy nooks flecked with the afternoon sunshine through the boughs: I was in the midst of such scenes, and in all of them one presence seemed to weigh on me in all these mighty shapes—the presence of something unknown and pitiless. For continual suffering had annihilated my religious faith: to the utterly miserable—the unloving and the unloved—there is no religion possible, no worship but a worship of devils. And beyond all these, and continually recurring, was the vision of my death—the pangs, the suffocation, the last struggle, when life would be grasped at in vain.

Things were in this state near the end of the seventh year. I had become entirely free from insight, from my abnormal cognizance of any other consciousness than my own, and instead of intruding involuntarily into the world of other minds, was living continually in my own solitary future. Bertha was aware that I was greatly changed. To my surprise she had of late seemed to seek opportunities of remaining in my society, and had cultivated that kind of distant yet familiar talk which is customary between a husband and wife who live in polite and irrevocable alienation. I bore this with languid submission, and without feeling enough interest in her motives to be roused into keen observation; yet I could not help perceiving something triumphant and excited in her carriage and the expression of her face—something too subtle to express itself in words or tones, but giving one the idea that she lived in a state of expectation or hopeful suspense. My chief feeling was satisfaction that her inner self was once more shut out from me; and I almost revelled for the moment in the absent melancholy that made me answer her at cross purposes, and betray utter ignorance of what she had been saying. I remember well the look and the smile with which she one day said, after a mistake of this kind on my part: "I used to think you were a clairvoyant, and that was the reason why you were so bitter against other clairvoyants, wanting to keep your monopoly; but I see now you have become rather duller than the rest of the world."

I said nothing in reply. It occurred to me that her recent obtrusion of herself upon me might have been prompted by the wish to test my power of detecting some of her secrets; but I let the thought drop again at once; her motives and her deeds had no interest for me, and whatever pleasures she might be seeking, I had no wish to balk her. There was still pity in my soul for every living thing, and Bertha was living—was surrounded with possibilities of misery.

Just at this time there occurred an event which roused me somewhat from my inertia, and gave me an interest in the passing moment that I had thought impossible for me. It was a visit from Charles Meunier, who had written me word that he was coming to England for relaxation from too strenuous labor, and would like to see me. Meunier had now a European reputation; but his letter to me expressed that keen remembrance of an early regard, an early debt of sympathy, which is inseparable from nobility of character; and I, too, felt as if his presence would be to me like a transient resurrection into a happier pre-existence.

He came, and as far as possible, I renewed our old pleasure of making *tête-à-tête* excursions, though, instead of mountains and glaciers and the wide blue lake, we had to content ourselves with mere slopes and ponds and artificial plantations. The years had changed us both, but with what different result! Meunier was now a brilliant figure in society, to whom elegant women pretended to listen, and whose acquaintance was boasted of by noblemen ambitious of brains. He repressed with the utmost delicacy all betrayal of the shock which I am sure he must have received from our meeting, or of a desire to penetrate into my condition and circumstances, and sought by the utmost exertion of his charming social powers to make our reunion agreeable. Bertha was much struck by the unexpected fascinations of a visitor whom she had expected to find presentable only on the score of his celebrity, and put forth all her coquetries and accomplishments. Apparently she succeeded in attracting his admiration, for his manner toward her was attentive and flattering. The effect of his presence on me was so benignant, especially in those renewals of our old *tête-à-tête* wanderings, when he poured forth to me wonderful narratives of his professonal experience, that more than once, when his talk turned on the psychological relations of disease, the thought crossed my mind that, if his stay with me were long enough, I might possibly bring myself to tell this man the secrets of my lot. Might there not lie some remedy for *me*, too, in his science? Might there not at least lie some comprehension and sympathy ready for me in his large and susceptible mind? But the thought only flickered feebly now and then, and died out before it could become a wish. The horror I had of again breaking in on the privacy of another soul, made me, by an irrational instinct, draw the shroud of concealment more closely around my own, as we automatically perform the gesture we feel to be wanting in another.

When Meunier's visit was approaching its conclusion, there happened an event which caused some excitement in our household, owing to the surprisingly strong effect it appeared to produce on Bertha—on Bertha, the self-possessed, who usually seemed inaccessible to feminine agitations, and did even her hate in a self-restrained hygienic manner. This event was the sudden severe illness of her maid, Mrs. Archer. I have reserved to this moment the mention of a circumstance which had forced itself on my notice shortly before Meunier's arrival, namely, that there had been some quarrel between Bertha and this maid, apparently during a visit to a distant family, in which she had accompanied her mistress. I had overheard Archer speaking in a tone of bitter insolence, which I should have thought an adequate reason for immediate dismissal. No dismissal followed; on the contrary, Bertha seemed to be silently putting up with personal inconveniences from the exhibitions of this woman's temper. I was the more astonished to observe that her illness seemed a cause of strong solicitude to Bertha; that she was at the bedside night and day, and would allow no one else to officiate as head nurse. It happened that our family doctor was out on a holiday, an accident which made Meunier's presence in the house doubly welcome, and he apparently entered into the case with an interest which seemed so much stronger than the ordinary professional feeling, that one day when he had fallen into a long fit of silence after visiting her, I said to him—

"Is this a very peculiar case of disease, Meunier?"

"No," he answered, "it is an attack of peritonitis,[23] which will be fatal, but which does not differ physically from many other cases that have come under my observation. But I'll tell you what I have on my mind. I want to make an experiment on this woman, if you will give me permission. It can do her no harm—will give her no pain—for I shall not make it until life is extinct to all purposes of sensation. I want to try the effect of transfusing blood into her arteries after the heart has ceased to beat for some minutes. I have tried the experiment again and again with animals that have died of this disease, with astounding results, and I want to try it on a human subject. I have the small tubes necessary, in a case I have with me, and the rest of the apparatus could be prepared readily. I should use my own blood—take it from my own arm. This woman won't live through the night, I'm convinced, and I want you to promise me your assistance in making the experiment. I can't do without another hand, but it would perhaps not be well to call in a medical assistant from among your provincial doctors. A disagreeable foolish version of the thing might get abroad."

"Have you spoken to my wife on the subject?" I said, "Because she appears to be peculiarly sensitive about this woman: she has been a favorite maid."

"To tell you the truth," said Meunier, "I don't want her to know about it. There are always insuperable difficulties with women in these matters, and the effect on the supposed dead body may be startling. You and I will sit up together, and be in readiness. When certain symptoms appear I shall take you in, and at the right moment we must manage to get every one else out of the room."

I need not give our farther conversation on the subject. He entered very fully into the details, and overcame my repulsion from them, by exciting in me a mingled awe and curiosity concerning the possible results of his experiment.

We prepared everything, and he instructed me in my part as assistant. He had not told Bertha of his absolute conviction that Archer would not survive through the night, and endeavored to persuade her to leave the patient and take a night's rest. But she was obstinate, suspecting the fact that death was at hand, and supposing that he wished merely to save her nerves. She refused to leave the sickroom. Meunier and I sat up together in the library, he making frequent visits to the sickroom and returning with the information that the case was taking precisely the course he expected. Once he said to me, "Can you imagine any cause of ill feeling this woman has against her mistress, who is so devoted to her?"

"I think there was some misunderstanding between them before her illness. Why do you ask?"

"Because I have observed for the last five or six hours—since, I fancy, she has lost all hope of recovery—there seems a strange prompting in her to say something which pain and failing strength forbid her to utter; and there is a look of hideous meaning in her eyes, which she turns continually toward her mistress. In this disease the mind often remains singularly clear to the last."

"I am not surprised at an indication of malevolent feeling in her," I said. "She is a woman who has always inspired me with distrust and dislike, but she managed to insinuate herself into her mistress's favor." He was silent after this, looking at the fire with an air of absorption, till he went upstairs again. He stayed away longer than usual, and on returning, said to me quietly, "Come now."

I followed him to the chamber where death was hovering. The dark hangings of the large bed

23. ***peritonitis*** (per′ə tə nī′təs), an inflammation of the thin, transparent tissue that lines the walls of the abdomen and covers the organs in it.

made a background that gave a strong relief to Bertha's pale face as I entered. She started forward as she saw me enter, and then looked at Meunier with an expression of angry inquiry; but he lifted up his hand as if to impose silence, while he fixed his glance on the dying woman and felt her pulse. The face was pinched and ghastly, a cold perspiration was on the forehead, and the eyelids were lowered so as almost to conceal the large dark eyes. After a minute or two, Meunier walked round to the other side of the bed where Bertha stood, and with his usual air of gentle politeness toward her begged her to leave the patient under our care—everything should be done for her—she was no longer in a state to be conscious of an affectionate presence. Bertha was hesitating, apparently almost willing to believe his assurance and to comply. She looked round at the ghastly dying face, as if to read the confirmation of that assurance, when for a moment the lowered eyelids were raised again, and it seemed as if the eyes were looking toward Bertha, but blankly. A shudder passed through Bertha's frame, and she returned to her station near the pillow, tacitly implying that she would not leave the room.

The eyelids were lifted no more. Once I looked at Bertha as she watched the face of the dying one. She wore a rich *peignoir*,[24] and her blonde hair was half covered by a lace cap: in her attire she was, as always, an elegant woman, fit to figure in a picture of modern aristocratic life: but I asked myself how that face of hers could ever have seemed to me the face of a woman born of woman, with memories of childhood, capable of pain, needing to be fondled? The features at that moment seemed so preternaturally sharp, the eyes were so hard and eager—she looked like a cruel immortal, finding her spiritual feast in the agonies of a dying race. For across those hard features there came something like a flash when the last hour had been breathed out, and we all felt that the dark veil had completely fallen. What secret was there between Bertha and this woman? I turned my eyes from her with a horrible dread lest my insight should return, and I should be obliged to see what had been breeding about two unloving women's hearts. I felt that Bertha had been watching for the moment of death as the sealing of her secret: I thanked Heaven it could remain sealed for me.

Meunier said quietly: "She is gone." He then gave his arm to Bertha, and she submitted to be led out of the room.

I suppose it was at her order that two female attendants came into the room, and dismissed the younger one who had been present before. When they entered, Meunier had already opened the artery in the long, thin neck that lay rigid on the pillow, and I dismissed them, ordering them to remain at a distance till we rang: the doctor, I said, had an operation to perform—he was not sure about the death. For the next twenty minutes I forgot everything but Meunier and the experiment in which he was so absorbed, that I think his senses would have been closed against all sounds or sights which had no relation to it. It was my task at first to keep up the artificial respiration in the body after the transfusion had been effected, but presently Meunier relieved me, and I could see the wondrous slow return of life; the breast began to heave, the inspirations became stronger, the eyelids quivered, and the soul seemed to have returned beneath them. The artificial respiration was withdrawn: still the breathing continued, and there was a movement of the lips.

Just then I heard the handle of the door moving: I suppose Bertha had heard from the women that they had been dismissed: probably a vague fear had arisen in her mind, for she entered with a look of alarm. She came to the foot of the bed and gave a stifled cry.

The dead woman's eyes were wide open, and met hers in full recognition—the recognition of hate. With a sudden strong effort, the hand that Bertha had thought for ever still was pointed toward her, and the haggard face moved. The gasping eager voice said—

"You mean to poison your husband——the poison is in the black cabinet—— I got it for you——you laughed at me, and told lies about me behind my back, to make me disgusting——because you were jealous——are you sorry——now?"

The lips continued to murmur, but the sounds were no longer distinct. Soon there was no

24. *peignoir* (pān wär′), a loose dressing gown or negligee for women.

sound—only a slight movement: the flame had leaped out, and was being extinguished the faster. The wretched woman's heartstrings had been set to hatred and vengeance; the spirit of life had swept the chords for an instant, and was gone again for ever. Great God! Is this what it is to live again——to wake up with our unstilled thirst upon us, with our unuttered curses rising to our lips, with our muscles ready to act out their half-committed sins?

Bertha stood pale at the foot of the bed, quivering and helpless, despairing of devices, like a cunning animal whose hiding-places are surrounded by swift-advancing flame. Even Meunier looked paralyzed; life for that moment ceased to be a scientific problem to him. As for me, this scene seemed of one texture with the rest of my existence: horror was my familiar, and this new revelation was only like an old pain recurring with new circumstances.

Since then Bertha and I have lived apart—she in her own neighborhood, the mistress of half our wealth, I as a wanderer in foreign countries, until I came to this Devonshire nest to die. Bertha lives pitied and admired; for what had I against that charming woman, whom every one but myself could have been happy with? There had been no witness of the scene in the dying room except Meunier, and while Meunier lived his lips were sealed by a promise to me.

Once or twice, weary of wandering, I rested in a favorite spot, and my heart went out toward the men and women and children whose faces were becoming familiar to me: but I was driven away again in terror at the approach of my old insight—driven away to live continually with the one Unknown Presence revealed and yet hidden by the moving curtain of the earth and sky. Till at last disease took hold of me and forced me to rest here—forced me to live in dependence on my servants. And then the curse of insight—of my double consciousness, came again, and has never left me. I know all their narrow thoughts, their feeble regard, their half-wearied pity.

It is the twentieth of September, 1850. I know these figures I have just written, as if they were a long familiar inscription. I have seen them on this page in my desk unnumbered times, when the scene of my dying struggle has opened upon me. □□

Discussion

Chapter I

1. **(a)** In what ways does Latimer, the narrator of "The Lifted Veil," differ from his brother Alfred? **(b)** Why does their father prefer Alfred?

2. When does Latimer's ability to foresee future experiences first appear? Why does the author introduce it in this way?

3. **(a)** What characteristics make Bertha seem dangerous? **(b)** Why does she wear Latimer's ring, while she is planning to marry his brother?

4. Why does Latimer find his ability to read the thoughts of others painfully wearing?

5. Why does the author end the first chapter with the scene in Prague?

Chapter II

1. In what ways does the relationship between Latimer and Bertha change as the years of their married life go by? Why does it change?

2. **(a)** What scene in his married life does Latimer foresee years earlier, in Vienna, after looking at a portrait of Lucrezia Borgia? **(b)** In this scene, why does Bertha think, "Fool, idiot, why don't you kill yourself, then?" **(c)** For what reason is this scene directly linked with the news that Mrs. Archer is coming to serve as Bertha's new maid?

3. Many have wanted to see into the future. **(a)** Once he has this ability, does Latimer want to keep it? **(b)** Why does he reach this conclusion?

4. **(a)** What does Mrs. Archer do when Meunier artificially revives her after death? **(b)** What conclusions does this suggest about the ways death affects a person's character? **(c)** Why does Latimer fear his own impending death, given the misery of his current life?

Extension • Writing

Since Latimer, who tells the story of "The Lifted Veil," is our only source for the facts, everything that he says is open to question. Perhaps he is a madman or a liar. Or, perhaps, he is just confused, and exaggerates coincidences. Consider the way he describes what is happening and then write a short essay defending one of the two opposing positions which follow: **(a)** Latimer is simply confused. Everything he describes can be explained rationally. He had no special mental powers. **(b)** Latimer is correct. There is no other way to account for what has happened to him. He must have been able to see into the future.

Vocabulary • Dictionary

Determine whether the italicized words in each item below are synonyms or antonyms. Then select, from the pairs of words that follow, the words that are related in the same way as the words in the first pair. Write your choice on a separate sheet of paper. In each item, there is a word in each pair that you will probably have to check in the Glossary.

1. *incipient: beginning* as **(a)** captious : tolerant; **(b)** latent : concealed; **(c)** antipathy : liking.

2. *puzzle : enigma* as **(a)** disrespect : homage; **(b)** cruel : benignant; **(c)** careful : assiduous.

3. *reprobation : praise* as **(a)** prosaic : extraordinary; **(b)** superannuate: retire; **(c)** badinage : joking.

4. *clear : opaque* as **(a)** stroll : saunter; **(b)** skillful : dexterous; **(c)** false : veracious.

5. *cognizant : aware* as **(a)** odious : pleasant; **(b)** affinity : liking; **(c)** insolence : politeness.

6. *seriousness : frivolity* as **(a)** shorten : protract; **(b)** comfort : solace; **(c)** misfortune : affliction.

7. *presentiment : foreboding* as **(a)** tumult : calm; **(b)** strenuous : inactive; **(c)** haggard : careworn.

8. *discourtesy : civility* as **(a)** continual : incessant; **(b)** temporary : perpetual; **(c)** appeal : entreaty.

Mary Ann Evans (George Eliot)
1819 • 1880

Mary Ann Evans broke through most of the conventions of the Victorian era. Yet she was not temperamentally rebellious. Rather, for the highest motives, she found herself again and again defying the expectations of her society.

When she was twenty-one Evans's father moved the family to the provincial town of Coventry. There she met two young men who had written books sceptical of traditional Christian beliefs. Evans, who had gone through a period of adolescent religious fervor, now became convinced that conventional religion was fallacious. This, of course, deeply pained her father. For his sake she decided not to act on her doubts, but rather to live the role of the young Victorian woman.

But after her father's death Evans moved to London (1850), taking rooms by herself—an unusual and socially questionable decision. She soon obtained work as assistant editor to one of the era's most progressive journals, *The Westminster Review.* Now she met numbers of people as gifted as she was. Soon she fell in love with one of them, the writer and editor G. H. Lewes.

But Lewes was married, and, though his wife had deserted him, she refused to divorce him. In 1854 Mary Ann Evans and Lewes began living together. They considered themselves husband and wife and defied the legal technicalities of the day. To ordinary English people their life seemed immoral and most refused to have anything to do with them.

Lewes encouraged Evans to try her hand at writing fiction. She was nearly forty when her first stories appeared. Her work enjoyed immediate success with readers and critics. To protect it from the controversy surrounding her private life, Mary Ann Evans made up the pen name George Eliot and for some time preserved the secret of her identity. It might fairly be stated that she is the most intelligent and, in some ways, the most serious of the Victorian novelists.

Unit Review Tests 6: The Victorians

CONTENT REVIEW

1. Explain how both "The Lifted Veil" and "Alice's Adventures Under Ground" explore, each in its own way, experiences beyond the reach of science and the analytic powers of human reason.

2. Tennyson, Robert Browning, Elizabeth Barrett Browning, Christina Rossetti and George Eliot all write about death. Compare and contrast what they have to say about it. Do you find such widespread interest in this topic surprising for the Victorian era? Explain.

3. Describe the variety of reasons for living found in Tennyson's "Ulysses," Matthew Arnold's "Dover Beach," Emily Brontë's "Ah! why, because . . ." and Elizabeth Barrett Browning's sonnet forty-three.

4. Most Victorian writers were well-educated and acutely conscious of past history. Of the authors you have read, which try to re-create a moment from the past? In each case, can you see a timeless human experience the writer is exploring through this historical approach?

5. List the works from this unit that describe a journey from one place to another. What does each of the journeys seem to symbolize?

Unit 6, Test I
INTERPRETATION: NEW MATERIAL

from The Subjection of Women

John Stuart Mill

John Stuart Mill (1806–1873) thought deeply and wrote forcefully on all manner of social, political, economic, and philosophical issues. The possessor of a brilliant, analytical mind, he was one of the leading intellectual figures of the Victorian age. Influenced by his wife, Harriet Taylor, he became an advocate for the rights of women, an unpopular cause at the time. Mill viewed the subjection of women as one part of the general tyranny he opposed. He was elected to parliament and proposed the first legislation ever submitted to that body on the rights of women. The Subjection of Women *was the last work published by Mill. It aroused a great deal of opposition when it appeared in 1869. After you have read the selection, answer the questions that follow on a separate sheet of paper. You may have to reread parts of this excerpt in order to answer the questions.*

1. The object of this Essay is to explain, as clearly as I am able, the grounds of an opinion which I have held from the very earliest period when I had formed any opinions at all on social or political matters, and which, instead of being weakened or modified, has been constantly growing stronger by the progress of reflection and the experience of life: That the principle which regulates the existing social relations between the two sexes—the legal subordination of one sex to the other—is wrong in itself, and now one of the chief hindrances to human improvement; and that it ought to be replaced by a principle of perfect equality, admitting no power or privilege on the one side, nor disability on the other. . . .

2. In the first place, the opinion in favour of the present system, which entirely subordinates the weaker sex to the stronger, rests upon theory only; for there never has been trial made of any other; so that experience, in the sense in which it is vulgarly[1] opposed to theory, cannot be pretended to have pronounced any verdict. And in the second place, the adoption of this system of inequality never was the result of deliberation, or forethought, or any social ideas, or any notion whatever of what conduced[2] to the benefit of humanity or the good order of society. It arose simply from the fact that from the very earliest twilight of human society, every woman (owing to the value attached to her by men, combined with her inferiority in muscular strength) was found in a state of bondage to some man. Laws and systems of polity[3] always begin by recognizing the relations they find already existing between individuals. They convert what was a mere physical fact into a legal right, give it the sanction of society, and principally aim at the substitution of public and organized means of asserting and protecting these rights, instead of the irregular and lawless conflict of physical strength. Those who had already been compelled to obedience became in this manner legally bound to it. Slavery, from being a mere affair of force between the master and the slave, became regularized and a matter of compact among the masters, who, binding themselves to one another for common protection, guaranteed by their collective strength the private possessions of each, including his slaves. In early times, the great majority of the male sex were slaves, as well as the whole of the female. And many ages elapsed, some of them ages of high cultivation, before any thinker was bold enough to question the rightfulness, and the absolute social necessity, either of the one slavery or of the other. By degrees such thinkers did arise: and (the general progress of society assisting) the slavery of the male sex has, in all the countries of Christian Europe at least (though, in one of them, only within the last few years) been at length abolished, and that of the female sex has been gradually changed into a milder form of dependence. But this dependence, as it exists at present, is not an original institution, taking a fresh start from considerations of justice and social expediency—it is the primitive state of slavery lasting on, through successive mitigations and modifications occasioned by the same causes which have softened the general manners, and brought all human relations more under the control of justice and the influence of humanity. It has not lost the taint of its brutal origin. . . . The inequality of rights between men and women has no other source than the law of the strongest. . . .

3. Men do not want solely the obedience of women, they want their sentiments. All men, except the most brutish, desire to have, in the woman most nearly connected with them, not a forced slave but a willing one; not a slave merely, but a favourite. They have therefore put everything in practice to enslave their minds. The masters of all other slaves rely, for maintaining obedience, on fear; either fear of themselves, or religious fears. The masters of women wanted more than simple obedience, and they turned the whole force of education to effect their purpose. All women are brought up from the very earliest years in the belief that their ideal of character is the very opposite to that of men; not self-will, and government by self-control, but submission, and yielding to the control of others. All the moralities tell them that it is the duty of women, and all the current sentimentalities that it is their nature to live for others; to make complete abnegation[4] of themselves, and to have no life but in their affections. And by their affections are meant the only ones they are allowed to have—those to the men with whom they are connected, or to the children who constitute an additional and indefeasible[5] tie between them and a man. When we put together three things—first, the natural attraction between opposite sexes; secondly, the wife's entire dependence on the husband, every privilege or pleasure she has being either his gift, or depending entirely on his will; and lastly, that the principal object of human pursuit, consideration, and all objects of social ambition, can in general be sought or obtained by her only through him—it would be a miracle if the object of being attractive to men had not

---

1. ***vulgarly,*** commonly, popularly, generally.
2. ***conduced,*** contributed, led.
3. ***polity*** (pol′ə tē), government.
4. ***abnegation*** (ab′nə gā′shən), denial, renunciation.
5. ***indefeasible,*** not capable of being annulled, made void, or done away with.

become the polar star of feminine education and formation of character. And, this great means of influence over the minds of women having been acquired, an instinct of selfishness made men avail themselves of it to the utmost as a means of holding women in subjection, by representing to them meekness, submissiveness, and resignation of all individual will into the hands of a man, as an essential part of sexual attractiveness. . . .

4. What is now called the nature of women is an eminently artificial thing—the result of forced repression in some directions, unnatural stimulation in others. It may be asserted without scruple, that no other class of dependents have had their character so entirely distorted from its natural proportions by their relation with their masters; for, if conquered and slave races have been, in some respects, more forcibly repressed, whatever in them has not been crushed down by an iron heel has generally been let alone, and if left with any liberty of development, it has developed itself according to its own laws; but in the case of women, a hot-house and stove cultivation has always been carried on of some of the capabilities of their nature, for the benefit and pleasure of their masters. . . .

5. Hence, in regard to that most difficult question, what are the natural differences between the two sexes—a subject on which it is impossible in the present state of society to obtain complete and correct knowledge—while almost everybody dogmatizes[6] upon it, almost all neglect and make light of the only means by which any partial insight can be obtained into it. This is, an analytic study of the most important department of psychology, the laws of the influence of circumstances on character. . . . The profoundest knowledge of the laws of the formation of character is indispensable to entitle any one to affirm even that there is any difference, much more what the difference is, between the two sexes considered as moral and rational beings; and since no one, as yet, has that knowledge (for there is hardly any subject which, in proportion to its importance, has been so little studied), no one is thus far entitled to any positive opinion on the subject. Conjectures are all that can at present be made; conjectures more or less probable, according as more or less authorized by such knowledge as we yet have of the laws of psychology, as applied to the formation of character.

6. Even the preliminary knowledge, what the differences between the sexes now are, apart from all question as to how they are made what they are, is still in the crudest and most incomplete state. Medical practitioners and physiologists[7] have ascertained, to some extent, the differences in bodily constitution; and this is an important element to the psychologist; but hardly any medical practitioner is a psychologist. Respecting the mental characteristics of women: their observations are of no more worth than those of common men. It is a subject on which nothing final can be known, so long as those who alone can really know it, women themselves, have given but little testimony, and that little, mostly suborned.[8] It is easy to know stupid women. Stupidity is much the same all the world over. A stupid person's notions and feelings may confidently be inferred from those which prevail in the circle by which the person is surrounded. Not so with those whose opinions and feelings are an emanation[9] from their own nature and faculties. It is only a man here and there who has any tolerable knowledge of the character even of the women of his own family. I do not mean, of their capabilities; these nobody knows, not even themselves, because most of them have never been called out. I mean their actually existing thoughts and feelings. . . .

---

6. ***dogmatizes,*** asserts opinions in a positive or authoritative manner.

7. ***physiologists*** (fiz′ē ol′ə jists), experts in a branch of biology dealing with the normal functions of living things and their parts.

8. ***suborned*** (sə bôrnd′), persuaded, bribed, or caused to give false testimony.

9. ***emanation*** (em′ə nā′shən), something that originates, comes, or spreads from a person or thing as a source.

1. In the first paragraph, what principle does Mill say regulates the relations between the sexes?

2. What principle does he propose to replace the above-mentioned principle?

3. In the second paragraph, what two reasons are given (in a parenthetical comment) for women being in a state of bondage to men?

4. In the same paragraph, what primitive or original state does the author say lies behind women's present "milder form of dependence"?

5. In the third paragraph, what force is described as used by men to reconcile women to their condition by enslaving their minds?

6. In the same paragraph, what three things when put together does the author say made it almost certain that being attractive to men would be the goal of feminine education?

7. At the beginning of the fourth paragraph, what two reasons for the artificial nature of women does the author mention?

8. In the fifth paragraph, where does the author say that we must look to discover the natural differences (if any) between the sexes?

9. In the final paragraph, whose testimony does the writer say is essential in determining the mental characteristics of women?

10. What does the author say is the relationship between a stupid person's thoughts and feelings and those of such a person's circle of family, friends, and acquaintances?

Unit 6, Test II
COMPOSITION

You may choose any *one* of the following assignments. Assume that you are writing for your classmates.

1. This is the first unit in which women writers are widely represented. Discuss why this might be so in the light of *The Subjection of Women* (Test I). What might the fact that such an essay was written in the same period in which female writers began to emerge tell us about changing values?

2. Compare and contrast the views of the world expressed in Tennyson's "Ulysses" and Arnold's "Dover Beach."

3. Discuss the attitudes toward faith or belief in Tennyson's *In Memoriam* (#34) and Arnold's "Dover Beach."

4. What is the proper relationship between self and world as described in Arnold's "Self-Dependence"?

5. Describe the element of the odd or mad in "Porphyria's Lover" and "My Last Duchess," and "The Lifted Veil."

6. Discuss the relationship between Latimer and Bertha in Eliot's "The Lifted Veil" in the light of Mill's remarks concerning relationships between men and women in *The Subjection of Women* (Test I).

7. Write about various aspects of the opposed qualities of selfishness and selflessness as reflected in Robert Browning's "My Last Duchess," Arnold's "Self-Dependence," Elizabeth Barrett Browning's sonnet forty-three, and Mill's *The Subjection of Women.*

8. Compare and contrast the quality of command or authority in the Duke in Browning's "My Last Duchess" and in Arthur in Tennyson's "The Passing of Arthur."

9. Despite the seeming assurance of much of Victorian culture and literature, a note of doubt is evident in some of the writing that balances this self-confidence. Discuss those works from the unit that you think reflect the element of unease in nineteenth-century English life.

Unit 7

1880 | 1885 | 1890 | 1895

- Morris: *News from Nowhere*
- *Boys' Own Paper* started
- Pater: *Marius the Epicurean*
- Wells: *The Time Machine*
- Browning Society founded
- Farm laborers win vote
- Gissing: *New Grub Street*
- Stevenson: *New Arabian Nights*
- Hardy: *The Mayor of Casterbridge*
- Hardy: *Tess of the D'Urbervilles*
- Shaw: *An Unsocial Socialist*
- Doyle: *A Study in Scarlet*
- Housman: *A Shropshire Lad*
- Fabian Society founded
- Kipling: *Plain Tales from the Hills*
- Morris: *The Well at the World's End*
- First volume of the *Oxford English Dictionary*
- Yeats: *The Countess Cathleen*
- Death of Hopkins
- Hardy: *Jude the Obscure*
- Yeats: *The Wanderings of Oisin*
- Frazer: *The Golden Bough*
- Wilde: *The Importance of Being Earnest*

New Directions 1880-1915

1900 1905 1910 1915

- Shaw: *Major Barbara*
- Sinking of *Titanic*
- Conrad: *Lord Jim*
- Marconi transmits transatlantic radio signals
- Conrad: *The Secret Agent*
- Kipling: *Kim*
- Yeats: *Responsibilities*
- National Insurance Act
- Shaw: *Man and Superman*
- Hardy: *The Dynasts*
- Wells: *Tono Bungay*
- Hardy: *Wessex Poems*
- Queen Victoria's Diamond Jubilee
- The Boer War

Background: New Directions 1880-1915

The End of an Era

Victoria's England was a nation confident of its imperial role in the world—a role characterized by global power and accomplishment. On the verge of the twentieth century, England was the most economically powerful country in the world. The vast empire, on which "the sun never set," was protected by an unchallenged naval supremacy. As political, social, and cultural model, England's influence was inescapable.

The Victorian period had contained the controversy, conflict, and sobering reality that are always present at a time of great social change. During the nineteenth century, the number of offenses punishable by death was reduced from over two hundred to four. The major voting reform bills in 1832, 1867, and 1884 gave the vote to almost all male adults, but not to women, who would have to wait until 1928 to acquire full and equal voting rights. The House of Commons, whose members are elected, gained control of Parliament from the House of Lords, whose members are not elected. The rise of the Commons reflected the shift of power from the land-owning aristocracy to the middle-class factory owners, bankers, and professionals, who were proud of England's status as "the workshop of the world." However, the condition of most of the working class was still a matter of exploitation and poverty. The country had already begun to suffer from the negative aspects of the factory system—grimy towns and cities with overcrowded slums, and an oppressive sense of domination by institutions and machines. Reforms in education—such as the Education Act of 1870, which could require children to attend school until the age of thirteen—helped to create an even larger literate public than the audience which had received Dickens so enthusiastically, but this increasing audience was met by the new writers' revolt against Victorian values.

It was perhaps to be expected that the end of the nineteenth century—often referred to by the French term, *fin de siècle* ("end of the century")—would be a period of disillusionment, a period in which English dependence on manners, morals, and traditions would inevitably be tested. It may have come as a shock to some, however, that England's confidence in both its oldest beliefs and its most recent achievements was not only challenged, but changed by the scientific claims of Charles Darwin and the economic and political theories of newly-formed Socialist organizations, especially the Fabian Society, whose ideas were to become the basis for the British Labour Party.

There were, of course, other influences on English thought and writing at this time, but many changes brought about were the result of interaction with people and ideas from beyond the English Channel—and beyond the secure center of the nineteenth-century English mind. In short, the Victorian sense of unity and integrity, of identity and a shared destiny was, by the 1880s, a waning spirit in the face of new realities.

It would be fair to say, then, that the period known as "Victorian" had been drawing to a close for at least a decade before the death, in 1901, of the woman for which it is named.

The Modern Spirit

Nowhere can the contrast between the essentially Victorian and the characteristically modern be more sharply drawn than in the contrast between Charles Dickens and Joseph Conrad, perhaps the most important novelists of their respective periods. While Dickens himself suffered as a child from the misery and helplessness of labor which was forced upon him, he nevertheless found it possible to write novels which contain humor, sentiment, and happy endings. A characteristic plot in his fiction, that of the orphan in search of a family, is a plot he shared with numerous other Victorian novelists. As in *Oliver Twist*, these orphan figures often find the place in society which they so earnestly believe is theirs. In contrast there is Joseph Conrad, whose life and work reflect the fragmented and unsettling conditions of modern life. Conrad was Polish by birth, but an exile in his youth, later becoming a British citizen. He was first a seaman and only later a novelist, writing in a language he did not learn until he was twenty. As an artist he possessed a vision of irony, the darkly comic, and the grotesque. He was obsessed by the destructive and primitive nature that lies behind the civilized exterior of the individual.

The England reflected in the literature of the period between 1880 and World War I is an empire in the process of self-discovery and acknowledging that while progress and change in human affairs are vital, they can also be unpredictable, excessive, uncontrollable, and destructive. And insofar as this was a period of social, cultural, and ideological change, it nurtured a wide range of artistic responses by writers who also shared, almost without exception, an insistent sense of exploration.

One of these responses was aestheticism. The Aesthetic Movement embodied a philosophy of artistic freedom from conventional expectations of content and form with a belief in "art for art's sake"; its emphasis was on sensory perception, the appreciation of beauty, the presentation of mood, and the perfection of technical expression, rather than an attempt to serve as a moral guide. Another, more enduring artistic development was the absorption of the concepts of French Symbolism into modern writing. The Symbolists explored the subtle changes in the human psyche and conveyed them with symbol and metaphor rather than by direct statement. Most remarkable in this context was William Butler Yeats, who began his career with the Aesthetic writers but gradually developed a magnificent personal vision of history and myth, which in its poetic

W. B. Yeats

richness and power has few equals. Symbolism went on to become the dominant mode of twentieth-century poetry, and Yeats became the greatest poet in English of our time.

Yet perhaps the single most significant characteristic of the early modern period in English literature, a characteristic which unites these and other writers and groups in a common spirit, was the deliberate testing and expansion of genre and style on the part of poets and novelists alike. Yeats, whose work involved continuous experimentation with language, rhythm, and symbol, was one example of this. Another was Gerard Manley Hopkins, a Jesuit priest who wrote in relative isolation from other poets and cannot properly be considered a member of any literary group. Hopkins believed deeply in the distinctiveness of things—in nature, in human affairs, in the world of the spirit—and felt that this distinctiveness could only be conveyed in a unique, arresting manner. For this reason he reacted against the bulky, ornate, and "proper" in verse by writing poetry characterized by a striking use of colloquial diction, a manipulation of syntax and the poetic line, and a unique theory of flexible or "sprung" rhythm. And Joseph Conrad, taking up the psychological emphasis of modern thought, projected it into his greatest stories and novels, among them *Heart of Darkness*, "The Secret Sharer," and *Lord Jim.* Specifically, Conrad experimented with multiple, sometimes "unreliable" narrators and with disruptions of chronological order in the telling of his tales.

Gerard Manley Hopkins

Modern Literature

Of even more pervasive importance, however, than individual experiments and styles, was the fact that such manipulation of traditional literary forms, whether poetry, drama, or fiction, abruptly altered what had usually been a comfortable relationship between English writers and their readers. The shared aim of Conrad and his contemporaries was not simply to educate or amuse or even to shock but, as he put it, to present a "rescued fragment" of life and to "reveal the substance of its truth." It was a conviction of these writers that the revelation of truth required both new techniques and the manipulation of old ones on the part of the writer, and thus much more critical and interpretive skill on the part of modern readers. It is not simple nostalgia, then, which makes even the relatively sophisticated contemporary reader of their works long occasionally for the more straightforward and approachable voices of such novelists as Thackeray, George Eliot, and Dickens, and such poets as Tennyson and the Brownings.

Beyond this conscious shift to new or modified styles and forms, English literature between 1880 and 1915 is characterized by its content, often a sharp departure from the subject matter of earlier writing. Here the most relevant contrast is perhaps that between Rudyard Kipling and H. G. Wells, who differed from each other as much as both differed from their predecessors. Particularly in such early work as *Barrack Room Ballads* and *Plain Tales from the Hills,* Kipling recorded with honesty and sympathy the emotions and events which humanized life in distant corners of the Empire. He conveyed the heroism of the British "Tommy," the valor of his "Fuzzy-Wuzzy" Sudanese adversary, and the loyalty of his Indian comrade, "Gunga Din." In his essential sympathy and adherence to the traditional, as well as his belief in the "white man's burden," as justification for the British presence in India and Africa, Kipling was clearly a product of late Victorianism. Wells, on the other hand, reflected the England of Victoria's successor, Edward VII, which shared both materialism and a sense of stability with the preceding era, but also saw some prophetic intellectual forays into the modern age. In particular Wells was a social critic, unafraid to direct irony and satire at "modern" failings;

Rudyard Kipling

and he was a man trained in science, aware of the implications of modern weaponry, airplanes and airships, and travel into space—in the end one of the pioneer science-fiction writers of our time. His writing reflects the shift from modern, industrial England to the world of the technological future.

Between Kipling and Wells as writers with new subjects and themes were numerous others, such as George Gissing, A. E. Housman, and Thomas Hardy. Gissing was concerned with the increasingly depressing conditions of urban existence, and especially the tenuous, peripheral status of the alienated writer; he voiced these concerns in such novels as *New Grub Street.* Housman, a classics scholar and poet who seemed equally doomed by love and fate, confronted the sense of fatality he shared with Gissing, Conrad, and others with a subdued stoicism which he found necessary despite the compensations of human society and the consolations of the natural world. Hardy, often as pessimistic in spirit as Gissing and as devoted to the English rural landscape as Housman, wrote several remarkable novels which treated earthy and, to some audiences, shocking themes and subjects; *The Mayor of Casterbridge* and *Tess of the D'Urbervilles* contain several cases in point. And then, as if to assert his independence even of his own success, Hardy devoted the rest of his career to the writing of a large and varied body of poetry which is equally earthy, ironic, colloquial, and dark.

Thomas Hardy

Finally, though, the most fully representative author of this rich and crucial period of new directions in English literature was the playwright, Bernard Shaw. As a dramatic artist Shaw led the revolt against the "well-made" but often contrived and sentimental play, and against the coercion of drama by convention and censorship. As a thinker, Shaw addressed himself to modern issues before they came into fashion and rejected old ideas which had become dogma. For example, he rejected theatrical realism and championed psychological realism, and he rejected society's notions of femininity in order to present women in such plays as *Candida, Pygmalion,* and *Saint Joan* as clever, intelligent, gifted, and strong—in short, worthy individuals and companions. In fact, Shaw is most significant as an author of "discussion plays," drama which creates a provocative, probing dialogue with an eye toward enlightenment and reform. At times he slipped into preaching and pronouncements, but he seldom failed to address with an honest eye and a witty tongue not only the perennially engaging themes and issues—money and status, love and sex, ignorance and education—but also the key concerns of his day, including socialism and democracy, aestheticism and Ibsen. The years of Shaw's artistic maturity and achievement coincide almost exactly with those of "new directions," so in this respect too he is a key figure of his time; but as an ironist, social critic, and believer in reform Shaw, who died in 1950 at the age of 94, no doubt took delight in seeing a number of his insights and ideas eventually embraced, not so much in his own time as in ours.

Bernard Shaw

Gerard Manley Hopkins

"Nant y Benglog, dawn" from *Eryri, the Mountains of Longing*, photographs by Philip H. Evans. Copyright Friends of the Earth.

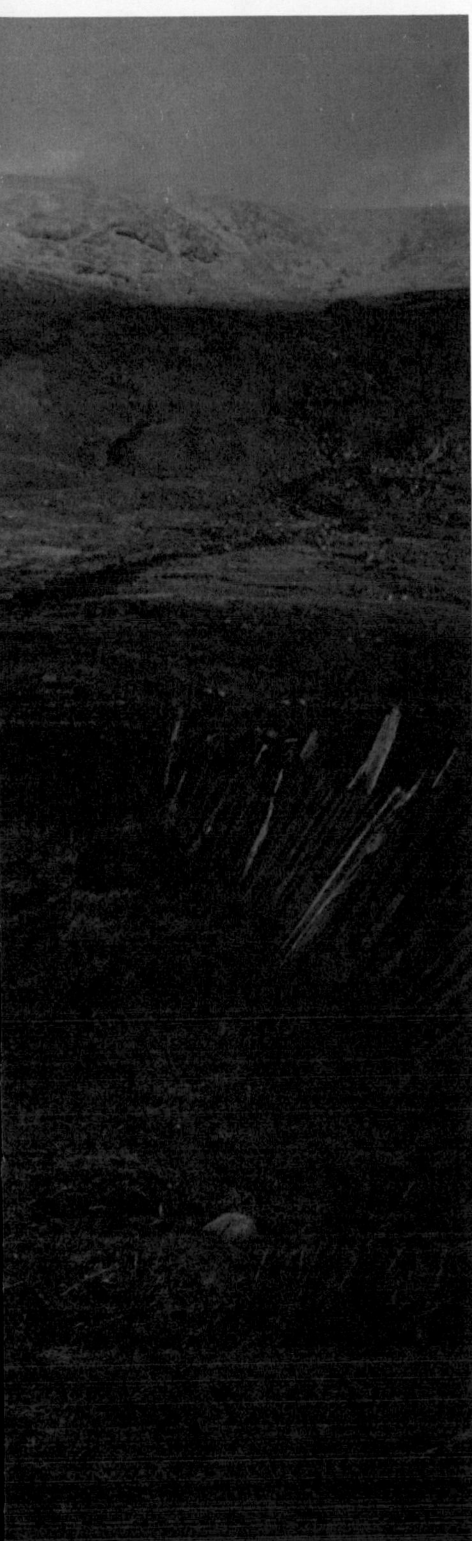

Pied Beauty

Glory be to God for dappled things—
For skies of couple-color as a brinded[1] cow;
For rose-moles all in stipple[2] upon trout that swim;
Fresh-firecoal chestnut-falls;[3] finches' wings;
Landscape plotted and pieced—fold, fallow, and plow;[4]
And all trades, their gear and tackle and trim.

All things counter,[5] original, spare, strange;
Whatever is fickle, freckled (who knows how?)
With swift, slow; sweet, sour; adazzle, dim;
He fathers-forth whose beauty is past change:
Praise him.

"Pied Beauty," "God's Grandeur," "Spring and Fall," and "Thou Art Indeed Just, Lord," from POEMS OF GERARD MANLEY HOPKINS, 4th Edition, Edited by W. H. Gardner and N. H. Mackenzie, 1967, published by Oxford University Press by arrangement with the Society of Jesus.

1. ***brinded,*** streaked with different colors. An early form of "brindled."
2. ***stipple.*** In graphic arts, areas of color or shade are sometimes rendered by masses of tiny dots, called stipples.
3. ***Fresh-firecoal chestnut-falls.*** Newly fallen nuts stripped of their husks look like fresh coals.
4. ***Landscape . . . plow.*** Seen from a distance, a landscape can look as if an architect laid it out in square sections—"plotted" it out; or a tailor sewed it together out of square bits of cloth—"pieced" it together. Different sections can be set aside as pastures—"folds"; to sit idly regaining fertility—"fallow" fields; or under cultivation—plowed.
5. ***counter,*** contrary to expectation.

God's Grandeur

The world is charged with the grandeur of God.
It will flame out, like shining from shook foil;
It gathers to a greatness, like the ooze of oil
Crushed. Why do men then now not reck his rod?
Generations have trod, have trod, have trod;
And all is seared with trade; bleared, smeared with toil;
And wears man's smudge and shares man's smell: the soil
Is bare now, nor can foot feel, being shod.

And for[1] all this, nature is never spent;
There lives the dearest freshness deep down things;
And though the last lights off the black West went
Oh, morning, at the brown brink eastward, springs—
Because the Holy Ghost over the bent
World broods with warm breast and with ah! bright wings.

---

1. ***for,*** despite.

Spring and Fall

to a young child

Márgarét, are you gríeving
Over Goldengrove unleaving?
Leáves, líke the things of man, you
With your fresh thoughts care for, can you?
Áh! ás the heart grows older
It will come to such sights colder
By and by, nor spare a sigh
Though worlds of wanwood leafmeal[1] lie;
And yet you wíll weep and know why.
Now no matter, child, the name:
Sórrow's spríngs áre the same.
Nor mouth had, no nor mind, expressed
What heart heard of, ghost guessed:
It ís the blight man was born for,
It is Margaret you mourn for.

1. ***wanwood leafmeal,*** palely colored autumn leaves ("wan") have fallen to the ground where they lie matted and already disintegrating ("leafmeal").

Thou Art Indeed Just, Lord

Righteous art thou, O Lord, when I plead with thee; yet let me talk with thee of thy judgments: Wherefore doth the way of the wicked prosper? (Jeremiah 12:1)

Thou art indeed just, Lord, if I contend
With thee; but, sir, so what I plead is just.
Why do sinners' ways prosper? and why must
Disappointment all I endeavour end?
Wert thou my enemy, O thou my friend,
How wouldst thou worse, I wonder, than thou dost
Defeat, thwart me? Oh, the sots and thralls of lust
Do in spare hours more thrive than I that spend,
Sir, life upon thy cause. See, banks and brakes[1]
Now, leavèd how thick! lacèd they are again
With fretty chervil,[2] look, and fresh wind shakes
Them; birds build—but not I build; no, but strain,
Time's eunuch, and not breed one work that wakes.
Mine, O thou lord of life, send my roots rain.

1. ***brakes,*** thickets.
2. ***fretty chervil,*** a kind of parsley.

Discussion

Pied Beauty

1. What particular characteristic of natural things does this poem celebrate? List several examples.

2. In what way, according to the poem, is God different from this aspect of His creation?

3. Why does the poem's speaker tell us to praise God?

God's Grandeur

1. What different characteristics of divine power do the first two sentences describe?

2. According to the poem, what has obscured human perception of the divine?

3. What does Hopkins mean by the word "spent" in line nine, and the word "bent" in thirteen?

4. Where does the speaker turn for hope?

Spring and Fall

1. What is the symbolic meaning of the autumn woods in this poem?

2. Why are Margaret's thoughts called "fresh" (line 4)?

3. How has young Margaret reacted to the falling leaves?

Thou Art Indeed Just, Lord

1. What problem does this poem describe?

2. What is the emotional relationship between the poem's speaker and his God? Why does he address Him as "sir" (line 2)?

3. At the poem's conclusion, to whom does the speaker turn? For what does he ask?

Imagery in "God's Grandeur"

In an early prose essay Hopkins wrote, "All things . . . are charged with God, and if we know how to touch them, give off sparks and take fire . . ." The imagery here is electrical, and refers to a battery, or to the static electricity which can build up in cloth or hair. Touching such objects strikes sparks, —shocks and surprises you. The first line of this poem expresses this idea in its image of a "charged" world. The second is related to it. Here we have an image of flaming light rays which Hopkins himself explained in a letter to a friend. "I mean foil in its sense of leaf or tinsel. . . . Shaken gold foil gives off broad glares like sheet lightning and also, and this is true of nothing else, owing to its zigzag dints and creasings and network of small many cornered facets, a sort of forked lightning too."

In lines three and four the initial images of electrical sparks and lightning are replaced by their opposites. If you put a puddle of heavy oil, like olive oil, between two surfaces and squeeze them together, the oil will be crushed into a thin ooze. But if you then separate the surfaces the tension within the oil itself will pull oil droplets back together. It is this kind of internal force drawing things back together which Hopkins here contrasts with the radiating energy of the first lines. He sees both as typical of God's power, reflected in His creation.

In line four the poet wonders why people no longer fear God's authority—fear the birch rod which God, like an angry father beating his children, could use to punish evil. This "rod" also suggest the lightning rod which carries the electrical energy of the divine storm to earth and links the first lines of the poem with this passage, as the "smear" of line six and "smudge" of line seven link with the oil of line three—though in six and seven the oil is the defiling oil of industrial society.

The imagery of the first eight lines, then, describes a god of power and wrath, and an earth sullied by a senseless civilization. The last six lines of the sonnet turn to very different images—a spring of fresh water (line 10), sunset and sunrise (11–12), with a double use of the verb "spring" in 12, and finally, a multiple image in which God the Holy Ghost, the spiritual dimension of the Christian God, is seen as the dawn of both a new day and a new, regenerated life, and also a dove, a benevolent bird of peace hovering over the world.

Gerard Manley Hopkins

1844 • 1889

The individuality of his abilities as a poet and thinker and the nature of his intellectual convictions forced Gerard Manley Hopkins into a solitary and frequently unhappy life.

Born into a large (seven children), prosperous and intelligent family, Hopkins seemed perfectly fashioned for the life of an Anglican minister, the vocation he thought he was following when he went to Oxford in 1863. However, as a student Hopkins's innate attraction to both the aesthetic splendor as well as the ascetic self-denial of the Roman Catholic Church led him to convert to that faith in 1866 and to join one of its most exacting religious orders, the Jesuits. These decisions partly alienated Hopkins from his family, cut him off from most of his college friends and teachers and, in excess of enthusiastic self-denial, moved him to burn all of his youthful poetry and resolve to never write again.

However, after seven years away, Hopkins seized upon a chance remark by his religious superior as a kind of permission to return to poetry, and thereafter he continued to work at his art for the rest of his life. But his responsibilities, first as a missionary (1877–1882), later as a professor of Greek (1884–1889), prevented him from spending much time or effort on poetry. The poems which survive are small in size and few in number.

Thomas Hardy

The Man He Killed

"Had he and I but met
By some old ancient inn,
We should have sat us down to wet
Right many a nipperkin![1]

"But ranged as infantry,
And staring face to face,
I shot at him as he at me,
And killed him in his place.

"I shot him dead because—
Because he was my foe,
Just so: my foe of course he was;
That's clear enough; although

"He thought he'd 'list, perhaps,
Off-hand like—just as I—
Was out of work—had sold his traps[2]—
No other reason why.

"Yes; quaint and curious war is!
You shoot a fellow down
You'd treat if met where any bar is,
Or help to half-a-crown."[3]

1. ***nipperkin,*** a half-pint of ale.
2. ***traps,*** simple personal belongings.
3. ***half-a-crown,*** an English coin worth about sixty-three cents in Hardy's day.

Ellen Siddons/Stock, Boston

Epitaph on a Pessimist

I'm Smith of Stoke, aged sixty-odd,
I've lived without a dame
From youth-time on; and would to God
My dad had done the same.

"Ah, Are You Digging on My Grave?"

"Ah, are you digging on my grave
    My loved one?—planting rue?"
—"No: yesterday he went to wed
One of the brightest wealth has bred.
'It cannot hurt her now,' he said,
    'That I should not be true.'"

"Then who is digging on my grave?
    My nearest dearest kin?"
—"Ah, no: they sit and think, 'What use!
What good will planting flowers produce?
No tendance of her mound can loose
    Her spirit from Death's gin.'"[1]

"But some one digs upon my grave?
    My enemy?—prodding sly?"
—"Nay: when she heard you had passed the Gate
That shuts on all flesh soon or late,
She thought you no more worth her hate,
    And cares not where you lie."

"Then, who is digging on my grave?
    Say—since I have not guessed!"
—"O it is I, my mistress dear,
Your little dog, who still lives near,
And much I hope my movements here
    Have not disturbed your rest?"

"Ah, yes! *You* dig upon my grave . . .
    Why flashed it not on me
That one true heart was left behind!
What feeling do we ever find
To equal among human kind
    A dog's fidelity!"

"Mistress, I dug upon your grave
    To bury a bone, in case
I should be hungry near this spot
When passing on my daily trot.
I am sorry, but I quite forgot
    It was your resting-place."

---

1. ***gin,*** a snare or trap for game.

At Castle Boterel

As I drive to the junction of lane and highway,
  And the drizzle bedrenches the waggonette,
I look behind at the fading byway,
  And see on its slope, now glistening wet,
    Distinctly yet

Myself and a girlish form benighted
  In dry March weather. We climb the road
Beside a chaise. We had just alighted
  To ease the sturdy pony's load
    When he sighed and slowed.

What we did as we climbed, and what we talked of
  Matters not much, nor to what it led—
Something that life will not be balked of
  Without rude reason till hope is dead,
    And feeling fled.

It filled but a minute. But was there ever
  A time of such quality, since or before,
In that hill's story? To one mind never,
  Though it has been climbed, foot-swift, foot-sore,
    By thousands more.

Primaeval rocks form the road's steep border,
  And much have they faced there, first and last,
Of the transitory in Earth's long order;
  But what they record in colour and cast
    Is—that we two passed.

And to me, though Time's unflinching rigour,
  In mindless rote, has ruled from sight
The substance now, one phantom figure
  Remains on the slope, as when that night
    Saw us alight.

I look and see it there, shrinking, shrinking,
  I look back at it amid the rain
For the very last time; for my sand is sinking,
  And I shall traverse old love's domain
    Never again.

Discussion

"Ah, Are You Digging . . ."

1. What does the dead girl hope for? Is there any specific order to her questions?

2. What does the poem imply, through the answers to each question?

3. How would you describe the overall effect of this poem on you as a reader?

4. Compare this poem with "The Unquiet Grave" (page 61). In what ways is Hardy's poem similar to that traditional ballad?

The Man He Killed

1. How wealthy do you think the speaker is? What leads you to this conclusion? In particular, does he use any words which suggest his social class?

2. Why does the speaker repeat himself in stanza three?

3. For what reasons does he go to war? Are these unusual motives, do you think?

At Castle Boterel

1. How does the present weather differ from that on the speaker's past visit? Why would Hardy use this contrast?

2. How much does the speaker tell us of what went on that day? Why?

3. What is the ultimate problem which faces this speaker?

Epitaph on a Pessimist

Comment on the character of Smith of Stoke in "Epitaph on a Pessimist." Limit yourself to 48 words—twice the number in the poem.

Afterwards

When the Present has latched its postern[1] behind my tremulous stay,
And the May month flaps its glad green leaves like wings,
Delicate-filmed as new-spun silk, will the neighbors say,
"He was a man who used to notice such things"?

If it be in the dusk when, like an eyelid's soundless blink,
The dewfall-hawk comes crossing the shades to alight
Upon the wind-warped upland thorn, a gazer may think,
"To him this must have been a familiar sight."

If I pass during some nocturnal blackness, mothy and warm,
When the hedgehog travels furtively over the lawn,
One may say, "He strove that such innocent creatures should come to no harm,
But he could do little for them; and now he is gone."

If, when hearing that I have been stilled at last, they stand at the door,
Watching the full-starred heavens that winter sees,
Will this thought rise on those who will meet my face no more,
"He was one who had an eye for such mysteries"?

And will any say when my bell of quittance[2] is heard in the gloom,
And a crossing breeze cuts a pause in its outrollings,
Till they rise again, as they were a new bell's boom,
"He hears it not now, but used to notice such things"?

1. ***postern,*** back gate.
2. ***bell of quittance,*** tolling of the church bells to commemorate his death.

Discussion

1. What aspect of his past life does the speaker hope his friends will remember? How does this poem reflect that interest?

2. Compare "Afterwards" with "Ah, Are You Digging on My Grave?" Do Hardy's hopes about the way we remember the dead differ in these two poems?

Thomas Hardy 1840 • 1928

Thomas Hardy's literary reputation rests on his abilities both as a poet and as a writer of fiction. (For Hardy's career as a novelist see page 491.)

Hardy began his literary career with the dream of being a poet, and although for many years he was known primarily as a novelist, to the end of his life he saw his poetry as "the more individual part" of his achievement. When his first poems could not find a receptive publisher, Hardy turned to writing fiction, enjoying a success mixed with controversy.

Finally tiring of the controversy, Hardy simply stopped writing fiction after 1896, devoting the final thirty-two years of his long life entirely to poetry. In the end he wrote nearly one thousand lyric poems, whose composition spans his entire life. His poems, he asserted, were fragmentary, their purpose ". . . to record impressions, not convictions . . . a series of feelings and fancies . . . in widely differing moods and circumstances." He frequently turns to the rhythm and the impersonal tone of the old ballads. His poetry has had persistant influence in our century on writers as diverse as W. H. Auden and Ted Hughes.

A. E. Housman

When I Was One-and-Twenty

When I was one-and-twenty
I heard a wise man say,
"Give crowns and pounds and guineas
But not your heart away;
Give pearls away and rubies
But keep your fancy free."
But I was one-and-twenty,
No use to talk to me.

When I was one-and-twenty
I heard him say again,
"The heart out of the bosom
Was never given in vain;
'Tis paid with sighs a plenty
And sold for endless rue."
And I am two-and-twenty,
And oh, 'tis true, 'tis true.

Loveliest of Trees

Loveliest of trees, the cherry now
Is hung with bloom along the bough,
And stands about the woodland ride,
Wearing white for Eastertide.

Now, of my threescore years and ten,
Twenty will not come again,
And take from seventy springs a score,
It only leaves me fifty more.

And since to look at things in bloom
Fifty springs are little room,
About the woodlands I will go
To see the cherry hung with snow.

To an Athlete Dying Young

The time you won your town the race
We chaired you through the market place;
Man and boy stood cheering by,
And home we brought you shoulder-high.

Today, the road all runners come,
Shoulder-high we bring you home,
And set you at your threshold down,
Townsman of a stiller town.

Smart lad, to slip betimes away
From fields where glory does not stay,
And early though the laurel grows
It withers quicker than the rose.

Eyes the shady night has shut
Cannot see the record cut,
And silence sounds no worse than cheers
After earth has stopped the ears.

Now you will not swell the rout
Of lads that wore their honors out,
Runners whom renown outran
And the name died before the man.

So set, before its echoes fade,
The fleet foot on the sill of shade,
And hold to the low lintel up
The still-defended challenge cup.

And round that early-laureled head
Will flock to gaze the strengthless dead,
And find unwithered on its curls
The garland briefer than a girl's.

Into My Heart an Air that Kills

Into my heart an air that kills
  From yon far country blows:
What are those blue remembered hills,
  What spires, what farms are those?

That is the land of lost content,
  I see it shining plain,
The happy highways where I went
  And cannot come again.

Far in a Western Brookland

Far in a western brookland
  That bred me long ago
The poplars stand and tremble
  By pools I used to know.

There, in the windless night-time,
  The wanderer, marvelling why,
Halts on the bridge to hearken
  How soft the poplars sigh.

He hears: no more remembered
  In fields where I was known,
Here I lie down in London
  And turn to rest alone.

There, by the starlit fences,
  The wanderer halts and hears
My soul that lingers sighing
  About the glimmering weirs.

Discussion

When I Was One-and-Twenty

1. Note the verbs the "wise man" uses to describe young love. What do they imply?

2. Why won't the young man listen?

Loveliest of Trees

1. Why does the speaker think the cherry the loveliest of trees?

2. What is the speaker doing in the second stanza? Why?

To an Athlete Dying Young

1. The poem describes two processions. Compare and contrast them.

2. What does the speaker mean by "a stiller town"? List all the details he gives which describe it.

3. Why does the speaker consider the athlete a "Smart lad" (line 9)?

Into My Heart . . .

Why does the air of line 1 "kill"?

Far in a Western Brookland

1. Why did Housman set the action of this poem in the nighttime?

2. What sounds and movements does this poem describe? In what ways are they appropriate?

Housman on Writing His Poetry

Late in his life A. E. Housman accepted an invitation to lecture on poetry at Cambridge. At the end of his remarks he turned to the definition of the term. "Poetry," he said, ". . . seems to me more physical than intellectual . . ." and he went on to describe the physical "symptoms" which it "provokes": "Experience has taught me, when I am shaving of a morning, to keep watch over my thoughts, because, if a line of poetry strays into my memory, my skin bristles so that the razor ceases to act. This particular symptom is accompanied by a shiver down the spine . . ." Housman's description of how his poems began is equally physical: "Having drunk a pint of beer at luncheon—beer is a sedative to the brain, and my afternoons are the least intellectual portion of my life—I would go out for a walk of two or three hours. As I went along, thinking of nothing in particular, only looking at things around me and following the progress of the seasons, there would flow into my mind, with sudden and unaccountable emotion, sometimes a line or two of verse, sometimes a whole stanza at once, accompanied, not preceded, by a vague notion of the poem which they were destined to form a part of. Then there would usually be a lull of an hour or so, then perhaps the spring would bubble up again . . . When I got home I wrote them down, leaving gaps, and hoping that further inspiration might be forthcoming another day."

A. E. Housman 1859 • 1936

Housman grew up in the rural England his poetry re-creates. For him, life there was lonely and unhappy. His mother died when he was twelve and his father turned to drink for consolation, squandering what property he owned. Housman was intelligent enough to win a scholarship to Oxford (1877) but for complex emotional reasons failed his final examination and left in 1881 without a degree.

Clearly determined to turn his failure into success Housman got a job at the patent office in London but devoted his energy to private study of Latin and Greek literature. During the next ten years (1882–1892) he trained himself to be one of the most learned classical scholars of his day, and in 1892 he won the chair of Professor of Latin at the University of London.

A life of rigid self-discipline led to this achievement, and yet the inner pressure of his emotional life continued to disturb him. He turned to poetry as a release, writing most of his brief lyrics between 1892 and 1895. In 1896 he published his first volume, *A Shropshire Lad.* Public response was tepid. But as the years passed the book's popularity grew, and within ten years it enjoyed wide readership and critical acclaim.

By this time Housman had quieted his inner turmoil, and though the subsequent years of his life saw mounting success for his books of classical scholarship, he wrote few poems.

Housman's art is the art of simplicity. In short lyrics of traditional rhyme scheme and meter he describes a few favorite themes: young love, violent death, the changing seasons. His language is intentionally plain; it resembles the speech of the common people whose lives and emotions he describes. His poetic achievement is modest in size and scope, but the particular characteristics of his work, its simplicity, its music, its rueful melancholy, have won for him a wide and permanent audience.

William Butler Yeats

The Lake Isle of Innisfree

I will arise and go now, and go to Innisfree,
And a small cabin build there, of clay and wattles made;
Nine bean rows will I have there, a hive for the honeybee,
And live alone in the bee-loud glade.

And I shall have some peace there, for peace comes
dropping slow,
Dropping from the veils of the morning to where the cricket
sings;
There midnight's all a-glimmer, and noon a purple glow,
And evening full of the linnet's wings.[1]

I will arise and go now, for always night and day
I hear lake water lapping with low sounds by the shore;
While I stand on the roadway, or on the pavements gray,
I hear it in the deep heart's core.

(1893)

1. ***linnet's wings.*** The linnet is a small songbird.

Discussion

1. Yeats described this poem as his first lyric with the "rhythm of my own music." Repetition plays a major role in this movement. **(a)** What words does the poet repeat? **(b)** What sounds—consonants and vowels—does this poem repeat?

2. What kind of life does the speaker dream about? What do you think his everyday life might be like?

notes and comments

W. B. Yeats on "Innisfree"

". . . Sometimes I told myself very adventurous love-stories with myself for hero, and at other times I planned a life of lonely austerity, and at other times mixed the ideals and planned a life of lonely austerity mitigated by periodical lapses. I had still the ambition, formed in Sligo in my teens, of living in imitation of Thoreau on Innisfree, a little island in Lough Gill, and when walking through Fleet Street very homesick I heard a little tinkle of water and saw a fountain in a shop-window which balanced a little ball upon its jet, and began to remember lake water. From the sudden remembrance came my poem *Innisfree,* my first lyric with anything in its rhythm of my own music."

from *The Trembling of the Veil* (1922).

"Portrait of Maud Gonne" by Sarah Purser. Courtesy of The Municipal Gallery of Modern Art, Dublin; photograph The National Gallery of Ireland.

When You Are Old

When you are old and gray and full of sleep,
And nodding by the fire, take down this book,
And slowly read, and dream of the soft look
Your eyes had once, and of their shadows deep;

How many loved your moments of glad grace,
And loved your beauty with love false or true,
But one man loved the pilgrim soul in you,
And loved the sorrows of your changing face;

And bending down beside the glowing bars,
Murmur, a little sadly, how Love fled
And paced upon the mountains overhead
And hid his face amid a crowd of stars.

(1893)

Discussion

1. What do you think is the speaker's attitude toward old age? Find words or phrases to support your answer.

2. **(a)** Which man loved "the pilgrim soul in you"? **(b)** What happened to this love and why?

3. Tell the "story" of this poem in your own words.

According to the story of creation in Genesis (see pages 204–207), God cursed Adam and Eve for their disobedience. Eve's portion is the pain of childbirth and the rule of her husband. Adam's curse is lifelong toil and final death: "In the sweat of thy face shalt thou eat bread, till thou return unto the ground; for out of it wast thou taken: for dust thou art, and unto dust thou shalt return." (Genesis 3: 17–19).

Adam's Curse

We sat together at one summer's end,
That beautiful mild woman, your close friend,
And you[1] and I, and talked of poetry.
I said, "A line will take us hours maybe;
Yet if it does not seem a moment's thought,
Our stitching and unstitching has been naught.
Better go down upon your marrow-bones[2]
And scrub a kitchen pavement, or break stones
Like an old pauper, in all kinds of weather;
For to articulate sweet sounds together
Is to work harder than all these, and yet
Be thought an idler by the noisy set
Of bankers, schoolmasters, and clergymen
The martyrs call the world."

And thereupon
That beautiful mild woman for whose sake
There's many a one shall find out all heartache
On finding that her voice is sweet and low
Replied, "To be born woman is to know—
Although they do not talk of it at school—
That we must labour to be beautiful."
I said, "It's certain there is no fine thing
Since Adam's fall but needs much labouring.
There have been lovers who thought love should be
So much compounded of high courtesy
That they would sigh and quote with learned looks
Precedents out of beautiful old books;
Yet now it seems an idle trade enough."

We sat grown quiet at the name of love;
We saw the last embers of daylight die,
And in the trembling blue-green of the sky
A moon, worn as if it had been a shell
Washed by time's waters as they rose and fell
About the stars and broke in days and years.

I had a thought for no one's but your ears:
That you were beautiful, and that I strove
To love you in the old high way of love;[3]
That it had all seemed happy, and yet we'd grown
As weary-hearted as that hollow moon.

(1904)

1. ***you,*** Maud Gonne (1865-1953), the Irish actress, painter, and revolutionary patriot whom Yeats loved and proposed to in vain, and to whom he refers in many of his poems. Her portrait appears opposite.
2. ***marrow-bones,*** knees.
3. ***the old high way of love,*** "courtly love," the medieval conventions governing aristocratic sexuality, described in lines 23–26.

Discussion

1. In Genesis Adam's curse describes the hard life of the farmer. In the poem Yeats lists three other kinds of labor. What are they? Why doesn't "the world" (line 14) consider these efforts true work? What is it about them that commands the poet's respect?

2. What is the end result of these labors, according to the poem? In what ways does the moon described in the poem resemble the person who has worked hard at these kinds of labor?

The Wild Swans at Coole[1]

The trees are in their autumn beauty,
The woodland paths are dry,
Under the October twilight the water
Mirrors a still sky;
Upon the brimming water among the stones
Are nine-and-fifty swans.

The nineteenth autumn has come upon me
Since I first made my count;
I saw, before I had well finished,
All suddenly mount
And scatter wheeling in great broken rings
Upon their clamorous wings.

I have looked upon those brilliant creatures,
And now my heart is sore.
All's changed since I, hearing at twilight,
The first time on this shore,
The bell-beat of their wings above my head,
Trod with a lighter tread.

Unwearied still, lover by lover,
They paddle in the cold
Companionable streams or climb the air;
Their hearts have not grown old;
Passion or conquest, wander where they will,
Attend upon them still.

But now they drift on the still water,
Mysterious, beautiful;
Among what rushes will they build,
By what lake's edge or pool
Delight men's eyes when I awake some day
To find they have flown away?

(1919)

---

1. ***Coole,*** Coole Park, the home of Yeats's friend Lady Augusta Gregory (1859-1932), the Irish playwright and folklorist.

Discussion

The Wild Swans at Coole

1. How old do you think the poem's speaker is? Where does the poem suggest his age?

2. In what ways is the season of the year appropriate for its speaker?

3. What are the crucial differences between the swans and this man?

4. What is the symbolic force of the action which the swans take?

The Second Coming

1. In the first eight lines of this poem Yeats tries to describe the characteristics of our era in history. Distinguish what it is that terrifies him by giving close scrutiny to the words and images which he employs in the following phrases: **(a)** "the centre cannot hold" **(b)** "The blood-dimmed tide is loosed" **(c)** "The ceremony of innocence is drowned" **(d)** "The best lack all conviction" **(e)** "the worst / Are full of passionate intensity."

2. What does the description of the "rough beast" suggest about its nature? What will life be like, do you think, once it becomes god?

The Second Coming

This phrase alludes to a complicated and emotionally charged idea in Christianity. In the Gospels Jesus warns his disciples that he will be crucified but assures them that he will return again to the earth after an indeterminate length of time. This return, or "second coming," will be preceded by cataclysmic violence and destruction, and Christ will then come to end the world.

Yeats intends his readers to remember this Christian tradition, clearly alluding to the destruction which foreshadows Christ's return in lines 4 to 8 and to his first coming in the reference to Bethlehem (line 22).

But Yeats is no Christian, and he alters the traditional story in a particular way, to make it fit his own theory of history. In his version it is not Jesus who returns, but rather some other divinity, too alien to be fully comprehended. The poet's knowledge of this new god comes from a vision he has had, a vision which rises out of the shared unconscious mind in which all human beings participate and to which Yeats refers by its Latin name, *Spiritus Mundi,* "the soul of the world." The vision this creates in the poet's mind is vague but menacing—the poet tries to describe it in lines 13–18, but soon loses it, and "darkness drops again" (line 18). He is still so unsure of its meaning that he ends his poem with a question.

What he does understand (lines 18–20) is that during the past two thousand years (an even number, suggesting a complete era in earthly history) this new beast-god has been in stony sleep (line 19), waiting to be born, and angered ("vexed") by the more gentle god of Christianity, symbolized in the "rocking cradle" (line 20) of the infant Jesus. Now this "rough beast" (line 21) is moving towards it own birth, its own, ominous Bethlehem.

The Second Coming[1]

Turning and turning in the widening gyre[2]
The falcon cannot hear the falconer;
Things fall apart; the centre cannot hold;
Mere anarchy is loosed upon the world,
The blood-dimmed tide is loosed, and everywhere
The ceremony of innocence is drowned;
The best lack all conviction, while the worst
Are full of passionate intensity.
  Surely some revelation is at hand;
Surely the Second Coming is at hand.
The Second Coming! Hardly are those words out
When a vast image out of *Spiritus Mundi*[3]
Troubles my sight: somewhere in sands of the desert
A shape with lion body and the head of a man,
A gaze blank and pitiless as the sun,
Is moving its slow thighs, while all about it
Reel shadows of the indignant desert birds.
The darkness drops again; but now I know
That twenty centuries of stony sleep
Were vexed to nightmare by a rocking cradle,
And what rough beast, its hour come round at last,
Slouches towards Bethlehem to be born?

(1921)

1. ***Second Coming.*** Here Yeats borrows a Christian conception—the Second Coming of Christ at the end of the world—in order to develop his own notions of historical cycles.
2. ***gyre*** (jir), a symbol used by Yeats in much of his later writing, describing a circular or spiral motion; a cone.
3. ***Spiritus Mundi,*** "soul of the world." [Latin]

Sailing to Byzantium[1]

I

That is no country for old men. The young
In one another's arms, birds in the trees,
—Those dying generations—at their song,
The salmon-falls, the mackerel-crowded seas,
Fish, flesh, or fowl, commend all summer long
Whatever is begotten, born, and dies.
Caught in that sensual music all neglect
Monuments of unaging intellect.

II

An aged man is but a paltry thing,
A tattered coat upon a stick, unless
Soul clap its hands and sing, and louder sing
For every tatter in its mortal dress,
Nor is there singing school but studying
Monuments of its own magnificence;
And therefore I have sailed the seas and come
To the holy city of Byzantium.

III

O sages standing in God's holy fire
As in the gold mosaic of a wall
Come from the holy fire, perne in a gyre,[2]
And be the singing-masters of my soul.
Consume my heart away; sick with desire
And fastened to a dying animal
It knows not what it is; and gather me
Into the artifice of eternity.

(continued on page 464)

Sixteenth-century illustration of Istanbul. Courtesy of the Istanbul University Library. Photo: Erkin Emiroğlu.

1. ***Byzantium,*** ancient name for the city that became Constantinople and then Istanbul. For Yeats, however, it was not so much a place as an ideal, a symbol for the timeless world of art and the intellect as opposed to the natural world of biological change. It was a "holy city," literally because it was the capital of Eastern Christendom, symbolically because it fostered that development of intellect and imagination which produces artistic perfection. Byzantine art was highly stylized, abandoning all naturalistic representation.
2. ***perne in a gyre,*** whirl or spin in a spiral motion.

IV

Once out of nature I shall never take
My bodily form from any natural thing,
But such a form as Grecian goldsmiths make[3]
Of hammered gold and gold enameling
To keep a drowsy Emperor awake;
Or set upon a golden bough to sing
To lords and ladies of Byzantium
Of what is past, or passing, or to come.

(1927)

---

3. ***such a form . . . make.*** Yeats said: "I have read somewhere that in the Emperor's palace at Byzantium was a tree of gold and silver, and artificial birds that sang."

Discussion

In "Sailing to Byzantium" the first two stanzas describe a country the speaker has left, and the last two describe the country (Byzantium) to which he is going. Both countries are symbolic only. Keeping this in mind, consider the following questions: **(a)** What images does Yeats use in stanza one to describe the first "country"? What is missing in the lives of those who live there? **(b)** Why does the speaker sail to Byzantium? What does he hope to lose before he reaches his destination? **(c)** What does the old man wish to do when he reaches Byzantium? Do you have respect for his goal? Explain your evaluation.

notes and comments

"Sailing to Byzantium"

Elder Olson

In "Sailing to Byzantium," an old man faces the problem of old age, of death, and of regeneration, and gives his decision. Old age, he tells us, excludes a man from the sensual joys of youth; the world appears to belong completely to the young, it is no place for the old; indeed, an old man is scarcely a man at all—he is an empty artifice, an effigy merely, of a man; he is a tattered coat upon a stick. This would be very bad, except that the young also are excluded from something; rapt in their sensuality, they are ignorant utterly of the world of the spirit. Hence if old age frees a man from sensual passion, he may rejoice in the liberation of the soul; he is admitted into the realm of the spirit; and his rejoicing will increase according as he realizes the magnificence of the soul. But the soul can best learn its own greatness from the great works of art; hence he turns to those great works, but in turning to them, he finds that these are by no means mere effigies, or monuments, but things that have souls also; these live in the noblest element of God's fire, free from all corruption; hence he prays for death, for release from his mortal body; and since the insouled monuments exhibit the possibility of the soul's existence in some other matter than flesh, he wishes reincarnation, not now in a mortal body, but in the immortal and changeless embodiment of art. . . ."

Vocabulary • Dictionary

Use your Glossary to answer the following questions about the italicized words. Write your answers on a separate sheet of paper. Be sure you know the meaning, spelling, and pronunciation of each word.

1. (a) From what specific Scandinavian language does *thwart* come? (b) What is the spelling and meaning of the original word from which *thwart* comes?

2. What are the three Latin words given in the development of the word *fidelity*?

3. (a) What is the spelling of the Greek word from which *anarchy* comes? (b) What is the meaning of the prefix and root that form the Greek word?

4. Look at the entry for *blight* and tell why it is or is not an appropriate word to describe humanity in the concluding lines of Hopkins's "Spring and Fall."

5. (a) In Hardy's poem "Castle Boterel," he uses a different spelling (*primaeval*) for a word we spell *primeval*. Check the entry under the latter spelling. Which of the two Latin root words given contains the letter *a* as in the variant spelling of *primeval?* (b) When the meanings of the two roots are joined, what phrase do they make up?

6. What religious meanings does the word *revelation* have?

7. (a) What do the Latin root words in *artifice* mean? (b) How many syllables does the word have? (c) Write one rhyme word each for the first and third syllables.

8. From what language does *rote* come?

William Butler Yeats

1865 • 1939

Unlike Hopkins, Hardy, and Housman, who lived quiet, solitary lives dedicated to study and writing, W. B. Yeats engaged strenuously and successfully in many different kinds of activity and integrated all of them into his art.

The early years of his maturity are typical. As a young man in the London of the nineties he edited an edition of Blake's poetry (1893), did research into Irish folklore and legend (e.g., *The Celtic Twilight*, 1893), wrote plays (his first, *The Countess Cathleen,* appeared in 1892), studied mysticism and occult knowledge in secret societies, fell into a passion for a beautiful woman, Maud Gonne, who refused to marry him, and, with some friends, started the Irish Literary Theatre (1899). At the same time, of course, he published collections of his poems at regular intervals.

These diverse interests grew from Yeats's ceaseless efforts to make sense out of his life and times. An Irishman, he rebelled against British dominance over his homeland and worked towards Irish independence, particularly by trying to rediscover lost Irish culture in his studies of folklore, and to renew it through such institutions as the Abbey Theatre. Raised without religious convictions (his father was an atheist) he sought for some systematic explanation of life in mysticism and the occult, finally developing his own elaborate theory of personality and history in *A Vision* (1925).

The wide range of Yeats's concerns, and the intensity of his involvement in them, appear in his poetry, which remained throughout his life highly personal and idiosyncratic.

As he matured as a man Yeats grew in power as a poet. The nature of his subjects and the character of his style changed radically. Influenced partly by the need to write clearly and dramatically for his stage plays, Yeats moved towards a sharply defined and simply stated poetry.

This later phase in Yeats's development began at a remarkably late age. He was forty-nine when his *Responsibilities* (1914), the first book clearly written in his new style, appeared. During the last twenty-five years of his life, a time when many artists are already played out, Yeats continued to explore the limits of poetic expression.

Rudyard Kipling

The Miracle of Purun Bhagat

The night we felt the earth would move
  We stole and plucked him by the hand,
Because we loved him with the love
  That knows but cannot understand.

And when the roaring hillside broke,
  And all our world fell down in rain,
We saved him, we the Little Folk;
  But lo! he does not come again!

Mourn now, we saved him for the sake
  Of such poor love as wild ones may.
Mourn ye! Our brother will not wake,
  And his own kind drive us away!

Dirge of the Langurs

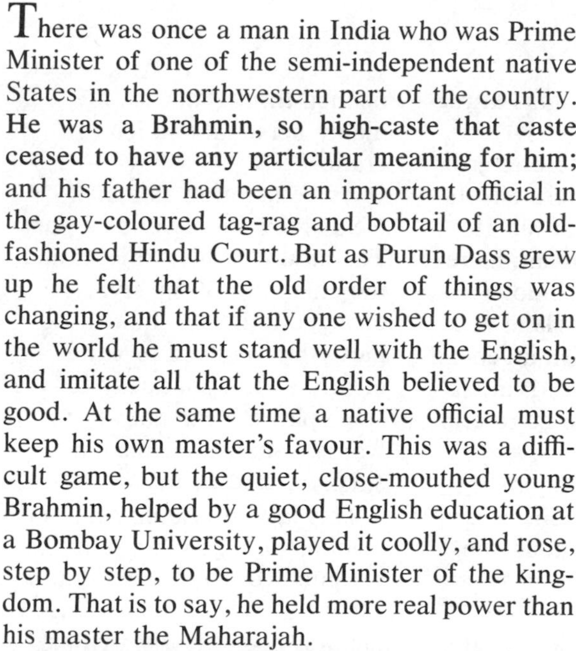

There was once a man in India who was Prime Minister of one of the semi-independent native States in the northwestern part of the country. He was a Brahmin, so high-caste that caste ceased to have any particular meaning for him; and his father had been an important official in the gay-coloured tag-rag and bobtail of an old-fashioned Hindu Court. But as Purun Dass grew up he felt that the old order of things was changing, and that if any one wished to get on in the world he must stand well with the English, and imitate all that the English believed to be good. At the same time a native official must keep his own master's favour. This was a difficult game, but the quiet, close-mouthed young Brahmin, helped by a good English education at a Bombay University, played it coolly, and rose, step by step, to be Prime Minister of the kingdom. That is to say, he held more real power than his master the Maharajah.

When the old king—who was suspicious of the English, their railways and telegraphs—died, Purun Dass stood high with his young successor, who had been tutored by an Englishman; and between them, though he always took care that his master should have the credit, they established schools for little girls, made roads, and started State dispensaries and shows of agricultural implements, and published a yearly blue-book on the "Moral and Material Progress of the State," and the Foreign Office and the Government of India were delighted. Very few native States take up English progress altogether, for they will not believe, as Purun Dass showed he did, that what was good for the Englishman must be twice as good for the Asiatic. The Prime Minister became the honoured friend of Viceroys, and Governors, and Lieutenant-Governors, and medical missionaries, and common missionaries, and hard-riding English officers who came to shoot in the State preserves, as well as of whole hosts of tourists who travelled up and down India in the cold weather, showing how things ought to be managed. In his spare time he would endow scholarships for the study of medicine and manufactures on strictly English lines, and write letters to the *Pioneer,* the greatest Indian daily paper, explaining his master's aims and objects.

At last he went to England on a visit, and had to pay enormous sums to the priests when he came back; for even so high-caste a Brahmin as Purun Dass lost caste by crossing the black sea.

In London he met and talked with every one worth knowing—men whose names go all over the world—and saw a great deal more than he said. He was given honorary degrees by learned universities, and he made speeches and talked of Hindu social reform to English ladies in evening dress, till all London cried, "This is the most fascinating man we have ever met at dinner since cloths were first laid."

When he returned to India there was a blaze of glory, for the Viceroy himself made a special visit to confer upon the Maharajah the Grand Cross of the Star of India—all diamonds and ribbons and enamel; and at the same ceremony, while the cannon boomed, Purun Dass was made a Knight Commander of the Order of the Indian Empire; so that his name stood Sir Purun Dass, K.C.I.E.

That evening, at dinner in the big Viceregal tent, he stood up with the badge and the collar of the Order on his breast, and replying to the toast of his master's health, made a speech few Englishmen could have bettered.

Next month, when the city had returned to its sun-baked quiet, he did a thing no Englishman would have dreamed of doing; for, so far as the world's affairs went, he died. The jewelled order of his knighthood went back to the Indian Government, and a new Prime Minister was appointed to the charge of affairs, and a great game of General Post[1] began in all the subordinate appointments. The priests knew what had happened, and the people guessed; but India is the one place in the world where a man can do as he pleases and nobody asks why; and the fact that Dewan Sir Purun Dass, K.C.I.E., had resigned position, palace, and power, and taken up the begging-bowl and ochre-coloured dress of a Sunnyasi, or holy man, was considered nothing extraordinary. He had been, as the Old Law recommends, twenty years a youth, twenty years a fighter,—though he had never carried a weapon in his life,—and twenty years head of a household. He had used his wealth and his power for what he knew both to be worth; he had taken honour when it came his way; he had seen men and cities far and near, and men and cities had stood up and honoured him. Now he would let those things go, as a man drops the cloak he no longer needs.

Behind him, as he walked through the city gates, an antelope skin and brass-handled crutch under his arm, and a begging-bowl of polished brown *coco-de-mer*[2] in his hand, barefoot, alone, with eyes cast on the ground—behind him they were firing salutes from the bastions in honour of his happy successor. Purun Dass nodded. All that life was ended; and he bore it no more ill will or goodwill than a man bears to a colourless dream of the night. He was a Sunnyasi—a houseless, wandering mendicant, depending on his neighbours for his daily bread; and so long as there is a morsel to divide in India, neither priest nor beggar starves. He had never in his life tasted meat, and very seldom eaten even fish. A five-pound note would have covered his personal expenses for food through any one of the many years in which he had been absolute master of millions of money. Even when he was being lionised in London he had held before him his dream of peace and quiet—the long, white, dusty Indian road, printed all over with bare feet, the incessant, slow-moving traffic, and the sharp-smelling wood smoke curling up under the fig-trees in the twilight, where the wayfarers sit at their evening meal.

When the time came to make that dream true the Prime Minister took the proper steps, and in three days you might more easily have found a bubble in the trough of the long Atlantic seas than Purun Dass among the roving, gathering, separating millions of India.

At night his antelope skin was spread where the darkness overtook him—sometimes in a Sunnyasi monastery by the roadside; sometimes by a mud-pillar shrine of Kala Pir, where the Yogis, who are another misty division of holy men, would receive him as they do those who know what castes and divisions are worth; sometimes on the outskirts of a little Hindu village, where the children would steal up with the food their parents had prepared; and sometimes on the pitch of the bare grazing-grounds, where the flame of his stick fire waked the drowsy camels. It was all one to Purun Dass—or Purun Bhagat, as he called himself now. Earth, people, and food were all one. But unconsciously his feet drew

1. ***General Post,*** a game like blind man's bluff.
2. ***coco-de-mer,*** "sea coconut," the large nut of a palm native to the Seychelles Islands in the Indian Ocean.

him away northward and eastward; from the south to Rohtak; from Rohtak to Kurnool; from Kurnool to ruined Samanah, and then up-stream along the dried bed of the Gugger river that fills only when the rain falls in the hills, till one day he saw the far line of the great Himalayas.

Then Purun Bhagat smiled, for he remembered that his mother was of Rajput Brahmin birth, from Kulu way—a Hill-woman, always homesick for the snows—and that the least touch of Hill blood draws a man in the end back to where he belongs.

"Yonder," said Purun Bhagat, breasting the lower slopes of the Sewaliks, where the cacti stand up like seven-branched candlesticks—"yonder I shall sit down and get knowledge"; and the cool wind of the Himalayas whistled about his ears as he trod the road that led to Simla.

The last time he had come that way it had been in state, with a clattering cavalry escort, to visit the gentlest and most affable of Viceroys; and the two had talked for an hour together about mutual friends in London, and what the Indian common folk really thought of things. This time Purun Bhagat paid no calls, but leaned on the rail of the Mall, watching that glorious view of the Plains spread out forty miles below, till a native Mohammedan policeman told him he was obstructing traffic; and Purun Bhagat salaamed reverently to the Law, because he knew the value of it, and was seeking for a Law of his own. Then he moved on, and slept that night in an empty hut at Chota Simla, which looks like the very last end of the earth, but it was only the beginning of his journey.

He followed the Himalaya-Tibet road, the little ten-foot track that is blasted out of solid rock, or strutted out on timbers over gulfs a thousand feet deep; that dips into warm, wet, shut-in valleys, and climbs out across bare, grassy hill-shoulders where the sun strikes like a burning-glass; or turns through dripping, dark forests where the tree-ferns dress the trunks from head to heel, and the pheasant calls to his mate. And he met Tibetan herdsmen with their dogs and flocks of sheep, each sheep with a little bag of borax on his back, and wandering wood-cutters, and cloaked and blanketed Lamas[3] from Tibet, coming into India on pilgrimage, and envoys of little solitary Hill-states, posting furiously on ring-streaked and piebald ponies, or the cavalcade of a Rajah paying a visit; or else for a long, clear day he would see nothing more than a black bear grunting and rooting below in the valley. When he first started, the roar of the world he had left still rang in his ears, as the roar of a tunnel rings long after the train has passed through; but when he had put the Mutteeanee Pass behind him that was all done, and Purun Bhagat was alone with himself, walking, wondering, and thinking, his eyes on the ground, and his thoughts with the clouds.

One evening he crossed the highest pass he had met till then—it had been a two-days' climb—and came out on a line of snow-peaks that banded all the horizon—mountains from fifteen to twenty thousand feet high, looking almost near enough to hit with a stone, though they were fifty or sixty miles away. The pass was crowned with dense, dark forest—deodar, walnut, wild cherry, wild olive, and wild pear, but mostly deodar, which is the Himalayan cedar; and under the shadow of the deodars stood a deserted shrine to Kali—who is Durga, who is Sitala,[4] who is sometimes worshipped against the smallpox.

Purun Bhagat swept the stone floor clean, smiled at the grinning statue, made himself a little mud fireplace at the back of the shrine, spread his antelope skin on a bed of fresh pine-needles, tucked his *bairagi*—his brass-handled crutch—under his armpit, and sat down to rest.

Immediately below him the hillside fell away, clean and cleared for fifteen hundred feet, where a little village of stone-walled houses, with roofs of beaten earth, clung to the steep tilt. All round it the tiny terraced fields lay out like aprons of patchwork on the knees of the mountain, and cows no bigger than beetles grazed between the smooth stone circles of the threshing-floors. Looking across the valley, the eye was deceived by the size of things, and could not at first realise that what seemed to be low scrub, on the oppo-

3. ***Lamas,*** Tibetan priests or monks.

4. ***Kali . . . Durga . . . Sitala,*** names given to three of the numerous forms of the Hindu goddess Devi. The first two are malignant: as Kali, "the black one," she is pictured garlanded with skulls; as Durga, "the inaccessible," she rides a tiger. However, as Sitala she is invoked against smallpox.

site mountain-flank, was in truth a forest of hundred-foot pines. Purun Bhagat saw an eagle swoop across the gigantic hollow, but the great bird dwindled to a dot ere it was half-way over. A few bands of scattered clouds strung up and down the valley, catching on a shoulder of the hills, or rising up and dying out when they were level with the head of the pass. And "Here shall I find peace," said Purun Bhagat.

Now, a Hill-man makes nothing of a few hundred feet up or down, and as soon as the villagers saw the smoke in the deserted shrine, the village priest climbed up the terraced hillside to welcome the stranger.

When he met Purun Bhagat's eyes—the eyes of a man used to control thousands—he bowed to the earth, took the begging-bowl without a word, and returned to the village, saying, "We have at last a holy man. Never have I seen such a man. He is of the Plains—but pale-coloured—a Brahmin of the Brahmins." Then all the housewives of the village said, "Think you he will stay with us?" and each did her best to cook the most savoury meal for the Bhagat. Hill-food is very simple, but with buckwheat and Indian corn, and rice and red pepper, and little fish out of the stream in the valley, and honey from the fluelike hives built in the stone walls, and dried apricots, and turmeric, and wild ginger, and bannocks of flour, a devout woman can make good things, and it was a full bowl that the priest carried to the Bhagat. Was he going to stay? asked the priest. Would he need a *chela*—a disciple—to beg for him? Had he a blanket against the cold weather? Was the food good?

Purun Bhagat ate, and thanked the giver. It was in his mind to stay. That was sufficient, said the priest. Let the begging-bowl be placed outside the shrine, in the hollow made by those two twisted roots, and daily should the Bhagat be fed; for the village felt honoured that such a man—he looked timidly into the Bhagat's face—should tarry among them.

That day saw the end of Purun Bhagat's wanderings. He had come to the place appointed for him—the silence and the space. After this, time stopped, and he, sitting at the mouth of the shrine, could not tell whether he were alive or dead; a man with control of his limbs, or a part of the hills, and the clouds, and the shifting rain and sunlight. He would repeat a Name softly to himself a hundred hundred times, till, at each repetition, he seemed to move more and more out of his body, sweeping up to the doors of some tremendous discovery; but, just as the door was opening, his body would drag him back, and, with grief, he felt he was locked up again in the flesh and bones of Purun Bhagat.

Every morning the filled begging-bowl was laid silently in the crutch of the roots outside the shrine. Sometimes the priest brought it; sometimes a Ladakhi trader, lodging in the village, and anxious to get merit, trudged up the path; but, more often, it was the woman who had cooked the meal overnight; and she would murmur, hardly above her breath: "Speak for me before the gods, Bhagat. Speak for such a one, the wife of so-and-so!" Now and then some bold child would be allowed the honour, and Purun Bhagat would hear him drop the bowl and run as fast as his little legs could carry him, but the Bhagat never came down to the village. It was laid out like a map at his feet. He could see the evening gatherings, held on the circle of the threshing-floors, because that was the only level ground; could see the wonderful unnamed green of the young rice, the indigo blues of the Indian corn, the dock-like patches of buckwheat, and, in its season, the red bloom of the amaranth, whose tiny seeds, being neither grain nor pulse, make a food that can be lawfully eaten by Hindus in time of fasts.

When the year turned, the roofs of the huts were all little squares of purest gold, for it was on the roofs that they laid out their cobs of the corn to dry. Hiving and harvest, rice-sowing and husking, passed before his eyes, all embroidered down there on the many-sided plots of fields, and he thought of them all, and wondered what they all led to at the long last.

Even in populated India a man cannot a day sit still before the wild things run over him as though he were a rock; and in that wilderness very soon the wild things, who knew Kali's Shrine well, came back to look at the intruder. The *langurs*, the big grey-whiskered monkeys of the Himalayas, were, naturally, the first, for they are alive with curiosity; and when they had upset the begging-bowl, and rolled it round the floor, and tried their teeth on the brass-handled crutch, and made faces at the antelope skin, they decid-

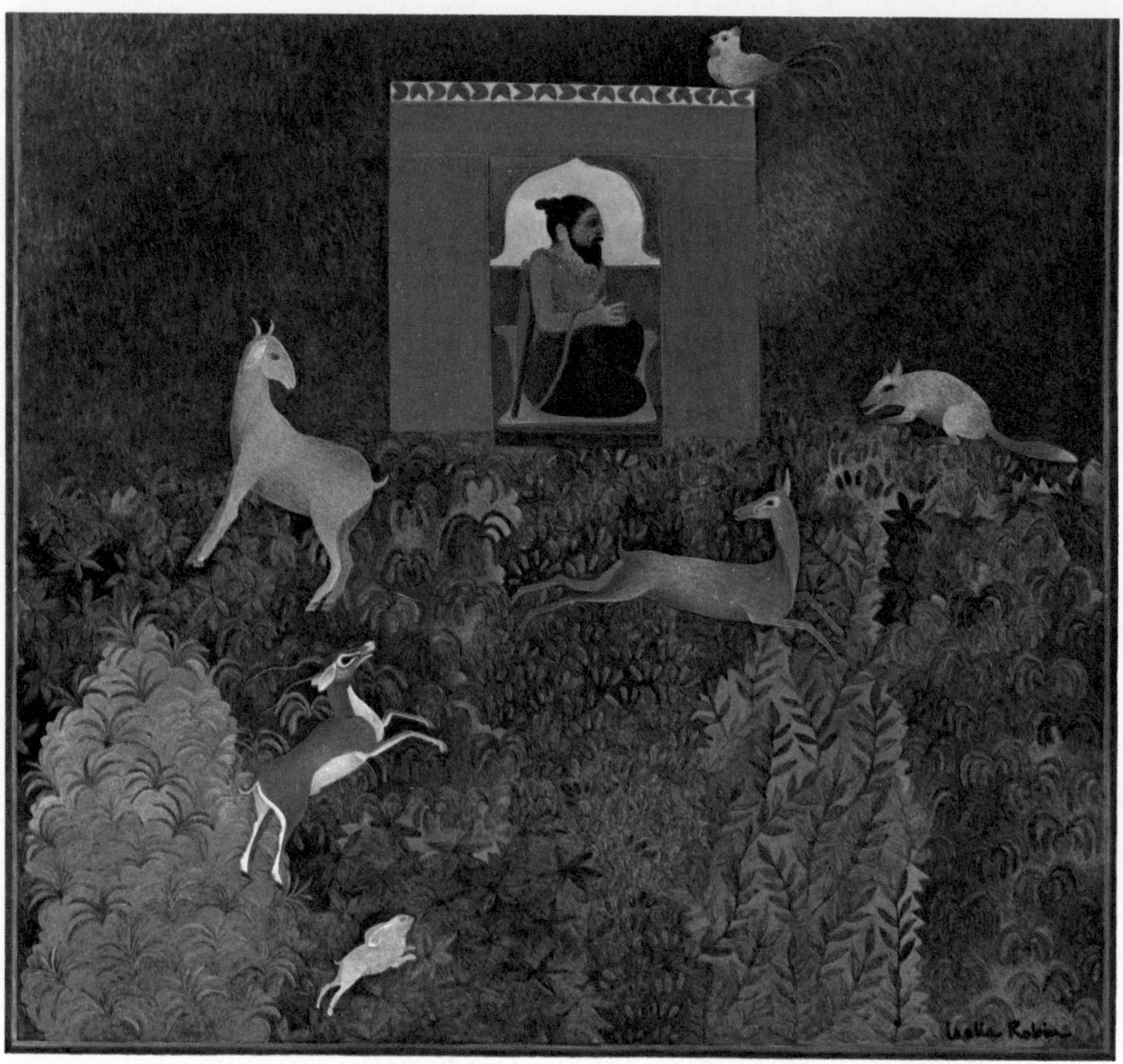

ed that the human being who sat so still was harmless. At evening, they would leap down from the pines, and beg with their hands for things to eat, and then swing off in graceful curves. They liked the warmth of the fire, too, and huddled round it till Purun Bhagat had to push them aside to throw on more fuel; and in the morning, as often as not, he would find a furry ape sharing his blanket. All day long, one or other of the tribe would sit by his side, staring out at the snows, crooning and looking unspeakably wise and sorrowful.

After the monkeys came the *barasingh*, that big deer which is like our red deer, but stronger. He wished to rub off the velvet of his horns against the cold stones of Kali's statue, and stamped his feet when he saw the man at the shrine. But Purun Bhagat never moved, and, little by little, the royal stag edged up and nuzzled his shoulder. Purun Bhagat slid one cool hand along the hot antlers, and the touch soothed the fretted beast, who bowed his head, and Purun Bhagat very softly rubbed and ravelled off the velvet. Afterward, the *barasingh* brought his doe and fawn—gentle things that mumbled on the holy man's blanket—or would come alone at night, his eyes green in the fire-flicker, to take his share of fresh walnuts. At last, the musk-deer, the shyest and almost the smallest of the deerlets, came, too, her big rabbity ears erect; even brindled, silent *mushicknabha* must needs find out what the light in the shrine meant, and drop out her moose-like nose into Purun Bhagat's lap, coming and going with the shadows of the fire. Purun Bhagat called them all "my brothers," and his low call of *"Bhai! Bhai!"* would draw them from the forest at noon if they were within earshot. The Himalayan black bear, moody and suspicious—Sona, who has the V-shaped white mark under his chin—passed that way more than once; and since the Bhagat showed no fear, Sona showed no anger, but watched him, and came closer, and begged a share of the caresses, and a dole of bread or wild berries. Often, in the still dawns, when the Bhagat would climb to the very crest of the pass to watch the red day walking along the peaks of the snows, he would find Sona shuffling and grunting at his heels, thrusting a curious fore-paw under fallen trunks, and bringing it away with a *whoof* of impatience; or his early steps would wake Sona where he lay curled up, and the great brute, rising erect, would think to fight, till he heard the Bhagat's voice and knew his best friend.

Nearly all hermits and holy men who live apart from the big cities have the reputation of being able to work miracles with the wild things, but all the miracle lies in keeping still, in never making a hasty movement, and, for a long time, at least, in never looking directly at a visitor. The villagers saw the outline of the *barasingh* stalking like a shadow through the dark forest behind the shrine; saw the *minaul*, the Himalayan pheasant, blazing in her best colours before Kali's statue; and the *langurs* on their haunches, inside, playing with the walnut shells. Some of the children, too, had heard Sona singing to himself, bear-fashion, behind the fallen rocks, and the Bhagat's reputation as miracle-worker stood firm.

Yet nothing was farther from his mind than miracles. He believed that all things were one big Miracle, and when a man knows that much he knows something to go upon. He knew for a certainty that there was nothing great and nothing little in this world: and day and night he strove to think out his way into the heart of things, back to the place whence his soul had come.

So thinking, his untrimmed hair fell down about his shoulders, the stone slab at the side of the antelope skin was dented into a little hole by the foot of his brass-handled crutch, and the place between the tree trunks, where the begging-bowl rested day after day, sunk and wore into a hollow almost as smooth as the brown shell itself; and each beast knew his exact place at the fire. The fields changed their colours with the seasons; the threshing-floors filled and emptied, and filled again and again; and again and again, when winter came, the *langurs* frisked among the branches feathered with light snow, till the mother-monkeys brought their sad-eyed little babies up from the warmer valleys with the spring. There were few changes in the village. The priest was older, and many of the little children who used to come with the begging-dish sent their own children now; and when you asked of the villagers how long their holy man had lived in Kali's Shrine at the head of the pass, they answered, "Always."

Then came such summer rains as had not been known in the Hills for many seasons. Through three good months the valley was wrapped in cloud and soaking mist—steady, unrelenting downfall, breaking off into thunder-shower after thunder-shower. Kali's Shrine stood above the clouds, for the most part, and there was a whole month in which the Bhagat never caught a glimpse of his village. It was packed away under a white floor of cloud that swayed and shifted and rolled on itself and bulged upward, but never broke from its piers—the streaming flanks of the valley.

All that time he heard nothing but the sound of a million little waters, overhead from the trees, and underfoot along the ground, soaking through the pine-needles, dripping from the tongues of draggled fern, and spouting in newly-torn muddy channels down the slopes. Then the sun came out, and drew forth the good incense of the deodars and the rhododendrons, and that far-off, clean smell which the Hill people call "the smell of the snows." The hot sunshine lasted for a week, and then the rains gathered together for their last downpour, and the water fell in sheets that flayed off the skin of the ground and leaped back in mud. Purun Bhagat heaped his fire high that night, for he was sure his brothers would need warmth; but never a beast came to the shrine, though he called and called till he dropped asleep, wondering what had happened in the woods.

It was in the black heart of the night, the rain drumming like a thousand drums, that he was roused by a plucking at his blanket, and, stretching out, felt the little hand of a *langur*. "It is better here than in the trees," he said sleepily, loosening a fold of blanket; "take it and be warm." The monkey caught his hand and pulled hard. "Is it food, then?" said Purun Bhagat. "Wait awhile, and I will prepare some." As he kneeled to throw fuel on the fire the *langur* ran to the door of the shrine, crooned and ran back again, plucking at the man's knee.

"What is it? What is thy trouble, Brother?" said Purun Bhagat, for the *langur's* eyes were full of things that he could not tell. "Unless one of thy caste be in a trap—and none set traps here—I will not go into that weather. Look, Brother, even the *barasingh* comes for shelter!"

The deer's antlers clashed as he strode into the shrine, clashed against the grinning statue of Kali. He lowered them in Purun Bhagat's direction and stamped uneasily, hissing through his half-shut nostrils.

"Hai! Hai! Hai!" said the Bhagat, snapping his fingers. "Is *this* payment for a night's lodging?" But the deer pushed him toward the door, and as he did so Purun Bhagat heard the sound of something opening with a sigh, and saw two slabs of the floor draw away from each other, while the sticky earth below smacked its lips.

"Now I see," said Purun Bhagat. "No blame to my brothers that they did not sit by the fire to-night. The mountain is falling. And yet—why should I go?" His eye fell on the empty begging-bowl, and his face changed. "They have given me good food daily since—since I came, and, if I am not swift, to-morrow there will not be one mouth in the valley. Indeed, I must go and warn them below. Back there, Brother! Let me get to the fire."

The *barasingh* backed unwillingly as Purun Bhagat drove a pine torch deep into the flame, twirling it till it was well lit. "Ah! ye came to warn me," he said, rising. "Better than that we shall do; better than that. Out, now, and lend me thy neck, Brother, for I have but two feet."

He clutched the bristling withers of the *barasingh* with his right hand, held the torch away with his left, and stepped out of the shrine into the desperate night. There was no breath of wind, but the rain nearly drowned the flare as the great deer hurried down the slope, sliding on his haunches. As soon as they were clear of the forest more of the Bhagat's brothers joined them. He heard, though he could not see, the *langurs* pressing about him, and behind them the *uhh! uhh!* of Sona. The rain matted his long white hair into ropes; the water splashed beneath his bare feet, and his yellow robe clung to his frail old body, but he stepped down steadily, leaning against the *barasingh*. He was no longer a holy man, but Sir Purun Dass, K.C.I.E, Prime Minister of no small State, a man accustomed to command, going out to save life. Down the steep, plashy path they poured all together, the Bhagat and his brothers, down and down till the deer's feet clicked and stumbled on the wall of a threshing-floor, and he snorted because he smelt Man. Now they were at the head of the one crooked village street, and the Bhagat beat with his crutch on the barred windows of the blacksmith's house, as his torch blazed up in the shelter of the eves. "Up and out!" cried Purun Bhagat; and he did not know his own voice, for it was years since he had spoken aloud to a man. "The hill falls! The hill is falling! Up and out, oh, you within!"

"It is our Bhagat," said the blacksmith's wife. "He stands among his beasts. Gather the little ones and give the call."

It ran from house to house, while the beasts, cramped in the narrow way, surged and huddled round the Bhagat, and Sona puffed impatiently.

The people hurried into the street—they were no more than seventy souls all told—and in the glare of the torches they saw their Bhagat holding back the terrified *barasingh*, while the monkeys plucked piteously at his skirts, and Sona sat on his haunches and roared.

"Across the valley and up the next hill!" shouted Purun Bhagat. "Leave none behind! We follow!"

Then the people ran as only Hill folk can run,

for they knew that in a landslip you must climb for the highest ground across the valley. They fled, splashing through the little river at the bottom, and panted up the terraced fields on the far side, while the Bhagat and his brethren followed. Up and up the opposite mountain they climbed, calling to each other by name—the roll-call of the village—and at their heels toiled the big *barasingh,* weighted by the failing strength of Purun Bhagat. At last the deer stopped in the shadow of a deep pine-wood, five hundred feet up the hillside. His instinct, that had warned him of the coming slide, told him he would be safe here.

Purun Bhagat dropped fainting by his side, for the chill of the rain and that fierce climb were killing him; but first he called to the scattered torches ahead, "Stay and count your numbers"; then, whispering to the deer as he saw the lights gather in a cluster: "Stay with me, Brother. Stay—till—I—go!"

There was a sigh in the air that grew to a mutter, and a mutter that grew to a roar, and a roar that passed all sense of hearing, and the hillside on which the villagers stood was hit in the darkness, and rocked to the blow. Then a note as steady, deep, and true as the deep C of the organ drowned everything for perhaps five minutes, while the very roots of the pines quivered to it. It died away, and the sound of the rain falling on miles of hard ground and grass changed to the muffled drum of water on soft earth. That told its own tale.

Never a villager—not even the priest—was bold enough to speak to the Bhagat who had saved their lives. They crouched under the pines and waited till the day. When it came they looked across the valley and saw that what had been forest, and terraced field, and track-threaded grazing-ground was one raw, red, fan-shaped smear, and a few trees flung head-down on the scarp. That red ran high up the hill of their refuge, damming back the little river, which had begun to spread into a brick-coloured lake. Of the village, of the road to the shrine, of the shrine itself, and the forest behind, there was no trace.

For one mile in width and two thousand feet in sheer depth the mountain-side had come away bodily, planed clean from head to heel.

And the villagers, one by one, crept through the wood to pray before their Bhagat. They saw the *barasingh* standing over him, who fled when they came near, and they heard the *langurs* wailing in the branches, and Sona moaning up the hill; but their Bhagat was dead, sitting cross-legged, his back against a tree, his crutch under his armpit, and his face turned to the north-east.

The priest said: "Behold a miracle after a miracle, for in this very attitude must all Sunnyasis be buried! Therefore where he now is we will build the temple to our holy man."

They built the temple before a year was ended—a little stone-and-earth shrine—and they called the hill the Bhagat's hill, and they worship there with lights and flowers and offerings to this day. But they do not know that the saint of their worship is the late Sir Purun Dass, K.C.I.E., D.C.L., Ph.D., etc., once Prime Minister of the progressive and enlightened State of Mohiniwala, and honorary or corresponding member of more learned and scientific societies than will ever do any good in this world or the next. □□

Discussion

1. (a) What is Kipling's attitude toward Indian manners and customs as implied through the story of Purun Bhagat? **(b)** What is Kipling's attitude toward England and its manners and customs?

2. How is time measured in Kipling's story? How does this affect the story's tone and meaning?

3. What is the significance of the Himalayan setting of the story?

4. How does Purun Bhagat's closeness to the animals affect the action and reflect the theme of the story?

5. Discuss the nature of Purun Bhagat's death. Is it pathetic? tragic? heroic? sad? Explain.

Extension • Reading

Read Kipling's poem "The White Man's Burden," written several years after "The Miracle of Purun Bhagat." Compare Kipling's attitude toward India (and other colonial countries) in the poem to his attitude in the story.

Rudyard Kipling 1865 • 1936

Kipling was born in Bombay, India; his father was a teacher, museum curator, and illustrator. At the age of six, the boy was sent to England for schooling, which in its brutality and overbearing pressure became one of the most harrowing experiences of his life. He returned to India in 1882 as a journalist, but by the end of that decade had given this up to concentrate on the stories and verse which were to make him one of the most popular writers in the English-speaking world.

Much of Kipling's most admired work was written early in his career. The work collected in volumes such as *Departmental Ditties* and *Plain Tales from the Hills* grew out of his sensitive observation of the ordinary people, both native and British, whose lives were affected by the imposing and sometimes insensitive progress of British imperialism. Kipling's stories are sometimes more striking than psychologically deep, and his verse can contain more rhythm than insight, but at their best both combine essential emotions and simple facts to convey not only the exotic but also the familiarly human in the life of British India.

In 1897 Kipling returned to England, where he wrote several novels, including *Captains Courageous* and *Kim*, and drew increasingly apart from the India of his early career. His work continued to reflect his sense of integrity and the values of loyalty and courage which informed his stories of Mowgli, Sher Khan, and Rikki-tikki-tavi, but it also reflected an uncritical allegiance to the spirit of imperialism.

Joseph Conrad

The Lagoon

The white man, leaning with both arms over the roof of the little house in the stern of the boat, said to the steersman—

"We will pass the night in Arsat's clearing. It is late."

The Malay only grunted, and went on looking fixedly at the river. The white man rested his chin on his crossed arms and gazed at the wake of the boat. At the end of the straight avenue of forests cut by the intense glitter of the river, the sun appeared unclouded and dazzling, poised low over the water that shone smoothly like a band of metal. The forests, sombre and dull, stood motionless and silent on each side of the broad stream. At the foot of big, towering trees, trunkless nipa palms rose from the mud of the bank, in bunches of leaves enormous and heavy, that hung unstirring over the brown swirl of eddies. In the stillness of the air every tree, every leaf, every bough, every tendril of creeper and every petal of minute blossoms seemed to have been bewitched into an immobility perfect and final. Nothing moved on the river but the eight paddles that rose flashing regularly, dipped together with a single splash; while the steersman swept right and left with a periodic and sudden flourish of his blade describing a glinting semicircle above his head. The churned-up water frothed alongside with a confused murmur. And the white man's canoe, advancing upstream in the short-lived disturbance of its own making, seemed to enter the portals of a land from which the very memory of motion had forever departed.

The white man, turning his back upon the setting sun, looked along the empty and broad expanse of the sea-reach. For the last three miles of its course the wandering, hesitating river, as if enticed irresistibly by the freedom of an open horizon, flows straight into the sea, flows straight to the east—to the east that harbours both light and darkness. Astern of the boat the repeated call of some bird, a cry discordant and feeble, skipped along over the smooth water and lost itself, before it could reach the other shore, in the breathless silence of the world.

The steersman dug his paddle into the stream, and held hard with stiffened arms, his body thrown forward. The water gurgled aloud; and suddenly the long straight reach seemed to pivot on its centre, the forests swung in a semicircle, and the slanting beams of sunset touched the broadside of the canoe with a fiery glow, throwing the slender and distorted shadows of its crew upon the streaked glitter of the river. The white man turned to look ahead. The course of the boat had been altered at right-angles to the stream, and the carved dragon-head of its prow was pointing now at a gap in the fringing bushes of the bank. It glided through, brushing the overhanging twigs, and disappeared from the river like some slim and amphibious creature leaving the water for its lair in the forests.

The narrow creek was like a ditch: torturous, fabulously deep; filled with gloom under the thin strip of pure and shining blue of the heaven. Immense trees soared up, invisible behind the festooned draperies of creepers. Here and there, near the glistening blackness of the water, a twisted root of some tall tree showed amongst the tracery of small ferns, black and dull, writhing and motionless, like an arrested snake. The short words of the paddlers reverberated loudly between the thick and sombre walls of vegetation. Darkness oozed out from between the trees, through the tangled maze of the creepers, from behind the great fantastic and unstirring leaves; the darkness, mysterious and invincible; the darkness scented and poisonous of impenetrable forests.

"The Lagoon" from TALES OF UNREST by Joseph Conrad. Published 1898.

The men poled in the shoaling water. The creek broadened, opening out into a wide sweep of a stagnant lagoon. The forests receded from the marshy bank, leaving a level strip of bright green, reedy grass to frame the reflected blueness of the sky. A fleecy pink cloud drifted high above, trailing the delicate colouring of its image under the floating leaves and the silvery blossoms of the lotus. A little house, perched on high piles, appeared black in the distance. Near it, two tall nibong palms, that seemed to have come out of the forests in the background, leaned slightly over the ragged roof, with a suggestion of sad tenderness and care in the droop of their leafy and soaring heads.

The steersman, pointing with his paddle, said, "Arsat is there. I see his canoe fast between the piles."

The polers ran along the sides of the boat glancing over their shoulders at the end of the day's journey. They would have preferred to spend the night somewhere else than on this lagoon of weird aspect and ghostly reputation. Moreover, they disliked Arsat, first as a stranger, and also because he who repairs a ruined house, and dwells in it, proclaims that he is not afraid to live amongst the spirits that haunt the places abandoned by mankind. Such a man can disturb the course of fate by glances or words; while his familiar ghosts are not easy to propitiate by casual wayfarers upon whom they long to wreak the malice of their human master. White men care not for such things, being unbelievers and in league with the Father of Evil, who leads them unharmed through the invisible dangers of this world. To the warnings of the righteous they oppose an offensive pretence of disbelief. What is there to be done?

So they thought, throwing their weight on the end of their long poles. The big canoe glided on swiftly, noiselessly, and smoothly, towards Arsat's clearing, till, in a great rattling of poles thrown down, and the loud murmurs of "Allah be praised!" it came with a gentle knock against the crooked piles below the house.

The boatmen with uplifted faces shouted discordantly, "Arsat! O Arsat!" Nobody came. The white man began to climb the rude ladder giving access to the bamboo platform before the house. The juragan[1] of the boat said sulkily, "We will cook in the sampan, and sleep on the water."

"Pass my blankets and the basket," said the white man, curtly.

He knelt on the edge of the platform to receive the bundle. Then the boat shoved off, and the white man, standing up, confronted Arsat, who had come out through thc low door of his hut. He was a man young, powerful, with broad chest and muscular arms. He had nothing on but his sarong.[2] His head was bare. His big, soft eyes stared eagerly at the white man, but his voice and demeanour were composed as he asked, without any words of greeting—

"Have you medicine, Tuan[3]?"

"No," said the visitor in a startled tone. "No. Why? Is there sickness in the house?"

"Enter and see," replied Arsat, in the same calm manner, and turning short round, passed

1. ***juragan*** (ju′rä gän), the rower chiefly responsible for steering the boat.
2. ***sarong*** (sə rông′), a brightly colored cloth, wrapped around the waist and worn as a skirt by both men and women of the Malay Archipelago and the Pacific Islands.
3. ***Tuan***, (tü än′), "lord," a Malay term or deference or respect.

again through the small doorway. The white man, dropping his bundles, followed.

In the dim light of the dwelling he made out on a couch of bamboos a woman stretched on her back under a broad sheet of red cotton cloth. She lay still, as if dead; but her big eyes, wide open, glittered in the gloom, staring upwards at the slender rafters, motionless and unseeing. She was in a high fever, and evidently unconscious. Her cheeks were sunk slightly, her lips were partly open, and on the young face there was the ominous and fixed expression—the absorbed, contemplating expression of the unconscious who are going to die. The two men stood looking down at her in silence.

"Has she been long ill?" asked the traveller.

"I have not slept for five nights," answered the Malay, in a deliberate tone. "At first she heard voices calling her from the water and struggled against me who held her. But since the sun of to-day rose she hears nothing—she hears not me. She sees nothing. She sees not me—me!"

He remained silent for a minute, then asked softly—

"Tuan, will she die?"

"I fear so," said the white man, sorrowfully. He had known Arsat years ago, in a far country in times of trouble and danger, when no friendship is to be despised. And since his Malay friend had come unexpectedly to dwell in the hut on the lagoon with a strange woman, he had slept many times there, in his journeys up and down the river. He liked the man who knew how to keep faith in council and how to fight without fear by the side of his white friend. He liked him—not so much perhaps as a man likes his favourite dog—but still he liked him well enough to help and ask no questions, to think sometimes vaguely and hazily in the midst of his own pursuits, about the lonely man and the long-haired woman with audacious face and triumphant eyes, who lived together hidden by the forests—alone and feared.

The white man came out of the hut in time to see the enormous conflagration of sunset put out by the swift and stealthy shadows that, rising like a black and impalpable vapour above the tree-tops, spread over the heaven, extinguishing the crimson glow of floating clouds and the red brilliance of departing daylight. In a few moments all the stars came out above the intense blackness of the earth and the great lagoon gleaming suddenly with reflected lights resembled an oval patch of night sky flung down into the hopeless and abysmal night of the wilderness. The white man had some supper out of the basket, then collecting a few sticks that lay about the platform, made up a small fire, not for warmth, but for the sake of the smoke, which would keep off the mosquitos. He wrapped himself in the blankets and sat with his back against the reed wall of the house, smoking thoughtfully.

Arsat came through the doorway with noiseless steps and squatted down by the fire. The white man moved his outstretched legs a little.

"She breathes," said Arsat in a low voice, anticipating the expected question. "She breathes and burns as if with a great fire. She speaks not; she hears not—and burns!"

He paused for a moment, then asked in a quiet, incurious tone—

"Tuan . . . will she die?"

The white man moved his shoulders uneasily and muttered in a hesitating manner—

"If such is her fate."

"No, Tuan," said Arsat, calmly. "If such is my fate. I hear, I see, I wait. I remember . . . Tuan, do you remember the old days? Do you remember my brother?"

"Yes," said the white man. The Malay rose suddenly and went in. The other, sitting still outside, could hear the voice in the hut. Arsat said: "Hear me! Speak!" His words were succeeded by a complete silence. "O Diamelen!" he cried, suddenly. After that cry there was a deep sigh. Arsat came out and sank down again in his old place.

They sat in silence before the fire. There was no sound within the house, there was no sound near them; but far away on the lagoon they could hear the voices of the boatmen ringing fitful and distinct on the calm water. The fire in the bows of the sampan shone faintly in the distance with a hazy red glow. Then it died out. The voices ceased. The land and the water slept invisible, unstirring and mute. It was as though there had been nothing left in the world but the glitter of stars streaming, ceaseless and vain, through the black stillness of the night.

The white man gazed straight before him into

the darkness with wide-open eyes. The fear and fascination, the inspiration and the wonder of death—of death near, unavoidable, and unseen, soothed the unrest of his race and stirred the most indistinct, the most intimate of his thoughts. The ever-ready suspicion of evil, the gnawing suspicion that lurks in our hearts, flowed out into the stillness round him—into the stillness profound and dumb, and made it appear untrustworthy and infamous, like the placid and impenetrable mask of an unjustifiable violence. In that fleeting and powerful disturbance of his being the earth enfolded in the starlight peace became a shadowy country of inhuman strife, a battlefield of phantoms terrible and charming, august or ignoble, struggling ardently for the possession of our helpless hearts. An unquiet and mysterious country of inextinguishable desires and fears.

A plaintive murmur rose in the night; a murmur saddening and startling, as if the great solitudes of surrounding woods had tried to whisper into his ear the wisdom of their immense and lofty indifference. Sounds hesitating and vague floated in the air round him, shaped themselves slowly into words; and at last flowed on gently in a murmuring stream of soft and monotonous sentences. He stirred like a man waking up and changed his position slightly. Arsat, motionless and shadowy, sitting with bowed head under the stars, was speaking in a low and dreamy tone—

". . . for where can we lay down the heaviness of our trouble but in a friend's heart? A man must speak of war and of love. You, Tuan, know what war is, and you have seen me in time of danger seek death as other men seek life! A writing may be lost; a lie may be written; but what the eye has seen is truth and remains in the mind!"

"I remember," said the white man, quietly. Arsat went on with mournful composure—

"Therefore I shall speak to you of love. Speak in the night. Speak before both night and love are gone—and the eye of day looks upon my sorrow and my shame; upon my blackened face; upon my burnt-up heart."

A sigh, short and faint, marked an almost imperceptible pause, and then his words flowed on, without a stir, without a gesture.

"After the time of trouble and war was over and you went away from my country in the pursuit of your desires, which we, men of the islands, cannot understand, I and my brother became again, as we had been before, the sword-bearers of the Ruler. You know we were men of family, belonging to a ruling race, and more fit than any to carry on our right shoulder the emblem of power. And in the time of prosperity Si Dendring showed us favour, as we, in time of sorrow, had showed to him the faithfulness of our courage. It was a time of peace. A time of deer-hunts and cock-fights; of idle talks and foolish squabbles between men whose bellies are full and weapons are rusty. But the sower watched the young rice-shoots grow up without fear, and the traders came and went, departed lean and returned fat into the river of peace. They brought news, too. Brought lies and truth mixed together, so that no man knew when to rejoice and when to be sorry. We heard from them about you also. They had seen you here and had seen you there. And I was glad to hear, for I remembered the stirring times, and I always remembered you, Tuan, till the time came when my eyes could see nothing in the past, because they had looked upon the one who is dying there—in the house."

He stopped to exclaim in an intense whisper, "O Mara bahia! O Calamity!" then went on speaking a little louder:

"There's no worse enemy and no better friend than a brother, Tuan, for one brother knows another, and in perfect knowledge is strength for good or evil. I loved my brother. I went to him and told him that I could see nothing but one face, hear nothing but one voice. He told me: 'Open your heart so that she can see what is in it—and wait. Patience is wisdom. Inchi Midah may die or our Ruler may throw off his fear of a woman!' . . . I waited! . . . You remember the lady with the veiled face, Tuan, and the fear of our Ruler before her cunning and temper. And if she wanted her servant, what could I do? But I fed the hunger of my heart on short glances and stealthy words. I loitered on the path to the bath-houses in the daytime, and when the sun had fallen behind the forest I crept along the jasmine hedges of the women's courtyard. Unseeing, we spoke to one another through the scent of flowers, through the veil of leaves, through the blades of long grass that stood still before our lips; so great was our prudence, so faint was the murmur of our great longing. The time passed swiftly . . . and there were whispers amongst women—and our enemies watched—my brother was gloomy, and I began to think of killing and of a fierce death. . . . We are of a people who take what they want—like you whites. There is a time when a man should forget loyalty and respect. Might and authority are given to rulers, but to all men is given love and strength and courage. My brother said, 'You shall take her from their midst. We are two who are like one.' And I answered, 'Let it be soon, for I find no warmth in sunlight that does not shine upon her.' Our time came when the Ruler and all the great people went to the mouth of the river to fish by torchlight. There were hundreds of boats, and on the white sand, between the water and the forests, dwellings of leaves were built for the households of the Rajahs. The smoke of cooking-fires was like a blue mist of the evening, and many voices rang in it joyfully. While they were making the boats ready to beat up the fish, my brother came to me and said, 'To-night!' I looked to my weapons, and when the time came our canoe took its place in the circle of boats carrying the torches. The lights blazed on the water, but behind the boats there was darkness. When the shouting began and the excitement made them like mad we dropped out. The water swallowed our fire, and we floated back to the shore that was dark with only here and there the glimmer of embers. We could hear the talk of slavegirls amongst the sheds. Then we found a place deserted and silent. We waited there. She came. She came running along the shore, rapid and leaving no trace, like a leaf driven by the wind into the sea. My brother said gloomily, 'Go and take her; carry her into our boat.' I lifted her in my arms. She panted. Her heart was beating against my breast. I said, 'I take you from those people. You came to the cry of my heart, but my arms take you into my boat against the will of the great!' 'It is right,' said my brother. 'We are men who take what we want and can hold it against many. We should have taken her in daylight.' I said, 'Let us be off'; for since she was in my boat I began to think of our Ruler's many men. 'Yes. Let us be off,' said my brother. 'We are cast out and this boat is our country now—and the sea is our refuge.' He lingered with his foot on the shore, and I entreated him to hasten, for I remembered the strokes of her heart against my breast and thought that two men cannot withstand a hundred. We left, paddling downstream close to the bank; and as we passed by the creek where they were fishing, the great shouting had ceased, but the murmur of voices was loud like the humming of insects flying at noonday. The boats floated, clustered together, in the red light of torches, under a black roof of smoke; and men talked of their sport. Men that boasted, and praised, and jeered—men that would have been our friends in the morning, but on that night were already our enemies. We paddled swiftly past. We had no more friends in the country of our birth. She sat in the middle of the canoe with covered face; silent as she is now; unseeing as she is now—and I had no regret at what I was leaving because I could hear her breathing close to me—as I can hear her now."

He paused, listened with his ear turned to the doorway, then shook his head and went on:

"My brother wanted to shout the cry of challenge—one cry only—to let the people know we were freeborn robbers who trusted our arms and the great sea. And again I begged him in the name of our love to be silent. Could I not hear her breathing close to me? I knew the pursuit would come quick enough. My brother loved me. He dipped his paddle without a splash. He only said, 'There is half a man in you now—the other half is in that woman. I can wait. When you are a whole man again, you will come back with me here to shout defiance. We are sons of the same mother.' I made no answer. All my strength and all my spirit were in my hands that held the paddle—for I longed to be with her in a safe place beyond the reach of men's anger and of women's spite. My love was so great, that I thought it could guide me to a country where death was unknown, if I could only escape from Inchi Midah's fury and from our Ruler's sword. We paddled with haste, breathing through our teeth. The blades bit deep into the smooth water. We passed out of the river; we flew in clear channels amongst the shallows. We skirted the black coast; we skirted the sand beaches where

Conrad on the Sources of His Fiction

". . . I need not point out that I had to *make* material from my own life's incidents arranged, combined, coloured for artistic purposes. I don't think there's anything reprehensible in that. After all I *am* a writer of fiction; and it is not what actually happened, but the manner of presenting it that settles the literary and even the moral value of my work. My little vol. of autobiography of course is absolutely genuine. The rest is a more or less close approximation to facts and suggestions. What I claim as true are my mental and emotional reactions to life, to men, to their affairs and passions as I have seen them. I have in that sense kept always true to myself."

the sea speaks in whispers to the land; and the gleam of white sand flashed back past our boat, so swiftly she ran upon the water. We spoke not. Only once I said, 'Sleep, Diamelen, for soon you may want all your strength.' I heard the sweetness of her voice, but I never turned my head. The sun rose and still we went on. Water fell from my face like rain from a cloud. We flew in the light and heat. I never looked back, but I knew that my brother's eyes, behind me, were looking steadily ahead, for the boat went as straight as a bushman's dart, when it leaves the end of the sumpitan.[4] There was no better paddler, no better steersman than my brother. Many times, together, we had won races in that canoe. But we never had put out our strength as we did then—then, when for the last time we paddled together! There was no braver or stronger man in our country than my brother. I could not spare the strength to turn my head and look at him, but every moment I heard the hiss of his breath getting louder behind me. Still he did not speak. The sun was high. The heat clung to my back like a flame of fire. My ribs were ready to burst, but I could no longer get enough air into my chest. And then I felt I must cry out with my last breath, 'Let us rest!' . . . 'Good!' he answered; and his voice was firm. He was strong. He was brave. He knew not fear and no fatigue . . . My brother!"

A murmur powerful and gentle, a murmur vast and faint; the murmur of trembling leaves, of stirring boughs, ran through the tangled depths of the forests, ran over the starry smoothness of the lagoon, and the water between the piles lapped the slimy timber once with a sudden splash. A breath of warm air touched the two men's faces and passed on with a mournful sound—a breath loud and short like an uneasy sigh of the dreaming earth.

Arsat went on in an even, low voice.

"We ran our canoe on the white beach of a little bay close to a long tongue of land that seemed to bar our road; a long wooded cape going far into the sea. My brother knew that place. Beyond the cape a river has its entrance, and through the jungle of that land there is a narrow path. We made a fire and cooked rice. Then we lay down to sleep on the soft sand in the shade of our canoe, while she watched. No sooner had I closed my eyes than I heard her cry of alarm. We leaped up. The sun was halfway down the sky already, and coming in sight in the opening of the bay we saw a prau[5] manned by many paddlers. We knew it at once; it was one of our Rajah's praus. They were watching the shore, and saw us. They beat the gong, and turned the head of the prau into the bay. I felt my

4. ***sumpitan*** (sum′pi tan), a type of blowgun used to propel a (usually poisoned) dart by the natives of Borneo and nearby islands.
5. ***prau*** (prou), or *proa*, a swift Malay sailing boat.

heart become weak within my breast. Diamelen sat on the sand and covered her face. There was no escape by sea. My brother laughed. He had the gun you had given him, Tuan, before you went away, but there was only a handful of powder. He spoke to me quickly: 'Run with her along the path. I shall keep them back, for they have no firearms, and landing in the face of a man with a gun is certain death for some. Run with her. On the other side of that wood there is a fisherman's house—and a canoe. When I have fired all the shots I will follow. I am a great runner, and before they can come up we shall be gone. I will hold out as long as I can, for she is but a woman—that can neither run nor fight, but she has your heart in her weak hands.' He dropped behind the canoe. The prau was coming. She and I ran, and as we rushed along the path I heard shots. My brother fired—once—twice—and the booming of the gong ceased. There was silence behind us. That neck of land is narrow. Before I heard my brother fire the third shot I saw the shelving shore, and I saw the water again; the mouth of a broad river. We crossed a grassy glade. We ran down to the water. I saw a low hut above the black mud, and a small canoe hauled up. I heard another shot behind me. I thought, 'That is his last charge.' We rushed down to the canoe; a man came running from the hut, but I leaped on him, and we rolled together in the mud. Then I got up, and he lay still at my feet. I don't know whether I had killed him or not. I and Diamelen pushed the canoe afloat. I heard yells behind me, and I saw my brother run across the glade. Many men were bounding after him. I took her in my arms and threw her into the boat, then leaped in myself. When I looked back I saw that my brother had fallen. He fell and was up again, but the men were closing round him. He shouted, 'I am coming!' The men were close to him. I looked. Many men. Then I looked at her. Tuan, I pushed the canoe! I pushed it into deep water. She was kneeling forward looking at me, and I said, 'Take your paddle,' while I struck the water with mine. Tuan, I heard him cry. I heard him cry my name twice; and I heard voices shouting, 'Kill! Strike!' I never turned back. I heard him calling my name again with a great shriek, as when life is going out together with the voice—and I never turned my head. My own name! . . . My brother! Three times he called—but I was not afraid of life. Was she not there in that canoe? And could I not with her find a country where death is forgotten—where death is unknown!"

The white man sat up. Arsat rose and stood, an indistinct and silent figure above the dying embers of the fire. Over the lagoon a mist drifting and low had crept, erasing slowly the glittering images of the stars. And now a great expanse of white vapour covered the land; it flowed cold and gray in the darkness, eddied in noiseless whirls round the tree-trunks and about the platform of the house, which seemed to float upon a restless and impalpable illusion of a sea. Only far away the tops of the trees stood outlined on the twinkle of heaven, like a sombre and forbidding shore—a coast deceptive, pitiless and black.

Arsat's voice vibrated loudly in the profound peace.

"I had her there! I had her! To get her I would have faced all mankind. But I had her—and——"

His words went out ringing into the empty distances. He paused, and seemed to listen to them dying away very far—beyond help and beyond recall. Then he said quietly—

"Tuan, I loved my brother."

A breath of wind made him shiver. High above his head, high above the silent sea of mist the drooping leaves of the palms rattled together with a mournful and expiring sound. The white man stretched his legs. His chin rested on his chest, and he murmured sadly without lifting his head—

"We all love our brothers."

Arsat burst out with an intense whispering violence—

"What did I care who died? I wanted peace in my own heart."

He seemed to hear a stir in the house—listened—then stepped in noiselessly. The white man stood up. A breeze was coming in fitful puffs. The stars shone paler as if they had retreated into the frozen depths of immense space. After a chill gust of wind there were a few seconds of perfect calm and absolute silence. Then from behind the black and wavy line of the forests a column of golden light shot up into the heavens and spread over the semicircle of the eastern horizon. The sun had risen. The mist

lifted, broke into drifting patches, vanished into thin flying wreaths; and the unveiled lagoon lay, polished and black, in the heavy shadows at the foot of the wall of trees. A white eagle rose over it with a slanting and ponderous flight, reached the clear sunshine and appeared dazzlingly brilliant for a moment, then soaring higher, became a dark and motionless speck before it vanished into the blue as if it had left the earth forever. The white man, standing gazing upwards before the doorway, heard in the hut a confused and broken murmur of distracted words ending with a loud groan. Suddenly Arsat stumbled out with outstretched hands, shivered, and stood still for some time with fixed eyes. Then he said—

"She burns no more."

Before his face the sun showed its edge above the tree-tops rising steadily. The breeze freshened; a great brilliance burst upon the lagoon, sparkled on the rippling water. The forests came out of the clear shadows of the morning, became distinct, as if they had rushed nearer—to stop short in a great stir of leaves, of nodding boughs, of swaying branches. In the merciless sunshine the whisper of unconscious life grew louder, speaking in an incomprehensible voice round the dumb darkness of that human sorrow. Arsat's eyes wandered slowly, then stared at the rising sun.

"I can see nothing," he said half aloud to himself.

"There is nothing," said the white man, moving to the edge of the platform and waving his hand to his boat. A shout came faintly over the lagoon and the sampan began to glide towards the abode of the friend of ghosts.

"If you want to come with me, I will wait all the morning," said the white man, looking away upon the water.

"No, Tuan," said Arsat, softly. "I shall not eat or sleep in this house, but I must first see my road. Now I can see nothing—see nothing! There is no light and no peace in the world; but there is death—death for many. We are sons of the same mother—and I left him in the midst of enemies; but I am going back now."

He drew a long breath and went on in a dreamy tone:

"In a little while I shall see clear enough to strike—to strike. But she has died, and . . . now . . . darkness."

He flung his arms wide open, let them fall along his body, then stood still with unmoved face and stony eyes, staring at the sun. The white man got down into his canoe. The polers ran smartly along the sides of the boat, looking over their shoulders at the beginning of a weary journey. High in the stern, his head muffled up in white rags, the juragan sat moody, letting his paddle trail in the water. The white man, leaning with both arms over the grass roof of the little cabin, looked back at the shining ripple of the boat's wake. Before the sampan passed out of the lagoon into the creek he lifted his eyes. Arsat had not moved. He stood lonely in the searching sunshine; and he looked beyond the great light of a cloudless day into the darkness of a world of illusions. □□

Discussion

1. (a) Using the first seven paragraphs as a focus, identify some of the characteristic elements of Conrad's style. **(b)** What is Conrad's sense of Malaya—the Eastern setting of the story—as conveyed by his description of it in these opening paragraphs?

2. Discuss the significance of the white man in the story. What purpose does he serve? Would a nonwhite listener serve the same purpose? Explain.

3. Discuss the white man's relationship to Arsat. What are its key characteristics? How "close" are the two men, and how does this affect Arsat's situation?

4. Arsat speaks repeatedly of "love." **(a)** What is the nature of love in Conrad's story? **(b)** What forces arise in opposition to love in the story?

5. In what ways is the reader given premonitions of the end of Arsat's story?

6. What "crime" does Arsat acknowledge to his listener? What is his "punishment"? What is the connection between them?

7. Why does Arsat decide to return to the kingdom from which he has escaped?

Extension • Writing

At the end of "The Lagoon" Arsat looks into "the darkness of a world of illusions." Write an essay in which you identify and distinguish among several illusions revealed in Conrad's story.

Joseph Conrad 1857 • 1924

Jozef Teodore Konrad Nalecz Korzeniowski was born in the Polish Ukraine in December 1857. His father, a sensitive man of letters who had translated both Shakespeare and Victor Hugo into Polish, was also a fierce patriot, whose leadership in the resistance to czarist rule led to exile, illness, and death. Jozef was an orphan at the age of eleven.

When he was sixteen, Conrad left the guardianship of an uncle to begin what was to be a twenty-year career as a seaman. He started his sea years as an apprentice on a French ship, and emerged from them a master in the English Merchant Marine; he began his travels a Pole, and ended them a naturalized British subject—with a new name. His voyages took him to Marseilles and London, Monte Carlo and Spain, to the African Congo, South America, the Indian Ocean, the Malay peninsula, and the China seas. And they provided him with experiences and insights of such range and intensity that they were to sustain his entire career as a writer of fiction, from *Almayer's Folly* in 1895 to *The Rover* in 1923.

One of the key legacies of Conrad's sea years was his knowledge that the lives of even the most sensitive, courageous, and gifted men can be irrevocably altered by a single moment of hesitation, pride, cowardice, or misjudgment. This is the essential truth behind *Almayer's Folly* and *Lord Jim,* "The Lagoon," "Heart of Darkness," and "The Secret Sharer," perhaps the key truth of his many stories of moral isolation and the struggle of his protagonists to reenter the human community through redemptive gestures, heroic acts, and the process of confession.

Although Conrad's remarkable stories and the great novels which contain them—*The Nigger of the "Narcissus," Nostromo, The Secret Agent, Under Western Eyes,* and *Victory*—made him a widely honored figure in his own lifetime, the more crucial, sustaining influence was probably that of his literary friends, including John Galsworthy, H. G. Wells, Stephen Crane, and Henry James. For personal reasons Conrad declined, in the year of his death, one of the greatest of his public honors, a knighthood offered by his adopted country.

Thomas Hardy

The Grave by the Handpost

I never pass through Chalk-Newton without turning to regard the neighbouring upland, at a point where a lane crosses the lone straight highway dividing this from the next parish; a sight which does not fail to recall the event that once happened there; and, though it may seem superfluous, at this date, to disinter more memories of village history, the whispers of that spot may claim to be preserved.

It was on a dark, yet mild and exceptionally dry evening at Christmas time (according to the testimony of William Dewy of Mellstock, Michael Mail, and others), that the choir of Chalk-Newton—a large, parish situated about halfway between the towns of Ivell and Casterbridge, and now a railway station—left their homes just before midnight to repeat their annual harmonies under the windows of the local population. The band of instrumentalists and singers was one of the largest in the county; and, unlike the smaller and finer Mellstock string-band, which eschewed all but the catgut, it included brass and reed performers at full Sunday services, and reached all across the west gallery.

On this night there were two or three violins, two 'cellos, a tenor viol, double bass, hautboy, clarionets, serpent,[1] and seven singers. It was, however, not the choir's labours, but what its members chanced to witness, that particularly marked the occasion.

They had pursued their rounds for many years without meeting with any incident of an unusual kind, but to-night, according to the assertions of several, there prevailed, to begin with, an exceptionally solemn and thoughtful mood among two or three of the oldest in the band, as if they were thinking they might be joined by the phantoms of dead friends who had been of their number in earlier years, and now were mute in the churchyard under flattening mounds—friends who had shown greater zest for melody in their time than was shown in this; or that some past voice of a semi-transparent figure might quaver from some bedroom window its acknowledgment of their nocturnal greeting, instead of a familiar living neighbour. Whether this were fact or fancy, the younger members of the choir met together with their customary thoughtlessness and buoyancy. When they had gathered by the stone stump of the cross in the middle of the village, near the White Horse Inn, which they made their starting-point, some one observed that they were full[2] early, that it was not yet twelve o'clock. The local waits[3] of those days mostly refrained from sounding a note before Christmas morning had astronomically arrived, and not caring to return to their beer, they decided to begin with some outlying cottages in Sidlinch Lane, where the people had no clocks, and would not know whether it were night or morning. In that direction they accordingly went; and as they ascended to higher ground their attention was attracted by a light beyond the houses, quite at the top of the lane.

The road from Chalk-Newton to Broad Sidlinch is about two miles long, and in the middle of its course, where it passes over the ridge dividing the two villages, it crosses at right angles, as has been stated, the lonely monotonous old highway known as Long Ash Lane, which runs, straight as a surveyor's line, many miles north and south of this spot, on the foundation of a Roman road, and has often been mentioned in these narratives. Though now quite deserted and grass-

"The Grave by the Handpost" by Thomas Hardy from THE WAITING SUPPER AND OTHER TALES.

1. ***serpent,*** an old-fashioned wind instrument, with a trumpet-like mouthpiece and a long, twisting wooden tube. It produced a strong, coarse bass tone.
2. ***full,*** very; quite.
3. ***waits,*** carolers.

grown, at the beginning of the century it was well kept and frequented by traffic. The glimmering light appeared to come from the precise point where the roads intersected.

"I think I know what that mid[4] mean!" one of the group remarked.

They stood a few moments, discussing the probability of the light having origin in an event of which rumours had reached them, and resolved to go up the hill.

Approaching the high land their conjectures were strengthened. Long Ash Lane cut athwart them, right and left; and they saw that at the junction of the four ways, under the handpost, a grave was dug, into which, as the choir drew nigh, a corpse had just been thrown by the four Sidlinch men employed for the purpose. The cart and horse which had brought the body thither stood silently by.

The singers and musicians from Chalk-Newton halted, and looked on while the grave-diggers shovelled in and trod down the earth, till, the hole being filled, the latter threw their spades into the cart, and prepared to depart.

"Who mid ye be a-burying there?" asked Lot Swanhills in a raised voice. "Not the sergeant?"

The Sidlinch men had been so deeply engrossed in their task that they had not noticed the lanterns of the Chalk-Newton choir till now.

"What—be you the Newton carol-singers?" returned the representatives of Sidlinch.

"Ay, sure. Can it be that it is old Sergeant Holway you've a-buried there?"

"'Tis so. You've heard about it, then?"

The choir knew no particulars—only that he had shot himself in his apple-closet on the previous Sunday. "Nobody seem'th to know what 'a did it for, 'a b'lieve? Leastwise, we don't know at Chalk-Newton," continued Lot.

"O yes. It all came out at the inquest."

The singers drew close, and the Sidlinch men, pausing to rest after their labours, told the story. "It was all owing to that son of his, poor old man. It broke his heart."

"But the son is a soldier, surely; now with his regiment in the East Indies?"

"Ay. And it have been rough with the army over there lately. 'Twas a pity his father persuaded him to go. But Luke shouldn't have twyted[5] the sergeant o't, since 'a did it for the best."

The circumstances, in brief, were these: The sergeant who had come to this lamentable end, father of the young soldier who had gone with his regiment to the East, had been singularly comfortable in his military experiences, these having ended long before the outbreak of the great war with France. On his discharge, after duly serving his time, he had returned to his native village, and married, and taken kindly to domestic life. But the war in which England next involved herself had cost him many frettings that age and infirmity prevented him from being ever again an active unit of the army. When his only son grew to young manhood, and the question arose of his going out in life, the lad expressed his wish to be a mechanic. But his father advised enthusiastically for the army.

"Trade is coming to nothing in these days," he said. "And if the war with the French lasts, as it will, trade will be still worse. The army, Luke—that's the thing for 'ee. 'Twas the making of me, and 'twill be the making of you. I hadn't half such a chance as you'll have in these splendid hotter times."

Luke demurred, for he was a home-keeping, peace-loving youth. But, putting respectful trust in his father's judgment, he at length gave way, and enlisted in the —d Foot. In the course of a few weeks he was sent out to India to his regiment, which had distinguished itself in the East under General Wellesley.

But Luke was unlucky. News came home indirectly that he lay sick out there; and then on one recent day when his father was out walking, the old man had received tidings that a letter awaited him at Casterbridge. The sergeant sent a special messenger the whole nine miles, and the letter was paid for and brought home; but though, as he had guessed, it came from Luke, its contents were of an unexpected tenor.

The letter had been written during a time of deep depression. Luke said that his life was a burden and a slavery, and bitterly reproached his father for advising him to embark on a career for which he felt unsuited. He found himself suffering fatigues and illnesses without gaining glory, and engaged in a cause which he did not under-

4. ***mid,*** might.
5. ***twyted,*** reproached.

stand or appreciate. If it had not been for his father's bad advice he, Luke, would now have been working comfortably at a trade in the village that he had never wished to leave.

After reading the letter the sergeant advanced a few steps till he was quite out of sight of everybody, and then sat down on the bank by the wayside.

When he arose half-an-hour later he looked withered and broken, and from that day his natural spirits left him. Wounded to the quick by his son's sarcastic stings, he indulged in liquor more and more frequently. His wife had died some years before this date, and the sergeant lived alone in the house which had been hers. One morning in the December under notice the report of a gun had been heard on his premises, and on entering the neighbours found him in a dying state. He had shot himself with an old firelock that he used for scaring birds; and from what he had said the day before, and the arrangements he had made for his decease, there was no doubt that his end had been deliberately planned, as a consequence of the despondency into which he had been thrown by his son's letter. The coroner's jury returned a verdict of *felo-de-se*.[6]

"Here's his son's letter," said one of the Sidlinch men. "'Twas found in his father's pocket. You can see by the state o't how many times he read it over. Howsomever, the Lord's will be done, since it must, whether or no."

The grave was filled up and levelled, no mound being shaped over it. The Sidlinch men then bade the Chalk-Newton choir good-night, and departed with the cart in which they had brought the sergeant's body to the hill. When their tread had died away from the ear, and the wind swept over the isolated grave with its customary stiffle of indifference, Lot Swanhills turned and spoke to old Richard Toller, the hautboy player.

"'Tis hard upon a man, and he a wold sojer, to serve en so, Richard. Not that the sergeant was ever in a battle bigger than would go into a half-acre paddock, that's true. Still, his soul ought to hae as good a chance as another man's, all the same, hey?"

Richard replied that he was quite of the same opinion. "What d'ye say to lifting up a carrel over his grave, as 'tis Christmas, and no hurry to begin down in parish, and 'twouldn't take up ten minutes, and not a soul up here to say us nay, or know anything about it?"

Lot nodded assent. "The man ought to hae his chances," he repeated.

"Ye may as well spet upon his grave, for all the good we shall do en by what we lift up, now he's got so far," said Notton, the clarionet man and professed skeptic of the choir. "But I'm agreed if the rest be."

They thereupon placed themselves in a semicircle by the newly-stirred earth, and roused the dull air with the well-known Number Sixteen of their collection, which Lot gave out as being the one he thought best suited to the occasion and the mood:—

He comes' the pri'-soners to' re-lease',
In Sa'-tan's bon'-dage held'.

"Jown it—we've never played to a dead man afore," said Ezra Cattstock, when, having concluded the last verse, they stood reflecting for a breath or two. "But it do seem more merciful than to go away and leave en, as they t'other fellers have done."

"Now backalong to Newton, and by the time we get overright the pa'son's 'twill be half after twelve," said the leader.

They had not, however, done more than gather up their instruments when the wind brought to their notice the noise of a vehicle rapidly driven up the same lane from Sidlinch which the gravediggers had lately retraced. To avoid being run over when moving on, they waited till the benighted traveller, whoever he might be, should pass them where they stood in the wider area of the Cross.

In half a minute the light of the lanterns fell upon a hired fly, drawn by a steaming and jaded horse. It reached the handpost, when a voice from the inside cried, "Stop here!" The driver pulled rein. The carriage door was opened from within, and there leapt out a private soldier in the uniform of some line regiment. He looked around, and was apparently surprised to see the musicians standing there.

"Have you buried a man here?" he asked.

6. ***felo-de-se,*** suicide.

"No. We bain't Sidlinch folk, thank God; we be Newton choir. Though a man is just buried here, that's true; and we've raised a carrel over the poor mortal's natomy. What—do my eyes see before me young Luke Holway, that went wi' his regiment to the East Indies, or do I see his spirit straight from the battlefield? Be you the son that wrote the letter—"

"Don't—don't ask me. The funeral is over, then?"

"There wer no funeral, in a Christen manner of speaking. But's buried, sure enough. You must have met the men going back in the empty cart."

"Like a dog in a ditch, and all through me!"

He remained silent, looking at the grave, and they could not help pitying him. "My friends," he said, "I understand better now. You have, I suppose, in neighbourly charity, sung peace to his soul? I thank you, from my heart, for your kind pity. Yes; I am Sergeant Holway's miserable son—I'm the son who has brought about his father's death, as truly as if I had done it with my own hand!"

"No, no. Don't ye take on so, young man. He'd been naturally low for a good while, off and on, so we hear."

"We were out in the East when I wrote to him. Everything had seemed to go wrong with me. Just after my letter had gone we were ordered home. That's how it is you see me here. As soon as we got into barracks at Casterbridge I heard o' this—. . . . Damn me! I'll dare to follow my father, and make away with myself, too. It is the only thing left to do!"

"Don't ye be rash, Luke Holway, I say again; but try to make amends by your future life. And maybe your father will smile a smile down from heaven upon 'ee for 't."

He shook his head. "I don't know about that!" he answered bitterly.

"Try and be worthy of your father at his best. 'Tis not too late."

"D' ye think not? I fancy it is! . . . Well, I'll turn it over. Thank you for your good counsel. I'll live for one thing, at any rate. I'll move father's body to a decent Christian churchyard, if I do it with my own hands. I can't save his life, but I can give him an honourable grave. He shan't lie in this accursed place!"

"Ay, as our pa'son says, 'tis a barbarous custom they keep up at Sidlinch, and ought to be done away wi'. The man a' old soldier, too. You see, our pa'son is not like yours at Sidlinch."

"He says it is barbarous, does he? So it is!" cried the soldier. "Now hearken, my friends." Then he proceeded to inquire if they would increase his indebtedness to them by undertaking the removal, privately, of the body of the suicide to the churchyard, not of Sidlinch, a parish he now hated, but of Chalk-Newton. He would give them all he possessed to do it.

Lot asked Ezra Cattstock what he thought of it.

Cattstock, the 'cello player, who was also the sexton, demurred, and advised the young soldier to sound the rector about it first. "Mid be he would object, and yet 'a midn't. The pa'son o' Sidlinch is a hard man, I own ye, and 'a said if folk will kill theirselves in hot blood they must take the consequences. But ours don't think like that at all, and might allow it."

"What's his name?"

"The honourable and reverent Mr. Oldham, brother to Lord Wessex. But you needn't be afeard o' en on that account. He'll talk to 'ee like a common man, if so be you haven't had enough drink to gie 'ee bad breath."

"O, the same as formerly. I'll ask him. Thank you. And that duty done—"

"What then?"

"There's war in Spain. I hear our next move is there. I'll try to show myself to be what my father wished me. I don't suppose I shall—but I'll try in my feeble way. That much I swear—here over his body. So help me God."

Luke smacked his palm against the white handpost with such force that it shook. "Yes, there's war in Spain; and another chance for me to be worthy of father."

So the matter ended that night. That the private acted in one thing as he had vowed to do soon became apparent, for during the Christmas week the rector came into the churchyard when Cattstock was there, and asked him to find a spot that would be suitable for the purpose of such an interment, adding that he had slightly known the late sergeant, and was not aware of any law which forbade him to assent to the removal, the letter of the rule having been observed. But as he did not wish to seem moved by opposition to his

notes and comments

Pessimism in Literature

E. M. Forster

In his essay "Pessimism in Literature," novelist and critic E. M. Forster makes the following observations: ". . . Is there any happy situation on earth that does not contain the seeds of decay, or at all events of transformation? The modern mind is, in this respect, horribly acute, and perceives that the glorious, happy things are not the things that last. And therefore, for an ending, the modern author must go elsewhere, or leave his work unfinished. Separation—that is the end that really satisfies him—not simply the separation that comes through death, but the more tragic separation of people who part before they need, or who part because they have seen each other too closely. Here is something that does last—the note of permanence on which his soul was set. He has labored sincerely; he has told a story not untrue to life; he has said the last word about his characters, for he leaves them in a situation where they can never meet each other any more."

from *Albergo Empedocle* (1906)

neighbour at Sidlinch, he had stipulated that the act of charity should be carried out at night, and as privately as possible, and that the grave should be in an obscure part of the enclosure. "You had better see the young man about it at once," added the rector.

But before Ezra had done anything Luke came down to his house. His furlough had been cut short, owing to new developments of the war in the Peninsula,[7] and being obliged to go back to his regiment immediately, he was compelled to leave the exhumation and reinterment to his friends. Everything was paid for, and he implored them all to see it carried out forthwith.

With this the soldier left. The next day Ezra, on thinking the matter over, again went across to the rectory, struck with sudden misgiving. He had remembered that the sergeant had been buried without a coffin, and he was not sure that a stake had not been driven through him. The business would be more troublesome than they had at first supposed.

"Yes, indeed!" murmured the rector. "I am afraid it is not feasible after all."

The next event was the arrival of a headstone by carrier from the nearest town; to be left at Mr. Ezra Cattstock's; all expenses paid. The sexton and the carrier deposited the stone in the former's outhouse; and Ezra, left alone, put on his spectacles and read the brief and simple inscription:—

HERE LYETH THE BODY OF SAMUEL HOLWAY
LATE SERGEANT IN HIS MAJESTY'S
—D REGIMENT OF FOOT,
WHO DEPARTED THIS LIFE DECEMBER 20TH, 180—.
ERECTED BY L. H.
"I AM NOT WORTHY TO BE CALLED THY SON."

Ezra again called at the riverside rectory. "The stone is come, sir. But I'm afeard we can't do it nohow."

"I should like to oblige him," said the gentlemanly old incumbent. "And I would forgo all fees willingly. Still, if you and the others don't think you can carry it out, I am in doubt what to say."

"Well, sir; I've made inquiry of a Sidlinch woman as to his burial, and what I thought seems true. They buried en wi' a new six-foot hurdle-saul[8] drough's body, from the sheep-pen up in

7. ***war in the Peninsula,*** the campaign against Napoleon after his invasion of Spain, fought by Spain, Portugal, and England.
8. ***hurdle-saul,*** a stake to which hurdles, or sections of fencing, are fastened.

North Ewelease, though they won't own to it now. And the question is, Is the moving worth while, considering the awkwardness?"

"Have you heard anything more of the young man?"

Ezra had only heard that he had embarked that week for Spain with the rest of the regiment. "And if he's as desperate as 'a seemed, we shall never see him here in England again."

"It is an awkward case," said the rector.

Ezra talked it over with the choir; one of whom suggested that the stone might be erected at the cross-roads. This was regarded as impracticable. Another said that it might be set up in the churchyard without removing the body; but this was seen to be dishonest. So nothing was done.

The headstone remained in Ezra's outhouse till, growing tired of seeing it there, he put it away among the bushes at the bottom of his garden. The subject was sometimes revived among them, but it always ended with: "Considering how 'a was buried, we can hardly make a job o't."

There was always the consciousness that Luke would never come back, an impression strengthened by the disasters which were rumoured to have befallen the army in Spain. This tended to make their inertness permanent. The headstone grew green as it lay on its back under Ezra's bushes; then a tree by the river was blown down, and, falling across the stone, cracked it in three pieces. Ultimately the pieces became buried in the leaves and mould.

Luke had not been born a Chalk-Newton man, and he had no relations left in Sidlinch, so that no tidings of him reached either village throughout the war. But after Waterloo and the fall of Napoleon there arrived at Sidlinch one day an English sergeant-major covered with stripes and, as it turned out, rich in glory. Foreign service had so totally changed Luke Holway that it was not until he told his name that the inhabitants recognized him as the sergeant's only son.

He had served with unswerving effectiveness through the Peninsular campaigns under Wellington; had fought at Busaco, Fuentes d'Onoro, Ciudad Rodrigo, Badajoz, Salamanca, Vittoria, Quatre Bras, and Waterloo; and had now returned to enjoy a more than earned pension and repose in his native district.

He hardly stayed in Sidlinch longer than to take a meal on his arrival. The same evening he started on foot over the hill to Chalk-Newton, passing the handpost, and saying as he glanced at the spot, "Thank God: he's not there!" Nightfall was approaching when he reached the latter village; but he made straight for the churchyard. On his entering it there remained light enough to discern the headstones by, and these he narrowly scanned. But though he searched the front part by the road, and the back part by the river, what he sought he could not find—the grave of Sergeant Holway, and a memorial bearing the inscription: "I AM NOT WORTHY TO BE CALLED THY SON."

He left the churchyard and made inquiries. The honourable and reverend old rector was dead, and so were many of the choir; but by degrees the sergeant-major learnt that his father still lay at the crossroads in Long Ash Lane.

Luke pursued his way moodily homewards, to do which, in the natural course, he would be compelled to repass the spot, there being no other road between the two villages. But he could not now go by that place, vociferous with reproaches in his father's tones; and he got over the hedge and wandered deviously through the ploughed fields to avoid the scene. Through many a fight and fatigue Luke had been sustained by the thought that he was restoring the family honour and making noble amends. Yet his father lay still in degradation. It was rather a sentiment than a fact that his father's body had been made to suffer for his own misdeeds; but to his supersensitiveness it seemed that his efforts to retrieve his character and to propitiate the shade of the insulted one had ended in failure.

He endeavoured, however, to shake off his lethargy, and, not liking the associations of Sidlinch, hired a small cottage at Chalk-Newton which had long been empty. Here he lived alone, becoming quite a hermit, and allowing no woman to enter the house.

The Christmas after taking up his abode herein he was sitting in the chimney-corner by himself, when he heard faint notes in the distance, and soon a melody burst forth immediately outside his own window. It came from the carol-singers, as usual; and though many of the old hands, Ezra and Lot included, had gone to their rest, the same old carols were still played out of the same old books. There resounded through the sergeant-major's window shutters the familiar lines that the deceased choir had rendered over his father's grave:—

> He comes' the pri'-soners to' re-lease',
> In Sa'-tan's bon'-dage held'.

When they had finished they went on to another house, leaving him to silence and loneliness as before.

The candle wanted snuffing, but he did not snuff it, and he sat on till it had burnt down into the socket and made waves of shadow on the ceiling.

The Christmas cheerfulness of next morning was broken at breakfast-time by tragic intelligence which went down the village like wind. Sergeant-Major Holway had been found shot through the head by his own hand at the crossroads in Long Ash Lane where his father lay buried.

On the table in the cottage he had left a piece of paper, on which he had written his wish that he might be buried at the Cross beside his father. But the paper was accidentally swept to the floor, and overlooked till after his funeral, which took place in the ordinary way in the churchyard. □□

Discussion

1. (a) As a group, what is the Chalk-Newton choir like? **(b)** How does Hardy use the choir to help tell the story of the grave by the handpost?

2. (a) What decisions and choices does Sergeant Holway make which affect his relationship with his son? **(b)** What decisions and choices does Luke make in relation to his father?

3. How much is Luke's fate determined by his community? How much by his country? Explain.

4. (a) How do coincidence and chance come into Hardy's story? **(b)** How are coincidence and chance commentaries on human affairs as perceived by Hardy?

Extension • Reading and Writing

Read (or reread) Joseph Conrad's "The Lagoon." Write an essay in which you compare Hardy's sense of fate and choice in "The Grave by the Handpost" to Conrad's in "The Lagoon."

Thomas Hardy 1840 • 1928

Hardy's early education was slender, and beyond the most basic skills he was self-taught. At age 16 he became apprenticed to an architect, and later worked at that art on his own.

Most of Hardy's novels and stories appeared first in magazines. The notoriously timid editors and prudish readers of the late Victorian period disliked what they took to be the gloomy pessimism and graphic realism of his fiction. Hardy was continually forced to cut or tone down his strongest passages. Nevertheless he continued, partly because his fiction was building for him economic independence. The novels of these years, *Far From the Madding Crowd* (1874), *The Return of the Native* (1878), *The Mayor of Casterbridge* (1886), *Tess of the D'Urbervilles* (1891), and *Jude the Obscure* (1896), are rightly considered masterpieces.

Hardy is famous for his ironic and pessimistic view of life, but he himself rejected efforts to read his work as systematic philosophizing. ". . . what is to-day, in allusions to the present author's pages, alleged to be 'pessimism'" he wrote, "is, in truth, only 'questionings' in the exploration of reality"

As a boy Hardy lived close to the land. His father was a mason, and Hardy was always close to the life of the common man. His stories grow out of this youthful familiarity with simple, rural life. Hardy uses spare, conversational language, with now and then the odd, local dialect term to give a sense of place. His imagery is of the earth.

In his fiction we see and hear working people, and learn of the conflicts and sorrows of their daily lives.

Hardy's studied simplicity, his devotion to plain speaking and to seeing things clearly and without sentiment have had persistent influence on writers in our century. He has managed, despite his birth and training in the middle of the Victorian period, to remain a thoroughly contemporary artist.

H. G. Wells

The Star

It was on the first day of the new year that the announcement was made, almost simultaneously from three observatories, that the motion of the planet Neptune, the outermost[1] of all the planets that wheel about the sun, had become very erratic. Ogilvy had already called attention to a suspected retardation in its velocity in December. Such a piece of news was scarcely calculated to interest a world the greater portion of whose inhabitants were unaware of the existence of the planet Neptune, nor outside the astronomical profession did the subsequent discovery of a faint remote speck of light in the region of the perturbed planet cause any very great excitement. Scientific people, however, found the intelligence remarkable enough, even before it became known that the new body was rapidly growing larger and brighter, that its motion was quite different from the orderly progress of the planets, and that the deflection of Neptune and its satellite was becoming now of an unprecedented kind.

Few people without a training in science can realise the huge isolation of the solar system. The sun with its specks of planets, its dust of planetoids, and its impalpable comets, swims in a vacant immensity that almost defeats the imagination. Beyond the orbit of Neptune there is space, vacant so far as human observation has penetrated, without warmth or light or sound, blank emptiness, for twenty million times a million miles. That is the smallest estimate of the distance to be traversed before the very nearest of the stars is attained. And, saving a few comets more unsubstantial than the thinnest flame, no matter had ever to human knowledge crossed this gulf of space, until early in the twentieth century this strange wanderer appeared. A vast mass of matter it was, bulky, heavy, rushing without warning out of the black mystery of the sky into the radiance of the sun. By the second day it was clearly visible to any decent instrument, as a speck with a barely sensible diameter, in the constellation Leo near Regulus. In a little while an opera glass could attain it.

On the third day of the new year the newspaper readers of two hemispheres were made aware for the first time of the real importance of this unusual apparition in the heavens. "A Planetary Collision," one London paper headed the news, and proclaimed Duchaine's opinion that this strange new planet would probably collide with Neptune. The leader writers enlarged upon the topic. So that in most of the capitals of the world, on January 3rd, there was an expectation, however vague, of some imminent phenomenon in the sky; and as the night followed the sunset round the globe, thousands of men turned their eyes skyward to see—the old familiar stars just as they had always been.

Until it was dawn in London and Pollux setting and the stars overhead grown pale. The winter's dawn it was, a sickly filtering accumulation of daylight, and the light of gas and candles shone yellow in the windows to show where people were astir. But the yawning policeman saw the thing, the busy crowds in the markets stopped agape, workmen going to their work betimes, milkmen, the drivers of news-carts, dissipation going home jaded and pale, homeless wanderers, sentinels on their beats, and in the country, labourers trudging afield, poachers slinking home, all over the dusky quickening country it could be seen—and out at sea by seamen watching for the day—a great white star, come suddenly into the westward sky!

Brighter it was than any star in our skies; brighter than the evening star at its brightest. It still glowed out white and large, no mere twinkling spot of light, but a small round clear shining

1. ***outermost.*** The planet Pluto was not discovered until 1930.

disc, an hour after the day had come. And where science has not reached, men stared and feared, telling one another of the wars and pestilences that are foreshadowed by these fiery signs in the Heavens. Sturdy Boers, dusky Hottentots, Gold Coast negroes, Frenchmen, Spaniards, Portuguese, stood in the warmth of the sunrise watching the setting of this strange new star.

And in a hundred observatories there had been suppressed excitement, rising almost to shouting pitch, as the two remote bodies had rushed together, and a hurrying to and fro to gather photographic apparatus and spectroscope, and this appliance and that, to record this novel astonishing sight, the destruction of a world. For it was a world, a sister planet of our earth, far greater than our earth indeed, that had so suddenly flashed into flaming death. Neptune it was, had been struck, fairly and squarely, by the strange planet from outer space and the heat of the concussion had incontinently turned two solid globes into one vast mass of incandescence. Round the world that day, two hours before the dawn, went the pallid great white star, fading only as it sank westward and the sun mounted above it. Everywhere men marvelled at it, but of all those who saw it none could have marvelled more than those sailors, habitual watchers of the stars, who far away at sea had heard nothing of its advent and saw it now rise like a pigmy moon and climb zenithward and hang overhead and sink westward with the passing of the night.

And when next it rose over Europe everywhere were crowds of watchers on hilly slopes, on house-roofs, in open spaces, staring eastward for the rising of the great new star. It rose with a white glow in front of it, like the glare of a white fire, and those who had seen it come into existence the night before cried out at the sight of it. "It is larger," they cried. "It is brighter!" And, indeed the moon a quarter full and sinking in the west was in its apparent size beyond comparison, but scarcely in all its breadth had it as much brightness now as the little circle of the strange new star.

"It is brighter!" cried the people clustering in the streets. But in the dim observatories the watchers held their breath and peered at one another. *"It is nearer,"* they said. *"Nearer!"*

And voice after voice repeated, "It is nearer," and the clicking telegraph took that up, and it trembled along telephone wires, and in a thousand cities grimy compositors fingered the type. "It is nearer." Men writing in offices, struck with a strange realisation, flung down their pens; men talking in a thousand places suddenly came upon a grotesque possibility in those words, "It is nearer." It hurried along awakening streets, it was shouted down the frost-stilled ways of quiet villages, men who had read these things from the throbbing tape stood in yellow-lit doorways shouting the news to the passers-by. "It is nearer." Pretty women, flushed and glittering, heard the news told jestingly between the dances, and feigned an intelligent interest they did not feel. "Nearer! Indeed. How curious! How very, very clever people must be to find out things like that!"

Lonely tramps faring through the wintry night murmured those words to comfort themselves—looking skyward. "It has need to be nearer, for the night's as cold as charity. Don't seem much warmth from it if it *is* nearer, all the same."

"What is a new star to me?" cried the weeping woman kneeling beside her dead.

The schoolboy, rising early for his examination work, puzzled it out for himself—with the great white star, shining broad and bright through the frost-flowers of his window. "Centrifugal, centripetal," he said, with his chin on his fist. "Stop a planet in its flight, rob it of its centrifugal force, what then? Centripetal has it, and down it falls into the sun! And this—!"

"Do *we* come in the way? I wonder—"

The light of that day went the way of its brethren, and with the later watches of the frosty darkness rose the strange star again. And it was now so bright that the waxing moon seemed but a pale yellow ghost of itself, hanging huge in the sunset. In a South African city a great man had married, and the streets were alight to welcome his return with his bride. "Even the skies have illuminated," said the flatterer. Under Capricorn, two negro lovers, daring the wild beasts and evil spirits, for love of one another, crouched together in a cane brake where the fire-flies hovered. "That is our star," they whispered, and felt strangely comforted by the sweet brilliance of its light.

The master mathematician sat in his private room and pushed the papers from him. His calculations were already finished. In a small white phial there still remained a little of the drug that had kept him awake and active for four long nights. Each day, serene, explicit, patient as ever, he had given his lecture to his students, and then had come back at once to this momentous calculation. His face was grave, a little drawn and hectic from his drugged activity. For some time he seemed lost in thought. Then he went to the window, and the blind went up with a click. Half way up the sky, over the clustering roofs, chimneys and steeples of the city, hung the star.

He looked at it as one might look into the eyes of a brave enemy. "You may kill me," he said after a silence. "But I can hold you—and all the universe for that matter—in the grip of this little brain. I would not change. Even now."

He looked at the little phial. "There will be no need of sleep again," he said. The next day at noon, punctual to the minute, he entered his lecture theatre, put his hat on the end of the table as his habit was, and carefully selected a large piece of chalk. It was a joke among his students that he could not lecture without that piece of chalk to fumble in his fingers, and once he had been stricken to impotence by their hiding his supply. He came and looked under his grey eyebrows at the rising tiers of young fresh faces, and spoke with his accustomed studied commonness of phrasing. "Circumstances have arisen—circumstances beyond my control," he said and paused, "which will debar me from completing the course I had designed. It would seem, gentlemen, if I may put the thing clearly and briefly, that—Man has lived in vain."

The students glanced at one another. Had they heard aright? Mad? Raised eyebrows and grinning lips there were, but one or two faces remained intent upon his calm grey-fringed face. "It will be interesting," he was saying, "to devote this morning to an exposition, so far as I can make it clear to you, of the calculations that have led me to this conclusion. Let us assume—"

He turned towards the blackboard, meditating a diagram in the way that was usual to him. "What was that about 'lived in vain'?" whispered one student to another. "Listen," said the other, nodding towards the lecturer.

And presently they began to understand.

That night the star rose later, for its proper eastward motion had carried it some way across Leo towards Virgo, and its brightness was so great that the sky became a luminous blue as it rose, and every star was hidden in its turn, save only Jupiter near the zenith, Capella, Aldebaran, Sirius and the pointers of the Bear. It was very white and beautiful. In many parts of the world that night a pallid halo encircled it about. It was perceptibly larger; in the clear refractive sky of the tropics it seemed as if it were nearly a quarter the size of the moon. The frost was still on the ground in England, but the world was as brightly lit as if it were midsummer moonlight. One could see to read quite ordinary print by that cold clear light, and in the cities the lamps burnt yellow and wan.

Science Fiction

C. S. Lewis

In his essay "On Science Fiction," writer C. S. Lewis identifies several types, one of them the "Eschatological": [It] gives an imaginative vehicle to speculations about the ultimate destiny of our species. Examples are Wells's *Time Machine,* Olaf Stapledon's *Last and First Men,* or Arthur Clarke's *Childhood's End. . . .* Work of this kind gives expression to thoughts and emotions which I think it good that we should sometimes entertain. It is sobering and cathartic to remember, now and then, our collective smallness, our apparent isolation, the apparent indifference of nature, the slow biological, geological, and astronomical processes which may, in the long run, make many of our hopes (possibly some of our fears) ridiculous. . . . Hence the uneasiness which such stories arouse in those who, for whatever reason, wish to keep us wholly imprisoned in the immediate conflict. That perhaps is why people are so ready with the charge of "escape." I never fully understood it till my friend Professor Tolkien asked me the very simple question, "What class of men would you expect to be most preoccupied with, and most hostile to, the idea of escape?" and gave the obvious answer: jailers.

And everywhere the world was awake that night, and throughout Christendom a sombre murmur hung in the keen air over the countryside like the belling of bees in the heather, and this murmurous tumult grew to a clangour in the cities. It was the tolling of the bells in a million belfry towers and steeples, summoning the people to sleep no more, to sin no more, but to gather in their churches and pray. And overhead, growing larger and brighter as the earth rolled on its way and the night passed, rose the dazzling star.

And the streets and houses were alight in all the cities, the shipyards glared, and whatever roads led to high country were lit and crowded all night long. And in all the seas about the civilised lands, ships with throbbing engines, and ships with bellying sails, crowded with men and living creatures, were standing out to ocean and the north. For already the warning of the master mathematician had been telegraphed all over the world, and translated into a hundred tongues. The new planet and Neptune, locked in a fiery embrace, were whirling headlong, ever faster and faster towards the sun. Already every second this blazing mass flew a hundred miles, and every second its terrific velocity increased. As it flew now, indeed, it must pass a hundred million of miles wide of the earth and scarcely affect it. But near its destined path, as yet only slightly perturbed, spun the mighty planet Jupiter and his moons sweeping splendid round the sun. Every moment now the attraction between the fiery star and the greatest of the planets grew stronger. And the result of that attraction? Inevitably Jupiter would be deflected from his orbit into an elliptical path, and the burning star, swung by his attraction wide of its sunward rush, would "describe a curved path" and perhaps collide with, and certainly pass very close to, our earth. "Earthquakes, volcanic outbreaks, cyclones, sea waves, floods, and a steady rise in temperature to I know not what limit"—so prophesied the master mathematician.

And overhead, to carry out his words, lonely and cold and livid, blazed the star of the coming doom.

To many who stared at it that night until their eyes ached, it seemed that it was visibly approaching. And that night, too, the weather changed, and the frost that had gripped all Central Europe and France and England softened towards a thaw.

But you must not imagine because I have spoken of people praying through the night and people going aboard ships and people fleeing towards mountainous country that the whole world was already in a terror because of the star. As a matter of fact, use and wont still ruled the world, and save for the talk of idle moments and the splendour of the night, nine human beings out of ten were still busy at their common occupations. In all the cities the shops, save one here and there, opened and closed at their proper hours, the doctor and the undertaker plied their trades, the workers gathered in the factories, soldiers drilled, scholars studied, lovers sought one another, thieves lurked and fled, politicians planned their schemes. The presses of the newspapers roared through the nights, and many a priest of this church and that would not open his holy building to further what he considered a foolish panic. The newspapers insisted on the lesson of the year 1000—for then, too, people had anticipated the end. The star was no star—mere gas—a comet; and were it a star it could not possibly strike the earth. There was no precedent for such a thing. Common sense was sturdy everywhere, scornful, jesting, a little inclined to persecute the obdurate fearful. That night, at seven-fifteen by Greenwich time, the star would be at its nearest to Jupiter. Then the world would see the turn things would take. The master mathematician's grim warnings were treated by many as so much mere elaborate self-advertisement. Common sense at last, a little heated by argument, signified its unalterable convictions by going to bed. So, too, barbarism and savagery, already tired of the novelty, went about their mighty business, and save for a howling dog here and there, the beast world left the star unheeded.

And yet, when at last the watchers in the European States saw the star rise, an hour later it is true, but no larger than it had been the night before, there were still plenty awake to laugh at the master mathematician—to take the danger as if it had passed.

But hereafter the laughter ceased. The star grew—it grew with a terrible steadiness hour after hour, a little larger each hour, a little nearer the midnight zenith, and brighter and brighter, until it had turned night into a second day. Had it come straight to the earth instead of in a curved path, had it lost no velocity to Jupiter, it must have leapt the intervening gulf in a day, but as it was it took five days altogether to come by our planet. The next night it had become a third the size of the moon before it set to English eyes, and the thaw was assured. It rose over America near the size of the moon, but blinding white to look at, and *hot;* and a breath of hot wind blew now with its rising and gathering strength, and in Virginia, and Brazil, and down the St. Lawrence valley, it shone intermittently through a driving reek of thunder-clouds, flickering violet lightning, and hail unprecedented. In Manitoba was a thaw and devastating floods. And upon all the mountains of the earth the snow and ice began to melt that night, and all the rivers coming out of high country flowed thick and turbid, and soon—in their upper reaches—with swirling trees and the bodies of beasts and men. They rose steadily, steadily in the ghostly brilliance, and came trickling over their banks at last, behind the flying population of their valleys.

And along the coast of Argentina and up the South Atlantic the tides were higher than had ever been in the memory of man, and the storms drove the waters in many cases scores of miles inland, drowning whole cities. And so great grew the heat during the night that the rising of the sun was like the coming of a shadow. The earthquakes began and grew until all down America from the Arctic Circle to Cape Horn, hillsides were sliding, fissures were opening, and houses and walls crumbling to destruction. The whole side of Cotopaxi slipped out in one vast convulsion, and a tumult of lava poured out so high and broad and swift and liquid that in one day it reached the sea.

So the star, with the wan moon in its wake, marched across the Pacific, trailed the thunderstorms like the hem of a robe, and the growing tidal wave that toiled behind it, frothing and eager, poured over island and island and swept them clear of men. Until that wave came at last—in a blinding light and with the breath of a furnace, swift and terrible it came—a wall of water, fifty feet high, roaring hungrily, upon the long coasts of Asia, and swept inland across the plains of China. For a space the star, hotter now and larger and brighter than the sun in its

strength, showed with pitiless brilliance the wide and populous country; towns and villages with their pagodas and trees, roads, wide cultivated fields, millions of sleepless people staring in helpless terror at the incandescent sky; and then, low and growing, came the murmur of the flood. And thus it was with millions of men that night—a flight nowhither, with limbs heavy with heat and breath fierce and scant, and the flood like a wall swift and white behind. And then death.

China was lit glowing white, but over Japan and Java and all the islands of Eastern Asia the great star was a ball of dull red fire because of the steam and smoke and ashes the volcanoes were spouting forth to salute its coming. Above was the lava, hot gases and ash, and below the seething floods, and the whole earth swayed and rumbled with the earthquake shocks. Soon the immemorial snows of Thibet and the Himalaya were melting and pouring down by ten million deepening converging channels upon the plains of Burmah and Hindostan. The tangled summits of the Indian jungles were aflame in a thousand places, and below the hurrying waters around the stems were dark objects that still struggled feebly and reflected the blood-red tongues of fire. And in a rudderless confusion a multitude of men and women fled down the broad river-ways to that one last hope of men—the open sea.

Larger grew the star, and larger, hotter, and brighter with a terrible swiftness now. The tropical ocean had lost its phosphorescence, and the whirling steam rose in ghostly wreaths from the black waves that plunged incessantly, speckled with storm-tossed ships.

And then came a wonder. It seemed to those who in Europe watched for the rising of the star that the world must have ceased its rotation. In a thousand open spaces of down and upland the people who had fled thither from the floods and the falling houses and sliding slopes of hill watched for that rising in vain. Hour followed hour through a terrible suspense, and the star rose not. Once again men set their eyes upon the old constellations they had counted lost to them forever. In England it was hot and clear overhead, though the ground quivered perpetually, but in the tropics, Sirius and Capella and Aldebaran showed through a veil of steam. And when at last the great star rose near ten hours late, the sun rose close upon it, and in the centre of its white heart was a disc of black.

Over Asia it was the star had begun to fall behind the movement of the sky, and then suddenly, as it hung over India, its light had been veiled. All the plain of India from the mouth of the Indus to the mouths of the Ganges was a shallow waste of shining water that night, out of which rose temples and palaces, mounds and hills, black with people. Every minaret was a clustering mass of people, who fell one by one into the turbid waters, as heat and terror overcame them. The whole land seemed a-wailing, and suddenly there swept a shadow across that furnace of despair, and a breath of cold wind, and a gathering of clouds, out of the cooling air. Men looking up, near blinded, at the star, saw that a black disc was creeping across the light. It was the moon, coming between the star and the earth. And even as men cried to God at this respite, out of the East with a strange inexplicable swiftness sprang the sun. And then star, sun and moon rushed together across the heavens.

So it was that presently, to the European watchers, star and sun rose close upon each other, drove headlong for a space and then slower, and at last came to rest, star and sun merged into one glare of flame at the zenith of the sky. The moon no longer eclipsed the star but was lost to sight in the brilliance of the sky. And though those who were still alive regarded it for the most part with that dull stupidity that hunger, fatigue, heat and despair engender, there were still men who could perceive the meaning of these signs. Star and earth had been at their nearest, had swung about one another, and the star had passed. Already it was receding, swifter and swifter, in the last stage of its headlong journey downward into the sun.

And then the clouds gathered, blotting out the vision of the sky, the thunder and lightning wove a garment round the world; all over the earth was such a downpour of rain as men had never before seen, and where the volcanoes flared red against the cloud canopy there descended torrents of mud. Everywhere the waters were pouring off the land, leaving mud-silted ruins, and the earth littered like a storm-worn beach with all that had floated, and the dead bodies of the men and brutes, its children. For days the water streamed off the land, sweeping away soil and trees and houses in the way, and piling huge dykes and scooping out Titanic gullies over the country side. Those were the days of darkness that followed the star and the heat. All through them, and for many weeks and months, the earthquakes continued.

But the star had passed, and men, hunger-driven and gathering courage only slowly, might creep back to their ruined cities, buried granaries, and sodden fields. Such few ships as had escaped the storms of that time came stunned and shattered and sounding their way cautiously through the new marks and shoals of once familiar ports. And as the storms subsided men perceived that everywhere the days were hotter than of yore, and the sun larger, and the moon, shrunk to a third of its former size, took now fourscore days between its new and new.

But of the new brotherhood that grew presently among men, of the saving of laws and books and machines, of the strange change that had come over Iceland and Greenland and the shores of Baffin's Bay, so that the sailors coming there presently found them green and gracious, and could scarce believe their eyes, this story does not tell. Nor of the movement of mankind now that the earth was hotter, northward and southward towards the poles of the earth. It concerns itself only with the coming and the passing of the Star.

The Martian astronomers—for there are astronomers on Mars, although they are very different beings from men—were naturally profoundly interested by these things. They saw them from their own standpoint of course. "Considering the mass and temperature of the missile that was flung through our solar system into the sun," one wrote, "it is astonishing what a little damage the earth, which it missed so narrowly, has sustained. All the familiar continental markings and the masses of the seas remain intact, and indeed the only difference seems to be a shrinkage of the white discoloration (supposed to be frozen water) round either pole." Which only shows how small the vastest of human catastrophes may seem, at a distance of a few million miles. □□

Discussion

1. Look up the word *grotesque* in the Glossary. Why is the potential encounter of earth and star a "grotesque possibility"?

2. (a) What insights does the master mathematician provide in the story? **(b)** What human element does his presence add to the story?

3. (a) What purpose is served by the reference to "Christendom" and its responses to the star? **(b)** What purpose is served by the reference to "scornful, jesting" common sense?

4. How is your understanding of the story affected by your knowledge that the star actually passes "a hundred million of miles wide of the earth"?

5. Near the end of the story, when the star fails to rise, in what ways does relief come to the earth? Do you find this to be ironic? Explain.

6. In the next-to-last paragraph we are told of the "new brotherhood" which grew among men. In light of what you have just read in the story, do you find this a satisfying statement? Explain.

7. The events of this story supposedly occur "early in the twentieth century," but of course they never did—the star never came. Does this fact affect the value of Wells's story today? Explain.

Extension • Writing and Speaking

Assume that the master mathematician and his class are among those who survived the coming of the star. Write (and deliver) the first five minutes of his opening lecture on the first day of class. Keep in mind, among other things, that he has told them that "Man has lived in vain."

H. G. Wells 1866 • 1946

Herbert George Wells was born in Bromley, England. As a young man he received a scholarship to the Royal College of Science, which he attended during the 1880s; he studied under, among others, the great Thomas Henry Huxley. This formal training in science, linked with Wells's simultaneous discovery of great works of imaginative and philosophical literature, was perhaps the single most formative influence on his career.

Wells began writing in the 1890s, and from that point onward voiced the divided mixture of anxiety and enthusiasm which characterized his age. On one hand his work, most notably *The Time Machine* and *The War of the Worlds,* reflects a sense of catastrophe and doom, often at the hands of new inventions or alien phenomena. On the other hand Wells's work reflects the optimism of the new century, an optimism similarly dependent on imagination and invention, but based on a belief in the more positive aspects of human nature. After 1910, Wells's fiction became strongly didactic in nature; he wrote it with an eye toward the exposure and correction of social and political conditions. But as important as these books were to Wells and to his time, their significance has faded with age. Aside from the "scientific romances" and stories of the 1890s, including *The Island of Dr. Moreau* and *The Invisible Man,* his most enduring works are his "Edwardian" novels, especially *Kipps* (1905), in which comedy and sympathy mix with social commentary, and *Tono-Bungay* (1909), which is not only analytical but also imaginative and stylistically provocative.

In the end H. G. Wells was a gifted but troubled figure of scientific, social, and literary transition. He was born a Victorian, but lived to see both the invention of the airplane and the dropping of the atomic bomb; he possessed the vexing double vision of Utopia and apocalypse.

George Gissing

Spellbound

At the doors of the Free Library waited a dozen men and half as many women; the lucky ones, by squeezing very close, partly sheltered themselves from a cold drizzle; not a word of conversation passed among them, and the minutes seemed to drag interminably. Then the clock struck, and the doors opened. There was a breakneck rush down the stairs to the newspaper room, a scamper for the first sight of this or that morning paper. All the women, and a few of the men, were genuinely eager to search columns of advertisements, on the chance of finding employment; the rest came for betting news, or a murder trial, or some such matter of popular interest. In a very short time each of the favourite journals had its little crowd, waiting with impatience behind the two or three persons who managed to read simultaneously. Silent all, amid the sound of rustling pages, and of shoes on the bare boards. Without roared the torrent of multitudinous traffic.

One of the first to enter was a young man in a hard felt hat and fawn-coloured overcoat, his chin stubbly with three days' growth, his collar betraying a week or more of use, and his fingernails bitten to the quick. He looked ill-fed and anxious; one could imagine him a clerk or shopman badly in want of a place. Yet he exhibited no great energy in the hunt for likely advertisements. After holding the first place for a minute or two, he drew back from the newspaper, and stood apart, gazing idly about him. Then, with sauntering step, he approached one of the publications which no one else cared to examine—the new number of a religious weekly—and over this he spent about a quarter of an hour. The retirement of a man from the paper next in the row seemed to give him a desired opportunity; he stepped into the vacant place, and read for another quarter of an hour. And so all through the morning, from paper to paper, as his turn came. He read, it appeared, with languid interest, often staring vacantly at the windows, often gnawing the stumps of his nails, yet never seeming inclined to go away. He had a very common face, touched with amiability, suggestive of average intelligence; rarely—very rarely—it changed expression, but it never betokened a meditative or animated mood. Read he certainly did, for his hand turned the leaves; yet it was difficult to credit him with either pleasure or purpose in these hours of quasi-intellectual occupation.

At one o'clock he gave signs of weariness, and stood as though debating a question with himself; as a result, he left the reading-room, walked a little way along the street, and entered a coffee tavern. A sausage, with bread and butter and a cup of cocoa, made his midday meal; he ate with gusto, which perhaps was not surprising. As the rain had ceased, he digested his dinner in half an hour's ramble about the neighbourhood, smoking the latter half of a pipe which had served him after breakfast. Ultimately his steps turned again towards the Free Library, and again he entered; but this time he went up to the magazine-room. Here readers were supplied with chairs, and sat at tables; and just now all but every place was occupied. He sauntered along the floor until, unable to do better, he took a chair at the spot devoted to an organ of vegetarianism. This subject had no interest whatever for him, but he opened the periodical and read therein, until a departing neighbour enabled him to exchange it for the *Westminster Review*. And thus again, moving at intervals from seat to seat, he passed the afternoon.

With the visage and the gait of a somnambulist he at length betook himself homeward—that is to say, to a couple of small rooms in an unpleasant street near Euston Station. His wife was awaiting him; she had tea ready upon the table, and on her face a not unkindly look of

"Spellbound" From A VICTIM OF CIRCUMSTANCES, AND OTHER STORIES.

expectation. The man did not meet her eyes; after throwing his hat and coat on to a chair, he sat down with every sign of weariness, and waited for questions.

"Nothing?" asked his wife, in a voice which was meant to anticipate consolation.

Percy Dunn—that was the man's name—shook a dreary head.

"Oh, I've written letters, as usual—two or three letters—and called at a place or two. No good."

He spoke with eyes shifting about the floor, and hand rubbing his stubbly chin.

"Then how do you spend the time—all day?"

"Oh, I loaf about—sit in the reading-room—anything. What's the good of coming 'ome. I can't sit here and do nothing."

"Well, come and have your tea and then I'll tell you something."

Dunn glanced quickly at her, a ray of shamefaced hope on his countenance. In spite of hard times, these two had not quarrelled, and were not weary of each other; which is as much as to say that Mrs. Dunn was not quite the ordinary wife of a man in this station. Indeed, she looked a pleasant and capable little woman. Her dress, though poor enough, had a becoming neatness; she showed very clean hands, and knew how to arrange her hair. She had ideas, too, on the subject of laying a poor table, so as to make it seem less poor, and, in the true sense, altogether homely.

"What is it?" said the husband, trying not to smile.

"Have your tea."

But he could not, until he had heard what there was to be told; so Mrs. Dunn, with a jest at his familiar impatience, made known to him that she had "gone back to the mantles."[1] Twelve shillings a week, the best she could obtain just now, and much better than nothing. What choice had she? In two months of undesired leisure, Dunn had drawn near to the end of his resources; if he could not earn money, she must.

"Oh, be hanged to that!" muttered the young man, keeping his face down. "I don't want you to go."

"It's done, so there's no good talking about it. Get your tea."

They had been married three years, and, happily, had no child. Dunn was a draper's salesman, generally in good employment, though he had changed his shop more often than was desirable. His last place he had quitted involuntarily, and under circumstances which he did not fully explain to his wife; in fact, he was found guilty, on two occasions, of such gross carelessness at the counter, that his employers could neither keep him in their service nor recommend him to anyone else. Mr. Dunn had grown aweary of standing behind a counter; he entertained hopes—the vaguest—of entering upon some new career; his health was indifferent, and he talked of getting a country place. Or someone might engage him as traveller. Or he might hear of something fresh and new. He would look about a bit. He had looked about, though not very energetically, for the first two or three weeks; then he fell a prey to the Free Library.

"Well, see here, Maggie; it's only for a time, you know. I can't allow you to go back to work. That won't do at all. I don't believe in married women going to work-rooms."

"All right; get your tea."

"Well, but—look here, now. I'm not going to live on your earnings. That's not my sort; I'm not one of that kind. You don't think I am, do you?"

"Course I don't, Percy. What's the good of bothering? You'll get a place before long."

"Why, I must. How are we to live? Of course I must."

They had furniture of their own, and paid only eight shillings for the two rooms: of late, the total of their expenditure had been some fifteen shillings a week. Dunn, with no base intention, asked himself whether they could live on his wife's wages. Impossible, of course. To-morrow he would really "look about"; it was high time.

He ate his meal and enjoyed it. Good-humour shone upon his pasty visage. He drew Maggie to him, made her sit upon his knee, and talked affectionately.

"You're a good sort, old girl. And I've given you a lot o' worry. And—"

"Oh, shut up. What's the odds? I'd just as soon work as not. What's the good of sitting at 'ome all day, when it doesn't take me more than an hour or two to do all there is to do?"

---

1. ***back . . . mantles,*** returned to dressmaking.

Historical Picture Service, Inc., Chicago

"But you wouldn't want to go to the mantles if I earned good money again?"

"I don't know. Why not? Unless, of course, we had a 'ouse of our own."

"And so we will!" exclaimed Dunn fervently, a sanguine flush upon his cheeks.

"A nice little 'ouse somewhere out north. There's splendid little 'ouses for little enough; it's only making the start. I ought to have saved more. It's all my fault—don't say it isn't. I go buying this and that, and wasting coin every sort of way. There! we'll have a little 'ouse of our own."

He began to discuss localities, rents, the price of furniture; all with a dreamy satisfaction, as if the means were already in hand. His wife, though of more practical temper, found the dream pleasant, and encouraged it. And, just as they had decided upon a Brussels carpet for the best room, someone knocked at their door.

"All right; it's only me," said a boyish voice.

Willie Smith, Mrs. Dunn's brother, showed himself; a lad of eighteen, comely, like his sister, and very good-natured. Young as he was, Willie had for several years supported himself.

"Thought I'd just look in and tell you. Got another rise. It's a pound a week now!—and there's something else."

He spoke of family affairs, of certain changes which would affect his own position and make it necessary for him to find a new abode.

"Why, you'd better come and live with us," said Mrs. Dunn. "There's a room to let upstairs, if it would suit you. Things would cost you less than anywhere else."

The lad stood dubious. Hitherto under the eyes of relatives, he had looked forward with no little satisfaction to a life of independence in manly lodgings; his sister's suggestion disturbed him; he wished to put it aside, but knew not how to do so without giving offence. Mrs. Dunn again urged the advantages of his taking a room in this house; she could look after his comfort, and (as she said to herself) after his welfare in other respects. Being of a pliable disposition, Willie swallowed his private objections to the scheme, and all three agreed that nothing could be better.

So, a week later, the family had three members. Mrs. Dunn and her brother were absent at work all day; the husband, as usual, betook himself each morning to St. Martin's Lane, ostensibly to search the newspapers for a likely advertisement, but in reality to indulge the form of idleness which had taken an irresistible hold upon him; to moon for hours over columns and pages of print, stupefying himself as with a drug which lulled his anxieties, obscured his conscience.

The presence of a third person at home made it easier for him to avoid talking of his perilous situation, but in a fortnight's time, when he had nothing whatever to live upon save his wife's earnings, he was driven by very shame to a new confession of hopelessness. It was after Willie had left them for the night.

"How are you managing?" he asked with a timid glance at his wife.

"Oh, it's all right; we can just get along."

"Yes, but how?"

He insisted, and Maggie with some confusion made known to him at length that her brother had saved a few pounds, which he was willing to lend them until things improved.

"He just lets me have a shilling or two as I want it. He don't mind; he's a good boy."

"Look here, Maggie. I can't stand this," muttered Dunn, genuinely moved. "It's a mean thing to do."

"But you'll pay it all back. And what else can we do?"

"I tell you what," he exclaimed, "if I don't earn something tomorrow I won't come 'ome at all. You can get along well enough without me. I won't come 'ome till I've got something in my pocket—I swear I won't."

His voice and aspect alarmed the impressible wife. Of late she had observed a growing strangeness in him, a lethargy which held him mute, and seemed to weigh upon his limbs; he sometimes looked at her with disquieting eyes, a dull stare as though his wits were leaving him. Hearing him speak thus, she had visions of tragic calamity; he would drown himself, or commit ghastly suicide on the railway line. With all the animation of which she was capable, Maggie exhorted him to be more hopeful. When things were at the worst they always mended—and so on. Dunn allowed her to soothe him; he promised to come home as usual, even though with empty pockets; but his resolve to make some kind of effort expressed itself with vehemence. He would be idle no longer, even if he had to go and work at the docks or sweep a crossing.

And the next day he did, in fact, take a practical step. He applied at a city warehouse for an itinerant agency, and, after depositing a small sum (obtained from Willie Smith), was allowed to take samples of certain goods, for sale on commission. His wife lamented, but Dunn was heroically determined. One whole day he spent in house-to-house visitation of a likely suburb, and his earnings at the close amounted to fourpence. Well, it was a beginning: fourpence is better than nothing. On the second morning he set forth again with aching limbs and a sinking heart. As it happened, his route led him past the doors of a newly-opened Free Library. It was like the sight of a public house[2] to the habitual drinker; he quivered under the temptation, and whipped himself forward; but his weary legs were traitorous. The reading-room, with its smell of new print, once more drugged his conscience, and there he sat until nightfall.

After this he yielded utterly to his vice. Pretending at home that no discouragement should daunt him, that he would work on until his agency became remunerative, he stood every morning before the familiar doors in St. Martin's Lane, and entered with the first rush. But now he did not even glance at the advertisements. First of all he made for one or other of the journals little in demand, and read it through at his ease. On certain mornings of the week the illustrated papers were his leading attraction; he darted upon the *London News,* the *Graphic,* and the rest of them with breathless excitement; and having satisfied his curiosity, could relinquish them to others for the next six days, until, mere tattered, grimy rags, they gave place to the new issue. Knowing the moment when the evening papers would arrive, he stood ready to pounce upon this or that before anyone could anticipate him. No matter the subject, its display in fresh-smelling print sufficed to interest him, or, at all events, to hold his eyes; there he stood, spellbound, unresisting, oblivious of everything save his gratification in the mere act of reading.

Upstairs, in the magazine-room, he read through everything that did not utterly defy his intelligence, and at the end of an article in one of the grave monthlies he would sigh with satisfaction, persuading himself that he had enriched his mind. For thus had he now begun to justify himself: on his walk home, when conscience tried to speak, he replied that he had been "studying," making up for the defects of his education, preparing for "something better," when fortune should put it in his way. He wished he could tell his wife and get her to approve, but he feared Maggie would not understand him.

Before long it was necessary to avow that the agency had proved a failure.

"It won't do," he said gravely. "I'm wearing out shoe leather. I must have a try at something else. I've got an idea, but I won't say anything about it just yet."

And he nodded several times with owlish impressiveness.

Mrs. Dunn and her young brother held private talk.

"I don't know what to make of Percy," she said anxiously. "He doesn't seem quite right in his 'ead—what do you think?"

"He's queer sometimes, I *must* say."

"And I am so ashamed at taking your money—that I am. It isn't right—that it isn't."

"Oh, don't you make any fuss," answered the good-natured lad. "I've got no use for it; I can't see you hard up, can I?"

Their earnings, put together, amply sufficed for the week's expenses; and, but for her uneasiness on Dunn's account, Maggie would have found nothing to complain of. It relieved her from an increasing apprehension when, one evening, her husband came home more like his old self, and announced a new project. Having heard by chance that an old acquaintance of his, a fellow shopman, had started a drapery business at Croydon, he had been over there to have a talk, and not without result. The Croydon man had no particular need of an assistant, but was willing to take Dunn in that capacity, if board and lodging were all he asked.

"And I'm going," declared the out-of-work. "It's better than 'anging about doing nothing. I shall come 'ome on Saturday night and go back on the Monday morning. If the business does well, he'll be able to pay me before long; and if

2. ***public house,*** a tavern.

he can't I shall have time to look out for another place."

Maggie agreed that this sort of engagement was preferable to none at all, but it would be necessary for Dunn to have a new outfit of clothes. He had grown so shabby as to be quite unpresentable behind a counter. Maggie and her brother managed to find the money for this outlay, and in a day or two Dunn took leave of them. He possessed not a farthing of his own; the cost of his traveling backwards and forwards each week, with other small expenditures not to be avoided, would, of course, be borne by the faithful two who worked to keep up the home.

"I shall pay you back every penny, boy," said Dunn to his brother-in-law in an outburst of sanguine gratitude. "Mind you keep an account. Make him keep an account of every penny we have from him, Maggie. There's better days coming, don't you fear!"

In the course of the first week he wrote an encouraging letter, and late on Saturday night he was welcomed back. Undoubtedly he looked better already; his report of the Croydon business was very hopeful. What the shop wanted was just the energy and experience which he brought to it; why, Tomlinson admitted that the takings had already increased. Though it had never been his speciality, Dunn flattered himself that he knew better than most men how to dress a window, and Tomlinson, already convinced of this, promised him the control of that department. Of course in such a little shop one couldn't do much in the way of artistic exhibition, but one had only to watch the passers-by to see how great an improvement had already been effected. Thus, while eating the tasty supper provided for him, Dunn talked till long after midnight. Next morning, to complete the enjoyment of his holiday, he bought three Sunday newspapers, and abandoned himself to luxurious reading.

On his next return home, he did not report the serious differences which had arisen between him and his employer in the course of the week; all went well, he declared—save that the diet might be improved; in that respect Tomlinson and his wife were rather mean. As a matter of fact, Dunn already felt his duties so burdensome that he had begun to grumble at not being paid, a piece of ingratitude which Mrs. Tomlinson not unnaturally resented. "Words," had passed between the two; moreover, there had been "words" between Tomlinson and his wife, and Mrs. Tomlinson had made up her mind to starve out the intruder. Dunn, speedily aware of this female hostility, knew how it would end; there is no holding one's ground against the Mrs. Tomlinsons of small drapers' shops. But not a syllable of this was allowed to pass his lips, and on Monday morning he went off with a show of excellent spirits.

By Wednesday things came to a head. There was a three-cornered combat. Tomlinson abused Dunn for laziness and incompetence; Mrs. Tomlinson reviled her husband for foolish good nature, and the assistant for every conceivable fault; and Dunn fired away at both with the recklessness of a man who knows that he has nothing to gain by moderation. It ended in the only possible way: Dunn, bidden to pack his traps and be off, did so with all speed, and at midday was back in London.

His modest luggage he had despatched by the parcel delivery company; unencumbered, and rejoicing in recovered freedom, he strolled from Victoria Station up to Charing Cross, and thence into St. Martin's Lane. The direction was fatal. Though he had no such thing in mind, he became aware that he was passing the door of the Free Library; the old spell seized upon him; he was drawn across the threshold and down the stairs. The scent of newspapers, mingled with the odour of filthy garments and unwashed humanity, put him beside himself with joy; his nostrils quivered, his eyes sparkled, he strode towards the dinner hour throng which pressed about the illustrated weeklies. Between musty heads he caught a glimpse of the tatters of last Saturday's *London News;* in five minutes' time he found his opportunity and leapt to the front.

He ate with strict economy, and hurried back again, this time to the upper hall. As usual, it was not easy to find a vacant chair. The sight of a labourer fast asleep on the pages of the *Nineteenth Century* roused him to indignation; he touched the man, then shook him.

"Here, I say, you don't seem to be reading!"

"All right, Guv'nor," growled the individual disturbed; "you're welcome."

Dunn seized the chair, turned to the first page

of the review, and began to read an article on "Hypnotism."

Reaching home at supper time, he professed to have come straight from Croydon. He made known his wrongs, the disgraceful treatment to which he had been subjected.

"Look here, Maggie, could you stand it? What do you advise me to do? Am I to go back and beg them to keep me?"

"I should think not!" cried the indignant wife. "What do you say, Willie?"

"I should chuck it up," said the lad unconcernedly.

So on the morrow Dunn resumed his visits to St. Martin's Lane. Week after week went by, and he sat reading; spellbound, hypnotised. Month after month, and still he read. Maggie and her brother worked to keep up the home. □□

Discussion

1. Percy Dunn has not been blessed with the Victorian virtues, such as dedication to hard work, thrift, and a sharp sense of familial duty. Does Gissing blame his "hero's" failures on weakness of character alone, or does he imply that other circumstances have contributed to Dunn's situation? Cite passages from the text to support your answer.

2. Why is Dunn's belief that his avid reading has "enriched his mind" only a delusion?

3. After Dunn leaves the Tomlinsons' employment, he is, according to the author, "rejoicing in recovered freedom." **(a)** Describe Dunn's "freedom" when unemployed. **(b)** How would most people react to this type of freedom?

4. Why is Dunn's reading choice of an article on "Hypnotism" an ironic one?

Vocabulary
Context and Dictionary

Using context as an aid, write the most appropriate definition for each italicized word on a separate sheet of paper. If you cannot get the meaning from context, use your Glossary. Be sure you can pronounce and spell all italicized words.

1. "The short words of the paddlers *reverberated* loudly between the thick and sombre walls of vegetation." **(a)** died; **(b)** echoed; **(c)** fell; **(d)** shifted.

2. "Luke said that his life was a burden and a slavery, and bitterly *reproached* his father for advising him to embark on a career for which he felt unsuited." **(a)** praised; **(b)** ignored; **(c)** blamed; **(d)** defended.

3. "He was a Sunnyasi—a houseless, wandering *mendicant*, depending on his neighbours for his daily bread. . . ." **(a)** beggar; **(b)** farmer; **(c)** sailor; **(d)** businessman.

4. "'It will be interesting,' he was saying, 'to devote this morning to an *exposition*, so far as I can make it clear to you, of the calculations that have led me to this conclusion.'" **(a)** country fair; **(b)** movement; **(c)** disproof; **(d)** explanation.

5. "The Sidlinch men had been so deeply *engrossed* in their task that they had not noticed the lanterns of the Chalk-Newton choir till now." **(a)** nauseated; **(b)** occupied; **(c)** distracted; **(d)** humorous.

6. "Already every second this blazing mass flew a hundred miles, and every second its terrific *velocity* increased." **(a)** stillness; **(b)** coolness; **(c)** speed; **(d)** slowness.

Put a check on your paper beside each definition you had to look up.

George Gissing 1857 • 1903

George Gissing, a formidable member of the literary avant-garde in the 1880s and 1890s, was relegated to the ranks of the old-fashioned and unreadable soon after his death at forty-six. Sixty years later—despite high praise from Henry James, Virginia Woolf, and George Orwell—only two of his thirty books remained in print. Now, with renewed interest in Gissing's work, all of his books are expected to be back in print by the early 1980s.

He was born in Wakefield on November 22, 1857, the eldest son of a chemist. A brilliant scholastic career at Owens College (now the University of Manchester) was abruptly terminated, as the result of a college scandal, when he was eighteen. Fleeing to the New World in the autumn of 1876, the disgraced student obtained a position teaching French and German at Waltham High School, near Boston. Restless and lonely, he soon went west, as far as Chicago. There he sold his first stories, to the Chicago *Tribune.* By the end of 1877 he was in London, his base for most of the remaining twenty-six years of his life.

Now married to a woman from his university days, he was determined on a literary career. The poverty of these years was to leave a permanent mark on Gissing. A first novel, *Workers in the Dawn,* was published in 1880 and received scant notice. It did bring in some journalistic work, writing reviews for the local magazines and as London correspondent for the Russian monthly *The Messenger of Europe.* In 1884 his second novel, *The Unclassed,* established him as an important writer, specializing in a realistic treatment of the London poor. The next five years produced five more novels on this theme, all of them finely constructed and unremittingly pessimistic.

Turning to the middle classes, Gissing wrote his masterpiece *New Grub Street* in 1891. Frankly critical of the London literary world, it reflected the author's own experiences. Although producing a book a year, he was never able to gain an income that would ever allow him to rest. A disastrous second marriage didn't help matters.

Gissing wrote *The Odd Women* in 1893. It has been called "the first feminist novel." He wrote scores of short stories in the nineties, in addition to the yearly novels, and a superb book on Dickens, a predecessor in the presentation of London poverty. In ill health, Gissing lived in France fron 1899 on. He died there in 1903.

Bernard Shaw

PYGMALION

Greek mythology has always been a rich source of legend for writers to draw upon. One of the favorite myths is the story of Pygmalion (pig-mā′li ən), a sculptor who created a statue so beautiful that he fell in love with it. The goddess of love transformed the statue into a real woman, Galatea (gal′ə tē′ə), whom Pygmalion married.

Shaw uses the Pygmalion myth as the basis of his play about a man to whom phonetics is the dominant interest in life. In the preface to the play he writes: ". . . The English have no respect for their language, and will not teach their children to speak it. They spell it so abominably that no man can teach himself what it sounds like. It is impossible for an Englishman to open his mouth without making some other Englishman hate or despise him. German and Spanish are accessible to foreigners: English is not accessible even to Englishmen. The reformer England needs today is an energetic phonetic enthusiast: that is why I have made such a one the hero of a popular play. . . . if the play makes the public aware that there are such people as phoneticians, and that they are among the most important people in England at present, it will serve its turn. . . ."

Cast of Characters

THE DAUGHTER—Miss Eynsford Hill (Clara)
THE MOTHER—Mrs Eynsford Hill
FREDDY—Mr Eynsford Hill, *her son*
THE FLOWER GIRL—Eliza (Liza) Doolittle
THE GENTLEMAN—Colonel Pickering
THE NOTE TAKER—Henry Higgins, *a professor of phonetics*
A BYSTANDER
A SARCASTIC BYSTANDER
GENERAL BYSTANDERS
MRS PEARCE, *Henry Higgins's housekeeper*
ALFRED DOOLITTLE, *Eliza's father*
MRS HIGGINS, *Henry Higgins's mother*
THE PARLOR-MAID

Act One

London at 11.15 P.M. *Torrents of heavy summer rain. Cab whistles blowing frantically in all directions. Pedestrians running for shelter into the portico of St. Paul's Church (*not *Wren's cathedral but Inigo Jones's church in Covent Garden*[1] *vegetable market), among them a lady and her daughter in evening dress. They are all peering out gloomily at the rain, except one man with his back turned to the rest, who seems wholly preoccupied with a notebook in which he is writing busily.*

The church clock strikes the first quarter.

THE DAUGHTER *(in the space between the central pillars, close to the one on her left).* I'm getting chilled to the bone. What can Freddy be doing all this time? He's been gone twenty minutes.

THE MOTHER *(on her daughter's right).* Not so long. But he ought to have got us a cab by this.

A BYSTANDER *(on the lady's right).* He wont[2] get no cab not until half-past eleven, missus, when they come back after dropping their theatre fares.

THE MOTHER. But we must have a cab. We cant stand here until half-past eleven. It's too bad.

THE BYSTANDER. Well, it aint my fault, missus.

THE DAUGHTER. If Freddy had a bit of gumption, he would have got one at the theatre door.

THE MOTHER. What could he have done, poor boy?

THE DAUGHTER. Other people got cabs. Why couldnt he?

FREDDY *rushes in out of the rain from the Southampton Street side, and comes between them closing a dripping umbrella. He is a young man of twenty, in evening dress, very wet round the ankles.*

THE DAUGHTER. Well, havnt you got a cab?

---

1. ***Covent Garden,*** chief fruit, vegetable, and flower-market district of London. It originally was a "convent garden" of Westminster Abbey. The area also includes St. Paul's Church (not to be confused with St. Paul's Cathedral), and the famous theater, Covent Garden Opera House.
2. ***wont.*** One of the spelling reforms advocated by Shaw was the omission of apostrophes in contractions. He retained the punctuation when omission would be confusing (*I'll* rather than *Ill*), or if omission would change pronunciation *(he's* rather than *hes).* He also spells names phonetically, e.g., Shakespear.

FREDDY. Theres not one to be had for love or money.

THE MOTHER. Oh, Freddy, there must be one. You cant have tried.

THE DAUGHTER. It's too tiresome. Do you expect us to go and get one ourselves?

FREDDY. I tell you theyre all engaged. The rain was so sudden: nobody was prepared; and everybody had to take a cab. Ive been to Charing Cross one way and nearly to Ludgate Circus the other; and they were all engaged.

THE MOTHER. Did you try Trafalgar Square?

FREDDY. There wasnt one at Trafalgar Square.

THE DAUGHTER. Did you try?

FREDDY. I tried as far as Charing Cross Station. Did you expect me to walk to Hammersmith?

THE DAUGHTER. You havnt tried at all.

THE MOTHER. You really are very helpless, Freddy. Go again; and dont come back until you have found a cab.

FREDDY. I shall simply get soaked for nothing.

THE DAUGHTER. And what about us? Are we to stay here all night in this draught, with next to nothing on? You selfish pig—

FREDDY. Oh, very well: I'll go; I'll go. *(He opens his umbrella and dashes off Strandwards,*[3] *but comes into collision with a flower girl, who is hurrying in for shelter, knocking her basket out of her hands. A blinding flash of lightning, followed instantly by a rattling peal of thunder, orchestrates the incident).*

THE FLOWER GIRL. Nah then, Freddy: look wh' y' gowin, deah.

FREDDY. Sorry *(he rushes off).*

THE FLOWER GIRL *(picking up her scattered flowers and replacing them in the basket).* Theres menners f' yer! Te-oo banches o voylets trod into the mad. *(She sits down on the plinth of the column, sorting her flowers, on the lady's right. She is not at all a romantic figure. She is perhaps eighteen, perhaps twenty, hardly older. She wears a little sailor hat of black straw that has long been exposed to the dust and soot of London and has seldom if ever been brushed. Her hair needs washing rather badly: its mousy color can hardly be natural. She wears a shoddy black coat that reaches nearly to her knees and is shaped to her waist. She has a brown skirt with a coarse apron. Her boots are much the worse for wear. She is no doubt as clean as she can afford to be; but compared to the ladies she is very dirty. Her features are no worse than theirs; but their condition leaves something to be desired; and she needs the services of a dentist).*

THE MOTHER. How do you know that my son's name is Freddy, pray?

THE FLOWER GIRL. Ow, eez ye-ooa san, is e? Wal, fewd dan y' de-ooty bawmz a mather should, eed now bettern to spawl a pore gel's flahrzn than ran awy athaht pyin. Will ye-oo py me f' them? *(Here, with apologies, this desperate attempt to represent her dialect without a phonetic alphabet must be abandoned as unintelligible outside London).*

THE DAUGHTER. Do nothing of the sort, mother. The idea!

THE MOTHER. Please allow me, Clara. Have you any pennies?

THE DAUGHTER. No. Ive nothing smaller than sixpence.

THE FLOWER GIRL *(hopefully).* I can give you change for a tanner,[4] kind lady.

THE MOTHER *(to* CLARA*).* Give it to me. *(*CLARA *parts reluctantly).* Now *(to the girl)* this is for your flowers.

THE FLOWER GIRL. Thank you kindly, lady.

THE DAUGHTER. Make her give you the change. These things are only a penny a bunch.

THE MOTHER. Do hold your tongue, Clara. *(To the girl)* You can keep the change.

THE FLOWER GIRL. Oh, thank you, lady.

THE MOTHER. Now tell me how you know that young gentleman's name.

THE FLOWER GIRL. I didnt.

THE MOTHER. I heard you call him by it. Dont try to deceive me.

THE FLOWER GIRL *(protesting).* Who's trying to deceive you? I called him Freddy or Charlie same as you might yourself if you was talking to a stranger and wished to be pleasant.

THE DAUGHTER. Sixpence thrown away! Really, mamma, you might have spared Freddy that. *(She retreats in disgust behind the pillar). An elderly gentleman of the amiable military type rushes into the shelter, and closes a drip-*

3. ***Strandwards.*** The Strand is the main thoroughfare between the West End, the fashionable residential area, and the business and commercial center of London. St. Paul's Church is two blocks from the Strand.

4. ***tanner,*** sixpence. [British Slang]

ping umbrella. He is in the same plight as FREDDY, *very wet about the ankles. He is in evening dress, with a light overcoat. He takes the place left vacant by the daughter's retirement.*

THE GENTLEMAN. Phew!

THE MOTHER *(to the gentleman).* Oh, sir, is there any sign of its stopping?

THE GENTLEMAN. I'm afraid not. It started worse than ever about two minutes ago. *(He goes to the plinth beside the flower girl; puts up his foot on it; and stoops to turn down his trouser ends).*

THE MOTHER. Oh dear! *(She retires sadly and joins her daughter).*

THE FLOWER GIRL *(taking advantage of the military gentleman's proximity to establish friendly relations with him).* If it's worse, it's a sign it's nearly over. So cheer up, Captain; and buy a flower off a poor girl.

THE GENTLEMAN. I'm sorry. I havnt any change.

THE FLOWER GIRL. I can give you change, Captain.

THE GENTLEMAN. For a sovereign? Ive nothing less.

THE FLOWER GIRL. Garn! Oh do buy a flower off me, Captain. I can change half-a-crown. Take this for tuppence.

THE GENTLEMAN. Now dont be troublesome: theres a good girl. *(Trying his pockets)* I really havnt any change—Stop: heres three hapence, if thats any use to you *(he retreats to the other pillar).*

THE FLOWER GIRL *(disappointed, but thinking three half-pence better than nothing).* Thank you, sir.

THE BYSTANDER *(to the girl).* You be careful: give him a flower for it. Theres a bloke here behind taking down every blessed word youre saying. *(All turn to the man who is taking notes).*

THE FLOWER GIRL *(springing up terrified).* I aint done nothing wrong by speaking to the gentleman. Ive a right to sell flowers if I keep off the kerb. *(Hysterically)* I'm a respectable girl: so help me, I never spoke to him except to ask him to buy a flower off me.

(General hubbub, mostly sympathetic to the flower girl, but deprecating her excessive sensibility. Cries of Dont start hollerin. Who's hurting you? Nobody's going to touch you. Whats the good of fussing? Steady on. Easy easy, etc., *come from the elderly staid spectators, who pat her comfortingly. Less patient ones bid her shut her head, or ask her roughly what is wrong with her. A remoter group, not knowing what the matter is, crowd in and increase the noise with question and answer:* Whats the row? What-she do? Where is he? A tec[5] taking her down. What! him? Yes: him over there: Took money off the gentleman, etc.

THE FLOWER GIRL *(breaking through them to the gentleman, crying wildly).* Oh, sir, dont let him charge me.[6] You dunno what it means to me. Theyll take away my character and drive me on the streets for speaking to gentlemen. They—

Culver Pictures

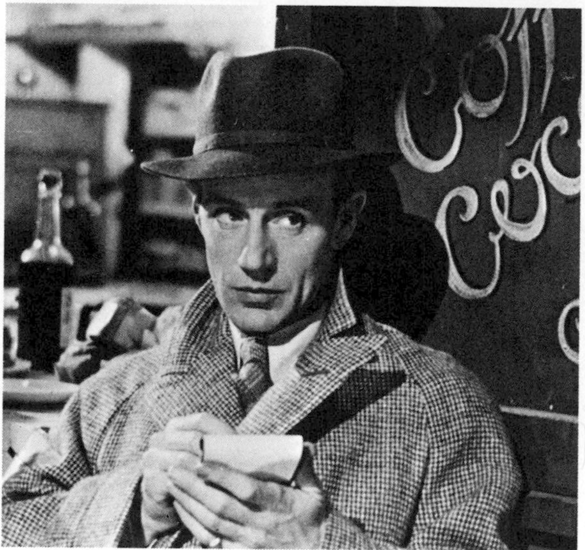

THE NOTE TAKER *(coming forward on her right, the rest crowding after him).* There, there, there, there! who's hurting you, you silly girl? What do you take me for?

THE BYSTANDER. It's all right: he's a gentleman: look at his boots. *(Explaining to the note taker)* She thought you was a copper's nark, sir.

THE NOTE TAKER *(with quick interest).* Whats a copper's nark?

---

5. ***tec,*** detective. [British Slang]
6. ***charge me,*** bring an accusation against me.

THE BYSTANDER *(inapt at definition).* It's a—well, it's a copper's nark, as you might say. What else would you call it? A sort of informer.

THE FLOWER GIRL *(still hysterical).* I take my Bible oath I never said a word—

THE NOTE TAKER *(overbearing but good-humored).* Oh, shut up, shut up. Do I look like a policeman?

THE FLOWER GIRL *(far from reassured).* Then what did you take down my words for? How do I know whether you took me down right? You just shew me what youve wrote about me. *(The note taker opens his book and holds it steadily under her nose, though the pressure of the mob trying to read it over his shoulders would upset a weaker man).* Whats that? That aint proper writing. I cant read that.

THE NOTE TAKER. I can. *(Reads, reproducing her pronunciation exactly)* "Cheer ap, Keptin; n' baw ya flahr orf a pore gel."

THE FLOWER GIRL *(much distressed).* It's because I called him Captain. I meant no harm. *(To the gentleman)* Oh, sir, dont let him lay a charge agen me for a word like that. You—

THE GENTLEMAN. Charge! I make no charge. *(To the note taker)* Really, sir, if you are a detective, you need not begin protecting me against molestation by young women until I ask you. Anybody could see that the girl meant no harm.

THE BYSTANDERS GENERALLY *(demonstrating against police espionage).* Course they could. What business is it of yours? You mind your own affairs. He wants promotion, he does. Taking down people's words! Girl never said a word to him. What harm if she did? Nice thing a girl cant shelter from the rain without being insulted, etc., etc., etc. *(She is conducted by the more sympathetic demonstrators back to her plinth, where she resumes her seat and struggles with her emotion).*

THE BYSTANDER. He aint a tec. He's a blooming busybody: thats what he is. I tell you, look at his boots.

THE NOTE TAKER *(turning on him genially).* And how are all your people down at Selsey?

THE BYSTANDER *(suspiciously).* Who told you my people come from Selsey?

THE NOTE TAKER. Never you mind. They did. *(To the girl)* How do you come to be up so far east? You were born in Lisson Grove.

THE FLOWER GIRL *(appalled).* Oh, what harm is there in my leaving Lisson Grove? It wasnt fit for a pig to live in; and I had to pay four-and-six a week. *(In tears)* Oh, boo—hoo—oo—

THE NOTE TAKER. Live where you like; but stop that noise.

THE GENTLEMAN *(to the girl).* Come, come! he cant touch you: you have a right to live where you please.

A SARCASTIC BYSTANDER *(thrusting himself between the note taker and the gentleman).* Park Lane, for instance. I'd like to go into the Housing Question with you, I would.

THE FLOWER GIRL *(subsiding into a brooding melancholy over her basket, and talking very low-spiritedly to herself).* I'm a good girl, I am.

THE SARCASTIC BYSTANDER *(not attending to her).* Do you know where *I* come from?

THE NOTE TAKER *(promptly).* Hoxton.

Titterings. Popular interest in the note taker's performance increases.

THE SARCASTIC ONE *(amazed).* Well, who said I didnt? Bly me! You know everything, you do.

THE FLOWER GIRL *(still nursing her sense of injury).* Aint no call to meddle with me, he aint.

THE BYSTANDER *(to her).* Of course he aint. Dont you stand it from him. *(To the note taker)* See here: what call have you to know about people what never offered to meddle with you?

THE FLOWER GIRL. Let him say what he likes. I dont want to have no truck with him.

THE BYSTANDER. You take us for dirt under your feet, dont you? Catch you taking liberties with a gentleman!

THE SARCASTIC BYSTANDER. Yes: tell him where he come from if you want to go fortune-telling.

THE NOTE TAKER. Cheltenham, Harrow, Cambridge, and India.

THE GENTLEMAN. Quite right.

(Great laughter. Reaction in the note taker's favor. Exclamations of He knows all about it. Told him proper. Hear him tell the toff where he come from? etc.).

THE GENTLEMAN. May I ask, sir, do you do this for your living at a music-hall?

THE NOTE TAKER. Ive thought of that. Perhaps I shall some day.

The rain has stopped; and the persons on the outside of the crowd begin to drop off.

THE FLOWER GIRL *(resenting the reaction).* He's no gentleman, he aint, to interfere with a poor girl.

THE DAUGHTER *(out of patience, pushing her way rudely to the front and displacing the gentleman, who politely retires to the other side of the pillar).* What on earth is Freddy doing? I shall get pneumownia if I stay in this draught any longer.

THE NOTE TAKER *(to himself, hastily making a note of her pronunciation of "monia").* Earlscourt.

THE DAUGHTER *(violently).* Will you please keep your impertinent remarks to yourself.

THE NOTE TAKER. Did I say that out loud? I didnt mean to. I beg your pardon. Your mother's Epsom, unmistakably.

THE MOTHER *(advancing between her daughter and the note taker).* How very curious! I was brought up in Largelady Park, near Epsom.

THE NOTE TAKER *(uproariously amused).* Ha! Ha! What a devil of a name! Excuse me. *(To the daughter)* You want a cab, do you?

THE DAUGHTER. Dont dare speak to me.

THE MOTHER. Oh please, please, Clara. *(Her daughter repudiates her with an angry shrug and retires haughtily).* We should be so grateful to you, sir, if you found us a cab. *(The note taker produces a whistle).* Oh, thank you. *(She joins her daughter).*

The note taker blows a piercing blast.

THE SARCASTIC BYSTANDER. There! I knowed he was a plain-clothes copper.

THE BYSTANDER. That aint a police whistle: thats a sporting whistle.

THE FLOWER GIRL *(still preoccupied with her wounded feelings).* He's no right to take away my character. My character is the same to me as any lady's.

THE NOTE TAKER. I dont know whether youve noticed it; but the rain stopped about two minutes ago.

THE BYSTANDER. So it has. Why didnt you say so before? and us losing our time listening to your silliness! *(He walks off towards the Strand).*

THE SARCASTIC BYSTANDER. I can tell where you come from. You come from Anwell. Go back there.

THE NOTE TAKER *(helpfully).* *H*anwell.

THE SARCASTIC BYSTANDER *(affecting great distinction of speech).* Thenk you, teacher. Haw haw! So long *(he touches his hat with mock respect and strolls off).*

THE FLOWER GIRL. Frightening people like that! How would he like it himself?

THE MOTHER. It's quite fine now, Clara. We can walk to a motor bus. Come. *(She gathers her skirts above her ankles and hurries off towards the Strand).*

THE DAUGHTER. But the cab—*(her mother is out of hearing).* Oh, how tiresome! *(She follows angrily). All the rest have gone except the note taker, the gentleman, and the flower girl, who sits arranging her basket and still pitying herself in murmurs.*

THE FLOWER GIRL. Poor girl! Hard enough for her to live without being worrited and chivied.

THE GENTLEMAN *(returning to his former place on the note taker's left).* How do you do it, if I may ask?

THE NOTE TAKER. Simply phonetics. The science of speech. Thats my profession: also my hobby. Happy is the man who can make a living by his hobby! You can spot an Irishman or a Yorkshireman by his brogue. *I* can place any man within six miles. I can place him within two miles in London. Sometimes within two streets.

THE FLOWER GIRL. Ought to be ashamed of himself, unmanly coward!

THE GENTLEMAN. But is there a living in that?

THE NOTE TAKER. Oh yes. Quite a fat one. This is an age of upstarts. Men begin in Kentish Town with £80 a year, and end in Park Lane with a hundred thousand. They want to drop Kentish Town; but they give themselves away every time they open their mouths. Now I can teach them—

THE FLOWER GIRL. Let him mind his own business and leave a poor girl—

THE NOTE TAKER *(explosively).* Woman: cease this detestable boohooing instantly; or else seek the shelter of some other place of worship.

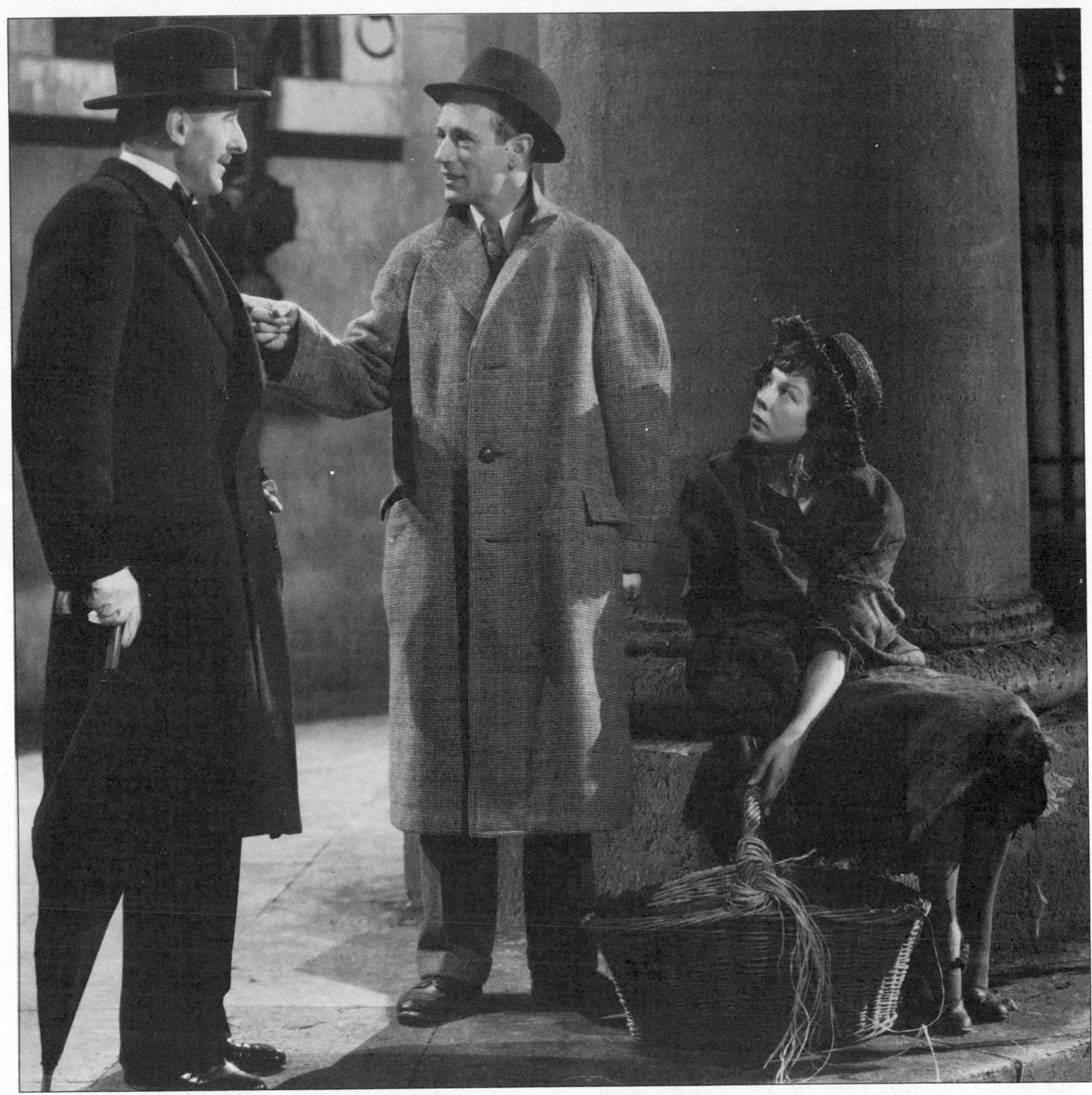

Culver Pictures

THE FLOWER GIRL *(with feeble defiance).* Ive a right to be here if I like, same as you.

THE NOTE TAKER. A woman who utters such depressing and disgusting sounds has no right to be anywhere—no right to live. Remember that you are a human being with a soul and the divine gift of articulate speech: that your native language is the language of Shakespear and Milton and The Bible: and dont sit there crooning like a bilious pigeon.

THE FLOWER GIRL *(quite overwhelmed, looking up at him in mingled wonder and deprecation without daring to raise her head).* Ah-ah-ah-ow-ow-ow-oo!

THE NOTE TAKER *(whipping out his book).* Heavens! what a sound! *(He writes; then holds out the book and reads, reproducing her vowels exactly)* Ah-ah-ah-ow-ow-ow-oo!

THE FLOWER GIRL *(tickled by the performance, and laughing in spite of herself).* Garn!

THE NOTE TAKER. You see this creature with her kerbstone English: the English that will keep her in the gutter to the end of her days. Well, sir, in three months I could pass that girl off as a duchess at an ambassador's garden party. I could even get her a place as lady's maid or shop assistant, which requires better English.

THE FLOWER GIRL. What's that you say?

THE NOTE TAKER. Yes, you squashed cabbage leaf, you disgrace to the noble architecture of these columns, you incarnate insult to the English language: I could pass you off as the Queen of Sheba. *(To the Gentleman)* Can you believe that?

THE GENTLEMAN. Of course I can. I am myself a student of Indian dialects; and—

THE NOTE TAKER *(eagerly).* Are you? Do you know Colonel Pickering, the author of Spoken Sanscrit?

THE GENTLEMAN. I am Colonel Pickering. Who are you?

THE NOTE TAKER. Henry Higgins, author of Higgins's Universal Alphabet.

PICKERING *(with enthusiasm).* I came from India to meet you.

HIGGINS. I was going to India to meet you.

PICKERING. Where do you live?

HIGGINS. 27A Wimpole Street. Come and see me to-morrow.

PICKERING. I'm at the Carlton. Come with me now and lets have a jaw over some supper.

HIGGINS. Right you are.

THE FLOWER GIRL *(to* PICKERING, *as he passes her).* Buy a flower, kind gentleman. I'm short for my lodging.

PICKERING. I really havnt any change. I'm sorry *(he goes away).*

HIGGINS *(shocked at the girl's mendacity).* Liar. You said you could change half-a-crown.

THE FLOWER GIRL *(rising in desperation).* You ought to be stuffed with nails, you ought. *(Flinging the basket at his feet)* Take the whole blooming basket for sixpence.

The church clock strikes the second quarter.

HIGGINS *(hearing in it the voice of God, rebuking him for his Pharisaic want of charity to the poor girl).* A reminder. *(He raises his hat solemnly; then throws a handful of money into the basket and follows* PICKERING*).*

THE FLOWER GIRL *(picking up a half-crown).* Ah-ow-ooh! *(Picking up a couple of florins)* Aaah-ow-ooh! *(Picking up several coins)* Aaaaaah-ow-ooh! *(Picking up a half-sovereign)* Aaaaaaaaaaaah-ow-ooh!!!

FREDDY *(springing out of a taxicab).* Got one at last. Hallo! *(To the girl)* Where are the two ladies that were here?

THE FLOWER GIRL. They walked to the bus when the rain stopped.

FREDDY. And left me with a cab on my hands! Damnation!

THE FLOWER GIRL *(with grandeur).* Never mind, young man. *I'm* going home in a taxi. *(She sails off to the cab. The driver puts his hand behind him and holds the door firmly shut against her. Quite understanding his mistrust, she shews him her handful of money).* A taxi fare aint no object to me, Charlie. *(He grins and opens the door).* Here. What about the basket?

THE TAXIMAN. Give it here. Tuppence extra.

LIZA. No: I dont want nobody to see it. *(She crushes it into the cab and gets in, continuing the conversation through the window)* Goodbye, Freddy.

FREDDY *(dazedly raising his hat)* Goodbye.

TAXIMAN. Where to?

LIZA. Bucknam Pellis (Buckingham Palace).

TAXIMAN. What d'ye mean—Bucknam Pellis?

LIZA. Dont you know where it is? In the Green Park, where the King lives. Goodbye, Freddy. Dont let me keep you standing there. Goodbye.

FREDDY. Goodbye. *(He goes).*

TAXIMAN. Here? Whats this about Bucknam Pellis? What business have you at Bucknam Pellis?

LIZA. Of course I havnt none. But I wasnt going to let him know that. You drive me home.

TAXIMAN. And wheres home?

LIZA. Angel Court, Drury Lane, next Meiklejohn's oil shop.

TAXIMAN. That sounds more like it, Judy. *(He drives off).*

Let us follow the taxi to the entrance to Angel Court, a narrow little archway between two shops, one of them Meiklejohn's oil shop. When it stops there, ELIZA *gets out, dragging her basket with her.*

LIZA. How much?

TAXIMAN. *(indicating the taximeter)* Cant you read? A shilling.

LIZA. A shilling for two minutes!!

TAXIMAN. Two minutes or ten: it's all the same.

LIZA. Well, I dont call it right.

TAXIMAN. Ever been in a taxi before?

LIZA *(with dignity)* Hundreds and thousands of times, young man.

TAXIMAN *(laughing at her)* Good for you, Judy. Keep the shilling, darling, with best love from all at home. Good luck! *(He drives off).*

LIZA *(humiliated)* Impidence!

She picks up the basket and trudges up the alley with it to her lodging: a small room with very old wall paper hanging loose in the damp places. A broken pane in the window is mended with paper. A portrait of a popular actor and a fashion plate of ladies' dresses, all wildly beyond poor ELIZA'*s means, both torn from newspapers, are pinned up on the wall. A birdcage hangs in the window; but its tenant died long ago: it remains as a memorial only.*

These are the only visible luxuries: the rest is the irreducible minimum of poverty's needs: a wretched bed heaped with all sorts of coverings that have any warmth in them, a draped packing case with a basin and jug on it and a little looking glass over it, a chair and a table, the refuse of some suburban kitchen, and an American alarm clock on the shelf above the unused fireplace: the whole lighted with a gas lamp with a penny in the slot meter. Rent: four shillings a week.

Here ELIZA, *chronically weary, but too excited to go to bed, sits, counting her new riches and dreaming and planning what to do with them, until the gas goes out, when she enjoys for the first time the sensation of being able to put in another penny without grudging it. This prodigal mood does not extinguish her gnawing sense of the need for economy sufficiently to prevent her from calculating that she can dream and plan in bed more cheaply and warmly than sitting up without a fire. So she takes off her shawl and skirt and adds them to the miscellaneous bedclothes. Then she kicks off her shoes and gets into bed without any further change.*

Act Two

Next day at 11 A.M. HIGGINS*'s laboratory in Wimpole Street. It is a room on the first floor, looking on the street, and was meant for the drawing room. The double doors are in the middle of the back wall; and persons entering find in the corner to their right two tall file cabinets at right angles to one another against the walls. In this corner stands a flat writing table, on which are a phonograph, a laryngoscope, a row of tiny organ pipes with bellows, a set of lamp chimneys for singing flames with burners attached to a gas plug in the wall by an indiarubber tube, several tuning-forks of different sizes, a lifesize image of half a human head, shewing in section the vocal organs, and a box containing a supply of wax cylinders for the phonograph.*

Further down the room, on the same side, is a fireplace, with a comfortable leather-covered easy-chair at the side of the hearth nearest the door, and a coal-scuttle. There is a clock on the mantelpiece. Between the fireplace and the phonograph table is a stand for newspapers.

On the other side of the central door, to the left of the visitor, is a cabinet of shallow drawers. On it is a telephone and the telephone directory. The corner beyond, and most of the side wall, is occupied by a grand piano, with the keyboard at the end furthest from the door, and a bench for the player extending the full length of the keyboard. On the piano is a dessert dish heaped with fruit and sweets, mostly chocolates.

The middle of the room is clear. Besides the easy-chair, the piano bench, and two chairs at the phonograph table, there is one stray chair. It stands near the fireplace. On the walls, engravings: mostly Piranesis and mezzotint portraits.[1] *No paintings.*

PICKERING *is seated at the table, putting down some cards and a tuning-fork which he has been using.* HIGGINS *is standing up near him, closing two or three file drawers which are hanging out. He appears in the morning light as a robust, vital, appetizing sort of man of forty or thereabouts,*

1. ***Piranesis and mezzotint portraits.*** Giovanni Battista Piranesi (1720–1778), an Italian draftsman and etcher, is noted for his large prints of buildings of classical and post-classical Rome, and views of Greek temples. A mezzotint is a picture engraved on a roughened copper or steel plate. Light areas are obtained by scraping away and burnishing parts of the plate.

dressed in a professional-looking black frock-coat with a white linen collar and black silk tie. He is of the energetic, scientific type, heartily, even violently interested in everything that can be studied as a scientific subject, and careless about himself and other people, including their feelings. He is, in fact, but for his years and size, rather like a very impetuous baby "taking notice" eagerly and loudly, and requiring almost as much watching to keep him out of unintended mischief. His manner varies from genial bullying when he is in a good humor to stormy petulance when anything goes wrong; but he is so entirely frank and void of malice that he remains likeable even in his least reasonable moments.

HIGGINS *(as he shuts the last drawer).* Well, I think thats the whole show.

PICKERING. It's really amazing. I havnt taken half of it in, you know.

HIGGINS. Would you like to go over any of it again?

PICKERING *(rising and coming to the fireplace, where he plants himself with his back to the fire).* No, thank you; not now. I'm quite done up for this morning.

HIGGINS *(following him, and standing beside him on his left).* Tired of listening to sounds?

PICKERING. Yes. It's a fearful strain. I rather fancied myself because I can pronounce twenty-four distinct vowel sounds; but your hundred and thirty beat me. I cant hear a bit of difference between most of them.

HIGGINS *(chuckling, and going over to the piano to eat sweets).* Oh, that comes with practice. You hear no difference at first; but you keep on listening, and presently you find theyre all as different as A from B. *(MRS PEARCE looks in: she is HIGGINS's housekeeper).* Whats the matter?

MRS PEARCE *(hesitating, evidently perplexed).* A young woman wants to see you, sir.

HIGGINS. A young woman! What does she want?

MRS PEARCE. Well, sir, she says youll be glad to see her when you know what she's come about. She's quite a common girl, sir. Very common indeed. I should have sent her away, only I thought perhaps you wanted her to talk into your machines. I hope Ive not done wrong; but really you see such queer people sometimes—youll excuse me, I'm sure, sir—

HIGGINS. Oh, thats all right, Mrs Pearce. Has she an interesting accent?

MRS PEARCE. Oh, something dreadful, sir, really. I dont know how you can take an interest in it.

HIGGINS *(to PICKERING).* Lets have her up. Shew her up, Mrs Pearce *(he rushes across to his working table and picks out a cylinder to use on the phonograph).*

MRS PEARCE *(only half resigned to it).* Very well, sir. It's for you to say. *(She goes downstairs).*

HIGGINS. This is rather a bit of luck. I'll shew you how I make records. We'll set her talking; and I'll take it down first in Bell's Visible Speech; then in broad Romic; and then we'll get her on the phonograph so that you can turn her on as often as you like with the written transcript before you.

MRS PEARCE *(returning).* This is the young woman, sir.

The flower girl enters in state. She has a hat with three ostrich feathers, orange, sky-blue, and red. She has a nearly clean apron, and the shoddy coat has been tidied a little. The pathos of this deplorable figure, with its innocent vanity and consequential air, touches PICKERING, who has already straightened himself in the presence of MRS PEARCE. But as to HIGGINS, the only distinction he makes between men and women is that when he is neither bullying nor exclaiming to the heavens against some feather-weight cross, he coaxes women as a child coaxes its nurse when it wants to get anything out of her.

HIGGINS *(brusquely, recognizing her with unconcealed disappointment, and at once, baby-like, making an intolerable grievance of it).* Why, this is the girl I jotted down last night. She's no use: Ive got all thc records I want of the Lisson Grove lingo; and I'm not going to waste another cylinder on it. *(To the girl)* Be off with you: I dont want you.

THE FLOWER GIRL. Dont you be so saucy. You aint heard what I come for yet. *(To MRS PEARCE, who is waiting at the door for further instructions)* Did you tell him I come in a taxi?

MRS PEARCE. Nonsense, girl! what do you

think a gentleman like Mr Higgins cares what you came in?

THE FLOWER GIRL. Oh, we are proud! He aint above giving lessons, not him: I heard him say so. Well, I aint come here to ask for any compliment; and if my money's not good enough I can go elsewhere.

HIGGINS. Good enough for what?

THE FLOWER GIRL. Good enough for ye-oo. Now you know, dont you? I'm come to have lessons, I am. And to pay for em too: make no mistake.

HIGGINS *(stupent).* Well!!! *(Recovering his breath with a gasp)* What do you expect me to say to you?

THE FLOWER GIRL. Well, if you was a gentleman, you might ask me to sit down, I think. Dont I tell you I'm bringing you business?

HIGGINS. Pickering: shall we ask this baggage to sit down, or shall we throw her out of the window?

THE FLOWER GIRL *(running away in terror to the piano, where she turns at bay).* Ah-ah-oh-ow-ow-ow-oo! *(Wounded and whimpering)* I wont be called a baggage when Ive offered to pay like any lady.

Motionless, the two men stare at her from the other side of the room, amazed.

PICKERING *(gently).* What is it you want, my girl?

THE FLOWER GIRL. I want to be a lady in a flower shop stead of selling at the corner of Tottenham Court Road. But they wont take me unless I can talk more genteel. He said he could teach me. Well, here I am ready to pay him—not asking any favor—and he treats me as if I was dirt.

MRS PEARCE. How can you be such a foolish ignorant girl as to think you could afford to pay Mr Higgins?

THE FLOWER GIRL. Why shouldnt I? I know what lessons cost as well as you do; and I'm ready to pay.

HIGGINS. How much?

THE FLOWER GIRL *(coming back to him, triumphant).* Now youre talking! I thought youd come off it when you saw a chance of getting back a bit of what you chucked at me last night. *(Confidentially)* Youd had a drop in, hadnt you?

HIGGINS *(peremptorily).* Sit down.

THE FLOWER GIRL. Oh, if youre going to make a compliment of it—

HIGGINS *(thundering at her).* Sit down.

MRS PEARCE *(severely).* Sit down, girl. Do as youre told.

THE FLOWER GIRL. Ah-ah-ah-ow-ow-oo! *(She stands, half rebellious, half bewildered).*

PICKERING *(very courteous).* Wont you sit down? *(He places the stray chair near the hearthrug between himself and* HIGGINS).

THE FLOWER GIRL *(coyly).* Dont mind if I do. *(She sits down.* PICKERING *returns to the hearthrug).*

HIGGINS. Whats your name?

THE FLOWER GIRL. Liza Doolittle.

HIGGINS *(declaiming gravely).*

Eliza, Elizabeth, Betsy and Bess,
They went to the woods to get a bird's nes':

PICKERING. They found a nest with four eggs in it:

HIGGINS. They took one apiece, and left three in it.

They laugh heartily at their own fun.

LIZA. Oh, dont be silly.

MRS PEARCE. *(placing herself behind* ELIZA'*s chair).* You mustnt speak to the gentleman like that.

LIZA. Well, why wont he speak sensible to me?

HIGGINS. Come back to business. How much do you propose to pay me for the lessons?

LIZA. Oh, I know whats right. A lady friend of mine gets French lessons for eighteenpence an hour from a real French gentleman. Well, you wouldnt have the face to ask me the same for teaching me my own language as you would for French; so I wont give more than a shilling. Take it or leave it.

HIGGINS *(walking up and down the room, rattling his keys and his cash in his pockets).* You know, Pickering, if you consider a shilling, not as a simple shilling, but as a percentage of this girl's income, it works out as fully equivalent to sixty or seventy guineas from a millionaire.

PICKERING. How so?

HIGGINS. Figure it out. A millionaire has about £150 a day. She earns about half-a-crown.

LIZA *(haughtily).* Who told you I only—

HIGGINS *(continuing).* She offers me two-fifths of her day's income for a lesson. Two-fifths of

Culver Pictures

a millionaire's income for a day would be somewhere about £60. It's handsome. By George, it's enormous! it's the biggest offer I ever had.

LIZA *(rising, terrified).* Sixty pounds! What are you talking about? I never offered you sixty pounds. Where would I get—

HIGGINS. Hold your tongue.

LIZA *(weeping).* But I aint got sixty pounds. Oh—

MRS PEARCE. Dont cry, you silly girl. Sit down. Nobody is going to touch your money.

HIGGINS. Somebody is going to touch you, with a broomstick, if you dont stop snivelling. Sit down.

LIZA *(obeying slowly).* Ah-ah-ah-ow-oo-o! One would think you was my father.

HIGGINS. If I decide to teach you, I'll be worse than two fathers to you. Here *(he offers her his silk handkerchief)*!

LIZA. Whats this for?

HIGGINS. To wipe your eyes. To wipe any part of your face that feels moist. Remember: thats your handkerchief; and thats your sleeve. Dont mistake the one for the other if you wish to become a lady in a shop.

LIZA, *utterly bewildered, stares helplessly at him.*

MRS PEARCE. It's no use talking to her like that, Mr. Higgins: she doesn't understand you. Besides, youre quite wrong: she doesnt do it that way at all *(she takes the handkerchief).*

LIZA *(snatching it).* Here! You give me that handkerchief. He give it to me, not to you.

PICKERING *(laughing).* He did. I think it must be regarded as her property, Mrs Pearce.

MRS PEARCE *(resigning herself).* Serve you right, Mr Higgins.

PICKERING. Higgins: I'm interested. What about the ambassador's garden party? I'll say youre the greatest teacher alive if you make that good. I'll bet you all the expenses of the experiment you cant do it. And I'll pay for the lessons.

LIZA. Oh, you are real good. Thank you, Captain.

HIGGINS *(tempted, looking at her).* It's almost irresistible. She's so deliciously low—so horribly dirty—

LIZA *(protesting extremely).* Ah-ah-ah-ah-ow-ow-oo-oo!!! I aint dirty: I washed my face and hands afore I come, I did.

PICKERING. Youre certainly not going to turn her head with flattery, Higgins.

MRS PEARCE *(uneasy).* Oh, dont say that, sir: theres more ways than one of turning a girl's head; and nobody can do it better than Mr Higgins, though he may not always mean it. I do hope, sir, you wont encourage him to do anything foolish.

HIGGINS *(becoming excited as the idea grows on him).* What is life but a series of inspired follies? The difficulty is to find them to do. Never lose a chance: it doesnt come every day. I shall make a duchess of this draggletailed guttersnipe.

LIZA *(strongly deprecating this view of her).* Ah-ah-ah-ow-ow-oo!

HIGGINS *(carried away).* Yes: in six months—in three if she has a good ear and a quick tongue—I'll take her anywhere and pass her off as anything. We'll start today: now! this moment! Take her away and clean her, Mrs Pearce. Monkey Brand, if it wont come off any other way. Is there a good fire in the kitchen?

MRS PEARCE *(protesting).* Yes; but—

HIGGINS *(storming on).* Take all her clothes off and burn them. Ring up Whiteley or somebody for new ones. Wrap her up in brown paper til they come.

LIZA. Youre no gentleman, youre not, to talk of such things. I'm a good girl, I am; and I know what the like of you are, I do.

HIGGINS. We want none of your Lisson Grove prudery here, young woman. Youve got to learn to behave like a duchess. Take her away, Mrs Pearce. If she gives you any trouble, wallop her.

LIZA *(springing up and running between* PICKERING *and* MRS PEARCE *for protection).* No! I'll call the police, I will.

MRS PEARCE. But Ive no place to put her.

HIGGINS. Put her in the dustbin.

LIZA. Ah-ah-ah-ow-ow-oo!

PICKERING. Oh come, Higgins! be reasonable.

MRS PEARCE *(resolutely).* You must be reasonable, Mr. Higgins: really you must. You cant walk over everybody like this.

HIGGINS, *thus scolded, subsides. The hurricane is succeeded by a zephyr of amiable surprise.*

HIGGINS *(with professional exquisiteness of modulation). I* walk over everybody! My dear Mrs Pearce, my dear Pickering, I never had the slightest intention of walking over anyone. All I propose is that we should be kind to this poor girl. We must help her to prepare and fit herself for her new station in life. If I did not express myself clearly it was because I did not wish to hurt her delicacy, or yours.

LIZA, *reassured, steals back to her chair.*

MRS PEARCE *(to* PICKERING*).* Well, did you ever hear anything like that, sir?

PICKERING *(laughing heartily).* Never, Mrs Pearce: never.

HIGGINS *(patiently).* Whats the matter?

MRS PEARCE. Well, the matter is, sir, that you cant take a girl up like that as if you were picking up a pebble on the beach.

HIGGINS. Why not?

MRS PEARCE. Why not! But you dont know anything about her. What about her parents? She may be married.

LIZA. Garn!

HIGGINS. There! As the girl very properly says, Garn! Married indeed! Dont you know that a woman of that class looks a worn out drudge of fifty a year after she's married?

LIZA. Whood marry me?

HIGGINS *(suddenly resorting to the most thrillingly beautiful low tones in his best elocutionary style).* By George, Eliza, the streets will be strewn with the bodies of men shooting themselves for your sake before Ive done with you.

MRS PEARCE. Nonsense, sir. You mustnt talk like that to her.

LIZA *(rising and squaring herself determinedly).* I'm going away. He's off his chump, he is. I dont want no balmies teaching me.

HIGGINS *(wounded in his tenderest point by her insensibility to his elocution).* Oh, indeed! I'm mad, am I? Very well, Mrs Pearce: you neednt order the new clothes for her. Throw her out.

LIZA *(whimpering).* Nah-ow. You got no right to touch me.

MRS PEARCE. You see now what comes of being saucy. *(Indicating the door)* This way, please.

LIZA *(almost in tears).* I didnt want no clothes. I wouldnt have taken them *(she throws away the handkerchief).* I can buy my own clothes.

HIGGINS *(deftly retrieving the handkerchief and intercepting her on her reluctant way to the door).* Youre an ungrateful wicked girl. This is my return for offering to take you out of the gutter and dress you beautifully and make a lady of you.

MRS PEARCE. Stop, Mr Higgins. I wont allow it. It's you that are wicked. Go home to your parents, girl; and tell them to take better care of you.

LIZA. I aint got no parents. They told me I was big enough to earn my own living and turned me out.

MRS PEARCE. Wheres your mother?

LIZA. I aint got no mother. Her that turned me out was my sixth stepmother. But I done without them. And I'm a good girl, I am.

HIGGINS. Very well, then, what on earth is all this fuss about? The girl doesnt belong to anybody—is no use to anybody but me. *(He goes to* MRS PEARCE *and begins coaxing).* You can adopt her, Mrs Pearce: I'm sure a daughter would be a great amusement to you. Now dont make any more fuss. Take her downstairs; and—

MRS PEARCE. But whats to become of her? Is she to be paid anything? Do be sensible, sir.

HIGGINS. Oh, pay her whatever is necessary: put it down in the housekeeping book. *(Impatiently)* What on earth will she want with money? She'll have her food and her clothes. She'll only drink if you give her money.

LIZA *(turning on him).* Oh you are a brute. It's a lie: nobody ever saw the sign of liquor on me. *(To Pickering)* Oh, sir: you're a gentleman: don't let him speak to me like that.

PICKERING *(in good-humored remonstrance).* Does it occur to you, Higgins, that the girl has some feelings?

HIGGINS *(looking critically at her).* Oh no, I dont think so. Not any feelings that we need bother about. *(Cheerily)* Have you, Eliza?

LIZA. I got my feelings same as anyone else.

HIGGINS *(to* PICKERING, *reflectively).* You see the difficulty?

PICKERING. Eh? What difficulty?

HIGGINS. To get her to talk grammar. The mere pronunciation is easy enough.

LIZA. I dont want to talk grammar. I want to talk like a lady in a flower-shop.

MRS PEARCE. Will you please keep to the point, Mr Higgins? I want to know on what terms the girl is to be here. Is she to have any wages? And what is to become of her when youve finished your teaching? You must look ahead a little.

HIGGINS *(impatiently).* Whats to become of her if I leave her in the gutter? Tell me that, Mrs Pearce.

MRS PEARCE. Thats her own business, not yours, Mr Higgins.

HIGGINS. Well, when Ive done with her, we can throw her back into the gutter; and then it will be her own business again; so thats all right.

LIZA. Oh, youve no feeling heart in you: you dont care for nothing but yourself *(she rises and takes the floor resolutely).* Here! Ive had enough of this. I'm going *(making for the door).* You ought to be ashamed of yourself, you ought.

HIGGINS *(snatching a chocolate cream from the piano, his eyes suddenly beginning to twinkle with mischief).* Have some chocolates, Eliza.

LIZA *(halting, tempted).* How do I know what might be in them? Ive heard of girls being drugged by the like of you.

HIGGINS *whips out his penknife; cuts a chocolate in two; puts one half into his mouth and bolts it; and offers her the other half.*

HIGGINS. Pledge of good faith, Eliza. I eat one half: you eat the other. *(*LIZA *opens her mouth to retort: he pops the half chocolate into it).* You shall have boxes of them, barrels of them, every day. You shall live on them. Eh?

LIZA *(who has disposed of the chocolate after being nearly choked by it).* I wouldnt have ate it, only I'm too ladylike to take it out of my mouth.

HIGGINS. Listen, Eliza. I think you said you came in a taxi.

LIZA. Well, what if I did? Ive as good a right to take a taxi as anyone else.

HIGGINS. You have, Eliza; and in future you shall have as many taxis as you want. You shall go up and down and round the town in a taxi every day. Think of that, Eliza.

MRS PEARCE. Mr Higgins: youre tempting the girl. It's not right. She should think of the future.

HIGGINS. At her age! Nonsense! Time enough to think of the future when you havnt any future to think of. No, Eliza: do as this lady does: think of other people's futures; but never think of your own. Think of chocolates, and taxis, and gold, and diamonds.

LIZA. No: I dont want no gold and no diamonds. I'm a good girl, I am. *(She sits down again, with an attempt at dignity).*

HIGGINS. You shall remain so, Eliza, under the care of Mrs Pearce. And you shall marry an officer in the Guards, with a beautiful moustache: the son of a marquis, who will disinherit him for marrying you, but will relent when he sees your beauty and goodness—

PICKERING. Excuse me, Higgins; but I really must interfere. Mrs Pearce is quite right. If this girl is to put herself in your hands for six months for an experiment in teaching, she must understand thoroughly what she's doing.

HIGGINS. How can she? She's incapable of understanding anything. Besides, do any of us understand what we are doing? If we did, would we ever do it?

PICKERING. Very clever, Higgins; but not to the present point. *(To* ELIZA*)* Miss Doolittle—

LIZA *(overwhelmed).* Ah-ah-ow-oo!

HIGGINS. There! Thats all youll get out of Eliza. Ah-ah-ow-oo! No use explaining. As a military man you ought to know that. Give her her orders: thats what she wants. Eliza: you are to live here for the next six months, learning how to speak beautifully, like a lady in a florist's shop. If youre good and do whatever youre told, you shall sleep in a proper bedroom, and have lots to eat, and money to buy chocolates and take rides in taxis. If youre naughty and idle you will sleep in the back kitchen among the black beetles, and be walloped by Mrs Pearce with a broomstick. At the end of six months you shall go to Buckingham Palace in a carriage, beautifully dressed. If the King finds out youre not a lady, you will be taken by the police to the Tower of London, where your head will be cut off as a warning to other presumptuous flower girls. If you are not found out, you shall have a present of seven-and-sixpence to start life with as a lady in a shop. If you refuse this offer you will be a most ungrateful and wicked girl; and the angels will weep for you. *(To* PICKERING*)* Now are you satisfied, Pickering? *(To* MRS PEARCE*)* Can I put it more plainly and fairly, Mrs Pearce?

MRS PEARCE *(patiently).* I think youd better let me speak to the girl properly in private. I dont know that I can take charge of her or consent to the arrangement at all. Of course I know you dont mean her any harm; but when you get what you call interested in people's accents, you never think or care what may happen to them or you. Come with me, Eliza.

HIGGINS. Thats all right. Thank you, Mrs Pearce. Bundle her off to the bathroom.

LIZA *(rising reluctantly and suspiciously).* Youre a great bully, you are. I wont stay here if I dont like. I wont let nobody wallop me. I never asked to go to Bucknam Palace, I didnt. I was never in trouble with the police, not me. I'm a good girl—

MRS PEARCE. Dont answer back, girl. You dont understand the gentleman. Come with me. *(She leads the way to the door, and holds it open for* ELIZA).

LIZA *(as she goes out).* Well, what I say is right. I wont go near the King, not if I'm going to have my head cut off. If I'd known what I was letting myself in for, I wouldnt have come here. I always been a good girl; and I never offered to say a word to him; and I dont owe him nothing; and I dont care; and I wont be put upon; and I have my feelings the same as anyone else—

MRS PEARCE *shuts the door; and* ELIZA*'s plaints are no longer audible.*

ELIZA *is taken upstairs to the third floor greatly to her surprise; for she expected to be taken down to the scullery. There* MRS PEARCE *opens a door and takes her into a spare bedroom.*

MRS PEARCE. I will have to put you here. This will be your bedroom.

LIZA. O-h, I couldnt sleep here, missus. It's too good for the likes of me. I should be afraid to touch anything. I aint a duchess yet, you know.

MRS PEARCE. You have got to make yourself

as clean as the room: then you wont be afraid of it. And you must call me Mrs Pearce, not missus. *(She throws open the door of the dress-ingroom, now modernized as a bathroom).*

LIZA. Gawd! whats this? Is this where you wash clothes? Funny sort of copper I call it.

MRS PEARCE. It is not a copper. This is where we wash ourselves, Eliza, and where I am going to wash you.

LIZA. You expect me to get into that and wet myself all over! Not me. I should catch my death. I knew a woman did it every Saturday night; and she died of it.

MRS PEARCE. Mr Higgins has the gentlemen's bathroom downstairs; and he has a bath every morning, in cold water.

LIZA. Ugh! He's made of iron, that man.

MRS PEARCE. If you are to sit with him and the Colonel and be taught you will have to do the same. They wont like the smell of you if you dont. But you can have the water as hot as you like. There are two taps: hot and cold.

LIZA. *(weeping).* I couldnt. I dursnt. Its not natural: it would kill me. Ive never had a bath in my life: not what youd call a proper one.

MRS PEARCE. Well, dont you want to be clean and sweet and decent, like a lady? You know you cant be a nice girl inside if youre a dirty slut outside.

LIZA. Boohoo!!!!

MRS PEARCE. Now stop crying and go back into your room and take off all your clothes. Then wrap yourself in this *(taking down a gown from its peg and handing it to her)* and come back to me. I will get the bath ready.

LIZA *(all tears).* I cant. I wont. I'm not used to it. Ive never took off all my clothes before. It's not right: it's not decent.

MRS PEARCE. Nonsense, child. Dont you take off all your clothes every night when you go to bed?

LIZA *(amazed).* No. Why should I? I should catch my death. Of course I take off my skirt.

MRS PEARCE. Do you mean that you sleep in the underclothes you wear in the daytime?

LIZA. What else have I to sleep in?

MRS PEARCE. You will never do that again as long as you live here. I will get you a proper nightdress.

LIZA. Do you mean change into cold things and lie awake shivering half the night? You want to kill me, you do.

MRS PEARCE. I want to change you from a frowzy slut to a clean respectable girl fit to sit with the gentlemen in the study. Are you going to trust me and do what I tell you or be thrown out and sent back to your flower basket?

LIZA. But you dont know what the cold is to me. You dont know how I dread it.

MRS PEARCE. Your bed wont be cold here: I will put a hot water bottle in it. *(Pushing her into the bedroom)* Off with you and undress.

LIZA. Oh, if only I'd a known what a dreadful thing it is to be clean I'd never have come. I didnt know when I was well off. I—(MRS PEARCE *pushes her through the door, but leaves it partly open lest her prisoner should take to flight).*

MRS PEARCE *puts on a pair of white rubber sleeves, and fills the bath, mixing hot and cold, and testing the result with the bath thermometer. She perfumes it with a handful of bath salts and adds a palmful of mustard. She then takes a formidable looking long handled scrubbing brush and soaps it profusely with a ball of scented soap.*

ELIZA *comes back with nothing on but the bath gown huddled tightly round her, a piteous spectacle of abject terror.*

MRS PEARCE. Now come along. Take that thing off.

LIZA. Oh I couldnt, Mrs Pearce: I reely couldnt. I never done such a thing.

MRS PEARCE. Nonsense. Here: step in and tell me whether its hot enough for you.

LIZA. Ah-oo! Ah-oo! It's too hot.

MRS PEARCE *(deftly snatching the gown away and throwing* ELIZA *down on her back)* It wont hurt you. *(She sets to work with the scrubbing brush).* ELIZA*'s screams are heartrending.*

Meanwhile the Colonel has been having it out with HIGGINS *about* ELIZA. PICKERING *has come from the hearth to the chair and seated himself astride of it with his arms on the back to cross-examine him.*

PICKERING. Excuse the straight question, Higgins. Are you a man of good character where women are concerned?

HIGGINS *(moodily).* Have you ever met a man of good character where women are concerned?

PICKERING. Yes: very frequently.

HIGGINS *(dogmatically, lifting himself on his hands to the level of the piano, and sitting on it with a bounce).* Well, I havnt. I find that the moment I let a woman make friends with me, she becomes jealous, exacting, suspicious, and a damned nuisance. I find that the moment I let myself make friends with a woman, I become selfish and tyrannical. Women upset everything. When you let them into your life, you find that the woman is driving at one thing and youre driving at another.

PICKERING. At what, for example?

HIGGINS *(coming off the piano restlessly).* Oh, Lord knows! I suppose the woman wants to live her own life; and the man wants to live his; and each tries to drag the other on to the wrong track. One wants to go north and the other south; and the result is that both have to go east, though they both hate the east wind. *(He sits down on the bench at the keyboard).* So here I am, a confirmed old bachelor, and likely to remain so.

PICKERING *(rising and standing over him gravely).* Come, Higgins! You know what I mean. If I'm to be in this business I shall feel responsible for that girl. I hope it's understood that no advantage is to be taken of her position.

HIGGINS. What! That thing! Sacred, I assure you. *(Rising to explain)* You see, she'll be a pupil; and teaching would be impossible unless pupils were sacred. Ive taught scores of American millionairesses how to speak English: the best looking women in the world. I'm seasoned. They might as well be blocks of wood. *I* might as well be a block of wood. It's—

MRS PEARCE *opens the door. She has* ELIZA*'s hat in her hand.* PICKERING *retires to the easy-chair at the hearth and sits down.*

HIGGINS *(eagerly).* Well, Mrs Pearce: is it all right?

MRS PEARCE *(at the door).* I just wish to trouble you with a word, if I may, Mr Higgins.

HIGGINS. Yes, certainly. Come in. *(She comes forward).* Dont burn that, Mrs Pearce. I'll keep it as a curiosity. *(He takes the hat).*

MRS PEARCE. Handle it carefully, sir, please. I had to promise her not to burn it; but I had better put it in the oven for a while.

HIGGINS *(putting it down hastily on the piano).* Oh! thank you. Well, what have you to say to me?

PICKERING. Am I in the way?

MRS PEARCE. Not at all, sir. Mr Higgins: will you please be very particular what you say before the girl?

HIGGINS *(sternly).* Of course. I'm always particular about what I say. Why do you say this to me?

MRS PEARCE *(unmoved).* No, sir: youre not at all particular when youve mislaid anything or when you get a little impatient. Now it doesnt matter before me: I'm used to it. But you really must not swear before the girl.

HIGGINS *(indignantly). I* swear! *(Most emphatically).* I never swear. I detest the habit. What the devil do you mean?

MRS PEARCE *(stolidly).* Thats what I mean, sir. You swear a great deal too much. I dont mind your damning and blasting, and what the devil and where the devil and who the devil—

HIGGINS. Mrs Pearce: this language from your lips! Really!

MRS PEARCE *(not to be put off).* —but there is a certain word I must ask you not to use. The girl has just used it herself because the bath was too hot. It begins with the same letter as bath. She knows no better: she learnt it at her mother's knee. But she must not hear it from your lips.

HIGGINS *(loftily).* I cannot charge myself with having ever uttered it, Mrs Pearce. *(She looks at him steadfastly. He adds, hiding an uneasy conscience with a judicial air)* Except perhaps in a moment of extreme and justifiable excitement.

MRS PEARCE. Only this morning, sir, you applied it to your boots, to the butter, and to the brown bread.

HIGGINS. Oh, that! Mere alliteration, Mrs Pearce, natural to a poet.

MRS PEARCE. Well, sir, whatever you choose to call it, I beg you not to let the girl hear you repeat it.

HIGGINS. Oh, very well, very well. Is that all?

MRS PEARCE. No, sir. We shall have to be very particular with this girl as to personal cleanliness.

HIGGINS. Certainly. Quite right. Most important.

MRS PEARCE. I mean not to be slovenly about her dress or untidy in leaving things about.

HIGGINS *(going to her solemnly).* Just so. I intended to call your attention to that. *(He passes on to* PICKERING, *who is enjoying the conversation immensely).* It is these little things that matter, Pickering. Take care of the pence and the pounds will take care of themselves is as true of personal habits as of money. *(He comes to anchor on the hearthrug, with the air of a man in an unassailable position).*

MRS PEARCE. Yes, sir. Then might I ask you not to come down to breakfast in your dressing-gown, or at any rate not to use it as a napkin to the extent you do, sir. And if you would be so good as not to eat everything off the same plate, and to remember not to put the porridge saucepan out of your hand on the clean tablecloth, it would be a better example to the girl. You know you nearly choked yourself with a fishbone in the jam only last week.

HIGGINS *(routed from the hearthrug and drifting back to the piano).* I may do these things sometimes in absence of mind; but surely I dont do them habitually. *(Angrily)* By the way: my dressing-gown smells most damnably of benzine.

MRS PEARCE. No doubt it does, Mr Higgins. But if you will wipe your fingers—

HIGGINS *(yelling).* Oh very well, very well: I'll wipe them in my hair in future.

MRS PEARCE. I hope youre not offended, Mr Higgins.

HIGGINS *(shocked at finding himself thought capable of an unamiable sentiment).* Not at all, not at all. Youre quite right, Mrs Pearce: I shall be particularly careful before the girl. Is that all?

MRS PEARCE. No sir. Might she use some of those Japanese dresses you brought from abroad? I really cant put her back into her old things.

HIGGINS. Certainly. Anything you like. Is that all?

MRS PEARCE. Thank you, sir. Thats all. *(She goes out).*

HIGGINS. You know, Pickering, that woman has the most extraordinary ideas about me. Here I am, a shy, diffident sort of man. Ive never been able to feel really grown-up and tremendous, like other chaps. And yet she's firmly persuaded that I'm an arbitrary overbearing bossing kind of person. I cant account for it.

MRS PEARCE *returns.*

MRS PEARCE. If you please, sir, the trouble's beginning already. Theres a dustman[2] downstairs, Alfred Doolittle, wants to see you. He says you have his daughter here.

PICKERING *(rising).* Phew! I say!

HIGGINS *(promptly).* Send the blackguard up.

MRS PEARCE. Oh, very well, sir. *(She goes out).*

PICKERING. He may not be a blackguard, Higgins.

HIGGINS. Nonsense. Of course he's a blackguard.

PICKERING. Whether he is or not, I'm afraid we shall have some trouble with him.

HIGGINS *(confidently).* Oh no: I think not. If theres any trouble he shall have it with me, not I with him. And we are sure to get something interesting out of him.

PICKERING. About the girl?

HIGGINS. No. I mean his dialect.

PICKERING. Oh!

MRS PEARCE *(at the door).* Doolittle, sir. *(She admits* DOOLITTLE *and retires).*

ALFRED DOOLITTLE *is an elderly but vigorous dustman, clad in the costume of his profession, including a hat with a black brim covering his neck and shoulders. He has well marked and rather interesting features, and seems equally free from fear and conscience. He has a remarkably expressive voice, the result of a habit of giving vent to his feelings without reserve. His present pose is that of wounded honor and stern resolution.*

DOOLITTLE *(at the door, uncertain which of the two gentlemen is his man).* Professor Iggins?

HIGGINS. Here. Good morning. Sit down.

DOOLITTLE. Morning, Governor. *(He sits down magisterially)* I come about a very serious matter, Governor.

HIGGINS *(to* PICKERING*).* Brought up in Hounslow. Mother Welsh, I should think. *(*DOOLITTLE *opens his mouth, amazed.* HIGGINS *continues)* What do you want, Doolittle?

2. ***dustman,*** trash or garbage collector.

DOOLITTLE *(menacingly).* I want my daughter: thats what I want. See?

HIGGINS. Of course you do. Youre her father, arnt you? You dont suppose anyone else wants her, do you? I'm glad to see you have some spark of family feeling left. She's upstairs. Take her away at once.

DOOLITTLE *(rising, fearfully taken aback).* What!

HIGGINS. Take her away. Do you suppose I'm going to keep your daughter for you?

DOOLITTLE *(remonstrating).* Now, now, look here, Governor. Is this reasonable? Is it fairity to take advantage of a man like this? The girl belongs to me. You got her. Where do I come in? *(He sits down again).*

HIGGINS. Your daughter had the audacity to come to my house and ask me to teach her how to speak properly so that she could get a place in a flower-shop. This gentleman and my housekeeper have been here all the time. *(Bullying him)* How dare you come here and attempt to blackmail me? You sent her here on purpose.

DOOLITTLE *(protesting).* No, Governor.

HIGGINS. You must have. How else could you possibly know that she is here?

DOOLITTLE. Dont take a man up like that, Governor.

HIGGINS. The police shall take you up. This is a plant—a plot to extort money by threats. I shall telephone for the police. *(He goes resolutely to the telephone and opens the directory).*

DOOLITTLE. Have I asked you for a brass farthing? I leave it to the gentleman here: have I said a word about money?

HIGGINS *(throwing the book aside and marching down on* DOOLITTLE *with a poser).* What else did you come for?

DOOLITTLE *(sweetly).* Well, what would a man come for? Be human, Governor.

HIGGINS *(disarmed).* Alfred: did you put her up to it?

DOOLITTLE. So help me, Governor, I never did. I take my Bible oath I aint seen the girl these two months past.

HIGGINS. Then how did you know she was here?

DOOLITTLE *("most musical, most melancholy"[3]).* I'll tell you, Governor, if you'll only let me get a word in. I'm willing to tell you. I'm wanting to tell you. I'm waiting to tell you.

HIGGINS. Pickering: this chap has a certain natural gift of rhetoric. Observe the rhythm of his native woodnotes wild. "I'm willing to tell you: I'm wanting to tell you: I'm waiting to tell you." Sentimental rhetoric! thats the Welsh strain in him. It also accounts for his mendacity and dishonesty.

PICKERING. Oh, please, Higgins: I'm west country myself. *(To* DOOLITTLE*)* How did you know the girl was here if you didnt send her?

DOOLITTLE. It was like this, Governor. The girl took a boy in the taxi to give him a jaunt. Son of her landlady, he is. He hung about on the chance of her giving him another ride home. Well, she sent him back for her luggage when she heard you was willing for her to stop here. I met the boy at the corner of Long Acre and Endell Street.

HIGGINS. Public house. Yes?

DOOLITTLE. The poor man's club, Governor: why shouldnt I?

PICKERING. Do let him tell his story, Higgins.

DOOLITTLE. He told me what was up. And I ask you, what was my feelings and my duty as a father? I says to the boy, "You bring me the luggage," I says—

PICKERING. Why didnt you go for it yourself?

DOOLITTLE. Landlady wouldnt have trusted me with it, Governor. She's that kind of woman: you know. I had to give the boy a penny afore he trusted me with it, the little swine. I brought it to her just to oblige you like, and make myself agreeable. Thats all.

HIGGINS. How much luggage?

DOOLITTLE. Musical instrument, Governor. A few pictures, a trifle of jewelry, and a birdcage. She said she didnt want no clothes. What was I to think from that, Governor? I ask you as a parent what was I to think?

HIGGINS. So you came to rescue her from worse than death, eh?

DOOLITTLE *(appreciatively: relieved at being so well understood).* Just so, Governor. Thats right.

PICKERING. But why did you bring her luggage if you intended to take her away?

---

3. ***most . . . melancholy,*** line 62 from Milton's "Il Penseroso."

The Bettman Archive, Inc.

DOOLITTLE. Have I said a word about taking her away? Have I now?

HIGGINS *(determinedly).* Youre going to take her away, double quick. *(He crosses to the hearth and rings the bell).*

DOOLITTLE *(rising).* No, Governor. Dont say that. I'm not the man to stand in my girl's light. Heres a career opening for her, as you might say; and—

MRS PEARCE *opens the door and awaits orders.*

HIGGINS. Mrs Pearce: this is Eliza's father. He has come to take her away. Give her to him. *(He goes back to the piano, with an air of washing his hands of the whole affair).*

DOOLITTLE. No. This is a misunderstanding. Listen here—

MRS PEARCE. He cant take her away, Mr Higgins: how can he? You told me to burn her clothes.

DOOLITTLE. Thats right. I cant carry the girl through the streets like a blooming monkey, can I? I put it to you.

HIGGINS. You have put it to me that you want your daughter. Take your daughter. If she has no clothes go out and buy her some.

DOOLITTLE *(desperate).* Wheres the clothes she come in? Did I burn them or did your missus here?

MRS PEARCE. I am the housekeeper, if you please. I have sent for some clothes for your girl. When they come you can take her away. You can wait in the kitchen. This way, please.

DOOLITTLE, *much troubled, accompanies her to the door; then hesitates; finally turns confidently to* HIGGINS.

DOOLITTLE. Listen here, Governor. You and me is men of the world, aint we?

HIGGINS. Oh! Men of the world, are we? Youd better go, Mrs Pearce.

MRS PEARCE. I think so, indeed, sir. *(She goes, with dignity).*

PICKERING. The floor is yours, Mr Doolittle.

DOOLITTLE *(to* PICKERING*).* I thank you, Governor. *(To* HIGGINS, *who takes refuge on the* *piano bench, a little overwhelmed by the proximity of his visitor; for* DOOLITTLE *has a professional flavor of dust about him).* Well, the truth is, Ive taken a sort of fancy to you, Governor; and if you want the girl, I'm not so set on having her back home again but what I might be open to an arrangement. Regarded in the light of a young woman, she's a fine handsome girl. As a daughter she's not worth her keep; and so I tell you straight. All I ask is my rights as a father; and youre the last man alive to expect me to let her go for nothing; for I can see youre one of the straight sort, Governor. Well, whats a five-pound note to you? And whats Eliza to me? *(He returns to his chair and sits down judicially).*

PICKERING. I think you ought to know, Doolittle, that Mr. Higgins's intentions are entirely honorable.

DOOLITTLE. Course they are, Governor. If I thought they wasnt, I'd ask fifty.

HIGGINS *(revolted).* Do you mean to say that you would sell your daughter for £50?

DOOLITTLE. Not in a general way I wouldnt; but to oblige a gentleman like you I'd do a good deal, I do assure you.

PICKERING. Have you no morals, man?

DOOLITTLE *(unabashed).* Cant afford them, Governor. Neither could you if you was as poor as me. Not that I mean any harm, you know. But if Liza is going to have a bit out of this, why not me too?

HIGGINS *(troubled).* I dont know what to do, Pickering. There can be no question that as a matter of morals it's a positive crime to give this chap a farthing. And yet I feel a sort of rough justice in his claim.

DOOLITTLE. Thats it, Governor. Thats all I say. A father's heart, as it were.

PICKERING. Well, I know the feeling; but really it seems hardly right—

DOOLITTLE. Dont say that, Governor. Dont look at it that way. What am I, Governors both? I ask you, what am I? I'm one of the undeserving poor: thats what I am. Think of what that means to a man. It means that he's up agen middle class morality all the time. If theres anything going, and I put in for a bit of it, it's always the same story: "Youre undeserving; so you cant have it." But my needs is as great as the most deserving widow's that ever got money out of six different charities in one week for the death of the same husband. I dont need less than a deserving man: I need more. I dont eat less hearty than him; and I drink a lot more. I want a bit of amusement, cause I'm a thinking man. I want cheerfulness and a song and a band when I feel low. Well, they charge me just the same for everything as they charge the deserving. What is middle class morality? Just an excuse for never giving me anything. Therefore, I ask you, as two gentlemen, not to play that game on me. I'm playing straight with you. I aint pretending to be deserving. I'm undeserving; and I mean to go on being undeserving. I like it; and thats the truth. Will you take advantage of a man's nature to do him out of the price of his own daughter what he's brought up and fed and clothed by the sweat of his brow until she's growed big enough to be interesting to you two gentlemen? Is five pounds unreasonable? I put it to you; and I leave it to you.

HIGGINS *(rising, and going over to* PICKERING*).* Pickering: if we were to take this man in hand for three months, he could choose between a seat in the Cabinet and a popular pulpit in Wales.

PICKERING. What do you say to that, Doolittle?

DOOLITTLE. Not me, Governor, thank you kindly. Ive heard all the preachers and all the prime ministers—for I'm a thinking man and game for politics or religion or social reform same as all the other amusements—and I tell you it's a dog's life any way you look at it. Undeserving poverty is my line. Taking one station in society with another, it's—it's—well, it's the only one that has any ginger in it, to my taste.

HIGGINS. I suppose we must give him a fiver.

PICKERING. He'll make a bad use of it, I'm afraid.

DOOLITTLE. Not me, Governor, so help me I wont. Dont you be afraid that I'll save it and spare it and live idle on it. There wont be a penny of it left by Monday: I'll have to go to work same as if I'd never had it. It wont pauperize me, you bet. Just one good spree for myself and the missus, giving pleasure to ourselves and employment to others, and satisfaction to you to think it's not been throwed away. You couldnt spend it better.

HIGGINS *(taking out his pocket book and coming between* DOOLITTLE *and the piano).* This is irresistible. Lets give him ten. *(He offers two notes to the dustman).*

DOOLITTLE. No, Governor. She wouldnt have the heart to spend ten; and perhaps I shouldnt neither. Ten pounds is a lot of money: it makes a man feel prudent like; and then goodbye to happiness. You give me what I ask you, Governor: not a penny more, and not a penny less.

PICKERING. Why dont you marry that missus of yours? I rather draw the line at encouraging that sort of immorality.

DOOLITTLE. Tell her so, Governor; tell her so. I'm willing. It's me that suffers by it. Ive no hold on her. I got to be agreeable to her. I got to give her presents. I got to buy her clothes something sinful. I'm a slave to that woman, Governor, just because I'm not her lawful husband. And she knows it too. Catch her marrying me! Take my advice, Governor: marry Eliza while she's young and dont know no better. If you dont youll be sorry for it after. If you do, she'll be sorry for it after; but better her than you, because youre a man, and she's only a woman and dont know how to be happy anyhow.

HIGGINS. Pickering: if we listen to this man another minute, we shall have no convictions left. *(To* DOOLITTLE*)* Five pounds I think you said.

DOOLITTLE. Thank you kindly, Governor.

HIGGINS. Youre sure you wont take ten?

DOOLITTLE. Not now. Another time, Governor.

HIGGINS *(handing him a five-pound note).* Here you are.

DOOLITTLE. Thank you, Governor. Good morning. *(He hurries to the door, anxious to get away with his booty. When he opens it he is confronted with a dainty and exquisitely clean young Japanese lady in a simple blue cotton kimono printed cunningly with small white jasmine blossoms.* MRS PEARCE *is with her. He gets out of her way deferentially and apologizes).* Beg pardon, miss.

THE JAPANESE LADY. Garn! Dont you know your own daughter?

DOOLITTLE	*exclaiming*	Bly me! it's Eliza!
HIGGINS	*simultaneously*	Whats that! This!
PICKERING		By Jove!

LIZA. Dont I look silly?

HIGGINS. Silly?

MRS PEARCE *(at the door).* Now Mr. Higgins, please dont say anything to make the girl conceited about herself.

HIGGINS *(conscientiously).* Oh! Quite right, Mrs Pearce. *(To* ELIZA*)* Yes: damned silly.

MRS PEARCE. Please, sir.

HIGGINS *(correcting himself).* I mean extremely silly.

LIZA. I should look all right with my hat on. *(She takes up her hat; puts it on; and walks across the room to the fireplace with a fashionable air).*

HIGGINS. A new fashion, by George! And it ought to look horrible!

DOOLITTLE *(with fatherly pride).* Well, I never thought she'd clean up as good looking as that, Governor. She's a credit to me, aint she?

LIZA. I tell you, it's easy to clean up here. Hot and cold water on tap, just as much as you like, there is. Woolly towels, there is; and a towel horse so hot, it burns your fingers. Soft brushes to scrub yourself, and a wooden bowl of soap smelling like primroses. Now I know why ladies is so clean. Washing's a treat for them. Wish they saw what it is for the like of me!

HIGGINS. I'm glad the bathroom met with your approval.

LIZA. It didnt: not all of it; and I dont care who hears me say it. Mrs Pearce knows.

HIGGINS. What was wrong, Mrs Pearce?

MRS PEARCE *(blandly).* Oh, nothing, sir. It doesnt matter.

LIZA. I had a good mind to break it. I didnt know which way to look. But I hung a towel over it, I did.

HIGGINS. Over what?

MRS PEARCE. Over the looking glass, sir.

HIGGINS. Doolittle: you have brought your daughter up too strictly.

DOOLITTLE. Me! I never brought her up at all, except to give her a lick of a strap now and again. Dont put it on me, Governor. She aint accustomed to it, you see: thats all. But she'll soon pick up your free-and-easy ways.

LIZA. I'm a good girl, I am; and I wont pick up no free-and-easy ways.

HIGGINS. Eliza: if you say again that youre a good girl, your father shall take you home.

LIZA. Not him. You dont know my father. All he come here for was to touch you for some money to get drunk on.

DOOLITTLE. Well, what else would I want money for? To put into the plate in church, I suppose. *(She puts out her tongue at him. He is so incensed by this that* PICKERING *presently finds it necessary to step between them).* Dont you give me none of your lip; and dont let me hear you giving this gentleman any of it neither, or youll hear from me about it. See?

HIGGINS. Have you any further advice to give her before you go, Doolittle? Your blessing, for instance.

DOOLITTLE. No, Governor, I aint such a mug as to put up my children to all I know myself. Hard enough to hold them in without that. If you want Eliza's mind improved, Governor, you do it yourself with a strap. So long, gentlemen. *(He turns to go).*

HIGGINS *(impressively).* Stop. Youll come regularly to see your daughter. It's your duty, you know. My brother is a clergyman; and he could help you in your talks with her.

DOOLITTLE *(evasively).* Certainly. I'll come, Governor. Not just this week, because I have a job at a distance. But later on you may depend on me. Afternoon, gentlemen. Afternoon, maam. *(He takes off his hat to* MRS PEARCE, *who disdains the salutation and goes out. He winks at* HIGGINS, *thinking him probably a fellow-sufferer from* MRS PEARCE*'s difficult disposition, and follows her).*

LIZA. Dont you believe the old liar. He'd as soon you set a bull-dog on him as a clergyman. You wont see him again in a hurry.

HIGGINS. I dont want to, Eliza. Do you?

LIZA. Not me. I dont want never to see him again, I dont. He's a disgrace to me, he is, collecting dust, instead of working at his trade.

PICKERING. What is his trade, Eliza?

LIZA. Taking money out of other people's pockets into his own. His proper trade's a navvy;[4] and he works at it sometimes too—for exercise—and earns good money at it. Aint you going to call me Miss Doolittle any more?

PICKERING. I beg your pardon, Miss Doolittle. It was a slip of the tongue.

LIZA. Oh, I dont mind; only it sounded so genteel. I should just like to take a taxi to the corner of Tottenham Court Road and get out there and tell it to wait for me, just to put the girls in their place a bit. I wouldnt speak to them, you know.

PICKERING. Better wait til we get you something really fashionable.

HIGGINS. Besides, you shouldnt cut your old friends now that you have risen in the world. Thats what we call snobbery.

LIZA. You dont call the like of them my friends now, I should hope. Theyve took it out of me often enough with their ridicule when they had the chance; and now I mean to get a bit of my own back. But if I'm to have fashionable clothes, I'll wait. I should like to have some. Mrs Pearce says youre going to give me some to wear in bed at night different to what I wear in the daytime; but it do seem a waste of money when you could get something to shew. Besides, I never could fancy changing into cold things on a winter night.

MRS PEARCE *(coming back).* Now, Eliza. The new things have come for you to try on.

LIZA. Ah-ow-oo-ooh! *(She rushes out).*

MRS PEARCE *(following her).* Oh, dont rush about like that, girl. *(She shuts the door behind her).*

HIGGINS. Pickering: we have taken on a stiff job.

PICKERING *(with conviction).* Higgins: we have.

There seems to be some curiosity as to what HIGGINS*'s lessons to* ELIZA *were like. Well, here is a sample: the first one.*

Picture ELIZA, *in her new clothes, and feeling her inside put out of step by a lunch, dinner, and breakfast of a kind to which it is unaccustomed, seated with* HIGGINS *and the Colonel in the study, feeling like a hospital out-patient at a first encounter with the doctors.*

HIGGINS, *constitutionally unable to sit still, discomposes her still more by striding restlessly*

4. ***navvy,*** unskilled laborer, especially one doing excavation or construction work.

about. But for the reassuring presence and quietude of her friend the Colonel she would run for her life, even back to Drury Lane.

HIGGINS. Say your alphabet.

LIZA. I know my alphabet. Do you think I know nothing? I dont need to be taught like a child.

HIGGINS *(thundering).* Say your alphabet.

PICKERING. Say it, Miss Doolittle. You will understand presently. Do what he tells you; and let him teach you in his own way.

LIZA. Oh well, if you put it like that—Ahyee, bəyee, cəyee, dəyee—

HIGGINS *(with the roar of a wounded lion).* Stop. Listen to this, Pickering. This is what we pay for as elementary education. This unfortunate animal has been locked up for nine years in school at our expense to teach her to speak and read the language of Shakespear and Milton. And the result is Ahyee, Bə-yee, Cə-yee, Də-yee. *(To Eliza)* Say A, B, C, D.

LIZA *(almost in tears).* But I'm sayin it. Ahyee, Bəyee, Cə-yee—

HIGGINS. Stop. Say a cup of tea.

LIZA. A cappətə-ee.

HIGGINS. Put your tongue forward until it squeezes against the top of your lower teeth. Now say cup.

LIZA. C-c-c—I cant. C-Cup.

PICKERING. Good. Splendid, Miss Doolittle.

HIGGINS. By Jupiter, she's done it at the first shot. Pickering: we shall make a duchess of her. *(To Eliza)* Now do you think you could possibly say tea? Not tə-yee, mind: if you ever say bə-yee cə-yee də-yee again you shall be dragged round the room three times by the hair of your head. *(Fortissimo)* T, T, T, T.

LIZA *(weeping).* I cant hear no difference cep that it sounds more genteel-like when you say it.

HIGGINS. Well, if you can hear that difference, what the devil are you crying for? Pickering: give her a chocolate.

PICKERING. No, no. Never mind crying a little, Miss Doolittle: you are doing very well; and the lessons wont hurt. I promise you I wont let him drag you round the room by your hair.

HIGGINS. Be off with you to Mrs Pearce and tell her about it. Think about it. Try to do it by yourself: and keep your tongue well forward in your mouth instead of trying to roll it up and swallow it. Another lesson at half-past four this afternoon. Away with you.

ELIZA, *still sobbing, rushes from the room.*

And that is the sort of ordeal poor ELIZA *has to go through for months before we meet her again on her first appearance in London society of the professional class.*

Act Three

It is MRS HIGGINS*'s at-home day. Nobody has yet arrived. Her drawing room, in a flat on Chelsea Embankment,*[1] *has three windows looking on the river; and the ceiling is not so lofty as it would be in an older house of the same pretension. The windows are open, giving access to a balcony with flowers in pots. If you stand with your face to the windows, you have the fireplace on your left and the door in the right-hand wall close to the corner nearest the windows.*

MRS HIGGINS *was brought up on Morris and Burne-Jones;*[2] *and her room, which is very unlike her son's room in Wimpole Street, is not crowded with furniture and little tables and nicknacks. In the middle of the room there is a big ottoman; and this, with the carpet, the Morris wall-papers, and the Morris chintz window curtains and brocade covers of the ottoman and its cushions, supply all the ornament, and are much too handsome to be hidden by odds and ends of useless things. A few good oil-paintings from the exhibitions in the Grosvenor Gallery thirty years ago (the Burne-Jones, not the Whistler side of them) are on the walls. The only landscape is a Cecil Lawson on the scale of a Rubens. There is a portrait of* MRS HIGGINS *as she was when she defied fashion in her youth in one of the beautiful Rossettian costumes which, when caricatured by people who did not understand, led to the absurdities of popular estheticism in the eighteen-seventies.*

---

1. ***Chelsea Embankment.*** Chelsea is a pleasant residential district along the bank of the Thames.
2. ***Morris and Burne-Jones.*** William Morris (1834–1896) and Edward Coley Burne-Jones (1833–1898) were members of a decorating firm noted for fine carvings, stained glass, metalwork, paper hangings, chintzes and carpets.

In the corner diagonally opposite the door MRS HIGGINS, *now over sixty and long past taking the trouble to dress out of the fashion, sits writing at an elegantly simple writing-table with a bell button within reach of her hand. There is a Chippendale chair further back in the room between her and the window nearest her side. At the other side of the room, further forward, is an Elizabethan chair roughly carved in the taste of Inigo Jones. On the same side a piano in a decorated case. The corner between the fireplace and the window is occupied by a divan cushioned in Morris chintz.*

It is between four and five in the afternoon.

The door is opened violently; and HIGGINS *enters with his hat on.*

MRS HIGGINS *(dismayed).* Henry *(scolding him)*! What are you doing here to-day? It is my at-home day: you promised not to come. *(As he bends to kiss her, she takes his hat off, and presents it to him).*

HIGGINS. Oh bother! *(He throws the hat down on the table).*

MRS HIGGINS. Go home at once.

HIGGINS *(kissing her).* I know, mother. I came on purpose.

MRS HIGGINS. But you mustnt. I'm serious, Henry. You offend all my friends: they stop coming whenever they meet you.

HIGGINS. Nonsense! I know I have no small talk; but people dont mind. *(He sits on the settee).*

MRS HIGGINS. Oh! dont they? Small talk indeed! What about your large talk? Really, dear, you mustnt stay.

HIGGINS. I must. Ive a job for you. A phonetic job.

MRS HIGGINS. No use, dear. I'm sorry; but I cant get round your vowels; and though I like to get pretty postcards in your patent shorthand, I always have to read the copies in ordinary writing you so thoughtfully send me.

HIGGINS. Well, this isnt a phonetic job.

MRS HIGGINS. You said it was.

HIGGINS. Not your part of it. Ive picked up a girl.

MRS HIGGINS. Does that mean that some girl has picked you up?

HIGGINS. Not at all. I dont mean a love affair.

MRS HIGGINS. What a pity!

HIGGINS. Why?

MRS HIGGINS. Well, you never fall in love with anyone under forty-five. When will you discover that there are some rather nice-looking young women about?

HIGGINS. Oh, I cant be bothered with young women. My idea of a lovable woman is something as like you as possible. I shall never get into the way of seriously liking young women: some habits lie too deep to be changed. *(Rising abruptly and walking about, jingling his money and his keys in his trouser pockets)* Besides, theyre all idiots.

MRS HIGGINS. Do you know what you would do if you really loved me, Henry?

HIGGINS. Oh bother! What? Marry, I suppose?

MRS HIGGINS. No. Stop fidgeting and take your hands out of your pockets.
(With a gesture of despair, he obeys and sits down again). Thats a good boy. Now tell me about the girl.

HIGGINS. She's coming to see you.

MRS HIGGINS. I dont remember asking her.

HIGGINS. You didnt. *I* asked her. If youd known her you wouldnt have asked her.

MRS HIGGINS. Indeed! Why?

HIGGINS. Well, it's like this. She's a common flower girl. I picked her off the kerbstone.

MRS HIGGINS. And invited her to my at-home!

HIGGINS *(rising and coming to her to coax her).* Oh, thatll be all right. Ive taught her to speak properly; and she has strict orders as to her behavior. She's to keep to two subjects: the weather and everybody's health—Fine day and How do you do, you know—and not to let herself go on things in general. That will be safe.

MRS HIGGINS. Safe! To talk about our health! about our insides! perhaps about our outsides! How could you be so silly, Henry?

HIGGINS *(impatiently).* Well, she must talk about something. *(He controls himself and sits down again).* Oh, she'll be all right: dont you fuss. Pickering is in it with me. Ive a sort of bet on that I'll pass her off as a duchess in six months. I started on her some months ago; and she's getting on like a house on fire. I shall win my bet. She has a quick ear; and she's been easier to teach than my middle class pupils because she's had to learn a complete new language. She talks English almost as you talk French.

MRS HIGGINS. Thats satisfactory, at all events.

HIGGINS. Well, it is and it isnt.

MRS HIGGINS. What does that mean?

HIGGINS. You see, Ive got her pronunciation all right; but you have to consider not only how a girl pronounces, but what she pronounces; and thats where—

They are interrupted by the parlor-maid, announcing guests.

THE PARLOR-MAID. Mrs and Miss Eynsford Hill. *(She withdraws).*

HIGGINS. Oh Lord! *(He rises; snatches his hat from the table; and makes for the door; but before he reaches it his mother introduces him).*

MRS *and* MISS EYNSFORD HILL *are the mother and daughter who sheltered from the rain in Covent Garden. The mother is well bred, quiet, and has the habitual anxiety of straitened means. The daughter has acquired a gay air of being very much at home in society: the bravado of genteel poverty.*

MRS EYNSFORD HILL *(to* MRS HIGGINS*).* How do you do? *(They shake hands).*

MISS EYNSFORD HILL. How d'you do? *(She shakes).*

MRS HIGGINS *(introducing).* My son Henry.

MRS EYNSFORD HILL. Your celebrated son! I have so longed to meet you, Professor Higgins.

HIGGINS *(glumly, making no movement in her direction).* Delighted. *(He backs against the piano and bows brusquely).*

MISS EYNSFORD HILL *(going to him with confident familiarity).* How do you do?

HIGGINS *(staring at her).* Ive seen you before somewhere. I havnt the ghost of a notion where; but Ive heard your voice. *(Drearily)* It doesnt matter. Youd better sit down.

MRS HIGGINS. I'm sorry to say that my celebrated son has no manners. You mustnt mind him.

MISS EYNSFORD HILL *(gaily).* I dont. *(She sits in the Elizabethan chair).*

MRS EYNSFORD HILL *(a little bewildered).* Not at all. *(She sits on the ottoman between her daughter and* MRS HIGGINS, *who has turned her chair away from the writing-table).*

HIGGINS. Oh, have I been rude? I didnt mean to be.

He goes to the central window, through which, with his back to the company, he contemplates the river and the flowers in Battersea Park on the opposite bank as if they were a frozen desert.

The parlor-maid returns, ushering in PICKERING.

THE PARLOR-MAID. Colonel Pickering. *(She withdraws).*

PICKERING. How do you do, Mrs Higgins?

MRS HIGGINS. So glad youve come. Do you know Mrs Eynsford Hill—Miss Eynsford Hill? *(Exchange of bows. The Colonel brings the Chippendale chair a little forward between* MRS HILL *and* MRS HIGGINS, *and sits down).*

PICKERING. Has Henry told you what weve come for?

HIGGINS *(over his shoulder).* We were interrupted: damn it!

MRS HIGGINS. Oh Henry, Henry, really!

MRS EYNSFORD HILL *(half rising).* Are we in the way?

MRS HIGGINS *(rising and making her sit down again).* No, no. You couldnt have come more fortunately: we want you to meet a friend of ours.

HIGGINS *(turning hopefully).* Yes, by George! We want two or three people. Youll do as well as anybody else.

The parlor-maid returns, ushering FREDDY.

THE PARLOR-MAID. Mr Eynsford Hill.

HIGGINS *(almost audibly, past endurance).* God of Heaven! another of them.

FREDDY *(shaking hands with* MRS HIGGINS). Ahdedo?

MRS HIGGINS. Very good of you to come. *(Introducing)* Colonel Pickering.

FREDDY *(bowing).* Ahdedo?

MRS HIGGINS. I dont think you know my son, Professor Higgins.

FREDDY *(going to* HIGGINS*).* Ahdedo?

HIGGINS *(looking at him much as if he were a pickpocket).* I'll take my oath Ive met you before somewhere. Where was it?

FREDDY. I dont think so.

HIGGINS *(resignedly).* It dont matter, anyhow. Sit down. *He shakes* FREDDY*'s hand, and almost slings him on to the ottoman with his face to the windows; then comes round to the other side of it.*

HIGGINS. Well, here we are, anyhow! *(He sits down on the ottoman next* MRS EYNSFORD HILL, *on her left).* And now, what the devil are we going to talk about until Eliza comes?

MRS HIGGINS. Henry: you are the life and soul of the Royal Society's soirees; but really youre rather trying on more commonplace occasions.

HIGGINS. Am I? Very sorry. *(Beaming suddenly)* I suppose I am, you know. *(Uproariously)* Ha, ha!

MISS EYNSFORD HILL *(who considers* HIGGINS *quite eligible matrimonially).* I sympathize. *I* havnt any small talk. If people would only be frank and say what they really think!

HIGGINS *(relapsing into gloom).* Lord forbid!

MRS EYNSFORD HILL *(taking up her daughter's cue).* But why?

HIGGINS. What they think they ought to think is bad enough, Lord knows; but what they really think would break up the whole show. Do you suppose it would be really agreeable if I were to come out now with what *I* really think?

MISS EYNSFORD HILL *(gaily).* Is it so very cynical?

HIGGINS. Cynical! Who the dickens said it was cynical? I mean it wouldnt be decent.

MRS EYNSFORD HILL *(seriously).* Oh! I'm sure you dont mean that, Mr Higgins.

HIGGINS. You see, we're all savages, more or less. We're supposed to be civilized and cultured—to know all about poetry and philosophy and art and science, and so on; but how many of us know even the meanings of these names? *(To* MISS HILL*)* What do you know of poetry? *(To* MRS HILL*)* What do you know of science? *(Indicating* FREDDY*)* What does he know of art or science or anything else? What the devil do you imagine I know of philosophy?

MRS HIGGINS *(warningly).* Or of manners, Henry?

THE PARLOR-MAID *(opening the door).* Miss Doolittle. *(She withdraws).*

HIGGINS *(rising hastily and running to* MRS HIGGINS*).* Here she is, mother. *(He stands on tiptoe and makes signs over his mother's head to* ELIZA *to indicate to her which lady is her hostess).*

ELIZA, *who is exquisitely dressed, produces an impression of such remarkable distinction and beauty as she enters that they all rise, quite fluttered. Guided by* HIGGINS*'s signals, she comes to* MRS HIGGINS *with studied grace.*

LIZA *(speaking with pedantic correctness of pronunciation and great beauty of tone).* How do you do, Mrs Higgins? *(She gasps slightly in making sure of the H in* HIGGINS, *but is quite successful).* Mr Higgins told me I might come.

MRS HIGGINS *(cordially).* Quite right: I'm very glad indeed to see you.

PICKERING. How do you do, Miss Doolittle?

LIZA *(shaking hands with him).* Colonel Pickering, is it not?

Culver Pictures

MRS EYNSFORD HILL. I feel sure we have met before, Miss Doolittle. I remember your eyes.

LIZA. How do you do? *(She sits down on the ottoman gracefully in the place just left vacant by* HIGGINS*).*

MRS EYNSFORD HILL *(introducing).* My daughter Clara.

LIZA. How do you do?

CLARA *(impulsively).* How do you do? *(She sits down on the ottoman beside* ELIZA, *devouring her with her eyes).*

FREDDY *(coming to their side of the ottoman).* Ive certainly had the pleasure.

MRS EYNSFORD HILL *(introducing).* My son Freddy.

LIZA. How do you do?

FREDDY *bows and sits down in the Elizabethan chair, infatuated.*

HIGGINS *(suddenly).* By George, yes: it all comes back to me! *(They stare at him).* Covent Garden! *(Lamentably)* What a damned thing!

MRS HIGGINS. Henry, please! *(He is about to sit on the edge of the table)* Dont sit on my writing-table: youll break it.

HIGGINS *(sulkily).* Sorry.

He goes to the divan, stumbling into the fender

and over the fire-irons on his way; extricating himself with muttered imprecations; and finishing his disastrous journey by throwing himself so impatiently on the divan that he almost breaks it. MRS HIGGINS *looks at him, but controls herself and says nothing.*

A long and painful pause ensues.

MRS HIGGINS *(at last, conversationally).* Will it rain, do you think?

LIZA. The shallow depression in the west of these islands is likely to move slowly in an easterly direction. There are no indications of any great change in the barometrical situation.

FREDDY. Ha! ha! how awfully funny!

LIZA. What is wrong with that, young man? I bet I got it right.

FREDDY. Killing!

MRS EYNSFORD HILL. I'm sure I hope it wont turn cold. Theres so much influenza about. It runs right through our whole family regularly every spring.

LIZA *(darkly).* My aunt died of influenza: so they said.

MRS EYNSFORD HILL *(clicks her tongue sympathetically)*!!!

LIZA *(in the same tragic tone).* But it's my belief they done the old woman in.

MRS HIGGINS *(puzzled).* Done her in?

LIZA. Y-e-e-e-es, Lord love you! Why should she die of influenza? She come through diphtheria right enough the year before. I saw her with my own eyes. Fairly blue with it, she was. They all thought she was dead; but my father he kept ladling gin down her throat til she came to so sudden that she bit the bowl off the spoon.

MRS EYNSFORD HILL *(startled).* Dear me!

LIZA *(piling up the indictment).* What call would a woman with that strength in her have to die of influenza? What become of her new straw hat that should have come to me? Somebody pinched it; and what I say is, them as pinched it done her in.

MRS EYNSFORD HILL. What does doing her in mean?

HIGGINS *(hastily).* Oh, thats the new small talk. To do a person in means to kill them.

MRS EYNSFORD HILL *(to* ELIZA, *horrified).* You surely dont believe that your aunt was killed?

LIZA. Do I not! Them she lived with would have killed her for a hat-pin, let alone a hat.

MRS EYNSFORD HILL. But it cant have been right for your father to pour spirits down her throat like that. It might have killed her.

LIZA. Not her. Gin was mother's milk to her. Besides, he'd poured so much down his own throat that he knew the good of it.

MRS EYNSFORD HILL. Do you mean that he drank?

LIZA. Drank! My word! Something chronic.

MRS EYNSFORD HILL. How dreadful for you!

LIZA. Not a bit. It never did him no harm what I could see. But then he did not keep it up regular. *(Cheerfully)* On the burst, as you might say, from time to time. And always more agreeable when he had a drop in. When he was out of work, my mother used to give him fourpence and tell him to go out and not come back until he'd drunk himself cheerful and loving-like. Theres lots of women has to make their husbands drunk to make them fit to live with. *(Now quite at her ease)* You see, it's like this. If a man has a bit of a conscience, it always takes him when he's sober; and then it makes him low-spirited. A drop of booze just takes that off and makes him happy. *(To* FREDDY, *who is in convulsions of suppressed laughter)* Here! what are you sniggering at?

FREDDY. The new small talk. You do it so awfully well.

LIZA. If I was doing it proper, what was you laughing at? *(To* HIGGINS*)* Have I said anything I oughtnt?

MRS HIGGINS *(interposing).* Not at all, Miss Doolittle.

LIZA. Well, thats a mercy, anyhow. *(Expansively)* What I always say is—

HIGGINS *(rising and looking at his watch).* Ahem!

LIZA *(looking round at him; taking the hint; and rising).* Well: I must go. *(They all rise,* FREDDY *goes to the door).* So pleased to have met you. Goodbye. *(She shakes hands with* MRS HIGGINS*).*

MRS HIGGINS. Goodbye.

LIZA. Goodbye, Colonel Pickering.

PICKERING. Goodbye, Miss Doolittle. *(They shake hands).*

LIZA *(nodding to the others).* Goodbye, all.

FREDDY *(opening the door for her).* Are you walking across the Park, Miss Doolittle? If so—

LIZA. Walk! Not bloody likely. *(Sensation).* I am going in a taxi. *(She goes out).*

PICKERING *gasps and sits down.* FREDDY *goes out on the balcony to catch another glimpse of* ELIZA.

MRS EYNSFORD HILL *(suffering from shock).* Well, I really cant get used to the new ways.

CLARA *(throwing herself discontentedly into the Elizabethan chair).* Oh, it's all right, mamma, quite right. People will think we never go anywhere or see anybody if you are so old-fashioned.

MRS EYNSFORD HILL. I daresay I am very old-fashioned; but I do hope you wont begin using that expression, Clara. I have got accustomed to hear you talking about men as rotters, and calling everything filthy and beastly; though I do think it horrible and unladylike. But this last is really too much. Dont you think so, Colonel Pickering?

PICKERING. Dont ask me. Ive been away in India for several years; and manners have changed so much that I sometimes dont know whether I'm at a respectable dinner-table or in a ship's forecastle.

CLARA. It's all a matter of habit. Theres no right or wrong in it. Nobody means anything by it. And it's so quaint, and gives such a smart emphasis to things that are not in themselves very witty. I find the new small talk delightful and quite innocent.

MRS EYNSFORD HILL *(rising).* Well, after that, I think it's time for us to go.

PICKERING *and* HIGGINS *rise.*

CLARA *(rising).* Oh yes: we have three at-homes to go to still. Goodbye, Mrs Higgins. Goodbye, Colonel Pickering. Goodbye, Professor Higgins.

HIGGINS *(coming grimly at her from the divan, and accompanying her to the door).* Goodbye. Be sure you try on that small talk at the three at-homes. Dont be nervous about it. Pitch it in strong.

CLARA *(all smiles).* I will. Goodbye. Such nonsense, all this early Victorian prudery!

HIGGINS *(tempting her).* Such damned nonsense!

CLARA. Such bloody nonsense!

MRS EYNSFORD HILL *(convulsively).* Clara!

CLARA. Ha! ha! *(She goes out radiant, conscious of being thoroughly up to date, and is heard descending the stairs in a stream of silvery laughter).*

FREDDY *(to the heavens at large).* Well, I ask you—*(He gives it up, and comes to* MRS HIGGINS*).* Goodbye.

MRS HIGGINS *(shaking hands).* Goodbye. Would you like to meet Miss Doolittle again?

FREDDY *(eagerly).* Yes, I should, most awfully.

MRS HIGGINS. Well, you know my days.

FREDDY. Yes. Thanks awfully. Goodbye. *(He goes out).*

MRS EYNSFORD HILL. Goodbye, Mr Higgins.

HIGGINS. Goodbye. Goodbye.

MRS EYNSFORD HILL *(to* PICKERING*).* It's no use. I shall never be able to bring myself to use that word.

PICKERING. Dont. It's not compulsory, you know. Youll get on quite well without it.

MRS EYNSFORD HILL. Only, Clara is so down on me if I am not positively reeking with the latest slang. Goodbye.

PICKERING. Goodbye.

(They shake hands).

MRS EYNSFORD HILL *(to* MRS HIGGINS*).* You mustnt mind Clara. *(*PICKERING, *catching from her lowered tone that this is not meant for him to hear, discreetly joins* HIGGINS *at the window).* We're so poor! and she gets so few parties, poor child! She doesnt quite know. *(*MRS HIGGINS, *seeing that her eyes are moist, takes her hand sympathetically and goes with her to the door).* But the boy is nice. Dont you think so?

MRS HIGGINS. Oh, quite nice. I shall always be delighted to see him.

MRS EYNSFORD HILL. Thank you, dear. Goodbye. *(She goes out).*

HIGGINS *(eagerly).* Well? Is Eliza presentable? *(He swoops on his mother and drags her to the ottoman, where she sits down in* ELIZA*'s place with her son on her left).*

PICKERING *returns to his chair on her right.*

MRS HIGGINS. You silly boy, of course she's not presentable. She's a triumph of your art and of her dressmaker's; but if you suppose for a moment that she doesnt give herself away in every sentence she utters, you must be perfectly cracked about her.

PICKERING. But dont you think something might be done? I mean something to eliminate the sanguinary element from her conversation.

MRS HIGGINS. Not as long as she is in Henry's hands.

HIGGINS *(aggrieved).* Do you mean that my language is improper?

MRS HIGGINS. No, dearest: it would be quite proper—say on a canal barge; but it would not be proper for her at a garden party.

HIGGINS *(deeply injured).* Well I must say—

PICKERING *(interrupting him).* Come, Higgins: you must learn to know yourself. I havnt heard such language as yours since we used to review the volunteers in Hyde Park twenty years ago.

HIGGINS *(sulkily).* Oh, well, if you say so, I suppose I dont always talk like a bishop.

MRS HIGGINS *(quieting* HENRY *with a touch).* Colonel Pickering: will you tell me what is the exact state of things in Wimpole Street?

PICKERING *(cheerfully: as if this completely changed the subject).* Well, I have come to live there with Henry. We work together at my Indian Dialects; and we think it more convenient—

MRS HIGGINS. Quite so. I know all about that: it's an excellent arrangement. But where does this girl live?

HIGGINS. With us, of course. Where should she live?

MRS HIGGINS. But on what terms? Is she a servant? If not, what is she?

PICKERING *(slowly).* I think I know what you mean, Mrs Higgins.

HIGGINS. Well, dash me if *I* do! Ive had to work at the girl every day for months to get her to her present pitch. Besides, she's useful. She knows where my things are, and remembers my appointments and so forth.

MRS HIGGINS. How does your housekeeper get on with her?

HIGGINS. Mrs Pearce? Oh, she's jolly glad to get so much taken off her hands; for before Eliza came, she used to have to find things and remind me of my appointments. But she's got some silly bee in her bonnet about Eliza. She keeps saying "You dont think, sir": doesnt she, Pick?

PICKERING. Yes: thats the formula. "You dont think, sir." Thats the end of every conversation about Eliza.

HIGGINS. As if I ever stop thinking about the girl and her confounded vowels and consonants. I'm worn out, thinking about her, and watching her lips and her teeth and her tongue, not to mention her soul, which is the quaintest of the lot.

MRS HIGGINS. You certainly are a pretty pair of babies, playing with your live doll.

HIGGINS. Playing! The hardest job I ever tackled: make no mistake about that, mother. But you have no idea how frightfully interesting it is to take a human being and change her into a quite different human being by creating a new speech for her. It's filling up the deepest gulf that separates class from class and soul from soul.

PICKERING *(drawing his chair closer to* MRS HIGGINS *and bending over to her eagerly).* Yes: it's enormously interesting. I assure you, Mrs Higgins, we take Eliza very seriously. Every week—every day almost—there is some new change. *(Closer again)* We keep records of every stage—dozens of gramophone disks and photographs—

HIGGINS *(assailing her at the other ear).* Yes, by George: it's the most absorbing experiment I ever tackled. She regularly fills our lives up: doesnt she, Pick?

PICKERING. We're always talking Eliza.

HIGGINS. Teaching Eliza.

PICKERING. Dressing Eliza.

MRS HIGGINS. What!

HIGGINS. Inventing new Elizas.

HIGGINS. *(speaking together).* You know, she has the most extraordinary quickness of ear:

PICKERING. I assure you, my dear Mrs Higgins, that girl

HIGGINS. just like a parrot. Ive tried her with every

PICKERING. is a genius. She can play the piano quite beautifully.

HIGGINS. possible sort of sound that a human being can make—

PICKERING. We have taken her to classical concerts and to music

HIGGINS. Continental dialects, African dialects, Hottentot

PICKERING. halls; and it's all the same to her: she plays everything

HIGGINS. clicks, things it took me years to get hold of; and

PICKERING. she hears right off when she comes home, whether it's

HIGGINS. she picks them up like a shot, right away, as if she had

PICKERING. Beethoven and Brahms or Lehar and Lionel Monckton;

HIGGINS. been at it all her life.

PICKERING. though six months ago, she'd never as much as touched a piano—

MRS HIGGINS *(putting her fingers in her ears, as they are by this time shouting one another down with an intolerable noise).* Sh-sh-sh-sh! *(They stop).*

PICKERING. I beg your pardon. *(He draws his chair back apologetically).*

HIGGINS. Sorry. When Pickering starts shouting nobody can get a word in edgeways.

MRS HIGGINS. Be quiet, Henry. Colonel Pickering: dont you realize that when Eliza walked into Wimpole Street, something walked in with her?

PICKERING. Her father did. But Henry soon got rid of him.

MRS HIGGINS. It would have been more to the point if her mother had. But as her mother didnt something else did.

PICKERING. But what?

MRS HIGGINS *(unconsciously dating herself by the word).* A problem.

PICKERING. Oh, I see. The problem of how to pass her off as a lady.

HIGGINS. I'll solve that problem. Ive half solved it already.

MRS HIGGINS. No, you two infinitely stupid male creatures; the problem of what is to be done with her afterwards.

HIGGINS. I dont see anything in that. She can go her own way, with all the advantages I have given her.

MRS HIGGINS. The advantages of that poor woman who was here just now! The manners and habits that disqualify a fine lady from earning her own living without giving her a fine lady's income! Is that what you mean?

PICKERING *(indulgently, being rather bored).* Oh, that will be all right, Mrs Higgins. *(He rises to go).*

HIGGINS *(rising also).* We'll find her some light employment.

PICKERING. She's happy enough. Dont you worry about her. Goodbye. *(He shakes hands as if he were consoling a frightened child, and makes for the door).*

HIGGINS. Anyhow, theres no good bothering now. The thing's done. Goodbye, mother. *(He kisses her, and follows* PICKERING*).*

PICKERING *(turning for a final consolation).* There are plenty of openings. We'll do whats right. Goodbye.

HIGGINS *(to* PICKERING *as they go out together).* Let's take her to the Shakespear exhibition at Earls Court.

PICKERING. Yes: lets. Her remarks will be delicious.

HIGGINS. She'll mimic all the people for us when we get home.

PICKERING. Ripping. *(Both are heard laughing as they go downstairs).*

MRS HIGGINS *(rises with an impatient bounce, and returns to her work at the writing table. She sweeps a litter of disarranged papers out of her way; snatches a sheet of paper from her stationery case; and tries resolutely to write. At the third line she gives it up; flings down her pen; grips the table angrily and exclaims).* Oh, men! men!! men!!!

Clearly ELIZA *will not pass as a duchess yet; and* HIGGINS*'s bet remains unwon. But the six months are not yet exhausted; and just in time* ELIZA *does actually pass as a princess. For a glimpse of how she did it imagine an Embassy in London one summer evening after dark. The hall door has an awning and a carpet across the sidewalk to the kerb, because a grand* *reception is in progress. A small crowd is lined up to see the guests arrive.*

A Rolls-Royce car drives up. PICKERING *in evening dress, with medals and orders, alights, and hands out* ELIZA, *in opera cloak, evening dress, diamonds, fan, flowers and all accessories.* HIGGINS *follows. The car drives off; and the three go up the steps and into the house, the door opening for them as they approach.*

Inside the house they find themselves in a spacious hall from which the grand staircase rises. On the left are the arrangements for the gentlemen's cloaks. The male guests are depositing their hats and wraps there.

On the right is a door leading to the ladies' cloakroom. Ladies are going in cloaked and coming out in splendor. PICKERING *whispers to* ELIZA *and points out the ladies' room. She goes into it.* HIGGINS *and* PICKERING *take off their overcoats and take tickets for them from the attendant.*

One of the guests, occupied in the same way, has his back turned. Having taken his ticket, he turns round and reveals himself as an important looking young man with an astonishingly hairy face. He has an enormous moustache, flowing out into luxuriant whiskers. Waves of hair cluster on his brow. His hair is cropped closely at the back, and glows with oil. Otherwise he is very smart. He wears several worthless orders. He is evidently a foreigner, guessable as a whiskered Pandour from Hungary; but in spite of the ferocity of his moustache he is amiable and genially voluble.

Recognizing HIGGINS, *he flings his arms wide apart and approaches him enthusiastically.*

WHISKERS. Maestro, maestro *(he embraces* HIGGINS *and kisses him on both cheeks).* You remember me?

HIGGINS. No I dont. Who the devil are you?

WHISKERS. I am your pupil: your first pupil, your best and greatest pupil. I am little Nepommuck, the marvellous boy. I have made your name famous throughout Europe. You teach me phonetic. You cannot forget ME.

HIGGINS. Why dont you shave?

NEPOMMUCK. I have not your imposing appearance, your chin, your brow. Nobody notice me when I shave. Now I am famous: they call me Hairy Faced Dick.

HIGGINS. And what are you doing here among all these swells?

NEPOMMUCK. I am interpreter, I speak 32 languages. I am indispensable at these international parties. You are great cockney specialist: you place a man anywhere in London the moment he open his mouth. I place any man in Europe.

A footman hurries down the grand staircase and comes to NEPOMMUCK.

FOOTMAN. You are wanted upstairs. Her Excellency cannot understand the Greek gentleman.

NEPOMMUCK. Thank you, yes, immediately.

The footman goes and is lost in the crowd.

NEPOMMUCK *(to* HIGGINS*).* This Greek diplomatist pretends he cannot speak nor understand English. He cannot deceive me. He is the son of a Clerkenwell watchmaker. He speaks English so villainously that he dare not utter a word of it without betraying his origin. I help him to pretend; but I make him pay through the nose. I make them all pay. Ha Ha! *(He hurries upstairs).*

PICKERING. Is this fellow really an expert? Can he find out Eliza and blackmail her?

HIGGINS. We shall see. If he finds her out I lose my bet. ELIZA *comes from the cloakroom and joins them.*

PICKERING. Well, Eliza, now for it. Are you ready?

LIZA. Are you nervous, Colonel?

PICKERING. Frightfully. I feel exactly as I felt before my first battle. It's the first time that frightens.

LIZA. It is not the first time for me, Colonel. I have done this fifty times—hundreds of times—in my little piggery in Angel Court in my daydreams. I am in a dream now. Promise me not to let Professor Higgins wake me; for if he does I shall forget everything and talk as I used to in Drury Lane.

PICKERING. Not a word, Higgins. *(To* ELIZA*)* Now, ready?

LIZA. Ready.

PICKERING. Go.

They mount the stairs, HIGGINS *last.* PICKERING *whispers to the footman on the first landing.*

FIRST LANDING FOOTMAN. Miss Doolittle, Colonel Pickering, Professor Higgins.

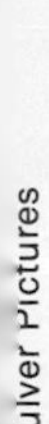

SECOND LANDING FOOTMAN. Miss Doolittle, Colonel Pickering, Professor Higgins.

At the top of the staircase the Ambassador and his wife, with NEPOMMUCK *at her elbow, are receiving.*

HOSTESS *(taking* ELIZA*'s hand).* How d'ye do?

HOST *(same play).* How d'ye do? How d'ye do, Pickering?

LIZA *(with a beautiful gravity that awes her hostess).* How do you do? *(She passes on to the drawingroom).*

HOSTESS. Is that your adopted daughter, Colonel Pickering? She will make a sensation.

PICKERING. Most kind of you to invite her for me. *(He passes on).*

HOSTESS *(to* NEPOMMUCK*).* Find out all about her.

NEPOMMUCK *(bowing).* Excellency—*(he goes into the crowd).*

HOST. How d'ye do, Higgins? You have a rival here tonight. He introduced himself as your pupil. Is he any good?

Culver Pictures

HIGGINS. He can learn a language in a fortnight—knows dozens of them. A sure mark of a fool. As a phonetician, no good whatever.

HOSTESS. How d'ye do, Professor?

HIGGINS. How do you do? Fearful bore for you this sort of thing. Forgive my part in it. *(He passes on).*

In the drawingroom and its suite of salons the reception is in full swing. ELIZA *passes through. She is so intent on her ordeal that she walks like a somnambulist in a desert instead of a débutante in a fashionable crowd. They stop talking to look at her, admiring her dress, her jewels, and her strangely attractive self. Some of the younger ones at the back stand on their chairs to see.*

The Host and Hostess come in from the staircase and mingle with their guests. HIGGINS, *gloomy and contemptuous of the whole business, comes into the group where they are chatting.*

HOSTESS. Ah, here is Professor Higgins: he will tell us. Tell us all about the wonderful young lady, Professor.

HIGGINS *(almost morosely).* What wonderful young lady?

HOSTESS. You know very well. They tell me there has been nothing like her in London since people stood on their chairs to look at Mrs Langtry.[3]

NEPOMMUCK *joins the group, full of news.*

HOSTESS. Ah, here you are at last, Nepommuck. Have you found out all about the Doolittle lady?

NEPOMMUCK. I have found out all about her. She is a fraud.

HOSTESS. A fraud! Oh no.

NEPOMMUCK. YES, yes. She cannot deceive me. Her name cannot be Doolittle.

HIGGINS. Why?

NEPOMMUCK. Because Doolittle is an English name. And she is not English.

HOSTESS. Oh, nonsense! She speaks English perfectly.

NEPOMMUCK. Too perfectly. Can you shew me any English woman who speaks English as it should be spoken? Only foreigners who have been taught to speak it speak it well.

HOSTESS. Certainly she terrified me by the way she said How d'ye do. I had a schoolmistress who talked like that; and I was mortally afraid of her. But if she is not English what is she?

---

3. ***Mrs. Langtry.*** Lily Langtry (1852–1929) was a famous actress.

NEPOMMUCK. Hungarian.

ALL THE REST. Hungarian!

NEPOMMUCK. Hungarian. And of royal blood. I am Hungarian. My blood is royal.

HIGGINS. Did you speak to her in Hungarian?

NEPOMMUCK. I did. She was very clever, She said "Please speak to me in English: I do not understand French." French! She pretends not to know the difference between Hungarian and French. Impossible: she knows both.

HIGGINS. And the blood royal? How did you find that out?

NEPOMMUCK. Instinct, maestro, instinct. Only the Magyar races can produce that air of the divine right, those resolute eyes. She is a princess.

HOST. What do you say, Professor?

HIGGINS. I say an ordinary London girl out of the gutter and taught to speak by an expert. I place her in Drury Lane.

NEPOMMUCK. Ha ha ha! Oh, maestro, maestro, you are mad on the subject of cockney dialects. The London gutter is the whole world for you.

HIGGINS *(to the Hostess).* What does your Excellency say?

HOSTESS. Oh, of course I agree with Nepommuck. She must be a princess at least.

HOST. Not necessarily legitimate, of course. Morganatic perhaps. But that is undoubtedly her class.

HIGGINS. I stick to my opinion.

HOSTESS. Oh, you are incorrigible.

The group breaks up, leaving HIGGINS *isolated.* PICKERING *joins him.*

PICKERING. Where is Eliza? We must keep an eye on her.

ELIZA *joins them.*

LIZA. I dont think I can bear much more. The people all stare so at me. An old lady has just told me that I speak exactly like Queen Victoria. I am sorry if I have lost your bet. I have done my best; but nothing can make me the same as these people.

PICKERING. You have not lost it, my dear. You have won it ten times over.

HIGGINS. Let us get out of this. I have had enough of chattering to these fools.

PICKERING. Eliza is tired; and I am hungry. Let us clear out and have supper somewhere.

Act Four

The Wimpole Street laboratory. Midnight. Nobody in the room. The clock on the mantelpiece strikes twelve. The fire is not alight: it is a summer night.

Presently HIGGINS *and* PICKERING *are heard on the stairs.*

HIGGINS *(calling down to* PICKERING*).* I say, Pick: lock up, will you? I shant be going out again.

PICKERING. Right. Can Mrs Pearce go to bed? We dont want anything more, do we?

HIGGINS. Lord, no!

ELIZA *opens the door and is seen on the lighted landing in all the finery in which she has just won* HIGGINS*'s bet for him. She comes to the hearth, and switches on the electric lights there. She is tired: her pallor contrasts strongly with her dark eyes and hair; and her expression is almost tragic. She takes off her cloak; puts her fan and flowers on the piano; and sits down on the bench, brooding and silent.* HIGGINS, *in evening dress, with overcoat and hat, comes in, carrying a smoking jacket which he has picked up downstairs. He takes off the hat and overcoat; throws them carelessly on the newspaper stand; disposes of his coat in the same way; puts on the smoking jacket; and throws himself wearily into the easy-chair at the hearth.* PICKERING, *similarly attired, comes in. He also takes off his hat and overcoat, and is about to throw them on* HIGGINS*'s when he hesitates.*

PICKERING. I say: Mrs Pearce will row if we leave these things lying about in the drawing room.

HIGGINS. Oh, chuck them over the bannisters into the hall. She'll find them there in the morning and put them away all right. She'll think we were drunk.

PICKERING. We are, slightly. Are there any letters?

HIGGINS. I didnt look. *(*PICKERING *takes the overcoats and goes downstairs.* HIGGINS *begins half singing half yawning an air from La Fanciulla del Golden West.*[1] *Suddenly he stops and*

---

1. ***La Fanciulla del Golden West,*** *The Girl of the Golden West,* an opera by Puccini that opened in New York in 1910.

exclaims) I wonder where the devil my slippers are!

ELIZA *looks at him darkly; then rises suddenly and leaves the room.*

HIGGINS *yawns again, and resumes his song.*

PICKERING *returns, with the contents of the letter-box in his hand.*

PICKERING. Only circulars, and this coroneted billet-doux for you. *(He throws the circulars into the fender, and posts himself on the hearthrug, with his back to the grate).*

HIGGINS *(glancing at the billet-doux).* Money-lender. *(He throws the letter after the circulars).*

ELIZA *returns with a pair of large down-at-heel slippers. She places them on the carpet before* HIGGINS, *and sits as before without a word.*

HIGGINS *(yawning again).* Oh Lord! What an evening! What a crew! What a silly tomfoolery! *(He raises his shoe to unlace it, and catches sight of the slippers. He stops unlacing and looks at them as if they had appeared there of their own accord).* Oh! Theyre there, are they?

PICKERING *(stretching himself).* Well, I feel a bit tired. It's been a long day. The garden party, a dinner party, and the opera! Rather too much of a good thing. But youve won your bet, Higgins. Eliza did the trick, and something to spare, eh?

HIGGINS *(fervently).* Thank God it's over!

ELIZA *flinches violently; but they take no notice of her; and she recovers herself and sits stonily as before.*

PICKERING. Were you nervous at the garden party! *I* was. Eliza didnt seem a bit nervous.

HIGGINS. Oh, she wasnt nervous. I knew she'd be all right. No: it's the strain of putting the job through all these months that has told on me. It was interesting enough at first, while we were at the phonetics; but after that I got deadly sick of it. If I hadnt backed myself to do it I should have chucked the whole thing up two months ago. It was a silly notion: the whole thing has been a bore.

PICKERING. Oh come! the garden party was frightfully exciting. My heart began beating like anything.

HIGGINS. Yes, for the first three minutes. But when I saw we were going to win hands down, I felt like a bear in a cage, hanging about doing nothing. The dinner was worse: sitting gorging there for over an hour, with nobody but a damned fool of a fashionable woman to talk to! I tell you, Pickering, never again for me. No more artificial duchesses. The whole thing has been simple purgatory.

PICKERING. Youve never been broken in properly to the social routine. *(Strolling over to the piano)* I rather enjoy dipping into it occasionally myself: it makes me feel young again. Anyhow, it was a great success: an immense success. I was quite frightened once or twice because Eliza was doing it so well. You see, lots of the real people cant do it at all: theyre such fools that they think style comes by nature to people in their position; and so they never learn. Theres always something professional about doing a thing superlatively well.

HIGGINS. Yes: thats what drives me mad: the silly people dont know their own silly business. *(Rising)* However, it's over and done with; and now I can go to bed at last without dreading tomorrow.

ELIZA*'s beauty becomes murderous.*

PICKERING. I think I shall turn in too. Still, it's been a great occasion: a triumph for you. Goodnight. *(He goes).*

HIGGINS *(following him).* Goodnight. *(Over his shoulder, at the door)* Put out the lights, Eliza; and tell Mrs Pearce not to make coffee for me in the morning: I'll take tea. *(He goes out).*

ELIZA *tries to control herself and feel indifferent as she rises and walks across to the hearth to switch off the lights. By the time she gets there she is on the point of screaming. She sits down in* HIGGINS*'s chair and holds on hard to the arms. Finally she gives way and flings herself furiously on the floor, raging.*

HIGGINS *(in despairing wrath outside).* What the devil have I done with my slippers? *(He appears at the door).*

LIZA *(snatching up the slippers, and hurling them at him one after the other with all her force).* There are your slippers. And there. Take your slippers; and may you never have a day's luck with them!

HIGGINS *(astounded).* What on earth—! *(He comes to her).* What's the matter? Get up. *(He pulls her up).* Anything wrong?

LIZA *(breathless).* Nothing wrong—with you.

The Bettman Archive, Inc.

Ive won your bet for you, havnt I? Thats enough for you. *I* dont matter, I suppose.

HIGGINS. You won my bet! You! Presumptuous insect! *I* won it. What did you throw those slippers at me for?

LIZA. Because I wanted to smash your face. I'd like to kill you, you selfish brute. Why didnt you leave me where you picked me out of—in the gutter? You thank God it's all over, and that now you can throw me back again there, do you? *(She crisps her fingers frantically).*

HIGGINS *(looking at her in cool wonder).* The creature is nervous, after all.

LIZA *(gives a suffocated scream of fury, and instinctively darts her nails at his face)*!!

HIGGINS *(catching her wrists).* Ah! would you? Claws in, you cat. How dare you shew your temper to me? Sit down and be quiet. *(He throws her roughly into the easy-chair).*

LIZA *(crushed by superior strength and weight).* Whats to become of me? Whats to become of me?

HIGGINS. How the devil do I know whats to become of you? What does it matter what becomes of you?

LIZA. You dont care. I know you dont care. You wouldnt care if I was dead. I'm nothing to you—not so much as them slippers.

HIGGINS *(thundering).* Those slippers.

LIZA *(with bitter submission).* Those slippers. I didnt think it made any difference now.

A pause. ELIZA *hopeless and crushed.* HIGGINS *a little uneasy.*

HIGGINS *(in his loftiest manner).* Why have you begun going on like this? May I ask whether you complain of your treatment here?

LIZA. No.

HIGGINS. Has anybody behaved badly to you? Colonel Pickering? Mrs Pearce? Any of the servants?

LIZA. No.

HIGGINS. I presume you dont pretend that *I* have treated you badly?

LIZA. No.

HIGGINS. I am glad to hear it. *(He moderates his tone).* Perhaps youre tired after the strain of the day. Will you have a glass of champagne? *(He moves toward the door).*

LIZA. No. *(Recollecting her manners)* Thank you.

HIGGINS *(good-humored again).* This has been coming on you for some days. I suppose it was natural for you to be anxious about the garden party. But thats all over now. *(He pats her kindly on the shoulder. She writhes).* Theres nothing more to worry about.

LIZA. No. Nothing more for you to worry about. *(She suddenly rises and gets away from him by going to the piano bench, where she sits and hides her face).* Oh God! I wish I was dead.

HIGGINS *(staring after her in sincere surprise).* Why? In heaven's name, why? *(Reasonably, going to her)* Listen to me, Eliza. All this irritation is purely subjective.

LIZA. I dont understand. I'm too ignorant.

HIGGINS. It's only imagination. Low spirits and nothing else. Nobody's hurting you. Nothing's wrong. You go to bed like a good girl and sleep it off. Have a little cry and say your prayers: that will make you comfortable.

LIZA. I heard your prayers. "Thank God it's all over!"

HIGGINS *(impatiently).* Well, dont you thank God it's all over? Now you are free and can do what you like.

LIZA *(pulling herself together in desperation).* What am I fit for? What have you left me fit for? Where am I to go? What am I to do? Whats to become of me?

HIGGINS *(enlightened, but not at all impressed).* Oh thats whats worrying you, is it? *(He thrusts his hands into his pockets, and walks about in his usual manner, rattling the contents of his pockets, as if condescending to a trivial subject out of pure kindness).* I shouldnt bother about it if I were you. I should imagine you wont have much difficulty in settling yourself somewhere or other, though I hadnt quite realized that you were going away. *(She looks quickly at him: he does not look at her, but examines the dessert stand on the piano and decides that he will eat an apple).* You might marry, you know. *(He bites a large piece out of the apple and munches it noisily).* You see, Eliza, all men are not confirmed old bachelors like me and the Colonel. Most men are the marrying sort (poor devils!); and youre not bad-looking: it's quite a pleasure to look at you sometimes—not now, of course, because youre crying and looking as ugly as the very devil; but when youre all right and quite yourself, youre what I should call attractive. That is, to the people in the marrying line, you understand. You go to bed and have a good nice rest; and then get up and look at yourself in the glass; and you wont feel so cheap.

ELIZA *again looks at him, speechless, and does not stir.*

The look is quite lost on him: he eats his apple with a dreamy expression of happiness, as it is quite a good one.

HIGGINS *(a genial afterthought occurring to him).* I daresay my mother could find some chap or other who would do very well.

LIZA. We were above that at the corner of Tottenham Court Road.

HIGGINS *(waking up).* What do you mean?

LIZA. I sold flowers. I didnt sell myself. Now youve made a lady of me I'm not fit to sell anything else. I wish youd left me where you found me.

HIGGINS *(slinging the core of the apple decisively into the grate).* Tosh, Eliza. Dont you insult human relations by dragging all this cant about buying and selling into it. You neednt marry the fellow if you dont like him.

LIZA. What else am I to do?

HIGGINS. Oh, lots of things. What about your old idea of a florist's shop? Pickering could set you up in one: he's lots of money. *(Chuckling)* He'll have to pay for all those togs you have been wearing to-day; and that, with the hire of the jewellery, you will make a big hole in two hundred pounds. Why, six months ago you would have thought it the millennium to have a flower shop of your own. Come! youll be all right. I must clear off to bed: I'm devilish sleepy. By the way, I came down for something: I forget what it was.

LIZA. Your slippers.

HIGGINS. Oh yes, of course. You shied them at me. *(He picks them up, and is going out when she rises and speaks to him).*

LIZA. Before you go, sir—

HIGGINS *(dropping the slippers in his surprise at her calling him Sir).* Eh?

LIZA. Do my clothes belong to me or to Colonel Pickering?

HIGGINS *(coming back into the room as if her question were the very climax of unreason).* What the devil use would they be to Pickering?

LIZA. He might want them for the next girl you pick up to experiment on.

HIGGINS *(shocked and hurt).* Is that the way you feel towards us?

LIZA. I dont want to hear anything more about that. All I want to know is whether anything belongs to me. My own clothes were burnt.

HIGGINS. But what does it matter? Why need you start bothering about that in the middle of the night?

LIZA. I want to know what I may take away with me. I dont want to be accused of stealing.

HIGGINS *(now deeply wounded).* Stealing! You shouldnt have said that, Eliza. That shews a want of feeling.

LIZA. I'm sorry. I'm only a common ignorant girl; and in my station I have to be careful. There cant be any feelings between the like of you and the like of me. Please will you tell me what belongs to me and what doesnt?

HIGGINS *(very sulky).* You may take the whole damned houseful if you like. Except the jewels. Theyre hired. Will that satisfy you? *(He turns on his heel and is about to go in extreme dudgeon).*

LIZA *(drinking in his emotion like nectar, and nagging him to provoke a further supply).* Stop, please. *(She takes off her jewels).* Will you take these to your room and keep them safe? I dont want to run the risk of their being missing.

HIGGINS *(furious).* Hand them over. *(She puts them into his hands).* If these belonged to me instead of to the jeweller, I'd ram them down your ungrateful throat. *(He perfunctorily thrusts them into his pockets, unconsciously*

decorating himself with the protruding ends of the chains).

LIZA *(taking a ring off).* This ring isnt the jeweller's: it's the one you bought me in Brighton. I dont want it now. *(*HIGGINS *dashes the ring violently into the fireplace, and turns on her so threateningly that she crouches over the piano with her hands over her face, and exclaims)* Dont you hit me.

HIGGINS. Hit you! You infamous creature, how dare you accuse me of such a thing? It is you who have hit me. You have wounded me to the heart.

LIZA *(thrilling with hidden joy).* I'm glad. Ive got a little of my own back, anyhow.

HIGGINS *(with dignity, in his finest professional style).* You have caused me to lose my temper: a thing that has hardly ever happened to me before. I prefer to say nothing more to-night. I am going to bed.

LIZA *(pertly).* Youd better leave a note for Mrs Pearce about the coffee; for she wont be told by me.

HIGGINS *(formally).* Damn Mrs Pearce; and damn the coffee; and damn you; and damn my own folly in having lavished hard-earned knowledge and the treasure of my regard and intimacy on a heartless guttersnipe. *(He goes out with impressive decorum, and spoils it by slamming the door savagely).*

ELIZA *goes down on her knees on the hearthrug to look for the ring. When she finds it she considers for a moment what to do with it. Finally she flings it down on the dessert stand and goes upstairs in a tearing rage.*

The furniture of ELIZA*'s room has been increased by a big wardrobe and a sumptuous dressing-table. She comes in and switches on the electric light. She goes to the wardrobe; opens it; and pulls out a walking dress, a hat, and a pair of shoes, which she throws on the bed. She takes off her evening dress and shoes; then takes a padded hanger from the wardrobe; adjusts it carefully in the evening dress; and hangs it in the wardrobe, which she shuts with a slam. She puts on her walking shoes, her walking dress, and hat. She takes her wrist watch from the dressing-table and fastens it on. She pulls on her gloves; takes her vanity bag; and looks into it to see that her purse is there before hanging it on her wrist. She makes for the door. Every movement expresses her furious resolution.*

She takes a last look at herself in the glass.

She suddenly puts out her tongue at herself; then leaves the room, switching off the electric light at the door.

Meanwhile, in the street outside, FREDDY EYNSFORD HILL, *lovelorn, is gazing up at the second floor, in which one of the windows is still lighted.*

The light goes out.

FREDDY. Goodnight, darling, darling, darling.

ELIZA *comes out, giving the door a considerable bang behind her.*

LIZA. Whatever are you doing here?

FREDDY. Nothing, I spend most of my nights here. It's the only place where I'm happy. Dont laugh at me, Miss Doolittle.

LIZA. Dont you call me Miss Doolittle, do you hear? Liza's good enough for me. *(She breaks down and grabs him by the shoulders)* Freddy: you dont think I'm a heartless guttersnipe, do you?

FREDDY. Oh no, no, darling: how can you imagine such a thing? You are the loveliest, dearest—

He loses all self-control and smothers her with kisses. She, hungry for comfort, responds. They stand there in one another's arms.

An elderly police constable arrives.

CONSTABLE *(scandalized).* Now then! Now then!! Now then!!!

They release one another hastily.

FREDDY. Sorry, constable. Weve only just become engaged.

They run away.

The constable shakes his head, reflecting on his own courtship and on the vanity of human hopes. He moves off in the opposite direction with slow professional steps.

The flight of the lovers takes them to Cavendish Square. There they halt to consider their next move.

LIZA *(out of breath).* He didnt half give me a fright, that copper. But you answered him proper.

FREDDY. I hope I havent taken you out of your way. Where were you going?

LIZA. To the river.

FREDDY. What for?

LIZA. To make a hole in it.

FREDDY *(horrified).* Eliza, darling. What do you mean? What's the matter?

LIZA. Never mind. It doesnt matter now. There's nobody in the world now but you and me, is there?

FREDDY. Not a soul.

They indulge in another embrace, and are again surpised by a much younger constable.

SECOND CONSTABLE. Now then, you two! What's this? Where do you think you are? Move along here, double quick.

FREDDY. As you say, sir, double quick.

They run away again, and are in Hanover Square before they stop for another conference.

FREDDY. I had no idea the police were so devilishly prudish.

LIZA. It's their business to hunt girls off the streets.

FREDDY. We must go somewhere. We cant wander about the streets all night.

LIZA. Cant we? I think it'd be lovely to wander about for ever.

FREDDY. Oh, darling.

They embrace again, oblivious of the arrival of a crawling taxi. It stops.

TAXIMAN. Can I drive you and the lady anywhere, sir?

They start asunder.

LIZA. Oh, Freddy, a taxi. The very thing.

FREDDY. But, damn it, I've no money.

LIZA. I have plenty. The Colonel thinks you should never go out without ten pounds in your pocket. Listen. We'll drive about all night; and in the morning I'll call on old Mrs. Higgins and ask here what I ought to do. I'll tell you all about it in the cab. And the police wont touch us there.

FREDDY. Righto! Ripping. *(To the Taximan)* Wimbledon Common. *(They drive off).*

Act Five

MRS HIGGINS*'s drawing room. She is at her writing-table as before. The parlor-maid comes in.*

THE PARLOR-MAID *(at the door).* Mr Henry, maam, is downstairs with Colonel Pickering.

MRS HIGGINS. Well, shew them up.

THE PARLOR-MAID. Theyre using the telephone, maam. Telephoning to the police, I think.

MRS HIGGINS. What!

THE PARLOR-MAID *(coming further in and lowering her voice).* Mr Henry is in a state, maam. I thought I'd better tell you.

MRS HIGGINS. If you had told me that Mr Henry was not in a state it would have been more surprising. Tell them to come up when theyve finished with the police. I suppose he's lost something.

THE PARLOR-MAID. Yes, maam *(going).*

MRS HIGGINS. Go upstairs and tell Miss Doolittle that Mr Henry and the Colonel are here. Ask her not to come down til I send for her.

THE PARLOR-MAID. Yes, maam.

HIGGINS *bursts in. He is, as the parlor-maid has said, in a state.*

HIGGINS. Look here, mother: heres a confounded thing!

MRS HIGGINS. Yes, dear. Good morning. *(He checks his impatience and kisses her, whilst the parlor-maid goes out).* What is it?

HIGGINS. Eliza's bolted.

MRS HIGGINS *(calmly continuing her writing).* You must have frightened her.

HIGGINS. Frightened her! nonsense! She was left last night, as usual, to turn out the lights and all that; and instead of going to bed she changed her clothes and went right off: her bed wasnt slept in. She came in a cab for her things before seven this morning; and that fool Mrs Pearce let her have them without telling me a word about it. What am I to do?

MRS HIGGINS. Do without, I'm afraid, Henry. The girl has a perfect right to leave if she chooses.

HIGGINS *(wandering distractedly across the room).* But I cant find anything. I dont know what appointments Ive got. I'm—*(*PICKERING *comes in.* MRS HIGGINS *puts down her pen and turns away from the writing-table).*

PICKERING *(shaking hands).* Good morning, Mrs Higgins. Has Henry told you? *(He sits down on the ottoman).*

HIGGINS. What does that ass of an inspector say? Have you offered a reward?

MRS HIGGINS *(rising in indignant amazement).* You dont mean to say you have set the police after Eliza.

HIGGINS. Of course. What are the police for? What else could we do? *(He sits in the Elizabethan chair).*

PICKERING. The inspector made a lot of difficulties. I really think he suspected us of some improper purpose.

MRS HIGGINS. Well, of course he did. What right have you to go to the police and give the girl's name as if she were a thief, or a lost umbrella, or something? Really! *(She sits down again, deeply vexed).*

HIGGINS. But we want to find her.

PICKERING. We cant let her go like this, you know, Mrs Higgins. What were we to do?

MRS HIGGINS. You have no more sense, either of you, than two children. Why—

The parlor-maid comes in and breaks off the conversation.

THE PARLOR-MAID. Mr Henry: a gentleman wants to see you very particular. He's been sent on from Wimpole Street.

HIGGINS. Oh, bother! I cant see anyone now. Who is it?

THE PARLOR-MAID. A Mr Doolittle, sir.

PICKERING. Doolittle! Do you mean the dustman?

THE PARLOR-MAID. Dustman! Oh no, sir: a gentleman.

HIGGINS *(springing up excitedly).* By George, Pick, it's some relative of hers that she's gone to. Somebody we know nothing about. *(To the parlor-maid)* Send him up, quick.

THE PARLOR-MAID. Yes, sir. *(She goes).*

HIGGINS *(eagerly, going to his mother).* Genteel relatives! now we shall hear something. *(He sits down in the Chippendale chair).*

MRS HIGGINS. Do you know any of her people?

PICKERING. Only her father: the fellow we told you about.

THE PARLOR-MAID *(announcing).* Mr Doolittle. *(She withdraws).*

DOOLITTLE *enters. He is resplendently dressed as for a fashionable wedding, and might, in fact, be the bridegroom. A flower in his buttonhole, a dazzling silk hat, and patent leather shoes complete the effect. He is too concerned with the business he has come on to notice* MRS HIGGINS. *He walks straight to* HIGGINS, *and accosts him with vehement reproach.*

DOOLITTLE *(indicating his own person).* See here! Do you see this? You done this.

HIGGINS. Done what, man?

DOOLITTLE. This, I tell you. Look at it. Look at this hat. Look at this coat.

PICKERING. Has Eliza been buying you clothes?

DOOLITTLE. Eliza! not she. Not half. Why would she buy me clothes?

MRS HIGGINS. Good morning, Mr Doolittle. Wont you sit down?

DOOLITTLE *(taken aback as he becomes conscious that he has forgotten his hostess).* Asking your pardon, maam. *(He approaches her and shakes her proffered hand).* Thank you. *(He sits down on the ottoman, on* PICKERING*'s right).* I am that full of what has happened to me that I cant think of anything else.

HIGGINS. What the dickens has happened to you?

DOOLITTLE. I shouldnt mind if it had only happened to me: anything might happen to anybody and nobody to blame but Providence, as you might say. But this is something that you done to me: yes, you, Enry Iggins.

HIGGINS. Have you found Eliza? Thats the point.

DOOLITTLE. Have you lost her?

HIGGINS. Yes.

DOOLITTLE. You have all the luck, you have. I aint found her; but she'll find me quick enough now after what you done to me.

MRS HIGGINS. But what has my son done to you, Mr Doolittle?

DOOLITTLE. Done to me! Ruined me. Destroyed my happiness. Tied me up and delivered me into the hands of middle class morality.

HIGGINS *(rising intolerantly and standing over* DOOLITTLE*).* Youre raving. Youre drunk.

Youre mad. I gave you five pounds. After that I had two conversations with you, at half-a-crown an hour. Ive never seen you since.

DOOLITTLE. Oh! Drunk! am I? Mad? am I? Tell me this. Did you or did you not write a letter to an old blighter in America that was giving five millions to found Moral Reform Societies all over the world, and that wanted you to invent a universal language for him?

HIGGINS. What! Ezra D. Wannafeller! He's dead. *(He sits down again carelessly).*

DOOLITTLE. Yes: he's dead; and I'm done for. Now did you or did you not write a letter to him to say that the most original moralist at present in England, to the best of your knowledge, was Alfred Doolittle, a common dustman.

HIGGINS. Oh, after your last visit I remember making some silly joke of the kind.

DOOLITTLE. Ah! you may well call it a silly joke. It put the lid on me right enough. Just give him the chance he wanted to shew that Americans is not like us: that they recognize and respect merit in every class of life, however humble. Them words is in his blooming will, in which, Henry Higgins, thanks to your silly joking, he leaves me a share in his Pre-digested Cheese Trust worth three thousand a year on condition that I lecture for his Wannafeller Moral Reform World League as often as they ask me up to six times a year.

HIGGINS. The devil he does! Whew! *(Brightening suddenly)* What a lark!

PICKERING. A safe thing for you, Doolittle. They wont ask you twice.

DOOLITTLE. It aint the lecturing I mind. I'll lecture them blue in the face, I will, and not turn a hair. It's making a gentleman of me that I object to. Who asked him to make a gentleman of me? I was happy. I was free. I touched pretty nigh everybody for money when I wanted it, same as I touched you, Enry Iggins. Now I am worrited; tied neck and heels; and everybody touches me for money. It's a fine thing for you, says my solicitor. Is it? says I. You mean it's a good thing for you, I says. When I was a poor man and had a solicitor once when they found a pram in the dust cart, he got me off, and got shut of me and got me shut of him as quick as he could. Same with the doctors: used to shove me out of the hospital before I could hardly stand on my legs, and nothing to pay. Now they finds out that I'm not a healthy man and cant live unless they looks after me twice a day. In the house I'm not let do a hand's turn for myself: somebody else must do it and touch me for it. A year ago I hadnt a relative in the world except two or three that wouldnt speak to me. Now Ive fifty, and not a decent week's wages among the lot of them. I have to live for others and not for myself: thats middle class morality. You talk of losing Eliza. Dont you be anxious: I bet she's on my doorstep by this: she that could support herself easy by selling flowers if I wasnt respectable. And the next one to touch me will be you, Enry Iggins. I'll have to learn to speak middle class language from you, instead of speaking proper English. Thats where youll come in; and I daresay thats what you done it for.

MRS HIGGINS. But, my dear Mr Doolittle, you need not suffer all this if you are really in earnest. Nobody can force you to accept this bequest. You can repudiate it. Isnt that so, Colonel Pickering?

PICKERING. I believe so.

DOOLITTLE *(softening his manner in deference to her sex).* Thats the tragedy of it, maam. It's easy to say chuck it; but I havnt the nerve. Which of us has? We're all intimidated. Intimidated, maam: thats what we are. What is there for me if I chuck it but the workhouse in my old age? I have to dye my hair already to keep my job as a dustman. If I was one of the deserving poor, and had put by a bit, I could chuck it; but then why should I, acause the deserving poor might as well be millionaires for all the happiness they ever has. They dont know what happiness is. But I, as one of the undeserving poor, have nothing between me and the pauper's uniform but this here blasted three thousand a year that shoves me into the middle class. (Excuse the expression, maam: youd use it yourself if you had my provocation.) Theyve got you every way you turn: it's a choice between the Skilly of the workhouse and the Char Bydis of the middle class;[1] and I

1. ***Skilly . . . class.*** *Scylla* (sil′ə) and *Charybdis* (kə rib′dis) were the names the Greeks gave to a dangerous rock and a whirlpool bracketing the strait between Sicily and Italy.

havnt the nerve for the workhouse. Intimidated: thats what I am. Broke. Brought up. Happier men than me will call for my dust, and touch me for their tip; and I'll look on helpless, and envy them. And thats what your son has brought me to. *(He is overcome by emotion).*

MRS HIGGINS. Well, I'm very glad youre not going to do anything foolish, Mr Doolittle. For this solves the problem of Eliza's future. You can provide for her now.

DOOLITTLE *(with melancholy resignation).* Yes, maam: I'm expected to provide for everyone now, out of three thousand a year.

HIGGINS *(jumping up).* Nonsense! he cant provide for her. He shant provide for her. She doesnt belong to him. I paid him five pounds for her. Doolittle: either youre an honest man or a rogue.

DOOLITTLE *(tolerantly).* A little of both, Henry, like the rest of us: a little of both.

HIGGINS. Well, you took that money for the girl; and you have no right to take her as well.

MRS HIGGINS. Henry: dont be absurd. If you want to know where Eliza is, she is upstairs.

HIGGINS *(amazed).* Upstairs!!! Then I shall jolly soon fetch her downstairs. *(He makes resolutely for the door).*

MRS HIGGINS *(rising and following him).* Be quiet, Henry. Sit down.

HIGGINS. I—

MRS HIGGINS. Sit down, dear; and listen to me.

HIGGINS. Oh very well, very well, very well. *(He throws himself ungraciously on the ottoman, with his face towards the windows).* But I think you might have told us this half an hour ago.

MRS HIGGINS. Eliza came to me this morning. She told me of the brutal way you two treated her.

HIGGINS *(bounding up again).* What!

PICKERING *(rising also).* My dear Mrs Higgins, she's been telling you stories. We didn't treat her brutally. We hardly said a word to her; and we parted on particularly good terms. *(Turning on* HIGGINS*)* Higgins: did you bully her after I went to bed?

HIGGINS. Just the other way about. She threw my slippers in my face. She behaved in the most outrageous way. I never gave her the slightest provocation. The slippers came bang into my face the moment I entered the room—before I had uttered a word. And used perfectly awful language.

PICKERING *(astonished).* But why? What did we do to her?

MRS HIGGINS. I think I know pretty well what you did. The girl is naturally rather affectionate, I think. Isnt she, Mr Doolittle?

DOOLITTLE. Very tender-hearted, maam. Takes after me.

MRS HIGGINS. Just so. She had become attached to you both. She worked very hard for you, Henry! I dont think you quite realize what anything in the nature of brain work means to a girl like that. Well, it seems that when the great day of trial came, and she did this wonderful thing for you without making a single mistake, you two sat there and never said a word to her, but talked together of how glad you were that it was all over and how you had been bored with the whole thing. And then you were surprised because she threw your slippers at you! *I* should have thrown the fire-irons at you.

HIGGINS. We said nothing except that we were tired and wanted to go to bed. Did we, Pick?

PICKERING *(shrugging his shoulders).* That was all.

MRS HIGGINS *(ironically).* Quite sure?

PICKERING. Absolutely. Really, that was all.

MRS HIGGINS. You didnt thank her, or pet her, or admire her, or tell her how splendid she'd been.

HIGGINS *(impatiently).* But she knew all about that. We didnt make speeches to her, if thats what you mean.

PICKERING *(conscience stricken).* Perhaps we were a little inconsiderate. Is she very angry?

MRS HIGGINS *(returning to her place at the writing-table).* Well, I'm afraid she wont go back to Wimpole Street, especially now that Mr Doolittle is able to keep up the position you have thrust on her; but she says she is quite willing to meet you on friendly terms and to let bygones be bygones.

HIGGINS *(furious).* Is she, by George? Ho!

MRS HIGGINS. If you promise to behave yourself, Henry, I'll ask her to come down. If not, go home; for you have taken up quite enough of my time.

HIGGINS. Oh, all right. Very well. Pick: you

behave yourself. Let us put on our best Sunday manners for this creature that we picked out of the mud. *(He flings himself sulkily into the Elizabethan chair).*

DOOLITTLE *(remonstrating).* Now, now, Enry Iggins! have some consideration for my feelings as a middle class man.

MRS HIGGINS. Remember your promise, Henry. *(She presses the bell-button on the writing-table).* Mr Doolittle: will you be so good as to step out on the balcony for a moment. I dont want Eliza to have the shock of your news until she has made it up with these two gentlemen. Would you mind?

DOOLITTLE. As you wish, lady. Anything to help Henry to keep her off my hands. *(He disappears through the window).*

The parlor-maid answers the bell. PICKERING *sits down in* DOOLITTLE*'s place.*

MRS HIGGINS. Ask Miss Doolittle to come down, please.

THE PARLOR-MAID. Yes, maam. *(She goes out).*

MRS HIGGINS. Now, Henry: be good.

HIGGINS. I am behaving myself perfectly.

PICKERING. He is doing his best, Mrs Higgins.

A pause. HIGGINS *throws back his head; stretches out his legs; and begins to whistle.*

MRS HIGGINS. Henry, dearest, you dont look at all nice in that attitude.

HIGGINS *(pulling himself together).* I was not trying to look nice, mother.

MRS HIGGINS. It doesnt matter, dear. I only wanted to make you speak.

HIGGINS. Why?

MRS HIGGINS. Because you cant speak and whistle at the same time.

HIGGINS *groans. Another very trying pause.*

HIGGINS *(springing up, out of patience).* Where the devil is that girl? Are we to wait here all day?

ELIZA *enters, sunny, self-possessed, and giving a staggeringly convincing exhibition of ease of manner. She carries a little work-basket, and is very much at home.* PICKERING *is too much taken aback to rise.*

LIZA. How do you do, Professor Higgins? Are you quite well?

HIGGINS *(choking).* Am I—*(He can say no more).*

LIZA. But of course you are: you are never ill. So glad to see you again, Colonel Pickering. *(He rises hastily; and they shake hands).* Quite chilly this morning, isnt it? *(She sits down on his left. He sits beside her).*

HIGGINS. Dont you dare try this game on me. I taught it to you; and it doesnt take me in. Get up and come home; and dont be a fool.

ELIZA *takes a piece of needlework from her basket, and begins to stitch at it, without taking the least notice of this outburst.*

MRS HIGGINS. Very nicely put, indeed, Henry. No woman could resist such an invitation.

HIGGINS. You let her alone, mother. Let her speak for herself. You will jolly soon see whether she has an idea that I havnt put into her head or a word that I havnt put into her mouth. I tell you I have created this thing out of the squashed cabbage leaves of Covent Garden; and now she pretends to play the fine lady with me.

MRS HIGGINS *(placidly).* Yes, dear; but youll sit down, wont you?

HIGGINS *sits down again, savagely.*

LIZA *(to* PICKERING, *taking no apparent notice of* HIGGINS, *and working away deftly).* Will you drop me altogether now that the experiment is over, Colonel Pickering?

PICKERING. Oh dont. You mustnt think of it as an experiment. It shocks me, somehow.

LIZA. Oh, I'm only a squashed cabbage leaf—

PICKERING *(impulsively).* No.

LIZA *(continuing quietly)*—but I owe so much to you that I should be very unhappy if you forgot me.

PICKERING. It's very kind of you to say so, Miss Doolittle.

LIZA. It's not because you paid for my dresses. I know you are generous to everybody with money. But it was from you that I learnt really nice manners; and that is what makes one a lady, isn't it? You see it was so difficult for me with the example of Professor Higgins always before me. I was brought up to be just like him, unable to control myself, and using bad language on the slightest provocation. And I should never have known that ladies and gentlemen didnt behave like that if you hadnt been there.

HIGGINS. Well!!

PICKERING. Oh, thats only his way, you know. He doesnt mean it.

LIZA. Oh, *I* didnt mean it either, when I was a flower girl. It was only my way. But you see I did it; and thats what makes the difference after all.

PICKERING. No doubt. Still, he taught you to speak; and I couldnt have done that, you know.

LIZA *(trivially).* Of course: that is his profession.

HIGGINS. Damnation!

LIZA *(continuing).* It was just like learning to dance in the fashionable way: there was nothing more than that in it. But do you know what began my real education?

PICKERING. What?

LIZA *(stopping her work for a moment).* Your calling me Miss Doolittle that day when I first came to Wimpole Street. That was the beginning of self-respect for me. *(She resumes her stitching).* And there were a hundred little things you never noticed, because they came naturally to you. Things about standing up and taking off your hat and opening doors—

PICKERING. Oh, that was nothing.

LIZA. Yes: things that shewed you thought and felt about me as if I were something better than a scullery-maid; though of course I know you would have been just the same to a scullery-maid if she had been let into the drawing room. You never took off your boots in the dining room when I was there.

PICKERING. You mustnt mind that. Higgins takes off his boots all over the place.

LIZA. I know. I am not blaming him. It is his way, isnt it? But it made such a difference to me that you didnt do it. You see, really and truly, apart from the things anyone can pick up (the dressing and the proper way of speaking, and so on), the difference between a lady and a flower girl is not how she behaves, but how she's treated. I shall always be a flower girl to Professor Higgins, because he always treats me as a flower girl, and always will; but I know I can be a lady to you, because you always treat me as a lady, and always will.

MRS HIGGINS. Please dont grind your teeth, Henry.

PICKERING. Well, this is really very nice of you, Miss Doolittle.

LIZA. I should like you to call me Eliza, now, if you would.

PICKERING. Thank you, Eliza, of course.

notes and comments

Comedy of Ideas

The main difference between the comedy of ideas and other forms of comedy is that it does not depend on situation or intrigue for its humor. Instead of laughing at an unexpected situation, we laugh at unexpected ideas which are cleverly expressed and developed. The humor, which appeals to the intellect, is created for a serious purpose. This form of comedy is especially appropriate for modern audiences since more people are able to read plays than to see them performed, and the humor depends more on a mental process than on a visual one.

The plot of *Pygmalion* advances but little in Act II, and it is Shaw's ideas that make the act exciting; ideas that are only incidentally related to the plot, although they are related to the theme. For instance, the plot in Act II consists of Eliza's decision to study phonetics with Professor Higgins and the arrangements under which this is to be accomplished. From such a small wedge Shaw leads his characters into critical conversations on Victorian ideas of manners, marriage, parenthood, and morals. Since the middle and upper classes, at whom these criticisms are aimed, comprise his audience, he softens his criticisms through comedy.

LIZA. And I should like Professor Higgins to call me Miss Doolittle.

HIGGINS. I'll see you damned first.

MRS HIGGINS. Henry! Henry!

PICKERING *(laughing).* Why dont you slang back at him? Dont stand it. It would do him a lot of good.

LIZA. I cant. I could have done it once; but now I cant go back to it. You told me, you know, that when a child is brought to a foreign country, it picks up the language in a few weeks, and forgets its own. Well, I am a child in your country. I have forgotten my own language, and can speak nothing but yours. Thats the real break-off with the corner of Tottenham Court Road. Leaving Wimpole Street finishes it.

PICKERING *(much alarmed).* Oh! but youre coming back to Wimpole Street, arnt you? Youll forgive Higgins?

HIGGINS *(rising).* Forgive! Will she, by George! Let her go. Let her find out how she can get on without us. She will relapse into the gutter in three weeks without me at her elbow.

DOOLITTLE *appears at the centre window. With a look of dignified reproach at* HIGGINS, *he comes slowly and silently to his daughter, who, with her back to the window, is unconscious of his approach.*

PICKERING. He's incorrigible, Eliza. You wont relapse, will you?

LIZA. No: not now. Never again. I have learnt my lesson. I dont believe I could utter one of the old sounds if I tried. *(*DOOLITTLE *touches her on her left shoulder. She drops her work, losing her self-possession utterly at the spectacle of her father's splendor)* A-a-a-a-a-ah-ow-ooh!

HIGGINS *(with a crow of triumph).* Aha! Just so. A-a-a-a-ahowooh! A-a-a-a-ahowooh! A-a-a-a-ahowooh! Victory! Victory! *(He throws himself on the divan, folding his arms, and spraddling arrogantly).*

DOOLITTLE. Can you blame the girl? Dont look at me like that, Eliza. It aint my fault. Ive come into some money.

LIZA. You must have touched a millionaire this time, dad.

DOOLITTLE. I have. But I'm dressed something special today. I'm going to St George's, Hanover Square. Your stepmother is going to marry me.

LIZA *(angrily).* Youre going to let yourself down to marry that low common woman!

PICKERING *(quietly).* He ought to, Eliza. *(To* DOOLITTLE*)* Why has she changed her mind?

DOOLITTLE *(sadly).* Intimidated, Governor. Intimidated. Middle class morality claims its victim. Wont you put on your hat, Liza, and come and see me turned off?

LIZA. If the Colonel says I must, I—I'll *(almost sobbing)* I'll demean myself. And get insulted for my pains, like enough.

DOOLITTLE. Dont be afraid: she never comes to words with anyone now, poor woman! respectability has broke all the spirit out of her.

PICKERING *(squeezing* ELIZA*'s elbow gently).* Be kind to them, Eliza. Make the best of it.

LIZA *(forcing a little smile for him through her vexation).* Oh well, just to shew theres no ill feeling. I'll be back in a moment. *(She goes out).*

DOOLITTLE *(sitting down beside* PICKERING*).* I feel uncommon nervous about the ceremony, Colonel. I wish youd come and see me through it.

PICKERING. But youve been through it before, man. You were married to Eliza's mother.

DOOLITTLE. Who told you that, Colonel?

PICKERING. Well, nobody told me. But I concluded—naturally—

DOOLITTLE. No: that aint the natural way, Colonel: it's only the middle class way. My way was always the undeserving way. But dont say nothing to Eliza. She dont know: I always had a delicacy about telling her.

PICKERING. Quite right. We'll leave it so, if you dont mind.

DOOLITTLE. And youll come to the church, Colonel, and put me through straight?

PICKERING. With pleasure. As far as a bachelor can.

MRS HIGGINS. May I come, Mr Doolittle? I should be very sorry to miss your wedding.

DOOLITTLE. I should indeed be honored by your condescension, maam; and my poor old woman would take it as a tremenjous compliment. She's been very low, thinking of the happy days that are no more.

MRS HIGGINS *(rising).* I'll order the carriage

and get ready. *(The men rise, except* HIGGINS*).* I shant be more than fifteen minutes. *(As she goes to the door* ELIZA *comes in, hatted and buttoning her gloves).* I'm going to the church to see your father married, Eliza. You had better come in the brougham with me. Colonel Pickering can go on with the bridegroom.

MRS HIGGINS *goes out.* ELIZA *comes to the middle of the room between the centre window and the ottoman.* PICKERING *joins her.*

DOOLITTLE. Bridegroom! What a word! It makes a man realize his position, somehow. *(He takes up his hat and goes towards the door).*

PICKERING. Before I go, Eliza, do forgive him and come back to us.

LIZA. I dont think papa would allow me. Would you, dad?

DOOLITTLE *(sad but magnanimous).* They played you off very cunning, Eliza, them two sportsmen. If it had been only one of them, you could have nailed him. But you see, there was two; and one of them chaperoned the other, as you might say. *(To* PICKERING*)* It was artful of you, Colonel; but I bear no malice: I should have done the same myself. I been the victim of one woman after another all my life; and I dont grudge you two getting the better of Eliza. I shant interfere. It's time for us to go, Colonel. So long, Henry. See you in St George's, Eliza. *(He goes out).*

PICKERING *(coaxing).* Do stay with us, Eliza. *(He follows* DOOLITTLE*).*

ELIZA *goes out on the balcony to avoid being alone with* HIGGINS. *He rises and joins her there. She immediately comes back into the room and makes for the door; but he goes along the balcony quickly and gets his back to the door before she reaches it.*

HIGGINS. Well, Eliza, youve had a bit of your own back, as you call it. Have you had enough? and are you going to be reasonable? Or do you want any more?

LIZA. You want me back only to pick up your slippers and put up with your tempers and fetch and carry for you.

HIGGINS. I havnt said I wanted you back at all.

LIZA. Oh, indeed. Then what are we talking about?

HIGGINS. About you, not about me. If you come back I shall treat you just as I have always treated you. I cant change my nature; and I dont intend to change my manners. My manners are exactly the same as Colonel Pickering's.

LIZA. Thats not true. He treats a flower girl as if she was a duchess.

HIGGINS. And I treat a duchess as if she was a flower girl.

LIZA. I see. *(She turns away composedly, and sits on the ottoman, facing the window).* The same to everybody.

HIGGINS. Just so.

LIZA. Like father.

HIGGINS *(grinning, a little taken down).* Without accepting the comparison at all points, Eliza, it's quite true that your father is not a snob, and that he will be quite at home in any station of life to which his eccentric destiny may call him. *(Seriously)* The great secret, Eliza, is not having bad manners or good manners or any other particular sort of manners, but having the same manner for all human souls: in short, behaving as if you were in Heaven, where there are no third-class carriages, and one soul is as good as another.

LIZA. Amen. You are a born preacher.

HIGGINS *(irritated).* The question is not whether I treat you rudely, but whether you ever heard me treat anyone else better.

LIZA *(with sudden sincerity).* I dont care how you treat me. I dont mind your swearing at me. I dont mind a black eye: Ive had one before this. But *(standing up and facing him)* I wont be passed over.

HIGGINS. Then get out of my way; for I wont stop for you. You talk about me as if I were a motor bus.

LIZA. So you are a motor bus: all bounce and go, and no consideration for anyone. But I can do without you: dont think I cant.

HIGGINS. I know you can. I told you you could.

LIZA *(wounded, getting away from him to the other side of the ottoman with her face to the hearth).* I know you did, you brute. You wanted to get rid of me.

HIGGINS. Liar.

LIZA. Thank you. *(She sits down with dignity).*

HIGGINS. You never asked yourself, I suppose, whether *I* could do without you.

LIZA *(earnestly)*. Dont you try to get round me. Youll have to do without me.

HIGGINS *(arrogant)*. I can do without anybody. I have my own soul: my own spark of divine fire. But *(with sudden humility)* I shall miss you, Eliza. *(He sits down near her on the ottoman)*. I have learnt something from your idiotic notions: I confess that humbly and gratefully. And I have grown accustomed to your voice and appearance. I like them, rather.

LIZA. Well, you have both of them on your gramophone and in your book of photographs. When you feel lonely without me, you can turn the machine on. It's got no feelings to hurt.

HIGGINS. I cant turn your soul on. Leave me those feelings; and you can take away the voice and the face. They are not you.

LIZA. Oh, you are a devil. You can twist the heart in a girl as easy as some could twist her arms to hurt her. Mrs Pearce warned me. Time and again she has wanted to leave you; and you always got round her at the last minute. And you dont care a bit for her. And you dont care a bit for me.

HIGGINS. I care for life, for humanity; and you are a part of it that has come my way and been built into my house. What more can you or anyone ask?

LIZA. I wont care for anybody that doesnt care for me.

HIGGINS. Commercial principles, Eliza. Like *(reproducing her Covent Garden pronunciation with professional exactness)* s'yolilin voylets *(selling violets)*, isn't it?

LIZA. Dont sneer at me. It's mean to sneer at me.

HIGGINS. I have never sneered in my life. Sneering doesnt become either the human face or the human soul. I am expressing my righteous contempt for Commercialism. I dont and wont trade in affection. You call me a brute because you couldnt buy a claim on me by fetching my slippers and finding my spectacles. You were a fool: I think a woman fetching a man's slippers is a disgusting sight: did I ever fetch your slippers? I think a good deal more of you for throwing them in my face. No use slaving for me and then saying you want to be cared for: who cares for a slave? If you come back, come back for the sake of good fellowship; for youll get nothing else. Youve had a thousand times as much out of me as I have out of you; and if you dare to set up your little dog's tricks of fetching and carrying slippers against my creation of a Duchess Eliza, I'll slam the door in your silly face.

LIZA. What did you do it for if you didnt care for me?

HIGGINS *(heartily)*. Why, because it was my job.

LIZA. You never thought of the trouble it would make for me.

HIGGINS. Would the world ever have been made if its maker had been afraid of making trouble? Making life means making trouble. Theres only one way of escaping trouble; and thats killing things. Cowards, you notice, are always shrieking to have troublesome people killed.

LIZA. I'm no preacher: I dont notice things like that. I notice that you dont notice me.

HIGGINS *(jumping up and walking about intolerantly)*. Eliza: youre an idiot. I waste the treasures of my Miltonic mind by spreading them before you. Once for all, understand that I go my way and do my work without caring twopence what happens to either of us. I am not intimidated, like your father and your stepmother. So you can come back or go to the devil: which you please.

LIZA. What am I to come back for?

HIGGINS *(bouncing up on his knees on the ottoman and leaning over it to her)*. For the fun of it. Thats why I took you on.

LIZA *(with averted face)*. And you may throw me out to-morrow if I dont do everything you want me to?

HIGGINS. Yes; and you may walk out to-morrow if I dont do everything you want me to.

LIZA. And live with my stepmother?

HIGGINS. Yes, or sell flowers.

LIZA. Oh! if I only could go back to my flower basket! I should be independent of both you and father and all the world! Why did you take my independence from me? Why did I give it up? I'm a slave now, for all my fine clothes.

HIGGINS. Not a bit. I'll adopt you as my daughter and settle money on you if you like. Or would you rather marry Pickering?

LIZA *(looking fiercely round at him).* I wouldnt marry you if you asked me; and youre nearer my age than what he is.

HIGGINS *(gently).* Than he is: not "than what he is."

LIZA *(losing her temper and rising).* I'll talk as I like. Youre not my teacher now.

HIGGINS *(reflectively).* I dont suppose Pickering would, though. He's as confirmed an old bachelor as I am.

LIZA. Thats not what I want; and dont you think it. Ive always had chaps enough wanting me that way. Freddy Hill writes to me twice and three times a day, sheets and sheets.

HIGGINS *(disagreeably surprised).* Damn his impudence! *(He recoils and finds himself sitting on his heels).*

LIZA. He has a right to if he likes, poor lad. And he does love me.

HIGGINS *(getting off the ottoman).* You have no right to encourage him.

LIZA. Every girl has a right to be loved.

HIGGINS. What! By fools like that?

LIZA. Freddy's not a fool. And if he's weak and poor and wants me, may be he'd make me happier than my betters that bully me and dont want me.

HIGGINS. Can he make anything of you? Thats the point.

LIZA. Perhaps I could make something of him. But I never thought of us making anything of one another; and you never think of anything else. I only want to be natural.

HIGGINS. In short, you want me to be as infatuated about you as Freddy? Is that it?

LIZA. No I dont. Thats not the sort of feeling I want from you. And dont you be too sure of yourself or of me. I could have been a bad girl if I'd liked. Ive seen more of some things than you, for all your learning. Girls like me can drag gentlemen down to make love to them easy enough. And they wish each other dead the next minute.

HIGGINS. Of course they do. Then what in thunder are we quarrelling about?

LIZA *(much troubled).* I want a little kindness. I know I'm a common ignorant girl, and you a book-learned gentleman; but I'm not dirt under your feet. What I done *(correcting herself)* what I did was not for the dresses and the taxis: I did it because we were pleasant together and I come—came—to care for you; not to want you to make love to me, and not forgetting the difference between us, but more friendly like.

HIGGINS. Well, of course. Thats just how I feel. And how Pickering feels. Eliza: youre a fool.

LIZA. Thats not a proper answer to give me *(she sinks on the chair at the writing-table in tears).*

HIGGINS. It's all youll get until you stop being a common idiot. If youre going to be a lady, youll have to give up feeling neglected if the men you know dont spend half their time snivelling over you and the other half giving you black eyes. If you cant stand the coldness of my sort of life, and the strain of it, go back to the gutter. Work til you are more a brute than a human being; and then cuddle and squabble and drink til you fall asleep. Oh, it's a fine life, the life of the gutter. It's real: it's warm: it's violent: you can feel it through the thickest skin: you can taste it and smell it without any training or any work. Not like Science and Literature and Classical Music and Philosophy and Art. You find me cold, unfeeling, selfish, dont you? Very well: be off with you to the sort of people you like. Marry some sentimental hog or other with lots of money, and a thick pair of lips to kiss you with and a thick pair of boots to kick you with. If you cant appreciate what youve got, youd better get what you can appreciate.

LIZA *(desperate).* Oh, you are a cruel tyrant. I cant talk to you: you turn everything against me: I'm always in the wrong. But you know very well all the time that youre nothing but a bully. You know I cant go back to the gutter, as you call it, and that I have no real friends in the world but you and the Colonel. You know well I couldnt bear to live with a low common man after you two; and it's wicked and cruel of you to insult me by pretending I could. You think I must go back to Wimpole Street because I have nowhere else to go but father's. But dont you be too sure that you have me under your feet to be trampled on and talked down. I'll marry Freddy, I will, as soon as he's able to support me.

HIGGINS *(thunderstruck).* Freddy!!! that young fool! That poor devil who couldn't get a job as an errand boy even if he had the guts to try for it! Woman: do you not understand that I have made you a consort for a king?

LIZA. Freddy loves me; that makes him king enough for me. I dont want him to work: he wasnt brought up to it as I was. I'll go and be a teacher.

HIGGINS. Whatll you teach, in heaven's name?

LIZA. What you taught me. I'll teach phonetics.

HIGGINS. Ha! ha! ha!

LIZA. I'll offer myself as an assistant to that hairy-faced Hungarian.

HIGGINS *(rising in a fury).* What! That impostor! that humbug! that toadying ignoramus! Teach him my methods! my discoveries! You take one step in his direction and I'll wring your neck. *(He lays hands on her).* Do you hear?

LIZA *(defiantly non-resistant).* Wring away. What do I care? I knew youd strike me some day. *(He lets her go, stamping with rage at having forgotten himself, and recoils so hastily that he stumbles back into his seat on the ottoman).* Aha! Now I know how to deal with you. What a fool I was not to think of it before! You cant take away the knowledge you gave me. You said I had a finer ear than you. And I can be civil and kind to people, which is more than you can. Aha! *(Purposely dropping her aitches to annoy him)* Thats done you, Enry Iggins, it has. Now I dont care that *(snapping her fingers)* for your bullying and your big talk. I'll advertize it in the papers that your duchess is only a flower girl that you taught, and that she'll teach anybody to be a duchess just the same in six months for a thousand guineas. Oh, when I think of myself crawling under your feet and being trampled on and called names, when all the time I had only to lift up my finger to be as good as you, I could just kick myself.

HIGGINS *(wondering at her).* You damned impudent slut, you! But it's better than snivelling; better than fetching slippers and finding spectacles, isnt it? *(Rising)* By George, Eliza, I said I'd make a woman of you; and I have. I like you like this.

LIZA. Yes: you turn round and make up to me now that I'm not afraid of you, and can do without you.

HIGGINS. Of course I do, you little fool. Five minutes ago you were like a millstone round my neck. Now youre a tower of strength: a consort battleship. You and I and Pickering will be three old bachelors together instead of only two men and a silly girl.

MRS HIGGINS *returns, dressed for the wedding.* ELIZA *instantly becomes cool and elegant.*

MRS HIGGINS. The carriage is waiting, Eliza. Are you ready?

LIZA. Quite. Is the Professor coming?

MRS HIGGINS. Certainly not. He cant behave himself in church. He makes remarks out loud all the time on the clergyman's pronunciation.

LIZA. Then I shall not see you again, Professor. Goodbye. *(She goes to the door).*

MRS HIGGINS *(coming to* HIGGINS*).* Goodbye, dear.

HIGGINS. Goodbye, mother. *(He is about to kiss her, when he recollects something).* Oh, by the way, Eliza, order a ham and a Stilton cheese, will you? And buy me a pair of reindeer gloves, number eights, and a tie to match that new suit of mine. You can choose the color. *(His cheerful, careless, vigorous voice shows that he is incorrigible).*

LIZA *(disdainfully).* Number eights are too small for you if you want them lined with lamb's wool. You have three new ties that you have forgotten in the drawer of your washstand. Colonel Pickering prefers double Gloucester to Stilton; and you dont notice the difference. I telephoned Mrs Pearce this morning not to forget the ham. What you are to do without me I cannot imagine. *(She sweeps out).*

MRS HIGGINS. I'm afraid youve spoilt that girl, Henry. I should be uneasy about you and her if she were less fond of Colonel Pickering.

HIGGINS. Pickering! Nonsense; she's going to marry Freddy. Ha ha! Freddy! Freddy!! Ha ha ha ha ha!!!!! *(He roars with laughter as the play ends).*

Epilogue

The rest of the story need not be shewn in action, and indeed, would hardly need telling if our imaginations were not so enfeebled by their lazy dependence on the ready-mades and reach-me-downs of the ragshop in which Romance keeps its stock of "happy endings" to misfit all stories. Now, the history of Eliza Doolittle, though called a romance because the transfiguration it records seems exceedingly improbable, is common enough. Such transfigurations have been achieved by hundreds of resolutely ambitious young women since Nell Gwynne set them the example by playing queens and fascinating kings in the theatre in which she began by selling oranges. Nevertheless, people in all directions have assumed, for no other reason than that she became the heroine of a romance, that she must have married the hero of it. This is unbearable, not only because her little drama, if acted on such a thoughtless assumption, must be spoiled, but because the true sequel is patent to anyone with a sense of human nature in general, and of feminine instinct in particular.

Eliza, in telling Higgins she would not marry him if he asked her, was not coquetting: she was announcing a well-considered decision. When a bachelor interests, and dominates, and teaches, and becomes important to a spinster, as Higgins with Eliza, she always, if she has character enough to be capable of it, considers very seriously indeed whether she will play for becoming that bachelor's wife, especially if he is so little interested in marriage that a determined and devoted woman might capture him if she set herself resolutely to do it. Her decision will depend a good deal on whether she is really free to choose; and that, again, will depend on her age and income. If she is at the end of her youth, and has no security for her livelihood, she will marry him because she must marry anybody who will provide for her. But at Eliza's age a good-looking girl does not feel that pressure: she feels free to pick and choose. She is therefore guided by her instinct in the matter. Eliza's instinct tells her not to marry Higgins. It does not tell her to give him up. It is not in the slightest doubt as to his remaining one of the strongest personal interests in her life. It would be very sorely strained if there was another woman likely to supplant her with him. But as she feels sure of him on that last point, she has no doubt at all as to her course, and would not have any, even if the difference of twenty years in age, which seems so great to youth, did not exist between them.

As our own instincts are not appealed to by her conclusion, let us see whether we cannot discover some reason in it. When Higgins excused his indifference to young women on the ground that they had an irresistible rival in his mother, he gave the clue to his inveterate old-bachelordom. The case is uncommon only to the extent that remarkable mothers are uncommon. If an imaginative boy has a sufficiently rich mother who has intelligence, personal grace, dignity of character without harshness, and a cultivated sense of the best art of her time to enable her to make her house beautiful, she sets a standard for him against which very few women can struggle, besides effecting for him a disengagement of his affections, his sense of beauty, and his idealism from his specifically sexual impulses. This makes him a standing puzzle to the huge number of uncultivated people who have been brought up in tasteless homes by commonplace or disagreeable parents, and to whom, consequently, literature, painting, sculpture, music, and affectionate personal relations come as modes of sex if they come at all. The word passion means nothing else to them; and that Higgins could have a passion for phonetics and idealize his mother instead of Eliza, would seem to them absurd and unnatural. Nevertheless, when we look round and see that hardly anyone is too ugly or disagreeable to find a wife or a husband if he or she wants one, whilst many old maids and bachelors are above the average in quality and culture, we cannot help suspecting that the disentanglement of sex from the associations with which it is so commonly confused, a disentanglement which persons of genius achieve by sheer intellectual analysis, is sometimes produced or aided by parental fascination.

Now, though Eliza was incapable of thus explaining to herself Higgins's formidable powers of resistance to the charm that prostrated Freddy at the first glance, she was instinctively aware that she could never obtain a complete grip of him, or come between him and his mother (the first necessity of the married woman). To put it shortly, she knew that for some mysterious reason he had not the makings of a married man in him, according to her conception of a husband as one to whom she would be his nearest and fondest and warmest interest. Even had there been no mother-rival, she would still have refused to accept an interest in herself that was secondary to philosophic interests. Had Mrs Higgins died, there would still have been Milton and the Universal Alphabet. Landor's remark that to those who have the greatest power of loving, love is a secondary affair, would not have recommended Landor to Eliza. Put that along with her resentment of Higgins's domineering superiority, and her mistrust of his coaxing cleverness in getting round her and evading her wrath when he had gone too far with his impetuous bullying, and you will see that Eliza's instinct had good grounds for warning her not to marry her Pygmalion.

And now, whom did Eliza marry? For if Higgins was a predestinate old bachelor, she was most certainly not a predestinate old maid. Well, that can be told very shortly to those who have not guessed it from the indications she has herself given them.

Almost immediately after Eliza is stung into proclaiming her considered determination not to marry Higgins, she mentions the fact that young Mr Frederick Eynsford Hill is pouring out his love for her daily through the post. Now Freddy is young, practically twenty years younger than Higgins: he is a gentleman (or, as Eliza would qualify him, a toff), and speaks like one; he is nicely dressed, is treated by the Colonel as an equal, loves her unaffectedly, and is not her master, nor ever likely to dominate her in spite of his advantage of social standing. Eliza has no use for the foolish romantic tradition that all women love to be mastered, if not actually bullied and beaten. "When you go to women," says Nietzsche, "take your whip with you." Sensible despots have never confined that precaution to women: they have taken their whips with them when they have dealt with men, and been slavishly idealized by the men over whom they have flourished the whip much more than by women. No doubt there are slavish women as well as slavish men: and women, like men, admire those that are stronger than themselves. But to admire a strong person and to live under that strong person's thumb are two different things. The weak may not be admired and hero-worshipped; but they are by no means disliked or shunned; and they never seem to have the least difficulty in marrying people who are too good for them. They may fail in emergencies; but life is not one long emergency: it is mostly a string of situations for which no exceptional strength is needed, and with which even rather weak people can cope if they have a stronger partner to help them out. Accordingly, it is a truth everywhere in evidence that strong people, masculine or feminine, not only do not marry stronger people, but do not shew any preference for them in selecting their friends. When a lion meets another with a louder roar "the first lion thinks the last a bore." The man or woman who feels strong enough for two, seeks for every other quality in a partner than strength.

The converse is also true. Weak people want to marry strong people who do not frighten them too much; and this often leads them to make the mistake we describe metaphorically as "biting off more than they can chew." They want too much for too little; and when the bargain is unreasonable beyond all bearing, the union becomes impossible: it ends in the weaker party being either discarded or borne as a cross, which is worse. People who are not only weak, but silly or obtuse as well, are often in these difficulties.

This being the state of human affairs, what is Eliza fairly sure to do when she is placed between Freddy and Higgins? Will she look forward to a lifetime of fetching Higgins's slippers or to a lifetime of Freddy fetching hers? There can be no doubt about the answer. Unless Freddy is biologically repulsive to her, and Higgins biologically attractive to a degree that overwhelms all her other instincts, she will, if she marries either of them, marry Freddy.

And that is just what Eliza did.

Complications ensued; but they were economic, not romantic. Freddy had no money and no occupation. His mother's jointure, a last relic of the opulence of Largelady Park, had enabled her to struggle along in Earlscourt with an air of gentility, but not to procure any serious secondary education for her children, much less give the boy a profession. A clerkship at thirty shillings a week was beneath Freddy's dignity, and extremely distasteful to him besides. His prospects consisted of a hope that if he kept up appearances somebody would do something for him. The something appeared vaguely to his imagination as a private secretaryship or a sinecure of some sort. To his mother it perhaps appeared as a marriage to some lady of means who could not resist her boy's niceness. Fancy her feelings when he married a flower girl who had become déclasseé under extraordinary circumstances which were now notorious!

It is true that Eliza's situation did not seem wholly ineligible. Her father, though formerly a dustman, and now fantastically disclassed, had become extremely popular in the smartest society by a social talent which triumphed over every prejudice and every disadvantage. Rejected by the middle class, which he loathed, he had shot up at once into the highest circles by his wit, his dustmanship (which he carried like a banner), and his Nietzschean transcendence of good and evil. At intimate ducal dinners he sat on the right hand of the Duchess; and in country houses he smoked in the pantry and was made much of by the butler when he was not feeding in the dining room and being consulted by cabinet ministers. But he found it almost as hard to do all this on three thousand a year as Mrs Eynsford Hill to live in Earlscourt on an income so pitiably smaller that I have not the heart to disclose its exact figure. He absolutely refused to add the last straw to his burden by contributing to Eliza's support.

Thus Freddy and Eliza, now Mr and Mrs Eynsford Hill, would have spent a penniless honeymoon but for a wedding present of £500 from the Colonel to Eliza. It lasted a long time because Freddy did not know how to spend money, never having had any to spend, and Eliza, socially trained by a pair of old bachelors, wore her clothes as long as they held together and looked pretty, without the least regard to their being many months out of fashion. Still, £500 will not last two young people for ever; and they both knew, and Eliza felt as well, that they must shift for themselves in the end. She could quarter herself on Wimpole Street because it had come to be her home; but she was quite aware that she ought not to quarter Freddy there, and that it would not be good for his character if she did.

Not that the Wimpole Street bachelors objected. When she consulted them, Higgins declined to be bothered about her housing problem when that solution was so simple. Eliza's desire to have Freddy in the house with her seemed of no more importance than if she had wanted an extra piece of bedroom furniture. Pleas as to Freddy's character, and the moral obligation on him to earn his own living, were lost on Higgins. He denied that Freddy had any character, and declared that if he tried to do any useful work some competent person would have the trouble of undoing it: a procedure involving a net loss to the community, and great unhappiness to Freddy himself, who was obviously intended by Nature for such light work as amusing Eliza, which, Higgins declared, was a much more useful and honorable occupation than working in the city. When Eliza referred again to her project of teaching phonetics, Higgins abated not a jot of his violent opposition to it. He said she was not within ten years of being qualified to meddle with his pet subject; and as it was evident that the Colonel agreed with him, she felt she could not go against them in this grave matter, and that she had no right, without Higgins's consent, to exploit the knowledge he had given her; for his knowledge seemed to her as much his private property as his watch: Eliza was no communist. Besides, she was superstitiously devoted to them both, more entirely and frankly after her marriage than before it.

It was the Colonel who finally solved the problem, which had cost him much perplexed cogitation. He one day asked Eliza, rather shyly, whether she had quite given up her notion of keeping a flower shop. She replied that she had thought of it, but had put it out of her head, because the Colonel had said, that day at Mrs Higgins's, that it would never do. The Colonel confessed that when he said that, he had not quite recovered from the dazzling impression of the day before. They broke the matter to Higgins that evening. The sole comment vouchsafed by him very nearly led to a serious quarrel with Eliza. It was to the effect that she would have in Freddy an ideal errand boy.

Freddy himself was next sounded on the subject. He said he had been thinking of a shop himself; though it had presented itself to his pennilessness as a small place in which Eliza should sell tobacco at one counter whilst he sold newspapers at the opposite one. But he agreed that it would be extraordinarily jolly to go early every morning with Eliza to Covent Garden and buy flowers on the scene of their first meeting: a sentiment which earned him many kisses from his wife. . . .

Now here is a last opportunity for romance. Would you not like to be assured that the shop was an immense success, thanks to Eliza's charms and her early business experience in Covent Garden? Alas! the truth is the truth: the shop did not pay for a long time, simply because Eliza and her Freddy did not know how to keep it. True, Eliza had not to begin at the very beginning: she knew the names and prices of the cheaper flowers; and her elation was unbounded when she found that Freddy, like all youths educated at cheap, pretentious, and thoroughly inefficient schools, knew a little Latin. It was very little, but enough to make him appear to her a Porson or Bentley,[1] and to put him at his ease with botanical nomenclature. Unfortunately he knew nothing else; and Eliza, though she could count money up to eighteen shillings or so, and had acquired a certain familiarity with the language of Milton from her struggles to qualify herself for winning Higgins's bet, could not write out a bill without utterly disgracing the establishment. Freddy's power of stating in Latin that Balbus built a wall and that Gaul was divided into three parts did not carry with it the slightest knowledge of accounts or business: Colonel Pickering had to explain to him what a cheque book and a bank account meant. And the pair were by no means easily teachable. Freddy backed up Eliza in her obstinate refusal to believe that they could save money by engaging a bookkeeper with some knowledge of the business. How, they argued, could you possibly save money by going to extra expense when you already could not make both ends meet? But the Colonel, after making the ends meet over and over again, at last gently insisted; and Eliza, humbled to the dust by having to beg from him so often, and stung by the uproarious derision of Higgins, to whom the notion of Freddy succeeding at anything was a joke that never palled, grasped the fact that business, like phonetics, has to be learned.

On the piteous spectacle of the pair spending their evenings in shorthand schools and polytechnic classes, learning bookkeeping and typewriting with incipient junior clerks, male and female, from the elementary schools, let me not dwell. There were even classes at the London School of Economics, and a humble personal appeal to the director of that institution to recommend a course bearing on the flower business. He, being a humorist, explained to them the method of the celebrated Dickensian essay on Chinese Metaphysics by the gentleman who read an article on China and an article on Metaphysics and combined the information. He suggested that they should combine the London School with Kew Gardens. Eliza, to whom the procedure of the Dickensian gentleman seemed perfectly correct (as in fact it was) and not in the least funny (which was only her ignorance), took his advice with entire gravity. But the effort that cost her the deepest humiliation was a request to Higgins, whose pet artistic fancy, next to Milton's verse, was calligraphy, and who himself wrote a most beautiful Italian hand, that he would teach her to write. He declared that she was congenitally incapable of forming a single letter worthy of the least of Milton's words; but she persisted; and again he suddenly threw himself into the task of teaching her with a combination of stormy intensity, concentrated patience, and occasional bursts of interesting disquisition on the beauty and nobility, the august mission and destiny, of human handwriting. Eliza ended by acquiring an extremely uncommercial script which was a positive extension of her personal beauty, and spending three times as much on stationery as anyone else because certain qualities and shapes of paper became indispensable to her. She could not even address an envelope in the usual way because it made the margins all wrong.

Their commercial schooldays were a period of disgrace and despair for the young couple. They seemed to be learning nothing about flower shops. At last they gave it up as hopeless, and shook the dust of the shorthand schools, and the polytechnics, and the London School of Economics from their feet for ever. Besides, the business was in some mysterious way beginning to take care of itself. They had somehow forgotten their objections to employing other people. They came to the conclusion that their own way

1. ***Porson or Bentley.*** Richard Porson (1759–1808), professor of Greek at Cambridge University, was a famous English scholar. Richard Bentley (1662–1742) was a well-known classical scholar.

was the best, and that they had really a remarkable talent for business. The Colonel, who had been compelled for some years to keep a sufficient sum on current account at his bankers to make up their deficits, found that the provision was unnecessary: the young people were prospering. It is true that there was not quite fair play between them and their competitors in trade. Their week-ends in the country cost them nothing, and saved them the price of their Sunday dinners; for the motor car was the Colonel's; and he and Higgins paid the hotel bills. Mr F. Hill, florist and greengrocer (they soon discovered that there was money in asparagus; and asparagus led to other vegetables), had an air which stamped the business as classy; and in private life he was still Frederick Eynsford Hill, Esquire. Not that there was any swank about him: nobody but Eliza knew that he had been christened Frederick Challoner. Eliza herself swanked like anything.

That is all. That is how it turned out. It is astonishing how much Eliza still manages to meddle in housekeeping at Wimpole Street in spite of the shop and her own family. And it is notable that though she never nags her husband, and frankly loves the Colonel as if she were his favorite daughter, she has never got out of the habit of nagging Higgins that was established on the fatal night when she won his bet for him. She snaps his head off on the faintest provocation, or on none. He no longer dares to tease her by assuming an abysmal inferiority of Freddy's mind to his own. He storms and bullies and derides: but she stands up to him so ruthlessly that the Colonel has to ask her from time to time to be kinder to Higgins; and it is the only request of his that brings a mulish expression into her face. Nothing but some emergency or calamity great enough to break down all likes and dislikes, and throw them both back on their common humanity—and may they be spared any such trial!—will ever alter this. She knows that Higgins does not need her, just as her father did not need her. The very scrupulousness with which he told her that day that he had become used to having her there, and dependent on her for all sorts of little services, and that he should miss her if she went away (it would never have occurred to Freddy or the Colonel to say anything of the sort) deepens her inner certainty that she is "no more to him than them slippers"; yet she has a sense, too, that his indifference is deeper than the infatuation of commoner souls. She is immensely interested in him. She has even secret mischievous moments in which she wishes she could get him alone, on a desert island, away from all ties and with nobody else in the world to consider, and just drag him off his pedestal and see him making love like any common man. We all have private imaginations of that sort. But when it comes to business, to the life that she really leads as distinguished from the life of dreams and fancies, she likes Freddy and she likes the Colonel; and she does not like Higgins and Mr Doolittle. Galatea never does quite like Pygmalion: his relation to her is too godlike to be altogether agreeable.

Discussion

Act One

1. How does the scene at Covent Garden provide a logical introduction to the main characters in the play?

2. (a) What social class is represented by the daughter, mother, and son Freddy? **(b)** Through what actions does Shaw reveal the character of the daughter in this scene?

3. (a) What class is represented by the bystander? **(b)** Why are they generally sympathetic to the flower girl? **(c)** What causes them to switch their sympathies to the note taker?

4. (a) What is the note taker's attitude toward the flower girl? **(b)** According to the note taker, what will keep the flower girl in the lower class?

Act Two

1. In the stage directions given for Eliza's entrance, what does Shaw say about Higgins's distinction between men and women?

2. Higgins says that he will

make a "duchess of this draggletailed guttersnipe." **(a)** What does he mean, and what does the statement reveal about him? **(b)** What arguments are put forth against using Eliza as a guinea pig, and how does Higgins answer each objection? **(c)** What do his arguments reveal about him?

3. How is Pickering's personality different from Higgins's?

4. **(a)** How does Doolittle define middle-class morality? **(b)** What does he mean when he says that he cannot afford to have morals?

5. What class or classes seem to be the main objects of Shaw's satire here?

Act Three

1. **(a)** Why has Higgins brought Eliza to his mother's at-home? **(b)** Describe Mrs. Higgins, drawing inferences from what she says and does in this act. **(c)** How is Higgins treated by his mother?

2. **(a)** How does Eliza reveal that she has not entirely mastered the social customs of the time? **(b)** To whom does Eliza seem a complete success? **(c)** What effect does Eliza produce on Clara?

3. What upper-class attitudes does Shaw criticize in this act?

4. Explain the reason for Mrs. Higgins's anger at the end of the act.

Act Four

1. How does Higgins react to Eliza's success at the garden party?

2. What comments does Pickering make about people's success in society?

3. Consider the relationship of Act Four to the development of the play. **(a)** Is it more important to the development of the plot, exposition of ideas, or creation of comic effects? **(b)** What two conflicts reach a climax in Act Four? **(c)** How are they resolved? **(d)** What problem must be resolved in the next act, and what are the possible solutions to the problems?

Act Five

1. **(a)** What circumstances have brought about Doolittle's change of fortune? **(b)** What is Doolittle's reaction to this change? **(c)** According to Doolittle, what is the difference between the middle class and the undeserving poor?

2. **(a)** Eliza says that it is manners that make one a lady; but what does she think is the biggest difference between a flower girl and a lady? **(b)** What explanation does Higgins give for his manners?

3. By the end of the act, has Eliza's problem been resolved?

The Epilogue

1. Why did Shaw think *Pygmalion* needed an epilogue?

2. Explain Shaw's reason for considering *Pygmalion* a romance.

3. Shaw explains that Eliza does not marry Higgins because she was "instinctively aware that she could never obtain a complete grip of him." What prevented her from getting a complete grip of him?

4. In Acts Two and Four, Higgins and Doolittle comment on marriage and the romantic notions of love. How does the "Epilogue" bear this out?

The Play

1. As the play progresses, Eliza emerges as a person rather than a character. Cite actions that show her emerging as a person.

2. Which characters does Shaw sketch in stage directions? Note the passages.

3. Much of Shaw's writing, like Sir Francis Bacon's, is aphoristic in style. Explain the main idea of each of the following aphorisms: **(a)** "What is middle class morality? Just an excuse for never giving me anything." (Alfred Doolittle, Act Two). **(b)** ". . . the difference between a lady and a flower girl is not how she behaves, but how she's treated." (Eliza, Act Five).

4. **(a)** Explain why Shaw called this play *Pygmalion.* **(b)** In what way is the title related to the theme?

Extension • Speaking

1. Choose a scene from the play and perform it for the class. Try to duplicate the language of the speakers.

2. Participate in a debate in which you argue for or against Eliza's marrying Professor Higgins.

Extension • Writing

1. Using the Pygmalion myth, write a one-act play or a film script set in the 1970s.

2. Write an essay comparing the characteristics of Higgins and Pickering.

3. Shaw called his play "a romance in Five Acts." In an essay, explain why you agree or disagree with Shaw.

4. Assume that you have not read Shaw's "Epilogue" to *Pygmalion* and write an essay explaining how you think the story ends.

Vocabulary
Pronunciation and Structure

A. Use your Glossary and its pronunciation key to answer the following questions about the pronunciation of the italicized words. Write your answers on a separate sheet of paper. Be sure you know the meaning of each italicized word.

1. Which syllable in *infamous* receives the primary accent or stress? **(a)** first; **(b)** second; **(c)** third.

2. Which of the following words rhymes with *draught?* **(a)** out; **(b)** ought; **(c)** raft; **(d)** straight.

3. How many syllables has *magisterially*? **(a)** three; **(b)** four; **(c)** five; **(d)** six; **(e)** seven.

4. The second vowel sound in *mendacity* rhymes with the vowel sound in which word? **(a)** hate; **(b)** mat; **(c)** car; **(d)** straw.

5. What is a rhyme word for the accented syllable in *soirée*? **(a)** flee; **(b)** cry; **(c)** stew; **(d)** bar; **(e)** clay.

B. Use the Glossary to answer the following questions about the structure of the words given below. Read each clue and then write on your paper the matching word from the list.

deprecate
incense
infatuate
magnanimous
perfunctory

6. Which word has a root that describes an act that is often performed in church?

7. Which has a root that describes how a light might burn?

8. Which is formed from two roots that mean something large but invisible?

9. Which has a root that can mean something done to criminals?

10. Which has a root with a meaning that might describe a dunce?

Bernard Shaw 1856 • 1950

"Things have not happened to me," Shaw once said; "on the contrary, it is I who have happened to things." To the public, Shaw was a witty and somewhat arrogant iconoclast, supporter of socialism, antivivisection, and vegetarianism. But under this mask of eccentricity was a man seriously concerned with solving mankind's problems.

Shaw was born in Dublin. For the first few years after his arrival in London in 1876, he earned a very meager living as an art critic, a music critic, and a literary editor and reviewer. When he began writing for the stage in 1885, most of his plays faced censorship problems and were banned. His caustic wit, directed at marriage, parenthood, and heroism, offended those who considered these traditions too sacred for ridicule. Shaw then, in an attempt to find readers rather than viewers, began including long prefaces, epilogues, and very detailed stage directions as vehicles to enable him to present his ideas. His sense of the comic and his skill in argumentation won him a reading public and ultimately aroused interest in seeing his works performed. By the time of World War I, his plays were enjoying successful runs on stage.

Among Shaw's avid followers were those who believe that things are not always what they seem, that what is conventionally considered to be bad or wicked may actually contain nobility, and that preconceived attitudes about human character may in reality be very far from the truth. For example, in his play *Arms and the Man*, a soldier demonstrates that military heroism is primarily the creation of the civilian mind. And in *Pygmalion*, he exposes the illusions of class distinctions.

In addition to his interest in the theater, Shaw advocated spelling reform that would include a phonetic alphabet of forty-four letters, each representing a sound. In his writing, he omitted apostrophes in some contractions. He stipulated in his will that the money in his estate was to be used to promote a system of English spelling that would implement his suggested reforms.

Unit Review Tests 7: New Directions

CONTENT REVIEW

1. British poetry written during this period of political and economic success is frequently about death. **(a)** In what ways does this subject appear in Hardy's poetry? Does death give any meaning to life in his poems? **(b)** Why does Housman actually praise a young man for dying? **(c)** And in Hopkins's poem, why does Margaret grieve? Does the speaker of that poem offer her any consolation? **(d)** In what ways can "The Second Coming" be considered a poem about death? What sort of future does it anticipate?

2. **(a)** In poem after poem Hopkins turns to nature. What does he find there? **(b)** How do Hardy and Housman differ in their approach to nature? Select one poem by each which seems to express most completely their relationship with nature, and point out how it develops their ideas. **(c)** What do the wild swans at Coole teach Yeats about nature?

3. **(a)** What kinds of isolation do you find in the poems of Hopkins, Hardy, Housman, and Yeats? List specific examples for each. **(b)** Which of these writers finds a solution to the problems of alienation? What are the solutions? **(c)** Which do not? How do they adjust?

4. **(a)** In the poetry of Housman one frequently encounters nostalgia for a lost past. What does he miss? Why are these things now lost to him? **(b)** Which Hardy poems deal with this same theme? What similarities do they share with Housman's poems on the same subject? **(c)** What are the poems by Yeats which take up this theme? In what way does Maud Gonne give shape and direction to some of these poems?

5. When it was first published in 1894, "The Miracle of Purun Bhagat" was titled "A Miracle of the Present Day." In light of what you know about the period of New Directions, explain why you believe Kipling changed the title of his story. Begin by citing some of the characteristics of England and its literature in the "present day"—i.e., the last decade of the nineteenth century.

6. Discuss ways in which Conrad's "The Lagoon" reflects the "loss of faith" in traditional beliefs which is characteristic of the period of New Directions. Begin by considering how Conrad treats concepts such as love, loyalty, and honor.

7. Discuss the extent to which Hardy's "The Grave by the Handpost" is a story of conscious human *choices*, and not simply the workings of chance.

8. Define as accurately as possible the central catastrophes in the stories by Kipling and Wells, respectively. Then compare and contrast the two stories as "optimistic" or "pessimistic" statements regarding the human potential for responding to catastrophe.

9. Most of George Gissing's life was spent in poverty and misery. **(a)** How is this reflected in his writing? **(b)** How does it influence his attitude toward his main protagonist?

10. Discuss the ways in which *Pygmalion* reflects Shaw's "New Directions" attitudes toward any two of the following: **(a)** the roles of women, **(b)** education, **(c)** social class.

from Major Barbara, Act One

Bernard Shaw

The title character in Shaw's play Major Barbara *(1906) is Barbara Undershaft, daughter of Lady Britomart and Andrew Undershaft, an arms merchant and millionaire. Barbara, one of three children, has shocked her upper-class mother by joining the Salvation Army. The parents live apart, and Andrew Undershaft has not seen his family in years. Lady Britomart invites him to her house to see the children because Barbara and her sister are to be married to young men who, although otherwise acceptable, have limited funds; therefore, the daughters will need larger allowances from their father. In the following excerpt from the play, Andrew Undershaft has just arrived for dinner and been introduced to his grown children and prospective sons-in-law. As the following scene opens Charles Lomax (see Cast of Characters) is about to play a tune on his concertina—a musical instrument somewhat like an accordion—for the group, assembled in the library. Answer the questions that follow this excerpt on a separate sheet of paper.*

Cast of Characters

ANDREW UNDERSHAFT
LADY BRITOMART UNDERSHAFT
BARBARA
SARAH *their children*
STEPHEN
CHARLES LOMAX (Cholly), engaged to Sarah
ADOLPHUS CUSINS, professor of Greek, engaged to Barbara

UNDERSHAFT. One moment, Mr. Lomax. I am rather interested in the Salvation Army. Its motto might be my own: Blood and Fire.
LOMAX *(shocked).* But not your sort of blood and fire, you know.
UNDERSHAFT. My sort of blood cleanses: my sort of fire purifies.
BARBARA. So do ours. Come down to-morrow to my shelter—the West Ham shelter—and see what we're doing. We're going to march to a great meeting in the Assembly Hall at Mile End. Come

and see the shelter and then march with us: it will do you a lot of good. Can you play anything?

UNDERSHAFT. In my youth I earned pennies, and even shillings occasionally, in the streets and in public house parlors by my natural talent for stepdancing.[1] Later on, I became a member of the Undershaft orchestral society, and performed passably on the tenor trombone.

LOMAX *(scandalized—putting down the concertina).* Oh I say!

BARBARA. Many a sinner has played himself into heaven on the trombone, thanks to the Army.

LOMAX *(to Barbara, still rather shocked).* Yes; but what about the cannon business, dont you know? *(To Undershaft).* Getting into heaven is not exactly in your line, is it?

LADY BRITOMART. Charles!!!

LOMAX. Well; but it stands to reason, dont it? The cannon business may be necessary and all that: we cant get on without cannons; but it isnt right, you know. On the other hand, there may be a certain amount of tosh[2] about the Salvation Army—I belong to the Established Church[3] myself—but still you cant deny that it's religion; and you cant go against religion, can you? At least unless youre downright immoral, dont you know.

UNDERSHAFT. You hardly appreciate my position, Mr. Lomax—

LOMAX *(hastily).* I'm not saying anything against you personally!

UNDERSHAFT. Quite so, quite so. But consider for a moment. Here I am, a profiteer in mutilation and murder. I find myself in a specially amiable humor just now because, this morning, down at the foundry, we blew twenty-seven dummy soldiers into fragments with a gun which formally destroyed only thirteen.

LOMAX *(leniently).* Well, the more destructive war becomes, the sooner it will be abolished, eh?

UNDERSHAFT. Not at all. The more destructive war becomes the more fascinating we find it. No, Mr. Lomax: I am obliged to you for making the usual excuse for my trade; but I am not ashamed of it. I am not one of those men who keep their morals and their business in watertight compartments. All the spare money my trade rivals spend on hospitals, cathedrals, and other receptacles for conscience money, I devote to experiments and researchs in improved methods of destroying life and property. I have always done so; and I always shall. Therefore your Christmas card moralities of peace on earth and goodwill among men are of no use to me. Your Christianity, which enjoins you to resist not evil, and to turn the other cheek, would make me a bankrupt. My morality—my religion—must have a place for cannons and torpedoes in it.

---

1. ***stepdancing,*** a solo dance characterized by intricate steps such as tapping or kicking, sometimes performed with the hands in the pockets.
2. ***tosh,*** nonsense.
3. ***Established Church,*** the Church of England, a national institution recognized and supported by the government.

STEPHEN *(coldly—almost sullenly).* You speak as if there were half a dozen moralities and religions to choose from, instead of one true morality and one true religion.

UNDERSHAFT. For me there is only one true morality; but it might not fit you, as you do not manufacture aerial battleships. There is only one true morality for every man; but every man has not the same true morality.

LOMAX *(overtaxed).* Would you mind saying that again? I didn't quite follow it.

CUSINS. It's quite simple. As Euripides[4] says, one man's meat is another man's poison morally as well as physically.

UNDERSHAFT. Precisely.

LOMAX. Oh, that. Yes, yes, yes. True. True.

STEPHEN. In other words, some men are honest and some are scoundrels.

BARBARA. Bosh.[5] There are no scoundrels.

UNDERSHAFT. Indeed? Are there any good men?

BARBARA. No. Not one. There are neither good men nor scoundrels: there are just children of one Father; and the sooner they stop calling one another names the better. You neednt talk to me: I know them. Ive had scores of them through my hands: scoundrels, criminals, infidels, philanthropists, missionaries, county councillors, all sorts. Theyre all just the same sort of sinner; and theres the same salvation ready for them all.

UNDERSHAFT. May I ask have you ever saved a maker of cannons?

BARBARA. No. Will you let me try?

UNDERSHAFT. Well, I will make a bargain with you. If I go to see you to-morrow in your Salvation Shelter, will you come the day after to see me in my cannon works?

BARBARA. Take care. It may end in your giving up the cannons for the sake of the Salvation Army.

UNDERSHAFT. Are you sure it will not end in your giving up the Salvation Army for the sake of the cannons?

BARBARA. I will take my chance of that.

UNDERSHAFT. And I will take my chance of the other. *(They shake hands on it).* Where is your shelter?

BARBARA. In West Ham. At the sign of the cross. Ask anybody in Canning Town. Where are your works?

UNDERSHAFT. In Perivale St Andrews. At the sign of the sword. Ask anybody in Europe.

LOMAX. Hadnt I better play something?

BARBARA. Yes. Give us Onward, Christian Soldiers.

LOMAX. Well, thats rather a strong order to begin with, dont you know. Suppose I sing Thourt passing hence, my brother. It's much the same tune.

---

4. ***Euripides*** (yü rip′ə dēz′), (480?-406? B.C.), Greek dramatist.
5. ***Bosh,*** nonsense.

BARBARA. It's too melancholy. You get saved, Cholly; and youll pass hence, my brother, without making such a fuss about it.

LADY BRITOMART. Really, Barbara, you go on as if religion were a pleasant subject. Do have some sense of propriety.

UNDERSHAFT. I do not find it an unpleasant subject, my dear. It is the only one that capable people really care for.

1. What do Undershaft's remarks about how he earned money as a youth and Lomax's scandalized response to his remarks say about the class origins of the two men?

2. The members of the upper classes in England sometimes used nonstandard language as an affectation. Sometimes they simply made mistakes. Cite an example of such nonstandard speech in the words of Lomax.

3. What different conclusions do Undershaft and Lomax draw from the increasing destructiveness of war, a fact they both acknowledge?

4. What different points of view do Undershaft and his son Stephen have on the nature of morality?

5. When Barbara denies the existence of good men and scoundrels, is she denying the existence of morality or religion? Explain.

6. **(a)** What is the bargain that Undershaft and Barbara strike? **(b)** What does each see as the possible consequence of the bargain?

7. What attitude does Lady Britomart express toward religion?

8. Explain Mr. Undershaft's statement at the end of this scene that religion is the only subject "that capable people really care for," in the light of his earlier statements on religion and morality.

9. What are some of Mr. Undershaft's outstanding qualities or characteristics?

10. In what ways, if any, does Barbara resemble her father?

Unit 7, Test II

COMPOSITION

You may choose any *one* of the following assignments. Assume that you are writing for your classmates.

1. Compare and contrast Hardy's and Hopkins's views of the world of nature as revealed in their poetry.

2. Compare and contrast Hardy's and Hopkins's views of the ultimate meaning of life as revealed in their poems.

3. Discuss Yeats's view of youth and old age in "Sailing to Byzantium" and "When You Are Old."

4. Discuss the skeptical element in Hardy's poetry and contrast it to the element of belief in the poetry of Yeats.

5. Discuss the importance and effect of family ties and relationships for Arsat in "The Lagoon" and Luke in "The Grave by the Handpost."

6. Compare and contrast the character of Purun Bhagat in "The Miracle of Purun Bhagat" with that of Luke in "The Grave by the Handpost" in terms of their leaving settled worlds and embarking upon new lives.

7. Interpret Wells's "The Star" in the light of the extended quote from C. S. Lewis in *notes and comments* ("Science Fiction") on page 496.

8. Contrast the life of Purun Bhagat with his earlier life as Purun Dass, and discuss the attitude toward worldly success implied in this transformation.

9. Discuss aspects of the class system in England as reflected in the various characters in *Pygmalion.*

10. In the poems, stories, and drama in this unit you have met with, on the one hand, a religious, idealistic, or sacred view of life, and, on the other, a pessimistic, secular, and skeptical view. Discuss the excerpt from Shaw's *Major Barbara* in Test I in terms of this opposition of values, and cite other works in the unit that reflect this opposition.

Unit 8:

1915 · 1925 · 1935 · 1945

- World War I begins
- Shaw: *Heartbreak House*
- Strachey: *Eminent Victorians*
- Peace of Versailles
- Owen: *Poems*
- Lawrence: *Women in Love*
- Irish Free State
- Joyce: *Ulysses*
- Forster: *A Passage to India*
- Shaw: *St. Joan*
- Woolf: *Mrs. Dalloway*
- General Strike
- Women win vote
- Fleming discovers penicillin
- Waugh: *Decline and Fall*
- Graves: *Goodbye to All That*
- Economic Depression
- Huxley: *Brave New World*
- Eliot: *Murder in the Cathedral*
- Abdication of Edward VIII
- The Spanish Civil War begins
- Yeats: *Last Poems*
- World War II begins
- Thomas: *New Poems*
- Orwell: *Animal Farm*
- Greene: *The Heart of the Matter*
- National Health Service Act

The Twentieth Century 1915

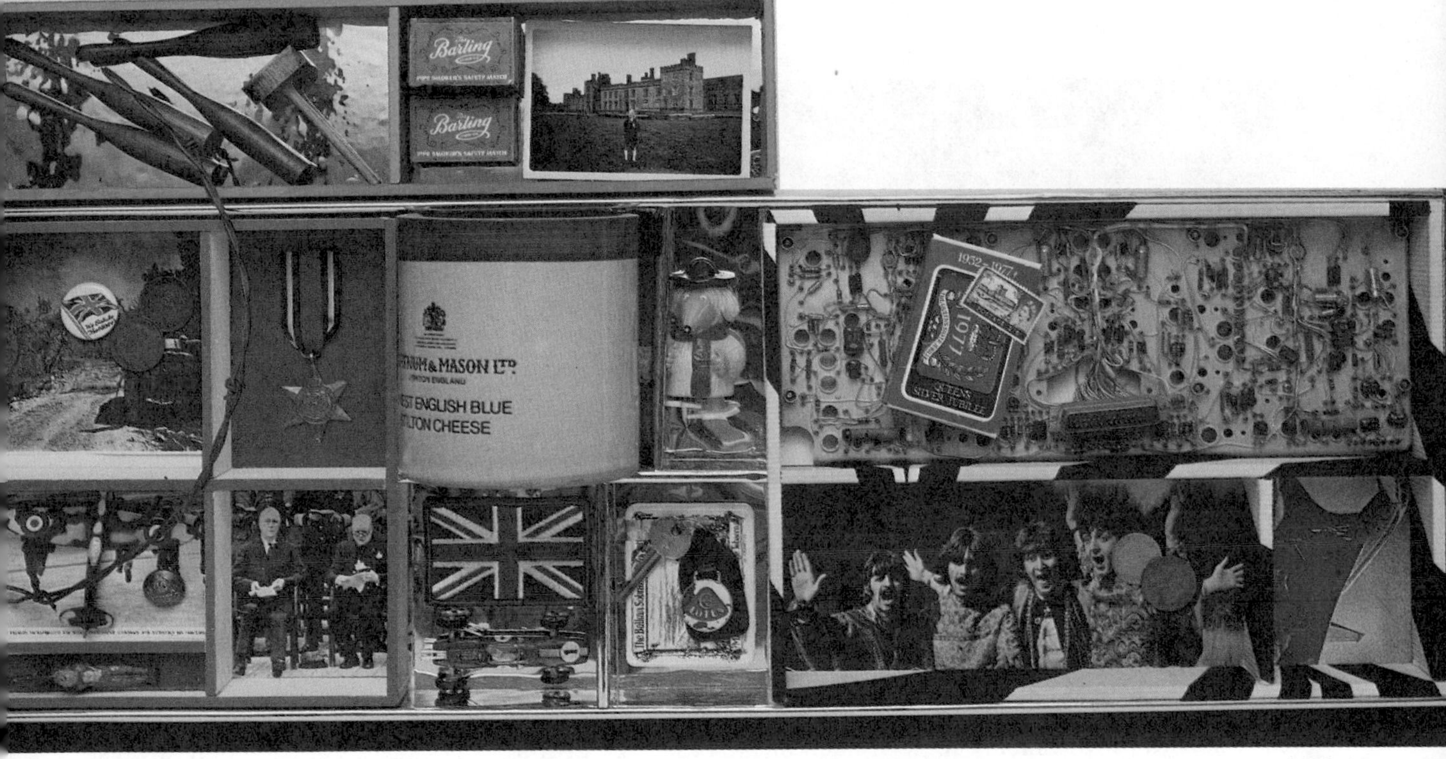

1955 | 1965 | 1975 | 1985

- Osborne: *Look Back in Anger*
- Pinter: *The Homecoming*
- Elizabeth II's Silver Jubilee
- Stoppard: *Rosencrantz and Guildenstern Are Dead*
- Murdoch: *The Bell*
- Pinter: *Old Times*
- The National theatre founded
- Sillitoe: *The Loneliness of the Long-Distance Runner*
- Beckett: *Waiting for Godot*
- Hughes: *Crow*
- Amis: *Lucky Jim*
- Larkin: *The Whitsun Weddings*
- Lessing: *The Golden Notebook*
- Greene: *The Honorary Consul*
- North Sea oil discovered
- Britain joins European Common Market

Background: The Twentieth Century 1915–

The Great War and Modern Literature

World War I marks the beginning of the modern era but, like the death of Queen Victoria, the war is a marker more useful in historical than literary terms. For example, the literary movement now commonly referred to as "Modernism" was well underway by the last decade of the nineteenth century. In the minds of those British writers who survived the conflict, the World War was more than a military and political event that changed the map of Europe. Beginning with the war poetry of Siegfried Sassoon, Wilfred Owen, and others, modern English literature took on pervasive tones of irony and intensity, and expressed moods of sobriety and pathos that writers believed were intrinsic to the human condition in the modern world. It would be incorrect to think of these qualities as uniquely modern, of course, but their increasing importance in literature suggests the movement away from the relatively self-confident view of the world that was characteristic of the nineteenth century.

For the "war poets" themselves, and for those who read their poetry, the harrowing experiences in the trenches of Europe marked the end of idealism and the stubborn faith in altruistic action which inspired much of the best work of the nineteenth century. For many writers it was simply the treacherous, crippling war, and the promises it did not fulfill, which defined "modern." "There is simply no poetry in war," wrote Wilfred Owen shortly before he himself was killed in the war. "The poetry is in the pity." In the end there were victors and vanquished, of course, but principally victims; some nations won, but individuals always lost. More than one reader has observed that Katherine Mansfield's stories of loneliness, deprivation, and injustice reflect the fact of her brother's death in the war as much as her awareness of the long illness which was to end her own life in 1923. Modern modes of expression might still be sensitive, and even tender, as Mansfield's own prose style shows, but in any case literature was obliged to reflect the harsher qualities of modern life.

It was undoubtedly perceptions akin to those of Mansfield and Owen which brought Virginia Woolf, granddaughter of the great Victorian novelist Thackeray, to argue that the primary responsibility of fiction was "to express character—not to preach doctrines, sing songs, or celebrate the glories of the British Empire."

Eliot, Joyce, Lawrence, and Woolf

One of those whose poetry is filled with unpoetic and unheroic characters and situations was T. S. Eliot, an American expatriate who became a British subject. His characters wander unattached and uncommitted, preoccupied with both the trivial and the overwhelming. They drift, usually without purpose or fulfillment, in a dry and cluttered world devoid of spiritual meaning. They are self-

T. S. Eliot

consciously modern, both obsessed with time and cut off from a vital relationship with the past. In Eliot's own imagination, however, conscious detachment from the nineteenth century was accompanied by a conscientious search for inspiration in literary and philosophical tradition, and in artistic concepts nurtured on the Continent. For Eliot, tradition included the literary tradition of English metaphysical poetry and, eventually, the religious tradition of the Anglican church, to which he became a convert.

Another expatriate, and another key writer of the modern period, was James Joyce, who exiled himself from Ireland and the city he thought of as "dear, dirty Dublin" in order to escape the restrictions of nationality, language, and religion. In Paris, Trieste, Rome, and Zurich, Joyce lived and wrote—most often about the people and places he had left behind—and became a principal figure in the development of the twentieth-century novel. Joyce began his work with the short stories collected in *Dubliners* (1914). The stories describe the cramped lives of inhabitants of Ireland's largest city. *A Portrait of the Artist as a Young Man* (1916), a sensitive and largely autobiographical novel, appeared two years later, and eventually Joyce completed the massive and difficult *Finnegans Wake* (1939), a blend of dream and reality, invention and translation, complex patterns and multiple puns. But perhaps his most widely acclaimed novel is *Ulysses* (1922), which employs a variety of prose styles and a story line which parallels that of Homer's *Odyssey* to recount the events of a single day in the life of a Dublin man, Leopold Bloom. *Ulysses* is perhaps the most influential novel of our time.

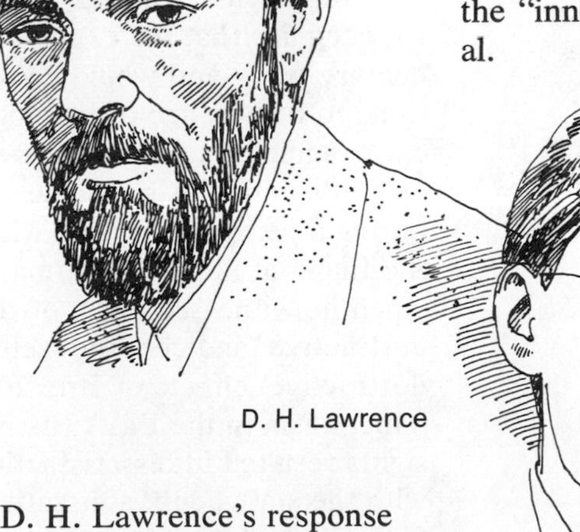

D. H. Lawrence

D. H. Lawrence's response to the repressiveness of industrialized society was to affirm the instincts and impulses of man. He believed the body was "wiser" than the intellect, and he trusted in "brute blood knowledge," a knowledge available to men and women at all social levels and essential to human life.

In Mexico, New Mexico, and Australia, among other places, he sought to escape modern industrial society and to explore the "primitive" in the individual and in culture. He pursued his vision of experience in his poetry and stories. The censors believed that Lawrence was preoccupied with sex and obsessed with destructive relationships. But in novels such as *Sons and Lovers, The Rainbow,* and *Women in Love,* Lawrence's focus was on how well or ill his characters understood their deepest human drives, especially as those drives were affected by personal demands and society's expectations. In this sense, Lawrence shared with Joyce and other modern writers a concern with the less conscious processes of the human mind, developing techniques to reveal the "inner life" of the individual.

James Joyce

Virginia Woolf was a perceptive literary theorist, critic, and reviewer. Her disapproval of several popular novelists of her day was based on her belief that they were too concerned with fiction as a social statement and not enough concerned with how fiction might reflect human character—especially the character of the mind. Woolf felt that writers could better speak to readers by recording the striking detail and conveying the telling moment in an individual's life rather than by informing readers of the individual's manners, wealth, or social status. And, like Conrad, Joyce, and Lawrence, she placed her stories as much in what the novelist Henry James called "the chamber of consciousness" as in the world of "things." She believed it was quality of mind which determined human uniqueness and vitality, rather than appearance, habitat, or social standing. It should come as no surprise, then, that one of Woolf's chief commitments—in novels such as *Mrs. Dalloway* and *To the Lighthouse* and stories such as "The Legacy"—was to the inner lives of women. Woolf knew that, "modern" as her age was, its economic, political, social, and intellectual habits created an environment in which the inner life was often the only true life that many women had. It was, then, by being a psychological novelist that Virginia Woolf was able to affirm the uniqueness and integrity of the individual, illuminate the lives of women, and fulfill the promise of her own artistic potential.

Virginia Woolf

The Thirties

In 1939 the coming of mass warfare for the second time in the century brought to an end all illusions that the conflicts which had torn Spain and Germany during the thirties were simply "internal" problems. One of the first British writers to recognize that the twentieth century was—and would continue to be—an age of ideological struggle was George Orwell. Orwell's initial insight came during a period of service with the Imperial Police in Burma, when he witnessed some of the destructive (and certainly self-destructive) effects of British imperialism in the East. His insights resulted in dissatisfaction with the status quo, a dissatisfaction which was fueled by his explorations of the world of poverty which he recorded in his novels and essays of the thirties. His dissatisfaction later became a commitment to fight fascism in the Spanish Civil War. In 1946 *Animal Farm* appeared, and three years later, *Nineteen Eighty-Four.* In these novels, Orwell articulated the case for democratic socialism and offered devastating critiques of totalitarian rule. In his essays Orwell argues with simplicity, directness, and a rare intellectual honesty. He established a standard for modern English prose.

W. H. Auden

Of course Orwell was not alone in recognizing the ideological implications of modern experience or in establishing literary standards. W. H. Auden, for example, was one of a number of poets whose careers began during the thirties, a period of energetic political and intellectual debate. The economic and political issues debated included the great Depression of 1929, and capitalism and its alternatives (such as fascism, communism, and democratic socialism). The "failure" of earlier intellectual movements led writers to adopt and combine in various ways the insights of psychology, political theory, and mythology, and the innovative techniques of individual predecessors. Auden, for example, wrote a number of "social action" poems, and he also showed (though not always in the same poems) how much he had learned from "teachers" such as Eliot, Hopkins, and Yeats. Stephen Spender, a close friend of Auden's, wrote social commentary in both poetry and prose, and like Orwell has been considered one of the most sensitive and eloquent voices of social conscience in his generation. In the end, however, it is more useful to consider Auden, Spender, and their close contemporaries, C. Day Lewis and Louis MacNeice, less in relation to the thirties than in relation to the forties and fifties, when their mature work emerged. And it is more useful to think of these men in terms of art rather than ideas, for two reasons. First, they cultivated an artistic understanding of irony, matter-of-factness, and overall economy of statement. Second, they responded to what Auden called "The Age of Anxiety" as artists of both individual and ecumenical imagination; they shared ideas, experimented with new techniques, and grew with the times.

Individual talent and drive simply resist, and usually outlive, any effort to place them within a "school"—as the careers of Edith Sitwell, Robert Graves, Stevie Smith, and Dylan Thomas prove. Sitwell and Thomas are particularly memorable cases in point. Sitwell began writing under the influence of T. S. Eliot and Symbolism, and created poetic blends of sight and sound, such as "The King of China's Daughter," which could be thought of as studies in perception. She continued to read and experiment, combined poetic and musical compositions, welcomed the new work of Dylan Thomas, and kept her imposing, controversial, and sometimes eccentric gifts—both personal and poetic—before the public through the sheer force of personality.

Dylan Thomas emerged from "dark" and provincial Welsh origins to invest the verse forms of the past with emotion and rhetorical energy, and to create poems "written for the love of Man and in praise of God." Thomas made his poetry reflect the paradoxes of experience, its overlaps and contradictions. He allowed his talent to express itself not only through poems, but also through stories, plays, and film scripts, the best known of which include "A Child's Christmas in Wales" and *Under Milk Wood.*

Some Contemporary Poets

Philip Larkin and Thom Gunn, among others, are thought of as original witnesses to modern melancholy and innovators of the conversational manner in poetry, but their work actually seems the product of a creative understanding of such varied predecessors as Hardy, Yeats, Owen, Eliot, and others. In considering English poetry since World War II it is more useful to focus on the *range* of modern poetry, rather than its coherence or consistency, as the contrast between the work of Elizabeth Jennings and Ted Hughes suggests. Jennings developed as a poet of the personal, internalized affections; her poetry is often concerned with the modest, overlooked, and set-aside. Hughes, on the other hand, is a poet of violent fact, of the wild, cruel, and even grotesque; his subjects are often creatures of the animal world. Between Jennings's poetry of perceived nuances and Hughes's poetry of fierce symbol lies the basic scope of poetry in our time.

English literature in the twentieth century reflects a world far different from that which Queen Victoria knew, far different from that which earlier centuries produced. It is a world not of the British Empire but of the Commonwealth, a world in which Canada, Australia, South Africa, and India, among others, are today independent nations. A world of international community has altered the idea of what being "English" is. Writers as different in origin and art as Graham Greene and Doris Lessing, for example, are among those now working in the long tradition which holds that the quality of life is enhanced by an ability to express ideas about it.

The modern world, in all its complexity, is described with compassion and bitterness, humor and irony, cynicism and hope in English literature of the twentieth century.

Siegfried Sassoon

Suicide in the Trenches

I knew a simple soldier boy
Who grinned at life in empty joy,
Slept soundly through the lonesome dark,
And whistled early with the lark.

In winter trenches, cowed and glum,
With crumps[1] and lice and lack of rum,
He put a bullet through his brain.
No one spoke of him again.

. . .

You smug-faced crowds with kindling eye
Who cheer when soldier lads march by,
Sneak home and pray you'll never know
The hell where youth and laughter go.

1. ***crumps,*** soldiers' slang for exploding shells, from the sound made by them.

Dreamers

Soldiers are citizens of death's gray land,
Drawing no dividend from time's tomorrows.
In the great hour of destiny they stand,
Each with his feuds, and jealousies, and sorrows.
Soldiers are sworn to action; they must win
Some flaming, fatal climax with their lives.
Soldiers are dreamers; when the guns begin
They think of firelit homes, clean beds, and wives.

I see them in foul dug-outs, gnawed by rats,
And in the ruined trenches, lashed with rain,
Dreaming of things they did with balls and bats,
And mocked by hopeless longing to regain
Bank-holidays, and picture shows, and spats,
And going to the office in the train.

Discussion

1. Describe the tone of each of the three stanzas in "Suicide in the Trenches."

2. **(a)** Identify the "you" in the last stanza. **(b)** Do you agree with the speaker's attitude in this stanza? Why or why not?

3. In "Dreamers": **(a)** Why might the soldiers become dreamers? **(b)** Can you relate these soldiers' dreams to the suicide described in the preceding poem? Explain.

Trench warfare, World War I. National Archives.

Wilfred Owen

The Next War

War's a joke for me and you,
While we know such dreams are true.
—SASSOON

Out there, we've walked quite friendly up to Death;
Sat down and eaten with him, cool and bland,—
Pardoned his spilling mess-tins in our hand.
We've sniffed the green thick odour of his breath,—
Our eyes wept, but our courage didn't writhe.
He's spat at us with bullets and he's coughed
Shrapnel. We chorused when he sang aloft;
We whistled while he shaved us with his scythe.

Oh, Death was never enemy of ours!
We laughed at him, we leagued with him, old chum.
No soldier's paid to kick against his powers.
We laughed, knowing that better men would come,
And greater wars; when each proud fighter brags
He wars on Death—for Life; not men—for flags.

---

4. In "The Next War": **(a)** Why does the speaker say that Death was never the soldiers' enemy? **(b)** Who, then, *was* their enemy? **(c)** What will be different about the "greater wars" of the future?

Siegfried Sassoon 1886 • 1967

Sassoon, who attended Cambridge University, was always more interested in poetry than in studies. He was twice wounded in World War I, received two medals for bravery, and rose to the rank of captain. However, his war experiences made him an outspoken pacifist, and as an antiwar protest he threw his Military Cross into the sea. Instead of being court-martialed as he hoped, he was judged temporarily insane and hospitalized. He met Wilfred Owen during one of his hospital stays, and encouraged him in his writing.

Wilfred Owen 1893 • 1918

Wilfred Owen enlisted in the British army in 1915, served ably as an officer in France, and earned the Military Cross for bravery. He was killed in action exactly a week before the Armistice was declared. He published very little during his lifetime—only four poems—but today is generally considered the best of the poets of World War I.

T. S. Eliot

The Hollow Men

Mistah Kurtz—he dead[1]

A penny for the Old Guy[2]

I

We are the hollow men
We are the stuffed men
Leaning together
Headpiece filled with straw. Alas!
Our dried voices, when
We whisper together
Are quiet and meaningless
As wind in dry grass
Or rats' feet over broken glass
In our dry cellar

Shape without form, shade without color,
Paralysed force, gesture without motion;

Those who have crossed
With direct eyes,[3] to death's other Kingdom[4]
Remember us—if at all—not as lost
Violent souls, but only
As the hollow men
The stuffed men.

II

Eyes[5] I dare not meet in dreams
In death's dream kingdom
These do not appear:
There, the eyes are
Sunlight on a broken column
There, is a tree swinging
And voices are
In the wind's singing
More distant and more solemn
Than a fading star.

Let me be no nearer
In death's dream kingdom
Let me also wear
Such deliberate disguises
Rat's coat, crowskin, crossed staves
In a field
Behaving as the wind behaves
No nearer—

Not that final meeting
In the twilight kingdom.

III

This is the dead land
This is catcus land
Here the stone images
Are raised, here they receive
The supplication of a dead man's hand
Under the twinkle of a fading star.

Is it like this
In death's other kingdom

---

1. ***Mistah Kurtz—he dead,*** a quotation from Joseph Conrad's novel *Heart of Darkness.* Mr. Kurtz was a European trader who had gone into "the heart of darkness"—the central African jungle—with European standards of life and conduct. Because he had no moral or spiritual strength to sustain him, he was soon turned into a barbarian. He differs, however, from Eliot's "hollow men": he is not paralyzed as they are, but commits acts of overwhelming evil; and he is not blind as they are, but on his death glimpses the nature of his actions when he exclaims, "The horror! The horror!" Kurtz is thus one of the "lost/Violent souls" mentioned in lines 15–16.
2. ***A penny . . . Guy,*** cry of English children soliciting money for fireworks to celebrate Guy Fawkes Day, November 5, which commemorates the thwarting of the "gunpowder plot" of 1605 in which Guy Fawkes and other conspirators planned to blow up both houses of Parliament. On this day—which of course celebrates the failure to produce an explosion—straw-stuffed images of Fawkes (the "Old Guy") are burned.
3. ***Those . . . direct eyes,*** those who have represented something positive (direct), either for good or bad.
4. ***death's other Kingdom,*** the afterlife; eternity.
5. ***Eyes,*** the eyes of those in the afterworld who had confident faith; those who represent positive spiritual force as opposed to spiritual stagnation or paralysis.

Waking alone
At the hour when we are
Trembling with tenderness
Lips that would kiss
Form prayers to broken stone.

IV

The eyes are not here
There are no eyes here
In this valley of dying stars
In this hollow valley
This broken jaw of our lost kingdoms

In this last of meeting places
We grope together
And avoid speech
Gathered on this beach of the tumid river

Sightless, unless
The eyes reappear
As the perpetual star
Multifoliate rose[6]
Of death's twilight kingdom
The hope only
Of empty men.

V

Here we go round the prickly pear
Prickly pear prickly pear
Here we go round the prickly pear
At five o'clock in the morning.

Between the idea
And the reality
Between the motion
And the act
Falls the Shadow

For Thine is the Kingdom

Between the conception
And the creation
Between the emotion
And the response
Falls the Shadow

Life is very long

Between the desire
And the spasm
Between the potency
And the existence
Between the essence
And the descent
Falls the Shadow

For Thine is the Kingdom

For Thine is
Life is
For Thine is the

This is the way the world ends
This is the way the world ends
This is the way the world ends
Not with a bang but a whimper.

6. ***Multifoliate rose,*** in Dante's *Divine Comedy* a symbol of Paradise, in which the saints are the many petals of the rose.

Discussion

1. In "The Hollow Men": **(a)** What images of human emptiness are conveyed in Section I? **(b)** Comment upon the appropriateness of the physical description of "death's dream kingdom," where the hollow men "grope together" (Sections II–IV).

2. Section V of the poem is an amplification of lines 11–12 of Section I. Cite evidence from Section V that the vital spark is missing in the hollow men.

3. **(a)** The last two lines of the poem are among the most quoted in twentieth-century poetry. What do they mean?
(b) How do they epitomize the spirit of the hollow men?
(c) Using the footnotes as a guide, explore the possible relevance of Eliot's epigraphs ("Mistah Kurtz—he dead" and "A penny for the Old Guy") in these last lines.

Detail, from "The Adoration of the Magi" by Gentile da Fabriano. SCALA/EPA.

Journey of the Magi[1]

"A cold coming we had of it,
Just the worst time of the year
For a journey, and such a long journey:
The ways deep and the weather sharp,
The very dead of winter."[2]
And the camels galled, sore-footed, refractory,
Lying down in the melting snow.
There were times we regretted
The summer palaces on slopes, the terraces,
And the silken girls bringing sherbet.
Then the camel men cursing and grumbling
And running away, and wanting their liquor and women,
And the night-fires going out, and the lack of shelters,
And the cities hostile and the towns unfriendly
And the villages dirty and charging high prices:
A hard time we had of it.
At the end we preferred to travel all night,
Sleeping in snatches,
With the voices singing in our ears, saying
That this was all folly.

---

1. ***Magi,*** the three wise men who journeyed to Bethlehem to see the infant Jesus.
2. ***"A cold . . . winter,"*** adapted from a Nativity sermon by the seventeenth-century divine Lancelot Andrews.

Discussion

1. In "The Journey of the Magi": **(a)** Who is the speaker? **(b)** How old do you think he is? **(c)** What sort of journey did he and the other magi have? **(d)** Why does he say: "this Birth was / Hard and bitter agony for us, like Death, our death"? **(e)** What does he mean when he says in the last line that he "should be glad of another death"? **(f)** Why then does he also say: "And I would do it again" (line 33)?

2. Did the magi find what they set out to find? Explain.

Then at dawn we came down to a temperate valley,
Wet, below the snow line, smelling of vegetation;
With a running stream and a water mill beating the darkness,
And three trees on the low sky,
And an old white horse galloped away in the meadow.
Then we came to a tavern with vine-leaves over the lintel,
Six hands at an open door dicing for pieces of silver,
And feet kicking the empty wineskins.[3]
But there was no information, and so we continued
And arrived at evening, not a moment too soon
Finding the place; it was (you may say) satisfactory.

All this was a long time ago, I remember,
And I would do it again, but set down
This set down
This: were we led all that way for
Birth or Death? There was a Birth, certainly,
We had evidence and no doubt. I had seen birth and death,
But had thought they were different; this Birth was
Hard and bitter agony for us, like Death, our death.
We returned to our places, these Kingdoms,
But no longer at ease here, in the old dispensation,[4]
With an alien people clutching their gods.
I should be glad of another death.

---

3. ***Then at dawn . . wineskins.*** Images in this passage suggest both renewal of life ("vegetation"; "running stream") and death, foreshadowing events in the life of Christ. The "three trees" suggest the Crucifixion; the men "dicing for pieces of silver" suggest both Judas's betrayal of Christ for thirty pieces of silver, and the soldiers who gambled for Christ's garments at the foot of the Cross. The white horse is mentioned in Revelation 6:2 and 19:11 in passages alluding to the end of the world.
4. ***the old dispensation,*** the old pagan religion.

Thomas Stearns Eliot
1888 • 1965

St. Louis-born Eliot wrote one of his most famous poems, "The Love Song of J. Alfred Prufrock," while still a student at Harvard. A formidable scholar, he did graduate work at Harvard, the Sorbonne in France, and Oxford. He settled in London in 1915, becoming a British subject in 1927. His writings attracted attention from the start, but because of financial pressures he taught school for a time, worked in a bank, and eventually became an editor and a director of a major British publishing house. He was awarded the Nobel Prize for literature in 1948.

As poet and critic, Eliot had an enormous influence on twentieth-century poetry. In his criticism he discussed his distaste for romanticism and the emotions it expresses. In his own poetry he made a complete break with the literary conventions of the Romantics and Victorians. Instead of using traditional "poetic diction," he turned to the idiom and rhythms of natural speech; instead of relying on abstractions and generalities, he expressed himself through sense impressions and concrete images.

In early poems such as "Prufrock," "The Hollow Men," and "The Waste Land," Eliot pictured the sterility, boredom, and spiritual emptiness of the modern world. In 1927, however, he became a convert to the Anglican Church, and in his later poetry turned to religion as the one possible hope for modern man.

Edith Sitwell

The King of China's Daughter

The King of China's daughter,
She never would love me
Though I hung my cap and bells upon
Her nutmeg tree.
For oranges and lemons,
The stars in bright blue air,
(I stole them long ago, my dear)
Were dangling there.
The Moon did give me silver pence,
The Sun did give me gold,
And both together softly blew
And made my porridge cold;
But the King of China's daughter
Pretended not to see,
When I hung my cap and bells upon
Her nutmeg tree.

Discussion

The King of China's Daughter

1. What do you think is most enjoyable about this poem: its story, theme, sound, meaning? Explain.

2. Although Sitwell also wrote serious poetry, she is best known as a "craftsman in nonsense." Which particular lines in this poem do you think most fit this description?

Edith Sitwell 1887 • 1964

Edith Sitwell became Dame Edith—Commander of the Order of the British Empire—in 1954. A member of an aristocratic and cultured family, she was privately educated at the family estate. She was a great eccentric, affecting the manner and dress of her conception of a poet. She towered six feet tall in brocaded, medieval-style gowns, strange headgear, and elaborate jewels. *Façade*, her innovative program of poems, with music by William Walton, was considered scandalously avant-garde at the time of its presentation in 1923.

Dame Edith once sent an owl to a critic whom she thought was too stuffy, and she objected to the Beat poets because of their smell.

Discussion

Intimates

1. Characterize the woman described in the poem.

2. Who are the "intimates" of the title?

3. Should the speaker have fled or stayed—or done something else? Why?

(For the biography of D.H. Lawrence see page 646.)

D. H. Lawrence

Intimates

Don't you care for my love? she said bitterly.

I handed her the mirror, and said:
Please address these questions to the proper person!
Please make all requests to head-quarters!
In all matters of emotional importance
please approach the supreme authority direct!—
So I handed her the mirror.

And she would have broken it over my head,
but she caught sight of her own reflection
and that held her spellbound for two seconds
while I fled.

Robert Graves

Read Me, Please!

If, as well may happen
  On an autumn day
When white clouds go scudding
  And winds are gay,

Some earth-bound spirit,
  A man lately dead
(Your fellow-clerk), should take it
  Into his crazed head

To adopt a more venturesome
  Shape than a dead leaf
And wish you a good morning,
  Abrupt and brief,

He will come disguised
  As a sheet of newspaper
Charging across the square
  With a clumsy caper,

To flatten himself out
  Across your shins and knees
In a suppliant posture:
  "Read me, please!"

Then, scanning every column
  On both sides, with care,
You will find the clerk's name
  Printed somewhere—

Unless, perhaps, in warning
  That sheet comes blown
And the name which you stumble on
  Is, alas, your own.

Discussion

1. In which column would the clerk's name probably appear?

2. What is the warning if the name is that of the reader?

3. Beneath the whimsy, does the poem have a more serious meaning? Explain.

Robert Graves 1895 •

Graves was born in London into a large family headed by a poet/ballad-writer. Though he had been accepted at Oxford, he went into the trenches of the First World War, serving in the same regiment as Siegfried Sassoon. He published three books of poetry while on active duty. After the war he finished his formal education, and upon recommendation of T. E. Lawrence (Lawrence of Arabia), spent a year as a professor at Cairo's Egyptian University. Except for a period during the Spanish Civil War, Graves has lived on the island of Majorca since 1929. He writes prodigiously in a variety of genres, including historical novels like *I Claudius* that have been described as "scholarly and mischievous."

Sullen Moods

Love, never count your labour lost
  Though I turn sullen or retired
Even at your side; my thought is crossed
  With fancies by no evil fired.

And when I answer you, some days
  Vaguely and wildly, never fear
That my love walks forbidden ways,
  Snapping the ties that hold it here.

If I speak gruffly, this mood is
  Mere indignation at my own
Shortcomings, plagues, uncertainties:
  I forget the gentler tone.

You, now that you have come to be
  My one beginning, prime and end,
I count at last as wholly me,
  Lover no longer nor yet friend.

Help me to see you as before
  When overwhelmed and dead, almost,
I stumbled on your secret door
  Which saves the live man from the ghost.

Be once again the distant light,
  Promise of glory, not yet known
In full perfection—wasted quite
  When on my imperfection thrown.

Discussion

1. **(a)** In "Sullen Moods," which of the stanzas best illustrates the speaker's love? Explain. **(b)** Discuss whether the alternating moods are typical of love.

2. In "She Tells Her Love . . .": **(a)** What does the Earth do that is the equivalent of the woman's telling her love? **(b)** What are the "dark hours" of the Earth? **(c)** State the meaning of the poem in your own words.

She Tells Her Love While Half Asleep

She tells her love while half asleep
  In the dark hours,
    With half-words whispered low:
As Earth stirs in her winter sleep
  And puts out grass and flowers
    Despite the snow,
    Despite the falling snow.

W. H. Auden

Musée des Beaux Arts[1]

About suffering they were never wrong,
The Old Masters: how well they understood
Its human position; how it takes place
While someone else is eating or opening a window or just walking dully along;
How, when the aged are reverently, passionately waiting
For the miraculous birth, there always must be
Children who did not specially want it to happen, skating
On a pond at the edge of the wood:
They never forgot
That even the dreadful martyrdom must run its course
Anyhow in a corner, some untidy spot
Where the dogs go on with their doggy life and the torturer's horse
Scratches its innocent behind on a tree.

In Brueghel's *Icarus,*[2] for instance: how everything turns away
Quite leisurely from the disaster; the ploughman may
Have heard the splash, the forsaken cry,
But for him it was not an important failure; the sun shone
As it had to on the white legs disappearing into the green
Water; and the expensive delicate ship that must have seen
Something amazing, a boy falling out of the sky,
Had somewhere to get to and sailed calmly on.

---

1. ***Musée des Beaux Arts,*** the Royal Museum of Fine Arts in Brussels.
2. ***Brueghel's Icarus.*** Brueghel was Pieter Brueghel the Elder (1525?–1569). His painting, "The Fall of Icarus," was inspired by the Greek myth which relates how the cunning artisan Daedalus made wings of feathers and wax for his son Icarus and himself in order to escape from imprisonment on the island of Crete. Despite his father's warnings, Icarus flew too close to the sun; his wings melted off, and he fell into the sea and was drowned.

"The Fall of Icarus" by Pieter Brueghel. Musée Royaux des Beaux-Arts de Belgique, Bruxelles.

The Unknown Citizen

(To JS/07/M/378
This Marble Monument
Is Erected by the State)

He was found by the Bureau of Statistics to be
One against whom there was no official complaint,
And all the reports on his conduct agree
That, in the modern sense of an old-fashioned word, he was a saint,
For in everything he did he served the Greater Community.
Except for the War till the day he retired
He worked in a factory and never got fired,
But satisfied his employers, Fudge Motors Inc.
Yet he wasn't a scab or odd in his views,
For his Union reports that he paid his dues,
(Our report on his Union shows it was sound)
And our Social Psychology workers found
That he was popular with his mates and liked a drink.
The Press are convinced that he bought a paper every day
And that his reactions to advertisements were normal in every way.
Policies taken out in his name prove that he was fully insured,
And his Health-card shows he was once in hospital but left it cured.
Both Producers Research and High-Grade Living declare
He was fully sensible to the advantages of the Instalment Plan
And had everything necessary to the Modern Man,
A phonograph, a radio, a car and a frigidaire.
Our researchers into Public Opinion are content
That he held the proper opinions for the time of year;
When there was peace, he was for peace; when there was war, he went.
He was married and added five children to the population,
Which our Eugenist says was the right number for a parent of his generation,
And our teachers report that he never interfered with their education.
Was he free? Was he happy? The question is absurd:
Had anything been wrong, we should certainly have heard.

Who's Who

A shilling life [1] will give you all the facts:
How Father beat him, how he ran away,
What were the struggles of his youth, what acts
Made him the greatest figure of his day:
Of how he fought, fished, hunted, worked all night,
Though giddy, climbed new mountains; named a sea:
Some of the last researchers even write
Love made him weep his pints like you and me.

With all his honours on, he sighed for one
Who, say astonished critics, lived at home;
Did little jobs about the house with skill
And nothing else; could whistle; would sit still
Or potter round the garden; answered some
Of his long marvellous letters but kept none.

---

1. ***shilling life,*** an inexpensive biography, often issued in series.

Discussion

1. As the first two lines in "Musée des Beaux Arts" indicate, this is a poem "about suffering." What is the point made "about suffering"?

2. Relate the point to your own experience.

3. **(a)** Why was no official complaint ever brought against the Unknown Citizen (line 2)? **(b)** In the next-to-last line we are asked: "Was he free? Was he happy?" Are these questions answered in the poem? How? **(c)** Reread the last line of the poem. Is it true? Explain. **(d)** In what sort of world would Citizen JS/07/M/378 merit a marble monument erected by the state? **(e)** Why is this poem titled "The Unknown Citizen"—how are we to read the word "Unknown"?

4. Lines 1–8 of the sonnet "Who's Who" deal with the great man; lines 9–14 deal with someone else. Who might that someone be? **(a)** Why might the great man sigh for him and write "long marvellous letters" to him? **(b)** Is it in keeping with the character of the recipient that he kept none of the letters? Explain. **(c)** From what the poem implies, what would you say might have made the great man so great?

W(ystan) H(ugh) Auden
1907 • 1973

At Oxford University, Auden was the nucleus of a group of young, socially concerned thinkers which included his friends Spender and MacNeice. Politically active, Auden spent 1928–1929 in Germany. He drove an ambulance for the anti-Franco Loyalists in the Spanish Civil War, but during the decade of the 1930s the orientation of his beliefs shifted from political to humanistic and Christian.

A diverse and prolific writer with a disciplined professional regard for his art, Auden wrote drama, criticism, and documentary films as well as poetry. He taught at Oxford and at various universities in the United States.

Auden became an American citizen in 1939, and for many years lived part of the year in New York City. Later, however, he returned to England and spent his last months in Oxford.

Stephen Spender

An Elementary School Class Room in a Slum

Far far from gusty waves, these children's faces.
Like rootless weeds the torn hair round their paleness.
The tall girl with her weighed-down head. The paper-
seeming boy with rat's eyes. The stunted unlucky heir
Of twisted bones, reciting a father's gnarled disease,
His lesson from his desk. At back of the dim class
One unnoted, sweet and young: his eyes live in a dream
Of squirrels' game, in tree room, other than this.

On sour cream walls, donations. Shakespeare's head
Cloudless at dawn, civilized dome riding all cities.
Belled, flowery, Tyrolese valley. Open-handed map
Awarding the world its world. And yet, for these
Children, these windows, not this world, are world,
Where all their future's painted with a fog,
A narrow street sealed in with a lead sky,
Far far from rivers, capes, and stars of words.

Surely Shakespeare is wicked, the map a bad example
With ships and sun and love tempting them to steal—
For lives that slyly turn in their cramped holes
From fog to endless night? On their slag heap, these children
Wear skins peeped through by bones and spectacles of steel
With mended glass, like bottle bits in slag.
Tyrol is wicked; map's promising a fable:
All of their time and space are foggy slum,
So blot their maps with slums as big as doom.

Unless, governor, teacher, inspector, visitor,
This map becomes their window and these windows
That open on their lives like crouching tombs
Break, O break open, till they break the town
And show the children to the fields and all their world
Azure on their sands, to let their tongues
Run naked into books, the white and green leaves open
The history theirs whose language is the sun.

Discussion

1. In the third stanza, what is the meaning of the words: "Shakespeare is wicked"; "Tyrol is wicked"?

2. In the last stanza, the speaker points to the possibility of the map becoming the window of the classroom and the actual windows breaking. What does he mean?

3. This poem was written nearly a half century ago. **(a)** How much of it is appropriate today? **(b)** What does the extent of its appropriateness tell us about our modern world?

Stephen Spender 1909 •

The son of a novelist-journalist, Spender became a literary journalist and critic. He was intensely concerned with social and political reform as a young man, and was in Germany in the early 1930s and in Spain during its civil war. As he grew older, he became less critic and more poet, especially after he made a significant break with organized politics.

C. Day Lewis

Walking Away

For Sean

It is eighteen years ago, almost to the day—
A sunny day with the leaves just turning,
The touch-lines new-ruled—since I watched you play
Your first game of football, then, like a satellite
Wrenched from its orbit, go drifting away

Behind a scatter of boys. I can see
You walking away from me towards the school
With the pathos of a half-fledged thing set free
Into a wilderness, the gait of one
Who finds no path where the path should be.

That hesitant figure, eddying away
Like a winged seed loosened from its parent stem,
Has something I never quite grasp to convey
About nature's give-and-take—the small, the scorching
Ordeals which fire one's irresolute clay.

I have had worse partings, but none that so
Gnaws at my mind. Perhaps it is roughly
Saying what God alone could perfectly show—
How selfhood begins with a walking away,
And love is proved in the letting go.

Discussion

1. About how old might Sean have been when his father watched him play his first game of football?

2. **(a)** How does line 19 apply to Sean? **(b)** How does line 20 apply to the speaker?

3. Why might the poet write eighteen years later about this "walking away"?

C(ecil) Day Lewis 1904 • 1972

The poet and critic C. Day Lewis, the former poet laureate, was an editor at the Ministry of Information and professor at various universities, including Harvard, Cambridge, and Oxford. In his student days at Oxford he was co-editor of the poetry magazine.

Like many other intellectuals of the thirties, C. Day Lewis was politically involved. His critical piece *A Hope for Poetry* (1934) was considered the manifesto of the Left Poetry Movement of that era.

He also wrote detective stories under the pseudonym Nicholas Blake.

Louis MacNeice

The British Museum Reading Room

Under the hive-like dome the stooping haunted readers
Go up and down the alleys, tap the cells of knowledge—
   Honey and wax, the accumulation of years—
Some on commission, some for the love of learning,
Some because they have nothing better to do
Or because they hope these walls of books will deaden
   The drumming of the demon in their ears.

Cranks, hacks, poverty-stricken scholars,
In pince-nez, period hats or romantic beards
   And cherishing their hobby or their doom
Some are too much alive and some are asleep
Hanging like bats in a world of inverted values,
Folded up in themselves in a world which is safe and silent:
   This is the British Museum Reading Room.

Out on the steps in the sun the pigeons are courting,
Puffing their ruffs and sweeping their tails or taking
   A sun-bath at their ease
And under the totem poles—the ancient terror—
Between the enormous fluted Ionic columns
There seeps from heavily jowled or hawk-like foreign faces
   The guttural sorrow of the refugees.

Discussion

1. **(a)** In the first three lines of this poem to what does the speaker compare the "Reading Room"? **(b)** Which words in these lines are involved in the comparison?

2. For what four different reasons are the "haunted readers" here?

3. To the readers, what is the most important aspect of the world of the reading room?

4. In stanza three, there is a contrast in tone between the, first three lines and the last four. Explain.

The Snow Man

His memory was shaped by forgetting
Into a snowman, handful by handful;
In the end two pebbles for eyes and a cherrywood
Pipe clamped in the thinlipped mouth.

But was this fellow really his past,
This white dummy in a white waste?
While the censor works, while the frost holds,
Perhaps he will pass—but then he will pass.

Yesterday was a dance of flakes
Waltzing down, around, and up,
But today is lull and smudge, today
Is a man with a pipe that will not draw.

Today is a legless day with head-on
Idiot eyes, a stranded deaf
Mute in a muted world. This lump
Is what he remembered when he forgot,

Already beginning to dribble. Tomorrow
Comes the complete forgetting, the thaw.
Or is it rather a dance of water
To replace, relive, that dance of white?

Discussion

1. This entire poem is a metaphor in which the memory is compared to a snow man. **(a)** Who or what is the "censor" (line 7)? **(b)** Explain the pun in line 8.

2. The last three stanzas describe, respectively, yesterday, today, and tomorrow. What will probably happen tomorrow?

Louis MacNeice 1907 • 1963

A classics scholar, MacNeice was a professor at universities in England and the United States, and director of the British Institute in Athens. He was a close friend of Auden and Spender, and one of the "poets of social protest" of the 1930s. He was a prolific writer whose work included poetry, criticism, radio scripts, and translations—most notably of Goethe's *Faust.*

Stevie Smith

The Frog Prince

I am a frog
I live under a spell
I live at the bottom
Of a green well

And here I must wait
Until a maiden places me
On her royal pillow
And kisses me
In her father's palace.

The story is familiar
Everybody knows it well
But do other enchanted people feel as nervous
As I do? The stories do not tell,

Ask if they will be happier
When the changes come,
As already they are fairly happy
In a frog's doom?

I have been a frog now
For a hundred years
And in all this time
I have not shed many tears.

I am happy, I like the life,
(When I have hopped to the river)
Can swim for many a mile
And am for ever agile.

And the quietness,
Yes, I like to be quiet,
I am habituated
To a quiet life.

But always when I think these thoughts
As I sit in my well
Another thought comes to me and says,
It is part of the spell

To be happy
To work up contentment
To make much of being a frog
To fear disenchantment

Says, It will be *heavenly*
To be set free
Cries, *Heavenly* the girl who disenchants
And the royal times, *heavenly,*
And I think it will be.

Come then, royal girl and royal times,
Come quickly,
I can be happy until you come
But I cannot be heavenly,
Only disenchanted people
Can be heavenly.

No Respect

I have no respect for you
For you would not tell the truth about your grief
But laughed at it
When the first pang was past
And made it a thing of nothing.
You said
That what had been
Had never been
That what was
Was not:
You have a light mind
And a coward's soul.

Not Waving But Drowning

Nobody heard him, the dead man,
But still he lay moaning:
I was much further out than you thought
And not waving but drowning.

Poor chap, he always loved larking
And now he's dead
It must have been too cold for him his heart gave way,
They said.

Oh no no no, it was too cold always
(Still the dead one lay moaning)
I was much too far out all my life
And not waving but drowning.

Alone in the Woods

Alone in the woods I felt
The bitter hostility of the sky and the trees
Nature has taught her creatures to hate
Man that fusses and fumes
Unquiet man
As the sap rises in the trees
As the sap paints the trees a violent green
So rises the wrath of Nature's creatures
At man
So paints the face of Nature a violent green.
Nature is sick at man
Sick at his fuss and fume
Sick at his agonies
Sick at his gaudy mind
That drives his body
Ever more quickly
More and more
In the wrong direction.

Discussion

The Frog Prince

1. (a) Why does the Frog Prince feel nervous? **(b)** Does he really want to be disenchanted? Explain.

2. What comment on life do you think the speaker is making in stanza four?

No Respect

Explain the last two lines of "No Respect" in the context of the rest of the poem.

Not Waving But Drowning

Compare what the "dead man" moans in the first stanza of "Not Waving but Drowning" with what he moans in the last stanza. If the poem describes a figurative drowning rather than an actual one, what is it all about?

Alone in the Woods

1. This poem presents an unusual approach—Nature hating man. Why might Nature feel as she does?

2. What is the "wrong direction" in which man is moving "ever more quickly"?

3. Explain why you agree or disagree with the speaker.

Stevie Smith 1902 • 1971

Only recently have we begun to realize the depth and versatility of Stevie Smith's poems. At times she resembles Emily Dickinson; at times her poetic voice is so clear and simple that it is chilling. A poet by vocation, Smith worked in an office while caring for her aged mother. Her range of subject matter, often tinged with loneliness, is testimony to her vivid imagination.

Dylan Thomas

The Force That Through the Green Fuse Drives the Flower

The force that through the green fuse drives the flower
Drives my green age; that blasts the roots of trees
Is my destroyer.
And I am dumb to tell the crooked rose
My youth is bent by the same wintry fever.

The force that drives the water through the rocks
Drives my red blood; that dries the mouthing streams
Turns mine to wax.
And I am dumb to mouth unto my veins
How at the mountain spring the same mouth sucks.

The hand that whirls the water in the pool
Stirs the quicksand; that ropes the blowing wind
Hauls my shroud sail.
And I am dumb to tell the hanging man
How of my clay is made the hangman's lime.

The lips of time leech to the fountain head;
Love drips and gathers, but the fallen blood
Shall calm her sores.
And I am dumb to tell a weather's wind
How time has ticked a heaven round the stars.

And I am dumb to tell the lover's tomb
How at my sheet goes the same crooked worm.

Discussion

1. The poem opens with a juxtaposition of creative and destructive forces, or forces of life and forces of death. Trace the linking of these forces throughout the poem and discuss the effect.

2. How does the poet relate these elements in nature to himself?

"The Force That Through the Green Fuse . . ."

The contending forces of growth and decay find their natural expression in antithetical imagery, one image posed against its opposite in imitation of the balance of forces. The gunpowder conceit of the first line (the flower seen as an explosion at the top of its stem, the fuse) supplies the "blasts" of the second line, which, however, utilizes the alternative meaning of *blasts* retained in *fever*; and *blasts* is recalled in *wintry*, a third connotation.

Antithetical form is very clear in the first stanza: the force that, on the one hand, brings the flowering of youth causes, on the other hand, destruction, which is then emphasized in the refrain. The second stanza repeats the form.

"Mouthing streams" are streams at the mouth, the estuary. The mouth sucking at the mountain spring can be thought of as the estuary, sucking down the whole course of the stream into the sea. The force that drives the water through the rocks is the same as that which sucks it in at the mouth: in short, the creating and destroying forces are identical. This same mouth, the estuary, sucks at the veins. The poet is leading up to a leech image in stanza four, but here the image is of the bloodstream, the stream of life, beginning in youth, with time slowly sucking away the vitality, pulling toward the estuary, death. The force that drives the blood also dries it; the force of youth pulls one on to age.

The same idea is represented differently in the next stanza. The force that whirls the water (positive action) stirs quicksand (betokening death). The force blows both the ship of life and the ship of death. The two forces are one.

Is this same kind of two-way cross current in the refrain? We certainly wouldn't see it unless we were looking for it. The poet's mortal clay is not only dead but is the receptor for dead flesh, doubly dead. Though the positive doesn't have much chance here, *lime* no doubt came down from *quicksand* (via quicklime) and shares the same implication of "quick." The lime pit is, in a sense, cleansing. Positive effects can, according to Thomas's way of looking at things, come out of the macabre.

This is the point of the next image. Time is a leech, which sucks at the fountain head of Love, making a sore wound. But the loss of blood, in keeping with archaic lore, is beneficial. The refrain of this stanza makes the same assertion of unexpected good coming from evil. *Heaven* must be positive; Thomas would not use it ironically here. When Time, usually the agent of destruction, ticks a heaven round the stars, it is unexpected, but that is the whole point—positive comes out of the usually negative.

The real subject of the poem is the idea of contending forces in nature and the vital role of destruction. Of course, the forces do cause dismay, and regret is the dominant response to the world of flux. The refrains communicate this tone, which is summed up in the final isolated couplet. The poet is expressing his identity with the dead lover, knowing himself to be mortal, the worm already at his sheet as though it were his shroud. The pathos here seems to set at nought the *heaven* of the previous lines. At the end of his celebration of the dual processes in nature, the poet emphasizes the negative. . . .

Abridged and slightly adapted from *Entrances to Dylan Thomas' Poetry* by Ralph Maud. By permission of the University of Pittsburgh Press.

Fern Hill

Now as I was young and easy under the apple boughs
About the lilting house and happy as the grass was green,
The night above the dingle starry,
Time let me hail and climb
Golden in the heydays of his eyes,
And honoured among wagons I was prince of the apple towns
And once below a time I lordly had the trees and leaves
Trail with daisies and barley
Down the rivers of the windfall light.

And as I was green and carefree, famous among the barns
About the happy yard and singing as the farm was home,
In the sun that is young once only,
Time let me play and be
Golden in the mercy of his means,
And green and golden I was huntsman and herdsman, the calves
Sang to my horn, the foxes on the hills barked clear and cold,
And the sabbath rang slowly
In the pebbles of the holy streams.

All the sun long it was running, it was lovely, the hay
Fields high as the house, the tunes from the chimneys, it was air
And playing, lovely and watery
And fire green as grass.
And nightly under the simple stars
As I rode to sleep the owls were bearing the farm away,
All the moon long I heard, blessed among stables, the night-jars
Flying with the ricks, and the horses
Flashing into the dark.

And then to awake, and the farm, like a wanderer white
With the dew, come back, the cock on his shoulder: it was all
Shining, it was Adam and maiden,
The sky gathered again
And the sun grew round that very day.
So it must have been after the birth of the simple light
In the first, spinning place, the spellbound horses walking warm
Out of the whinnying green stable
On to the fields of praise.

And honoured among foxes and pheasants by the gay house
Under the new made clouds and happy as the heart was long,
In the sun born over and over,
I ran my heedless ways,

My wishes raced through the house high hay
And nothing I cared, at my sky blue trades, that time allows
In all his tuneful turning so few and such morning songs
Before the children green and golden
Follow him out of grace.

Nothing I cared, in the lamb white days, that time would take me
Up to the swallow thronged loft by the shadow of my hand,
In the moon that is always rising,
Nor that riding to sleep
I should hear him fly with the high fields
And wake to the farm forever fled from the childless land.
Oh as I was young and easy in the mercy of his means,
Time held me green and dying
Though I sang in my chains like the sea.

notes and comments

"Fern Hill"

If one sought to describe this poem within the compass of a single phrase, it might be called "an elegy in praise of lost youth." Lament and celebration sound throughout the work: the latter strongly at the beginning, the former gaining tone as the poem progresses.

But, as with all great threnodies in English—with Milton's *Lycidas,* Gray's *Elegy,* Shelley's *Adonais,* and Arnold's *Thyrsis*—the particularity of the cause of grief is lost in a sorrow which speaks for all men. Nostalgic recollection of a child's farm holiday is the leaping-off point for the poem; but—once launched—so intense and poignant a memory overtakes the poet, that his words convey more than a merely topographical homesickness. The farm becomes Eden before the Fall, and time the angel with a flaming sword.

But no such intrusive personification operates within the poem. The farm is invested with a light as radiant as the unforfeited Garden, and time exercises its function as irrevocably as God's excluding angel. So, though at the end we are faced with nothing worse than a farmstead which cannot be revisited, in actual poetic terms we have experienced the states of innocence and eternity, and been subjected to corruption, time, and change.

The poem is constructed from six nine-line stanzas, with only an infrequent rhyme. The absence of rhyme suffices to make the lyrically undulating lines more natural. The artifice and architectonic of the poem consists not in the usual technical devices, but in the repetition, in later stanzas, of *motifs* established in the first. These *motifs* are not worked out with any mechanical regularity; and their place and precedence in the poem are not formally observed. The *motifs* I find to be mainly three: that of the unwitting situation of childhood; that of the delight in this situation; that of time's operation, by which the situation becomes a fate.

Do Not Go Gentle into That Good Night

Do not go gentle into that good night,
Old age should burn and rave at close of day;
Rage, rage against the dying of the light.

Though wise men at their end know dark is right,
Because their words had forked no lightning they
Do not go gentle into that good night.

Good men, the last wave by, crying how bright
Their frail deeds might have danced in a green bay,
Rage, rage against the dying of the light.

Wild men who caught and sang the sun in flight,
And learn, too late, they grieved it on its way,
Do not go gentle into that good night.

Grave men, near death, who see with blinding sight
Blind eyes could blaze like meteors and be gay,
Rage, rage against the dying of the light.

And you, my father, there on the sad height,
Curse, bless, me now with your fierce tears, I pray.
Do not go gentle into that good night.
Rage, rage against the dying of the light.

---

notes and comments

The Villanelle

"Do Not Go Gentle" is a villanelle, an intricate poetic form consisting of five or more three-line stanzas (tercets) and a final four-line stanza (quatrain), all relying on only two rhymes. The first and third lines of the poem alternate as the last lines of the three-line stanzas, and together end the quatrain. This exacting form is chiefly used in Medieval French poetry, although a few poets writing in English have used it. One is W. H. Auden, who has written a villanelle called "If I Could Tell You."

Discussion

1. "Fern Hill" recounts life from a child's innocent and egocentric viewpoint. **(a)** What are some examples of this? **(b)** What is meant by: "As I rode to sleep the owls were bearing the farm away" (line 24)? **(c)** Comment on the appropriateness of the description of the Garden of Eden in stanza 4. **(d)** Explain the last two lines: "Time held me green and dying / Though I sang in my chains like the sea."

2. When Dylan Thomas wrote "Do Not Go Gentle . . .", his father was ill and apparently had only a short time to live. The poem was not published until after the old man's death. **(a)** Stanzas 2–5 mention four kinds of men. How does each type meet death, and why? **(b)** Light and dark (night) are contrasted throughout the poem. What does each signify? **(c)** Explore the possible implications of the often-repeated phrase "good night." **(d)** It has been stated that this poem would not be half so moving without the ritualistic repetition with variation that the villanelle form demands. Discuss.

Dylan Thomas 1914 • 1953

Thomas was born in the seacoast town of Swansea in Wales and left school at 16. He tried reporting for a local newspaper for a year, but poetry-writing, which he had been doing since he was a small boy, was more to his taste than journalism. He published his first volume of poetry at 19 and continued to publish well-received books of verse during the 1930s. *Portrait of the Artist as a Young Dog,* a collection of stories about his childhood and youth, appeared in 1940. Another book of boyhood reminiscences, *Quite Early One Morning,* and a verse play, *Under Milk Wood,* were published after his death.

Thomas worked for the BBC during World War II as a documentary film editor and also as a radio broadcaster; his magnificent Welsh voice reading poetry or stories enchanted listeners. In the early 1950s he made several enormously successful lecture-poetry reading trips to the United States. On his third lecture tour, he died suddenly in New York.

Alastair Reid

The O-Filler

One noon in the library, I watched a man—
imagine!—filling in O's, a little, rumpled
nobody of a man, who licked his stub of pencil
and leaned over every O with a loving care,
shading it neatly, exactly to its edges
until the open pages
were pocked and dotted with solid O's, like towns
and capitals on a map. And yet, so peppered,
the book appeared inhabited and complete.

That whole afternoon as the light outside softened
and the library groaned woodenly,
he worked and worked, his O-so-patient shading
descending like an eyelid over each open O
for page after page. Not once did he miss one,
or hover even a moment over an *a*,
or an *e* or a *p* or a *g*. Only the O's—
oodles of O's, O's multitudinous, O's manifold,
O's italic and roman.
And what light on his crumpled face when he
discovered—
as I supposed—odd words like *zoo* and *ooze,*
polo, oolong and *odontology!*

Think now. In that limitless library,
all round the steep-shelved walls, bulging in their bind-
ings,
books stood, waiting. Heaven knows how many
he had so far filled, but still there remained
uncountable volumes of O-laden prose, and odes
with inflated capital O's (in the manner of Shelley),
O-bearing bibles and biographies,

even whole sections devoted to O alone,
all his for the filling. Glory, glory, glory!
How utterly open and endless the world must have
seemed to him,
how round and ample! Think of it. A pencil
was all he needed. Life was one wide O.

And, why, at the end of things, should O's not be
closed
as eyes are? I envied him, for in my place
across the table from him, had I accomplished
anything as firm as he had, or as fruitful?
What could I show? A handful of scrawled lines,
an afternoon yawned and wondered away,
and a growing realization that in time
even my scribbled words would come
under his grubby thumb, and the blinds be drawn
on all my O's, with only this thought for comfort—
that when he comes to this poem, a proper joy
may amaze his wizened face, and, O, a pure pleasure
make his meticulous pencil quiver.

Discussion

1. Explain the attitude, in the last stanza, of the speaker toward the O-filler.

2. Does this poem about O's contain an excessive number of O's? Explain.

Alastair Reid 1926 •

Born and educated in Scotland, Reid has taught in the U.S. (at Sarah Lawrence College) and is a correspondent for the *New Yorker.* He has traveled extensively, and was twice the recipient of a Guggenheim Fellowship.

Philip Larkin

At Grass

The eye can hardly pick them out
From the cold shade they shelter in.
Till wind distresses tail and mane;
Then one crops grass, and moves about
—The other seeming to look on—
And stands anonymous again.

Yet fifteen years ago, perhaps
Two dozen distances sufficed
To fable them: faint afternoons
Of Cups and Stakes and Handicaps,
Whereby their names were artificed
To inlay faded, classic Junes—

Silks at the start: against the sky
Numbers and parasols: outside,
Squadrons of empty cars, and heat,
And littered grass: then the long cry
Hanging unhushed till it subside
To stop-press columns on the street.

Do memories plague their ears like flies?
They shake their heads. Dusk brims the
shadows.
Summer by summer all stole away,
The starting-gates, the crowds and cries—
All but the unmolesting meadows,
Almanacked, their names live; they

Have slipped their names, and stand at ease,
Or gallop for what must be joy,
And not a fieldglass sees them home,
Or curious stop-watch prophesies:
Only the groom, and the groom's boy,
With bridles in the evening come.

The Explosion

On the day of the explosion
Shadows pointed towards the pithead:
In the sun the slagheap slept.

Down the lane came men in pitboots
Coughing oath-edged talk and pipe-smoke,
Shouldering off the freshened silence.

One chased after rabbits; lost them;
Came back with a nest of lark's eggs;
Showed them; lodged them in the grasses.

So they passed in beards and moleskins,
Fathers, brothers, nicknames, laughter,
Through the tall gates standing open.

At noon, there came a tremor; cows
Stopped chewing for a second; sun,
Scarfed as in a heat-haze, dimmed.

The dead go on before us, they
Are sitting in God's house in comfort,
We shall see them face to face—

Plain as lettering in the chapels
It was said, and for a second
Wives saw men of the explosion

Larger than in life they managed—
Gold as on a coin, or walking
Somehow from the sun towards them,

One showing the eggs unbroken.

Discussion

1. (a) Are the retired racehorses in "At Grass" satisfied with their fate? Cite evidence from the poem to support your answer. **(b)** What is meant by: "they / Have slipped their names" (lines 24-25)? **(c)** One critic has commented that the two racehorses have virtually faded away into oblivion, into nature itself. Explain why you agree or disagree.

2. (a) What in "The Explosion" turns out to be ironic in the miners' restoring the lark's eggs? **(b)** What is the "tremor" mentioned in line 13? **(c)** How do the women react to the words of the funeral service? **(d)** What is the point of the poem?

3. (a) Is the poem "Homage to a Government" in favor of war and armies of occupation? Explain. **(b)** What is meant by the last line? **(c)** What is the significance of the title? **(d)** What is the tone of the poem?

Philip Larkin 1922 •

Larkin received B.A. and M.A. degrees from Oxford, and since 1955 has been librarian at the University of Hull. He has written novels as well as poetry, and also writes on jazz for the London *Daily Telegraph.*

Homage to a Government

Next year we are to bring the soldiers home
For lack of money, and it is all right,
Places they guarded, or kept orderly,
Must guard themselves, and keep themselves orderly.
We want the money for ourselves at home
Instead of working. And this is all right.

It's hard to say who wanted it to happen,
But now it's been decided nobody minds.
The places are a long way off, not here,
Which is all right, and from what we hear
The soldiers there only made trouble happen.
Next year we shall be easier in our minds.

Next year we shall be living in a country
That brought its soldiers home for lack of money.
The statues will be standing in the same
Tree-muffled squares, and look nearly the same.
Our children will not know it's a different country.
All we can hope to leave them now is money.

Elizabeth Jennings

The Climbers

To the cold peak without their careful women
(Who watching children climbing into dreams
Go dispossessed at home). The mountain moves
Away at every climb and steps are hard
Frozen along the glacier. Every man
Tied to the rope constructs himself alone.

And not the summit reached nor any pole
Touched is the wished embrace, but still to move
And as the mountain climbs to see it whole
And each mind's landscape growing more complete
As sinews strain and all the muscles knot.

One at the peak is small. His disappointment
The coloured flag flown at the lonely top,
And all the valley's motive grown obscure.
He envies the large toilers halfway there
Who still possess the mountain by desire
And, not arriving, dream in no resentment.

Discussion

1. Who is it (in line 3) who goes "dispossessed at home"?

2. In stanza two, what is "the wished embrace"?

3. **(a)** What is the disappointment of the first man who reached the top, and why does he envy the toilers below him? **(b)** How can this man's reactions be paralleled to the events in many lives?

Discussion

1. (a) What place might "here" in the first line refer to? (b) Why do the guidebooks not refer to this place?
2. Why is a place like this good for visitors?

Elizabeth Jennings 1926 •

Conscious of being both a woman and a Roman Catholic, Jennings has avoided poetic movements, preferring to write as an individual rather than as a member of any poetic coterie. Her poetry is always imaginative, sometimes unusual, and nearly always illuminated by insights into the human condition.

Not in the Guide-Books

Nobody stays here long;
  Deliberate visitors know
There is nothing here the guide-books show,
  No ruin or statue to sustain
Some great emotion in their stone.
  So visitors soon go.

Some travellers stay a little
  To collect wine or corn
And here breathe in the over-subtle
  Smell of places worn
Not by a marvellous death or battle
  But by their insignificance brought down.

Yet good, a place like this,
  For one grown tired of histories
To shape a human myth,
  A story but for his
Delight, where he might make the place
  His own success
Building what no one else had bothered with—
  A simple life or death.

Thom Gunn

The Secret Sharer

Over the ankles in snow and numb past pain
I stared up at my window three stories high:
From a white street unconcerned as a dead eye,
I patiently called my name again and again.

The curtains were lit, through glass were lit by
doubt
And there was I, within the room alone.
In the empty wind I stood and shouted on:
But O, what if the strange head should peer out?

Suspended taut between two equal fears
I was like to be torn apart by their strong pull:
What, I asked, if I never hear my call?
And what if it reaches my insensitive ears?

Fixed in my socket of thought I saw them move
Aside, I saw that some uncertain hand
Had touched the curtains. Mine, I wondered? And,
At this instant, the wind turned in its groove.
The wind turns in its groove and I am here
Lying in bed, the snow and street outside;
Fire-glow still reassuring; dark defied.
The wind turns in its groove: I am still there.

Discussion

1. **(a)** What hint does the last stanza of "The Secret Sharer" give about the speaker, and thus—possibly—about the rest of the poem? **(b)** How do the tense changes in the last stanza function to help in understanding the poem? **(c)** The last line is ambiguous; how would you explain it? **(d)** The concept of the "doppelganger"—the physical manifestation of one part of a character's personality—is fairly common in literature. Comment upon its possible use here.

2. In "The Annihilation . . ." **(a)** what is the state of mind of the speaker? **(b)** what is meant by the **paradox** "infinite finitude" (line 17)?

Thom Gunn 1929 •

Thom Gunn was born in Gravesend, brought up in London, educated at Oxford, and has both studied and taught in California. He believes that his personal life should remain private.

The Annihilation of Nothing

Nothing remained: Nothing, the wanton name
That nightly I rehearsed till led away
To a dark sleep, or sleep that held one dream.

In this a huge contagious absence lay,
More space than space, over the cloud and slime,
Defined but by the encroachments of its sway.

Stripped to indifference at the turns of time,
Whose end I knew, I woke without desire,
And welcomed zero as a paradigm.

But now it breaks—images burst with fire
Into the quiet sphere where I have bided,
Showing the landscape holding yet entire:

The power that I envisaged, that presided
Ultimate in its abstract devastations,
Is merely change, the atoms it divided

Complete, in ignorance, new combinations.
Only an infinite finitude I see
In those peculiar lovely variations.

It is despair that nothing cannot be
Flares in the mind and leaves a smoky mark
Of dread.
Look upward. Neither firm nor free,

Purposeless matter hovers in the dark.

Ted Hughes

Fern

Here is the fern's frond, unfurling a gesture,
Like a conductor whose music will now be pause
And the one note of silence
To which the whole earth dances gravely.

The mouse's ear unfurls its trust,
The spider takes up her bequest,
And the retina
Reins the creation with a bridle of water.

And, among them, the fern
Dances gravely, like the plume
Of a warrior returning, under the low hills,

Into his own kingdom.

Bullfrog

With their lithe, long, strong legs,
Some frogs are able
To thump upon double-
Bass strings, though pond water deadens and clogs.

But you, bullfrog, you pump out
Whole fogs full of horn—a threat
As of a liner looming. True
That, first hearing you
Disgorging your gouts of darkness like a wounded god,
Not utterly fantastically, I expected
(As in some antique tale depicted)
A broken-down bull up to its belly in mud,
Sucking black swamp up, belching out black cloud

And a squall of gudgeon and lilies.
A surprise
Now, to see you, a boy's prize,
No bigger than a rat, with all dumb silence
In your little old woman hands.

Esther's Tomcat

Daylong this tomcat lies stretched flat
As an old rough mat, no mouth and no eyes,
Continual wars and wives are what
Have tattered his ears and battered his head.

Like a bundle of old rope and iron
Sleeps till blue dusk. Then reappear
His eyes, green as ringstones: he yawns wide red,
Fangs fine as a lady's needle and bright.

A tomcat sprang at a mounted knight,
Locked round his neck like a trap of hooks
While the knight rode fighting its clawing and bite.
After hundreds of years the stain's there

On the stone where he fell, dead of the tom:
That was at Barnborough. The tomcat still
Grallochs[1] odd dogs on the quiet,
Will take the head clean off your simple pullet,

Is unkillable. From the dog's fury,
From gunshot fired point-blank he brings
His skin whole, and whole
From owlish moons of bekittenings

Among ashcans. He leaps and lightly
Walks upon sleep, his mind on the moon.
Nightly over the round world of men,
Over the roofs go his eyes and outcry.

---

1. ***Grallochs*** (gral′əʜs), disembowels.

Discussion

1. (a) What might have occasioned the writing of the poem "Bullfrog"? **(b)** What is the speaker's attitude toward the bullfrog? **(c)** This poem is not traditionally rhymed, but there is a careful matching of end-of-line consonant sounds that approximates rhyme. What is your reaction to this modern technique?

2. The poem "Fern" has been called by one reader "a hymn to nature." Discuss the extent to which you agree with this statement.

3. (a) What does the speaker find surprising about Esther's tomcat? **(b)** How does this tomcat typify all tomcats? **(c)** How does he appear to be almost supernatural?

Young men in a National Guard Camp, 1910. Courtesy of the Collection of Mary Elizabeth Higgins.

Six Young Men

The celluloid of a photograph holds them well—
Six young men, familiar to their friends.
Four decades that have faded and ochre-tinged
This photograph have not wrinkled the faces or the hands.
Though their cocked hats are not now fashionable,
Their shoes shine. One imparts an intimate smile,
One chews a grass, one lowers his eyes, bashful,
One is ridiculous with cocky pride—
Six months after this picture they were all dead.

All are trimmed for a Sunday jaunt. I know
That bilberried bank, that thick tree, that black wall,
Which are there yet and not changed. From where these sit
You hear the water of seven streams fall
To the roarer in the bottom, and through all
The leafy valley a rumouring of air go.
Pictured here, their expressions listen yet,
And still that valley has not changed its sound
Though their faces are four decades under the ground.

This one was shot in an attack and lay
Calling in the wire, then this one, his best friend,
Went out to bring him in and was shot too;
And this one, the very moment he was warned
From potting at tin-cans in no man's land,
Fell back dead with his rifle-sights shot away.
The rest, nobody knows what they came to,
But come to the worst they must have done, and held it
Closer than their hope; all were killed.

Here see a man's photograph,
The locket of a smile, turned overnight
Into the hospital of his mangled last
Agony and hours; see bundled in it
His mightier-than-a-man dead bulk and weight;
And on this one place which keeps him alive
(In his Sunday best) see fall war's worst
Thinkable flash and rending, onto his smile
Forty years rotting into soil.

That man's not more alive whom you confront
And shake by the hand, see hale, hear speak loud,
Than any of these six celluloid smiles are,
Nor prehistoric or fabulous beast more dead;
No thought so vivid as their smoking blood:
To regard this photograph might well dement,
Such contradictory permanent horrors here
Smile from the single exposure and shoulder out
One's own body from its instant and heat.

Discussion

1. **(a)** What event does the photograph record? **(b)** What common fate did the young men share?

2. **(a)** Is the scene of the Sunday outing unchanged? **(b)** How does the poet convey this?

3. **(a)** In line 33, to what does the "one place" refer? **(b)** What instruction does the poet give in regard to it?

4. In stanza five, what contradiction does the poet connect with the photograph?

5. What seems to be the basic subject of this poem? Is it the horrors of war or the photograph as relic or something else?

Extension • Writing

Write a short essay defending your answer to question five above.

Ted Hughes 1930 •

Ted Hughes was born in Yorkshire and educated at Cambridge. His poetry shows the influences of, among others, Thomas Hardy, D. H. Lawrence, and Robert Graves. The poems in *Crow* (1970) seem the most complete expression of one important tendency—the mythological—in his work.

John Holloway

Journey Through the Night

At the first hour from dawn
The traveller in the window seat
Rubbed his eyes, woke from a daze,
Brushed his rough hair back with great
Podgy fingers, gave a yawn,
Cleared the pane's white dewy haze,
Then stared so eagerly, it might
Have been his home place come in sight.

But at the second hour from dawn
The traveller in the window seat
Suddenly turned away from the world
As though he saw some thing too sweet
Or too bitter to be borne;
And when he met my glance, he curled
His body to the wall, and wept
I thought; but it may be he slept.

At the third hour from dawn
The ticket man rolled back the door:
The traveller blurted out that he
Wanted another ticket for
Some other place, somewhere further on;
He spoke shortly, confusedly;
But I saw he did not know,
Now, where in the world to go.

Discussion

1. (a) In the first stanza, what does the behavior of the traveller suggest to the speaker? **(b)** What other explanations for the traveller's behavior might there be?

2. Continuing the speculation begun in the first stanza, what does the speaker suggest in lines 12–13 about the traveller's experience?

3. Continuing this same speculation, how does the speaker explain the traveller's behavior in the third stanza?

4. What does his preoccupation suggest about the speaker?

John Holloway 1920 •

John Holloway was educated at Oxford. He has travelled widely in Europe, the Near East, India, and America. He has taught at Oxford, Aberdeen, and Cambridge. His autobiography, *A London Childhood,* was published in 1966.

Roger McGough

P.C.[1] Plod Versus the Dale St Dog Strangler

For several months
Liverpool was held in the grip of fear
by a dogstrangler most devilish,
who roamed the streets after dark
looking for strays. Finding one
he would tickle it seductively
about the body to gain its confidence,
then lead it down a deserted backstreet
where he would strangle the poor brute.
Hardly a night passed without somebody's
faithful fourlegged friend being dispatched
to that Golden Kennel in the sky.

The public were warned,
At the very first sign
Of anything suspicious,
Ring Canine-nine-nine.

Nine o'clock on the evening of January 11th sees P.C. Plod
on the corner of Dale St and Sir Thomas St
disguised as a Welsh collie.
It is part of a daring plan to apprehend the strangler.
For though it is a wet and moonless night,
Plod is cheered in the knowledge
that the whole of the Liverpool City Constabulary
is on the beat that night disguised as dogs.
Not ten minutes earlier, a pekinese (Policewoman Hodges)
had scampered past on her way to Clayton Square.
For Plod, the night passed uneventfully
and so in the morning he was horrified to learn
that no less than fourteen policemen and policewomen
had been tickled and strangled during the night.

The public were horrified
The Commissioner aghast
Something had to be done
And fast.

---

1. ***P.C.,*** police constable.

P.C. Plod (wise as a brace of owls)
met the challenge magnificently
and submitted an idea so startling in its vision
so audacious in its conception
that the Commissioner gasped
before ordering all dogs in the city
to be thereinafter disguised as fuzz.
The plan worked
and the dogstrangler was heard of no more.

Cops and mongrels
Like P.C.s in a pod
To a grateful public
Plod was God.

So next time you're up in Liverpool
take a closer look at that
policeman on pointduty, he might
well be a cocker spaniel.

Discussion

1. This poem is sheer nonsense—but did you enjoy it? Explain.

2. Might the poem be spoofing something? If so, what?

Roger McGough 1937 •

A member of The Scaffold, a satirical pop group, McGough often writes poetry that is suitable for performance. His verse is noted for puns and other types of wordplay. In addition to his poetry, he has thus far written one full-length play and a number of shorter ones, some sketches, and a short novel.

Vocabulary • Structure

A. The prefix *sub*-comes from the Latin. Other forms of the prefix are *suc-, sup-, sus-,* and *suf-*. On a separate sheet of paper, write the word in which the prefix appears in each of the following passages. Then use your Glossary to give the original meaning of the prefix in each word. Finally, write a synonym for the meaning of the whole word as it is used in the passage.

1. "There is nothing here the guide-books show, / No ruin or statue to sustain / Some great emotion in their stone."

2. "Yet fifteen years ago, perhaps / Two dozen distances sufficed / To fable them . . . "

3. "This is the dead land / This is the cactus land / Here the stone images / Are raised, here they receive / The supplication of a dead man's hand / Under the twinkle of a fading star."

B. The common suffix *-ous* means "full of, having much, having." On your paper, write the word in which the suffix appears in the following passages. Then write how the word functions, or what part of speech it is, in each passage.

4. "P. C. Plod (wise as a brace of owls) / met the challenge magnificently / and submitted an idea so startling in its vision / so audacious in its conception / that the Commissioner gasped . . . "

5. "Only the O's— / oodles of O's, O's multitudinous, O's manifold, / O's italic and roman."

Saki

Tobermory

It was a chill, rain-washed afternoon of a late August day, that indefinite season when partridges are still in security or cold storage, and there is nothing to hunt—unless one is bounded on the north by the Bristol Channel, in which case one may lawfully gallop after fat red stags. Lady Blemley's house-party was not bounded on the north by the Bristol Channel, hence there was a full gathering of her guests round the tea table on this particular afternoon. And, in spite of the blankness of the season and the triteness of the occasion, there was no trace in the company of that fatigued restlessness which means a dread of the pianola and a subdued hankering for auction bridge. The undisguised open-mouthed attention of the entire party was fixed on the homely negative personality of Mr. Cornelius Appin. Of all her guests, he was the one who had come to Lady Blemley with the vaguest reputation. Some one had said he was "clever," and he had got his invitation in the moderate expectation, on the part of his hostess, that some portion at least of his cleverness would be contributed to the general entertainment. Until tea-time that day she had been unable to discover in what direction, if any, his cleverness lay. He was neither a wit nor a croquet champion, a hypnotic force nor a begetter of amateur theatricals. Neither did his exterior suggest the sort of man in whom women are willing to pardon a generous measure of mental deficiency. He had subsided into mere Mr. Appin, and the Cornelius seemed a piece of transparent baptismal bluff. And now he was claiming to have launched on the world a discovery beside which the invention of gunpowder, of the printing-press, and of steam locomotion were inconsiderable trifles. Science had made bewildering strides in many directions during recent decades, but this thing seemed to belong to the domain of miracle rather than to scientific achievement.

"And do you really ask us to believe," Sir Wilfrid was saying, "that you have discovered a means for instructing animals in the art of human speech, and that dear old Tobermory has proved your first successful pupil?"

"It is a problem at which I have worked for the last seventeen years," said Mr. Appin, "but only during the last eight or nine months have I been rewarded with glimmerings of success. Of course I have experimented with thousands of animals, but latterly only with cats, those wonderful creatures which have assimilated themselves so marvellously with our civilization while retaining all their highly developed feral instincts. Here and there among cats one comes across an outstanding superior intellect, just as one does among the ruck of human beings, and when I made the acquaintance of Tobermory a week ago I saw at once that I was in contact with a 'Beyond-cat' of extraordinary intelligence. I had gone far along the road to success in recent experiments; with Tobermory, as you call him, I have reached the goal."

Mr. Appin concluded his remarkable statement in a voice which he strove to divest of a triumphant inflection. No one said "Rats," though Clovis's lips moved in a monosyllabic contortion which probably invoked those rodents of disbelief.

"And do you mean to say," asked Miss Resker, after a slight pause, "that you have taught Tobermory to say and understand easy sentences of one syllable?"

"My dear Miss Resker," said the wonder-worker patiently, "one teaches little children and savages and backward adults in that piecemeal

---

"Tobermory" from THE SHORT STORIES OF SAKI by H. H. Munro (British title: THE BODLEY HEAD SAKI). Reprinted by permission of The Viking Press and The Bodley Head.

fashion; when one has once solved the problem of making a beginning with an animal of highly developed intelligence one has no need for those halting methods. Tobermory can speak our language with perfect correctness."

This time Clovis very distinctly said, "Beyond-rats!" Sir Wilfrid was more polite, but equally sceptical.

"Hadn't we better have the cat in and judge for ourselves?" suggested Lady Blemley.

Sir Wilfrid went in search of the animal, and the company settled themselves down to the languid expectation of witnessing some more or less adroit drawing-room ventriloquism.

In a minute Sir Wilfrid was back in the room, his face white beneath its tan and his eyes dilated with excitement.

"By Gad, it's true!"

His agitation was unmistakably genuine, and his hearers started forward in a thrill of awakened interest.

Collapsing into an armchair he continued breathlessly: "I found him dozing in the smoking-room, and called out to him to come for his tea. He blinked at me in his usual way, and I said, 'Come on, Toby; don't keep us waiting'; and, by Gad! he drawled out in a most horribly natural voice that he'd come when he dashed well pleased! I nearly jumped out of my skin!"

Appin had preached to absolutely incredulous hearers; Sir Wilfrid's statement carried instant conviction. A Babel-like chorus of startled exclamation arose, amid which the scientist sat mutely enjoying the first fruit of his stupendous discovery.

In the midst of the clamour Tobermory entered the room and made his way with velvet tread and studied unconcern across to the group seated round the tea table.

A sudden hush of awkwardness and constraint fell on the company. Somehow there seemed an element of embarrassment in addressing on equal terms a domestic cat of acknowledged mental ability.

"Will you have some milk, Tobermory?" asked Lady Blemley in a rather strained voice.

"I don't mind if I do," was the response, couched in a tone of even indifference. A shiver of suppressed excitement went through the listeners, and Lady Blemley might be excused for pouring out the saucerful of milk rather unsteadily.

"I'm afraid I've spilt a good deal of it," she said apologetically.

"After all, it's not my Axminster," was Tobermory's rejoinder.

Another silence fell on the group, and then Miss Resker, in her best district-visitor manner, asked if the human language had been difficult to learn. Tobermory looked squarely at her for a moment and then fixed his gaze serenely on the middle distance. It was obvious that boring questions lay outside his scheme of life.

"What do you think of human intelligence?" asked Mavis Pellington lamely.

"Of whose intelligence in particular?" asked Tobermory coldly.

"Oh, well, mine for instance," said Mavis, with a feeble laugh.

"You put me in an embarrassing position," said Tobermory, whose tone and attitude certainly did not suggest a shred of embarrassment. "When your inclusion in this house-party was suggested Sir Wilfrid protested that you were the most brainless woman of his acquaintance, and that there was a wide distinction between hospitality and the care of the feeble-minded. Lady Blemley replied that your lack of brain-power was the precise quality which had earned you your invitation, as you were the only person she could think of who might be idiotic enough to buy their old car. You know, the one they call 'The Envy of Sisyphus.'[1] because it goes quite nicely uphill if you push it."

Lady Blemley's protestations would have had greater effect if she had not casually suggested to Mavis only that morning that the car in question would be just the thing for her down at her Devonshire home.

Major Barfield plunged in heavily to effect a diversion.

"How about your carryings-on with the tortoiseshell puss up at the stables, eh?"

The moment he had said it everyone realized the blunder.

---

1. ***'The Envy of Sisyphus.'*** Sisyphus (sis′ə fəs) is a trickster from Greek mythology. He was finally punished in the Underworld for his crimes, being compelled to roll a great rock toward the top of a hill, where, nearing the top, the rock would break away and roll to the bottom again.

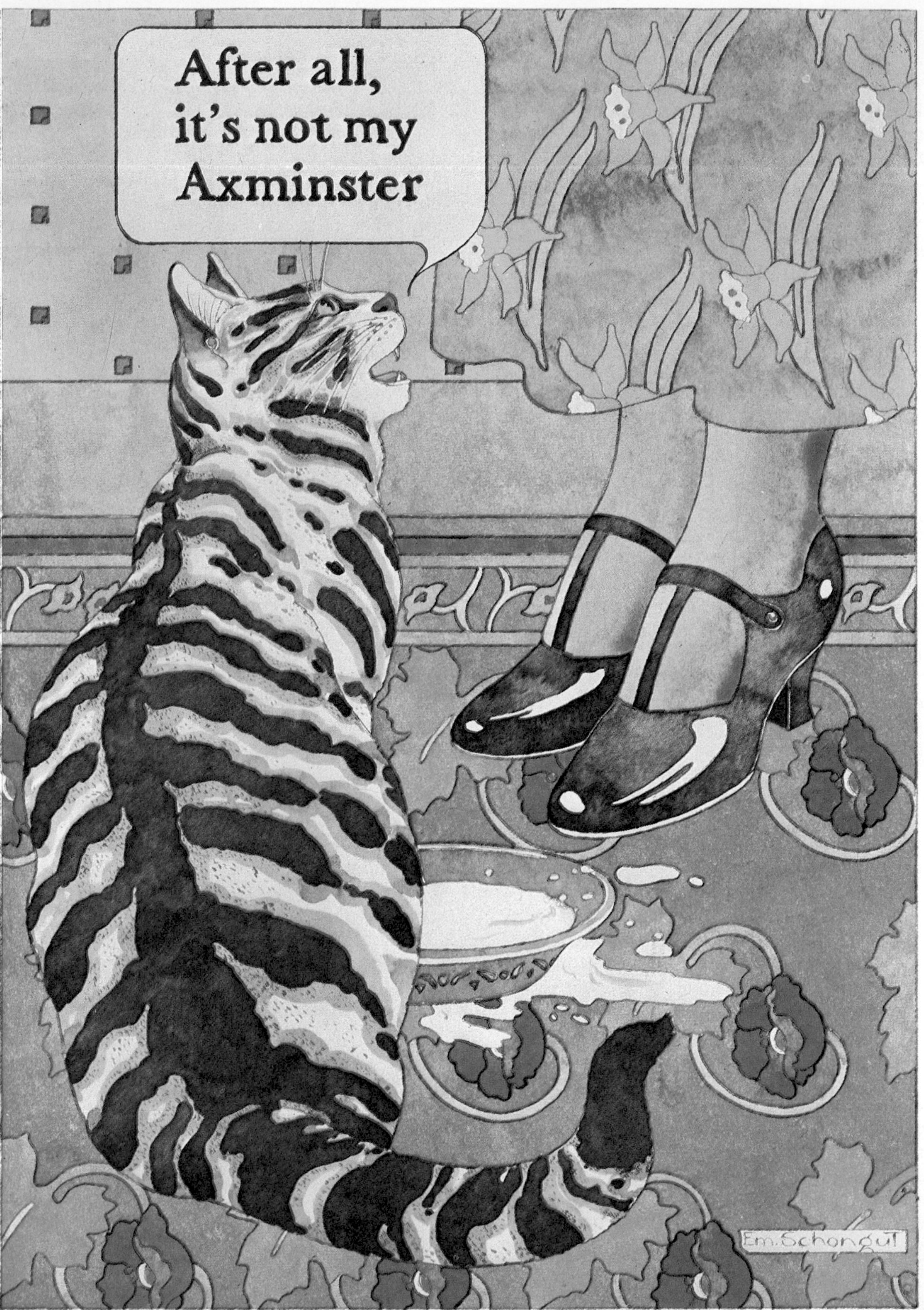
After all,
it's not my
Axminster
Em. Schongut

"One does not usually discuss these matters in public," said Tobermory frigidly. "From a slight observation of your ways since you've been in this house I should imagine you'd find it inconvenient if I were to shift the conversation on to your own little affairs."

The panic which ensued was not confined to the Major.

"Would you like to go and see if cook has got your dinner ready?" suggested Lady Blemley hurriedly, affecting to ignore the fact that it wanted at least two hours to Tobermory's dinner-time.

"Thanks," said Tobermory, "not quite so soon after my tea. I don't want to die of indigestion."

"Cats have nine lives, you know," said Sir Wilfrid heartily.

"Possibly," answered Tobermory; "but only one liver."

"Adelaide!" said Mrs. Cornett, "do you mean to encourage that cat to go out and gossip about us in the servants' hall?"

The panic had indeed become general. A narrow ornamental balustrade ran in front of most of the bedroom windows at the Towers, and it was recalled with dismay that this had formed a favourite promenade for Tobermory at all hours, whence he could watch the pigeons—and heaven knew what else besides. If he intended to become reminiscent in his present outspoken strain the effect would be something more than disconcerting. Mrs. Cornett, who spent much time at her toilet table, and whose complexion was reputed to be of a nomadic though punctual disposition, looked as ill at ease as the Major. Miss Scrawen, who wrote fiercely sensuous poetry and led a blameless life, merely displayed irritation; if you are methodical and virtuous in private you don't necessarily want every one to know it. Bertie van Tahn, who was so depraved at seventeen that he had long ago given up trying to be any worse, turned a dull shade of gardenia white, but he did not commit the error of dashing out of the room like Odo Finsberry, a young gentleman who was understood to be reading for the Church and who was possibly disturbed at the thought of scandals he might hear concerning other people. Clovis had the presence of mind to maintain a composed exterior; privately he was calculating how long it would take to procure a box of fancy mice through the agency of the *Exchange and Mart* as a species of hush-money.

Even in a delicate situation like the present, Agnes Resker could not endure to remain too long in the background.

"Why did I ever come down here?" she asked dramatically.

Tobermory immediately accepted the opening.

"Judging by what you said to Mrs. Cornett on the croquet-lawn yesterday, you were out for food. You described the Blemleys as the dullest people to stay with that you knew, but said they were clever enough to employ a first-rate cook; otherwise they'd find it difficult to get any one to come down a second time."

"There's not a word of truth in it! I appeal to Mrs. Cornett—" exclaimed the discomfited Agnes.

"Mrs. Cornett repeated your remark afterwards to Bertie van Tahn," continued Tobermory, "and said, 'That woman is a regular Hunger Marcher; she'd go anywhere for four square meals a day,' and Bertie van Tahn said—"

At this point the chronicle mercifully ceased. Tobermory had caught a glimpse of the big yellow Tom from the Rectory working his way through the shrubbery towards the stable wing. In a flash he had vanished through the open French window.

With the disappearance of his too brilliant pupil Cornelius Appin found himself beset by a hurricane of bitter upbraiding, anxious inquiry, and frightened entreaty. The responsibility for the situation lay with him, and he must prevent matters from becoming worse. Could Tobermory impart his dangerous gift to other cats? was the first question he had to answer. It was possible, he replied, that he might have initiated his intimate friend the stable puss into his new accomplishment, but it was unlikely that his teaching could have taken a wider range as yet.

"Then," said Mrs. Cornett, "Tobermory may be a valuable cat and a great pet; but I'm sure you'll agree, Adelaide, that both he and the stable cat must be done away with without delay."

"You don't suppose I've enjoyed the last quarter of an hour, do you?" said Lady Blemley bitterly. "My husband and I are very fond of Tobermory—at least, we were before this horrible accomplishment was infused into him; but now, of course, the only thing is to have him destroyed as soon as possible."

"We can put some strychnine in the scraps he always gets at dinnertime," said Sir Wilfrid, "and I will go and drown the stable cat myself. The coachman will be very sore at losing his pet, but I'll say a very catching form of mange has broken out in both cats and we're afraid of it spreading to the kennels."

"But my great discovery!" expostulated Mr. Appin; "after all my years of research and experiment—"

"You can go and experiment on the shorthorns at the farm, who are under proper control," said Mrs. Cornett, "or the elephants at the Zoological Gardens. They're said to be highly intelligent, and they have this recommendation, that they don't come creeping about our bedrooms and under chairs, and so forth."

An archangel ecstatically proclaiming the Millennium, and finding that it clashed unpardonably with Henley[2] and would have to be indefinitely postponed, could hardly have felt more crestfallen than Cornelius Appin at the reception of his wonderful achievement. Public opinion, however, was against him—in fact, had the general voice been consulted on the subject it is probable that a strong minority vote would have been in favour of including him in the strychnine diet.

Defective train arrangements and a nervous desire to see matters brought to a finish prevented an immediate dispersal of the party, but dinner that evening was not a social success. Sir Wilfrid had had rather a trying time with the stable cat and subsequently with the coachman. Agnes Resker ostentatiously limited her repast to a morsel of dry toast, which she bit as though it were a personal enemy; while Mavis Pellington maintained a vindictive silence throughout the meal. Lady Blemley kept up a flow of what she hoped was conversation, but her attention was fixed on the doorway. A plateful of carefully dosed fish scraps was in readiness on the sideboard, but sweets and savoury and dessert went their way, and no Tobermory appeared either in the dining-room or kitchen.

The sepulchral dinner was cheerful compared with the subsequent vigil in the smoking-room. Eating and drinking had at least supplied a distraction and cloak to the prevailing embarrassment. Bridge was out of the question in the general tension of nerves and tempers, and after Odo Finsberry had given a lugubrious rendering of "Melisande in the Wood" to a frigid audience, music was tacitly avoided. At eleven the servants went to bed, announcing that the small window in the pantry had been left open as usual for Tobermory's private use. The guests read steadily through the current batch of magazines, and fell back gradually on the "Badminton Library" and bound volumes of *Punch.* Lady Blemley made periodic visits to the pantry, returning each time with an expression of listless depression which forestalled questioning.

At two o'clock Clovis broke the dominating silence.

"He won't turn up tonight. He's probably in the local newspaper office at the present moment, dictating the first instalment of his reminiscences. Lady What's-her-name's book won't be in it. It will be the event of the day."

Having made this contribution to the general cheerfulness, Clovis went to bed. At long intervals the various members of the house-party followed his example.

The servants taking round the early tea made a uniform announcement in reply to a uniform question. Tobermory had not returned.

Breakfast was, if anything, a more unpleasant function than dinner had been, but before its conclusion the situation was relieved. Tobermory's corpse was brought in from the shrubbery, where a gardener had just discovered it. From the bites on his throat and the yellow fur which coated his claws it was evident that he had fallen in unequal combat with the big Tom from the Rectory.

By midday most of the guests had quitted the Towers, and after lunch Lady Blemley had sufficiently recovered her spirits to write an extremely nasty letter to the Rectory about the loss of her valuable pet.

Tobermory had been Appin's one successful

2. ***Henley,*** a place on the Thames River in Oxfordshire, the site of an annual regatta since 1839.

pupil, and he was destined to have no successor. A few weeks later an elephant in the Dresden Zoological Garden, which had shown no previous signs of irritability, broke loose and killed an Englishman who had apparently been teasing it. The victim's name was variously reported in the papers as Oppin and Eppelin, but his front name was faithfully rendered Cornelius.

"If he was trying German irregular verbs on the poor beast," said Clovis, "he deserved all he got." □□

Discussion

1. (a) What hadn't Cornelius Appin considered when he taught Tobermory to speak? **(b)** Can you think of any other "great" inventions or discoveries that had unexpected side effects?

2. (a) Where does the humor lie in this story? **(b)** To what extent is the story an attack on hypocrisy? **(c)** To what extent is it true to human nature?

Extension • Writing

1. Write about an adventure that might have happened to Cornelius Appin between Tobermory's death and his own.

2. Write on any of the following topics, or a similar one of your choice: "Tobermory Tells About ______ High School," "Tobermory Visits Congress," "Tobermory Goes to War."

H. H. Munro (Saki)
1870 • 1916

Hector Hugh Munro was born in Burma, the son of a police inspector-general. His mother died when he was two, and he was sent home to Scotland to live with relatives. His formal education ended with grammar school, but his father tutored him on extensive travels. In 1893 his father secured him a post with the Burma police, but his delicate health forced his return to Britain. There he took up a career in writing, and it was while doing political sketches for the *Westminster Gazette* that he adopted the pen name of Saki—the name of the cupbearer in the *Rubáiyát of Omar Khayyam.*

After serving for a time as a foreign correspondent for the *Morning Post*, he returned to London to devote himself to the writing of stories and novels. When World War I began, he enlisted as a private, declining several offers of commissions. He was killed in action in 1916.

James Joyce

Eveline

She sat at the window watching the evening invade the avenue. Her head was leaned against the window curtains and in her nostrils was the odor of dusty cretonne. She was tired.

Few people passed. The man out of the last house passed on his way home; she heard his footsteps clacking along the concrete pavement and afterwards crunching on the cinder path before the new red houses. One time there used to be a field there in which they used to play every evening with other people's children. Then a man from Belfast bought the field and built houses in it—not like their little brown houses but bright brick houses with shining roofs. The children of the avenue used to play together in that field—the Devines, the Waters, the Dunns, little Keogh the cripple, she and her brothers and sisters. Ernest, however, never played: he was too grown up. Her father used often to hunt them in out of the field with his blackthorn stick; but usually little Keogh used to keep *nix*[1] and call out when he saw her father coming. Still they seemed to have been rather happy then. Her father was not so bad then; and besides, her mother was alive. That was a long time ago; she and her brothers and sisters were all grown up; her mother was dead. Tizzie Dunn was dead, too, and the Waters had gone back to England. Everything changes. Now she was going to go away like the others, to leave her home.

Home! She looked round the room, reviewing all its familiar objects which she had dusted once a week for so many years, wondering where on earth all the dust came from. Perhaps she would never see again those familiar objects from which she had never dreamed of being divided. And yet during all those years she had never found out the name of the priest whose yellowing photograph hung on the wall above the broken harmonium beside the colored print of the promises made to Blessed Margaret Mary Alacoque. He had been a school friend of her father. Whenever he showed the photograph to a visitor her father used to pass it with a casual word: "He is in Melbourne now."

She had consented to go away, to leave her home. Was that wise? She tried to weigh each side of the question. In her home anyway she had shelter and food; she had those whom she had known all her life about her. Of course she had to work hard, both in the house and at business. What would they say of her in the Stores when they found out that she had run away with a fellow? Say she was a fool, perhaps; and her place would be filled up by advertisement. Miss Gavan would be glad. She had always had an edge on her, especially whenever there were people listening.

"Miss Hill, don't you see these ladies are waiting?"

"Look lively, Miss Hill, please."

She would not cry many tears at leaving the Stores.

But in her new home, in a distant unknown country, it would not be like that. Then she would be married—she, Eveline. People would treat her with respect then. She would not be treated as her mother had been. Even now, though she was over nineteen, she sometimes felt herself in danger of her father's violence. She knew it was that that had given her the palpitations. When they were growing up he had never gone for her, like he used to go for Harry and Ernest, because she was a girl; but latterly he had begun to threaten her and say what he would do to her only for her dead mother's sake. And now she had nobody to protect her. Ernest was dead and Harry, who was in the church decorating business, was nearly always down some-

---

1. ***nix,*** an old slang word, originally used by thieves, to refer to the member of a gang who kept watch.

where in the country. Besides, the invariable squabble for money on Saturday nights had begun to weary her unspeakably. She always gave her entire wages—seven shillings—and Harry always sent up what he could but the trouble was to get any money from her father. He said she used to squander the money, that she had no head, that he wasn't going to give her his hard-earned money to throw about the streets, and much more, for he was usually fairly bad on Saturday night. In the end he would give her the money and ask her had she any intention of buying Sunday's dinner. Then she had to rush out as quickly as she could and do her marketing, holding her black leather purse tightly in her hand as she elbowed her way through the crowds and returning home late under her load of provisions. She had hard work to keep the house together and to see that the two young children who had been left to her charge went to school regularly and got their meals regularly. It was hard work—a hard life—but now that she was about to leave it she did not find it a wholly undesirable life.

She was about to explore another life with Frank. Frank was very kind, manly, open-hearted. She was to go away with him by the night boat to be his wife and to live with him in Buenos Aires where he had a home waiting for her. How well she remembered the first time she had seen him; he was lodging in a house on the main road where she used to visit. It seemed a few weeks ago. He was standing at the gate, his peaked cap pushed back on his head and his hair tumbled forward over a face of bronze. Then they had come to know each other. He used to meet her outside the Stores every evening and see her home. He took her to see *The Bohemian Girl* and she felt elated as she sat in an unaccustomed part of the theater with him. He was awfully fond of music and sang a little. People knew that they were courting and, when he sang about the lass that loves a sailor, she always felt pleasantly confused. He used to call her Poppens out of fun. First of all it had been an excitement for her to have a fellow and then she had begun to like him. He had tales of distant countries. He had started as a deck boy at a pound a month on a ship of the Allan Line going out to Canada. He told her the names of the ships he had been on and the names of the different services. He had sailed through the Straits of Magellan and he told her stories of the terrible Patagonians. He had fallen on his feet in Buenos Aires, he said, and had come over to the old country just for a holiday. Of course, her father had found out the affair and had forbidden her to have anything to say to him.

"I know these sailor chaps," he said.

One day he had quarreled with Frank and after that she had to meet her lover secretly.

The evening deepened in the avenue. The white of two letters in her lap grew indistinct. One was to Harry; the other was to her father. Ernest had been her favorite but she liked Harry too. Her father was becoming old lately, she noticed; he would miss her. Sometimes he could be very nice. Not long before, when she had been laid up for a day, he had read her out a ghost story and made toast for her at the fire. Another day, when their mother was alive, they had all gone for a picnic to the Hill of Howth. She remembered her father putting on her mother's bonnet to make the children laugh.

Her time was running out but she continued to sit by the window, leaning her head against the window curtain, inhaling the odor of dusty cretonne. Down far in the avenue she could hear a street organ playing. She knew the air. Strange that it should come that very night to remind her of the promise to her mother, her promise to keep the home together as long as she could. She remembered the last night of her mother's illness; she was again in the close dark room at the other side of the hall and outside she heard a melancholy air of Italy. The organ player had been ordered to go away and given six-pence. She remembered her father strutting back into the sickroom saying: "Damned Italians! coming over here!"

As she mused the pitiful vision of her mother's life laid its spell on the very quick of her being—that life of commonplace sacrifices closing in final craziness. She trembled as she heard again her mother's voice saying constantly with foolish insistence: "Derevaun Seraun! Derevaun Seraun!"[2]

2. ***"Derevaun . . . Seraun."*** possibly corrupt Gaelic for "the end of pleasure is pain."

She stood up in a sudden impulse of terror. Escape! She must escape! Frank would save her. He would give her life, perhaps love, too. But she wanted to live. Why should she be unhappy? She had a right to happiness. Frank would take her in his arms, fold her in his arms. He would save her.

She stood among the swaying crowd in the station at the North Wall. He held her hand and she knew that he was speaking to her, saying something about the passage over and over again. The station was full of soldiers with brown baggages. Through the wide doors of the sheds she caught a glimpse of the black mass of the boat, lying in beside the quay wall, with illumined portholes. She answered nothing. She felt her cheek pale and cold and, out of a maze of distress, she prayed to God to direct her, to show her what was her duty. The boat blew a long mournful whistle into the mist. If she went, tomorrow she would be on the sea with Frank, steaming toward Buenos Aires. Their passage had been booked. Could she still draw back after all he had done for her? Her distress awoke a nausea in her body and she kept moving her lips in silent fervent prayer.

A bell clanged upon her heart. She felt him seize her hand:

"Come!"

All the seas of the world tumbled about her heart. He was drawing her into them: he would drown her. She gripped with both hands at the iron railing.

"Come!"

No! No! No! It was impossible. Her hands clutched the iron in frenzy. Amid the seas she sent a cry of anguish.

"Eveline! Evvy!"

He rushed beyond the barrier and called to her to follow. He was shouted at to go on but he still called to her. She set her white face to him, passive, like a helpless animal. Her eyes gave him no sign of love or farewell or recognition. □□

Discussion

1. Eveline thinks of Frank and his offer of marriage: "Escape! She must escape! Frank would save her. He would give her life, perhaps love, too." What would Frank save her from?

2. Why is Eveline attached to the hard life she wishes to leave?

3. **(a)** Point out some of the details that help create the atmosphere of Dublin of a half-century ago. **(b)** How do Joyce's details involve senses other than sight? Give examples.

4. Eveline, about to sail away from Ireland, thinks: "All the seas of the world tumbled about her heart. . . . Her eyes gave him no sign of love or farewell or recognition." What has happened to her?

Extension • Writing

In his biography of James Joyce, Richard Ellman reports that Eveline's real-life counterpart, Eveline Thornton, did not make the same decision as the girl in the story. Instead, Eveline Thornton married her sailor, settled down with him in Dublin, and had a number of children. Which version do you prefer, and why? Write an essay to explain your response.

James Joyce 1882 • 1941

Joyce was one of ten children. His father was a civil servant, continually in financial difficulties; his mother was conventionally pious. Joyce was a brilliant scholar, and at one time thought of entering the priesthood. At a crucial time in his life, however, he felt he had to renounce both his religion and his native land. In 1904 he went to Trieste and from then on lived on the continent.

Joyce was extremely gifted in languages—he was fluent in French, German, and Italian, and knew twelve other languages. He had taught himself Norwegian in order to read the plays of Ibsen.

In form and content much of Joyce's work was controversial. During his lifetime, publication was often delayed, and his works were banned, burned, pirated, and confiscated. The ruling of U.S. Federal Judge Woolsey in 1933 permitting the American publication of *Ulysses* was a landmark in the fight against literary censorship.

Virginia Woolf

The Legacy

For Sissy Miller." Gilbert Clandon, taking up the pearl brooch that lay among a litter of rings and brooches on a little table in his wife's drawing-room, read the inscription: "For Sissy Miller, with my love."

It was like Angela to have remembered even Sissy Miller, her secretary. Yet how strange it was, Gilbert Clandon thought once more, that she had left everything in such order—a little gift of some sort for every one of her friends. It was as if she had foreseen her death. Yet she had been in perfect health when she left the house that morning, six weeks ago; when she stepped off the kerb in Piccadilly and the car had killed her.

He was waiting for Sissy Miller. He had asked her to come; he owed her, he felt, after all the years she had been with them, this token of consideration. Yes, he went on, as he sat there waiting, it was strange that Angela had left everything in such order. Every friend had been left some little token of her affection. Every ring, every necklace, every little Chinese box—she had a passion for little boxes—had a name on it. And each had some memory for him. This he had given her; this—the enamel dolphin with the ruby eyes—she had pounced upon one day in a back street in Venice. He could remember her little cry of delight. To him, of course, she had left nothing in particular, unless it were her diary. Fifteen little volumes, bound in green leather, stood behind him on her writing table. Ever since they were married, she had kept a diary. Some of their very few—he could not call them quarrels, say tiffs—had been about that diary. When he came in and found her writing, she always shut it or put her hand over it. "No, no, no," he could hear her say. "After I'm dead—perhaps." So she had left it him, as her legacy. It was the only thing they had not shared when she was alive. But he had always taken it for granted that she would outlive him. If only she had stopped one moment, and had thought what she was doing, she would be alive now. But she had stepped straight off the kerb, the driver of the car had said at the inquest. She had given him no chance to pull up. . . . Here the sound of voices in the hall interrupted him.

"Miss Miller, Sir," said the maid.

She came in. He had never seen her alone in his life, nor, of course, in tears. She was terribly distressed, and no wonder. Angela had been much more to her than an employer. She had been a friend. To himself, he thought, as he pushed a chair for her and asked her to sit down, she was scarcely distinguishable from any other woman of her kind. There were thousands of Sissy Millers—drab little women in black carrying attaché cases. But Angela, with her genius for sympathy, had discovered all sorts of qualities in Sissy Miller. She was the soul of discretion; so silent; so trustworthy, one could tell her anything, and so on.

Miss Miller could not speak at first. She sat there dabbing her eyes with her pocket handkerchief. Then she made an effort.

"Pardon me, Mr. Clandon," she said.

He murmured. Of course he understood. It was only natural. He could guess what his wife had meant to her.

"I've been so happy here," she said, looking round. Her eyes rested on the writing table behind him. It was here they had worked—she and Angela. For Angela had her share of the duties that fall to the lot of a prominent politician's wife. She had been the greatest help to him in his career. He had often seen her and Sissy sitting at that table—Sissy at the typewriter, taking down letters from her dictation. No doubt

---

Miss Miller was thinking of that, too. Now all he had to do was to give her the brooch his wife had left her. A rather incongruous gift it seemed. It might have been better to have left her a sum of money, or even the typewriter. But there it was—"For Sissy Miller, with my love." And, taking the brooch, he gave it her with the little speech that he had prepared. He knew, he said, that she would value it. His wife had often worn it. . . . And she replied, as she took it almost as if she too had prepared a speech, that it would always be a treasured possession. . . . She had, he supposed, other clothes upon which a pearl brooch would not look quite so incongruous. She was wearing the little black coat and skirt that seemed the uniform of her profession. Then he remembered—she was in mourning, of course. She, too, had had her tragedy—a brother, to whom she was devoted, had died only a week or two before Angela. In some accident was it? He could not remember—only Angela telling him. Angela, with her genius for sympathy, had been terribly upset. Meanwhile Sissy Miller had risen. She was putting on her gloves. Evidently she felt that she ought not to intrude. But he could not let her go without saying something about her future. What were her plans? Was there any way in which he could help her?

She was gazing at the table, where she had sat at her typewriter, where the diary lay. And, lost in her memories of Angela, she did not at once answer his suggestion that he should help her. She seemed for a moment not to understand. So he repeated:

"What are your plans, Miss Miller?"

"My plans? Oh, that's all right, Mr. Clandon," she exclaimed. "Please don't bother yourself about me."

He took her to mean that she was in no need of financial assistance. It would be better, he realized, to make any suggestion of that kind in a letter. All he could do now was to say as he pressed her hand, "Remember, Miss Miller, if there's any way in which I can help you, it will be a pleasure. . . ." Then he opened the door. For a moment, on the threshold, as if a sudden thought had struck her, she stopped.

"Mr. Clandon," she said, looking straight at him for the first time, and for the first time he was struck by the expression, sympathetic yet searching, in her eyes. "If at any time," she continued, "there's anything I can do to help you, remember, I shall feel it, for your wife's sake, a pleasure. . . ."

With that she was gone. Her words and the look that went with them were unexpected. It was almost as if she believed, or hoped, that he would need her. A curious, perhaps a fantastic idea occurred to him as he returned to his chair. Could it be, that during all those years when he had scarcely noticed her, she, as the novelists say, had entertained a passion for him? He caught his own reflection in the glass as he passed. He was over fifty; but he could not help admitting that he was still, as the looking-glass showed him, a very distinguished-looking man.

"Poor Sissy Miller!" he said, half laughing. How he would have liked to share that joke with his wife! He turned instinctively to her diary. "Gilbert," he read, opening it at random, "looked so wonderful. . . ." It was as if she had answered his question. Of course, she seemed to say, you're very attractive to women. Of course Sissy Miller felt that too. He read on. "How proud I am to be his wife!" And he had always been very proud to be her husband. How often, when they dined out somewhere, he had looked at her across the table and said to himself, "She is the loveliest woman here!" He read on. That first year he had been standing for Parliament. They had toured his constituency. "When Gilbert sat down the applause was terrific. The whole audience rose and sang: 'For he's a jolly good fellow.' I was quite overcome." He remembered that, too. She had been sitting on the platform beside him. He could still see the glance she cast at him, and how she had tears in her eyes. And then? He turned the pages. They had gone to Venice. He recalled that happy holiday after the election. "We had ices at Florians." He smiled—she was still such a child; she loved ices. "Gilbert gave me a most interesting account of the history of Venice. He told me that the Doges . . ."[1] she had written it all out in her schoolgirl hand. One of the delights of travelling with Angela had been that she was so eager to learn. She was so terribly ignorant, she used to say, as if that were

1. ***the Doges,*** the elected chief magistrates of the former republics of Venice and Genoa.

not one of her charms. And then—he opened the next volume—they had come back to London. "I was so anxious to make a good impression. I wore my wedding dress." He could see her now sitting next old Sir Edward; and making a conquest of that formidable old man, his chief. He read on rapidly, filling in scene after scene from her scrappy fragments. "Dined at the House of Commons. . . . To an evening party at the Lovegroves'. Did I realize my responsibility, Lady L. asked me, as Gilbert's wife?" Then, as the years passed—he took another volume from the writing table—he had become more and more absorbed in his work. And she, of course, was more often home. . . . It had been a great grief to her, apparently, that they had had no children. "How I wish," one entry read, "that Gilbert had a son!" Oddly enough he had never much regretted that himself. Life had been so full, so rich as it was. That year he had been given a minor post in the government. A minor post only, but her comment was: "I am quite certain now that he will be Prime Minister!" Well, if things had gone differently, it might have been so. He paused here to speculate upon what might have been. Politics was a gamble, he reflected; but the game wasn't over yet. Not at fifty. He cast his eyes rapidly over more pages, full of the little trifles, the insignificant, happy, daily trifles that had made up her life.

He took up another volume and opened it at random. "What a coward I am! I let the chance slip again. But it seemed selfish to bother him with my own affairs, when he had so much to think about. And we so seldom have an evening alone." What was the meaning of that? Oh, here was the explanation—it referred to her work in the East End. "I plucked up courage and talked to Gilbert at last. He was so kind, so good. He made no objection." He remembered that conversation. She had told him that she felt so idle, so useless. She wished to have some work of her own. She wanted to do something—she had blushed so prettily, he remembered, as she said it, sitting in that very chair—to help others. He had bantered her a little. Hadn't she enough to do looking after him, after her home? Still, if it amused her, of course he had no objection. What was it? Some district? Some committee? Only she must promise not to make herself ill. So it seemed that every Wednesday she went to Whitechapel.[2] He remembered how he hated the clothes she wore on those occasions. But she had taken it very seriously, it seemed. The diary was full of references like this: "Saw Mrs. Jones. . . . She has ten children. . . . Husband lost his arm in an accident. . . . Did my best to find a job for Lily." He skipped on. His own name occurred less frequently. His interest slackened. Some of the entries conveyed nothing to him. For example: "Had a heated argument about socialism with B. M." Who was B. M.? He could not fill in the initials; some woman, he supposed, that she had met on one of her committees. "B. M. made a violent attack upon the upper classes. . . . I walked back after the meeting with B. M. and tried to convince him. But he is so narrow-minded." So B. M. was a man—no doubt one of those "intellectuals," as they call themselves, who are so violent, as Angela said, and so narrow-minded. She had invited him to come and see her apparently. "B. M. came to dinner. He shook hands with Minnie!" That note of exclamation gave another twist to his mental picture. B. M., it seemed, wasn't used to parlourmaids; he had shaken hands with Minnie. Presumably he was one of those tame working men who air their views in ladies' drawing-rooms. Gilbert knew the type, and had no liking for this particular specimen, whoever B. M. might be. Here he was again. "Went with B. M. to the Tower of London. . . . He said revolution is bound to come. . . . He said we live in a Fool's Paradise." That was just the kind of thing B. M. would say—Gilbert could hear him. He could also see him quite distinctly—a stubby little man, with a rough beard, red tie, dressed as they always did in tweeds, who had never done an honest day's work in his life. Surely Angela had the sense to see through him? He read on. "B. M. said some very disagreeable things about—." The name was carefully scratched out. "I told him I would not listen to any more abuse of—" Again the name was obliterated. Could it have been his own name? Was that why Angela covered the page so quickly when he came in? The thought added to his growing dislike of B. M. He had had the impertinence to discuss him in this very

2. ***Whitechapel,*** a poor district in East London.

room. Why had Angela never told him? It was very unlike her to conceal anything; she had been the soul of candour. He turned the pages, picking out every reference to B. M. "B. M. told me the story of his childhood. His mother went out charring. . . . When I think of it, I can hardly bear to go on living in such luxury. . . . Three guineas for one hat!" If only she had discussed the matter with him, instead of puzzling her poor little head about questions that were much too difficult for her to understand! He had lent her books. *Karl Marx, The Coming Revolution.* The initials B. M., B. M., B. M., recurred repeatedly. But why never the full name? There was an informality, an intimacy in the use of initials that was very unlike Angela. Had she called him B. M. to his face? He read on. "B. M. came unexpectedly after dinner. Luckily, I was alone." That was only a year ago. "Luckily"—why luckily?—"I was alone." Where had he been that night? He checked the date in his engagement book. It had been the night of the Mansion House dinner. And B. M. and Angela had spent the evening alone! He tried to recall that evening. Was she waiting up for him when he came back? Had the room looked just as usual? Were there glasses on the table? Were the chairs drawn close together? He could remember nothing—nothing whatever, nothing except his own speech at the Mansion House dinner. It became more and more inexplicable to him—the whole situation: his wife receiving an unknown man alone. Perhaps the next volume would explain. Hastily he reached for the last of the diaries—the one she had left unfinished when she died. There, on the very first page, was that cursed fellow again. "Dined alone with B. M. . . . He became very agitated. He said it was time we understood each other. . . . I tried to make him listen. But he would not. He threatened that if I did not . . ." the rest of the page was scored over. She had written "Egypt. Egypt. Egypt,"[3] over the whole page. He could not make out a single word; but there could be only one interpretation: the scoundrel had asked her to become his mistress. Alone in his room! The blood rushed to Gilbert Clandon's face. He turned the pages rapidly. What had been her answer? Initials had ceased. It was simply "he" now. "He came again. I told him I could not come to any decision. . . . I implored him to leave me." He had forced himself upon her in this very house. But why hadn't she told him? How could she have hesitated for an instant? Then: "I wrote him a letter." Then pages were left blank. Then there was this: "No answer to my letter." Then more blank pages; and then this: "He has done what he threatened." After that—what came after that? He turned page after page. All were blank. But there, on the very day before her death, was this entry: "Have I the courage to do it too?" That was the end.

Gilbert Clandon let the book slide to the floor. He could see her in front of him. She was standing on the kerb in Piccadilly. Her eyes stared; her fists were clenched. Here came the car. . . .

He could not bear it. He must know the truth. He strode to the telephone.

"Miss Miller!" There was silence. Then he heard someone moving in the room.

"Sissy Miller speaking"—her voice at last answered him.

"Who," he thundered, "is B. M.?"

He could hear the cheap clock ticking on her mantelpiece; then a long drawn sigh. Then at last she said:

"He was my brother."

He *was* her brother; her brother who had killed himself. "Is there," he heard Sissy Miller asking, "anything that I can explain?"

"Nothing!" he cried. "Nothing!"

He had received his legacy. She had told him the truth. She had stepped off the kerb to rejoin her lover. She had stepped off the kerb to escape from him. □□

3. ***"Egypt . . . Egypt,"*** probably an allusion to Shakespeare's *Antony and Cleopatra* (Act IV, scene xv), in which Antony, who has just stabbed himself, speaks these lines to the Egyptian queen: "I am dying Egypt, dying; only / I here importune death awhile, until / Of many thousand kisses the poor last / I lay upon thy lips." In Act V Cleopatra herself commits suicide.

Women and Fiction

Virginia Woolf

If one may generalize, not only do women submit less readily to observation than men, but their lives are far less tested and examined by the ordinary processes of life. Often nothing tangible remains of a woman's day. The food that has been cooked is eaten; the children that have been nursed have gone out into the world. Where does the accent fall? What is the salient point for the novelist to seize upon? It is difficult to say. Her life has an anonymous character which is baffling and puzzling in the extreme. For the first time, this dark country is beginning to be explored in fiction; and at the same moment a woman has also to record the changes in women's minds and habits which the opening of the professions has introduced. She has to observe how their lives are ceasing to run underground; she has to discover what new colours and shadows are showing in them now that they are exposed to the outer world.

If, then, one should try to sum up the character of women's fiction at the present moment, one would say that it is courageous; it is sincere; it keeps closely to what women feel. It is not bitter. It does not insist upon its femininity. But at the same time, a woman's book is not written as a man would write it. These qualities are much commoner than they were, and they give even to second- and third-rate work the value of truth and the interest of sincerity.

Discussion

1. **(a)** Describe Gilbert Clandon's social position as revealed in the story. **(b)** Discuss Clandon's attitude toward "drab little women in black carrying attaché cases."

2. How does Gilbert Clandon's attitude toward Sissy Miller affect his assessment of Sissy's relationship to his wife?

3. What do you feel are the most significant factors in Mrs. Clandon's relationship with Sissy Miller? Explain.

4. **(a)** Explain the ironic aspects of Gilbert Clandon's assumption that Sissy Miller "had entertained a passion for him." **(b)** What other lines or phrases in the story have an ironic ring once the reader knows what Clandon's legacy is? Explain your examples.

5. "The Legacy" can be thought of as a kind of detective story. If so, what is the crime? Who is the criminal? Who is the victim? Explain.

Extension

Reading and Writing

Read the excerpt from E. M. Forster's "Pessimism in Literature" which accompanies Thomas Hardy's "The Grave by the Handpost" in Unit 7. How do Forster's comments enhance your understanding of Woolf's story? Explain in a brief essay.

Virginia Woolf 1882 • 1941

A brilliant young woman, Virginia Woolf grew up in a literary atmosphere and was educated in her father Leslie Stephen's extensive library. The famous group of intellectuals which came to be known as the Bloomsbury Group originated in gatherings of Cambridge University graduates and their friends at the house where Virginia was living with her brother and sister. She married one of the young men, Leonard Woolf. A few years later, the Woolfs started the Hogarth Press.

In her writing Woolf experimented with new techniques. She believed that much imaginative literature is false to life because it relates episodes in a straight line, whereas our experiences actually flow together like a stream. She wrote novels, stories, criticism and essays.

D. H. Lawrence

Tickets, Please

There is in the Midlands a single-line tramway system which boldly leaves the county town and plunges off into the black, industrial countryside, up hill and down dale, through the long ugly villages of workmen's houses, over canals and railways, past churches perched high and nobly over the smoke and shadows, through stark, grimy cold little marketplaces, tilting away in a rush past cinemas and shops down to the hollow where the collieries are, then up again, past a little rural church, under the ash trees, on in a rush to the terminus, the last little ugly place of industry, the cold little town that shivers on the edge of the wild, gloomy country beyond. There the green and creamy coloured tram-car seems to pause and purr with curious satisfaction. But in a few minutes—the clock on the turret of the Co-operative Wholesale Society's shops gives the time—away it starts once more on the adventure. Again there are the reckless swoops downhill, bouncing the loops: again the chilly wait in the hill-top market place: again the breathless slithering round the precipitous drop under the church: again the patient halts at the loops, waiting for the outcoming car: so on and on, for two long hours, till at last the city looms beyond the fat gasworks, the narrow factories draw near, we are in the sordid streets of the great town, once more we sidle to a standstill at our terminus, abashed by the great crimson and cream-coloured city cars, but still perky, jaunty, somewhat dare-devil, green as a jaunty sprig of parsley out of a black colliery garden.

To ride on these cars is always an adventure. Since we are in war-time, the drivers are men unfit for active service: cripples and hunchbacks. So they have the spirit of the devil in them. The ride becomes a steeplechase. Hurray! we have leapt in a clear jump over the canal bridge—now for the four-lane corner. With a shriek and a trail of sparks we are clear again. To be sure, a tram often leaps the rails—but what matter! It sits in a ditch till other trams come to haul it out. It is quite common for a car, packed with one solid mass of living people, to come to a dead halt in the midst of unbroken blackness, the heart of nowhere on a dark night, and for the driver and the girl conductor to call: "All get off—car's on fire!" Instead, however, of rushing out in a panic, the passengers stolidly reply: "Get on—get on! We're not coming out. We're stopping where we are. Push on, George." So till flames actually appear.

The reason for this reluctance to dismount is that the nights are howlingly cold, black, and windswept, and a car is a haven of refuge. From village to village the miners travel, for a change of cinema, of girl, of pub. The trams are desperately packed. Who is going to risk himself in the black gulf outside, to wait perhaps an hour for another tram, then to see the forlorn notice "Depot Only," because there is something wrong! Or to greet a unit of three bright cars all so tight with people that they sail past with a howl of derision. Trams that pass in the night.

This, the most dangerous tram-service in England, as the authorities themselves declare, with pride, is entirely conducted by girls, and driven by rash young men, a little crippled, or by delicate young men, who creep forward in terror. The girls are fearless young hussies. In their ugly blue uniform, skirts up to their knees, shapeless old peaked caps on their heads, they have all the *sang-froid* of an old non-commissioned officer. With a tram packed with howling colliers, roaring hymns downstairs and a sort of antiphony of obscenities upstairs, the lasses are perfectly at their ease. They pounce on the youths who try to

---

evade their ticket-machine. They push off the men at the end of their distance. They are not going to be done in the eye—not they. They fear nobody—and everybody fears them.

"Hello, Annie!"

"Hello, Ted!"

"Oh, mind my corn, Miss Stone. It's my belief you've got a heart of stone, for you've trod on it again."

"You should keep it in your pocket," replies Miss Stone, and she goes sturdily upstairs in her high boots.

"Tickets, please."

She is peremptory, suspicious, and ready to hit first. She can hold her own against ten thousand. The step of that tram-car is her Thermopylae.[1]

Therefore, there is a certain wild romance aboard these cars—and in the sturdy bosom of Annie herself. The time for soft romance is in the morning, between ten o'clock and one, when things are rather slack: that is, except market-day and Saturday. Thus Annie has time to look about her. Then she often hops off her car and into a shop where she has spied something, while the driver chats in the main road. There is very good feeling between the girls and the drivers. Are they not companions in peril, shipments aboard this careering vessel of a tram-car, for ever rocking on the waves of a stormy land.

Then, also, during the easy hours, the inspectors are most in evidence. For some reason, everybody employed in this tram-service is young: there are no grey heads. It would not do. Therefore the inspectors are of the right age, and one, the chief, is also good looking. See him stand on a wet, gloomy morning, in his long oilskin, his peaked cap well down over his eyes, waiting to board a car. His face ruddy, his small brown moustache is weathered, he has a faint impudent smile. Fairly tall and agile, even in his waterproof, he springs aboard a car and greets Annie.

"Hello, Annie! Keeping the wet out?"

"Trying to."

There are only two people in the car. Inspecting is soon over. Then for a long and impudent chat on the foot-board, a good, easy, twelve-mile chat.

The inspector's name is John Thomas Raynor—always called John Thomas, except sometimes, in malice, Coddy. His face sets in fury when he is addressed, from a distance, with this abbreviation. There is considerable scandal about John Thomas in half a dozen villages. He flirts with the girl conductors in the morning, and walks out with them in the dark night, when they leave their tram-car at the depot. Of course, the girls quit the service frequently. Then he flirts and walks out with the newcomer: always providing she is sufficiently attractive, and that she will consent to walk. It is remarkable, however, that most of the girls are quite comely, they are all young, and this roving life aboard the car gives them a sailor's dash and recklessness. What matter how they behave when the ship is in port? To-morrow they will be aboard again.

Annie, however, was something of a Tartar, and her sharp tongue had kept John Thomas at arm's length for many months. Perhaps, therefore, she liked him all the more: for he always came up smiling, with impudence. She watched him vanquish one girl, then another. She could tell by the movement of his mouth and eyes, when he flirted with her in the morning, that he had been walking out with this lass, or the other, the night before. A fine cock-of-the-walk he was. She could sum him up pretty well.

In this subtle antagonism they knew each other like old friends, they were as shrewd with one another almost as man and wife. But Annie had always kept him sufficiently at arm's length. Besides, she had a boy of her own.

The Statutes fair, however, came in November, at Bestwood. It happened that Annie had the Monday night off. It was a drizzling ugly night, yet she dressed herself up and went to the fair-ground. She was alone, but she expected soon to find a pal of some sort.

The roundabouts were veering round and grinding out their music, the side-shows were making as much commotion as possible. In the coconut shies there were no coconuts, but artificial war-time substitutes, which the lads declared were fastened into the irons. There was a sad decline in brilliance and luxury. None the less,

---

1. ***Thermopylae,*** a narrow mountain pass in Greece where a small number of Greeks held back the Persian army in 480 B. C. until all the Greeks were slain.

the ground was muddy as ever, there was the same crush, the press of faces lighted up by the flares and the electric lights, the same smell of naphtha and a few potatoes, and of electricity.

Who should be the first to greet Miss Annie on the showground but John Thomas. He had a black overcoat buttoned up to his chin, and a tweed cap pulled down over his brows, his face between was ruddy and smiling and handy as ever. She knew so well the way his mouth moved.

She was very glad to have a "boy." To be at the Statutes without a fellow was no fun. Instantly, like the gallant he was, he took her on the Dragons, grim-toothed, roundabout switchbacks. It was not nearly so exciting as a tram-car actually. But, then, to be seated in a shaking, green dragon, uplifted above the sea of bubble faces, careering in a rickety fashion in the lower heavens, whilst John Thomas leaned over her, his cigarette in his mouth, was after all the right style. She was a plump, quick, alive little creature. So she was quite excited and happy.

John Thomas made her stay on for the next round. And therefore she could hardly for shame repulse him when he put his arm around her and drew her a little nearer to him, in a very warm and cuddly manner. Besides, he was fairly discreet, he kept his movement as hidden as possible. She looked down, and saw that his red, clean hand was out of sight of the crowd. And they knew each other so well. So they warmed up to the fair.

After the dragons they went on the horses. John Thomas paid each time, so she could but be complaisant. He, of course, sat astride on the outer horse—named "Black Bess"—and she sat sideways, towards him, on the inner horse—named "Wildfire." But of course John Thomas was not going to sit discreetly on "Black Bess," holding the brass bar. Round they spun and heaved, in the light. And round he swung on his wooden steed, flinging one leg across her mount, and perilously tipping up and down, across the space, half lying back, laughing at her. He was perfectly happy; she was afraid her hat was on one side, but she was excited.

He threw quoits on a table, and won for her two large, pale blue hat-pins. And then, hearing the noise of the cinemas, announcing another performance, they climbed the boards and went in.

Of course, during these performances pitch darkness falls from time to time, when the machine goes wrong. Then there is a wild whooping, and a loud smacking of simulated kisses. In these moments John Thomas drew Annie towards him. After all, he had a wonderfully warm, cosy way of holding a girl with his arm, he seemed to make such a nice fit. And, after all, it was pleasant to be so held: so very comforting and cosy and nice. He leaned over her and she felt his breath on her hair; she knew he wanted to kiss her on the lips. And, after all, he was so warm and she fitted in to him so softly. After all, she wanted him to touch her lips.

But the light sprang up; she also started electrically, and put her hat straight. He left his arm lying nonchalantly behind her. Well, it was fun, it was exciting to be at the Statutes with John Thomas.

When the cinema was over they went for a walk across the dark, damp fields. He had all the arts of love-making. He was especially good at holding a girl, when he sat with her on a stile in the black, drizzling darkness. He seemed to be holding her in space, against his own warmth and gratification. And his kisses were soft and slow and searching.

So Annie walked out with John Thomas, though she kept her own boy dangling in the distance. Some of the tram-girls chose to be huffy. But there, you must take things as you find them, in this life.

There was no mistake about it, Annie liked John Thomas a good deal. She felt so rich and warm in herself whenever he was near. And John Thomas really liked Annie, more than usual. The soft, melting way in which she could flow into a fellow, as if she melted into his very bones, was something rare and good. He fully appreciated this.

But with a developing acquaintance there began a developing intimacy. Annie wanted to consider him a person, a man: she wanted to take an intelligent interest in him, and to have an intelligent response. She did not want a mere nocturnal presence, which was what he was so far. And she prided herself that he could not leave her.

Here she made a mistake. John Thomas intended to remain a nocturnal presence; he had no idea of becoming an all-round individual to her. When she started to take an intelligent interest in him and his life and his character, he sheered off. He hated intelligent interest. And he knew that the only way to stop it was to avoid it. The possessive female was aroused in Annie. So he left her.

It is no use saying she was not surprised. She was at first startled, thrown out of her count. For she had been so *very* sure of holding him. For a while she was staggered, and everything became uncertain to her. Then she wept with fury, indignation, desolation, and misery. Then she had a spasm of despair. And then, when he came, still impudently, on to her car, still familiar, but letting her see by the movement of his head that he had gone away to somebody else for the time being, and was enjoying pastures new, then she determined to have her own back.

She had a very shrewd idea what girls John Thomas had taken out. She went to Nora Purdy. Nora was a tall, rather pale, but well-built girl, with beautiful yellow hair. She was rather secretive.

"Hey!" said Annie, accosting her; then softly: "Who's John Thomas on with now?"

"I don't know," said Nora.

"Why, tha does," said Annie, ironically lapsing into dialect. "Tha knows as well as I do."

"Well, I do, then," said Nora. "It isn't me, so don't bother."

"It's Cissy Meakin, isn't it?"

"It is, for all I know."

"Hasn't he got a face on him!" said Annie. "I don't half like his cheek. I could knock him off the foot-board when he comes round at me."

"He'll get dropped on one of these days," said Nora.

"Ay, he will, when somebody makes up their mind to drop it on him. I should like to see him taken down a peg or two, shouldn't you?"

"I shouldn't mind," said Nora.

"You've got quite as much cause to as I have," said Annie. "But we'll drop on him one of these days, my girl. What? Don't you want to?"

"I don't mind," said Nora.

But as a matter of fact, Nora was much more vindictive than Annie.

One by one Annie went the round of the old flames. It so happened that Cissy Meakin left the tramway service in quite a short time. Her mother made her leave. Then John Thomas was on the *qui vive.* He cast his eyes over his old flock. And his eyes lighted on Annie. He thought she would be safe now. Besides, he liked her.

She arranged to walk home with him on Sunday night. It so happened that her car would be in the depôt at half-past nine: the last car would come in at 10:15. So John Thomas was to wait for her there.

At the depôt the girls had a little waiting-room of their own. It was quite rough, but cosy, with a fire and an oven and a mirror, and table and wooden chairs. The half-dozen girls who knew John Thomas only too well had arranged to take service this Sunday afternoon. So, as the cars began to come in, early, the girls dropped into the waiting-room. And instead of hurrying off home, they sat around the fire and had a cup of tea. Outside was the darkness and lawlessness of war-time.

John Thomas came on the car after Annie, at about a quarter to ten. He poked his head easily into the girls' waiting-room.

"Prayer-meeting?" he asked.

"Ay," said Laura Sharp. "Ladies only."

"That's me!" said John Thomas. It was one of his favourite exclamations.

"Shut the door, boy," said Muriel Baggaley.

"Oh, which side of me?" said John Thomas.

"Which tha likes," said Polly Birkin.

He had come in and closed the door behind him. The girls moved in their circle, to make a place for him near the fire. He took off his great-coat and pushed back his hat.

"Who handles the teapot?" he said.

Nora Purdy silently poured him out a cup of tea.

"Want a bit o' my bread and drippin'?" said Muriel Baggaley to him.

"Ay, give us a bit."

And he began to eat his piece of bread.

"There's no place like home, girls," he said.

They all looked at him as he uttered this piece of impudence. He seemed to be sunning himself in the presence of so many damsels.

"Especially if you're not afraid to go home in the dark," said Laura Sharp.

"Me! By myself I am."

They sat till they heard the last tram come in. In a few minutes Emma Houselay entered.

"Come on, my old duck!" cried Polly Birkin.

"It *is* perishing," said Emma, holding her fingers to the fire.

"But—I'm afraid to, go home in, the dark," sang Laura Sharp, the tune having got into her mind.

"Who're you going with to-night, John Thomas?" asked Muriel Baggaley coolly.

"To-night?" said John Thomas. "Oh, I'm going home by myself to-night—all on my lonely-o."

"That's me!" said Nora Purdy, using his own ejaculation.

The girls laughed shrilly.

"Me as well, Nora," said John Thomas.

"Don't know what you mean," said Laura.

"Yes, I'm toddling," said he, rising and reaching for his overcoat.

"Nay," said Polly. "We're all here waiting for you."

"We've got to be up in good time in the morning," he said, in the benevolent official manner.

They all laughed.

"Nay," said Muriel. "Don't leave us all lonely, John Thomas. Take one!"

"I'll take the lot, if you like," he responded gallantly.

"That you won't, either," said Muriel. "Two's company; seven's too much of a good thing."

"Nay—take one," said Laura. "Fair and square, all above board and say which."

"Ay," cried Annie, speaking for the first time. "Pick, John Thomas; let's hear thee."

"Nay," he said. "I'm going home quiet tonight. Feeling good, for once."

"Whereabouts?" said Annie. "Take a good 'un, then. But tha's got to take one of us!"

"Nay, how can I take one," he said, laughing uneasily. "I don't want to make enemies."

"You'd only make *one*," said Annie.

"The chosen *one*," added Laura.

"Oh, my! Who said girls!" exclaimed John Thomas, again turning, as if to escape. "Well—goodnight."

"Nay, you've got to make your pick," said Muriel. "Turn your face to the wall, and say which one touches you. Go on—we shall only just touch your back—one of us. Go on—turn your face to the wall, and don't look, and say which one touches you."

He was uneasy, mistrusting them. Yet he had not the courage to break away. They pushed him to a wall and stood him there with his face to it. Behind his back they all grimaced, tittering. He looked so comical. He looked around uneasily.

"Go on!" he cried.

"You're looking—you're looking!" they shouted.

He turned his head away. And suddenly, with a movement like a swift cat, Annie went forward and fetched him a box on the side of the head that sent his cap flying and himself staggering. He started round.

But at Annie's signal they all flew at him, slapping him, pinching him, pulling his hair, though more in fun than in spite or anger. He, however, saw red. His blue eyes flamed with strange fear as well as fury, and he butted through the girls to the door. It was locked. He wrenched at it. Roused, alert, the girls stood round and looked at him. He faced them, at bay. At that moment they were rather horrifying to him, as they stood in their short uniforms. He was distinctly afraid.

"Come on, John Thomas! Come on! Choose!" said Annie.

"What are you after? Open the door," he said.

"We shan't—not till you've chosen!" said Muriel.

"Chosen what?" he said.

"Chosen the one you're going to marry," she replied.

He hesitated a moment.

"Open the blasted door," he said, "and get back to your senses." He spoke with official authority.

"You've got to choose!" cried the girls.

"Come on!" cried Annie, looking him in the eye. "Come on! Come on!"

He went forward, rather vaguely. She had taken off her belt, and swinging it, she fetched him a sharp blow over the head with the buckle end. He sprang and seized her. But immediately the other girls rushed upon him, pulling and tearing and beating him. Their blood was now thoroughly up. He was their sport now. They were going to have their own back, out of him. Strange, wild creatures, they hung on him and rushed at him to bear him down. His tunic was torn right up the back, Nora had hold at the back of his collar, and was actually strangling him. Luckily the button burst. He struggled in a wild frenzy of fury and terror, almost mad terror. His tunic was simply torn off his back, his shirt-sleeves were torn away, his arms were naked. The girls rushed at him, clenched their hands on him, and pulled at him: or they rushed at him and pushed him, butted him with all their might: or they struck him wild blows. He ducked and cringed and struck sideways. They became more intense.

At last he was down. They rushed on him, kneeling on him. He had neither breath nor strength to move. His face was bleeding with a long scratch, his brow was bruised.

Annie knelt on him, the other girls knelt and hung on to him. Their faces were flushed, their hair wild, their eyes were all glittering strangely. He lay at last quite still, with face averted, as an animal lies when it is defeated and at the mercy of the captor. Sometimes his eye glanced back at the wild faces of the girls. His breast rose heavily, his wrists were torn.

"Now, then, my fellow!" gasped Annie at length. "Now then—now—"

At the sound of her terrifying, cold triumph, he suddenly started to struggle as an animal might, but the girls threw themselves upon him with unnatural strength and power, forcing him down.

"Yes—now, then!" gasped Annie at length.

And there was a dead silence, in which the thud of heart-beating was to be heard. It was a suspense of pure silence in every soul.

"Now you know where you are," said Annie.

The sight of his white, bare arm maddened the girls. He lay in a kind of trance of fear and antagonism. They felt themselves filled with supernatural strength.

Suddenly Polly started to laugh—to giggle wildly—helplessly—and Emma and Muriel joined in. But Annie and Nora and Laura remained the same, tense, watchful, with gleaming eyes. He winced away from these eyes.

"Yes," said Annie, in a curious low tone, secret and deadly. "Yes! You've got it now. You know what you've done, don't you? You know what you've done."

He made no sound nor sign, but lay with bright, averted eyes, and averted, bleeding face.

"You ought to be *killed*, that's what you ought," said Annie, tensely. "You ought to be *killed.*" And there was a terrifying lust in her voice.

Polly was ceasing to laugh, and giving long-drawn Oh-h-hs and sighs as she came to herself.

"He's got to choose," she said vaguely.

"Oh, yes, he has," said Laura, with vindictive decision.

"Do you hear—do you hear?" said Annie. And with a sharp movement, that made him wince, she turned his face to her.

"Do you hear?" she repeated, shaking him.

But he was quite dumb. She fetched him a sharp slap on the face. He started, and his eyes widened. Then his face darkened with defiance, after all.

"Do you hear?" she repeated.

He only looked at her with hostile eyes.

"Speak!" she said, putting her face devilishly near his.

"What?" he said, almost overcome.

"You've got to *choose!*" she cried, as if it were some terrible menace, and as if it hurt her that she could not exact more.

"What?" he said, in fear.

"Choose your girl, Coddy. You've got to choose her now. And you'll get your neck broken if you play any more of your tricks, my boy. You're settled now."

There was a pause. Again he averted his face. He was cunning in his overthrow. He did not give in to them really—no, not if they tore him to bits.

"All right, then," he said, "I choose Annie." His voice was strange and full of malice. Annie let go of him as if he had been a hot coal.

"He's chosen Annie!" said the girls in chorus.

"Me!" cried Annie. She was still kneeling, but away from him. He was still lying prostrate, with averted face. The girls grouped uneasily around.

"Me!" repeated Annie, with a terrible bitter accent.

Then she got up, drawing away from him with strange disgust and bitterness.

"I wouldn't touch him," she said.

But her face quivered with a kind of agony, she seemed as if she would fall. The other girls turned aside. He remained lying on the floor, with his torn clothes and bleeding, averted face.

"Oh, if hc's chosen—" said Polly.

"I don't want him—he can choose again," said Annie, with the same rather bitter hopelessness.

"Get up," said Polly, lifting his shoulder. "Get up."

He rose slowly, a strange, ragged, dazed creature. The girls eyed him from a distance, curiously, furtively, dangerously.

"Who wants him?" cried Laura, roughly.

"Nobody," they answered, with contempt. Yet each one of them waited for him to look at her, hoped he would look at her. All except Annie, and something was broken in her.

He, however, kept his face closed and averted from them all. There was a silence of the end. He picked up the torn pieces of his tunic, without knowing what to do with them. The girls stood about uneasily, flushed, panting, tidying their hair and their dress unconsciously, and watching him. He looked at none of them. He espied his cap in a corner, and went and picked it up. He put it on his head, and one of the girls burst into a shrill, hysteric laugh at the sight he presented. He, however, took no heed, but went straight to where his overcoat hung on a peg. The girls moved away from contact with him as if he had been an electric wire. He put on his coat and buttoned it down. Then he rolled his tunic-rags into a bundle, and stood before the locked door, dumbly.

"Open the door, somebody," said Laura.

"Annie's got the key," said one.

Annie silently offered the key to the girls. Nora unlocked the door.

"Tit for tat, old man," she said. "Show yourself a man, and don't bear a grudge."

But without a word or sign he had opened the door and gone, his face closed, his head dropped.

"That'll learn him," said Laura.

"Coddy!" said Nora.

"Shut up, for God's sake!" cried Annie fiercely, as if in torture.

"Well, I'm about ready to go, Polly. Look sharp!" said Muriel.

The girls were all anxious to be off. They were tidying themselves hurriedly, with mute, stupefied faces. □□

Discussion

1. Describe the mood and tone created by the first paragraph of Lawrence's story.

2. **(a)** Does John Thomas deserve his fate? Explain. **(b)** Is John Thomas ever in any real danger?

3. What does the fact that the girls wear uniforms have to do with the events of the story?

4. **(a)** Why does Annie refuse John Thomas after he selects her? **(b)** At the end of the story, why do the six girls behave so strangely after they have humiliated John Thomas?

5. Of what significance to the story is the fact that "Outside was the darkness and lawlessness of wartime"?

D. H. Lawrence 1885 • 1930

Like the hero of his early novel *Sons and Lovers*, Lawrence was born in an English coal-mining town, the son of an uneducated miner and an ambitious mother who was a teacher. He himself taught school for a time before he established himself in London literary circles and became a writer. In 1912 he eloped with an aristocratic German, Frieda von Richthofen. She was married at the time, but eventually became his wife. They began a life of wandering, seeking for a place undamaged by modern civilization.

All his life, Lawrence revolted against puritanism, mediocrity, and the dehumanization of an industrial society. Since much of his work is an exploration of the primitive and sexual in human nature, he was often in trouble with the censors.

Katherine Mansfield

Doll house at Wenham built in 1884 by Benjamin Chamberlain for his daughters. Courtesy of the Wenham Historical Association.

The Doll's House

When dear old Mrs. Hay went back to town after staying with the Burnells she sent the children a doll's house. It was so big that the carter and Pat carried it into the courtyard, and there it stayed, propped up on two wooden boxes beside the feed-room door. No harm could come of it; it was summer. And perhaps the smell of paint would have gone off by the time it had to be taken in. For, really, the smell of paint coming from that doll's house ("Sweet of old Mrs. Hay, of course; most sweet and generous!")—but the smell of paint was quite enough to make any one seriously ill, in Aunt Beryl's opinion. Even before the sacking was taken off. And when it was . . .

There stood the doll's house, a dark, oily, spinach green, picked out with bright yellow. Its two solid little chimneys, glued on to the roof, were painted red and white, and the door, gleaming with yellow varnish, was like a little slab of toffee. Four windows, real windows, were divided into panels by a broad streak of green. There was actually a tiny porch, too, painted yellow, with big lumps of congealed paint hanging along the edge.

But perfect, perfect little house! Who could possibly mind the smell? It was part of the joy, part of the newness.

"Open it quickly, some one!"

The hook at the side was stuck fast. Pat pried it open with his pen-knife, and the whole house-front swung back, and—there you were, gazing at one and the same moment into the drawing-room and dining-room, the kitchen and two bedrooms. That is the way for a house to open! Why don't all houses open like that? How much more exciting than peering through the slit of a door into a mean little hall with a hatstand and two umbrellas! That is—isn't it?—what you long to know about a house when you put your hand on the knocker. Perhaps it is the way God opens houses at dead of night when He is taking a quiet turn with an angel. . . .

"O-oh!" The Burnell children sounded as though they were in despair. It was too marvellous; it was too much for them. They had never seen anything like it in their lives. All the rooms were papered. There were pictures on the walls, painted on the paper, with gold frames complete. Red carpet covered all the floors except the kitchen; red plush chairs in the drawing-room, green in the dining-room; tables, beds with real bedclothes, a cradle, a stove, a dresser with tiny plates and one big jug. But what Kezia liked more than anything, what she liked frightfully, was the lamp. It stood in the middle of the dining-room table, an exquisite little amber lamp with a white globe. It was even filled all ready for lighting, though, of course, you couldn't light it. But there was something inside that looked like oil, and that moved when you shook it.

The father and mother dolls, who sprawled very stiff as though they had fainted in the drawing-room, and their two little children asleep upstairs, were really too big for the doll's house. They didn't look as though they belonged. But the lamp was perfect. It seemed to smile at Kezia, to say, "I live here." The lamp was real.

The Burnell children could hardly walk to school fast enough the next morning. They burned to tell everybody, to describe, to—well—to boast about their doll's house before the school-bell rang.

"I'm to tell," said Isabel, "because I'm the eldest. And you two can join in after. But I'm to tell first."

There was nothing to answer. Isabel was bossy, but she was always right, and Lottie and Kezia knew too well the powers that went with being eldest. They brushed through the thick buttercups at the road edge and said nothing.

"And I'm to choose who's to come and see it first. Mother said I might."

For it had been arranged that while the doll's house stood in the courtyard they might ask the girls at school, two at a time, to come and look. Not to stay to tea, of course, or to come traipsing through the house. But just to stand quietly in the courtyard while Isabel pointed out the beauties, and Lottie and Kezia looked pleased. . . .

But hurry as they might, by the time they had reached the tarred palings of the boys' playground the bell had begun to jangle. They only just had time to whip off their hats and fall into line before the roll was called. Never mind. Isabel tried to make up for it by looking very important and mysterious and by whispering behind her hands to the girls near her, "Got something to tell you at playtime."

Playtime came and Isabel was surrounded. The girls of her class nearly fought to put their arms round her, to walk away with her, to beam flatteringly, to be her special friend. She held quite a court under the huge pine trees at the side of the playground. Nudging, giggling together, the little girls pressed up close. And the only two who stayed outside the ring were the two who were always outside, the little Kelveys. They knew better than to come anywhere near the Burnells.

For the fact was, the school the Burnell children went to was not at all the kind of place their parents would have chosen if there had been any choice. But there was none. It was the only school for miles. And the consequence was all the children in the neighbourhood, the Judge's little girls, the doctor's daughters, the storekeeper's children, the milkman's, were forced to mix together. Not to speak of there being an equal number of rude, rough little boys as well. But the line had to be drawn somewhere. It was drawn at the Kelveys. Many of the children, including the Burnells, were not allowed even to speak to them. They walked past the Kelveys with their heads in the air, and as they set the fashion in all matters of behaviour, the Kelveys were shunned by everybody. Even the teacher had a special voice for them, and a special smile for the other children when Lil Kelvey came up to her desk with a bunch of dreadfully common-looking flowers.

They were the daughters of a spry, hard-working little washerwoman, who went about from house to house by the day. This was awful enough. But where was Mr. Kelvey? Nobody knew for certain. But everybody said he was in prison. So they were the daughters of a washerwoman and a gaolbird. Very nice company for other people's children! And they looked it. Why Mrs. Kelvey made them so conspicuous was hard to understand. The truth was they were dressed in "bits" given to her by the people for whom she worked. Lil, for instance, who was a stout, plain child, with big freckles, came to school in a dress made from a green art-serge table-cloth of the Burnells', with red plush sleeves from the Logans' curtains. Her hat, perched on top of her high forehead, was a grown-up woman's hat, once the property of Miss Lecky, the postmistress. It was turned up at the back and trimmed with a large scarlet quill. What a little guy she looked! It was impossible not to laugh. And her little sister, our Else, wore a long white dress, rather like a nightgown, and a pair of little boy's boots. But whatever our Else wore she would have looked strange. She was a tiny wishbone of a child, with cropped hair and enormous solemn eyes—a little white owl. Nobody had ever seen her smile; she scarcely ever spoke. She went through life holding on to Lil, with a piece of Lil's shirt screwed up in her hand. Where Lil went our Else followed. In the playground, on the road going to and from school, there was Lil marching in front and our Else holding on behind. Only when she wanted anything, or when she was out of breath, our Else gave Lil a tug, a twitch, and Lil stopped and turned round. The Kelveys never failed to understand each other.

Now they hovered at the edge; you couldn't stop them listening. When the little girls turned round and sneered, Lil, as usual, gave her silly, shame-faced smile, but our Else only looked.

And Isabel's voice, so very proud, went on telling. The carpet made a great sensation, but so did the beds with real bedclothes, and the stove with an oven door.

When she finished Kezia broke in. "You've forgotten the lamp, Isabel."

"Oh, yes," said Isabel, "and there's a teeny little lamp, all made of yellow glass, with a white globe that stands on the dining-room table. You couldn't tell it from a real one."

"The lamp's best of all," cried Kezia. She thought Isabel wasn't making half enough of the little lamp. But nobody paid any attention. Isabel was choosing the two who were to come back with them that afternoon and see it. She chose Emmie Cole and Lena Logan. But when the others knew they were all to have a chance, they couldn't be nice enough to Isabel. One by one they put their arms round Isabel's waist and walked her off. They had something to whisper to her, a secret. "Isabel's *my* friend."

Only the little Kelveys moved away forgotten; there was nothing more for them to hear.

Days passed, and as more children saw the doll's house, the fame of it spread. It became the one subject, the rage. The one question was, "Have you seen Burnells' doll house? Oh, ain't it lovely!" "Haven't you seen it? Oh, I say!"

Even the dinner hour was given up to talking about it. The little girls sat under the pines eating their thick mutton sandwiches and big slabs of johnny cake spread with butter. While always, as near as they could get, sat the Kelveys, our Else holding on to Lil, listening too, while they chewed their jam sandwiches out of a newspaper soaked with large red blobs. . . .

"Mother," said Kezia, "can't I ask the Kelveys just once?"

"Certainly not, Kezia."

"But why not?"

"Run away, Kezia; you know quite well why not."

At last everybody had seen it except them. On that day the subject rather flagged. It was the dinner hour. The children stood together under the pine trees, and suddenly, as they looked at the Kelveys eating out of their paper, always by themselves, always listening, they wanted to be horrid to them. Emmie Cole started the whisper.

"Lil Kelvey's going to be a servant when she grows up."

"O-oh, how awful!" said Isabel Burnell, and she made eyes at Emmie.

Emmie swallowed in a very meaning way and nodded to Isabel as she'd seen her mother do on those occasions.

"It's true—it's true—it's true," she said.

Then Lena Logan's little eyes snapped. "Shall I ask her?" she whispered.

"Bet you don't," said Jessie May.

"Pooh, I'm not frightened," said Lena. Suddenly she gave a little squeal and danced in front of the other girls. "Watch! Watch me! Watch me now!" said Lena. And sliding, gliding, dragging one foot, giggling behind her hand, Lena went over to the Kelveys.

Lil looked up from her dinner. She wrapped the rest quickly away. Our Else stopped chewing. What was coming now?

"Is it true you're going to be a servant when you grow up, Lil Kelvey?" shrilled Lena.

Dead silence. But instead of answering, Lil only gave her silly, shame-faced smile. She didn't seem to mind the question at all. What a sell[1] for Lena! The girls began to titter.

Lena couldn't stand that. She put her hands on her hips; she shot forward. "Yah, yer father's in prison!" she hissed, spitefully.

This was such a marvellous thing to have said that the little girls rushed away in a body, deeply, deeply excited, wild with joy. Some one found a long rope, and they began skipping. And never did they skip so high, run in and out so fast, or do such daring things as on that morning.

In the afternoon Pat called for the Burnell children with the buggy and they drove home. There were visitors. Isabel and Lottie, who liked visitors, went upstairs to change their pinafores. But Kezia thieved out[2] at the back. Nobody was about; she began to swing on the big white gates of the courtyard. Presently, looking along the road, she saw two little dots. They grew bigger, they were coming towards her. Now she could see that one was in front and one close behind. Now she could see that they were the Kelveys. Kezia stopped swinging. She slipped off the gate as if she was going to run away. Then she hesitated. The Kelveys came nearer, and beside them stalked their shadows, very long, stretching right across the road with their heads in the buttercups. Kezia clambered back on the gate; she had made up her mind; she swung out.

"Hullo," she said to the passing Kelveys.

They were so astounded that they stopped. Lil gave her silly smile. Our Else stared.

"You can come and see our doll's house if you want to," said Kezia, and she dragged one toe on the ground. But at that Lil turned red and shook her head quickly.

"Why not?" asked Kezia.

Lil gasped, then she said. "Your ma told our ma you wasn't to speak to us."

"Oh, well," said Kezia. She didn't know what to reply. "It doesn't matter. You can come and see our doll's house all the same. Come on. Nobody's looking."

But Lil shook her head still harder.

"Don't you want to?" asked Kezia.

Suddenly there was a twitch, a tug at Lil's skirt. She turned round. Our Else was looking at her with big, imploring eyes; she was frowning; she wanted to go. For a moment Lil looked at our Else very doubtfully. But then our Else twitched her skirt again. She started forward. Kezia led the way. Like two little stray cats they followed across the courtyard to where the doll's house stood.

"There it is," said Kezia.

There was a pause. Lil breathed loudly, almost snorted; our Else was still as a stone.

"I'll open it for you," said Kezia kindly. She undid the hook and they looked inside.

"There's the drawing-room and the dining-room, and that's the—"

"Kezia!"

Oh, what a start they gave!

"Kezia!"

It was Aunt Beryl's voice. They turned round. At the back door stood Aunt Beryl, staring as if she couldn't believe what she saw.

"How dare you ask the little Kelveys into the courtyard?" said her cold, furious voice. "You know as well as I do, you're not allowed to talk to them. Run away, children, run away at once. And don't come back again," said Aunt Beryl. And she stepped into the yard and shooed them out as if they were chickens.

"Off you go immediately!" she called, cold and proud.

They did not need telling twice. Burning with shame, shrinking together, Lil huddling along like her mother, our Else dazed, somehow they

1. ***What a sell,*** what a come-down, disappointment.
2. ***thieved out,*** sneaked out, dallied.

crossed the big courtyard and squeezed through the white gate.

"Wicked, disobedient little girl!" said Aunt Beryl bitterly to Kezia, and she slammed the doll's house to.

The afternoon had been awful. A letter had come from Willie Brent, a terrifying, threatening letter, saying if she did not meet him that evening in Pulman's Bush, he'd come to the front door and ask the reason why! But now that she had frightened those little rats of Kelveys and given Kezia a good scolding, her heart felt lighter. That ghastly pressure was gone. She went back to the house humming.

When the Kelveys were well out of sight of Burnells', they sat down to rest on a big red drain-pipe by the side of the road. Lil's cheeks were still burning; she took off the hat with the quill and held it on her knee. Dreamily they looked over the hay paddocks, past the creek, to the group of wattles where Logan's cows stood waiting to be milked. What were their thoughts?

Presently our Else nudged up close to her sister. But now she had forgotten the cross lady. She put out a finger and stroked her sister's quill; she smiled her rare smile.

"I seen the little lamp," she said, softly.

Then both were silent once more. □□

Discussion

1. **(a)** What are the differences in personality between Isabel and Kezia? **(b)** What is the significance of the doll's house for Isabel? What is it for Kezia?

2. **(a)** What are Lil and Else like? How do they relate to one another? **(b)** How does their relationship affect the reader's response to them?

3. Why is so much attention given to the description of how the Kelvey girls are dressed?

4. When Lena asks Lil Kelvey about being a servant when she grows up, Lil just gives "her silly, shame-faced smile." **(a)** What reaction did Lena expect? **(b)** Why does Lil respond as she does? **(c)** What do you think of Lil's smile?

5. **(a)** How would the reader's response to the last statement in the story—"I seen the little lamp"—be different if the line were given to Lil instead of Else? Explain. **(b)** What is the significance of Else's having seen the little lamp?

Extension
Reading and Discussion

Discuss the attitudes toward social class reflected in "The Doll's House" and Woolf's "The Legacy."

Extension • Writing

1. Write an essay in which you explain why you believe Kezia invited the Kelvey girls to look at the doll's house.

2. Draw upon your own experience to write an essay or story involving prejudice, gossip, or both.

Katherine Mansfield
1888 • 1923

Katherine Mansfield was born in New Zealand, the daughter of a prominent banker. She went to London in 1902 to study music at Queens College. By the time she completed her studies, however, she had decided to become a writer.

Her first collection of stories, written in Germany and published in 1911, received little recognition. But it was in Germany that she met the literary critic John Middleton Murray, with whom she collaborated on a short-lived literary magazine and whom she married in 1918.

Mansfield was particularly impressed by the short fiction of the Russian writer Chekhov, and like him she wrote stories which depend more on atmosphere, character, and the nuances of language than on plot.

Katherine Mansfield's brother was killed in action in World War I. Her own mature years were lived in the shadow of tuberculosis, of which she died at the age of thirty-four. It has been suggested that her consciousness of the imminence of death heightened her awareness and helps account for the sensitivity for which her stories are noted.

Elizabeth Bowen

Tears, Idle Tears

Frederick burst into tears in the middle of Regent's Park. His mother, seeing what was about to happen, had cried: "Frederick, you *can't*—in the middle of Regent's Park!" Really, this was a corner, one of those lively corners just inside a big gate, where two walks meet and a bridge starts across the pretty winding lake. People were passing quickly; the bridge rang with feet. Poplars stood up like delicate green brooms; diaphanous willows whose weeping was not shocking quivered over the lake. May sun spattered gold through the breezy trees; the tulips though falling open were still gay; three girls in a long boat shot under the bridge. Frederick, knees trembling, butted towards his mother a crimson convulsed face, as though he had the idea of burying himself in her. She whipped out a handkerchief and dabbed at him with it under his grey felt hat, exclaiming meanwhile in fearful mortification: "You really haven't got to be such a *baby!*" Her tone attracted the notice of several people, who might otherwise have thought he was having something taken out of his eye.

He was too big to cry: the whole scene was disgraceful. He wore a grey flannel knickerbocker suit and looked like a schoolboy; though in fact he was seven, still doing lessons at home. His mother said to him almost every week: "I don't know what they will think when you go to school!" His tears were a shame of which she could speak to no one; no offensive weakness of body could have upset her more. Once she had got so far as taking her pen up to write to the Mother's Advice Column of a helpful woman's weekly about them. She began: "I am a widow; young, good tempered, and my friends all tell me that I have great control. But my little boy—" She intended to sign herself "Mrs. D., Surrey." But then she had stopped and thought no, no: after all, he is Toppy's son . . . She was a gallant-looking, correct woman, wearing to-day in London a coat and shirt, a silver fox, white gloves and a dark-blue toque put on exactly right—not the sort of woman you ought to see in a Park with a great blubbering boy belonging to her. She looked a mother of sons, but not of a son of this kind, and should more properly, really, have been walking a dog. "Come on!" she said, as though the bridge, the poplars, the people staring were to be borne no longer. She began to walk on quickly, along the edge of the lake, parallel with the park's girdle of trees and the dark, haughty windows of Cornwall Terrace looking at her over the red may. They had meant to go to the Zoo, but now she had changed her mind: Frederick did not deserve the Zoo.

Frederick stumbled along beside her, too miserable to notice. His mother seldom openly punished him, but often revenged herself on him in small ways. He could feel how just this was. His own incontinence in the matter of tears was as shocking to him, as bowing-down, as annulling, as it could be to her. He never knew what happened—a cold black pit with no bottom opened inside himself; a red-hot bellwire jagged up through him from the pit of his frozen belly to the caves of his eyes. Then the hot gummy rush of tears, the convulsion of his features, the terrible square grin he felt his mouth take all made him his own shameful and squalid enemy. Despair howled round his inside like a wind, and through his streaming eyes he saw everything quake. Anyone's being there—and most of all his mother—drove this catastrophe on him. He never cried like this when he was alone.

Crying made him so abject, so outcast from other people that he went on crying out of despair. His crying was not just reflex, like a baby's; it dragged up all unseemliness into view. No wonder everyone was repelled. There is something about an abject person that rouses cruelty in the kindest breast. The plate-glass windows of the lordly houses looked at him through the may-trees with judges' eyes. Girls with their knees crossed, reading on the park benches, looked up with unkind smiles. His apathetic stumbling, his not seeing or caring that they had given up their trip to the Zoo, became more than Mrs. Dickinson, his mother, could bear. She pointed out, in a voice tense with dislike: "I'm not taking you to the Zoo."

"Mmmph-mmph-mmph," sobbed Frederick.

"You know, I so often wonder what your father would think."

"Mmmph-mmph-mmph."

"He used to be so proud of you. He and I used to look forward to what you'd be like when you were a big boy. One of the last things he ever said was: 'Frederick will take care of you.' You almost make me glad he's not here now."

"Oough-oough."

"What do you say?"

"I'm t-t-trying to stop."

"Everybody's looking at you, you know."

She was one of those women who have an unfailing sense of what not to say, and say it: despair, perversity or stubborn virtue must actuate them. She had a horror, also, of the abnormal and had to hit out at it before it could hit at her. Her husband, an R.A.F.[1] pilot who had died two days after a ghastly crash, after two or three harrowing spaces of consciousness, had never made her ashamed or puzzled her. Their intimacies, then even his death, had had a bold naturalness.

"Listen, I shall walk on ahead," said Frederick's mother, lifting her chin with that noble, decided movement so many people liked. "You stay here and look at that duck till you've stopped that noise. Don't catch me up till you have. No, I'm really ashamed of you."

She walked on. He had not been making, really, so very much noise. Drawing choppy breaths, he stood still and looked at the duck that sat folded into a sleek white cypher on the green grassy margin of the lake. When it rolled one eye open over a curve, something unseeing in its expression calmed him. His mother walked away under the gay tree-shadows; her step quickened lightly, the tip of her fox fur swung. She thought of the lunch she had had with Major and Mrs. Williams, the party she would be going to at five. First, she must leave Frederick at Aunt Mary's, and what would Aunt Mary say to his bloated face? She walked fast; the gap between her and Frederick widened: she was a charming woman walking by herself.

Everybody had noticed how much courage she had; they said: "How plucky Mrs. Dickinson is." It was five years since her tragedy and she had not remarried, so that her gallantness kept on coming into play. She helped a friend with a little hat shop called *Isobel* near where they lived in Surrey, bred puppies for sale and gave the rest of her time to making a man of Frederick. She smiled nicely and carried her head high. Those two days while Toppy had lain dying she had hardly turned a hair, for his sake: no one knew when he might come conscious again. When she was not by his bed she was waiting about the hospital. The chaplain hanging about her and the doctor had given thanks that there were women like this; another officer's wife who had been her friend had said she was braver than could be good for anyone. When Toppy finally died the other woman had put the unflinching widow into a taxi and driven back with her to the Dickinsons' bungalow. She kept saying: "Cry, dear, cry: you'd feel better." She made tea and clattered about, repeating: "Don't mind me, darling: just have a big cry." The strain became so great that tears streamed down her own face. Mrs. Dickinson looked past her palely, with a polite smile. The empty-feeling bungalow with its rustling curtains still smelt of Toppy's pipe; his slippers were under a chair. Then Mrs. Dickinson's friend, almost tittering with despair, thought of a poem of Tennyson's she had learnt as a child. She said: "Where's Frederick? He's quiet. Do you think he's asleep?" The widow, rising, perfectly automatic, led her into the room where Frederick lay in his cot. A nursemaid rose from beside him, gave them one morbid look and scurried away. The two-year-old baby, flushed, and drawing up his upper lip in his sleep as his father used to do, lay curved under his blue

1. ***R.A.F.,*** Royal Air Force of Britain.

blanket, clenching one fist on nothing. Something suddenly seemed to strike his mother, who, slumping down by the cot, ground her face and forehead into the fluffy blanket, then began winding the blanket round her two fists. Her convulsions, though proper, were fearful: the cot shook. The friend crept away into the kitchen, where she stayed an half-hour, muttering to the maid. They made more tea and waited for Mrs. Dickinson to give full birth to her grief. Then extreme silence drew them back to the cot. Mrs. Dickinson knelt asleep, her profile pressed to the blanket, one arm crooked over the baby's form. Under his mother's arm, as still as an image, Frederick lay wide awake, not making a sound. In conjunction with a certain look in his eyes, the baby's silence gave the two women the horrors. The servant said to the friend: "You would think he knew."

Mrs. Dickinson's making so few demands on pity soon rather alienated her women friends, but men liked her better for it: several of them found in her straight look an involuntary appeal to themselves alone, more exciting than coquetry, deeply, nobly exciting: several wanted to marry her. But courage had given her a new intractable kind of virgin pride: she loved it too much; she could never surrender it. "No, don't ask me that," she would say, lifting her chin and with that calm, gallant smile. "Don't spoil things. You've been splendid to me: such a support. But you see, there's Frederick. He's the man in my life now. I'm bound to put him first. That wouldn't be fair, would it?" After that, she would simply go on shaking her head. She became the perfect friend for men who wished to wish to marry but were just as glad not to, and for married men who liked just a little pathos without being upset.

Frederick had stopped crying. This left him perfectly blank, so that he stared at the duck with abstract intensity, perceiving its moulded feathers and porcelain-smooth neck. The burning, swirling film had cleared away from his eyes, and his diaphragm felt relief, as when retching has stopped. He forgot his focus of grief and forgot his mother, but saw with joy a quivering bough of willow that, drooping into his gaze under his swollen eyelids, looked as pure and strong as something after the Flood.[2] His thought clutched at the willow, weak and wrecked but happy. He knew he was now qualified to walk after his mother, but without feeling either guilty or recalcitrant did not wish to do so. He stepped over the rail—no park keeper being at hand to stop him—and, tenderly and respectfully, attempted to touch the white duck's tail. Without a blink, with automatic uncoyness, the duck slid away from Frederick into the lake. Its lovely white china body balanced on the green glass water as it propelled itself gently round the curve of the bank. Frederick saw with a passion of observation its shadowy webbed feet lazily striking out.

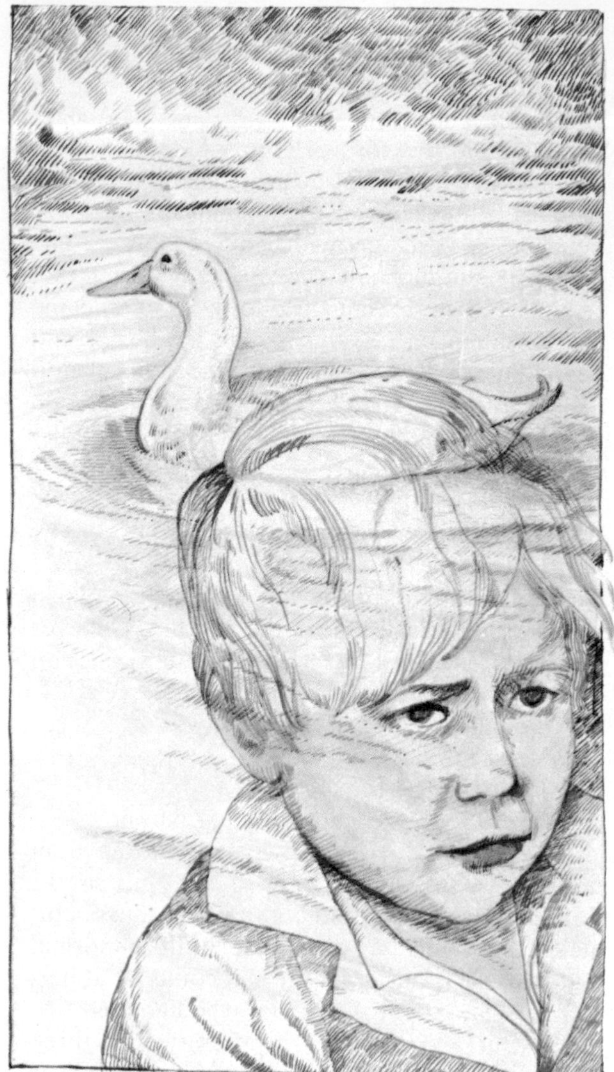

2. ***the Flood,*** the deluge that covered the earth in the time of Noah, as described in the Bible.

"The keeper'll eat you," said a voice behind him.

Frederick looked cautiously round with his bunged-up eyes. The *individual* who had spoken sat on a park bench; it was a girl with a despatch case beside her. Her big bony knee-joints stuck out through her thin crepe-de-chine dress; she was hatless and her hair made a frizzy, pretty outline, but she wore spectacles, her skin had burnt dull red: her smile and the cock of her head had about them something pungent and energetic, not like a girl's at all. "Whatcher mean, eat me?"

"You're on his grass. And putting salt on his duck's tail."[3]

Frederick stepped back carefully over the low rail. "I haven't got any salt." He looked up and down the walk: his mother was out of sight but from the direction of the bridge a keeper was approaching, still distant but with an awesome gait. "My goodness," the girl said. "What's been biting you?" Frederick was at a loss. "Here," she said, "have an apple." She opened her case, which was full of folded grease-paper that must have held sandwiches, and rummaged out an apple with a waxy, bright skin. Frederick came up, tentative as a pony, and finally took the apple. His breath was still hitching and catching; he did not wish to speak.

"Go on," she said, "swallow: it'll settle your chest. Where's your mother gone off to? What's all the noise about?" Frederick only opened his jaws as wide as they would go, then bit slowly, deeply into the apple. The girl re-crossed her legs and tucked her thin crepe-de-chine skirt round the other knee. "What had you done—cheeked her?"

Frederick swept the mouthful of apple into one cheek. "No," he said shortly. "Cried."

"I should say you did. Bellowed. I watched you all down the path." There was something ruminative in the girl's tone that made her remark really not at all offensive; in fact, she looked at Frederick as though she were meeting an artist who had just done a turn. He had been standing about, licking and biting the apple, but now he came and sat down at the other end of the bench. "How do you do it?" she said.

Frederick only turned away: his ears began burning again.

"What gets at you?" she said.

"Don't know."

"Someone coming it over you? I know another boy who cries like you, but he's older. He knots himself up and bellows."

"What's his name?"

"George."

"Does he go to school?"

"Oh, lord, no; he's a boy at the place where I used to work." She raised one arm, leaned back, and watched four celluloid bangles, each of a different colour, slide down it to her elbow joint, where they stuck. "He doesn't know why he does it," she said, "but he's got to. It's as though he saw something. You can't ask him. Some people take him that way: girls do. I never did. It's as if he knew about something he'd better not. I said once, well what just *is* it, and he said if he *could* tell me he wouldn't do it. I said, well, what's the *reason*, and he said, well, what's the reason not to? I knew him well at one time."

Frederick spat out two pips, looked round cautiously for the keeper, then dropped the apple-core down the back of the seat. "Where's George live?"

"I don't know now," she said, "I often wonder. I got sacked from that place where I used to work, and he went right off and I never saw him again. You snap out of that, if you can, before you are George's age. It does you no good. It's all in the way you see things. Look, there's your mother back. Better move, or there'll be *more* trouble." She held out her hand to Frederick, and when he put his in it shook hands so cheerfully, with such tough decision, that the four celluloid bangles danced on her wrist. "You and George," she said. "Funny to meet two of you. Well, good-bye, Henry: cheer up."

"I'm Frederick."

"Well, cheer up, Freddie."

As Frederick walked away, she smoothed down the sandwich papers inside her despatch case and snapped the case shut again. Then she put a finger under her hair at each side, to tuck her spectacles firmly down on her ears. Her mouth, an unreddened line across her harsh-burnt face, still wore the same truculent, homely

3. ***putting salt . . . tail.*** Since as early as the sixteenth century, children have been given the joking advice that the best way to catch birds is to put salt on their tails.

smile. She crossed her arms under the flat chest, across her stomach, and sat there holding her elbows idly, wagging one foot in its fawn sandal, looking fixedly at the lake through her spectacles wondering about George. She had the afternoon, as she had no work. She saw George's face lifted abjectly from his arms on a table, blotchy over his clerk's collar. The eyes of George and Frederick seemed to her to be wounds in the world's surface, through which its inner, terrible, unassuageable, necessary sorrow constantly bled away and as constantly welled up.

Mrs. Dickinson came down the walk under the band of trees, carefully unanxious, looking lightly at objects to see if Frederick were near them; he had been a long time. Then she saw Frederick shaking hands with a sort of girl on a bench and starting to come her way. So she quickly turned her frank, friendly glance on the lake, down which, as though to greet her, a swan came swimming. She touched her fox fur lightly, sliding it up her shoulder. What a lovely mother to have. "Well, Frederick," she said, as he came into earshot, "coming?" Wind sent a puff of red mayflowers through the air. She stood still and waited for Frederick to come up. She could not think what to do now: they had an hour to put in before they were due at Aunt Mary's. But this only made her manner calmer and more decisive.

Frederick gave a great skip, opened his mouth wide, shouted: "Oo, I say, mother, I nearly caught a duck!"

"Frederick, dear, how silly you are: you couldn't."

"Oo, yes, I could, I could. If I'd had salt for its tail!" Years later, Frederick could still remember, with ease, pleasure and with a sense of lonely shame being gone, that calm white duck swimming off round the bank. But George's friend with the bangles, and George's trouble, fell through a cleft in his memory and were forgotten soon. □□

Discussion

1. In the first paragraph of the story, Mrs. Dickinson chides Frederick for being "such a *baby*!" How is this significant in light of other facts about Frederick and his mother as revealed in the story?

2. At one point in the story the reader is told that Mrs. Dickinson spends much of her time "making a man of Frederick." What are her methods for doing this?

3. **(a)** What is Frederick's reaction to the young woman's telling him of her friend George? **(b)** What does the reader gain from knowing that George, who is several years older than Frederick, also cries for inexplicable reasons? Explain.

4. The reader is told that Mrs. Dickinson "often revenged herself" on Frederick in small ways. Why do you feel she does this? Offer evidence from the story for your response.

5. **(a)** Explain why his crying makes Frederick "his own shameful and squalid enemy." How did Frederick come to understand the idea of "shame"? **(b)** In the context of this story, how is the reader to respond to the terms "shame" and "courage"?

Elizabeth Bowen 1899 • 1973

Elizabeth Bowen, born in Ireland, was raised and educated in England. During World War I she returned to Ireland to work as a nurse in a hospital for shell-shocked patients near Dublin. After the war she returned to England, where she studied at the London Council of Arts, married, and began to publish short stories.

During World War II Bowen and her husband lived in Regent's Park, London. She worked in the Ministry of Information during the day, served as an air-raid warden at night, and continued to write. Her knowledge of the psychological effects of war on the civilian mind is reflected in the stories in *Ivy Gripped the Steps* (1946) and the novel *The Heat of the Day* (1949).

Bowen is a writer of sensitive, sometimes delicate prose—especially in the creation of landscape and setting. Her principal themes are betrayal and disillusionment, disappointment and loss of innocence. Among the best of her many volumes of fiction are *The House in Paris* (1936), *The Death of the Heart* (1939), *The Demon Lover* (1945), and *The Little Girls* (1964).

Graham Greene

A Shocking Accident

1

Jerome was called into his housemaster's room in the break between the second and the third class on a Thursday morning. He had no fear of trouble, for he was a warden—the name that the proprietor and headmaster of a rather expensive preparatory school[1] had chosen to give to approved, reliable boys in the lower forms[2] (from a warden one became a guardian and finally before leaving, it was hoped for Marlborough or Rugby,[3] a crusader). The housemaster, Mr Wordsworth, sat behind his desk with an appearance of perplexity and apprehension. Jerome had the odd impression when he entered that he was a cause of fear.

"Sit down, Jerome," Mr Wordsworth said. "All going well with the trigonometry?"

"Yes, sir."

"I've had a telephone call, Jerome. From your aunt. I'm afraid I have bad news for you."

"Yes, sir?"

"Your father has had an accident."

"Oh."

Mr Wordsworth looked at him with some surprise. "A serious accident."

"Yes, sir?"

Jerome worshipped his father: the verb is exact. As man re-creates God, so Jerome re-created his father—from a restless widowed author into a mysterious adventurer who travelled in far places—Nice, Beirut, Majorca, even the Canaries. The time had arrived about his eighth birthday when Jerome believed that his father either "ran guns" or was a member of the British Secret Service. Now it occurred to him that his father might have been wounded in "a hail of machine-gun bullets."

Mr Wordsworth played with the ruler on his desk. He seemed at a loss how to continue. He said, "You know your father was in Naples?"

"Yes, sir."

"Your aunt heard from the hospital today."

"Oh."

Mr Wordsworth said with desperation, "It was a street accident."

"Yes, sir?" It seemed quite likely to Jerome that they would call it a street accident. The police of course had fired first; his father would not take human life except as a last resort.

"I'm afraid your father was very seriously hurt indeed."

"Oh."

"In fact, Jerome, he died yesterday. Quite without pain."

"Did they shoot him through the heart?"

"I beg your pardon. What did you say, Jerome?"

"Did they shoot him through the heart?"

"Nobody shot him, Jerome. A pig fell on him." An inexplicable convulsion took place in the nerves of Mr Wordsworth's face; it really looked for a moment as though he were going to laugh. He closed his eyes, composed his features and said rapidly as though it were necessary to expel the story as quickly as possible, "Your father was walking along a street in Naples when a pig fell on him. A shocking accident. Apparently in the poorer quarters of Naples they keep pigs

---

1. ***preparatory school,*** a private elementary school.
2. ***lower forms,*** lower grades.
3. ***Marlborough or Rugby,*** two famous public schools. The English public school is a private boarding school for the sons of the well-to-do classes.

on their balconies. This one was on the fifth floor. It had grown too fat. The balcony broke. The pig fell on your father."

Mr Wordsworth left his desk rapidly and went to the window, turning his back on Jerome. He shook a little with emotion.

Jerome said, "What happened to the pig?"

2

This was not callousness on the part of Jerome, as it was interpreted by Mr Wordsworth to his colleagues (he even discussed with them whether, perhaps, Jerome was yet fitted to be a warden). Jerome was only attempting to visualize the strange scene to get the details right. Nor was Jerome a boy who cried; he was a boy who brooded, and it never occurred to him at his preparatory school that the circumstances of his father's death were comic—they were still part of the mystery of life. It was later, in his first term at his public school, when he told the story to his best friend, that he began to realize how it affected others. Naturally after that disclosure he was known, rather unreasonably, as Pig.

Unfortunately his aunt had no sense of humour. There was an enlarged snapshot of his father on the piano; a large sad man in an unsuitable dark suit posed in Capri with an umbrella (to guard him against sunstroke), the Faraglione rocks forming the background. By the age of sixteen Jerome was well aware that the portrait looked more like the author of *Sunshine and Shade* and *Rambles in the Balearics* than an agent of the Secret Service. All the same he loved the memory of his father: he still possessed an album filled with picture-postcards (the stamps had been soaked off long ago for his other collection), and it pained him when his aunt embarked with strangers on the story of his father's death.

"A shocking accident," she would begin, and the stranger would compose his or her features into the correct shape for interest and commiseration. Both reactions, of course, were false, but it was terrible for Jerome to see how suddenly, midway in her rambling discourse, the interest would become genuine. "I can't think how such things can be allowed in a civilized country," his aunt would say. "I suppose one has to regard Italy as civilized. One is prepared for all kinds of things abroad, of course, and my brother was a great traveller. He always carried a water-filter with him. It was far less expensive, you know, than buying all those bottles of mineral water. My brother always said that his filter paid for his dinner wine. You can see from that what a careful man he was, but who could possibly have expected when he was walking along the Via Dottore Manuele Panucci on his way to the Hydrographic Museum that a pig would fall on him?" That was the moment when the interest became genuine.

Jerome's father had not been a very distinguished writer, but the time always seems to come, after an author's death, when somebody thinks it worth his while to write a letter to the *Times Literary Supplement* announcing the preparation of a biography and asking to see any letters or documents or receive any anecdotes from friends of the dead man. Most of the biographies, of course, never appear—one wonders whether the whole thing may not be an obscure form of blackmail and whether many a potential writer of a biography or thesis finds the means in this way to finish his education at Kansas or Nottingham. Jerome, however, as a chartered accountant, lived far from the literary world. He did not realize how small the menace really was, or that the danger period for someone of his father's obscurity had long passed. Sometimes he rehearsed the method of recounting his father's death so as to reduce the comic element to its smallest dimensions—it would be of no use to refuse information, for in that case the biographer would undoubtedly visit his aunt who was living to a great old age with no sign of flagging.

It seemed to Jerome that there were two possible methods—the first led gently up to the accident, so that by the time it was described the listener was so well prepared that the death came really as an anti-climax. The chief danger of laughter in such a story was always surprise. When he rehearsed this method Jerome began boringly enough.

"You know Naples and those high tenement buildings? Somebody once told me that the Neapolitan always feels at home in New York just as the man from Turin feels at home in London

because the river runs in much the same way in both cities. Where was I? Oh, yes. Naples, of course. You'd be surprised in the poorer quarters what things they keep on the balconies of those sky-scraping tenements—not washing, you know, or bedding, but things like livestock, chickens or even pigs. Of course the pigs get no exercise whatever and fatten all the quicker." He could imagine how his hearer's eyes would have glazed by this time. "I've no idea, have you, how heavy a pig can be, but these old buildings are all badly in need of repair. A balcony on the fifth floor gave way under one of those pigs. It struck the third floor balcony on its way down and sort of ricochetted into the street. My father was on the way to the Hydrographic Museum when the pig hit him. Coming from that height and that angle it broke his neck." This was really a masterly attempt to make an intrinsically interesting subject boring.

The other method Jerome rehearsed had the virtue of brevity.

"My father was killed by a pig."

"Really? In India?"

"No, in Italy."

"How interesting. I never realized there was pig-sticking[4] in Italy. Was your father keen on polo?"

In course of time, neither too early nor too late, rather as though, in his capacity as a chartered accountant, Jerome had studied the statistics and taken the average, he became engaged to be married: to a pleasant fresh-faced girl of twenty-five whose father was a doctor in Pinner. Her name was Sally, her favourite author was still Hugh Walpole,[5] and she had adored babies ever since she had been given a doll at the age of five which moved its eyes and made water. Their relationship was contented rather than exciting, as became the love-affair of a chartered accountant; it would never have done if it had interfered with the figures.

One thought worried Jerome, however. Now that within a year he might himself become a father, his love for the dead man increased; he realized what affection had gone into the picture-postcards. He felt a longing to protect his memory, and uncertain whether this quiet love of his would survive if Sally were so insensitive as to laugh when she heard the story of his father's death. Inevitably she would hear it when Jerome brought her to dinner with his aunt. Several times he tried to tell her himself, as she was naturally anxious to know all she could that concerned him.

"You were very small when your father died?"

"Just nine."

"Poor little boy," she said.

"I was at school. They broke the news to me."

"Did you take it very hard?"

"I can't remember."

"You never told me how it happened."

"It was very sudden. A street accident."

"You'll never drive fast, will you, Jemmy?" (She had begun to call him "Jemmy".) It was too late then to try the second method—the one he thought of as the pig-sticking one.

They were going to marry quietly in a registry-office and have their honeymoon at Torquay. He avoided taking her to see his aunt until a week before the wedding, but then the night came, and he could not have told himself whether his apprehension was more for his father's memory or the security of his own love.

The moment came all too soon. "Is that Jemmy's father?" Sally asked, picking up the portrait of the man with the umbrella.

"Yes, dear. How did you guess?"

"He has Jemmy's eyes and brow, hasn't he?"

"Has Jerome lent you his books?"

"No."

"I will give you a set for your wedding. He wrote so tenderly about his travels. My own favourite is *Nooks and Crannies*. He would have had a great future. It made that shocking accident all the worse."

"Yes?"

Jerome longed to leave the room and not see that loved face crinkle with irresistible amusement.

"I had so many letters from his readers after the pig fell on him." She had never been so abrupt before.

---

4. ***pig-sticking,*** the hunting of wild boars with a spear, especially in India.

5. ***Hugh Walpole,*** a popular English novelist in the 1920s and 1930s. The author is making the point that Sally is a person of conventional tastes.

And then the miracle happened. Sally did not laugh. Sally sat with open eyes of horror while his aunt told her the story, and at the end, "How horrible," Sally said. "It makes you think, doesn't it? Happening like that. Out of a clear sky."

Jerome's heart sang with joy. It was as though she had appeased his fear for ever. In the taxi going home he kissed her with more passion than he had ever shown and she returned it. There were babies in her pale blue pupils, babies that rolled their eyes and made water.

"A week today," Jerome said, and she squeezed his hand. "Penny for your thoughts, my darling."

"I was wondering," Sally said, "what happened to the poor pig?"

"They almost certainly had it for dinner," Jerome said happily and kissed the dear child again. □□

Discussion

1. Aren't all accidents "shocking"? Why is Greene's title an apt one for this story?

2. "What happened to the pig?" Do you feel that Jerome's question is a reasonable one? Explain.

3. What is the significance in the story of Jerome's occupation?

4. Which of the following is the most important to Jerome: His confusion regarding death, his affection for his father, his embarrassment over the pig? Explain your answer.

5. Did Jerome overestimate the comic nature of the accident or underestimate Sally? Explain.

Graham Greene 1904 •

Greene was born in Hertfordshire, England. He was the son of a headmaster and attended Berkhamsted School. In an autobiography, *A Sort of Life,* Greene recalls that, as a child growing up in the years before World War I, his idea of happiness was going to London: "Once a year we were all taken to *Peter Pan.* I loved it

wholeheartedly. My favorite scene was the one where Peter Pan fought alone against the pirates with his sword, and narrowly second to it was the moment of enjoyable horror when the green-lit face of Captain Hook appeared at a service hatch and put poison in Peter's glass. The dying Tinker Bell touched me, but never would I consent to call out with the audience that I believed in fairies. It would have been dishonest, for I had never believed in them, except for the period of the play. There was one scene with attractive mermaids which to my great disappointment was cut, for reasons, I think, of wartime economy, from later productions. I could have dispensed more easily with the house in the treetops, for I never cared for Wendy, but 'To die will be an awfully big adventure' was a line which echoed through all my adolescence; it only really faded from my mind when death became for all of us a common everyday risk."

Greene attended Oxford, was on the staff of the London *Times* from 1926 to 1930, and from 1937 to 1941 was a movie critic and literary editor for the *Spectator.* During World War II he served in the Foreign Office.

His themes are alienation and faith in the modern world—in Sweden, Mexico, Africa, Vietnam, Haiti. He conveys these themes through fast-moving, inventive stories of violence and suspense. Among Greene's most important and serious novels are those which reflect his Roman Catholicism.

In addition to his many novels and short stories, Greene has written plays, screenplays, film criticism, and travel books.

From A SORT OF LIFE, by Graham Greene. Simon and Schuster, New York, 1971.

Frank O'Connor

My Oedipus Complex

Father was in the army all through the war—the first war, I mean—so, up to the age of five, I never saw much of him, and what I saw did not worry me. Sometimes I woke and there was a big figure in khaki peering down at me in the candlelight. Sometimes in the early morning I heard the slamming of the front door and the clatter of nailed boots down the cobbles of the lane. These were Father's entrances and exits. Like Santa Claus he came and went mysteriously.

In fact, I rather liked his visits, though it was an uncomfortable squeeze between Mother and him when I got into the big bed in the early morning. He smoked, which gave him a pleasant musty smell, and shaved, an operation of astounding interest. Each time he left a trail of souvenirs—model tanks and Gurkha knives with handles made of bullet cases, and German helmets and cap badges and button-sticks, and all sorts of military equipment—carefully stowed away in a long box on top of the wardrobe, in case they ever came in handy. There was a bit of the magpie about Father; he expected everything to come in handy. When his back was turned, Mother let me get a chair and rummage through his treasures. She didn't seem to think so highly of them as he did.

The war was the most peaceful period of my life. The window of my attic faced southeast. My mother had curtained it, but that had small effect. I always woke with the first light and, with all the responsibilities of the previous day melted, feeling myself rather like the sun, ready to illumine and rejoice. Life never seemed so simple and clear and full of possibilities as then. I put my feet out from under the clothes—I called them Mrs. Left and Mrs. Right—and invented dramatic situations for them in which they discussed the problems of the day. At least Mrs. Right did; she was very demonstrative, but I hadn't the same control of Mrs. Left, so she mostly contented herself with nodding agreement.

They discussed what Mother and I should do during the day, what Santa Claus should give a fellow for Christmas, and what steps should be taken to brighten the home. There was that little matter of the baby, for instance. Mother and I could never agree about that. Ours was the only house in the terrace without a new baby, and Mother said we couldn't afford one till Father came back from the war because they cost seventeen and six. That showed how simple she was. The Geneys up the road had a baby, and everyone knew they couldn't afford seventeen and six. It was probably a cheap baby, and Mother wanted something really good, but I felt she was too exclusive. The Geneys' baby would have done us fine.

Having settled my plans for the day, I got up, put a chair under the attic window, and lifted the frame high enough to stick out my head. The window overlooked the front gardens of the terrace behind ours, and beyond these it looked over a deep valley to the tall, red-brick houses terraced up the opposite hillside, which were all still in shadow, while those at our side of the valley were all lit up, though with long strange shadows that made them seem unfamiliar; rigid and painted.

After that I went into Mother's room and climbed into the big bed. She woke and I began to tell her of my schemes. By this time, though I never seem to have noticed it, I was petrified in my nightshirt, and I thawed as I talked until, the last frost melted, I fell asleep beside her and woke again only when I heard her below in the kitchen, making the breakfast.

After breakfast we went into town; heard Mass at St. Augustine's and said a prayer for Father, and did the shopping. If the afternoon was fine we either went for a walk in the country or a visit to Mother's great friend in the convent, Mother St. Dominic. Mother had them all praying for Father, and every night, going to bed, I asked God to send him back safe from the war to us. Little, indeed, did I know what I was praying for!

One morning, I got into the big bed, and there, sure enough, was Father in his usual Santa Claus manner, but later, instead of uniform, he put on his best blue suit, and Mother was as pleased as anything. I saw nothing to be pleased about, because, out of uniform, Father was altogether less interesting, but she only beamed, and explained that our prayers had been answered, and off we went to Mass to thank God for having brought Father safely home.

The irony of it! That very day when he came in to dinner he took off his boots and put on his slippers, donned the dirty old cap he wore about the house to save him from colds, crossed his legs, and began to talk gravely to Mother, who looked anxious. Naturally, I disliked her looking anxious, because it destroyed her good looks, so I interrupted him.

"Just a moment, Larry!" she said gently.

This was only what she said when we had boring visitors, so I attached no importance to it and went on talking.

"Do be quiet, Larry!" she said impatiently. "Don't you hear me talking to Daddy?"

This was the first time I had heard those ominous words, "talking to Daddy," and I couldn't help feeling that if this was how God answered prayers, he couldn't listen to them very attentively.

"Why are you talking to Daddy?" I asked with as great a show of indifference as I could muster.

"Because Daddy and I have business to discuss. Now, don't interrupt again!"

In the afternoon, at Mother's request, Father took me for a walk. This time we went into town instead of out to the country, and I thought at first, in my usual optimistic way, that it might be an improvement. It was nothing of the sort. Father and I had quite different notions of a walk in town. He had no proper interest in trams, ships, and horses, and the only thing that seemed to divert him was talking to fellows as old as himself. When I wanted to stop he simply went on, dragging me behind him by the hand; when he wanted to stop I had no alternative but to do the same. I noticed that it seemed to be a sign that he wanted to stop for a long time whenever he leaned against a wall. The second time I saw him do it I got wild. He seemed to be settling himself forever. I pulled him by the coat and trousers, but, unlike Mother who, if you were too persistent, got into a wax and said: "Larry, if you don't behave yourself, I'll give you a good slap," Father had an extraordinary capacity for amiable inattention. I sized him up and wondered would I cry, but he seemed to be too remote to be annoyed even by that. Really, it was like going for a walk with a mountain! He either ignored the wrenching and pummeling entirely, or else glanced down with a grin of amusement from his peak. I had never met anyone so absorbed in himself as he seemed.

At teatime, "talking to Daddy" began again, complicated this time by the fact that he had an evening paper, and every few minutes he put it down and told Mother something new out of it. I felt this was foul play. Man for man, I was prepared to compete with him any time for Mother's attention, but when he had it all made up for him by other people it left me no chance. Several times I tried to change the subject without success.

"You must be quiet while Daddy is reading, Larry," Mother said impatiently.

It was clear that she either genuinely liked talking to Father better than talking to me, or else that he had some terrible hold on her which made her afraid to admit the truth.

"Mummy," I said that night when she was tucking me up, "do you think if I prayed hard God would send Daddy back to the war?"

She seemed to think about that for a moment.

"No, dear," she said with a smile. "I don't think he would."

"Why wouldn't he, Mummy?"

"Because there isn't a war any longer, dear."

"But, Mummy, couldn't God make another war, if he liked?"

"He wouldn't like to, dear. It's not God who makes wars, but bad people."

"Oh!" I said.

I was disappointed about that. I began to think that God wasn't quite what he was cracked up to be.

Next morning I woke at my usual hour, feeling like a bottle of champagne. I put out my feet and invented a long conversation in which Mrs. Right talked of the trouble she had with her own father till she put him in the Home. I didn't quite know what the Home was but it sounded the right place for Father. Then I got my chair and stuck my head out of the attic window. Dawn was just breaking, with a guilty air that made me feel I had caught it in the act. My head bursting with stories and schemes, I stumbled in next door, and in the half-darkness scrambled into the big bed. There was no room at Mother's side so I had to get between her and Father. For the time being I had forgotten about him, and for several minutes I sat bolt upright, racking my brains to know what I could do with him. He was taking up more than his fair share of the bed, and I couldn't get comfortable, so I gave him several kicks that made him grunt and stretch. He made room all right, though. Mother waked and felt for me. I settled back comfortably in the warmth of the bed with my thumb in my mouth.

"Mummy!" I hummed, loudly and contentedly.

"Sssh! dear," she whispered. "Don't wake Daddy!"

This was a new development, which threatened to be even more serious than "talking to Daddy." Life without my early-morning conferences was unthinkable.

"Why?" I asked severely.

"Because poor Daddy is tired."

This seemed to me a quite inadequate reason, and I was sickened by the sentimentality of her "poor Daddy." I never liked that sort of gush; it always struck me as insincere.

"Oh!" I said lightly. Then in my most winning tone: "Do you know where I want to go with you today, Mummy?"

"No, dear," she sighed.

"I want to go down the Glen and fish for thornybacks with my new net, and then I want to go out to the Fox and Hounds, and—"

"Don't-wake-Daddy!" she hissed angrily, clapping her hand across my mouth.

But it was too late. He was awake, or nearly so. He grunted and reached for the matches. Then he stared incredulously at his watch.

"Like a cup of tea, dear?" asked Mother in a meek, hushed voice I had never heard her use before. It sounded almost as though she were afraid.

"Tea?" he exclaimed indignantly. "Do you know what the time is?"

"And after that I want to go up the Rathcooney Road," I said loudly, afraid I'd forget something in all those interruptions.

"Go to sleep at once, Larry!" she said sharply.

I began to snivel. I couldn't concentrate, the way that pair went on, and smothering my early-morning schemes was like burying a family from the cradle.

Father said nothing, but lit his pipe and sucked it, looking out into the shadows without minding Mother or me. I knew he was mad. Every time I made a remark Mother hushed me irritably. I was mortified. I felt it wasn't fair; there was even something sinister in it. Every time I had pointed out to her the waste of making two beds when we could both sleep in one, she had told me it was healthier like that, and now here was this man, this stranger, sleeping with her without the least regard for her health!

He got up early and made tea, but though he brought Mother a cup he brought none for me.

"Mummy," I shouted, "I want a cup of tea, too."

"Yes, dear," she said patiently. "You can drink from Mummy's saucer."

That settled it. Either Father or I would have to leave the house. I didn't want to drink from Mother's saucer; I wanted to be treated as an equal in my own home, so, just to spite her, I drank it all and left none for her. She took that quietly, too.

But that night when she was putting me to bed she said gently: "Larry, I want you to promise me something."

"What is it?" I asked.

"Not to come in and disturb poor Daddy in the morning. Promise?"

"Poor Daddy" again! I was becoming suspicious of everything involving that quite impossible man.

"Why?" I asked.

"Because poor Daddy is worried and tired and he doesn't sleep well."

"Why doesn't he, Mummy?"

"Well, you know, don't you, that while he was at the war Mummy got the pennies from the Post Office?"

"From Miss MacCarthy?"

"That's right. But now, you see, Miss MacCarthy hasn't any more pennies, so Daddy must go out and find us some. You know what would happen if he couldn't?"

"No," I said, "tell us."

"Well, I think we might have to go out and beg for them like the poor old woman on Fridays. We wouldn't like that, would we?"

"No," I agreed. "We wouldn't."

"So you'll promise not to come in and wake him?"

"Promise."

Mind you, I meant that. I knew pennies were a serious matter, and I was all against having to go out and beg like the old woman on Fridays. Mother laid out all my toys in a complete ring round the bed so that, whatever way I got out, I was bound to fall over one of them.

When I woke I remembered my promise all right. I got up and sat on the floor and played—for hours, it seemed to me. Then I got my chair and looked out the attic window for more hours. I wished it was time for Father to wake; I wished someone would make me a cup of tea. I didn't feel in the least like the sun; instead, I was bored and so very, very cold! I simply longed for the warmth and depth of the big featherbed.

At last I could stand it no longer. I went into the next room. As there was still no room at Mother's side I climbed over her and she woke with a start.

"Larry," she whispered, gripping my arm very tightly, "what did you promise?"

"But I did, Mummy," I wailed, caught in the very act. "I was quiet for ever so long."

"Oh, dear, and you're perished!" she said sadly, feeling me all over. "Now, if I let you stay will you promise not to talk?"

"But I want to talk, Mummy," I wailed.

"That has nothing to do with it," she said with a firmness that was new to me. "Daddy wants to sleep. Now, do you understand that?"

I understood it only too well. I wanted to talk, he wanted to sleep—whose house was it, anyway?

"Mummy," I said with equal firmness, "I think it would be healthier for Daddy to sleep in his own bed."

That seemed to stagger her, because she said nothing for a while.

"Now, once for all," she went on, "you're to be perfectly quiet or go back to your own bed. Which is it to be?"

The injustice of it got me down. I had convicted her out of her own mouth of inconsistency and unreasonableness, and she hadn't even attempted to reply. Full of spite, I gave Father a kick, which she didn't notice but which made him grunt and open his eyes in alarm.

"What time is it?" he asked in a panic-stricken voice, not looking at Mother but the door, as if he saw someone there.

"It's early yet," she replied soothingly. "It's only the child. Go to sleep again. . . . Now, Larry," she added, getting out of bed, "you've wakened Daddy and you must go back."

This time, for all her quiet air, I knew she meant it, and knew that my principal rights and privileges were as good as lost unless I asserted them at once. As she lifted me, I gave a screech, enough to wake the dead, not to mind Father. He groaned.

"That damn child! Doesn't he ever sleep?"

"It's only a habit, dear," she said quietly, though I could see she was vexed.

"Well, it's time he got out of it," shouted Father, beginning to heave in the bed. He suddenly gathered all the bedclothes about him, turned to the wall, and then looked back over his shoulder with nothing showing only two small, spiteful, dark eyes. The man looked very wicked.

To open the bedroom door, Mother had to let me down, and I broke free and dashed for the farthest corner, screeching. Father sat bolt upright in bed.

"Shut up, you little puppy!" he said in a choking voice.

I was so astonished that I stopped screeching. Never, never had anyone spoken to me in that tone before. I looked at him incredulously and saw his face convulsed with rage. It was only then that I fully realized how God had codded me, listening to my prayers for the safe return of this monster.

"Shut up, you!" I bawled, beside myself.

"What's that you said?" shouted Father, making a wild leap out of bed.

"Mick, Mick!" cried Mother. "Don't you see the child isn't used to you?"

"I see he's better fed than taught," snarled Father, waving his arms wildly. "He wants his bottom smacked."

All his previous shouting was as nothing to these obscene words referring to my person. They really made my blood boil.

"Smack your own!" I screamed hysterically. "Smack your own! Shut up! Shut up!"

At this he lost his patience and let fly at me. He did it with the lack of conviction you'd expect of a man under Mother's horrified eyes, and it ended up as a mere tap, but the sheer indignity of being struck at all by a stranger, a total stranger who had cajoled his way back from the war into our big bed as a result of my innocent intercession, made me completely dotty. I shrieked and shrieked, and danced in my bare feet, and Father, looking awkward and hairy in nothing but a short grey army shirt, glared down at me like a

mountain out for murder. I think it must have been then that I realized he was jealous too. And there stood Mother in her nightdress, looking as if her heart was broken between us. I hoped she felt as she looked. It seemed to me that she deserved it all.

From that morning out my life was a hell. Father and I were enemies, open and avowed. We conducted a series of skirmishes against one another, he trying to steal my time with Mother and I his. When she was sitting on my bed, telling me a story, he took to looking for some pair of old boots which he alleged he had left behind him at the beginning of the war. While he talked to Mother I played loudly with my toys to show my total lack of concern. He created a terrible scene one evening when he came in from work and found me at his box, playing with his regimental badges, Gurkha knives and buttonsticks. Mother got up and took the box from me.

"You mustn't play with Daddy's toys unless he lets you, Larry," she said severely. "Daddy doesn't play with yours."

For some reason Father looked at her as if she had struck him and then turned away with a scowl.

"Those are not toys," he growled, taking down the box again to see had I lifted anything. "Some of those curios are very rare and valuable."

But as time went on I saw more and more how he managed to alienate Mother and me. What made it worse was that I couldn't grasp his method or see what attraction he had for Mother. In every possible way he was less winning than I. He had a common accent and made noises at his tea. I thought for a while that it might be the newspapers she was interested in, so I made up bits of news of my own to read to her. Then I thought it might be the smoking, which I personally thought attractive, and took his pipes and went round the house dribbling into them till he caught me. I even made noises at my tea, but Mother only told me I was disgusting. It all seemed to hinge round that unhealthy habit of sleeping together, so I made a point of dropping into their bedroom and nosing round, talking to myself, so that they wouldn't know I was watching them, but they were never up to anything that I could see. In the end it beat me. It seemed to depend on being grownup and giving people rings, and I realized I'd have to wait.

But at the same time I wanted him to see that I was only waiting, not giving up the fight. One evening when he was being particularly obnoxious, chattering away and well above my head, I let him have it.

"Mummy," I said, "do you know what I'm going to do when I grow up?"

"No, dear," she replied. "What?"

"I'm going to marry you," I said quietly.

Father gave a great guffaw out of him, but he didn't take me in. I knew it must only be pretense. And Mother, in spite of everything was pleased. I felt she was probably relieved to know that one day Father's hold on her would be broken.

"Won't that be nice?" she said with a smile.

"It'll be very nice," I said confidently. "Because we're going to have lots and lots of babies."

"That's right, dear," she said placidly. "I think we'll have one soon, and then you'll have plenty of company."

I was no end pleased about that because it showed that in spite of the way she gave in to Father she still considered my wishes. Besides, it would put the Geneys in their place.

It didn't turn out like that, though. To begin with, she was very preoccupied—I supposed about where she would get the seventeen and six—and though Father took to staying out late in the evenings it did me no particular good. She stopped taking me for walks, became as touchy as blazes, and smacked me for nothing at all. Sometimes I wished I'd never mentioned the confounded baby—I seemed to have a genius for bringing calamity on myself.

And calamity it was! Sonny arrived in the most appalling hullabaloo—even that much he couldn't do without a fuss—and from the first moment I disliked him. He was a difficult child—so far as I was concerned he was always difficult—and demanded far too much attention. Mother was simply silly about him, and couldn't see when he was only showing off. As company he was worse than useless. He slept all day, and I had to go round the house on tiptoe to avoid waking him. It wasn't any longer a question of not waking Father. The slogan now was "Don't-wake-Sonny!" I couldn't understand why the child wouldn't sleep at the proper time, so whenever Mother's back was turned I woke him. Sometimes to keep him awake I pinched him as well. Mother caught me at it one day and gave me a most unmerciful flaking.

One evening, when Father was coming in from work, I was playing trains in the front garden. I let on not to notice him; instead, I pretended to be talking to myself, and said in a loud voice: "If another bloody baby comes into this house, I'm going out."

Father stopped dead and looked at me over his shoulder.

"What's that you said?" he asked sternly.

"I was only talking to myself," I replied, trying to conceal my panic. "It's private."

He turned and went in without a word. Mind you, I intended it as a solemn warning, but its effect was quite different. Father started being quite nice to me. I could understand that, of course. Mother was quite sickening about Sonny. Even at mealtimes she'd get up and gawk at him in the cradle with an idiotic smile, and tell Father to do the same. He was always polite about it, but he looked so puzzled you could see he didn't know what she was talking about. He complained of the way Sonny cried at night, but she only got cross and said that Sonny never cried except when there was something up with him—which was a flaming lie, because Sonny never had anything up with him, and only cried for attention. It was really painful to see how simple-minded she was. Father wasn't attractive, but he had a fine intelligence. He saw through Sonny, and now he knew that I saw through him as well.

One night I woke with a start. There was someone beside me in the bed. For one wild moment I felt sure it must be Mother, having come to her senses and left Father for good, but then I heard Sonny in convulsions in the next room, and Mother saying: "There! There! There!" and I knew it wasn't she. It was Father. He was lying beside me, wide awake, breathing hard and apparently as mad as hell.

After a while it came to me what he was mad about. It was his turn now. After turning me out of the big bed, he had been turned out himself. Mother had no consideration now for anyone but that poisonous pup, Sonny. I couldn't help feeling sorry for Father. I had been through it all myself, and even at that age I was magnanimous. I began to stroke him down and say: "There! There!" He wasn't exactly responsive.

"Aren't you asleep either?" he snarled.

"Ah, come on and put your arm around us, can't you?" I said, and he did, in a sort of way. Gingerly, I suppose, is how you'd describe it. He was very bony but better than nothing.

At Christmas he went out of his way to buy me a really nice model railway. □□

Discussion

1. What is the basic source of conflict between father and son in O'Connor's story?

2. Much of the humor in this story depends on the narrator's innocence and the irony that stems from his naivete. Give some key examples of this.

3. Comment on the use of a first-person narrator in this story. Why is this more effective than a third-person narrative?

4. What happens when the family triangle is squared by the arrival of Sonny?

5. Nowadays stories that show a healthy family relationship seem to be as rare as humorous stories. This combines both types. **(a)** Comment on the story's effectiveness. **(b)** How appropriate is its title?

Extension • Reading

Read Part I of Frank O'Connor's autobiography, *An Only Child.* Compare and contrast his father's behavior to that of Larry's father in "My Oedipus Complex."

Extension • Writing

1. Reread Elizabeth Bowen's "Tears, Idle Tears," then write an essay in which you compare and contrast Larry and Frederick and their relationships to their mothers.

2. Write a dialogue in which the following people exchange opinions on how to rear children: Larry's father in "My Oedipus Complex," Frederick's mother in "Tears, Idle Tears," and the mother of Lil and Else in "The Doll's House."

Frank O'Connor 1903 • 1966

In his autobiography, *An Only Child*, Frank O'Connor, who was christened Michael O'Donovan, traces his life from his birth in a slum in Cork to his release in 1923 from imprisonment as a revolutionary during the Irish fight for independence. His early life was hard, unhappy, and poverty-stricken, yet he was able to look back on it with humor and compassion—qualities that are dominant in most of his stories.

He had learned Gaelic from his grandmother, and his knowledge of this language enabled him to collaborate with William Butler Yeats on translations of Gaelic poems. He began writing as a boy, but was undecided whether to become a painter or a writer. He abandoned painting, he claimed, because it was too expensive. O'Connor toured Ireland on a bicycle, and this made him intimately acquainted with the manners and speech of the Irish people and provided him with the scenes and subjects for his many stories.

O'Connor served for several years as director of the Abbey Theatre, and became a member of the Irish Academy of Letters. In 1952 he moved permanently to the United States, where he published *The Stories of Frank O'Connor* and other collections, wrote for *The New Yorker*, and taught writing courses at Stanford, Harvard, and Northwestern.

Leslie Norris

Three Shots for Charlie Betson

We moved into this village fifteen years ago, a week before Christmas. Our furniture was taken away in the early morning and we had followed by leisurely train after lunch. It was already dark when we reached Brighton and it was bitterly cold. We got on the bus which was to take us to our new house and we were the only passengers. A wind off the bleak sea came unchecked through the body of the coach and we sat huddled against fatigue and numbing cold in the faulty havens of our greatcoats. It took an hour and a half to reach the village, a distance of only twelve miles.

I couldn't find the key when we arrived at the house, but the back door was open and we tumbled in, regretting that we'd ever heard of the place. But a huge fire was burning in the grate, a loaf of bread and two bottles of milk stood on the kitchen table, and soon we began to recognize our nomadic furniture in its strange corners. I found the key in a briefcase I'd carried with me. I opened the front door and there on the step was a cabbage, a bag of potatoes, and a bunch of mimosa. I couldn't see anyone about and there wasn't a sound. In those days the village street had no lighting and we had no very near neighbors. The school building opposite was merely a dark bulk against a dark sky.

I picked up the vegetables and the mimosa and carried them in to my wife. She was enchanted, warmed by anonymous generosity. We reinforced our hot milk with big slugs of whiskey, made toast by the lovely fire, and went happy to bed. We talked before sleep of the people who had so tactfully welcomed us, because we knew nobody in the village.

Old Bill Francis had done it all himself, trudging sturdily over the three fields between our house and his, but I didn't know that until months later.

The next morning was full of rain and we worked away indoors, eating a sketchy meal about midday. Afterwards, in a break in the rain, I dressed against the weather and went out. I found a cinder path running between two high thorn hedges. It led to a lane very little wider than itself, but properly surfaced and serving a scatter of small houses along its length. A sign called it Crook Lane.

I still hadn't seen anyone since our arrival in the place, and it was a relief to find a man trying to prop open a field gate with a fallen branch.

"Here," said the man, "you've come just in time. Hold the gate open while I drive these cows across the lane and into this other field of mine."

He was a huge old man, his large red face carrying an ample nose. I held the gate and he drove his three amicable heifers across the road and into his other field. The old man was lame, one leg deformed, stiff at the bent knee joint. He came up to me as I closed the gate, looking at me for a long time. He was inspecting me, his expression cheerful and sardonic, his little blue eyes alight and curious.

"Them cows," he said, "they can be real cantankerous, so you came in very handy. Just come to live here, have you?"

I said I had. I pointed across the fields to the roof of my house. It was the first house we'd ever owned.

"Saw your lights come on," said the old man, "last night. You won't stay long, you won't like it here. We're a close lot in this village, keep ourselves to ourselves. No, you won't find it easy in this village, I can tell you. We don't take to strangers."

He was Bill Francis, and he smiled at me with enormous friendship and satisfaction.

"Come down the house," he said, "and have a cup of tea."

He jerked his head toward our house.

"My father used to live in that one," he said, "that house of yours. Pretty as a picture it used to be."

"You'll have hard work of it," he said sternly, "If you want that house to look as it did in my father's day."

We walked together down Crook Lane toward his house. He told me that his brother was a retired sergeant of police, that he himself had more than £3000 in the bank, that he had been very fond of boxing when he was young.

"I loved it, I did," he said. His great wide laughter rang in the empty lane. "I liked nothing better of a Sunday morning than to get the gloves on with a good boy and to belt ourselves tired. Many's the time I've come home with my face swollen up twice its size."

He shook his large head sadly.

"My wife didn't like it though," he said. "She didn't like it, and in the end I gave it up. She's been dead now these five years, a lovely woman she was."

Bill Francis's garden was a delight. Although it was winter, there was about it an air of plenty: it seemed merely awaiting some signal to blossom into miraculous fecundity. It was an artist's garden; not only was it immaculately neat, but it's proportions were immediately satisfying, the branches of his apple trees pruned so that they made clear and perfect shapes in the air, the patterns of his flower beds coherent and full of interest. Bill's house was the same, the furniture good and glowingly cared for. The cups we drank from were old, fragile, very beautiful.

It became a habit for me to walk across the cinder path in the afternoons, unless I was into something very important, to hold open old Bill's gate and walk on down to have a cup of tea with him. Years later, when he was in his eighties and grown frail, I used to go over and see to his heifers myself. He always had two or three running on, to sell when they were down-calving. I liked him.

It was inevitable that I should have come across the Betsons sooner or later, for they were so large a family that everyone in the village was in some way or other connected with them. Physically, too, they were so positive and vigorous that it would have been impossible to ignore them. I'd seen the children, without knowing who they were, on their way to school. They walked up the road as far as my garden wall, silent, tall boys, very fair and upright, and crossed over the road there. There must have been half a dozen of them—in fact, there were seven, and now that I put my mind to it I can give a name to every one of them. They never laughed or played and they ranged between six years old and fifteen.

A busy main road ran the straggling length of the village and I was often anxious about the safety of children as they went to and from the school, but not the Betsons. Casually and with dignity they walked, crossing the road when it was absolutely clear. The youngest boys were the children of the two Betson sisters, but I didn't know that. None of them spoke to me, nor did they show they were aware of me as I began, in the drier afternoons, to set my garden to rights. Lord, how they must have laughed in the village as I cut, tore, and burned. I killed a long bank of Albertine roses, the pride of the garden, through pure ignorance.

Occasionally, if it was too cold for digging, or if I was thinking of something, I'd cut through the school playground and over a couple of fields. A small river ran through a shallow valley there, and the light was so clear it gave the heart a lift even on intransigent days. Often, wild ducks flew honking over the water, or landed noisily, feathering the surface with their braced feet. It's all built over now. Everything changes.

One afternoon I walked through the school fields as the older boys were playing football. I'd not long given up playing myself, had played for good clubs. I walked through the intent boys as a high ball came upfield in an inviting parabola, made entirely for me. I was rising to it in an instinct of joy, neck and shoulders taut, knowing my forehead would meet the ball perfectly. Out of the corner of my eye I saw someone come up with me, and I turned slightly so that my shoulder would smother out impact. Even so he almost got the ball before me. Amused and ashamed, I challenged more fiercely than was at all necessary. Hell, I wasn't even supposed to be playing. But the boy dropped cleverly away, landing easily and breaking at once into his stride. He was the biggest of the fair Betson boys I'd seen, he was Charlie Betson.

Hodges, the schoolmaster, came over, a round, gentle, smiling man, the most comfortable looking man I've ever known. When I think of him now I see his dark, smooth face and imagine him with a pipe in his mouth. In reality, he didn't smoke at all, I got to know him well before he moved away to a bigger school in Lancashire. He's dead now, died unnecessarily in a stupid car smash, in fog, about three years back.

"That was nicely done," he said. "I wish I were able to get up like that, but I was never a games player."

I grinned at him. He was about my own age, couldn't have been much more.

"I hope you didn't mind," I said. "I'm just passing through to the river."

"No trouble," he said. "It's a public footpath anyway."

I walked on and was climbing the stile when he called me.

It turned out that he was the only man on the staff of that small school, his colleagues being two elderly ladies who taught the younger children, and he felt the boys were not getting the games coaching he would have liked. In the end I said I'd go across once a week and take the bigger boys for football. I did it for almost ten years. It helped to keep me fit and I used to enjoy showing off. Old Bill Francis, who was on the school committee, was delighted with me.

I've never seen another boy with such quick and accurate reflexes as Charlie Betson. He was already taller than I am, but very thin, as some adolescent boys are. He could kick a ball with either foot without thinking, he could catch marvelously well. I thought I had found a great player in the making, but it was all physical. He hadn't an idea in his head. It took me some time to realize this, since Charlie was so shy he didn't speak to me. I talked to Hodges about him.

"The Betsons are all the same," he said. "I've had dozens of them in the school, and Charlie is the archetypal Betson. Beautiful to look at, quiet and hardworking, but stupid. Charlie, for example, can't read at all. He's had special tutoring for years, but he gets nowhere."

Not long after this I was in my garden when Charlie looked over the wall. I asked him in. In about two minutes it became obvious that Charlie knew more about gardening than I ever would. He came to work for me on Saturday mornings and I taught him to read out of seed catalogues.

Spring comes early to this part of the country, and it was particularly lovely that year, the first year we lived in the village. Toward the end of April, the sun already warm, cuckoos shouting, I was in Crook Lane talking to Bill Francis. It was Sunday, and the church bells were floating their traditional messages over the fields. My wife's birthday was that day, and I'd mentioned this to Bill some days earlier.

"Why, that'll be Primrose Sunday, look," he'd said, "a good day for a birthday."

I had only laughed, but that morning we found a small bunch of primroses on the doorstep, in an exquisite tiny jug. Afterwards he never forgot her birthday, never failed to leave her such a gift. We have the jugs still. We used to find it very moving, imagining his enormous hands plucking with such delicacy among the threadlike stalks of the flowers, placing them artfully with a few of their puckered leaves in the little jugs. I went over to tell Bill of her delight, and we carried on talking in the renewing warmth.

But something drew Bill's attention as we spoke. He looked down the lane, an expression at once stern, surprised, and disapproving on his face. I turned to see what could have caused this. A strange little procession was moving toward us, ceremonious, quiet, celebrating ritually, it seemed, the spring of the year.

A group of young Betsons, tall and silent, were walking up the lane toward us, the smaller boys forming the erratic edges of the party. The older fellows, those who were at work and whom I had not seen before, were carrying on their shoulders a simple throne, adapted from a wooden armchair. Chestnut poles were fastened to clamps on each side of the chair, and the young men held the poles on their strong shoulders, their identical golden heads tilted away. They walked in unison, easily, unconcernedly. There was something noble in the way they walked, theirs was a willing submission.

Seated up in the chair, a plaid blanket neatly over his knees, was an old man. Up high there, his head above the uncut hedges, he had accepted his elevation as entirely natural. He wore an old hat, and a thick scarf, its ends tucked into his coat, was crossed over his chest. As he passed us, the old man lifted a hand in greeting. He was completely at ease, relaxed as if he were sitting at his own fireside. He smiled directly at Bill Francis and his smile was full and subtle, as amused and meaningful as an hour of speech.

"Bill," he said.

His voice was deep, gentle, and mocking. Bill Francis stood unmoving at my side, the corners of his mouth pulled down and his face stony. He nodded once, a brisk hard butt of the head, in response to the old man's greeting. The old man was very ill. Long gray hair hung below his hat and lay on his pale cheeks. The skin of his face was thick and coarse, pitted and lumped like the skin of an orange. He was obviously the father of the tribe, the patriarch Betson. Nobody else said a word, not even Charlie. As they passed us, Charlie took his place among the bearers, moving in to relieve one of his brothers. I could feel his eyes slide remotely away from me. Behind the men two or three little girls quarreled and scrambled along. These were the old man's granddaughters. The only one of his daughters I ever knew was Sarah Betson, a great slashing creature tall as an Amazon, two or three years older than Charlie. She moved away to London when she was nineteen, came home at Christmas for a few years and walked through the village in her vivid clothes before disappearing from our lives forever. Facially she was very like Charlie, but bolder and more confident.

We watched Mr. Betson and his splendid phalanx around the bend in the lane. He turned once and waved a hand from his dipping throne as he went, and old Bill Francis breathed deeply through his nose.

"Them owdacious Betsons," he said, his disapproval palpable. "There always have been Betsons in this village, and by the look of it there always will be."

I thought it admirable that his sons should take the sick old man out in his carried chair in the first good sun of the year, and I said so. I was shocked at Bill Francis's anger. He turned on me, fairly hissing, white spittle on his lower lip, two hectic lights on his cheekbones.

"You ain't been here long enough to know anything," he said, "and you ain't got enough sense to look about you. While the Betsons increase and flourish, what's happening to the decent people, eh? What's to happen to the decent people, just think of that!"

He wheeled like a great ship of state and marched solemnly away. He didn't ask me down to his house. That was the only time we ever approached a disagreement.

In the summer Mr. Betson died, in great agony. Charlie left school and went to work on one of the farms. I didn't see him often, and when I did it would be on a Saturday, or on some holiday, when he'd be dressed in his finery. He grew rapidly. Tall when I first knew him, he was well over six feet by the time he was seventeen, and he walked like a guardsman. Colonel Fletcher gave Charlie one of his Labradors. Sometimes I'd see him at a distance, walking one of the hedges with his dog, a gun under his arm. He was great on rabbits, was Charlie, fast, cool, invariably accurate.

One Friday afternoon I heard a frightening scream of brakes outside the house. I was in the kitchen. I put down a cup so slowly and carefully that I was driven to anger by my cautious body, and then I ran outside. Two little girls were clinging together against the wall, their voices inhumanly high as they shrieked. A truck, heavily loaded with timber, was stopped halfway across the road, it's front wheels wrenched at a despairing angle, and a little brown dog lay near the offside wheel. It was pitifully broken, blood and fragments of bone everywhere, but it was still alive. I knew the little girls. They were sisters who lived higher up the village and they owned the dog. I ran toward them, not knowing what to do, and held them in my arms. The young driver was getting out of his cab. He was white and shaking, his mouth opening and shutting without words. Everything seemed to be happening slowly and with a dreadful clarity. I could see Charlie Betson leaping over the gate on the other side of the road, landing lightly, his face expressionless and remote.

"Take the little girls away," he said to me. "Take them into your house. I'll see to this."

As we went inside I heard the crack of Charlie's gun, but I don't think the girls did. Children are remarkable, so resilient. Those little girls were shocked and genuinely heartbroken, and they sobbed for an hour, but afterward they ate a good meal with us and we played a riotous game of cards before we took them home. The road was clean, all evidence of the small tragedy washed and swept away. The kids' parents were out, I remember, and we had to leave them with a neighbor. I've not thought of it for years. It happened the year Bill Francis took to his bed and I became a member of the parish council in his place.

Charlie moved from the village when he got married. His wife came from a little place about ten miles away and they found a house there. I saw them together once or twice, Charlie and his wife, and they looked marvelous. She was a tall girl, athletic and fair, with an open smiling face, a generous face. They had two children quite quickly. I was amused to think of Charlie suddenly so mature and responsible. Time goes, of course; I had not seen the sudden quickening of the years.

Last year, in June, I awoke very early one morning. I sleep less and less these days, and most mornings I'm alert by seven o'clock. But that day I was up and padding about before five. About six-thirty I walked up the village looking for something to do. We've a new recreation ground, and I turned in there. The place has grown a lot during the last few years, new houses, new young people, and somehow it was decided that we ought to have a recreation field: tennis courts, football fields, swings and roundabouts for the little ones, the lot. I'm on the committee for the provision of this field, and I thought I might look at what progress was being made.

The place lies behind houses and there's a drive of about a hundred and fifty yards to reach it. The work had been nicely done, and I walked along admiring the rolled surface, the neat fencing. A little parking lot stands at the end of the drive, next to the hard courts, and a car was already there. I assumed that it belonged to someone living nearby, that it had been left there overnight. I began to walk along the field's boundary, near the hedge. The light dew was almost off the grass and cuttings from the mower were dry and flaky on the surface, although you could still see where a bird had disturbed the direction of the grass earlier. I hadn't gone far when I heard a shout. Someone climbed out of the parked car and waved to me. It was Charlie Betson. He came up to me, grinning.

At first I thought there was something wrong with him, but he was all right. He was very thin and he walked loosely, arms dangling and feet planting themselves aimlessly at the end of the irregular strides. He held his head far back, as if to compensate for the loss of his old, controlled, straight-backed dignity. This worried me for a while, but he spoke well and naturally, telling me of his job. He was felling a stand of beech on an estate some miles away; I knew the trees well. We walked along the mixed hedge at the end of the field, blackthorn mainly, with a bit of scrub oak and some maple, and we heard something rustling on the other side.

"Heron," said Charlie, "that's a heron in the wet ditch. There's always one there, between the old gravel pond and the mill. Good picking in the ditch for herons, plenty of frogs and that."

He smiled.

"My old dad," he said, "told me about him when I was small. Finest poacher in the country was my dad, and he told me about the heron. There was one in the ditch when he was a boy, and I reckon there always will be one. After my day, I expect."

We poked a branch through the hedge and the long heron rose slowly, his legs trailing, and flew toward the mill. We watched him go.

"What was between your father," I asked carefully, "and Bill Francis?"

"Well," said Charlie, "much of an age, weren't they? Went to school together, grew up together, young men together. Bill Francis could beat my dad all along the line. He was stronger, he could fight better, people liked him more. And even with a gun, why, Bill could always beat my dad. Best shot I ever see was Bill Francis. My dad always gave him credit. Rivals, they were."

He cocked an amused eye down at me.

"Of course," he said, "in the end, my father won."

"How's that?" I said.

"We've always been here," said Charlie, "Betson and Francis. Those are the true names in this village. My father had nine boys, counting Archie who got killed in the war; Bill Francis never had any. There ain't no Francis left."

We walked quietly back down the field.

"Old Bill liked you, didn't he?" asked Charlie.

"He did," I said. "He wanted to leave me his fields."

"Yeah, well," Charlie picked up a stone and flung it away, "understandable, that is. You should have let him. You're about the same age as my oldest brother."

We reached his car and I looked inside. It was perfectly neat and clean, Charlie's racing paper open on the seat the one untidy object.

"It's the wife," said Charlie. "She cleans everything, car, house, kids, me . . . there's no rest."

"Charlie," I said, "why are you down here so early? It's not seven o'clock."

He lowered his head, suddenly heavy and obstinate. The skin of his face was thickening and coarsening as his father's had, and deep folds were appearing at the sides of his nose and under his cheekbones. When he looked up, I saw that his teeth were lined and spotted.

He got into the car and picked up his paper, folding it uneasily. I could see in him so clearly the silent, shy boy he had been.

"It's quieter," he said. "It's much quieter. I get up most mornings and go on down to my mother's for breakfast. Then I bring the paper up here and pick a few winners."

He sat there uncomfortably, as if he didn't care, his face sad and heavy, looking at something far away.

"You don't know what it's like," he said, "living somewhere else. Do you know who lives next door to me? Gypsies, that's who. And it's the same everywhere, all strangers. Down here, it's quieter and I know everybody. My family, and that. It's nicer."

I didn't say anything.

"It's lovely here," said Charlie, "in the morning, in the early morning."

"What are your runners today?" I said loudly. "What do you fancy?"

He began to read some names out of his paper.

"Is there a gray in the big race?" I said.

I was wasting time. I would have been glad to leave. I wanted some neat conclusion to our meeting.

"You like grays?" Charlie asked.

"Yes," I said. "A couple of years ago I went to a breeding stables in Yorkshire where they had a gray stallion. Abernant was his name—he had a lot of gray offspring, you couldn't miss them. Beautiful size, wonderful clean round bone and such neat intelligent heads. Good stuff, they were."

Charlie laughed. The life was back in his eyes.

"You don't want to bother about color," he said. "A good horse is never a bad color. I'll be better off picking my own winners."

I went away down the road, The morning was beautiful, the afternoon cloudless and very hot. About eight that evening, as a small, cool wind began, Charlie came into the garden. He was waving a thin bundle of notes.

"Here you are," he called. "Two pounds at eight to one, that's sixteen pounds!"

He was delighted with himself.

"What's all this?" I said.

I was astonished at the change in Charlie. He was inches taller than he had been that morning, he moved with all his remembered certainty and assurance.

"I put two pounds on the gray for you," he said, "and five for myself. We've had a good day."

"What gray?" I said, bewildered.

"Ah, you're a sly one," he said. "You're as cunning as a cartload. You knew all the time a gray by Abernant was going in that race. Well, you've done us both a bit of good."

He pushed the notes at me.

"I can't take these, Charlie," I said. "Give them to the children."

"They're yours," he said, roughly. "The kids get plenty. Take the money—if the horse had lost I'd have been around here for the two pounds stake, don't worry."

"If you're sure," I said.

I took the money from him and at once he moved away, waving as he went. He was full of bounce. I wondered how, that morning, I had thought him changed in any way, how anything could have so filled me with false foreboding.

That was the last time I spoke to Charlie.

Last week I heard that Charlie was missing, hadn't been seen for two days. I can't remember how I learned this; by the sort of osmosis that happens in a village, I expect. I was neither surprised nor had I expected this news. I was just filled with an unthinking certainty. As soon as I heard I took the car out and went to the recreation field. I drove through the parking lot and across the field itself, right to the far end. When I got out I was moving very stiffly, as if my body were a strange and intricate mechanism come newly to me. I remember my eyes so tight and stiff that it would have been impossible to blink without single-minded and deliberate effort. I broke through the hedge and the heron got up about fifty yards away. A single flap of his wings turned him into the wind and he vanished over the elms.

Charlie was there, almost at my feet. He was lying quite peacefully, untouched almost, if you didn't look too closely. His gun was at his side, the muzzle under his chest. I slid it out and walked down the ditch. One barrel was still loaded. A pigeon flew up from the noise of my walking and I shot it casually, brought it back, and put it obviously in the field about ten yards from Charlie. Then I placed the gun near his fallen hand. We're a close lot in his village, look after our own. Almost the first thing old Bill Francis said to me, that was.

When I got home, I thought about it, hard. I wasn't shocked, or stunned; I was just completely sad. I'd recognized something in Charlie that last day without knowing it, some intuition had prepared me. I got it all clear in my mind and walked over to the police station. Sergeant Watson is a sensible man, made no fuss, and the official business began.

Yesterday I went to the funeral, simple enough. Charlie's mother asked me. She came up to the house early this week, sat on the edge of a chair, and said that she expected to see me there. The church was full of young men. Charlie's friends, and in front sat a row of Betsons, tall and hard-faced. Afterward Charlie's wife asked me back to his mother's house to have a meal. I thought of refusing, but at her side was Charlie's oldest sister, fair-haried and implacable. The enormous Betson men were already there when I arrived, talking in their quiet, heavy voices. One by one they came up to me, shook my hand, told me that Charlie had spoken of me often, always boasted of how I had taught him to read.

"He liked you," they said. "Charlie liked you. He always gave you credit."

I sat there, my plate on my knee, drinking the strong, hot tea. After a while Charlie's mother came over. She was a very old lady and she sat silent and upright opposite me. I tried to tell her that it had been a good occasion, that Charlie would have been glad to know that so many of his friends had come to wish him goodbye. Her face was calm and without expression, but there was that in her eyes which would not be comforted.

"He was a good boy," she said, "but he was lost. He needed safety. All my boys need safety, like their father before them. People think when they see my lovely boys, strong and proud, that nothing could every worry them. But it's not true."

One of the daughters stood by the table warily, listening carefully.

"When Archie went to the war," said Mrs. Betson, "when he was eighteen, the oldest of them. I watched him going nearly mad away from us. My boys need to be in the fields about us, nearby, where their father walked before them, where they feel safe. They need a house where their brothers are only a shout away and there's food and drink without fuss, any time of the day or night."

The room was very still. Charlie's brothers, listening uncomfortably to their mother's unlikely eloquence, stared blankly about.

"I knew he was going lost," said Mrs. Betson. "I knew Charlie was going lost when he started coming over here every morning, six o'clock, five o'clock. He never went to Brighton, did you know that? In all his life Charlie never went as far away as Brighton."

The sisters began to move about, making things orderly. They gave tea and food to brothers and nephews, they arranged them in little groups, they sent them into the garden to walk between the rows of beans and potatoes. The world began to look safe and normal.

"We won't forget what you've done," said Mrs. Betson. "We've guessed what you've done, and we shan't forget it."

I stood up and said goodbye. The whole house was suddenly more cheerful and brisk, the day brighter. One or two of the men lifted a hand to me as I left, but most of them smoked and talked together, ignoring me.

And all day I've sat here in the garden thinking of the handsome Betson men, golden as Vikings, walking safe in the little world of our one street and its handful of fields. I thought of Charlie, who might be dead because he had left that simple and limited world for one where he had been forced to make decisions and live in a frightening freedom. But most of all I've been thinking of old Bill Francis, who had spent his life watching over the village and who hadn't any sons at all. □□

Discussion

1. Create a portrait of Charlie Betson from the following incidents: the narrator's encounter with him on the soccer field; the conversation between the narrator and the schoolmaster; the small dog's death; and the winning bet on a gray horse.

2. **(a)** What do we learn about the Betson family from the scene where the young members carry the old Betson "on a simple throne"? **(b)** Why does Bill Francis comment disapprovingly, "There always were Betsons in this village, and by the look of it there always will be"?

3. Mrs. Betson tells the narrator, "We've guessed what you've done, and we shan't forget it." What does she mean?

4. Charlie Betson has strong senses of identity and belonging. How then do you explain his tragic end?

Leslie Norris 1921 •

Poet, short-story writer, and teacher, Leslie Norris was born and reared in the industrial town of Merthyr in South Wales. Merthyr has a strong literary tradition and Norris was encouraged to write in school from an early age. Much of his material is drawn from the surrounding rural areas, which are among the most scenic in Wales, through which he roamed as a schoolboy.

During World War II Norris served in the Royal Air Force. Since 1949 he has taught at various English universities and has been a visiting professor of English at the University of Washington, Seattle.

Norris has written several volumes of poetry—his most popular poem being "The Ballad of Billy Rose," a moving tribute to a blind boxer. Apart from his poetry, short stories, and radio plays, he has translated poetry from medieval Welsh. In all his works he blends compassion and intelligence with a gift for sharp observation.

Elizabeth Jane Howard

Three Miles Up

There was absolutely nothing like it.

An unoriginal conclusion, and one that he had drawn a hundred times during the last fortnight. Clifford would make some subtle and intelligent comparison, but he, John, could only continue to repeat that it was quite unlike anything else. It had been Clifford's idea, which, considering Clifford, was surprising. When you looked at him, you would not suppose him capable of it. However, John reflected, he had been ill, some sort of breakdown these clever people went in for, and that might account for his uncharacteristic idea of hiring a boat and travelling on canals. On the whole, John had to admit, it was a good idea. He had never been on a canal in his life, although he had been in almost every kind of boat, and thought he knew a good deal about them; so much, indeed, that he had embarked on the venture in a light-hearted, almost a patronizing manner. But it was not nearly as simple as he had imagined. Clifford, of course, knew nothing about boats; but he had admitted that almost everything had gone wrong with a kind of devilish versatility which had almost frightened him. However, that was all over, and John, who had learned painfully all about the boat and her engine, felt that the former at least had run her gamut of disaster. They had run out of food, out of petrol, and out of water; had dropped their windlass into the deepest lock, and, more humiliating, their boathook into the side-pond. The head had come off the hammer. They had been disturbed for one whole night by a curious rustling in the cabin, like a rat in a paper bag, when there was no paper, and, so far as they knew, no rat. The battery had failed and had to be recharged. Clifford had put his elbow through an already cracked window in the cabin. A large piece of rope had wound itself round the propeller with a malignant intensity which required three men and half a morning to unravel. And so on, until now there was really nothing left to go wrong, unless one of them drowned, and surely it was impossible to drown in a canal.

"I suppose one might easily drown in a lock?" he asked aloud.

"We must be careful not to fall into one," Clifford replied.

"What?" John steered with fierce concentration, and never heard anything people said to him for the first time, almost on principle.

"I said we must be careful not to fall *into* a lock."

"Oh. Well there aren't any more now until after the Junction. Anyway, we haven't yet, so there's really no reason why we should start now. I only wanted to know whether we'd drown if we did."

"Sharon might."

"What?"

"Sharon might."

"Better warn her then. She seems agile enough." His concentrated frown returned, and he settled down again to the wheel. John didn't mind where they went, or what happened, so long as he handled the boat, and all things considered, he handled her remarkably well. Clifford planned and John steered: and until two days ago they had both quarrelled and argued over a smoking and unusually temperamental primus. Which reminded Clifford of Sharon. Her advent and the weather were really their two unadulterated strokes of good fortune. There had been no rain, and Sharon had, as it were, dropped from the blue on to the boat, where she speedily restored domestic order, stimulated evening conversation, and touched the whole venture with her attractive being: the requisite number of miles each day were achieved, the boat behaved herself, and admirable meals were steadily and regularly prepared. She had, in fact, identified herself with the journey, without making the slightest effort to control it: a talent which many women were supposed in theory to possess, when, in fact, Clifford reflected gloomily, most of them were bored with the whole thing, or tried to dominate it.

Her advent was a remarkable, almost a miraculous, piece of luck. He had, after a particularly ill-fed day, and their failure to dine at a small hotel, desperately telephoned all the women he knew who seemed in the least suitable (and they were surprisingly few), with no success. They had spent a miserable evening, John determined to argue about everything, and he, Clifford, refusing to speak; until, both in a fine state of emotional tension, they had turned in for the night. While John snored, Clifford had lain distraught, his resentment and despair circling round John and then touching his own smallest and most random thoughts; until his mind found no refuge and he was left, divided from it, hostile and afraid, watching it in terror racing on in the dark like some malignant machine utterly out of his control.

The next day things had proved no better between them, and they had continued throughout the morning in a silence which was only occasionally and elaborately broken. They had tied up for lunch beside a wood, which hung heavy and magnificent over the canal. There was a small clearing beside which John then proposed to moor, but Clifford failed to achieve the considerable leap necessary to stop the boat; and they had drifted helplessly past it. John flung him a line, but it was not until the boat was secured, and they were safely in the cabin, that the storm had broken. John, in attempting to light the primus, spilt a quantity of paraffin on Clifford's bunk. Instantly all his despair of the previous evening had contracted. He hated John so much that he could have murdered him. They both lost their tempers, and for the ensuing hour and a half had conducted a blazing quarrel which, even at the time, secretly horrified them both in its intensity.

It had finally ended with John striding out of the cabin, there being no more to say. He had returned almost at once, however.

"I say, Clifford. Come and look at this."

"At what?"

"Outside, on the bank."

For some unknown reason Clifford did get up and did look. Lying face downwards quite still on the ground, with her arms clasping the trunk of a large tree, was a girl.

"How long has she been there?"

"She's asleep."

"She can't have been asleep all the time. She must have heard some of what we said."

"Anyway, who is she? What is she doing here?"

Clifford looked at her again. She was wearing a dark twill shirt and dark trousers, and her hair hung over her face, so that it was almost invisible. "I don't know. I suppose she's alive?"

John jumped cautiously ashore. "Yes, she's alive all right. Funny way to lie."

"Well, it's none of our business anyway. Anyone can lie on a bank if they want to."

"Yes, but she must have come in the middle of our row, and it does seem queer to stay, and then go to sleep."

"Extraordinary," said Clifford wearily. Nothing was really extraordinary, he felt, nothing. "Are we moving on?"

"Let's eat first. I'll do it."

"Oh, I'll do it."

The girl stirred, unclasped her arms, and sat up. They had all stared at each other for a moment, the girl slowly pushing the hair from her forehead. Then she had said: "If you will give me a meal, I'll cook it."

Afterwards they had left her to wash up, and had walked about the wood, while Clifford suggested to John that they ask the girl to join them. "I'm sure she'd come," he said. "She didn't seem at all clear about what she was doing."

"We can't just pick somebody up out of a wood," said John, scandalized.

"Where do you suggest we pick them up? If we don't have someone, this holiday will be a failure."

"We don't know anything about her."

"I can't see that that matters very much. She seems to cook well. We can at least ask her."

"All right. Ask her then. She won't come."

When they returned to the boat, she had finished the washing-up, and was sitting on the floor of the cockpit, with her arms stretched

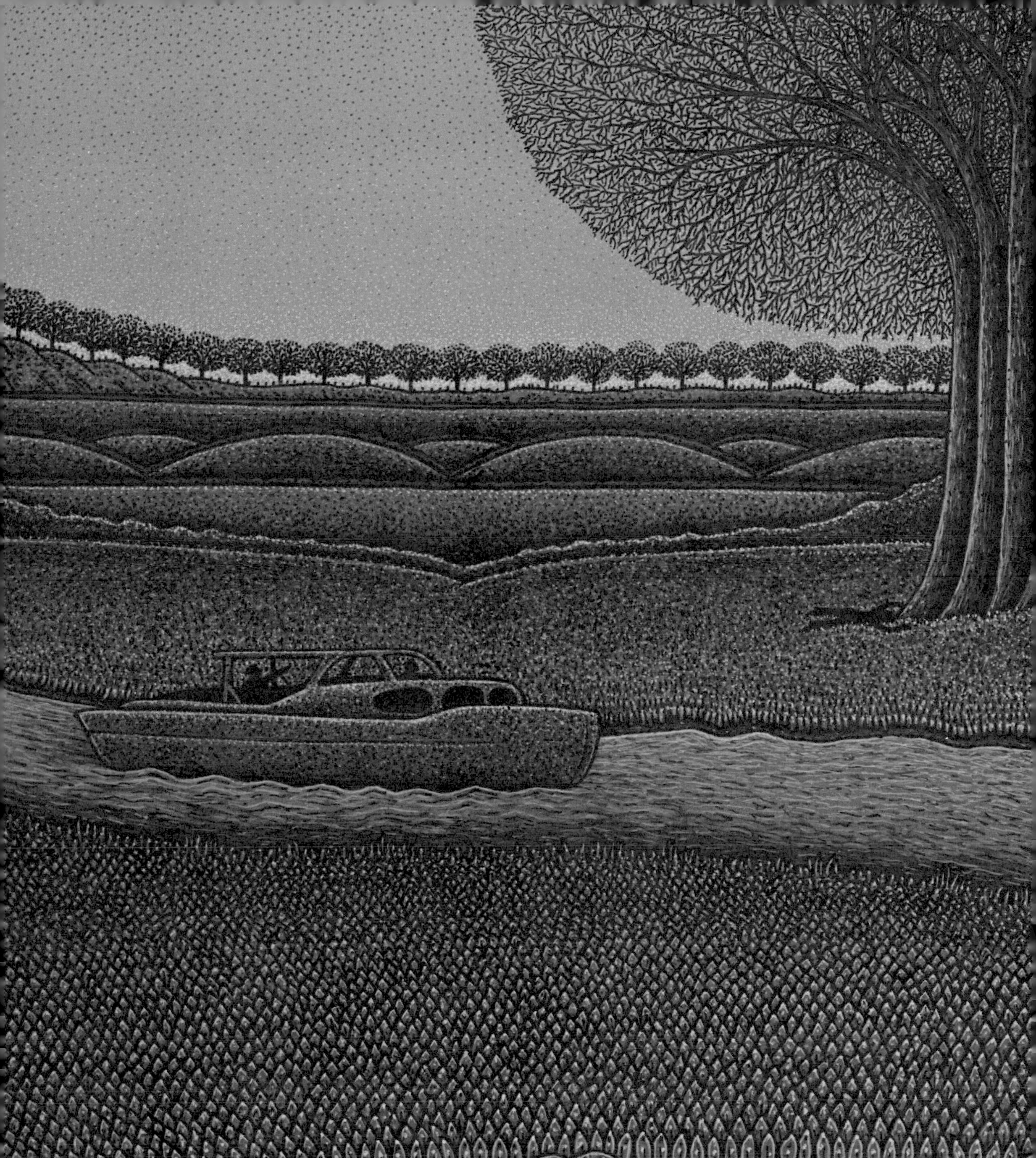

behind her head. Clifford asked her; and she accepted as though she had known them a long time and they were simply inviting her to tea.

"Well, but look here," said John, thoroughly taken aback. "What about your things?"

"My things?" she looked inquiringly and a little defensively from one to the other.

"Clothes and so on. Or haven't you got any? Are you a gipsy or something? Where do you come from?"

"I am not a gipsy," she began patiently; when Clifford, thoroughly embarrassed and ashamed, interrupted her.

"Really, it's none of our business who you are, and there is absolutely no need for us to ask you anything. I'm very glad you will come with us, although I feel we should warn you that we are new to this life, and anything might happen."

"No need to warn me," she said, and smiled gratefully at him.

After that, they both felt bound to ask her nothing; John because he was afraid of being made to look foolish by Clifford, and Clifford because he had stopped John.

"Good Lord, we shall never get rid of her; and she'll fuss about condensation," John had muttered aggressively as he started the engine. But she was very young, and did not fuss about anything. She had told them her name, and settled down, immediately and easily: gentle, assured and unselfconscious to a degree remarkable in one so young. They were never sure how much she had overheard them, for she gave no sign of having heard anything. A friendly but uncommunicative creature.

The map on the engine box started to flap, and immediately John asked, "Where are we?"

"I haven't been watching, I'm afraid. Wait a minute."

"We just passed under a railway bridge," John said helpfully.

"Right. Yes. About four miles from the Junction, I think. What's the time?"

"Five-thirty."

"Which way are we going when we get to the Junction?"

"We haven't time for the big loop. I must be back in London by the fifteenth."

"The alternative is to go up as far as the basin, and then simply turn round and come back, and who wants to do that?"

"Well, we'll know the route then. It'll be much easier coming back."

Clifford did not reply. He was not attracted by the route being easier, and he wanted to complete his original plan.

"Let us wait till we get there." Sharon appeared with tea and marmalade sandwiches.

"All right, let's wait." Clifford was relieved.

"It'll be almost dark by five-thirty. I think we ought to have a plan," John said. "Thank you, Sharon."

"Have tea first." She curled herself on to the floor with her back to the cabin doors and a mug in her hands.

They were passing rows of little houses with gardens that backed on to the canal. They were long narrow strips, streaked with cinder paths, and crowded with vegetables and chicken-huts, fruit trees and perambulators; sometimes ending with fat white ducks, and sometimes in a tiny patch of grass with a bench on it.

"Would you rather keep ducks or sit on a bench?" asked Clifford.

"Keep ducks," said John promptly. "More useful. Sharon wouldn't mind which she did. Would you, Sharon?" He liked saying her name, Clifford noticed. "You could be happy anywhere, couldn't you?" He seemed to be presenting her with the widest possible choice.

"I might *be* anywhere," she answered after a moment's thought.

"Well you happen to be on a canal, and very nice for us."

"In a wood, and then on a canal," she replied contentedly, bending her smooth dark head over her mug.

"Going to be fine tomorrow," said John. He was always a little embarrassed at any mention of how they found her and his subsequent rudeness.

"Yes. I like it when the whole sky is so red and burning and it begins to be cold."

"*Are* you cold?" said John, wanting to worry about it: but she tucked her dark shirt into her trousers and answered composedly:

"Oh no. I am never cold."

They drank their tea in a comfortable silence. Clifford started to read his map, and then said they were almost on to another sheet. "New country," he said with satisfaction. "I've never been here before."

"You make it sound like an exploration; doesn't he, Sharon?" said John.

"Is that a bad thing?" She collected the mugs. "I am going to put these away. You will call me if I am wanted for anything." And she went into the cabin again.

There was a second's pause, a minute tribute to her departure; and, lighting cigarettes, they settled down to stare at the long silent stretch of water ahead.

John thought about Sharon. He thought rather desperately that really they still knew nothing about her, and that when they went back to London they would in all probability never see her again. Perhaps Clifford would fall in love with her, and she would naturally reciprocate, because she was so young and Clifford was reputed to be so fascinating and intelligent, and because women were always foolish and loved the wrong man. He thought all these things with equal intensity, glanced cautiously at Clifford, and supposed he was thinking about her; then wondered what she would be like in London, clad in anything else but her dark trousers and shirt. The engine coughed; and he turned to it in relief.

Clifford was making frantic calculations of time and distance; stretching their time, and diminishing the distance, and groaning that with the utmost optimism they could not be made to fit. He was interrupted by John swearing at the engine, and then for no particular reason he remembered Sharon, and reflected with pleasure how easily she left the mind when she was not present, how she neither obsessed nor possessed one in her absence, but was charming to see.

The sun had almost set when they reached the Junction, and John slowed down to neutral while they made up their minds. To the left was the straight cut which involved the longer journey originally planned; and curving away to the right was the short arm which John advocated. The canal was fringed with rushes, and there was one small cottage with no light in it. Clifford went into the cabin to tell Sharon where they were, and then, as they drifted slowly in the middle of the Junction, John suddenly shouted: "Clifford! What's the third turning?"

"There are only two." Clifford reappeared. "Sharon is busy with dinner."

"No, look. Surely that is another cut."

Clifford stared ahead. "Can't see it."

"Just to the right of the cottage. Look. It's not so dark as all that."

Then Clifford saw it very plainly. It seemed to wind away from the cottage on a fairly steep curve, and the rushes shrouding it from anything but the closest view were taller than the rest.

"Have another look at the map. I'll reverse for a bit."

"Found it. It's just another arm. Probably been abandoned," said Clifford eventually.

The boat had swung round; and now they could see the continuance of the curve dully gleaming ahead, and banked by reeds.

"Well, what shall we do?"

"Getting dark. Let's go up a little way, and moor. Nice quiet mooring."

"With some nice quiet mudbanks," said John grimly. "Nobody uses that."

"How do you know?"

"Well look at it. All those rushes, and it's sure to be thick with weed."

"Don't go up it then. But we shall go aground if we drift about like this."

"*I* don't mind going up it," said John doggedly. "What about Sharon?"

"What about her?"

"Tell her about it."

"We've found a third turning," Clifford called above the noise of the primus through the cabin door.

"One you had not expected?"

"Yes. It looks very wild. We were thinking of going up it."

"Didn't you say you wanted to explore?" she smiled at him.

"You are quite ready to try it? I warn you we shall probably run hard aground. Look out for bumps with the primus."

"I am quite ready, and I am quite sure we shan't run aground," she answered with charming confidence in their skill.

They moved slowly forward in the dusk. Why they didn't run aground, Clifford could not imagine: John really was damned good at it. The canal wound and wound, and the reeds grew not only thick on each bank, but in clumps across the canal. The light drained out of the sky into the water and slowly drowned there; the trees and the banks became heavy and black.

Clifford began to clear things away from the

heavy dew which had begun to rise. After two journeys he remained in the cabin, while John crawled on, alone. Once, on a bend, John thought he saw a range of hills ahead with lights on them, but when he was round the curve and had time to look again he could see no hills: only a dark indeterminate waste of country stretched ahead.

He was beginning to consider the necessity of mooring, when they came to a bridge; and shortly after he saw a dark mass which he took to be houses. When the boat had crawled for another fifty yards or so, he stopped the engine, and drifted in absolute silence to the bank. The houses, about half a dozen of them, were much nearer than he had at first imagined, but there were no lights to be seen. Distance is always deceptive in the dark, he thought, and jumped ashore with a bow line. When, a few minutes later, he took a sounding with the boathook, the water proved unexpectedly deep; and he concluded that by incredible good fortune they had moored at the village wharf. He made everything fast, and joined the others in the cabin with mixed feelings of pride and resentment; that he should have achieved so much under such difficult conditions, and that they (by 'they' he meant Clifford), should have contributed so little towards the achievement. He found Clifford reading *Bradshaw's Guide to the Canals and Navigable Rivers* in one corner and Sharon, with her hair pushed back behind her ears, bending over the primus with a knife. Her ears are pale, exactly the colour of her face, he thought; wanted to touch them; then felt horribly ashamed, and hated Clifford.

"Let's have a look at Bradshaw," he said, as though he had not noticed Clifford reading it.

But Clifford handed him the book in the most friendly manner, remarking that he couldn't see where they were. "In fact you have surpassed yourself with your brilliant navigation. We seem to be miles from anywhere."

"What about your famous ordnance?"

"It's not on any sheet I have. The new one I thought we should use only covers the loop we planned. There is precisely three-quarters of a mile of this canal shown on the present sheet and then we run off the map. I suppose there must once have been trade here, but I cannot imagine what, or where."

"I expect things change," said Sharon. "Here is the meal."

"How can you see to cook?" asked John, eyeing his plate ravenously.

"There is a candle."

"Yes, but we've selfishly appropriated that."

"Should I need more light?" she asked, and looked troubled.

"There's no should about it. I just don't know how you do it, that's all. Chips[1] exactly the right colour, and you never drop anything. It's marvellous."

She smiled a little uncertainly at him and lit another candle. "Luck, probably," she said, and set it on the table.

They ate their meal, and John told them about the mooring. "Some sort of village. I think we're moored at the wharf. I couldn't find any rings without the torch, so I've used the anchor." This small shaft was intended for Clifford, who had dropped the spare torch-battery in the washing-up bowl, and forgotten to buy another. But it was only a small shaft, and immediately afterwards John felt much better. His aggression slowly left him, and he felt nothing but a peaceful and well-fed affection for the other two.

"Extraordinarily cut off this is," he remarked over coffee.

"It's very pleasant in here. Warm, and extremely full of us."

"Yes. I know. A quiet village, though, you must admit."

"I shall believe in your village when I see it."

"Then you would believe it?"

"No he wouldn't, Sharon. Not if he didn't want to, and couldn't find it on the map. That map!"

The conversation turned again to their remoteness, and to how cut off one liked to be and at what point it ceased to be desirable; to boats, telephones, and, finally, canals: which, Clifford maintained, possessed the perfect proportions of urbanity and solitude.

Hours later, when they had turned in for the night, Clifford reviewed the conversation, together with others they had had, and remembered with surprise how little Sharon had actually

1. ***Chips,*** french fried potatoes.

said. She listened to everything and occasionally, when they appealed to her, made some small composed remark which was oddly at variance with their passionate interest. "She has an elusive quality of freshness about her," he thought, "which is neither naive nor stupid nor dull, and she invokes no responsibility. She does not want us to know what she was, or why we found her as we did, and curiously, I, at least, do not want to know. She is what women ought to be," he concluded with sudden pleasure: and slept.

He woke the next morning to find it very late, and stretched out his hand to wake John.

"We've all overslept. Look at the time."

"Good Lord! Better wake Sharon."

Sharon lay between them on the floor, which they had ceded her because, oddly enough, it was the widest and most comfortable bed. She seemed profoundly asleep, but at the mention of her name sat up immediately, and rose, almost as though she had not been asleep at all.

The morning routine, which, involving the clothing of three people and shaving of two of them, was necessarily a long and complicated business, began. Sharon boiled water, and Clifford, grumbling gently, hoisted himself out of his bunk and repaired with a steaming jug to the cockpit. He put the jug on a seat, lifted the canvas awning, and leaned out. It was absolutely grey and still; a little white mist hung over the canal, and the country stretched out desolate and unkempt on every side with no sign of a living creature. The village, he thought; suddenly: John's village: and was possessed of a perilous uncertainty and fear. I am getting worse, he thought, this holiday is doing me no good. I am mad. I imagined that he said we moored by a village wharf. For several seconds he stood gripping the gunwale, and searching desperately for anything, huts, a clump of trees, which could in the darkness have been mistaken for a village. But there was nothing near the boat except tall rank rushes which did not move at all. Then, when his suspense was becoming unbearable, John joined him with another steaming jug of water.

"We shan't get anywhere at this rate," he began; and then . . . "Hullo! Where's my village?"

"I was wondering that," said Clifford. He could almost have wept with relief, and quickly began to shave, deeply ashamed of his private panic.

"Can't understand it," John was saying. It was no joke, Clifford decided, as he listened to his hearty puzzled ruminations.

At breakfast John continued to speculate upon what he had or had not seen, and Sharon listened intently while she filled the coffee-pot and cut bread. Once or twice she met Clifford's eye with a glance of discreet amusement.

"I must be mad, or else the whole place is haunted," finished John comfortably. These two possibilities seemed to relieve him of any further anxiety in the matter, as he ate a huge breakfast and set about greasing the engine.

"Well," said Clifford, when he was alone with Sharon. "What do you make of that?"

"It is easy to be deceived in such matters," she answered perfunctorily.

"Evidently. Still, John is an unlikely candidate, you must admit. Here, I'll help you dry."

"Oh no. It is what I am here for."

"Not entirely, I hope."

"Not entirely." She smiled and relinquished the cloth.

John eventually announced that they were ready to start. Clifford, who had assumed that they were to retrace their journey, was surprised, and a little alarmed, to find John intent upon continuing it. He seemed undeterred by the state of the canal, which, as Clifford immediately pointed out, rendered navigation both arduous and unrewarding. He announced that the harder it was, the more he liked it, adding very firmly, "Anyway we must see what happens."

"We shan't have time to do anything else."

"Thought you wanted to explore."

"I do, but . . . What do you think, Sharon?"

"I think John will have to be a very good navigator to manage that." She indicated the rush- and weed-ridden reach before them. "Do you think it's possible?"

"Of course it's possible. I'll probably need some help though."

"I'll help you," she said.

So on they went.

They made incredibly slow progress. John enjoys showing off his powers to her, thought

Clifford, half amused, half exasperated, as he struggled for the fourth time in an hour to scrape weeds off the propeller.

Sharon eventually retired to cook lunch.

"Surprising amount of water here," John said suddenly.

"Oh?"

"Well, I mean, with all this weed and stuff, you'd expect the canal to have silted up. I'm sure nobody uses it."

"The whole thing is extraordinary."

"Is it too late in the year for birds?" asked Clifford later.

"No, I don't think so. Why?"

"I haven't heard one, have you?"

"Haven't noticed, I'm afraid. There's someone anyway. First sign of life."

An old man stood near the bank watching them. He was dressed in corduroy and wore a straw hat.

"Good morning," shouted John, as they drew nearer.

He made no reply, but inclined his head slightly. He seemed very old. He was leaning on a scythe, and as they drew almost level with him, he turned away and began slowly cutting rushes. A pile of them lay neatly stacked beside him.

"Where does this canal go? Is there a village further on?" Clifford and John asked simultaneously. He seemed not to hear, and as they chugged steadily past, Clifford was about to suggest that they stop and ask again, when he called after them: "Three miles up you'll find the village. Three miles up that is," and turned away to his rushes again.

"Well now we know something, anyway," said John.

"We don't even know what the village is called."

"Soon find out. Only three miles."

"Three miles!" said Clifford darkly. "That might mean anything."

"Do you want to turn back?"

"Oh no, not now. I want to see this village now. My curiosity is thoroughly aroused."

"Shouldn't think there'll be anything to see. Never been in such a wild spot. Look at it."

Clifford looked at it. Half wilderness, half marsh, dank and grey and still, with single trees bare of their leaves; clumps of hawthorn that might once have been hedge, sparse and sharp with berries; and, in the distance, hills and an occasional wood: these were all one could see, beyond the lines of rushes which edged the canal winding ahead.

They stopped for a lengthy meal, which Sharon described as lunch and tea together, it being so late; and then, appalled at how little daylight was left, continued.

"We've hardly been any distance at all," said John forlornly. "Good thing there were no locks. I shouldn't think they'd have worked if there were."

"*Much* more than three miles," he said, about two hours later. Darkness was descending and it was becoming very cold.

"Better stop," said Clifford.

"Not yet. I'm determined to reach that village."

"Dinner is ready," said Sharon sadly. "It will be cold."

"Let's stop."

"You have your meal. I'll call if I want you."

Sharon looked at them, and Clifford shrugged his shoulders. "Come on. I will. I'm tired of this."

They shut the cabin doors. John could hear the pleasant clatter of their meal, and just as he was coming to the end of the decent interval which he felt must elapse before he gave in, they passed under a bridge, the first of the day, and, clutching at any straw, he immediately assumed that it prefaced the village. "I think we're nearly there," he called.

Clifford opened the door. "The village?"

"No, a bridge. Can't be far now."

"You're mad, John. It's pitch dark."

"You can see the bridge though."

"Yes. Why not moor under it?"

"Too late. Can't turn round in this light, and she's not good at reversing. Must be nearly there. You go back, I don't need you."

Clifford shut the door again. He was beginning to feel irritated with John behaving in this childish manner and showing off to impress Sharon. It was amusing in the morning, but really he was carrying it a bit far. Let him manage the thing himself then. When, a few minutes later, John shouted that they had reached the sought-after village, Clifford merely pulled back the little curtain over a cabin window, rubbed the condensation, and remarked that he could see nothing. "No light at least."

"He is happy anyhow," said Sharon peaceably.

"Going to have a look around," said John, slamming the cabin doors and blowing his nose.

"Surely you'll eat first?"

"If you've left anything. My God, it's cold! It's *unnaturally* cold."

"We won't be held responsible if he dies of exposure will we?" said Clifford.

She looked at him, hesitated a moment, but did not reply, and placed a steaming plate in front of John. She doesn't want us to quarrel, Clifford thought, and with an effort of friendliness he asked: "What does tonight's village look like?"

"Much the same. Only one or two houses you know. But the old man called it a village." He seemed uncommunicative; Clifford thought he was sulking. But after eating the meal, he suddenly announced, almost apologetically, "I don't think I shall walk round. I'm absolutely worn out. You go if you like. I shall start turning in."

"All right. I'll have a look. You've had a hard day."

Clifford pulled on a coat and went outside. It was, as John said, incredibly cold and almost overwhelmingly silent. The clouds hung very low over the boat, and mist was rising everywhere from the ground, but he could dimly discern the black huddle of cottages lying on a little slope above the bank against which the boat was moored. He did actually set foot on shore, but his shoe sank immediately into a marshy hole. He withdrew it, and changed his mind. The prospect of groping round those dark and silent houses became suddenly distasteful, and he joined the others with the excuse that it was too cold and that he also was tired.

A little later, he lay half-conscious in a kind of restless trance, with John sleeping heavily opposite him. His mind seemed full of foreboding, fear of something unknown and intangible: he thought of them lying in warmth on the cold secret canal with desolate miles of water behind and probably beyond; the old man and the silent houses; John, cut off and asleep, and Sharon, who lay on the floor beside him. Immediately he was filled with a sudden and most violent desire for her, even to touch her, for her to know that he was awake.

"Sharon," he whispered; "Sharon, Sharon," and stretched down his fingers to her in the dark.

Instantly her hand was in his, each smooth and separate finger warmly clasped. She did not move or speak, but his relief was indescribable and for a long while he lay in an ecstasy of delight and peace, until his mind slipped imperceptibly with her fingers into oblivion.

When he woke he found John absent and Sharon standing over the primus. "He's outside," she said.

"Have I overslept again?"

"It is late. I am boiling water for you now."

"We'd better try and get some supplies this morning."

"There is no village," she said, in a matter-of-fact tone.

"What?"

"John says not. But we have enough food, if you don't mind this queer milk from a tin."

"No, I don't mind," he replied, watching her affectionately. "It doesn't really surprise me," he added after a moment.

"The village?"

"No village. Yesterday I should have minded awfully. Is that you, do you think?"

"Perhaps."

"It doesn't surprise you about the village at all, does it? Do you love me?"

She glanced at him quickly, a little shocked, and said quietly: "Don't you know?" then added: "It doesn't surprise me."

John seemed very disturbed. "I don't like it," he kept saying as they shaved. "Can't understand it at all. I could have sworn there were houses last night. You saw them didn't you?"

"Yes."

"Well, don't you think it's very odd?"

"I do."

"Everything looks the same as yesterday morning. I don't like it."

"It's an adventure, you must admit."

"Yes, but I've had enough of it. I suggest we turn back."

Sharon suddenly appeared, and, seeing her, Clifford knew that he did not want to go back. He remembered her saying: "Didn't you say you wanted to explore?" She would think him weak-hearted if they turned back all those dreary miles with nothing to show for it. At breakfast, he exerted himself in persuading John to the same opinion. John finally agreed to one more day, but, in turn, extracted a promise that they would then go back whatever happened. Clifford agreed to this, and Sharon for some inexplicable reason laughed at them both. So that eventually they prepared to set off in an atmosphere of general good humour.

Sharon began to fill the water-tank with their four-gallon can. It seemed too heavy for her, and John dropped the starter and leapt to her assistance.

She let him take the can and held the funnel for him. Together they watched the rich, even stream of water disappear.

"You shouldn't try to do that," he said. "You'll hurt yourself."

"Gipsies do it," she said.

"I'm awfully sorry about that. You know I am."

"I shouldn't have minded if you had thought I was a gipsy."

"I do like you," he said, not looking at her. "I do like you. You won't disappear altogether when this is over, will you?"

"You probably won't find I'll disappear for good," she replied comfortingly.

"Come on," shouted Clifford.

It's all right for *him* to talk to her, John thought, as he struggled to swing the starter. He just doesn't like me doing it; and he wished, as he had often begun to do, that Clifford was not there.

They had spasmodic engine trouble in the morning, which slowed them down; and the consequent halts, with the difficulty they experienced of mooring anywhere (the banks seemed nothing but marsh), were depressing and cold. Their good spirits evaporated: by lunch-time John was plainly irritable and frightened, and Clifford had begun to hate the grey silent land on either side, with the woods and hills which remained so consistently distant. They both wanted to give it up by then, but John felt bound to stick to his promise, and Clifford was secretly sure that Sharon wished to continue.

While she was preparing another late lunch, they saw a small boy who stood on what once had been the towpath watching them. He was bare-headed, wore corduroy, and had no shoes. He held a long reed, the end of which he chewed as he stared at them.

"Ask him where we are," said John; and Clifford asked.

He took the reed out of his mouth, but did not reply.

"Where do you live then?" asked Clifford as they drew almost level with him.

"I told you. Three miles up," he said; and then he gave a sudden little shriek of fear, dropped the reed, and turned to run down the bank the way they had come. Once he looked back, stumbled and fell, picked himself up sobbing, and ran raster. Sharon had appeared with lunch a moment before, and together they listened to his gasping cries growing fainter and fainter, until he had run himself out of their sight.

"What on earth frightened him?" said Clifford.

"I don't know. Unless it was Sharon popping out of the cabin like that."

"Nonsense. But he was a very frightened little boy. And, I say, do you realize . . ."

"He was a very foolish little boy," Sharon interrupted. She was angry, Clifford noticed with surprise, really angry, white and trembling, and with a curious expression which he did not like.

"We might have got something out of him," said John sadly.

"Too late now," Sharon said. She had quite recovered herself.

They saw no one else. They journeyed on throughout the afternoon; it grew colder, and at the same time more and more airless and still. When the light began to fail, Sharon disappeared as usual to the cabin. The canal became more tortuous, and John asked Clifford to help him with the turns. Clifford complied unwillingly: he did not want to leave Sharon, but as it had been he who had insisted on their continuing, he could hardly refuse. The turns were nerve-racking, as the canal was very narrow and the light grew worse and worse.

"All right if we stop soon?" asked John eventually.

"Stop now if you like."

"Well, we'll try and find a tree to tie up to. This swamp is awful. Can't think how that child ran."

"That child . . ." began Clifford anxiously; but John, who had been equally unnerved by the incident, and did not want to think about it, interrupted. "Is there a tree ahead anywhere?"

"Can't see one. There's a hell of a bend coming though. Almost back on itself. Better slow a bit more."

"Can't. We're right down as it is."

They crawled round, clinging to the outside bank, which seemed always to approach them, its rushes to rub against their bows, although the wheel was hard over. John grunted with relief, and they both stared ahead for the next turn.

They were presented with the most terrible spectacle. The canal immediately broadened, until no longer a canal but a sheet, an infinity, of water stretched ahead; oily, silent, and still, as far as the eye could see, with no country edging it, nothing but water to the low grey sky above it. John had almost immediately cut out the engine, and now he tried desperately to start it again, in order to turn round. Clifford instinctively glanced behind them. He saw no canal at all, no inlet, but grasping and close to the stern of the boat, the reeds and rushes of a marshy waste closing in behind them. He stumbled to the cabin doors and pulled them open. It was very neat and tidy in there, but empty. Only one stern door of the cabin was free of its catch, and it flapped irregularly backwards and forwards with their movements in the boat.

There was no sign of Sharon at all. □□

Discussion

1. (a) What is strange about Sharon's arrival and how does it help set the tone of the story? **(b)** Why does Clifford consider her coming aboard as a stroke of good luck?

2. (a) What do the incidents with the old man and the young boy have in common? **(b)** How do the two incidents and Sharon's reaction to the latter one add to the mystery and suspense of the story?

3. In Greek mythology sirens were sea goddesses whose singing lured sailors to their destruction. Discuss the similarities between the myth and the story.

Vocabulary • Dictionary

Determine whether the italicized words in each item below are synonyms or antonyms. Then select, from the pairs of words that follow, the words that are related in the same way as the words in the first pair. Write your choice on a separate sheet of paper. In each item, there is a word in each pair that you will probably have to check in the Glossary.

1. *precipitous: flat* as **(a)** stolid: dull; **(b)** impudent: courteous; **(c)** fervent: earnest.

2. *incongruous: inappropriate* as **(a)** obnoxious: unpleasant; **(b)** haughty: humble; **(c)** commotion: calm.

3. *forgiving: vindictive* as **(a)** strong: formidable; **(b)** wretched: squalid; **(c)** upset: appease.

4. *peaceful: truculent* as **(a)** stubborn: intractable; **(b)** unfriendly: amiable; **(c)** coax: cajole.

5. *tentative: final* as **(a)** forlorn: cheerful; **(b)** apathetic: indifferent; **(c)** recalcitrant: disobedient.

6. *pretend: simulate* as **(a)** claim: allege; **(b)** humor: pathos; **(c)** clean: sordid.

7. *peremptory: indecisive* as **(a)** benevolent: kind; **(b)** nocturnal: nightly; **(c)** callous: sensitive.

8. *diaphanous: transparent* as **(a)** vanquish: lose; **(b)** squander: waste; **(c)** ominous: favorable.

Elizabeth Jane Howard • 1923

Elizabeth Jane Howard is the author of several novels and short stories. Her first novel, *The Beautiful Visit,* published in 1950, won her England's John Llewellyn Rhys Memorial Prize. In addition she has written many television plays, including one episode in the series of *Upstairs, Downstairs.*

An intelligent and perceptive writer, Howard has had considerable success in the creation of macabre and eerie situations. It will come as no surprise to readers of "Three Miles Up" that she is a highly skilled sailor. She is married to the novelist and critic Kingsley Amis.

Virginia Woolf

Three Pictures

The First Picture

It is impossible that one should not see pictures; because if my father was a blacksmith and yours was a peer of the realm,[1] we must needs be pictures to each other. We cannot possibly break out of the frame of the picture by speaking natural words. You see me leaning against the door of the smithy with a horseshoe in my hand and you think as you go by: "How picturesque!" I, seeing you sitting so much at your ease in the car, almost as if you were going to bow to the populace, think what a picture of old luxurious aristocratical England! We are both quite wrong in our judgments no doubt, but that is inevitable.

So now at the turn of the road I saw one of these pictures. It might have been called "The Sailor's Homecoming" or some such title. A fine young sailor carrying a bundle; a girl with her hand on his arm; neighbours gathering round; a cottage garden ablaze with flowers; as one passed one read at the bottom of that picture that the sailor was back from China, and there was a fine spread waiting for him in the parlour; and he had a present for his young wife in his bundle; and she was soon going to bear him their first child. Everything was right and good and as it should be, one felt about that picture. There was something wholesome and satisfactory in the sight of such happiness; life seemed sweeter and more enviable than before.

So thinking I passed them, filling in the picture as fully, as completely as I could, noticing the colour of her dress, of his eyes, seeing the sandy cat slinking round the cottage door.

For some time the picture floated in my eyes, making most things appear much brighter, warmer, and simpler than usual; and making some things appear foolish; and some things wrong and some things right, and more full of meaning than before. At odd moments during that day and the next the picture returned to one's mind, and one thought with envy, but with kindness, of the happy sailor and his wife; one wondered what they were doing, what they were saying now. The imagination supplied other pictures springing from that first one, a picture of the sailor cutting firewood, drawing water; and they talked about China; and the girl set his present on the chimney-piece where everyone who came could see it; and she sewed at her baby clothes, and all the doors and windows were open into the garden so that the birds were flittering and the bees humming, and Rogers—that was his name—could not say how much to his liking all this was after the China seas. As he smoked his pipe, with his foot in the garden.

The Second Picture

In the middle of the night a loud cry rang through the village. Then there was a sound of something scuffling; and then dead silence. All that could be seen out of the window was the branch of lilac tree hanging motionless and ponderous across the road. It was a hot still night. There was no moon. The cry made everything seem ominous. Who had cried? Why had she cried? It was a woman's voice, made by some extremity of feeling almost sexless, almost expressionless. It was as if human nature had cried out against some iniquity, some inexpressible horror. There was dead silence. The stars shone perfectly steadily. The fields lay still. The trees were motionless. Yet all seemed guilty, convicted, ominous. One felt that something ought to be done. Some light ought to appear tossing, moving agitatedly. Someone ought to come running down the road. There should be lights in the cottage windows. And then perhaps another cry, but less sexless, less wordless, comforted,

1. ***peer . . . realm,*** a member of the British nobility.

appeased. But no light came. No feet were heard. There was no second cry. The first had been swallowed up, and there was dead silence.

One lay in the dark listening intently. It had been merely a voice. There was nothing to connect it with. No picture of any sort came to interpret it, to make it intelligible to the mind. But as the dark arose at last all one saw was an obscure human form, almost without shape, raising a gigantic arm in vain against some overwhelming iniquity.

The Third Picture

The fine weather remained unbroken. Had it not been for that single cry in the night one would have felt that the earth had put into harbour; that life had ceased to drive before the wind; that it had reached some quiet cove and there lay anchored, hardly moving, on the quiet waters. But the sound persisted. Wherever one went, it might be for a long walk up into the hills, something seemed to turn uneasily beneath the surface, making the peace, the stability all round one seem a little unreal. There were the sheep clustered on the side of the hill; the valley broke in long tapering waves like the fall of smooth waters. One came on solitary farmhouses. The puppy rolled in the yard. The butterflies gambolled over the gorse. All was as quiet, as safe could be. Yet, one kept thinking, a cry had rent it; all this beauty had been an accomplice that night; had consented; to remain calm, to be still beautiful; at any moment it might be sundered again. This goodness, this safety were only on the surface.

And then to cheer oneself out of this apprehensive mood one turned to the picture of the sailor's homecoming. One saw it all over again producing various little details—the blue colour of her dress, the shadow that fell from the yellow flowering tree—that one had not used before. So they had stood at the cottage door, he with his bundle on his back, she just lightly touching his sleeve with her hand. And a sandy cat had slunk round the door. Thus gradually going over the picture in every detail, one persuaded oneself by degrees that it was far more likely that this calm and content and good will lay beneath the surface than anything treacherous, sinister. The sheep grazing, the waves of the valley, the farmhouse, the puppy, the dancing butterflies were in fact like that all through. And so one turned back home, with one's mind fixed on the sailor and his wife, making up picture after picture of them so that one picture after another of happiness and satisfaction might be laid over that unrest, that hideous cry, until it was crushed and silenced by their pressure out of existence.

Here at last was the village, and the churchyard through which one must pass; and the usual thought came, as one entered it, of the peacefulness of the place, with its shady yews, its rubbed tombstones, its nameless graves. Death is cheerful here, one felt. Indeed, look at that picture! A man was digging a grave, and children were picnicking at the side of it while he worked. As the shovels of yellow earth were thrown up, the children were sprawling about eating bread and jam and drinking milk out of large mugs. The gravedigger's wife, a fat fair woman, had propped herself against a tombstone and spread her apron on the grass by the open grave to serve as a tea-table. Some lumps of clay had fallen among the tea things. Who was going to be buried, I asked. Had old Mr. Dodson died at last? "Oh! no. It's for young Rogers, the sailor," the woman answered, staring at me. "He died two nights ago, of some foreign fever. Didn't you hear his wife? She rushed into the road and cried out. . . . Here, Tommy, you're all covered with earth!"

What a picture it made! □□

Discussion

1. What does the narrator mean in the final paragraph of "The First Picture" when she says that the picture made "most things appear much . . . simpler than usual"?

2. In the first paragraph of "The Third Picture," what disturbs the seeming calm?

3. **(a)** What is the effect that the third picture at first produces in the narrator? **(b)** What is the final effect of the picture on her?

George Orwell

Why I Write

From a very early age, perhaps the age of five or six, I knew that when I grew up I should be a writer. Between the ages of about seventeen and twenty-four I tried to abandon this idea, but I did so with the consciousness that I was outraging my true nature and that sooner or later I should have to settle down and write books.

I was the middle child of three, but there was a gap of five years on either side, and I barely saw my father before I was eight. For this and other reasons I was somewhat lonely, and I soon developed disagreeable mannerisms which made me unpopular throughout my schooldays. I had the lonely child's habit of making up stories and holding conversations with imaginary persons, and I think from the very start my literary ambitions were mixed up with the feeling of being isolated and undervalued. I knew that I had a facility with words and a power of facing unpleasant facts, and I felt that this created a sort of private world in which I could get my own back for my failure in everyday life. Nevertheless the volume of serious—*i.e.* seriously intended—writing which I produced all though my childhood and boyhood would not amount to half a dozen pages. I wrote my first poem at the age of four or five, my mother taking it down to dictation. I cannot remember anything about it except that it was about a tiger and the tiger had "chair-like teeth"—a good enough phrase, but I fancy the poem was a plagiarism of Blake's "Tiger, Tiger." At eleven, when the war of 1914–18 broke out, I wrote a patriotic poem which was printed in the local newspaper, as was another, two years later, on the death of Kitchener.[1] From time to time, when I was a bit older, I wrote bad and usually unfinished "nature poems" in the Georgian style.[2] I also, about twice, attempted a short story which was a ghastly failure. That was the total of the would-be serious work that I actually set down on paper during all those years.

However, throughout this time I did in a sense engage in literary activities. To begin with there was the made-to-order stuff which I produced quickly, easily and without much pleasure to myself. Apart from school work, I wrote *vers d'occasion,* semi-comic poems which I could turn out at what now seems to me astonishing speed—at fourteen I wrote a whole rhyming play, in imitation of Aristophanes,[3] in about a week—and helped to edit school magazines, both printed and in manuscript. These magazines were the most pitiful burlesque stuff that you could imagine, and I took far less trouble with them than I now would with the cheapest journalism. But side by side with all this, for fifteen years or more, I was carrying out a literary exercise of a quite different kind: this was the making up of a continuous "story" about myself, a sort of diary existing only in the mind. I believe this is a common habit of children and adolescents. As a very small child I used to imagine that I was, say, Robin Hood, and picture myself as the hero of thrilling adventures, but quite soon my "story" ceased to be narcissistic in a crude way and became more and more a mere description of what I was doing and the things I saw. For minutes at a time this kind of thing would be running through my head: "He pushed the door open and entered the room. A yellow beam of sunlight, filtering through the muslin curtains,

1. ***Kitchener,*** Horatio Herbert, 1850–1916, a British military leader and colonial official in Africa and India. He was drowned during World War I when his ship was torpedoed.
2. ***Georgian style,*** the quiet and traditional literary style characteristic of the period between 1910 and the end of World War I. The name comes from King George V, whose reign began in 1910.
3. ***Aristophanes*** (ar′ə stof′ə nēz′), 448?–385 B.C., Greek writer of comedies.

slanted on to the table, where a matchbox, half open, lay beside the inkpot. With his right hand in his pocket he moved across to the window. Down in the street a tortoiseshell cat was chasing a dead leaf," etc., etc. This habit continued till I was about twenty-five, right through my non-literary years. Although I had to search, and did search, for the right words, I seemed to be making this descriptive effort almost against my will, under a kind of compulsion from outside. The "story" must, I suppose, have reflected the syles of the various writers I admired at different ages, but so far as I remember it always had the same meticulous descriptive quality.

When I was about sixteen I suddenly discovered the joy of mere words, *i.e.* the sounds and associations of words. The lines from *Paradise Lost*—

> So hee with difficulty and labour hard
> Movcd on: with difficulty and labour hee,

which do not now seem to me so very wonderful, sent shivers down my backbone; and the spelling "hee" for "he" was an added pleasure. As for the need to describe things, I knew all about it already. So it is clear what kind of books I wanted to write, in so far as I could be said to want to write books at that time. I wanted to write enormous naturalistic novels with unhappy endings, full of detailed descriptions and arresting similes, and also full of purple passages in which words were used partly for the sake of their sound. And in fact my first completed novel, *Burmese Days*, which I wrote when I was thirty but projected much earlier, is rather that kind of book.

I give all this background information because I do not think one can assess a writer's motives without knowing something of his early development. His subject matter will be determined by the age he lives in—at least this is true in tumultuous, revolutionary ages like our own—but before he ever begins to write he will have acquired an emotional attitude from which he will never completely escape. It is his job, no doubt, to discipline his temperament and avoid getting stuck at some immature stage, or in some perverse mood: but if he escapes from his early influences altogether, he will have killed his impulse to write. Putting aside the need to earn a living, I think there are four great motives for writing, at any rate for writing prose. They exist in different degrees in every writer, and in any one writer the proportions will vary from time to time, according to the atmosphere in which he is living. They are:

(1) Sheer egoism. Desire to seem clever, to be talked about, to be remembered after death, to get your own back on grownups who snubbed you in childhood, etc., etc. It is humbug to pretend that this is not a motive, and a strong one. Writers share this characteristic with scientists, artists, politicians, lawyers, soldiers, successful businessmen—in short, with the whole top crust of humanity. The great mass of human beings are not acutely selfish. After the age of about thirty they abandon individual ambition—in many cases, indeed, they almost abandon the sense of being individuals at all—and live chiefly for others, or are simply smothered under drudgery. But there is also the minority of gifted, wilful people who are determined to live their own lives to the end, and writers belong in this class. Serious writers, I should say, are on the whole more vain and self-centered than journalists, though less interested in money.

(2) Esthetic enthusiasm. Perception of beauty in the external world, or, on the other hand, in words and their right arrangement. Pleasure in the impact of one sound on another, in the firmness of good prose or the rhythm of a good story. Desire to share an experience which one feels is valuable and ought not to be missed. The esthetic motive is very feeble in a lot of writers, but even a pamphleteer or a writer of textbooks will have pet words and phrases which appeal to him for non-utilitarian reasons; or he may feel strongly about typography, width of margins, etc. Above the level of a railway guide, no book is quite free from esthetic considerations.

(3) Historical impulse. Desire to see things as they are, to find out true facts and store them up for the use of posterity.

(4) Political purpose—using the word "political" in the widest possible sense. Desire to push the world in a certain direction, to alter other people's idea of the kind of society that they should strive after. Once again, no book is genuinely free from political bias. The opinion that art

should have nothing to do with politics is itself a political attitude.

It can be seen how these various impulses must war against one another, and how they must fluctuate from person to person and from time to time. By nature—taking your "nature" to be the state you have attained when you are first adult—I am a person in whom the first three motives would outweigh the fourth. In a peaceful age I might have written ornate or merely descriptive books, and might have remained almost unaware of my political loyalties. As it is I have been forced into becoming a sort of pamphleteer. First I spent five years in an unsuitable profession (the Indian Imperial Police, in Burma), and then I underwent poverty and the sense of failure. This increased my natural hatred of authority and made me for the first time fully aware of the existence of the working classes, and the job in Burma had given me some understanding of the nature of imperialism: but these experiences were not enough to give me an accurate political orientation. Then came Hitler, the Spanish civil war, etc. By the end of 1935 I had still failed to reach a firm decision. I remember a little poem that I wrote at that date, expressing my dilemma:

A happy vicar I might have been
Two hundred years ago,
To preach upon eternal doom
And watch my walnuts grow;

But born, alas, in an evil time,
I missed that pleasant haven,
For the hair has grown on my upper lip
And the clergy are all clean-shaven.

And later still the times were good,
We were so easy to please,
We rocked our troubled thoughts to sleep
On the bosoms of the trees.

All ignorant we dared to own
The joys we now dissemble;
The greenfinch on the apple bough
Could make my enemies tremble.

But girls' bellies and apricots,
Roach in a shaded stream,
Horses, ducks in flight at dawn,
All these are a dream.

It is forbidden to dream again;
We maim our joys or hide them;
Horses are made of chromium steel
And little fat men shall ride them.

I am the worm who never turned,
The eunuch without a harem;
Between the priest and the commissar
I walk like Eugene Aram,[4]

And the commissar is telling my fortune
While the radio plays,
But the priest has promised an Austin Seven,[5]
For Duggie always pays.[6]

I dreamed I dwelt in marble halls,
And woke to find it true;
I wasn't born for an age like this;
Was Smith? Was Jones? Were you?

The Spanish war and other events in 1936–7 turned the scale and thereafter I knew where I stood. Every line of serious work that I have written since 1936 has been written, directly or indirectly, *against* totalitarianism and *for* democratic socialism, as I understand it. It seems to me nonsense, in a period like our own, to think that one can avoid writing of such subjects. Everyone writes of them in one guise or another. It is simply a question of which side one takes and what approach one follows. And the more one is conscious of one's political bias, the more chance one has of acting politically without sacrificing one's esthetic and intellectual integrity.

What I have most wanted to do throughout the past ten years is to make political writing into an art. My starting point is always a feeling of partisanship, a sense of injustice. When I sit down to write a book, I do not say to myself, "I am going to produce a work of art." I write it because there is some lie that I want to expose, some fact to which I want to draw attention, and my initial concern is to get a hearing. But I could not do the work of writing a book, or even a long magazine article, if it were not also an esthetic

4. ***Eugene Aram,*** the principal character—a scientist and scholar convicted and executed for murder—in the novel of the same name, written by Edward Bulwer-Lytton and first published in 1832.

5. ***Austin Seven,*** an influential model of automobile produced by the Austin Motor Company of England.

6. ***Duggie always pays,*** the advertising slogan of Doug Stewart, a well-known firm of bookmakers.

experience. Anyone who cares to examine my work will see that even when it is downright propaganda it contains much that a full-time politician would consider irrelevant. I am not able, and I do not want, completely to abandon the world-view that I acquired in childhood. So long as I remain alive and well I shall continue to feel strongly about prose style, to love the surface of the earth, and to take a pleasure in solid objects and scraps of useless information. It is no use trying to suppress that side of myself. The job is to reconcile my ingrained likes and dislikes with the essentially public, non-individual activities that this age forces on all of us.

It is not easy. It raises problems of construction and of language, and it raises in a new way the problem of truthfulness. Let me give just one example of the cruder kind of difficulty that arises. My book about the Spanish civil war,[7] *Homage to Catalonia*, is, of course, a frankly political book, but in the main it is written with a certain detachment and regard for form. I did try very hard in it to tell the whole truth without violating my literary instincts. But among other things it contains a long chapter, full of newspaper quotations and the like, defending the Trotskyists who were accused of plotting with Franco. Clearly such a chapter, which after a year or two would lose its interest for any ordinary reader, must ruin the book. A critic whom I respect read me a lecture about it. "Why did you put in all that stuff?" he said. "You've turned what might have been a good book into journalism." What he said was true, but I could not have done otherwise. I happened to know what very few people in England had been allowed to know, that innocent men were being falsely accused. If I had not been angry about that I should never have written the book.

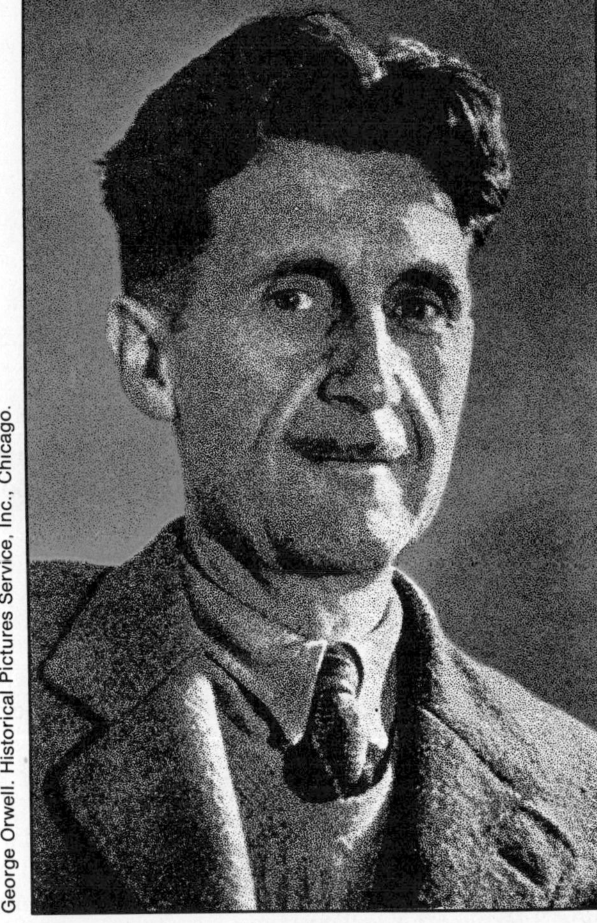
George Orwell. Historical Pictures Service, Inc., Chicago.

In one form or another this problem comes up again. The problem of language is subtler and would take too long to discuss. I will only say that of late years I have tried to write less picturesquely and more exactly. In any case I find that by the time you have perfected any style of writing, you have always outgrown it. *Animal Farm*[8] was the first book in which I tried, with full consciousness of what I was *doing*, to fuse political purpose and artistic purpose into one whole. I have not written a novel for seven years, but I hope to write another fairly soon. It is bound to be a failure, every book is a failure, but I do know with some clarity what kind of book I want to write.

Looking back through the last page or two, I see that I have made it appear as though my motives in writing were wholly public-spirited. I don't want to leave that as the final impression. All writers are vain, selfish and lazy, and at the very bottom of their motives there lies a mystery. Writing a book is a horrible, exhausting

---

7. ***Spanish civil war.*** Orwell fought in the Spanish civil war (1936–39) on the side of the Republicans against the Nationalist forces led by General Franco. Since Franco's armies were aided by troops and supplies from Hitler's Germany and Mussolini's Italy, Orwell saw the war as a struggle against fascism. He was, however, disillusioned by the bloody conflicts that occurred on the Republican side between the Communists and other left-wing groups. Orwell described his war experiences in *Homage to Catalonia.*

8. ***Animal Farm,*** a political satire by Orwell on Soviet Russia, in the form of an animal fable.

struggle, like a long bout of some painful illness. One would never undertake such a thing if one were not driven on by some demon whom one can neither resist nor understand. For all one knows that demon is simply the same instinct that makes a baby squall for attention. And yet it is also true that one can write nothing readable unless one constantly struggles to efface one's own personality. Good prose is like a window pane. I cannot say with certainty which of my motives are the strongest, but I know which of them deserve to be followed. And looking back through my work, I see that it is invariably where I lacked a *political* purpose that I wrote lifeless books and was betrayed into purple passages, sentences without meaning, decorative adjectives and humbug generally. □□

Discussion

1. What does Orwell tell us about himself in this essay which convinces the reader that he is being candid?

2. **(a)** What does the poem have to do with Orwell's subject and purpose here? **(b)** Would the essay be better or worse if the poem were omitted? Explain.

3. "The opinion that art should have nothing to do with politics is itself a political attitude." Explain Orwell's remark.

4. Why does Orwell think information about a writer's background is useful to the reader?

5. Does Orwell believe a writer should try to be objective and free of political bias?

6. In the next-to-last paragraph, what quality does the writer say he has tried to capture in his writing?

Extension • Writing

1. Write a one-paragraph summary of the advice Orwell gives to prospective writers in the course of this essay.

2. In the light of Orwell's essay, interpret the political elements and attitudes contained in Virginia Woolf's "The Legacy."

George Orwell (Eric Blair)
1903 • 1950

Eric Blair, who later changed his name to George Orwell, was born in Bengal, India. He was the son of a minor official in the Bengal Civil service. He received scholarships for his education, and attended private schools from the age of eight until he graduated from Eton in 1921.

It could be said, however, that Blair's education began when he left school for five years of service with the Imperial Police in Burma. He returned to Europe deeply disillusioned by what he had seen of imperialism, a vision which he was later to convey in essays such as "Shooting an Elephant" and "A Hanging." He began to write, but without success. In 1927 he began a six-year succession of odd jobs: dishwasher, tramp, tutor, bookstore assistant. He went through the experiences which are recorded in his first book, *Down and Out in Paris and London* (1933), and obtained the critical understanding of society which changed him into George Orwell.

Like the novels of Graham Greene, Orwell's novels—especially *Animal Farm* (1946) and *Nineteen Eighty-Four* (1949)—made for their author a reputation of international scope. But it is at least as much for his clear, direct, intelligent, and deeply-felt essays on social issues that he has been identified as "the conscience of his generation." *Homage to Catalonia* (1938), for example, is one of the key statements on the meaning of the Spanish civil war, and his *Collected Essays* continue to reveal how well Orwell understood the basic conflicts of the modern world—totalitarianism, communism, socialism, and democracy.

The respect paid to Orwell's work is that due to a writer who always had a clear purpose in his writing, and who achieved that purpose through clear and honest thinking and a prose style based on substance rather than frills.

Dylan Thomas

Reminiscences of Childhood

I like very much people telling me about their childhood, but they'll have to be quick or else I'll be telling them about mine.

I was born in a large Welsh town at the beginning of the Great War[1]—an ugly, lovely town (or so it was and is to me), crawling, sprawling by a long and splendid curving shore where truant boys and sandfield boys and old men from nowhere, beachcombed, idled and paddled, watched the dock-bound ships or the ships steaming away into wonder and India, magic and China, countries bright with oranges and loud with lions; threw stones into the sea for the barking outcast dogs; made castles and forts and harbors and race tracks in the sand; and on Saturday summer afternoons listened to the brass band, watched the Punch and Judy,[2] or hung about on the fringes of the crowd to hear the fierce religious speakers who shouted at the sea, as though it were wicked and wrong to roll in and out like that, white-horsed and full of fishes.

One man, I remember, used to take off his hat and set fire to his hair every now and then, but I do not remember what it proved, if it proved anything at all, except that he was a very interesting man.

This sea-town was my world; outside a strange Wales, coal-pitted, mountained, river-run, full, so far as I knew, of choirs and football teams and sheep and storybook tall hats and red flannel petticoats, moved about its business which was none of mine.

Beyond that unknown Wales with its wild names like peals of bells in the darkness, and its mountain men clothed in the skins of animals perhaps and always singing, lay England which was London and the country called the Front,[3] from which many of our neighbors never came back. It was a country to which only young men traveled.

At the beginning, the only "front" I knew was the little lobby before our front door. I could not understand how so many people never returned from there, but later I grew to know more, though still without understanding, and carried a wooden rifle in the park and shot down the invisible unknown enemy like a flock of wild birds. And the park itself was a world within the world of the sea-town. Quite near where I lived, so near that on summer evenings I could listen in my bed to the voices of older children playing ball on the sloping paper-littered bank, the park was full of terrors and treasures. Though it was only a little park, it held within its borders of old tall trees, notched with our names and shabby from our climbing, as many secret places, caverns and forests, prairies and deserts, as a country somewhere at the end of the sea.

And though we would explore it one day, armed and desperate, from end to end, from the robbers' den to the pirates' cabin, the highwayman's inn to the cattle ranch, or the hidden room in the undergrowth, where we held beetle races, and lit the wood fires and roasted potatoes and talked about Africa, and the makes of motor cars, yet still the next day, it remained as unexplored as the Poles—a country just born and always changing.

There were many secret societies but you could belong only to one; and in blood or red ink, and a rusty pocketknife, with, of course, an instrument to remove stones from horses' feet, you signed your name at the foot of a terrible document, swore death to all the other societies, crossed your heart that you would divulge no

1. ***Great War,*** World War I (1914–1918).
2. ***Punch and Judy,*** a popular puppet show for children named after its two main characters.
3. ***the Front.*** A reference to the battle line in France during World War I, where British and French troops suffered enormous casualties in containing the German armies.

secret and that if you did, you would consent to torture by slow fire, and undertook to carry out by yourself a feat of either daring or endurance. You could take your choice: would you climb to the top of the tallest and most dangerous tree, and from there hurl stones and insults at grown-up passers-by, especially postmen, or any other men in uniform? Or would you ring every doorbell in the terrace, not forgetting the doorbell of the man with the red face who kept dogs and ran fast? Or would you swim in the reservoir, which was forbidden and had angry swans, or would you eat a whole jam jar full of mud?

There were many more alternatives. I chose one of endurance and for half an hour, it may have been longer or shorter, held up off the ground a very heavy broken pram we had found in a bush. I thought my back would break and the half hour felt like a day, but I preferred it to braving the red face and the dogs, or to swallowing tadpoles.

We knew every inhabitant of the park, every regular visitor, every nursemaid, every gardener, every old man. We knew the hour when the alarming retired policeman came in to look at the dahlias and the hour when the old lady arrived in the Bath chair[4] with six Pekinese, and a pale girl to read aloud to her. I think she read the newspaper, but we always said she read the *Wizard*.[5] The face of the old man who sat summer and winter on the bench looking over the reservoir, I can see clearly now and I wrote a poem long long after I'd left the park and the sea-town called:

The Hunchback in the Park

The hunchback in the park
A solitary mister
Propped between trees and water
From the opening of the garden lock
That lets the trees and water enter
Until the Sunday sombre bell at dark

Eating bread from a newspaper
Drinking water from the chained cup
That the children filled with gravel
In the fountain basin where I sailed my ship
Slept at night in a dog kennel
But nobody chained him up.

Like the park birds he came early
Like the water he sat down
And Mister they called Hey mister
The truant boys from the town
Running when he had heard them clearly
On out of sound

Past lake and rockery
Laughing when he shook his paper
Hunchbacked in mockery
Through the loud zoo of the willow groves
Dodging the park keeper
With his stick that picked up leaves.

And the old dog sleeper
Alone between nurses and swans
While the boys among willows
Made the tigers jump out of their eyes
To roar on the rockery stones
And the groves were blue with sailors

Made all day until bell time
A woman figure without fault
Straight as a young elm
Straight and tall from his crooked bones
That she might stand in the night
And the locks and the chains

All night in the unmade park
After the railings and shrubberies
The birds the grass the trees and the lake
And the wild boys innocent as strawberries
Had followed the hunchback
To his kennel in the dark.

And that park grew up with me; that small world widened as I learned its secrets and boundaries, as I discovered new refuges and ambushes in its woods and jungles; hidden homes and lairs for the multitudes of imagination, for cowboys and Indians, and the tall terrible half-people who rode on nightmares through my bedroom. But it was not the only world—that world of rockery, gravel path, playbank, bowling green, bandstands, reservoir, dahlia garden, where an ancient keeper, known as Smoky, was the whiskered snake in the grass one must keep off. There was another world where with my friends I used to dawdle on half holidays along the bent and Devon-facing seashore, hoping for gold watches or the skull of a sheep or a message in a bottle to be washed up with the tide; and another where we used to wander whistling through the packed streets, stale as station sand-

---

4. ***Bath chair,*** wheel chair.
5. ***Wizard,*** a weekly magazine for young schoolboys.

wiches,[6] round the impressive gasworks and the slaughter house, past by the blackened monuments and the museum that should have been in a museum. Or we scratched at a kind of cricket on the bald and cindery surface of the recreation ground, or we took a tram that shook like an iron jelly down to the gaunt pier, there to clamber under the pier, hanging perilously on to its skeleton legs or to run along to the end where patient men with the seaward eyes of the dockside unemployed capped and mufflered, dangling

6. ***stale . . . sandwiches.*** The staleness of sandwiches at railroad station cafeterias is a standing joke in Britain.

from their mouths pipes that had long gone out, angled over the edge for unpleasant tasting fish.

Never was there such a town as ours, I thought, as we fought on the sandhills with rough boys or dared each other to climb up the scaffolding of half-built houses soon to be called Laburnum Beaches. Never was there such a town, I thought, for the smell of fish and chips on Saturday evenings; for the Saturday afternoon cinema matinees where we shouted and hissed our threepences away; for the crowds in the streets with leeks[7] in their hats on international nights; for the park, the inexhaustible and mysterious, bushy red-Indian hiding park where the hunchback sat alone and the groves were blue with sailors. The memories of childhood have no order, and so I remember that never was there such a dame school[8] as ours, so firm and kind and smelling of galoshes, with the sweet and fumbled music of the piano lessons drifting down from upstairs to the lonely schoolroom, where only the sometimes tearful wicked sat over undone sums, or to repeat a little crime—the pulling of a girl's hair during geography, the sly shin kick under the table during English literature. Behind the school was a narrow lane where only the oldest and boldest threw pebbles at windows, scuffled and boasted, fibbed about their relations—

"My father's got a chauffeur."

"What's he want a chauffeur for? He hasn't got a car."

"My father's the richest man in the town."

"My father's the richest man in Wales."

"My father owns the world."

And swapped gob-stoppers[9] for slings, old knives for marbles, kite strings for foreign stamps.

The lane was always the place to tell your secrets; if you did not have any, you invented them. Occasionally now I dream that I am turning out of school into the lane of confidences when I say to the boys of my class, "At last, I have a real secret."

"What is it—what is it?"

"I can fly."

And when they do not believe me, I flap my arms and slowly leave the ground only a few inches at first, then gaining air until I fly waving my cap level with the upper windows of the school, peering in until the mistress at the piano screams and the metronome falls to the ground and stops, and there is no more time.

And I fly over the trees and chimneys of my town, over the dockyards skimming the masts and funnels, over Inkerman Street, Sebastopol Street, and the street where all the women wear men's caps, over the trees of the everlasting park, where a brass band shakes the leaves and sends them showering down on to the nurses and the children, the cripples and the idlers, and the gardeners, and the shouting boys: over the yellow seashore, and the stone-chasing dogs, and the old men, and the singing sea.

The memories of childhood have no order, and no end. □□

---

7. ***leeks,*** the national flower of Wales. The Welsh wear a sprig of leek on St. David's Day, March 1.

8. ***dame school,*** an elementary school kept by a *dame*, usually an old woman or widow.

9. ***gob-stoppers,*** large, ball-shaped candies. *Gob* is a slang word for mouth.

Discussion

1. What is the relationship of the "Hunchback" poem to Thomas's essay as a whole?

2. Do you feel that these reminiscences are exaggerations? Explain.

3. Why might Thomas, after telling the reader about "the country called the Front," then drop the subject?

4. Is Thomas serious when he tells his friends, "I can fly"? Is the description of flying that follows his words a factual account (for example, of an airplane ride), or a fantasy? Explain.

Extension • Writing

1. Write an essay, which contains as much concrete detail as possible, in which you describe a place where you played as a child.

2. Write a narrative essay about some "feat of either daring or endurance" which you once accomplished.

3. Write an imaginative excuse, which involves neither illness nor death, for missing school or for not having done your homework.

Doris Lessing

from Going Home

Over the plains of Ethiopia the sun rose as I had not seen it in seven years. A big, cool, empty sky flushed a little above a rim of dark mountains. The landscape 20,000 feet below gathered itself from the dark and showed a pale gleam of grass, a sheen of water. The red deepened and pulsed, radiating streaks of fire. There hung the sun, like a luminous spider's egg, or a white pearl, just below the rim of the mountains. Suddenly it swelled, turned red, roared over the horizon and drove up the sky like a train engine. I knew how far below in the swelling heat the birds were an orchestra in the trees about the villages of mud huts; how the long grass was straightening while dangling flocks of dewdrops dwindled and dried; how the people were moving out into the fields about the business of herding and hoeing.

Here is where the sun regulates living in a twelve-hour cycle. Here the sun is a creature of the same stuff as oneself; powerful and angry, but at least responsive, and no mere dispenser of pale candlepower.

When I was first in England I was disturbed all the time in my deepest sense of probability because the sun went down at four in the middle of an active afternoon, filling a cold, damp remote sky with false pathos. Or, at eleven in the morning, instead of blazing down direct, a hand's-span from centre, it would appear on a slant and in the wrong place, at eight o'clock position, a swollen, misshapen, watery ghost of a thing peering behind chimneypots. The sun in England should be feminine, as it is in Germany.

During that first year in England, I had a vision of London I cannot recall now. Recently I found some pages I wrote then: it was a nightmare city that I lived in for a year; endless miles of heavy, damp, dead building on a dead, sour earth, inhabited by pale, misshapen, sunless creatures under a low sky of grey vapour.

Then, one evening, walking across the park, the light welded buildings, trees and scarlet buses into something familiar and beautiful, and I knew myself to be at home. Now London is to me the pleasantest of cities, full of the most friendly and companionable people. But that year of horrible estrangement from everything around me was real enough. It was because, bred in Africa, I needed to be in direct physical touch with what I saw; I needed the cycle of hot, strong light, of full, strong dark.

One does not look at London, but at a pretty house, a glimpse of trees over rooftops, the remains of an old street, a single block of flats. The eye learns to reject the intolerable burden of the repetition of commercialization. It is the variegated light of London which creates it; at night, the mauvish wet illumination of the city sky; or the pattern of black shadow-leaves on a wall; or, when the sun emerges, the instant gaiety of a pavement.

On that morning over Africa I learned that I had turned myself inwards, had become a curtain-drawer, a fire-hugger, the inhabitant of a cocoon. Easy enough to turn outwards again: I felt I had never left at all. This was my air, my landscape, and above all, my sun.

Africa belongs to the Africans; the sooner they take it back the better. But—a country also belongs to those who feel at home in it. Perhaps it may be that the love of Africa the country will be strong enough to link people who hate each other now. Perhaps.

On this trip home a man with whom I had been arguing bitterly about politics said to me suddenly: Where did I come from? I said Lomagundi. He knew it well, he said. He liked the

---

highveld, he remarked, defensively. For the highveld is reaches of pale, dry grass, studded with small, dry, stunted trees—wide, empty, barren country. I said yes, and the Kalahari, too. Yes, he said; and the Karroo.[1] The Kalahari and the Karroo are stages nearer desert of the highveld, full of bitter shrubs, cacti, lizards and hot stones. They are enormous, with a scarifying, barren beauty. They, too, are almost empty.

For a moment we shared the understanding of people who have been made by the same landscape.

But I am not sure whether this passion for emptiness, for space, only has meaning in relation to Europe. Africa is scattered all over with white men who push out and away from cities and people, to remote farms and outposts, seeking solitude. But perhaps all they need is to leave the seethe and the burden of Europe behind.

I remember an old prospector came to our farm one evening when I was a child. He had spent all his life wandering around Africa. He said he had just gone home to England for a holiday of six months; but left at the end of a week. Too many people, he said; a tame little country, catching trains and keeping to timetables. He had learned his lesson; he would never leave the highveld again. 'People,' he said, shouting at himself—for he was certainly arguing against his own conscience—"people are mad, wanting to change Africa. Why don't they leave it alone? A man can breathe here, he can be himself. And," he went on, getting angrier and angrier, "when we've filled Africa up, what then? The world is only tolerable because of the empty places in it—millions of people all crowded together, fighting and struggling, but behind them, somewhere, enormous, empty places. I tell you what I think," he said, "when the world's filled up, we'll have to get hold of a star. Any star. Venus, or Mars. Get hold of it and leave it empty. Man needs an empty space somewhere for his spirit to rest in."

That's what he said. I remember every word, for he made a great impression on me.

Next morning he went away, and we heard he had gone up over the Zambezi[2] escarpment into the bush with his bearer. On the verge of one of the hills overlooking the river he built a hut and thatched it, and settled to live there, entirely alone. But he got black-water fever, and the news traveled back, as news does in these parts, and at last reached his wife in the city, who—a bush-widow[3] these many years—got herself a lorry and went off after him until she reached the end of the road, and then inquired of some passing Africans who took her to the hill where her husband was. Between one bout of fever and another, he sat on a candle-box under a tree, an old man of fifty or so, looking at the gorges of the river and the hills. Africans from a neighbouring village had set water and some meat by him, and were waiting at a little distance in the shade of a tree. He was very ill.

"And now," said she, "enough of this nonsense: it's time you came back and let me look after you."

"Go away," he said. "I want to die alone."

"But there's no need to die. You'll get better in hospital."

A look of revulsion came over his face, which she understood too well. "Oh, all right," she said. "I'll look after you myself."

He turned his face from her, and looked out and down to the river. And so she went to examine the inside of the mud hut which had nothing in it but a case of whisky and a roll of bedding and some quinine and a rifle; and then went over to the young men, who got to their feet as she approached.

"Now, look after the baas[4] nicely," she said.

"Yes, Nkosikaas,"[5] they said.

She walked away down along the Kaffir paths several miles to the road, climbed back into the lorry and drove back to town. And when he died, which was several days later, the people of the village buried him and sang their mourning songs over him.

That was the story as we heard it from a group of young men travelling through our farm

---

1. ***Kalahari . . . Karroo.*** The Kalahari is a vast desert in Botswana and South West Africa. The Karroo is a barren plateau in the Republic of South Africa.
2. ***Zambezi,*** the fourth largest river in Africa. It has its source in Zambia (formerly Northern Rhodesia).
3. ***bush widow,*** a woman who lives in the city while her husband works or travels in jungle or rural areas.
4. ***baas,*** an Afrikaans word that means "master." Afrikaans is a language spoken in South Africa that developed from the Dutch of the colonists.
5. ***Nkosikaas,*** "mistress" in Afrikaans.

on their way to find work in the gold mines of the Rand.[6]

It seems to me that this story of the man who preferred to die alone rather than return to the cities of his own people expresses what is best in the older type of white men who have come to Africa. He did not come to take what he could get from the country. This man loved Africa for its own sake, and for what is best in it: its emptiness, its promise. It is still uncreated.

Yet it is only when one flies over Africa that one can see it, as such solitary people do, as the empty continent. The figures are eloquent enough—that is, if one possesses the kind of mind that makes figures live. In Central Africa there are seven million Africans and two hundred thousand white people. It sounds like quite a lot of people from one point of view, if one tries to imagine the word *million* in terms of a crowd of people. And if one has lived in a city there, one remembers the pressure of people. Yet it seems seven million people are nothing, not enough—this enormous area could hold hundreds of millions.

But now, steadily flying south for hour after hour, one sees forest, mountain and lake; river and gorge and swamp; and the great reaches of the flat, tree-belted grassland. The yellow flanks of Africa lie beneath the moving insect-like plane, black-maned with forest, twitching in the heat. A magnificent country, with all its riches in the future. Because it is so empty we can dream. We can dream of cities and a civilization more beautiful than anything that has been seen in the world before. □□

6. ***the Rand,*** Witwatersrand, a region in the Republic of South Africa noted for its deposits of gold and other minerals.

Discussion

1. What does the story of the old prospector add to Lessing's essay?

2. "Man needs an empty space somewhere for his spirit to rest in." Do you find this an odd statement? Explain.

Vocabulary • Context

Using context as an aid, write the most appropriate definition for each italicized word on a separate sheet of paper. Be sure you can pronounce and spell all italicized words.

1. "It can be seen how these various impulses must war against one another, and how they must *fluctuate* from person to person and from time to time." **(a)** envy; **(b)** glow; **(c)** change; **(d)** belong.

2. "It was a woman's voice, made by some extremity of feeling almost sexless, almost expressionless. It was as if human nature had cried out against some *iniquity*, some inexpressible horror." **(a)** happiness; **(b)** honor; **(c)** injustice; **(d)** freedom.

3. ". . . you signed your name at the foot of a terrible document, swore death to all the other societies, crossed your heart that you would *divulge* no secret and that if you did, you would consent to torture by slow fire. . . ." **(a)** invent; **(b)** reveal; **(c)** respect; **(d)** ignore.

4. "Although I had to search, and did search, for the right words, I seemed to be making this descriptive effort almost against my will, under a kind of *compulsion* from outside." **(a)** force; **(b)** laziness; **(c)** foolishness; **(d)** joke.

5. "There hung the sun, like a *luminous* spider's egg, or a white pearl, just below the rim of the mountains." **(a)** dark; **(b)** expensive; **(c)** quiet; **(d)** shining.

Doris Lessing 1919 •

Lessing was born in Kermanshah, Persia, lived on a farm in Southern Rhodesia, and moved permanently to London in 1949.

Much of Lessing's work has autobiographical overtones, beginning with *Going Home* (1957), which concerns a return visit to Africa, and continuing through the Martha Quest novels, which are deeply concerned with male-female relationships and the personal pattern of change and growth in the character of Martha Quest. Beginning with *In Pursuit of the English* (1960), a record of her initial experiences in dark and alien London after World War II, Lessing's work reflects a growing vision of cataclysm, and a sense that the supposedly "mad" or insane may, through extra-sensory perception, provide the modern world with vital messages. Her best novel in this context is *Briefing for a Descent into Hell* (1970).

Unit Review Tests

8: The Twentieth Century

Content Review

1. (**a**) What details of trench warfare do Sassoon and Owen include in their poems? (**b**) What effect do these details have on the feelings these poems generate?

2. Eliot's "The Journey of the Magi" deals with the conflict of faith and doubt. Compare Eliot's treatment of this conflict with (**a**) John Donne's in Sonnet 14 from *Holy Sonnets*; (**b**) Matthew Arnold's in "Dover Beach"; (**c**) Gerard Manley Hopkins's in "Thou Art Indeed Just, Lord."

3. Contrast the treatment of love in D. H. Lawrence's "Intimates" and Robert Graves's "Sullen Moods."

4. Both W. H. Auden's "The Unknown Citizen" and Stephen Spender's "An Elementary School Class Room in a Slum" deal with the impact of government efforts at welfare. What attitude do they have in common? Explain.

5. In one of his poems W. B. Yeats wrote "The innocent and beautiful / have no enemy but time . . ." Discuss the attitudes toward time expressed in the poems by Dylan Thomas in this unit.

6. What historical process is reflected in Philip Larkin's poem "Homage to a Government"?

7. Compare Ted Hughes's treatment of natural objects with (**a**) Robert Burns's in "To a Mouse"; (**b**) Gerard Manley Hopkins's in "Pied Beauty"; Thomas Hardy's in "Afterwards."

8. The stories by Mansfield, Bowen, Greene, and O'Connor contain children. How are the children used in the respective stories to shed light on adult values and behavior?

9. Identify (**a**) some key characteristics and (**b**) some important effects of consciousness of social class as it is reflected in the stories by Joyce, Woolf, and Mansfield. Cite specific examples from the stories to illustrate your points.

10. Compare and contrast the attitudes toward death reflected in the stories by Woolf, Bowen, and Greene.

11. In several of the stories in this unit, male/female relationships are severely tested, and some run into trouble. Identify as succinctly and precisely as possible, the source of the difficulty in the stories by Joyce, Woolf, Lawrence, Greene, and O'Connor.

Unit 8, Test I
Interpretation: New Material

The following story takes place at a health spa or resort in Germany. Read it and write your answers to the questions that follow on a separate sheet of paper. Do not write in your book.

Germans at Meat

Katherine Mansfield

Bread soup was placed upon the table. "Ah," said the Herr[1] Rat, leaning upon the table as he peered into the tureen, "that is what I need. My 'magen'[2] has not been in order for several days. Bread soup, and just the right consistency. I am a good cook myself"—He turned to me.

"How interesting," I said, attempting to in-

1. ***Herr*** (her), German for "Mister" or "sir."
2. ***magen*** (mäh′gən), German for "stomach."

fuse just the right amount of enthusiasm into my voice.

"Oh yes—when one is not married it is necessary. As for me, I have had all I wanted from women without marriage." He tucked his napkin into his collar and blew upon his soup as he spoke. "Now at nine o'clock I made myself an English breakfast, but not much. Four slices of bread, two eggs, two slices of cold ham, one plate of soup, two cups of tea—that is nothing to you."

He asserted the fact so vehemently that I had not the courage to refute it.

All eyes were suddenly turned upon me. I felt I was bearing the burden of the nation's preposterous breakfast—I who drank a cup of coffee while buttoning my blouse in the morning.

"Nothing at all," cried Herr Hoffman from Berlin. "Ach,[3] when I was in England in the morning I used to eat."

He turned up his eyes and his moustache, wiping the soup drippings from his coat and waistcoat.

"Do they really eat so much?" asked Fräulein[4] Stiegelauer. "Soup and baker's bread and pig's flesh, and tea and coffee and stewed fruit, and honey and eggs, and cold fish and kidneys, and hot fish and liver. All the ladies eat, too, especially the ladies?"

"Certainly. I myself have noticed it, when I was living in a hotel in Leicester Square," cried the Herr Rat. "It was a good hotel, but they could not make tea—now—"

"Ah, that's one thing I *can* do," said I, laughing brightly. I can make very good tea. The great secret is to warm the teapot."

"Warm the teapot," interrupted the Herr Rat, pushing away his soup plate. "What do you warm the teapot for? Ha! Ha! that's very good! One does not eat the teapot, I suppose?"

He fixed his cold blue eyes upon me with an expression which suggested a thousand premeditated invasions.

"So that is the great secret of your English tea? All you do is to warm the teapot."

I wanted to say that was only the preliminary canter, but could not translate it, and so was silent.

The servant brought in veal, with sauerkraut and potatoes.

"I eat sauerkraut with great pleasure," said the Traveller from North Germany, "but now I have eaten so much of it that I cannot retain it. I am immediately forced to—"

"A beautiful day," I cried, turning to Fräulein Stiegelauer. "Did you get up early?"

"At five o'clock. I walked for ten minutes in the wet grass. Again in bed. At half-past five, I fell asleep, and woke at seven, when I made an 'overbody' washing! Again in bed. At eight o'clock I had a cold-water poultice,[5] and at half-past eight I drank a cup of mint tea. At nine I drank some malt coffee, and began my 'cure.' Pass me the sauerkraut, please. You do not eat it?"

"No, thank you. I still find it a little strong."

"Is it true," asked the Widow, picking her teeth with a hairpin as she spoke, "that you are a vegetarian?"

"Why, yes; I have not eaten meat for three years."

"Impossible! Have you any family?"

"No."

"There now, you see, that's what you're coming to! Who ever heard of having children upon vegetables? It is not possible. But you never have large families in England now; I suppose you are too busy with your suffragetting.[6] Now I have nine children, and they are all alive, thank God. Fine, healthy babies—though after the first one was born I had to—"

"How *wonderful!*" I cried.

"Wonderful," said the Widow contemptuously, replacing the hairpin in the knob which was balanced on the top of her head. "Not at all! A friend of mine had four at the same time. Her husband was so pleased he gave a supper-party and had them placed on the table. Of course she was very proud."

"Germany," boomed the Traveller, biting round a potato which he had speared with his knife, "is the home of the Family."

Followed an appreciative silence.

The dishes were changed for beef, red currants and spinach. They wiped their forks upon black bread and started again.

---

3. ***Ach*** (äkh), German for "ah" or "alas."
4. ***Fräulein*** (froi′lin), German for "Miss."
5. ***poultice*** (pōl′tis), a soft, moist mixture of mustard, herbs, etc., applied to the body as a medicine.
6. ***suffragetting*** (suf′rə jet′ing), campaigning for the right of women to vote.

"How long are you remaining here?" asked the Herr Rat.

"I do not know exactly. I must be back in London in September."

"Of course you will visit München?"[7]

"I am afraid I shall not have time. You see, it is important not to break in my 'cure.'"

"But you *must* go to München. You have not seen Germany if you have not been to München. All the Exhibitions, all the Art and Soul life of Germany are in München. There is the Wagner Festival in August, and Mozart and a Japanese collection of pictures—and there is the beer! You do not know what good beer is until you have been to München. Why, I see fine ladies every afternoon, but fine ladies, I tell you, drinking glasses so high." He measured a good washstand pitcher in height, and I smiled.

"If I drink a great deal of München beer I sweat so," said Herr Hoffman. "When I am here, in the fields or before my bath, I sweat, but I enjoy it; but in the town it is not all the same thing."

Prompted by the thought, he wiped his neck and face with his dinner napkin and carefully cleaned his ears.

A glass dish of stewed apricots was placed upon the table.

"Ah, fruit!" said Fräulein Stiegelauer, "that is so necessary to health. The doctor told me this morning that the more fruit I could eat the better."

She very obviously followed the advice.

Said the Traveller: "I suppose you are frightened of an invasion, too, eh? Oh, that's good. I've been reading all about your English play in a newspaper. Did you see it?"

"Yes." I sat upright. "I assure you we are not afraid."

"Well, then, you ought to be," said the Herr Rat. "You have got no army at all—a few little boys with their veins full of nicotine poisoning."

"Don't be afraid," Herr Hoffman said. "We don't want England. If we did we would have had her long ago. We really do not want you."

He waved his spoon airily, looking across at me as though I were a little child whom he would keep or dismiss as he pleased.

"We certainly do not want Germany," I said.

"This morning I took a half bath. Then this afternoon I must take a knee bath and an arm bath," volunteered the Herr Rat; "then I do my exercises for an hour, and my work is over. A glass of wine and a couple of rolls with some sardines—"

They were handed cherry cake with whipped cream.

"What is your husband's favorite meat?" asked the Widow.

"I really do not know," I answered.

"You really do not know? How long have you been married?"

"Three years."

"But you cannot be in earnest? You would not have kept house as his wife for a week without knowing that fact."

"I really never asked him; he is not at all particular about his food."

A pause. They all looked at me, shaking their heads, their mouths full of cherry stones.

"No wonder there is a repetition in England of that dreadful state of things in Paris," said the Widow, folding her dinner napkin. "How can a woman expect to keep her husband if she does not know his favorite food after three years?"

"Mahlzeit!"[8]

"Mahlzeit!"

I closed the door after me. □□

---

7. München (mün′kən), German spelling for city of Munich (myu′nik).

8. *Mahlzeit* (mahl′tsit), a German expression that here means something like "May you enjoy your meal!"

1. What do you infer is the tone of the narrator's voice in the second paragraph? **(a)** harsh; **(b)** ironic; **(c)** kind. **(d)** angry.

2. In the third paragraph, what stereotype of the English does Herr Rat refer to?

3. Does the narrator conform to or differ from Herr Rat's generalization?

4. What main trait of Herr Rat does the narrator emphasize? **(a)** humor; **(b)** bitterness; **(c)** grossness; **(d)** wisdom.

5. What stereotyped views of Englishwomen does the Widow display?

6. In the same paragraph, what does the Widow imply is the proper role of the woman?

7. When the narrator says that the Traveller's boast that Germany is the home of the family is followed by "an appreciative silence," do you think she shares in the appreciation?

8. When the narrator says "She very obviously followed the advice", is her tone: **(a)** sarcastic; **(b)** outraged; **(c)** gentle; **(d)** sad?

9. What shift occurs in the story on page 706?

10. In discussing tea with Herr Rat, the narrator says of him that "He fixed his cold blue eyes upon me with an expression which suggested a thousand premeditated invasions." In this context, she is referring to invasions of her privacy, reserve or personal integrity. Considering the shift that takes place on page 706, how does the earlier reference to "invasion" function in the story?

11. What statement does Herr Rat make against the young men who make up the English army?

12. When Herr Hoffman says "Don't be afraid," what is his tone most likely to be? **(a)** concerned; **(b)** meek; **(c)** bitter; **(d)** condescending.

13. The German characters are frequently revealed as holding stereotypical views of the English. How does the author make the German characters stereotypes?

14. Throughout this story the narrator knows what the Germans think of the English, because they tell her. Does she tell them what she thinks of them?

15. Does the narrator explicitly tell the reader what she thinks of the Germans? How does she reveal her dislike to us?

16. What kind of future is forecast by the narrator's perceptions of the Germans and the Germans' perceptions of the narrator (and the English she represents to them)?

Unit 8, Test II

Composition

You may choose any *one* of the following assignments. Assume that you are writing your essay for your classmates.

1. Various views of home, childhood, and a sense of belonging are presented in Joyce's "Eveline," Mansfield's "The Doll's House," Thomas's "Reminiscences of Childhood," and Lessing's "Going Home." Write your own reminiscences of home, childhood, or belonging—or a combination of these. Try to make your language as concrete and specific as possible.

2. Discuss the possible sources and nature of the antagonism between men and women in Lawrence's "Tickets, Please."

3. Discuss the relationship between husband and wife described in Woolf's story "The Legacy" in regard to the way the relationship is perceived by each of the partners in terms of appearance and reality.

4. Compare and contrast Eliot's "The Hollow Men" and "Journey of the Magi" in their attitudes toward faith, despair, and the life of the spirit.

5. Discuss Auden's view of the relationship between the world of poetry and art and the world of suffering as revealed in "Musée des Beaux Arts."

6. Discuss the bonds between parents and children described in Lewis's "Walking Away" and Thomas's "Do Not Go Gentle Into That Good Night."

7. Discuss the views of nature in Smith's "Alone in the Woods," and Thomas's "Fern Hill" and "The Force that Through the Green Fuse Drives the Flower."

8. Discuss the relationship between the human and the animal in Smith's "The Frog Prince," Hughes's "Bullfrog" and "Esther's Tomcat," and Larkin's "At Grass."

Definitions of Literary Terms

Words within entries in SMALL CAPITAL LETTERS refer you to other entries in the *Definitions of Literary Terms.* Numbers after a title or example refer to pages in the text where the selection referred to can be found.

alexandrine (See HEXAMETER.)

allegory (al′ə gôr′ē), a NARRATIVE either in VERSE or prose, in which characters, action, and sometimes SETTING represent abstract concepts apart from the literal meaning of the story. The underlying meaning has moral, social, religious, or political significance, and the characters are often PERSONIFICATIONS of abstract ideas such as charity, hope, greed, or envy. Spenser's *The Faerie Queen*, page 121, is a good example of allegory.

alliteration (ə lit′ə rā′shən), the repetition of consonant sounds at the beginnings of words or within words, particularly in accented syllables. It can be used to reinforce meaning, unify thought, or simply for musical effect. "This *gr*uesome *c*reature was *c*alled *Gr*endel." *(Beowulf*, page 6, line 82.)

allusion (ə lü′zhən), a brief reference to a person, event, or place, real or fictitious, or to a work of art. In Dryden's "To the Memory of Mr. Oldham," page 247, the reference to Marcellus, the promising young nephew of the emperor Augustus who died before he could succeed his uncle, is an allusion. In Auden's "Musée Des Beaux Arts," page 592, there is an allusion to *Icarus,* a painting by Brueghel and to the Greek myth which inspired the painting.

analogy (ə nal′ə jē), a comparison made between two items, situations, or ideas that are somewhat alike but unlike in most respects. Frequently an unfamiliar or complex object or idea will be explained through comparison to a familiar or simpler one. In "Of Studies," page 209, Bacon makes an analogy between the growth of natural human abilities and that of plants in nature.

anapest (an′ə pest), a three-syllable metrical FOOT consisting of two unaccented syllables followed by an accented syllable. In the following line, the feet are divided by slashes, and since there are four feet, the line can be described as *anapestic* TETRAMETER.

> Like a child / from the womb, / like a ghost /
> from the tomb . . .
>
> Shelley, "Cloud"

anastrophe (ə nas′trə fē), inversion of the usual order of the parts of a sentence, primarily for emphasis or to achieve a certain rhythm or rhyme. "About the woodlands I will go" ("Loveliest of Trees," page 454) is a reversal or inversion of the normal order of subject-verb-object (complement), "I will go about the woodlands."

antagonist (an tag′ə nist), a character in a story or play who opposes the chief character or PROTAGONIST. In *Beowulf*, page 6, Grendel is an antagonist, as is the Devil in *Paradise Lost*, page 226.

aphorism (af′ə riz′əm), a brief saying embodying a moral, such as Pope's "Some praise at morning what they blame at night, / But always think the last opinion right," from the *Essay on Criticism*, page 272.

apostrophe (ə pos′trə fē), a figure of speech in which an absent person, an abstract concept, or an inanimate object is directly addressed. "Milton! thou shouldst be living at this hour . . ." is an example of the first (Wordsworth's "London, 1802," page 311); "Death, be not proud . . ." is an example of the second (Donne, page 214); and "O sylvan Wye! thou wanderer through the woods . . ." is an example of the third (Wordsworth's "Tintern Abbey," page 312).

archetype (är′kə tīp), an image, story-pattern, or character type which recurs frequently in literature and evokes strong, often unconscious, associations in the reader. For example, the wicked witch, the enchanted prince, and the sleeping beauty are character types widely dispersed throughout folk tales and literature. "Kubla Khan," page 317, derives much of its power from its use of archetypal images such as the "deep romantic chasm," the "demon lover," the "sacred river," "ancestral voices prophesying war," and the "damsel with a dulcimer." The story of a hero who undertakes a dangerous quest (see *Beowulf*, page 6, or *Sir Gawain and the Green Knight*, pagc 104) is a recurrent story pattern.

argument, a prose summary or synopsis of what is in a poem or play, both with regard to PLOT and meaning. Shaw's Epilogue to *Pygmalion* (page 511) may be regarded as an argument.

assonance (as′n əns), the repetition of similar vowel sounds followed by different consonant sounds in stressed syllables or words. It is often used instead of RHYME. *Hate* and *great* are examples of rhyme; *hate* and *grade* are examples of assonance. In ". . . that hoard, and sleep, and feed, and know not me" the words *sleep, feed,* and *me* are assonant. ("Ulysses" by Tennyson, page 362).

atmosphere, the MOOD of a literary work. An author establishes atmosphere partly through description of SETTING or landscape, and partly by the objects chosen to be described, as in the first eighteen lines of *The Prologue* to *The Canterbury Tales*, page 66, where an atmosphere of rebirth and renewal is created by Chaucer.

autobiography (See BIOGRAPHY.)

ballad, a NARRATIVE passed on in the oral tradition. It often makes use of repetition and dialogue. See "Lord Randal," page 60, or "Sir Patrick Spence," page 64. A ballad whose author is unknown is called a *folk ballad.* If the author is known, the ballad is called a *literary ballad.*

ballad stanza, a STANZA usually consisting of four alternating lines of IAMBIC TETRAMETER and TRIMETER and rhyming the second and fourth lines.

> The wind sae cauld blew south and north,
>   And blew into the floor;
> Quoth our goodman to our goodwife,
>   "Gae out and bar the door."
>
> "Get Up and Bar the Door," page 62

biography, any account of a person's life. See Johnson's life of *Milton,* page 278, or Boswell's life of *Johnson,* page 283. *Autobiography* is the story of all or part of a person's life written by the person who lived it. See Thomas's "Reminiscences," page 697, or Lessing's "Going Home," page 701.

blank verse, unrhymed IAMBIC PENTAMETER, a line of five feet. The Shakespeare play, page 136, and Milton's *Paradise Lost,* page 226, are written in blank verse.

> Ĭ máy / ăssért / Ĕtér- / năl Próv- / ĭdénce,
> Ănd jús- / tĭfý / thĕ wáys / ŏf Gód / tŏ mén.
>
> Milton, *Paradise Lost,* page 227, lines 25–26

burlesque (See SATIRE.)

cacophony (kə kof′ə nē), a succession of harsh, discordant sounds in either poetry or prose, used to achieve a specific effect. Note the harshness of sound and difficulty of articulation in these lines:

> And all is seared with trade; bleared, smeared
>   with toil;
> And wears man's smudge and shares man's smell:
>   the soil
> Is bare now, nor can foot feel, being shod.
>
> Hopkins, "God's Grandeur," page 447

caesura (si zhůr′ə, si zyür′ə), a pause usually near the middle in a line of verse, usually indicated by the sense of the line, and often greater than a normal pause. For purposes of study, the mark indicating a caesura is two short vertical lines (||). A caesura can be indicated by punctuation, the grammatical construction of a sentence, or the placement of lines on a page. It is used to add variety to regular METER and therefore to add emphasis to certain words.

> Born but to die,|| and reas'ning but to err;
> Alike in ignorance,|| his reason such,
> Whether he thinks too little,|| or too much:
> Chaos of thought and passion,|| all confused;
> Still by himself abused, ||or disabused . . .
>
> Pope, from *An Essay on Man,* page 274

The caesura was a particularly important device in Anglo-Saxon poetry, where each line had a caesura in the middle, but it is a technique used in most forms of poetry, such as the SONNET, the HEROIC COUPLET, and BLANK VERSE.

caricature (kar′ə kə chůr), exaggeration of prominent features of appearance or character, as in "Germans at Meat," page 704.

carpe diem (kär′pe dē′əm), Latin for "seize the day," the name applied to a THEME frequently found in LYRIC poetry: enjoy life's pleasures while you are able. See "To the Virgins, To Make Much of Time," page 219.

catastrophe, the final stage of a tragedy in which the hero meets his unhappy fate. See the final act of the Shakespeare play, page 136.

characterization, the method an author uses to acquaint a reader with his or her characters. A character's physical traits and personality may be described, as are those of John Thomas in "Tickets, Please," page 640; a character's speech and behavior may be described, as are those of the father in "My Oedipus Complex," page 662; or the thoughts and feelings of a character or the reactions of other characters to an individual may be shown, as in "A Shocking Accident," page 657. Any or all of these methods may be used in the same work.

cliché (kli shā′), an expression or phrase that is so overused as to become trite and meaningless: *white as snow, black as coal, cold as ice* are examples. A line from a famous writer may be quoted so often that it becomes a cliché. For example, Pope's "A little learning is a dangerous thing . . ." from the *Essay on Criticism,* page 272.

climax, as a term of dramatic structure, the decisive or turning point in a story or play when the action changes course and begins to resolve itself. In *Hamlet,* the hesitation and failure of the hero to kill Claudius at prayer in Act III is often regarded as the climax of the play. In *Macbeth,* the banquet scene in Act III where the ghost of Banquo appears to Macbeth is often regarded as the climax. Not every story or play has this kind of dramatic climax. Sometimes a character may simply resolve a problem in his or her mind. At times there is no resolution of the PLOT; the climax then comes when a character realizes that a resolution is impossible. (See also PLOT.) The term is also used to mean the point of greatest interest in a work, where the reader or audience has the most intense emotional response.

comedy, a play written primarily to amuse the audience. In addition to arousing laughter, comic writing often appeals to the intellect. Thus the comic mode has often been used to "instruct" the audience about the follies of certain social conventions and human foibles, as is done in *Pygmalion*, page 511. When so used, the comedy tends toward SATIRE.

comedy of ideas, a comedy in which the humor lies in ideas more than in situations. See *Pygmalion*, page 511.

conceit, an elaborate and surprising *figure of speech* comparing two very dissimilar things. It usually involves intellectual cleverness and ingenuity. In the last three STANZAS of "A Valediction: Forbidding Mourning," page 213, Donne compares his soul and that of his love to the two legs or branches of a draftsman's compass used to make a circle. The previously unseen likeness as developed by the poet helps us to see and understand the subject described (the relationship of the lovers' souls) more clearly.

conflict, the struggle between two opposing forces. The four basic kinds of conflict are: (1) a person against another person or opponent (*Beowulf,* page 6, or "My Oedipus Complex," page 662); (2) a person against nature ("The Seafarer," page 53, or "The Star," page 492); (3) a person against society (*Pygmalion,* page 511); and (4) two elements within a person struggling for mastery (Joyce's "Eveline," page 632).

connotation (kon′ə tā′shən), the emotional associations surrounding a word, as opposed to its literal meaning or DENOTATION. Some connotations are fairly general, others quite personal. Shakespeare's Sonnet 30, page 131, uses the connotative powers of language to create a mood of longing for lost beauties of the past that survive only in the poet's memory. Many of the words used by Shakespeare in this sonnet suggest associations that cluster around a sense of loss.

consonance (kon′sə nəns), the repetition of consonant sounds that are preceded by different vowel sounds.

> For*l*orn! the very word is like a be*ll*
> To to*ll* me back from thee to my so*l*e se*lf*.
>
> Keats, "Ode to a Nightingale," page 334.

Consonance is an effective device for linking sound, mood, and meaning. In the lines above, the *l* sounds reinforce the melancholy mood.

couplet, a pair of rhyming lines with identical meter.

> Know then thyself, presume not God to scan:
> The proper study of mankind is man.
>
> Pope, from *An Essay on Man*, page 274

dactyl (dak′tl), a three-syllable metrical FOOT consisting of an accented syllable followed by two unaccented syllables. In the following lines the feet are divided by slashes, and since there are six feet, the basic RHYTHM is *dactylic* HEXAMETER.

> Loósĭng hĭs / árms frŏm hĕr / waíst hĕ flĕw /
> úpwărd, ă- / waítĭng thĕ / séa beást.
>
> Charles Kingsley, *Andromeda*

denotation (dē nō tā′shən), the strict, literal meaning of a word. (See CONNOTATION.)

denouement (dā′nü mäN′), the resolution of the PLOT. The word is derived from a French word meaning literally "to untie." In "The Legacy," page 635, the denouement involves the revelation of the fact and identity of Angela's lover, and the explanation of her death.

dialogue, the conversation between two or more people in a literary work. Dialogue can serve many purposes, among them: (1) CHARACTERIZATION of those speaking and those spoken about, as in "Tears, Idle Tears," page 652; (2) the creation of MOOD or ATMOSPHERE, as in "The Lagoon," page 475; (3) the advancement of the PLOT, as in "The Legacy," page 635; and (4) the development of a THEME, as in "Tickets, Please," page 640.

diary, a record of daily happenings written by a person for his or her own use. The diarist is moved by a need to record daily routine and confess innermost thoughts. The diary makes up in immediacy and frankness what it lacks in artistic shape and coherence. See the diary of Pepys, page 249.

diction, the author's choice of words or phrases in a literary work. This choice involves both the CONNOTATIVE and denotative meaning of a word as well as levels of usage. In *Pygmalion,* page 511, the playwright makes use of a wide variety of dictions when he has each character speak in a way that is appropriate to his or her education and background.

dramatic convention, any of several devices which the audience accepts as a substitution for reality in a dramatic work. For instance, the audience accepts that an interval between acts may represent hours, days, weeks, months, or years; that a bare stage may be a meadow; that an invisible scaffold rather than a house supports a balcony; that an audible dialogue is supposed to represent whispered conversation; or that a rosy spotlight signals the dawn.

dramatic irony (See IRONY.)

dramatic monologue (mon′l ôg), a LYRIC poem in which the speaker addresses someone whose replies are not recorded. Sometimes the one addressed seems to be present, sometimes not. See "Porphyria's Lover," page 373, or "My Last Duchess," page 374.

elegy, a solemn, reflective poem, usually about death, written in a formal style. See Gray's "Elegy Written in a Country Churchyard," page 288.

end rhyme, the rhyming of words at the ends of lines of poetry. (See RHYME.)

end-stopped line, a line of poetry that contains a complete thought, thus necessitating the use of a semicolon, colon, or period at the end:

Good nature and good sense must ever join;
To err is human, to forgive divine.

Pope, *An Essay on Criticism*, page 272

(See also RUN-ON LINE.)

epic, a long NARRATIVE poem (originally handed down in oral tradition, later a literary form) dealing with great heroes and adventures, having a national, worldwide, or cosmic setting, involving supernatural forces, and written in a deliberately ceremonial STYLE. See *Beowulf,* page 6, or *Paradise Lost,* page 226.

epigram, any short, witty verse or saying, often ending with a wry twist.

'Tis with our judgments as our watches; none
Go just alike, yet each believes his own.

Pope, *An Essay on Criticism*, page 272

epilogue, concluding section added to a work, serving to round out or interpret it. See the Epilogue to *Pygmalion,* page 511.

essay, a brief composition that presents a personal point of view. An essay may present a viewpoint through formal analysis and argument, as in "Of Studies," page 209, or it may be more informal in style, as in "Going Home," page 701.

euphony (yü′fə nē), a combination of pleasing sounds in poetry or prose.

I cannot see what flowers are at my feet,
Nor what soft incense hangs upon the boughs,
But, in embalmèd darkness, guess each sweet
Wherewith the seasonable month endows
The grass, the thicket, and the fruit tree wild . . .

Keats, "Ode to a Nightingale," page 334

(See also CACOPHONY.)

extended metaphor, a figure of speech that is developed at great length, often through a whole work or a great part of it. It is common in poetry but is used in prose as well. Wyatt's "Whoso List to Hunt," page 116, contains an extended metaphor, with the hunter representing the love-struck poet and the deer representing the poet's beloved. (See METAPHOR.)

fable, a brief tale, in which the characters are often animals, told to point out a moral truth. Dryden's *The Hind and the Panther,* page 244, is an example of a fable.

fantasy, a work that takes place in an unreal world, concerns incredible characters, or employs physical and scientific principles not yet discovered. Thus, there are elements of fantasy in "The Lifted Veil," page 409, *Alice's Adventures under Ground,* page 386, and "The Star," page 492.

figurative language, language used in a nonliteral way to express a suitable relationship between essentially unlike things. When, in "Going Home," page 701, the writer says that the sun hung in the sky "like a luminous spider's egg, or a white pearl," she is using figurative language or a *figure of speech.* The more common figures of speech are SIMILE, METAPHOR, PERSONIFICATION, HYPERBOLE, and SYNECHDOCHE.

flashback, interruption of the narrative to show an episode that happened before that particular point in the story. In "Tears, Idle Tears," page 652, the description of Mrs. Dickinson's grief at the loss of her husband is an example of flashback.

foil, a character whose traits are the opposite of those of another character and who thus points up the strengths or weaknesses of another character. Henry Higgins and Liza Doolittle are foils to one another in *Pygmalion,* page 511.

folk ballad (See BALLAD.)

folklore, the customs, legends, songs, and tales of a people or nation. The popular ballads, page 60, are examples of folklore.

foot, a group of syllables in VERSE usually consisting of one accented syllable and the unaccented syllable(s) associated with it. (A foot may occasionally, for variety, have two accented syllables—see SPONDEE—or two unaccented syllables—the *pyrrhic.*) In the following lines the feet are divided by slashes:

C˘ome líve/ w˘ith mé / ˘and bé / m˘y Lóve,
˘And wé / w˘ill áll / th˘e pléa- / s˘ures próve.

Marlow, "The Passionate Shepherd," page 126

The most common line lengths are five feet (PENTAMETER), four feet (TETRAMETER), and three feet (TRIMETER). The quoted lines above are IAMBIC TETRAMETER. (See also RHYTHM.)

foreshadowing, a hint given to the reader of what is to come. In "Lord Randal," page 60, the reader begins to suspect, because of the dinner and the bloodhounds, that Lord Randal has been poisoned before his mother explicitly says so in the final STANZA.

frame, a NARRATIVE device presenting a story or group of stories within the frame of a larger narrative. The frame provides continuity for the group of stories. The pilgrimage in Chaucer's *The Canterbury Tales,* page 66, is the frame unifying the stories told by the pilgrims.

free verse, a type of poetry that differs from conventional VERSE forms in being "free" from a fixed pattern of METER and RHYME, but using RHYTHM and other poetic devices. See Eliot's "The Hollow Men," page 584.

genre (zhän′rə), a form or type of literary work. For example, the novel, the short story, and the poem are all genres. The term is a very loose one, however, so that subheadings under these would themselves also be called genres, for instance, EPIC.

heroic couplet, a pair of rhymed verse lines in IAMBIC PENTAMETER.

Trust not yourself: but your defects to know,
Make use of every friend—and every foe.

Pope, from *An Essay on Criticism*, page 272

heroic simile, a SIMILE sustained for several lines and suggesting the heroic in nature or quality. See *Paradise Lost*, page 226, lines 100–113.

hexameter (hek sam′ə tər), a verse line of six feet. Spenser, in *The Faerie Queen*, uses a STANZA consisting of nine lines, the first eight of which are IAMBIC PENTAMETER and the last of which is a hexameter.

> Most loath- / some, filth- / y, foul, /
> and full / of vile / disdain.
>
> Spenser, *The Faerie Queen*, page 121

homily (hom′ə lī), a sermon, or serious moral talk. See "Meditation 17," page 215.

hyperbole (hī pėr′bə lē), a figure of speech involving great exaggeration. The effect may be serious or comic. Byron uses hyperbole for comic effect in *Don Juan* (see stanza 17, page 323).

iamb (ī′amb), a two-syllable metrical FOOT consisting of one unaccented syllable followed by one accented syllable. The *iambic* foot is the most common meter in English poetry.

> For God's / sake, hold / your tongue, /
> and let / me love . . .
>
> Donne, "The Canonization," page 212

imagery, the sensory details that provide vividness in a literary work and tend to arouse emotions or feelings in a reader which abstract language does not. Shakespeare's Sonnet 130, page 130, is rich in specific, concrete details that appeal to the senses.

inference, a reasonable conclusion about the behavior of a character or the meaning of an event drawn from the limited information presented by the author.

in medias res (in mā′dē äs rās′), Latin for "in the middle of things." In a traditional EPIC the opening scene often begins in the middle of the action. *Paradise Lost,* page 226, opens with Satan and his angels already defeated and in Hell; later in the poem the story of the battle between Satan and the forces of Heaven, which led to this defeat, is told. This device may be used in any NARRATIVE form, not just the epic.

internal rhyme, rhyming words or accented syllables within a line which may or may not have a rhyme at the end of the line as well: "We three shall flee across the sea to Italy."

inversion (See ANASTROPHE.)

invocation (in′və kā′shən), the call on a deity or muse (classical goddess that inspired a poet) for help and inspiration found at the beginning of traditional EPIC poems. Milton, in *Paradise Lost*, page 226, instead of invoking one of the traditional muses of poetry calls upon the "Heavenly Muse."

irony, the term used to describe a contrast between what appears to be and what really is. In *verbal irony*, the intended meaning of a statement or work is different from (often the opposite of) what the statement or work literally says, as in Swift's "A Modest Proposal," page 259. *Understatement,* in which an opinion is expressed less emphatically than it might be, is a form of verbal irony, often used for humorous or cutting effect; for example, Johnson's remark in his "Letter to Chesterfield," page 277: "To be so distinguished [by Chesterfield's praise of Johnson's *Dictionary* in the press] is an honor which, being very little accustomed to favors from the great, I know not well how to receive." *Irony of situation* refers to an occurrence that is contrary to what is expected or intended, as in Hardy's "Ah, Are You Digging on My Grave," page 451. *Dramatic irony* refers to a situation in which events or facts not known to a character on stage or in a fictional work are known to another character and the audience or reader. In "The Lifted Veil," page 409, events known to Latimer (and the reader) are not known to the other characters.

journal, a formal record of a person's daily experiences. It is less intimate or personal than a DIARY and more chronological than an autobiography. See *Journal of the Plague Year,* page 294, for a fictional attempt to create the impression of an actual journal.

kenning, metaphorical compound word used as a poetic device. In *Beowulf,* page 6, there are many examples of kennings. The king is the "ring-giver," the rough sea is the "whale-road," and the calm sea is the "swan-road."

literary ballad (See BALLAD.)

lyric, a poem, usually short, that expresses some basic emotion or state of mind. It usually creates a single impression and is highly personal. It may be rhymed or unrhymed. SONNETS are lyric poems. Other examples of lyrics are Burns's "A Red, Red Rose," page 292, and most of the shorter poems of the Romantics.

main idea (See THEME.)

maxim (See APHORISM.)

memoir (mem′wär, mem′wôr), a form of autobiography that is more concerned with personalities, events, and actions of public importance than with the private life of the writer. "Why I Write," page 692, and "Going Home," page 701, have some of the qualities of memoir.

metaphor, a figure of speech involving an implied comparison. In "Meditation 17," page 215, Donne compares the individual to a chapter in a book and, later, to a piece of a continent. (See also SIMILE and FIGURATIVE LANGUAGE.)

metaphysical (met′ə fiz′ə kəl) **poetry,** poetry exhibiting a highly intellectual style that is witty, subtle, and sometimes fantastic, particularly in the use of CONCEITS. See especially the work of Donne, page 211.

meter, the pattern of stressed and unstressed syllables in poetry. (See RHYTHM.)

metonomy (mə ton′ə mē), a figure of speech in which a specific term naming an object is substituted for another word with which it is closely associated. For example, in "The Creation of the World," page 204, it is said, "In the sweat of thy face shalt thou eat bread," in which the term "sweat" represents hard physical labor.

mock-heroic (also called *mock-epic*), a SATIRE using the form and style of an EPIC poem to treat a trivial incident. There are mock-heroic elements in *Don Juan*, page 322.

monologue (See SOLILOQUY and DRAMATIC MONOLOGUE.)

mood, the overall ATMOSPHERE or prevailing emotional aura of a work. "The Eve of St. Agnes," page 336, might be described as having a hypnotic, dreamlike atmosphere or mood. (See TONE for a comparison.)

motif (mō tēf′), a character, incident, idea, or object that recurs in various works or in various parts of the same work. In Shakespeare's sonnets, page 130, the nature and effect of time is a recurrent motif.

myth, a traditional story connected with the religion of a people, usually attempting to account for something in nature. Milton's *Paradise Lost*, page 226, has mythic elements in its attempts to interpret aspects of the universe.

narrative, a story or account of an event or a series of events. It may be told either in poetry or prose; it may be either fictional or true. Defoe's *Journal of the Plague Year*, page 294, is a narrative, as is *Paradise Lost*, page 226.

narrator, the teller of a story. The teller may be a character in the story, as in "My Oedipus Complex," page 662; the author herself, as in "Going Home," page 701; or an anonymous voice outside the story, as in "The Legacy," page 635. A narrator's attitude toward his or her subject is capable of much variation; it can range from one of apparent indifference to one of extreme conviction and feeling. When a narrator appears to have some bias regarding his or her subject, as in "Germans at Meat," page 704, it becomes especially important not to automatically assume that the narrator and the author are to be regarded as the same person. (See also PERSONA and POINT OF VIEW.)

naturalism, writing that depicts events as rigidly determined by the forces of heredity and environment. The world described tends to be bleak. There are elements of naturalism in the work of Thomas Hardy, George Eliot, and D. H. Lawrence.

neo-classicism, writing that shows the influence of the Greek and Roman classics. The term is often applied to English literature of the eighteenth century. (See Unit 4, page 240.)

novel, a long work of NARRATIVE prose fiction dealing with characters, situations, and SETTINGS that imitate those of real life. Among the authors in this text who have written novels are George Eliot, Thomas Hardy, Joseph Conrad, D. H. Lawrence, James Joyce, Virginia Woolf, Graham Greene, and Doris Lessing. Eliot's "The Lifted Veil," page 409, is considered a short novel by some, although it is more properly classified as a long short story.

ode, a long LYRIC poem, formal in style and complex in form, often written in commemoration or celebration of a special quality, object, or occasion. See "Ode to the West Wind," page 330, "Ode on a Grecian Urn," page 333, and "Ode to a Nightingale," page 334.

onomatopoeia (on′ə mat′ə pē′ə), word(s) used in such a way that the sound of the word(s) imitates the sound of the thing spoken of. Some single words in which sound suggests meaning: "hiss," "smack," "buzz," and "hum." An example where sound echoes sense throughout the whole phrase: "The murmurous haunt of flies on summer eves." ("Ode to a Nightingale," page 334.)

ottava rima (ō tä′və rē′mə), a STANZA pattern consisting of eight IAMBIC PENTAMETER lines rhyming *abababcc*. *Don Juan*, page 322, is written in ottava rima.

parable, a brief fictional work which concretely illustrates an abstract idea or teaches some lesson or truth. It differs from a FABLE in that the characters in it are generally people rather than animals; it differs from an ALLEGORY in that its characters do not necessarily represent abstract qualities. *The Wife of Bath's Tale*, page 81, has elements of the parable.

paradox, a statement, often metaphorical, that seems to be self-contradictory but which has valid meaning:

> When I lie tangled in her hair
> And fettered to her eye,
> The birds that wanton in the air
> Know no such liberty.
>
> Lovelace, "To Althea, from Prison," page 218

parody (See SATIRE.)

pastoral poetry, a conventional form of LYRIC poetry presenting an idealized picture of rural life. See "The Passionate Shepherd to His Love," page 126.

pentameter (pen tam′ə tər), a metrical line of five feet. (See also FOOT.)

> Whén tŏ / thĕ sés- / siŏns óf / swĕet sí- /
> lĕnt thóught . . .
>
> Shakespeare, Sonnet 30, page 131

persona (pər sō′nə), the mask or voice of the author or the author's creation in a particular work. George Eliot is of course the author of "The Lifted Veil," page 409, but even though the narrative is told from the *first-person* POINT OF VIEW, we are not to assume that Eliot is expressing her personal opinions. Rather, she has created a persona in the form of a narrator, Latimer, who can see into the future. "A Shocking Accident," page 657, is told from the *omniscient* POINT OF VIEW, but Greene has assumed a voice or persona—detached, witty, ironic—in telling the story. (See also NARRATOR and POINT OF VIEW.)

personification (pər son′ə fə kā′shən), the representation of abstractions, ideas, animals, or inanimate objects as human beings by endowing them with human qualities. Death is personified in Donne's "Holy Sonnet 10," page 214. Personification is one kind of FIGURATIVE LANGUAGE.

Petrarchan sonnet (See SONNET.)

plot, in the simplest sense, a series of happenings in a literary work; but it is often used to refer to the action as it is organized around a CONFLICT and builds through complication to a CLIMAX followed by a DENOUEMENT or resolution. See the Shakespeare play, page 136.

point of view, the relation between the teller of the story and the characters in it. The teller, or NARRATOR, may be a character in the story, in which case it is told from the *first-person* point of view, as in "The Lifted Veil," page 409. A writer who describes, in the *third person,* the thoughts and actions of any or all of the characters as the need arises is said to use the *omniscient* (om nish′ənt) point of view, as in "Tickets, Please," page 640. A writer who, in the *third person,* follows along with one character and tends to view events from that person's perspective is said to use a *limited omniscient* point of view, as in "Eveline," page 632. An author who describes only what can be seen, like a newspaper reporter, is said to use the *dramatic* point of view. (See also NARRATOR and PERSONA.)

prologue, section which precedes the main body of a work and serves as an introduction. See *The Prologue* to *The Canterbury Tales,* page 67.

propaganda (prop′ə gan′də), writing that directly advocates a certain doctrine as the solution to some social or political problem. Orwell's "Why I Write," page 692, sheds interesting light on the nature of propaganda.

prose poem, a piece of writing set down as prose but having some of the rhythms, language, and imaginative quality usually associated with poetry. "The Creation of the World," page 204, and Thomas's "Reminiscences of Childhood," page 697, have elements of prose poetry.

protagonist (prō tag′ə nist), the leading character in a literary work. Purun Bhagat (Purun Dass) is the protagonist of "The Miracle of Purun Bhagat," page 466. (See ANTAGONIST.)

quatrain (kwot′rān), verse STANZA of four lines. This stanza may take many forms, according to line lengths and RHYME patterns.

To plead my faith where faith had no reward,
To move remorse where favor is not borne,
To heap complaints where she doth not regard—
Were fruitless, bootless, vain, and yield but scorn.

Earl of Essex, "To Plead My Faith," page 119

realism, a way of representing life that emphasizes ordinary people in everyday experiences. "My Oedipus Complex," page 662, provides an example of realism.

refrain, the repetition of one or more lines in each STANZA of a poem. See "Lord Randal," page 60.

rhyme, exact repetition of sounds in at least the final accented syllables of two or more words.

Let such teach others who themselves ex*cel,*
And censure freely who have written *well.*

Pope, *An Essay on Criticism*, page 272

(See also RHYME SCHEME, INTERNAL RHYME, END RHYME, and SLANT RHYME.)

rhyme scheme, any pattern of rhyme in a STANZA. For purposes of study, the pattern is labeled as shown below, with the first rhyme labeled *a,* as are all the words rhyming with it; the second rhyme labeled *b,* the third rhyme *c,* and so on.

Queen and huntress, chaste and fair, *a*
Now the sun is laid to sleep, *b*
Seated in thy silver chair *a*
State in wonted manner keep; *b*
Hesperus entreats thy light, *c*
Goddess excellently bright. *c*

Jonson, "To Cynthia," page 216

rhythm, the arrangement of stressed and unstressed sounds in speech or writing into patterns. Rhythm, or meter, may be regular or it may vary within a line or work. The four most common meters are IAMB or *iambus* (⏑ /), TROCHEE (/ ⏑), ANAPEST (⏑⏑/), and DACTYL (/⏑⏑).

romance, a long narrative in VERSE or prose that originated in the Middle Ages. Its main elements are adventure, love, and magic. There are elements of romance in "The Day of Destiny," page 96, *Sir Gawain and the Green Knight,* page 104, and *The Faerie Queen,* page 121, particularly in its ATMOSPHERE and SETTING.

romanticism, unlike REALISM, romanticism tends to portray the uncommon. The material selected tends to deal with extraordinary people in unusual experiences. In romantic literature there is often a stress on the past and an emphasis on nature. See Unit 5 for many examples of romanticism.

run-on line, a line in which the thought continues beyond the end of the poetic line. There should be no pause after *thine* in the first line:

For sure our souls were near allied, and thine
Cast in the same poetic mould with mine.

Dryden, "To the Memory of Mr. Oldham," page 247

sarcasm (sar′kaz′əm), the use of language to hurt or ridicule. It is less subtle in TONE than IRONY. Boswell, in the *Life of Johnson,* page 283, reports that when he first met Johnson he said (knowing Johnson's aversion to Scotland): "I do indeed come from Scotland, but I cannot help it." To which Johnson replied: "That, Sir, I find is what a very great many of your countrymen cannot help." Johnson's retort is an example of sarcasm.

satire, the technique that employs wit to ridicule a subject, usually some social institution or human foible, with the intention to inspire reform. SARCASM and IRONY are often used in writing satire. *Burlesque* and *parody* are closely related to satire. *Burlesque* is a literary or dramatic work that ridicules people, actions, or their literary works by mimickry and exaggeration. *Parody,* a kind of burlesque, is humorous imitation of serious writing, usually for the purpose of making the style of an author appear ridiculous. Swift's poetry and prose, page 256, Byron's *Don Juan,* page 322, and Shaw's *Pygmalion,* page 511, all provide good examples of satire.

scansion (skan′shən), the marking off of lines of poetry into feet, indicating the stressed and unstressed syllables. (See RHYTHM and FOOT.)

setting, the time (both time of day and period in history) and place in which the action of a narrative occurs. The setting may be suggested through dialogue and action, or it may be described by the NARRATOR or one of the characters. Setting contributes strongly to the MOOD or ATMOSPHERE and plausibility of a work. Setting is important in "Lines Composed a Few Miles Above Tintern Abbey," page 312, and "The Lagoon," page 475.

Shakespearean sonnet (See SONNET.)

simile (sim′ə lē), a *figure of speech* involving a comparison using *like* or *as:*

> And now, like amorous birds of prey,
> Rather at once our time devour . . .
>
> Marvell, "To His Coy Mistress," page 221

In this example the similarity between the lovers and the birds of prey is their hungry appetite. (See METAPHOR for comparison.)

slant rhyme, rhyme in which the vowel sounds are not quite identical, as in the first and third lines below.

> And I untightened next the tress
> About her neck; her cheek once more
> Blushed bright beneath my burning kiss:
> I propped her head up as before,
> Only, this time my shoulder bore . . .
>
> Browning, "Porphyria's Lover," page 373

soliloquy (sə lil′ə kwē), a DRAMATIC CONVENTION that allows a character alone on stage to speak his or her thoughts aloud. If someone else is on stage, and the character's words are unheard, the soliloquy becomes an *aside.* See the Shakespeare play, page 136, for examples. (Compare with DRAMATIC MONOLOGUE.)

sonnet, a LYRIC poem with a traditional form of fourteen IAMBIC PENTAMETER lines. Sonnets fall into two groups, according to their RHYME SCHEMES. The *Italian* or *Petrarchan* (after the Italian poet Petrarch) sonnet is usually rhymed *abbaabba/cdecde* (with variations permitted in the *cdecde* rhyme scheme), forming basically a two-part poem of eight lines (*octave*) and six lines (*sestet*) respectively. These two parts are played off against each other in a great variety of ways. See "Whoso List to Hunt," page 116. The *English* or *Shakespearean* sonnet is usually rhymed *abab/cdcd/efef/gg,* presenting a four-part structure in which an idea or theme is developed in three stages and then brought to a conclusion in the COUPLET. See Shakespeare's sonnets, page 130.

speaker (See NARRATOR.)

Spenserian stanza (See HEXAMETER.)

spondee (spon′dē), a metrical FOOT of two accented syllables (/ /). It serves occasionally as a substitute foot to vary the meter, as in the third foot below.

> As yet / but knock, / breathe, shine, / and
> seek / to mend . . .
>
> Donne, Holy Sonnet 14, page 214

The opposite of the spondee is the *pyrrhic,* a metrical foot of two unaccented syllables (⌣⌣). It is rare in English poetry and is not even accepted as a foot by some experts.

sprung rhythm, metrical form which consists of scanning the accented or stressed syllables without regard to the number of unstressed syllables in a FOOT. A foot may have from one to four syllables, with the accent always on the first syllable of the foot. The term was invented and the technique developed by Gerard Manley Hopkins. The following line is scanned according to Hopkins's theory:

> And for all / this, / nature is / never /
> spent . . .
>
> Hopkins, "God's Grandeur," page 447

The first foot has three syllables, the second foot one, the third foot three, the fourth foot two, and the fifth foot one, with the accent on the first syllable of each foot.

stanza, a group of lines which are set off and form a division in a poem, sometimes linked with other stanzas by RHYME. Hopkins's "Pied Beauty," page 446, has two stanzas.

stereotype (ster′ē ə tīp′, stir′ē ə tīp), a conventional character, PLOT, or SETTING, which thus possesses little or no individuality, but which may be used for a purpose. "Germans at Meat," page 704, makes use of stereotyped characters.

stream of consciousness, the recording or re-creation of a character's flow of thought. Raw images, perceptions, memories come and go in seemingly random, but actually controlled, fashion, much as they do in people's minds. There are elements of stream of consciousness in the excerpt from Gardner's *Grendel,* page 33.

style, the distinctive handling of language by an author. It involves the specific choices made with regard to DICTION, syntax, FIGURATIVE LANGUAGE, etc. For a comparison of two very different styles, see Orwell's

"Why I Write," page 692, and Thomas's "Reminiscences of Childhood," page 697.

subject, the topic about which an author is writing. (See THEME for a comparison.)

surrealism (sə rē′ə liz′əm), a term used in both painting and literature to apply to incongruous and dreamlike IMAGERY and sequences which are associated with the unconscious. "The Hollow Men," page 584, and "The King of China's Daughter," page 588, contain examples of surrealism.

symbol, something relatively concrete, such as an object, action, character, or scene, which signifies something relatively abstract, such as a concept or idea. In "Sailing to Byzantium," page 462, the city is a symbol of the ideal unity of all aspects of life—religious, aesthetic, practical, intellectual.

synecdoche (si nek′də kē), a *figure of speech* in which a part stands for the whole, as in "hired *hands*," in which *hands* (the part) stands for the whole (those who do manual labor—labor with their hands). The term also refers to a figurative expression in which the whole stands for a part, as in "call the *law*," in which *law* (the whole) represents the police (a part of the whole system of law).

tercet (tėr′sit), also called *triplet*, a STANZA of three rhyming lines.

> Whenas in silks my Julia goes,
> Then, then (methinks) how sweetly flows
> That liquefaction of her clothes.
>
> Herrick, "Upon Julia's Clothes"

terza rima (ter′tsä rē′mä), a verse form with a three-line STANZA rhyming *aba*, *bcb*, *cdc*, etc.

> Thou who didst waken from his summer dreams
> The blue Mediterranean, where he lay,
> Lulled by the coil of his crystalline streams,
>
> Beside a pumice isle in Baiae's bay,
> And saw in sleep old palaces and towers
> Quivering within the wave's intenser day . . .
>
> Shelley, "Ode to the West Wind," page 330

tetrameter (te tram′ə tər), a metrical line of four feet.

> Hăd wé / bŭt wórld / ĕnóugh, / ănd tíme . . .
>
> Marvell, "To His Coy Mistress," page 221

theme, the main idea or underlying meaning of a literary work. A theme may be directly stated but more often is implied. In "The Doll's House," page 647, the TOPIC or subject is described, at least in part, in the title, but an important theme is the pain of childhood.

tone, the author's attitude toward his or her subject matter and toward the audience. In *The Prologue* to *The Canterbury Tales*, page 67, Chaucer's tone is both sympathetic and ironic. He pretends to be an innocent observer, supplying details about each pilgrim in haphazard manner; yet these details, when carefully weighed, have a telling ironic force. The irony, however, is blended with humor and compassion.

topic, the subject about which an author writes. (See THEME.)

tragedy, dramatic or narrative writing in which the main character suffers disaster after a serious and significant struggle but faces his or her downfall in such a way as to attain heroic stature. See Shakespeare play, page 136.

trimeter (trim′ə tər), metrical line of three feet.

> Dówn tŏ / ă sún- / lĕss séa.
>
> Coleridge, "Kubla Khan," page 317

triplet (See TERCET.)

trochee (trō′kē), metrical foot made up of one accented syllable followed by an unaccented syllable.

> Dóublĕ, / dóublĕ / tóil ănd / tróublĕ;
> Fírĕ / búrn ănd / cáldrŏn / búbblĕ.
>
> *Macbeth*, IV, 1

verbal irony (See IRONY.)

verse, in its most general sense a synonym for *poetry*. Verse may also be used to refer to poetry carefully composed as to RHYTHM and RHYME SCHEME, but of inferior literary value. Sometimes the word *verse* is used to mean a *line* or STANZA of poetry.

vignette (vi nyet′), a literary sketch or verbal description, a brief incident or scene. "Three Pictures," page 690, may be considered a vignette.

voice (See PERSONA.)

GLOSSARY

Full pronunciation key

The pronunciation of each word is shown just after the word, in this way: **ab bre vi ate** (ə brē′vē āt). The letters and signs used are pronounced as in the words below. The mark ′ is placed after a syllable with primary or heavy accent, as in the example above. The mark ′ after a syllable shows a secondary or lighter accent, as in **ab bre vi a tion** (ə brē′vē ā′shən).

Some words, taken from foreign languages, are spoken with sounds that do not otherwise occur in English. Symbols for these sounds are given in the key as "foreign sounds."

a	hat, cap
ā	age, face
ä	father, far
b	bad, rob
ch	child, much
d	did, red
e	let, best
ē	equal, be
ėr	term, learn
f	fat, if
g	go, bag
h	he, how
i	it, pin
ī	ice, five
j	jam, enjoy
k	kind, seek
l	land, coal
m	me, am
n	no, in
ng	long, bring
o	hot, rock
ō	open, go
ô	order, all
oi	oil, voice
ou	house, out
p	paper, cup
r	run, try
s	say, yes
sh	she, rush
t	tell, it
th	thin, both
ᴛʜ	then, smooth
u	cup, butter
u̇	full, put
ü	rule, move
v	very, save
w	will, woman
y	young, yet
z	zero, breeze
zh	measure, seizure
ə	represents: a in about, e in taken, i in pencil, o in lemon, u in circus

foreign sounds

ʏ as in French *du.* Pronounce (ē) with the lips rounded as for (ü).

à as in French *ami.* Pronounce (ä) with the lips spread and held tense.

œ as in French *peu.* Pronounce (ā) with the lips rounded as for (ō).

ɴ as in French *bon.* The ɴ is not pronounced, but shows that the vowel before it is nasal.

ʜ as in German *ach.* Pronounce (k) without closing the breath passage.

Grammatical key

adj.	adjective
adv.	adverb
conj.	conjunction
interj.	interjection
n.	noun
sing.	singular
prep.	preposition
pron.	pronoun
v.	verb
v.i.	intransitive verb
v.t.	transitive verb
pl.	plural

ab-, *prefix.* from; away; away from; off.

a base (ə bās′), *v.t.,* **a based, a bas ing.** make lower in rank, condition, or character; degrade. [< Old French *abaissier* < *a-* to + *baissier* lower] **—a base′ment,** *n.*

a bate (ə bāt′), *v.,* **a bat ed, a bat ing.** —*v.t.* 1 lessen in force or intensity; reduce or decrease. 2 put an end to; stop. —*v.i.* become less in force or intensity; diminish.

a bate ment (ə bāt′mənt), *n.* 1 a decrease; lessening. 2 amount abated; reduction. 3 a putting an end to.

ab hor (ab hôr′), *v.t.,* **-horred, -hor ring.** regard with horror or disgust; hate completely: detest; loathe.

a bide (ə bīd′), *v.,* **a bode** or **a bid ed, a bid ing.** —*v.t.* 1 put up with; endure; tolerate. 2 submit to. 3 await or withstand defiantly. 4 ARCHAIC. wait for. —*v.i.* 1 stay; remain. 2 continue to live (in a place); dwell; reside. [Old English *ābīdan* stay on, and *onbīdan* wait for]

ab ject (ab′jekt, ab jekt′), *adj.* 1 so low or degraded as to be hopeless; wretched; miserable. 2 deserving contempt; despicable. 3 slavish.

ab jure (ab jůr′), *v.t.,* **-jured, -jur ing.** 1 swear to give up; renounce. 2 retract formally or solemnly; repudiate. 3 refrain from; avoid. [< Latin *abjurare* < *ab-* away + *jurare* swear]

-able, *suffix forming adjectives from verbs and nouns.*

a bom i na ble (ə bom′ə nə bəl), *adj.* 1 arousing disgust and hatred; detestable; loathsome. 2 very unpleasant; disagreeable. **—a bom′i na bly,** *adv.*

ab so lu tion (ab′sə lü′shən), *n.* 1 a freeing from sin, guilt, or blame. 2 declaration that frees a person from guilt or punishment for sin.

ab ste mi ous (ab stē′mē əs), *adj.* 1 sparing in eating, drinking, etc.; moderate; temperate. 2 very plain; restricted.

ab struse (ab strüs′), *adj.* hard to understand; difficult; recondite.

a bys mal (ə biz′məl), *adj.* 1 too deep or great to be measured; bottomless. 2 of the lowest depths of the ocean.

a byss (ə bis′), *n.* 1 a bottomless or very great depth; chasm. 2 anything too deep or great to be measured; lowest depth. 3 the chaos before the Creation. [< Greek *abyssos* < *a-* without + *byssos* bottom]

ac crue (ə krü′), *v.i.,* **-crued, -cru ing.** 1 come as a natural product or result. 2 grow or arise as the product of money invested. [< Old French *acreüe* an increase < *acreistre* to increase < Latin *accrescere* < *ad-* to + *crescere* grow] **—ac crue′ment,** *n.*

ac quit (ə kwit′), *v.t.,* **-quit ted, -quit ting.** 1 declare not guilty; set free after considering evidence; exonerate. 2 **acquit oneself,** do one's part; behave.

ac quit tance (ə kwit′ns), *n.* a written release from a debt or obligation.

ac ri mo ni ous (ak′rə mō′nē əs), *adj.* bitter and irritating in disposition or manner; caustic.

ac tu ate (ak′chü āt), *v.t.,* **-at ed, -at ing.** influence to act; impel.

ad age (ad′ij), *n.* a well-known proverb.

ad a man tine (ad′ə man′tēn′, ad′ə man′tīn), *adj.* unyielding; firm; immovable.

ad ver sar y (ad′vər ser′ē), *n., pl.* **-sar ies.** 1 person or group opposing or resisting another or others; antagonist; enemy. 2 person or group on the other side in a contest; opponent.

ad ver si ty (ad vėr′sə tē), *n., pl.* **-ties.** 1 condition of being in unfavorable circumstances, especially unfavorable financial circumstances; misfortune; distress. 2 a particular misfortune; calamity.

af fa ble (af′ə bəl), *adj.* 1 courteous and pleasant in receiving and responding to the conversation or approaches of others. 2 gracious.

af fec ta tion (af′ek tā′shən), *n.* 1 behavior that is not natural, but assumed to impress others; pretense. 2 mannerism, choice of language, etc., that indicates a tendency toward this.

af fin i ty (ə fin′ə tē), *n., pl.* **-ties.** 1 a natural attraction to a person or liking for a thing. 2 relation; connection.

af flic tion (ə flik′shən), *n.* 1 condition of continued pain or distress; misery. 2 cause of continued pain or distress; misfortune.

a gape (ə gāp′, ə gap′), *adj.* open-mouthed with wonder or surprise; gaping.

a ghast (ə gast′), *adj.* struck with surprise or horror; filled with shocked amazement. [past participle of obsolete *agast* terrify < Old English *on-* on + *gæstan* frighten. Related to GHOST.]

a gue (ā′gyü), *n.* 1 a malarial fever with chills and sweating that alternate at regular intervals. 2 any fit of shaking or shivering; chill.

-al¹, *suffix forming adjectives from nouns.* Also, **-ial.**

-al², *suffix forming nouns from verbs.*

al be it (ôl bē′it), *conj.* even though; even if; although.

al ien ate (ā′lyə nāt, ā′lē ə nāt), *v.t.,* **-at ed, -at ing.** turn away the normal feelings, fondness, or devotion of anyone; make unfriendly; estrange.

al lay (ə lā′), *v.t.,* **-layed, -lay ing.** 1 put at rest; quiet. 2 relieve (pain, trouble, thirst, etc.); alleviate. [Old English *ālecgan* < *ā-* away, off + *lecgan* to lay]

al lege (ə lej′), *v.t.,* **-leged, -leg ing.** 1 state positively; assert; declare. 2 assert without proof; claim. 3 give or bring forward as a reason, argument, or excuse.

al lude (ə lüd′), *v.i.,* **-lud ed, -lud ing.** refer indirectly *(to);* mention slightly in passing.

al lure (ə lůr′), *v.,* **-lured, -lur ing,** *n.* —*v.t.* tempt or attract very strongly; fascinate; charm. —*n.* great charm; fascination.

al lu sion (ə lu′zhən), *n.* act of alluding; slight or incidental mention of something.

a main (ə mān′), *adv.* 1 at full speed. 2 with full force; violently. 3 in haste; at once.

am big u ous (am big′yü əs), *adj.* 1 having or permitting more than one interpretation or explanation; equivocal. 2 of doubtful position or classification. 3 not clearly defined; doubtful; uncertain.

a mi a ble (ā′mē ə bəl), *adj.* having a good-natured and friendly disposition; pleasant and agreeable.

am i ty (am′ə tē), *n., pl.* **-ties.** peace and friendship, especially between nations; friendly relations; friendliness.

am phib i ous (am fib′ē əs), *adj.* able to live both on land and in water.

-an, *suffix forming adjectives and nouns, especially from proper nouns.*

an ar chy (an′ər kē), *n.* 1 absence of a system of government and law. 2 disorder and confusion; lawlessness. [< Greek *anarchia* < *an-* without + *archos* ruler]

-ance, *suffix forming nouns chiefly from verbs.*

an ec dote (an′ik dōt), *n.* a short account of some interesting incident or single event, especially one in the life of a person.

an i mad ver sion (an′ə mad ver′zhən), *n.* 1 comment, criticism, or remark expressing censure. 2 censure; blame.

an i mos i ty (an′ə mos′ə tē), *n., pl.* **-ties.** keen hostile feelings; active dislike or enmity; ill will.

an nals (an′lz), *n.pl.* 1 historical events; history. 2 a written account of events year by year.

an ni hi late (ə nī′ə lāt), *v.t.,* **-lat ed, -lat ing.** destroy completely; wipe out of existence.

an nul (ə nul′), *v.t.,* **-nulled, -nul ling.** 1 destroy the force of; make void; nullify. 2 do away with; cancel. 3 reduce to nothing; annihilate.

a nom a ly (ə nom′ə lē), *n., pl.* **-lies.** 1 something anomalous. 2 deviation from the rule; irregularity.

-ant, *suffix forming adjectives and nouns from verbs.*

ante-, *prefix.* 1 before. 2 in front of.

anti-, *prefix.* 1 against; opposed to. 2 not; the opposite of. 3 rival. 4 reducing or counteracting. 5 preventing, curing, or alleviating.

an ti cli max (an′ti klī′maks), *n.* 1 an abrupt descent from the important to the trivial or unimportant. 2 descent (in importance, interest, etc.) contrasting sharply with a previous rise or high point.

an tip a thy (an tip′ə thē), *n., pl.* **-thies.** 1 a strong or fixed dislike; feeling against; aversion. 2 object of aversion or dislike.

an tiph o ny (an tif′ə nē), *n.* alternating response between groups (for example, of singers).

ap a thet ic (ap′ə thet′ik), *adj.* 1 lacking interest or desire for action; indifferent. 2 lacking in feeling; unemotional.

ap pa ri tion (ap′ə rish′ən), *n.* 1 a supernatural sight or thing; ghost or phantom. 2 the appearance of something strange, remarkable, or unexpected.

ap pease (ə pēz′), *v.t.,* **-peased, -peas ing.** 1 put an end to by satisfying (an appetite or desire). 2 make calm or quiet; pacify. 3 give in to the demands of (especially those of a potential enemy).

ap pre hen sion (ap′ri hen′shən), *n.* 1 expectation of misfortune; dread of impending danger; fear. 2 understanding.

ap pro ba tion (ap′rə bā′shən), *n.* favorable opinion; approval.

ap pur te nance (ə pėrt′n əns), *n.* addition to something more important; added thing; accessory.

ar bi trar y (är′bə trer′ē), *adj.* 1 based on one's own wishes, notions, or will; not going by rule or law. 2 fixed or determined by chance. 3 using or abusing unlimited power; tyrannical; despotic.

ar bi trate (är′bə trāt), *v.,* **-trat ed, -trat ing.** —*v.i.* give a decision in a dispute; act as arbiter; mediate. —*v.t.* settle by arbitration.

ar gent (är′jənt), *n.* silver. —*adj.* silvery.

ar rant (ar′ənt), *adj.* thoroughgoing; downright.

ar ras (ar′əs), *n.* curtain, screen, or hangings of tapestry.

ar rears (ə rirz′), *n.pl.* 1 money due but not paid. 2 unfinished work. 3 **in arrears,** behind in payments, work, etc.

ar ti fice (är′tə fis), *n.* 1 a clever device or trick. 2 trickery; craft. 3 skill or ingenuity.

[< Latin *artificium* < *artem* art + *facere* make]

-ary, *suffix forming nouns and adjectives.*

as per i ty (a sper′ə tē), *n., pl.* **-ties.** harshness or sharpness of temper, especially as shown in tone or manner.

as sid u ous (ə sij′ü əs), *adj.* careful and attentive; diligent.

as suage (ə swāj′), *v.t.,* **-suaged, -suaging.** 1 make (angry or excited feelings, etc.) less intense; calm or soothe. 2 make (physical or mental pain) easier or milder; relieve or lessen. 3 satisfy or appease (appetites or desires).

-ate, *suffix forming adjectives, verbs, and nouns.*

a thwart (ə thwôrt′), *adv.* across from side to side; crosswise. *—prep.* 1 across. 2 in opposition to; against.

-ation, *suffix forming nouns chiefly from verbs.*

a troc i ty (ə tros′ə tē), *n., pl.* **-ties.** 1 monstrous wickedness or cruelty. 2 a very cruel or brutal act.

at test (ə test′), *v.t.* 1 give proof or evidence of; certify. 2 bear witness to; testify to. *—v.i.* bear witness; testify. [< Latin *attestari* < *ad-* to + *testis* witness]

at trib ute (*v.* ə trib′yüt; *n.* at′rə byüt), *v.,* **-ut ed, -ut ing,** *n.* *—v.t.* 1 regard as an effect or product of; think of as caused by. 2 think of as belonging to or appropriate to. *—n.* 1 an object considered appropriate to a person, rank, or office; symbol. 2 a quality considered as belonging to a person or thing; characteristic.

au da cious (ô dā′shəs), *adj.* having the courage to take risks; recklessly daring; bold.

au dac i ty (ô das′ə tē), *n.* 1 reckless daring; boldness. 2 rude boldness; impudence; presumption.

aught (ôt), *n.* anything. Also, **ought.**

aug ment (ôg ment′), *v.t., v.i.* make or become greater in size, number, amount, or degree; increase or enlarge.

au gur y (ô′gyər ē), *n., pl.* **-gur ies.** 1 prediction; sign; omen. 2 art or practice of foretelling events by interpreting such signs and omens as the flight of birds, thunder and lightning, etc.

au gust (ô gust′), *adj.* inspiring reverence and admiration; majestic; venerable.

a vail (ə vāl′), *v.t.* be of use or value to; help. *—v.i.* be of use or value; help. [< Old French *a-* to + *vail-*, a form of *valoir* be worth < Latin *valere* be worth]

av ar ice (av′ər is), *n.* too great a desire for money or property; greed for wealth.

av a ri cious (av′ə rish′əs), *adj.* greatly desiring money or property; greedy for wealth.

a vaunt (ə vônt′, ə vänt′), *interj.* ARCHAIC. begone! get out! go away!

av id (av′id), *adj.* extremely eager; greatly desirous.

a vouch (ə vouch′), *v.t.* 1 declare positively to be true; affirm. 2 vouch for; guarantee: *I can avouch her honesty.* 3 acknowledge; avow. [< Old French *avochier* < *a-* to + *vochier* to call] **—a vouch′ment,** *n.*

az ure (azh′ər), *n.* the clear blue color of the unclouded sky; sky blue. *—adj.* sky-blue.

bad i nage (bad′n äzh′), *n.* good-natured joking; banter. [< French]

bait (bāt), *v.t.* 1 put bait on (a hook) or in (a trap). 2 tempt; attract. 3 set dogs to attack. 4 attack; torment. 5 torment or worry by unkind or annoying remarks. [< Scandinavian (Old Icelandic) *beita* cause to bite]

bal dric (bôl′drik), *n.* belt, usually of leather and richly ornamented, hung from one shoulder to the opposite side of the body to support the wearer's sword, bugle, etc.

bale (bāl), *n.* ARCHAIC. 1 evil; harm. 2 sorrow; pain. [Old English *bealu*]

bale ful (bāl′fəl), *adj.* 1 full of hurtful or deadly influence; destructive. 2 full of misfortune; disastrous.

balm (bäm, bälm), *n.* an ointment or similar preparation that heals or soothes.

bard (bärd), *n.* 1 a Celtic minstrel and poet who from earliest times to the Middle Ages sang his own poems, usually to harp accompaniment, celebrating martial exploits, etc. 2 any poet. [< Irish and Scottish Gaelic]

bar row (bar′ō), *n.* mound of earth or stones over an ancient grave.

bas tion (bas′chən, bas′tē ən), *n.* a projecting part of a fortification made so that the defenders can fire at attackers from several angles.

bat tle ment (bat′l mənt), *n.* a low wall for defense at the top of a tower or wall, with indentations and loopholes through which soldiers could shoot.

bea dle (bē′dl), *n.* a minor parish officer in the Church of England whose duties include keeping order and waiting on the clergy. [< Old French *bedel*]

be hest (bi hest′), *n.* command; order.

be hight (bē hīt′), *v.* ARCHAIC. promise.

be hoove (bi hüv′), *v.,* **-hooved, -hooving.** *—v.t.* 1 be necessary for. 2 be proper for. *—v.i.* be proper or due.

be lie (bi lī′), *v.t.,* **-lied, -ly ing.** give a false idea of; misrepresent.

ben e dic tion (ben′ə dik′shən), *n.* the asking of God's blessing, as at the end of a church service or a marriage ceremony.

ben e fice (ben′ə fis), *n.* a permanent office or position in the church created by proper ecclesiastical authority and consisting of a sacred duty and the income that goes with it.

be nev o lent (bə nev′ə lənt), *adj.* wishing or intended to promote the happiness of others; kindly; charitable.

be night ed (bi nī′tid), *adj.* 1 not knowing right from wrong; ignorant. 2 ARCHAIC. overtaken by darkness.

be nign (bi nīn′), *adj.* 1 kindly in feeling; benevolent; gracious. 2 showing a kindly feeling; gentle. 3 favorable; propitious. 4 mild. 5 not dangerous to health; not malignant.

be nig nant (bi nig′nənt), *adj.* 1 having or showing a kindly feeling toward inferiors and dependents; benevolent: *a benignant ruler.* 2 having a good effect; beneficial.

be queath (bi kwēᴛʜ′, bi kwēth′), *v.t.* 1 give or leave (especially money or other personal property) by a will. 2 hand down or leave to posterity; pass along.

be quest (bi kwest′), *n.* 1 something bequeathed; legacy. 2 act of bequeathing.

be reave (bi rēv′), *v.t.,* **-reaved** or **-reft, -reav ing.** 1 leave desolate and alone. 2 deprive ruthlessly; rob. [Old English *berēafian* < *be-* away + *rēafian* rob]

be shrew (bi shrü′), *v.t.* ARCHAIC. curse (used as a mild exclamation).

bil ious (bil′yəs), *adj.* 1 suffering from or caused by some trouble with bile or the liver. 2 peevish; bad-tempered.

bil let-doux (bil′ē dü′, bil′ā dü′), *n., pl.* **bil lets-doux** (bil′ē düz′, bil′ā düz′). a love letter.

bit tern (bit′ərn), *n.* any of several small herons found chiefly in marshes, characterized by a peculiar booming cry.

black guard (blag′ärd, blag′ərd), *n.* a low, contemptible man; scoundrel.

blanch (blanch), *v.t.* 1 make white or pale. 2 whiten or prevent from becoming green by excluding the light, as the stems or leaves of plants such as celery or lettuce. *—v.i.* turn white or pale. [< Old French *blanchir* < *blanc* white]

blas phe my (blas′fə mē), *n., pl.* **-mies.** abuse or contempt for God or sacred things; profanity.

blench (blench), *v.i., v.t.* turn white or pale; blanch. [variant of *blanch*]

blight (blīt), *n.* 1 disease of plants that causes leaves, stems, fruits, and tissues to wither and die. 2 bacterium, fungus, or virus that causes such a disease. 3 anything that withers hope or causes destruction or ruin. 4 decay; deterioration. *—v.t.* 1 cause to wither and die. 2 destroy; ruin.

blithe (blīᴛʜ, blīth), *adj.* 1 happy and cheerful; gay; joyous. 2 heedless.

boon (bün), *n.* 1 great benefit; blessing. 2 ARCHAIC. something asked for or granted as a favor. [< Scandinavian (Old Icelandic) *bōn* petition]

boor (bůr), *n.* 1 a rude, bad-mannered person. 2 a clumsy person, especially from the country; bumpkin. 3 OBSOLETE. a farm laborer; peasant. [< Low German *bur* or Dutch *boer* farmer]

brake (brāk), *v.* ARCHAIC. a pt. of **break.**

bran dish (bran′dish), *v.t.* wave or shake threateningly; flourish. *—n.* a threatening shake; flourish. [< Old French *brandiss-*, a form of *brandir* to brand < *brand* sword]

bra va do (brə vä′dō), *n., pl.* **-does** or **-dos.** a show of courage or boldness without much real courage; defiant or blustering behavior.

broach (brōch), *v.t.* 1 begin conversation or discussion about; introduce. 2 open by making a hole.

bruit (brüt), *v.t.* spread a report or rumor of.

brusque (brusk), *adj.* abrupt in manner or speech; blunt.

buf fet (buf′it), *n.* 1 a blow of the hand or fist. 2 a knock, stroke, or hurt.

bur gess (bėr′jis), *n.* citizen.

buss (bus), *v.t., v.i., n.* INFORMAL. kiss.

ca dence (kād′ns), *n.* 1 the measure or beat of music, dancing, marching, or any movement regularly repeating itself; rhythm. 2 a rising and falling sound; modulation.

ca jole (kə jōl′), *v.t.,* **-joled, -jol ing.** persuade by pleasant words, flattery, or false promises; coax.

cal lous (kal′əs), *adj.* 1 hard or hardened, as parts of the skin that are exposed to constant

---

hat, āge, fär; let, ēqual, tėrm;
it, īce; hot, ōpen, ôrder;
oil, out; cup, pu̇t, rüle;
ch, child; ng, long; sh, she;
th, thin; ᴛʜ, then; zh, measure;

ə represents *a* in about, *e* in taken, *i* in pencil, *o* in lemon, *u* in circus.

< = from, derived from, taken from.

---

pressure and friction. 2 unfeeling; insensitive.

ca lum ni ous (kə lum′nē əs), *adj.* slanderous.

cant (kant), *n.* 1 insincere talk; moral or religious statements that many people make, but few really believe or follow out. 2 the peculiar language of a special group, using many strange words; jargon; argot. —*adj.* peculiar to a special group. —*v.i.* 1 use cant; talk in cant. 2 speak in the manner of a beggar; whine; beg. [< Latin *cantus* song]

ca price (kə prēs′), *n.* 1 a sudden change of mind without reason; unreasonable notion or desire; whim. 2 tendency to change suddenly and without reason.

ca pri cious (kə prish′əs, kə prē′shəs), *adj.* likely to change suddenly without reason; changeable; fickle.

cap tious (kap′shəs), *adj.* 1 hard to please; faultfinding. 2 that entraps or entangles by subtlety.

ca reer (kə rir′), *n.* 1 way of living; occupation; profession. 2 a run at full speed; going with force; speed. —*v.i.* rush along wildly; dash. [< Middle French *carrière* race course < Latin *carrus* wagon]

car nage (kär′nij), *n.* slaughter of a great number of people. [< Middle French < Italian *carnaggio,* ultimately < Latin *carnem* flesh]

ca rouse (kə rouz′), *v.,* **-roused, -rous ing,** *n.* —*v.i.* drink heavily; take part in noisy revels. —*n.* a noisy revel or drinking party. [< German *gar aus(trinken)* (drink) all up]

car rel or **car ol** (kar′əl), *n.* 1 song of joy. 2 hymn of joy sung at Christmas.

car ri on (kar′ē ən), *n.* 1 dead and decaying flesh. 2 rottenness; filth. —*adj.* 1 dead and decaying. 2 feeding on dead and decaying flesh. [< Old French *caroine* carcass < Popular Latin *caronia* < Latin *carnem* flesh]

casque (kask), *n.* a piece of armor to cover the head; helmet.

caste (kast), *n.* 1 one of the social classes into which Hindus are divided. 2 an exclusive social group; distinct class. 3 a social system having distinct classes separated by differences of birth, rank, wealth, or position.

cat er waul (kat′ər wôl), *v.i.* howl like a cat; screech. —*n.* such a howl or screech. [Middle English *caterwrawe* < *cater* cat + *wrawe* wail, howl]

cav ern ous (kav′ər nəs), *adj.* 1 like a cavern; large and hollow. 2 full of caverns.

ce les tial (sə les′chəl), *adj.* 1 of the sky; having to do with the heavens. 2 of or belonging to heaven as the place of God and the angels; heavenly; divine.

cen trif u gal (sen trif′yə gəl, sen trif′ə gəl), *adj.* moving or tending to move away from a center. [< Latin *centrum* center + *fugere* flee]

cen trip e tal (sen trip′ə təl), *adj.* moving or tending toward a center. [< Latin *centrum* center + *petere* seek]

cere ment (sir′mənt), *n.* Often, **cerements,** *pl.* cloth or garment in which a dead person is wrapped for burial.

chafe (chāf), *v.,* **chafed, chaf ing,** *n.* —*v.t.* 1 rub so as to wear away, scrape, or make sore. 2 wear away by rubbing. 3 make angry. —*v.i.* 1 become worn away by rubbing. 2 become irritated by rubbing. 3 become angry.

chaise (shāz), *n.* a light, open carriage, usually with a folding top, especially a one-horse, two-wheeled carriage for two persons.

chan cel (chan′səl), *n.* the space around the altar of a church, used by the clergy and the choir.

chan son (shäN sôN′), *n.* FRENCH. song.

char ac ter y (kar′ik tə rē), *n.* signs or symbols used to express ideas.

char y (cher′ē, char′ē), *adj.,* **char i er, char i est.** 1 showing caution; careful; wary. 2 shy. 3 sparing; stingy.

cher ub (cher′əb), *n., pl.* **cher u bim.** one of the second highest order of angels.

chid (chid), *v.* a pt. and a pp. of **chide.**

chide (chīd), *v.,* **chid ed, chid, chid ing.** —*v.t.* find fault with; reproach or blame; scold.

chol er ic (kol′ər ik), *adj.* 1 having an irritable disposition; easily made angry. 2 enraged; angry; wrathful.

chron ic (kron′ik), *adj.* 1 lasting a long time. 2 suffering long from an illness. 3 never stopping; constant; habitual.

chron i cle (kron′ə kəl), *n., v.,* **-cled, -cling.** —*n.* record of events in the order in which they took place; history; story. —*v.t.* write the history of; tell the story of.

chrys a lis (kris′ə lis), *n., pl.* **chrys a lis es, chry sal i des** (krə sal′ə dēz′). 1 the stage in the development of moths, butterflies, and most other insects between the larva and the adult, when the larva lives in a hard case or cocoon; pupa. 2 the case or cocoon. 3 stage of development or change.

cic a trice (sik′ə tris), *n.* cicatrix.

cic a trix (sik′ə triks, sə kā′triks), *n., pl.* **cic a tri ces** (sik′ə trī′sēz′). scar left by a healed wound.

cir cum scribe (sėr′kəm skrīb′, sėr′kəm-skrīb), *v.t.,* **-scribed, -scrib ing.** 1 draw a line around; mark the boundaries of; bound. 2 surround. 3 limit; restrict.

cis tern (sis′tərn), *n.* an artificial reservoir for storing water, especially a tank below ground. [< Latin *cisterna* < *cista* box]

ci vil i ty (sə vil′ə tē), *n., pl.* **-ties.** 1 polite behavior; courtesy. 2 act or expression of politeness or courtesy.

clair voy ant (kler voi′ənt, klar voi′ənt), *n.* person who has, or claims to have, the power of seeing or knowing things that are out of sight.

clar i on (klar′ē ən), *n.* 1 a trumpet with clear, shrill tones. 2 a clear, shrill sound like it.

cleave[1] (klēv), *v.,* **cleft** or **cleaved** or **clove, cleft** or **cleaved** or **clo ven, cleav ing.** —*v.t.* 1 cut, divide, or split open. 2 pass through; pierce; penetrate. 3 make by cutting. —*v.i.* 1 split, especially into layers. 2 pass; penetrate.

cleave[2] (klēv), *v.i.,* **cleaved** or (ARCHAIC) **clave, cleav ing.** hold fast; cling; adhere.

cleft (kleft), *v.* a pt. and a pp. of **cleave.**[1] —*adj.* split; divided. —*n.* space or opening made by splitting; crack; fissure.

clois ter (kloi′stər), *n.* 1 a covered walk, often along the wall of a building, with a row of pillars on the open side or sides. 2 place of religious retirement; convent or monastery. —*v.t.* shut away in a quiet place.

cloy (kloi), *v.t., v.i.* 1 make or become weary by too much, too sweet, or too rich food. 2 make or become weary by too much of anything pleasant.

co-, *prefix.* 1 with; together. 2 joint. 3 equally.

cog ni zance (kog′nə zəns, kon′ə zəns), *n.* knowledge; perception; awareness.

cog ni zant (kog′nə zənt, kon′ə zənt), *adj.* having cognizance; aware.

coign of vantage, a good location for watching or doing something.

col lat er al (kə lat′ər əl), *adj.* 1 related but less important; secondary; indirect. 2 side by side; parallel. 3 in a parallel line of descent; descended from the same ancestors, but in a different line. Cousins are collateral relatives. 4 additional. 5 secured by stocks, bonds, etc.

col lier (kol′yər), *n.* 1 ship for carrying coal. 2 a coal miner.

col lier y (kol′yər ē), *n., pl.* **-lier ies.** a coal mine and its buildings and equipment.

com-, *prefix.* with; together; altogether.

com bus ti ble (kəm bus′tə bəl), *adj.* capable of taking fire and burning; easily burned.

com mis e rate (kə miz′ə rāt′), *v.t., v.i.,* **-rat ed, -rat ing.** feel or express sorrow for another's suffering or trouble; sympathize with; pity. **—com mis′e ra′tion,** *n.*

com mo tion (kə mō′shən), *n.* 1 violent movement; agitation; turbulence. 2 bustle or stir; confusion.

com plai sant (kəm plā′znt, kom′plə zant), *adj.* 1 obliging; gracious; courteous. 2 compliant.

com pos i tor (kəm poz′ə tər), *n.* typesetter.

com pound (*adj.* kom′pound, kom pound′; *n.* kom′pound; *v.* kom pound′, kəm pound′), *adj.* 1 having more than one part. 2 formed of many similar parts combined into a single structure. —*n.* something made by combining parts; mixture. —*v.t.* 1 mix; combine. 2 add to; increase; multiply. [< Old French *compondre* put together < Latin *componere* < *com-* together + *ponere* put]

com pul sion (kəm pul′shən), *n.* 1 a compelling or a being compelled; use of force; force; coercion. 2 impulse that is hard to resist.

con-, *prefix.* form of **com-** before *n,* as in *connote,* and before consonants except *b, h, l, m, p, r, w,* as in *concern.*

con cil i ate (kən sil′ē āt), *v.t.,* **-at ed, -at ing.** 1 win over; soothe. 2 gain (good will, regard, favor, etc.) by friendly acts. 3 bring into harmony; reconcile.

con cu bine (kong′kyə bīn, kon′kyə bīn), *n.* woman who lives with a man without being legally married to him.

con du it (kon′dü it, kon′dit), *n.* channel or pipe for carrying liquids long distances.

con fla gra tion (kon′flə grā′shən), *n.* a great and destructive fire.

con flu ence (kon′flü əns), *n.* 1 a flowing together. 2 place where two or more rivers, streams, etc., come together. 3 a coming together of people or things; throng.

con found (kon found′, kən found′ *for 1, 2, 4, 5;* kon′found′ *for 3*), *v.t.* 1 confuse; mix up. 2 surprise and puzzle. 3 damn. 4 ARCHAIC. make uneasy and ashamed. 5 ARCHAIC. defeat; overthrow.

con fute (kən fyüt′), *v.t.,* **-fut ed, -fut ing.** 1 prove (an argument, testimony, etc.) to be false or incorrect. 2 prove (a person) to be wrong; overcome by argument.

con ju ra tion (kon′jə rā′shən), *n.* 1 an invoking by a sacred name; conjuring. 2 the practice of magic. 3 a magic form of words used in conjuring; magic spell. 4 ARCHAIC. a solemn appeal.

con jure (kon′jər, kən jür′), *v.,* **-jured, -jur ing.** —*v.t.* 1 compel (a spirit, devil, etc.) to appear or disappear by a set form of words. 2 make a solemn appeal to; request earnestly; entreat.

con se quen tial (kon′sə kwen′shəl), *adj.* self-important; pompous.
con sort (*n.* kon′sôrt; *v.* kən sôrt′), *n.* 1 husband or wife. 2 an associate. —*v.i.* 1 keep company; associate. 2 agree; accord.
con stit u en cy (kən stich′ü ən sē), *n., pl.* **-cies.** the voters in a district; constituents.
con sum ma tion (kon′sə mā′shən), *n.* completion; fulfillment.
con tig u ous (kən tig′yü əs), *adj.* 1 in actual contact; touching. 2 adjoining; near.
con ti nence (kon′tə nəns), *n.* 1 control of one's actions and feelings; self-restraint; moderation. 2 chastity.
con ti nent (kon′tə nənt), *adj.* 1 showing restraint with regard to the desires or passions; using self-control; temperate. 2 chaste. [< Latin *continentem* holding in, refraining < *com-* in + *tenere* to hold]
con tu me ly (kən tü′mə lē, kən tyü′mə lē; kon′tü mə lē, kon′tyə mə lē), *n., pl.* **-lies.** 1 insolent contempt; insulting words or actions; humiliating treatment. 2 a humiliating insult.
con vey ance (kən vā′əns), *n.* 1 a carrying; transmission; transportation. 2 thing that carries people and goods; vehicle. 3 communication. 4 transfer of ownership. 5 document showing such a transfer; deed.
con vo ca tion (kon′və kā′shən), *n.* 1 a calling together; assembling by a summons. 2 assembly.
copse (kops), *n.* thicket of small trees, bushes, shrubs, etc.; coppice.
co que try (kō′kə trē, kō ket′rē), *n., pl.* **-tries.** 1 flirting. 2 trifling.
cor por al (kôr′pər əl), *adj.* of the body.
cor po re al (kôr pôr′ē əl, kôr pōr′ē əl), *adj.* 1 of or for the body; bodily. 2 material; tangible.
cor ro sive (kə rō′siv), *adj.* producing corrosion; tending to corrode. —*n.* substance that corrodes.
corse let (kôrs′lit), *n.* armor for the upper part of the body. Also, **corslet.**
coun te nance (koun′tə nəns), *n., v.,* **-nanced, -nanc ing.** —*n.* 1 expression of the face. 2 face; features. 3 approval; encouragement. 4 calmness; composure. —*v.t.* approve or encourage; sanction.
cour ti er (kôr′tē ər, kōr′tē ər), *n.* person often present at the court of a king, emperor, etc.; court attendant.
cov e nant (kuv′ə nənt), *n.* 1 a solemn agreement between two or more persons or groups to do or not to do a certain thing; compact. 2 a formal agreement that is legal; legal contract.
cov ert (kuv′ərt, kō′vərt), *adj.* kept from sight; concealed; secret; hidden. —*n.* 1 a hiding place; shelter. 2 thicket in which animals hide.
cov et (kuv′it), *v.t.* desire eagerly (something that belongs to another).
cox comb (koks′kōm′), *n.* 1 a vain, empty-headed man; conceited dandy. 2 cockscomb.
cra ven (krā′vən), *adj.* cowardly. —*n.* coward.
cre dent (krē′dənt), *adj.* believing.
cred u lous (krej′ə ləs), *adj.* too ready to believe; easily deceived.
cre tonne (kri ton′, krē′ton), *n.* a strong cotton, linen, or rayon cloth with designs printed in colors on one or both sides.
cuck old (kuk′əld), *n.* husband of an unfaithful wife.
cudg el (kuj′əl), *n., v.,* **-eled, -el ing** or **-elled, -el ling.** —*n.* a short, thick stick used as a weapon; club. —*v.t.* beat with a cudgel.
cuisse (kwis), *n.* piece of armor to protect the thigh.
cu ta ne ous (kyü tā′nē əs), *adj.* of or having to do with the skin; on the skin.
cy pher or **ci pher** (sī′fər), *n.* zero.

da is (dā′is; *British* dās), *n.* a raised platform at one end of a hall or large room for a throne, seats of honor, a lectern, etc.
dal li ance (dal′ē əns), *n.* 1 a dallying; trifling. 2 flirtation.
dam a scene (dam′ə sēn′, dam′ə sēn′), *v.t.,* **-scened, -scen ing.** ornament (metal) with inlaid gold or silver or with a wavy design.
dap ple (dap′əl), *adj., v.,* **-pled, -pling,** *n.* —*adj.* marked with spots; spotted. —*v.t., v.i.* mark or become marked with spots. —*n.* 1 a spotted appearance or condition. 2 animal with a spotted or mottled skin.
daunt (dônt, dänt), *v.t.* 1 overcome with fear; frighten; intimidate. 2 lessen the courage of; discourage; dishearten.
daunt less (dônt′lis, dänt′lis), *adj.* not to be frightened or discouraged; brave.
dearth (dėrth), *n.* 1 too small a supply; great scarcity or lack. 2 scarcity of food; famine. [Middle English *derthe*]
de claim (di klām′), *v.i.* 1 recite in public; make a formal speech. 2 speak in a loud and emotional manner; speak or write for effect.
de co rum (di kôr′əm, di kōr′əm), *n.* 1 proper behavior; good taste in conduct, speech, dress, etc. 2 observance or requirement of polite society.
de cus sate (di kus′āt), *adj.* crossed; intersecting.
def er ence (def′ər əns), *n.* 1 a yielding to the judgment, opinion, wishes, etc., of another. 2 great respect. 3 **in deference to,** out of respect for the wishes or authority of.
def e ren tial (def′ə ren′shəl), *adj.* showing deference; respectful. —**def′e ren′tial ly,** *adv.*
deft (deft), *adj.* quick and skillful in action; nimble. —**deft′ly,** *adv.*
deg ra da tion (deg′rə dā′shən), *n.* a degraded condition; debasement; degeneracy.
de lib er ate (di lib′ə rāt′), *v.,* **-at ed, -at ing.** —*v.i., v.t.* 1 think over carefully; consider. 2 discuss reasons for and against something; debate.
de lude (di lüd′), *v.t.,* **-lud ed, -lud ing.** mislead the mind or judgment of; trick or deceive. [< Latin *deludere* < *de-* + *ludere* to play]
de lu sive (di lü′siv), *adj.* misleading the mind or judgment; deceptive.
de mean (di mēn′), *v.t.* lower in dignity or standing; humble; degrade.
de mur (di mėr′), *v.,* **-murred, -mur ring,** *n.* —*v.i.* 1 show disapproval or dislike; take exception; object. 2 OBSOLETE. hesitate. —*n.* a demurring; objection; exception.
dep o si tion (dep′ə zish′ən, dē′pə zish′ən), *n.* 1 the giving of testimony under oath. 2 testimony, especially a sworn statement in writing.
dep re cate (dep′rə kāt), *v.t.,* **-cat ed, -cat ing.** express strong disapproval of. [< Latin *deprecatum* pleaded in excuse, averted by prayer < *de-* + *precari* pray]
dep re ca tion (dep′rə kā′shən), *n.* a strong expression of disapproval.
dep re da tion (dep′rə dā′shən), *n.* act of plundering; robbery; ravaging.
des cant (*v.* des kant′, dis kant′; *n.* des′kant), *v.i.* 1 talk at great length; discourse. 2 sing or play a melody with another melody.

hat, āge, fär; let, ēqual, tėrm;
it, īce; hot, ōpen, ôrder;
oil, out; cup, pu̇t, rüle;
ch, child; ng, long; sh, she;
th, thin; ᴛʜ, then; zh, measure;

ə represents *a* in about, *e* in taken, *i* in pencil, *o* in lemon, *u* in circus.

< = from, derived from, taken from.

de scry (di skrī′), *v.t.,* **-scried, -scry ing.** 1 catch sight of; be able to see; make out. 2 discover by observation; detect.
des e crate (des′ə krāt), *v.t.,* **-crat ed, -crat ing.** treat or use without respect; disregard the sacredness of; profane.
des o late (*adj.* des′ə lit; *v.* des′ə lāt), *adj., v.,* **-lat ed, -lat ing.** —*adj.* 1 laid waste; devastated; barren. 2 not lived in; deserted. 3 unhappy; forlorn; wretched. 4 left alone; solitary; lonely. 5 dreary; dismal. —*v.t.* 1 make unfit to live in; lay waste. 2 make unhappy. 3 deprive of inhabitants. [< Latin *desolatum* < *de-* + *solus* alone]
de spoil (di spoil′), *v.t.* strip of possessions; rob; plunder.
de spond en cy (di spon′dən sē), *n.* loss of heart, courage, or hope; discouragement; dejection.
det ri ment (det′rə mənt), *n.* 1 loss, damage, or injury done, caused to, or sustained by a person or thing; harm. 2 something that causes loss, damage, or injury.
de vi a tion (dē′vē ā′shən), *n.* 1 act of turning aside; swerving. 2 divergence from a policy or course of action.
dex ter ous (dek′stər əs), *adj.* 1 skillful in using the hands or body. 2 having or showing skill in using the mind; clever.
di aph a nous (dī af′ə nəs), *adj.* transparent.
dif fi dent (dif′ə dənt), *adj.* lacking in self-confidence; shy.
di gress (də gres′, dī gres′), *v.i.* 1 turn aside from the main subject in talking or writing. 2 swerve.
di lec tion (di lek′shən), *n.* ARCHAIC. love; choice.
dil i gence (dil′ə jəns), *n.* constant and earnest effort to accomplish what is undertaken; industry.
dil i gent (dil′ə jənt), *adj.* 1 hard-working; industrious. 2 careful and steady.
di min u tive (də min′yə tiv), *adj.* very small; tiny; minute.
din gle (ding′gəl), *n.* a small, deep, shady valley.
dirge (dėrj), *n.* a funeral song or tune.
dirk (dėrk), *n.* dagger. —*v.t.* stab with a dirk.
dis-, *prefix.* 1 opposite of; lack of; not. 2 do the opposite of. 3 apart; away.
dis burse (dis bėrs′), *v.t.,* **-bursed, -burs ing.** pay out; expend. [< Old French *desbourser* < *des-* dis- + *bourse* purse]
dis cern (də zėrn′, də sėrn′), *v.t.* see clearly; perceive the difference between (two or more things); distinguish or recognize. [< Latin *discernere* < *dis-* off + *cernere* to separate] —**dis cern′er,** *n.*
dis cern ment (də zėrn′mənt, də sėrn′mənt), *n.* keenness in seeing and understanding; good judgment; shrewdness.
dis com fit (dis kum′fit), *v.t.* 1 defeat com-

pletely; rout. 2 embarrass greatly; confuse, disconcert.

dis course (*n.* dis′kôrs, dis′kōrs; *v.* dis-kôrs′, dis kōrs′), *n., v.,* **-coursed, -cours-ing.** —*n.* 1 a formal or extensive speech or writing. 2 talk; conversation. —*v.i.* 1 speak or write formally or at length on some subject. 2 talk; converse. [< Latin *discursus* a running about < *dis-* + *cursus* a running]

dis par age (dis par′ij), *v.t.,* **-aged, -ag ing.** 1 speak slightingly of; belittle. 2 lower the reputation of; discredit. [< Old French *desparagier* match unequally < *des-* dis- + *parage* rank, lineage < *par* peer]

dis patch (dis pach′), *v.t.* send off to some place or for some purpose. —*n.* promptness in doing anything; speed.

dis perse (dis pėrs′), *v.,* **-persed, -pers-ing.** —*v.t.* 1 send or drive off in different directions; scatter. 2 scatter throughout another substance or a mixture. —*v.i.* spread in different directions; scatter. [< Latin *dispersum* dispersed < *dis-* apart + *spargere* to scatter]

dis port (dis pôrt′, dis pōrt′), *v.t., v.i.* amuse or entertain (oneself); play; sport.

dis po si tion (dis′pə zish′ən), *n.* 1 one's habitual ways of acting toward others or of thinking about things; nature. 2 tendency; inclination. 3 a putting in a proper or desired order or position; arrangement. 4 a disposing; settlement. 5 disposal.

dis sem ble (di sem′bəl), *v.,* **-bled, -bling.** —*v.t.* 1 hide (one's real feelings, thoughts, plans, etc.); disguise. 2 pretend; feign. —*v.i.* conceal one's opinions, motives, etc.

dis sev er (di sev′ər), *v.t.* cut into parts; sever; separate. —*v.i.* separate.

dis si pate (dis′ə pāt), *v.,* **-pat ed, -pat ing.** —*v.t.* 1 spread in different directions; scatter. 2 cause to disappear; dispel. 3 spend foolishly; waste on things of little value; squander. —*v.i.* 1 scatter so as to disappear; disperse. 2 indulge excessively in sensual or foolish pleasures.

dis traught (dis trôt′), *adj.* 1 in a state of mental conflict and confusion; distracted. 2 crazed.

di ur nal (dī ėr′nl), *adj.* 1 occurring every day; daily. 2 of or belonging to the daytime.

di vert (də vėrt′, dī vėrt′), *v.t.* 1 turn aside. 2 amuse; entertain.

di vulge (də vulj′, dī vulj′), *v.t.,* **-vulged, -vulg ing.** make known or tell openly (something private or secret); reveal.

dole (dōl), *n., v.,* **doled, dol ing.** —*n.* 1 portion of money, food, etc., given in charity. 2 a small portion. —*v.t.* 1 give as a dole; distribute in charity. 2 give in small portions.

dole ful (dōl′fəl), *adj.* very sad or dreary; mournful; dismal.

do lor (dō′lər), *n.* sorrow; grief.

dol or ous (dol′ər əs, dō′lər əs), *adj.* 1 full of or expressing sorrow; mournful. 2 causing or giving rise to sorrow; grievous; painful.

-dom, *suffix forming nouns.*

do min ion (də min′yən), *n.* 1 power or right of governing and controlling; rule; control. 2 territory under the control of one ruler or government. 3 a self-governing territory.

dot age (dō′tij), *n.* a weak-minded and childish condition that sometimes accompanies old age; senility.

dot ard (dō′tərd), *n.* person who is weak-minded and childish because of old age.

dote (dōt), *v.i.,* **dot ed, dot ing.** 1 be weak-minded and childish because of old age. 2 **dote on** or **dote upon,** be foolishly fond of; be too fond of.

dou blet (dub′lit), *n.* 1 a man's close-fitting jacket. Men in Europe wore doublets from the 1400's to the 1600's. 2 one of two or more words in a language, derived from the same original source but coming by different routes.

dow er (dou′ər), *n.* 1 a widow's share for life of her dead husband's property. 2 dowry.

dow ry (dou′rē), *n., pl.* **-ries.** 1 money or property that a woman brings to her husband when she marries him. 2 natural gift, talent, or quality; natural endowment.

drag gle (drag′əl), *v.,* **-gled, -gling.** become wet or dirty by dragging through mud, water, dust, etc.

draught (draft), *n., v.t., adj.* draft.

dudg eon (duj′ən), *n.* a feeling of anger or resentment.

dul ci mer (dul′sə mər), *n.* a musical instrument with metal strings, played by striking the strings with two hammers. [< Old French *doulcemer, doulcemele* < Latin *dulcis* sweet + *melos* song]

du ly (dü′lē, dyü′lē), *adv.* 1 according to what is due; as due; rightly; suitably. 2 when due; at the proper time.

dun (dun), *adj.* dull, grayish-brown. —*n.* a dull, grayish brown.

du ress (dů res′, dyů res′; důr′es, dyůr′es), *n.* 1 use of force; compulsion. 2 imprisonment; confinement.

ed dy (ed′ē), *n., pl.* **-dies,** *v.,* **-died, -dy ing.** —*n.* water, air, smoke, etc., moving against the main current, especially when having a whirling motion; small whirlpool or whirlwind. —*v.i., v.t.* move against the main current in a whirling motion; whirl.

-eer, *suffix added to nouns to form nouns and verbs.*

ef face (ə fās′), *v.t.,* **-faced, -fac ing.** 1 rub out; blot out; wipe out; obliterate. 2 keep (oneself) from being noticed; make inconspicuous.

ef fec tu al (ə fek′chü əl), *adj.* 1 producing or capable of producing the desired effect. 2 valid.

ef fi ca cious (ef′ə kā′shəs), *adj.* producing the desired results; effective. **—ef′fi ca′cious ly,** *adv.*

ef fi gy (ef′ə jē), *n., pl.* **-gies.** image or statue, usually of a person.

e late (i lāt′), *v.t.,* **e lat ed, e lat ing.** raise the spirits of; make joyful or proud. [< Latin *elatum* carried away < *ex-* out, away + *latum* carried]

el lip ti cal (i lip′tə kəl), *adj.* 1 of or shaped like an ellipse. 2 of or showing ellipsis.

em bow er (em bou′ər), *v.t.* enclose in a shelter of leafy branches.

em i nent (em′ə nənt), *adj.* 1 above all or most others; outstanding; distinguished. 2 conspicuous; noteworthy. 3 high; lofty. 4 standing out above other things; prominent. [< Latin *eminentem* standing out, prominent < *ex-* out + *minere* jut]

em pir i cal (em pir′ə kəl), *adj.* based on experiment and observation.

em u late (em′yə lāt), *v.t.,* **-lat ed, -lat ing.** 1 strive to equal or excel (a person, his achievements, or qualities); copy or imitate in order to equal or excel. 2 vie with; rival. **—em′u la′tion,** *n.*

-en, *suffix forming verbs from adjectives and nouns.*

-ence, *suffix forming nouns chiefly from verbs.*

en croach (en krōch′), *v.i.* 1 go beyond proper or usual limits; make gradual inroads on. 2 trespass upon the property or rights of another, especially stealthily or by gradual advances; intrude.

en cum ber (en kum′bər), *v.t.* 1 hold back (from running, doing, etc.); hinder; hamper. 2 block up; fill. 3 burden with weight, difficulties, cares, debt, etc. [< Old French *encombrer* < *en-* in + *combre* barrier]

en due (en dü′, en dyü′), *v.t.,* **-dued, -du ing.** 1 provide with a quality or power; furnish; supply. 2 clothe.

en gen der (en jen′dər), *v.t.* 1 bring into existence; produce; cause. 2 beget.

en gross (en grōs′), *v.t.* occupy wholly; take up all the attention of.

e nig ma (i nig′mə), *n.* 1 a baffling or puzzling problem, situation, person, etc. 2 a puzzling statement; riddle.

en join (en join′), *v.t.* 1 order, direct, or urge. 2 (in law) require or forbid by an authoritative command.

en mi ty (en′mə tē), *n., pl.* **-ties.** the feeling that enemies have for each other; hostility or hatred. [< Old French *enemistie* < Popular Latin *inimicitatem* < Latin *inimicus.*]

en sign (en′sīn, en′sən), *n.* 1 a flag or banner. 2 sign of one's rank, position, or power; symbol of authority.

en sue (en sü′), *v.i.,* **-sued, -su ing.** 1 come after; follow. The ensuing year means the year following this. 2 happen as a result.

-ent, *suffix added to verbs.*

en tail (en tāl′), *v.t.* impose or require.

en trails (en′trālz, en′trəlz), *n.pl.* 1 the inner parts of the body of a man or animal. 2 the intestines; bowels.

en treat y (en trē′tē), *n., pl.* **-treat ies.** an earnest request; prayer or appeal.

e phem er al (i fem′ər əl), *adj.* 1 lasting for only a very short time; very short-lived; transitory. 2 lasting for only a day. [< Greek *ephēmeros* < *epi-* upon + *hēmera* day]

ep i cure (ep′ə kyůr), *n.* person who has a refined taste in eating and drinking and who is very particular in choosing fine foods, wines, etc. [< *Epicurus*]

ep i taph (ep′ə taf), *n.* a short statement in memory of a dead person, usually put on a gravestone or tombstone.

ep i thet (ep′ə thet), *n.* 1 a descriptive expression; word or phrase expressing some quality or attribute. 2 an insulting or contemptuous word or phrase used in place of a person's name.

e pit o mize (i pit′ə mīz), *v.t.,* **-mized, -miz-ing.** 1 give an epitome of; summarize. 2 be typical or representative of.

ep och (ep′ək, ē′pok), *n.* 1 period of time; era; age. 2 period of time in which striking things happened. 3 the starting point of such a period.

e qui nox (ē′kwə noks), *n.* 1 either of the two times in the year when the center of the sun crosses the celestial equator, and day and night are of equal length in all parts of the earth, occurring about March 21 **(vernal equinox)** and about September 22 **(autumnal equinox).** 2 winds or storms that occur at these times.

e quiv o cate (i kwiv′ə kāt), *v.i.,* **-cat ed, -cat ing.** use expressions of double meaning in order to mislead.

e quiv o ca tion (i kwiv′ə kā′shən), *n.*

1 the use of expressions with double meaning in order to mislead. 2 an equivocal expression.

-er, *suffix forming nouns.*

es carp ment (e skärp′mənt), *n.* a steep slope; cliff.

es chew (es chü′), *v.t.* keep away from; avoid; shun.

-ess, *suffix forming nouns from other nouns.*

es say (*n.* es′ā, *also* e sā′ *for 2; v.* e sā′), *n.* 1 a literary composition written on a certain subject. 2 a try; attempt. —*v.t.* try; attempt. [< Old French *essai* < Latin *exagium* a weighing < *ex-* out + *agere* do, act]

es thet ic or **aes thet ic** (es thet′ik), *adj.* having or showing an appreciation of beauty in nature or art.

es ti ma ble (es′tə mə bəl), *adj.* worthy of esteem; deserving high regard.

es trange ment (e strānj′mənt), *n.* a turning away in feeling; becoming distant or unfriendly.

e ther e al (i thir′ē əl), *adj.* 1 light; airy; delicate. 2 not of the earth; heavenly. 3 of or having to do with the upper regions of space.

eu nuch (yü′nək), *n.* 1 a castrated man. 2 a castrated man in charge of a harem or the household of an Oriental ruler.

ex-, *prefix.* 1 former; formerly. 2 out of; from; out.

ex e cra tion (ek′sə krā′shən), *n.* 1 act of execrating. 2 a curse.

ex er tion (eg zėr′shən), *n.* strenuous action; effort.

ex hort (eg zôrt′), *v.t.* urge strongly; advise or warn earnestly.

ex hor ta tion (eg′zôr tā′shən, ek′sôr-tā′shən), *n.* 1 strong urging; earnest advice or warning. 2 speech, sermon, etc., that exhorts.

ex hu ma tion (eks′hyə mā′shən), *n.* act of exhuming.

ex hume (eks hyüm′, eg zyüm′), *v.t.*, **-humed, -hum ing.** dig (a dead body) out of a grave or the ground; disinter.

ex pe di en cy (ek spē′dē ən sē), *n., pl.* **-cies.** 1 a helping to bring about a desired result; desirability or fitness under the circumstances; usefulness. 2 personal advantage; self-interest.

ex pe di ent (ek spē′dē ənt), *adj.* 1 helping to bring about a desired result; desirable or suitable under the circumstances; useful; advantageous. 2 giving or seeking personal advantage. —*n.* means of bringing about a desired result.

ex po si tion (ek′spə zish′ən), *n.* 1 a detailed explanation. 2 speech or writing explaining a process, thing, or idea.

ex pos tu late (ek spos′chə lāt), *v.i.*, **-lat ed, -lat ing.** reason earnestly with a person, protesting against something he means to do or has done; remonstrate in a friendly way.

ex pound (ek spound′), *v.t.* 1 make clear; explain, interpret, etc. 2 set forth or state in detail.

ex pur gate (ek′spər gāt), *v.t.*, **-gat ed, -gat ing.** remove objectionable passages or words from (a book, letter, etc.).

ex ten u a tion (ek sten′yü ā′shən), *n.* partial excuse.

ex tin guish (ek sting′gwish), *v.t.* 1 put out; quench. 2 bring to an end; snuff out; destroy. [< Latin *exstinguere* < *ex-* out + *stinguere* quench]

ex tol or **ex toll** (ek stōl′, ek stol′), *v.t.*, **-tolled, -tol ling.** praise highly; commend. **—ex tol′ler,** *n.* **—ex tol′ment,** *n.*

ex tort (ek stôrt′), *v.t.* obtain (money, a promise, etc.) by threats, force, fraud, or illegal use of authority. [< Latin *extortum* twisted out < *ex-* + *torquere* twist]

extra-, *prefix.* outside ___; beyond ___.

fa cil i ty (fə sil′ə tē), *n., pl.* **-ties.** 1 absence of difficulty; ease. 2 power to do anything easily and quickly; skill in using the hands or mind.

fac ti tious (fak tish′əs), *adj.* developed by effort; not natural; artificial.

fain (fān), ARCHAIC. —*adv.* gladly; willingly.

farce (färs), *n.* 1 a play full of ridiculous happenings, absurd actions, and unreal situations, meant to be very funny. 2 a ridiculous mockery; absurd pretense; sham.

fas tid i ous (fa stid′ē əs), *adj.* hard to please; dainty in taste; easily disgusted.

fawn (fôn), *v.i.* 1 try to get favor or notice by slavish acts. 2 (of dogs, etc.) show fondness by crouching, wagging the tail, licking the hand, etc.

fe al ty (fē′əl tē), *n., pl.* **-ties.** 1 loyalty and duty owed by a vassal to his feudal lord. 2 loyalty; faithfulness; allegiance.

feign (fān), *v.t.* 1 put on a false appearance of; make believe; pretend. 2 make up to deceive; invent falsely. —*v.i.* make oneself appear; pretend (to be).

fe lic i ty (fə lis′ə tē), *n., pl.* **-ties.** 1 great happiness; bliss. 2 good fortune; blessing. 3 a pleasing ability in expression; appropriateness or gracefulness.

fell (fel), *adj.* 1 fierce; savage; ruthless. 2 deadly; destructive.

fen (fen), *n.* low, marshy land covered wholly or partially with shallow, often stagnant water. [Old English *fenn*]

fer vent (fėr′vənt), *adj.* 1 showing great warmth of feeling; very earnest; ardent. 2 hot; glowing; intense.

fes tive (fes′tiv), *adj.* of or suitable for a feast, festival, or holiday; merry; joyous.

fes toon (fe stün′), *n.* a string or chain of flowers, leaves, ribbons, etc., hanging in a curve between two points. —*v.t.* 1 decorate with festoons. 2 form into festoons; hang in curves.

fet ter (fet′ər), *n.* chain or shackle for the feet to prevent escape. —*v.t.* 1 bind with fetters; chain the feet of. 2 bind; restrain. [Old English *feter.* Related to FOOT.]

fi del i ty (fī del′ə tē, fə del′ə tē), *n., pl.* **-ties.** 1 steadfast faithfulness; loyalty. 2 exactness, as in a copy; accuracy. [< Latin *fidelitatem* < *fidelis* faithful < *fides* faith]

fil i al (fil′ē əl), *adj.* of a son or daughter; due from a son or daughter toward a mother or father.

fir ma ment (fėr′mə mənt), *n.* arch of the heavens; sky.

fis sure (fish′ər), *n., v.*, **-sured, -sur ing.** —*n.* 1 a long, narrow opening; split; crack. 2 a splitting apart; division into parts.

flag on (flag′ən), *n.* container for liquids, usually having a handle, a spout, and a cover.

fledg ling or **fledge ling** (flej′ling), *n.* 1 a young bird that has just grown feathers needed for flying. 2 a young, inexperienced person.

flout (flout), *v.t.* treat with contempt or scorn; scoff at; mock. —*v.i.* show contempt or scorn; scoff.

fluc tu ate (fluk′chü āt), *v.i.*, **-at ed, -at ing.** 1 rise and fall; change continually; vary irregularly; waver; vacillate. 2 move in waves.

flute (flüt), *n., v.*, **flut ed, flut ing.** —*n.* 1 a long, slender, pipelike musical instrument. 2 a long, round groove, especially one of a parallel series cut in a column. —*v.i.* 1 play on a flute. 2 sing or whistle so as to sound like a flute. —*v.t.* 1 play (a melody, etc.) on a flute. 2 sing, whistle, say, etc., in flutelike tones.

hat, āge, fär; let, ēqual, tėrm;
it, īce; hot, ōpen, ôrder;
oil, out; cup, pu̇t, rüle;
ch, child; ng, long; sh, she;
th, thin; ᴛʜ, then; zh, measure;
ə represents *a* in about, *e* in taken, *i* in pencil, *o* in lemon, *u* in circus.
< = from, derived from, taken from.

for lorn (fôr lôrn′), *adj.* 1 left alone and neglected; deserted; abandoned. 2 wretched in feeling or looks; unhappy. 3 hopeless; desperate.

for mi da ble (fôr′mə də bəl), *adj.* hard to overcome; hard to deal with; to be dreaded.

fret (fret), *n., v.*, **fret ted, fret ting.** —*n.* an ornamental pattern made of straight lines bent or combined at angles. —*v.t.* decorate with fretwork.

frieze (frēz), *n.* a horizontal band, often ornamented with sculpture, between the cornice and architrave of a building.

fri vol i ty (fri vol′ə tē), *n., pl.* **-ties.** 1 a being frivolous; silly behavior; trifling. 2 a frivolous act or thing.

-ful, *suffix added to nouns to form adjectives or other nouns.*

fus tian (fus′chən), *n.* a coarse, heavy cloth made of cotton and flax, used for clothing in Europe throughout the Middle Ages. —*adj.* made of fustian.

-fy, *suffix forming verbs chiefly from adjectives.*

gad (gad), *v.i.*, **gad ded, gad ding.** move about restlessly; go about looking for pleasure or excitement.

gall[1] (gôl), *n.* 1 bile of animals. 2 anything very bitter or harsh. 3 bitterness; hate. 4 SLANG. too great boldness; impudence.

gall[2] (gôl), *v.t.* 1 make sore by rubbing. 2 annoy; irritate. —*v.i.* become sore by rubbing. —*n.* 1 a sore spot on the skin caused by rubbing, especially one on a horse's back. 2 cause of annoyance or irritation.

gam bol (gam′bəl), *n.* a running and jumping about in play; caper; frolic. —*v.i.* run and jump about in play; frolic. [earlier *gambade* < Middle French < Italian *gambata* < *gamba* leg < Late Latin *camba* < Greek *kampē* a bend]

gar ner (gär′nər), *v.t.* 1 gather and store away. 2 collect or deposit. —*n.* 1 storehouse for grain. 2 a store of anything. [< Old French *gernier, grenier* < Latin *granarium* granary]

gar nish (gär′nish), *v.t.* 1 decorate (food). 2 decorate; trim.

gar ret (gar′it), *n.* 1 space in a house just below a sloping roof; attic. 2 room or apartment in such a place.

gar ru lous (gar′ə ləs, gar′yə ləs), *adj.* 1 talking too much; talkative. 2 using too many words; wordy.

gen ial (jē′nyəl), *adj.* 1 smiling and pleasant;

cheerful and friendly; kindly. 2 helping growth; pleasantly warming; comforting. [< Latin *genialis,* literally, belonging to the genius < *genius*]

gen teel (jen tēl′), *adj.* 1 belonging or suited to polite society. 2 polite; well-bred; fashionable; elegant. 3 artificially polite and courteous.

gen til i ty (jen til′ə tē), *n., pl.* **-ties.** 1 gentle birth; being of good family and social position. 2 good manners. 3 refinement.

gib ber (jib′ər, gib′ər), *v.i.* chatter senselessly; talk in a confused, meaningless way.

gib bet (jib′it), *n.* 1 an upright post with a projecting arm at the top, from which the bodies of criminals were hung after execution. 2 gallows.

gird (gėrd), *v.t.,* **gird ed** or **girt, gird ing.** 1 put a belt or girdle around. 2 fasten with a belt or girdle. 3 surround; enclose. 4 get ready. 5 clothe; furnish; endue.

glean (glēn), *v.t.* 1 gather (grain) left on a field by reapers. 2 gather little by little.

goad (gōd), *n.* 1 a sharp-pointed stick for driving cattle; gad. 2 anything which drives or urges one on.

gob bet (gob′it), *n.* lump; mass.

gorge (gôrj), *n., v.,* **gorged, gorg ing.** —*n.* 1 contents of a stomach. 2 ARCHAIC. throat.

gorse (gôrs), *n.* a low, prickly, evergreen shrub of the pea family, having yellow flowers, common on waste lands in Europe.

gout (gout), *n.* 1 a painful disease, characterized by inflammation of the joints, especially of the big toe. 2 drop, splash, or clot.

gra da tion (grā dā′shən), *n.* 1 a change by steps or stages; gradual change. 2 step, stage, or degree in a series.

greave (grēv), *n.* Often, **greaves,** *pl.* armor for the leg below the knee.

griev ous (grē′vəs), *adj.* 1 hard to bear; causing great pain or suffering; severe. 2 very evil or offensive; outrageous. 3 causing grief. 4 full of grief; showing grief.

gri mace (grə mās′, grim′is), *n., v.,* **-maced, -mac ing.** —*n.* a twisting of the face; ugly or funny smile. —*v.i.* make grimaces.

gro tesque (grō tesk′), *adj.* 1 odd or unnatural in shape, appearance, manner, etc.; fantastic; queer. 2 ridiculous; absurd. [< French < Italian *grottesco,* literally, of caves, cavelike < *grotta*]

grov el (gruv′əl, grov′əl), *v.i.,* **-eled, -el ing** or **-elled, -el ling.** 1 lie face downward; crawl at someone's feet; cringe. 2 abase or humble oneself. 3 enjoy low, mean, or contemptible things. [Middle English *groveling,* originally an adverb, in a prone position]

gru el (grü′əl), *n.* a thin, almost liquid food made by boiling oatmeal, etc., in water or milk.

gudg eon (guj′ən), *n.* a small Eurasian freshwater fish of the same family as the carp, that is easy to catch and is often used for bait.

guile (gīl), *n.* crafty deceit; sly tricks; cunning.

guin ea (gin′ē), *n.* a British gold coin, not made since 1813, worth 21 shillings. [< *Guinea,* because the coins were originally made of gold from Guinea]

guise (gīz), *n.* 1 style of dress; garb. 2 outward appearance; aspect; semblance. 3 assumed appearance; pretense.

gu los i ty (gü los′ə tē), *n.* greediness.

guy (gī), *n., v.,* **guyed, guy ing.** —*n.* rope, chain, or wire attached to something to steady or secure it.

haft (haft), *n.* handle, especially that of a knife, sword, dagger, etc.

hag gard (hag′ərd), *adj.* looking worn from pain, fatigue, worry, hunger, etc.; careworn; gaunt.

hale (hāl), *adj.,* **hal er, hal est.** free from infirmity; strong and well; healthy.

hal low (hal′ō), *v.t.* 1 make holy; make sacred; sanctify. 2 honor as holy or sacred.

hap ly (hap′lē), *adv.* ARCHAIC. by chance; perhaps.

har bin ger (här′bən jər), *n.* one that goes ahead to announce another's coming; forerunner. —*v.t.* announce beforehand; foretell. [< Old French *herbergere* provider of shelter (hence, one who goes ahead), ultimately < *herberge* lodging, of Germanic origin. Related to HARBOR.]

har row (har′ō), *n.* a heavy frame with iron teeth or upright disks, used by farmers to break up plowed ground. —*v.t.* 1 draw a harrow over (land, etc.). 2 hurt; wound. 3 cause pain or torment to; distress.

hatch ment (hach′mənt), *n.* a square tablet set diagonally, bearing the coat of arms of a dead person.

haugh ty (hô′tē), *adj.,* **-ti er, -ti est.** too proud and scornful of others.

haw ser (hô′zər, hô′sər), *n.* a large, stout rope or thin steel cable, used for mooring or towing ships.

hea then (hē′ᴛʜən), *n., pl.* **-thens** or **-then,** *adj.* —*n.* 1 person who does not believe in the God of the Bible; person who is not a Christian, Jew, or Moslem; pagan. 2 people who are heathens.

heave (hēv), *v.,* **heaved** or **hove, heav ing,** *n., interj.* —*v.i.* 1 pull with force or effort; haul. 2 rise and fall alternately. 3 breathe hard; pant; gasp. 4 be raised, thrown, or forced up; rise; swell; bulge.

her mit age (hėr′mə tij), *n.* 1 dwelling place of a hermit. 2 a solitary or secluded dwelling place.

hid e ous (hid′ē əs), *adj.* very ugly; frightful; horrible.

hom age (hom′ij, om′ij), *n.* 1 dutiful respect; reverence. 2 (in the Middle Ages) a formal acknowledgment by a vassal that he owed loyalty and service to his lord.

hone (hōn), *n., v.,* **honed, hon ing.** —*n.* a fine-grained whetstone on which to sharpen cutting tools, especially razors. —*v.t.* sharpen on a hone. [Old English *hān* stone]

host (hōst), *n.* 1 a large number; multitude. 2 army of soldiers.

hove (hōv), *v.* a pt. and a pp. of **heave.**

hum bug (hum′bug′), *n., v.,* **-bugged, -bug ging.** —*n.* 1 person who pretends to be what he is not; fraud; impostor. 2 cheat; sham. 3 nonsense or pretense.

hus band ry (huz′bən drē), *n.* 1 farming. 2 careful management; thrift.

-ible, *suffix added to verbs to form adjectives.*

-ic, *suffix added to nouns to form adjectives.*

-ical, *suffix.*

ig no ble (ig nō′bəl), *adj.* 1 without honor; disgraceful; base. 2 not of noble birth or position; humble.

im me mo ri al (im′ə môr′ē əl, im′ə-mōr′ē əl), *adj.* extending back beyond the bounds of memory; ancient beyond record or knowledge; extremely old.

im mi nent (im′ə nənt), *adj.* likely to happen soon; about to occur. [< Latin *imminentem* overhanging, threatening]

imp (imp), *n.* 1 a young or small devil; little demon. 2 a mischievous child.

im pal pa ble (im pal′pə bəl), *adj.* 1 that cannot be felt by touching; intangible. 2 very hard to understand; that cannot be grasped by the mind.

im ped i ment (im ped′ə mənt), *n.* hindrance; obstruction.

im per a tive (im per′ə tiv), *adj.* 1 not to be avoided; that must be done; urgent. 2 expressing a command or request. **—im per′a tive ly,** *adv.*

im per ti nent (im pėrt′n ənt), *adj.* 1 rudely bold; impudent; insolent. 2 not pertinent; not to the point; out of place.

im pi ous (im′pē əs, im pī′əs), *adj.* not pious; not having or not showing reverence for God; wicked; profane.

im por tu nate (im pôr′chə nit), *adj.* asking repeatedly; annoyingly persistent; urgent.

im por tune (im′pôr tün′, im′pôr tyün′, im pôr′chən), *v.,* **-tuned, -tun ing,** *adj.* —*v.t.* ask urgently or repeatedly; annoy with pressing demands. —*adj.* importunate. [< Latin *importunus* inconvenient]

im pos ture (im pos′chər), *n.* deception; fraud.

im pre ca tion (im′prə kā′shən), *n.* 1 an imprecating; cursing. 2 curse.

im preg na ble (im preg′nə bəl), *adj.* able to resist attack; not yielding to force, persuasion, etc.

im pu dent (im′pyə dənt), *adj.* shamelessly bold; very rude and insolent.

im pu ta tion (im′pyə tā′shən), *n.* a charge or hint of wrongdoing.

im pute (im pyüt′), *v.t.,* **-put ed, -put ing.** consider as belonging; attribute; charge to a person or a cause; blame.

in-[1], *prefix.* not; the opposite of; the absence of.

in-[2], *prefix.* in; into; on; upon.

in can des cence (in′kən des′ns), *n.* a being incandescent.

in can des cent (in′kən des′nt), *adj.* 1 heated to such a high temperature that it gives out light; glowing with heat; red-hot or white-hot. 2 shining brightly; brilliant.

in can ta tion (in′kan tā′shən), *n.* 1 set of words spoken as a magic charm or to cast a magic spell. 2 the use of such words.

in cense (in sens′), *v.t.,* **-censed, -cens ing.** make very angry; fill with rage. [< Latin *incensum* inflamed, enraged, set on fire < *in-* (intensive) + *candere* glow white]

in ces sant (in ses′nt), *adj.* never stopping; continued or repeated without interruption; continual.

in cip i ent (in sip′ē ənt), *adj.* just beginning; in an early stage; commencing.

in clem en cy (in klem′ən sē), *n., pl.* **-cies.** inclement condition or quality; severity; harshness.

in clem ent (in klem′ənt), *adj.* 1 rough or stormy. 2 not merciful or kindly; severe.

in con gru ous (in kong′grü əs), *adj.* 1 out of keeping; not appropriate; out of place. 2 lacking in agreement or harmony; not consistent.

in con ti nence (in kon′tə nəns), *n.* 1 lack of self-control. 2 lack of chastity.

in con ti nent (in kon′tə nənt), *adj.* 1 without self-control. 2 not chaste; licentious. **—in con′ti nent ly,** *adv.*

in cor ri gi ble (in kôr′ə jə bəl, in kor′ə jə-bəl), *adj.* 1 too firmly fixed in bad ways, an annoying habit, etc., to be reformed or changed. 2 so fixed that it cannot be changed or cured.

in cred u lous (in krej′ə ləs), *adj.* 1 not ready to believe; doubting; skeptical. 2 showing a lack of belief. **—in cred′u lous ly,** *adv.*

in cum bent (in kum′bənt), *adj.* lying, leaning, or pressing on something.

in dict (in dīt′), *v.t.* charge with an offense or crime; accuse.

in dict ment (in dīt′mənt), *n.* 1 a formal written accusation, especially one presented by a grand jury. 2 accusation.

in di gence (in′də jəns), *n.* extreme need; poverty.

in dig nant (in dig′nənt), *adj.* angry at something unworthy, unjust, unfair, or mean.

in dig na tion (in′dig nā′shən), *n.* anger at something unworthy, unjust, unfair, or mean; anger mixed with scorn; righteous anger.

in dis sol u ble (in′di sol′yə bəl), *adj.* that cannot be dissolved, undone, or destroyed; lasting; firm.

in do lent (in′dl ənt), *adj.* disliking work; lazy; idle.

in duce ment (in düs′mənt, in dyüs′mənt), *n.* 1 something that influences or persuades; incentive. 2 act of influencing or persuading.

in ef fec tu al (in′ə fek′chü əl), *adj.* 1 without effect; useless. 2 not able to produce the effect wanted; powerless.

in ert (in ėrt′), *adj.* 1 having no power to move or act; lifeless. 2 inactive; slow; sluggish.

in er tia (in ėr′shə), *n.* tendency to remain in the state one is in, and not start changes.

in ex or a ble (in ek′sər ə bəl), *adj.* not influenced by pleading or entreaties; relentless; unyielding.

in ex plic a ble (in′ik splik′ə bəl, in-ek′splə kə bəl), *adj.* that cannot be explained, understood, or accounted for; mysterious.

in fa mous (in′fə məs), *adj.* 1 deserving or causing a very bad reputation; shamefully bad; disgraceful. 2 having a very bad reputation; in public disgrace.

in fat u ate (in fach′ü āt), *v.t.*, **-at ed, -at ing.** 1 inspire with a foolish or extreme passion. 2 make foolish. [< Latin *infatuatum* made foolish < *in-* + *fatuus* foolish]

in fer nal (in fėr′nl), *adj.* 1 of or having to do with hell. 2 of the lower world which the ancient Greeks and Romans thought of as the abode of the dead. 3 fit to have come from hell; hellish; diabolical.

in firm (in fėrm′), *adj.* 1 lacking strength or health; physically weak or feeble, especially through age. 2 without a firm purpose; not steadfast; faltering.

in fir mi ty (in fėr′mə tē), *n., pl.* **-ties.** 1 weakness; feebleness. 2 sickness; illness.

in gen ious (in jē′nyəs), *adj.* 1 skillful in making; good at inventing. 2 cleverly planned or made. [< Latin *ingeniosus* < *ingenium* natural talent < *in-* in + *gignere* beget, be born]

in gen u ous (in jen′yü əs), *adj.* 1 free from restraint or reserve; frank and open; sincere. 2 simple and natural; innocent; naïve.

in iq ui ty (in ik′wə tē), *n., pl.* **-ties.** 1 gross injustice or unrighteousness; wickedness; sin. 2 a wicked or unjust act.

in quis i tive (in kwiz′ə tiv), *adj.* 1 asking many questions; curious. 2 prying into other people's affairs; too curious.

in scru ta ble (in skrü′tə bəl), *adj.* that cannot be understood; so mysterious or obscure that one cannot make out its meaning; incomprehensible.

in sid i ous (in sid′ē əs), *adj.* 1 seeking to entrap or ensnare; wily or sly; crafty; tricky. 2 working secretly or subtly; developing without attracting attention. [< Latin *insidiosus* < *insidiae* ambush < *insidere* sit in < *in-* in + *sedere* sit]

in sin u ate (in sin′yü āt), *v.*, **-at ed, -at ing.** *—v.t.* 1 suggest in an indirect way; hint. 2 push in or get in by an indirect, subtle way. *—v.i.* make insinuations.

in sip id (in sip′id), *adj.* 1 without any particular flavor; tasteless. 2 lacking interest or spirit; dull, colorless, or weak.

in so lence (in′sə ləns), *n.* bold rudeness; insulting behavior or speech.

in su per a ble (in sü′pər ə bəl), *adj.* that cannot be passed over or overcome; insurmountable.

inter-, *prefix.* 1 one with the other; together. 2 between.

in ter fuse (in′tər fyüz′), *v.t., v.i.*, **-fused, -fus ing.** 1 spread through; be diffused through; permeate. 2 fuse together; blend; mix. [< Latin *interfusum* poured between < *inter-* between + *fundere* pour]

in ter ment (in tėr′mənt), *n.* act of interring; burial.

in ter mit (in′tər mit′), *v.t., v.i.*, **-mit ted, -mit ting.** stop for a time; discontinue; suspend. [< Latin *intermittere* < *inter-* between + *mittere* to leave]

in ter sperse (in′tər spėrs′), *v.t.*, **-spersed, -spers ing.** 1 vary with something put here and there. 2 scatter or place here and there among other things. [< Latin *interspersum* scattered < *inter-* between + *spargere* to scatter]

in ter stice (in tėr′stis), *n., pl.* **-sti ces** (-stə sēz′). a small or narrow space between things or parts; narrow chink, crack, or opening.

in tes tate (in tes′tāt, in tes′tit), *adj.* 1 having made no will. 2 not disposed of by a will.

intra-, *prefix.* within; inside; on the inside.

in trac ta ble (in trak′tə bəl), *adj.* 1 hard to manage; stubborn. 2 not easily treated.

in trep id (in trep′id), *adj.* very brave; fearless; dauntless; courageous. [< Latin *intrepidus* < *in-* not + *trepidus* alarmed]

in tu i tive (in tü′ə tiv, in tyü′ə tiv), *adj.* 1 perceiving or understanding by intuition. 2 acquired by intuition; instinctive; natural.

in ure (in yůr′), *v.*, **-ured, -ur ing.** *—v.t.* toughen or harden; accustom; habituate.

in vert (in vėrt′), *v.t.* 1 turn upside down. 2 turn the other way; reverse in position, direction, order, etc.

-ion, *suffix forming nouns chiefly from verbs.*

ire (īr), *n.* anger; wrath.

ir res o lute (i rez′ə lüt), *adj.* not resolute; unable to make up one's mind; not sure of what one wants; hesitating; vacillating.

ir rev o ca ble (i rev′ə kə bəl), *adj.* 1 not able to be revoked; final. 2 impossible to call or bring back.

-ish, *suffix forming adjectives from other adjectives and from nouns.*

-ist, *suffix forming nouns chiefly from other nouns.*

isth mus (is′məs), *n.* a narrow strip of land with water on both sides, connecting two larger bodies of land.

-ity, *suffix forming nouns from adjectives.*

-ive, *suffix forming adjectives from nouns.*

hat, āge, fär; let, ēqual, tėrm;
it, īce; hot, ōpen, ôrder;
oil, out; cup, pu̇t, rüle;
ch, child; ng, long; sh, she;
th, thin; ᴛʜ, then; zh, measure;

ə represents *a* in about, *e* in taken, *i* in pencil, *o* in lemon, *u* in circus.

< = from, derived from, taken from.

-ize, *suffix forming verbs from adjectives and nouns.*

jeop ar dy (jep′ər dē), *n.* 1 risk; danger; peril. 2 (in law) the danger of being convicted and punished when tried for a crime. [< Old French *jeu parti* an even or divided game]

joc und (jok′ənd, jō′kənd), *adj.* feeling, expressing, or communicating mirth or cheer; cheerful; merry. [< Latin *jocundus, jucundus* pleasant < *juvare* please]

joust (just, joust, jüst), *n.* combat between two knights on horseback, armed with lances, especially as part of a tournament. *—v.i.* fight with lances on horseback.

jo vi al (jō′vē əl), *adj.* good-hearted and full of fun; good-humored and merry. [< Latin *Jovialis* of the planet Jupiter (those born under the planet's sign being supposedly cheerful) < *Jovis* Jove]

ju di cious (jü dish′əs), *adj.* having, using, or showing good judgment; wise; sensible.

ken (ken), *n., v.*, **kenned** or **kent** (kent), **ken ning.** *—n.* 1 range of sight. 2 range of knowledge. *—v.t.* SCOTTISH. know. *—v.i.* SCOTTISH. have knowledge.

kern (kėrn), *n.* 1 ARCHAIC. an Irish or Scottish foot soldier carrying light weapons. 2 an Irish peasant.

knave (nāv), *n.* a tricky, dishonest man; rogue; rascal.

knell (nel), *n.* 1 sound of a bell rung slowly after a death or at a funeral. 2 a warning sign of death, failure, etc. 3 a mournful sound.

knick er bock ers (nik′ər bok′ərz), *n.pl.* knickers.

knick ers (nik′ərz), *n.pl.* short, loose-fitting trousers gathered in at, or just below, the knee.

la i ty (lā′ə tē), *n., pl.* **-ties.** the people who are not members of the clergy or of a professional class; laymen collectively.

la ment (lə ment′), *v.t.* 1 express grief for; mourn for. 2 regret. *—v.i.* express grief; mourn; weep. *—n.* 1 expression of grief or sorrow; wail. 2 poem, song, or tune that expresses grief.

lan guid (lang′gwid), *adj.* 1 without energy; drooping; weak; weary. 2 without interest or enthusiasm; indifferent; listless. 3 not brisk or lively; sluggish; dull. [< Latin *languidus* < *languere* be faint]

lan guish (lang′gwish), *v.i.* 1 become weak or weary; lose energy; droop. 2 suffer under any unfavorable conditions. 3 grow dull, slack, or less intense. 4 long or pine *(for).* 5 assume a soft, tender look for effect.

las si tude (las′ə tüd, las′ə tyüd), *n.* lack of energy; weariness; languor.

la tent (lāt′nt), *adj.* present but not active; hidden; concealed.

lat tice (lat′is), *n., v.,* **-ticed, -tic ing.** —*n.* 1 structure of crossed wooden or metal strips with open spaces between them. 2 window, gate, etc., having a lattice.

laud a ble (lô′də bəl), *adj.* worthy of praise; commendable.

lave (lāv), *v.,* **laved, lav ing.** —*v.t.* 1 wash; bathe. 2 wash or flow against. —*v.i.* ARCHAIC. bathe.

lay (lā), *n.* 1 a short lyric or narrative poem to be sung. 2 song; tune.

lea (lē), *n.* a grassy field; meadow; pasture.

lech er ous (lech′ər əs), *adj.* lewd; lustful.

lees (lēz), *n.pl.* dregs; sediment.

-less, *suffix forming adjectives from verbs and nouns.*

leth ar gy (leth′ər jē), *n., pl.* **-gies.** drowsy dullness; lack of energy; sluggish inactivity.

li ber ti cide (li bėr′ti sīd), *n.* the destruction of liberty.

lib er tine (lib′ər tēn′), *n.* person without moral restraints; immoral or licentious person. —*adj.* without moral restraints; dissolute; licentious.

liege (lēj), *n.* in the Middle Ages: 1 lord having a right to the homage and loyal service of his vassals; liege lord. 2 vassal obliged to give homage and loyal service to his lord; liegeman. —*adj.* 1 having a right to the homage and loyal service of vassals. 2 obliged to give homage and loyal service to a lord.

lin den (lin′dən), *n.* 1 any of a genus of shade trees with heart-shaped leaves and clusters of small, fragrant, yellowish flowers. 2 the light, white wood of any of these trees.

lin e age (lin′ē ij), *n.* 1 descent in a direct line from a common ancestor. 2 the descendants of a common ancestor. 3 family or race.

lin tel (lin′tl), *n.* a horizontal beam or stone over a door, window, etc., to support the structure above it.

li ti gious (lə tij′əs), *adj.* 1 having the habit of going to law. 2 that can be disputed in a court of law.

loath (lōth, lōᴛʜ), *adj.* unwilling or reluctant; averse.

low (lō), *v.i., v.t.* make the sound of a cow; moo. —*n.* the sound a cow makes; mooing.

lub ber (lub′ər), *n.* 1 a big, clumsy, stupid fellow. 2 a clumsy sailor.

lu mi nous (lü′mə nəs), *adj.* 1 shining by its own light. 2 full of light; shining; bright. 3 easily understood; clear; enlightening.

-ly[1], *suffix forming adverbs from adjectives.*

-ly[2], *suffix forming adjectives from nouns.*

mag is ter i al (maj′ə stir′ē əl), *adj.* 1 of a magistrate; suited to a magistrate. 2 showing authority; authoritative. 3 imperious; domineering; overbearing.

mag nan i mous (mag nan′ə məs), *adj.* 1 noble in soul or mind; generous in forgiving; free from mean or petty feelings or acts; unselfish. 2 showing or arising from a generous spirit. [< Latin *magnanimus* < *magnus* great + *animus* spirit]

mal e fac tion (mal′ə fak′shən), *n.* an evil deed; crime.

ma lev o lence (mə lev′ə ləns), *n.* the wish that evil may happen to others; ill will; spite.

mal ice (mal′is), *n.* 1 active ill will; wish to hurt or make suffer; rancor.

ma lig ni ty (mə lig′nə tē), *n., pl.* **-ties.** 1 great malice; extreme hate or ill will. 2 great harmfulness; dangerous quality; deadliness. 3 a malignant feeling or act.

man a cle (man′ə kəl), *n., v.,* **-cled, -cling.** —*n.* 1 Usually, **manacles,** *pl.* fetter for the hands; handcuff. 2 anything that fetters; restraint.

man dar in (man′dər ən), *n.* 1 an official of any of nine ranks under the Chinese empire. 2 any great official. [< Portuguese *mandarim* < Malay *mantrī* < Sanskrit *mantrin* advisor]

man date (*n.* man′dāt, man′dit; *v.* man′dāt), *n., v.,* **-dat ed, -dat ing.** —*n.* 1 an order or command. 2 order from a higher court or official to a lower one.

man i fold (man′ə fōld), *adj.* 1 of many kinds; many and various. 2 having many parts or forms. 3 doing many things at the same time. —*v.t.* make many copies of.

man ner ism (man′ə riz′əm), *n.* 1 too much use of some manner in speaking, writing, or behaving; affectation. 2 an odd little trick; queer habit; a peculiar way of acting.

mar (mär), *v.t.,* **marred, mar ring.** spoil the beauty of; damage; injure; ruin.

ma raud (mə rôd′), *v.i.* go about in search of plunder. —*v.t.* plunder.

marl (märl), *n.* 1 a loose, crumbly soil or earthy deposit containing clay and calcium carbonate, used as a fertilizer. 2 ARCHAIC. earth.

mar tial (mär′shəl), *adj.* 1 of war; suitable for war. 2 such as war requires; brave; valiant. 3 given to fighting; warlike.

mauve (mōv), *adj.* delicate, pale purple. —*n.* a delicate, pale purple.

mead (mēd), *n.* an alcoholic drink made from fermented honey and water.

me an der (mē an′dər), *v.i.* 1 follow a winding course. 2 wander aimlessly. —*n.* 1 a winding course. 2 aimless wandering. 3 a looplike turn in a river or stream. [< Latin *maeander* a winding course < Greek *Maiandros* (now, *Menderes*) a winding river in Asia Minor]

men dac i ty (men das′ə tē), *n., pl.* **-ties.** 1 habit of telling lies; untruthfulness. 2 a lie; falsehood.

men di cant (men′də kənt), *adj.* begging. Mendicant friars ask alms for charity. —*n.* 1 beggar. 2 member of a mendicant religious order.

-ment, *suffix added to verbs to form nouns.*

mete (mēt), *v.t.,* **met ed, met ing.** give to each his share or what is due him; distribute; allot.

me tic u lous (mə tik′yə ləs), *adj.* extremely or excessively careful about small details. [< Latin *meticulosus* fearful, timid < *metus* fear]

met tle (met′l), *n.* 1 quality of disposition or temperament. 2 spirit; courage. [variant of *metal*]

met tle some (met′l səm), *adj.* full of mettle; spirited; courageous.

mick le (mik′əl), *adj., adv., n.* ARCHAIC or DIALECT. much. [Old English *micel*]

mil len ni um (mə len′ē əm), *n., pl.* **-len ni ums, -len ni a** (-len′ē ə). 1 period of a thousand years. 2 (in the Bible) the period of a thousand years during which Christ is expected to reign on earth. 3 period of righteousness and happiness, of just government, of peace and prosperity, etc.

min a ret (min′ə ret′), *n.* a slender, high tower of a Moslem mosque with one or more projecting balconies.

mince (mins), *v.,* **minced, minc ing,** *n.* —*v.t.* 1 chop up into very small pieces; shred; hash. 2 speak or do in an affectedly polite or elegant manner.

min ion (min′yən), *n.* 1 servant or follower willing to do whatever he is ordered; servile or obsequious person. 2 a darling; favorite.

mi nu ti ae (mi nü′shē ē, mi nyü′shē ē), *n.pl.* very small matters; trifling details.

mis-, *prefix.* 1 bad. 2 badly. 3 wrong.

mit i gate (mit′ə gāt), *v.t., v.i.,* **-gat ed, -gat ing.** make or become mild or milder; make or become less harsh; soften.

mit i ga tion (mit′ə gā′shən), *n.* 1 a mitigating. 2 a being mitigated.

mor ti fy (môr′tə fī), *v.,* **-fied, -fy ing.** —*v.t.* 1 wound the feelings of; make feel humbled and ashamed; humiliate. 2 overcome (bodily desires and feelings) by pain and self-denial.

mote (mōt), *n.* speck of dust.

moun te bank (moun′tə bangk), *n.* person who sells quack medicines in public, appealing to his audience by tricks, stories, jokes, etc.

mul ti tu di nous (mul′tə tüd′n əs, mul′tə-tyüd′n əs), *adj.* 1 forming a multitude; very numerous; existing or occurring in great numbers. 2 including many parts, elements, items, or features.

mu nif i cence (myü nif′ə səns), *n.* very great generosity. [< Latin *munificentia,* ultimately < *munus* gift + *facere* to make]

myr i ad (mir′ē əd), *n.* 1 ten thousand. 2 a very great number. —*adj.* 1 ten thousand. 2 countless; innumerable.

nar cis sism (när′sə siz′əm, när sis′iz′əm), *n.* excessive love or admiration of oneself.

nar cis sis tic (när′sə sis′tik), *adj.* of or characterized by narcissism.

nec tar (nek′tər), *n.* 1 (in Greek and Roman myths) the drink of the gods. 2 any delicious drink. 3 a sweet liquid found in many flowers. Bees gather nectar and make it into honey.

neg li gent (neg′lə jənt), *adj.* 1 given to or showing neglect; neglectful. 2 careless; indifferent.

-ness, *suffix added to adjectives to form nouns.*

net tle (net′l), *n., v.,* **-tled, -tling.** —*n.* any of a genus of herbs having sharp hairs on the leaves and stems that sting the skin when touched. —*v.t.* sting the mind of; irritate; provoke; vex.

nig gard (nig′ərd), *n.* a stingy person; miser. —*adj.* stingy.

noc tur nal (nok tėr′nl), *adj.* 1 of the night. 2 in the night. 3 active in the night. 4 closed by day, open by night.

non-, *prefix.* not; not a; opposite of; lack of; failure of.

nose gay (nōz′gā′), *n.* bunch of flowers; bouquet.

nox ious (nok′shəs), *adj.* 1 very harmful to life or health; pernicious; poisonous. 2 morally hurtful; corrupting.

nul li ty (nul′ə tē), *n., pl.* **-ties.** 1 condition of being null; futility; nothingness. 2 a mere nothing.

hat, āge, fär; let, ēqual, tėrm;
it, īce; hot, ōpen, ôrder;
oil, out; cup, pu̇t, rüle;
ch, child; ng, long; sh, she;
th, thin; ᴛʜ, then; zh, measure;

ə represents *a* in about, *e* in taken, *i* in pencil, *o* in lemon, *u* in circus.

< = from, derived from, taken from.

ob dur ate (ob′dər it, ob′dyər it), *adj.* 1 stubborn or unyielding; obstinate. 2 hardened in feelings or heart; not repentant. [< Latin *obduratum* hardened < *ob-* against + *durare* harden]

o blique (ə blēk′; *military* ə blīk′), *adj., v.,* **o bliqued, o bliqu ing.** —*adj.* 1 neither perpendicular to nor parallel with a given line or surface; not straight up and down or straight across; slanting. 2 not straightforward; indirect. —*v.i., v.t.* have or take an oblique direction; slant.

o bliq ui ty (ə blik′wə tē), *n., pl.* **-ties.** 1 indirectness or crookedness of thought, speech, or behavior, especially conduct that is not upright and moral. 2 a being oblique. 3 inclination, or degree of inclination.

o blit e rate (ə blit′ə rāt′), *v.t.,* **-rat ed, -rat ing.** 1 remove all traces of; blot out; efface. 2 blot out so as to leave no distinct traces; make unrecognizable.

o bliv i on (ə bliv′ē ən), *n.* 1 condition of being entirely forgotten. 2 fact of forgetting; forgetfulness.

o bliv i ous (ə bliv′ē əs), *adj.* 1 not mindful; forgetful. 2 bringing or causing forgetfulness.

ob nox ious (əb nok′shəs), *adj.* very disagreeable; offensive; hateful.

ob se quies (ob′sə kwēz), *n.pl.* funeral rites or ceremonies; stately funeral.

ob sti na cy (ob′stə nə sē), *n., pl.* **-cies.** a being obstinate; stubbornness.

ob sti nate (ob′stə nit), *adj.* 1 not giving in; stubborn. 2 hard to control, treat, or remove; persistent.

ob trude (əb trüd′), *v.,* **-trud ed, -trud ing.** —*v.t.* 1 put forward unasked and unwanted; force. 2 push out; thrust forward. —*v.i.* come unasked and unwanted; force oneself; intrude.

ob tru sion (əb trü′zhən), *n.* 1 an obtruding. 2 something obtruded.

o chre or **o cher** (ō′kər), *n.* a pale brownish yellow.

o di ous (ō′dē əs), *adj.* very displeasing; hateful; offensive.

of fi cious (ə fish′əs), *adj.* too ready to offer services or advice; minding other people's business; meddlesome.

om i nous (om′ə nəs), *adj.* of bad omen; unfavorable; threatening.

om nip o tent (om nip′ə tənt), *adj.* 1 having all power; almighty. 2 having very great power or influence. —*n.* **the Omnipotent,** God. **—om nip′o tent ly,** *adv.*

o paque (ō pāk′), *adj.* 1 not letting light through; not transparent or translucent. 2 not conducting heat, sound, electricity, etc. 3 not shining; dark; dull. 4 hard to understand; obscure. 5 stupid.

o pi ate (ō′pē it, ō′pē āt), *n.* 1 any medical preparation containing opium or a derivative of opium and used especially to dull pain or bring sleep. 2 anything that quiets, soothes, etc.

-or, *suffix forming nouns from verbs.*

o ra cle (ôr′ə kəl, or′ə kəl), *n.* 1 (in ancient Greece and Rome) an answer believed to be given by a god through a priest or priestess to some question. 2 place where the god was believed to give such answers. 3 the priest, priestess, or other means by which the god's answer was believed to be given. 4 a very wise person.

orb (ôrb), *n.* 1 anything round like a ball; sphere; globe. 2 sun, moon, planet, or star. 3 the eyeball or eye.

or di nance (ôrd′n əns), *n.* rule or law made by authority, especially one adopted and enforced by a municipal or other local authority; decree.

o ri son (ôr′ə zən, or′ə zən; ôr′ə sən, or′ə-sən), *n.* ARCHAIC. prayer.

os ten ta tion (os′ten tā′shən), *n.* a showing off; display intended to impress others.

-ous, *suffix forming adjectives from nouns.*

pal ate (pal′it), *n.* 1 roof of the mouth. 2 sense of taste. 3 a liking; relish.

pal frey (pôl′frē), *n., pl.* **-freys.** ARCHAIC. a gentle riding horse, especially one used by ladies.

pal pa ble (pal′pə bəl), *adj.* 1 readily seen or heard and recognized; obvious. 2 that can be touched or felt; tangible.

pal pi tate (pal′pə tāt), *v.i.,* **-tat ed, -tat ing.** 1 beat very rapidly, as from emotion, exercise, or disease; throb. 2 quiver; tremble. [< Latin *palpitare* to throb < *palpare* to pat]

pal sy (pôl′zē), *n., pl.* **-sies,** *v.,* **-sied, -sy ing.** —*n.* paralysis, especially a form of paralysis occurring with Parkinson's disease.

pal ter (pôl′tər), *v.i.* 1 talk or act insincerely; trifle deceitfully. 2 act carelessly; trifle.

pal try (pôl′trē), *adj.,* **-tri er, -tri est.** 1 almost worthless; trifling; petty; mean. 2 of no worth; despicable; contemptible. [probably related to Low German *paltrig* ragged, torn]

par a digm (par′ə dim, par′ə dīm), *n.* pattern; example. [< Greek *paradeigma* pattern, ultimately < *para-* + *deiknynai* to show]

par a gon (par′ə gon), *n.* model of excellence or perfection.

par ley (pär′lē), *n., pl.* **-leys.** 1 conference or informal talk. 2 an informal discussion with an enemy during a truce about terms of surrender, exchange of prisoners, etc. —*v.i.* 1 discuss terms, especially with an enemy. 2 ARCHAIC. speak; talk. [< Old French *parlee,* past participle of *parler* speak < Late Latin *parabolare* < *parabola* speech, story. Doublet of PALAVER, PARABLE, PARABOLA, PAROLE.]

par ri cide (par′ə sīd), *n.* 1 act of killing one's parent or parents. 2 person who kills his parent or parents.

par si mo ny (pär′sə mō′nē), *n.* extreme economy; stinginess.

pass ing (pas′ing), *adj.* 1 that goes by or passes. 2 fleeting; transitory. 3 cursory; incidental. 4 that is now happening. 5 allowing a person to pass an examination, course, etc. —*n.* 1 act of one that passes; going by; departure. 2 means or place of passing. 3 death. —*adv.* surpassingly; very.

pa thos (pā′thos), *n.* 1 quality in speech, writing, music, events, or a scene that arouses a feeling of pity or sadness; power of evoking tender or melancholy emotion. 2 a pathetic expression or utterance.

pat ri mo ni al (pat′rə mō′nē əl), *adj.* having to do with a patrimony; inherited from one's father or ancestors.

pe dan tic (pi dan′tik), *adj.* 1 displaying one's knowledge more than is necessary. 2 tediously learned; scholarly in a dull and narrow way. **—pe dan′ti cal ly,** *adv.*

peer (pir), *n.* 1 person of the same rank, ability, etc., as another; equal. 2 man belonging to the nobility.

peer less (pir′lis), *adj.* without an equal; matchless.

pend ent (pen′dənt), *adj.* 1 hanging; suspended. 2 overhanging. 3 pending.

pen i tent (pen′ə tənt), *adj.* sorry for sinning or doing wrong; repenting; repentant. —*n.* person who confesses and does penance for his sins under the direction of a church. **—pen′i tent ly,** *adv.*

pen sive (pen′siv), *adj.* 1 thoughtful in a serious or sad way. 2 melancholy.

pe nur i ous (pi nu̇r′ē əs, pi nyu̇r′ē əs), *adj.* 1 mean about spending or giving money; stingy. 2 in a condition of penury; extremely poor.

per ad ven ture (pėr′əd ven′chər), *adv.* ARCHAIC. maybe; perhaps.

per chance (pər chans′), *adv.* perhaps.

per di tion (pər dish′ən), *n.* 1 loss of one's soul and the joys of heaven; damnation. 2 hell. 3 utter loss or destruction; complete ruin.

pe remp tor y (pə remp′tər ē, per′əmp-tôr′ē, per′əmp tōr′ē), *adj.* 1 leaving no choice; decisive; final; absolute. 2 allowing no denial or refusal. 3 imperious; dictatorial.

per fid i ous (pər fid′ē əs), *adj.* deliberately faithless; treacherous.

per func tor y (pər fungk′tər ē), *adj.* 1 done merely for the sake of getting rid of the duty; done from force of habit; mechanical; indifferent. 2 acting in a perfunctory way. [< Late Latin *perfunctorius* < Latin *per-* through + *fungi* execute]

per il (per′əl), *n., v.,* **-iled, -il ing** or **-illed, -il ling.** —*n.* 1 chance of harm or loss; exposure to danger. 2 cause of peril or danger. —*v.t.* put in danger. [< Old French < Latin *periculum*]

per il ous (per′ə ləs), *adj.* full of peril; dangerous.

per ni cious (pər nish′əs), *adj.* 1 that will destroy or ruin; causing great harm or damage; very injurious. 2 fatal; deadly.

per pe trate (pėr′pə trāt), *v.t.,* **-trat ed, -trat ing.** do or commit (a crime, fraud, trick, or anything bad or foolish).

per pet u al (pər pech′ü əl), *adj.* 1 lasting forever; eternal. 2 lasting throughout life. 3 never ceasing; continuous; constant. 4 being in bloom more or less continuously throughout the year or the season.

per plex i ty (pər plek′sə tē), *n., pl.* **-ties.** 1 a perplexed condition; being puzzled; confusion; bewilderment. 2 an entangled or confused state. 3 something that perplexes.

per turb (pər tėrb′), *v.t.* 1 disturb greatly; make uneasy or troubled; distress. 2 cause disorder or irregularity in; agitate.

per tur ba tion (pėr′tər bā′shən), *n.* 1 a perturbing. 2 a perturbed condition. 3 thing, act, or event that causes disturbance or agitation.

pe rus al (pə rü′zəl), *n.* a perusing; reading.

pe ruse (pə rüz′), *v.t.,* **-rused, -rus ing.** read, especially thoroughly and carefully.

pes ti lence (pes′tl əns), *n.* 1 any infectious or contagious epidemic disease that spreads rapidly, often causing many deaths. 2 the bubonic plague.

pes ti lent (pes′tl ənt), *adj.* 1 often causing death. 2 harmful to morals, destroying peace; pernicious. 3 troublesome; annoying.

pet rel (pet′rəl), *n.* any of various sea birds, especially the storm petrel.

pet u lance (pech′ə ləns), *n.* a being petulant; peevishness.

pet u lant (pech′ə lənt), *adj.* likely to have little fits of bad temper; irritable over trifles; peevish.

pha lanx (fā′langks, fal′angks), *n., pl.* **phalanx es** or **pha lan ges** (fə lan′jēz). 1 (in ancient Greece) a special battle formation of infantry fighting in close ranks with their shields joined and long spears overlapping each other. 2 any body of troops in close array.

Phar i sa ic (far′ə sā′ik), *adj.* 1 of or having to do with the Pharisees. 2 **pharisaic,** making an outward show of religion or morals without the real spirit.

phi al (fī′əl), a small glass or plastic bottle for holding medicines or the like.

phos pho res cence (fos′fə res′ns), *n.* 1 act or process of giving out light without burning or by very slow burning without noticeable heat. 2 light given out in this way.

pine (pīn), *v.i.,* **pined, pin ing.** 1 long eagerly; yearn. 2 waste away with pain, hunger, grief, or desire.

pi quan cy (pē′kən sē), *n.* piquant quality.

pi quant (pē′kənt), *adj.* 1 stimulating to the mind, interest, etc. 2 pleasantly sharp; stimulating to the taste.

pith (pith), *n.* 1 the important or essential part. 2 strength; energy.

pit tance (pit′ns), *n.* 1 a small allowance of money. 2 a small amount or share.

plac id (plas′id), *adj.* pleasantly calm or peaceful; quiet.

plain tive (plān′tiv), *adj.* expressive of sorrow; mournful; sad.

plait (plāt, plat *for 1;* plāt, plēt *for 2*), *n., v.t.* 1 braid. 2 pleat.

plat i tude (plat′ə tüd, plat′ə tyüd), *n.* a dull or commonplace remark, especially one given out solemnly as if it were fresh and important.

Pla ton ic (plə ton′ik), *adj.* 1 of or having to do with Plato or his philosophy. 2 Also, **platonic.** designating love or affection of a purely spiritual character, free from sensual desire.

plight (plīt), *n.* condition or situation, usually bad.

plinth (plinth), *n.* the lower, square part of the base of a column.

ploy (ploi), *n.* gambit or maneuver by which an advantage is or may be gained over another. [short for *employ*]

pol i tic (pol′ə tik), *adj.* 1 wise in looking out for one's own interests; prudent; shrewd. 2 showing wisdom or shrewdness. 3 scheming; crafty. 4 political.

pom mel (pum′əl, pom′əl), *n., v.,* **-meled, -mel ing** or **-melled, -mel ling.** —*n.* 1 part of a saddle that sticks up at the front. 2 a rounded knob on the hilt of a sword, dagger, etc.

por tal (pôr′tl, pōr′tl), *n.* door, gate, or entrance, usually an imposing one.

post-, *prefix.* 1 after in time; later. 2 after in space; behind.

pos tern (pō′stərn, pos′tərn), *n.* 1 a back door or gate. 2 any small or private entrance.

pos tu late (*n.* pos′chə lit; *v.* pos′chə lāt), *n., v.,* **-lat ed, -lat ing.** —*n.* something taken for granted or assumed as a basis for reasoning; fundamental principle; necessary condition. —*v.t.* 1 assume as a postulate; take for granted. 2 require; demand; claim.

prate (prāt), *v.,* **prat ed, prat ing,** *n.* —*v.i.* talk a great deal in a foolish way. —*v.t.* say in an empty or foolish way.

pre-, *prefix.* 1 before in time, rank, etc. 2 before in position, space, etc.; in front of.

pre am ble (prē′am′bəl), *n.* 1 a preliminary statement; introduction to a speech or a writing. 2 a preliminary or introductory fact or circumstance, especially one showing what is to follow. [< Medieval Latin *praeambulum* < Late Latin, walking before < Latin *prae-* pre- + *ambulare* to walk]

pre cept (prē′sept), *n.* rule of action or behavior; maxim.

pre cep tor (pri sep′tər, prē′sep tər), *n.* instructor; teacher; tutor.

pre cip i tous (pri sip′ə təs), *adj.* 1 like a precipice; very steep. 2 hasty; rash. 3 rushing headlong; very rapid.

pre curse (prē kėrs′), *n.* ARCHAIC. a foreshadowing.

pre fer ment (pri fėr′mənt), *n.* 1 advancement; promotion. 2 position or office giving social or financial advancement, especially one in the church.

prel ate (prel′it), *n.* clergyman of high rank, such as a bishop.

pres age (pres′ij; *also* pri sāj′ *for v.*), *n., v.,* **pre saged, pre sag ing.** —*n.* sign felt as a warning; omen. —*v.t.* give warning of; predict.

pre sen ti ment (pri zen′tə mənt), *n.* a feeling or impression that something, especially something evil, is about to happen; vague sense of approaching misfortune; foreboding.

pre ter nat ur al (prē′tər nach′ər əl), *adj.* 1 out of the ordinary course of nature; abnormal. 2 due to something above or beyond nature; supernatural.

pre var i ca tion (pri var′ə kā′shən), *n.* a prevaricating; turning aside from the truth; lie.

pri mal (prī′məl), *adj.* 1 of early times; first; primeval. 2 chief; fundamental.

pri me val (prī mē′vəl), *adj.* 1 of or having to do with the first age or ages, especially of the world. 2 ancient. [< Latin *primaevus* early in life < *primus* first + *aevum* age]

pris tine (pris′tēn′, pris′tən, *or* pris′tīn), *adj.* as it was in its earliest time or state; original; primitive.

priv y (priv′ē), *adj., n., pl.* **priv ies.** —*adj.* 1 private. 2 ARCHAIC. secret; hidden. 3 **privy to,** having secret or private knowledge of.

pro-¹, *prefix.* 1 forward. 2 forth; out. 3 on the side of; in favor of. 4 in place of; acting as.

pro-², *prefix.* 1 before; preceding; prior to. 2 in front of; anterior.

pro cre ant (prō′krē ant), *adj.* concerning procreation.

pro cure (prə kyůr′), *v.t.,* **-cured, -cur ing.** 1 obtain by care or effort; secure. 2 bring about; cause.

prod i gal (prod′ə gəl), *adj.* 1 given to extravagant or reckless spending; wasteful. 2 abundant; lavish. —*n.* person who is wasteful or extravagant; spendthrift.

pro di gious (prə dij′əs), *adj.* 1 very great; huge; vast. 2 wonderful; marvelous.

prof a na tion (prof′ə nā′shən), *n.* act of profaning.

pro fane (prə fān′), *adj., v.,* **-faned, -fan ing.** —*adj.* 1 characterized by contempt or disregard for God or holy things; irreverent. 2 not sacred; worldly; secular. 3 ritually unclean or polluted. —*v.t.* 1 treat (holy things) with contempt or disregard; desecrate. 2 put to wrong or unworthy use. [< Latin *profanus* not sacred < *pro-* in front (outside) of + *fanum* temple, shrine]

prog nos tic (prog nos′tik), *adj.* indicating something in the future. —*n.* 1 indication; sign. 2 forecast; prediction.

pro lif ic (prə lif′ik), *adj.* 1 producing offspring or fruit abundantly. 2 highly productive; fertile. 3 conducive to growth, fruitfulness, etc.

prom on to ry (prom′ən tôr′ē, prom′əntōr′ē), *n., pl.* **-ries.** a high point of land extending from the coast into the water; headland.

prop a ga tion (prop′ə gā′shən), *n.* 1 the breeding of plants or animals. 2 a spreading; getting more widely believed; making more widely known.

proph e sy (prof′ə sī), *v.,* **-sied, -sy ing.** —*v.i.* 1 tell what will happen. 2 speak when or as if divinely inspired. —*v.t.* 1 foretell; predict. 2 utter in prophecy.

pro pi ti ate (prə pish′ē āt), *v.t.,* **-at ed, -at ing.** prevent or reduce the anger of; win the favor of; appease or conciliate (one offended or likely to be).

pro pri e tor (prə prī′ə tər), *n.* person who owns something as his possession or property; owner.

pro pri e ty (prə prī′ə tē), *n., pl.* **-ties.** 1 quality or condition of being proper; fitness. 2 proper behavior.

pro sa ic (prō zā′ik), *adj.* like prose; matter-of-fact; ordinary; not exciting.

pro tract (prō trakt′), *v.t.* 1 draw out; lengthen in time; prolong. 2 slide out; thrust out; extend.

prov i dence (prov′ə dəns), *n.* 1 God's care and help. 2 **Providence,** God. 3 instance of God's care and help.

prov i dent (prov′ə dənt), *adj.* 1 having or showing foresight; careful in providing for the future; prudent. 2 economical; frugal.

prow ess (prou′is), *n.* 1 bravery; daring. 2 unusual skill or ability.

prox im i ty (prok sim′ə tē), *n.* nearness; closeness.

prud er y (prü′dər ē), *n., pl.* **-er ies.** extreme modesty or propriety, especially when not genuine.

pu er ile (pyü′ər əl), *adj.* 1 foolish for a grown person to say or do; childish. 2 youthful; juvenile.

pu e ril i ty (pyü′ə ril′ə tē), *n., pl.* **-ties.** 1 childishness; foolishness. 2 a foolish act, idea, or statement.

pun gent (pun′jənt), *adj.* 1 sharply affecting the organs of taste and smell. 2 sharp; biting. 3 stimulating to the mind; keen; lively.

pur ga to ry (pėr′gə tôr′ē, pėr′gə tōr′ē), *n., pl.* **-ries.** 1 (in Roman Catholic belief) a temporary condition or place in which the souls of those who have died penitent are purified from venial sin or the effects of sin by punishment. 2 any condition or place of temporary suffering or punishment.

purl (pėrl), *v.i.* 1 flow with rippling motions and a murmuring sound. 2 pass with a sound like this. —*n.* a purling motion or sound.

pur port (*v.* pər pôrt′, pər pōrt′; pėr′pôrt,

pėr′pōrt; *n.* pėr′pôrt, pėr′pōrt), *v.t.* 1 claim or profess. 2 have as its main idea; mean. —*n.* meaning; main idea.

pyre (pīr), *n.* pile of wood for burning a dead body as a funeral rite.

quaff (kwäf, kwaf, kwôf), *v.i., v.t.* drink in large swallows; drink deeply and freely.

quail (kwāl), *v.i.* be afraid; lose courage; shrink back in fear.

quay (kē), *n.* a solid landing place where ships load and unload, often built of stone.

quell (kwel), *v.t.* 1 put down (disorder, rebellion, etc.). 2 put an end to; overcome.

quer u lous (kwer′ə ləs, kwer′yə ləs), *adj.* complaining; fretful; peevish.

quin tes sence (kwin tes′ns), *n.* 1 the purest form of some quality; pure essence. 2 the most perfect example of something.

qui vive? (kē vēv′), 1 who goes there? 2 **on the qui vive,** watchful; alert. [< French, literally, (long) live who?; expecting such a reply as *Vive le roi!* Long live the king!]

quoit (kwoit), *n.* 1 a heavy, flattish iron or rope ring thrown to encircle a peg or to come as close to it as possible. 2 **quoits,** *pl. in form, sing. in use.* game so played.

rail ler y (rā′lər ē), *n., pl.* **-ler ies.** good-humored ridicule; joking; teasing.

rai ment (rā′mənt), *n.* clothing; garments.

ran cor (rang′kər), *n.* bitter resentment or ill will; extreme hatred or spite.

rank (rangk), *adj.* 1 large and coarse. 2 having a strong, bad smell or taste. 3 strongly marked; extreme. 4 not decent; coarse; obscene.

ran kle (rang′kəl), *v.,* **-kled, -kling.** —*v.i.* be sore; cause soreness; continue to give pain. —*v.t.* cause pain or soreness in or to.

rapt (rapt), *adj.* 1 lost in delight. 2 so busy thinking of or enjoying one thing that one does not know what else is happening.

rav el (rav′əl), *v.,* **-eled, -el ing** or **-elled, -el ling,** *n.* —*v.i.* 1 fray out; separate into threads. 2 become tangled, involved, or confused. —*v.t.* separate the threads of; fray.

rav en ous (rav′ə nəs), *adj.* 1 very hungry. 2 greedy. 3 rapacious.

raze (rāz), *v.t.,* **razed, raz ing.** tear down; destroy completely; demolish.

re-, *prefix.* 1 again; anew; once more. 2 back.

re buke (ri byük′), *v.,* **-buked, -buk ing,** *n.* —*v.t.* express disapproval of; reprove. —*n.* expression of disapproval; scolding.

re cal ci trant (ri kal′sə trənt), *adj.* resisting authority or control; disobedient.

reck (rek), *v.i.* ARCHAIC. care; heed.

rec om pense (rek′əm pens), *v.,* **-pensed, -pens ing,** *n.* —*v.t.* 1 pay (a person); pay back; reward. 2 make a fair return for. —*n.* 1 payment; reward. 2 return; amends.

re doubt a ble (ri dou′tə bəl), *adj.* that should be feared or dreaded; formidable.

re dress (*v.* ri dres′; *n.* rē′dres, ri dres′), *v.t.* set right; repair; remedy.

re fec tor y (ri fek′tər ē), *n., pl.* **-tor ies.** a room for meals, especially in a monastery, convent, or school.

re fract (ri frakt′), *v.t.* bend (a ray, waves, etc.) from a straight course.

re frac tive (ri frak′tiv), *adj.* having power to refract; refracting.

re frac tor y (ri frak′tər ē), *adj.* 1 hard to manage; stubborn; obstinate. 2 not yielding readily to treatment.

re it e rate (rē it′ə rāt′), *v.t.,* **-rat ed, -rat ing.** say or do several times; repeat (an action, demand, etc.) again and again.

re lapse (ri laps′), *v.,* **-lapsed, -laps ing,** *n.* —*v.i.* 1 fall or slip back. 2 fall back into wrongdoing; backslide.

re miss (ri mis′), *adj.* 1 careless or slack in doing what one has to do; neglectful; negligent. 2 characterized by carelessness, negligence, or inattention.

re mon strance (ri mon′strəns), *n.* protest; complaint.

re mon strate (ri mon′strāt), *v.i.,* **-strat ed, -strat ing.** speak, reason, or plead in complaint or protest.

re morse (ri môrs′), *n.* deep; painful regret for having done wrong; compunction; contrition. [< Late Latin *remorsum* tormented, bit again < Latin *re-* back + *mordere* to bite]

rend (rend), *v.t.,* **rent, rend ing.** 1 pull apart violently; tear. 2 split. 3 disturb violently.

re nown (ri noun′), *n.* a being widely celebrated or held in high repute; fame.

rent (rent), *n.* a torn place; tear; split. —*adj.* torn; split. —*v.* pt. and pp. of **rend.**

rep ar tee (rep′ər tē′), *n.* 1 a witty reply or replies. 2 talk characterized by clever and witty replies.

re plen ish (ri plen′ish), *v.t.* fill again; provide a new supply for; renew.

re pose (ri pōz′), *n., v.,* **-posed, -pos ing.** —*n.* 1 rest or sleep. 2 quietness; ease. 3 peace; calmness. —*v.i.* 1 lie at rest. 2 rest from work or toil; take a rest. —*v.t.* lay to rest.

re prieve (ri prēv′), *v.,* **-prieved, -priev ing,** *n.* —*v.t.* 1 postpone the punishment of (a person), especially the execution of (a person condemned to death). 2 give relief from any evil or trouble. —*n.* 1 delay in carrying out a punishment, especially of the death penalty. 2 temporary relief from any evil or trouble.

re proach (ri prōch′), *n.* 1 blame or censure. 2 a cause of blame or disgrace; discredit. 3 object of blame, censure, or disapproval. 4 expression of blame, censure, or disapproval. —*v.t.* 1 blame or censure; upbraid. 2 disgrace; shame.

rep ro ba tion (rep′rə bā′shən), *n.* condemnation; censure.

re prove (ri prüv′), *v.t.,* **-proved, -prov ing.** show disapproval of; find fault with; blame. [< Old French *reprover* < Late Latin *reprobare* < Latin *re-* + *probare* to test]

re pug nance (ri pug′nəns), *n.* strong dislike, distaste, or aversion.

re pug nant (ri pug′nənt), *adj.* 1 disagreeable or offensive; distasteful; objectionable. 2 objecting; averse; opposed.

req ui em or **Req ui em** (rek′wē əm, rē′kwē əm), *n.* 1 Mass for the dead; musical church service for the dead. 2 music for it. 3 any musical service or hymn for the dead.

re quite (ri kwīt′), *v.t.,* **-quit ed, -quit ing.** 1 pay back; make return for. 2 make return to; reward. 3 make retaliation for; avenge.

res pite (res′pit), *n., v.,* **-pit ed, -pit ing.** —*n.* 1 time of relief and rest; lull. 2 a putting off; delay, especially in carrying out a sentence of death; reprieve.

re splend ent (ri splen′dənt), *adj.* very bright; shining; splendid.

re tic u late (*adj.* ri tik′yə lit, ri tik′yə lāt; *v.* ri tik′yə lāt), *adj., v.,* **-lat ed, -lat ing.** —*adj.* covered with a network; netlike. —*v.t.* cover or mark with a network. —*v.i.* form a network.

hat, āge, fär; let, ēqual, tėrm;
it, īce; hot, ōpen, ôrder;
oil, out; cup, pu̇t, rüle;
ch, child; ng, long; sh, she;
th, thin; ᴛʜ, then; zh, measure;

ə represents *a* in about, *e* in taken, *i* in pencil, *o* in lemon, *u* in circus.

< = from, derived from, taken from.

ret i nue (ret′n ü, ret′n yü), *n.* group of attendants or retainers; following.

retro-, *prefix.* backward; back; behind.

rev el (rev′əl), *v.,* **-eled, -el ing** or **-elled, -el ling,** *n.* —*v.i.* 1 take great pleasure *(in).* 2 make merry. —*n.* a noisy good time; merrymaking.

rev e la tion (rev′ə lā′shən), *n.* 1 act of making known. 2 the thing made known. 3 God's disclosure of Himself and of His will to His creatures. 4 **Revelation,** the last book of the New Testament, supposed to have been written by the apostle John.

rev el ry (rev′əl rē), *n., pl.* **-ries.** boisterous reveling or festivity.

re ver be rate (ri vėr′bə rāt′), *v.,* **-rat ed, -rat ing.** —*v.i.* 1 echo back. 2 be cast back; be reflected a number of times, as light or heat. —*v.t.* 1 reecho (a sound or noise). 2 cast back; reflect (light or heat).

rind (rīnd), *n.* 1 the firm outer covering of oranges, melons, cheeses, etc. 2 the bark of a tree or plant. 3 the skin.

ro bus tious (rō bus′chəs), *adj.* ARCHAIC. 1 rough; rude. 2 robust; strong.

ro guish (rō′gish), *adj.* 1 having to do with or like rogues; dishonest; rascally. 2 playfully mischievous.

rook (ru̇k), *n.* 1 a common European bird, of the same genus as and closely resembling the crow, that often nests in large flocks in trees near buildings. 2 person who cheats at cards, dice, etc.

rote (rōt), *n.* a set, mechanical way of doing things. [Middle English]

rout (rout), *n.* 1 flight of a defeated army in disorder. 2 a complete defeat. 3 a noisy, disorderly crowd; mob; rabble. 4 riot; disturbance. —*v.t.* 1 put to flight in disorder. 2 defeat completely.

ru bric (rü′brik), *n.* 1 title or heading of a chapter, a law, etc., written or printed in red or in special lettering. 2 direction for the conducting of religious services inserted in a prayer book, ritual, etc. 3 any heading, rule, or guide.

ru di ment (rü′də mənt), *n.* 1 part to be learned first; beginning. 2 something in an early stage; undeveloped or imperfect form.

rue[1] (rü), *v.,* **rued, ru ing,** *n.* —*v.t.* be sorry for; regret. —*n.* sorrow; regret.

rue[2] (rü), *n.* a strong-smelling, woody herb of the same family as the citrus, with yellow flowers, and bitter leaves.

ru mi nant (rü′mə nənt), *n.* any of a suborder of even-toed, hoofed, herbivorous mammals which chew the cud and have a stomach with four separate cavities, including cattle, deer, sheep, goats, giraffes, and camels.

ru mi na tive (rü′mə nā′tiv), *adj.* meditative; inclined to ruminate.

rune (rün), *n.* 1 any letter of an ancient Germanic alphabet used from the A.D. 200's

to the 1200's. 2 mark that looks like a rune and has some mysterious, magic meaning.
ru nic (rü′nik), *adj.* consisting of runes; written in runes; marked with runes.
rus set (rus′it), *adj.* yellowish-brown or reddish-brown. *—n.* 1 a yellowish brown or a reddish brown. 2 a coarse, russet-colored cloth.

sac ri le gious (sak′rə lij′əs, sak′rə lē′jəs), *adj.* injurious or insulting to sacred persons or things.
sa ga cious (sə gā′shəs), *adj.* 1 wise in a keen, practical way; shrewd. 2 intelligent. [< Latin *sagacem*]
sage (sāj), *adj.,* **sag er, sag est,** *n.* *—adj.* 1 showing wisdom or good judgment. 2 wise. 3 wise-looking; grave; solemn. *—n.* a very wise man.
sa laam (sə läm′), *n.* 1 a greeting that means "Peace," used especially in Moslem countries. 2 a very low bow, with the palm of the right hand placed on the forehead. *—v.t.* greet with a salaam. *—v.i.* make a salaam.
sal ly (sal′ē), *v.,* **-lied, -ly ing,** *n., pl.* **-lies.** *—n.* 1 a sudden attack on an enemy made from a defensive position; sortie. 2 a sudden rushing forth. 3 a going forth; trip; excursion.
sal u ta tion (sal′yə tā′shən), *n.* a greeting; saluting.
sal ver (sal′vər), *n.* tray.
sanc ti fy (sangk′tə fī), *v.t.,* **-fied, -fy ing.** 1 make holy; make legitimate or binding by a religious sanction. 2 set apart as sacred; observe as holy. 3 make right; justify or sanction.
sang-froid (sang frwä′; *French* säɴ frwȧ′), *n.* coolness of mind; calmness; composure. [< French *sang froid,* literally, cold blood]
san gui nar y (sang′gwə ner′ē), *adj.* 1 with much blood or bloodshed; bloody. 2 delighting in bloodshed; bloodthirsty.
san guine (sang′gwən), *adj.* 1 naturally cheerful and hopeful. 2 confident; hopeful. 3 having a healthy red color; ruddy. [< Latin *sanguineus* < *sanguinem* blood]
sau cy (sô′sē), *adj.,* **-ci er, -ci est.** 1 showing lack of respect; impudent; rude. 2 pert; smart.
saun ter (sôn′tər, sän′tər), *v.i.* walk along slowly and happily; stroll. *—n.* 1 a leisurely or careless gait. 2 a stroll.
scarp (skärp), *n.* 1 a steep slope. 2 the inner slope or side of a ditch surrounding a fortification.
scathe (skāᴛʜ), *v.,* **scathed, scath ing,** *n.* *—v.t.* 1 blast or sear with abuse or invective. 2 sear; scorch. 3 ARCHAIC. injure; damage.
scin til late (sin′tl āt), *v.i.,* **-lat ed, -lat ing.** sparkle; flash.
screed (skrēd), *n.* a long speech or writing.
scrive ner (skriv′nər), *n.* ARCHAIC. a public writer of letters or documents for others; clerk; notary.
scru ple (skrü′pəl), *n., v.,* **-pled, -pling.** *—n.* 1 a feeling of doubt about what one ought to do. 2 a feeling of uneasiness that keeps a person from doing something.
scru pu lous (skrü′pyə ləs), *adj.* 1 very careful to do what is right; conscientious. 2 attending thoroughly to details; very careful.
scud (skud), *v.,* **scud ded, scud ding,** *n.* *—v.i.* 1 run or move swiftly. 2 (of a boat, etc.) run before a storm with little or no sail set. *—n.* 1 a scudding. 2 clouds or spray driven by the wind.
sear (sir), *v.t.* 1 burn or char the surface of. 2 make hard or unfeeling. 3 dry up; wither. *—v.i.* become dry, burned, or hard. *—n.* mark made by searing.
sec u lar (sek′yə lər), *adj.* 1 not religious or sacred; worldly. 2 living in the world; not belonging to a religious order.
sedge (sej), *n.* any of a large family of herbs growing chiefly in wet places, resembling grasses.
semi-, *prefix.* 1 half. 2 partly; incompletely. 3 twice.
sep ul cher (sep′əl kər), *n.* 1 place of burial; tomb; grave. 2 structure or recess in some old churches in which sacred relics were deposited.
se ques ter (si kwes′tər), *v.t.* 1 remove or withdraw from public use or from public view; seclude. 2 take away (property) for a time from an owner until a debt is paid or some claim is satisfied. 3 seize by authority; take and keep.
se ros i ty (si ros′i tē), *n.* secretion of serum or something resembling serum.
ser ous (sir′əs), *adj.* 1 of, having to do with, or producing serum. 2 like serum; watery.
ser vile (sėr′vəl), *adj.* 1 like that of slaves; mean; base. 2 of or having to do with slaves. 3 fit for a slave. 4 yielding through fear, lack of spirit, etc.
shift (shift), *n.* 1 change of direction, position, attitude, etc. 2 **make shift, a** manage to get along; do as well as one can. **b** manage with effort or difficulty.
shoal (shōl), *n.* 1 place in a sea, lake, or stream where the water is shallow. 2 sandbank or sandbar that makes the water shallow, especially one which can be seen at low tide. *—adj.* shallow. *—v.i.* become shallow.
shrift (shrift), *n.* ARCHAIC. 1 confession to a priest, followed by the imposing of penance and the granting of absolution. 2 act of shriving.
shrive (shrīv), *v.,* **shrove** or **shrived, shriv en** or **shrived, shriv ing.** ARCHAIC. *—v.t.* hear the confession of, impose penance on, and grant absolution to. *—v.i.* 1 make confession. 2 hear confessions.
shut tle (shut′l), *n., v.,* **-tled, -tling.** *—n.* 1 device that carries the thread from one side of the web to the other in weaving. 2 a similar device on which thread is wound, used in knitting, tatting, and embroidery.
shy (shī), *v.,* **shied, shy ing.** *—v.t., v.i.* throw; fling.
sim u late (sim′yə lāt), *v.t.,* **-lat ed, -lat ing.** 1 put on a false appearance of; pretend; feign. 2 act like; look like; imitate.
sin ew (sin′yü), *n.* 1 tendon. 2 strength; energy; force. 3 means of strength; source of power. *—v.t.* furnish with sinews. [Old English *sionu*]
sin u ous (sin′yü əs), *adj.* 1 having many curves or turns; winding. 2 indirect; devious. 3 morally crooked. [< Latin *sinuosus* < *sinus* a curve]
slav ish (slā′vish), *adj.* 1 of or having to do with a slave or slaves. 2 like a slave; mean; base. 3 weakly submitting. 4 like that of slaves; fit for slaves. 5 lacking originality and independence.
sloth (slôth, slōth), *n.* unwillingness to work or exert oneself; laziness; idleness.
slov en ly (sluv′ən lē), *adj.,* **-li er, -li est,** *adv.* *—adj.* untidy, dirty, or careless in dress, appearance, habits, work, etc.
soi ree or **soi rée** (swä rā′), *n.* an evening party or social gathering.
so journ (*v.* sō′jėrn′, sō jėrn′; *n.* sō′jėrn′), *v.i.* stay for a time. *—n.* a brief stay.
sol ace (sol′is), *n., v.,* **-aced, -ac ing.** *—n.* 1 comfort or relief. 2 that which gives comfort or consolation. *—v.t.* comfort or relieve; cheer.
sole (sōl), *adj.* 1 one and only; single. 2 only. 3 of or for only one person or group and not others; exclusive. 4 without help; alone.
so lem ni ty (sə lem′nə tē), *n., pl.* **-ties.** solemn feeling; seriousness; impressiveness.
so lic it (sə lis′it), *v.t.* 1 ask earnestly; try to get. 2 influence to do wrong; tempt; entice. *—v.i.* 1 make appeals or requests. 2 accost a person with immoral offers.
so lic i tor (sə lis′ə tər), *n.* lawyer in Britain who can advise clients and prepare cases, but can plead only in a lower court.
so lic i tous (sə lis′ə təs), *adj.* 1 showing care or concern; anxious; concerned. 2 desirous; eager.
sol i tude (sol′ə tüd, sol′ə tyüd), *n.* 1 a being alone. 2 a lonely place. 3 loneliness.
sor did (sôr′did), *adj.* 1 dirty; filthy. 2 caring too much for money; meanly selfish; greedy. 3 mean; low; base; contemptible. 4 of a dull or dirty color.
sot (sot), *n.* person who commonly or habitually drinks too much alcoholic liquor; confirmed drunkard. [Old English, a fool]
spe cious (spē′shəs), *adj.* 1 seeming desirable, reasonable, or probable, but not really so; apparently good or right, but without real merit. 2 making a good outward appearance in order to deceive.
spec ter (spek′tər), *n.* 1 phantom or ghost, especially one of a terrifying nature or appearance. 2 thing causing terror or dread. Also, **spectre.**
spec u late (spek′yə lāt), *v.i.,* **-lat ed, -lat ing.** 1 think carefully; reflect; meditate; consider. 2 guess; conjecture. 3 buy or sell when there is a large risk, with the hope of making a profit from future price changes.
spec u la tion (spek′yə lā′shən), *n.* 1 careful thought; reflection. 2 a guessing; conjecture.
spoor (spür), *n.* trail of a wild animal; track.
spor tive (spôr′tiv, spōr′tiv), *adj.* playful; merry. **—spor′tive ly,** *adv.*
squal id (skwol′id), *adj.* 1 foul through neglect or want of cleanliness; dirty; filthy. 2 morally repulsive or wretched; degraded.
squan der (skwon′dər), *v.t.* spend foolishly; waste.
staid (stād), *adj.* 1 having a settled, quiet character; sober; sedate. 2 settled; unchanging; fixed.
stat ute (stach′üt), *n.* 1 law enacted by a legislative body. 2 a formally established rule; law; decree.
stave (stāv), *n., v.,* **staved** or **stove, stav ing.** *—n.* stick, rod, bar, pole, staff, or the like.
stealth (stelth), *n.* secret or sly action.
stealth y (stel′thē), *adj.,* **stealth i er, stealth i est.** done in a secret manner; secret; sly.
stip u late (stip′yə lāt), *v.,* **-lat ed, -lat ing.** *—v.t.* arrange definitely; demand as a condition of agreement. *—v.i.* make an express demand or arrangement *(for).*
stol id (stol′id), *adj.* hard to arouse; not easily excited; showing no emotion; seeming dull; impassive.

stoup (stüp), *n.* a drinking vessel of varying size for liquids, such as a cup, flagon, or tankard.

strait en (strāt/n), *v.t.* 1 limit by the lack of something; restrict. 2 make narrow; contract.

stren u ous (stren/yü əs), *adj.* 1 very active. 2 full of energy. 3 requiring much energy.

sub-, *prefix.* 1 under; below. 2 down; further; again. 3 near; nearly. 4 lower; subordinate. 5 resulting from further division. 6 slightly; somewhat.

suc cor (suk/ər), *n.* person or thing that helps or assists; help; aid. —*v.t.* help, assist, or aid (a person, etc.). Also, BRITISH **succour.**

suf fer ance (suf/ər əns), *n.* 1 permission or consent given only by a failure to object or prevent. 2 power to bear or endure; patient endurance.

suf fice (sə fīs/), *v.,* **-ficed, -fic ing.** —*v.i.* be enough; be sufficient. —*v.t.* make content; satisfy. [< Latin *sufficere* < *sub-* near + *facere* to make]

sul ly (sul/ē), *v.t., v.i.,* **-lied, -ly ing.** make or become soiled, stained, or tarnished.

sump tu ous (sump/chü əs), *adj.* lavish and costly; magnificent; rich.

sun dry (sun/drē), *adj.* several; various.

super-, *prefix.* 1 over; above. 2 besides; further. 3 in high proportion; to excess; exceedingly. 4 surpassing.

su per an nu ate (sü/pər an/yü āt), *v.t., v.i.,* **-at ed, -at ing.** 1 retire or be retired on a pension because of age or infirmity. 2 make or become old-fashioned or out of date.

su per flu i ty (sü/pər flü/ə tē), *n., pl.* **-ties.** a greater amount than is needed; excess.

su per flu ous (sù pėr/flü əs), *adj.* 1 more than is needed. 2 needless; unnecessary.

su per nal (sù pėr/nl), *adj.* 1 heavenly; divine. 2 lofty; exalted.

su pine (*adj.* sü pīn/; *n.* sü/pīn), *adj.* 1 lying flat on the back. 2 lazily inactive; listless. —*n.* a Latin verbal noun formed from the stem of the past participle.

sup ple (sup/əl), *adj.,* **-pler, -plest,** *v.,* **-pled, -pling.** —*adj.* 1 bending or folding easily. 2 moving easily or nimbly. 3 readily adaptable to different ideas, circumstances, people, etc.; yielding. —*v.t., v.i.* make or grow supple. [< Old French *souple* < Latin *supplex* submissive < *supplicare* bend down, supplicate]

sup pli ance (sup/lē əns), *n.* supplication.

sup pli ant (sup/lē ənt), *adj.* asking humbly and earnestly. —*n.* person who asks humbly and earnestly.

sup pli cate (sup/lə kāt), *v.,* **-cat ed, -cat ing.** —*v.t.* beg humbly and earnestly. —*v.i.* pray humbly. [< Latin *supplicatum* bent down, suppliant < *sub-* down + *plicare* to bend]

sup pli ca tion (sup/lə kā/shən), *n.* 1 a supplicating. 2 Usually, **supplications,** *pl.* a humble prayer addressed to God or a deity.

sur feit (sėr/fit), *n.* 1 too much; excess. 2 disgust or nausea caused by this. —*v.t.* feed or supply to excess. —*v.i.* eat, drink, or indulge in something to excess.

sur mise (*v.* sər mīz/; *n.* sər mīz/, sėr/mīz), *v.,* **-mised, -mis ing,** *n.* —*v.t., v.i.* infer or guess. —*n.* formation of an idea with little or no evidence; a guessing.

sus pi ra tion (sus/pə rā/shən), *n.* a sigh.

sus tain (sə stān/), *v.t.* 1 keep up; keep going. 2 supply with food, provisions, etc. 3 hold up; support. 4 bear; endure. 5 suffer; experience. 6 allow; admit; favor. 7 agree with; confirm. [< Old French < Latin *sustinere* < *sub-* up + *tenere* to hold]

sus te nance (sus/tə nəns), *n.* 1 food or provisions; nourishment. 2 means of living; support.

swain (swān), *n.* ARCHAIC. 1 lover. 2 a young man who lives in the country.

swill (swil), *n.* 1 kitchen refuse, especially when partly liquid; slops. 2 a deep drink. —*v.t.* 1 drink greedily. 2 fill with drink. —*v.i.* drink greedily; drink too much.

syl van (sil/vən), *adj.* of, in, or having woods.

syn co pe (sing/kə pē), *n.* a fainting.

syn od (sin/əd), *n.* 1 assembly called together under authority to discuss and decide church affairs; a church council. 2 any assembly, convention, or council.

tar ry (tar/ē), *v.,* **-ried, -ry ing.** —*v.i.* 1 delay leaving; remain; stay. 2 be tardy; hesitate: *Why do you tarry so long?* —*v.t.* ARCHAIC. wait for.

te di ous (tē/dē əs, tē/jəs), *adj.* long and tiring; boring, wearisome.

teem (tēm), *v.i.* be full (of); abound; swarm.

ten ant (ten/ənt), *n.* 1 person paying rent for the temporary use of the land or buildings of another person. 2 person or thing that occupies. —*v.t.* hold or occupy as a tenant; inhabit.

ten dril (ten/drəl), *n.* a threadlike part of a climbing plant that attaches itself to something and helps support the plant.

ten or (ten/ər), *n.* 1 the general tendency; course. 2 the general meaning or drift; gist; purport.

ten ta tive (ten/tə tiv), *adj.* 1 done as a trial or experiment; experimental. 2 hesitating.

ten ure (ten/yər), *n.* 1 a holding or possessing. 2 length of time of holding or possessing. 3 manner of holding land, buildings, etc., from a feudal lord or superior. 4 conditions, terms, etc., on which anything is held or occupied.

tes sel late (*v.* tes/ə lāt; *adj.* tes/ə lit, tes/ə lāt), *v.,* **-lat ed, -lat ing,** *adj.* —*v.t.* make of small squares or blocks, or in a checkered pattern. —*adj.* made in small squares or blocks or in a checkered pattern.

thane (thān), *n.* (in early English history) a man who ranked between an earl and an ordinary freeman. Thanes held lands of the king or lord and gave military service in return.

thews (thüz), *n.pl.* 1 muscles. 2 sinews. 3 bodily force; might; strength.

thwart (thwôrt), *v.t.* prevent from doing something, particularly by blocking the way; oppose and defeat. —*adj.* lying or passing across. —*adv.* across; crosswise; athwart. [< Scandinavian (Old Icelandic) *thvert* across]

tier (tir), *n.* one of a series of rows arranged one above another.

-tion, *suffix added to verbs to form nouns.*

tip ple (tip/əl), *v.,* **-pled, -pling,** *n.* —*v.t., v.i.* drink (alcoholic liquor) often or too much. —*n.* an alcoholic liquor.

toad y (tō/dē), *n., pl.* **toad ies,** *v.,* **toad ied, toad y ing.** —*n.* a fawning flatterer. —*v.i.* act like a toady. —*v.t.* fawn upon; flatter.

toque (tōk), *n.* hat without a brim or with a very small brim, worn by women.

tor rid (tôr/id, tor/id), *adj.* 1 very hot; burning; scorching. 2 exposed or subject to great heat. 3 very ardent; passionate.

tram mel (tram/əl), *n., v.,* **-meled, -mel ing** or **-melled, -mel ling.** —*v.t.* 1 hinder; restrain. 2 catch in or as if in a trammel; entangle.

trans-, *prefix.* 1 across; over; through. 2 on the other side of; beyond. 3 to a different place, condition, etc.

tran sient (tran/shənt), *adj.* 1 passing soon; fleeting; not lasting. 2 passing through and not staying long. —*n.* visitor or boarder who stays for a short time. [< Latin *transientem* going through < *trans-* + *ire* go]

tran si to ry (tran/sə tôr/ē, tran/sə tōr/ē), *adj.* passing soon or quickly; lasting only a short time; fleeting; transient.

tra vail (trə vāl/, trav/āl), *n.* 1 toil; labor. 2 trouble, hardship, or suffering. 3 severe pain; agony; torture. —*v.i.* 1 toil; labor. 2 suffer the pains of childbirth; be in labor. [< Old French < Late Latin *trepalium* torture device, ultimately < Latin *tri-* three + *palus* stake]

trem u lous (trem/yə ləs), *adj.* 1 trembling; quivering. 2 timid; fearful. 3 that wavers; shaky.

trench ant (tren/chənt), *adj.* 1 sharp; keen; cutting. 2 vigorous; effective. 3 clear-cut; distinct. [< Old French, cutting]

trep i da tion (trep/ə dā/shən), *n.* 1 nervous dread; fear; fright. 2 a trembling.

trib u la tion (trib/yə lā/shən), *n.* great trouble; severe trial; affliction.

trough (trôf, trof), *n.* a long hollow between two ridges, especially the hollow between two waves or two hills.

truc u lent (truk/yə lənt, trü/kyə lənt), *adj.* 1 fierce, savage, or violent. 2 brutally harsh or scathing.

tu mult (tü/mult, tyü/mult), *n.* 1 noise or uproar; commotion. 2 a violent disturbance or disorder. 3 a violent disturbance of mind or feeling; confusion or excitement.

tur bid (tėr/bid), *adj.* 1 muddy; thick; not clear. 2 (of air, smoke, etc.) thick; dense; dark. 3 confused; disordered.

un-¹, *prefix.* not; the opposite of.

un-², *prefix.* do the opposite of; do what will reverse the act.

unc tion (ungk/shən), *n.* 1 an anointing with oil, ointment, or the like, for medical purposes or as a religious rite. 2 the oil, ointment, or the like, used for anointing. 3 something soothing or comforting. 4 fervor; earnestness. 5 affected earnestness, sentiment, etc.; smoothness and oiliness of language, manner, etc.

up braid (up brād/), *v.t.* find fault with; blame; reprove.

u surp (yü zėrp/, yü sėrp/), *v.t.* seize and hold (power, position, authority, etc.) by force or without right. —*v.i.* commit usurpa-

hat, āge, fär; let, ēqual, tėrm;
it, īce; hot, ōpen, ôrder;
oil, out; cup, pu̇t, rüle;
ch, child; ng, long; sh, she;
th, thin; ᴛʜ, then; zh, measure;

ə represents *a* in about, *e* in taken, *i* in pencil, *o* in lemon, *u* in circus.

< = from, derived from, taken from.

tion. [< Latin *usurpare* < *usu* through use + *rapere* seize]

u sur pa tion (yü′zər pā′shən, yü′sər pā′shən), *n.* a usurping; the seizing and holding of the place or power of another by force or without right.

u til i tar i an (yü til′ə ter′ē ən), *adj.* 1 of or having to do with utility. 2 aiming at or designed for usefulness rather than beauty, style, etc.

van quish (vang′kwish, van′kwish), *v.t.* 1 conquer, defeat, or overcome in battle or conflict. 2 overcome or subdue by other than physical means.

var i e gat ed (ver′ē ə gā′tid, ver′i gā′tid; var′ē ə gā′tid, var′i gā′tid), *adj.* 1 varied in appearance; marked with different colors. 2 having variety.

var let (vär′lit), *n.* ARCHAIC. a low fellow; rascal.

vaunt (vônt, vänt), *v.t.* boast of. —*v.i.* brag or boast. —*n.* a boasting assertion or speech; brag.

vel li cate (vel′ə kāt), *v.,* **-cated, -cating.** to pluck, twitch, move with convulsions.

ve loc i ty (və los′ə tē), *n., pl.* **-ties.** 1 quickness of motion; speed; swiftness. 2 rate of motion in a particular direction. 3 the absolute or relative rate of operation or action.

ve ra cious (və rā′shəs), *adj.* 1 truthful. 2 true.

ver dur ous (vėr′jər əs), *adj.* green and fresh.

ver i ty (ver′ə tē), *n., pl.* **-ties.** 1 truth. 2 a true statement or fact. 3 reality.

vice roy (vīs′roi), *n.* person ruling a country or province as the deputy of the sovereign.

vict ual (vit′l), *n., v.,* **-ualed, -ual ing** or **-ualled, -ual ling.** —*n.* **victuals,** *pl.* food or provisions. —*v.t.* supply with food or provisions. —*v.i.* 1 take on a supply of food or provisions. 2 eat or feed.

vile (vīl), *adj.,* **vil er, vil est.** 1 very bad. 2 foul; disgusting; obnoxious. 3 evil; low; immoral. 4 poor; mean; lowly. 5 of little worth or account; trifling.

vin dic tive (vin dik′tiv), *adj.* 1 feeling a strong tendency toward revenge; bearing a grudge. 2 showing a strong tendency toward revenge.

vint ner (vint′nər), *n.* dealer in wine; wine merchant.

vis age (viz′ij), *n.* 1 face. 2 appearance or aspect.

vi tal (vī′tl), *adj.* 1 of or having to do with life. 2 necessary to life. —*n.* **vitals,** *pl.* parts or organs necessary to life. The brain, heart, lungs, and stomach are vitals.

vi vac i ty (vī vas′ə tē, vi vas′ə tē), *n., pl.* **-ties.** liveliness; sprightliness; animation; gaiety.

vo cif er ous (vō sif′ər əs), *adj.* loud and noisy; shouting; clamoring.

vol u ble (vol′yə bəl), *adj.* 1 tending to talk much; fond of talking; talkative. 2 having a smooth, rapid flow of speech.

waist coat (wāst′kōt, wes′kət), *n.* BRITISH. a man's vest.

wane (wān), *v.,* **waned, wan ing,** *n.* —*v.i.* 1 lose size; become smaller gradually. 2 decline in power, influence, or importance. 3 decline in strength or intensity. 4 draw to a close.

wan ton (won′tən), *adj.* 1 reckless, heartless, or malicious. 2 without reason or excuse. 3 not moral; not chaste. 4 frolicsome; playful. 5 not restrained. —*n.* a wanton person. —*v.i.* act in a wanton manner. —*v.t.* waste foolishly; squander. [Middle English *wantowen* < Old English *wan-* not, lacking + *togen* brought up]

war rant (wôr′ənt, wor′ənt), *n.* 1 that which gives a right; authority. 2 a written order giving authority to do something. 3 a good and sufficient reason; promise; guarantee.

was sail (wos′əl, was′əl), *n.* 1 a drinking party; revelry with drinking of healths. 2 spiced ale or other liquor drunk at a wassail. [< Scandinavian (Old Icelandic) *ves heill* be healthy!]

wat tle (wot′l), *n., v.,* **-tled, -tling.** —*n.* Also, **wattles,** *pl.* sticks interwoven with twigs or branches; framework of wicker.

wax (waks), *v.i.,* **waxed, waxed** or **wax en, wax ing.** 1 grow bigger or greater; increase. 2 become. [Old English *weaxan*]

weal (wēl), *n.* well-being; prosperity. ARCHAIC. society; the state.

weft (weft), *n.* the threads running from side to side across a fabric; woof.

wel ter (wel′tər), *v.i.* 1 roll or tumble about; wallow. 2 lie soaked; be drenched. 3 be sunk or deeply involved (in).

whet (hwet), *v.,* **whet ted, whet ting.** —*v.t.* 1 sharpen by rubbing. 2 make keen or eager; stimulate. 3 rub vigorously together.

wile (wīl), *n., v.,* **wiled, wil ing.** —*n.* 1 a trick to deceive; cunning way. 2 subtle trickery; slyness; craftiness. —*v.t.* coax; lure; entice.

wil y (wī′lē), *adj.,* **wil i er, wil i est.** using wiles or subtle tricks to deceive; crafty; cunning; sly.

with ers (wiᴛʜ′ərz), *n.pl.* the highest part of a horse's or other animal's back, between the shoulder blades.

wiz ened (wiz′nd, wē′znd), *adj.* dried up; withered; shriveled.

wold (wōld), *n.* high, rolling country, bare of woods.

wont (wunt, wōnt), *adj.* accustomed. —*n.* custom; habit.

woof (wüf), *n.* the threads running from side to side across a woven fabric. The woof crosses the warp.

wreak (rēk), *v.t.* 1 give expression to; work off (feelings, desires, etc.). 2 inflict (vengeance, punishment, etc.).

-y, *suffix forming adjectives chiefly from nouns.*

yeo man (yō′mən), *n., pl.* **-men.** 1 (in the United States Navy) a petty officer who performs clerical duties. 2 (formerly, in Great Britain) a person who owned land, but not a large amount, and usually farmed it himself. 3 ARCHAIC. servant or attendant of a lord or king.

zeal ous (zel′əs), *adj.* full of zeal; eager; earnest; enthusiastic.

ze nith (zē′nith), *n.* 1 the point in the heavens directly overhead. 2 the highest point; apex.

zeph yr (zef′ər), *n.* 1 the west wind. 2 any soft, gentle wind; mild breeze. [< *Zephyrus*]

Time Line Notes

The two pages preceding each unit introduction are occupied by time lines, presenting graphically some of the important events of each period. Events occurring at one specific date, e.g., the Battle of Hastings, are marked with a dot. Events of uncertain date, e.g., the Sutton Hoo ship burial, or events occurring over a period of time, e.g., the reign of Alfred the Great, are not marked in this way.

At the top of each time line is a construction composed of objects suggestive of the period. The paragraphs that follow briefly discuss each construction.

(pages 2-3) The objects to the left recall the life of the Roman province of Britannia: a Roman spoon found near Chester; two coins from the reign of the emperor Claudius (41–54), whose armies added Britannia to the Empire; an oil lamp (viewed from above). The objects to the right suggest the varied ethnic makeup of the England that is shaping during this period: Viking chess pieces of walrus ivory; some Celtic jewelry; a fragment of the Bayeux Tapestry depicting the Norman invasion of England.

(pages 56–57) The weapon at the center of the construction is a crossbow. The grains in the jars are rye, wheat, and barley. The map to the right is of Jerusalem, the goal of the Crusading knights of the Middle Ages.

(pages 110–111) The figures to the left are Henry VIII and his six wives. To the right is a letter dated May, 1555, written by Mary Tudor, Henry's daughter by Catherine of Aragon, who reigned briefly as Mary I from 1553 to 1558. The figure within the porthole is Sir Francis Drake, who plundered the Spanish and sailed around the world (1577–80).

(pages 238–239) The silver pot to the left of the British lion is a characteristic product of eighteenth-century ingenuity. Called an *argyll*, it is a double-jacketed serving pot (a kind of thermos bottle), for serving hot or cold liquids. The figure surrounded by various views of London is Sir Christopher Wren (1632–1723), who rebuilt London's churches, including St. Paul's Cathedral, after the Great Fire of 1666.

(pages 298–299) To the left is a picture of the *Victory*, the flagship of the British admiral Lord Horatio Nelson (1758–1805), who defeated Napoleon and his Spanish allies at Trafalgar. The document to the right of it is an agreement of indenture, dated 1804, by which a European emigrant to the United States "sold" himself to an owner for a period of years in exchange for his passage money. The candle (viewed from above) was called a "wax-jack." As the waxed wick burns down, it can be pulled up again.

(pages 358–359) The portrait of a woman in profile, in the center on the left, is of Emily Brontë. The jump rope at the top is of a kind made by the children employed in the textile mills in the North of England from the bobbins of the looms they tended. To the right is a picture of Queen Victoria taken in 1876, the year she became Empress of India. The jar contains potpourri, a mixture of flower petals and spices often used to scent rooms.

(pages 440–441) The construction is dominated by a large dart board, a typical amusement found in public houses. At the top of the page is a copy of the *Boy's Own Paper*, the first of a very successful series of weekly newspapers for children, which started publication in 1879. The man at the far left is the Prince of Wales, who reigned as Edward VII from 1901 to 1910.

(pages 576–577) To the left at the bottom, a soldier has quoted from Tennyson in an autograph book: "Kind hearts are more than coronets, / And simple faith than Norman blood" (from stanza seven of "Lady Clara de Vere").

The editors would like to thank Charles Schultz of Kings 3 and Acme Rentals, Inc., for their assistance in this project.

Index of Authors and Titles

Adam's Curse, 459
Addison, Joseph; from *The Spectator,* 265
Afterwards, 453
Ah, Are You Digging on My Grave? 451
Ah! Why, Because the Dazzling Sun, 379
Alexander, Michael (trans.); *Anglo-Saxon Riddles,* 48
Alice's Adventures Under Ground, 386
Allegory, (Notes and Comments), 125
Alone In The Woods, 603
Amoretti, Sonnet 30, 127
Anglo-Saxon Riddles, 48
Annihilation of Nothing, The, 617
Arnold, Matthew; *Dover Beach,* 377; *Self-Dependence,* 378
Astrophel and Stella, Sonnet 31, 127
At Castle Boterel, 452
At Grass, 612
Auden, W. H.; *The Wanderer* (Notes and Comments), 43; *Musée Des Beaux Arts,* 592; *The Unknown Citizen,* 594; *Who's Who,* 595.

Bacon, Sir Francis; *Of Studies,* 209
Bait, The, 211
Ballad, The (Notes and Comments), 65
Battle of Brunanburh, The, 37
Bede's History (excerpt), 49
Ben Jonson's Vision of His Son (Notes and Comments), 216
Beowulf, Part I, 6
Beowulf (Notes and Comments), 35
Blake, William; *Introduction* from *Songs of Innocence,* 302; *Introduction* from *Songs of Experience,* 302; *The Lamb,* 303; *The Tyger,* 303; *Holy Thursday* from *Songs of Innocence,* 304; *Holy Thursday* from *Songs of Experience,* 304; *The Divine Image,* 305; *The Human Abstract,* 305; *Proverbs of Hell,* 306
Borges, Jorge Luis; *Brunanburh A.D. 937* (Notes and Comments), 38
Boswell, James; from *The Life of Samuel Johnson,* 283
Bowen, Elizabeth; *Tears, Idle Tears,* 652
Bradley, A. C.; *The Witch-Scenes in* MACBETH (Notes and Comments), MACBETH edition, 172; *The Character of Macbeth* (Notes and Comments), MACBETH edition, 199
British Museum Reading Room, The, 598
Brontë, Emily; *Ah! Why, Because the Dazzling Sun,* 379; *The Night Wind,* 380; *I'll Not Weep,* 381
Browning, Elizabeth Barrett; from *Sonnets from the Portuguese: I thought once how . . .,* 382; *Unlike are we . . .,* 382; *When our two souls . . .,* 383; *My letter, all dead paper . . .,* 383; *How do I love thee . . .,* 383
Browning, Robert; *Porphyria's Lover,* 373; *My Last Duchess,* 374
Brunanburh A. D. 937 (Notes and Comments), 38
Bullfrog, 618
Burns, Robert; *To a Mouse,* 291; *A Red, Red Rose,* 292
Byron, Lord (George Gordon); *When We Two Parted,* 320; *She Walks in Beauty,* 321; *So, We'll Go No More A-Roving,* 321; from *Canto 1, Don Juan,* 322

Campion, Thomas; *The Man of Life Upright,* 129; *Never Love Unless You Can,* 129; *When to Her Lute Corinna Sings,* 129
Canonization, The, 212
Carroll, Lewis; *Alice's Adventures Under Ground,* 386
Certain Books of Virgil's AENEID (excerpt), 117
Character of Macbeth, The (Notes and Comments), MACBETH edition 199
Chaucer, Geoffrey; *Prologue to the Canterbury Tales,* 66; *The Wife of Bath's Tale,* 81
Chaucer the Satirist (Notes and Comments), 73
Chaucer's Words to His Scribe (Notes and Comments), 76
Climbers, The, 614
Coghill, Nevill (trans.); *Prologue to the Canterbury Tales,* 66; *The Wife of Bath's Tale,* 81
Coleridge, Samuel Taylor; *Frost at Midnight,* 316; *Kubla Khan,* 317
Coleridge's Remarks about KUBLA KHAN (Notes and Comments), 318
Comedy of Ideas, The (Notes and Comments), 558
Composed Upon Westminster Bridge, September 3, 1802, 310
Conrad, Joseph; *The Lagoon,* 475
Conrad on the Sources of His Fiction (Notes and Comments), 481
Constant Lover, The, 219
Creation of the World, The, 204
Crossley-Holland, Kevin (trans.); *Beowulf, Part I,* 6; *The Wanderer,* 39
Cummings, E. E.; *i carry your heart* (Notes and Comments), 128

Dark Age Glosses on the Venerable Bede (Notes and Comments), 51
Day of Destiny, The, from *Morte Darthur,* 96
Death of Raleigh, The (Notes and Comments), 119
Defoe, Daniel; from *A Journal of the Plague Year,* 294
De Quincey, Thomas; *On the Knocking at the Gate in* MACBETH, 344
Description of a City Shower, A, 257
Devereux, Robert (see **Essex, Earl of**)
Diary of Samuel Pepys, The (excerpt), 249
Dictionary of the English Language, (excerpts), 275
Divine Image, The, 305

Doll's House, The, 647
Don Juan, Canto I (excerpts), 322
Donne, John; *Song,* 211; *The Bait,* 211; *The Canonization,* 212; *A Valediction Forbidding Mourning,* 213; from *Holy Sonnets: No. 7,* 214, *No. 10,* 214; *No. 14,* 214; *Meditation* 17, 215;
Donne's Puns (Notes and Comments), 213
Do Not Go Gentle into That Good Night, 608
Dover Beach, 377
Dramatic Monologue, The (Notes and Comments), 376
Dreamers, 582
Dryden, John; from *The Hind and the Panther,* 244; *To the Memory of Mr. Oldham,* 247
Dryden and the Heroic Couplet (Notes and Comments), 248

Elegy Written in a Country Churchyard, 288
Elementary School Class Room in a Slum, An, 596
Eliot, George; *The Lifted Veil,* 409
Eliot, T. S.; *The Hollow Men,* 584; *The Journey of the Magi,* 586
Elizabeth I; *When I Was Fair and Young,* 118
England in 1819, 329
Epic, The (Notes and Comments), 9
Epistle to Miss Blount, 271
Epitaph on a Pessimist, 450
Essay on Criticism, An (excerpts) 272
Essay on Man, An (excerpt), 274
Essex, Earl of (Robert Devereux); *To Plead My Faith,* 119
Esther's Tomcat, 619
Eveline, 632
Eve of St. Agnes, The, 336
Exeter Book, The (Notes and Comments), 50
Explosion, The, 612

Faerie Queene, The (excerpt), 121
Far in a Western Brookland, 455
Fern, 618
Fern Hill, 606
Fern Hill (Notes and Comments), 607
First Folio, The (Notes and Comments), HAMLET edition, 178
Force That Through the Green Fuse . . . (Notes and Comments), 605
Force That Through the Green Fuse Drives the Flower, The, 604
Forster, E. M.; *Pessimism in Literature* (Notes and Comments), 489
Frog Prince, The, 600
Frost at Midnight, 316

Garden, The, 223
Gardner, John; from *Grendel* (Notes and Comments), 33
Germans at Meat, 705
Get Up and Bar the Door, 62
Gissing, George; *Spellbound,* 502
Globe Theater, The (Notes and Comments) MACBETH edition, 188
God's Grandeur, 447
Going Home, 701
Gordon, George (see **Byron, Lord)**
Grave by the Handpost, The, 485
Graves, Robert; *Read Me, Please,* 590; *Sullen Moods,* 591; *She Tells Her Love While Half Asleep,* 591
Gray, Thomas; *Elegy Written in a Country Churchyard,* 288; *Sonnet on the Death of Richard West,* 290
Greene, Graham; *A Shocking Accident,* 657
Grendel (excerpt) (Notes and Comments), 33
Gunn, Thom; *The Secret Sharer,* 616; *The Annihilation of Nothing,* 617

Hamlet, 136
Hardy, Thomas; *The Man He Killed,* 450; *Epitaph on a Pessimist,* 450; *Ah, Are You Digging on My Grave?* 451; *At Castle Boterel,* 452; *Afterwards,* 453; *The Grave by the Handpost,* 485
Heart Exchange, 128
Herrick, Robert; *To the Virgins, to Make Much of Time,* 219
Hind and the Panther, The (excerpt), 244
Holloway, John; *Journey Through the Night,* 622
Hollow Men, The, 584
Holy Sonnets (excerpts), No. *7,* 214; No. *10,* 214; No. *14,* 214
Holy Thursday, from *Songs of Experience,* 304
Homage to a Government, 613
Hopkins, Gerard Manley; *Pied Beauty,* 447; *God's Grandeur,* 447; *Spring and Fall,* 448; *Thou Art Indeed Just, Lord,* 448
Housman, A. E.; *When I Was One-and-Twenty,* 454; *Loveliest of Trees,* 454; *To an Athlete Dying Young,* 454; *Into My Heart an Air That Kills,* 455; *Far in a Western Brookland,* 455
Housman on Writing His Poetry (Notes and Comments), 456
Howard, Elizabeth Jane; *Three Miles Up,* 679
Howard, Henry (see **Surrey, Earl of)**
How do I love thee . . ., from *Sonnets from the Portuguese,* 383
How Original was Chaucer? (Notes and Comments), 89
Hughes, Ted; *Bullfrog,* 618; *Fern,* 618; *Esther's Tomcat,* 619; *Six Young Men,* 620
Human Abstract, The, 305
Husband's Message, The, 44

i carry your heart (Notes and Comments), 128
I'll Not Weep, 381
Imagery in GOD'S GRANDEUR (Notes and Comments), 449
In Memoriam (excerpts), 364
Intimates, 589
Into My Heart an Air That Kills, 455
Introduction from *Songs of Experience,* 302
Introduction from *Songs of Innocence,* 302
I thought once how . . ., from *Sonnets from the Portuguese,* 382
It Is a Beauteous Evening, 309
It was a Beauty that I Saw, 217

Jennings, Elizabeth; *The Climbers,* 614; *Not in the Guidebooks,* 615
Johnson, Samuel; from the *Dictionary of the English Language,* 275; *Letter to Chesterfield,* 277; from the *Life of Milton,* 278; *On the Death of Mr. Robert Levet,* 281
Jonson, Ben; *On My First Son,* 216; *To Cynthia,* 216; *It was a Beauty That I Saw,* 217; *Song, To Celia,* 217
Journal of the Plague Year, A (excerpt) 294
Journey of the Magi, The, 586
Journey Through the Night, 622
Joyce, James; *Eveline,* 632

Keats, John; *When I Have Fears,* 332; *This Living Hand,* 332; *Ode on a Grecian Urn,* 333; *Ode to a Nightingale,* 334; *The Eve of St. Agnes,* 336
Kennedy, Charles (trans.); *The Wife's Lament,* 45
King of China's Daughter, The, 588
Kipling, Rudyard; *The Miracle of Purun Bhagat,* 466
Kubla Khan, 317

Lagoon, The, 475
Lake Isle of Innisfree, The, 457
Lamb, The, 303
Larkin, Philip; *At Grass,* 612; *The Explosion,* 612; *Homage to a Government,* 613
Lawrence, D. H.; *Intimates,* 589; *Tickets, Please,* 640
Legacy, The, 635
Lessing, Doris; *Going Home,* 701
Letter to Chesterfield, 277
Lewis, C. Day; *Walking Away,* 597
Lewis, C. S.; *Science Fiction* (Notes and Comments), 496
Life of Milton (excerpt), 278
Life of Samuel Johnson, The (excerpts), 283
Lifted Veil, The, 409
Lines Composed a Few Miles Above Tintern Abbey, 312
London, 1802, 310
Lord Randal, 60
Lovelace, Richard; *To Althea, from Prison,* 218; *To Lucasta, on Going to the Wars,* 218
Loveliest of Trees, 454
Lover's Vow, A, 116

Macbeth, 136
MacLeish, Archibald; *You, Andrew Marvell* (Notes and Comments), 222
MacNeice, Louis; *Dark Age Glosses on the Venerable Bede* (Notes and Comments), 51; *The British Museum Reading Room,* 596; *The Snow Man,* 597
Major Barbara, Act I (excerpt), 570
Malory, Sir Thomas; *The Day of Destiny* from *Morte Darthur,* 96
Man He Killed, The, 450
Man of Life Upright, The, 129
Mansfield, Katherine; *The Doll's House,* 647; *Germans at Meat,* 696
Marlowe, Christopher; *The Passionate Shepherd to his Love,* 126
Marvell, Andrew; *To His Coy Mistress,* 221; *The Garden,* 223
Mary Wollstonecraft (Notes and Comments), 350
McGough, Roger; *P. C. Plod Vs. the Dale St. Dog Strangler,* 624
Meditation 17, 215
Mill, John Stuart; from *On the Subjection of Women,* 436
Milton, John; *On His Having Arrived at the Age of Twenty-three,* 225; *On His Blindness,* 225; from *Paradise Lost, Book 1,* 226
Miracle of Purun Bhagat, The, 466
Modest Proposal, A, 259
Monna Innominata, Sonnet 2, 384
Munro, H. H. (see **Saki**)
Musée des Beaux Arts, 592
My Last Duchess, 374
My letter, all dead paper . . ., from *Sonnets from the Portuguese,* 383
My Oedipus Complex, 662

Never Love Unless You Can, 129
Next War, The, 583
Night Wind, The, 380
No Respect, 602
Norris, Leslie; *Three Shots for Charlie Betson,* 670
Not in the Guidebooks, 615
Not Waving but Drowning, 602
Nymph's Reply to the Shepherd, The, 126

O'Connor, Frank; *My Oedipus Complex,* 662
Ode on a Grecian Urn, 333
Ode to a Nightingale, 334
Ode to the West Wind, 330
O'Filler, The, 610
Of Studies, 209
Olson, Elder; *Sailing to Byzantium* (Notes and Comments), 464
On His Blindness, 225
On His Having Arrived at the Age of Twenty-three, 225
On My First Son, 216
On the Death of Mr. Robert Levet, 281
On the Knocking at the Gate in MACBETH, 344
On the Subjection of Women (excerpt), 436
Opinions of the Wife (Notes and Comments), 85
Orwell, George; *Why I Write,* 692
Owen, Wilfred; *The Next War,* 583
Ozymandias, 329

Paley, Morton D.; *What Did Blake Mean by Innocence and Experience?* (Notes and Comments), 307
Paradise Lost, Book 1 (excerpt), 226
Passing of Arthur, The, from *Idylls of the King,* 365
Passionate Shepherd to his Love, The, 126
P. C. Plod Vs. the Dale St. Dog Strangler, 624
Pepys, Samuel; from *The Diary of Samuel Pepys,* 249
Pessimism in Literature (Notes and Comments), 489
Physiognomists, The (Notes and Comments), 68
Pied Beauty, 447

Poetry of BEOWULF, *The* (Notes and Comments), 13
Pope, Alexander; *Epistle to Miss Blount,* 271; from *An Essay on Criticism,* 272; from *An Essay on Man,* 274
Porphyria's Lover, 373
Prelude, Book 1, The (excerpt), 354
Prologue to The Canterbury Tales, The, 66
Proverbs of Hell, 306
Pygmalion, 511

Raffel, Burton (trans.); *The Battle of Brunanburh,* 38; *The Husband's Message,* 44; *The Seafarer,* 53
Raleigh, Sir Walter; *What Is Our Life?* 119; *To Queen Elizabeth,* 120; *The Nymph's Reply to the Shepherd,* 126
Read Me, Please, 590
Red, Red Rose, A, 292
Reid, Alastair; *The O-Filler,* 610
Reminiscences, 697
Richard II, Act Three (excerpt), 235
Role of Lady Macbeth, The (Notes and Comments) MACBETH edition, 154
Rossetti, Christina; from *Monna Innominata, Sonnet 2,* 384; *Shut Out,* 384

Sailing to Byzantium, 462
Sailing to Byzantium (Notes and Comments), 464
Saki (H. H. Munro); *Tobermory,* 626
Sassoon, Siegfried; *Suicide in the Trenches,* 582; *Dreamers,* 582
Satirical Elegy on the Death of a Late Famous General, A, 256
Science Fiction (Notes and Comments), 496
Seafarer, The, 53
Second Coming, The, 461
Second Coming, The (Notes and Comments) 461
Secret Sharer, The, 616
Self-Dependence, 378
Shakespeare, William; Sonnets: *18, Shall I compare thee . . .,* 130; *130, My Mistress' eyes . . .,* 130; *29, When in disgrace . . .,* 131; *30, When to the sessions . . .,* 131; *55, Not marble . . .,* 131; *71, No longer mourn for me . . .,* 131; *73, That time of year . . .,* 132; *116, Let me not to the marriage . . .,* 132; *Hamlet,* 136; *Macbeth,* 136; from *Richard II, Act Three,* 235
Shaw, Bernard; *Pygmalion,* 511; from *Major Barbara, Act One,* 570
Shelley, Percy Bysshe; *England in 1819,* 329; *Ozymandias,* 329; *Ode to the West Wind,* 330
She Tells Her Love While Half Asleep, 591
Sherley-Price, Leo (trans.); from *Bede's History,* 49
Shocking Accident, A, 657
Shut Out, 384
Sidney, Sir Philip; *Sonnet 31* from *Astrophel and Stella,* 127; *Heart Exchange,* 128
Sir Gawain and the Green Knight (excerpt), 104
Sir Patrick Spence, 64
Sitwell, Edith; *The King of China's Daughter,* 588
Six Young Men, 620
Smith, Stevie; *The Frog Prince,* 600; *No Respect,* 602; *Not Waving but Drowning,* 602; *Alone in the Woods,* 603
Snow Man, The, 599
Song (Donne), 211
Song, to Celia, 217
Sonnet 30, from *Amoretti,* 127
Sonnet 31, from *Astrophel and Stella,* 127
Sonnet on the Death of Richard West, 290
Sonnets from the Portuguese (excerpts), 382
Sonnets (Shakespeare): 18, Shall I compare thee . . ., 130; *130, My mistress's eyes . . .,* 130; *29, When in disgrace . . .,* 131; *30, When to the sessions . . .,* 131; *55, Not marble . . .,* 131; *71, No longer mourn for me . . .,* 73; *That time of year . . .,* 132; *116, Let me not to the marriage . . .,* 132
So, We'll Go No More A-Roving, 321
Spectator, The (excerpts), 265
Spellbound, 502
Spender, Stephen; *An Elementary School Class Room in a Slum,* 596
Spenser, Edmund; from *The Faerie Queene,* 121; *Sonnet 30* from *Amoretti,* 127
Spenserian Stanza, The (Notes and Comments), 124
Spring and Fall, 448
Star, The, 493
Steele, Richard; from *The Spectator,* 265
Stone, Brian; from *Sir Gawain and the Green Knight,* 104
Suckling, Sir John; *The Constant Lover,* 219
Suicide in the Trenches, 582
Sullen Moods, 591
Surrey, Earl of (Henry Howard); *A Lover's Vow,* 116; from *Certain Books of Virgil's* AENEID, 117
Swift, Jonathan; *A Satirical Elegy on the Death of a Late Famous General,* 256; *A Description of a City Shower,* 257; *A Modest Proposal,* 259

Tears, Idle Tears, 652
Tennyson, Alfred, Lord; *Ulysses,* 362; from *In Memoriam,* 364; *The Passing of Arthur* from *Idylls of the King,* 365
This Living Hand, 332
Thomas, Dylan; *The Force That Through the Green Fuse,* 604; *Fern Hill,* 606; *Do Not Go Gentle into That Good Night,* 608; *Reminiscences,* 697
Thou Art Indeed Just, Lord, 448
Three Miles Up, 679
Three Pictures, 690
Three Shots for Charlie Betson, 670
Tickets, Please, 640
To Althea, from Prison, 218
To a Mouse, 291
To an Athlete Dying Young, 454
Tobermory, 626
To Cynthia, 216
To His Coy Mistress, 221
To Lucasta, on Going to the Wars, 218
To the Memory of Mr. Oldham, 247
To Plead My Faith, 119

To Queen Elizabeth, 120
To the Virgins, to Make Much of Time, 219
Twenty-third Psalm, The, from *The Great Bible,* 208; from *The King James Bible,* 208; from *The Bay Psalm Book,* 208; from *The New English Bible,* 208
Tyger, The, 303

Ulysses, 362
Unknown Citizen, The, 594
Unlike are we . . . from *Sonnets from the Portuguese,* 382
Unquiet Grave, The, 61

Valediction: Forbidding Mourning, A, 213
Villanelle, The (Notes and Comments), 609
Vindication of the Rights of Woman, A (excerpts), 347

Walking Away, 597
Wanderer, The, 39
Wanderer, The (Notes and Comments), 43
Wells, H. G.; *The Star,* 492
What Care I? 220
What Did Blake Mean by Innocence and Experience? (Notes and Comments), 307
What Is Our Life? 119
When I Have Fears, 332
When I Was Fair and Young, 118
When I Was One-and-Twenty, 454
When our two souls . . . from *Sonnets from the Portuguese,* 383
When to Her Lute Corinna Sings, 129
When We Two Parted, 320
When You Are Old, 458
Whoso List to Hunt, 116
Who's Who, 595
Why I Write, 692
Wife's Lament, The, 45
Witch-Scenes in MACBETH, *The* (Notes and Comments), 172
Wife of Bath's Tale, The, 81
Wilbur, Richard; *Beowulf* (Notes and Comments), 35
Wild Swans at Coole, The, 460
Wither, George; *What Care I?,* 220
Woolf, Virginia; *Mary Wollstonecraft* (Notes and Comments), 350; *The Legacy,* 635; *Women and Fiction* (Notes and Comments), 639; *Three Pictures,* 690
Wollstonecraft, Mary; from *A Vindication of the Rights of Woman,* 347
Women and Fiction (Notes and Comments), 639
Wordsworth, William; *The World Is Too Much With Us,* 309; *It Is a Beauteous Evening,* 309; *Composed Upon Westminster Bridge, September 3, 1802,* 310; *London, 1802,* 310; *Lines Composed a Few Miles Above Tintern Abbey,* 312; from *The Prelude, Book 1,* 354
World Is Too Much With Us, The, 309
Wyatt, Sir Thomas; *Whoso List to Hunt,* 116

Yeats on Innisfree (Notes and Comments), 457
Yeats, William Butler; *The Lake Isle of Innisfree,* 457; *When You Are Old,* 458; *Adam's Curse,* 459; *The Wild Swans at Coole,* 460; *The Second Coming,* 461; *Sailing to Byzantium,* 462
You, Andrew Marvell, (Notes and Comments), 222

Index of Extension Assignments

Reading: 255, 474, 491, 639, 651, 669

Speaking: 32, 127, 203 (both plays), 231, 305, 501, 569

Writing: 32, 34, 38, 42, 52, 65, 103, 120, 127, 133, 202 (Hamlet), 203 (Macbeth), 210, 220, 231, 255, 270, 272, 304, 307, 309, 315, 328, 343, 349, 353, 434, 484, 491, 501, 569, 621, 631, 634, 639, 651, 669, 696, 700

Index of Vocabulary Exercises

Context: 32, 80, 202 (Hamlet), 231, 264, 343, 508, 703

Structure: 32, 52, 95, 132, 202 (Hamlet), 319, 343, 385, 570, 625

Pronunciation: 32, 52, 103, 202 (Hamlet), 231, 293, 385, 570

Dictionary: 32, 52, 80, 95, 103, 132, 203 (Macbeth), 231, 264, 282, 319, 353, 385, 435, 465, 508, 689